NINTH EDITION

Exceptional Learners

Introduction to Special Education

Daniel P. Hallahan

University of Virginia

James M. Kauffman

University of Virginia

Allyn and Bacon

Boston   New York   San Francisco
Mexico City   Montreal   Toronto   London   Madrid   Munich   Paris
Hong Kong   Singapore   Tokyo   Cape Town   Sydney

Senior Editor: Virginia Lanigan
Editorial Assistant: Erin Leidel, Robert Champagne
Developmental Editor: Alicia R. Reilly
Marketing Manager: Amy Cronin
Production Administrator: Deborah Brown

Editorial-Production Service: Barbara Gracia
Copyeditor: William Heckman
Text Designer: Mark Bergeron
Manufacturing Buyer: Megan Cochran
Cover Administrator: Linda Knowles
Photo Researcher: Kathy Smith

Library of Congress Cataloging-in-Publication Data

Hallahan, Daniel P., 1944–
    Exceptional learners: introduction to special education / Daniel P. Hallahan, James M. Kauffman.—9th ed.
        p.   cm.
    Includes bibliographical references and indexes.
    ISBN 0-205-35029-1
    1. Special education—United States.   I. Kauffman, James M.   II. Title.

LC3981.H34 2003
371.9'0973—dc21   2002016435

Printed in the United States of America
10 9 8 7 6 5 4 3 2 1—VHP—08 07 06 05 04 03 02

Chapter-Opening Quotes
Page 3 from Richard H. Hungerford, 1950, "On Locusts," *American Journal of Mental Deficiency, 54*, pp. 415–418. **Page 39** from Bob Dylan, "The Times They Are A-Changin'." Copyright © 1963, 1964 by Warner Bros., Inc. Copyright renewed 1991 by Special Rider Music. All rights reserved. International copyright secured. Reprinted by permission. **Page 79** from *The Measure of Our Success* by Marian Wright Edelman. Copyright © 1992 by Marian Wright Edelman. Reprinted by permission of Beacon Press. **Page 109** from S. Z. Kaufman (1999). *Retarded Isn't Stupid, Mom!* (Rev. ed.). Baltimore, MD: Paul H. Brookes. **Page 148** from L. Pelkey (2001). In the LD bubble. In P. Rodis, A. Garrod, & M. L. Boscardin (Eds.), *Learning Disabilities and Life Stories*. Boston: Allyn & Bacon. **Page 185** from Heinrich Hoffmann, "The Story of Fidgety Philip" in (Author) *Slovenly Peter or Cheerful Stories and Funny Pictures for Good Little Folks* (Philadelphia: John C. Winston, 1940). **Page 221** from Anonymous, 1994, "First Person Account: Schizophrenia with Childhood Onset," *Schizophrenia Bullet, 20*, 287–288. **Page 263** from David Shields, *Dead Languages* (New York: Alfred A. Knopf, Inc., 1989). **Page 299** from M. Sheridan (2001). *Inner Lives of Deaf Children: Interviews and Analysis*. Washington, DC: Gallaudet University Press. **Page 337** from *Planet of the Blind: A Memoir* by Stephen Kuusisto, copyright © 1998 by Stephen Kuusisto. Used by permission of The Dial Press/Dell Publishing, a division of Random House, Inc. **Page 373** from *Exiting Nirvana: A Daughter's Life with Autism* by C. C. Park. Copyright © 2001 by Clara Claiborne Park. By permission of Little, Brown, and Company, Inc. **Page 419** from *Jim the Boy* by Tony Early. Copyright © 2000. Boston: Little, Brown and Company, Inc.

Page 453 from *The Autobiography of Mark Twain*, edited by Charles Neider. Copyright © 1927, 1940, 1958, 1959 by the Mark Twain Company, copyright 1924, 1952, 1955 by Clara Clemens Somossoud, copyright 1959 by Charles Neider. Reprinted by permission of HarperCollins Publishers, Inc. **Page 485** from E. K. Gerlach (1999). *Just This Side of Normal: Glimpses into Life with Autism*. Eugene, Oregon: Four Leaf Press.

Photo Credits
Chapter 1 Bob Daemmrich/The Image Works: p. 4; DKR Photo: p. 7; Jamie Bloomquist: p. 8; Courtesy of Blair Smith: 9; Will Hart: pp. 14, 37; David Young-Wolff/PhotoEdit: p. 20; Spencer Grant/PhotoEdit: p. 23; Lyle Ahern: p. 24; North Wind Picture Archives: p. 25; L.M. Otero/AP/Wide World Photos: p. 28. *Chapter 2* Jonathan Nourok/PhotoEdit: p. 42; Mark Richards/PhotoEdit: p. 43; Courtesy of the Carroll Center: p. 45; Steven Rubin/The Image Works: p. 48; Courtesy of Kathy Buckley: p. 49; Ellen Senisi/The Image Works: pp. 52, 57; PhotoEdit: p. 61; Will Faller: p. 64; James L. Shaffer: p. 69. *Chapter 3* Will Hart: pp. 84, 91, 98; Will Faller: pp. 86, 90, 102; Bob Daemmrich/The Image Works: p. 94; Ellen Senisi/The Image Works: p. 97; David Young-Wolff: p. 106. *Chapter 4* Will Hart: pp. 113, 114, 118, 125, 132; Getty Images, Inc./Photo Disc, Inc.: p. 120; Courtesy of Williams Syndrome Association: p. 127; Will Faller: p. 131; James Shaffer/PhotoEdit: p. 134; Paul Conklin/PhotoEdit: p. 138. *Chapter 5* Will Faller: pp. 150, 159, 176; Brian Smith: p. 154; Will and Deni McIntyre/Photo Researchers, Inc.: p. 156;

(Photo credits are continued on page 591 and are considered an extension of the copyright page.)

Brief Contents

Chapter 1   Exceptionality and Special Education   3

Chapter 2   Current Trends and Issues   39

Chapter 3   Multicultural and Bilingual Aspects of Special Education   79

Chapter 4   Learners with Mental Retardation   109

Chapter 5   Learners with Learning Disabilities   147

Chapter 6   Learners with Attention Deficit Hyperactivity Disorder   185

Chapter 7   Learners with Emotional or Behavioral Disorders   221

Chapter 8   Learners with Communication Disorders   263

Chapter 9   Learners Who Are Deaf or Hard of Hearing   299

Chapter 10   Learners with Blindness or Low Vision   337

Chapter 11   Learners with Low Incidence, Multiple, and Severe
             Disabilities: Autistic Spectrum, Traumatic Brain Injury,
             and Deaf-Blindness   373

Chapter 12   Learners with Physical Disabilities   419

Chapter 13   Learners with Special Gifts and Talents   453

Chapter 14   Parents and Families   485

Contents

Preface   xxiii

Chapter 1   Exceptionality and Special Education   3

Educational Definition of Exceptional Learners   7
Prevalence of Exceptional Learners   10
Definition of Special Education   13
Providing Special Education   13
Teachers' Roles   18
  Relationship Between General and Special Education   18
  Expectations for All Educators   19
  Expectations for Special Educators   22
Origins of Special Education   23
  People and Ideas   23
  Growth of the Discipline   25
  Professional and Parent Organizations   25
  Legislation   26
Trends in Legislation and Litigation   26
  Trends in Legislation   26
  Relationship of Litigation to Legislation   28
  Trends in Litigation   28
  The Intent of Legislation: An Individualized Educational Program   30
A Perspective on the Progress of Special Education   34
Summary   36

Chapter 2   Current Trends and Issues   39

Integration into the Larger Society   40
  *Philosophical and Historical Roots: Normalization, Deinstitutionalization,
  and Full Inclusion*   40
  Deinstitutionalization   42
  Self-Determination   43
  Full Inclusion   44

Current Trends 44

Mainstreaming Practices 56

Continuing Issues 58

Participation in General Assessments of Progress **59**

Current Trends 59

Continuing Issues 61

Access to New Technologies **62**

Current Trends 63

Continuing Issues 63

Early Intervention **63**

Types of Programs 65

Current Trends 66

Continuing Issues 67

Transition to Adulthood **68**

Federal Initiatives 68

Current Trends 69

Continuing Issues 72

Discipline of Students with Disabilities **72**

Current Trends 73

Continuing Issues 74

Some Concluding Thoughts Regarding Trends and Issues **75**

Summary **75**

Chapter 3   Multicultural and Bilingual Aspects of Special Education   79

Education and Cultural Diversity: Concepts for Special Education **85**

Implementing Multicultural and Bilingual Special Education **90**

Assessment 93

Instruction 95

Socialization 103

Summary **107**

Chapter 4   Learners with Mental Retardation   109

Definition **112**

The AAMR Definition 112

The AAMR Classification Scheme 113

Criticisms of the AAMR Classification Scheme 114

Prevalence **114**

Causes **115**

Prenatal Causes *115*

Perinatal Causes *120*

Postnatal Causes *121*

Assessment **123**

Intelligence Tests *123*

Adaptive Skills *124*

Psychological and Behavioral Characteristics **124**

Linking Genetic Syndromes to Particular Behavioral Phenotypes *125*

Educational Considerations **126**

Inclusion and Useful Skills *126*

Self-Determination *127*

Instructional Methods *131*

Service Delivery Models *134*

Early Intervention **136**

Early Childhood Programs Designed for Prevention *137*

Early Childhood Programs Designed to Further Development *138*

Transition to Adulthood **138**

Community Adjustment *139*

Employment *141*

Prospects for the Future *143*

Summary **143**

Chapter 5   Learners with Learning Disabilities   147

Definition **148**

Factors to Consider in Definitions of Learning Disabilities *150*

The Federal Definition *152*

The National Joint Committee for Learning Disabilities (NJCLD) Definition *153*

Similarities and Differences in the Federal and NJCLD Definitions *154*

Toward a New or Revised Definition of Learning Disabilities? *154*

Prevalence **155**

Causes **155**

Genetic Factors *157*

Teratogenic Factors *158*

Medical Factors *158*

Assessment **158**

Standardized Achievement Assessment *158*

Formative Assessment *159*

Informal Assessment *161*

Authentic Assessment *161*

Psychological and Behavioral Characteristics **161**

Interindividual Variation	*162*
Intraindividual Variation	*162*
Academic Achievement Problems	*162*
Perceptual, Perceptual-Motor, and General Coordination Problems	*164*
Disorders of Attention and Hyperactivity	*165*
Memory, Cognitive, and Metacognitive Problems	*165*
Social-Emotional Problems	*166*
Motivational Problems	*167*
The Child with Learning Disabilities as an Inactive Learner with Strategy Deficits	*167*
Educational Considerations	**169**
Cognitive Training	*169*
Direct Instruction	*173*
Best Practices in Teaching Students with Learning Disabilities	*173*
Service Delivery Models	*175*
Early Intervention	**176**
Transition to Adulthood	**177**
Factors Related to Successful Transition	*179*
Secondary Programming	*180*
Postsecondary Programming	*181*
Summary	**182**

Chapter 6 Learners with Attention Deficit Hyperactivity Disorder 185

Brief History	**186**
Still's Children with "Defective Moral Control"	*186*
Goldstein's Brain-Injured Soldiers of World War I	*188*
The Strauss Syndrome	*188*
Cruickshank's Work	*188*
Minimal Brain Injury and Hyperactive Child Syndrome	*189*
Definition	**189**
Prevalence	**189**
Assessment	**192**
Causes	**193**
Areas of the Brain Affected: Frontal Lobes, Basal Ganglia, and Cerebellum	*193*
Neurotransmitter Involved: Dopamine	*195*
Hereditary Factors	*195*
Toxins and Medical Factors	*195*
Psychological and Behavioral Characteristics	**196**
Barkley's Model of ADHD	*196*
Adaptive Skills	*198*

Problems Socializing with Peers	*198*
Coexisting Conditions	*199*
Educational Considerations	**200**
Classroom Structure and Teacher Direction	*201*
Functional Assessment and Contingency-Based Self-Management	*204*
Service Delivery Models	*207*
Medication Considerations	**207**
Opposition to Ritalin	*207*
The Research Evidence	*208*
Cautions Regarding Ritalin	*212*
Early Intervention	**213**
Transition to Adulthood	**214**
Diagnosis in Adulthood	*214*
Adult Outcomes	*216*
Importance of Coaching	*216*
Summary	**218**

Chapter 7   Learners with Emotional or Behavioral Disorders   221

Terminology	**224**
Definition	**225**
Definitional Problems	*225*
Current Definitions	*225*
Classification	**228**
Prevalence	**229**
Causes	**230**
Biological Factors	*231*
Family Factors	*232*
School Factors	*234*
Cultural Factors	*235*
Identification	**236**
Psychological and Behavioral Characteristics	**237**
Intelligence and Achievement	*238*
Social and Emotional Characteristics	*238*
Educational Considerations	**245**
Contrasting Conceptual Models	*245*
Balancing Behavioral Control with Academic and Social Learning	*250*
Importance of Integrated Services	*251*
Strategies That Work	*251*
Service Delivery Models	*252*
Instructional Considerations	*253*

Special Disciplinary Considerations   *254*

Functional Behavioral Assessment and Positive Behavioral Supports   *255*

Early Intervention   **256**

Transition to Adulthood   **259**

Summary   **260**

Chapter 8   Learners with Communication Disorders   263

Definitions   **264**

Prevalence   **266**

Language Development and Language Disorders   **267**

Classification of Language Disorders   *270*

Strategies for Assessment and Intervention   *273*

Delayed Language Development   *275*

Language Disorders Associated with Emotional and Behavioral Disorders   *276*

Educational Considerations   **277**

Communication Variations   **283**

Speech Disorders   **288**

Voice Disorders   *288*

Articulation Disorders   *289*

Fluency Disorders   *290*

Speech Disorders Associated with Neurological Damage   *291*

Early Intervention   **291**

Transition to Adulthood   **294**

Summary   **296**

Chapter 9   Learners Who Are Deaf or Hard of Hearing   299

Definition and Classification   **300**

Prevalence   **303**

Anatomy and Physiology of the Ear   **303**

The Outer Ear   *303*

The Middle Ear   *304*

The Inner Ear   *304*

Measurement of Hearing Ability   **305**

Screening Tests   *305*

Pure-Tone Audiometry   *305*

Speech Audiometry   *305*

Tests for Young and Hard-to-Test Children   *306*

Causes   **306**

Conductive, Sensorineural, and Mixed Hearing Loss	306
Hearing Loss and the Outer Ear	307
Hearing Loss and the Middle Ear	307
Hearing Loss and the Inner Ear	307
Psychological and Behavioral Characteristics	**308**
English Language and Speech Development	308
Intellectual Ability	308
Academic Achievement	309
Social Adjustment	310
Educational Considerations	**316**
Oral Approach: Auditory-Verbal Approach and Speechreading	319
Total Communication	320
The Bicultural-Bilingual Approach	323
Service Delivery Models	324
Technological Advances	326
Early Intervention	**330**
Transition to Adulthood	**331**
Postsecondary Education	332
Family Issues	333
Summary	**334**

Chapter 10   Learners with Blindness or Low Vision   337

Definition and Classification	**340**
Legal Definition	340
Educational Definition	341
Prevalence	**341**
Anatomy and Physiology of the Eye	**341**
Measurement of Visual Ability	**342**
Causes	**343**
Psychological and Behavioral Characteristics	**346**
Language Development	346
Intellectual Ability	346
Orientation and Mobility	347
Academic Achievement	348
Social Adjustment	348
Stereotypic Behaviors	351
Educational Considerations	**352**
Braille	352
Use of Remaining Sight	356
Listening Skills	357
Orientation and Mobility (O & M) Training	357

Technological Aids	*360*
Educational Placement Models	**364**
Early Intervention	**365**
Transition to Adulthood	**367**
Independent Living	*367*
Employment	*369*
Summary	**370**

Chapter 11   Learners with Low Incidence, Multiple, and Severe Disabilities: Autistic Spectrum, Traumatic Brain Injury and Deaf-Blindness   373

Autism and Related Disorders—Autistic Spectrum Disorder	374
Definitions and Characteristics	**376**
Impaired Social Responsiveness	*378*
Impaired Communication	*378*
Stereotyped and Ritualistic Behavior	*378*
Preoccupation with Objects and Restricted Range of Interests	*378*
Range of Severity of Symptoms	*378*
Asperger Syndrome (AS)	*379*
Internal States	*379*
Prevalence	**380**
Causes	**380**
Educational Considerations	**382**
Traumatic Brain Injury (TBI)	384
Definition and Characteristics	**384**
Prevalence	**386**
Causes	**386**
Educational Considerations	**387**
Language Disorders	*388*
Social and Emotional Problems	*389*
Deaf-Blindness	391
Definition	**392**
Prevalence	**393**
Causes	**393**
Genetic/Chromosomal Syndromes	*393*
Prenatal Conditions	*394*
Postnatal Conditions	*394*
Psychological and Behavioral Characteristics	**396**

Problems Accessing Information   396
Problems Communicating   396
Problems Navigating the Environment   397
Educational Considerations   **397**
The Importance of Direct Teaching   397
The Importance of Structured Routines   397
Communication   398
Orientation and Mobility   399
Special Considerations for Students with Usher Syndrome   401

Considerations for All Low Incidence, Multiple, and Severe Disabilities   401
Augmentative and Alternative Communication   **402**
Behavior Problems   **406**
Self-Stimulation   406
Self-Injury   407
Tantrums   407
Aggression Toward Others   407
Lack of Daily Living Skills   407
Functional Behavioral Assessment and Positive Behavioral Support   407
Early Intervention   **410**
Research-or Value-Based Practices   410
Family-Centered Practices   411
Multicultural Perspective   411
Cross-Disciplinary Collaboration   411
Developmentally and Chronologically Age-Appropriate Practices   412
Principle of Normalization   412
Transition to Adulthood   **413**
Changing Philosophy   413
Vocational Programming   414
Community and Domestic Living Skills   415
Summary   **415**

Chapter 12   Learners with Physical Disabilities   419

Definition and Classification   **420**
Prevalence and Need   **422**
Neuromotor Impairments   **422**
Cerebral Palsy   423
Seizure Disorder (Epilepsy)   425
Spina Bifida and Other Spinal Cord Injuries   427
Orthopedic and Musculoskeletal Disorders   **428**
Other Conditions Affecting Health or Physical Ability   **428**
Prevention of Physical Disabilities   **431**

Psychological and Behavioral Characteristics — **432**

Academic Achievement — *432*

Personality Characteristics — *432*

Prosthetics, Orthotics, and Adaptive Devices for Daily Living — **435**

Educational Considerations — **437**

Individualized Planning — *439*

Educational Placement — *439*

Educational Goals and Curricula — *441*

Links with Other Disciplines — *444*

Early Intervention — **445**

Transition to Adulthood — **446**

Choosing a Career — *447*

Sociosexuality — *448*

Summary — **449**

Chapter 13   Learners with Special Gifts and Talents   453

Definition — **454**

Prevalence — **461**

Origins of Giftedness — **461**

Identification of Giftedness — **463**

Psychological and Behavioral Characteristics — **463**

Cultural Values Regarding Student with Special Gifts or Talents and Their Education — **465**

Neglected Groups of Students with Special Gifts or Talents — **468**

Underachievers with Special Gifts or Talents — *468*

Students with Special Gifts from Cultural- and Ethnic-Minority Groups — *468*

Students with Disabilities and Special Gifts or Talents — *470*

Females with Special Gifts or Talents — *473*

Educational Considerations — **474**

Acceleration — *479*

Enrichment — *479*

Early Intervention — **479**

Transition to Adulthood — **481**

Summary — **482**

Chapter 14   Parents and Families   485

Professionals' Changing Views of Parents — **486**

The Effects of a Child with a Disability on the Family — **488**

Parental Reactions — *489*

Contents   XV

Sibling Reactions   493
Family Involvement in Treatment and Education   **494**
Family Systems Theory   495
Social Support for Families   501
Communication Between Parents and Professionals   502
In Conclusion   **508**
Summary   **510**

Glossary   513

References   525

Name Index   565

Subject Index   575

Special Features

General Interest

CHAPTER 1

A Focus on Abilities: Erik Weihenmayer and Blair Smith · 8

Where Needs Are Great, the Needs Go Untended: Failings of Special Ed System Extract a High Price · 10

An IEP for Alice: What Can Happen When Special Education Works · 11

What Should I Do Before I Make a Referral? · 21

Major Provisions of IDEA · 29

CHAPTER 2

Cutting Through Prejudicial Barriers with Humor · 46

Laughing Out Loud: Turning a Deaf Ear to Comedy · 49

Parents' Thoughts on Inclusion of Their Children with Severe Disabilities · 53

Case Study: Sarah · 70

CHAPTER 3

The Color of Water: School · 83

In Living Black and White · 84

Plan to Teach in Spanish Upsets Some in Arlington · 89

It's OK to Be Different · 100

CHAPTER 4

The Humane Genome Project: Ethical Issues Pertaining to Mental Retardation · 116

Down Syndrome and Alzheimer's Disease · 117

The Nature-Nurture Controversy · 122

Williams Syndrome: An Inspiration for Some Pixie Legends? · 127

AAMR Policy Statement on Self-Determination · 130

CHAPTER 5

Reauthorization of IDEA: Implications for the Definition and Identification Procedures for Learning Disabilities · 153

Neuroimaging and Reading Disabilities: Major Findings · 157

Ms. Lopez Conducts an Error Analysis   160

Dyslexia: Same Brains, Different Language   163

CHAPTER 6

How Many Students with ADHD Are Served in Special Education?   191

Use of Ritalin Leads to Lawsuits   210

Is Medication Effective for Children with ADHD?   211

Ritalin Sold in Playgrounds   212

An Adult with ADHD: Ann's Story   214

CHAPTER 7

Personal Reflection: Family Factors   233

CHAPTER 8

Definitions of the American Speech-Language-Hearing Association   268

Disorders of the Five Subsystems of Language   272

The Speech-Language Pathologist   289

Identifying Possible Language-Related Problems   295

CHAPTER 9

The National Theatre of the Deaf   311

Making Peace with a Threat to "Deaf Culture"   314

American Sign Language as a True Language   322

Tips for Working with Sign Language Interpreters   332

CHAPTER 10

Social Interaction with People Who Are Blind: Points of Etiquette   340

Signs of Possible Eye Troubles in Children   343

Captain Charles Barbier de la Serre and Louis Braille   354

Stephen Kuusisto and His Guide Dog, Corky   359

CHAPTER 11

TBI: Often a Hidden Disability   386

The Genetics of Usher Syndrome and Its Geographic Distribution   395

Laura Bridgman and Her Teacher, Samuel Gridley Howe   398

Braille Is Not Just for People Who Are Already Blind   402

Simplified Sign Language   403

Life with Cerebral Palsy   404

CHAPTER 12

First Aid for Epileptic Seizures   426

The Importance of Family and School in Coping with Asthma   430

Overcoming a Health Challenge   434

Accommodations and Self-Advocacy in the Classroom   439

Weighing the Issue of Placement: One Student's Perspective   442

CHAPTER 13

Prodigies   466

Disabilities Do Not Preclude Giftedness   472

CHAPTER 14

Fighting Prejudice   496

Facilitating Involvement of Culturally and/or Linguistically Diverse Families   498

Homework: Tips for Teachers   505

Advocacy in Action: You Can Advocate for Your Child   509

Making It Work

Collaboration and Co-Teaching for Students with Disabilities   26

Collaboration and Co-Teaching for Students with Mental Retardation   136

Collaboration and Co-Teaching for Students with Learning Disabilities   176

Collaboration and Co-Teaching for Students with ADHD   208

Collaboration and Co-Teaching for Students with Emotional/Behavioral Disorders   250

Collaboration and Co-Teaching with Speech-Language Pathologists: 284

Collaboration and Co-Teaching for Students Who Are Deaf or Hard of Hearing   324

Collaboration and Co-Teaching for Students with Blindness or Low Vision   364

Collaboration and Co-Teaching for Students with Severe and Profound Disabilities   412

Collaboration and Co-Teaching for Students with Physical Disabilities   444

Collaboration and Co-Teaching for Students with Special Gifts and Talents   474

Misconceptions About

Exceptional Learners   5

Learners with Disabilities   41

Multicultural and Bilingual Aspects of Special Education   81

Learners with Mental Retardation   111

Learners with Learning Disabilities   149

Learners with Attention Deficit Hyperactivity Disorder   187

Learners with Emotional or Behavioral Disorders   223

Learners with Communication Disorders   265

Learners Who Are Deaf or Hard of Hearing   301

Learners with Blindness or Low Vision   339

Learners with Low Incidence, Multiple, and Severe Disabilities   375

Learners with Physical Disabilities   421

Learners with Special Gifts or Talents   455

Persons and Families of Persons with Disabilities   487

Responsive Instruction

MEETING THE NEEDS OF STUDENTS WITH MENTAL RETARDATION

Strategies for Effective Instruction in Mathematics   133

Classwide Peer-Tutoring   135

Community-Based Instruction: Shopping for Groceries   140

MEETING THE NEEDS OF STUDENTS WITH LEARNING DISABILITIES

Mnemonics   170

Direct Instruction   174

PALS—Peer-Assisted Learning Strategies   178

MEETING THE NEEDS OF STUDENTS WITH ATTENTION DEFICIT HYPERACTIVITY DISORDER

Task Switching: Preparing Students with ADHD for Change   197

Planning for Students with ADHD in the General Education Classroom   202

The Benefits of Self-Monitoring and Group Contingency   206

MEETING THE NEEDS OF STUDENTS WITH EMOTIONAL OR BEHAVIORAL DISORDERS

Approaches to Reducing Bullying in Schools   239

Strategies for Students with Oppositional Defiant Disorder   240

Strategies for Reducing Cursing   242

MEETING THE NEEDS OF STUDENTS WITH COMMUNICATION DISORDERS

Working with the Speech-Language Pathologist   280

Collaboration in an Inner-City Classroom   286

MEETING THE NEEDS OF STUDENTS WHO ARE DEAF OR HARD OF HEARING

Advances in Instructional Practices   318

Assistive Technology   327

MEETING THE NEEDS OF STUDENTS WITH BLINDNESS OR LOW VISION

Instructional Adaptations   353

Strategies for Working with Young Children   366

MEETING THE NEEDS OF STUDENTS WITH AUTISTIC SPECTRUM DISORDERS

Instructional Strategies   381

MEETING THE NEEDS OF STUDENTS WITH MULTIPLE OR SEVERE DISABILITIES

The Importance of Establishing Structured Routines   400

Positive Behavioral Support   409

MEETING THE NEEDS OF STUDENTS WITH PHYSICAL DISABILITIES

Adapted Physical Education   438

Integrating Physical and Occupational Therapy in General Education Settings   443

MEETING THE NEEDS OF STUDENTS WITH SPECIAL GIFTS OR TALENTS

Strategies for the Indentification and Instruction of Twice Exceptional Students 471

Acceleration   478

Success Stories: Special Educators at Work

Molly Berry, Lisa Douville, and Mike Morcom   128

Eliot Danner, Nancy Cushen White, and Mia Callahan Russell   168

Josh Bishop and Jane Warner   200

Christina Issacs and Teresa Zutter   246

Ryan McGarr and Nancy Maher-Maxwell   278

Najia Elyoumni-Pinedo and Wanda Frankel   316

Patrick Pugh and Ricki Curry   350

David Womack   390

Danielle Durrance and Leigh-Anne Williams   440

Noshua Watson and Celeste Rhodes   476

Preface

*E*xceptional Learners: Introduction to Special Education, Ninth Edition is a general introduction to the characteristics of exceptional learners and their education. (*Exceptional* is the term that traditionally has been used to refer to persons with disabilities as well as to those who are gifted.) This book emphasizes classroom practices as well as the psychological, sociological, and medical aspects of disabilities and giftedness.

We have written this text with two primary audiences in mind: those individuals who are preparing to be special educators and those who are preparing to be general educators. Given the current movement toward including students with disabilities in general education classrooms, general educators must be prepared to understand this special student population and be ready to work with special educators to provide appropriate educational programming for these students. This book also is appropriate for professionals in other fields who work with exceptional learners (e.g., speech-language pathologists, audiologists, physical therapists, occupational therapists, adapted physical educators, counselors, and school psychologists).

In Chapter 1, we begin with an overview of exceptionality and special education, including definitions, basic legal requirements, and the history and development of the field. In Chapter 2, we discuss major current issues and trends, such as inclusion, early childhood programming, transition to adulthood programming, inclusion of students with disabilities in general assessments of progress, discipline of students with disabilities, and access of persons with disabilities to new technologies. In Chapter 3, we address multicultural and bilingual aspects of special education. In the next ten chapters we examine each of the major categories of exceptionality—4: mental retardation; 5: learning disabilities; 6: attention deficit hyperactivity disorder; 7: emotional or behavioral disorders; 8: communication disorders; 9: deaf or hard of hearing; 10: blindness or low vision; 11: low incidence, multiple, and severe disabilities: autistic spectrum, traumatic brain injury, and deaf-blindness; 12: physical disabilities; and 13: special gifts and talents. Finally, in Chapter 14, we consider the significant issues pertaining to parents and families of persons with disabilities.

We believe that we have written a text that reaches the heart as well as the mind. It is our conviction that professionals working with exceptional learners need to develop not only a solid base of knowledge but also a healthy attitude toward their work and the people whom they serve. Professionals must constantly challenge themselves to learn more theory, research, and practice in special education and develop an ever more sensitive understanding of exceptional learners and their families.

Major Changes for This Edition

In revising this text over the years, we have learned that there is a fine line between making too many versus too few changes. As teachers, we recognize that change simply for the sake of change in a text can be distracting and end up causing instructors unnecessary work. Therefore, we have tried hard to strike the right balance between including new information and features that truly add to the text's currency and clarity while maintaining those features that our readers tell us they have liked about previous editions.

In making revisions, we have also been attentive to the overall length of the text. Again, as teachers, we know the value of a concisely written text. Instructors and students consistently tell us they appreciate our text's being many pages shorter than others without sacrificing important content. Thus, we are pleased that through careful consolidation of this revision we were able to incorporate a new chapter plus many important content updates throughout the text while maintaining the same length as the previous edition.

NEW CHAPTER—LOW INCIDENCE, MULTIPLE, AND SEVERE DISABILITIES: AUTISTIC SPECTRUM, TRAUMATIC BRAIN INJURY, AND DEAF-BLINDNESS

In previous editions, we covered these low incidence disabilities in multiple chapters. In this edition for the sake of clarity, we have combined them into one chapter—Chapter 11. Although autistic spectrum disorders and TBI may range from mild to severe disabilities, they are low incidence disabilities and always entail multiple problems. Neither normal development nor disabilities are often neatly packaged with clear lines of demarcation from all other conditions. However, we see the logic and necessity of clustering certain disabilities under categorical labels for purposes of discussion. To us, it makes sense to have a chapter devoted to the types of disabilities we discuss in Chapter 11. We hope you enjoy reading this chapter as much as we enjoyed writing it.

NEW FEATURE—RESPONSIVE INSTRUCTION: MEETING THE NEEDS OF STUDENTS

It is our firm belief that most students with disabilities require intensive instruction in order to maximize their potential. Sprinkled throughout the 10 categorical chapters (4–13) are 25 boxes that feature a variety of research-based strategies for teaching students with disabilities. Although they cannot possibly take the place of a full-blown course and text in teaching methods, we think these strategies offer practical suggestions for begin-

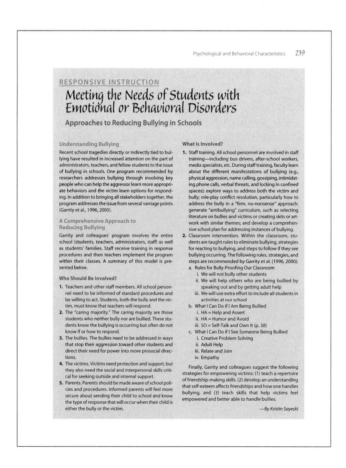

ning to meet the needs of exceptional learners through intensive instruction. In keeping with this era of accountability, the author of these boxes, Dr. Kristin Sayeski of the University of Virginia, has stressed teaching practices having a sound research base.

NEW FEATURE—MAKING IT WORK: COLLABORATION AND CO-TEACHING

Each of the categorical chapters (4–13) includes a feature, authored by Dr. Margaret Weiss of the University of North Carolina, devoted to co-teaching and collaboration between special and general education teachers. The first section of each box includes information about knowledge and skills special educators should possess as they enter the field, as identified by the Council for Exceptional Children (CEC) in its *Performance-Based Professional Standards* (2001). We believe it is important for all teachers to understand what expertise special educators can contribute to collaborative, general education classrooms. The second section contains examples of research-based instructional practices that teachers can use when collaborating or descriptions of successful collaborations in real classrooms. Each box contains specifics about how to get more information about the strategy or classroom described.

MAKING IT WORK
Collaboration and Co-teaching for Students with Visual Impairments

"I don't have time to learn braille!"

What Does It Mean to Be a Teacher of Students with Visual Impairments?

Collaboration for students with visual impairments often takes the form of working with itinerant special education teachers. This can be frustrating for general educators in that they are left "on their own" when the special educator is at another building. Therefore, in planning for collaboration, it is important that the general educator and itinerant teacher have time to plan for student needs that may arise at any time. Working with the general educator to plan for instruction, the teacher of students with visual impairments can offer expertise in:

1. Designing multisensory learning environments that encourage active participation in group and individual activities.
2. Creating learning environments that encourage self-advocacy and independence.

3. Teaching individuals with visual impairments to use thinking, problem-solving, and other cognitive strategies.
4. Preparing individuals with visual impairments to respond constructively to societal attitudes and actions.
5. Obtaining and organizing special materials (including technologies) to implement instructional goals. (Council for Exceptional Children, 2001)

Successful Strategies for Co-teaching

Ricki Curry (an itinerant teacher) and Jenny Garrett (a fourth-grade teacher) talk about how they collaborated to fully include Dennis, a student with a severe visual impairment.

Jenny: My fourth-grade class consisted of 23 nine- and ten-year-old children, including two children with learning disabilities, one with severe behavior disorders, and Den-

nis. They began the year reading anywhere from a first-to a sixth-grade level.

Ricki: Although he has some usable vision, Dennis can see no details from a distance of more than about two feet and uses large-print texts for reading.

Jenny: Dennis has some difficulty making friends because of his immaturity, his compulsive talking, and his inability to listen. On the other hand, Dennis has a good sense of humor and is quick with language. Dennis was in my class all day long for every academic subject. Ricki worked with him during language arts block, teaching braille. She would come to school during the last half of my planning period, which gave us a daily opportunity to discuss assignments, homework, curricular adaptations, equipment, and the like. Homework was an enormous issue. Ricki helped him set up a notebook with a homework contract enclosed and a special highlighter, which he used to mark off completed assignments. He had to write down the assignments himself, remember to take the notebook home, complete the assignments, get a parent's signature, and get it back to school. The hardest part of working with Dennis was the start-up period. I had to get to know him, his visual capabilities, his strengths and weaknesses, his coping strategies. I began

adapting my teaching style, using an easel rather than the blackboard so that he could scoot up to it. I had to decide how hard to push, what to expect from his parents, and what to demand from Dennis.

Ricki: I often found myself overwhelmed by the number of things that Jenny and/or Dennis needed help with in the short time that I was in the building. And so many things seemed to go wrong in the time between when I left one day and arrived again the next day! Although I was frustrated by the limitations imposed by time constraints, the beauty of the inclusion model was that I was very aware of the true gestalt of Dennis's program and knew exactly what he was involved in all the time. Had I not had an almost daily view of Dennis's classroom performance, I might not have believed how hard it was to integrate this very bright, verbal, personable child into Jenny's class.

Jenny: Collaboration works best when there is a match of personalities as well as energy, enthusiasm for teaching, and professionalism.

More information about visual impairments and their impact on the classroom can be found at the Web site of the Division on Visual Impairments of the Council for Exceptional Children, www.ed.arizona.edu/dvi/welcome.htm.

A particular problem for those who are blind is their ability to access the wealth of information that is now available via computers and the World Wide Web. As computers have moved more and more toward graphic displays of information on the screen, users with visual impairments have become concerned about how this affects their access to that information. For example, a graphics-based interface requires the user to move a mouse to a relatively precise position on the screen in order to click on the desired function. There are screen-reading programs available that allow those who are visually impaired to access information nonvisually, but cooperation is required from Web site developers to ensure that their Web sites are compatible with these programs (Wunder, 2000). Some progress has been made on this front. The National Federation of the Blind filed a lawsuit against America Online (AOL) and then withdrew it, in July of 2000, after reaching an agreement that AOL would make its service and content accessible to those who are blind.

Educational Placement Models

Itinerant teacher services. Services for students who are visually impaired in which the special education teacher visits several different schools to work with students and their general education teachers; the students attend their local schools and remain in general education classrooms.

The four major educational placements for students with visual impairment, from most to least segregated, are (1) residential school, (2) special class, (3) resource room, and (4) regular class with itinerant teacher help. In the early 1900s virtually all children who were blind were educated in residential institutions. Today, however, **itinerant teacher services,** wherein a vision teacher visits several different schools to work with students and their general education classrooms, is the most popular placement for students with visual impairment. The fact is, there are so few students with visual impairment that most schools find it difficult to provide services through special classes or resource rooms.

Residential placement, however, is still a relatively popular placement model compared to other areas of disability. For example, about 7 percent of students with vision loss between the ages of six and twenty-one years are placed in a residential institution,

whereas only about .5 percent of students with mental retardation are so placed. The advantage of residential placement is that services can be concentrated to this relatively low-incidence population. In the past, most children who were blind attended institutions for several years; today some may attend on a short-term basis (e.g., one to four years). The prevailing philosophy of integrating children with visual impairments with the sighted is also reflected in the fact that many residential facilities have established cooperative arrangements with local public schools wherein the staff of the residential facility usually concentrates on training for independent living skills such as mobility, personal grooming, and home management, while local school personnel emphasize academics.

Early Intervention

For many years psychologists and educators believed that the sighted infant was almost totally lacking in visual abilities during the first half-year or so of life. We now know that the young sighted infant is able to take in a great deal of information through the visual system. This fact makes it easy to understand why intensive intervention should begin as early as possible to help the infant with visual impairment begin to explore the environment. As we noted earlier, many infants who are blind lag behind their peers in motor development. Consequently, O & M training should be a critical component of preschool programming.

Although many advocate that preschoolers with visual impairments should be educated in inclusive settings with sighted children, it is critical that teachers facilitate interactions between the children. We know from research that merely placing preschoolers who are visually impaired with sighted preschoolers does not lead to their interacting with one another (McGaha & Farran, 2001).

Most authorities agree that it is extremely important to involve parents of infants with visual impairment in early intervention efforts. Parents can become actively involved in

---

Extensive Revisions and Updates

In addition to the new chapter on low incidence, multiple, and severe disabilities, we have made extensive revisions to virtually every aspect of the remaining thirteen chapters. We have included over 400 new references bearing a copyright date from 2000 and beyond. Approximately 20 percent of the main text in these thirteen chapters is new. These chapters also now include 63 new glossary terms, 9 new tables, and 14 new figures.

EXPANDED COVERAGE OF MAJOR ISSUES

This edition includes material in Chapter 1 on IDEA 1997, the development of IEPs, and the March '99 federal regulations related to IDEA '97. The Amendments to IDEA in 1997 were significant, and we bring students up to date on the new features of federal law and IEP requirements. In Chapter 2, we have added discussions of self-determination and person-centered planning to our coverage of integration. Consistent with trends toward more collaborative teaching, we have added a feature in Chapter 2 on teachers working together, setting up the issue of collaborative teaching for the subsequent categorical chapters. We also revised our discussion of the inclusion of students with disabilities in general assessments of educational progress and on the discipline of students with disabilities. IDEA 1997 requires appropriate inclusion of students with disabilities in general assessments of educational progress as part of schools' movement toward setting higher academic standards. This requirement raises many questions for most teachers and prospective teachers, and our revisions address the most common of these. Probably the most controversial and adversarial aspect of IDEA 1997 is the law related to disciplinary action involving students with disabilities. Consequently, we have added discussion of two important issues: functional behavioral assessment and positive behavioral supports. Issues in special education are ever changing, but some controversies and problems will undoubtedly extend well into the new century. As this edition goes to press, IDEA is undergoing yet another reauthorization. Consult the Companion Web site for changes.

CHAPTER-OPENING QUOTES AND ART

Going back to our first edition is the practice of opening each chapter with an excerpt from literature or song. We draw on this quote in the opening paragraphs to begin our discussion of the topics covered in the chapter. Students continue to tell us that they find this use of quotes to be an effective method of grabbing their attention and leading them

Rebecca Bella Rich

The Family, Ink, watercolor on rag paper. 15 × 11 in.

Ms. Rich, who was born in 1960 in Cambridge, Massachusetts, has a dramatic sensibility. Her life, art, and poetry have an extravagent and flamboyant quality. She has produced an autobiographical performance video and a book of interviews with artists who are challenged by disabilities.

CHAPTER

5

Learners with Learning Disabilities

As much as I want to find the perfect words to express what it is like to be dyslexic, I cannot. I can no more make you understand what it is like to be dyslexic than you can make me understand what it is like not to be. I can only guess and imagine. For years, I have looked out, wanting to be normal, to shed the skin that limits me, that holds me back. All the while, others have looked upon me, as well. There were those who have pitied me and those who have just given up on me, those who stood by, supporting me and believing in me, and those who looked at me as if I were an exhibit in a zoo. But, in general, people have shown a desire to understand what dyslexia is and how to teach those afflicted with it. Each side, it seems, longs to understand the other.

LYNN PELKEY
"In the LD Bubble"

into some of the issues contained in the text. Five chapters (mental retardation; learning disabilities; deafness or hard of hearing; physical disabilities; and parents and families) include new chapter-opening quotes.

The chapter opening art is the work of adult artists with disabilities and is supplied by Gateway Arts in Brookline, Massachusetts. Gateway is a vocational art service and workshop of the nonprofit human service agency Vinfen. Adults with developmental and other disabilities attend the program, which has an on-site fine art gallery and craft store. Gateway participants make their careers in art through the facilitation of a staff of artists. Their work is exhibited nationally and abroad. Individuals receive funding from the Massachusetts Department of Mental Retardation, the Massachusetts Department of Mental Health, the Massachusetts Rehabilitation Commission, the Massachusetts Commission for the Blind, and private funding sources.

MISCONCEPTIONS ABOUT EXCEPTIONAL LEARNERS: MYTHS AND FACTS BOXES

We start each chapter with a box that juxtaposes several myths and facts about the subject of the chapter. This popular feature, familiar to longtime users (it dates back to our first edition in 1978) serves as an excellent advance organizer for the material to be covered. We have added seven new myths and facts to the thirteen retained chapters.

SPECIAL TOPICS BOXES

Inserted throughout the text are several types of boxes (see an example on page xxviii, top): some highlight research findings and their applicability to educational practice; some discuss issues facing educators in the field; and some present the human side of having a disability. We have added 32 new boxes.

A Focus on Abilities

Erik Weihenmayer

Erik Weinhenmayer ■

It was at this camp [Khumbu Icefall, elevation 21,300 feet on Mt. Everest] one night in May that Erik Weihenmayer sat in his tent as a lightening storm moved across the mountain face.

"It was amazingly beautiful," recalls Weihenmayer (pronounced WINE-mare), sitting in a downtown hotel suite during a recent visit to Boston.

"Every time the lightening cracked, it would echo off the mountains," he says. "And I would have a view of the way the mountains looked by the echo. I could *feel* the beauty of it." . . .

As most everyone on the planet knows by now, Weihenmayer, 32, became the first blind person to reach the summit of Everest when he accomplished the feat May 25 [2001]. The achievement put the Boston College graduate and former grade-school teacher on top of the media world, including the cover of *Time* magazine.

It also put to rest any lingering doubts that a climber of Weihenmayer's ability—he has summited five of the seven continents' highest peaks, along with the likes of Yosemite's imposing El Capitan—could pull off something that has cost 170 climbers their lives over the past half-century. . . .

Weihenmayer was born with a rare degenerative eye condition known as retinoschisis. His pre-school years were "a two-year nightmare of doctor visits around the country," he writes in his book, as specialists told the Weihenmayers that Erik would be totally blind by his teenage years. . . .

Despite—or maybe because of—his impairment, he grew into a rebellious, even angry, kid. For a long time, he refused to try a cane or to learn Braille. He took up wrestling and became a high-school champion at one of the few sports that allowed him equal footing with sighted athletes. As he would later conquer the world's most challenging mountains, he won his independence gradually, one halting step at a time.

"Only 10 percent of blind people are literate in Braille," Weihenmayer says, looking back on his own period of frustration and denial. "It took me two years to master it, but when I realized I could read Braille, I realized I could do a lot of normal things. I just needed to do them in a different way. Rock climbing was the same deal."[1]

Note: For more details on the climb, see Pierce (2001).

Blair Smith

Blair Smith ■

Blair Smith is different . . . Her legs look like they could snap beneath her at any moment, and she is so short that her perspective barely changes when she rises from her wheelchair.

Still, she always rises.

Smith is among the 20,000 to 50,000 people in the United States with the bone disorder osteogenesis imperfecta (OI). She is also a relentlessly giddy cheerleader at Monticello High School.

There are at least four forms of OI, representing extreme variations in severity from one individual to another. Smith's case falls somewhere in the fairly severe category. OI has rendered her bones soft and brittle, leaving her literally fragile. When she walks she relies on the support of her crutches and leg braces to keep from breaking a leg or two. Her growth was stunted drastically. . . .

As a ninth-grader at Albemarle High School, Smith cheered from the stands like most of the other Patriot students. But for her sophomore year, she moved to brand-new Monticello . . . and joined the junior varsity team for the Mustangs.

And as a junior this past fall, Smith made the varsity squad, serving as a headliner for Monticello's act from September to February. She takes the floor in her wheelchair—Smith's parents had to solicit the aid of [her physical education teacher] to make her use the chair—and participates in the routines in her own way. Stunts are definitely out, but Smith manages to make her indelible mark on the show without the tools of gymnastic display. . . .

"It's been unbelievable," Debbie Smith [Blair's mother] said. "The kids have just been wonderful. They have been wonderful the whole time she has been in school about accepting her for the way she is."

Added Ralph Smith [Blair's father]: "People are always pushing her forward and letting her do things and not putting her in a shell." . . .

She is just another young girl full of life.

That is all. And that makes you want to stand up and cheer.[2]

SOURCES: [1]"Touching the Sky" by Joseph P. Kahn. *Boston Globe*, June 27, 2001, pp. F1, F5. Reprinted with permission.

[2]"Something to Cheer About" by Tom Gresham, *The Daily Progress*, May 7, 2000, pp. E1, E6, Charlottesville, VA. Reprinted with permission.

the child's development. The box on page 10 describes two such cases. In spite of federal laws requiring appropriate education and the existence of a special education system, Willie and Anthony received no special education at all or extremely poor special education services. The consequences of the neglect of their need for special education are profoundly negative. Although early identification and intervention hold the promise of preventing many disabilities from becoming worse, preventive action is often not taken (Kauffman, 1999b).

When special education works as it should, a student's disability is identified early and effective special education is provided in the least restrictive environment. The student's parents are involved in the decision about how to address the student's needs, and the outcome of special education is the student's improved achievement and behavior. Consider the case of Alice, presented in the box on page 11.

Students with exceptionalities are an extraordinarily diverse group compared to the general population, and relatively few generalizations apply to all exceptional individuals. Their exceptionalities may involve sensory, physical, cognitive, emotional, or communication abilities or any combination of these. Furthermore, exceptionalities may vary greatly in cause, degree, and effect on educational progress, and the effects may vary greatly depending on the individual's age, sex, and life circumstances. Any individual we might present as an example of our definition is likely to be representative of exceptional learners in some respects but unrepresentative in others.

The typical student who receives special education has no immediately obvious disability. He—more than half of the students served by special education are males—is in elementary or middle school and has persistent problems in learning and behaving appropriately in school. His problems are primarily academic and social or behavioral. These difficulties are not apparent to many teachers until they have worked with the student for a period of weeks or months. His problems persist despite teachers' efforts to meet his needs in the regular school program in which most students succeed. He is most likely to be described as having a learning disability or to be designated by an even broader label

SUCCESS STORIES: SPECIAL EDUCATORS AT WORK

Special educators work in a variety of settings, ranging from general education classrooms to residential institutions. Although their main function involves teaching, these professionals also engage in a variety of roles, such as counseling, collaborating, consulting, and

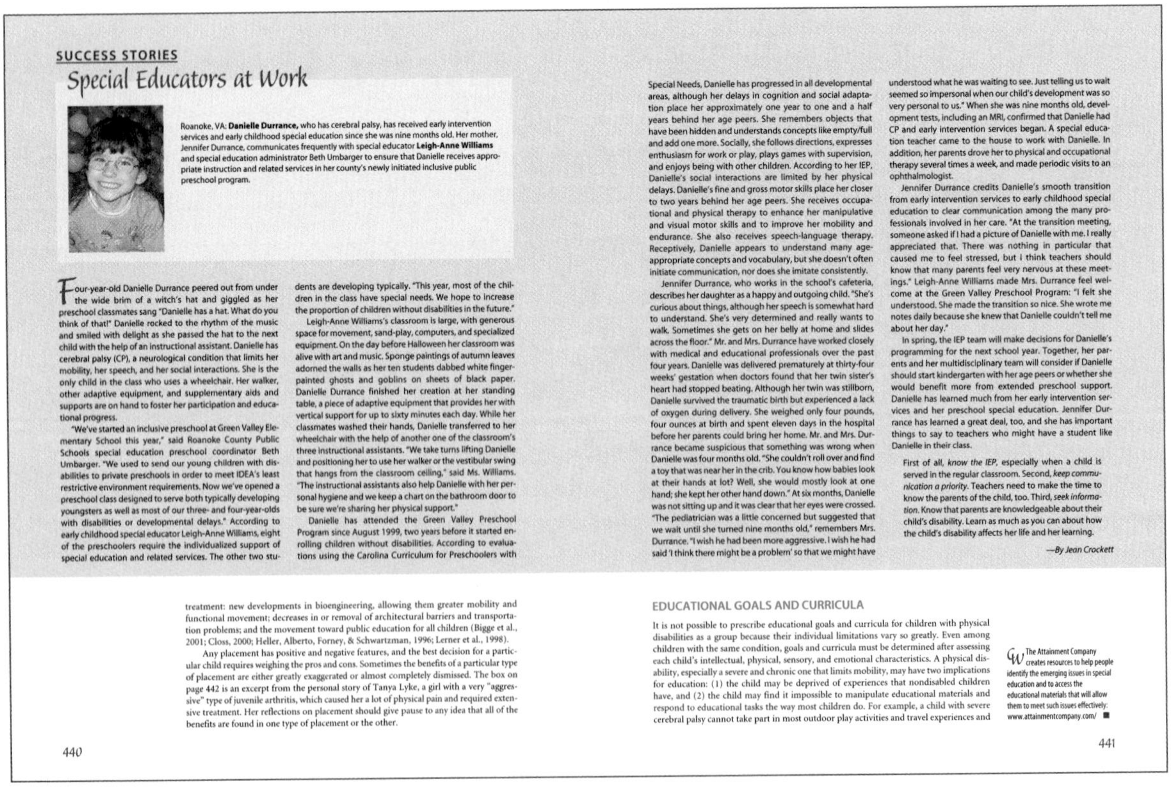
SUCCESS STORIES

Special Educators at Work

Roanoke, VA: **Danielle Durrance,** who has cerebral palsy, has received early intervention services and early childhood special education since she was nine months old. Her mother, Jennifer Durrance, communicates frequently with special educator **Leigh-Anne Williams** and special education administrator Beth Umbarger to ensure that Danielle receives appropriate instruction and related services in her county's newly initiated inclusive public preschool program.

Four-year-old Danielle Durrance peered out from under the wide brim of a witch's hat and giggled as her preschool classmates sang "Danielle has a hat. What do you think of that!" Danielle rocked to the rhythm of the music and smiled with delight as she passed the hat to the next child with the help of an instructional assistant. Danielle has cerebral palsy (CP), a neurological condition that limits her mobility, her speech, and her social interactions. She is the only child in the class who uses a wheelchair. Her walker, other adaptive equipment, and supplementary aids and supports are on hand to foster her participation and educational progress.

"We've started an inclusive preschool at Green Valley Elementary School this year," said Roanoke County Public Schools special education preschool coordinator Beth Umbarger. "We used to send our young children with disabilities to private preschools in order to meet IDEA's least restrictive environment requirements. Now we've opened a preschool class designed to serve both typically developing youngsters as well as most of our three- and four-year-olds with disabilities or developmental delays." According to early childhood special educator Leigh-Anne Williams, eight of the preschoolers require the individualized support of special education and related services. The other two students are developing typically. "This year, most of the children in the class have special needs. We hope to increase the proportion of children without disabilities in the future."

Leigh-Anne Williams's classroom is large, with generous space for movement, sand-play, computers, and specialized equipment. On the day before Halloween her classroom was alive with art and music. Sponge paintings of autumn leaves adorned the walls as her ten students dabbed white finger-painted ghosts and goblins on sheets of black paper. Danielle Durrance finished her creation at her standing table, a piece of adaptive equipment that provides her with vertical support for up to sixty minutes each day. While her classmates washed their hands, Danielle transferred to her wheelchair with the help of another one of the classroom's three instructional assistants. "We take turns lifting Danielle and positioning her to use her walker or the vestibular swing that hangs from the classroom ceiling," said Ms. Williams. "The instructional assistants also help Danielle with her personal hygiene and we keep a chart on the bathroom door to be sure we're sharing her physical support."

Danielle has attended the Green Valley Preschool Program since August 1999, two years before it started enrolling children without disabilities. According to evaluations using the Carolina Curriculum for Preschoolers with Special Needs, Danielle has progressed in all developmental areas, although her delays in cognition and social adaptation place her approximately one year to one and a half years behind her age peers. She remembers objects that have been hidden and understands concepts like empty/full and add one more. Socially, she follows directions, expresses enthusiasm for work or play, plays games with supervision, and enjoys being with other children. According to her IEP, Danielle's social interactions are limited by her physical delays. Danielle's fine and gross motor skills place her closer to two years behind her age peers. She receives occupational and physical therapy to enhance her manipulative and visual motor skills and to improve her mobility and endurance. She also receives speech-language therapy. Receptively, Danielle appears to understand many age-appropriate concepts and vocabulary, but she doesn't often initiate communication, nor does she imitate consistently.

Jennifer Durrance, who works in the school's cafeteria, describes her daughter as a happy and outgoing child. "She's curious about things, although her speech is somewhat hard to understand. She's very determined and really wants to walk. Sometimes she gets on her belly at home and slides across the floor." Mr. and Mrs. Durrance have worked closely with medical and educational professionals over the past four years. Danielle was delivered prematurely at thirty-four weeks' gestation when doctors found that her twin sister's heart had stopped beating. Although her twin was stillborn, Danielle survived the traumatic birth but experienced a lack of oxygen during delivery. She weighed only four pounds, four ounces at birth and spent eleven days in the hospital before her parents could bring her home. Mr. and Mrs. Durrance became suspicious that something was wrong when Danielle was four months old. "She couldn't roll over and find a toy that was near her in the crib. You know how babies look at their hands at lot? Well, she would mostly look at one hand; she kept her other hand down." At six months, Danielle was not sitting up and it was clear that her eyes were crossed. "The pediatrician was a little concerned but suggested that we wait until she turned nine months old," remembers Mrs. Durrance. "I wish he had been more aggressive. I wish he had said 'I think there might be a problem' so that we might have understood what he was waiting to see. Just telling us to wait seemed so impersonal when our child's development was so very personal to us." When she was nine months old, development tests, including an MRI, confirmed that Danielle had CP and early intervention services began. A special education teacher came to the house to work with Danielle. In addition, her parents drove her to physical and occupational therapy several times a week, and made periodic visits to an ophthalmologist.

Jennifer Durrance credits Danielle's smooth transition from early intervention services to early childhood special education to clear communication among the many professionals involved in her care. "At the transition meeting, someone asked if I had a picture of Danielle with me. I really appreciated that. There was nothing in particular that caused me to feel stressed, but I think teachers should know that many parents feel very nervous at these meetings." Leigh-Anne Williams made Mrs. Durrance feel welcome at the Green Valley Preschool Program: "I felt she understood. She made the transition so nice. She wrote me notes daily because she knew that Danielle couldn't tell me about her day."

In spring, the IEP team will make decisions for Danielle's programming for the next school year. Together, her parents and her multidisciplinary team will consider if Danielle should start kindergarten with her age peers or whether she would benefit more from extended preschool support. Danielle has learned much from her early intervention services and her preschool special education. Jennifer Durrance has learned a great deal, too, and she has important things to say to teachers who might have a student like Danielle in their class.

> First of all, *know the IEP*, especially when a child is served in the regular classroom. Second, *keep communication a priority*. Teachers need to make the time to know the parents of the child, too. Third, *seek information*. Know that parents are knowledgeable about their child's disability. Learn as much as you can about how the child's disability affects her life and her learning.

—*By Jean Crockett*

treatment: new developments in bioengineering, allowing them greater mobility and functional movement; decreases in or removal of architectural barriers and transportation problems; and the movement toward public education for all children (Bigge et al., 2001; Closs, 2000; Heller, Alberto, Forney, & Schwartzman, 1996; Lerner et al., 1998).

Any placement has positive and negative features, and the best decision for a particular child requires weighing the pros and cons. Sometimes the benefits of a particular type of placement are either greatly exaggerated or almost completely dismissed. The box on page 442 is an excerpt from the personal story of Tanya Lyke, a girl with a very "aggressive" type of juvenile arthritis, which caused her a lot of physical pain and required extensive treatment. Her reflections on placement should give pause to any idea that all of the benefits are found in one type of placement or the other.

EDUCATIONAL GOALS AND CURRICULA

It is not possible to prescribe educational goals and curricula for children with physical disabilities as a group because their individual limitations vary so greatly. Even among children with the same condition, goals and curricula must be determined after assessing each child's intellectual, physical, sensory, and emotional characteristics. A physical disability, especially a severe and chronic one that limits mobility, may have two implications for education: (1) the child may be deprived of experiences that nondisabled children have, and (2) the child may find it impossible to manipulate educational materials and respond to educational tasks the way most children do. For example, a child with severe cerebral palsy cannot take part in most outdoor play activities and travel experiences and

CW The Attainment Company creates resources to help people identify the emerging issues in special education and to access the educational materials that will allow them to meet such issues effectively: www.attainmentcompany.com/ ■

so forth. To illustrate this variety, each of the ten categorical chapters includes an example of a special educator at work. Written by Dr. Jean B. Crockett of Virginia Tech University, an experienced special education administrator and teacher educator, each story focuses on a special educator's work with an individual student. These boxes show readers the wide range of challenges faced by special educators, the dynamic nature of their positions, and the competent, hopeful practice of special education.

MARGIN NOTES

The marginal glossary of key terms and concepts continues to appear in this new edition. We have also added new margin notes that provide information about interesting and relevant Web sites. *All* of these Web sites are also included as hot links on the Companion Web site for the 9th edition.

PHOTOGRAPHY

Over half of the photographs for this edition were supplied by Allyn and Bacon's photo library. The photo library is a compilation of images from photo shoots that were set up at schools around the country, including California, Connecticut, Florida, Maryland, Massachusetts, Missouri, New Mexico, Utah, and Canada. Photos for our ninth edition were selected from the most recent photo sessions. Allyn and Bacon's photo department is aware of the rapid changes that are occurring in special education and is committed to reflecting those changes in its library.

Allyn and Bacon solicited our guidance for the shoots. All the photographs we chose are reproduced with the consent of the individual depicted.

Supplements

STUDENT STUDY GUIDE

Written by Paula Crowley of Illinois State University, and reviewed by Dan Hallahan and Jim Kauffman, the study guide reinforces for students conceptual and factual text material and includes key points, learning objectives, exercises, practice tests, and enrichment activities.

COMPANION WEBSITE PLUS, WITH ONLINE STUDY GUIDE

Prepared by Paige Pullen of the University of Virginia, this dynamic, interactive Companion Website includes an online study guide for students that provides, on a chapter-by-chapter basis, learning objectives, study questions with text page references, "live" links to relevant Website (including those referenced and highlighted in the text), audio and video clips, and additional enrichment material. The Companion Website also features a "syllabus builder" that allows instructors to create and customize course syllabi online. [www.abacon.com/hallahan9e]

INSTRUCTOR'S RESOURCE MANUAL AND TEST BANK

The Instructor's Resource Manual section of this supplement was prepared by Melody Tankersley of Kent State University, along with Dan Hallahan and Jim Kauffman. For each chapter of the text, it provides a Chapter Outline, a Chapter Overview, and an Annotated Outline wherein the major headings of the chapter are summarized in detail. Included in the Annotated Outline are suggestions for Lecture Ideas, Discussion Points, and Activities. The IRM also keys each chapter to appropriate videos, transparencies, and digital images available with this text. Also included are references to Related Media, Films, Journals, and Web sites.

The Test Bank section, written by Kerri Martin of East Tennessee State University consists of over 1000 test questions, including multiple choice, true/false, and essay formats. Also included are quizzes and comprehensive tests for each chapter.

NEW! POWERPOINT ELECTRONIC SLIDE PACKAGE

The PowerPoint package, created by Virginia Dudgeon of the State University of New York at Cortland to accompany the ninth edition, is easily accessed from the Allyn & Bacon Web site. More than 100 slides are organized by chapter for use as lecture presentation and/or handouts for students. Those instructors who already use PowerPoint as a lecture presentation tool, will find this new supplement a convenient way to incorporate new slides into their existing slide package. Those instructors who have not used Power-Point (and perhaps have no intention of doing so!) and/or do not have the PowerPoint program on their computers can rest assured these slides can be easily downloaded onto the hard drive and printed out for use as traditional overhead transparencies and handouts. [www.ablongman.com/ppt]

COMPUTERIZED TEST BANK

A computerized version of the Test Bank is available to adopters in CD-ROM for both PC and Macintosh machines. Please ask your Allyn & Bacon representative for details.

THE "SNAPSHOTS" VIDEO SERIES FOR SPECIAL EDUCATION

Snapshots: Inclusion Video (© 1995; 22 minutes) profiles three students of different ages and with various levels of disability in inclusive class settings.

Snapshots 2: Video for Special Education (categorical organization) (© 1995; 20–25 minutes) is a set of six videotaped segments designed specifically for use in your college classroom. It is also available in closed-captioned format. The topics explored are:

- traumatic brain injury
- behavior disorders
- learning disabilities
- mental retardation
- hearing impairment
- visual impairment

Each segment profiles three individuals, their families, teachers, and experiences. These programs will be of great interest to your students. Instructors who have used the tapes in their courses have found that they help in disabusing students of stereotypical viewpoints, and put a "human face" on course material. Teaching notes for both *Snapshots: Inclusion* and *Snapshots 2* are provided in corresponding chapters of the Instructor's Resource Manual.

THE ALLYN AND BACON "PROFESSIONALS IN ACTION" VIDEO SERIES: "TEACHING STUDENTS WITH SPECIAL NEEDS"

Available with the ninth edition of the text, the *Professionals in Action* video is approximately two hours in length, consisting of five 15–30 minute modules. These modules present several viewpoints and approaches to teaching students of various disabilities in general education classrooms, separate education settings, and several combinations of the two. Each module explores its topic through actual classroom footage and interviews with students, general and special education teachers, and parents. The five modules are:

1. Working Together: The Individualized Education Plan (IEP)
2. Working Together: The Collaborative Process
3. Instruction and Behavior Management
4. Technology for Inclusion
5. Working with Families

ALLYN & BACON TRANSPARENCY PACKAGE FOR SPECIAL EDUCATION

The Transparency Package includes approximately 100 acetates, over half of which are full color.

ISEARCH: SPECIAL EDUCATION

This resource guide for the Internet covers the basics of using the Internet, conducting Web searches, and critically evaluating and documenting Internet sources. It also contains Internet activities and URLs specific to the discipline of Special Education. This practical booklet is available *only* as part of a "value pack," shrinkwrapped with an Allyn & Bacon textbook. Please ask your Allyn & Bacon representative for details and ordering information.

COURSECOMPASS AND BLACKBOARD FOR EXCEPTIONAL LEARNERS, NINTH EDITION

CourseCompass is a dynamic, interactive eLearning program powered by Blackboard. Flexible, easy-to-use course management tools allow you to combine content created for *Exceptional Learners*, Ninth Edition, with your own. Putting your online resources in one place has never been easier and it just got better. An updated CourseCompass design now includes a new Course home page and other features to help you create a better online learning experience for your students. Ask your local Allyn & bacon representative for more information or go to www.ablongman.com/coursecompass.

CASES FOR REFLECTION AND ANALYSIS—NEW EDITION

The past few editions of *Exceptional Learners* have included a free booklet of case studies with every new copy of the text purchased from Allyn & Bacon. The overwhelming popularity of this supplement motivated us to revise it for the 9th edition. Four of the nine cases are new to this edition. These cases reflect both the joy and the pain teachers experience while working with exceptional children. What professors of education and commentators in the popular press write about teaching is often wondrously abstract, hypothetical, or idealistic, and does not always ring true for those who teach in classrooms every day. These cases are neither abstract descriptions nor conjecture, nor do they reflect an idealism detached from the realities of the classroom. These are true stories—what really happened as told from the perspectives of real teachers and how they thought and felt about what was happening. We hope you will enjoy reading and discussing them as much as we have.

ACKNOWLEDGMENTS

We are grateful to those individuals who provided valuable comments on the eighth edition and the drafts of our ninth edition chapters:

Jose Luis Alvarado, San Diego State University
Peggy L. Anderson, Metropolitan State College of Denver
William N. Bender, University of Georgia
David F. Conway, University of Nebraska at Omaha
Rhoda Cummings, University of Nevada
Gary A. Davis, University of Wisconsin at Madison
Beverly A. Doyle, Creighton University
Mary K. Dykes, University of Florida at Gainesville
Cynthia Ewers, Wilmington College
Laura Gaudet, Towson State University
Herbert Grossman, University of Wisconsin at Platteville
Craig Kennedy, Vanderbilt University
Festus E. Obiakor, University of Wisconsin at Milwaukee
Thomas F. Reilly, Chicago State University
Michael A Rettig, Washburn University
Karen E. Santos, James Madison University
Phillip Waldrop, Middle Tennessee State University
George J. Yard, University of Missouri at St. Louis

We thank Elizabeth Martinez, who oversaw the tedious task of securing permissions for quoted material. We are thankful for the wonderful support and assistance we have received for this and other editions from the folks at Allyn and Bacon. Alicia Reilly continues to amaze us with her ability to balance family responsibilities while attending to all the details of our book. She is a gem. Deborah Brown's professionalism, as always, brought order to moments of chaos. Erin Leidel's responsiveness to our e-mails and phone calls was critical to our meeting deadlines. We thank Barbara Gracia for gracefully coordinating the many eyes that pored over the page proofs. Thanks, also to Bill Heckman for a terrific job of keeping us stylistically and grammatically correct. And, finally, we thank our editor, Virginia Lanigan. She is one of those rare individuals with competence, professionalism, sensitivity, and a sense of humor. She is first class.

This may well be the most extensive overall revision we have made in the twenty-five-year history of this text. For those loyal users of previous editions, we assure you that we weighed carefully each change or update. We hope you agree that our revisions reflect the myriad changes in the field of special education over the past few years as well as the information explosion brought about by ever more accessible computer databases and the Internet. We also hope you will agree that we have not failed in our continuing commitment to bring you the best that research has to offer with regard to educating exceptional learners.

DPH
JMK

Exceptional Learners

Introduction to Special Education

Claude Fourel

Fish, Watercolor on rag paper. 22 × 30 in.

Ms. Fourel, who was born in 1937 in Brookline, Massachusetts, creates colorful, nature-based paintings. She enjoys an independent life style. She is proud of her mother's French heritage and her father's background as a violinist with the Boston Symphony Orchestra.

Exceptionality and Special Education

Only the brave dare look
upon the gray—
upon the things which
cannot be explained easily,
upon the things which often
engender mistakes,
upon the things whose cause
cannot be understood,
upon the things we must
accept and live with.
And therefore only the brave
dare look upon difference
without flinching.

RICHARD H. HUNGERFORD
"On Locusts"

The study of exceptional learners is the study of *differences*. The exceptional learner is different in some way from the average. In very simple terms, such a person may have problems or special talents in thinking, seeing, hearing, speaking, socializing, or moving. More often than not, he or she has a combination of special abilities or disabilities. Today, over five million such different learners have been identified in public schools throughout the United States. About one out of every ten students in U.S. schools is considered exceptional. The fact that even many so-called normal students also have school-related problems makes the study of exceptionality very demanding.

The study of exceptional learners is also the study of *similarities*. Exceptional individuals are not different from the average in every way. In fact, most exceptional learners are average in more ways than they are not. Until recently, professionals and laypeople as well, tended to focus on the differences between exceptional and nonexceptional learners, almost to the exclusion of the ways in which all individuals are alike. Today, we give more attention to what exceptional and nonexceptional learners have in common—to similarities in their characteristics, needs, and ways of learning. As a result, the study of exceptional learners has become more complex, and many so-called facts about children and youths with disabilities and those who have special gifts or talents have been challenged.

Students of one of the "hard" sciences may boast of the difficulty of the subject matter because of the many facts they must remember and piece together. The plight of students of special education is quite different. To be sure, they study facts, but the facts are relatively few compared to the unanswered questions. Any study of human beings must take into account inherent ambiguities, inconsistencies, and unknowns. In the case of the individual who deviates from the norm, we must multiply all the mysteries of normal human behavior and development by those pertaining to the person's exceptionalities. Because there is no single accepted theory of normal development, it is not at all surprising that relatively few definite statements can be made about exceptional learners.

There are, however, patches of sunshine in the bleak gray painted by Hungerford (see p. 3). It is true that in the vast majority of cases we are unable to identify the exact reason why a person is exceptional, but progress is being made in determining the causes of some disabilities. In a later chapter, for example, we discuss the detection of causal factors in Down syndrome—a condition resulting in the largest number of children classified as having moderate mental retardation. Likewise, the incidence of **retinopathy of prematurity (ROP)**—at

Retinopathy of prematurity (ROP). A condition resulting from administration of an excessive concentration of oxygen at birth; causes scar tissue to form behind the lens of the eye.

The goal of special education is to prepare individuals with disabilities for success and a high quality of life in mainstream society. ■

MISCONCEPTIONS ABOUT
Exceptional Learners

MYTH Public schools may choose not to provide education for some students with disabilities.

FACT Federal legislation specifies that to receive federal funds, every school system must provide a free, appropriate education for every student regardless of any disabling condition.

MYTH By law, the student with a disability must be placed in the least restrictive environment (LRE). The LRE is always the regular classroom.

FACT The law does require the student with a disability to be placed in the LRE. However, the LRE is *not* always the regular classroom. What the LRE does mean is that the student shall be separated as little as possible from home, family, community, and the regular class setting while appropriate education is provided. In many but not all instances, this will mean placement in the regular classroom.

MYTH The causes of most disabilities are known, but little is known about how to help individuals overcome or compensate for their disabilities.

FACT In most cases, the causes of disabilities are not known, although progress is being made in pinpointing why many disabilities occur. More is known about the treatment of most disabilities than about their causes.

MYTH People with disabilities are just like everyone else.

FACT First, no two people are exactly alike. People with disabilities, just like everyone else, are unique individuals. Most of their abilities are much like those of the average person who is not considered to have a disability. Nevertheless, a disability is a characteristic not shared by most people. It is important that disabilities be recognized for what they are, but individuals with disabilities must be seen as having many abilities— other characteristics that they share with the majority of people.

MYTH A disability is a handicap.

FACT A *disability* is an inability to do something, the lack of a specific capacity. A *handicap*, on the other hand, is a disadvantage that is imposed on an individual. A disability may or may not be a handicap, depending on the circumstances. For example, the inability to walk is not a handicap in learning to read, but it can be a handicap in getting into the stands at a ball game. Sometimes handicaps are needlessly imposed on people with disabilities. For example, a student who cannot write with a pen but can use a typewriter or word processor would be needlessly handicapped without such equipment.

5

Phenylketonuria (PKU).
A metabolic genetic disorder caused by the inability of the body to convert phenylalanine to tyrosine; an accumulation of phenylalanine results in abnormal brain development.

Cystic fibrosis.
An inherited disease affecting primarily the gastrointestinal (GI) tract and respiratory organs; characterized by thick, sticky mucous that often interferes with breathing or digestion.

Hydrocephalus.
A condition characterized by enlargement of the head because of excessive pressure of the cerebrospinal fluid.

𝒢𝒲 A variety of information and links related to people with disabilities can be found at file:///E|/welcome.html
    You can also visit the site of the virtual world congress and exposition on disability at http://www.vwcdexpo.com
    For news about special education, see www.specialednews.com/ ∎

one time a leading cause of blindness—has been greatly reduced since the discovery of its cause. The cause of mental retardation associated with a metabolic disorder—**phenylketonuria (PKU)**—has been discovered. Soon after birth, infants are now routinely tested for PKU so that mental retardation can be prevented if they should have the disorder. More recently, the gene responsible for **cystic fibrosis,** an inherited disease characterized by chronic respiratory and digestive problems, has been identified. And in the future, the specific genes governing many other diseases and disorders will also likely be located. The location of such genes raises the possibility of gene therapy to prevent or correct many disabling conditions. Surgery to correct some identifiable defects can now sometimes be done on a fetus before birth (in utero), completely avoiding some conditions like **hydrocephalus** (an accumulation of fluid around the brain that can cause mental or physical disabilities if not corrected). And research may before long lead to the ability to grow new organs from tissues taken from a person or from stem cells, perhaps allowing a poorly functioning lung or pancreas or other internal organ to be replaced and the associated physical disabilities to be avoided.

Besides these and other medical breakthroughs, research is bringing us a more complete understanding of the ways in which the individual's psychological, social, and educational environments are related to learning. For example, special educators, psychologists, and pediatricians are increasingly able to identify environmental conditions that increase the likelihood that a child will have learning or behavior problems (Bolger & Patterson, 2001; Hart & Risley, 1995; Patterson, Reid, & Dishion, 1992; Werner, 1986).

Educational methodology has also made strides. In fact, compared to what we know about causes, we know a lot about how exceptional learners can be taught and managed effectively in the classroom. Although special educators constantly lament that all the questions have not been answered, we do know considerably more today about how to educate exceptional learners than we did ten or fifteen years ago (e.g., Hallahan, Kauffman, & Lloyd, 1999; Kauffman, Mostert, Trent, & Hallahan, 2002; Lloyd, Forness, & Kavale, 1998; Stein & Davis, 2000).

Before moving to the specific subject of exceptional learners, we must point out that we vehemently disagree with Hungerford on an important point: We must certainly learn to live with disabling exceptionalities, but we must never accept them. We prefer to think there is hope for the eventual eradication of many of the disabling forms of exceptionality. In addition, we believe it is of paramount importance to realize that even individuals whose exceptionalities are extreme can be helped to lead fuller lives than they would without appropriate education.

We must not let people's *disabilities* keep us from recognizing their *abilities*. Many people with disabilities have abilities that go unrecognized because their disabilities become the focus of our concern and we do not give enough attention to what they can do. We must study the disabilities of exceptional children and youths if we are to learn how to help them make maximum use of their abilities in school. Some students with disabilities that are not obvious to the casual observer need special programs of education and related services to help them live full, happy, productive lives. However, we must not lose sight of the fact that *the most important characteristics of exceptional learners are their abilities*.

Most exceptional individuals have disabilities, and they have often been referred to as "handicapped" in laws, regulations, and everyday conversations. In this book, we make an important distinction between *disability* and *handicap*. A disability is an inability to do something, a diminished capacity to perform in a specific way. A handicap, on the other hand, is a disadvantage imposed on an individual. Thus, a disability may or may not be a handicap, depending on the circumstances. Likewise, a handicap may or may not be caused by a disability.

For example, blindness is a disability that can be anything but a handicap in the dark. In fact, in the dark, the person who has sight is the one who is handicapped. Needing to use a wheelchair may be a handicap in certain circumstances, but the disadvantage may be a result of architectural barriers or other people's reactions, not the inability to walk. Oth-

ers can handicap people who are different from them (in color, size, appearance, language, and so on) by stereotyping them or not giving them opportunities to do the things they are able to do. When working and living with exceptional individuals who have disabilities, we must constantly strive to separate their disabilities from the handicaps. That is, our goal should be to confine their handicaps to those characteristics and circumstances that cannot be changed, and to make sure that we impose no further handicaps by our attitudes or our unwillingness to accommodate their disabilities.

One major challenge for special education is to teach individuals with disabilities—as well as those around them—to focus on abilities: what they can do as opposed to what they cannot. ■

Educational Definition of Exceptional Learners

For purposes of their education, *exceptional learners are those who require special education and related services if they are to realize their full human potential.* They require special education because they are markedly different from most students in one or more of the following ways: They may have mental retardation, learning or attention disabilities, emotional or behavioral disorders, physical disabilities, disorders of communication, autism, traumatic brain injury, impaired hearing, impaired sight, or special gifts or talents. In the chapters that follow, we define as exactly as possible what it means to have an exceptionality.

Two concepts are important to our educational definition of exceptional learners: (1) diversity of characteristics and (2) need for special education. The concept of diversity is inherent in the definition of exceptionality; the need for special education is inherent in an educational definition.

Consider the two cases described in the box on page 8. Their stories illustrate a matter we have mentioned and discuss further in Chapter 2—how our focus on persons with disabilities must be on what they *can* do and how they should be integrated into the larger society as much as possible.

Erik Weihenmayer is an outstanding athlete—mountain climber, skydiver, wrestler, runner, biker, scuba diver—and a former elementary school teacher. He lost his sight gradually, becoming totally blind by the time he was 13. The fact that he is blind does not prevent him from doing many things done by only a few who have sight (see Pierce, 2001 for description of his climbing of Mt. Everest). Like some others who are blind, he had difficulty coming to terms with the fact that he cannot see and at first resisted using some of the devices that are essential for blind people—braille for reading and a cane or dog for everyday mobility (see also Kuusisto, 1998 and Chapter 10). But he did learn to use these devices, which are often part of the special educational curriculum for children with extremely low vision.

Blair Smith typically, but not always, uses a wheel chair because of a physical disability. However, that does not stop her from being a high school cheerleader or from being included with her peers in many typical teenage activities. For her, appropriate education requires a few reasonable accommodations that allow her access to places and activities. Most of all, she needs—and receives—an attitude of acceptance on the part of teachers and peers.

Sometimes seemingly obvious disabilities are never identified, and the consequences for the person and his or her family, as well as the larger society, are tragic. Sometimes disabilities are identified but special education is not provided, squandering opportunities for

A Focus on Abilities

Erik Weihenmayer

Erik Weinhenmayer ■

It was at this camp [Khumbu Icefall, elevation 21,300 feet on Mt. Everest] one night in May that Erik Weihenmayer sat in his tent as a lightening storm moved across the mountain face.

"It was amazingly beautiful," recalls Weihenmayer (pronounced WINE-mare), sitting in a downtown hotel suite during a recent visit to Boston.

"Every time the lightening cracked, it would echo off the mountains," he says. "And I would have a view of the way the mountains looked by the echo. I could *feel* the beauty of it." . . .

As most everyone on the planet knows by now, Weihenmayer, 32, became the first blind person to reach the summit of Everest when he accomplished the feat May 25 [2001]. The achievement put the Boston College graduate and former grade-school teacher on top of the media world, including the cover of *Time* magazine.

It also put to rest any lingering doubts that a climber of Weihenmayer's ability—he has summited five of the seven continents' highest peaks, along with the likes of Yosemite's imposing El Capitan—could pull off something that has cost 170 climbers their lives over the past half-century. . . .

Weihenmayer was born with a rare degenerative eye condition known as retinoschisis. His pre-school years were "a two-year nightmare of doctor visits around the country," he writes in his book, as specialists told the Weihenmayers that Erik would be totally blind by his teenage years. . . .

Despite—or maybe because of—his impairment, he grew into a rebellious, even angry, kid. For a long time, he refused to try a cane or to learn Braille. He took up wrestling and became a high-school champion at one of the few sports that allowed him equal footing with sighted athletes. As he would later conquer the world's most challenging mountains, he won his independence gradually, one halting step at a time.

"Only 10 percent of blind people are literate in Braille," Weihenmayer says, looking back on his own period of frustration and denial. "It took me two years to master it, but when I realized I could read Braille, I realized I could do a lot of normal things. I just needed to do them in a different way. Rock climbing was the same deal."[1]

Note: For more details on the climb, see Pierce (2001).

---

the child's development. The box on page 10 describes two such cases. In spite of federal laws requiring appropriate education and the existence of a special education system, Willie and Anthony received no special education at all or extremely poor special education services. The consequences of the neglect of their need for special education are profoundly negative. Although early identification and intervention hold the promise of preventing many disabilities from becoming worse, preventive action is often not taken (Kauffman, 1999b).

When special education works as it should, a student's disability is identified early and effective special education is provided in the least restrictive environment. The student's parents are involved in the decision about how to address the student's needs, and the outcome of special education is the student's improved achievement and behavior. Consider the case of Alice, presented in the box on page 11.

Students with exceptionalities are an extraordinarily diverse group compared to the general population, and relatively few generalizations apply to all exceptional individuals.

Blair Smith

Blair Smith ■

Blair Smith is different . . . Her legs look like they could snap beneath her at any moment, and she is so short that her perspective barely changes when she rises from her wheelchair.

Still, she always rises.

Smith is among the 20,000 to 50,000 people in the United States with the bone disorder osteogenesis imperfecta (OI). She is also a relentlessly giddy cheerleader at Monticello High School.

There are at least four forms of OI, representing extreme variations in severity from one individual to another. Smith's case falls somewhere in the fairly severe category. OI has rendered her bones soft and brittle, leaving her literally fragile. When she walks she relies on the support of her crutches and leg braces to keep from breaking a leg or two. Her growth was stunted drastically. . . .

As a ninth-grader at Albemarle High School, Smith cheered from the stands like most of the other Patriot students. But for her sophomore year, she moved to brand-new Monticello . . . and joined the junior varsity team for the Mustangs.

And as a junior this past fall, Smith made the varsity squad, serving as a headliner for Monticello's act from September to February. She takes the floor in her wheelchair—Smith's parents had to solicit the aid of [her physical education teacher] to make her use the chair—and participates in the routines in her own way. Stunts are definitely out, but Smith manages to make her indelible mark on the show without the tools of gymnastic display. . . .

"It's been unbelievable," Debbie Smith [Blair's mother] said. "The kids have just been wonderful. They have been wonderful the whole time she has been in school about accepting her for the way she is."

Added Ralph Smith [Blair's father]: "People are always pushing her forward and letting her do things and not putting her in a shell." . . .

She is just another young girl full of life.

That is all. And that makes you want to stand up and cheer.[2]

SOURCES: [1]"Touching the Sky" by Joseph P. Kahn. *Boston Globe,* June 27, 2001, pp. F1, F5. Reprinted with permission.

[2]"Something to Cheer About" by Tom Gresham, *The Daily Progress,* May 7, 2000, pp. E1, E6, Charlottesville, VA. Reprinted with permission.

Their exceptionalities may involve sensory, physical, cognitive, emotional, or communication abilities or any combination of these. Furthermore, exceptionalities may vary greatly in cause, degree, and effect on educational progress, and the effects may vary greatly depending on the individual's age, sex, and life circumstances. Any individual we might present as an example of our definition is likely to be representative of exceptional learners in some respects but unrepresentative in others.

The typical student who receives special education has no immediately obvious disability. He—more than half of the students served by special education are males—is in elementary or middle school and has persistent problems in learning and behaving appropriately in school. His problems are primarily academic and social or behavioral. These difficulties are not apparent to many teachers until they have worked with the student for a period of weeks or months. His problems persist despite teachers' efforts to meet his needs in the regular school program in which most students succeed. He is most likely to be described as having a learning disability or to be designated by an even broader label

Where Needs Are Great, the Needs Go Untended: Failings of Special Ed System Extract a High Price

A lost childhood ago, Willie Williamson was forgotten in the D.C. schools. He flunked kindergarten and first grade. His speech was a muddled slur. He never learned to read. He heard his father kill his brother with a shotgun in the next room. His life cried out for help.

Willie was declared mildly retarded when he was 7, tested again at 10 and then never reevaluated for eight years. He was bumped up from grade to grade. Now 18, angry and illiterate, Willie hides in an overlarge jacket and watches the world with suspicion.

"He was lost in the system," said his guardian, Cynthia Savage. "Nobody cared enough to say, 'We will help this child.'"

Fighting for a Grandson

Rosemary McKinney, like many others, has had to learn the jargon and intricacies of the special education system to try to get D.C. schools to provide proper service for her grandson, Anthony.

Born of a mother who used PCP and other drugs, according to school social worker evaluations, Anthony stuttered badly and had a poor attention span. His grandmother helped get him speech therapy in elementary school. For a while, the system was working.

"He was coming along fine—learning his ABC's and counting real good," McKinney said of the 7-year-old. When she moved to the neighborhood served by Webb Elementary School in Northeast Washington in September, she asked the school to enroll him in its special education class. Seven months later, she found school officials had misplaced Anthony's records.

"They just put him in a regular class and left him there," she said "Now, he writes backwards. He doesn't say anything about school. He's missed a whole year, now. I don't know what's going to happen to him."

A request to school authorities for a response from Webb was not answered.

McKinney, who lives with a son and three grandchildren, is often exhausted by the chore of fighting the schools. "You need a lawyer just to get them to do anything."

SOURCE: Struck, D. (1997, February 19). Where needs are great, the needs go untended: Failings of special ed system extract a high price. *The Washington Post,* pp. A1, A9. ©**1997, The Washington Post. Reprinted with permission.**

indicating that his academic and social progress in school are unsatisfactory due to a disability.

By federal law, an exceptional student is not to be identified as eligible for special education until careful assessment indicates that he or she is unable to make satisfactory progress in the regular school program without special services designed to meet his or her extraordinary needs. Federal special education laws and regulations include definitions of several conditions (categories such as learning disability, mental retardation, hearing impairment, and so on) that might create a need for special education. These laws and regulations require that special services be provided to meet whatever special needs are created by a disabling condition and cannot be met in the regular educational program. They do not require that special education be provided simply because a student has a disability.

Prevalence of Exceptional Learners

Prevalence refers to the percentage of a population or number of individuals having a particular exceptionality. The prevalence of mental retardation, for example, might be estimated at 2.3 percent, which means that 2.3 percent of the population, or twenty-three people in every thousand, are assumed to have mental retardation. If the prevalence of giftedness is assumed to be between 3 percent and 5 percent, we would expect somewhere between thirty and fifty people in a sample of a thousand to have special gifts of some kind. Obviously, accurate estimates of prevalence depend on our ability to count the number of people in a given population who have a certain exceptionality.

An IEP for Alice: What Can Happen When Special Education Works

Alice's first-grade teacher called about five minutes after the educational planner left my room. Both the first-grade teacher and the educational planner informed me that at the eligibility meeting the day before, it was determined that Alice qualified for services in my class for children with mild mental retardation.

"It would be great if you could write the IEP for Alice soon, so we could have her start right after Christmas," her teacher suggested. "She cries so much. I feel so bad for her. She's no problem, but she just *can't* do the work."

Legally, I had thirty days before an educational plan had to be approved by the parents. It was just a few days before Christmas break, all the kids in the school had decided to have a nervous breakdown, and all the teachers were tired and cranky—especially me. And my aide and I had the added fatigue of trying to insure that all the students in my class received some presents for Christmas. I wasn't keen to add to my stress or my responsibilities. But both the supervisor and the first-grade teacher had pleaded with me to arrange a meeting with the parents as quickly as I could.

I spent the evening reading Alice's psychological folder. She had been in the preschool program for three years. The preceding spring, when there had been an eligibility meeting, the school staff felt Alice qualified for services in my class beginning in September. But the parents felt otherwise. *Retardation* is such a dirty word. The present euphemism "class for children with mild mental disabilities" didn't disguise the fact for the parents that this was what some would call the "dummy class."

The father flatly refused to have her placed in my class. "Alice can do the work. I know she can," he said.

So Alice started out the year with new clothes, a smile, and the fine-motor skills of a two-year-old. And although she was from a loving, attentive family that read to her and paid a lot of attention to her, her skills were seriously delayed compared to the other students in the first grade. It wasn't that she didn't learn. She just took *so much longer* than the other children in her class. Even though Alice participated in the resource program, the speech program, the occupational therapy program (all done in the general education classroom and including other classmates in her lessons), she could not keep up with even the slowest group in her class.

It wasn't long before Alice was asking her mother, "Why can't I do what the other kids do? I *want* to do it." Motivation did not seem to be a problem initially, but after a few months, Alice decided not to try to try. Can't say that I much blame her. After a while, she made her misery known to all, both at home and at school. She became a helpless blob that cried most of the time. Her teacher said, "As far as I know, no one in my class has ever been mean to Alice. She just purely hates school now," she sighed. Alice's mother agreed with the teacher. "I've asked her over and over again if anyone has been mean to her. She says no, and I believe her."

After reading her folder and talking with teachers who worked with Alice, I felt bad for her too. The parents and I wrote an educational plan for Alice, stating that she would begin attending my class after Christmas. Dad still wasn't so sure that he approved, but knew that *something* had to be done. "But you have to promise to push her. She can be really manipulative," he warned.

After a few weeks of Alice's placement in my room, the parents and I met again. They seemed much happier. "Alice enjoys coming to school now," they let me know. The dad, much to his credit, wished that he had not denied her services in the fall. "She feels so much better about herself now," he said.

Two years later, Alice's father and I talked about his reaction to the eligibility meeting (the one deciding that Alice qualified for my services). "There were so many people," he said, "and they were all saying that there was something terribly wrong with my daughter. I wondered who in the hell they were talking about! My pretty little girl is so loving and funny. How could they say she was retarded?"

"Does it matter what label they put on her? Isn't she still a pretty, funny, loving little girl?"

"Yeah," he laughed. "Except now she can read!"

SOURCE: Kauffman, J. M., & Pullen, P. L. (1996). Eight myths about special education. *Focus on Exceptional Children, 28*(5), 7–8. Reprinted with permission.

At first thought, the task of determining the number of students who have exceptionalities seems simple enough, yet the prevalence of most exceptionalities is uncertain and a matter of considerable controversy. A number of factors make it hard to say with great accuracy and confidence just how many exceptional individuals there are, including vagueness in definitions, frequent changes in definitions, and the role of schools in determining exceptionality—matters we discuss in later chapters.

Government figures show that about ten students out of every hundred were receiving special education in the late 1990s (U.S. Department of Education, 2000). Beginning in the mid-1970s, there was steady growth in the number of students served by special education, from about 3.75 million in 1976 to about 5 million in the late 1990s. Most of the children and youths served by special education are between the ages of six and seventeen. Although preschoolers and youths eighteen to twenty-one are being identified with increasing frequency as having disabilities, school-age children and youths in their early teens make up the bulk of the identified population.

The percentage of the special education population identified as having certain disabilities has changed considerably over several decades. For example, the number of students identified as having learning disabilities has more than doubled since the mid-1970s and now makes up about half of the number of students receiving special education. In contrast, the percentage of students whose primary disability is "speech or language impairments" has declined substantially, and the percentage identified as having "mental retardation" is now about half of what it was in 1976. No one has an entirely satisfactory explanation of these changes. However, they may in part reflect alterations in definitions and diagnostic criteria for certain disabilities and the social acceptability of the "learning disabilities" label. In subsequent chapters we discuss the prevalence of specific categories of exceptionality.

Figure 1.1 shows the increase in the number of children served in various low-incidence categories according to the *Twenty-second Annual Report to Congress on Implementation of the Individuals with Disabilities Education Act* (U.S. Department of Education, 2000). This federal law is usually referred to as IDEA. Annual reports and other information about IDEA are available online at www.ideapractices.org/. The annual reports can be accessed on the Internet.

As Figure 1.1 shows, the most dramatic changes of the past decade have been in the number of children identified as having **autism** and the number with **traumatic brain**

Ѻ For additional information about annual reports to Congress on IDEA, see www.ed.gov/offices/OSERS/OSEP/Products/OSEP2000AnlRpt/index.html

You can visit the general site for the Office of Special Education Programs at www.ed.gov/offices/OSERS/OSEP/index.html or change the year in the first address to see more recent reports. ■

FIGURE 1.1

Growth reported in low-incidence disabilities from 1989–90 to 1998–99.

SOURCE: U.S. Department of Education, Office of Special Education Programs, Data Analysis System (DANS). Washington, DC: Author.

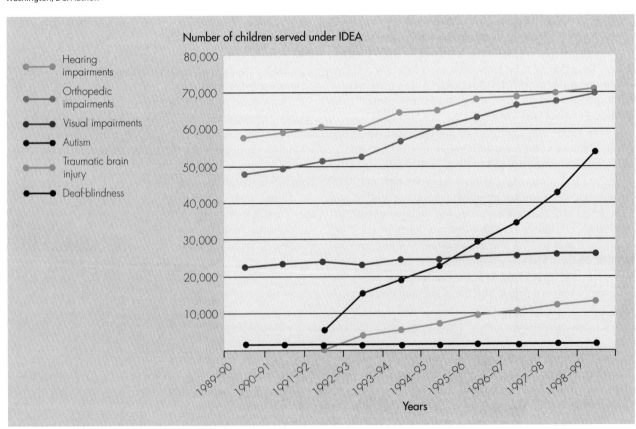

Number of children served under IDEA

Hearing impairments
Orthopedic impairments
Visual impairments
Autism
Traumatic brain injury
Deaf-blindness

Years

injury (TBI). It is important to note that only in 1990 did these two disabilities become separate categories for reporting data under federal law. Although both disabilities existed prior to that date, the graph begins showing those disabilities only for the first reporting year under federal special education law (i.e., 1991–92). In prior years, these two disabilities were subsumed under other categories.

Much of the increase in autism shown in Figure 1.1 probably represents improved identification procedures and identification of milder cases of autism, not an epidemic (National Research Council, 2001). Although some of the increase in TBI may represent better diagnosis, it may also reflect actual increases in brain injuries, as we discuss in Chapter 11. The increases in orthopedic impairments may reflect the increasing survival rate of infants born with significant physical anomalies and children who have been involved in accidents. Increases in hearing and vision impairments may represent better diagnosis of these disabilities. Finally, Figure 1.1 indicates that deaf-blindness is an extremely low-incidence disability. Deaf-blindness is a severe and multiple disability that is seldom overlooked or misdiagnosed, which probably accounts for the fact that the figure shows no growth in this category.

Definition of Special Education

Special education means specially designed instruction that meets the unusual needs of an exceptional student. Special materials, teaching techniques, or equipment and/or facilities may be required. For example, students with visual impairments may require reading materials in large print or braille; students with hearing impairments may require hearing aids and/or instruction in sign language; those with physical disabilities may need special equipment; those with emotional or behavioral disorders may need smaller and more highly structured classes; and students with special gifts or talents may require access to working professionals. Related services—special transportation, psychological assessment, physical and occupational therapy, medical treatment, and counseling—may be necessary if special education is to be effective. The single most important goal of special education is finding and capitalizing on exceptional students' abilities.

Providing Special Education

Several administrative plans are available for the education of exceptional learners, from a few special provisions made by the student's regular teacher to twenty-four-hour residential care in a special facility. Who educates exceptional students and where they receive their education depends on two factors: (1) how and how much the student differs from average students, and (2) what resources are available in the school and community. We describe various administrative plans for education according to the degree of physical integration—the extent to which exceptional and nonexceptional students are taught in the same place by the same teachers.

Beginning with the most integrated intervention, the *regular classroom teacher* who is aware of the individual needs of students and skilled at meeting them may be able to acquire appropriate materials, equipment, and/or instructional methods. At this level, the direct services of specialists may not be required—the expertise of the regular teacher may meet the student's needs.

At the next level, the regular classroom teacher may need consultation with a *special educator* or other professional (e.g., school psychologist) in addition to acquiring the special materials, equipment, or methods. The special educator may instruct the regular teacher, refer the teacher to other resources, or demonstrate the use of materials, equipment, or methods.

Going a step further, a special educator may provide *itinerant services* to the exceptional student and/or the regular classroom teacher. The itinerant teacher establishes a

Autism.
A pervasive developmental disability characterized by extreme withdrawal, cognitive deficits, language disorders, self-stimulation, and onset before the age of thirty months.

Traumatic brain injury (TBI).
Injury to the brain (not including conditions present at birth, birth trauma, or degenerative diseases or conditions) resulting in total or partial disability or psychosocial maladjustment that affects educational performance; may affect cognition, language, memory, attention, reasoning, abstract thinking, judgment, problem solving, sensory or perceptual and motor disabilities, psychosocial behavior, physical functions, information processing, or speech.

Individuals with disabilities are as diverse a group as any other; thus, a major emphasis of special education is to tailor services to meet individual needs. ■

consistent schedule, moving from school to school and visiting classrooms to instruct students individually or in small groups. This teacher provides materials and teaching suggestions for the regular teacher to carry out and consults with the regular teacher about special problems.

At the next level, a *resource teacher* provides services for the students and teachers in only one school. The students being served are enrolled in the regular classroom and are seen by the specially trained teacher for a length of time and at a frequency determined by the nature and severity of their particular problems. The resource teacher continually assesses the needs of the students and their teachers, and usually works with students individually or in small groups in a special classroom where special materials and equipment are available. Typically, the resource teacher serves as a consultant to the regular classroom teacher, advising on the instruction and management of the student in the classroom and perhaps demonstrating instructional techniques. The flexibility of the plan and the fact that the student remains with nondisabled peers most of the time make this a particularly attractive and popular alternative.

Diagnostic-prescriptive centers go beyond the level of intervention represented by resource teachers and rooms. In this plan, students are placed for a short time in a special class in a school or other facility so their needs can be assessed and a plan of action can be determined on the basis of diagnostic findings. After an educational prescription has been written for the pupil, the recommendations for placement may include anything from institutional care to placement in a regular classroom with a particularly competent teacher who can carry out the plan.

Hospital or homebound instruction is most often required by students who have physical disabilities, although it is sometimes employed for those with emotional or behavioral disorders or other disabilities when no alternative is readily available. Typically, the youngster is confined to the hospital or the home for a relatively short time, and the hospital or homebound teacher maintains contact with the regular teacher.

One of the most visible—and in recent years, controversial—service alternatives is the *special self-contained class.* Such a class typically enrolls fifteen or fewer exceptional students with particular characteristics or needs. The teacher ordinarily has been trained as a special educator and provides all or most of the instruction. Those assigned to such classes usually spend most or all of the school day separated from their nondisabled peers. Often students with disabilities are integrated with nondisabled students during part of the day (perhaps for physical education, music, or some other activity in which they can participate well).

Special day schools provide an all-day special placement for exceptional learners. The day school is usually organized for a specific category of exceptional students and may contain special equipment necessary for their care and education. These students return to their homes during nonschool hours.

The final level of intervention is the *residential school*. Here, exceptional students receive twenty-four-hour care away from home, often at a distance from their communities. These children and youths may make periodic visits home or return each weekend, but during the week they are residents of the institution, where they receive academic instruction in addition to management of their daily living environment.

The major features of each type of placement or service alternative, examples of the types of students most likely to be served in each, and the primary roles of the special educators who work with them are shown in Table 1.1 (pp. 16 and 17). Note that although these are the major administrative plans for delivery of special education, variations are possible. For example, special day schools and residential schools may help students make the transition to regular schools as they are able to return. Many school systems, in the process of trying to find more effective and economical ways of serving exceptional students, combine or alter these alternatives and the roles special educators and other professionals play in service delivery. Furthermore, the types of students listed under each service alternative are *examples only;* there are wide variations among school systems in the kinds of placements made for particular kinds of students. Note also that what any special education teacher may be expected to do includes a variety of items not specified in Table 1.1. We discuss these expectations for teachers in the following section.

As noted earlier, special education law requires placement of the student in the **least restrictive environment (LRE).** What is usually meant is that the student should be separated from nondisabled classmates and from home, family, and community as little as possible. That is, his or her life should be as normal as possible, and the intervention should be consistent with individual needs and not interfere with individual freedom any more than is absolutely necessary. For example, students should not be placed in special classes if they can be served adequately by resource teachers, and they should not be placed in institutions if a special class will serve their needs just as well.

Although this movement toward placement of exceptional students in the least restrictive environment is laudable, the definition of *least restrictive* is not as simple as it seems. Cruickshank (1977; see also Crockett & Kauffman, 2001) has pointed out that greater restriction of the physical environment does not necessarily mean greater restriction of psychological freedom or human potential. In fact, it is conceivable that some students could be more restricted in the long run in a regular class where they are rejected by others and fail to learn necessary skills than in a special class or day school where they learn happily and well. It is important to keep the ultimate goals for the students in mind and to avoid letting "least restrictive" become a hollow slogan that results in shortchanging them in their education (Crockett & Kauffman, 1999, 2001; Kauffman, 1995). As Morse has noted, "The goal should be to find the most productive setting to provide the maximum assistance for the child" (1984, p. 120).

Although considerable variation in the placement of students with disabilities is found from state to state and among school systems within a given state, most exceptional students are educated in regular classes. Nationwide, over 40 percent of exceptional children and youths are served primarily in regular classes. Most of these students receive special instruction for part of the school day from special education resource teachers. In the United States, about one-fourth of all students in special education spend most of their school day in a resource room. Most of these students spend a significant part of their school day in regular classes. Slightly over 20 percent of all children and youths with disabilities are placed in separate special classes, and many of these students are mainstreamed into regular classes for some part of the school day. Only about 5 percent are placed in separate schools or other special environments (e.g., residential facilities,

Least restrictive environment (LRE). A legal term referring to the fact that exceptional children must be educated in as normal an environment as possible.

TABLE 1.1   Examples of Service Alternatives for Special Education

Most Physically Integrated ←

Type of Placement	Regular Class Only	Special Educator Consultation	Itinerant Teacher	Resource Teacher
Major features of placement alternatives	Regular teacher meets all needs of student; student may not be officially identified or labeled; student totally integrated	Regular teacher meets all needs of student with only occasional help from special education consultant(s); student may not be officially identified or labeled; student totally integrated	Regular teacher provides most or all instruction; special teacher provides intermittent instruction of student and/or consultation with regular teacher; student integrated except for brief instructional sessions	Regular teacher provides most instruction; special teacher provides instruction part of school day and advises regular teacher; student integrated most of school day
Types of students typically served	Student with mild learning disability, emotional/behavioral disorder, or mild mental retardation; student with physical disability	Student with mild learning disability, emotional/behavioral disorder, or mild mental retardation	Student with visual impairment or physical disability; student with communication disorder	Student with mild to moderate emotional/behavioral, learning, or communication disorder or hearing impairment
Primary role of special education teacher	None	To offer demonstration and instruction and to assist regular class teacher as requested	To visit classroom regularly and see that appropriate instruction, materials, and other services are provided; to offer consultation, demonstration, and referral for regular teacher and assessment and instruction of student as needed; to work toward total integration of student	To assess student's needs for instruction and management; to provide individual or small-group instruction on set schedule in regular class or resource room; to offer advice and demonstration for regular teacher; to handle referral to other agencies for additional services; to work toward total integration of student

hospital schools, and homebound instruction; see Figure 1.2 on p. 18). Since the late 1980s, there has been a steady trend toward placing more students with disabilities in regular classes and a corresponding trend toward placing fewer students with disabilities in resource rooms, separate classes, and separate facilities (U.S. Department of Education, 1995, 1997, 2000). Placing more students in regular classes and schools reflects educational reform in the 1990s, a topic to which we return later in this chapter and in Chapter 2.

Children under the age of six less often receive education in regular classes, and more often attend separate schools than do children who have reached the usual school age. Special classes, separate schools, and other environments such as homebound instruction are used more often for older teenagers and young adults than for students of elementary and high school age. We can explain these differences by several facts:

1. Preschoolers and young adults who are identified for special education tend to have more severe disabilities than students in kindergarten through grade 12.

Least Physically Integrate

Diagnostic-Prescriptive Center	Hospital or Homebound Instruction	Self-Contained Class	Special Day School	Residential School
Special teacher in center provides most or all instruction for several days or weeks and develops plan or prescription for regular or special education teacher; following diagnosis and prescription, student may be partially or totally integrated into regular school or class	Special teacher provides all instruction in hospital or home until student is able to return to usual school classes (regular or special) from which he or she has been temporarily withdrawn; student totally separated from regular school for short period	Special teacher provides most or all instruction in special class of students; regular teacher may provide instruction in regular class for part of school day; student mostly or totally separated from regular class	Special teacher provides instruction in separate school; also may work with teachers in regular or special classes of regular school; student totally or mostly separated from regular school	Same as special day school; special teacher also works with other staff to provide a total therapeutic environment or milieu; student totally or mostly in special setting
Student with mild disability who has been receiving no services or inadequate services	Student with physical disability; student undergoing treatment or medical tests	Student with moderate to severe mental retardation or emotional/ behavioral disorder	Student with severe or profound physical or mental disability	Student with severe or profound mental retardation or emotional/ behavioral disorder
To make comprehensive assessment of student's educational strengths and weaknesses; to develop written prescription for instruction and behavior management for receiving teacher; to interpret prescription for receiving teacher and assess and revise prescription as needed	To obtain records from student's school of attendance; to maintain contact with teachers (regular or special) and offer instruction consistent with student's school program; to prepare student for return to school (special or regular)	To manage and teach special class; to offer instruction in most areas of curriculum; to work toward integration of students in regular classes	To manage and teach individuals and/or small groups of students with disabilities; to work toward integration of students in regular school	Same as special day school; also to work with residential staff to make certain school program is integrated appropriately with nonschool activities

2. Some school systems do not have regular classes for preschoolers and young adults, and thus placements in other than regular classes are typically more available and more appropriate.
3. Curriculum and work-related educational programs for older teens and young adults with disabilities are frequently offered off the campuses of regular high schools.

The environment that is least restrictive depends in part on the individual's exceptionality. There is almost never a need to place in a separate class or separate school a student whose primary disability is a speech impairment. Likewise, most students with learning disabilities can be appropriately educated primarily in regular classes. On the other hand, the resources needed to teach students with severe impairments of hearing and vision may require that they attend separate schools or classes for at least part of their school careers.

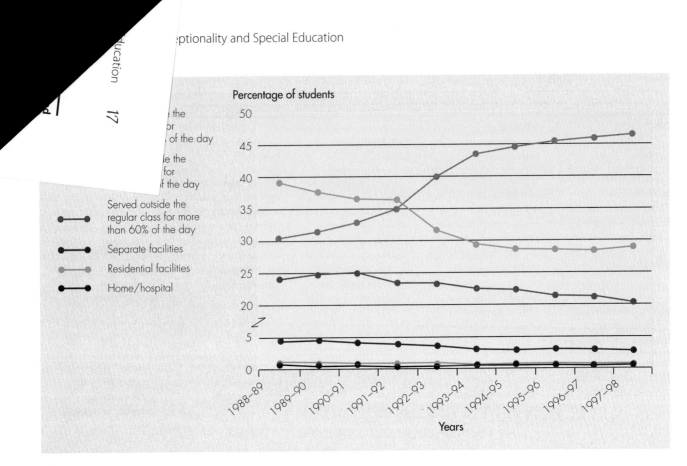

Served outside the regular class for more than 60% of the day

Separate facilities

Residential facilities

Home/hospital

FIGURE 1.2

Percentage of students ages 6 through 21 in different education environments during 1988–89 through 1997–98.

SOURCE: U.S. Department of Education, Office of Special Education Programs, Data Analysis System (DANS). Washington, DC: Author.

Regular education initiative (REI).
A philosophy that maintains that general education, rather than special education, should be primarily responsible for the education of students with disabilities.

Inclusive schools movement.
A reform movement designed to restructure general education schools and classrooms so they better accommodate all students, including those with disabilities.

Teachers' Roles

We have noted that most students in public schools who have been identified as exceptional are placed in regular classrooms for at least part of the school day. Furthermore, there is good reason to believe that a large number of public school students not identified as disabled or gifted share many of the characteristics of those who are exceptional. Thus, all teachers must obviously be prepared to deal with exceptional students, although it is unreasonable to expect *all* teachers to teach *all* exceptional students (Mock & Kauffman, 2002).

The roles of general and special education teachers are not always clear in a given case. Sometimes uncertainty about the division of responsibility can be extremely stressful; for example, teachers may feel uneasy because it is not clear whose job it is to make special adaptations for a pupil or just what they are expected to do in cooperating with other teachers.

RELATIONSHIP BETWEEN GENERAL AND SPECIAL EDUCATION

During the 1980s, the relationship between general and special education became a matter of great concern to policymakers, researchers, and advocates for exceptional children. Proposals for changing the relationship between general and special education, including radical calls to restructure or merge the two, came to be known in the 1980s as **the regular education initiative (REI).** In the 1990s, reform proposals have been called the **inclusive schools movement.** Moderate proponents of reform suggest that general educators take more responsibility for many students with mild or moderate disabilities, with special educators serving more as consultants or resources to regular classroom teachers and less as special teachers. More radical reformers recommend that special education be eliminated as a separate, identifiable part of education. They call for a single, unified educational system in which all students are viewed as unique and special and entitled to the same quality of education. Although many of the suggested reforms have great appeal and some could produce benefits for exceptional students, the basis for the integration of special and general education and the ultimate consequences they might bring have been questioned (Crockett & Kauffman, 1999, 2001; Fuchs & Fuchs, 1994; Hockenbury, Kauffman, & Hallahan, 1999–2000; Kauffman, 1995, 1999–2000; Lloyd, Singh, & Repp, 1991; Martin, 1995; Mock & Kauffman, 2002).

One reason behind reform proposals is concern for pupils who are considered at risk. *At risk* is often not clearly defined, but it generally refers to students who perform or behave poorly in school and appear likely to fail or fall far short of their potential. Some advocates of reform suggest that at-risk students cannot be or should not be distinguished from those with mild disabilities. Others argue that the problems of at-risk students tend to be ignored because special education siphons resources from general education. Should special education and general education merge for the purpose of making general education better able to respond to students at risk? Or should special education maintain its separate identity and be expanded to include these students? Should general education be expected to develop new programs for at-risk students without merging with special education? There are no ready answers to these and other questions about the education of students at risk.

We discuss inclusion and its implications further in Chapter 2. Regardless of one's views, the controversy about the relationship between special and general education has made teachers more aware of the problems of deciding just which students should be taught specific curricula, which students should receive special attention or services, and where and by whom these should be provided (Crockett & Kauffman, 1999, 2001; Kauffman & Hallahan, 1995, 1997). There are no pat answers to the questions about how special and general education should work together to see that every student receives an appropriate education. Yet it is clear that the relationship between them must be one of cooperation and collaboration. They must not become independent or mutually exclusive educational tracks. Neither can we deny that general and special educators have somewhat different roles to play. With this in mind, we summarize some of the major expectations for all teachers, and for special education teachers in particular.

EXPECTATIONS FOR ALL EDUCATORS

Regardless of whether a teacher is specifically trained in special education, he or she may be expected to participate in educating exceptional students in any one of the following ways:

1. *Make maximum effort to accommodate individual students' needs.* Teaching in public schools requires dealing with diverse students in every class. All teachers must make an effort to meet the needs of individuals who may differ in some way from the average or typical student. Flexibility, adaptation, accommodation, and special attention are to be expected of every teacher. Special education should be considered necessary only when a teacher's best efforts to meet a student's individual needs are not successful.

2. *Evaluate academic abilities and disabilities.* Although a psychologist or other special school personnel may give a student formal standardized tests in academic areas, adequate evaluation requires the teacher's assessment of the student's performance in the classroom. Teachers must be able to report specifically and precisely how students can and cannot perform in all academic areas for which they are responsible.

3. *Refer for evaluation.* By law, all public school systems must make extensive efforts to screen and identify all children and youths of school age who have disabilities. Teachers must observe students' behavior and refer those they suspect of having disabilities for evaluation by a multidisciplinary team. *We stress here that a student should not be referred for special education unless extensive and unsuccessful*

efforts have been made to accommodate his or her needs in regular classes. Before referral, school personnel must document the strategies that have been used to teach and manage the student in general education. Referral is justified only if these strategies have failed. (See the box on p. 21.)

4. *Participate in eligibility conferences.* Before a student is provided special education, his or her eligibility must be determined by an interdisciplinary team. Therefore, teachers must be ready to work with other teachers and with professionals from other disciplines (psychology, medicine, or social work, for example) in determining a student's eligibility for special education.

5. *Participate in writing individualized education programs.* A written individualized education program (IEP) must be on file in the records of every student with a disability. Teachers must be ready to participate in a conference (possibly including the student and/or parents, as well as other professionals) in which the program is formulated.

6. *Communicate with parents or guardians.* Parents (sometimes surrogate parents) or guardians must be consulted during the evaluation of their child's eligibility for special education, formulation of the individualized education program, and reassessment of any special program that may be designed for their child. Teachers must contribute to the school's communication with parents about their child's problems, placement, and progress.

7. *Participate in due process hearings and negotiations.* When parents, guardians, or students with disabilities themselves are dissatisfied with the school's response to educational needs, they may request a due-process hearing or negotiations regarding appropriate services. Teachers may be called on to offer observations, opinions, or suggestions in such hearings or negotiations.

8. *Collaborate with other professionals in identifying and making maximum use of exceptional students' abilities.* Finding and implementing solutions to the challenges of educating exceptional students is not the exclusive responsibility of any one professional group. General and special education teachers are expected to share responsibility for educating students with special needs. In addition, teachers may need to collaborate with other professionals, depending on the given student's exceptionality. Psychologists, counselors, physicians, physical therapists, and a variety of other specialists may need teachers' perspectives on students' abilities and disabilities, and they may rely on teachers to implement critical aspects of evaluation or treatment.

A high level of professional competence and ethical judgment is required to conform to these expectations. Teaching demands a thorough knowledge of child development

Special education referrals very often begin with the recommendations of general education teachers. ■

What Should I Do Before I Make a Referral?

If you are thinking about referring a student, probably the most important thing you should do is contact his or her parents. If you cannot reach them by phone, try a home visit or ask the visiting teacher (or school social worker, psychologist, or other support personnel) to help you set up a conference. It is very important that you discuss the student's problems with the parents *before* you refer. Parents should never be surprised to find that their child has been referred; they should know well in advance that their child's teachers have noticed problems. One of the most important things you can do to prevent conflict with parents is to establish and maintain communication with them regarding their child's progress.

Before making a referral, check *all* the student's school records. Look for information that could help you understand the student's behavioral or academic problems. Has the student ever:

- Had a psychological evaluation?
- Qualified for special services?
- Been included in other special programs (e.g., programs for disadvantaged children or speech or language therapy)?
- Scored far below average on standardized tests?
- Been retained?

Do the records indicate:

- Good progress in some areas, poor progress in others?
- Any physical or medical problem?
- That the student is taking medication?

Talk to the student's other teachers and professional support personnel about your concern for him or her. Have other teachers:

- Also had difficulty with the student?
- Found ways of dealing successfully with the student?

The analysis of information obtained in these ways may help you teach and manage the student successfully, or help you justify to the parents why you believe their child may need special education.

Before making a referral, you will be expected to document the strategies that you have used in your class to meet the student's educational needs. Regardless of whether the student is later found to have a disabling condition, your documentation will be useful in the following ways:

1. You will have evidence that will be helpful to or required by the committee of professionals who will evaluate the student.
2. You will be better able to help the student's parents understand that methods used for other students in the class are not adequate for their child.
3. You will have records of successful and/or unsuccessful methods of working with the student that will be useful to you and any other teacher who works with the student in the future.

Your documentation of what you have done may appear to require a lot of paperwork, but careful record keeping will pay off. If the student is causing you serious concern, then you will be wise to demonstrate your concern by keeping written records. Your notes should include items such as the following:

- Exactly what you are concerned about
- Why you are concerned about it
- Dates, places, and times you have observed the problem
- Precisely what you have done to try to resolve the problem
- Who, if anyone, helped you devise the plans or strategies you have used
- Evidence that the strategies have been successful or unsuccessful

In summary, make certain that you have accomplished the following before you make a referral:

1. Held at least one conference to discuss your concerns with the parents (or made extensive and documented efforts to communicate with the parents)
2. Checked all available school records and interviewed other professionals involved with the child
3. Documented the academic and behavioral management strategies that you have tried

Remember that you should refer a student only if you can make a convincing case that the student may have a disability and probably cannot be served appropriately without special education. Referral for special education begins a time-consuming, costly, and stressful process that is potentially damaging to the student and has many legal ramifications.

and expertise in instruction. Furthermore, teachers are sometimes faced with serious professional and ethical dilemmas in trying to serve the needs of students and their parents, on the one hand, and in attempting to conform to legal or administrative pressures, on the other (Crockett & Kauffman, 1999; Howe & Miramontes, 1992). For example, when there are indications that a student may have a disability, should the teacher refer that student for evaluation and possible placement in special education, knowing that only inadequate or inappropriate services will be provided? Should a teacher who believes strongly that teenage students with mild retardation need sex education refrain from giving students any information because sex education is not part of the prescribed curriculum and is frowned on by the school board?

EXPECTATIONS FOR SPECIAL EDUCATORS

In addition to being competent enough to meet the preceding expectations, special education teachers must attain special expertise in the following areas:

1. *Academic instruction of students with learning problems.* The majority of students with disabilities have more difficulty learning academic skills than do those without disabilities. This is true for all categories of disabling conditions because sensory impairments, physical disabilities, and mental or emotional disabilities all tend to make academic learning more difficult. Often, the difficulty is slight; sometimes it is extreme. Special education teachers must have more than patience and hope, though they do need these qualities; they must also have the technical skill to present academic tasks so that students with disabilities will understand and respond appropriately. Exceptional instruction is the key to improving special education (Zigmond, 1997).
2. *Management of serious behavior problems.* Many students with disabilities have behavior problems in addition to their other exceptionalities. Some, in fact, require special education primarily because of their inappropriate or disruptive behavior. Special education teachers must have the ability to deal effectively with more than the usual troublesome behavior of students. Besides understanding and empathy, special education teachers must master the techniques that will allow them to draw out particularly withdrawn students, control those who are hyperaggressive and persistently disruptive, and teach critical social skills. Federal law now requires, in fact, that positive, proactive behavior intervention plans be written for all students who receive special education and exhibit serious behavior problems, regardless of their diagnostic label or classification (Bateman & Linden, 1998; Kauffman et al., 2002; Yell, 1998).
3. *Use of technological advances.* Technology is increasingly being applied to the problems of teaching exceptional students and improving their daily lives. New devices and methods are rapidly being developed, particularly for students with sensory and physical disabilities. Special education teachers need more than mere awareness of the technology available; they must also be able to evaluate its advantages and disadvantages for teaching the exceptional children and youths with whom they work.
4. *Knowledge of special education law.* For good or ill, special education today involves many details of law. The rights of students with disabilities are spelled out in considerable detail in federal and state legislation. The laws, as well as the rules and regulations that accompany them, are constantly being interpreted by new court decisions, some of which have widespread implications for the practice of special education. Special education teachers do not need to be lawyers, but they do need to be aware of the law's requirements and prohibitions if they are to be adequate advocates for students with disabilities (see Bateman & Linden, 1998; Huefner, 2000; Yell, 1998).

The knowledge and skills that every special education teacher is expected to master have been detailed by the primary professional organization of special educators (Council for Exceptional Children, 1998). We caution here that the specific day-to-day expectations for special education teachers vary from school system to school system and from state to state. What are listed here are the general expectations and areas of competence with which every special educator will necessarily be concerned. Nevertheless, we emphasize that special educators have the responsibility to offer not just good instruction but instruction that is highly individualized, intensive, relentless, urgent, and goal directed (Zigmond, 1997; Zigmond & Baker, 1995).

Origins of Special Education

The voice synthesizer is one of the technological devices available to special education learners. ■

There have always been exceptional learners, but there have not always been special educational services to address their needs. During the closing years of the eighteenth century, following the American and French Revolutions, effective procedures were devised for teaching children with sensory impairments—those who were blind or deaf (Winzer, 1986, 1993, 1998). Early in the nineteenth century, the first systematic attempts were made to educate "idiotic" and "insane" children—those who today are said to have mental retardation and emotional or behavioral disorders.

In the prerevolutionary era, the most society had offered children with disabilities was protection—asylum from a cruel world into which they did not fit and in which they could not survive with dignity, if they could survive at all. But as the ideas of democracy, individual freedom, and egalitarianism swept America and France, there was a change in attitude. Political reformers and leaders in medicine and education began to champion the cause of children and adults with disabilities, urging that these "imperfect" or "incomplete" individuals be taught skills that would allow them to become independent, productive citizens. These humanitarian sentiments went beyond a desire to protect and defend people with disabilities. The early leaders sought to normalize exceptional people to the greatest extent possible and confer on them the human dignity they presumably lacked.

The historical roots of special education are found primarily in the early 1800s. Contemporary educational methods for exceptional children can be traced directly to techniques pioneered during that era. And many (perhaps most) of today's vital, controversial issues have been issues ever since the dawn of special education. Some contemporary writers feel that the history of special education is critically important to understanding today's issues and should be given more attention for the lessons we can learn from our past (e.g., Kauffman, 1999a; Smith, 1998a, 1998b). In our discussion of some of the major historical events and trends since 1800, we comment briefly on the history of people and ideas, the growth of the discipline, professional and parent organizations, and legislation.

PEOPLE AND IDEAS

Most of the originators of special education were European physicians. They were primarily young, ambitious people who challenged the wisdom of the established authorities, including their own friends and mentors (Kanner, 1964; see also Winzer, 1998).

Jean-Marc-Gaspard Itard (1775–1838), a French physician who was an authority on diseases of the ear and on the education of students who were deaf, is the person to whom most historians trace the beginning of special education as we know it today. In the early

Jean-Marc-Gaspard Itard
(1775–1838) ∎

years of the nineteenth century, this young doctor began to educate a boy of about twelve who had been found roaming naked and wild in the forests of France. Itard's mentor, Philippe Pinel (1745–1826), a prominent French physician who was an early advocate of humane treatment of insane persons, advised him that his efforts would be unsuccessful because the boy, Victor, was a "hopeless idiot." But Itard persevered. He did not eliminate Victor's disabilities, but he did dramatically improve the wild child's behavior through patient, systematic educative procedures (Itard, 1962).

Itard's student, Édouard Séguin (1812–1880), immigrated to the United States in 1848. Before that, Séguin had become famous as an educator of so-called idiotic children, even though most thinkers of the day were convinced that such children could not be taught anything of significance.

The ideas of the first special educators were truly revolutionary for their times. These are a few of the revolutionary ideas of Itard, Séguin, and their successors that form the foundation for present-day special education:

- *Individualized instruction,* in which the child's characteristics, rather than prescribed academic content, provide the basis for teaching techniques
- *A carefully sequenced series of educational tasks,* beginning with tasks the child can perform and gradually leading to more complex learning
- *Emphasis on stimulation and awakening of the child's senses,* the aim being to make the child more aware of and responsive to educational stimuli
- *Meticulous arrangement of the child's environment,* so that the structure of the environment and the child's experience of it lead naturally to learning
- *Immediate reward for correct performance,* providing reinforcement for desirable behavior
- *Tutoring in functional skills,* the desire being to make the child as self-sufficient and productive as possible in everyday life
- *Belief that every child should be educated to the greatest extent possible,* the assumption being that every child can improve to some degree

So far we have mentioned only European physicians who figured prominently in the rise of special education. Although it is true that much of the initial work took place in Europe, many U.S. researchers contributed greatly during those early years. They stayed informed of European developments as best they could, some of them traveling to Europe for the specific purpose of obtaining firsthand information about the education of children with disabilities.

Among the young U.S. thinkers concerned with the education of students with disabilities was Samuel Gridley Howe (1801–1876), an 1824 graduate of Harvard Medical School. Besides being a physician and an educator, Howe was a political and social reformer, a champion of humanitarian causes and emancipation. He was instrumental in founding the Perkins School for the Blind in Watertown, Massachusetts, and was also a teacher of students who were deaf and blind. His success in teaching Laura Bridgman, who was deaf and blind, greatly influenced the education of Helen Keller. In the 1840s, Howe was also a force behind the organization of an experimental school for children with mental retardation and was personally acquainted with Séguin.

When Thomas Hopkins Gallaudet (1787–1851), a minister, was a student at Andover Theological Seminary, he tried to teach a girl who was deaf. He visited Europe to learn about educating the deaf and in 1817 established the first American residential school, in Hartford, Connecticut, for students who were deaf (now known as the American School of the Deaf). Gallaudet University in Washington, D.C., the only liberal-arts college for students who are deaf, was named in his honor.

The early years of special education were vibrant with the pulse of new ideas. It is not possible to read the words of Itard, Séguin, Howe, and their contemporaries without being captivated by the romance, idealism, and excitement of their exploits. The results they achieved were truly remarkable for their era. Today special education remains a vibrant field in which innovations, excitement, idealism, and controversies are the norm. Teachers of exceptional children—and that includes, as discussed earlier, all teachers—must understand how and why special education emerged as a discipline.

GROWTH OF THE DISCIPLINE

Special education did not suddenly spring up as a new discipline, nor did it develop in isolation from other disciplines. The emergence of psychology and sociology, and especially the beginning of the widespread use of mental tests in the early years of the twentieth century, had enormous implications for the growth of special education. Psychologists' study of learning and their prediction of school failure or success by means of tests helped focus attention on children with special needs. Sociologists, social workers, and anthropologists drew attention to the ways in which exceptional children's families and communities responded to them and affected their learning and adjustment. Anecdotal accounts of mental retardation or other mental disabilities can be found in the nineteenth-century literature, but they are not presented within the conceptual frameworks that we recognize today as psychology, sociology, or special education (see, for example, Hallahan & Kauffman, 1977; Kauffman, 1976; Richards & Singer, 1998). Even in the early twentieth century, the concepts of disability seem crude by today's standards (see Trent, 1998).

Thomas Hopkins Gallaudet (1787–1851) ■

As the education profession itself matured and as compulsory school attendance laws became a reality, there was a growing realization among teachers and school administrators that a large number of students must be given something beyond the ordinary classroom experience. Elizabeth Farrell, a teacher in New York City in the early twentieth century, was highly instrumental in the development of special education as a profession. She and the New York City superintendent of schools attempted to use information about child development, social work, mental testing, and instruction to address the needs of children and youths who were being ill served in or excluded from regular classes and schools. Farrell was a great advocate for services for students with special needs (see Safford & Safford, 1998). Her motives and those of the teachers and administrators who worked with her were to see that every student—including every exceptional child or youth—had an appropriate education and received the related health and social services necessary for optimum learning in school (Hendrick & MacMillan, 1989; MacMillan & Hendrick, 1993). In 1922, Farrell and a group of other special educators from across the United States and Canada founded the Council for Exceptional Children, today still the primary professional organization of special educators.

Contemporary special education is a professional field with roots in several academic disciplines—especially medicine, psychology, sociology, and social work—in addition to professional education. It is a discipline sufficiently different from the mainstream of professional education to require special training programs but sufficiently like the mainstream to maintain a primary concern for schools and teaching.

PROFESSIONAL AND PARENT ORGANIZATIONS

Individuals and ideas have played crucial roles in the history of special education, but it is accurate to say that much of the progress made over the years has been achieved primarily by the collective efforts of professionals and parents. Professional groups were organized first, beginning in the nineteenth century. Effective national parent organizations have existed in the United States only since 1950.

The earliest professional organizations having some bearing on the education of children with disabilities were medical associations founded in the 1800s. With the organization of the Council for Exceptional Children (CEC) and its many divisions, educators had a professional association devoted to special education. Today the CEC has a national membership of over 50,000, including about 10,000 students. There are state CEC organizations and hundreds of local chapters. Divisions of the CEC have been organized to meet the interests and needs of members who specialize in a particular area.

GW You may want to explore the web site of the Council for Exceptional Children at www.cec. sped.org/ or the Eric Clearing House on Disabilities and Gifted Education at http://ericec.org/

For more information about the history of special education, see www.npr.org/programs/disability and www.disabilityhistory.org/ ■

Education for All Handicapped Children Act.
Also known as Public Law 94–142, which became law in 1975 and is now known as the Individuals with Disabilities Education Act (IDEA).

Individuals with Disabilities Education Act (IDEA).
The Individuals with Disabilities Education Act of 1990 and its amendments of 1997; replaced PL 94–142. A federal law stating that to receive funds under the act, every school system in the nation must provide a free, appropriate public education for every child between the ages of three and twenty-one, regardless of how or how seriously he or she may be disabled.

Americans with Disabilities Act (ADA).
Civil rights legislation for persons with disabilities ensuring nondiscrimination in a broad range of activities.

Although parent organizations offer membership to individuals who do not have exceptional children of their own, they are made up primarily of parents who do have such children and concentrate on issues of special concern to them. Parent organizations have typically served three essential functions: (1) providing an informal group for parents who understand one another's problems and needs and help one another deal with anxieties and frustrations; (2) providing information regarding services and potential resources; and (3) providing the structure for obtaining needed services for their children. Some of the organizations that came about primarily as the result of parents' efforts include the ARC (formerly the Association for Retarded Citizens), the National Association for Gifted Children, the Learning Disabilities Association, the Autism Society of America, and the Federation of Families for Children's Mental Health.

LEGISLATION

Laws have played a major role in the history of special education. In fact, much of the progress in meeting the educational needs of children and youths with disabilities is attributable to laws requiring states and localities to include students with special needs in the public education system. We focus here on recent legislation that represents a culmination of decades of legislative history.

A landmark federal law was passed in 1975, the **Education for All Handicapped Children Act,** also commonly known as PL 94–142.* In 1990 this law was amended to become the **Individuals with Disabilities Education Act (IDEA).** In 1997 the law was amended again, but its name was not changed (see Bateman & Linden, 1998; Huefner, 2000; and Yell, 1998, for details). IDEA ensures that all children and youths with disabilities have the right to a free, appropriate public education.

Another landmark federal law, enacted in 1990, is the **Americans with Disabilities Act (ADA).** ADA ensures the right of individuals with disabilities to nondiscriminatory treatment in other aspects of their lives; it provides protections of civil rights in the specific areas of employment, transportation, public accommodations, state and local government, and telecommunications.

IDEA and another federal law focusing on intervention in early childhood (PL 99–457) now mandate a free, appropriate public education for every child or youth between the ages of three and twenty-one regardless of the nature or severity of the disability he or she may have. PL 99–457 also provides incentives for states to develop early intervention programs for infants with known disabilities and those considered at risk. Together, these laws require public school systems to identify all children and youths with disabilities and to provide the special education and related services they may need.

The law we know today as IDEA was revolutionary. It was the first federal law mandating free, appropriate public education for all children with disabilities. Its basic provisions, as amended in 1997, are described in the box on p. 29.

Trends in Legislation and Litigation

TRENDS IN LEGISLATION

℠ You can access current information about IDEA at the following Web address: http://www.ideapractices.org/ and at www.ed.gov/inits/commissionsboards/whspecialeducation/index.html ∎

Legislation historically has been increasingly specific and mandatory. In the 1980s, however, the renewed emphasis on states' rights and local autonomy, plus a political strategy of federal deregulation, led to attempts to repeal some of the provisions of IDEA (then still known as PL 94–142) and loosen federal rules and regulations. Federal disinvestment in

---

*Legislation is often designated PL (for public law), followed by a hyphenated numeral, the first set of digits representing the number of the Congress that passed the bill and the second set representing the number of that bill. Thus, PL 94–142 was the 142nd public law passed by the 94th Congress.

education and deregulation of education programs were hallmarks of the Reagan administration (Clark & Astutó, 1988; Verstegen & Clark, 1988), so it is not surprising that federal mandates for special education came under fire during that time. Dissatisfaction with federal mandates is due in part to the fact that the federal government contributes relatively little to the funding of special education. Although the demands of IDEA are detailed, state and local governments must pay most of the cost of special education programs. Some have characterized the legal history of special education as a long, strange trip (Yell, Rogers, & Rogers, 1998). Special education law is highly controversial; not surprisingly, Congressional battles over IDEA are ongoing.

The amendment and continuation of IDEA in 1997 represented a sustained commitment to require schools, employers, and government agencies to recognize the abilities of people with disabilities. IDEA and ADA (the Americans with Disabilities Act) require reasonable accommodations that will allow those who have disabilities to participate to the fullest extent possible in all the activities of daily living that individuals without disabilities take for granted. The requirements of ADA are intended to grant equal opportunities to people with disabilities in employment, transportation, public accommodations, state and local government, and telecommunications.

ADA was as revolutionary for business in the 1990s as PL 94–142 (now IDEA) was for education when it was enacted in the 1970s. ADA has had great implications for many young adults with disabilities as they have left high school for work or higher education, and for the everyday lives of all individuals with disabilities who live in our communities. Yet ADA has not been without controversy. In fact, the controversy was reflected in a

MAKING IT WORK

Collaboration and Co-Teaching for Students with Disabilities

I have to do what?!

According to the *Seventeenth Annual Report to Congress,* 40.53 percent of students with disabilities in the United States were served in regular classrooms in the 1992–93 school year (U.S. Department of Education, 1995). In the *Twenty-second Annual Report to Congress,* 46.97 percent of all students with disabilities spent less than 21 percent of their school time outside of the general education classroom, the most inclusive category reported (U.S. Department of Education, 2000). With the inclusion of more students with disabilities in the general education classroom, special educators are asking a greater number of general educators to work with them to deliver instruction. This collaboration can take many forms, such as collaborative consultation, working with itinerant teachers or paraprofessionals, and co-teaching. According to the National Center on Educational Restructuring and Inclusion (1995), co-teaching is the collaborative model used most often by schools.

To address the issues of collaboration and co-teaching, we have included a feature called Making It Work to give readers some "how-tos" and "cautions." These boxes, which you will find in most of the chapters, contain two separate sections: (a) What Does It Mean to Be a Teacher of Students with . . . , and (b) Successful Strategies for Co-teaching or Collaboration. The first section includes information about knowledge and skills special educators should possess as they enter the field, as identified by the Council for Exceptional Children (CEC) in its Performance Based Professional Standards (2001). CEC is the largest professional organization for special educators and is made up of smaller divisions representing professionals and parents from all disability categories. We believe it is important for all teachers to understand what expertise special educators can contribute to collaborative classrooms. For more information, try www.cec.sped.org.

The second section contains examples of research-based instructional practices that teachers could use when collaborating or descriptions of successful collaborations in real classrooms. Each box contains specifics about how to get more information about the strategy or collaboration described.

—*By Margaret P. Weiss*

Golfer Casey Martin is shown here in the first round of the Nike Greater Austin Open in Texas after a court ruling allowed him to use a golf cart. ■

special-issue forum in the *Washington Post* on July 18, 1995, called "Year Five of the ADA" (Taylor, 1995). Some critics of ADA have claimed that it has not lived up to its promise of more employment for people with disabilities, whereas others have described it as too expensive and its regulations as too oppressive to business. To some, support for ADA may seem to come primarily from legislators and people with disabilities. However, a 1995 survey by Louis Harris and the National Organization on Disability (NOD) found overwhelming support for ADA among business owners (Taylor, 1995).

ADA was intended to "level the playing field" for people with disabilities in earning their livelihood and participating in community life. Just where the boundaries of fairness are in making accommodations for disabilities will likely be a matter of continuing controversy. Perhaps the most talked-about issue to date has been related to a U.S. Supreme Court decision in 2001 that professional golfer Casey Martin must, under ADA, be allowed to use a golf cart in Professional Golf Association (PGA) tournaments. Martin has Klippel-Trenaunay-Weber syndrome, a rare congenital abnormality of the circulatory system that makes it extremely difficult for him to walk. After years of legal wrangling between Martin and the PGA, the Supreme Court finally decided the case. The court's decision was followed by a flurry of editorials pro and con. Some see allowing Martin to use a golf cart as only common sense, a reasonable accommodation of an obvious disability. Others think the decision forever changes the game of golf and that the Supreme Court's decision opens the door to all kinds of frivolous claims of disability in sports.

RELATIONSHIP OF LITIGATION TO LEGISLATION

Legislation requires or gives permission to provide special education, but it does not necessarily result in what legislators intended. Whether the laws are administered properly is a legal question for the courts. That is, laws may have little or no effect on the lives of individuals with disabilities until courts interpret exactly what the laws require in practice. Exceptional children, primarily through the actions of parent and professional organizations, have been getting their day in court more frequently since IDEA and related federal and state laws were passed. Thus, we must examine trends in litigation to complete the picture of how the U.S. legal system may safeguard or undermine appropriate education for exceptional children.

TRENDS IN LITIGATION

For updates on legal issues in special education, see the Web site maintained by legal expert Dixie Snow Huefner and click on "Chapter Updates": www.gse.utah.edu/sped/huefner/spdlawbk.htm or www.wrightslaw.com ■

Zelder (1953) noted that in the early days of public education, school attendance was seen as a privilege that could be awarded or withheld from an individual child at the discretion of local school officials. During the late nineteenth and early twentieth centuries, the courts typically found that disruptive children or those with mental retardation could be excluded from school for the sake of preserving order, protecting the teacher's time from excessive demands, and sparing children the "pain" of seeing others who are disabled. In the first half of the twentieth century, the courts tended to defend the majority of schoolchildren from a disabled minority. But now the old excuses for excluding students with disabilities from school are no longer thought to be valid. Today the courts must interpret laws that define school attendance as the *right* of every child, regardless of his or her disability. Litigation is now focused on ensuring that every child receives an education *appropriate for his or her individual needs*. As some legal scholars have pointed out, this does not

Major Provisions of IDEA

	Each state and locality must have a plan to ensure:
Identification	Extensive efforts to screen and identify all children and youths with disabilities.
Free, Appropriate Public Education (FAPE)	Every student with a disability has an appropriate public education at no cost to the parents or guardian.
Due Process	The student's and parents' rights to information and informed consent before the student is evaluated, labeled, or placed, and the right to an impartial due process hearing if they disagree with the school's decisions.
Parent/Guardian Surrogate Consultation	The student's parents or guardian are consulted about the student's evaluation and placement and the educational plan; if the parents or guardian are unknown or unavailable, a surrogate parent must be found to act for the student.
Least Restrictive Environment (LRE)	The student is educated in the least restrictive environment consistent with his or her educational needs and, insofar as possible, with students without disabilities.
Individualized Education Program (IEP)	A written individualized education program is prepared for each student with a disability, including levels of functioning, long- and short-term goals, extent to which the student will *not* participate in the general education classroom and curriculum, services to be provided, plans for initiating and evaluating the services, and needed transition services (from school to work or continued education).
Nondiscriminatory Evaluation	The student is evaluated in all areas of suspected disability and in a way that is not biased by his or her language or cultural characteristics or disabilities. Evaluation must be by a multidisciplinary team, and no single evaluation procedure may be used as the sole criterion for placement or planning.
Confidentiality	The results of evaluation and placement are kept confidential, though the student's parents or guardian may have access to the records.
Personnel Development, Inservice	Training for teachers and other professional personnel, including inservice training for regular teachers, in meeting the needs of students with disabilities.

Detailed federal rules and regulations govern the implementation of each of these major provisions. The definitions of some of these provisions—LRE and nondiscriminatory evaluation, for example—are still being clarified by federal officials and court decisions. See related Web sites.

mean that laws or litigation support full inclusion of all children with disabilities in general education (Dupre, 1997).

Litigation may involve legal suits filed for either of two reasons: (1) because special education services are not being provided for students whose parents want them, or (2) because students are being assigned to special education when their parents believe they should not be. Suits filed *for* special education have been brought primarily by parents whose children are unquestionably disabled and are being denied any education at all or are being given very meager special services. The parents who file these suits believe that the advantages of their children's identification for special education services clearly outweigh the disadvantages. Suits *against* special education have been brought primarily by parents of students who have mild or questionable disabilities and who are already attending school. These parents believe that their children are being stigmatized and discriminated against rather than helped by special education. Thus, the courts today are asked to make decisions in which individual students' characteristics are weighed against specific educational programs.

Parents want their children with disabilities to have a free public education that meets their needs but does not stigmatize them unnecessarily and that permits them to be taught in the regular school and classroom as much as possible. The laws governing education recognize parents' and students' rights to such an education. In the courts today, the burden of proof is ultimately on local and state education specialists, who must show in every instance that the student's abilities and disabilities have been completely and accurately assessed and that appropriate educational procedures are being employed. Much of the special education litigation has involved controversy over the use of IQ and other standardized testing to determine students' eligibility for special education. Although there has been much acrimony in the debate about IQ tests, some scholars have found that IQ scores themselves have not been the primary means of classifying children as eligible for special education (MacMillan & Forness, 1998).

One historic court case of the 1980s deserves particular consideration. In 1982, the U.S. Supreme Court made its first interpretation of PL 94–142 (now IDEA) in *Hudson v. Rowley,* a case involving Amy Rowley, a child who was deaf. The Court's decision was that appropriate education for a deaf child with a disability does not necessarily mean education that will produce the maximum possible achievement. Amy's parents had contended that she might be able to learn more in school if she were provided with a sign language interpreter. But the Court decided that because the school had designed an individualized program of special services for Amy and she was achieving at or above the level of her nondisabled classmates, the school system had met its obligation under the law to provide an appropriate education. Future cases will undoubtedly help to clarify what the law means by *appropriate education* and *least restrictive environment* (Crockett & Kauffman, 1999; Huefner, 1994; Yell, 1998).

THE INTENT OF LEGISLATION: AN INDIVIDUALIZED EDUCATION PROGRAM

Individualized education program (IEP).
IDEA requires an IEP to be drawn up by the educational team for each exceptional child; the IEP must include a statement of present educational performance, instructional goals, educational services to be provided, and criteria and procedures for determining that the instructional objectives are being met.

The primary intent of the special education laws passed during the past two decades has been to require educators to focus on the needs of individual students with disabilities. The **individualized education program (IEP)** is the most important aspect of this focus; it spells out just what teachers plan to do to meet an exceptional student's needs, and the plan must be approved by the student's parents or guardian. IEPs vary greatly in format and detail and from one school district to another. Some school districts use computerized IEP systems to help teachers determine goals and instructional objectives and to save time and effort in writing the documents. Legally, such cut-and-paste IEPs may be questionable because they lack sufficient attention to the particular needs of individuals (see Bateman & Linden, 1998). Many school systems, however, still rely on teachers' knowledge of students and curriculum to complete handwritten IEPs on the district's forms. Federal and state regulations do not specify exactly how much detail must be included in an IEP, only that it must be a written statement developed in a meeting of a representative of the local school district, the teacher, the parents or guardian, and, whenever appropriate, the child—and that it must include certain elements (see Table 1.2 on page 31).

The IEPs written in most schools contain much information related to the technical requirements of IDEA in addition to the heart of the plans—their instructional components. Figure 1.3 is an IEP provided by Bateman and Linden (1998). Curt "is a ninth-grade low achiever who was considered by the district to be a poorly motivated disciplinary problem student with a 'bad attitude.' His parents recognized him as a very discouraged, frustrated student who had learning disabilities, especially in language arts" (Bateman & Linden, 1998, p. 126).

TABLE 1.2   IEP Components

For All Students:	For Some Students:
• Present levels of performance • Measurable goals and objectives • Assessment status • Nonparticipation with nondisabled students • All needed services fully described (amount, frequency, etc.) • Progress reporting	• Transition—including transfer of parental rights to students • Behavior plan • ESL needs • Braille • Communication needs • Assistive technology

As mentioned earlier, there is no standard IEP format used by all schools. An entire IEP may be a document of ten pages or more, depending on the format and the extent and complexity of the student's disabilities. The emphasis should be on writing IEPs that are clear, useful, and legally defensible, not on the IEP format (Bateman & Linden, 1998). Clear and explicit relationships among IEP components are required to make sure that the focus of the individualized program—special, individually tailored instruction to meet unique needs—is not lost. In Curt's IEP (Figure 1.3), the relationships among the components are maintained by the alignment of information across columns. Reading across the form, we first read a description of the unique characteristic or need and present level of performance, then the special services and modifications needed to address that need, and then the annual goals and short-term objectives or benchmarks related to the need.

The process of writing an IEP and the document itself are perhaps the most important features of compliance with the spirit and letter of IDEA. Bateman and Linden (1998) summarize compliance with both the spirit and the letter of the law as the "IDEA Commandments," as shown in Table 1.3 on page 35. When the IEP is prepared as intended by the law, it means that:

- The student's needs have been carefully assessed.
- A team of professionals and the parents have worked together to design a program of education to best meet the student's needs.
- Goals and objectives are clearly stated so that progress in reaching them can be evaluated.

Government regulation of the IEP process has always been controversial. Some of the people who were influential in formulating the basic law (IDEA) have expressed great disappointment in the results of requiring IEPs (Goodman & Bond, 1993, p. 413). Others question whether the requirement of long-term and short-term objectives is appropriate:

The IEP assumes that instructors know in advance what a child should and can learn, and the speed at which he or she will learn. . . . This is a difficult projection to make with nondisabled children of school age—for preschool children with cognitive, emotional, and social disabilities, it is near impossible. (Goodman & Bond, 1993, p. 415)

A major problem is that the IEP—the educational *program*—is too often written at the wrong time and for the wrong reason (Bateman & Linden, 1998). As illustrated in Figure 1.4 (p. 35), the legal IEP is written following evaluation and identification of the student's disabilities and before a placement decision is made; what the student needs is determined first, and then a decision is made about placement in the least restrictive environment in which the needed services can be provided. Too often, we see the educationally wrong (and illegal) practice of basing the IEP on an available placement; that is, the student's IEP is written *after* available placements and services are considered.

Individualized Education Program

Student: _Curt_____   Age: _15_____   Grade: _9_____   Date: _1998_____

Unique Educational Needs, Characteristics, and Present Levels of Performance (PLOPs) *(including how the disability affects the student's ability to progress in the general curriculum)*	Special Education, Related Services, Supplemental Aids & Services, Assistive Technology, Program Modifications, Support for Personnel *(including frequency, duration, and location)*	Measurable Annual Goals & Short-Term Objectives or Benchmarks • To enable student to participate in the general curriculum • To meet other needs resulting from the disability *(including how progress toward goals will be measured)*
Present Level of Social Skills: Curt lashes out violently when not able to complete work, uses profanity, and refuses to follow further directions from adults. Social Needs: • To learn anger management skills, especially regarding swearing • To learn to comply with requests	1. Teacher and/or counselor consult with behavior specialist regarding techniques and programs for teaching skills, especially anger management. 2. Provide anger management instruction to Curt. Services 3 times/week, 30 minutes. 3. Establish a peer group which involves role playing, etc., so Curt can see positive role models and practice newly learned anger management skills. Services 2 times/week, 30 minutes. 4. Develop a behavioral plan for Curt which gives him responsibility for charting his own behavior. 5. Provide a teacher or some other adult mentor to spend time with Curt (talking, game playing, physical activity, etc.). Services 2 times/week, 30 minutes. 6. Provide training for the mentor regarding Curt's needs/goals.	*Goal:* During the last quarter of the academic year, Curt will have 2 or fewer detentions for any reason. Obj. 1: At the end of the 1st quarter, Curt will have had 10 or fewer detentions. Obj. 2: At the end of the 2nd quarter, Curt will have had 7 or fewer detentions. Obj. 3: At the end of the 3rd quarter, Curt will have had 4 or fewer detentions. *Goal:* Curt will manage his behavior and language in a reasonably acceptable manner as reported by faculty and peers. Obj. 1: At 2 weeks, asked at the end of class if Curt's behavior and language were acceptable or unacceptable, 3 out of 6 teachers will say "acceptable." Obj. 2: At 6 weeks, asked the same question, 4 out of 6 teachers will say "acceptable." Obj. 3: At 12 weeks, asked the same question, 6 out of 6 teachers will say "acceptable."

FIGURE 1.3

An IEP for Curt.

SOURCE: Reprinted with permission from Bateman, B. D., & Linden, M. A. (1998). *Better IEPs: How to develop legally correct and educationally useful programs* (3rd ed.). Longmont, CO: Sopris West. All rights reserved.

Writing IEPs that meet all the requirements of the law and that are also educationally useful is no small task. Computerized IEPs and those based only on standardized testing or developmental inventories are likely to violate the requirements of the law, or be of little educational value, or both (Bateman & Linden, 1998; Goodman & Bond, 1993). However, much of the controversy about IEPs and the disappointment in them appear to result from misunderstanding of the law, or lack of instructional expertise, or both. Within the framework of IDEA and other regulations, it is possible to write IEPs that are both legally correct and educationally useful. Bateman and Linden (1998) summarize do's and don'ts in the form of IEP "sins" and "virtues," as illustrated in Table 1.4 (p. 36).

Legislation and litigation were initially used in the 1960s and 1970s to include exceptional children in public education with relatively little regard for quality. In the 1980s and 1990s, laws and lawsuits have been used to try to ensure individualized education, coop-

Individualized Education Program *(continued)*

Unique Educational Needs, Characteristics, and Present Levels of Performance (PLOPs) *(including how the disability affects the student's ability to progress in the general curriculum)*	Special Education, Related Services, Supplemental Aids & Services, Assistive Technology, Program Modifications, Support for Personnel *(including frequency, duration, and location)*	Measurable Annual Goals & Short-Term Objectives or Benchmarks • To enable student to participate in the general curriculum • To meet other needs resulting from the disability *(including how progress toward goals will be measured)*

Study Skills/ Organizational Needs:
 	
How to read text
 	
Note taking
 	
How to study notes
 	
Memory work
 	
Be prepared for class, with materials
 	
Lengthen and improve attention span and on-task behavior
 	
Present Level:
 	
Curt currently lacks skill in all these areas.
	1. Speech/lang. therapist, resource room teacher, and content area teachers will provide Curt with direct and specific teaching of study skills, i.e.
	
	    Note taking from lectures
	
	    Note taking while reading text
	
	    How to study notes for a test
	
	    Memorization hints
	
	    Strategies for reading text to retain information
	
	2. Assign a "study buddy" for Curt in each content area class.
	
	3. Prepare a motivation system for Curt to be prepared for class with all necessary materials.
	
	4. Develop a motivational plan to encourage Curt to lengthen his attention span and time on task.
	
	5. Provide aide to monitor on-task behaviors in first month or so of plan and teach Curt self-monitoring techniques.
	
	6. Provide motivational system and self-recording form for completion of academic tasks in each class.
		Goal: At the end of academic year, Curt will have better grades and, by his own report, will have learned new study skills.
		
		Obj. 1: Given a 20–30 min. lecture/oral lesson, Curt will take appropriate notes as judged by that teacher.
		
		Obj. 2: Given 10–15 pgs. of text to read, Curt will employ an appropriate strategy for retaining info.—i.e., mapping, webbing, outlining, notes, etc.—as judged by the teacher.
		
		Obj. 3: Given notes to study for a test, Curt will do so successfully as evidenced by his test score.
		
		Goal: Curt will improve his on-task behavior from 37% to 80% as measured by a qualified observer at year's end.
		
		Obj. 1: By 1 month, Curt's on-task behavior will increase to 45%.
		
		Obj. 2: By 3 months, Curt's on-task behavior will increase to 60%.
		
		Obj. 3: By 6 months, Curt's on-task behavior will increase to 80% and maintain or improve until end of the year.

(continued)

eration, and collaboration among professionals; parental participation; and accountability of educators for providing high-quality, effective programs.

IDEA, for example, is noteworthy for its expansion of the idea of individualized planning and collaboration among disciplines. PL 99–457 mandated an individualized family service plan (IFSP) for infants and toddlers with disabilities. An IFSP is similar to an IEP for older children in that it requires assessment and statement of goals, needed services, and plans for implementation. As we discuss in Chapter 2, an IFSP also requires more involvement of the family, coordination of services, and plans for making the transition into preschool. IDEA mandated the inclusion of plans for transition from school to work for older students as part of their IEPs. Other provisions of IDEA are intended to improve the quality of services received by children and youths with disabilities.

In the early twenty-first century, some have expressed considerable unhappiness with

Individualized Education Program *(continued)*

Unique Educational Needs, Characteristics, and Present Levels of Performance (PLOPs) *(including how the disability affects the student's ability to progress in the general curriculum)*	Special Education, Related Services, Supplemental Aids & Services, Assistive Technology, Program Modifications, Support for Personnel *(including frequency, duration, and location)*	Measurable Annual Goals & Short-Term Objectives or Benchmarks • To enable student to participate in the general curriculum • To meet other needs resulting from the disability *(including how progress toward goals will be measured)*
Academic Needs/ Written Language: Curt needs strong remedial help in spelling, punctuation, capitalization, and usage. Present Level: Curt is approximately 2 grade levels behind his peers in these skills.	1. Provide direct instruction in written language skills (punctuation, capitalization, usage, spelling) by using a highly structured, well-sequenced program. Services provided in small group of no more than four students in the resource room, 50 minutes/day. 2. Build in continuous and cumulative review to help with short-term rote memory difficulty. 3. Develop a list of commonly used words in student writing (or use one of many published lists) for Curt's spelling program.	*Goal:* Within one academic year, Curt will improve his written language skills by 1.5 or 2 full grade levels. Obj. 1: Given 10 sentences of dictation at his current level of instruction, Curt will punctuate and capitalize with 90% accuracy (checked at the end of each unit taught). Obj. 2: Given 30 sentences with choices of usage, at his current instructional level, Curt will perform with 90% accuracy. Obj. 3: Given a list of 150 commonly used words in writing. Curt will spell with 90% accuracy.

Adaptations to Regular Program:

- In all classes, Curt should sit near the front of the class.
- Curt should be called on often to keep him involved and on task.
- All teachers should help Curt with study skills as trained by spelling/language specialist and resource room teacher.
- Teachers should monitor Curt's work closely in the beginning weeks/months of his program.

FIGURE 1.3
(Continued)

the results of federal legislation and litigation. Critics have charged that laws intended to ensure the appropriate education of students with disabilities have gone awry and that new legislation and federal rules are required (e.g., Finn, Rotherham, & Hokanson, 2001).

A Perspective on the Progress of Special Education

Special education has come a long way since it was introduced into American public education over a century ago. It has become an expected part of the U.S. public education system, a given rather than an exception or an experiment. Much progress has been made since PL 94–142 (now IDEA) was enacted a quarter century ago. Now parents and their children have legal rights to free, appropriate education; they are not powerless in the face of school administrators who do not want to provide appropriate education and related services. The enactment of PL 94–142 was one of very few events in the twentieth century that altered the power relationship between schools and parents (Sarason, 1990).

TABLE 1.3   IDEA Commandments

I.   THOU SHALT BASE ALL ELIGIBILITY DECISIONS ON PROFESSIONAL JUDGMENT, NOT ON QUANTITATIVE FORMULAE.
II.   THOU SHALT OPEN WIDE THE DOOR UNTO EVERY NEEDED SERVICE AND PLACEMENT FOR EACH ELIGIBLE CHILD.
III.   REMEMBER THOU THAT CATEGORICAL DELIVERY OF SERVICES IS AN ABOMINATION.
IV.   EACH IEP SHALL BE BASED SOLELY UPON THE CHILD'S NEEDS. HE OR SHE WHO LOOKS INSTEAD TO AVAILABILITY OF SERVICES SHALL KNOW THE INFERNO.
V.   MAKETH EVERY IEP IN THE IMAGE OF ITS CHILD. AN IEP LIKE UNTO ANOTHER IS A GRAVEN IMAGE, DESPISED BY ALL WHO KNOW IDEA.
VI.   PLACE NOT ALL CHILDREN IN THE SAME SETTING, BUT MAKE AVAILABLE THE ENTIRE CONTINUUM OF ALTERNATIVE PLACEMENTS.
VII.   THOU SHALT NOT EXCLUDE PARENTS FROM DECISIONS THAT AFFECT THEIR CHILDREN.
VIII.   THOU SHALT NOT BURDEN PARENTS WITH THE COST OF THEIR CHILDREN'S SPECIAL EDUCATION AND SERVICES.

SOURCE: Reprinted with permission from Bateman, B. D., & Linden, M. A. (1998). *Better IEPs: How to develop legally correct and educationally useful programs* (3rd ed.). Longmont, CO: Sopris West. All rights reserved.

In spite of the fact that IDEA and related laws and court cases have not resulted in flawless programs for exceptional children, they have done much to move American public schools toward providing better educational opportunities for those with disabilities. Laws enacted in the twentieth century have helped ensure that all infants and toddlers with disabilities will receive early intervention. Laws like ADA help ensure that children and adults with disabilities will not be discriminated against in U.S. society. Laws and court cases cannot eliminate all problems in our society, but they can certainly be of enormous help in our efforts to equalize opportunities and minimize handicaps for people with disabilities.

We have made much progress in special education, but making it all that we hope for is—and always will be—a continuing struggle. In Chapter 2 we discuss current trends and issues that highlight dissatisfaction with the way things are and represent hope for what special education and related services might become.

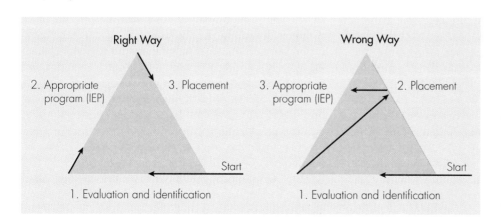

FIGURE 1.4

The right and wrong routes to placement.

SOURCE: Reprinted with permission from Bateman, B. D., & Linden, M. A. (1998). *Better IEPs: How to develop legally correct and educationally useful programs* (3rd ed., p. 66.). Longmont, CO: Sopris West. All rights reserved.

TABLE 1.4   Do's and Don'ts for IEPs

IEP Sins	IEP Virtues
• Failure to individualize the program to fit the student • Failure to address all the student's needs • Failure to sufficiently describe and specify all necessary services • Failure to write clear, objective, meaningful, and reasonable PLOPs, objectives, and goals	• Full and equal parental participation • Truly individualized to fit the student • Present levels of performance (PLOPs) and needs/characteristics carefully specified • All services, modifications, and supports to meet the student's needs fully detailed • Goals and objectives measurable, real, and taken seriously

SOURCE: Reprinted with permission from Bateman, B. D., & Linden, M. A. (1998). *Better IEPs: How to develop legally correct and educationally useful programs* (3rd ed.). Longmont, CO: Sopris West. All rights reserved.

Summary

The study of exceptional learners is the study of similarities and differences among individuals. Exceptional learners differ from most others in specific ways, but they are also similar to most others in most respects. Exceptionalities—differences—must not be allowed to obscure the ways in which exceptional learners are like others. We distinguish between an exceptionality that is a *disability* and one that is a *handicap*. A disability is an inability to do something. A handicap is a disadvantage that may be imposed on an individual. A disability may or may not be a handicap.

For purposes of education, *exceptional learners* are defined as those who require special education and related services if they are to realize their full human potential. Special education strives to make certain that students' handicaps are confined to those characteristics that cannot be changed.

Current government figures show that approximately one student in ten is identified as exceptional and receiving special education services. Most children and youths identified as exceptional are between the ages of six and seventeen, although identification of infants and young adults with disabilities is increasing.

Special education refers to specially designed instruction that meets the unusual needs of exceptional learners. The single most important goal of special education is finding and capitalizing on exceptional students' abilities. Special education may be provided under a variety of administrative plans. The regular classroom teacher, sometimes in consultation with other professionals, such as psychologists or teachers with more experience or training, is expected to serve many exceptional students in her or his regular classroom. Some exceptional students are served by an itinerant teacher who moves from school to school or by a resource teacher. Itinerant and resource teachers may teach students individually or in small groups for certain periods of the school day and provide assistance to regular

classroom teachers. Sometimes students are placed in a diagnostic-prescriptive center so their special needs can be determined. The special self-contained class is used for a small group of students, who are usually taught in the special class all or most of the day. Special day schools are sometimes provided for students whose disabilities necessitate special equipment and methods for care and education. Hospital and homebound instruction are provided when the student is unable to go to regular classes. Finally, the residential school provides educational services and management of the daily living environment for students with disabilities who must receive full-time care.

Present law requires that every exceptional child and youth be placed in the *least restrictive environment (LRE)* so that educational intervention will be consistent with individual needs and not interfere with individual freedom and the development of potential. Today, therefore, most students with exceptionalities are educated primarily in regular classes.

All teachers need to be prepared to some extent to deal with exceptional students because many of these students are placed for part of the day in regular classrooms. Furthermore, many students not identified as exceptional share some of the characteristics of disability or giftedness. Although the relationship between general and special education must be one of collaboration and shared responsibility for exceptional learners, the roles of special and general educators are not always clear. Both may be involved in educating exceptional students by making maximum efforts to accommodate individual students' needs, evaluating academic abilities and disabilities, referring students for further evaluation, participating in eligibility conferences, writing individualized education programs (IEPs), communicating with parents, participating in due-process hearings, and collaborating with other professionals. In addition, special educators must have particular

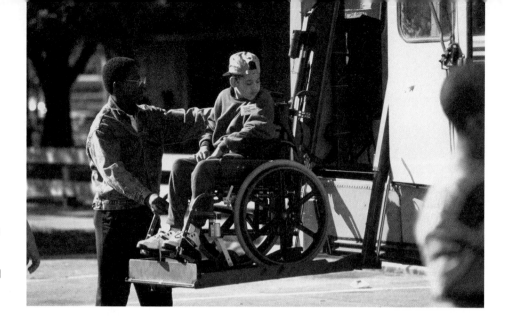

The Individuals with Disabilities Act (IDEA), passed in 1990, and renewed in 1997, requires public schools to provide equal education opportunities for all students with disabilities. ■

expertise in instructing students with learning problems, managing serious behavioral problems, using technological aids, and interpreting special education law.

Systematic attempts to educate learners with disabilities, especially those with mental retardation and emotional and behavioral disorders, began in the early 1800s. European physicians like Itard, Pinel, and Séguin pioneered in these educational efforts. Their revolutionary ideas included individualized instruction, carefully sequenced series of educational tasks, emphasis on stimulation and the awakening of the child's senses, meticulous arrangement of the child's environment, immediate reward for correct performance, tutoring in functional skills, and the belief that every child should be educated to the greatest extent possible. Howe and Gallaudet brought special education techniques and ideas to the United States.

Many other disciplines, especially psychology and sociology, were involved in the emergence of special education as a profession. Much of the progress in special education has resulted from the efforts of professional and parent organizations. The Council for Exceptional Children (CEC) is an influential group with many divisions devoted to such things as the study of specific exceptionalities; the administration, supervision, and implementation of special programs; teacher training and placement; and research. Organizations such as the ARC provide parents, schools, and the public with information about exceptionalities and the structure for obtaining needed services.

The legal basis of special education has evolved over the years, from permissive legislation allowing public funding of special programs for exceptional learners, to mandatory legislation requiring such expenditures. The contemporary commitment to the principle that every individual has the right to as normal a life and education as possible prompted much legislation and litigation in the 1970s and 1980s. Special education legislation has historically been increasingly specific and mandatory. The Individuals with Disabilities Education Act (IDEA) mandated that in order to receive funds under the act, *every school sys-* *tem in the country must make provision for a free, appropriate education for every child and youth with a disability.*

Laws and regulations may have little effect until the courts, through litigation, interpret their meanings. Litigation today focuses on ensuring that every exceptional child and youth receives an education that is appropriate for his or her individual needs. Lawsuits *for* special education tend to be filed on behalf of students who are unquestionably disabled but are receiving no education at all or only meager services. Lawsuits *against* special education tend to be filed on behalf of students whose disabilities are mild or questionable and for whom special education is thought to be more stigmatizing and discriminatory than helpful. Future court cases will undoubtedly result in clarification of the term *appropriate* with reference to education for exceptional students.

The primary intent of special education legislation has been to require educators to focus on the needs of individual students. Thus, a central feature of IDEA is the requirement that every student receiving special education under the law must have an individualized education program (IEP). An IEP is a written plan, which must be approved by the child's parents or guardian, that specifies the following for each area of disability: (1) the student's current level of performance; (2) annual goals; (3) short-term instructional objectives or benchmarks; (4) special services to be provided and the extent to which the student will participate in regular education; (5) plans for starting services and their expected duration; (6) plans for evaluation; and (7) for older students, the services needed to ensure a successful transition from school to work or higher education. These goals are based on the view that special education must *be individualized, intensive, relentless, urgent, and goal directed.*

Special education has made much progress during the past century. It is now an expected part of American public education, not an exception or experiment. Parents of students with disabilities now have more involvement in their children's education. In part, this progress has occurred because of laws requiring appropriate education and other services for individuals with disabilities.

Susan Jean Semple

Birds, Pencil, acrylic on rag paper. 14 × 17 in.

Ms. Semple, who was born in 1949 in Stillwater, Oklahoma, holds a Bachelor of Fine Arts degree from the University of Oklahoma and is proud of her three adult children. She traveled around the United States as an itinerant portrait artist before settling in Cambridge, Massachusetts. She is a creative and innovative artist working in many mediums.

Current Trends and Issues

Come writers and critics
Who prophesy with your pen
And keep your eyes wide,
The chance won't come again.
And don't speak too soon
For the wheel's still in spin
And there's no tellin' who
That it's namin'
For the loser now
Will be later to win
For the times they are a-changin'.

BOB DYLAN
"The Times They Are A-Changin' "

Bob Dylan could have written his song "The Times They Are A-Changin'" (see excerpt on p. 39) for the field of special education, which has a rich history of controversy and change. In fact, controversy and change are what make the teaching and study of people with disabilities so challenging and exciting. The history of special education is replete with unexpected twists and turns. Many of today's events and conditions will undoubtedly have consequences that we do not foresee (see Jakubecy, Mock, & Kauffman, 2003; Kauffman, 1999a, 1999-2000; Mock, Jakubecy, & Kauffman, 2003; Smith, 1998).

The 1980s and 1990s have seen especially dramatic changes in the education of people with disabilities, and current thinking indicates that the field is poised for still more changes in the early twenty-first century. One critically important trend and issue for the new century is movement toward multicultural special education. Because this topic is so important, it is the subject of Chapter 3.

In this chapter, we explore six major trends in special education and the related issues that the field is facing:

1. Integration of people with disabilities into the larger, nondisabled society
2. Participation of students with disabilities in general assessments of educational progress
3. Access of people with disabilities to new technologies
4. Early intervention with children who have disabilities
5. Transition from secondary school to adulthood
6. Discipline of students with disabilities

You can search major newspaper Web sites for articles about issues in special education. For example, the *Washington Post* carried an article on February 18, 2002, about lawyers in special education at www.washingtonpost.com/wp-dyn/articles/A259982002Feb17.html. The *New York Times* site is at www.nytimes.com and the *Washington Post* site is www.washingtonpost.com/ ■

Integration into the Larger Society

The trend of integrating people with disabilities into the larger society began in the 1960s and continues stronger than ever today. Champions of integration are proud of the fact that they have reduced the number of people with disabilities who reside in institutions and the number of special education students who attend special schools and special self-contained classes. Some of today's more radical proponents of integration, however, will not be satisfied until virtually all institutions, special schools, and special classes are eliminated. These proponents recommend that all students with disabilities be educated in regular classes. And even today's more conservative advocates of integration recommend a much greater degree of interaction between students with and without disabilities than was ever dreamed of by most special educators in the 1960s and 1970s.

PHILOSOPHICAL AND HISTORICAL ROOTS: NORMALIZATION, DEINSTITUTIONALIZATION, AND FULL INCLUSION

A key principle behind the trend toward more integration of people with disabilities into society is normalization. First espoused in Scandinavia (Bank-Mikkelsen, 1969) before being popularized in the United States, **normalization** is the philosophical belief that we should use "means which are as culturally normative as possible, in order to establish and/or maintain personal behaviors and characteristics which are as culturally normative as possible" (Wolfensberger, 1972, p. 28). In other words, under the principle of normalization, both the means and the ends of education for students with disabilities should be as much like those for nondisabled students as possible. Regarding the means, for example, we should place students with disabilities in educational settings as similar to those of nondisabled students as possible. And we should use treatment approaches that are as close as possible to the ones we use with the rest of the student population. Regarding the ends, we should strive to weave people with disabilities into the larger fabric of society.

Normalization.
A philosophical belief in special education that every individual, even the most disabled, should have an educational and living environment as close to normal as possible.

Learners with Disabilities

MYTH Normalization, the principle that the means and ends of education for students with disabilities should be as culturally normative as possible, is straightforward, needing little interpretation.

FACT There are many disagreements pertaining to the interpretation of the normalization principle. As just one example, some educators have interpreted it to mean that all people with disabilities must be educated in regular classes, whereas others maintain that a continuum of placements (residential schools, special schools, special classes, resource rooms, regular classes) should remain available as options.

MYTH All professionals agree that technology should be used to its fullest to aid people with disabilities.

FACT Some believe that technology should be used cautiously because it can lead people with disabilities to become too dependent on it. Some professionals believe that people with disabilities can be tempted to rely on technology rather than develop their own abilities.

MYTH All students with disabilities must now be included in standardized testing, just like students without disabilities.

FACT Most students with disabilities will be included in standardized testing procedures, but for some a given test will be judged inappropriate. Some students will require adaptations of the testing procedure to accommodate their specific disabilities. However, students with disabilities can no longer be automatically excluded from participation in standardized assessment procedures.

MYTH Research has established beyond a doubt that special classes are ineffective and that mainstreaming is effective.

FACT Research comparing special versus mainstream placement has been inconclusive because most of these studies have been methodologically flawed. Researchers are now focusing on finding ways of making mainstreaming work more effectively.

MYTH Professionals agree that labeling people with disabilities, (e.g., "retarded," "blind," "behavior disordered") is more harmful than helpful.

FACT Some professionals maintain that labels help them communicate, explain the atypical behavior of some people with disabilities to the public, and spotlight the special needs of people with disabilities for the general public.

MYTH People with disabilities are pleased with the media's portrayal, especially about their extraordinary achievements.

FACT Some disability rights advocates are disturbed by what they believe are too frequent overly negative and overly positive portrayals in the media.

MYTH Everyone agrees that teachers in early intervention programs need to assess parents as well as their children.

FACT Some authorities now believe that although families are an important part of intervention programming and should be involved in some way, special educators should center their assessment efforts primarily on the child, not the parents.

MYTH Everyone agrees that good early childhood programming for students with or without disabilities should be the same.

FACT There is considerable disagreement about whether early intervention programming for children with disabilities should be child directed, as is typical of regular preschool programs, or more teacher directed.

MYTH Professionals agree that all students with disabilities in secondary school should be given a curriculum focused on vocational preparation.

FACT Professionals are in conflict over how much vocational versus academic instruction students with mild disabilities should receive.

MYTH There are completely different rules of discipline for students with disabilities.

FACT In most cases, the same discipline rules apply to students with and without disabilities. However, the law does not allow discontinuation of education for a student with a disability. Even if the student is not allowed to return to the school, education must be provided in an alternative setting.

Deinstitutionalization.
A social movement of the 1960s and 1970s whereby large numbers of persons with mental retardation and/or mental illness were moved from large mental institutions into smaller community homes or into the homes of their families; recognized as a major catalyst for integrating persons with disabilities into society.

Although on its face the principle of normalization seems simple enough, numerous controversies have swirled around the implementation of this important concept. Many of these controversies have involved deinstitutionalization, self-determination, and—particularly important for teachers—full inclusion. Here we shall mention four of the more hotly contested issues regarding normalization:

1. The phrase as *culturally normative as possible* is open to interpretation. Even though the originators of the normalization principle saw the need for a variety of service delivery options—including residential institutions, special schools, and special classes—more recently, some have interpreted normalization to mean abolishing all such separate settings.

2. Some groups of people with disabilities are leery about being too closely integrated with nondisabled society. For example, some people who are deaf, because of their difficulty in communicating with the hearing world, prefer associating with other people who are deaf. For them, normalization does not translate into integration with the larger society. Others have pointed out that a diversity of different settings and groupings of people is itself normative in most societies (Kauffman & Hallahan, 1997).

3. Some disability rights advocates suggest that the assessment of normalization is wrongheaded, as it begins with the idea that nondisabled people should be seen as the norm to which those with disabilities are compared. For example, a representative of the organization Disabled People's International has called for "the elimination of the value concept of normalization as a measurement and the use of non-disabled people as the norm" (Mathiason, 1997, p. 2).

4. Some have questioned whether the rapidly expanding use of technology to assist people with disabilities actually works against the goal of normalization. Certainly, there is little doubt that technology has made it possible for more and more people with disabilities to take part in activities that previously were inaccessible to them. Thus, in many instances, technology serves as a means for achieving normalization. Some people with disabilities, however, have expressed concern that individuals might be too quick to rely on technology instead of working to improve their own abilities. Reliance on artificial means of interacting with the environment when more natural means are possible could jeopardize a person's quest for normalization.

DEINSTITUTIONALIZATION

At one time it was common to place children and adults with mental retardation and/or mental illness in residential institutions, especially if they had relatively severe problems. The 1960s and 1970s, however, witnessed a systematic drive to move people out of institutions and back into closer contact with the community. Referred to as **deinstitutionalization,** this movement caused more and more children with disabilities to be raised by their families. Today, smaller facilities, located within local neighborhoods, are now common. Halfway houses exist as placements for individuals with emotional difficulties who no longer need the more isolated environment of a large institution. For people with mental retardation, group homes house small numbers of individuals whose retardation may range from mild to severe. More and more

It is much more common today to find individuals with disabilities participating fully in everyday activities. This man uses a specialized chair to enjoy downhill skiing at a public resort. ■

people with disabilities are now working, with assistance from "job coaches," in competitive employment situations.

Some professionals assert that deinstitutionalization has been implemented, in certain cases, without much forethought (Crissey & Rosen, 1986; Landesman & Butterfield, 1987; Zigler, Hodapp, & Edison, 1990). They maintain that although deinstitutionalization has the potential to improve the quality of life for most people who, in previous generations, would have been lifelong residents of institutions, it has failed other people because of poor planning. Some individuals, for instance, have been turned out of institutions onto the streets. Moreover, institutions can be humane, effective alternative placements for some individuals.

A review of research on deinstitutionalization between 1980 and 1999 suggested that many people with intellectual disabilities have improved their adaptive behavior by moving into small community homes (University of Minnesota, 1999). However, research also indicates that much still needs to be done to improve the quality of life for some persons with disabilities who have been released from institutions. Studies of deinstitutionalization in California, where it has become a common practice, indicate that mortality (the death rate) is considerably higher among people with mental retardation who have been returned from institutions to community settings than among those who have remained in institutions (Strauss & Kastner, 1996; Strauss, Shavelle, Baumeister, & Anderson, 1998).

SELF-DETERMINATION

The movement of individuals with disabilities out of institutions and into communities has fostered increasing recognition that people with and without disabilities have a right to exercise self-determination. **Self-determination** refers to making one's own decisions about important aspects of one's life—for example, where to work and live, with whom to become friends, and what education to pursue. Individuals with disabilities may need to be taught how to plan for their self-determination, and thus **person-centered planning** has become an important aspect of self-determination.

Schwartz, Jacobson, and Holburn (2000) suggest that the primary hallmark of person centeredness is that "the person's activities, services and supports are based upon his or her dreams, interests, preferences, strengths, and capacities" (p. 238). The main idea is that people with disabilities, like those without disabilities, should exercise personal control of their lives (Stancliffe, Abery, & Smith, 2000). Other people, such as psychologists, counselors, physicians, parents, teachers, and administrators, should not make decisions for people with disabilities, as they often have in the past.

There is growing recognition that self-determination is learned and should be taught in schools (Agran, Blanchard, & Wehmeyer, 2000; Browder, Wood, Test, Karvonen, & Algozzine, 2001; Wehmeyer, Palmer, Agran, Mithaug, & Martin, 2000). Making schools places where all children have a significant voice or say in important decisions is seen as critical.

> In general, self-determination means taking charge of one's life. Teachers can play an important role in promoting the abilities and attitudes individuals will need in order to take charge of their lives through both providing instruction in self-determination skills and creating school environments where these skills can be practiced. (Browder et al., 2001, p. 233)

Some professional organizations now have policy statements regarding self-determination. For example, you might want to

Self-determination.
The ability to make personal choices, regulate one's own life, and be a self-advocate; a prevailing philosophy in education programming for persons with mental retardation.

Person-centered planning.
Planning for a person's self-determination; planning activities and services based on a person's dreams, aspirations, interests, preferences, strengths, and capacities.

A key goal for individuals with disabilities is to develop self-determination skills so that they "have a say" in their own lives, rather than being told what to do by others. ■

Full inclusion.
All students with disabilities are placed in their neighborhood schools in general education classrooms for the entire day; general education teachers have the primary responsibility for students with disabilities.

Individuals with Disabilities Education Act (IDEA).
The Individuals with Disabilities Education Act of 1990 and its amendments of 1997; replaced PL 94–142.

Least restrictive environment (LRE).
A legal term referring to the fact that exceptional children must be educated in as normal an environment as possible.

Continuum of alternative placements (CAP).
The full range of alternative placements, from those assumed to be least restrictive to those considered most restrictive; the continuum ranges from regular classrooms in neighborhood schools to resource rooms, self-contained classes, special day schools, residential schools, hospital schools, and home instruction.

Free appropriate public education (FAPE).
The primary intent of federal special education law, that the education of all children with disabilities will in all cases be free of cost to parents (i.e., at public expense) and appropriate for the particular student.

visit the home page of the American Association on Mental Retardation for statements on self-determination and other issues of interest.

The idea of self-determination, like so many other concepts related to ability and disability, is culturally embedded. In working toward self-determination, as well as any other goal, we must be aware of cultural differences in the meaning of self, independence, and success, as we discuss further in Chapter 3 (see also Cronin, 2000).

FULL INCLUSION

Writers have different ideas about exactly what **full inclusion** means (Laski, 1991; Sailor, 1991; Stainback & Stainback, 1992). However, most definitions contain the following key elements:

1. *All* students with disabilities—no matter the types or severities of disabilities—attend only classes in general education. In other words, there are no separate special education classes.
2. *All* students with disabilities attend their neighborhood schools (i.e., the ones they would normally go to if they had no disabilities).
3. General education, not special education, assumes primary responsibility for students with disabilities.

With regard to this last point, some full-inclusionists propose the total elimination of special education. Others hold that professionals such as special educators and speech therapists are still needed but that their main duties should be carried out in general education classrooms along with general education teachers.

CURRENT TRENDS

Integration has involved an array of controversial issues. Normalization, deinstitutionalization, self-determination, and inclusion are all ideas that some contend have not been pushed far enough and others feel can be pushed to harmful extremes. We focus here on issues around full inclusion, as it is the topic most directly affecting classroom teachers.

Controversies about full inclusion include debates about whether a continuum of placement options should be maintained, the legitimacy of claims for and against full inclusion, and a variety of arguments regarding the implementation of inclusion, pro and con.

Full Inclusion versus a Continuum of Alternative Placements   Educational programming for students with disabilities has historically been built on the assumption that a variety of service delivery options need to be available (Crockett & Kauffman, 1999, 2001). As mentioned in Chapter 1, federal special education law (the **Individuals with Disabilities Education Act,** known as **IDEA**) stipulates that schools place students with disabilities in the **least restrictive environment (LRE),** which is to be chosen from a **continuum of alternative placements (CAP).**

Most people have conceptualized LRE as involving only a physical location of the child, with alternatives along a continuum of restrictiveness ranging from residential institutions on one end to regular classes on the other. They have viewed the LRE concept as subordinate to the concept of a **free appropriate public education (FAPE).** Before LRE was enacted into law, school personnel were free to claim that they did not have services for children with disabilities and to deny these children access to regular classes. Now, however, some of the advocates of full inclusion would like to make FAPE subordinate to LRE—to do away with the concept of LRE and deny access to special classes or schools to children with disabilities (Laski, 1991). The argument of Laski and some of the others who advocate full inclusion is that the general education classroom is the LRE for *all* students, whether they have disabilities or not. In fact, it is our observation that in some school districts, special classes have been closed down in favor of full inclusion, leaving no continuum of placement options.

Some have suggested that the restrictiveness of an environment is not simply a matter of location. Restrictiveness also is determined by what is taught and how it is presented—the instructional and social contexts of a place (e.g., Crockett & Kauffman, 2001; Cruickshank, 1977; Rueda, Gallego, & Moll, 2000). The argument can then be made that some special classes or schools are, for some students, less restrictive of their academic, emotional, and social development than is a general education classroom (e.g., Carpenter & Bovair, 1996; Kauffman, Bantz, & McCullough, 2002; Mock & Kauffman, 2002).

Premises of Full Inclusion   Those who advocate full inclusion base their position on at least the following four premises:

1. Labeling people is harmful.
2. Special education pull-out programs have been ineffective.
3. People with disabilities should be viewed as a minority group.
4. Ethics are more important than empirical evidence.

We consider each of these premises in the sections that follow.

Labeling Is Harmful   Some people fear that a "special education" label can cause a child to feel unworthy or to be viewed by the rest of society as a deviant and hence grow to feel unworthy. This fear is not entirely unfounded, as any label designating students as needing special education carries negative connotations. Being so described may lower a person's self-esteem or cause others to behave differently toward him or her. Consequently, advocates for people with disabilities have suggested using different labels or, to the extent possible, avoiding labels altogether.

Antilabeling sentiment is based, in part, on the theory that disabilities are a matter of social perceptions and values, not inherent characteristics. Bogdan (1986) suggests that disability is a socially created construct. Its existence depends on social interaction. Only in a very narrow sense, according to Bogdan, does a person *have* a disability. For example, the fact that a person cannot see only sets the stage for his or her being labeled "blind."

Once we call a person "blind," a variety of undesirable consequences occur. Our interactions are different because of the label. That is, we view the person primarily in

When the use of labels takes precedence over recognizing individual characteristics, labels themselves can become disabling. For instance, if we view these sailors only in terms of their blindness, we might overlook things about them that don't fit our stereotype of blind people. ■

Cutting Through Prejudicial Barriers with Humor

Most special education professionals and people with disabilities would agree that there are many ways to break down attitudinal barriers toward those who have disabilities. Humor may be one of the most effective weapons against such prejudices, especially if humor and disability are merely coincidental. In her syndicated cartoon feature "For Better or For Worse," Lynn Johnston occasionally includes a teacher who uses a wheelchair. This teacher experiences the frustrations and successes of any other in managing and teaching students, and her use of a wheelchair is typical of humor in this vein.

Others make frontal attacks on attitudinal barriers through humor in which disability is central, not incidental. One of the best-known cartoonists taking this approach is John Callahan, who is quadriplegic (as a result of an auto accident) and a recovering alcoholic. His cartoons, which often feature so-called black humor about disability, have appeared in *The New Yorker, Penthouse, National Lampoon, American Health,* and a variety of other magazines, newspapers, and books. Callahan's autobiography, *Don't Worry, He Won't Get Far on Foot,* is a book that some may find offensive but others find liberating in its irreverence and ability to make people laugh at disability.

FOR BETTER OR FOR WORSE®   **Lynn Johnston**

SOURCE: "For Better or For Worse." Copyright © United Feature Syndicate. Reprinted by permission.

terms of the blindness. We tend to interpret everything he or she can or cannot do in terms of the blindness, and the label takes precedence over other things we may know about the individual. This labeling opens the door for viewing the person in a stereotypical and prejudicial manner because, once labeled, we tend to think of all people with blindness as being similar to one another but different from the rest of society.

Research on the effects of labeling has been inconclusive. On the one hand, studies indicate that people tend to view labeled individuals differently from nonlabeled ones. People are more likely both to expect deviant behavior from labeled individuals and to see abnormality in nondisabled individuals if told (incorrectly) that nondisabled persons are deviant. On the other hand, labels may also make nondisabled people more tolerant of those with disabilities. That is, labels may provide explanations or justifications for differences in appearance or behavior for which the person with a disability otherwise might be blamed or stigmatized even more (Fiedler & Simpson, 1987). For example, it is probably fairly common for the nondisabled adult to tolerate a certain degree of socially immature behavior in a child with mental retardation while finding the same behavior unacceptable in a nondisabled child.

In addition to serving as an explanation for unusual behavior, the use of labels is defended on other grounds by some special educators. First, they argue that the elimination of one set of labels would only prompt development of another set. In other words, they believe that individuals with special problems will always be perceived as different. Second, these special educators contend that labels help professionals communicate with one another. In talking about a research study, for example, it helps to know with what type of population the study was conducted. Third, they assert that labels help spotlight the special needs of people with disabilities for the general public: "Like it or not, it is a fine mixture of compassion, guilt, and social consequence that has been established over these many years as a conditioned response to the label 'mental retardation' that brings forth . . . resources [monies for specialized services]" (Gallagher, 1972, p. 531). The taxpayer is more likely to react sympathetically to something that can be labeled. Finally, they point out that anytime we use an intervention that is not universal—used with all students regardless of their characteristics—we automatically apply a label. That is, labels are an inescapable part of preventive practices unless those practices are universal—applied to all children without regard to their individual characteristics (Kauffman, 2001, 1999b).

Special Education Pull-Out Programs Have Been Ineffective

Some special educators assert that research shows **pull-out programs** to be ineffective. These educators maintain that students with disabilities have better, or at least no worse, scores on cognitive and social measures if they stay in regular classes than if they are pulled out for all (self-contained classes) or part (resource rooms) of the school day. Adding fuel to this argument are studies showing that the instruction received in pull-out programs is not what one would expect if special education were being implemented appropriately (e.g., Vaughn, Moody, & Schumm, 1998).

Many research studies have compared students with disabilities in more and less segregated settings; over the past thirty years, there have been more than fifty such studies. Results, when taken at face value, have not been very supportive of pull-out programs. Critics of this research, however, argue that taking these investigations at face value is highly questionable (Kauffman & Hallahan, 1992). The biggest problem with this line of research is that most of the studies are methodologically flawed. Furthermore, some studies do show that some students with disabilities make better progress in more specialized settings and that full inclusion does not serve all children best.

> These findings challenge the idea that one type of placement (full inclusion) is best for all children. By limiting placement for special education children to mainstreamed classrooms only, some children may experience a less than optimal learning environment. As Bricker (1995) reminds us, the needs of the child should not be lost in a movement to advocate one type of placement over all other considerations. (Mills, Cole, Jenkins, & Dale, 1998, p. 89)

People with Disabilities as a Minority

Advocates of full inclusion tend to see people with disabilities as members of a minority group, rather than as individuals who have difficulties as an inherent result of their disabilities. In other words, the problems that people with disabilities face are seen as the result of society's discrimination and prejudice. The Stainbacks typify this point of view:

> In the past, educators have assumed a "functional limitations" approach to services. This paradigm locates the difficulty within students with disabilities when they experience problems in learning or adapting in general education classrooms. From this perspective, the primary task of educators is to remediate these students' functional deficits to the maximum extent possible. That is, educators attempt to fix, improve, or make ready the students who are being unsuccessful by providing them with the skills to be able to succeed in a mainstreamed educational environment that is not adapted to meet their particular needs, interests, or capabilities. And if this is not possible, they must be relegated to special, separate learning settings. In the "functional limitations" paradigm the student is expected to fit into the existing or educational environment.
>
> This paradigm is gradually being replaced by a minority group paradigm. The minority group paradigm of school operation locates the principle [sic] difficulties of students with disabilities as not residing in the student, but rather in

Pull-out programs. Special education programs in which students with disabilities leave the general education classroom for part or all of the school day (e.g., to go to special classes or resource room).

Protests by disability rights activists are reminiscent of and perhaps direct descendants of the Civil Rights protests of the 1960s. ■

the organization of the general education environment. That is, school failure is the result of such things as educational programs, settings, and criteria for performance that do not meet the diverse needs of students. From this perspective, the problem is with the educational organization or environment that needs to be fixed, improved, or made ready to address the diverse needs of all students. (Stainback & Stainback, 1992, p. 32)

The notion of people with disabilities as a minority is consistent with the views of disability rights activists. These activists are a part of the **disability rights movement,** which is patterned after the civil rights movement of the 1960s. Disability activists claim that they, like African Americans and other ethnic minority groups, are an oppressed minority. They have coined the term *handicapism,* a parallel of racism. **Handicapism** is a "set of assumptions and practices that promotes the differential and unequal treatment of people because of apparent or assumed physical, mental, or behavioral differences" (Bogdan & Biklen, 1977, p. 14).

Although more and more people with disabilities—and nondisabled professionals too—are supporting the disability rights movement, there are several impediments to its achieving the same degree of impact as the civil rights movement. Some believe that the political climate in the United States has not been conducive to fostering yet another rights movement. Whereas the civil rights movement of the 1960s was spawned in an era of liberal ideology, the disability rights movement has coincided with a more conservative climate (Gartner & Joe, 1986).

The disability rights movement is now international and is addressing a wide range of issues. Like other political or social movements, the disability rights movement includes a spectrum of views on controversial topics, and not every statement of every person with a disability is representative of the majority of people with disabilities. For example, some express negative sentiments about finding a "cure" for spinal cord injuries that would allow people with paralysis to walk; others find optimism about reversing the effects of spinal cord injuries laudable and heartening (Kastor, 1997).

Activists themselves have been unable to agree on the best ways to meet the movement's general goals. For example, some believe that individuals with disabilities should receive special treatment in such things as tax exemptions or reduced public transportation fares. Others maintain that such preferential treatment fosters the image that people with disabilities are dependent on the nondisabled for charity (Gartner & Joe, 1986).

Disability rights movement.
Patterned after the civil rights movement of the 1960s, this is a loosely organized effort to advocate for the rights of people with disabilities through lobbying legislators and other activities. Members view people with disabilities as an oppressed minority.

Handicapism.
A term used by activists who fault the unequal treatment of individuals with disabilities. This term is parallel to the term *racism,* coined by those who fault unequal treatment based on race.

𝒢𝓌 Disability rights issues are discussed in an on-line magazine called *Ragged Edge*, which may be found at www.ragged-edge-mag.com/ You can also use the resource at www.links2go.com/topic/Disability_Rights ■

Laughing Out Loud: Turning a Deaf Ear to Comedy

When it comes to comedy, Kathy Buckley takes center stage. Billed as "America's First Hearing Impaired Comedienne," she was nominated "Best Female Stand-Up Comedienne" for the 1997 American Comedy Awards, the third year in a row Buckley has made the award list.

On a Wing and a Dare

Buckley never aspired to be a comedienne. "I didn't know what I wanted to do," she says. "I wanted to be a nurse when I was a kid, but because of my hearing impairment they said I couldn't." Actually, her performing career started almost by accident.

"I did it on a dare," Buckley admits, speaking of the first time she performed on stage. It was in 1988 at a charity benefit called "Stand-up Comics Take a Stand" in Encino, California. "I was a nervous wreck," she admits. Even though she could not hear the audience's laughter except by feeling the stage floor vibrations, Buckley says what really made her nervous was competing against other comedians with years of experience. Despite that, she won fourth place.

Since then Kathy Buckley has turned the comedy world "on its ear." She is popular at "Catch a Rising Star" in Las Vegas, "The Improv" and "The Comedy Store" in Hollywood, and has appeared several times on HBO comedy specials and such television shows as "The Tonight Show Starring Jay Leno," "The Howard Stern Show," and "Phil Donahue." Much of her comic material is based on her hearing loss.

Kathy Buckley's Humor

On personal relationships: "I haven't had a date in over two and a half years. I don't know if it's just me or because I couldn't hear the phone ring."

On hearing: "One of the first sounds I ever heard were the birds, and I thought "Birds are hard to lip read, they've got these tiny little beaks!"

On rehabilitation: "I spent 13 years learning how to talk, and now everyone thinks I'm from New York."

On celebrities: Howard Stern asked me if I would consider dating a man who had a disability and I said, 'Sure, I'd consider dating you.'"

On intimacy: "I love it when a man kisses me on the neck. When he sticks his tongue in my ear he gets electrocuted."

Childhood Diagnosis

Buckley says it is wonderful how parents have learned to embrace a child's disability. She was not so lucky as a child. Her own parents never questioned their daughter's hearing impairment and could not accept that she had a disability.

Buckley recalls the years it took teachers and administrators to realize she was deaf. Her grades were poor; there seemed no way to stimulate her academically. "People weren't educated then," she says. "My parents just did what the doctor told them and never asked any questions." What they were told was to put Buckley in a school for children with mental retardation. It took almost a year after that before doctors realized her disability. "And they called *me* slow?" she laughs.

"My parents went into denial that I even had a problem. The doctors saw I had a problem, but told my parents that this or that device would 'fix' me. I ended up in denial as well because no one ever talked to me about it." Buckley says it was not until she was 34 years old that a specialist explained her condition to her. "It was the first time anyone talked to me about it."

"You cannot bond or love unconditionally in denial," Kathy says. "The best gift parents can give their children is joy. Teach that to your children."

Embracing Individuality

"My comedy disarms people. I truly believe that the only disability out there today is attitude," she says. "I love to make people laugh, but I love even more if I can teach them something at the same time."

And that is just what she does. In her nightly performance she jokes about what it is like to be hearing impaired and about how others treat her. She performs for many charity events and benefits.

Buckley says that although she tries to entertain and enlighten all kinds of people, her heart belongs to children. "Kids mean everything to me," she says. "Every single child deserves to have a real childhood, and they should have healthy role models to show them that people do care about them deeply."

SOURCE: D'Agostino, D. (1997). Laughing out loud: Turning a deaf ear to comedy. *Exceptional Parent, 27*(3), 44–45. Reprinted by permission.

People with disabilities are an incredibly heterogeneous population. Although general goals can be the same for all people with disabilities, specific needs vary greatly, depending to a large extent on the particular type and severity of disability the person has. Clearly, the *particular* problems an adolescent with severe mental retardation and blindness faces are considerably different from those of a Vietnam veteran who has lost the use of his or her legs. Although activists admit it would not be good for the public to believe that all people with disabilities are alike—any more than they already do (Gartner & Joe, 1986)—this heterogeneity does make it more difficult for people with disabilities to join forces on specific issues.

Consider the case of Kathy Buckley, described in the box on page 49. Her deafness is obviously not as important as her positive self-perception, can-do attitude, personal charm, and keen wit. Kathy Buckley's story has less to say about special education than about changing the image of disability, the importance of focusing on abilities, and the movement toward including people with disabilities in show business and other aspects of everyday life. Her autobiography and PBS special highlight the way she has turned potentially negative experiences as a minority into assets.

Kathy Buckley exhibits what perhaps has been missing most and is hardest to achieve in the disability rights movement—a sense of happiness with oneself, of satisfaction, if not pride, in one's identity, a recognition that one's difference from the dominant or standard group is not necessarily limiting.

People in the disability rights movement have been active on a variety of fronts, ranging from lobbying legislators and employers to criticizing the media for being guilty of representing people with disabilities in stereotypical and inaccurate ways. Disability activists have been particularly critical of television and movies (Klobas, 1985; Longmore, 1985; see also Longmore & Umansky, 2001; Safran, 1998, 2001). They argue that the depictions are typically overly negative or overly positive. On the negative side, electronic media often treat people with disabilities as criminals, monsters, potential suicides, maladjusted people, or sexual deviants. These portrayals offer the viewer absolution for any difficulties faced by persons with disabilities and allow the nondisabled to "blame the victims" for their own problems. Rarely do movie themes acknowledge society's role in creating attitudinal barriers for people with disabilities.

When television attempts to portray people with disabilities in a positive light, it often ends up highlighting phenomenal accomplishments—a one-legged skier, a wheelchair marathoner, and so forth. The superhero image, according to some disability activists, is a mixed blessing. It does promote the notion that being disabled does not automatically limit achievement. Such human interest stories, however, may make other more ordinary people with disabilities somehow feel inferior because they have not achieved such superhuman goals. These stories also imply that people with disabilities can prove their worth only by achieving superhuman goals and reinforce "the view that disability is a problem of individual emotional coping and physical overcoming, rather than an issue of social discrimination against a stigmatized minority" (Longmore, 1985, p. 35).

Although disability activists, for the most part, have been extremely displeased with television's handling of disabilities, they have been more complimentary of TV advertising that uses characters with disabilities. Beginning in the mid-1980s, advertisers began to experiment with the use of persons with disabilities. In the last years of the twentieth century, there was a dramatic increase in actors with disabilities in TV advertising, whether out of corporate America's desire to be more socially responsive or their recognition of the large market of buyers with disabilities.

Ethics over Evidence   Full-inclusion proponents emphasize that people with disabilities are a minority group who have undergone discrimination. Thus, these proponents tend to approach issues of integration from an ethical, rather than an empirical, evidentiary perspective. Many proponents of full inclusion are not interested in pursuing the question of whether full inclusion is effective. For them, empirical data on the comparative effectiveness of full inclusion versus pull-out programs are irrelevant. Apparently,

ᏟᏔ Information about disability related to jobs, shopping, and other issues can be found at www.wemedia.com/
A resource for people with disabilities in the entertainment industry can be found at www.mediaaccessoffice.com/index.html ■

even if one were to find, through well-controlled research, that pull-out programs lead to better academic and social outcomes than do full-inclusion programs, these advocates would still favor full inclusion on ethical grounds (see Kavale & Forness, 2000; Sasso, 2001 for comment on this tactic). For them,

> by far the most important reason for including all students into the mainstream is that it is the fair, ethical, and equitable thing to do. It deals with the value of EQUALITY. As was decided in the *Brown versus Board of Education* decision, SEPARATE IS NOT EQUAL. All children should be part of the educational and community mainstream.
>
> It is discriminatory that some students, such as those labeled disabled, must earn the right or be prepared to be in the general education mainstream or wait for educational researchers to prove that students with disabilities can profit from the mainstream, when other students are allowed unrestricted access simply because they have no label. No one should have to pass anyone's test or prove anything in a research study to live and learn in the mainstream of school and community life. It is a basic right, not something one has to earn. (Stainback & Stainback, 1992, p. 31)

Arguments Against Full Inclusion   The notion of full inclusion has met with considerable resistance. At least six arguments against full inclusion have been offered:

1. General educators, special educators, and parents are largely satisfied with and see the continuing need for the continuum of alternative placements.
2. General educators are unwilling and/or unable to cope with all students with disabilities.
3. Justifying full inclusion by asserting that people with disabilities are a minority is flawed.
4. Full-inclusion proponents' unwillingness to consider empirical evidence is professionally irresponsible.
5. The available empirical evidence does not support full inclusion.
6. In the absence of data to support one service delivery model, special educators must preserve the continuum of placements.

Satisfaction with and Need for the Continuum of Placements   Defenders of the full continuum point out that, for the most part, teachers, parents, and students are satisfied with the degree of integration into general education now experienced by children with disabilities and see the need to maintain it. Repeated polls, surveys, and interviews have indicated that the vast majority of parents of students with disabilities, as well as students themselves, were satisfied with the special education system and placement options (e.g., Guterman, 1995; Semmel, Abernathy, Butera, & Lesar, 1991). Many students themselves say they prefer pull-out to in-class services, which may be interpreted to support the preservation of a full continuum of placement options (Klinger, Vaughn, Schumm, Cohen, & Forgan, 1998). Although many students are no doubt unhappy with the stigma the label of learning disabilities brings with it, the majority seem not to regret that they are not educated in general education classes. As one student summed up:

> [Full inclusion] would make it worse. Basically it would be embarrassing for that person (a student with learning disabilities). It (an inclusive classroom) would be egging it more. People would be getting into a lot more fights because somebody is always going to joke around and say something like, "He's a retard." (Guterman, 1995, p. 120)

Critics of full inclusion assert that it is unrealistic to expect the general education system, with its fast, competitive pace and whole-group focus, to provide individualized instruction that is sustained and intensive, which is so often required by learners with disabilities. ∎

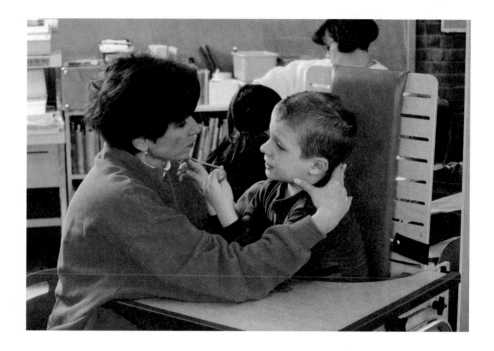

Critics of full inclusion claim that the idea of full inclusion is being championed by only a few radical special educators, primarily those who teach the most severely disabled children (Fuchs & Fuchs, 1994). As some have pointed out, most students with severe disabilities continue to be taught primarily in special classes; students with the most mild disabilities are those most likely to be fully included (Palmer, Fuller, Arora, & Nelson, 2001). Palmer et al. studied the comments of parents of children with severe disabilities about inclusion, finding that although some were supportive of inclusion, others were skeptical of inclusion for their children. Given parents' thoughts on the matter, it is not surprising to encounter the argument that parents' thinking has been ignored by those who push hardest for full inclusion. Consider the responses of parents in the box on page 53.

Although a majority of parents of children with disabilities—if one includes the entire range of disabilities from none to severe—may have positive attitudes toward inclusion, there are parents with serious reservations and concerns (Duhaney & Salend, 2000).

> These concerns are related to the availability of qualified personnel and individualized and specialized services, especially for their children in early childhood inclusive programs. Furthermore, the results of some of the studies show that parents of children with severe disabilities who moved from integrated [at least some mainstreaming] to inclusion programs believe that their children lost services, were mistreated, and were isolated by peers who were not disabled. Additional concerns expressed by parents of children with disabilities included those about excess demands on their time, frustrations in getting schools to provide inclusive programs for their children, and a lack of administrators and teachers with the expertise necessary to implement inclusion. (Duhaney & Salend, 2000, p. 126)

Those who question full inclusion do not oppose inclusion in all cases, but see it as inappropriate for *some* students. The italicized phrase in the second response in the box on page 53—that inclusion must decided *on a case-by-case basis*—is the position of those who question the inclusion of *all* students in general education, and it is also a statement of one of the requirements of IDEA (Bateman & Linden, 1998).

Parents' Thoughts on Inclusion of Their Children with Severe Disabilities

Parents of children with severe disabilities have suggested the following reasons for supporting inclusion:

1. The child acquires more academic or functional skills because of higher expectations and greater stimulation in the regular classroom.
2. Nondisabled students benefit by learning to know children with disabilities; they become more sensitive to people with disabilities.
3. Being around "normal" kids helps students with disabilities acquire social skills.
4. Siblings with and without disabilities go to the same school.
5. Segregation of any kind is morally wrong; inclusion is morally right.

Parents of children with severe disabilities have suggested the following reasons for *not* supporting inclusion:

1. The type or severity of the child's disability precludes benefits from inclusion.
2. Inclusion would overburden or negatively affect regular classroom teachers and students.
3. The curriculum of the general education classroom doesn't match the needs of the child.
4. The child does not get the needed teacher attention or services in general education.
5. The child is unlikely to be treated well by nondisabled children in the regular classroom.
6. The child is not likely to benefit but to be overwhelmed by the surroundings in the regular classroom.
7. The child is too young (and needs more supervision or structure) or too old (having become used to a special class) to benefit from inclusion.
8. The child needs to be around other children with similar disabilities; he or she fits in better, feels less stigmatized or different, and has more real friends in a special setting.
9. The child is too disruptive or aggressive or has too many behavior problems for a regular class.
10. Teachers and others in general education don't have the appropriate training for dealing with the child's needs.

Following are two responses from parents who have more than one child with disabilities and made different decisions for their own children, depending on their characteristics and needs.

First Response

I think I have a pretty good perspective on full inclusion because I have three children, all with different needs. I have a "normal" 10-year-old son in regular ed. Then I have 6-year-old twins with cerebral palsy. My daughter will be fully included in public school in kindergarten. . . . She talks and is very bright but is in a wheelchair and has deficits in fine motor. My son, on the other hand, is severely handicapped. He does not talk, walk, or communicate to us. He is very unhappy and cries a lot. So he would be extremely disruptive in a regular educational setting. His needs are best met in a special ed classroom. I would not like a kid like him to be fully included in either my other son's class or my daughter's class (his twin).

Second Response

I have two children with disabilities; this survey is about one. He is uncomfortable around other children and in close spaces. He expresses dislikes of normal students. He is also disliked by them and they tell me about his behavior when I'm on campus. Mainstreaming to a large extent would not do anyone service in this case.

My other son has been fully and successfully mainstreamed for years. I know the downfalls, I know the up side. I consider mainstreaming as something that *must be decided on a case-by-case basis*. Like any other fad, it is being evangelized as a cure-all. It isn't. It is terrific in some cases. In others, it is child abuse.

SOURCE: From Taking sides: Parent views on inclusion for their children with severe disabilities by D. S. Palmer, K. Fuller, T. Arora, & M. Nelson, *Exceptional Children, 67,* 2001, 467–484 Copyright © 2001 by the Council for Exceptional Children. Reprinted with permission.

General Educators Are Unwilling and/or Unable to Cope   The attitudes of many general educators toward including students with disabilities in regular classes have been less than enthusiastic. In a synthesis of over two dozen surveys of general educators' views on integrating students with disabilities into their classes, only about half thought that integration could provide some benefits (Scruggs & Mastropieri, 1996). Furthermore, only about one-fourth to one-third thought they had sufficient time, skills, training, and resources for working with students with disabilities. Most critics of full inclusion sympathize with the classroom teacher's already arduous job. Although some critics blame teachers for their unwillingness to accommodate more students with disabilities, many agree that their hesitation to do so is justified and that training all teachers to be able to meet the needs of all students with disabilities is simply impossible from a practical standpoint (see Lieberman, 1992; Mock & Kauffman, 2002; Palmer et al., 2001).

Asserting That People with Disabilities Are a Minority Is Flawed   Many critics of full inclusion do not deny that, in many ways, people with disabilities have been treated similarly to oppressed minority groups, such as African Americans, Hispanics, and women. They have experienced discrimination on the basis of their disability and thus can be considered an oppressed minority group.

These critics, however, do not see that this minority group status translates into the same educational placement decisions as it does for African Americans, Hispanics, and women (Dupre, 1997; Hallahan & Kauffman, 1994; Kauffman & Hallahan, 1993; Kauffman & Lloyd, 1995). They argue that for the latter groups, separation from the mainstream cannot be defended on educational grounds, but for students with disabilities, separation can. Students with disabilities are sometimes placed in special classes or resource rooms to better accommodate their educational needs. Placement in separate educational environments is inherently unequal, these critics maintain, when it is done for factors irrelevant to learning (e.g., skin color), but such placements may result in equality when done for instructionally relevant reasons (e.g., student's ability to learn, difficulty of material being presented, preparation of the teacher).

Finally, critics of full inclusion argue that the most important civil right of the minority in question—students with disabilities and their parents—is the right to choose. That is, the Individuals with Disabilities Education Act gives parents and students themselves, when appropriate, the right to choose the environment they, not advocates of total inclusion, consider most appropriate and least restrictive (Crockett & Kauffman, 1998, 1999, 2001).

Unwillingness to Consider Empirical Evidence Is Professionally Irresponsible
Some professionals see as folly the disregard of empirical evidence espoused by some proponents of full inclusion (Fuchs & Fuchs, 1991; Kauffman, 1989, 1999a; Kauffman & Hallahan, 1997; Kauffman, Lloyd, Hallahan, & Astuto, 1995; Kavale & Forness, 2000). These professionals believe that ethical actions are always of the utmost importance. They assert, however, that decisions about what is ethical should be informed by research. In the case of mainstreaming, they think it is important to have as much data as possible on its advantages and disadvantages and how best to implement it before deciding if and how it should be put into practice. Some critics maintain that full-inclusion proponents have gone too far in championing their cause, that they have resorted to rhetoric rather than reason. These critics assert that backers of full inclusion have traded in their credentials as scientific researchers in favor of becoming advocates and lobbyists (Sasso, 2001).

Available Empirical Evidence Does Not Support Full Inclusion   There are few rigorous studies of full inclusion, but those available suggest that full inclusion has not led to social or academic benefits for all students, according to critics. For example, one study found that students with disabilities in full-inclusion classrooms were not very well liked by their general education peers (Sale & Carey, 1995); another, that attempts to implement full inclusion did not produce the expected results (Fox & Ysseldyke, 1997); and others, that full inclusion does not serve *all* children appropriately (Baxter, Woodward, & Olson, 2001; Cook, Gerber, & Semmel, 1997; Mills et al., 1998; Vaughn, Elbaum, & Boardman, 2001). The authors concluded that their results were similar to those of previous studies of students with disabilities who were served in resource rooms. With respect to academics, the combined results of three longitudinal studies indicate that, even after investing tremendous amounts of financial and professional resources, 40 percent of fully included students with learning disabilities "were slipping behind at what many would consider a disturbing rate" (Zigmond et al., 1995, p. 539). More recent research has found that teachers tend to have unmanageable case loads in resource rooms and that the instruction teachers are able to give in such circumstances leaves children with learning disabilities without important skills in reading (Moody, Vaughn, Hughes, & Fischer, 2000).

In perhaps the most extensive study of full inclusion, researchers interviewed school personnel and students and observed in classrooms in five full-inclusion sites around the United States (Baker & Zigmond, 1995; Zigmond, 1995; Zigmond & Baker, 1995). Based on their data, the researchers claimed that teachers did not individualize instruction or plan ahead for how to accommodate the needs of students with disabilities. In fact, the individualization that did occur was most often carried out by peers (using peer tutoring—see page 58) or paraprofessionals (teacher aides). The researchers concluded:

> Regardless of how well prepared a general educator is, the focus of general education practice is on the group: managing instruction for a large group of students, managing behavior within a large group of students, designing assessments suitable for a large group, and so forth. The special educator's focus has always been, and should continue to be, on the individual, providing unique and response-contingent instruction, teaching socially appropriate behavior, designing tailored assessments that are both diagnostic and summative, and so forth. (Zigmond & Baker, 1995, pp. 249–250)

"Students with severe reading-related LD [learning disabilities] require *specific, intensive, and explicit reading instruction individually or in small groups* if they are to make significant progress" (McCray, Vaughn, & Neal, 2001, p. 17, emphasis added). McCray et al. studied middle school students with reading disabilities, finding that most did not receive such instruction but, instead, received instructional "supports" in the form of tutoring or strategy training designed to help them survive in the general middle school curriculum. Yet McCray et al. note that "intensive and highly structured reading programs can make a qualitative difference in students' reading performance, even for students with a history of reading failure" (p. 29). Regarding socialization, Vaughn et al. (2001) found that although inclusion may be appropriate for some students with learning disabilities, for others it is ill advised, making matters worse rather than better. There appears to be no substitute for case-by-case determination of the best placement of students with disabilities.

Based on research to date, we conclude that intensive instruction is required for many students with disabilities if they are to make substantial progress. Such intensive instruction will sometimes need to be delivered in separate special education settings, such as special classes or resource rooms. Unfortunately, teachers in general education classrooms often find it difficult to provide enough intensive instruction, even with "supports" intended to help students survive the general education curriculum. The current structure of resource room programs, in which teachers have high case loads and cannot provide the instruction students need, is a setup for failure (Moody et al., 2000).

Preserving the Continuum of Placements   Critics of full inclusion argue that, given that empirical evidence is scant and that what is available does not support any one service delivery option, it is wise to be cautious about changing the current configuration too quickly or drastically. They admit that there are problems with the current special education system and that there may even be a need for more integration of students with disabilities, including the use of full inclusion. They are leery, however, about eliminating the range of service delivery options currently available to school personnel and parents (e.g., Crockett & Kauffman, 1999, 2001; Gallagher, 1994; Martin, 1994; Vaughn et al., 2001).

MAINSTREAMING PRACTICES

Whether or not one supports the concept of full inclusion, the fact is that most special educators are in favor of some degree of **mainstreaming**—integrating students with disabilities with nondisabled students. Educators have devised a number of strategies for implementing mainstreaming. Most of these practices are still in the experimental stages; that is, we do not have a wealth of evidence indicating their effectiveness. However, various authorities have recommended the following four basic strategies:

1. Prereferral teams
2. Collaborative consultation
3. Cooperative teaching and other team arrangements
4. Curricula and instructional strategies

In the following sections, we briefly describe each of these approaches.

Prereferral Teams   Groups of professionals called **prereferral teams** (**PRTs**) (sometimes called **preassessment teams** or **PATs**) work with general education teachers to recommend different strategies for working with children who exhibit academic and/or behavioral problems (Ormsbee, 2001). One of the primary goals is to establish "ownership" of these children by general and not special educators. In other words, PRTs try to keep down the number of referrals to special education by stressing that general educators try as many alternative strategies as possible before deciding that difficult-to-teach students need to become the primary responsibility of special educators. Although PRTs have become popular, there is very little research on their effectiveness (see Hallahan, Kauffman, & Lloyd, 1999; Vaughn, Bos, & Schumm, 1997).

Collaborative Consultation   Cooperation between general and special education is a key concept in providing appropriate special education (Bateman & Linden, 1998). In **collaborative consultation,** the special education teacher or psychologist acts as an expert in providing advice to the general education teacher. The special education teacher may see the child with disabilities in a resource room, or the student may receive all of his or her instruction in the general education class. Like PRTs, collaborative consultation can be used to keep teachers from referring difficult-to-teach students to special education or after the child has been identified for special education. Research suggests that collaborative consultation is a promising approach to meeting the needs of many students with disabilities in general education settings if the consultant provides frequent follow-up and feedback on intervention (Noell et al., 2000). Nevertheless, much remains unknown about what makes consultation effective or ineffective in meeting students' needs.

Cooperative Teaching and Other Team Arrangements   Sometimes referred to as collaborative teaching or co-teaching, **cooperative teaching** takes the notions of mutuality and reciprocity in collaborative consultation one step further (see Fennick, 2001; Vaughn, Schumm, & Arguelles, 1997). In cooperative teaching, general educators and special educators jointly teach in the same general education classroom composed of students with and without disabilities. In other words, the special educator comes out of his or her separate classroom (sometimes permanently) to teach in the regular class setting. In addition to promoting the notions of mutuality and reciprocity, one of the advantages that proponents of this model point out is that it helps the special educator know the everyday curricular demands faced by the student with disabilities. The special educator sees the context within which the student must function to succeed in the mainstream.

Cooperative teaching can vary with regard to who has the primary instructional responsibility in the classroom: the general educator, the special educator, or both. In some arrangements, the general educator assumes primary responsibility for instruction of academic content, while the special educator teaches academic survival skills, such as

---

Mainstreaming.
The placement of students with disabilities in general education classes for all or part of the day and for all or only a few classes; special education teachers maintain the primary responsibility for students with disabilities.

Prereferral teams (PRTs).
Teams made up of a variety of professionals, especially regular and special educators, who work with regular class teachers to come up with strategies for teaching difficult-to-teach children. Designed to influence regular educators to take ownership of difficult-to-teach students and to minimize inappropriate referrals to special education.

Preassessment teams (PATs).
Teams made up of a variety of professionals, especially regular and special educators, who work with regular class teachers to devise strategies for teaching difficult-to-teach children before they are formally assessed for special education.

Collaborative consultation.
An approach in which a special educator and a general educator collaborate to come up with teaching strategies for a student with disabilities. The relationship between the two professionals is based on the premises of shared responsibility and equal authority.

Cooperative teaching.
An approach in which general educators and special educators teach together in the general classroom; it helps the special educator know the context of the regular classroom better.

note taking and organizing homework assignments. This form of cooperative teaching is popular at the secondary level because it is difficult for special educators to have expertise in all content areas (history, biology, chemistry, Spanish, French, and so forth). In another arrangement, which is more popular at the elementary level, the special educator and general educator practice team teaching. They jointly plan and teach all content to all students, taking turns being responsible for different aspects of the curriculum. Under this model, a person walking into the classroom would have a difficult time telling which of the two teachers is the special educator.

Research on cooperative teaching is in its infancy. Researchers are consistently finding, however, that its success is dependent on at least two factors. First, enough time needs to be built into the general and special educators' schedules for cooperative planning. Second, the two teachers' personalities and working styles need to be compatible (Kauffman, Mostert, Trent, & Hallahan, 2002). Because of the importance of interpersonal skills in making cooperative teaching and collaborative consultation successful, some researchers have cautioned teachers against neglecting the actual teaching of the students (Vaughn, Bos, & Schumm, 1997). In other words, teachers engaged in cooperative teaching or collaborative consultation need to work on getting along together, but not to the neglect of the students they are teaching.

Besides working with other educators, special educators are often expected to work on a team comprised of parents and people from multiple disciplines (Ogletree, Bull, Drew, & Lunnen, 2001). A major idea underlying team-based services is that people with training and expertise in many different areas are required to understand and address all aspects of a child's life. In inclusion programs, as well as in many special classes and schools, there is considerable emphasis on working not only with other teachers but parents and members of a variety of professions.

Curricula and Instructional Strategies   Over several decades, authors have developed curriculum materials to enlighten nondisabled students about students with disabilities. These materials often involve activities constructed to teach children about differences, including disabilities. Some curricula are focused on multicultural differences (e.g., Thompson, 1993). Others are materials produced and disseminated by organizations such as the Easter Seal Society (see Arizona Easter Seal Society). Many of these approaches involve a variety of media and activities. Although more and more schools are using materials designed to teach children in regular education about students with disabilities, very few efforts have been mounted to evaluate these curricular modifications systematically.

Cooperative learning is an instructional strategy that many proponents of inclusion stress is an effective way of integrating students with disabilities into groups of nondisabled peers. In cooperative learning, students work together in heterogeneous small groups to solve problems or practice responses. The emphasis is on assisting each other in learning rather than on competition. Some educators have suggested that cooperative learning leads to better attitudes on the part of nondisabled students toward their peers with disabilities as well as to better attitudes of students with disabilities toward themselves. However, studies of cooperative groups also indicate that some students with disabilities, particularly those with emotional or behavioral disorders and those with mental impairments, do not work very well with others in groups that demand cooperation (Pomplun, 1997).

Involving peers in instruction is generally referred to as **peer-mediated instruction** or intervention (King-Sears, 2001). Peer-mediated instruction may refer to peer tutoring, the use of peer confederates in managing behavior problems, or any other arrangement in which peers are deliberately recruited and trained to help teach an academic or social skill to a classmate (Falk & Wehby, 2001). **Peer tutoring** is often recommended as a method of integrating students with disabilities into the mainstream (Fuchs et al., 2001; Gardner et al., 2001; Maheady, Harper, & Mallette, 2001; see also Fulk & King, 2001 and the web sites they list). Professionals have advocated using children with disabilities as tutors as well as tutees. When a child with a disability assumes the role of tutor, the tutee is usually a younger peer.

When the whole class is involved, the strategy is referred to as **classwide peer tutoring (CWPT)**. In this procedure, peer tutoring is routinely done by all students in the general education classroom for particular subject matter, such as reading or math (Greenwood et al., 2001). CWPT does not mean that the teacher provides no instruction but that peers tutor each other to provide drill and practice. Researchers are continuing to test new combinations of cooperative learning and peer tutoring (e.g., Klinger & Vaughn, 1998).

Research on the effectiveness of various peer tutoring and cooperative learning strategies suggests that these methods may be very helpful for some students with disabilities and virtually useless for others (see Utley, Mortweet, & Greenwood, 1997; Greenwood et al., 2001). This leads us to emphasize the importance of monitoring carefully the progress of each individual student to assess the effectiveness of any instructional approach.

Partial participation means having students with disabilities participate, on a reduced basis, in virtually all activities experienced by all students in the general education classroom. It questions the assumption that including students with severe mental and physical limitations is a waste of time because they cannot benefit from them in the same way that nondisabled students can. Instead of excluding anyone from these activities, advocates of partial participation recommend that the teacher accommodate the student with disabilities by such strategies as "providing assistance for more difficult parts of a task, changing the 'rules' of the game or activity to make it less difficult, or changing the way in which a task or activity is organized or presented" (Raynes, Snell, & Sailor, 1991, p. 329). The objectives of partial participation are twofold. First, proponents maintain that it provides exposure to academic content that the student with disabilities might otherwise miss. Second, it helps students with disabilities achieve a greater degree of social interaction with nondisabled peers.

CONTINUING ISSUES

As the twenty-first century unfolds, the full-inclusion controversy is being sharpened by emphasis on school reform, especially reforms setting higher standards that all students are expected to meet. The direction the controversy will take is anyone's guess (see Kauffman, 1999a, 1999–2000). However, three dimensions of the controversy appear likely to dominate.

Cooperative learning.
A teaching approach in which the teacher places students with heterogeneous abilities (for example, some might have disabilities) together to work on assignments.

Peer-mediated instruction.
The deliberate use of a student's classroom peer(s) to assist in teaching an academic or social skill.

Peer tutoring.
A method that can be used to integrate students with disabilities in general education classrooms, based on the notion that students can effectively tutor one another. The role of learner or teacher may be assigned to either the student with a disability or the nondisabled student.

Classwide peer tutoring (CWPT).
An instructional procedure in which all students in the class are involved in tutoring and being tutored by classmates on specific skills as directed by their teacher.

Partial participation.
An approach in which students with disabilities, while in the general education classroom, engage in the same activities as nondisabled students but on a reduced basis; the teacher adapts the activity to allow each student to participate as much as possible.

𝒞𝒲 For more on peer-assisted or peer-mediated learning, see www.vanderbilt.edu/kennedy/pals/index.html ■

First, there is the question of the legitimacy of atypical placements: Do special classes and special schools have a legitimate, defensible place in the alternatives provided to students with disabilities at public expense? If the answer to this question is "yes," then we are likely to see renewed emphasis on the advantages such special placements offer.

Second, if a student is not able to function adequately in the general education curriculum—achieving what is judged to be "success" in general education—then should he or she remain in the general education environment or be taught in an alternative place with students having similar learning needs? If the answer to this question is "remain in the general education environment," then ways must be found to remove the stigma of failure in that environment from both the student and the teacher, who may be judged to have failed to measure up to expectations.

Third, for students placed in alternative environments, increasing attention must be given to the quality of instruction that is provided there. Vaughn et al. (1998) and Moody et al. (2000) found that the instruction offered in the resource rooms they studied was not the intensive, individualized, relentless, and effective instruction that should characterize special education. The critical problem of today's special education may not be that students with disabilities are sometimes taught in separate settings but that special education teachers too seldom use the opportunity of such settings to offer the instruction students need. *We cannot overemphasize the importance of intensive instruction in meeting the needs of children with disabilities.* In our opinion, children with disabilities should be placed where such instruction is most likely to be provided.

Participation in General Assessments of Progress

In the 1990s, state and federal policy makers became very concerned about what they perceived as a general decline in students' educational achievement. As a result, they emphasized "standards-based" reforms. These reforms involve setting standards of learning or achievement that are measured through standardized tests or other assessment procedures. The reformers felt that teachers' expectations have been too low and that all students should be held to higher standards of performance (see Finn, Rotherham, & Hokanson, 2001; Pugach & Warger, 2001; Thurlow, 2000; Thurlow, Nelson, Teelucksingh, & Draper, 2001).

CURRENT TRENDS

Because special education is an integral part of the system of public education in America, students with disabilities were included in the concern expressed for higher standards. That is, the feeling was that expectations have been too low for students in special education and that they should not only be expected to learn the general curriculum but be expected to perform at a level comparable to that of students without disabilities on assessments of progress. Moreover, reformers argued, no school or state should be allowed to avoid responsibility for demonstrating that its students with disabilities are making acceptable progress in the general education curriculum.

The standards-based reform movement of the 1990s brought with it a heavy emphasis on *access to the general education curriculum* by students with disabilities (Pugach & Warger, 2001; Thurlow, 2000). The curriculum for students with disabilities often has been different from the curriculum in general education. Failure to teach students with disabilities the same things that are taught in general education has been interpreted to mean that the expectations for these students are lower, resulting in their low achievement and failure to make a successful transition to adult life.

Furthermore, students with disabilities often have not been included in statewide or national assessments of educational progress. Consequently, we have little information about how they have been progressing compared to the normative group or how education reforms might affect them (Gronna, Jenkins, & Chin-Chance, 1998; Vanderwood, McGrew, & Ysseldyke, 1998). The standards-based reform movement of the 1990s resulted in projects designed to include students with disabilities in national and state assessments of educational progress. The 1997 amendments of the federal Individuals with Disabilities Education Act (IDEA) required the inclusion of students with disabilities in such assessments (Bateman & Linden, 1998; Huefner, 2000; McDonnell, McLaughlin, & Morison, 1997; Pugach & Warger, 2001; Thurlow, 2000; Yell, 1998).

Understandably, the standards-based reform movement has generated much controversy: What constitutes curriculum? What *should* be the curriculum? What should the standards be (just how high should they be, and in what areas of the curriculum should they be set)? Who should set the standards? How should achievement of or progress toward the standards be measured? What should be the consequences for students—and for schools or states—if standards are not met? What is a "watered-down" curriculum? Under what circumstances is a different curriculum than the general education curriculum warranted?

For students with disabilities, additional questions arise: Should all standards apply to all students, regardless of their disability? What should be the consequences of failing to meet a given standard if the student has a disability? Under what circumstances are alternative standards appropriate? Under what circumstances should special accommodations be made in assessing progress toward a standard? Answering questions like these requires professional judgment in the individual case, and such judgment is required by law (see Bateman & Linden, 1998; Huefner, 2000; Thurlow, 2000; Yell, 1998).

The inclusion of students with disabilities in assessments of progress in the general education curriculum must now be addressed in every IEP. Although the law recognizes that some students with disabilities have educational needs that are not addressed in the general education curriculum, each student's IEP must include:

> A statement of measurable annual goals, including benchmarks or short-term objectives related to—
>
> **(i)** meeting the child's needs that result from the child's disability to enable the child to be involved in and progress in the general curriculum; and
>
> **(ii)** *meeting each of the child's other educational needs that result from the child's disability* [authors' emphasis].

Thus, the IEP team for each child with a disability must make an individualized determination regarding how the child will participate in the general curriculum, and what, if any, educational needs that will not be met through involvement in the general curriculum should be addressed in the IEP. This includes children who are educated in separate classrooms or schools. (Bateman & Linden, 1998, pp. 192–193)

Yell and Shriner (1997) explain further:

> The IEP team must document which portions of the curriculum, and therefore which goals and standards, are relevant to each student in special education. It may be that all curricular goals are pertinent regardless of where instruction is provided. In this case, the student should take part in the general state assessment even if accommodations are needed. If the student's instruction addresses only some of the curricular goals, partial participation is indicated. In this case, the student has a modified assessment plan. If the student is working on performance goals and standards unique to his or her situation, because no portion of the curriculum is appropriate (even with modification), participation in the general assessment . . . is not the appropriate course in these circumstances. A plan for how the student will be assessed must be part of the IEP. (p. 7)

ᏯᎳ For updates on legal issues in special education, see the Web site maintained by legal expert Dixie Snow Huefner and click on "Chapter Updates": www.gse.utah.edu/sped/huefner/spdlawbk.htm or www.wrightslaw.com ∎

TABLE 2.1   Examples of Accommodations for Assessments

Flexible Time	Flexible Setting	Alternative Presentation Format	Alternative Response Format
Extended time	Test alone in test carrel or separate room	Braille or large-print edition	Pointing to response
Alternating lengths of test sections (e.g., shorter and longer)	Test in small-group setting	Signing of directions	Using template for responding
More frequent breaks	Test at home (with accountability)	Interpretation of directions	Giving response in sign language
Extended testing sessions over several days	Test in special education classroom	Taped directions	Using a computer
	Test in room with special lighting	Highlighted keywords	Allow answers in test book

SOURCE: Yell, M. L., & Shriner, J. G. (1997). The IDEA amendments of 1997: Implications for special and general education teachers, administrators, and teacher trainers. *Focus on Exceptional Children, 30*(1), p. 8. Reprinted with permission.

Accommodations for evaluation procedures might involve altering the time given for responding, changing the setting in which the assessment is done, or using an alternative format for either the presentation of tasks or the type of response required. Examples of the kinds of accommodations that might be made for students with disabilities who are taking tests are shown in Table 2.1. Such accommodations may make a significant difference in how students with some disabilities are able to perform on standardized tests (Tindal, Heath, Hollenbeck, Almond, & Harniss, 1998). Therefore, making sure that students are assessed with appropriate accommodations for their disabilities will be extremely important when they are included in evaluations of progress.

CONTINUING ISSUES

No doubt the current standards-based reform movement will entail enormous difficulties related to all students, but particularly to those with disabilities. Moreover, although some argue that uniform standards or expectations will result in greater equity for students, others worry that new inequalities for ethnic minority students and those with disabilities will be created by standards-based reforms (e.g., McNeil, 2000; Thurlow, 2000; Thurlow et al., 2001).

In any area of performance, setting a standard that very few individuals fail will be perceived, eventually, as "low." Setting a standard that many individuals cannot reach will be perceived, at least after a time, as "high." Who will be blamed for a given person's failure to meet a standard—and who will be congratulated when someone meets or exceeds a standard—depends on our assessment of the effort expended by teacher and student. However, one thing seems certain: Standards will not homogenize achievement or expectations. The consequences of standards-based reform for students with and without disabilities will become clearer as reforms are implemented and standards are set. Requiring all students with disabilities and those for whom the tests are inappropriate for other reasons to take state exams may be considered by some to be cruel to both students and teachers.

The goal of universal design is to consider the needs of all potential users when developing architectural design, tools, technologies, instruction, etc. ■

Special education teacher Pixie Holbrook describes the agony of a state-mandated test for herself and one of her pupils, Sarah, a fourth-grader with a learning disability. She describes Sarah as a good and diligent student, but because of her learning disability Sarah hasn't the skills required for the test.

> She knows she doesn't know. And she knows that I know she doesn't know. This is so very humiliating.
>
> Her eyes are wet now, but she's silent and stoic. I check in, and she reassures me she's fine. She appears to be on the verge of weeping, but she will not be deterred. I cannot help her in any way; I can only sit nearby and return a false smile. I can offer a break, nothing more. Later, I calculated the reading level of this selection. Sarah reads like a second-grader, and the poem is at the high end of the fifth-grade scale. Her eyes are not just scanning the paragraphs. I know she has stopped reading and is just glancing and gazing. It's meaningless, and it hurts. Yet she attempts to answer every question.
>
> It is now 2½ hours, and my anger is growing. This is immoral and has become intolerable. And it's only the first day. (Holbrook, 2001, p. 783)

The potential for bias in testing must be taken seriously. However, objecting to all testing and standards is likely to be counterproductive. As Thurlow et al. remarked:

> Despite the potential hazards of results-based education systems, there are some potential benefits for all students, including those students with disabilities from multicultural backgrounds. Only with information on how these students are doing, information like that obtained on other students, will we know that our education system is or is not working. This information appears necessary as we begin to adjust and improve the educational opportunities provided to these students, so that they achieve all of the important educational outcomes. (2001, p. 169)

Access to New Technologies

As technology becomes ever more sophisticated, the issue of independence will become ever more important. One general guideline might be that if the technology allows people with disabilities to do something they could not do without it, then the technology is in their best interest. If, however, it allows them to do something new or better but at the same time imposes new limitations, then one might need to rethink the technology's benefits.

Technological advances of all types may have implications for people with disabilities, but two types stand out as particularly important: advances in medical and communications technologies. Some of these advances, particularly those in the medical field, are very controversial. The controversy is typically about whether something that *can* be done *should* be done. For example, should **cochlear implantations**—artificial inner ears, which we discuss further in Chapter 9—be used to allow deaf children to hear whenever possible? Should disabilities be corrected surgically before birth (*in utero*) if that is possible? Should the findings of fetal stem cell research be applied to cure or correct physical disabilities if it is possible? These are some of the controversial, ethical issues that we discuss in following chapters.

Communication technologies sometimes overlap with medical technologies (e.g., cochlear implants), but ordinarily they do not. Usually, they involve hardware or software applications that allow someone to use equipment or media. Perhaps the most obvious issue today is making the World Wide Web accessible to people with disabilities. For some, this means adaptations that allow a person to use a keyboard or mouse or read a visual display. We discuss some of these adaptations in Chapters 11 and 12.

Cochlear implantation. A surgical procedure that allows people who are deaf to hear some environmental sounds; an external coil fitted on the skin by the ear picks up sound from a microphone worn by the person and transmits it to an internal coil implanted in the bone behind the ear, which carries it to an electrode implanted in the cochlea of the inner ear.

CURRENT TRENDS

As the pace of technology quickens, so do applications of these technologies to the daily lives of people with disabilities (Condon & Tobin, 2001; Wyer, 2001). In many ways, technologies expand the abilities of persons without disabilities to access information, communicate, travel, and accomplish many other everyday tasks. The current trend is toward considering the needs of all potential users when developing a technology. This is often called **universal design** (Pisha & Coyne, 2001). In architecture, the design of new tools and the design of instructional programs, the trend is toward making technologies or products useable by the widest possible population of potential users.

Access to the World Wide Web by people with disabilities is a current trend with significant implications for design. You may want to visit the Web site of the Web Accessibility Initiative (WAI) sponsored by the U.S. Department of Education's National Institute on Disability and Rehabilitation Research and other agencies.

For information about universal design, see www.cec.sped.org/spotlight/udl/ ■

Universal design. The design of new buildings, tools, and instructional programs to make them usable by the widest possible population of potential users.

CONTINUING ISSUES

One of the major issues concerning technologies is cost. Technologically advanced equipment or surgical procedures typically are very costly at first. Their immediate application to people of any description is beyond the financial reach of most consumers. However, as technological advances are incorporated into everyday life and mass produced, their cost typically falls dramatically.

An issue likely to become more controversial is whether we *should* do things that we *can* with new technologies. The moral and ethical dilemmas created by the availability of the means to eliminate limitations, whether they are considered disabilities or not—for example, being unable to hear, see, walk, or communicate—will increase in years to come.

Another issue bound to arise as new technologies are created is when to assume that the limits of universal design have been reached and go ahead with production. Inventors and designers may do their best to be "smart from the start" (Pisha & Coyne, 2001), but perhaps no one can be certain that no potential user's needs have been overlooked. At some point, someone decides to put a gadget or technology into production under the assumption that the design is as universal as it can be made at that time. Perhaps *universal*, like *all*, must not be taken too literally or it becomes self-defeating.

Issues related to accessibility of the World Wide Web to people with disabilities are found at www.w3.org/WAI/. You may also want to visit SERI, the site of Special Education Resources on the Internet, at http://seriweb.com/.
For Web sites and radio related to disability, see www.ican.com/channels/on_a_roll/index.cfm ■

Early Intervention

Many educators and social scientists believe that the earlier in life a disability is recognized and a program of education or treatment is started, the better the outcome for the child. They also see an important federal role in ensuring early intervention (e.g., Bailey, 2000; Feil, Walker, Severson, & Ball, 2000; Gallagher, 2000; Serna, Nielsen, Lambros, & Forness, 2000; Smith, 2000; Sprague & Walker, 2000; Zigler & Styfco, 2000). Three basic arguments underlie early intervention (see Bricker, 1986; Kaiser, 2000):

1. A child's early learning provides the foundation for later learning, so the sooner a special program of intervention is begun, the further the child is likely to go in learning more complex skills.
2. Early intervention is likely to provide support for the child and family that will help prevent the child from developing additional problems or disabilities.
3. Early intervention can help families adjust to having a child with disabilities; give parents the skills they need to handle the child effectively at home; and help families find the additional support services they may need, such as counseling, medical assistance, or financial aid.

Public Law 99-457, passed in 1986, stipulates that states must provide preschool services to all children between the ages of three and five who have disabilities. This law also provides incentives for establishing special education programs for infants and toddlers. ■

Developmental delay.
A term often used to encompass a variety of disabilities of infants or young children indicating that they are significantly behind the norm for development in one or more areas such as motor development, cognitive development, or language.

Children whose disabilities are diagnosed at a very young age tend to be those with specific syndromes (Down syndrome, for example) or obvious physical disabilities. Many have severe and multiple disabilities. Up through the primary grades, children with disabilities may be categorized under the broad label **developmental delay** rather than identified as having a more specific disability (e.g., mental retardation, learning disability, or emotional disturbance). Typically, such a child's needs cannot be met by a single agency or intervention, so many professionals must work together closely if the child is to be served effectively. If the child's disabilities are recognized at an early age and intervention by all necessary professionals is well coordinated, the child's learning and development can often be greatly enhanced.

In the area of emotional and behavioral disorders, particularly involving children who are highly oppositional or disobedient and aggressive from a young age, early intervention shows enormous promise (Sprague & Walker, 2000). Long-term follow-up data suggest that the life course of children at high risk for becoming aggressive and disruptive can be changed dramatically through early behavioral intervention (Strain & Timm, 2001).

Individualized family service plan (IFSP).
A plan mandated by PL 99–457 to provide services for young children with disabilities (under three years of age) and their families; drawn up by professionals and parents; similar to an IEP for older children.

Federal laws now require that a variety of early intervention services be available to all infants and toddlers who are identified as having disabilities. Such services include special education instruction, physical therapy, speech and language therapy, and medical diagnostic services. In addition, laws require the development of an **individualized family service plan (IFSP)** (see Bateman & Linden, 1998). As discussed in Chapter 1, an IFSP is similar to an individualized education program (IEP) for older children, but it broadens the focus to include the family as well as the child. In fact, federal regulations stipulate that the family be involved in the development of the IFSP. Other important requirements are that the IFSP must contain statements of the:

- child's present levels of functioning in cognitive, physical, language and speech, psychosocial, and self-help development
- family's resources, priorities, and concerns relating to the child's development
- major expected outcomes for the child and family, including criteria, procedures, and time lines for assessing progress
- specific early intervention services necessary to meet the child's and the family's needs, including frequency, intensity, location, and method of delivery

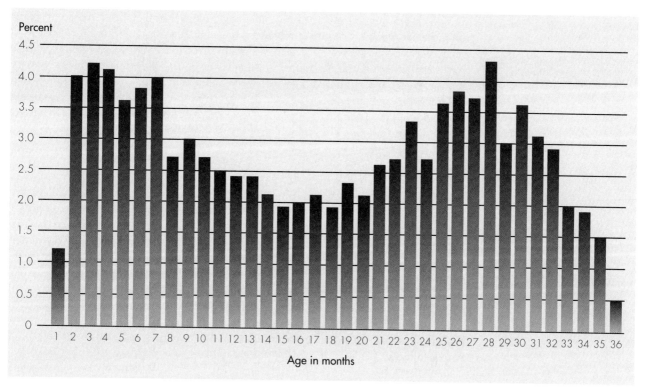

FIGURE 2.1

Age at time of Individualized Family Service Plan (IFSP).

SOURCE: National Early Intervention Longitudinal Study. (2000).

- projected dates for initiating and ending the services
- name of the case manager
- steps needed to ensure a smooth transition from the early intervention program into a preschool program

Figure 2.1 shows the relationship between age of children in months and the writing of IFSPs. The figure shows that although children first had IFSPs at every age from one month through 36 months, most first had IFSPs very soon after birth or soon after their second birthday. Likely, this is because the disabilities of young children tend on the one hand to be obvious at birth or very soon thereafter or, on the other hand, to become obvious when the child is not learning to talk or walk. If a child is not talking and walking by age two, then a developmental delay is suspected.

TYPES OF PROGRAMS

One common way of categorizing the variety of early intervention programs is to consider whether the primary location of the services is in a center, a home, or a combination of the two. The earliest early intervention programs for children with disabilities were **center-based.** In center-based programs, the child and the family come to the center for training and/or counseling. One advantage of center-based programs is that center staff can see more children. Furthermore, some professionals believe that this program allows center staff to have more influence over what goes on in the interaction between parent and child.

In more recent years, authorities have advocated **home-based** programs or a combination of center- and home-based approaches. There are several advantages to approaches that take place in the home. A couple of the most important are that (1) with the increase

Center-based.
A program implemented primarily in a school or center, not in the student's home.

Home-based.
A program delivered primarily in a student's home rather than in a school or center.

in mothers working outside the home and single-parent families, home-based programs are more convenient for more family members, and (2) skills and techniques learned by children and adults at the center need to be transferred to the home, but when these skills are learned in the natural environment—that is, the home—this transfer is not necessary.

As preschool programs and day care become more pervasive, more and more young children with disabilities are being included in "natural" environments with their nondisabled or typically developing peers (U.S. Department of Education, 2000). The integrated or inclusionary day care or preschool program is thus another type of program.

CURRENT TRENDS

Compared to special education in general, special education for infants, toddlers, and preschoolers has had few controversial issues. This is probably because so many professionals have fought for so long to get the needs of very young children recognized that they have not had time to engage in many debates about specific details concerning early intervention. In a sense, early childhood special educators have been bound together by the common goal of securing legislation and programming for young children with disabilities. Nevertheless, there have been and continue to be some areas of disagreement among early childhood special education professionals. Three of the most compelling issues relate to (1) the appropriate role of the family in early intervention, (2) whether it is better to have a child- or a adult-directed curriculum, and (3) whether full inclusion is best for all young children.

CW Resources for Early Childhood Special Education has a useful site at http://www.mcps.k12.md.us/curriculum/pep/pz.html ∎

Appropriate Role of the Family   A significant issue is how the family should be involved in early intervention programming (Bruder, 2000; McCabe, Hernandez, Lara, & Brooks-Gunn, 2000; Thompson, Lobb, Elling, Herman, Jurkiewicz, & Hulleza, 1998). One characteristic of recent early intervention programming, and indeed one of the hallmarks of the IFSP, has been the involvement of parents. Federal regulations, however, have not specifically directed how parents should be included in early intervention programming.

For example, some special educators hold that parents should be trained to use intervention techniques with their preschoolers. Research on the effectiveness of this approach is scant, but one team of researchers found that preschoolers with language disorders made comparable progress whether they received intervention from professionals or from their parents who had been trained to deliver the intervention (Eiserman, Weber, & McCoun, 1995). Strain and Timm (2001) trained parents to intervene in the behavior of their oppositional preschoolers and to train other parents in how to intervene. Other educators are concerned that the notion of including parents may be being misinterpreted to mean that professionals should focus more on changing the family than the child. Closely related is the larger issue of who should be in control over decision making for the family. The consensus is that families should be trusted to make many decisions regarding their children (Lerner et al., 1998).

Child-Directed Versus Adult-Directed Programs   For some time, tension has existed between early childhood educators concerned with nondisabled populations and those focused on children with disabilities over the degree of adult direction that is most appropriate, whether the adult is a parent or teacher. Heavily influenced by the theories of Piaget, most early childhood teachers are oriented toward a curriculum that allows children to explore their environment relatively freely. These teachers advocate a developmental approach that assumes that children's development will unfold naturally with encouragement, guidance, and support from the teacher (Position Statement of National Association for the Education of Young Children and National Association of Early Childhood Specialists in State Departments of Education, 1991).

Many early interventionists, on the other hand, come from a tradition that assumes children with disabilities need a heavy dose of direction from adults if they are to learn the skills they lack. Furthermore, early childhood special educators have generally had a greater focus on individualizing instruction for preschoolers through task analysis, adaptation of materials and activities, and systematic assessment (Carta, 1995; Carta & Greenwood, 1997). As more and more children with disabilities have been integrated with nondisabled preschoolers, the issues of adult direction and individualization have come to the fore.

A major task facing early childhood special educators is to reach agreement with mainstream early childhood educators regarding programming for preschoolers with disabilities. Both sides can undoubtedly learn from each other. On the one hand, researchers have known for a long time that preschoolers with disabilities do better in highly structured, teacher-directed, individualized programs (Abt Associates, 1976–1977). On the other hand, authorities have noted that moving from a highly structured preschool intervention program to a traditional kindergarten can present problems.

Inclusive Education   Virtually all early childhood educators suggest that children with identifiable disabilities and those considered at risk for school failure should be included in programs designed to serve diverse groups of learners, including young children without disabilities (Bowman, 1994; Katz, 1997; Sainato & Strain, 1993). Over half of preschoolers with disabilities now receive their education totally or primarily in regular classrooms (U.S. Department of Education, 2000). However, the extent to which the practices in programs for typically developing young children are appropriate for children with disabilities has been a matter of considerable controversy (Bricker, 1995; McLean & Odom, 1993; Odom, 2000).

Bricker's observation that a radical philosophy of inclusive education may not necessarily serve all young children well seems borne out by research (Garrett, Thorp, Behrmann, & Denham, 1998; Mills et al., 1998). However, other research has suggested that with proper adjustment for the individual needs of children, inclusion of young children with disabilities is always or nearly always beneficial (Odom, 2000; Strain, 2001). Certainly, there is more evidence supporting the inclusion of very young children in groups with typically developing students than there is supporting the inclusion of older students.

CONTINUING ISSUES

We hope that early childhood education will continue to play an important role in eliminating and lessening the impact of disability on children and their families. We caution, however, not to assume that early intervention alone will mean fewer children with disabilities. Although educators are devising more effective programs of early intervention, the number of children with disabilities is increasing. The reasons for this increase are many and complex and are related to changes in economic and social conditions in the United States. Today, we know that at the beginning of the twenty-first century:

- A high percentage of young children and their mothers live in poverty, have poor nutrition, and are exposed to environmental conditions likely to cause disease and disability.
- Many babies are born to teenage mothers.
- Many babies are born to mothers who receive inadequate prenatal care, have poor nutrition during pregnancy, and abuse substances that can harm the fetus.
- Many babies are born with a low birthweight.
- Environmental hazards, both chemical and social, are increasing.
- Millions of children are subjected to abuse and an environment in which violence and substance abuse are pervasive.
- Substantial cuts in and revisions of social programs have widened the gap between needs and the availability of social services.

Early intervention seems to hold great promise for prevention of disabilities, but there are strong forces working against prevention, including the revulsion many people

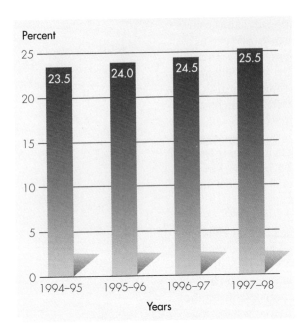

FIGURE 2.2

Percentage of Students Ages 17 Through 21+ with Disabilities Graduating with a Standard Diploma: 1994–95 to 1997–98

SOURCE: U.S. Department of Education, Office of Special Education Programs, Data Analysis System (DANS). Washington, DC: Author.

The National Information Center for Children and Youth with Disabilities has a useful Web site at http://www.nichcy.org ■

feel for labels and propositions of education reformers that work against identifying problems early and intervening to stop them from getting worse (Kauffman, 1999b). Besides issues surrounding prevention, other issues for the new millennium include the use of computer technology with young children, the changing roles of special educators, emerging philosophies of early childhood education, cultural and linguistic diversity, and access to community resources (Lerner et al., 1998).

Transition to Adulthood

Preparing students for continued education, adult responsibilities, independence, and employment have always been goals of public secondary education. Most students complete high school and find jobs, enter a vocational training program, or go to college without experiencing major adjustment difficulties. We know that dropout and unemployment rates are far too high for all youths, especially in economically depressed communities, but the outlook for students with disabilities may be even worse (Hendrick, MacMillan, & Balow, 1989; Sitlington, Clark, & Kolstoe, 2000; U.S. Department of Education, 2000).

Published figures on dropout rates must be viewed with caution because there are many different ways of defining *dropout* and computing the statistics (MacMillan et al., 1992). Studies of what happens to students with disabilities during and after their high school years strongly suggest, however, that a higher percentage of them, compared to students without disabilities, have difficulty in making the transition from adolescence to adulthood and from school to work. Many students with disabilities drop out of school, experience great difficulty in finding and holding jobs, do not find work suited to their capabilities, do not receive further training or education, or become dependent on their families or public assistance programs (Collet-Klingenberg, 1998; Heal & Rusch, 1995; Sinclair, Christenson, Evelo, & Hurley, 1998).

Figure 2.2 shows the gradual increase in students with disabilities graduated from high school with a standard diploma. These overall rates of graduation with a diploma mask the outcomes for particular categories of disability. Overall outcomes for students with disabilities are disappointing, but those in some categories of disability fare much better than others. Students with severe and multiple disabilities and those with emotional or behavioral disorders typically have the poorest outcomes. Those with specific learning disabilities or speech and language impairments tend to have comparatively better outcomes (U.S. Department of Education, 2000).

FEDERAL INITIATIVES

Federal laws, including IDEA, now require attention to transition plans for older students, and these must be incorporated in students' IEPs (Bateman & Linden, 1998; Huefner, 2000; Yell, 1998). The federal government defines transition services as:

a coordinated set of activities for a student, designed within an outcome-oriented process, which promotes movement from school to post-school activities, including post-secondary education, vocational training, integrated employment (including supported employment), continuing and adult education, adult services, independent living, or community participation.

Students with disabilities must have preparation for life after high school, including further education, work, and independent living. Working with a job coach and with the cooperation of a local business, a student is integrated into this work staff ■

Each student's IEP must contain a statement of needed transition services for him or her, beginning no later than sixteen years of age and annually thereafter. (For students for whom it is appropriate, the statement is to be included in the IEP at a younger age.) In addition, the IEP must include a statement of the linkages and/or responsibilities of each participating agency before the student leaves the school setting.

An important aspect of this legislation is that it recognizes that transition involves more than just employment. The box on page 70 illustrates how multiple agencies and individuals may be involved in planning for the transition of a high school student with disabilities. This broad emphasis on independent living, community adjustment, and so forth has been applauded by many authorities. For example, some have championed the idea that transition programming should be aimed at increasing the quality of life for people with disabilities (e.g., Chadsey-Rusch & Heal, 1995). Although quality of life is difficult to define, Halpern (1993) points to personal choice as its underlying principle. He also identifies three important quality-of-life domains: (1) physical and material well-being; (2) performance of adult roles (e.g., employment, leisure, personal relationships, social responsibility); and (3) personal fulfillment (e.g., happiness).

An increase in supported employment has come with the federal mandate for transition services. **Supported employment** is designed to assist persons with disabilities who cannot function independently in competitive employment. It is a method of ensuring that they are able to work in integrated work settings alongside people without disabilities. In a typical supported employment situation, an employment specialist, or **job coach,** places the individual in a job with a business. The job coach then provides on-site training that is gradually reduced as the worker is able to function more independently on the job. Competitive employment is usually defined as working at least twenty hours per week at a type of job usually filled by a person without disabilities.

Although employment is a goal, some adults with disabilities attend activity centers or day care. Table 2.2 describes the range of adult service and community employment alternatives that might be considered for an individual with severe disabilities.

CURRENT TRENDS

Like early intervention programming, little controversy surrounds the basic premise of transition programming for students as they move from secondary school to work or

Supported employment. A method of integrating people with disabilities who cannot work independently into competitive employment; includes use of an employment specialist, or job coach, who helps the person with a disability function on the job.

Job coach. A person who assists adult workers with disabilities (especially those with mental retardation), providing vocational assessment, instruction, overall planning, and interaction assistance with employers, family, and related government and service agencies.

Case Study: Sarah

Sarah is a junior at East Side High School. She was in an accident in 3rd grade that left her with a learning disability and without the use of her legs; she uses a wheelchair for mobility. Sarah has use of both arms and hands, but she experiences weakness in them after prolonged use. Sarah is interested in a career in the retail fashion industry, both in sales and clothing design. She plans to live independently and wants to work with youth programs in her spare time.

Her IEP team this year is headed by one of the school's guidance counselors and consists of Sarah, her parents, her LD teacher, a vocational rehabilitation counselor, the OT/PT, her marketing and distributive education (DE) teacher, and the district's transition specialist. Based on an assessment of Sarah's needs, goals, and preferences, her educational program for 11th grade will consist of the following courses: art (drawing), computers (graphic design), marketing and distribution (two class periods), English, math, and physical education.

The guidance counselor and LD teacher are working with the general academic teachers to assist Sarah in applying strategies to facilitate her learning in these classes. Through her marketing and distributive education class (a regular vocational education cooperative program), Sarah will begin working at the Gap store in the local mall. She will leave school at the end of sixth period and will work 20 hours per week. She will ride the transit system bus from school to work. Her parents will provide transportation home, although Sarah expects to arrange rides with co-workers in the mall once she gets to know them.

The DE teacher has worked with Sarah and her new supervisor to develop a training plan that identifies her work tasks and the competencies she is to develop through the work experience. The VR counselor is helping the employer modify the cashiering station to accommodate Sarah's wheelchair, as well as the storage areas and store aisles. In the future, the VR counselor will assist Sarah in developing a PASS plan (Plan to Achieve Self-Support) to purchase a computer needed for the graphic arts program at the community college—her immediate postschool training goal. The DE teacher has also invited and encouraged Sarah to join the DE club that meets every Wednesday after school.

Through the help of her parents and the district transition specialist, Sarah worked half days during the previous summer, and will do so next year, in the summer youth program doing arts and crafts activities with elementary school children. To help Sarah gain strength in her hands and arms, the OT/PT is working with Sarah and her PE teacher to develop a weight-lifting program. She has also helped to identify strategies that Sarah can use when drawing and working on the computer so that her arms and hands become less fatigued.

At home, Sarah has specific chores and responsibilities involving cleaning, cooking, laundry, and helping to care for the family pet. With her parents' assistance and cooperation, Sarah developed a schedule that fits together school, work, and home responsibilities as well as provides time to just hang out with her friends.

SOURCE: Kohler, P. D. (1998). Implementing a transition perspective of education: A comprehensive approach to planning and delivering secondary education and transition services. From *Beyond high school: Transition from school to work, 1st edition,* by F. R. Rusch and J. G. Chadsey © 1998. Reprinted with permission of Wadsworth, an imprint of the Wadsworth Group, a division of Thompson Learning. Fax 800 730-2215.

postsecondary education. All special educators agree that transition programming is critical for the successful adjustment of adults with disabilities (see Kohler, 1998; Moon & Inge, 2000; Sitlington et al., 2000). However, there is some controversy regarding the specifics of transition. Much of this has to do with trying to meet the diverse requirements of the federal mandate. A few states have achieved a high degree of compliance with federal law and have implemented excellent transition policies, but many others have not (Furney, Hasazi, & DeStefano, 1997). Many IEPs are in technical compliance with the IDEA mandate for transition but lack key elements, reflecting a lack of thoughtful planning (Grigal, Test, Beattie, & Wood, 1997).

Some professionals are debating how best to build a curriculum that covers education, employment, independent living, and community participation. This concern for meeting the diverse needs of students is manifested somewhat differently for students with more severe disabilities than for those with milder disabilities.

TABLE 2.2   Typical Adult Service and Community Employment Alternatives

1. *Competitive (unsupported) employment*—on company payroll with benefits and without trainer or support from a human services agency.

2. *Job placement, or transitional support into regular employment*—short-term help from an agency, such as the state vocational rehabilitation agency, in finding and getting adjusted to a job.

3. *Supported employment*—job placement, training, and continuing support for as long as necessary in an integrated community business. Supported employment can be in the form of an individual placement or a group model of several workers, such as an enclave or mobile work crew. Workers earn minimum wage or better.

4. *Volunteer work*—unpaid work that is preferred or chosen by an individual for reasons other than "daily support." This is usually done for community service organizations, such as the SPCA, a hospital, or the National Cancer Society. Labor laws define what types of work are considered volunteer. Workers with disabilities cannot volunteer to do work that would pay a wage to employees without disabilities.

5. *Sheltered work*—work done in a sheltered workshop where the majority of workers are disabled and earn subminimum wages. Sheltered workshops can offer a variety of employment and evaluation services, such as work activity, work adjustment training, vocational evaluation, long-term sheltered employment, and work activity programs.

6. *Work activity center–based or nonintegrated day programs*—focus on "prevocational" skills, such as motor tasks or self-care skills.

7. *Day activity or adult day care center–based, nonintegrated programs*—usually have a therapeutic or nonvocational emphasis, depending on the funding source.

SOURCE: Moon, M. S., & Inge, K. (2000). Vocational preparation and transition. In M. E. Snell & F. Brown (Eds.), *Instruction of students with severe disabilities* (5th ed., p. 595). Upper Saddle River, NJ: Merrill. Reprinted with permission.

Students with Severe Disabilities   For students with severe disabilities, much of the concern focuses on the coordination and linkage of the many agencies outside the school setting (Moon & Inge, 2000). Many special education personnel are unaccustomed to working with nonschool agencies. For example, the relationship between vocational and special education has traditionally been ambiguous. Federal regulations, however, now require that special education work with vocational education as well as with other agencies in the community.

For a number of years, special educators at the secondary level have been moving toward more involvement in the community, but the federal transition mandate has hastened the need for these outreach efforts. Approaches such as supported employment, for example, require that special educators work with local employers in setting up and instituting training and working environments for students with disabilities. Not all special educators have been trained for this expanded role, however. We are still in the infancy stage of knowing how best to accomplish this interface between the school and community environments. There is a need for experimentation with approaches to educating special educators for this broader role.

Students with Mild Disabilities   For students with mild disabilities, much of the concern centers on attempting to meet their academic as well as their vocational needs. Teachers of secondary students are constantly faced with the decision of how much to stress academics versus vocational preparation. Because their disabilities are milder, many children with learning disabilities, for example, may be able to go on to postsecondary educational institutions, such as community colleges or universities. It is often difficult to tell as early as tenth grade (when such decisions need to be made) whether to steer students with learning disabilities toward college preparatory or more vocationally oriented curricula. Co-teaching is one approach to helping students with disabilities in general education settings learn skills related to employment (Fennick, 2001). That is, general and special education teachers can work together to help students learn about career possibilities, prepare their resumes, search for jobs, write letters of application, interview for jobs, and so on.

Some authorities believe that too many students with learning disabilities have been "sold short" on how much they can achieve academically. These authorities believe that such students are written off as academic failures who can never achieve at the college level. This diminished expectation for academic success translates into a curriculum that makes few academic demands on students. For example, one study of students in learning disabilities classrooms at the secondary level found an "environmental press against academic content" (Zigmond & Miller, 1992, p. 25); hence the recent emphasis we have already discussed on access to and progress in the general education academic curriculum.

Other authorities maintain that an overemphasis on academics leaves many students with learning disabilities unprepared to enter the world of work upon leaving school. They believe that the learning problems of students with learning disabilities tend to be minimized. These authorities assert that just because students with learning disabilities are characterized as having mild disabilities, they do not necessarily have insignificant learning impairments.

Along these same lines, some professionals think that far too few support services are available to students with mild disabilities. Whereas transition services such as supported employment are available to persons with severe disabilities, individuals with milder disabilities are often left to fend for themselves once they graduate from secondary school.

CONTINUING ISSUES

It is still too early to tell how much impact the emphasis on standards-based reform and the inclusion of students with disabilities in general education curriculum and assessment procedures (as mandated by the 1997 amendments to IDEA) will have on students with disabilities. However, despite some of the unresolved issues, we can be encouraged by all the attention that special educators have given to the area of transition. A variety of transition opportunities are available now that were unavailable just a few years ago. However, it is increasingly clear that successful transition takes early and sustained effort, and it is not clear just how such support can best be provided (see Moon & Inge, 2000; Sitlington et al., 2000).

In considering transition issues, it is helpful to keep in mind that a smooth and successful transition to adult life is difficult for any adolescent. Individuals find many different routes to adulthood, and we would be foolish to prescribe a single pattern of transition. Our goal must be to provide the special assistance needed by adolescents and young adults with disabilities that will help them achieve the most rewarding, productive, independent, and integrated adult lives possible. This goal cannot be achieved by assuming that all adolescents and young adults with disabilities, or even all individuals falling into a given special education category, will need the same special transition services or that all will achieve the same level of independence and productivity. One of education's great challenges is to devise an effective array of programs that will meet the individual needs of students on their paths to adulthood.

Zero tolerance.
A school policy, supported by federal and state laws, that having possession of any weapon or drug on school property will automatically result in a given penalty (usually suspension or expulsion) regardless of the nature of the weapon or drug or any extenuating circumstances.

Discipline of Students with Disabilities

In the 1990s, safe schools and orderly learning environments became paramount concerns of many school administrators and legislators (e.g., Dupre, 2000; Dwyer, Osher, & Hoffman, 2000; Skiba & Peterson, 2000; Sprague & Walker, 2000; Smith, 2000; Yell, Rozalski, & Dragow, 2001). Dramatic shootings in schools, plus statistics on the presence of weapons, violence, and drugs in schools, led to severe measures intended to improve discipline, decrease violence, and eliminate drugs in schools.

One of the most dramatic and controversial measures involving discipline for serious offenses is known as *zero tolerance*. **Zero tolerance** was introduced by the federal Gun-Free

Schools Act of 1994, which led to corresponding state legislation. Under most of these state laws, school boards and other school administration may choose to use discretion in applying the zero-tolerance policy, although sometimes they do not. In the case of discipline, zero tolerance means that the circumstances surrounding a particular incident are not weighed in deciding what the consequences should be; only the act itself is to be questioned. For example, if a student brings a weapon to school, the circumstances leading up to the incident are not considered relevant in determining the punishment (see Kauffman & Brigham, 2000; Skiba & Peterson, 2000).

In many ways, zero tolerance is parallel to **mandatory sentencing** in the legal system. Mandatory sentencing, which requires a particular sentence for a particular offense without consideration of circumstances, was passed into law because judges were thought to be often too lenient. In essence, judges were assumed to be abusing their authority to use discretion, so their discretion was removed by legislators; the judge's only role, under mandatory sentencing laws, is to determine whether or not a particular criminal offense was committed by the defendant. Predictably, mandatory sentencing has resulted in outrageous miscarriages of justice, as judges have no discretion in taking facts other than the commission of the offense into consideration in determining punishment. For example, a defendant might be sentenced to twenty years or more in prison for an offense that he or she did not understand.

Similar observations led to the institution of zero tolerance in school discipline, and the outcomes have been similar. In education, school administrators and teachers have been assumed to abuse their discretion in determining the punishment for certain serious offenses, such as bringing a weapon to school. Therefore, higher authorities (e.g., boards of education) have in many cases removed discretion from the hands of teachers and lower administrators, prescribing a given punishment (e.g., long-term suspension or expulsion) for a particular offense (e.g., bringing a knife or a drug to school) regardless of the circumstances surrounding the act. For example, if an elementary school child accidentally brings a paring knife to school in her lunch box, then she will be expelled. If a high school boy forgets to remove a roofing knife from his pocket and turns it in at the office because he knows he should not have it in school, then he will be expelled. If a toy gun is brought to school by a mentally retarded student who does not understand that a gun is a weapon and even toy weapons are forbidden in school, or if a child is found to possess a single dose of a commonly used nonprescription drug, then he or she will be expelled. Decisions like these have actually been made by school authorities under the zero-tolerance rationale.

Violence, disorder, and drugs in schools are serious problems that must be addressed. However, the current movement toward zero tolerance and standardization of penalties presents particular problems for special education. Special educators recognize the need for schoolwide discipline that brings a high degree of uniformity to consequences for particular acts (e.g., Nelson, Martella, & Galand, 1999; Sugai, 1996). Nevertheless, special educators also argue for, and the 1997 amendments to IDEA require, that exceptions be made based on the relevance of the student's disability to the event in question (see Skiba & Peterson, 2000; Zurkowski, Kelly, & Griswold, 1998; Yell et al., 2001).

Mandatory sentencing. Laws requiring specific sentences for specific violations, removing the discretion of the judge in sentencing based on circumstances of the defendant or other considerations.

CURRENT TRENDS

The discipline of students with disabilities is highly controversial, and many teachers and school administrators are confused about what is legal. Special rules apply to managing some of the serious misbehavior of students who are identified as having disabilities. In some cases, the typical school rules apply, but in others they do not (see Bateman & Linden, 1998; Huefner, 2000; Yell, 1998; Yell & Shriner, 1997; Yell et al., 2001). In any case, much of the special education advocacy regarding discipline is based on finding alternatives to suspension and expulsion for bringing weapons or drugs to school or for endangering others, as keeping students out of school is not an effective way of helping them learn to behave acceptably (Bock, Tapscott, & Savner, 1998).

Manifestation determination.
Determination that a student's misbehavior is or is not a manifestation of a disability.

Three concepts and related procedures provide the basis for much of the controversy surrounding the discipline of students with disabilities: (1) determining whether the behavior is or is not a manifestation of the student's disability, (2) providing an alternative placement for the student's education for an interim period if temporary removal from the student's present placement is necessary, and (3) developing positive, proactive behavior intervention plans. We discuss these issues further in Chapter 7, as they most frequently arise in the case of students with emotional or behavioral disorders.

Deciding whether a student's misbehavior is or is not a manifestation of disability is called a **manifestation determination.** The idea behind this part of the law is that it would be unfair to punish a student for engaging in a misbehavior that is part of his or her disability. However, if the misbehavior is not a manifestation of disability, then the usual punishment for students without disabilities should apply. For example, if a misbehavior is the result of a seizure or other neurological disorder or a manifestation of mental incapacity or emotional disturbance, then the student should not be punished for doing it. The manifestation determination is a highly controversial issue, and some writers believe it is more political than educational in purpose (Dupre, 2000; Katsiyannis & Maag, 2001). Some people argue that the process actually undermines fairness because the rules or procedures for the manifestation determination are not entirely objective, requiring subjective judgment about the causes of misbehavior.

Functional behavioral assessment (FBA).
Evaluation that consists of finding out the consequences (purposes), antecedents (what triggers the behavior), and setting events (contextual factors) that maintain inappropriate behaviors; this information can help teachers plan educationally for students.

Perhaps the most critical part of the discipline provisions of IDEA 1997 is the requirement that teachers must devise positive behavioral intervention plans for students with disabilities who have behavior problems. The emphasis of this requirement is on creating proactive and positive interventions (Artesani & Millar, 1998; Buck, Polloway, Kirkpatrick, Patton, & Fad, 2000; Ruef, Higgins, Glaeser, & Patnode, 1998; Sugai & Horner, 1999–2000; Sugai et al., 2000). When special discipline is involved, the school must reevaluate the student's IEP and make efforts to address the misconduct that led to the problem. Also required is a **functional behavioral assessment (FBA),** in which educators attempt to determine and alter the factors that account for the student's misconduct (Condon & Tobin, 2001; McConnell, Hilvitz, & Cox, 1998). Although the notion of functional assessment is itself a controversial issue, it is clear that the intent of the legal requirement is to encourage proactive problem solving rather than reactive punishment of misconduct (Nelson, Roberts, Mather, & Rutherford, 1999; Sasso, Conroy, Stichter, & Fox, 2001).

Positive behavioral supports (PBS) or Positive behavioral intervention and supports (PBIS).
Positive reinforcement (rewarding) procedures intended to support a student's appropriate or desirable behavior.

Positive behavioral supports (PBS) (also known as **positive behavioral intervention and supports (PBIS)** are procedures required under IDEA to help students behave as desired (Bradley, 2001). The emphasis is on positive (rewarding) consequences for appropriate behavior rather than punishment for misbehavior.

PBS uses systemic and individualized strategies to prevent problem behavior and achieve positive social and learning outcomes. It integrates valued outcomes, the science of human behavior, validated procedures, and systems change to enhance quality of life and reduce problem behavior. Its primary goal is to improve the link between research-validated practices and the environments in which teaching and learning occur. This behaviorally based systems approach enhances the capacity of schools, families, and communities to design effective teaching and learning environments that improve lifestyle results (personal, health, social, family, work, recreation, etc.) for all children and youth. These environments apply contextually and culturally appropriate interventions to make problem behavior less effective, efficient, and relevant, and to make desired behavior more functional (Sugai et al., 2000).

CONTINUING ISSUES

The struggle to resolve discipline issues involving students with disabilities is ongoing. On the one hand, school administrators want the highest possible degree of uniformity of expectations (i.e., the same high expectations for all students). On the other hand, special educators and other advocates for students with disabilities see the uniformity of disciplinary rules as failure to accommodate students' individual abilities and needs. The legal requirements regarding discipline, including suspension and expulsion, will continue to evolve as educators find more productive ways of dealing with serious misconduct.

Some Concluding Thoughts Regarding Trends and Issues

If you are feeling a bit overwhelmed at the controversial nature of special education, then we have achieved our objective. We, too, are constantly amazed at the number of unanswered questions our field faces. It seems that just as we find what we think are the right answers to a certain set of questions about how to educate students with disabilities, another set of questions emerges. And each new collection of questions is as complex and challenging as the last.

It would be easy to view this inability to reach definitive conclusions as indicative of a field in chaos. We disagree. We prefer to view this constant state of questioning as a sign of health and vigor. The controversial nature of special education is what makes it exciting and challenging. We would be worried (and we believe people with disabilities and their families would be worried, too) if the field were suddenly to decide that it had reached complete agreement on most of the important issues. We should constantly be striving to find better ways to provide education and related services for persons with disabilities. In doing this, it is inevitable that there will be differences of opinion.

Summary

Special education has changed dramatically during its history, and the field appears poised for more changes. Six major trends and issues are integration, access to technology, participation in assessments of progress, early intervention, transition from secondary school to adulthood, and discipline.

The trend toward integration of people with disabilities into the larger society began in the 1960s and continues stronger than ever today. Much of the philosophical rationale for integration comes from the principle of normalization. Normalization dictates that both the means and ends of education for people with disabilities should be as normal as possible. Controversies have surrounded implementation of the normalization principle. There is disagreement about whether it means the abolition of residential programs and special classes. Members of some groups, such as those who are deaf, have questioned whether normalization should mean integration for them. And some have cautioned that the overuse of technology may go against the concept of normalization.

Three important movements in the drive toward more integration have been deinstitutionalization, self-determination, and the full-inclusion movement. Started in the 1960s, deinstitutionalization is a trend to move people with disabilities into closer contact with the community and home. Some researchers question the wisdom of complete deinstitutionalization, as some people who return to community placements do not fare well and the death rate may be higher for these people in community placements than in institutions. Self-determination is based on the philosophy that people with disabilities should make decisions about their own lives. Advocates of full inclusion contend that there should be no separate special education classes, that students should attend their neighborhood schools, and that the general education system should have the primary responsibility for all students. Others believe that although mainstreaming should be employed more than is currently the case, what's needed is a continuum of placements (e.g., residential institutions, special schools, special classes, resource rooms, general classes) from which parents and professionals can choose.

Full inclusion is based on four premises: (1) labeling of people is harmful; (2) special education pull-out programs have been ineffective; (3) people with disabilities should be viewed as a minority group; and (4) ethics should take precedence over empiricism.

Sentiment against labeling arose out of the fear that labeling students for special education stigmatizes them and makes them feel unworthy. Research on the effects of labeling is inconclusive. People do tend to view labeled individuals differently than they do those without labels. Some educators maintain, however, that labels may provide an explanation for atypical behavior.

Over the past thirty years, more than fifty studies have compared outcomes for students with disabilities placed in special education versus regular classes, or resource rooms versus general education classes. The results have not been very supportive of special education. Critics of this research, however, point out that virtually all these studies have been methodologically flawed.

Advocates of full inclusion tend to believe that the problems people with disabilities face are due to their being members of a minority group, rather than the result of their disability. This view is consistent with that of the disability rights movement, whose members have advocated for a variety of civil rights for persons with disabilities and have been influential in lobbying legislators and promoting more appropriate media portrayals of people with disabilities.

Some full-inclusion advocates do not care if full inclusion is more or less effective than pull-out special education programs; they believe in full inclusion because they think it is the ethical thing to do.

Opponents of full inclusion argue that (1) professionals and parents are largely satisfied with the current level of integration; (2) general educators are unwilling and/or unable to cope with all students with disabilities; (3) although equating disabilities with minority group status is in many ways legitimate, it has limitations when it comes to translation into educational programming recommendations; (4) an unwillingness to consider empirical evidence is professionally irresponsible; (5) available empirical evidence does not support full inclusion; and (6) in the absence of data to support one service delivery model, special educators must preserve the continuum of placements.

Even those special educators who do not believe in full inclusion believe there needs to be more integration of students into general classes and more research on better ways to implement mainstreaming. Some of the most popular mainstreaming practices are prereferral teams, collaborative consultation, cooperative teaching, and curricula and instructional strategies. Among the curricula and instructional strategies employed to further inclusion are curricula designed to change attitudes toward disabilities, cooperative learning, peer tutoring, and partial participation.

The standards-based reform movement of the 1990s has been expanded to include students with disabilities. Standards-based reform emphasizes higher expectations for all students and measuring progress toward academic goals through standardized tests or other assessment procedures. Students with disabilities have often been excluded from participation in the general education curriculum and from standardized tests of educational progress. IDEA now requires that students with disabilities have access to the general curriculum studied by nondisabled students and be included in systemwide or statewide assessments of educational progress, with appropriate adaptations or accommodations as necessary. Accommodations for assessment might involve altering the time given to respond, changing the setting of the assessment, or using an alternative format for presenting tasks or responding.

Access by individuals with disabilities to new technologies is being increasingly emphasized. The major technologies that become controversial for people with disabilities involve medical advances and communications. The controversy is often over whether we *should* do something that we *can*. New technologies are often created with concern for universal design—the principle that the technological device or program should be workable for as many potential users as possible.

Early intervention programs for children with disabilities and their families are now mandated by law. A cornerstone of early intervention is the individualized family service plan (IFSP). The IFSP is like an IEP, but it broadens the focus to include the family. There are several types of early intervention programs. A common way of categorizing them is according to whether they are center-based, home-based, or a combination of the two. Three issues pertaining to early childhood intervention are (1) the appropriate role of the family, (2) whether the curriculum should be teacher or child centered, and (3) whether full inclusion is best for all young children.

Federal law now also stipulates programming for transition from secondary school to adulthood. Transition is defined as including a variety of postschool activities, including postsecondary education, vocational training, integrated employment, continuing and adult education, adult services, independent living, or community participation. The law mandates that transition plans must be incorporated into the IEPs of students with disabilities. The law emphasizes both employment and issues pertaining to the quality of life of people with disabilities.

Supported employment is one way to integrate persons with disabilities into the workplace. In a typical supported employment situation, a job coach provides on-site training, which gradually tapers off as the worker learns to perform the job independently.

Issues pertaining to implementing transition from secondary school to adulthood for people with severe disabilities focus largely on coordinating and linking the many agencies outside the school setting. For people with mild disabilities, many of the issues center on providing programming that balances their vocational and academic needs. Some educators are concerned that the recent press for more rigorous academic standards generally will result in the disregard of the needs of students with disabilities.

Concern for safe and orderly schools has resulted in controversial policies related to the discipline of students with disabilities. Much of the controversy regarding discipline has to do with zero tolerance for certain behaviors that might result in the student's suspension or expulsion, such as bringing a weapon or drugs to school. The disciplinary action the school may take might depend on determining whether the student's misbehavior was or was not a manifestation of his or her disability.

In most cases, the same rules of discipline apply to students with disabilities as apply to all other students. However, federal law does not allow the discontinuation of education for students with disabilities, even if they are expelled. If a student with disabilities is disciplined by suspension or expulsion, then his or her education must continue in an alternative setting.

The 1997 amendments to IDEA that relate to discipline emphasize problem solving rather than punishment. Educators must develop proactive and positive behavioral intervention plans and complete a functional assessment of the student's behavior designed to solve or prevent problems.

Carmen Martinez

Untitled (Figure), Marker on paper. 14 × 17 in.

Ms. Martinez, who was born in 1978 in New York City, is an engaging young woman who enjoys watching wrestling on television. Her work seems to command attention. She is a leader among her peers.

Multicultural and Bilingual Aspects of Special Education

Remember and help America remember that the fellowship of human beings is more important than the fellowship of race and class and gender in a democratic society. . . . All children need [a] pride of heritage and sense of history of their own people and of all the people who make up the mosaic of this great nation. African American and Latino and Asian American and Native American children should know about European history and cultures, and white children should know about the histories and cultures of diverse peoples of color with whom they share a city, a nation, and a world. I believe in integration. But that does not mean I become someone else or ignore or deny who I am. I learned the Negro National anthem, "Lift Every Voice and Sing," at the same time I learned "The Star Spangled Banner" and "America the Beautiful" and I love them all. I have raised you, my children, to respect other people's children, not to become their children but to become yourselves at your best. I hope others will raise their children to respect you.

MARIAN WRIGHT EDELMAN
The Measure of Our Success: A Letter to My Children and Yours

In the last decade of the twentieth century and in the early years of the twenty-first, many nations and regions have splintered into factions, clans, tribes, and gangs. In some cases, this splintering has been accompanied by extreme cruelty of individuals or groups toward others. Differences—especially those of religion, ethnic origin, color, custom, and social class—are too often the basis for viciousness toward other people. This has been the case throughout human history, and it remains a central problem of humankind. In the early twenty-first century, slavery still is practiced in some nations of the world. All cultures and ethnic groups of the world can take pride in much of their heritage, but most, if not all, also bear a burden of shame because at some time in their history, they have engaged in the ruthless treatment or literal enslavement of others. Sometimes this treatment has extended to certain minority members of their own larger group whose differences have been viewed as undesirable or intolerable.

In virtually every nation, society, religion, ethnic group, tribe, or clan, discrimination exists against those who are different in some dimension of human identity. The discrimination that we practice or experience stems from and perpetuates fear, hatred, and abusive relationships. If a group feels discriminated against or oppressed and sees no hope of becoming valued and being treated fairly, it inevitably will seek to become separate and autonomous, sometimes threatening or subjugating others in the process.

Views of our shared history are often told from only one point of view and are so unrealistic that they promise only more misunderstanding and conflict. As Roger Wilkins (2001) has written:

> Ancient pains are summoned up to cloak contemporary arguments in the self-righteousness of victimhood. So we divide up our past and use simplistic bits selectively—avoiding real human complexity—in order to fuel the argument of the moment or to meet urgent but unrelated needs. But in so dividing and simplifying history—for example, maintaining that the Confederate flag is merely the symbol of past honor and gallantry or that all blacks were innocent and noble victims—we ensure that our future will be rent along the same jagged seams that wound us so grievously today.
>
> Tales of the republic's founding—mythic national memories used to bind us together—are often told in ways that exclude and diminish all of us. They diminish the founders by denying them rich human complexity and giving us instead monumental heroes whose actual lives cannot possibly live up to the marble facades that have come down to us through the generations; and they diminish blacks either by simply excluding us or by minimizing our humanity and our contributions to the richness, strength, and vibrancy of the nation. (pp. 6–7)

It is critically important, therefore, that we learn and help others learn both the actual facts of history and contemporary life and tolerance for those who differ from us—not *toleration* in the sense rightfully scorned by Roger Wilkins (2001), but understanding and acceptance of the principle that those who differ from us are equals as human beings. Furthermore, it is necessary for special educators, as well as general educators, to understand the purpose of **multicultural education.** Namely, multicultural education aims to change educational institutions and curricula so that they will provide equal educational opportunities to students regardless of their gender, social class, ethnicity, race, disability, or other cultural identity. It also seeks to socialize students to a multicultural norm—tolerance of and respect for those whose culture is different from one's own and knowledge of our *shared* history.

Our desire as Americans is to build a diverse but just society in which the personal freedom and pride of all cultural groups and respect for others' cultural heritage are the norm, a society in which fear, hate, and abuse are eliminated (see Banks & Banks, 1997; Glazer, 1997, 1998; Spencer, 1997; Utley & Obiakor, 2001a). Working toward this ideal demands a multicultural perspective, one from which we can simultaneously accomplish two tasks. First, as a nation of increasing cultural diversity, we must renew our efforts to

Multicultural education.
Aims to change educational institutions and curricula so they will provide equal educational opportunities to students regardless of their gender, social class, ethnicity, race, disability, or other cultural identity.

Multicultural and Bilingual Aspects of Special Education

MYTH Multicultural education addresses the concerns of ethnic minorities who want their children to learn more about their history and the intellectual, social, and artistic contributions of their ancestors.

FACT This is a partial truth. In FACT, multicultural education seeks to help the children of all ethnic groups appreciate their own and others' cultural heritages—plus our common American culture that sustains multiculturalism.

MYTH Everyone agrees that multicultural education is critical to our nation's future.

FACT Some people, including some who are members of ethnic minorities, believe that multicultural education is misguided and diverts attention from our integration in a distinctive, cohesive American culture.

MYTH Implementing multicultural education is a relatively simple matter of including information about all cultures in the curriculum and teaching respect for them.

FACT Educators and others are struggling with how to construct a satisfactory multicultural curriculum and multicultural instructional methods. Nearly every aspect of the task is controversial—which cultures to include, how much attention to give to each, and what and how to teach about them.

MYTH Multiculturalism includes only the special features and contributions of clearly defined ethnic groups.

FACT Ethnicity is typically the focal point of discussions of multiculturalism, but ethnicity is sometimes a point of controversy if it is defined too broadly (for example, by lumping all Asians, all Africans, or all Europeans together). Besides ethnic groups, other groups and individuals—such as people identified by gender, sexual orientation, religion, and disability—need consideration in a multicultural curriculum.

MYTH Disproportionate representation of ethnic minorities in special education is no longer a problem.

FACT Some ethnic minorities are still underrepresented or overrepresented in certain special education categories. For example, African American students, especially males, are overrepresented in programs for students with emotional disturbance and underrepresented in programs for gifted and talented students.

MYTH Disability is never related to ethnicity.

FACT Some disabilities are genetically linked and therefore more prevalent in some ethnic groups. For example, sickle cell disease (a severe, chronic, hereditary blood disease) occurs disproportionately in children with ancestry from Africa, Mediterranean and Caribbean regions, Saudi Arabia, and India.

MYTH If students speak English, there is no need to be concerned about bilingual education.

FACT Conversational English is not the same as the more formal and sometimes technical language used in academic curriculum and classroom instruction. Educators must make sure that students understand the language used in teaching, not just informal conversation.

achieve social justice and take specific steps to understand and appreciate one another's cultures. Second, in doing so we must pledge our first loyalty to common cultural values that make diversity a strength rather than a fatal flaw. We seek a commitment to our common humanity and to democratic ideals that bind people together for the common good and give all freedom for the rightful honoring of their heritage. These two tasks of multicultural education in a multicultural nation are expressed in the words of Marian Wright Edelman in her letter to her children and others (see excerpt on p. 79).

Nevertheless, multicultural education has its critics, some of whom see it as eroding the moral foundations of society and undermining the central purpose of schooling—ensuring the academic competence of students. For example, one newspaper columnist wrote, "For 40 years, American public education has pressed children into a humanistic, secular, multicultural mold" (Thomas, 1998, p. A8). Although multiculturalism may sometimes be distorted into indefensible ideology, we do not understand how the multicultural education we advocate can be anything but helpful in students' academic learning and socialization to American ideals.

Since the civil rights movement of the 1960s, educators have become increasingly aware of the extent to which differences among cultural and ethnic groups affect children's schooling. Gradually, educators and others are coming to understand that the cultural diversity of the United States and the world demands multicultural education. Progress in constructing multicultural education has been slow, however, in part because of the way all cultural groups tend to view themselves as the standard against which others should be judged (Rogoff & Morelli, 1989).

Education that takes full advantage of the cultural diversity in our schools and the larger world requires much critical analysis and planning. It may be very difficult for all cultural or ethnic groups to find common satisfaction in any specific curriculum, even if they are all seeking what they consider the multicultural ideal. Moreover, some argue that the more important goal is finding the common American culture and ensuring that our children have a common cultural literacy (see Hirsch, 1987, 1996; Kennedy, 1997; Rodriguez, 1982, 1992). Even the metaphors we use for dealing with cultural diversity and cultural unity are points of controversy. The United States has often been called a "cultural melting pot," but some now reject the notion of total melding or amalgamation—they reject the metaphor of an alloy in which metals are dissolved in each other and fused into a new substance (Price, 1992; see also Spencer, 1997). For example, one teacher in a videotaped case study of multicultural education comments about the American melting pot, "I have no desire to melt, but I would love to enrich. But I do not want to melt! . . . Back to my stew, if I'm going in as a carrot, I want to be tasted as a carrot and then still add to the flavor of the entire . . ." (McNergney, 1992). To continue with the "stew" metaphor, there is controversy regarding how "chunky" our American culture should be.

That racism and discrimination remain serious problems in the United States and most other societies is obvious. These problems have no simple resolution, and they are found among virtually all ethnic groups. People of every cultural description struggle with the meaning of differences that may seem trivial or superficial to some but elicit powerful emotional responses and discrimination from others. Russell (1992) describes color discrimination that is practiced not only between whites and African Americans but also among African Americans of varied hues. Consider the hostilities and suffering associated with differences in color as well as in gender, religion, sexual orientation, abilities and disabilities, and political beliefs. In the box on page 83, the Jewish mother of a black man, James McBride, recalls the racial and religious prejudices she experienced and observed as a child in the 1930s. Anti-Semitism and other racist attitudes still exist in all regions of America as well as in all nations of the world, and no cultural group is entirely free of prejudice and other racist sentiments. Consider the experience of Susie Kay, a Jewish teacher in a Washington, D.C., high school where all the students are African American:

Kay's students say they know about white culture mainly from television shows; hardly any interact regularly with whites—"Caucasians," as they call them. Most have never met a Jewish person, except for Miss Kay, who wears her Star of David necklace every day. Prompting students to ask, "Isn't that the star of the Devil?"

"And what's the difference between a white person and a Jew anyway?" asks another. Both are rich, right? (Horwitz, 1998, p. F1)

The solution is not as simple as becoming sensitized to differences. Too often, Eurocentrism is met with Europhobia, Afrocentrism with Afrophobia, homocentrism with homophobia, sensitivity to difference with hypersensitivity about being different. Nor is the solution to become "blind" to difference, as the box "In Living Black and White" on page 84 illustrates (see Schofield, 1997; Williams, 1998a, 1998b). In discussing people of color, Spencer (1997) concludes that "we need the current racial classifications in order to fight racism, because as soon as we discard the racial classifications black people are still going to be discriminated against" (p. 148). Glazer (1997, 1998) also observes that loss of racial identity in the service of equal opportunity for minorities cannot work. Likewise, eliminating labels for individuals with disabilities inevitably results in the loss of their

The Color of Water: School

The Jewish school didn't really count with the white folks, so I went to the white school, Thomas Jefferson Elementary. If it was up to Tateh [my father] he would have kept me out of school altogether. "That gentile school won't teach you anything you can use," he scoffed. He paid for us to take private lessons in sewing and knitting and record keeping from other people. He was tight with his money, but when it came to that kind of thing, he wasn't cheap, I'll say that for him. He would rather pay for us to study privately than to go to school with gentiles, but the law was the law, so I had to go to school with the white folks. It was a problem from the moment I started, because the white kids hated Jews in my school. "Hey, Ruth, when did you start being a dirty Jew?" they'd ask. I couldn't stand being ridiculed. I even changed my name to try to fit in more. My real name was Rachel, which in Yiddish is Ruckla, which is what my parents called me—but I used the name Ruth around white folk, because it didn't sound so Jewish, though it never stopped the other kids from teasing me.

Nobody liked me. That's how I felt as a child. I know what it feels like when people laugh at you walking down the street, or snicker when they hear you speaking Yiddish, or just look at you with hate in their eyes. You know a Jew living in Suffolk when I was coming up could be lonely even if there were fifteen of them standing in the room, I don't know why; it's that feeling that nobody likes you; that's how I felt, living in the South. You were different from everyone and liked by very few. There were white sections of Suffolk, like the Riverview section, where Jews weren't allowed to own property. It said that on the deeds and you can look them up. They'd say "for

White Anglo-Saxon Protestants only." That was the law there and they meant it. The Jews in Suffolk did stick together, but even among Jews my family was low because we dealt with *shvartses* [blacks]. So I didn't have a lot of Jewish friends either.

When I was in the fourth grade, a girl came up to me in the schoolyard during recess and said, "You have the prettiest hair. Let's be friends." I said, "Okay." Heck, I was glad someone wanted to be my friend. Her name was Frances. I'll never forget Frances for as long as I live. She was thin, with light brown hair and blue eyes. She was a quiet gentle person. I was actually forbidden to play with her because she was a gentile, but I'd sneak over to her house anyway and sneak her over to mine. Actually I didn't have to sneak into Frances's house because I was always welcome there. She lived past the cemetery on the other side of town in a frame house that we entered from the back door. It seemed that dinner was always being served at Frances's house. Her mother would serve it on plates she took out of a wooden china closet; ham, bread, and hot biscuits with lots of butter—and I couldn't eat any of it. It was *treyf*, not kosher for a Jew to eat. The first time her mother served dinner I said, "I can't eat this," and I was embarrassed until Frances piped out, "I don't like this food either. My favorite food is mayonnaise on white bread." That's how she was. She'd do little things to let you know she was on your side. It didn't bother her one bit that I was Jewish, and if she was around, no one in school would tease me.

SOURCE: From *The Color of Water*, pp. 80–82, by James McBride. Copyright © 1996 by James McBride. Used by permission of Riverhead Books, a division of Penguin Putnam Inc.

In Living Black and White

My son used to attend a small nursery school. Over the course of a year, three different teachers in his school assured me that he was colorblind. Resigned to this diagnosis, I took my son to an ophthalmologist who tested him and pronounced his vision perfect. I could not figure out what was going on until I began to listen carefully to what he was saying about color.

As it turned out, my son did not misidentify color. He resisted identifying color at all. "I don't know," he would say when asked what color the grass was; or, most peculiarly, "It makes no difference." This latter remark, this assertion of the greenness of grass making no difference, was such a precociously cynical retort that I began to suspect some social complication in which he somehow was invested.

The long and short of it is that the well-meaning teachers at his predominantly white school had valiantly and repeatedly assured their charges that color makes no difference. "It doesn't matter," they told the children, "whether you're black or white or red or green or blue." Yet upon further investigation, the very reason that the teachers had felt it necessary to impart this lesson in the first place was that it did matter, and in predictably cruel ways: Some of the children had been fighting about whether black people could play "good guys."

My son's anxious response was redefined by his teachers as physical deficiency—illustrative, perhaps, of the way in which the liberal ideal of colorblindness is too often confounded. That is to say, the very notion of blindness about color constitutes an ideological confusion at best, and denial at its very worst. I recognize, certainly, that the teachers were inspired by a desire to make whole a division in the ranks. But there is much overlooked in the move to undo that which clearly and unfortunately matters just by labeling it that which "makes no difference." The dismissiveness, however unintentional, leaves those in my son's position pulled between the clarity of their own experience and the often alienating terms in which they must seek social acceptance.

SOURCE: Excerpt from *Seeing a Color-Blind Future: The Paradox of Race* by Patricia J. Williams. Copyright © 1997 by Patricia J. Williams. Reprinted with permission of Farrar, Strauss & Giroux, Inc.

equal educational opportunity (Hallahan & Kauffman, 1994; Kauffman, 1999, 2001); we cannot accommodate what we do not see and label. Perhaps the solution must include both engendering sensitivity to differences and building confidence that one's own differences will not be threatened by others'. The solution may also require transforming the curriculum in ways that help students understand how knowledge is constructed and how to view themselves and others from different perspectives.

An individual's membership in any cultural, ethnic, racial, regional, gender, social class, or disability group should not affect what education opportunities are available to him or her. ■

Perhaps we *can* find a uniquely American culture, one that celebrates valued diversities within a framework of clearly defined common values, one that sees "our problems" rather than the problems of particular racial or ethnic groups or other subgroups of our common culture (see Kennedy, 1997). This perspective recognizes that not all diversity is valued, that tolerance has its limits, and that American culture is dynamic and continuously evolving:

> There are limits to cultural tolerance, a lesson the 20th century has repeatedly taught us. There are, among some cultures, deeply held convictions—about women and their bodies; about races; about children; about authority; about lawbreakers, the sick, the weak, the poor and the rich—that we absolutely deplore. The fact is, we need absolutes. Where a plurality of cultures exists, we need an overarching set of values cherished by all. Otherwise what begins as multicultural harmony inevitably descends into balkanization or chaos. . . .
>
> The simple truth, which is either denied or distorted by the prevailing orthodoxies, is that a thriving national culture does exist. It is neither a salad bowl nor static, received tradition, but an ever-evolving national process which selects, unrepresentatively, from the marketplace of raw, particular identities, those that everyone finds it useful and gratifying to embrace and transform into their own. (Patterson, 1993, p. C2)

We are optimistic about multicultural education because it is an opportunity to face our shared problems squarely and to extract the best human qualities from each cultural heritage. Without denying any culture's inhumanity to others or to its own members, we have the opportunity to develop an appreciation of our individual and shared cultural treasures and to engender tolerance, if not love, of all differences that are not destructive of the human spirit. We concur with Price (1992) that the best antidote for cultural insularity is inclusiveness and that insularity will be overcome by adherence to truly American values.

Multiculturalism is now a specialized field of study and research in education, and its full exploration is far beyond the scope of this chapter. Of particular concern to special educators is how exceptionalities are related to cultural diversity and the way in which special education fits within the broader general education context in a multicultural society (Artiles & Trent, 1997a, 1997b; Trent & Artiles, 1998; Utley & Obiakor, 2001a). Cultural diversity presents particular challenges for special educators in three areas: (1) assessment of abilities and disabilities, (2) instruction, and (3) socialization. Before discussing each of these challenges, we summarize some of the major concepts about education and cultural diversity that set the context for multicultural and bilingual special education.

Education and Cultural Diversity: Concepts for Special Education

Culture has many definitions. As Banks (1994) points out, however, "Most contemporary social scientists view culture as consisting primarily of the symbolic, ideational, and intangible aspects of human societies" (p. 83). Banks suggests six major components or elements of culture:

1. Values and behavioral styles
2. Languages and dialects
3. Nonverbal communication
4. Awareness (of one's cultural distinctiveness)
5. Frames of reference (normative world views or perspectives)
6. Identification (feeling part of the cultural group)

For information about diversity issues, you can access file:/// E|/welcome.html

Many of the other general Web sites listed contain information about diversity issues. ▦

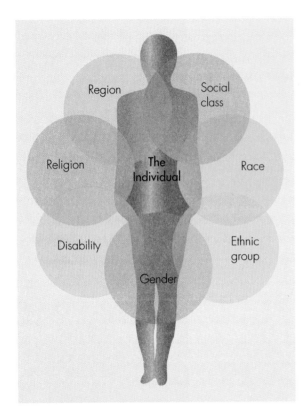

FIGURE 3.1

Individuals belong to many different microcultural groups.

SOURCE: From J. A. Banks, *Multiethnic education: Theory and practice,* 3rd ed., p. 89. Copyright © 1994 by Allyn & Bacon. Reprinted/adapted with permission.

These elements may together make up a national or shared culture, sometimes referred to as a **macroculture.** Within the larger macroculture are **microcultures**—smaller cultures that share the common characteristics of the macroculture but have their unique values, styles, languages and dialects, nonverbal communication, awareness, frames of reference, and identities. An individual may identify with the macroculture and also belong to many different microcultures, as shown in Figure 3.1. The variety of microcultures to which a person belongs affects his or her behavior. Macroculture in the United States consists of certain overarching values, symbols, and ideas, such as justice, equality, and human dignity. Microcultures within the U.S. macroculture may share these common values but differ in many additional ways. The number of microcultures represented in U.S. schools has increased in recent decades because of the variety of immigrants from other countries, particularly Southeast Asia.

The national census of 2000 as well as many other sources have noted enormous demographic changes in the United States. The number and percentage of nonwhite citizens is increasing rapidly, but our society is becoming more diverse in many ways. "The most detailed demographic snapshot in a decade describes a nation where nearly 1 in 5 Americans does not speak English at home, more than 2 million grandparents are raising their grandchildren, and the number of adults who work solely out of their homes has grown a third since 1990" (Cohn & Cohen, 2001, p. A1). Cohn and Cohen also provide many other figures: for example, 1 in 6 children lives in poverty and the nation gained more immigrants in the 1990s than in any previous decade. Poverty clearly places children at higher risk of disability compared to children reared in conditions of economic advantage (Fujiura & Yamaki, 2000). America is increasingly home to refugees from other nations (Harrison, 2000), and many urban children spend a great deal of time on the streets or are homeless (Walker, 2000). Thus the United States of the twenty-first century is more diverse than ever in the microcultures it includes—diverse in ethnic groups, economic status, lifestyles, *and* disabilities.

Family support (or the lack thereof) is recognized as a key factor in children's academic success. ∎

Students from some microcultures in U.S. society do extremely well in school, but others do not. The factors accounting for the school performance of microcultural minorities are complex, and social scientists are still searching for the attitudes, beliefs, behavioral styles, and opportunities that foster the success of specific microcultural groups. Researchers have reported that Southeast Asian (Indochinese) refugee families adopting an orientation to certain American values—acquiring material possessions and seeking fun and excitement—have children whose academic performance is lower than that of children from families maintaining traditional Southeast Asian values—persistence, achievement, and family support (Caplan, Choy, & Whitmore, 1992). This finding suggests that schools and teachers may face an impossible task unless changes occur in students' home cultures. "It is clear that the U.S. educational system can work—if the requisite familial and social supports are provided for the students outside school" (Caplan et al., 1992, p. 36). Ogbu (1992) also notes the critical role played by different minority communities in encouraging academic success among their children and youth. He differentiates between immigrant, or voluntary, minorities—those who have come to the United States primarily for their own economic and social benefit—and castelike, or involuntary, minorities who were originally brought to the United States against their will. Most Chinese and Punjabi Indians, for example, are voluntary minorities; African American children and youths are, for the most part, members of an involuntary minority. Ogbu concludes that "minority children do not succeed or fail only because of what schools do or do not do, but also because of what the community does" (1992, p. 12).

Ogbu's suggestion of the importance of community as well as individual influences has been expanded in **sociocultural theory.** Rueda and Kim (2001) have depicted sociocultural theory as shown in Figure 3.2, which they explain as follows:

> A complete account of learning and development must take into account three levels. First, the *individual or personal plane* involves individual cognition, emotion, behavior, values, and beliefs. In educational research, this might correspond with studies of individual student or teacher actions, psychological characteristics, or competence. Second, the *interpersonal or social plane* includes communication, role performances, dialogue, cooperation, conflict, assistance, and assessment. In educational research, this is often addressed in studies of teaching/learning interactions, such as a study of cooperative learning groups. And third, the *community or institutional plane* involves shared history, languages, rules, values, beliefs, and identities. This is sometimes addressed in studies of entire schools, districts, professions, neighborhoods, tribes, or cultures. This last plane of development, often overlooked in behavioral science, focuses on factors such as past and current power relationships among various groups under consideration, including (a) how these are embedded in social institutions; and (b) how these are perceived and experienced by individuals and their communities. . . . Sociocultural theory, in general, emphasizes that these three planes are inseparable: moreover, language is the primary force that defines and connects the planes. (p. 80)

Although there is considerable evidence that various ethnic minority communities have a strong influence on students' achievement and school behavior, we offer three cautions:

1. We need to guard against stereotypes—assumptions that one's cultural identity is sufficient to explain academic achievement or economic success. The "Doonesbury" cartoon makes the point rather well, we feel.

Macroculture.
A nation or other large social entity with a shared culture.

Microculture.
A smaller group existing within a larger cultural group and having unique values, style, language, dialect, ways of communicating nonverbally, awareness, frame of reference, and identification.

Sociocultural theory.
The theory that the individual, interpersonal or social experiences, and community or institution are all important and inseparable causes of human behavior and that language ties all of these aspects of development together.

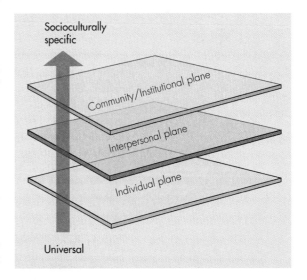

FIGURE 3.2

The interrelated planes of learning and development

SOURCE: From Rueda, R., & Kim, S. (2001). Cultural and linguistic diversity as a theoretical framework for understanding multicultural learners with mild disabilities. In C. A. Utley & F. E. Obiakor (Eds.), *Special education, multicultural education, and school reform: Components of quality education for learners with mild disabilities,* p. 81. Courtesy of Charles C. Thomas, Publisher, Ltd., Springfield, IL.

2. The fact that minority communities may have a strong influence on school success does not relieve schools of the obligation to provide a multicultural education. All students need to feel that they and their cultural heritage are included in the mainstream of American culture and schooling.

3. Unless teachers and other school personnel value minority students—see value and promise in them and act accordingly by setting demanding but not unreachable expectations—the support of families and the minority community may be insufficient to improve the academic success of minority students. Too often, minority students are devalued in school, regardless of their achievements and behaviors.

The general purposes of multicultural education are (1) to promote pride in one's own cultural heritage and understanding of microcultures different from one's own, (2) to foster positive attitudes toward cultural diversity, and (3) to ensure equal educational opportunities for all students. These purposes cannot be accomplished unless students develop an understanding and appreciation of their own cultural heritage, as well as an awareness and acceptance of cultures different from their own. Understanding and appreciation are not likely to develop automatically through unplanned contact with members of other microcultures. Rather, teachers must plan experiences that teach about culture and provide models of cultural awareness and acceptance and the appreciation of cultural diversity.

On the surface, teaching about cultures and engendering an acceptance and appreciation of cultural diversity appear to be simple tasks. However, two questions immediately complicate the matter when we get below the surface and address the actual practice of multiculturalism in education: (1) Which cultures shall we include? (2) What and how shall we teach about them? The first question demands that we consider all the microcultures that might be represented in the school and the difficulties inherent in including them all. The United States has more than 100 distinct microcultures based on national origin alone. In some urban school districts with large numbers of immigrant children, more than twenty different languages may be spoken in students' homes. But ethnic or national origin is only one dimension of cultural diversity, one branch of many in the multicultural program. Ethnicity is not the only representation of culture, and there is much variation of culture within any ethnic group (Keogh, Gallimore, & Weisner, 1997). In fact, assuming that all individuals of a particular racial or ethnic group have the same values and perspectives is a form of stereotyping.

Many advocates of multiculturalism consider gender, sexual orientation, religion, disability, and so on to be additional dimensions of cultural diversity that require explicit attention. Moreover, some microcultural groups find the traditions, ceremonies, values, holidays, and other characteristics of other microcultures unacceptable or even offensive. That is, when it comes to what and how to teach about other cultures, the stage may be set

Doonesbury 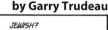 **by Garry Trudeau**

SOURCE: "Doonesbury." Copyright © 1992 G. B. Trudeau. Reprinted with permission of Universal Press Syndicate. All rights reserved.

Plan to Teach in Spanish Upsets Some in Arlington

A proposal by Arlington school administrators to teach Spanish-speaking kindergartners at four schools in their native language for two hours a day has drawn heated opposition from some county residents, who say it will make it harder for the children to learn English.

The County's School Board this week postponed voting on the plan after 12 residents spoke against it at a board meeting and two spoke in favor. Only one of the five board members, E. T. "Libby" Garvey, expressed strong support for the bilingual experiment, whose aim is to boost the academic performance of Spanish-speaking children. Other board members said they wanted to learn more about it.

The program would be the first of its kind in the Washington area. Most area public schools put students with weak English skills in English as a Second Language (ESL) classes, which are conducted in English.

Under the Arlington proposal, the special Spanish language classes would be an option for about 120 kindergartners this fall at Barcroft, Barrett, Glencarlyn and Henry elementary schools. The students' families, if they preferred, could instead have their children placed in ESL classes or in regular classes.

The two hours a day of instruction in Spanish would cover basic subjects such as reading concepts, science, math and social studies. The program would continue until the third grade, with more kindergartners being added each year.

Leaders of Arlington's Republican Party have been among the chief critics of the plan. They argue that giving some students Spanish-language instruction would produce the same parental dissatisfaction that has led to a June ballot measure in California designed to kill bilingual education in that state.

"Native-language programs simply trap children in a cycle of government dependency by denying them the opportunity to learn English," Henriette Warfield, chairman of the Arlington Republican Party, told the board.

But Kathleen F. Grove, Arlington's assistant school superintendent for instruction, said the proposed pilot program is simply a small part of the school system's effort to raise the academic achievement level of Spanish-speaking students to match that of their classmates who speak English at home.

On the Stanford 9 test, for example, the average scores of Hispanic students in Arlington are 29 to 40 percentile points lower than the average scores of non-Hispanic white students in the county, depending on the grade level. The test is one of five nationally recognized standardized achievement tests.

Criticisms of the proposal, Grove said, "sounded as if they were motivated more by the desire to identify an inflammatory issue than discuss what is the best thing to do."

In California, many Hispanic parents have objected to instructing children in Spanish. At Tuesday night's Arlington School Board meeting, the residents who criticized the proposal did not include any Spanish-speaking residents with children in the county schools. Grove said she has not notified Hispanic parents about the program. She said she wanted to get board approval first so as not to raise the hopes of parents who might want to try it.

Jose R. Oyola, a member of the Arlington Hispanic Parents Association, said he has read the proposal and thought "it had merit in its structure."

Some studies show bilingual education to be effective, and some do not. In California and other states that have such programs, increasing numbers of educators and Hispanic parents have argued that the Spanish-language lessons, after a year or so, become a crutch that keeps students from developing the English skills they need in high school and college.

A recent report by Wayne Thomas and Virginia Collier, of the Graduate School of Education at George Mason University, noted that the number of students from non-English-speaking families had quadrupled in Arlington in the last two decades. About 31 percent of Arlington public school children are Hispanic.

The GMU researchers found that the county's efforts to build English skills through ESL lessons put most of the students into regular classes fairly quickly. But after that, the students generally lagged far behind native English speakers, particularly in high school, the study said.

Arlington, like several other Washington area school districts, has a voluntary Spanish immersion program, in which all the students at one elementary school are taught in Spanish for about half the school day and taught in English for the other half.

The report by Thomas and Collier recommended more immersion programs, which depend on voluntary participation by significant numbers of English-speaking parents. The report said national studies show that such programs are the most effective approach for students with poor English.

SOURCE: Mathews. J. (1998, April 17) Plan to teach in Spanish upsets some in Arlington. *The Washington Post*, pp. C–1, C–5. **© 1998 The Washington Post. Reprinted with permission.**

One of the most controversial aspects of multicultural education is whether English and non-English languages should be combined in classrooms and how. ◼

for conflict. Treating all cultures with equal attention and respect may present substantial or seemingly insurmountable logistical and interpersonal problems.

One of the most controversial aspects of multicultural education is the use of language. For instance, is it appropriate to refer to a *minority* or *minorities* when the group or aggregates to which we refer constitute half or more of the population in a given school, district, region, or state? What labels and terms are acceptable for designating various groups? What languages or dialects should be used for instruction? With the arrival of many immigrants to the United States, the issue of bilingual education and its relationship to multiculturalism has become increasingly important. The box on page 89 illustrates how controversial the issue of language can be. As we discuss later, bilingual education is of even greater concern when children with disabilities are considered (Gersten & Baker, 2000; Gersten, Brengelman, & Jimenez, 1994).

Given the multiplicity of microcultures, each wanting—if not demanding—its precise and fair inclusion in the curriculum, it is not surprising that educators sometimes feel caught in a spiral of factionalism and feuding. Furthermore, additional questions about cultural values inevitably must be addressed: Which cultural values and characteristics should we embrace? Which, if any, should we shun? Would we, if we could, fully sustain some cultures, alter some significantly, and eliminate others? Consider, for example, cultures in which women are treated as chattel, as well as the drug culture, the culture of street gangs, the culture of poverty. To what extent does every culture have a right to perpetuate itself? How should we respond to some members of the Deaf culture, for example, who reject the prevention of deafness or procedures and devices that enable deaf children to hear, preferring deafness to hearing and wishing to sustain the Deaf culture deliberately? Depending on how we define culture, the values of our own cultural heritage, and our role in multicultural education, we may find ourselves embroiled in serious cultural conflicts. No wonder that some describe the late twentieth and early twenty-first centuries as an era of "culture wars." To deal effectively with the multicultural challenge, we must focus on the challenges most pertinent to special education.

Implementing Multicultural and Bilingual Special Education

For more information about bilingual education and linguistic diversity in education, see www.ed.gov/offices/OBEMLA/ ◼

The microcultures of particular importance for special education are ethnic groups and exceptionality groups. Banks (1997) notes that an *ethnic group* "has a historic origin and a shared heritage and tradition" (p. 66). It has value orientations, behavioral patterns, and often political and economic interests that differ from those of other groups in the larger society. An ethnic group may be a majority or a minority of people in a given country or region. We define an *exceptionality group* as a group sharing a set of specific abilities or disabilities that are especially valued or that require special accommodation within a given microculture. Thus, a person may be identified as exceptional in one ethnic group (or other microculture defined by gender, social class, religion, etc.) but not in another. Being unable to read or speak standard English, for example, may identify a student as having a

Teachers must recognize and confront their own attitudes about people from various cultural groups, or they may inadvertently discriminate against their own students. Achieving this awareness is a key factor in the success or failure of multicultural education. ■

disability in an Anglo-dominated microculture, although the same student would not be considered disabled in a microculture in which English-language skills are unimportant. In certain cultures, children avoid direct eye contact with adults in positions of authority. Given this, a child who does not look directly at the teacher may mistakenly be assumed to be inattentive or oppositional by adults from cultures in which eye contact between the teacher and pupil is expected. This child could be inappropriately identified as having a disability requiring special education.

We still do not know much about how best to train teachers to be aware of their own cultural histories and biases. However, because of the relatively poor performance of many students of color in schools, many parents and policy makers, as well as teacher educators, see better teacher education as critically important. Part of the better training of teachers is helping them to be more knowledgeable about and responsive to both their own and their students' cultures. Some teacher educators suggest that this can be accomplished only if teachers are helped to understand their own culture's history of community, rules, ways of handling tasks, language, and values related to people and outcomes (Artiles, Trent, Hoffman-Kipp, & Lopez-Torres, 2000).

Ethnicity and exceptionality are distinctly different concepts. In fact, multicultural special education must focus on two primary objectives that go beyond the general purposes of multicultural education:

1. Ensuring that ethnicity is not mistaken for educational exceptionality
2. Increasing understanding of the microculture of exceptionality and its relationship to other microcultures

Ethnicity may be mistaken for exceptionality when one's own ethnic group is viewed as setting the standard for all others. For example, patterns of eye contact, physical contact, use of language, and ways of responding to persons in positions of authority may vary greatly from one ethnic group to another. Members of each ethnic group must realize that what they see as deviant or unacceptable in their own group may be normal and adaptive in another ethnic group. That is, we must not mistakenly conclude that a student has a disability or is gifted just because he or she is different.

Members of minority ethnic groups are more apt to be identified as disabled because their differences are not well understood or valued by others. In part, this higher risk may be a result of prejudice—unreasonable or irrational negative attitudes, feelings, judgments, or behaviors based on ignorance or misunderstanding. Prejudice may cause individuals to be judged as deviant or disabled on the basis of characteristics that are typical for their ethnic group or from stereotyping. That is, an individual's identity as a member of a particular group may result in the automatic assumption that he or she will behave in certain ways.

Students may be particularly likely to be identified or not identified as having certain disabilities depending on their gender and ethnicity. The disproportional representation of males and ethnic minority students in special education is a problem of long standing. Boys make up considerably more than half of the students with certain disabilities (e.g., about 75 percent of those with emotional disturbance), and the percentage of students with certain disabilities who are ethnic minorities is disproportionately high—or, in some cases, disproportionately low. Table 3.1 shows the discrepancies between the percentages of all public school students who are white, black, Asian/Pacific Islander, Hispanic, and American Indian and the percentages of these minorities identified as having certain disabilities. Notice that white, Asian/Pacific Islander, and Hispanic students receive special education at percentages somewhat below their representation in the general population, while black and American Indian students are overrepresented in special education. One has to be careful not to misinterpret these figures. For example, a common misinterpretation is that 20 percent of black students are receiving special education (MacMillan & Reschly, 1998; Reschly, 2001). Such grotesque misinterpretations demean the image of minority students and undermine the seriousness of the problem of overrepresentation. The actual meaning of the figures shown in Table 3.1 is that about *20 percent of the students receiving special education* are black, a far different matter than the common misinterpretation.

It is also important to recognize that disproportionality is not an equal problem in all special education categories, schools, localities, or states for any given ethnic group. The problem of overrepresentation varies with ethnic group and the proportion of the school population that is minority (see Artiles & Zamora-Duran, 1997; Coutinho & Oswald, 2000; Oswald & Coutinho, 2001). The U.S. Department of Education (1992, 1996, 1997, 2000) has shown particular concern about the disproportional representation of ethnic minorities in special education. Important civil rights are involved in the issue. On the one hand, children with disabilities have a right to appropriate education regardless of their ethnicity, even if their ethnic group is statistically overrepresented in special education. On the other hand, however, children also have a right to freedom from discrimination and segregation. The disproportional placement of ethnic minority students in special education strongly suggests that in some cases students are misidentified and wrongly placed (and stigmatized and segregated) in special education, while in other cases ethnic minority students' disabilities are ignored (and the students thus denied appropriate education).

The reasons for the disproportional representation of certain groups in special education may involve assessment of students' abilities, but other factors such as community standards and resources may be implicated as well. In commenting on the disproportion-

TABLE 3.1 Percentage of Students of Various Ethnic Groups in the Total School Population and Their Percentage of Those Receiving Special Education

	White	Black	Asian/Pacific Islander	Hispanic	American Indian
Percent of total school population	66.2	14.8	3.8	14.2	1.0
Percent of those receiving special education	63.6	20.2	1.7	13.2	1.3

SOURCE: U.S. Department of Education (2000). *Twenty-second annual report to Congress on the implementation of the Individuals with Disabilities Education Act.* Washington, DC: Author.

ately high representation of black students in most special education categories, the Department of Education commented, "It is possible that black youth were more likely than their white counterparts to have experienced poor prenatal, perinatal, or postnatal health care and early childhood nutrition which may have resulted in actual disabilities" (1992, p. 15). In its 1996 report to Congress on the implementation of IDEA, the Department of Education focused on the problems of urban schools and the relationship of urban factors to disproportional placement in special education. It has become clear that the problem of disproportionality is very complex and that there are no simple solutions (Oswald & Coutinho, 2001).

The complexity of this issue requires an integrated and multifaceted effort to promote greater educational access and excellence for racial/ethnic minority students that involves policy makers, educators, researchers, parents, advocates, students, and community representatives. The disproportionate representation of racial/ethnic minority students in special education programs and classes points to the need to:

- make available strong academic programs that foster success for all students in regular and special education;
- implement effective and appropriate special education policies and procedures for referral, assessment, eligibility, classification, placement, and re-evaluation;
- increase the level of home/school/community involvement in the educational process; and
- use diverse community resources to enhance and implement educational programs. (U.S. Department of Education, 1997, p. I-47)

Disproportionality is not the only multicultural issue in special education. People with certain exceptionalities can develop their own microcultures (Gollnick & Chinn, 1994). Those with severe hearing impairments, for example, are described by some as belonging to a Deaf culture that is not well understood by most normally hearing people and that results in feelings of isolation or separation from people with normal hearing (Padden & Humphries, 1988). An important aspect of multicultural special education is developing an increased awareness, understanding, and appreciation of cultural differences involving disabilities. Multicultural special education is not merely a matter of overcoming students' prejudice and stereotyping. We must also educate ourselves as teachers to improve methods of assessment, provide effective instruction, and foster appropriate socialization.

We now turn to specific problems in assessment, instruction, and socialization involving microcultural groups, including students with exceptionalities.

ASSESSMENT

Assessment is a process of collecting information about individuals or groups for the purpose of making decisions. In education, assessment ordinarily refers to testing, interviewing, and observing students. The results of assessment should help us decide whether problems exist in a student's education and, if problems are identified, what to do about them (Taylor, 1997). Clearly, assessment often results in important decision about people's lives, and therefore in the U.S. macroculture there is great concern for accuracy, justice, and fairness.

Unfortunately, the accuracy, justice, and fairness of many educational assessments, especially those involving special education, are open to question (McDonnell, McLaughlin, & Morison, 1997; Utley & Obiakor, 2001b). Particularly when ethnic microcultures are involved, traditional assessment practices have frequently violated the U.S. ideals of fairness and equal opportunity regardless of ethnic origin, gender, or disability. That is, the assessment practices of educators and psychologists have frequently come under attack as

Some of the limitations of standardized tests include that they do not take cultural differences into account, that they focus on deficits rather than strengths, and that they do not always provide useful information for teachers. ■

being (1) biased, resulting in misrepresentation of the abilities and disabilities of ethnic minorities and exceptional students, and (2) useless, resulting only in labeling or classification rather than improved educational programming (Council for Exceptional Children, 1997; Ford, 1998). Even prereferral practices, in which the objective is to find solutions to educational problems *before* referral for evaluation, are subject to bias (see Katsiyannis, 1994).

The problems of assessing students to qualify for special education are numerous and complex, and there are no simple solutions (MacMillan, & Reschly, 1998; MacMillan, Gresham, Lopez, & Bocian, 1996; Thurlow, Nelson, Teelucksingh, & Draper, 2001; Utley & Obiakor, 2001b). Many of the problems are centered on traditional standardized testing approaches to assessment that have serious limitations: (1) they do not take cultural diversity into account, (2) they focus on deficits in the individual alone, and (3) they do not provide information useful in teaching. Although these problems have not been entirely overcome, awareness of them and the use of more appropriate assessment procedures for diverse learners are increasing (Lopez-Reyna & Bay, 1997). Assessment must not result in the misidentification of children whose language or other characteristics are merely different, but it must also identify those whose differences represent disabilities (Ortiz, 1997; Van Keulen, Weddington, & DeBose, 1998; Utley & Obiakor, 2001b).

Standardized tests may be biased because most of the test items draw on specific experiences that students from different microcultures may not have had. Tests may, for example, be biased toward the likely experiences of white, middle-class students or be couched in language unfamiliar to members of a certain microculture (Singh, Baker, Winton, & Lewis, 2000). Tests may be administered in ways that penalize students with impaired vision, hearing, or ability to answer in a standard way. Because test scores are often the basis for deciding that a student qualifies for special education, many scholars suspect that test bias accounts for the disproportionate representation of certain groups in special education, especially males and children of color, and the neglect of many children of color who are gifted (see Artiles & Zamora-Duran, 1997; Ford, 1998; U.S. Department of Education, 1996, 1997).

At best, test scores represent a sample of an individual's ability to respond to a standard set of questions or tasks; they do not tell us *all* the important things an individual has learned or how much he or she *can* learn. Controversy over the biases inherent in standardized tests and the search for so-called culture-free and culture-fair tests continue (Taylor, 1997). Three cautions are in order:

1. Tests give only clues about what a student has learned.
2. Test scores must be interpreted with recognition of the possible biases the test contains.
3. Testing alone is an insufficient basis for classifying a student or planning an instructional program.

Traditional assessment procedures focus on the student, not on the environment in which he or she is being taught. Critics of traditional assessment have decried the assumption that any deficit identified will be a deficit of the student. So in addition to assessing the student's behavior or performance, many educators now suggest assessing the instructional environment. This may involve classroom observation and interviews with the student and teacher. It focuses on such items as whether instruction is presented clearly and effectively, the classroom is effectively controlled, the teacher's expectations are appropriate, appropriate curriculum modifications are made, thinking skills are being taught, effective motivational strategies are used, the student is actively engaged in academic responding and given adequate practice and feedback on performance, and progress is directly and frequently evaluated. The purpose of assessing the instructional environment is to make sure that the student is not mistakenly identified as the source of the learning problem (see Hallahan, Kauffman, & Lloyd, 1999; Utley & Obiakor, 2001b). An underlying assumption is that this approach will decrease the likelihood that cultural differences will be mistaken for disabilities.

Traditional assessment procedures result in test scores that may be useful in helping to determine a student's eligibility for special education or other special services. These testing procedures do not, however, typically provide information that is useful in planning for instruction. A variety of alternative assessment procedures were devised in the late 1980s and early 1990s, focusing on students' performance in the curriculum or on tasks in everyday contexts, as opposed to how well they did on standardized tests (see Rueda, 1997; Rueda & Garcia, 1997; Rueda & Kim, 2001). The intent of these procedures is to avoid the artificiality and biased nature of traditional testing and obtain a more fair and instructionally useful assessment of students' abilities. These procedures may be useful in some respects, but they are not a solution to all problems of assessment (Terwilliger, 1997; Utley & Obiakor, 2001b).

One particularly useful alternative approach that emerged in the 1980s is **curriculum-based assessment** (**CBA**) (Choate, Enright, Miller, Poteet, & Rakes, 1995; Fuchs & Fuchs, 1997; Jones, 2001a, 2001b). This method of assessment contrasts sharply with traditional testing, in which students are tested infrequently and may never before have seen the specific items on the test. CBA involves students' responses to their usual instructional materials; it entails direct and frequent samples of performance from the curriculum in which students are being instructed. (We discuss curriculum-based assessment in more detail in Chapter 5.) This form of assessment is thought to be more useful for teachers than traditional testing and to decrease the likelihood of cultural bias.

Finally, we note that fair and accurate assessment is an issue in identifying special gifts and talents as well as disabilities. Too often, the extraordinary abilities of students of color or other ethnic difference and those with disabilities are overlooked because of bias or ignorance on the part of those responsible for assessment. In Chapter 1, we emphasized the importance of identifying the abilities as well as the disabilities of students. To that we want to add the importance of being aware of culturally relevant gifts and talents and recognizing and valuing the abilities of minority students (Ford, 1998; Patton, 1997).

INSTRUCTION

A major objective of multicultural education is ensuring that all students are instructed in ways that do not penalize them because of their cultural differences and that, in fact, capitalize on their cultural heritage (see Council for Exceptional Children, 2000). The methods used to achieve this objective are among the most controversial topics in education

Curriculum-based assessment (CBA). A formative evaluation method designed to evaluate performance in the particular curriculum to which students are exposed; usually involves giving students a small sample of items from the curriculum in use in their schools; proponents argue that CBA is preferable to comparing students with national norms or using tests that do not reflect the curriculum content learned by students.

today. All advocates of multicultural education are concerned with the problem of finding instructional methods that help equalize educational opportunity and achievement for all microcultural groups—that is, methods that break down the inequities and discrimination that have been part of the U.S. public education system. Yet there is considerable debate over the question of what instructional methods are most effective in achieving this goal.

The controversy regarding instruction is generated by what Minow (1985) calls "the dilemma of difference." The dilemma is that either ignoring or recognizing students' linguistic or cultural differences can perpetuate them and maintain inequality of social power and opportunity among ethnic or other microcultural groups. If students' differences are ignored, the students will probably be given instruction that is not suited to their cultural styles or needs. They will then likely fail to learn many skills, which will in turn deny them power and opportunity in the dominant culture. For example, if we ignore non-English-speaking students' language and cultural heritage and force them to speak English, they may have great difficulty in school. "This story [of the harm children experience when their language and cultural differences are not recognized] manifests one half of the difference dilemma: nonacknowledgment of difference reiterates difference" (p. 838).

However, the answer to this problem is not necessarily recognition of students' differences, for instruction geared to individual students' cultural styles may teach only skills valued by their own microcultures. Because the dominant culture does not value these skills, the students' difference will be perpetuated. For example, if non-English-speaking students are taught in their native language and are not required to learn English, then their progress in the English-speaking society will be slowed. As the *Washington Post* put it in an editorial, some children with limited English have spent years in bilingual programs, "turning them into a trap rather than a steppingstone" ("Teach English," 2001, p. A18).

Should a student who speaks no English be forced to give up his or her native language in school and learn to use only English (ignoring the cultural-linguistic difference)? Or should the student's native language be used as the primary vehicle of instruction, while English is taught as a second language (acknowledging the cultural-linguistic difference)? We could pose similar questions for students with severe hearing impairments: Should we teach them by using primarily sign language or spoken language? And the same dilemma of difference appears in providing instruction for students with other disabilities: To what extent should they be treated as different and provided with special accommodations, and to what extent should they be treated just like everyone else?

To a great extent, the controversy over the dilemma of difference has to do with how students fare in society after their school years, not just how they are treated in school. Delpit (1988, 1995) examines a variety of perspectives on the problem of multicultural education, including the following position:

> Children have the right to their own language, their own culture. We must fight cultural hegemony and fight the system by insisting that children be allowed to express themselves in their own language and style. It is not they, the children, who must change, but the schools. (1988, p. 291)

Delpit's response to this perspective acknowledges both the benefit of recognizing and valuing different cultural styles and the necessity of accepting the realities of the society in which we live:

> I believe in diversity of style, and I believe the world will be diminished if cultural diversity is ever obliterated. Further, I believe strongly . . . that each cultural group should have the right to maintain its own language style. When I speak, therefore, of the culture of power, I don't speak of how I wish things to be but of how they are.

Cultural diversity should be fostered and accepted but must not diminish the importance of teaching students the skills they need to survive and prosper in the larger context of the macroculture. ■

> I further believe that to act as if power does not exist is to ensure that the power status quo remains the same. To imply to children or adults . . . that it doesn't matter how you talk or how you write is to ensure their ultimate failure. I prefer to be honest with my students. Tell them that their language and cultural style is unique and wonderful but that there is a political power game that is also being played, and if they want to be in on that game there are certain games that they too must play. . . . They [my colleagues] seem to believe that if we accept and encourage diversity within classrooms of children, then diversity will automatically be accepted at gatekeeping points. . . .
>
> I believe that will never happen. What will happen is that the students who reach the gatekeeping points . . . will understand that they have been lied to and react accordingly. (1988, p. 292)

The gatekeeping points to which Delpit refers are admission to higher education and employment.

Clearly, the problem of instruction in multicultural education is not easily resolved, especially for bilingual students in special education (Gersten & Baker, 2000). Most authorities now agree, however, that accepting and fostering cultural diversity must not be used as an excuse for not teaching students the skills they need to survive and prosper in the larger context of American macroculture.

Among the multicultural controversies of our time are Afrocentric instruction and special African American programs and schools. Afrocentric instruction is an alternative to the Eurocentrism of the prevailing curriculum and methods of instruction; it highlights African culture and seeks distinctively African modes of teaching and learning. Some suggest that Afrocentrism is a regressive practice that detaches students from the realities of their American social environment (Wortham, 1992). Others call for instructional practices that are culturally sensitive—attuned to the particular cultural characteristics of African American learners (Ford, Obiakor, & Patton, 1995; Franklin, 1992; Van Keulen et al., 1998). The assumption underlying culturally sensitive instruction is that students with different cultural backgrounds need to be taught differently, that certain aspects of a student's cultural heritage determine to a significant extent how he or she learns best. For example, Franklin (1992) suggests that African American students differ from others in the cultural values of their homes and families, their language and patterns of movement, their responses to variety and multiplicity of stimulation, and their preference for divergent thinking.

Perhaps it is understandable that when emphasis is placed on differences in the ways students learn, there is also emphasis on devising special programs and schools that cater to these differences. Furthermore, the greater the diversity of cultural backgrounds of students in one class, the greater the difficulty in teaching all students effectively—if we

Classwide peer tutoring.
An instructional procedure in
which all students in the class
are involved in tutoring and
being tutored by classmates on
specific skills as directed by
their teacher.

assume that cultural background determines how students are best taught. Of course, we might hypothesize that certain methods of instruction are equally effective for all students in a culturally diverse group (see Council for Exceptional Children, 2000; Singh, Ellis, Oswald, Wechsler, & Curtis, 1997). That is, some instructional approaches (e.g., direct instruction, cooperative learning, peer tutoring, and cross-age grouping) may allow teachers to provide culturally sensitive instruction to all members of a diverse group at once. **Classwide peer tutoring** may, in fact, be particularly useful in helping children at the elementary school level who are not proficient in English learn English more efficiently (Fulk & King, 2001; Greenwood, Arrega-Mayer, Utley, Gavin, & Terry, 2001).

Nevertheless, the notion that certain curricula and instructional practices are more appropriate for students of one ethnic origin than another may be used to justify distinctive programs, including African American immersion schools, in which all instruction is geared to the presumed particular learning characteristics of a single ethnic group (see Ascher, 1992; Leake & Leake, 1992). Such schools are often said to be segregationist in practice and intent, but Leake and Leake (1992) suggest that their philosophy opposes the concept of segregation:

> True integration occurs naturally when the differences between peers are minimal. Therefore, the bane of segregation is a culturally and ethnically diverse population of academically competent and self-confident individuals. The African-American immersion schools were designed to provide academically challenging and culturally appropriate experiences for their students. It was hoped that the anticipated increase in student achievement would work to vitiate the African-American students' feelings of inadequacy and impotence. (p. 784)

Do special programs designed with specific learning characteristics in mind help students learn more than they otherwise would and increase their self-esteem? This is a central controversy for both special education and multicultural general education, and research has not provided a clear answer for special programs of either type. Given that ethnicity and disability are two separate dimensions of human difference, however, special programming might be much more appropriate and effective for one dimension of difference than the other.

Hilliard (1992) poses the question of differential programming for students with disabilities as follows: "Can learning impediments be overcome or eliminated, allowing the formerly impaired student to perform significantly better than he or she would have without the services, or allowing the student to perform well in the mainstream academic program?" (p. 171). Research does not answer this question resoundingly—either affirmatively or negatively—for any model of delivering special education services. The question remains open as to whether making special education multicultural in its best sense will add to the weight of evidence regarding special education's effectiveness in improving disabled students' academic performance and success in the mainstream.

What is not an open question, however, is this: Must both special and general education adopt instructional programs that value all students and help all to be as successful as possible in American society, regardless of their specific cultural heritage? This question has been answered resoundingly in the affirmative, not by research but by our common commitment to the American values of equality of opportunity and fairness for all (see

Schools should be places where students from different cultural and ethnic groups can learn about themselves and one another in natural, nonintimidating ways. ∎

Singh, 1996). The pursuit of equality and fairness has led educational reformers toward four instructional goals:

1. Teaching tolerance and appreciation of difference
2. Working cooperatively with families
3. Improving instruction for language-minority students
4. Adopting effective teaching practices

Teaching Tolerance and Appreciation   Noted historian Ronald Takaki (1994), whose grandparents were Japanese immigrant plantation laborers in Hawaii, suggests that the American promise of equality and fairness can become a reality only if we free ourselves from a legacy of racism and prejudice. We can do so by acknowledging the reality of our past and learning more about ourselves and our heritage. Historian and African American civil rights leader Roger Wilkins makes the same point in *Jefferson's Pillow* (2001). Takaki argues that schools have a special responsibility in achieving this knowledge:

> I think schools are a crucial—probably the most crucial—site for inviting us to view ourselves in a different mirror. I think schools have the responsibility to teach Americans about who we are and who we have been. This is where it's important for schools to offer a more accurate, a more inclusive multicultural curriculum. The classroom is the place where students who come from different ethnic or cultural communities can learn not only about themselves but about one another in an informed, systematic and non-intimidating way. I think the schools offer us our best hope for working it out. I would be very reluctant to depend upon the news media or the entertainment media, which do not have a responsibility to educate. (1994, p. 15)

Overcoming prejudice and teaching students to appreciate those who are different from themselves will be by no means easy. Moreover, this is not an area in which research can provide definitive guidelines. Yet proposed methods for how teachers can help students learn both self-esteem and tolerance of difference seem promising (Artiles & Zamora-Duran, 1997; Banks, 1997; Utley & Obiakor, 2001a). Some schools are focusing on how to incorporate diversity by design or organizing anti-bias clubs that encourage understanding and tolerance of others (e.g., Bennett, 2000; Collins, 2000; McAfee, 2000).

Teaching tolerance is not, of course, limited to ethnic, regional, sexual orientation, or language differences but includes differences of all types, including disabilities. By teaching tolerance, we hope to overcome the kind of prejudice Angie Erickson describes in the box on pages 100–101. In addition, we hope to teach the self-acceptance and pride in identity that Angie articulates. For more ideas about how to teach tolerance, you may want to visit the Web site www.tolerance.org/teach.

Teaching Tolerance magazine and teaching ideas can be found at www.tolerance.org/teach/ ■

Working with Families   Schools have always depended, in part, on family involvement and support for their success. The ability of teachers to understand and communicate with their students' parents has been particularly important. Different cultural traditions mean that parents have different views of exceptionality and disability and different ways of accommodating these differences in their children (Cho, Singer, & Brenner, 2000). An understanding of the cultural basis for parents' attitudes and wishes is therefore critical, particularly for families that have recently come to the United States.

The increasing separation of economic and social classes, along with the increasing diversity of racial and ethnic groups in public schools, have created greater demands on teachers' understanding of their students' parents and families. "As the experiential gap between teachers and their students increases, so does teachers' fear of crossing what they perceive as barriers to communication with poor families, and, in particular, families from racial groups other than their own" (Harry, Torguson, Katkavich, & Guerrero, 1993, p. 48).

It's OK to Be Different

Stop Making Fun of My Disability

Why me? I often ask myself. Why did I have to be the one? Why did I get picked to be different? Why are people mean to me and always treating me differently? These are the kinds of questions that I used to ask myself. It took more than 10 years for me to find answers and realize that I'm not more different than anyone else.

I was born on June 29, 1978. Along with me came my twin sister, Stephanie. She was born with no birth defects, but I was born with cerebral palsy. For me, CP made it so I shake a little; when my sister began to walk, I couldn't. The doctors knew it was a minor case of cerebral palsy. But they didn't know if I'd ever walk straight or do things that other kids my age could do.

At first my disability did not bother me, because when you're a toddler, you do things that are really easy. When it took me a little longer to play yard games, because I couldn't run that well, my friends just thought I was slow. My disability was noticed when other children were learning how to write and I couldn't. Kids I thought were my friends started to stay away from me because they said I was different. Classmates began commenting on my speech. They said I talked really weird. Every time someone was mean to me, I would start to cry and I would always blame myself for being different.

People thought I was stupid because it was hard for me to write my own name. So when I was the only one in the class to use a typewriter, I began to feel I was different. It got worse when the third graders moved on to fourth grade and I had to stay behind. I got held back

because the teachers thought I'd be unable to type fast enough to keep up. Kids told me that was a lie and the reason I got held back was because I was a retard. It really hurt to be teased by those I thought were my friends.

After putting up with everyone making fun of me and me crying about it, I started sticking up for myself when I was 10, in fourth grade. I realized if I wanted them to stop, I would have to be the person who made them stop. I finally found out who my real friends were, and I tried to ignore the ones who were mean. Instead of constantly thinking about the things I couldn't do, I tried to think about the things I *could* do, and it helped others, and myself, understand who I really was. When there was something I couldn't do such as play Pictionary, I sat and I watched or I would go find something else to do. A few people still called me names and made fun of me, but after a while, when they saw they didn't get a reaction, they quit, because it wasn't fun anymore. What they didn't know was that it did still hurt me. It hurt me a lot more than they could ever imagine.

When I was 12, my family moved. I kept this fairy tale in my head that, at my next school, no one would be mean to me or would see that I had a disability. I'd always wished I could be someone other than myself. I found out the hard way that I wasn't going to change, that I'd never be able to write and run with no problems. When kids in my new school found out that I couldn't write and my talking and walking were out of the ordinary, they started making fun of me. They never took time to know me.

Everything went back to the way it was before. I went

Teachers should realize that the parents of low-income and minority children may feel alienated from schools, especially if their children have disabilities or histories of school problems. In fact, any parent who associates schools with failure, anxiety, or rejection is likely to shy away from involvement with teachers and avoid participation in school activities. Even very bright parents who are highly involved with their children's development and who are not ethnic minorities can be intimidated by the process of getting special education for their child with a disability (see the case "My Son Is Not Average!" in Kauffman, Mostert, Trent, & Hallahan, 2002). Given this avoidance or anxiety, teachers may perceive that parents have low expectations for their children. Even in cases in which parents seem unconcerned and do not participate in parent–teacher conferences or other school activities, it is important for teachers to maintain high expectations for students. Teachers must reach out to parents—visiting parents' homes, if possible—even if they are skeptical or fearful of what they will encounter (Harry et al., 1993). Building two-way communication, sharing concern for the child's welfare, and focusing on the student's

back to blaming myself and thinking that, since I was different, I'd never fit in. I would cry all the time, because it was so hard for me to make friends again. I didn't know whether I should trust anyone—I thought that if people knew that I had a disability they would not like me anymore. It took me a long time to understand that I had to return to not caring about what other people say.

People make fun of others because of insecurity. They have to show off to feel better about themselves. When a person made fun of me everyone thought it was just a big joke. After a while I just started laughing along with them or walking away. It really made some kids mad that they weren't getting any reaction out of me. Yeah, it still hurt a lot. I wanted to break down and start crying right then and there, but I knew I didn't want them to get their pleasure out of my hurt feelings. I couldn't cry.

I still get really frustrated when I can't do certain things, and I probably always will. I thought I should give people a better chance to get to know me, but I knew that I would probably get hurt. I never thought that anyone would want to be friends with somebody who had cerebral palsy. At times I have trouble dealing with kids making fun of me, but these are people who need help figuring out things in life and need to be treated better themselves. Maybe then they'll treat others the same. They look disappointed when I walk away or laugh when they try to make fun of me. Perhaps they're hurting more than I am.

It took a lot of willpower on my part and a lot of love from family and friends to get where I am today. I learned that no one was to blame for my disability. I realize that I can do things and I can do them very well. Some things I can't do, like taking my own notes in class or running in a race, but I will have to live with that. At 16, I believe I've learned more than many people will learn in their whole lives. I have worked out that some people are just mean because they're afraid of being nice. They try to prove to themselves and others that they are cool, but, sooner or later, they're going to wish they hadn't said some of those hurtful things. A lot of people will go through life being mean to those with disabilities because they don't know how to act or what to say to them—they feel awkward with someone who's different.

Parents need to teach their children that it's all right to be different and it's all right to be friends with those who are. Some think that the disabled should be treated like little kids for the rest of their lives. They presume we don't need love and friends, but our needs are the same as every other human being's.

There are times when I wish I hadn't been born with cerebral palsy, but crying about it isn't going to do me any good. I can only live once, so I want to live the best I can. I am glad I learned who I am and what I am capable of doing. I am happy with who I am. Nobody else could be the Angela Marie Erickson who is writing this. I could never be, or ever want to be, anyone else.

SOURCE: By Angie Erickson, "It's OK to Be Different," from *Newsweek*, October 24, 1994. © 1994, Newsweek, Inc. All rights reserved. Reprinted by permission.

strengths, particularly in initial meetings with parents, are critically important (Kalyanpur & Harry, 1997; Kauffman et al., 2002).

Improving Instruction for Language-Minority Students   Students for whom English is a second language face the simultaneous demands of learning a new language and mastering traditional subject matter. Those who have disabilities encounter the third demand of coping with the additional hurdles imposed by their exceptionalities. Bilingual special education is therefore particularly controversial, presenting difficult dilemmas and paradoxes.

We have already discussed the dilemma of difference—the fact that both recognizing and ignoring linguistic or other differences can put children at a disadvantage (Minow, 1985). In addition, language-minority students with disabilities face the paradox of simultaneous overrepresentation and underrepresentation. Ethnic- and language-minority students may be overrepresented in special education if they are referred and misidentified

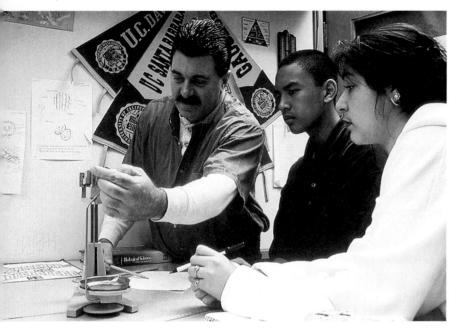

Educational programming must challenge all learners to stretch their abilities. History warns teachers not to "underteach" minority learners. ■

for problems that are not disabilities. At the same time, students from language-minority groups may be underreferred (see Ortiz, 1997; U.S. Department of Education, 2000). They may "truly need specialized assistance, but . . . languish in general education classrooms, benefiting little from conventional instruction" (Gersten & Woodward, 1994, p. 312). Addressing these issues effectively demands that we examine different approaches to second-language instruction.

One approach to teaching language-minority students is to emphasize use of their native languages. In this approach, all academic instruction is initially provided in each student's native language, and English is taught as a separate subject. Later, when the student has demonstrated adequate fluency in English, he or she makes the transition to instruction in English in all academic subjects. A different approach is to offer content-area instruction in English from the beginning of the student's schooling but at a level that is "sheltered," or constantly modified to make sure the student understands it. The goal of this approach is to help the student learn English while learning academic subjects as well.

In the first approach—**native-language emphasis**—students are taught for most of the day in their native languages and later make a transition to English. In the second, the **sheltered-English approach,** students receive instruction in English for most of the school day from the beginning of their schooling. The question as to which approach is better for students with disabilities has not been answered, although it is clear that changing from one approach to the other when students change schools creates particular difficulties (Gersten & Baker, 2000; Gersten & Woodward, 1994).

Another issue for language-minority instruction is whether an emphasis on the natural uses of language or, alternatively, on skills such as vocabulary and pronunciation is most effective. However, this controversy may be based on a false dichotomy. What students need is an effective balance between skill building and language that is meaningful and relevant to their lives and interests (Gersten & Baker, 2000; Ovando, 1997; Van Keulen et al., 1998). Instructional materials must make sense to students and provide explicit links to their own experiences. While teaching specific language skills, teachers must use language and create language variations that students understand. And students must be encouraged to learn to express complex ideas and feelings using increasingly complex sentences as they acquire fluency in English. In short, language-minority instruction needs to be constructed in the context of what we know about effective teaching.

Native-language emphasis.
An approach to teaching language-minority pupils in which the student's native language is used for most of the day and English is taught as a separate subject.

Sheltered-English approach.
A method in which language-minority students are taught all their subjects in English at a level that is modified constantly according to individuals' needs.

Adopting Effective Teaching Practices   In a sense, effective multicultural education requires only that we implement what we know about effective instruction. Namely, effective teaching practices are sensitive to each student's cultural heritage, sense of self, view of the world, and acquired knowledge and skills. Teaching about various cultures, individual differences, and the construction of knowledge should permeate and transform the curriculum (Banks, 1993, 1994, 1997). Nonetheless, for language-minority students—indeed, for all students—we can articulate more specific components of effective teaching. We offer the following description of six components of effective teaching outlined by Gersten et al. (1994, p. 9):

1. *Scaffolding and strategies.* Students learn more efficiently when they are provided a "scaffold," or structure, for ideas and strategies for problem solving. In

scaffolded instruction, the teacher assists the student in learning a task and then phases out the help as the student learns to use the strategy independently. (See Chapter 5 for further discussion.) Means of helping students learn more easily include stories, visual organizers (e.g., pictures, diagrams, outlines), **mnemonics** (tactics that aid memory, such as rhymes or images), and **reciprocal teaching** (in which the student sees the teacher use a learning strategy and then tries it out).

2. *Challenge.* Too much of education, even special education, is not appropriately challenging for students. All students—including those who are from cultural minorities, who are at high risk for failure, and who have disabilities—need to be given challenging tasks. *Appropriately challenging tasks* are those that a given student finds just manageable. While these tasks are not impossible, they do require serious effort and stretch the student's capabilities. Too often, teachers underestimate the capabilities of minority and exceptional students and underteach them (Delpit, 1995; Ford, 1998; Patton, 1997).

3. *Involvement.* Students must be engaged in extended conversations, in which they use complex linguistic structures. Verbal exchanges between teachers and pupils must not always be short, simple, and direct (although such exchanges have their place). Rather, teachers must probe with questions, share experiences, and elicit from pupils the kind of language that demonstrates their active involvement in learning (Kline, Simpson, Blesz, Myles, & Carter, 2001).

4. *Success.* Students at the highest risk of failure and dropping out are those who have low rates of success in daily school activities. *All* students need to experience frequent success, and teachers must present challenging tasks at which the student can be successful (Kauffman et al., 2002). Failure should not be perpetuated.

5. *Mediation and feedback.* Too often, students work for long periods without receiving feedback, or are given feedback that is not comprehensible, or are asked for rote responses to which they attach little or no meaning. Providing frequent, comprehensible feedback on performance is vital to effective teaching, as is focusing on the meanings of responses—how evidence and logic are used to construct questions and their answers.

6. *Responsiveness to cultural and individual diversity.* The content of instruction must be related to students' experiences, including those as individuals and as members of various cultural groups. The issues of cultural and individual diversity cannot be adequately considered in a few special lessons; rather, they must be included routinely in all curriculum areas.

As Banks (1997) points out, a viable multicultural curriculum cannot be created and handed out to teachers. Teachers must be invested in the endeavor, as their values, perspectives, and teaching styles will affect what is taught and how. The effective implementation of a multicultural curriculum requires teaching strategies that are involvement oriented, interactive, personalized, and cooperative.

This perspective applies to our own teaching and writing as well. In any textbook, the adequate treatment of multicultural issues cannot be confined to a single chapter. A chapter like this one—devoted specifically to multicultural education—may be necessary to ensure that the topic is given sufficient focused attention. Our intention in this book, however, is to prompt consideration of multicultural issues in every chapter.

SOCIALIZATION

Academic instruction is one of two primary purposes of education. The other, socialization, involves helping students develop appropriate social perceptions and interactions with others and learn how to work for desirable social change. Socializing the student does not mean that any kind of behavior or attitude is acceptable in school; neither does it mean ignoring the student's cultural heritage. Cartledge and Loe (2001) offer these challenging conclusions about the necessity of teaching social skills in a multicultural society:

Scaffolded instruction.
A cognitive approach to instruction in which the teacher provides temporary structure or support while students are learning a task; the support is gradually removed as the students are able to perform the task independently.

Mnemonics.
Techniques that aid memory, such as using rhymes, songs, or visual images to remember information.

Reciprocal teaching.
A method in which students and teachers are involved in a dialogue to facilitate learning.

> The commonalities among our children are greater than their differences. Nevertheless, many children from [culturally and linguistically different] backgrounds, especially those reared under impoverished conditions, may be socialized in ways that present special school challenges for these students and their middle-class teachers. Behaviors rooted in this diversity portend to undermine the child's school success and overall social adjustment. As schools struggle to help all students acquire the requisite skills to become competent in the larger society, they must become aware of the disconnect between the culture of the school and that of the learner. Educators must become cross-culturally competent and skilled in the basic principles of culturally relevant teaching. Among other things, teachers must learn ways to discern behavior problems from cultural differences, create positive and affirming environments, communicate and foster desired classroom behaviors, and use the child's culture as the basis for critical social learnings. (p. 44).

In some cases, helping children learn appropriate social skills may require helping parents learn how to teach their children (Elksnin & Elksnin, 2000). This requires understanding the cultural and linguistic diversity of families.

Destructive and stereotypic social perceptions and interactions among differing microcultural groups are long-standing problems in schools and communities in the United States, particularly when there are cultural differences among students in language and social behavior (Ishii-Jordan, 1997). The cartoon on this page illustrates how stereotypes have affected the way we describe people and are embedded in our language. Part of the process of multicultural socialization is giving students experiences that make them question the way we have described other cultures.

The most obvious examples involve racial discrimination, although sex discrimination and discrimination against people of differing religions and disabilities are also common in our society. Teachers must become keenly aware of their own cultural heritages, identities, and biases before they can help their students deal with cultural diversity in ways that enhance democratic ideals, such as human dignity, justice, and equality (Banks, 1997). Becoming comfortable with one's own identity as a member of microcultural groups is an important objective for both teachers and students. Depending on the cultural context, accepting and valuing one's identity can be quite difficult.

Cooperative learning.
A teaching approach in which the teacher places students with heterogeneous abilities (for example, some might have disabilities) together to work on assignments.

Teaching about different cultures and their value may be important in reducing racial and ethnic conflict and promoting respect for human differences. Equally important, however, is structuring classroom interactions to promote the understanding and appreciation of others. One of the most effective ways of breaking down prejudice and encouraging appropriate interaction among students with different characteristics is **cooperative learning.** In cooperative learning, students of different abilities and cultural characteristics work together as a team, fostering interdependence. In *Among Schoolchildren,* Tracy

For Better or for Worse   **Lynn Johnston**

SOURCE: "For Better or For Worse." Copyright © 2001 United Feature Syndicate. Reprinted by permission.

Kidder describes this approach to socialization as it was used by a fifth-grade teacher, Chris Zajac:

> Then came fifteen minutes of study, during which teams of two children quizzed each other. Chris paired up good spellers with poor ones. She also made spelling an exercise in socialization, by putting together children who did not seem pre-disposed to like each other. She hoped that some would learn to get along with classmates they didn't think they liked. At least they'd be more apt to do some work than if she paired them up with friends. Her guesses were good. Alice raised her eyes to the florescent-lit ceiling at the news that she had Claude for a spelling partner. Later she wrote, "Today is the worst day of my life." Clarence scowled at the news that he had Ashley, who was shy and chubby and who didn't look happy either. A little smile collected in one corner of Chris's mouth as she observed the reactions. "Now, you're not permanently attached to that person for the rest of your life," she said to the class. (1989, pp. 28–29)

Teachers of exceptional children and youths must be aware of the variety of microcultural identities their students may be developing and struggling with. Review the multiple aspects of cultural identity suggested by Figure 3.1 (page 86) and reflect on the combinations of these and other subcultures that a given student might adopt. One of the microcultural identities not included in Figure 3.1 is sexual orientation. Yet many children and adolescents, including many with educational exceptionalities, experience serious difficulties with what some have called the "invisible culture" of gay and lesbian youth. Students who are "straight" may struggle with their own prejudices against homosexuals, prejudices all too often fostered by both their peers and adults and sometimes given justification by identification with a religious or political microculture. Gay and lesbian students are often harassed and abused verbally and physically in school and may suffer from serious depression or other psychological disorders as a result (McIntyre, 1992; Uribe & Harbeck, 1992). Gay students need to be able to be themselves without fear of harassment or discrimination (Elliot, 2000). Consider also that a student might be both gay or lesbian and gifted, physically disabled, mentally retarded, or have any other educational exceptionality.

Our point is that the task of socialization in a multicultural society demands attention to the multitude of identities that students may assume. It also demands an awareness that any of these identities may carry the consequence of social rejection, isolation, and alienation. Many children with disabilities are lonely and need to develop friendships (Pavri, 2001). Our task as educators is to promote understanding of cultural differences and acceptance of individuals whose identities are different from one's own. Building pride in one's cultural identity is a particular concern in teaching exceptional students. As we have noted elsewhere (Hallahan & Kauffman, 1994), many people in the Deaf community prefer to be called "the Deaf," which runs contrary to the current use of terms such as *hearing impaired*. Deaf people and blind people have begun to express pride in their identities and microcultures and, at the same time, foster multicultural experiences involving other languages and customs (Gallucci, 2000). In fact, for increasing numbers of people with disabilities, labels are to be embraced, not hidden. For example, one adult with learning disabilities said in an interview, "I need to be proud of myself. As long as I was ashamed of being LD [learning disabled], it was difficult to proceed" (Gerber, Ginsberg, & Reiff, 1992, p. 481).

People from many segments of society, or microcultures—such as parents of children with disabilities, senior citizens, religious groups, recovering alcoholics, and so on—find that congregating for mutual support and understanding enhances their feelings of self-worth. Educators need to consider the possible value of having students with disabilities congregate for specific purposes. As Edgar and Siegel (1995) have noted:

> In a naive and overzealous rush to implement fully inclusive school environments, we risk overlooking and discarding the discovery of identity, common will, and support that comes from the opportunity to congregate with those

engaged in struggles that share characteristics of ability, culture, status, or environment. (p. 274)

By trying to avoid labels and insisting that students with disabilities always be placed with those who do not have disabilities, perhaps we risk giving the message that those who have disabilities are less desirable or even not fit to associate with as peers. Bateman (1994) suggests that "something is terribly and not very subtly insulting about saying a bright learning disabled student ought not attend a special school with other students who have learning disabilities because he needs to be with non-disabled students" (p. 516). In striving for true multicultural awareness, we may learn that it is more productive in the long run to embrace identities associated with exceptionalities, while working to increase tolerance and understanding of differences, than it is to avoid labels or refrain from congregating students with specific characteristics.

One of the most difficult tasks of teaching is socializing students through classroom discipline—that is, through the management of classroom behavior. Managing classroom behavior presents a serious challenge for nearly all teachers and a particularly difficult challenge for most special education teachers (Kauffman at al., 2002). Two considerations are critical: (1) the relationship between the teacher's approach to classroom discipline and the parents' childrearing practices, and (2) the sensitivity of the teacher to cultural differences in responses to discipline.

Middle-class American teachers may have an approach to classroom discipline that they consider effective and humane but that differs radically from some cultures' accepted childrearing practices. Educators, like everyone else, are often ethnocentric, believing that their views are correct and those of others are not. In a given case they may be right, in that their view is more humane or effective, but they may also be biased and wrong. In the case of discipline involving students of culturally diverse backgrounds, the teacher may face difficult ethical decisions about child abuse or neglect. When do one's own beliefs about the treatment of children demand that a culturally condoned disciplinary practice be confronted as abuse or neglect? Answering this question is not easy.

Finally, we note that education should not merely socialize students to fit into the existing social order. The goals of multicultural education include teaching students to work for social change, which entails helping students who are members of oppressed minorities become advocates for themselves and other members of their microcultures (Banks, 1997; Banks & Banks, 1997; Utley & Obiakor, 2001c).

Multicultural education may teach us to understand and embrace individual differences, rather than try to erase them. ■

Summary

Education for cultural diversity involves managing tension between microcultural diversity, on the one hand, and common macrocultural values, on the other. Many microcultures are found in the U.S. macroculture, which values justice, equality, and human dignity. Progress in multicultural education is difficult because each microculture tends to see many of its own values as the standards against which others should be judged. Special educators and general educators alike must understand how to provide an education that gives equal opportunity to students regardless of gender, socioeconomic status, ethnic group, disability, or other cultural identity. Doing so may require that educators change students' knowledge construction of their own and others' cultural identities. Devising a multicultural curriculum that is satisfactory to all groups is difficult, and not everyone agrees that understanding cultural diversity is as important as building the common culture. Although multiculturalism is fraught with conflicts, it offers an opportunity to practice American values of tolerance, justice, equality, and individualism.

Communities and families contribute much to students' attitudes toward education and academic achievement. Minority communities can encourage academic success among students by highlighting values consistent with school achievement. However, we must guard against ethnic stereotypes of achievement or failure and understand that community and family attitudes toward schooling do not excuse educators from their responsibility to provide an effective and multicultural education for all students.

Multicultural education may at first seem a relatively simple matter, but it is complicated by questions about what cultures to include and what and how to teach about them. Many distinct microcultures exist, and some have values or customs that others find unacceptable or offensive. Microcultural groups may be distinguished not only by gender and ethnicity but also by religious or political affiliation and sexual orientation. Finding a balance among cultural values and traditions that satisfies all groups is often quite difficult. Moreover, this balance may vary from school to school. Controversy often exists in communities where so-called minorities constitute well over half the school population. Issues such as language differences and bilingual education have become divisive within many such communities.

The types of cultural diversity most relevant to special education are ethnicity and disability or giftedness. We must remember, however, that students may be members of a variety of microcultural groups besides those designating educational exceptionality. Multicultural special education must give special attention to ensuring that ethnicity is not mistaken for educational exceptionality and to increasing the understanding of educational exceptionality and its relationship to other microcultures. Members of ethnic minority groups may be mistakenly identified as disabled or overlooked in attempts to identify special gifts and talents if their cultural practices and languages are not understood by teachers. Disproportional representation of ethnic minority students in special education is a long-standing and complex problem with no obvious solution. Individuals with certain exceptionalities (deafness, for example) may develop their own microcultures, and it is important to help others understand and appreciate these cultures.

Three specific problems in multicultural special education are assessment, instruction, and socialization. Assessment is a particularly critical issue because it forms the basis for decisions about instruction and placement; therefore, it is imperative that assessment be accurate, fair, and directly related to designing effective instruction. Traditional testing procedures, such as standardized tests, are problematic for members of many ethnic minorities. Curriculum-based assessment and performance assessment are gaining wide acceptance as alternatives. Assessment of the learning environment may be as important as assessment of students' skills.

Instruction presents many points of controversy for multicultural and bilingual special education. One of the great and pervasive problems of special education is the dilemma of difference. Recognizing students' differences and providing special services of any kind may be helpful, but identification and special programming may also carry stigmas and perpetuate the differences. Some leading scholars in multicultural education suggest that instruction should help students understand and preserve their own microcultures while at the same time help students learn to function successfully in the American macroculture. The pursuit of equality and fairness has led educators to four instructional goals: (1) teaching tolerance and appreciation of differences; (2) working cooperatively with families; (3) improving the instruction of language-minority students; and (4) adopting effective teaching practices.

Socialization is an aspect of education that some believe is as important as academic instruction. Multicultural special education must seek to improve students' understanding and acceptance of others' differences and to help students develop pride in their own cultural identities. Teachers may encounter particular multicultural problems in managing classroom behavior because of differences between their own views of discipline and childrearing and those of their students and students' parents.

Bohill Wong

Still Life with Dinosaur Pot, Ink, watercolor on rag paper. 15 × 11 in.

Bohill Wong was born in 1934 in Hong Kong, China. When he immigrated to this country in the early '30s, Mr. Wong drew and painted mostly Chinese themes. As time passed, he began to introduce more popular themes into his work. Now, his many fans are intrigued by the quirky and zany elements of his art and personality.

4

Learners with Mental Retardation

Whenever I step back and consider how "normal" ... Nicole's life is, I am struck by how different her adulthood is from what Matt and I had thought it would be. I must have been 10 years old when my mother informed me that a "retarded boy" lived in the house on the corner. We kids had played around that house, yet we never knew he existed. ... When Matt and I were told Nicole was retarded, I assumed she would be kept out of sight, too. But that was 1957, 2 years after Nicole's birth. The change in approaches to and supports for people with mental retardation in the ensuing 40+ years ... can only be described as revolutionary. ...

I paid a visit to the Regional Center. ... I intentionally arrived early so I would have some time to look around ...

What a different world it is out there these days, I mused. Parents of a baby or child who is identified as having—or even at risk of having—developmental delays can turn to the Regional Center system for assessments, counseling, intervention therapies, respite care, and a host of other programs for both family and child. ...

A mother with a crying baby entered the library. As I watched her trying to talk with the volunteer over the din, I thought of the things that haven't changed at all: the gut-wrenching adjustment to the actuality of giving birth to an "imperfect" infant, the exhaustion of caring for the vulnerable son or daughter, and the toll the child ... can exact on a family. ...

I followed [Colleen Mock] upstairs, and we soon settled into her office where I learned that she has 25 years of experience as a service delivery provider and is also the mother of a young adult daughter with mental retardation. ... She segued into an explanation of the current perspective among professionals. Rather than view children or adults as "discrete sets of problems to be fixed, needs to be met, and issues to be addressed" (Nisbet, 1992, p. 2), professionals try to regard children or adults they see as whole people, capable of making decisions for themselves about things that affect their lives. Consumers ... are encouraged—are empowered—to set goals and make choices. ... When the appropriate supports are in place as a child grows older, his or her role as the determiner of what is wanted supplants the parents' function as advocate. Support services continue, but consumers are encouraged to use community resources to solve problems that arise, the rationale being that the process of engaging "natural supports"—family members, friends, neighbors, or fellow employees—is controlled by the consumer and integrates him or her in the community far more than dependence on service personnel.

SANDRA KAUFMAN
Retarded Isn't Stupid, Mom!

As Sandra Kaufman points out (see p. 109), in many ways there is a world of differ-ence in the quantity and quality of services for persons with mental retardation now, compared to just a few years ago. At the same time, though, she poignantly reminds us that some things related to mental retardation are likely never to change. For parents, having a child with mental retardation means facing a set of lifelong challenges. The main difference, however, is that today, although parents of a child with mental retar-dation are very likely to feel overwhelmed initially, they can look around them and see signs of hope. They can see examples of adults with mental retardation who are leading relatively independent lives, holding jobs in competitive or semi-competitive work envi-ronments and living independently or semi-independently in the community.

As Mock explains to Kaufman, much of the current success being achieved by persons with mental retardation is attributed to a change in philosophy that includes respecting their rights to be a part of decisions affecting their lives and that involves the use of **nat-ural supports.** Later in the chapter we discuss the important philosophical changes that have brought about the emphasis on self-determination and natural supports.

It takes more than well-intentioned philosophies, however, to ensure that persons with mental retardation do in fact reach their full potential with respect to independent employment and community living. We hasten to point out that it often takes years of intensive instruction from special educators, working in tandem with other professionals, including general educators, to put the philosophies of self-determination and natural supports into effect.

There have been other changes, too, that have had a profound effect on the field of mental retardation in the past several years, perhaps the most significant of which is the fact that designating someone as mentally retarded has become much more difficult. Today, professionals are more reluctant to apply the label of mental retardation than they once were. At least three reasons account for this more cautious attitude toward identifi-cation of students as mentally retarded:

1. Professionals became concerned about the misdiagnosis of children from ethnic minority groups as mentally retarded. Twenty to thirty years ago it was much more common for children from ethnic minorities, especially African American and Hispanic students, to be labeled mentally retarded because they did not achieve well in school and they scored poorly on intelligence tests.
2. Another reason for using more stringent criteria for determining mental retar-dation is related to the fear that the stigma of such a diagnosis can have harmful consequences for the individual. Some believe that the label of mental retarda-tion causes children to have poor self-concepts and to be viewed negatively by others.
3. Some professionals now believe that, to a certain extent, mental retardation is a socially constructed condition. For example, the American Association on Men-tal Retardation (AAMR) Ad Hoc Committee on Terminology and Classification (1992) has conceived of mental retardation not as a trait residing in the individ-ual but as the product of the interaction between a person and his or her envi-ronment. This point of view has not gone uncontested, with some authorities thinking that the AAMR has gone too far in denying the existence of mental retardation as an essential feature within a person.

In fact, there has been recent discussion within the AAMR, the major professional organization concerned with mental retardation, about doing away with the label *mental retardation* altogether and renaming the organization (Luckasson & Reeve, 2001; Smith & Mitchell, 2001). There are those vehemently opposed to such a change. However, even if the name change does not occur, the fact that it is being debated indicates the level of con-cern about terminology and definition, topics to which we now turn.

Natural supports.
Resources in person's environment that can be used for support, such as friends, family, co-workers.

An example of an organization that has changed its name to avoid using the term, *mental retarda-tion*, is the Arc. Although formerly known as the Association for Retarded Citizens, it also uses the acronym, the Arc, as its name. The Arc is primarily a parent organization and a strong advocate for rights for those with mental retardation: http://www.thearc.org/ ■

MISCONCEPTIONS ABOUT
Learners with Mental Retardation

MYTH Mental retardation is defined by how a person scores on an IQ test.	**FACT** The most commonly used definition specifies that in order for a person to be considered mentally retarded, he or she must meet two criteria: (1) low intellectual functioning *and* (2) low adaptive skills.
MYTH Once diagnosed as mentally retarded, a person remains within this classification for life.	**FACT** A person's level of mental functioning does not necessarily remain stable; this is particularly true for those individuals who are mildly mentally retarded. With intensive educational programming, some persons can improve to the point that they are no longer mentally retarded.
MYTH In most cases, we can identify the cause of mental retardation.	**FACT** In most cases, especially those of people who are mildly mentally retarded or who require less intensive support, we cannot specify the cause. For many children who are mildly mentally retarded, poor environment may be a causal factor, but it is extremely difficult to document.
MYTH Most children with mental retardation look different from nondisabled children.	**FACT** The majority of children with mental retardation are mildly mentally retarded (or require less intensive support), and most of these look like nondisabled children.
MYTH We can identify most cases of mental retardation in infancy.	**FACT** Most children with mental retardation are not identified as such until they go to school, for several reasons: (1) because most children with mental retardation are mildly mentally retarded; (2) because infant intelligence tests are not very reliable and valid; and (3) because intellectual demands on the child increase greatly upon entrance to school.
MYTH Persons with mental retardation tend to be gentle people who have an easy time making friends.	**FACT** Because of a variety of behavioral characteristics and because they sometimes live and work in relatively isolated situations, some persons with mental retardation have difficulty making and holding friends.
MYTH The teaching of vocational skills to students with mental retardation is best reserved for secondary school and beyond.	**FACT** Many authorities now believe it appropriate to introduce vocational content in elementary school to students with mental retardation.
MYTH When workers with mental retardation fail on the job, it is usually because they do not have adequate job skills.	**FACT** When they fail on the job, it is more often because of poor job responsibility (poor attendance and lack of initiative) and social incompetence (interacting inappropriately with co-workers) than because of incompetence in task production.
MYTH Persons with mental retardation should not be expected to work in the competitive job market.	**FACT** More and more persons who are mentally retarded hold jobs in competitive employment. Many are helped through supportive employment situations, in which a job coach helps them and their employer adapt to the workplace.

Definition

Founded in 1876, the American Association on Mental Retardation is one of the oldest professional organizations focused on mental retardation in the world. Its mission is to "promote progressive policies, sound research, effective practices, and universal human rights for people with intellectual disabilities." Visit its Web site at http://www.aamr.org/index.shtml for information related to mental retardation. For example, you can access past issues of AAMR's newsletter, *News & Notes*. ■

A more conservative approach to identifying students as mentally retarded is reflected in changes in definition that have occurred over the years. Since 1950, seven official definitions of mental retardation have been endorsed by the AAMR.

THE AAMR DEFINITION

The current AAMR definition reads:

> Mental retardation refers to substantial limitations in present functioning. It is characterized by significantly subaverage intellectual functioning, existing concurrently with related limitations in two or more of the following applicable adaptive skill areas: communication, self-care, home living, social skills, community use, self-direction, health and safety, functional academics, leisure, and work. Mental retardation manifests before age 18. (AAMR Ad Hoc Committee on Terminology and Classification, 1992, p. 5)

In making this definition operational, the professional is to rely on assessment of two areas: **intellectual functioning** and **adaptive skills.** Intellectual functioning, usually estimated by an IQ test, refers primarily to ability related to academic performance. Adaptive skills, usually estimated by adaptive behavior surveys, refer to abilities related to coping with one's environment.

The definition, like each of its predecessors, continues three trends consistent with a more cautious approach to diagnosing students as mentally retarded:

Intellectual functioning.
The ability to solve problems related to academics; usually estimated by an IQ test; one of two major components (the other is adaptive skills) of the AAMR definition.

Adaptive skills.
Skills needed to adapt to one's living environment (e.g., communication, self-care, home living, social skills, community use, self-direction, health and safety, functional academics, leisure, and work); usually estimated by an adaptive behavior survey; one of two major components (the other is intellectual functioning) of the AAMR definition.

1. A broadening of the definition beyond the single criterion of an IQ score
2. A lowering of the IQ score used as a cutoff for qualification as mentally retarded
3. A conceptualization of mental retardation as a condition that can be improved and that is not necessarily permanent

Broadening the Definition   At one time it was common practice to diagnose individuals as mentally retarded solely on the basis of an IQ score. Today we recognize that IQ tests are far from perfect and that they are but one indication of a person's ability to function. Professionals came to consider adaptive skills in addition to IQ in defining retardation because they began to recognize that some students might score poorly on IQ tests but still be "streetwise"—able to cope, for example, with the subway system, with an after-school job, with peers.

Lowering the IQ Score Cutoff   It was also common at one time for practitioners to use a cutoff score of 85 on an IQ test as an indicator of mental retardation. This cutoff score was endorsed by the AAMR until the mid-1970s, when they made it more difficult for people to be identified as mentally retarded by establishing a cutoff score of 70 to 75. The current AAMR definition also sanctions this cutoff of 70 to 75. A five-point spread of 70 to 75 has been established to reinforce the notion that IQ scores should not be regarded as precise measurements, that professionals should use some clinical judgment in interpreting IQ scores.

Mental Retardation as Improvable and Possibly Nonpermanent   In the past many authorities held little hope for significantly enhancing the functioning of people with mental retardation and essentially believed mental retardation to be incurable. Over the years, however, professionals have become more optimistic about the beneficial effects of educational programming. Not only do they believe that the functioning of virtually all persons with mental retardation can be improved, but they have forwarded the notion that some persons with mental retardation, especially those with mild mental retardation, can eventually improve to the point that they are no longer classified as mentally retarded.

In agreement with the notion that mental retardation is improvable and not necessarily permanent, the developers of the current and proposed AAMR definitions hold that how well a person with mental retardation functions is directly related to the amount of support he or she receives from the environment. With enough support, he or she can improve and possibly overcome the mental retardation. The importance of support, in fact, is underscored in the AAMR's classification scheme, to which we now turn.

THE AAMR CLASSIFICATION SCHEME

Professionals have typically classified persons with mental retardation according to the severity of their problems. For many years, the AAMR promoted the use of the terms **mild, moderate, severe,** and **profound mental retardation,** with each of these levels keyed to approximate IQ levels. For example, mild mental retardation is from a score of 50–55 to approximately 70, and severe mental retardation is from 20–25 to 35–40. Most school systems now classify their students with mental retardation using these terms or a close approximation of them.

In 1992, however, the AAMR recommended a radical departure from this system of classification (AAMR Ad Hoc Committee on Terminology and Classification, 1992). Rather than categorize students based on their IQ scores, the AAMR recommended that professionals classify them according to how much support they need to function as competently as possible. Table 4.1 depicts these **levels of support.**

The authors of the AAMR classification scheme believe categorization based on support needed is better than categorization based on IQ because it (1) implies that persons with mental retardation can achieve positive outcomes with appropriate support services,

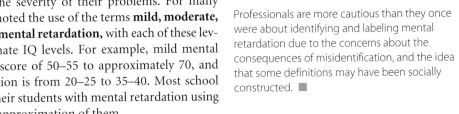

Professionals are more cautious than they once were about identifying and labeling mental retardation due to the concerns about the consequences of misidentification, and the idea that some definitions may have been socially constructed. ■

Mild mental retardation.
A classification used to specify an individual whose IQ is approximately 55–70.

Moderate mental retardation.
A classification used to specify an individual whose IQ is approximately 40–55.

Severe mental retardation.
A classification used to specify an individual whose IQ is approximately 25–40.

Profound mental retardation.
A classification used to specify an individual whose IQ is below approximately 25.

Levels of support.
The basis of the AAMR classification scheme; characterizes the amount of support needed for someone with mental retardation to function as competently as possible as (1) intermittent, (2) limited, (3) extensive, or (4) pervasive.

TABLE 4.1   AAMR Classification Scheme for Mental Retardation Based on Levels of Support

Intermittent	Supports on an "as needed basis." Characterized by episodic nature, person not always needing the support(s), or short-term supports needed during life-span transitions (e.g., job loss or an acute medical crisis). Intermittent supports may be high or low intensity when provided.
Limited	An intensity of supports characterized by consistency over time and time-limited but not of an intermittent nature, may require fewer staff members and less cost than more intense levels of support (e.g., time- limited employment training or transitional supports during the school-to-adult period).
Extensive	Supports characterized by regular involvement (e.g., daily) in at least some environments (such as work or home) and not time-limited (e.g., long-term home living support).
Pervasive	Supports characterized by their constancy, high intensity, provided across environments; potential life-sustaining nature. Pervasive supports typically involve more staff members and intrusiveness than do extensive or time-limited supports.

SOURCE: From AAMR Ad Hoc Committee on Terminology and Classification. (1992). *Mental retardation: Definition, classification, and systems of support.* Copyright © 1992 by American Association on Mental Retardation. Reprinted with permission.

Adaptive skills refer to abilities related to coping with one's everyday environment, including social skills and the ability to function in different communities. ■

Ⓦ As of the printing of 9th edition of *Exceptional Learners*, the AAMR has not yet reached a decision on a new definition. In the fall of 2001, it published a proposed definition and invited its membership to comment on it. You can see this definition in the Sept/Oct, 2001 issue of AAMR's *News & Notes* at http://www.aamr.org/ Periodicals/N&N/n&n_14_5.pdf. You should consult the AAMR's main web site at http://www.aamr.org/index. shtml to see if it has adopted a new definition. ■

Conceptual intelligence. The traditional conceptualization of intelligence, emphasizing problem solving related to academic material; what IQ tests primarily assess.

Practical intelligence. The ability to solve problems related to activities of daily living.

Social intelligence. The ability to understand social expectations and to cope in social situations.

(2) avoids reliance on a single IQ score, and (3) can result in descriptions that are more meaningful when considered in combination with adaptive skills. Rather than saying, for example, that a person has "severe mental retardation," one might say the person has mental retardation that requires "extensive supports in self-care, home living, and work."

CRITICISMS OF THE AAMR DEFINITION AND CLASSIFICATION SCHEME

As we noted above, some critics believe that the notion that mental retardation does not reside in the individual may be too radical. And, notably, many of these critics are also members of AAMR. They suggest that believing that mental retardation is a condition that a person has does not necessarily mean that it is permanent and immutable. Some question the utility of a classification system based on levels of support (Greenspan, 1997; MacMillan, Gresham, & Siperstein, 1993; Smith, 1994). They point to the long tradition of classifying individuals based on severity and argue that it is difficult to develop ways of reliably measuring the levels of support different people need. Still others think that the entire notion of intelligence versus adaptive skills needs to be rethought. For example, Greenspan has proposed three types of intelligence: conceptual, practical, and social (Greenspan, 1997). **Conceptual intelligence** is the traditional view of intelligence, the one assessed primarily by IQ tests. **Practical intelligence** refers to the ability to act independently and manage daily living activities. **Social intelligence** is the ability to interpret the social behavior of others and to interact in a socially appropriate manner.

The AAMR has formed a committee to review its definition and classification system (see Luckasson, 2000). Given the number of criticisms of the 1992 definition, it is very likely that there will be changes.

Two other prominent professional organizations have adopted definitions and classification schemes that are essentially the same as that of the AAMR's definition *prior to* 1992. Both the American Psychological Association (Jacobson & Mulick, 1996) and the American Psychiatric Association (2000) define mental retardation as involving deficits in intellectual functioning and adaptive functioning. And most significant, they use the categories of mild, moderate, severe, and profound mental retardation.

Given the highly sensitive issue of identifying people as mentally retarded, the effort to come up with a definition that will please everyone is perhaps futile. However, virtually all authorities agree on one thing: Mental retardation should not be defined solely on the basis of a single IQ score. That many professionals are now not relying solely on an IQ score is evident from current prevalence figures, which we consider next.

Prevalence

The average (mean) score on an IQ test is 100. Theoretically, we expect 2.27 percent of the population to fall two standard deviations (IQ = 70 on the Wechsler Intelligence Scale for Children–Revised, or WISC-III) or more below this average. This expectation is based on the assumption that intelligence, like so many other human traits, is distributed along a normal curve. Figure 4.1 shows the hypothetical normal curve of intelligence. This curve is split into eight areas by means of standard deviations. On the latest edition of the Wechsler, the WISC-III, where one standard deviation equals 15 IQ points, 2.14 percent of the population scores between 55 and 70 and 0.13 percent scores below 55. Thus it would seem that 2.27 percent should fall between 0 and 70. (See p. 123 for more on intelligence tests.)

However, the actual prevalence figures for students identified as mentally retarded are much lower. In recent years they have been somewhere around 1 to 1.5 percent. Authorities surmise that this lower prevalence figure is due to school personnel considering adaptive behavior or a broader definition of intelligence in addition to an IQ score to diagnose mental retardation. As well, there is evidence that in cases in which the student's IQ score is in the 70s, thus making identification as mentally retarded a close call, parents and school officials may be more likely to identify children as learning disabled than as mentally retarded because "learning disabled" is perceived as a less stigmatizing label (MacMillan, Gresham, Bocian, & Lambros, 1998).

Causes

As recently as the mid-1990s, most experts estimated that only in about 10 to 15 percent of cases was the cause of mental retardation known. However, the mapping of the human genetic code by the Human Genome Project has brought a wealth of information related to causes of mental retardation. (These advances have also engendered a number of thorny controversies; see the box on p. 116.) As we soon discuss, however, not all causes of mental retardation are genetically related, so there still remains a large percentage of cases (probably over 50 percent) in which we are not able to pinpoint the cause of a child's mental retardation.

The AAMR categorizes causes of mental retardation according to the time at which the cause occurs: (1) **prenatal** (before birth), (2) **perinatal** (at the time of birth), and (3) **postnatal** (after birth) (AAMR Ad Hoc Committee on Terminology and Classification, 1992).

PRENATAL CAUSES

We can group prenatal causes into (1) **chromosomal disorders,** (2) inborn errors of metabolism, (3) developmental disorders affecting brain formation, and (4) environmental influences.

Prenatal causes of mental retardation.
Causes occurring during fetal development; some examples include chromosomal disorders, inborn errors of metabolism, developmental disorders affecting brain formation, and environmental influences.

Perinatal causes of mental retardation.
Causes at birth; some examples are anoxia, low birthweight, and infections such as syphilis and herpes simplex.

Postnatal causes of mental retardation.
Causes occurring after birth; can be biological (e.g., traumatic brain injury, infections) or psychosocial (an unstimulating environment).

Chromosomal disorder.
Any of several syndromes resulting from abnormal or damaged chromosome(s); can result in mental retardation.

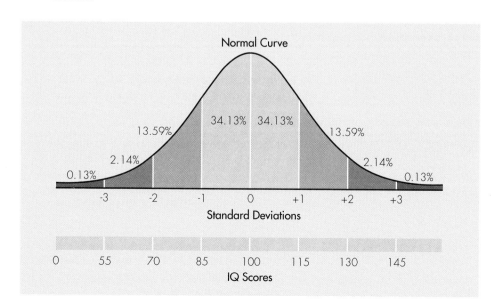

FIGURE 4.1
Theoretical distribution of IQ scores based on normal curve.

The Human Genome Project: Ethical Issues Pertaining to Mental Retardation

Started in 1990, the U.S. Human Genome Project is a fifteen-year undertaking of the U.S. Department of Energy and the National Institutes of Health to:

- Identify all the estimated 80,000 genes in human DNA
- Determine the sequences of the 3 billion chemical bases that make up human DNA, store this information in data bases, and develop tools for data analysis (Human Genome Management Information System, 1998)

The mapping of the human genome was completed in the summer of 2000.

One of the practical benefits noted by the project's administrators is the development of revolutionary ways to diagnose, treat, and eventually prevent genetic conditions. However, such potential breakthroughs have made some uneasy. For example, some have asserted that to use genetic information to prevent mental retardation devalues the lives of those who are mentally retarded:

Then, in a world where disability is not valued, people with disabilities are also not valued, rendering our efforts towards "normalization" impossible. How do we cope with a culture that teaches us, with an emphasis on "success," to devalue individuals whose disabilities render their chances of achievement, in its usual meaning, as less than likely? What of the ethical issues surrounding potential genetic therapies that may eventually "cure" mental retardation? Do people with disabilities lead fulfilling lives with their disability or in spite of it? How do professionals . . . assist and support individuals when the shifting climate indicates more than ever their worth, or lack thereof, in society? (Kuna, 2001, pp. 159–160)

Not all who raise concerns about the Human Genome Project are totally against it. But they have called for careful consideration of the ethical ramifications of its work. Below are excerpts from an address identifying issues of concern to The Arc of the United States, a national organization on mental retardation (Davis, 1997):

Issues of concern include the following: Must a physician offer prenatal genetic screening to all pregnant women or risk medical malpractice liability if he doesn't? Should a woman have a right to refuse prenatal screening? What if she's already had a child with a serious genetic condition? One of our workshop participants reported that her 3-year-old son's serious genetic condition had already cost more than $1 million, paid for by the state. She expressed her intention to have another child and her strong belief that she would refuse prenatal screening. What about testing infants and children for genetic conditions when there is no treatment available? . . .

Arguments in Favor of Gene Therapy. The major argument in favor of gene therapy is based on its potential for treating individuals severely affected by their condition. A perfect example is Lesch-Nyhan disease, which is characterized by communication deficits, writhing movements, and involuntary self-injurious behavior. Males who have this disorder have to be restrained constantly to prevent them from inflicting severe damage on themselves. Most have their teeth removed to keep from biting their lips off. If we have a new medical technology that will cure this condition, don't we have an obligation to use it?

Arguments Against Gene Therapy. A number of arguments are offered against gene therapy, including the concern about the potential for harmful abuse if we don't distinguish between good and bad uses of gene therapy. The eugenics movement of the 1920s to the 1940s found people with mental retardation being involuntarily sterilized. . . . Another concern is that in mental retardation gene-therapy research, many candidates are likely to be children who are too young or too disabled to understand ramifications of the treatment. Finally, gene therapy is very expensive and may never be sufficiently cost-effective to merit high social priority. Opponents say that if those who can afford gene therapy are the only ones to receive it, the distribution of desirable biological traits will widen the differences among various socioeconomic groups.

To see the complete address of Sharon Davis, a representative from the Arc, visit: http://www.ornl.gov/hgmis/resource/arc.html
For further information on the Human Genome Project visit: http://www.ornl.gov/hgmis/ ∎

Chromosomal Disorders   As noted above, scientists are making great strides in identifying genetic causes of mental retardation. There are now at least 750 genetic syndromes that have been identified as causes of mental retardation (Dykens, Hodapp, & Finucane, 2000). Just a few of the most common of these genetic syndromes are Down syndrome, Williams syndrome, fragile X syndrome, and Prader-Willi syndrome.

Down Syndrome   Many, but not all, genetic syndromes are transmitted hereditarily. In fact, by far the most common of these syndromes, **Down syndrome,** is usually not an inherited condition. Down syndrome involves an anomaly at the twenty-first pair of chromosomes. In the vast majority of cases of Down syndrome, the twenty-first set of **chromosomes** (the normal human cell contains twenty-three pairs of chromosomes) is a triplet rather than a pair; hence, Down syndrome is also referred to as **trisomy 21.** Estimated to account for about 5 to 6 percent of all cases of mental retardation (Beirne-Smith, Ittenbach, & Patton, 1998), Down syndrome is the most common form of mental retardation present at birth.

Down syndrome is associated with a range of distinctive physical characteristics that vary considerably in number from one individual to another. Persons with Down syndrome may have thick epicanthal folds in the corners of the eyes, making them appear to slant upward slightly. Other common characteristics include small stature, decreased muscle tone (hypotonia), hyperflexibility of the joints, a small oral cavity that can result in a protruding tongue, short and broad hands with a single palmar crease, heart defects, and susceptibility to upper respiratory infections and leukemia (Hunter, 2001). There is also evidence of a link between Down syndrome and Alzheimer's disease (see the box below).

The degree of mental retardation varies widely among people with Down syndrome; most individuals fall in the moderate range. In recent years, more children with Down

Down syndrome.
A condition resulting from an abnormality with the twenty-first pair of chromosomes; the most common abnormality is a triplet rather than a pair (the condition sometimes referred to as trisomy 21); characterized by mental retardation and such physical signs as slanted-appearing eyes, hypotonia, a single palmar crease, shortness, and a tendency toward obesity.

Chromosome.
A rod-shaped entity in the nucleus of the cell; contains genes, which convey hereditary characteristics; each cell in the human body contains 23 pairs of chromosomes.

Trisomy 21.
A type of Down syndrome in which the twenty-first chromosome is a triplet, making forty-seven, rather than the normal forty-six, chromosomes in all.

Down Syndrome and Alzheimer's Disease

It has been well over a century since researchers first noted a high prevalence of senility in persons with Down syndrome (Fraser & Mitchell, 1876, cited in Evenhuis, 1990). And it was in the early twentieth century that postmortem studies of the brains of people with Down syndrome revealed neuropathological signs similar to those of people with Alzheimer's disease (Carr, 1994). It was not until the 1980s and 1990s, however, that scientists started to address this correlation seriously.

Part of the reason for this shift in priority was the observation that the life expectancy for people with Down syndrome had increased dramatically over the twentieth century. In the first half of the century, very few people with Down syndrome lived until adulthood. But today, due to medical advances, the average life expectancy for people with Down syndrome is about fifty years, with many surviving into their sixties (Slomka & Berkey, 1997).

Postmortem studies of the brains of people with Down syndrome indicate that virtually all who reach the age of thirty-five have brain abnormalities very similar to those of persons with Alzheimer's disease (Wisniewski, Silverman, & Wegiel, 1994; Hof et al., 1995). Behavioral symptoms such as memory and speech problems are more difficult to document because of the low cognitive ability of persons with Down syndrome in the first place. However, research generally shows that (1) the prevalence of senility in people with Down syndrome is about 10 to 15 percent for those between the ages of forty and fifty; (2) the average age of onset is about fifty to fifty-five years; and (3) the prevalence is over 75 percent for those between the ages of sixty and seventy (Slomka & Berkey, 1997; Visser et al., 1997).

Findings that link Down syndrome to Alzheimer's disease have made researchers optimistic about uncovering the genetic underpinnings of both conditions. For example, researchers have found that some types of Alzheimer's are related to mutations of the twenty-first pair of chromosomes (Pinel, 2000).

Amniocentesis.
A medical procedure that allows examination of the amniotic fluid around the fetus; sometimes recommended to determine the presence of abnormality.

Chorionic villus sampling (CVS).
A method of testing the unborn fetus for a variety of chromosomal abnormalities, such as Down syndrome; a small amount of tissue from the chorion (a membrane that eventually helps form the placenta) is extracted and tested; can be done earlier than amniocentesis but the risk of miscarriage is slightly higher.

Sonography.
A medical procedure in which high-frequency sound waves are converted into a visual picture; used to detect major physical malformations in the unborn fetus.

Maternal serum screening (MSS).
A method of screening the fetus for developmental disabilities such as Down syndrome or spina bifida; a blood sample is taken from the mother and analyzed; if it is positive, a more accurate test such as amniocentesis or CVS is usually recommended.

Spina bifida.
A congenital midline defect resulting from failure of the bony spinal column to close completely during fetal development.

Williams syndrome.
A condition resulting from deletion of material in the seventh pair of chromosomes; often results in mild to moderate mental retardation, heart defects, and elfin facial features; people affected often display surprising strengths in spoken language and sociability while having severe deficits in spatial organization, reading, writing, and math.

Down syndrome is associated with certain physical characteristics: slightly slanted eyes, decreased muscle tone, and broad hands. Children with Down syndrome have shown an increase in IQ scores into the mildly mentally retarded range since special education programming. ∎

syndrome have achieved IQ scores in the mildly mentally retarded range than previously, presumably because of intensive special education programming.

The likelihood of having a child with Down syndrome increases with the age of the mother. For example, for mothers forty-five years of age, there is about a 1 in 30 chance of giving birth to a child with Down syndrome (Beirne-Smith et al., 1998). In addition to the age of the mother, researchers are pointing to other variables as possible causes, such as age of the father, exposure to radiation, and exposure to some viruses (Beirne-Smith et al., 1998). Research on these factors is still preliminary, however.

Methods are available for screening for Down syndrome and some other birth defects during pregnancy. Four such methods are **amniocentesis, chorionic villus sampling (CVS), sonography,** and **maternal serum screening (MSS):**

- In amniocentesis, the physician takes a sample of amniotic fluid from the sac around the fetus and analyzes the fetal cells for chromosomal abnormalities. In addition, the amniotic fluid can be tested for the presence of proteins that may have leaked out of the fetus's spinal column, indicating the presence of **spina bifida** (a condition in which the spinal column fails to close properly).
- In CVS, the physician takes a sample of villi (structures that later become the placenta) and tests them for chromosomal abnormalities. One advantage of CVS is that it can be done earlier than amniocentesis.
- In sonography, high-frequency sound waves are converted into pictures of the fetus, allowing the physician to detect physical malformations, such as spina bifida. Although not as accurate as amniocentesis or CVS, sonography also allows detection of Down syndrome through measurements of the spine.
- In MSS, a blood sample is taken from the mother and screened for the presence of certain elements that indicate the possibility of spina bifida or Down syndrome. If the results are positive, the physician can recommend a more accurate test such as amniocentesis or CVS.

Williams Syndrome   **Williams syndrome** is caused by the absence of material on the seventh pair of chromosomes. The average IQ of people with Williams syndrome is somewhere around 50 to 60; however, there are cases of individuals with IQs much lower or much higher, and some rare cases with IQs close to the normal range (Dykens et al., 2000). In addition, they often exhibit heart defects, an unusual sensitivity to sounds, and "elfin" facial features.

Fragile X Syndrome   **Fragile X syndrome** is the most common known hereditary cause of mental retardation (Hagerman, 2001). In association with mental retardation, it occurs in 1 in 4,000 males and at least half as many females (Turner, Webb, Wake, & Robinson, 1996). In association with milder cognitive deficits, such as learning disabilities, the prevalence may be as high as 1 in 2,000 (Hagerman, 2001). It is associated with the X chromosome in the twenty-third pair of chromosomes. In males, the twenty-third pair consists of an X and a Y chromosome; in females, it consists of two X chromosomes. This disorder is called *fragile X* syndrome because in affected individuals the bottom of the X chromosome is pinched off in some of the blood cells. Fragile X occurs less often in females because they have an extra X chromosome, giving them better protection if one of their X chromosomes is damaged. Persons with fragile X syndrome may have a number of physical features such as a large head; large, flat ears; long, narrow face; prominent forehead; broad nose; prominent, square chin; large testicles; and large hands with nontapering fingers. Although this condition usually results in moderate rather than severe mental retardation, the effects are highly variable, with some persons having less severe cognitive deficiencies and some, especially females, scoring in the normal range of intelligence (Dykens et al., 2000).

Prader-Willi Syndrome   Persons with **Prader-Willi syndrome** have inherited from their father a lack of genetic material on the fifteenth pair of chromosomes (Dykens et al., 2000). There are two distinct phases to Prader-Willi. Infants are lethargic and have difficulty eating. Starting at about one year of age, however, they become obsessed with food. In fact, Prader-Willi is the leading genetic cause of obesity. Although a vulnerability to obesity is usually their most serious medical problem, persons with Prader-Willi are also at risk for a variety of other health problems, including short stature due to growth hormone deficiencies; heart defects; sleep disturbances, such as excessive daytime drowsiness and **sleep apnea** (cessation of breathing while sleeping); and **scoliosis** (curvature of the spine). The degree of mental retardation varies, but the majority fall within the mildly mentally retarded range.

Inborn Errors of Metabolism

Inborn errors of metabolism result from inherited deficiencies in enzymes used to metabolize basic substances in the body, such as amino acids, carbohydrates, vitamins, or trace elements (Thomas, 1985). One of the most common of these is **phenylketonuria (PKU).** PKU involves the inability of the body to convert a common dietary substance—phenylalanine—to tyrosine; the consequent accumulation of phenylalanine results in abnormal brain development. All states routinely screen babies for PKU before they leave the hospital. Babies with PKU are immediately put on a special diet, which prevents the occurrence of mental retardation. At one time it was thought that the diet could be discontinued in middle childhood. However, authorities now recommend that it be continued indefinitely, for two important reasons: (1) Those who stop the diet are at risk for developing learning disabilities or other behavioral problems. (2) Over 90 percent of babies born to women with PKU who are no longer on the diet will have mental retardation and may also have heart defects (The Arc, 2001).

Developmental Disorders of Brain Formation

There are a number of conditions, some of which are hereditary and accompany genetic syndromes and some of which are caused by other conditions such as infections, that can affect the structural development of the brain and cause mental retardation. Two examples are **microcephalus** and **hydrocephalus.** In the former, the head is abnormally small and conical in shape. The mental retardation that results usually ranges from severe to profound. There is no specific treatment for microcephaly and life expectancy is low (National Institute of Neurological Disorders and Stroke, 2001). Hydrocephalus results from an accumulation of cerebrospinal fluid inside or outside the brain. The blockage of the circulation of the fluid results in a buildup of excessive pressure on the brain and enlargement of the skull. The degree of mental retardation depends on how early the condition is diagnosed and treated.

Fragile X syndrome.
A condition in which the bottom of the X chromosome in the twenty-third pair of chromosomes is pinched off; can result in a number of physical anomalies as well as mental retardation; occurs more often in males than females; thought to be the most common hereditary cause of mental retardation.

Prader-Willi syndrome.
Caused by inheriting from one's father a lack of genetic material on the fifteenth pair of chromosomes; leading genetic cause of obesity; degree of mental retardation varies, but the majority fall within the mildly mentally retarded range.

Sleep apnea.
Cessation of breathing while sleeping.

Scoliosis.
Curvature of the spine.

Inborn errors of metabolism.
Deficiencies in enzymes used to metabolize basic substances in the body, such as amino acids, carbohydrates, vitamins, or trace elements; can sometimes result in mental retardation; PKU is an example.

Phenylketonuria (PKU).
A metabolic genetic disorder caused by the inability of the body to convert phenylalanine to tyrosine; an accumulation of phenylalanine results in abnormal brain development.

Microcephalus.
A condition causing development of a small, conical-shaped head; proper development of the brain is prevented, resulting in mental retardation.

Hydrocephalus.
A condition characterized by enlargement of the head because of excessive pressure of the cerebrospinal fluid.

A variety of environmental factors can affect a woman who is pregnant and, thereby, affect the development of the fetus she is carrying. ■

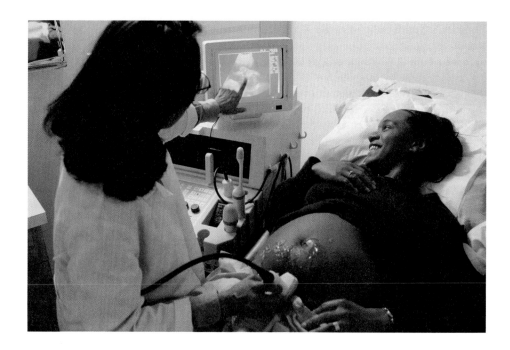

Treatment consists of surgical placement of a shunt (tube) that drains the excess fluid away from the brain and into a vein behind the ear or in the neck.

Environmental Influences There are a variety of environmental factors that can affect a woman who is pregnant and thereby affect the development of the fetus she is carrying. One example is maternal malnutrition. If the mother-to-be does not maintain a healthy diet, fetal brain development may be compromised. Although mental retardation resulting from maternal malnutrition is more common in developing countries, it is also evident in the United States, especially among those who are poor.

We are also now much more aware of the harmful effects of a variety of substances, from obvious toxic agents, such as cocaine and heroin, to more subtle potential poisons, such as tobacco and alcohol. In particular, researchers have exposed **fetal alcohol syndrome (FAS)** as a significant health problem for the unborn children of expectant mothers who consume large quantities of alcohol (Baumeister & Woodley-Zanthos, 1996; see also Chapter 12). Children with FAS are characterized by a variety of physical deformities as well as mental retardation. There is evidence that women who drink moderately during pregnancy may have babies who, although not exhibiting full-blown FAS, nevertheless show more subtle behavioral abnormalities.

We have recognized the hazards of radiation to the unborn fetus for some time. Physicians, for example, are cautious not to expose pregnant women to X rays unless absolutely necessary. Since the mid-to-late 1970s, however, the public has become even more concerned over the potential dangers of radiation from improperly designed or supervised nuclear power plants.

Infections in the mother-to-be can also affect the developing fetus and result in mental retardation. **Rubella (German measles),** in addition to being a potential cause of blindness, can also result in mental retardation. Rubella is most dangerous during the first trimester (three months) of pregnancy.

PERINATAL CAUSES

A variety of problems that can happen during the process of giving birth can result in brain injury and mental retardation. For example, if the child is not positioned properly in the uterus, brain injury can result during delivery. One problem that sometimes occurs because of difficulty during delivery is **anoxia** (complete deprivation of oxygen).

Fetal alcohol syndrome (FAS).
Abnormalities associated with the mother's drinking alcohol during pregnancy; defects range from mild to severe.

Rubella (German measles).
A serious viral disease, which, if it occurs during the first trimester of pregnancy, is likely to cause deformity in the fetus.

Anoxia.
Deprivation of oxygen; can cause brain injury.

Another condition that the AAMR categorizes as a perinatal cause is low birthweight. **Low birthweight (LBW)** can result in a variety of behavioral and medical problems, including mental retardation (Taylor, Klein, Minich, & Hack, 2000). Because most babies with LBW are premature, the two terms—LBW and premature—are often used synonymously. LBW is usually defined as 5.5 pounds or lower, and it is associated with a number of factors—poor nutrition, teenage pregnancy, drug abuse, and excessive cigarette smoking.

Infections such as **syphilis** and **herpes simplex** can be passed from mother to child during childbirth. These venereal diseases can potentially result in mental retardation. (Herpes simplex, which shows as cold sores or fever blisters, is not usually classified as a venereal disease unless it affects the genitals.)

POSTNATAL CAUSES

We can group causes of mental retardation occurring after birth into two very broad categories—those biological in nature and those psychosocial in nature.

Biological Postnatal Causes   Examples of biological postnatal causes are **traumatic brain injury (TBI),** infections, malnutrition, and toxins. TBI refers to head injuries that result from such things as blows to the head, vehicular accidents, or violent shaking. (We discuss TBI in more detail in Chapter 11.) **Meningitis** and **encephalitis** are two examples of infections that can cause mental retardation. Meningitis is an infection of the covering of the brain that may be caused by a variety of bacterial or viral agents. Encephalitis, an inflammation of the brain, results more often in mental retardation and usually affects intelligence more severely. One of the toxins, or poisons, that has been linked to mental retardation is lead. Although lead in paint is now prohibited, infants still become poisoned by eating lead-based paint chips, particularly in impoverished areas. Lead poisoning varies in its effect on children; high levels can result in death. The federal government now requires that automobile manufacturers produce cars that use only lead-free gasoline to lower the risk of inhaling lead particles from auto exhaust.

Psychosocial Postnatal Causes   Children raised in poor environmental circumstances are at risk for mental retardation. It should be obvious that extreme cases of abuse, neglect, or understimulation can result in mental retardation. However, most authorities believe that less severe forms of environmental deprivation can also result in mild mental retardation. In fact, many authorities implicate an unstimulating environment as one of the leading causes, if not the leading cause, of mild mental retardation. And because many persons who are mentally retarded fall in the mildly retarded range, this means that psychosocial disadvantage is considered one of the leading causes of mental retardation.

Although the environment is undeniably critical in fostering intellectual development, we hasten to point out that it is often impossible to disentangle its influence from that of genetics or heredity. **Cultural-familial mental retardation** is an important term with respect to environmental and/or hereditary causes of mental retardation. Some use this term to refer to a person with a mild degree of retardation who, among other things, (1) has no evidence of brain damage, (2) has parents who are also mildly mentally retarded, (3) has siblings who are mildly mentally retarded (if he or she has siblings), and (4) is likely to produce children who are mildly mentally retarded (Zigler & Hodapp, 1986). Today professionals use the term broadly to indicate mild mental retardation that may be due to an unstimulating environment (possibly but not necessarily specifically caused by poor parenting) and/or nonspecific hereditary factors. Just which factor is most influential—environment or heredity—has been the subject of debate for years (see the box on p. 122).

For many years it has been assumed that cultural-familial mental retardation is the cause of the vast majority of cases of mild mental retardation, whereas organic, or biological, factors are the cause of more severe mental retardation. In recent years, however,

Low birthweight (LBW).
Babies who are born weighing less than 5.5 pounds; usually premature; at risk for behavioral and medical conditions, such as mental retardation.

Syphilis.
A venereal disease that can cause mental subnormality in a child, especially if it is contracted by the mother-to-be during the latter stages of fetal development.

Herpes simplex.
A viral disease that can cause cold sores or fever blisters; if it affects the genitals and is contracted by the mother-to-be in the later stages of fetal development, it can cause mental subnormality in the child.

Traumatic brain injury (TBI).
Injury to the brain (not including conditions present at birth, with trauma, or degenerative diseases or conditions) resulting in total or partial disability or psychosocial maladjustment that affects educational performance; may affect cognition, language, memory, reasoning, abstract thinking, judgment, problem solving, sensory or perceptual and motor abilities, psychosocial behavior, physical functions, information processing, or speech.

Meningitis.
A bacterial or viral infection of the linings of the brain or spinal cord.

Encephalitis.
An inflammation of the brain; can affect the child's mental development adversely.

Cultural-familial mental retardation.
Today, a term used to refer to mild mental retardation due to an unstimulating environment and/or hereditary factors.

The Nature–Nurture Controversy

In the early part of this century, the predominant viewpoint among educators was that genetics determines intellectual development. The classic study of Skeels and Dye (1939), however, did much to strengthen the position of the environmentalists. Skeels and Dye investigated the effects of stimulation on the development of infants and young children in an orphanage, many of whom were classified as mentally retarded. One group of children remained in the typical orphanage environment, while the other group was given stimulation. For the latter group, nurturance was provided by teenage girls who were mentally retarded. The effects were clear-cut: IQs for members of the group given stimulation increased, whereas the other children's IQs decreased. Even more dramatic were the results of Skeels's follow-up study, done twenty-one years later (Skeels, 1966). Among other things, the experimental group on average had completed the twelfth grade, with some having one or more years of college and one completing a B.A. degree.

By the 1960s, many educators supported the environmental (nurture) position. During this time, for example, the federal government established the Head Start program, which was based on the premise that the negative effects of poverty could be reduced through educational and medical services during the preschool years.

For many years, theoreticians tended to view the nature–nurture issue from an either/or perspective—either you believed that heredity held the key to determining intellectual development or you held that the environment was the all-important factor. Today, however, most authorities hold that both heredity and the environment are critical determinants of intelligence. Some scientists have tried to discover how much of intelligence is determined by heredity versus the environment, but many view this quest as futile. They assert that heredity and environment do not combine in an additive fashion to produce intelligence. Instead, the interaction between genes and environment results in intelligence.

The following exchange between a professor of biopsychology and his student points out the importance of viewing intelligence in this way—that is, as the result of an interaction between genetics and experience and not a simple addition of the two:

One of my students told me that she had read that intelligence was one-third genetic and two-thirds experience, and she wondered whether this was true. She must have been puzzled when I began my response by describing an alpine experience. "I was lazily wandering up a summit ridge when I heard an unexpected sound. Ahead, with his back to me, was a young man sitting on the edge of a precipice, blowing into a peculiar musical instrument. I sat down behind him on a large sun-soaked rock, and shared his experience with him. Then, I got up and wandered back down the ridge, leaving him undisturbed.

I put the following question to my student: "If I wanted to get a better understanding of the musician, would it be reasonable for me to begin by asking how much of it came from the musician and how much of it came from the instrument?"

"That would be dumb," she said, "The music comes from both; it makes no sense to ask how much comes from the musician and how much comes from the instrument. Somehow the music results from the interaction of the two, and you would have to ask about the interaction."

"That's exactly right," I said. "Now, do you see why . . ."

"Don't say any more," she interrupted. "I see what you're getting at. Intelligence is the product of the interaction of genes and experience, and it is dumb to try to find how much comes from genes and how much comes from experience." (Pinel, 2000, p. 24)

authorities are beginning to suspect that many cases of mild mental retardation may be caused by specific genetic syndromes (Dykens et al., 2000). They point to the many cases of persons with Prader-Willi syndrome and Williams syndrome, as well as females with fragile X syndrome, who have mild mental retardation, and they speculate that in the near future new genetic syndromes will be discovered as causes of mild mental retardation:

The prevalence rates of [cultural-familial] mental retardation may not be anywhere near the 75% figure widely held. . . . The actual prevalence of true [cultural-familial] mental retardation seems likely to be significantly lower, as people with even the mildest degrees of intellectual impairment are increasingly being diagnosed with specific genetic syndromes. . . . Thus, the formerly clear-cut linking of "lower IQ–organic" and "higher IQ–environmental" retardation is no longer so straightforward. (Dykens et al., 2000, pp. 26–27)

Assessment

Two major areas are assessed to determine whether a person is mentally retarded: intelligence and adaptive skills. To assess intelligence, a professional administers an intelligence test to the person. To assess adaptive skills, a parent or professional who is familiar with the person responds to a survey about different adaptive skills.

INTELLIGENCE TESTS

There are many types of IQ tests. Because of their accuracy and predictive capabilities, practitioners prefer individually administered tests to group tests. Two of the most common individual IQ tests for children are the Stanford-Binet (4th ed.; Thorndike, Hagen, & Sattler, 1986) and the Wechsler Intelligence Scale for Children–Third Edition (WISC-III) (Wechsler, 1991). Both of these tests are verbal, although the WISC-III is intended to assess both verbal and performance aspects of intelligence. It has a verbal and a performance scale with a number of subtests. The full-scale IQ, a statistical composite of the verbal and performance IQ measures, is used when a single overall score for a child is desired.

Another relatively common IQ test is the Kaufman Assessment Battery for Children (K-ABC) (Kaufman & Kaufman, 1983). Some psychologists recommend using the K-ABC with African American students because they believe it is less culturally biased (Kamphaus & Reynolds, 1987).

Although not all IQ tests call for this method of calculation, we can get a rough approximation of a person's IQ by dividing **mental age** (the age level at which a person is functioning) by **chronological age** and multiplying by 100. For example, a ten-year-old student who performs on an IQ test as well as the average eight-year-old (and thus has a mental age of eight years) would have an IQ of 80.

Compared to most psychological tests, IQ tests such as the Stanford-Binet, WISC-III, and K-ABC are among the most reliable and valid. By reliability, we mean that a person will obtain relatively similar scores if given the test on two separate occasions that are not too close or far apart in time. Validity generally answers the question of whether the instrument measures what it is supposed to measure. A good indicator of the validity of an IQ test is the fact that it is generally considered the best single index of how well a student will do in school. It is wise to be wary, however, of placing too much faith in a single score from any IQ test. There are at least four reasons for caution:

1. Even on very reliable tests, an individual's IQ can change from one testing to another, and sometimes the change can be dramatic.
2. All IQ tests are culturally biased to a certain extent. Largely because of differences in language and experience, persons from minority groups are sometimes at a disadvantage in taking such tests.
3. The younger the child, the less validity and reliability the test has. Infant intelligence tests are particularly questionable.
4. IQ tests are not the absolute determinant when it comes to assessing a person's ability to function in society. A superior IQ does not guarantee a successful and happy life, nor does a low IQ doom a person to a miserable existence. Other variables are also important determinants of a person's coping skills in society. That is why, for example, professionals also assess adaptive skills.

Mental age.
Age level at which a person performs on an IQ test; used in comparison to chronological age to determine IQ. IQ = (mental age ÷ chronological age) × 100.

Chronological age.
Refers to how old a person is; used in comparison to mental age to determine IQ. IQ = (mental age ÷ chronological age) × 100.

ADAPTIVE SKILLS

There are a number of commonly used adaptive behavior measures, including the Vineland Adaptive Behavior Scales (Sparrow, Balla, & Cicchetti, 1984); the Adaptive Behavior Inventory for Children (Mercer & Lewis, 1982); the AAMR Adaptive Behavior Scale–School, Second Edition (Lambert, Nihira, & Leland, 1993); and the AAMR Adaptive Behavior Scale–Residential and Community Edition (Nihira, Leland, & Lambert, 1993). In addition, the Assessment of Adaptive Areas (Bryant, Taylor, & Rivera, 1996) combines the last two and is the only one that covers all ten of the adaptive skills in the AAMR definition (communication, self-care, home living, social skills, community use, self-direction, health and safety, functional academics, leisure, and work). The basic format of these instruments requires that a parent, teacher, or other professional answer questions related to the subject's ability to perform adaptive skills.

Psychological and Behavioral Characteristics

Some of the major areas in which persons with mental retardation are likely to experience deficits are attention, memory, language development, self-regulation, social development, and motivation. In considering the psychological and behavioral characteristics of persons with mental retardation, we hasten to point out that a given individual with mental retardation may not display all of these characteristics.

The importance of attention for learning is critical. A person must be able to attend to the task at hand before she or he can learn it. For years, researchers have posited that we can attribute many of the learning problems of persons with mental retardation to attention problems (Tomporowski & Tinsley, 1997). Often attending to the wrong things, they have difficulty allocating their attention properly.

One of the most consistent research findings is that persons with mental retardation have difficulty remembering information. Their deficits are widespread, but they often have particular problems with working memory (Bray, Fletcher, & Turner, 1997). **Working memory** involves the ability to keep information in mind while simultaneously doing another cognitive task. Trying to remember an address while listening to instructions on how to get there is an example of working memory.

In general, the language of persons who are mentally retarded follows the same developmental course as that of nonretarded persons, but their language development starts later, progresses at a slower rate, and ends up at a lower level of development (Warren & Yoder, 1997). They often experience problems with the ability both to understand and to produce language.

Self-regulation is a broad term referring to an individual's ability to regulate his or her own behavior. Persons who are mentally retarded also have difficulties with metacognition, which is closely connected to the ability to self-regulate (Bebko & Luhaorg, 1998). **Metacognition** refers to a person's awareness of what strategies are needed to perform a task, the ability to plan how to use the strategies, and the evaluation of how well the strategies are working. Self-regulation is, thus, a component of metacognition. (We discuss metacognition again in Chapter 5.)

People with mental retardation are candidates for a variety of social problems. They often have problems making and keeping friends, for at least two reasons: First, many do not seem to know how to strike up social interactions with others, and this difference is evident as early as preschool (Kasari & Bauminger, 1998). Second, even when not attempting to interact with others, they may exhibit behaviors that "turn off" their peers. For example, they display higher rates of inattention and disruptive behavior than their nonretarded classmates.

Many of the problems pertaining to attention, memory, language development, self-regulation, and social development place persons who are mentally retarded at risk to develop problems of motivation. If these individuals have experienced a long history of

Working memory.
The ability to remember information while also performing other cognitive operations.

Self-regulation.
Refers generally to a person's ability to regulate his or her own behavior (e.g., to employ strategies to help in a problem-solving situation); an area of difficulty for persons who are mentally retarded.

Metacognition.
A person's (1) awareness of what strategies are necessary to perform a task and (2) ability to use self-regulation strategies.

The self-concepts of children with mental retardation are influenced by their relationships with their peers. Positive personal interaction is as important to these individuals as to anyone. ■

failure, they can be at risk to develop **learned helplessness**—the feeling that no matter how hard they try, they will still fail. Believing they have little control over what happens to them and that they are primarily controlled by other people and events, some persons with mental retardation tend to give up easily when faced with challenging tasks. Professionals recognize that a good educational or vocational program for persons with mental retardation needs to contain a component focused on motivational problems.

LINKING GENETIC SYNDROMES TO PARTICULAR BEHAVIORAL PHENOTYPES

Until recently, most authorities paid little attention to the type of mental retardation a person had in considering behavioral characteristics. However, researchers have begun to find general patterns of behavioral characteristics associated with some of the genetic syndromes. These patterns of behavior are referred to as behavioral phenotypes. A **behavioral phenotype** is

> specific and characteristic behavior repertoire exhibited . . . with a genetic or chromosomal disorder. It includes a wide range of developmental and behavioral characteristics including cognitive, language, and social aspects as well as behavioral problems and psychopathology (Finegan, 1998). (Moldavsky, Lev, & Lerman-Sagie, 2001, p. 749)

Researchers have identified the four genetic syndromes we discussed under prenatal causes of mental retardation—Down syndrome, Williams syndrome, fragile X syndrome, and Prader-Willi syndrome—as being ones that have relatively distinctive behavioral phenotypes (Dykens, 2001; Dykens et al., 2000; Hodapp & Fidler, 1999; Moldavsky et al., 2001). For example, persons with Down syndrome often have significant impairments in expressive language and grammar compared to visual-spatial skills, whereas for individuals with Williams syndrome the reverse is often true. In fact, the storytelling ability of the latter, including their ability to modulate the pitch and volume of their voices to interject emotional tone in their stories, together with their sociability and elflike faces, have led some to speculate that people with Williams syndrome are the pixies or fairies depicted in folktales (see the box on p. 127).

Learned helplessness.
A motivational term referring to a condition wherein a person believes that no matter how hard he or she tries, failure will result.

Behavioral phenotype.
A collection of behaviors, including cognitive, language, and social behaviors as well as psychopathological symptoms that tend to occur together in persons with a specific genetic syndrome.

TABLE 4.2   Links Between Genetic Syndromes and Behavioral Phenotypes

Genetic Syndrome	Behavioral Phenotype	
	Relative Weaknesses	Relative Strengths
Down syndrome	Verbal skills, especially grammar	Visual-spatial skills
	Problems interpreting facial emotions	
	Cognitive skills tend to worsen over time	
	Early onset of Alzheimer's	
Williams syndrome	Visual-spatial skills	Expressive language, vocabulary
	Fine-motor control	Facial recognition and memory
	Anxieties, fears, phobias	Musical interests and skills
	Overly friendly	
Fragile X syndrome	Short-term memory	Verbal skills, including vocabulary
	Sequential processing	Long-term memory for information already acquired
	Repetitive speech patterns	
	Social anxiety and withdrawal	
Prader-Willi syndrome	Auditory processing	Relatively high IQ (average about 70)
	Feeding problems in infancy	Visual processing
	Overeating, obesity in childhood and adulthood	Facility with jigsaw puzzles
	Sleep disturbances	
	Compulsive behaviors	

SOURCE: Based on the following studies and reviews: Belser & Sudhalter, 2001; Dimitropoulos, Feurer, Butler, & Thompson, 2001; Dykens, Hodapp, & Finucane, 2000; Kasari, Freeman, & Hughes, 2001; Mervis, Klein-Tasman, & Mastin, 2001; Moldavsky, Lev, & Lerman-Sagie, 2001

CW The National Association for Down Syndrome (NADS), was founded in 1961 by a group of parents. Its Web site at http://www.nads.org/index.html provides information on resources as well as links to other sites devoted to Down syndrome.

The Williams Syndrome Association is devoted to providing information to affected families: http://www.williams-syndrome.org/

The National Fragile X Foundation is devoted to providing information to affected families: http://www.fragilex.org/home.htm

The Prader-Willi Association (USA) is devoted to providing information to affected families: http://www.pwsausa.org/
    The propensity for those with Prader-Willi to crave food has raised ethical issues pertaining to allowing then to eat and the concept of least restrictive environment. The Prader-Willi Association (USA) has issued a policy statement on the subject. See: http://www.pwsausa.org/position/ps002.htm ■

Table 4.2 lists some of the major behavioral characteristics associated with Down syndrome, Williams syndrome, fragile X syndrome, and Prader-Willi syndrome. Although much research has been done to link these behavioral phenotypes with each of the syndromes, there is far from a one-to-one correspondence between the diagnosis and the characteristics. Not all individuals in each of these conditions will have all of the symptoms. In other words, not all persons within these syndromes are exactly alike.

Educational Considerations

In recent years there has been a dramatic philosophical change toward educational programming for students with mental retardation. This change has involved two related movements—a greater emphasis on (1) inclusion and the teaching of useful skills and (2) self-determination (Westling & Fox, 2000).

INCLUSION AND USEFUL SKILLS

As we noted above, more and more students with mental retardation are being educated in regular schools alongside students without disabilities. Advocates of inclusion also believe that, in cases in which they are taught in separate classrooms for a portion of the time, the primary "home room" should be the regular classroom.
    To help facilitate inclusion in the mainstream environment, inclusion advocates note the importance of teaching students with mental retardation using a curriculum that promotes practical, age-appropriate skills. In the past, the tendency was to provide such

Williams Syndrome: An Inspiration for Some Pixie Legends?

Folktales from many cultures feature magical "little people"—pixies, elves, trolls and other fairies. A number of physical and behavioral similarities suggest that at least some of the fairies in the early yarns were modeled on people who have Williams syndrome. Such a view is in keeping with the contention of historians that a good deal of folklore and mythology is based on real life.

The facial traits of Williams people are often described as pixielike. In common with pixies in folklore and art, many with Williams syndrome have small, upturned noses, a depressed nasal bridge, "puffy" eyes, oval ears and broad mouths with full lips accented by a small chin. Indeed, those features are so common that Williams children tend to look more like one another than their relatives, especially as children. The syndrome also is accompanied by slow growth and development, which leads most Williams individuals to be relatively short.

The "wee, magical people" of assorted folktales often are musicians and storytellers. Fairies are said to "repeat the songs they have heard" and can "enchant" humans with their melodies. Much the same can be said of people with Williams syndrome, who in spite of typically having subnormal IQs, usually display vivid narrative skills and often show talent for music. (The large pointed ears so often associated with fairies may symbolically represent the sensitivity of those mythical individuals—and of Williams people—to music and to sound in general.)

As a group, Williams people are loving, trusting, caring and extremely sensitive to the feelings of others. Similarly, fairies are frequently referred to as the "good people" or as kind and gentle-hearted souls. Finally, Williams individuals, much like the fairies of legend, require order and predictability. In Williams people this need shows up as rigid adherence to daily routines and a constant need to keep abreast of future plans.

In the past, storytellers created folktales about imaginary beings to help explain phenomena that they did not understand—perhaps including the distinguishing physical and behavioral traits of Williams syndrome. Today researchers turn to Williams people in a quest to understand the unknown, hoping to decipher some of the secrets of how the brain functions.

The children in the photograph, who are unrelated, display elfin facial features that clinicians associate with Williams syndrome. ■

SOURCE: Adapted from article Williams syndrome and the brain by Howard M. Lenhoff, Paul P. Wang, Frank Greenberg, & Ursula Bellugi (1997 December) p. 73. Copyright © 1997 by Scientific American, Inc. All rights reserved.

students with a curriculum that was more suited to their mental age than their chronological age. Most authorities agree that this is demeaning. In addition, it does not prepare the students for functioning alongside their nondisabled peers.

SELF-DETERMINATION

Because people with mental retardation have reduced cognitive capacity, professionals and parents alike have traditionally considered them incapable of making decisions on their own. In a sense, this paternalistic attitude often resulted in a self-fulfilling prophecy by not providing persons with mental retardation an opportunity to take more control over their lives. However, many professionals and parents now champion the notion of promoting self-determination in persons who are mentally retarded. In fact, the major parent organization in the field, The Arc, and the major professional organization, the AAMR, have each adopted position statements supporting the idea of self-determination. (See the box on p. 130 for an excerpt from AAMR's policy.)

SUCCESS STORIES
Special Educators at Work

Orono, ME: Thirteen-year-old **Molly Berry** is helpful and energetic, much like her parents, Karen and Dave. As a fifth grader, Molly is a student council representative at her school. Because of her drive (and despite her limitations), the Berrys have advocated for Molly to be included in general education classes since pre-school. Special educator **Lisa Douville** and general educator **Mike Morcom** are collaborating to maximize Molly's learning before she leaves elementary school.

Mike Morcom readied his class for the totem pole project and rehearsed positive behaviors for cooperative learning groups. As Molly listened to reminders about sound levels and cleaning up, she seemed eager to start. "I'm going to make a unicorn for my totem pole," she said, and started to paint an ice-cream container white. She never sat still for long, as she repeatedly left her project to inspect others. She told a friend, "When you finish painting, you'll need some glue."

Karen and Dave Berry agree that Molly is distractible, but they feel she has made significant social gains in the mainstream classroom. Special educator Lisa Douville also sees improvement in Molly's ability to focus. "She has a good attitude and responds without much grumbling! She hasn't needed sticker reinforcement so far this year."

The Berrys have what they call a "healthy adversarial relationship" with Molly's school district. They are strong advocates for parents being closely involved in the educational decisions affecting their children. According to Dave Berry, "When parents and professionals are both well informed, then they're on even ground." The Berrys have received training in individualized education program (IEP) develop-

ment and how to exercise their rights. Karen Berry says, "I always ask that IEPs be available to all Molly's teachers. Then, I check to see if they are being used."

For the Berrys, the key issue in Molly's education is effective communication and teamwork from year to year. This means that teachers exchange information and that parents and educators listen carefully to each other. "Everyone needs to know it's okay to speak up for the real needs of the child, despite the costs or inconveniences," says Dave Berry. "We've all worked hard to help Molly make progress."

In June, Molly will graduate from the pine-paneled elementary school where she has attended general education classes since grade 1. Triennial testing has been completed and a meeting will soon be held to determine how Molly can best make the transition to middle school for grade 6.

When the Pupil Evaluation Team meets, Lisa Douville and Mike Morcom will attend, along with Dave and Karen Berry. Molly's social goals will be reviewed to determine her progress toward independence in beginning work, attention to task, and use of appropriate behaviors in managing stress. New academic goals will be set and supports will be updated to reflect any changes in modifications, such as

Self-determination.
The ability to make personal choices, regulate one's own life, and be a self-advocate; a prevailing philosophy in educational programming for persons with mental retardation.

Self-determination involves the ability to make personal choices, to regulate one's life, and to be a self-advocate (Westling & Fox, 2000). A person who is self-determined exhibits four characteristics:

Autonomy, acting according to one's own preferences, interests, and abilities, independently and free from undue external influences

Self-regulation, deciding what strategies and tactics to use in particular situations, in setting goals, in problem solving, and in monitoring one's own performance in these tasks

Psychological empowerment, a belief that one has control over important circumstances, and a belief that one has the skills to achieve desired outcomes, and that by applying those skills the desired outcome will occur

shortened written assignments or notes copied from a sheet on her desk, rather than from the board.

Karen and Dave Berry are committed advocates for Molly and have worked closely with a psychologist to obtain an objective assessment of her abilities and potential for successful inclusion. Together with the team, they have crafted an IEP that describes areas that interfere with Molly's learning:

Molly exhibits delays in the development of perceptual-motor skills, a mild to moderate phonological disorder, a moderate to severe expressive language delay, and difficulties comprehending complex verbal material. When compared to her peers, Molly has difficulties in the following areas: working independently and initiating and completing tasks. Off-task behaviors consist of unpredictable episodes of physical and visual wandering and ignoring teacher requests. This behavior is compounded in situations when Molly perceives tasks as being difficult. Her levels of performance are consistent with test results and classroom observations.

This year Molly, her best friend Jenny, and two other special-needs students are among the twenty-two members of Mike Morcom's fifth-grade class. "I don't want the kids to patronize Molly, and they don't seem to," says Mike. "We work on building sensitivity to differences and modeling ways of interacting."

Mike acknowledges that it would be hard to manage instructionally without a classroom aide, and he sees this as a key to Molly's success. Janet Metcalf, a certified teacher, has worked as the educational technician with Molly's class for two years. So has special educator Lisa Douville, who supervises Janet, works directly with Molly on reading and math skills in the resource room, and manages her educational plan. Lisa and Mike jointly track Molly's progress.

Molly's math program is carried out by the educational technician in the classroom and guided by individualized packets of materials assembled by Lisa Douville. If the class is working as a group or taking a test, Janet Metcalf will often adapt the activity, pull the next item from Molly's packet, or develop a criterion-referenced test, based on Molly's third-grade-level goals. For social studies and science, Janet adapts Mike Morcom's materials and activities for the special-needs students in the class. Janet also keeps a daily school/home journal with the Berrys.

Like her math program, Molly's reading and spelling programs are directed by Lisa Douville and similarly carried out in the classroom. However, these are areas in which Molly has less confidence and fears failure. She is stronger at receiving information orally but has difficulty decoding words when reading. Says Lisa, "Molly is embarrassed to be seen with the second–third-grade-level books she is able to read. She is aware of her social environment and needs help with handling sensitive issues appropriately."

In reflecting on his daughter's progress, Dave Berry recalls that once Molly was provided with a well-trained aide and resource support, the role of her general educators changed. "We started to work as a team when the second-grade teacher wisely identified the supports Molly needed in the classroom. Her fourth- and fifth-grade teachers have been terrific at working closely with special educators. We don't expect the classroom teachers to do it all, but we do expect them to have help."

As they plan for Molly's future, this team of parents and professionals hopes that she will be able to remain in classes with her nondisabled peers as much as is appropriate for her. Says Dave Berry, "I work with students every day, and I think it must be said that while this approach works for my child, inclusion in a regular class might not be appropriate for someone else's child." Karen Berry agrees: "I don't want Molly just to be *included*. It's what is *done* for her in the classroom that counts."

—By Jean Crockett

Self-realization, one has a reasonably accurate knowledge of himself[/herself] and his[/her] strengths and his[/her] limitations, and acts in a way that capitalizes on this knowledge (Westling & Fox, 2000, p. 34)

We should not assume that self-determination will develop on its own in persons who are mentally retarded. Based on our previous discussion of their history of learning deficits and vulnerability for developing learned helplessness, it should be obvious that persons with mental retardation will find it difficult to become self-determined. Investigators have just begun to look into ways of fostering self-determination (e.g., Wehmeyer, Palmer, Agran, Mithaug, & Martin, 2000), but much more research is needed to determine the best ways to cultivate self-determination in students with mental retardation. In the meantime, it is important that the philosophy of self-determination not be interpreted to mean

AAMR Policy Statement on Self-Determination

The following are excerpts from the American Association on Mental Retardation's Self-Determination Policy Statement:

Issue

There is a well-documented history of discrimination, exploitation, and custodial treatment of persons with mental retardation. These individuals have not been participants in choices involving many important aspects of their lives such as living arrangements, personal relationships, employment, and community participation. As a result, many persons with mental retardation have difficulty in making choices and display characteristics of dependency and learned helplessness. It is for these reasons that the self-determination movement is so essential. . . .

Position

- AAMR will uphold the right to self-determination as the right to act as the primary causal agent in one's life, to pursue self-defined goals and to participate fully in society. Self-determining individuals control their lives, make choices and decisions based on their interests, abilities and preferences, and take responsibility for their lives.

- People with mental retardation must have the opportunity to advocate for themselves, without fear of punishment, and with the knowledge that their demands and suggestions will be heard and given fair consideration.

- AAMR recognizes and supports the right of individuals with mental retardation to self-determination in every aspect of decision making that affects them as individuals, including living arrangements, work, religious participation, personal relationships and control of their private funds and public funds designated for the purchase of services for them as individuals. . . .

SOURCE: American Association on Mental Retardation, 1998 (revised 2000), posted on the World Wide Web: aamr.org/Policies/Pol_self_determination.shtml. Reprinted with permission.

CW The Arc has also issued a policy statement on self-determination: http://www.thearc.org/posits/selfdetpos.html ■

that persons who are mentally retarded should be left totally to their own devices. As the 1999–2000 president of the AAMR warned in his presidential address:

> We cannot let choice become excuse for neglect. Let me tell you two real stories. . . . One is a gentleman by the name of Robert, who moved out of one of our . . . community homes into his own apartment. It became obvious after a couple of months that Robert was not eating properly. He was beginning to lose weight and was spending his limited funds on junk food and some questionable recreational activity. Our staff debated at length about Robert's right to eat poorly versus our responsibility for Robert's well-being. The decision we eventually came to was that to simply allow the situation to continue would be allowing choice to become an excuse for neglect. So we did intervene. We arranged a budget, and scheduled staff was there at dinnertime to make sure that Robert ate more appropriately.
>
> A second example, a fellow by the name of Jimmy, posed a similar kind of situation. Jimmy moved out of one of our . . . community group homes into his own apartment. Very quickly after moving out, he got a job as a dishwasher in a local restaurant. Jimmy took great delight in walking to and from work. In fact, he took great pride and delight in walking all over. I think he probably loved to walk because of the independence he gained by walking, not having to rely on arranged transportation. He had spent many years in institutional settings waiting for the institution bus or community home van. . . . The staff was very concerned about Jimmy walking home late at night, 10:30 or 11:00 o'clock, when he was through with his dishwasher job. Jimmy insisted, however, that he wanted to walk home. The end to this tragic story is that one night, while he was walking home from work, a drunk driver left the road, went up 10 yards onto the side of the road, hit and killed Jimmy. Needless to say, we went through a tremendous

Educational approaches for children with mental retardation depend on the degree of retardation or the need for support. The most popular placement continues to be the special class, but more and more students are being educated in the general education classroom. ■

amount of soul searching as to whether or not we had made a tragic mistake of letting choice become an excuse for neglect. In this particular case, we finally decided that we had not.

I do not necessarily expect you to agree with my conclusions about Robert or Jimmy. What I do encourage, however, is that you take these examples as indicators of the very fine line that we walk at times between choice and safety concerns. (Wagner, 2000, pp. 436–437)

As we discussed in Chapter 3, we also need to keep in mind that self-determination will be defined differently depending on the particular culture of the individual. Some cultures are more oriented toward valuing individuality and autonomy; others are less so (Cronin, 2000).

INSTRUCTIONAL METHODS

Although there is some overlap, in general the focus of educational programs varies according to the degree of the student's mental retardation, or how much he or she requires support services. For example, the lesser the degree of mental retardation, the more the teacher emphasizes academic skills; and the greater the degree of mental retardation, the more stress there is on self-help, community living, and vocational skills. Keep in mind, however, that this distinction is largely a matter of emphasis. In practice, all students who are mentally retarded, no matter the severity level, need instruction in academic, self-help, community living, and vocational skills. We focus on the elementary school level here; we discuss preschool and secondary programming in later sections.

Students with Mild Mental Retardation, or Those Requiring Less Intensive Support   Early elementary education is heavily oriented toward providing children who are mildly mentally retarded with **readiness skills:** abilities that are prerequisites for later learning. These include such things as the ability to sit still and attend to the teacher, follow directions, hold a pencil or cut with a pair of scissors, tie shoes, button and unbutton, zip and unzip, use the toilet, and interact with peers in a group situation.

In the later elementary years, emphasis is greater on academics, usually on what are known as **functional academics.** Whereas the nonretarded child is taught academics, such as reading, in order to learn other academic content, such as history, the child with mental retardation is often taught reading in order to learn to function independently. In

Readiness skills.
Skills deemed necessary before academics can be learned (e.g., attending skills, ability to follow directions, knowledge of letter names).

Functional academics.
Practical skills (e.g., reading a newspaper or telephone book) rather than academic learning skills.

Systematic instruction.
Teaching that involves instructional prompts, consequences for performance, and transfer of stimulus control; often used with students with mental retardation.

Constant time delay.
An instructional procedure whereby the teacher makes a request while simultaneously prompting the student and then over several occasions makes the same request and waits a constant period of time before prompting; often used with students with mental retardation.

Progressive time delay.
An instructional procedure whereby the teacher makes a request while simultaneously prompting the student and then over several occasions gradually increases the latency between the request and the prompt; often used with students with mental retardation.

Research shows consistently that positive reinforcement leads to improved learning. For students with mental retardation, the more immediate the reinforcement, the more effective. ■

functional academics, the child learns academics in order to do such things as read a newspaper, read the telephone book, read labels on goods at the store, make change, and fill out job applications.

Although the rudiments of community and vocational living skills are emphasized much more in high school, some children are taught these skills in later elementary school (Morse & Schuster, 2000). Because some students who are mentally retarded take a relatively long time to learn particular skills, it is best to acquaint them with these skills as early as elementary school.

Students with More Severe Mental Retardation, or Those Requiring More Intensive Support

Educational programming for students with mental retardation, especially those with more severe mental retardation, often includes the following three features: (1) systematic instruction, (2) instruction in real-life settings with real materials, and (3) functional behavioral assessment and positive behavioral support.

Systematic Instruction   **Systematic instruction** involves the use of instructional prompts, consequences for performance, and strategies for the transfer of stimulus control (Davis & Cuvo, 1997). Students who are mentally retarded often need to be prompted or cued to respond in the appropriate manner. These prompts can be verbal, gestural, physical, or modeling may be used (Davis & Cuvo, 1997). A verbal prompt can be a question, such as "What do you need to do next?" or a command, such as "Put your socks in the top dresser drawer." A gestural prompt might involve pointing to the socks and/or the dresser drawer while stating the question or the command. Taking the student's hand and placing it on the socks and/or drawer would be an example of a physical prompt. And the adult might also model putting the socks in the drawer before then asking the student to do it.

With respect to consequences, research has consistently shown that students who are positively reinforced for correct responses learn faster. Positive reinforcers can range from verbal praise to tokens that can be traded for prizes or other rewards. For students with severe mental retardation, the more immediate the reinforcement, the more effective. Once the student demonstrates the desired behavior consistently, the goal is to wean the student from reliance on external reinforcers as soon as possible.

The goal of transfer of stimulus control is to reach a point at which the student does not have to rely on prompts and can be more independent. In order to transfer the control away from the prompts to more naturally occurring stimuli, several techniques are used, including delaying the time between a request and the prompt (Browder & Snell, 2000; Wolery & Schuster, 1997). For example, with **constant time delay,** the adult starts by making a request ("Please put your clothes away") and giving a prompt simultaneously ("Put your clothes in the top dresser drawer"). Then the adult might wait a set period of time (e.g., five seconds) between the request and the prompt. With **progressive time delay,** the adult also starts with a simultaneous prompt and request, but then the latency period between the two is increased gradually.

Instruction in Real-Life Settings with Real Materials   Instruction can take place in the classroom, under simulated conditions, or in real-life settings. It is generally better to teach students who are mentally retarded daily living skills in the actual settings where they will be using these skills. Because it is easier to hold instruction in classrooms than in real-life settings, the teacher may start out with instruction in the classroom and then supplement it with *in vivo* instruction (Browder & Snell, 2000). For example, the teacher might use

Meeting the Needs of Students with Mental Retardation

Strategies for Effective Instruction in Mathematics

What the Research Says

Although many professionals use the catchall term "mildly disabled" when referring to both students with learning disabilities and students with mild-to-moderate mental retardation, research on instruction for these two groups reveals differences in learning that have implications for classroom practices (Butler, Miller, Lee, & Pierce, 2001; Parmar, Cawley, & Miller, 1994). Current research demonstrates quantitative and qualitative differences between the performances of students with mental retardation and students with learning disabilities (Parmar et al., 1994; Scott, Greenfield, & Partridge, 1991). Questions about what topics should be taught, when topics should be introduced, how much time should be spent on certain topics, and if students with different IQ levels can be equally served by the same methods drive this current research.

Research Study

A study conducted with large groups of students with mental retardation and learning disabilities (206 and 295, respectively) revealed differences between the groups in the areas of basic concepts, listening vocabulary, problem solving/reasoning, and fractions (Parmar et al., 1994). The students with mental retardation scored lower on all subtest areas (concepts, vocabulary, problem solving, and fractions) when compared to the students with learning disabilities. Overall, *both groups* performed poorly on the problem-solving and application-of-concepts problems. Researchers attributed problem-solving difficulties to lack of instruction in "real-world problem solving." The general depressed scores of the students with mental retardation, however, reflect the need for more intense and differentiated instructional practices for this group of students.

Research Findings

In answer to the questions of when, how, and with what intensity certain mathematics topics should be taught, the students with mental retardation scored significantly lower than the students with learning disabilities (e.g., 14-year-old students with mental retardation performed at levels similar to or lower than those of 10-year-olds with learning disabilities). They also failed to attain the same steady growth rates exhibited by students with learning disabilities (e.g., gains in problem solving/reasoning by students with learning disabilities were more than twice those of students with mental retardation (Parmar et al., 1994). Thus, it is reasonable to conclude that instruction for these groups of students should differ in terms of pace, type of instruction, and level of practice.

Applying the Research to Teaching

Historically, mathematics instruction for students with mental retardation emphasized memorization of algorithms and abstract routines—a practice clearly reflected in the above study. Yet a recent review of studies on mathematics instruction for students with mental retardation identified specific instructional practices that resulted in increased competence in both basic-skills computation and problem solving/application (Butler et al., 2001).

Based upon recommended practices, a team of researchers designed the following instructional sequence that could be implemented in a general education classroom that includes students with mental retardation (Butler et al., 2001):

1. A one-minute math time trial to promote fluency and retention of previously learned facts. These trials would be specific to the particular skills a student is working on.
2. Step-by-step strategy instruction provided to the whole class using direct instruction.
3. Small-group work that involves applying the strategy. Problems for each group would be commensurate with the computational skill level of students within the group. Work at the concrete, representational, and abstract levels would be introduced during this time at the appropriate pace and sequence.
4. Final individual instruction in basic skills or computation could be provided via the computer, peers, or teacher-directed methods such as constant time delay or multisensory methods.

—By Kristin L. Sayeski

Community-based instruction focuses on everyday living skills learned in actual settings. ■

worksheets and photos of various shopping activities in class or set up a simulated "store" with shelves of products and a cash register. These classroom activities could then be supplemented with periodic visits to real grocery stores. Likewise, it is preferable to use real cans of food and real money in teaching students to read product labels and to make change.

Functional Behavioral Assessment and Positive Behavioral Support One of the major reasons some students with mental retardation have difficulty being included in general education classrooms is that they sometimes exhibit inappropriate behavior, such as hitting, biting, or screaming. Authorities recommend that teachers use a combination of **functional behavioral assessment (FBA)** and **positive behavioral support (PBS)** to reduce or eliminate these behaviors. (We discuss FBA and PBS more fully in Chapters 7 and 11.) FBA involves determining the consequences, antecedents, and setting events that maintain such behaviors (Horner, Albin, Sprague, & Todd, 2000). *Consequences* refer to the purpose the behavior serves for the person. For example, some students behave inappropriately in order to gain attention. *Antecedents* refer to things that trigger the behavior. For example, the student might become aggressive only toward certain peers. *Setting events* take into account broader contextual factors. For example, the student might be more likely to exhibit inappropriate behavior when sick or in hot, humid weather. Based on a functional assessment, the teacher can make changes in consequences, antecedents, and/or contextual factors and monitor the effectiveness of these changes.

Based on results from FBA, teachers can develop a PBS plan for students. PBS involves finding ways to support positive behaviors of students instead of punishing negative behaviors. PBS focuses on the total environment of the student, including instruction. Some proponents of PBS place an emphasis on implementing schoolwide plans to promote positive behavior in all students, not just those with disabilities (Sugai et al., 2000). Under such a plan, all school personnel are prepared to deliver positive reinforcement to for appropriate behavior in virtually all settings—classrooms, cafeteria, hallways, playground, school buses, etc.

Functional behavioral assessment.
The practice of determining the consequences (what purpose the behavior serves), antecedents (what triggers the behavior), and setting events (in what contexts the behavior occurs) of inappropriate behavior.

Positive behavioral support (PBS).
Systematic use of the science of behavior to find ways of supporting the desirable behavior of an individual rather than punishing the undesirable behavior.

SERVICE DELIVERY MODELS

Placements for school-age students with mental retardation range from general education classes to residential facilities. Although special classes for these students tend to be the

Meeting the Needs of Students with Mental Retardation

Classwide Peer-Tutoring

What the Research Says

In an effort to meet the instructional needs of students with mild mental retardation within inclusive settings, researchers have explored instructional methods that provide the necessary structure, individualization, and level of corrective feedback critical for success for this population. One such method is classwide peer tutoring (CWPT) (Delquadri, Greenwood, Stretton, & Hall, 1983). CWPT involves the use of peers to provide instruction and feedback in a reciprocal format. That is, paired students have the opportunity to serve as a tutor and as a tutee during each session. CWPT procedures were designed to address the need for higher levels of active, academic engagement for all students, but particularly for students with the greatest academic deficits (Greenwood, 1991).

Research Study

A team of researchers conducted a study to examine the effectiveness of CWPT on the spelling performance of eight students (four students with mild mental retardation and four nondisabled students) participating in a general education class (Mortweet et al., 1999). The students with mild mental retardation were included in general education classrooms for spelling, a social activity period, and lunch. The CWPT model was compared to traditional teacher-led instruction during the spelling period.

The investigators used the following structure for the CWPT sessions:

1. Each student with mild mental retardation was paired with a nondisabled peer.
2. Tutoring sessions occurred four times a week for twenty minutes per day.
3. Tutoring materials included: the list of spelling words, point sheets, and practice sheets.
4. The teacher assigned each pair to one of two competing classroom teams. (Points earned by the pairs contributed to daily "team point" totals.) Partners and teams were reassigned on a weekly basis.
5. During each session, students served as the "tutor" for ten minutes and the "tutee" for the other ten minutes.
6. Instruction consisted of the tutor reading the spelling word to the tutee. The tutee wrote the spelling word while saying each letter aloud. If the word was spelled correctly, the tutor awarded the tutee two points; if the word was spelled incorrectly, the tutor spelled the word correctly and the tutee wrote the word three times while naming each letter. The tutee could receive one point for correctly spelling the practice word. After ten minutes, the roles were reversed.
7. The teacher assigned bonus points for pairs that were working cooperatively and following the instructional protocol.
8. When the twenty-minute session was over, the teacher calculated team points based upon partner points. The winning team received such privileges as lining up for recess first.
9. Modifications made for the students with mild mental retardation included: shortened word lists, enlarged practice sheets, and "tutee" reading of words when the student with mild mental retardation was the tutor and was unable to read the word.

Research Findings

When compared to the teacher-led condition, the CWPT resulted in increased academic performance for all students, increased amount of engaged academic time (approximately five to ten minutes more per student per session), and positive acceptance from the teachers and students. Thus, CWPT provides teachers with a flexible instructional strategy to meet the varying needs of an inclusive classroom.

Applying the Research to Teaching

Given the effectiveness of CWPT, teachers can establish similar procedures in their classes. Tasks such as math facts, spelling, letter sounds, and word identification make great CWPT topics. Following the model established in the study, teachers can create their own tutoring materials. Key features of CWPT include: (a) partnering of a higher and lower skilled student, (b) explicit instruction in the tutoring activities (i.e., ample training prior to independent partner work), (c) structured tasks for the tutor to guide the tutee in completing, (d) reciprocal roles so the tutee has the opportunity to be a tutor, and (e) use of points to reward desired behavior.

—*By Kristin L. Sayeski*

Collaboration and Co-Teaching for Students with Mental Retardation

"Why should this student be in my classroom?"

What Does It Mean to Be a Teacher of Students with Mental Retardation?

Collaboration for students with mental retardation can include general and special educators and, often, other related service personnel and parents. Coordinating all of these participants is the responsibility of the special educator and this requires both management and interpersonal skills. Teachers of students with mental retardation are expected to:

1. Plan instruction in a variety of placement settings
2. Use and maintain assistive technologies
3. Select and use specialized instructional strategies appropriate for students with mental retardation
4. Plan and implement age- and ability-appropriate instruction
5. Design, implement, and evaluate instructional programs

that enhance social participation across environments (Council for Exceptional Children, 2001)

Successful Strategies for Collaboration

Pat Daniels is the mother of Will, a high school student with Down syndrome. She collaborated with Will's teachers and coaches to make his experience in general and special education successful. Will received his special education diploma and was awarded one of the school's ten Faculty Awards. Pat describes their experiences.

Open lines of communication between the teachers and the parent were extremely important. I made a point to meet each teacher before the school year began. French was one of the more successful classes. The teacher was unaware of what she was getting with Will, but she was willing and eager to learn. She began by getting to know him, not his weaknesses.

CW For more information on classwide peer tutoring visit: http://www.lso.ku.edu/~tech%20grant/CWPTLMS/

TASH, an organization that has been, perhaps, the most vocal in advocating for full inclusion of students with disabilities, identifies itself as a "civil rights organization for, and of, people with mental retardation, autism, cerebral palsy, physical disabilities and other conditions that make full integration a challenge": http://www.tash.org/ ■

norm, more and more students with mental retardation are being placed in more integrated settings. The degree of integration tends to be determined by the level of severity, with students who are less severely mentally retarded being the most integrated. However, as we discussed in Chapter 2, some professionals believe that all students with mental retardation should be educated in the general education classroom and that schools should provide the necessary support services (e.g., a special aide or special education teacher) in the class.

Although not all authorities agree on how much inclusion should be practiced, virtually all agree that placement in a self-contained class with no opportunity for interaction with nondisabled students is inappropriate. At the same time, even parents who favor integrated settings often believe that it is good for their children to interact with other children with disabilities, too, and that being the only student in the class with a disability has its drawbacks (Guralnick, Connor, & Hammond, 1995). And although parents of students with severe mental retardation enthusiastically believe in the social benefits of having their children in full-inclusion settings, they are more apprehensive about inclusion's impact on the quality of educational programming received by their children (Palmer, Borthwick-Duffy, & Widaman, 1998).

Early Intervention

We can categorize preschool programs for children with mental retardation as (1) those whose purpose is to prevent retardation and (2) those designed to further the development of children already identified as retarded. In general, the former address children who are at risk for mild mental retardation, and the latter are for children with more severe mental retardation.

She let him try activities, putting him in situations where he was successful and challenged. He had a textbook and did homework with the class, taking tests aimed at what he had learned. She helped find a volunteer "study-buddy." This teacher understood that he was working at his own level but she, like others, was often surprised and delighted by his contributions to the class.

The general education teachers and I communicated most frequently about tests and special projects. For example, one history teacher would call me before a test and we would generate specific review questions. Another teacher would send the class's study sheets home with specific items highlighted. Phone calls by teachers describing class projects helped establish exactly what Will was expected to accomplish (Will was not always accurate about the specific instructions given orally in class). When the special education teachers knew of a project, they incorporated time to work on that project into Will's special classes.

Will's drama class was also successful. The teacher let him participate as he was able, even performing at a teacher's meeting. Students' positive attitudes were important to both the French and drama classes. These teachers set the example. Will sat among other students, teachers called upon him, and they assigned him to teams to participate in activities. Will's participation was valued, as was every other student's.

Will was also the manager for two girls' varsity teams and was a member of the track team. The special education teacher was the assistant coach of the volleyball team so she was able to work with the coach to teach Will the duties of a manager. The basketball coach saw Will in action and asked for his help. The coaches expected Will to do what any manager would do, including filling in at practice for missing players and riding the bus to away games. The coaches would communicate with me and I would discuss any of Will's frustrations with them. The coaches made decisions based on Will's abilities, resulting in two "good finishes" each meet. At many track meets, the encouragement to "RUN" came from teammates and from participants and spectators from the opposing team. Our collaboration with coaches encouraged a student with a hearing impairment and his interpreter to join the team!

—By Margaret P. Weiss

EARLY CHILDHOOD PROGRAMS DESIGNED FOR PREVENTION

The 1960s witnessed the birth of infant and preschool programs for at-risk children and their families. Three such projects are the Perry Preschool Project, the Chicago Child–Parent Center (CPC) Program, and the Abecedarian Project. The first two focused on preschool children from low-income environments who were at risk for a variety of negative outcomes, including mental retardation. Both have demonstrated that early intervention can have positive long-term effects on participants, including reduction in rates of mental retardation. In the case of the Perry Preschool Project (Schweinhart & Weikart, 1993), when students who had received preschool intervention were studied again at age 27, a number of differences favored them over those who had not received the intervention:

- More had completed the twelfth grade
- Fewer had been arrested
- More owned their own homes
- Fewer had ever been on welfare
- They had a lower teenage pregnancy rate
- They earned a better-than-average income
- Classification as disabled or mentally retarded was less likely

Furthermore, a cost–benefit analysis—taking into account such things as costs of welfare and the criminal justice system and benefits of taxes on earnings—showed a return of $7.16 for every dollar invested in the Perry Preschool Project.

The most recent follow-up of participants in the CPC Program, at age 20, indicates similar results: higher school completion rates, lower juvenile arrest rates, and lower rates of grade retention and identification for special education. In fact, the rate of identification for special education was almost half that of the comparison group, which had not received early intervention (Reynolds, Temple, Robertson, & Mann, 2001).

Early intervention programs can have positive long-term effects on participants, including reduction in rates of mental retardation. ■

One of the best-known infant stimulation programs is the Abecedarian Project (Ramey & Campbell, 1984, 1987). Participants were identified before birth by selecting children from a pool of pregnant women living in poverty. After birth, the infants were randomly assigned to one of two groups: half to a day-care group that received special services, and half to a control group that received no such services. The day-care group participated in a program that provided experiences to promote perceptual-motor, intellectual, language, and social development. The families of these children also received a number of social and medical services. Results of the Abecedarian Project, reported through the age of 21, indicate that the infants from the day-care group have attained better cognitive scores and are more likely to have attended college (Campbell & Pungello, 2000).

EARLY CHILDHOOD PROGRAMS DESIGNED TO FURTHER DEVELOPMENT

Unlike preschool programs for children at risk, in which the goal is to prevent mental retardation from occurring, programs for infants and preschoolers who are already identified as mentally retarded are designed to help them achieve as high a cognitive level as possible. These programs place a great deal of emphasis on language and conceptual development. Because these children often have multiple disabilities, other professionals—for example, speech therapists and physical therapists—are frequently involved in their education. Also, many of the better programs include opportunities for parent involvement. Through practice with their children, parents can reinforce some of the skills that teachers work on. For example, parents of infants with physical disabilities, such as cerebral palsy, can learn from physical therapists the appropriate ways of handling their children to further their physical development. Similarly, parents can learn appropriate feeding techniques from speech therapists.

Transition to Adulthood

Most authorities agree that although the degree of emphasis on transition programming should be greater for older than for younger students, such programming should begin in the elementary years. Table 4.3 (see below) depicts some examples of curriculum activities across the school years pertaining to domestic, community living, leisure, and vocational skills. Transition programming for individuals with mental retardation involves two related areas—community adjustment and employment.

COMMUNITY ADJUSTMENT

For persons with mental retardation to adjust to living in the community, they need to acquire a number of skills, many of which are in the area of self-help. For example, they

TABLE 4.3   Examples of Curriculum Activities across the School Years for Domestic, Community Living, Leisure, and Vocational Skills

Skill Area			
Domestic	**Community Living**	**Leisure**	**Vocational**
Elementary school student: Tim			
Picking up toys Washing dishes Making bed Dressing Grooming Eating skills Toileting skills Sorting clothes Vacuuming	Eating meals in a restaurant Using restroom in a local restaurant Putting trash into container Choosing correct change to ride city bus Giving the clerk money for an item he wants to purchase	Climbing on swing set Playing board games Playing tag with neighbors Tumbling activities Running Playing kickball	Picking up plate, silverware, and glass after a meal Returning toys to appropriate storage space Cleaning the room at the end of the day Working on a task for a designated period (15–20 minutes)
Junior high school student: Mary			
Washing clothes Cooking a simple hot meal (soup, salad, and sandwich) Keeping bedroom clean Making snacks Mowing lawn Raking leaves Making a grocery list Purchasing items from a list Vacuuming and dusting living room	Crossing streets safely Purchasing an item from a department store Purchasing a meal at a restaurant Using local transportation system to get to and from recreational facilities Participating in local scout troop Going to neighbor's house for lunch on Saturday	Playing volleyball Taking aerobics classes Playing checkers with a friend Playing miniature golf Cycling Attending high school or local college basketball games Playing softball Swimming	Waxing floors Cleaning windows Filling lawn mower with gas Hanging and bagging clothes Bussing tables Working for 1–2 hours Operating machinery (such as dishwasher, buffer, etc.) Cleaning sinks, bathtubs, and fixtures Following a job sequence
High school student: Sandy			
Cleaning all rooms in place of residence Developing a weekly budget Cooking meals Operating thermostat to regulate heat or air conditioning Doing yard maintenance Maintaining personal needs Caring for and maintaining clothing	Utilizing bus system to move about the community Depositing checks into bank account Using community department stores Using community grocery stores Using community health facilities (physician, pharmacist)	Jogging Archery Boating Watching college basketball Video games Card games (Uno) Athletic club swimming class Gardening Going on a vacation trip	Performing required janitorial duties at J.C. Penney Performing housekeeping duties at Days Inn Performing grounds keeping duties at VCU campus Performing food service at K St. Cafeteria Performing laundry duties at Moon's Laundromat Performing photography at Virginia National Bank Headquarters

SOURCE: Adapted from P. Wehman, M. S. Moon, J. M. Everson, W. Wood, & J. M. Barcus, (1988) *Transition from school to work: New challenges for youth with severe disabilities* (Baltimore: Paul H. Brookes), pp. 140–142. Reprinted with permission.

Meeting the Needs of Students with Mental Retardation

Community-Based Instruction: Shopping for Groceries

What the Research Says

The goals for many students with mental retardation, after graduation, focus on (1) obtaining a job, (2) maintaining independent or semi-independent living, and (3) integrating themselves into the community (Patton et al., 1996). One strategy long heralded as important for supporting such goals is community-based instruction (CBI) (Browder & Snell, 2000). In CBI students first learn the skills needed to function in community settings and then, have the opportunity to apply those skills in real-life (in vivo) situations. Common elements of CBI include: task analysis of the community-based skill, instruction in the classroom prior to application in the community, and support for generalization of the classroom-taught skill to the community (Hughes & Agran, 1993).

Research Study

One team of investigators used CBI to teach students with moderate mental retardation how to shop for groceries (Morse & Schuster, 2000). The ability to grocery shop encompasses important subskills such as math computation and problem-solving skills, social interaction skills, and fine and gross motor skills. In this study, instruction took place in the classroom and in a local grocery store. Prior to instruction, the researchers created a twenty-eight-step task analysis—a step-by-step sequence of skills the students would need to follow in order to successfully retrieve and purchase the items in a grocery store. The task analysis served as a blueprint for instruction.

During classroom-based training, students used a pictorial storyboard to help them learn about the location of the items they were to purchase at the grocery store. Students were systematically taught the step-by-step procedures for grocery shopping by learning to correctly place thirteen pictures that represented the task analysis on a storyboard. While students were in the grocery store, the teacher used a constant time delay procedure (Schuster et al., 1998) to support instruction. In this case,

the constant time delay was a 0-second delay during the first two training trials and a 4-second delay in subsequent trials. That is, when the students were first in the store the teacher would provide a prompt (e.g., "Pick up a handbasket") and then wait 0 seconds to deliver the controlling prompt, in this case modeling the desired activity. In the subsequent trials, the teacher waited 4 seconds before modeling.

Research Findings

The majority of students in the study were not only able to purchase items successfully from the grocery store, they maintained these skills six weeks after the intervention and were able to generalize the skills to a different grocery store. Studies such as this one demonstrate the effectiveness of classroom-based instruction supported by in vivo application, particularly when teachers employ such features as task analysis, constant time delay, and pictorial storyboards.

Applying the Research to Teaching

Classroom teachers can apply the strategies used in the study to teach many different skills. To implement this model of instruction, teachers first identify the skill/task they would like to teach. In many cases, IEP goals serve as an excellent guide for identifying educationally relevant tasks. Teachers should then conduct a task analysis. This requires identifying all the subskills that lead to completing the task successfully. Using the task analysis as a guide, the teacher teaches the subskills in isolation or as a part of the sequence until the student has mastered the task. Finally, the student should practice the task in real-life settings or situations. The constant time delay procedure has been shown to be extremely effective in supporting skill development and can be used by classroom teachers in both the classroom setting and in community settings.

—By Kristin L. Sayeski

need to be able to manage money, use public transportation, and keep themselves well groomed and their living quarters well maintained. They also need to have good social skills so they can get along with persons in the community. In general, research has shown that attempts to train for community survival skills can be successful, especially when the training occurs within the actual setting in which the individuals live.

Although large residential facilities for persons with mental retardation still exist, they are fast disappearing. There is a trend toward smaller **community residential facilities (CRFs).** CRFs, or group homes, accommodate small groups (three to ten people) in houses under the direction of "house parents." Placement can be permanent, or it can serve as a temporary arrangement to prepare them for independent living. In either case, the purpose of the CRF is to teach independent living skills in a more normal setting than a large institution offers.

Some professionals are questioning whether CRFs go far enough in offering opportunities for integration into the community. They are recommending **supported living,** whereby persons with mental retardation receive supports to live in more natural, noninstitutional settings such as their own home or apartment. Supported living means

> rejecting the notion of a continuum of residential services, with its attendant focus on "care and treatment" designed to teach people skills that will result in their moving to the next less restrictive residential setting, in favor of supporting people to experience community presence and participation in homes of their own. . . . Rather than fitting people into existing residential facilities (e.g., group homes) that offer prepackaged services of a particular kind and level, supported living involves developing support that is matched to a person's specific needs and preferences and changing that support as the person's needs and preferences change. . . . (Howe, Horner, & Newton, 1998, pp. 1–2)

There is some evidence that supported living arrangements lead to a higher level of self-determination in persons with mental retardation than do CRFs (Stancliffe, Abery, & Smith, 2000).

More and more authorities point to the family as a critical factor in whether persons with mental retardation will be successful in community adjustment and employment. Even though many hold up supported living as an ideal, the fact is that the vast majority of adults with mental retardation live with their families (MR/DD Data Brief, 2001). And even for those who live away from home, the family can still be a significant source of support for living in the community and finding and holding jobs.

EMPLOYMENT

Traditionally, employment figures for adults with mental retardation have been appalling. For example, in the most thorough national survey, researchers found that three to five years after exiting secondary school only 37 percent of persons with mental retardation were competitively employed (Blackorby & Wagner, 1996).

Even though employment statistics for workers who are retarded have been uncouraging, most professionals working in this area are optimistic about the potential for providing training programs that will lead to meaningful employment for these adults. Research indicates that with appropriate training, persons with mental retardation can hold down jobs with a good deal of success, measured by such things as attendance, employer satisfaction, and length of employment (Brown et al., 1986; Nietupski, Hamre-Nietupski, VanderHart, & Fishback, 1996; Stodden & Browder, 1986).

When persons with mental retardation are not successful on the job, the cause more often involves behaviors related to job responsibility and social skills than to job performance per se (Butterworth & Strauch, 1994; Heal, Gonzalez, Rusch, Copher, & DeStefano, 1990; Salzberg, Lignugaris/Kraft, & McCuller, 1988). In other words, the problem

Community residential facility (CRF).
A place, usually a group home, in an urban or residential neighborhood where about three to ten adults with mental retardation live under supervision.

Supported living.
An approach to living arrangements for those with mental retardation that stresses living in natural settings rather than institutions, big or small.

Sheltered workshop.
A facility that provides a structured environment for persons with disabilities in which they can learn skills; can be either a transitional placement or a permanent arrangement.

Competitive employment.
A workplace that provides employment that pays at least minimum wage and in which most workers are nondisabled.

Supported competitive employment.
A workplace where adults who are disabled earn at least minimum wage and receive ongoing assistance from a specialist or job coach; the majority of workers in the workplace are nondisabled.

Job coach.
A person who assists adult workers with disabilities (especially those with mental retardation), providing vocational assessment, instruction, overall planning, and interaction assistance with employers, family, and related government and service agencies.

is not so much that people with mental retardation cannot perform the job as it is that they have difficulty with such issues as attendance, initiative, responding to criticism, and interacting socially with co-workers and supervisors. This latter problem—social interaction—most consistently distinguishes workers who are mentally retarded from those who are not.

A variety of vocational training and employment approaches for individuals with mental retardation are available. Most of these are subsumed under two very different kinds of arrangements—the sheltered workshop and supported competitive employment.

Sheltered Workshops   The traditional job-training environment for adults with mental retardation, especially those classified as more severely mentally retarded, has been the sheltered workshop. A **sheltered workshop** is a structured environment where a person receives training and works with other workers with disabilities on jobs requiring relatively low skills. This can be either a permanent placement or a transitional placement before a person obtains a job in the competitive job market.

More and more authorities are voicing dissatisfaction with sheltered workshops. Among the criticisms are the following:

1. Workers make very low wages because sheltered workshops rarely turn a profit. Usually managed by personnel with limited business management expertise, they rely heavily on charitable contributions.
2. There is no integration of workers who are disabled with those who are nondisabled. This restricted setting makes it difficult to prepare workers who are mentally retarded for working side by side with nondisabled workers in the competitive workforce.
3. Sheltered workshops offer only limited job-training experiences. A good workshop should provide opportunities for trainees to learn a variety of new skills. All too often, however, the work is repetitive and does not make use of current industrial technology.

Supported Competitive Employment   In contrast to sheltered employment, **competitive employment** is an approach that provides jobs for at least the minimum wage in integrated work settings in which most of the workers are not disabled. In **supported competitive employment,** the person with mental retardation has a competitive employment position but receives ongoing assistance, often from a **job coach.** In addition to on-the-job training, the job coach may provide assistance in related areas, such as finding an appropriate job, interactions with employers and other employees, use of transportation, and involvement with other agencies.

In comparison to sheltered workshops, supported competitive employment is more in keeping with the philosophy of self-determination, which we discussed in Chapter 2 and earlier in this chapter. However, in order to achieve the goal of self-determination, it is important that clients not become too dependent on their job coach. For this reason, the role of the job coach has been changing in recent years. Many now advocate that the job coach involve co-workers of persons with mental retardation as trainers and/or mentors (Mank, Cioffi, & Yovanoff, 2000). After a period of time, the worker can be weaned from relying on the job coach and can learn to use more natural supports. Recall the quotation at the beginning of the chapter (p. 109), in which Sandra Kaufman talks about the change in philosophy toward the use of natural supports in the form of relatives, neighbors, friends, and co-workers rather than social agency personnel.

Not surprisingly, workers who are mentally retarded report higher job satisfaction in supported competitive employment than in sheltered workshops (Test, Carver, Ewers, Haddad, & Person, 2000). Researchers have found that movement from sheltered work environments to supported employment has proved cost-effective for society; moreover, this approach has resulted in a 500 percent increase in salaries for workers with mental retardation (McCaughrin, Ellis, Rusch, & Heal, 1993; Revell, Wehman, Kregel, West, & Rayfield, 1994). Although the ultimate goal for some adults with mental retardation may be competitive employment, many will need supported employment for a period of time or even permanently.

The use of supported competitive employment has grown dramatically. However, the number of workers in sheltered workshops still far outnumbers those in competitive employment. According to a recent study of national data on persons with mental retardation receiving vocational services, only 16 percent were in competitive employment, whereas 50 percent were in noncompetitive employment (Olney & Kennedy, 2001).

PROSPECTS FOR THE FUTURE

Current employment figures and living arrangements for adults with mental retardation may look bleak, but there is reason to be optimistic about the future. Evidence shows that employers are taking a more favorable attitude toward hiring workers who are mentally retarded (Nietupski et al., 1996). And outcomes for adults with mental retardation are improving, albeit slowly, with respect to employment and living arrangements (Frank & Sitlington, 2000). As Kaufman noted at the beginning of the chapter, with the development of innovative transition programs, many persons with mental retardation are achieving levels of independence in community living and employment that were never thought possible.

Summary

Professionals are generally more cautious about identifying students as mentally retarded than they once were because (1) there has been a history of misidentifying students from minority groups, (2) the label "mental retardation" may have harmful consequences for students, and (3) some believe that, to a certain extent, mental retardation is socially constructed. Changes in the definition of the American Association on Mental Retardation over the years reflect this cautious attitude toward identification. The current AAMR definition continues three trends: (1) a broadening of the definition beyond the single criterion of an IQ score (adaptive skills are also considered), (2) a lowering of the IQ score used as a cutoff, and (3) a view of mental retardation as a condition that can be improved.

The AAMR has traditionally classified persons as having *mild, moderate, severe,* or *profound* retardation based on their IQ scores. Currently, however, the AAMR recommends classification according to the level of support needed: *intermittent, limited, extensive,* or *pervasive.* Several authorities have been critical of the AAMR classification system on the grounds that it goes too far in denying the existence of mental retardation within a person and that it is more straightforward to classify individuals based on levels of severity. Two other definitions have been offered, those of the American Psychological Association and the American Psychiatric Association. They are essentially the same as the current AAMR definition, with one important exception:

They retain the use of the traditional classifications of mild, moderate, severe, and profound.

From a purely statistical-theoretical perspective, 2.27 percent of the population should score low enough on an IQ test (below about 70) to qualify as mentally retarded. Figures indicate, however, that about 1 to 1.5 percent of the population is identified as mentally retarded. The discrepancy may be due to school personnel using low adaptive behavior as well as low IQ as criteria for mental retardation, plus the tendency to prefer to have students labeled "learning disabled" rather than "mentally retarded" because they perceive it as less stigmatizing.

There are a variety of causes of mental retardation. The AAMR categorizes them according to time of occurrence: prenatal (before birth), perinatal (at time of birth), and postnatal (after birth). Prenatal causes can be grouped into (1) chromosomal disorders, (2) inborn errors of metabolism, (3) developmental disorders affecting brain formation, and (4) environmental influences. Some of the most common chromosome disorders are Down syndrome, Williams syndrome, fragile X syndrome, and Prader-Willi syndrome. Down syndrome and Williams syndrome result from chromosomal abnormalities but are not inherited as such. Fragile X and Prader-Willi are inherited. PKU is an example of a cause due to an inborn error of metabolism—the inability of the body to convert phenylalanine to tyrosine. Microcephalus and hydrocephalus are examples of disorders of brain formation. Examples of causes due to environmental influences are maternal malnutrition, fetal alcohol syndrome, and rubella (German measles). Using amniocentesis, chorionic villus sampling, sonography, and maternal serum screening, physicians are now able to detect a variety of defects in the unborn fetus.

Perinatal causes include anoxia (lack of oxygen), low birthweight, and infections such as syphilis and herpes simplex.

Postnatal causes can be grouped into biological and psychosocial causes. Biological causes include traumatic brain injury and infections such as meningitis and encephalitis. Psychosocial causes, involving an unstimulating environment, are thought to be the most common reasons for mild mental retardation. Some use the term *cultural-familial mental retardation* to refer to causes related to poor environmental and/or hereditary factors. Although the nature–nurture debate has raged for years, most authorities now believe that the interaction between heredity and the environment is important in determining intelligence.

Two of the most common IQ tests are the Stanford-Binet and the Wechsler Intelligence Scale for Children. The latter has verbal and performance subscales. Some professionals recommend using the Kauffman Assessment Battery for Children (K–ABC) with African American students because they believe it less culturally biased.

There are several cautions in using and interpreting IQ tests: (1) an individual's IQ score can change; (2) all IQ tests are culturally biased to some extent; (3) the younger the child, the less reliable the results; and (4) a person's ability to live a successful and fulfilling life does not depend solely on his or her IQ. In addition to IQ tests, several adaptive behavior scales are available.

Persons with mental retardation have learning problems related to attention, memory (especially working memory), language development, academic achievement, self-regulation, social development, and motivation. An important concept related to self-regulation is metacognition—the awareness of what strategies are needed to perform a task and the ability to use self-regulatory mechanisms before, during, and after performing a task.

Researchers are beginning to link genetic syndromes to particular behavioral patterns, or phenotypes. For example, Down syndrome is characterized by poor expressive language but relatively strong visual-spatial skills, whereas Williams syndrome is associated with relatively high verbal skills and relatively low visual-spatial skills.

Education for students with mental retardation has been heavily influenced by the related philosophies of inclusion and self-determination. Self-determination—the ability to make personal choices, to regulate one's life, and to be a self-advocate—does not come easily for students who are mentally retarded and must be taught.

Educational goals for students with mild mental retar-

dation emphasize readiness skills at younger ages and functional academics, community adjustment, and vocational training at older ages. Functional academics are for the purpose of enabling the person to function independently. Educational programs for students with more severe mental retardation are characterized by (1) systematic instruction, (2) instruction in real-life settings with real materials, and (3) functional behavioral assessment and positive behavioral support. Systematic instruction includes instructional prompts, consequences for performance, and transfer of stimulus control, including constant and progressive time delay. *In vivo* instruction using real materials is preferable to instruction that only occurs in the classroom. Functional behavioral assessment involves determining the consequences, antecedents, and setting events of behaviors. Positive behavioral support emphasizes modifying the total environment to support positive behavior of all students rather than focusing on punishing inappropriate behavior.

Depending to a large extent on the degree of mental retardation or the need for support, students with mental retardation may be in learning environments ranging from regular classrooms to residential institutions. The most popular placement continues to be the special class, but more and more students are being educated in the general education classroom.

Preschool programs differ in their goals according to whether they are aimed at preventing mental retardation or furthering the development of children already identified as mentally retarded. For the most part, the former types of programs are aimed at children at risk of developing mild mental retardation, whereas the latter are for children with more severe mental retardation. Research supports the clear link between such interventions and success later in life.

Programming for transition to adulthood includes goals related to domestic living, community living, leisure, and vocational skills. Although the emphasis on transition programming increases with age, authorities recommend that such efforts begin in elementary school. Large residential institutions are on the decline. Most adults with mental retardation living outside the family usually live in community-based facilities, or group homes, which accommodate from three to ten persons with mental retardation. However, there is a trend toward supported living arrangements, in which they live in more natural settings such as their own home or apartment. Even with these efforts toward more independent living, however, most adults who are mentally retarded live with their families.

The employment picture for workers with mental retardation is changing. Although sheltered work environments remain the most common setting, authorities have pointed out their weaknesses: (1) wages are very low, (2) there is no integration with nondisabled workers, and (3) they offer only limited job-training experiences. Placement of workers who are mentally retarded in supported competitive employment has increased dramatically since its inception in the early 1980s. The role of the job coach is critical to the success of supported competitive employment arrangements. The job coach provides on-the-job training as well as such things as helping the worker with job selection, interactions with other workers and the employer, use of transportation, and using other agencies.

The job coach's role is changing to take advantage of natural supports. To reduce reliance on the job coach, nondisabled co-workers are being trained to be mentors and trainers of employees who are mentally retarded. Although employment figures are still discouraging, the growth in innovative programs gives reason to be hopeful about the future of community living and employment for adults with mental retardation.

Rebecca Bella Rich

The Family, Ink, watercolor on rag paper. 15 × 11 in.

Ms. Rich, who was born in 1960 in Cambridge, Massachusetts, has a dramatic sensibility. Her life, art, and poetry have an extravagant and flamboyant quality. She has produced an autobiographical performance video and a book of interviews with artists who are challenged by disabilities.

Learners with Learning Disabilities

As much as I want to find the perfect words to express what it is like to be dyslexic, I cannot. I can no more make you understand what it is like to be dyslexic than you can make me understand what it is like not to be. I can only guess and imagine. For years, I have looked out, wanting to be normal, to shed the skin that limits me, that holds me back. All the while, others have looked upon me, as well. There were those who have pitied me and those who have just given up on me, those who stood by, supporting me and believing in me, and those who looked at me as if I were an exhibit in a zoo. But, in general, people have shown a desire to understand what dyslexia is and how to teach those afflicted with it. Each side, it seems, longs to understand the other.

LYNN PELKEY
"In the LD Bubble"

For other first-person accounts of having a learning disability, visit http://www.ldonline.org/first_person/first_person_archives.html

This is a page contained on the LD-Online Web site. LD-Online is a service of the Learning Project of WETA in Washington, DC. Visit the LD-Online home page for more information on learning disabilities: http://www.ldonline.org/ ■

ynn Pelkey's comment about having dyslexia, or reading disability (see p. 147), should provide some degree of solace to researchers, teachers, parents, and policy makers, who have struggled to define *learning disabilities* since its formal recognition by the federal government in the 1960s. Pelkey has one specific, albeit the most common, form of learning disabilities—a reading disability. Yet even after having lived with the condition for 35 years, she is still unable to articulate its essence.

That she and the best of theoreticians and practitioners are unable to define *learning disabilities* in precise language, however, does not mean her disability is not real. If you were to go on to read the rest of her story, you would find that like the millions of others who have learning disabilities, she faced tremendous challenges not only academically but also socially.

Reading the rest of her story, you would also find that Pelkey was able eventually to overcome her feelings of rejection, successfully hold a job, and receive an associate's degree with honors from a community college. Her success, however, came not only from hard work and the support of others (as she notes in the quote on p. 147), but also from coming to terms with her learning disability: "Not long ago, it became very clear to me that I would have to come face-to-face with my feelings about being stupid if I was going to find peace within myself" (Pelkey, 2001, p. 27). As we discuss later in this chapter, being able to take control of one's life is what often separates persons with learning disabilities who function successfully as adults from those who do not.

The struggle to elucidate the nature of learning disabilities has traditionally led to professional turmoil over the best ways to educate such students. At least two factors have contributed to this confusion:

1. The enigma of children who are not mentally retarded but who have severe academic problems has often led parents of these children, as well as professionals, to seek quick-and-easy "miracle" cures. We now recognize that in most cases learning disability is a lifelong condition with which a person must learn to cope.
2. The field of learning disabilities is a relatively new category of special education, having been recognized by the federal government in 1969. It is also now the largest category, constituting over half of all students identified as eligible for special education. Much professional and popular media exposure has focused on this rapidly expanding category, creating a hotbed in which controversies can ferment.

Although the field of learning disabilities has had to struggle to overcome its penchant for questionable practices and to survive the intense scrutiny of professionals and the lay public, most who work within this field are happy to be part of it. For them, controversy and ambiguity only add excitement to the already challenging task of educating students with learning disabilities. And as the field has matured, there is now much more consensus regarding key issues. For example, research evidence has converged to help us understand the causes of learning disabilities, as well as the best educational treatment approaches.

Two related controversies, however, that have continued to nag the field are those of definition and identification procedures.

Definition

At a parents' meeting in New York City in the early 1960s, Samuel Kirk proposed the term *learning disabilities* as a compromise because of the confusing variety of labels then used to describe the child with relatively normal intelligence who was having learning problems. Such a child was likely to be referred to as *minimally brain injured,* a *slow learner, dyslexic,* or *perceptually disabled.*

Learners with Learning Disabilities

MYTH IQ–achievement discrepancies are easily calculated.	**FACT** A complicated formula determines a discrepancy between a student's IQ and his or her achievement.
MYTH All students with learning disabilities are brain damaged.	**FACT** Many authorities now refer to students with learning disabilities as having central nervous system (CNS) *dysfunction*, which suggests a malfunctioning of the brain rather than actual tissue damage.
MYTH The fact that so many definitions of *learning disabilities* have been proposed is an indicator that the field is in chaos.	**FACT** Although there have been at least eleven definitions proposed at one time or another, professionals have settled on two—the federal definition and the National Joint Committee on Learning Disabilities definition. And although they differ in some ways, these two definitions have a lot in common.
MYTH The rapid increase in the prevalence of learning disabilities is due solely to sloppy diagnostic practices.	**FACT** Although poor diagnostic practices may account for some of the increase, there are plausible social/cultural reasons for the increase. In addition, there is evidence that school personnel may "bend" the rules to identify students as learning disabled instead of the more stigmatizing identification of "mentally retarded."
MYTH We know very little about what causes learning disabilities.	**FACT** Although there is no simple clinical test for determining the cause of learning disabilities in individual cases, recent research strongly suggests causes related to neurological dysfunction resulting from genetic, teratogenic, or medical factors.
MYTH Standardized achievement tests are the most useful kind of assessment for teachers of students with learning disabilities.	**FACT** Standardized achievement tests do not provide much information about *why* a student has achievement difficulties. Formative, informal, and authentic assessments give teachers a better idea of the particular strengths and weaknesses of a student.
MYTH Math disabilities are relatively rare.	**FACT** Math disabilities are second only to reading as an area of academic difficulty for students with learning disabilities.
MYTH We need not be concerned about the social-emotional well-being of students with learning disabilities because their problems are in academics.	**FACT** Many students with learning disabilities also develop problems in the social-emotional area.
MYTH Most children with learning disabilities outgrow their disabilities as adults.	**FACT** Learning disabilities tend to endure into adulthood. Most individuals with learning disabilities who are successful must learn to cope with their problems and make extraordinary efforts to gain control of their lives.
MYTH For persons with learning disabilities, IQ and achievement are the best predictors of success in adulthood.	**FACT** The best predictors of success for adults with learning disabilities are perseverance, goal-setting, realistic acceptance of weaknesses and ability to build on strengths, exposure to intensive and long-term educational intervention, and especially the ability to take control of their lives.

Educators have struggled to formulate a clear and comprehensive definition of the term *learning disability*, which generally describes children of seemingly normal intelligence who, nevertheless, have learning problems. ■

Minimal brain injury.
A term used to describe a child who shows behavioral but not neurological signs of brain injury; the term is not as popular as it once was, primarily because of its lack of diagnostic utility (i.e., some children who learn normally show signs indicative of minimal brain injury).

ₘ The Learning Disabilities Association of America remains the major parent organization for learning disabilities. Its Web site at http://www.ldanatl.org/ contains a variety of information on learning disabilities for parents and professionals. ■

Many parents as well as teachers, however, believed the label "minimal brain injury" to be problematic. **Minimal brain injury** refers to individuals who show behavioral but not neurological signs of brain injury. They exhibit behaviors (e.g., distractibility, hyperactivity, and perceptual disturbances) similar to those of people with real brain injury, but their neurological examinations are indistinguishable from those of nondisabled individuals.

Historically, the diagnosis of minimal brain injury was sometimes dubious because it was based on questionable behavioral evidence rather than on more solid neurological data. Moreover, minimal brain injury was not an educationally meaningful term because such a diagnosis offered little real help in planning and implementing treatment. The term *slow learner* described the child's performance in some areas but not in others—and besides, intelligence testing indicated that the ability to learn existed. *Dyslexic,* too, fell short as a definitive term because it described only reading disabilities, and many of these children had problems in other academic areas, such as math. To describe a child as *perceptually disabled* just confused the issue further, for perceptual problems might be only part of a puzzling inability to learn. So the New York parents' group finally agreed on the educationally oriented term *learning disabilities*. Accordingly, they founded the Association for Children with Learning Disabilities, now known as the Learning Disabilities Association of America. A few years later, following the lead of the parents, professionals and the federal government officially recognized the term as well.

The interest in learning disabilities evolved as a result of a growing awareness that a large number of children were not receiving needed educational services. Because they were within the normal range of intelligence, these children did not qualify for placement in classes for children with mental retardation. And although many of them did show inappropriate behavior disturbances, some of them did not. Thus, it was felt that placement in classes for students with emotional disturbance was inappropriate. Parents of children who were not achieving at their expected potential—children who are learning disabled—wanted their children's academic achievement problems corrected.

FACTORS TO CONSIDER IN DEFINITIONS OF LEARNING DISABILITIES

Eleven different definitions of learning disabilities have enjoyed some degree of acceptance since the field's inception in the early 1960s (Hammill, 1990). Created by individual professionals and committees of professionals and lawmakers, each definition provides a slightly different slant. Three factors—each of which is included in some definitions, but not all—have historically caused considerable controversy:

1. Presumption of central nervous system dysfunction
2. Psychological processing disorders
3. IQ–achievement discrepancy

The first two are now less controversial than they once were, but the last one remains contentious.

Central Nervous System Dysfunction   Many of the theoretical concepts and teaching methods associated with the field of learning disabilities grew out of work done in the 1930s and 1940s with children who were mentally retarded and brain injured (Werner & Strauss, 1941). When the field of learning disabilities was emerging, professionals noted that many of these children displayed behavioral characteristics (e.g., distractibility, hyperactivity, language problems, perceptual disturbances) similar to those exhibited by persons known to have brain damage, such as, those having suffered a stroke or a head wound.

In the case of most children with learning disabilities, however, there is little neurological evidence of actual *damage* to brain tissues. Therefore, today, the term *dysfunction* has come to replace *injury* or *damage*. Thus, a child with learning disabilities is now often referred to as having central nervous system (CNS) dysfunction rather than brain injury. Dysfunction does not necessarily mean tissue damage; instead, it signifies a malfunctioning of the brain, or central nervous system.

At one time, there was little evidence, other than the behavioral symptoms noted above, that children with learning disabilities actually had CNS dysfunction. However, as we discuss in the section on causes (see pp. 155–158), with the advent of neuroimaging technology, that picture is changing.

Psychological Processing Disorders   The field of learning disabilities was founded on the assumption that children with such disabilities have deficits in the ability to perceive and interpret visual and auditory stimuli—that is, they have psychological processing problems. These problems are not the same as the visual and auditory acuity problems evidenced in blindness or deafness. Rather, they are difficulties in organizing and interpreting visual and auditory stimuli.

Many of the early advocates of this viewpoint, however, also believed that training students in visual- and auditory-processing skills in isolation from academic material would help them conquer their reading problems (Frostig & Horne, 1964; Kephart, 1971; Kirk & Kirk, 1971). For instance, such training might involve finding and tracing figures embedded within other lines or connecting dots as a teacher draws them on a chalkboard. Researchers ultimately determined that these perceptual and perceptual-motor exercises did not result in benefits for students' reading achievement (see Hallahan, 1975; Hallahan & Cruickshank, 1973 for reviews); thus, very few teachers use these practices today.

Even though perceptual training was found to be ineffective, researchers have found that many students with learning disabilities do indeed have such information-processing problems. For example, as we discuss in the section on behavioral characteristics (see pp. 161–168), particular processing skills are associated with reading disabilities (Torgesen, 2001).

IQ–Achievement Discrepancy   A child with an **IQ–achievement discrepancy** is not achieving up to potential as measured by a standardized intelligence test. Professionals have used a number of methods to determine such a discrepancy. For many years they simply compared the mental age obtained from an intelligence test to the grade-age equivalent taken from a standardized achievement test. A difference of two years was often con-

IQ–achievement discrepancy. Academic performance markedly lower than would be expected based on a student's intellectual ability.

sidered enough to indicate a learning disability. Two years below expected grade level is not equally serious at different grade levels, however. For example, a child who tests two years below grade 8 has a less severe deficit than one who tests two years below grade 4. So professionals have developed formulas that take into account the relative ages of the students.

Although some states and school districts have adopted different formulas for identifying IQ–achievement discrepancies, many authorities have advised against their use. Some of the formulas are statistically flawed and lead to inaccurate judgments, and those that are statistically adequate are difficult and expensive to implement. Furthermore, they give a false sense of precision. That is, they tempt school personnel to reduce to a single score the complex and important decision of identifying a learning disability.

In addition to the problem of using formulas, some authorities have objected to using an IQ–achievement discrepancy to identify learning disabilities on other conceptual grounds (Fletcher et al., 2001). For example, some authorities have pointed out that IQ is not a very strong predictor of reading ability. And IQ scores of students with learning disabilities are subject to underestimation because performance on IQ tests is dependent on reading ability, to some extent. In other words, students with poor reading skills have difficulty expanding their vocabularies and learning about the world. As a result, they obtain lower-than-average scores on IQ tests, which lessens the discrepancy between IQ and achievement. Finally, some educators have pointed out that the idea of discrepancy is practically useless in the earliest elementary grades. In the first or second grade, a child is not expected to have achieved very much in reading or math, so it would be difficult to find a discrepancy.

Even with all these problems, the vast majority of states use some kind of IQ–achievement discrepancy in order to identify students as learning disabled, probably because of the observation that there continue to be children who have normal intelligence yet do not achieve up to their expected performance. As we discuss later (see the box on p. 153), there is some doubt about whether school personnel will continue to use a discrepancy in identifying learning disabilities. However, if they do so, the most reasonable position is not to use the IQ–achievement discrepancy as the sole criterion for determining a learning disability (Kavale, 2001) and to shy away from the use of formulas to calculate discrepancies.

We turn now to two of the most popular definitions: The federal definition and the National Joint Committee for Learning Disabilities definition.

THE FEDERAL DEFINITION

The majority of states use a definition based on the definition of the federal government. This definition, first signed into law in 1977, was—with a few minor wording changes—adopted again in 1997 by the federal government:

A. GENERAL—The term "specific learning disability" means a disorder in one or more of the basic psychological processes involved in understanding or in using language, spoken or written, which disorder may manifest itself in an imperfect ability to listen, think, speak, read, write, spell, or do mathematical calculations.

B. DISORDERS INCLUDED—Such term includes such conditions as perceptual disabilities, brain injury, minimal brain dysfunction, dyslexia, and developmental aphasia.

C. DISORDERS NOT INCLUDED—Such term does not include a learning problem that is primarily the result of visual, hearing, or motor disabilities, of mental retardation, of emotional disturbance, or of environmental, cultural, or economic disadvantage. [Individuals with Disabilities Education Act Amendments of 1997, Sec. 602(26), p. 13.]

Reauthorization of IDEA: Implications for the Definition and Identification Procedures for Learning Disabilities

There have been many questions raised about the federal definition of learning disabilities and even more questions raised regarding the federal regulations' reference to an IQ–achievement discrepancy criterion for use in identifying students as learning disabled. These questions, coupled with concerns about the growing numbers of students identified as learning disabled, led officials at the U.S. Department of Education's Office of Special Education Programs (OSEP) to mount a Learning Disabilities Initiative beginning in 2000. The purpose of the initiative was to arrive at agreement among researchers, parents, and practitioners about identification procedures that could become part of the impending reauthorization of IDEA scheduled for 2002 or 2003.

OSEP commissioned nine White Papers on topics pertaining to identification of learning disabilities:

- Jenkins, J., & O'Connor, R. (2001, August). *Early identification and intervention for children with reading/ learning disabilities.*
- Fletcher, J.M., Lyon, G.R., Barnes, M., Stuebing, K.K., Francis, D.J., Olson, R.K., Shaywitz, S.E., & Shaywitz, B.A. (2001, August). *Classification of learning disabilities: An evidence-based evaluation.*
- Hallahan, D.P., & Mercer, C.D. (2001, August). *Learning disabilities: Historical perspectives.*
- MacMillan, D.L., & Siperstein, G.N. (2001, August). *Learning disabilities as operationally defined by schools.*
- Kavale, K.A. (2001, August). *Discrepancy models in the identification of learning disability.*
- Gresham, F. (2001, August). *Responsiveness to intervention: An alternative approach to the identification of learning disabilities.*
- Torgesen, J. (2001, August). *Empirical and theoretical support for direct diagnosis of learning disabilities by assessment of intrinsic processing weaknesses.*
- Wise, B.W., & Snyder, L. (2001, August). *Judgments in identifying and teaching children with language-based reading difficulties.*

- Fuchs, D., Fuchs, L.S., Mathes, P.G., Lipsey, M.W., & Roberts, P.H. (2001, August). *Is "learning disabilities" just a fancy term for low achievement? A meta-analysis of reading differences between low achievers with and without the label.*

These papers, along with respondents' comments, were presented in August 2001 at the Learning Disabilities Summit: Building a Foundation for the Future, which was keynoted by the U.S. Secretary of Education, Rod Paige, and broadcast on C-Span 2. Over 200 representatives from parent, professional, and government ranks were in attendance.

At this time it is difficult to predict what specific recommendations from these papers OSEP will use in the reauthorization process. The following are some of the possibilities:

- *Retain the use of the IQ–achievement discrepancy.* However, make sure that statistically appropriate methods are used and that discrepancy is not used as the sole criterion for identification as learning disabled. In other words, treat IQ–achievement discrepancy as a necessary but not sufficient criterion (Kavale, 2001).
- *Eliminate IQ-achievement and use measures of psychological processing.* In the area of reading, in particular, administer tests of phonological awareness. This processing domain has been found deficient in many students with reading problems (Torgesen, 2001). (We discuss phonological awareness, the ability to understand the rules by which sounds go with letters to make up words, more fully on p. 162.)
- *Eliminate IQ-achievement and use "failure to respond to intervention."* Using this approach, students would not be identified as learning disabled until after they were provided with an effective instructional intervention in the general education classroom but still failed to achieve at a rate and level equal, or nearly equal, to peers in that classroom (Fuchs & Fuchs, 1998a; Gresham, 2001).

THE NATIONAL JOINT COMMITTEE FOR LEARNING DISABILITIES (NJCLD) DEFINITION

The National Joint Committee on Learning Disabilities (NJCLD), made up of representatives of several professional organizations, has issued an alternative definition:

Much of the research on learning disabilities has focused on psychological processing problems, or deficits in the ability to perceive and interpret visual and auditory stimuli. ■

"Learning disabilities is a general term that refers to a heterogeneous group of disorders manifested by significant difficulties in the acquisition and use of listening, speaking, reading, writing, reasoning, or mathematical abilities. These disorders are intrinsic to the individual, presumed to be due to central nervous system dysfunction, and may occur across the life span. Problems in self-regulatory behaviors, social perception and social interaction may exist with learning disabilities but do not by themselves constitute a learning disability.

Although learning disabilities may occur concomitantly with other handicapping conditions (for example, sensory impairment, mental retardation, serious emotional disturbance) or with extrinsic influences (such as cultural differences, insufficient or inappropriate instruction), they are not the result of those conditions or influences." (National Joint Committee on Learning Disabilities, 1989, p. 1)

SIMILARITIES AND DIFFERENCES IN THE FEDERAL AND NJCLD DEFINITIONS

There are some important similarities in the federal and NJCLD definitions. Both view central nervous system dysfunction as a potential cause; specify that listening, speaking, reading, writing, and math can be affected; and exclude learning problems due primarily to other conditions (e.g., mental retardation, emotional disturbance, cultural differences).

There are also some important differences between the two definitions. The authors of the NJCLD definition point out that it does not use the phrase *basic psychological processes,* which has been so controversial (because such processes are not observable and hence difficult to measure), and does not mention perceptual handicaps, dyslexia, or minimal brain dysfunction, which have been so difficult to define (Hammill, Leigh, McNutt, & Larsen, 1981). Furthermore, the NJCLD definition clearly states that a learning disability may be a lifelong condition.

As of the printing of this text, the federal government's conceptualization of learning disabilities also stressed the notion of an IQ–achievement discrepancy, as discussed earlier. Although such a discrepancy is not part of the definition, the federal regulations for identifying learning disabilities refer to a severe discrepancy between intellectual ability and academic achievement. And it is the practice of using an IQ–achievement discrepancy that has led many authorities to reconsider what procedures we should use to determine whether students have learning disabilities.

TOWARD A NEW OR REVISED DEFINITION OF LEARNING DISABILITIES?

As the ninth edition of this book goes to press, the future of the 1997 federal definition of learning disabilities and, especially, the use of an IQ–achievement discrepancy for identification of learning disabilities are uncertain. The Individuals with Disabilities Education Act is scheduled for congressional reauthorization sometime in 2002 or 2003. The reauthorization may result in a change in definition and/or identification procedures for learning disabilities (see the box on p. 153). (Consult our companion Web site www.ablongman.com/hallahan9e for the most up-to-date information regarding the reauthorization, generally, and the learning disabilities definition, specifically.)

ʕⱳ To see an executive summary of each of the papers from the Learning Disabilities Summit, as well as videos of the presenters, visit: http://www.air.org/LDsummit/default .htm

The full papers, as well as those of respondents, are included in: Danielson, L., Bradley, R., & Hallahan, D.P. (Eds.), (2002). *Identification of learning disabilities: Research to practice.* Mahwah, NJ: Lawrence Erlbaum. ■

ʕⱳ For the most up-to-date information on the reauthorization of IDEA visit:

http://www.ed.gov/offices/OSERS/

http://www.ed.gov/inits/commissionsboards/whspecialeducation/index .html ■

Prevalence

According to figures kept by the U.S. government, the public schools have identified as learning disabled between 5 and 6 percent of students six to seventeen years of age. Learning disabilities is by far the largest category of special education. More than half of all students identified by the public schools as needing special education are learning disabled. The size of the learning disabilities category has more than doubled since 1976–1977, when prevalence figures first started being kept by the federal government.

Many authorities maintain that the rapid expansion of the learning disabilities category reflects poor diagnostic practices. They believe that children are being overidentified, that teachers are too quick to label students with the slightest learning problem as "learning disabled" rather than entertain the possibility that their teaching practices are at fault. Some, however, argue that some of the increase may be due to social/cultural changes that have raised children's vulnerability to developing learning disabilities (Hallahan, 1992). For example, an increase in poverty has placed children at greater risk for biomedical problems, including central nervous system dysfunction (Baumeister, Kupstas, & Klindworth, 1990). The number of children living in poverty, for example, has grown by 15 to 19 percent since the 1970s (U.S. Department of Education, 1997). Furthermore, even families who are not in poverty are under more stress than ever before, which takes its toll on the time children have for concentrating on their schoolwork and on their parents' ability to offer social support.

Still others maintain that there is a causal relationship between the decrease in the numbers of students being identified as mentally retarded and the increase in the numbers of students being identified as learning disabled. There is suggestive evidence that school personnel, when faced with a student who could qualify as mentally retarded, often "bend" the rules to apply the label of "learning disabilities" rather than the more stigmatizing label of "mental retardation" (MacMillan, Gresham, & Bocian, 1998; MacMillan & Siperstein, 2001).

Boys outnumber girls by about three to one in the learning disabilities category. Some researchers have suggested that the prevalence of learning disabilities among males is due to their greater biological vulnerability. The infant mortality rate for males is higher than that for females, and males are at greater risk than females for a variety of biological abnormalities. Other researchers have contended, however, that the higher prevalence of learning disabilities among males may be due to referral bias. They suggest that academic difficulties are no more prevalent among boys than among girls, but that boys are more likely to be referred for special education when they do have academic problems because of other behaviors that bother teachers, such as hyperactivity. Research on this issue is mixed (Clarizio & Phillips, 1986; Leinhardt, Seewald, & Zigmond, 1982; Shaywitz, Shaywitz, Fletcher, & Escobar, 1990). So at this point, it is probably safest to conclude that

> some bias does exist but that the biological vulnerability of males also plays a role. For example, the federal government's figures indicate that all disabilities are more prevalent in males, including conditions that are difficult to imagine resulting from referral or assessment bias, such as hearing impairment (53% are males), orthopedic impairment (54% are males), and visual impairment (56% are males). (Hallahan, Kauffman, & Lloyd, 1999, pp. 31–32)

Causes

In many cases, the cause of a child's learning disabilities remains a mystery. For years many professionals suspected that neurological factors were a major cause of learning disabilities. Not all agreed, however, because the evidence for a neurological cause was based on relatively crude neurological measures. In recent years researchers have begun to

The operator views computer-generated pictures of the brain during a scan procedure. ■

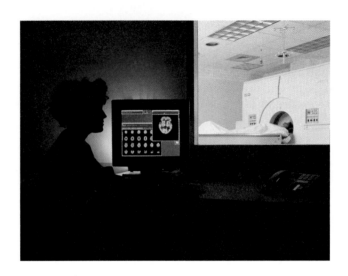

Computerized axial tomographic (CAT) scans.
A neuroimaging technique whereby X rays of the brain are compiled by a computer to produce a series of pictures of the brain.

Magnetic resonance imaging (MRI).
A neuroimaging technique whereby radio waves are used to produce cross-sectional images of the brain; used to pinpoint areas of the brain that are dysfunctional.

Functional magnetic resonance imaging (fMRI).
An adaptation of the MRI used to detect changes in the brain while it is in an active state; unlike a PET scan, it does not involve using radioactive materials.

Functional magnetic resonance spectroscopy (fMRS).
An adaptation of the MRI used to detect changes in the brain while it is in an active state; unlike a PET scan, it does not involve using radioactive materials.

Positron emission tomography (PET) scans.
A computerized method for measuring bloodflow in the brain; during a cognitive task, a low amount of radioactive dye is injected in the brain; the dye collects in active neurons, indicating which areas of the brain are active.

harness advanced technology to assess brain activity more accurately. The most recent technology being used by researchers to document neurological dysfunction in some persons with learning disabilities includes **computerized axial tomographic (CAT) scans, magnetic resonance imaging (MRI), functional magnetic resonance imaging (fMRI), functional magnetic resonance spectroscopy (fMRS),** and **positron emission tomography (PET) scans.**

- A CAT scan involves placing the patient's head in a large ring and then taking a series of X rays. The X rays are then fed into a computer that plots a series of pictures of the brain.
- An MRI uses radio waves instead of radiation to create cross-sectional images of the brain.
- fMRI and fMRS are adaptations of the MRI. Unlike an MRI, they are used to detect changes in brain activity while a person is engaged in a task, such as reading.
- A PET scan, like an fMRI or fMRS, is used while the person is performing a task. The subject is injected with a substance containing a low amount of radiation, which collects in active neurons. Using a scanner to detect the radioactive substance, researchers can tell which parts of the brain are actively engaged during various tasks.

Using these neuroimaging techniques, researchers are accumulating evidence for structural and functional differences in the brains of those with and without learning disabilities, especially reading disabilities (Kibby & Hynd, 2001; Richards, 2001). Structural differences refer to such things as the size of the various areas of the brain. Function refers to activity in the brain. With respect to the functional differences, for example, researchers have found that different areas of the brain are activated during reading tasks for individuals with dyslexia versus nondyslexics. See the box on p. 157 for a summary of the major findings.

Taken as a whole, these studies are not definitive evidence of a neurological basis for *all* students identified as learning disabled. Some researchers have noted that, for the most part, the studies have been conducted on individuals with severe learning disabilities. The results, however, have turned many who were formerly skeptical into believers that central nervous system dysfunction may be the cause of many cases of learning disabilities.

Even in cases in which one can be fairly certain that the person with learning disabilities has neurological dysfunction, the question still remains: How did he or she come to have the neurological dysfunction? Possible reasons fall into three general categories: (1) genetic, (2) teratogenic, and (3) medical factors.

Neuroimaging and Reading Disabilities: Major Findings

Several teams of researchers have been studying the structural and functional differences between the brains of those with and without reading disabilities. These scientists have used different neuroimaging methods, different measures of reading, and studied different populations, adults as well as children.

Even with these many methodological differences among research teams, their conclusions have been remarkably consistent. It appears that the left side of the brain is the site of abnormal structure and function in most individuals with severe reading disabilities. Scientists have also begun to pinpoint specific areas within the left side. Figure A depicts *some* of the areas that have

generally received the most support as being abnormal in individuals with severe reading disabilities. (See Richards, 2001, for a review of some of this research.) We should be cautious, however, about concluding that any of these is (are) *the* site(s) of dysfunction in individual cases. Not all of those studied have had abnormalities in the same areas. Furthermore, some have shown an abnormality in only one area, whereas others have had disturbances in several of the areas. As neuroimaging techniques are perfected further, researchers will undoubtedly refine their conclusions with respect to the areas of the brain responsible for reading disabilities.

Angular gyrus[1]
Broca's area[2]
Temporal lobe[3]
Wernicke's area[4]

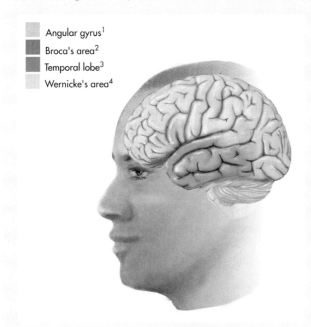

FIGURE A

Areas of the Brain Associated with Reading Difficulties

Studies supporting these sites as involved in individuals with reading disabilities:

[1]*Angular gyrus:* Flowers, Wood, & Naylor, 1991; Pugh et al., 2000; Rumsey et al., 1999; Shaywitz et al., 1998

[2]*Broca's area:* Georgiewa et al., 1999; Shaywitz et al., 1998

[3]*Temporal lobe:* Hagman et al., 1992; McCrory et al., 2000; Paulesu et al., 2001

[4]*Wernicke's area:* Brunswick, McCrory, Price, Frith, & Frith, 1999; Flowers, 1993; Flowers, Wood, & Naylor, 1991; Kushch et al., 1993; Shaywitz et al., 1998

GENETIC FACTORS

Over the years, evidence has accumulated that learning disabilities can be inherited. The two most common types of studies used to look at the genetic basis of learning disabilities are familiality studies and heritability studies.

Familiality studies examine the degree to which a certain condition, such as a learning disability, occurs in single family (i.e., the tendency for it to "run in a family"). Researchers have found that about 35 to 45 percent of first-degree relatives of persons with reading disabilities—that is, the immediate birth family (parents and siblings)—have reading disabilities (Hallgren, 1950; Olson, Wise, Conners, Rack, & Fulker, 1989; Pennington, 1990). And the risk for having reading disabilities goes up for children who have both parents with reading disabilities (Raskind, 2001). The same degree of familiality has also been found in families of people with speech and language disorders (Beichtman, Hood, &

Familiality studies.
A method of determining the degree to which a given condition is inherited; looks at the prevalence of the condition in relatives of the person with the condition.

Inglis, 1992; Lewis, 1992) and spelling disabilities (Schulte-Korne, Deimel, Muller, Gutenbrunner, & Remschmidt, 1996).

The tendency for learning disabilities to run in families may also be due to environmental factors. For example, it is possible that parents with learning disabilities may pass on their disabilities to their children through their childrearing practices. Given this, a more convincing method of determining whether learning disabilities are inherited is **heritability studies**—comparing the prevalence of learning disabilities in identical (*monozygotic,* from the same egg) versus fraternal (*dizygotic,* from two eggs) twins. Researchers have found that identical twins are more concordant than fraternal twins for reading disabilities and speech and language disorders (DeFries, Gillis, & Wadsworth, 1993; Lewis & Thompson, 1992; Reynolds et al., 1996). In other words, if an identical twin and a fraternal twin each has a learning disability, the second identical twin is more likely to have a learning disability than the second fraternal twin.

There have also been studies attempting to pinpoint the precise gene or genes involved in learning disabilities. Although there is some research implicating genes located on chromosomes 6 and 15, this evidence is only suggestive at this time (Raskind, 2001).

TERATOGENIC FACTORS

Teratogens are agents that can cause malformations or defects in the developing fetus. In Chapter 4, we discussed **fetal alcohol syndrome** and lead as two potential causes of mental retardation. Authorities have also speculated that some people may be exposed to levels of these substances that are not high enough to result in mental retardation but do meet a threshold high enough to cause learning disabilities.

MEDICAL FACTORS

There are several medical conditions that can have such a negative impact on children that they develop learning disabilities. Again, many of these can also result in mental retardation, depending on the severity of the condition. For example, premature birth places children at risk for neurological dysfunction. And pediatric AIDS can also result in neurological damage such that learning disabilities result.

Assessment

Four types of assessment are popular in the field of learning disabilities:

1. Standardized achievement assessment
2. Formative assessment
3. Informal assessment
4. Authentic assessment

STANDARDIZED ACHIEVEMENT ASSESSMENT

Teachers and psychologists commonly use **standardized achievement assessment** with students who are learning disabled because achievement deficits are the primary characteristic of these students. Several standardized achievement tests are currently in use. For example, the Wechsler Individual Achievement Test (WIAT) (Psychological Corporation, 1992) assesses achievement in all the areas pertaining to the federal definition of learning disabilities: basic reading, reading comprehension, spelling, written expression, mathematics reasoning, numerical operations, listening comprehension, and oral expression. The developers of the WIAT designed the test so it could be used in conjunction with the Wechsler Intelligence Scale for Children (WISC) in order to look for discrepancies between achievement and ability. There are also examples of achievement tests focused on specific areas, among them the Key Math, Revised (Connolly, 1997) and the Test of Written Language, Third Edition (Hammill & Larsen, 1996).

One limitation of most standardized instruments is that they cannot be used to gain much insight into why students have difficulty. Teachers and clinicians use these tests primarily to identify students with learning problems and to provide gross indicators of academic strengths and weaknesses.

The notion of using assessment information to help plan educational strategies has gained much of its popularity from professionals working in the area of learning disabilities. Three methods of assessment—formative assessment, informal assessment, and authentic assessment—are better suited to the philosophy that evaluation is more useful to teachers if it can be translated into educational recommendations. We discuss each in following sections.

FORMATIVE ASSESSMENT

Formative assessment directly measures a student's behavior to keep track of his or her progress (Choate, Enright, Miller, Poteet, & Rakes, 1995; Deno, 1985; Fuchs & Fuchs, 1997). Formative evaluation is less concerned with how the student's performance compares with that of other students and more concerned with how the student performs in light of his or her abilities. Although there are a variety of formative evaluation models, at least five features are common to all of them:

1. The assessment is usually done by the child's teacher, rather than a school psychologist or diagnostician.
2. The teacher assesses classroom behaviors directly. For instance, if the teacher is interested in measuring the student's pronunciation of the letter *l,* he or she looks at that particular behavior and records whether the child can pronounce that letter.
3. The teacher observes and records the student's behavior frequently and over a period of time. Most other kinds of tests are given once or twice a year at the most. In formative evaluation, performance is measured at least two or three times a week.

Formative assessment. Measurement procedures used to monitor an individual student's progress; they are used to compare how an individual performs in light of his or her abilities, in contrast to standardized tests, which are primarily used to compare an individual's performance to that of other students.

Informal assessment includes having students do academic work in order to analyze where they might have problems. Error analyses help identify what skills need to be remediated ■

Criterion-referenced testing.
Assessment wherein an individual's performance is compared to a goal or standard of mastery, differs from norm-referenced testing wherein an individual's performance is compared to the performance of others.

Curriculum-based assessment (CBA).
A formative evaluation method designed to evaluate performance in the particular curriculum to which students are exposed; usually involves giving students a small sample of items from the curriculum in use in their schools; proponents argue that CBA is preferable to comparing students with national norms or using tests that do not reflect the curriculum content learned by students.

4. The teacher uses formative evaluation to assess the pupil's progress toward educational goals. After an initial testing, the teacher establishes goals for the student to reach in a given period of time. For example, if the student can orally read 25 words correctly in one minute out of a certain book, the teacher may set a goal, or criterion, of being able to read 100 words correctly per minute after one month. This aspect of formative evaluation is sometimes referred to as **criterion-referenced testing.**

5. The teacher uses formative evaluation to monitor the effectiveness of educational programming. For instance, in the preceding example, if after a few days the teacher realizes it is unlikely that the child will reach the goal of 100 words, the teacher can try a different educational intervention.

One particular model of formative evaluation is **curriculum-based assessment (CBA).** Although it draws heavily on earlier research, CBA was largely developed by Deno and his colleagues (Deno, 1985; Fuchs, Deno, & Mirkin, 1984).

Because it is a type of formative evaluation, CBA has the five features just listed. In addition, it has two other distinguishing characteristics:

1. It is designed to measure students' performances on the particular curriculum to which they are exposed. In spelling, for example, a typical CBA assessment strategy is to give children two-minute spelling samples, using dictation from a random selection of words from the basal spelling curriculum. The number of words or letter sequences correctly spelled serves as the performance measure. In math, the teacher may give students two minutes to compute samples of problems from the basal text and record the number of digits computed correctly. Proponents of CBA state that this reliance on the curriculum is an advantage over commercially available standardized achievement tests, which are usually not keyed to the curriculum in any particular school.

2. CBA compares the performance of students with disabilities to that of their peers in their own school or school division. Deno and his colleagues suggest that the

Ms. Lopez Conducts an Error Analysis

Teachers often use curriculum-based assessment and student work samples to analyze student errors and plan for instruction. Let's listen to a conversation in Ms. Lopez's room during a spelling lesson with Travis:

Ms. Lopez: Travis, let's look at the work you completed yesterday in spelling.

Travis: Okay.

Ms. Lopez: It looks like you had some trouble with the new vowel pattern we've been working on this week. What is your new vowel pattern?

Travis: Uh . . . the "ay?"

Ms. Lopez: That's right. Tell me the rule for the "ay" pattern.

Travis: Um . . . a long /a/ sound is spelled A-Y.

Ms. Lopez: Travis, a long /a/ sound *at the end of a one-syllable word* is spelled A-Y.

Travis: Oh yeah!

Ms. Lopez: Tell me some words on the list that have the "ay" pattern.

Travis: Um . . . "hay" and "play."

Ms. Lopez: Good. Those are some of the words with the "ay" pattern. Let's look through your spelling list again. The "ay" words are the only words that gave you trouble. I think you've figured out the "ee" words pretty well. We'll do a practice activity tomorrow on just the "ay" words, and I'll test you on just those words before we do the whole spelling list again. Okay, now let's take another look at those tricky "ay" words. . . .

SOURCE: Meese, R.L. (2001). *Teaching learners with mild disabilities: Integrating research and practice* (2nd ed., p. 137). Stamford, CT: Wadsworth.

teacher take CBA measures on a random sample of nondisabled students so this comparison can be made. Comparison with a local reference group is seen as more relevant than comparison with the national norming groups used in commercially developed standardized tests.

INFORMAL ASSESSMENT

A common method of assessment used by teachers is to ask students to work on their academic assignments and take note of what they do well and where they have difficulty. In the area of reading, for example, teachers can use an **informal reading inventory (IRI),** a series of reading passages or word lists graded in order of difficulty. The teacher has the student read from the series, beginning with a list or passage that is likely to be easy for the student. The student continues to read increasingly more difficult lists or passages while the teacher monitors his or her performance. After the results of the IRI have been compiled, the teacher can use them to estimate the appropriate difficulty level of reading material for the student.

In using an IRI or other means of informal assessment, the teacher can also do an error analysis of the student's work (Lopez-Reyna & Bay, 1997). Sometimes referred to as miscue analysis, an **error analysis** is a way of pinpointing particular areas in which the student has difficulty. In reading, for example, it might show that the student typically substitutes one vowel for another or omits certain sounds when reading aloud. See the box on p. 160 for an example of an error analysis.

AUTHENTIC ASSESSMENT

Some educators question the authenticity of typical test scores—especially those from standardized tests—asserting that they do not reflect what students do in situations in which they work with, or receive help from, teachers, peers, parents, or supervisors. The purpose behind **authentic assessment** is to assess students' critical-thinking and problem-solving abilities in real-life situations.

An example of authentic assessment is portfolios. **Portfolios** are a collection of samples of a student's work done over time. Students of music or art have used portfolios, but their use in academic areas is more recent (Meese, 2001). Portfolios allow for a broader-based evidence of students' work, evidence that is more closely related to "real-life" skills. For example, the following might be included:

- Essays or other writing samples, such as letters, instructions, or stories
- Video- or audiotapes of speeches, or oral responses to questions
- Audio- or videotapes of recitals or other performances
- Experiments and their results or reports

Portfolio assessment, however, is more difficult and time consuming than many educators realize (Hallahan et al., 1999). Teachers need to help students decide what to put in their portfolios and need to give careful attention to criteria for evaluating them. However, when done properly, they can be a rich source of information about a student's strengths and interests. Furthermore, portfolios can be of particular value for culturally diverse students for whom traditional standardized tests may not reflect their true abilities (Rueda & Garcia, 1997).

Psychological and Behavioral Characteristics

Before discussing some of the most common characteristics of persons with learning disabilities, we point out two important features of this population: Persons with learning disabilities exhibit a great deal of both interindividual and intraindividual variation.

Informal reading inventory (IRI). A method of assessing reading in which the teacher has the student read progressively more difficult series of passages or word lists; the teacher notes the difficulty level of the material read and the types of errors the student makes.

Error analysis. An informal method of teacher assessment that involves the teacher noting the particular kinds of errors a student makes when doing academic work.

Authentic assessment. A method that evaluates a student's critical-thinking and problem-solving ability in real-life situations in which he or she may work with or receive help from peers, teachers, parents, or supervisors.

Portfolios. A collection of samples of a student's work done over time; a type of authentic assessment.

INTERINDIVIDUAL VARIATION

In any classroom of students with learning disabilities, some will have problems in reading, some will have problems in math, some will have problems in spelling, some will be inattentive, and so on. One term for such interindividual variation is *heterogeneity*. Although heterogeneity is a trademark of children from all the categories of special education, the old adage "No two are exactly alike" is particularly appropriate for students with learning disabilities. This heterogeneity makes it a challenge for teachers to plan educational programs for the diverse group of children they find in their classrooms.

INTRAINDIVIDUAL VARIATION

In addition to differences among one another, children with learning disabilities also tend to exhibit variability within their own profiles of abilities. For example, a child may be two or three years above grade level in reading but two or three years behind grade level in math. Such uneven profiles account for references to specific learning disabilities in the literature on learning disabilities. Some children have specific deficits in just one or a few areas of achievement or development.

Some of the pioneers in the field of learning disabilities alerted colleagues to what is termed *intraindividual* variation. Samuel Kirk was one of the most influential in advocating the notion of individual variation in students with learning disabilities. He developed the Illinois Test of Psycholinguistic Abilities, which purportedly measured variation in processes important for reading. Researchers ultimately found that Kirk's test did not measure processes germane to reading (Hallahan & Cruickshank, 1973; Hammill & Larsen, 1974), and the test is rarely used today. Nonetheless, most authorities still recognize intraindividual differences as a feature of many students with learning disabilities.

We now turn to a discussion of some of the most common characteristics of persons with learning disabilities.

ACADEMIC ACHIEVEMENT PROBLEMS

Academic deficits are the hallmark of learning disabilities. By definition, if there is no academic problem, a learning disability does not exist.

Phonological awareness.
The ability to understand that speech flow can be broken into smaller sound units such as words, syllables, and phonemes; generally thought to be the reason for the reading problems of many students with learning disabilities.

Reading   Reading poses the most difficulty for most students with learning disabilities. Most authorities believe that this problem is related to deficient language skills, especially **phonological awareness**—the ability to understand that speech flow can be broken into smaller sound units such as words, syllables, and phonemes (Torgesen, 2001). It is easy to understand why problems with phonology would be at the heart of many reading difficulties. If a person has problems breaking words into their component sounds, he or she will have trouble learning to read. And there is suggestive evidence that readers of English are more susceptible than readers of some other languages to problems with phonological awareness. Some have speculated that this is why reading disabilities are more prevalent in English-speaking countries than in some other countries (see the box on p. 163).

Written Language   People with learning disabilities often have problems in one or more of the following areas: handwriting, spelling, and composition (Hallahan et al., 1999). Although even the best students can have less-than-perfect handwriting, the kinds of problems manifested by some students with learning disabilities are much more severe. These children are sometimes very slow writers and their written products are sometimes illegible. Spelling can be a significant problem because of the difficulty (noted in the previous section) in understanding the correspondence between sounds and letters.

In addition to the more mechanical areas of handwriting and spelling, students with learning disabilities also frequently have difficulties in the more creative aspects of composition (Montague & Graves, 1992). For example, compared to nondisabled peers, stu-

Dyslexia: Same Brains, Different Languages

Pity the poor speakers of English. New research suggests that they may be especially prone to manifest dyslexia, the language disorder that makes reading and writing a struggle, simply because their language is so tricky.

The distinctive pattern of spelling and memory problems that characterizes dyslexia has a strong genetic basis, suggesting that some neurological oddity underlies the disorder. But there appears to be a cultural component to the [condition] as well, because dyslexia is more prevalent in some countries than others; for instance, about twice as many people fit the definition of dyslexic in the United States as in Italy. Researchers have suspected that certain languages expose the disorder while others allow dyslexics to compensate. Now a brain imaging study backs this theory up.

A multinational team of researchers used positron emission tomography (PET) scans to observe brain activity in British, French, and Italian adults while they read [Paulesu et al., 2001]. Regardless of language, . . . people with symptoms of dyslexia showed less neural activity in a part of the brain that's vital for reading.

"Neurologically, the disease looks very much the same" in people who speak different languages, says neurologist Eraldo Paulesu of the University of Milan Biocca in Italy. "Therefore, the difference in prevalence of clinical manifestations [among different countries] must be attributed to something else." The researchers blame language.

English consists of just 40 sounds, but these phonemes can be spelled, by one count, in 1120 different ways. French spelling is almost as maddening. Italian speakers, in contrast, must map 25 different speech sounds to just 33 combinations of letters. Not surprisingly, Italian schoolchildren read faster and more accurately than do those in Britain. And it's no surprise that people have a harder time overcoming reading disorders if their language, like English or French, has a very complex, arbitrary system for spelling. . . .

Compared to normal readers, dyslexics from all three countries showed less activation in parts of the [left] temporal lobe while reading. [See the figure in the box on p. 157.] The underutilized areas are familiar to neurologists: Patients with strokes in this area often lose the ability to read and spell, even though they still speak fluently. . . .

This research doesn't supply ready solutions for how to help dyslexic students overcome their reading disability, Paulesu says, short of moving to Italy, Turkey, or Spain, where spelling is simple and straightforward. So sympathize when English- or French-speaking students complain about having to memorize arbitrarily spelled words; they're right to feel wronged.

SOURCE: Reprinted with permission from Helmuth, L. (2001). Dyslexia: Same brains, different languages. *Science, 291,* 2064–2065. Copyright © 2001 by American Association for the Advancement of Science.

CW To see the full text for the Helmuth article from *Science,* see: http://www.sciencemag.org/content/vol291/issue5511/index.shtml ■

---

dents with learning disabilities use less complex sentence structures; include fewer types of words; write paragraphs that are less well organized; include fewer ideas in their written products; and write stories that have fewer important components, such as introducing main characters, setting scenes, describing a conflict to be resolved (Hallahan et al., 1999).

Spoken Language   Many students with learning disabilities have problems with the mechanical and social uses of language. Mechanically, they have trouble with **syntax** (grammar), **semantics** (word meanings), and, as we have already noted, **phonology** (the ability to break words into their component sounds and blend individual sounds together to make words).

With regard to social uses of language—commonly referred to as **pragmatics**—students with learning disabilities are often inept in the production and reception of discourse. In short, they are not very good conversationalists. They are unable to engage in the mutual give-and-take that conversations between individuals require.

For instance, conversations of individuals with learning disabilities are frequently marked by long silences because they do not use the relatively subtle strategies that their

Syntax.
The way words are joined together to structure meaningful sentences (i.e., grammar).

Semantics.
The study of the meanings attached to words.

Phonology.
The study of how individual sounds make up words.

Pragmatics.
The study within psycholinguistics of how people use language in social situations; emphasizes the functional use of language, rather than mechanics.

The term pragmatics refers to the social uses of language. Individuals with learning disabilities who have problems with pragmatics may find it difficult to carry on conversations. ■

nondisabled peers do to keep conversations going. They are not skilled at responding to others' statements or questions and tend to answer their own questions before their companions have a chance to respond. They tend to make task-irrelevant comments and make those with whom they talk uncomfortable. In one often-cited study, for example, children with and without learning disabilities took turns playing the role of host in a simulated television talk show (Bryan, Donahue, Pearl, & Sturm, 1981). Analysis of the verbal interactions revealed that in contrast to nondisabled children, children with learning disabilities playing the host role allowed their nondisabled guests to dominate the conversation. Also, their guests exhibited more signs of discomfort during the interview than did the guests of nondisabled hosts.

Math   Although disorders of reading, writing, and language have traditionally received more emphasis than problems with mathematics, the latter are now gaining a great deal of attention. Authorities now recognize that math difficulties are second only to reading disabilities as an academic problem area for students with learning disabilities. The types of problems these students have include difficulties with computation of math facts (Cawley, Parmar, Yan, & Miller, 1998) as well as word problems (Woodward & Baxter, 1997); trouble with the latter is often due to the inefficient application of problem-solving strategies.

PERCEPTUAL, PERCEPTUAL-MOTOR, AND GENERAL COORDINATION PROBLEMS

Studies indicate that some children with learning disabilities exhibit visual and/or auditory perceptual disabilities (see Hallahan, 1975, and Willows, 1998, for reviews). A child with visual perceptual problems might, for example, have trouble solving puzzles or seeing and remembering visual shapes, or he or she might have a tendency to reverse letters (e.g., mistake a *b* for a *d*). A child with auditory perceptual problems might have difficulty discriminating between two words that sound nearly alike (e.g., *fit* and *fib*) or following orally presented directions.

Teachers and parents have also noted that some students with learning disabilities have difficulty with physical activities involving motor skills. They describe some of these children as having "two left feet" or "ten thumbs." The problems may involve both fine motor (small motor muscles) and gross motor (large motor muscles) skills. Fine motor skills often involve coordination of the visual and motor systems.

DISORDERS OF ATTENTION AND HYPERACTIVITY

Students with attention problems display such characteristics as distractibility, impulsivity, and hyperactivity. Teachers and parents of these children often characterize them as being unable to stick with one task for very long, failing to listen to others, talking nonstop, blurting out the first things on their minds, and being generally disorganized in planning their activities in and out of school.

Individuals with learning disabilities often have attention problems (Kotkin, Forness, & Kavale, 2001), and they are often severe enough to be diagnosed as having **attention deficit hyperactivity disorder (ADHD).** ADHD, characterized by severe problems of inattention, hyperactivity, and/or impulsivity, is a diagnosis made by a psychiatrist or psychologist, using criteria established by the American Psychiatric Association (1994). (See Chapter 6 for a full discussion of ADHD.) Although estimates vary, researchers have consistently found an overlap of 10 to 25 percent between ADHD and learning disabilities (Forness & Kavale, 2002).

MEMORY, COGNITIVE, AND METACOGNITIVE PROBLEMS

We discuss memory, cognitive, and metacognitive problems together because they are closely related. A person who has problems in one of these areas is likely to have problems in the other two as well.

Memory   Parents and teachers are well aware that students with learning disabilities have problems remembering such things as assignments and appointments. In fact, they often exclaim in exasperation that they can't understand how a child so smart could forget things so easily. And early researchers in learning disabilities documented that many students with learning disabilities have a real deficit in memory (Hallahan, 1975; Hallahan, Kauffman, & Ball, 1973; Swanson, 1987; Torgesen, 1988; Torgesen & Kail, 1980).

Students with learning disabilities have problems that affect at least two types of memory: **short-term memory (STM)** and **working memory (WM)** (Swanson & Sachse-Lee, 2001). Problems with STM involve difficulty recalling information shortly after having seen or heard it. A typical STM task requires a person to repeat a list of words presented visually or aurally. Problems with WM affect a person's ability to keep information in mind while simultaneously doing another cognitive task. Trying to remember an address while listening to instructions on how to get there is an example of WM.

Researchers have found that one of the major reasons that children with learning disabilities perform poorly on memory tasks is that, unlike their nondisabled peers, they do not use strategies. For example, when presented with a list of words to memorize, most children will rehearse the names to themselves. They will also make use of categories by rehearsing words in groups that go together. Students with learning disabilities are not likely to use these strategies spontaneously.

Cognition   The deficiency in the use of strategies on memory tasks also indicates that children with learning disabilities demonstrate problems in cognition. **Cognition** is a broad term covering many different aspects of thinking and problem solving. Students with learning disabilities often exhibit disorganized thinking that results in problems with planning and organizing their lives at school and at home.

Metacognition   Closely related to these cognitive problems are problems in metacognition. **Metacognition** has at least three components—the ability to: (1) recognize task requirements, (2) select and implement appropriate strategies, and (3) monitor and adjust performance (Butler, 1998).

Regarding the first component—ability to recognize task requirements—students with learning disabilities frequently have problems judging how difficult tasks can be. For example, they may approach the reading of highly technical information with the same level of intensity as reading for pleasure.

Attention deficit hyperactivity disorder (ADHD). A condition characterized by severe problems of inattention, hyperactivity, and/or impulsivity; often found in persons with learning disabilities.

Short-term memory. The ability to recall information after a short period of time.

Working memory. The ability to remember information while also performing other cognitive operations.

Cognition. The ability to solve problems and use strategies; an area of difficulty for many persons with learning disabilities.

Metacognition. One's understanding of the strategies available for learning a task and the regulatory mechanisms needed to complete the task.

An example of problems with the second component—ability to select and implement appropriate strategies—is when students with learning disabilities are asked questions such as "How can you remember to take your homework to school in the morning?" they do not come up with as many strategies (e.g., writing a note to oneself, placing the homework by the front door) as students without disabilities.

An example of the third component of metacognition—ability to monitor or adjust performance—is comprehension monitoring. **Comprehension monitoring** refers to the abilities employed while one reads and attempts to comprehend textual material. Many students with reading disabilities, have problems, for example, in being able to sense when they are not understanding what they are reading (Butler, 1998). Good readers are able to sense this and make necessary adjustments, such as slowing down and/or rereading difficult passages. Students with reading problems are also likely to have problems picking out the main ideas of paragraphs.

Comprehension monitoring.
The ability to keep track of one's own comprehension of reading material and to make adjustments to comprehend better while reading; often deficient in students with learning disabilities.

SOCIAL-EMOTIONAL PROBLEMS

Although not all, perhaps not even a majority, of children with learning disabilities have significant social-emotional problems, they do run a greater risk than their nondisabled peers of having these types of problems. For those who do experience behavioral problems, the effects can be long-lasting and devastating. In their early years they are often rejected by their peers and have poor self-concepts (Sridhar & Vaughn, 2001). And in adulthood, the scars from years of rejection can be painful and not easily forgotten (McGrady, Lerner, & Boscardin, 2001). The following excerpt, written by an a 34-year-old man, is testimony to the depth of the emotional scars experienced by some persons with learning disabilities:

> Making new friends was a most difficult process, one I rarely attempted. I had been so shy in the first grade that the other kids saw me as a freak and avoided contact with me. I was socially blackballed from the get-go. When my father, a man without many friends, heard of my social problems he passed along some less than sage advice. He said, "If they don't like you, dazzle them with bullshit." Once I was clear on what bullshit was, I embarked on a destructive path that ruined my prospects of making true friends. In order to keep people interested in maintaining a friendship, I jazzed myself up. When given the opportunity to advance my image in someone else's eyes, I leapt on it, no matter how outrageous the lie. After the divorce, my father's absence lent itself to a plethora of lies, everything from being an astronaut or a super-spy to being president of the United States. No lie, so long as it led to some measure of social acceptance, was too great, and I told them all.
>
> All too soon, the practice began to backfire as my peers, not nearly as stupid as I believed, began to challenge my lies. For a while, I stood by my stories, unable to address why I told them or the effect they might have on others. But time and the constant doubt of my classmates eventually wore me down. By the third grade, I was beaten, defenseless, and had nowhere to retreat, so I publicly recanted. After that, word of my confession spread like pink eye through the school yard, and I was left alone. No one at school would befriend the known liar, the boy who could not tell the truth. As my peers rolled down the path of socialization, I was left standing in their dust. Early on, I had tried being myself and it had gotten me alienated. I tried being everything to everyone, and it cost me any hope of social acceptance. I was left with nothing, both socially and emotionally. (Queen, 2001, p. 5)

One plausible reason for the social problems of some students with learning disabilities is that they have deficits in social cognition. That is, they misread social cues and may misinterpret the feelings and emotions of others. Most children, for example, are able to tell when their behavior is bothering others. Students with learning disabilities sometimes act as if they are oblivious to the effect their behavior is having on their peers. They also have difficulty taking the perspective of others, of putting themselves in someone else's shoes.

Researchers have noted that problems with social interaction tend to be more evident in children who also have problems in math, visual-spatial tasks, tactual tasks, and self-regulation and organization (Rourke, 1995; Worling, Humphries, & Tannock, 1999). In laypersons' terms, such children are sometimes described as "spacey" or "in a fog." Persons with this constellation of behaviors are referred to as having **nonverbal learning disabilities.** However, the term is somewhat of a misnomer because they often exhibit subtle problems in using language, especially in social situations. Researchers have speculated that nonverbal learning disabilities are caused by malfunctioning of the right half of the brain because of known linkages of math, visual-spatial, and tactual skills to the right cerebral hemisphere.

There is also evidence that individuals with nonverbal learning disabilities are at risk for depression, presumably because of the social rejection and isolation they may experience. In extreme cases they have an increased risk of suicide (Bender, Rosenkrans, & Crane, 1999).

MOTIVATIONAL PROBLEMS

Another source of problems for many persons with learning disabilities is their motivation, or feelings about their abilities to deal with life's many challenges and problems. People with learning disabilities may appear content to let events happen without attempting to control or influence them. These individuals have what is referred to as an *external,* rather than an *internal,* **locus of control.** In other words, they believe their lives are controlled by external factors such as luck or fate, rather than by internal factors such as determination or ability (Hallahan, Gajar, Cohen, & Tarver, 1978; Short & Weissberg-Benchell, 1989). People with this outlook sometimes display **learned helplessness:** a tendency to give up and expect the worst because they think that no matter how hard they try, they will fail (Seligman, 1992).

What makes these motivational problems so difficult for teachers, parents, and individuals with learning disabilities to deal with is the interrelationship between cognitive and motivational problems (Montague, 1997). A vicious cycle develops: The student learns to expect failure in any new situation, based on past experience. This expectancy of failure, or learned helplessness, may then cause him or her to give up too easily when faced with a difficult or complicated task. As a result, not only does the student fail to learn new skills; she or he also has another bad experience, reinforcing feelings of helplessness and even worthlessness—and so the cycle goes.

THE CHILD WITH LEARNING DISABILITIES AS AN INACTIVE LEARNER WITH STRATEGY DEFICITS

Many of the psychological and behavioral characteristics we have described can be summed up by saying that the student with learning disabilities is an inactive learner, lacking in strategies for attacking academic problems (Hallahan & Bryan, 1981; Hallahan & Reeve, 1980; Torgesen, 1977). Specifically, research describes the student with learning disabilities as someone who does not believe in his or her own abilities (learned helplessness), has an inadequate grasp of what strategies are available for problem solving (poor metacognitive skills), and has problems producing appropriate learning strategies spontaneously.

The practical implications of this constellation of characteristics is that students with learning disabilities may have difficulties working independently. They are not likely to be "self-starters." Assignments or activities requiring them to work on their own may cause

GW In 1999, two mothers of daughters with nonverbal learning disabilities started a Web site devoted to information on nonverbal learning disabilities: http://www.nldontheweb.org/ ■

Nonverbal learning disabilities.
A term used to refer to individuals who have a cluster of disabilities in social interaction, math, visual-spatial tasks, and tactual tasks.

Locus of control.
A motivational term referring to how people explain their successes or failures; people with an internal locus of control believe they are the reason for success or failure, whereas people with an external locus of control believe outside forces influence how they perform.

Learned helplessness.
A motivational term referring to a condition in which a person believes that no matter how hard he or she tries, failure will result.

problems, unless the teacher carefully provides an appropriate amount of support. Homework, for example, is a major problem for many students with learning disabilities (Bryan & Sullivan-Burstein, 1998; Epstein, Munk, Bursuck, Polloway, & Jayanthi, 1998). Students' difficulties range from failing to bring home their homework, to being distracted while doing homework, to forgetting to turn in their homework. Some useful strategies for teachers include:

- Assigning homework whereby students can practice proficiency in skills they already possess, rather than learning new skills
- Making sure that students understand the assignment
- Giving assignments on which students can receive help while in school
- Providing frequent reminders about homework due dates
- Allowing multiple ways of completing assignments (e.g., audiotaped oral responses)

We discuss the topic of homework again in Chapter 14 (see p. 505).

SUCCESS STORIES
Special Educators at Work

San Francisco, CA: Like many students across the country, eleven-year-old **Eliot Danner** attends a private school that does not provide any special education services. His parents had to look elsewhere for specialized training to help him learn to read. They found that help with special educators **Nancy Cushen White** and **Mia Callahan Russell**.

Eliot met Nancy Cushen White, a clinical faculty member at the University of California at San Francisco and a learning specialist for the San Francisco City Schools, in the summer before second grade, when he first attended an intense special education program designed to address language disabilities. Up to that point, perceptually oriented therapies had been tried with Eliot, but without clear success. Everyone knew he had trouble reading, but no one was sure what to do about it.

Since kindergarten, Eliot has attended independent schools designed for high academic achievers, not for students with learning disabilities. In the early grades, he had passionate interests and easily memorized stories read to him, but for all his curiosity and interest, Eliot could not read by himself. A psychological evaluation identified problems with spatial orientation, word attack, spelling, and composi-

tion skills. After one year of tutoring in phonological awareness to complement his school's whole-language approach, Eliot was still anxious and unsure if he would ever learn to read. "We needed to respond to that, or we feared we would lose him as a reader," says his mother, Nancy Pietrefesa.

Eliot's parents considered enrolling him in another school but kept him in place following an assessment that suggested he would do best in this challenging but relaxed atmosphere. Says Nancy Cullen White, "This wasn't a question of settings but of strategies. Eliot is a child with dyslexia who needed to learn how to read."

"Teaching kids with learning disabilities is not a casual engagement," says Nancy Pietrefesa. She believes her son's success began the summer he met Nancy White and Mia Callahan Russell, both teachers trained to address language disabilities. They could accurately describe Eliot's problems,

Educational Considerations

In this section we consider two major approaches to alleviating the academic problems of students with learning disabilities—cognitive training and Direct Instruction (DI)—as well as service delivery models. Although we look at these approaches individually, in practice they are often combined.

COGNITIVE TRAINING

The approach termed **cognitive training** involves three components: (1) changing thought processes, (2) providing strategies for learning, and (3) teaching self-initiative. Whereas behavior modification focuses on modifying observable behaviors, cognitive training is concerned with modifying unobservable thought processes, prompting observable changes in behavior. Cognitive training has proven successful in helping a

GW The Division for Learning Disabilities of the Council for Exceptional Children maintains a Web site devoted to research-based, teaching practices: www.TeachingLD.org

Another professional organization providing information on learning disabilities is the Council for Learning Disabilities: http://www.cldinternational.org/ ■

Cognitive training.
A group of training procedures designed to change thoughts or thought patterns.

---

clearly articulate his strengths and weaknesses, and prescribe intense remedial instruction. Through that process, Eliot assumed greater control and self-acceptance. He began to understand himself as a reader.

It was Nancy White who specifically described his problem:

Eliot does not have a weakness in any one modality. He has great difficulty with auditory, visual, and kinesthetic integration, particularly in association with his long-term visual memory. In the summer of 1992, his phonological awareness was poor and he was not able to segment syllables into individual sounds for spelling or to blend sounds into syllables for decoding. In addition, he had difficulties with visual discrimination and both short-term and long-term visual memory for words. Unable to rely on his memory, it all became a jumble when he had to write things down.

That July, eight-year-old Eliot began an intensive regimen of language training and educational therapy that has paid off. Along with a group of ten other students from public and private schools, he attended a three-week summer program for three-and-one-half hours of daily direct instruction in language skills. Says Nancy White, "What some folks learn on their own, these kids need to be taught."

Getting students to think through the process of language is the program's goal. Skills are taught in specific sequence to foster automatic use, and students are given the rationale so they can see how the rules of the English language fit together. "There is emphasis on repetition and practice, much like in sports or in music," says Nancy Pietrefesa. "Have you ever seen how football coaches make kids practice plays over and over?"

Nancy White trains teachers to keep sessions lively. Emphasis is on the active student, self-checking and always thinking. "Nobody should just sit!" she says. "Success hinges on developing the simultaneous association of hearing, saying, seeing, and writing. Students are taught there is a system and they can use it!"

According to Eliot, it was all "fiddle-faddle" until the end of the first summer, when he began to see himself improve. "He was immersed daily," says his mother, "and this intense immersion is what enabled him to see the fruits of his labors." To keep up this pace for grades two and three, a creative schedule was developed with Eliot's private school. Monday through Thursday, he attended classes from 9 to 12 and was tutored at home daily for two and a half hours. He was present for a full day on Friday. Teacher Mia Russell was trained by Nancy White as an educational therapist, and her intensive tutorial work with Eliot was tailored specifically to his individual patterns and errors. After several summers of training, in the fourth grade, Eliot worked with Mia eight hours a week in a room provided for them at his school. The sessions were reduced to three hours a week in grade five. "The staff at the school is very cooperative," says Mia. "They see Eliot as a bright, articulate student who needs specific interventions they are not equipped to offer."

Eliot has worked hard to become an expert on how he learns, and he is eager to start sixth grade. "He has really knocked himself out," says his mom. He is an independent learner, conscious of which strategies he needs to follow to get to what he wants to know. Says Eliot, "Learning that stuff is not fun, but it works!"

—By Jean Crockett

Meeting the Needs of Students with Learning Disabilities

Mnemonics

What Are Mnemonics?

The term *mnemonic* comes from the name of the Greek goddess of memory, Mnemosyne. Mnemosyne's name was derived from *mnemon,* meaning mindful. Today, a mnemonic refers to any memory-enhancing strategy. Everyone has used a mnemonic at one time or another. To remember the order of the planets, many students learn the phrase "My Very Educated Mother Just Served Us Nine Pizzas." Music students trying to remember scales learn "Every Good Boy Deserves Fudge." Rhymes are another form of mnemonic—"I before E, except after C, or when pronounced as A as in neighbor and weigh." Mnemonics come in a variety of forms, but what defines a mnemonic is its ability to aid in the retention of certain information.

What the Research Says

It is well documented that many students with learning disabilities have difficulty remembering information and do not spontaneously engage in memory-enhancing strategies, such as rehearsal (Mastropieri & Scruggs, 1998). By the early 1980s, researchers had begun conducting studies to identify strategies that would address these deficit areas. Although rehearsal was found to be an effective tool for increasing the retention of information, researchers found that memory strategies involving pictures and elaboration had greater potential (Mastropieri & Scruggs, 1998). Using *mnemonic strategies* to help children with memory problems remember curriculum content, the teacher transforms abstract information into a concrete picture that depicts the material in a more meaningful way.

Researchers have studied mnemonics and students with learning disabilities in both laboratory settings (i.e., one-to-one with trained experimenters rather than classroom teachers) and in classroom settings. Findings from these studies reveal the following gains made by students who were taught using mnemonics:

1. Mnemonic keyword method resulted in increased recall of information.

2. Small groups of students with learning disabilities could be taught using a variety of mnemonic strategies over a period of days without diminishing the effectiveness of the specific mnemonics.

3. Mnemonic pictures aided in the comprehension and recall of information presented in science and history texts.

4. Students with learning disabilities could be taught to create their own mnemonics and apply them successfully.

5. Students with learning and behavior disorders benefited from teacher-created mnemonics and were able to retain the information longer than students who were not provided mnemonics.

6. Mnemonics appeared to result in increased motivation, efficacy, and willingness to learn. (Mastropieri & Scruggs, 1998)

Implementing Mnemonics in the Classroom

Two effective mnemonic techniques are the keyword and pegword methods (Lasley, Matczynski, & Rowley, 2002). When using a keyword approach, students are taught how to transform an unfamiliar word to a familiar word. For example, the word *accolade* could be associated with the keyword *Kool-Aid*. To associate Kool-Aid with the definition of accolade, students can think of someone making a toast to a guest of honor with a cup of Kool-Aid. Thus, the definition "giving praise" will be closely associated with *accolade* (Levin, 1993).

To use the pegword strategy, students learn to correlate numbers with familiar rhyming words. The teacher creates a picture that incorporates the pegword along with the content associations. Teachers use this strategy when students need to remember the order of information or when there is a number association with the fact. For example, a student trying to remember that Monroe was the fifth president could combine the keyword *money* for Monroe and the pegword *hive* for five. The image of bees carrying money to a hive would be the mnemonic (Mastropieri & Scruggs, 1998).

Teachers working in inclusive settings find that mnemonics can be a useful strategy for both their special needs and general education students (see Mastropieri, Sweda, & Scruggs, 2000 for examples of inclusive classroom implementations).

Example Mnemonic

Figure A is an example of a mnemonic based upon the keyword *purse* for Franklin Pierce and the pegword *fork-*ing for fourteen. The "action" of the fork piercing the purse reinforces the connection between the two items and enhances the association students will need to recall.

—*By Kristin L. Sayeski*

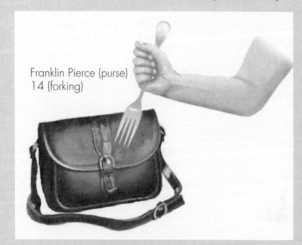

Franklin Pierce (purse)
14 (forking)

FIGURE A
Mnemonic Representation of Franklin Pierce, Fourteenth President of the United States.
SOURCE: Adapted from Mastropieri, M.A., Scruggs, T.E., & Whedon, C. (1997). Using mnemonic strategies to teach information about U.S. Presidents: A classroom-based investigation. *Learning Disability Quarterly, 20,* 13–21. Copyright 1994 by Thomas E. Scruggs and Margo A. Mastropieri.

variety of academic problems for many students with learning disabilities (Hallahan et al., 1999).

Authorities give at least two reasons as to why cognitive training is particularly appropriate for students with learning disabilities. Namely, it aims at helping them overcome:

1. Cognitive and metacognitive problems, by providing them with specific strategies for solving problems
2. Motivational problems of passivity and learned helplessness, by stressing self-initiative and involving them as much as possible in their own treatment

A variety of specific techniques and approaches fall under the heading of cognitive training. We briefly discuss four: (1) self-instruction, (2) self-monitoring, (3) scaffolded instruction, and (4) reciprocal teaching.

Self-Instruction   The purpose of **self-instruction** is to make students aware of the various stages of problem-solving tasks while they are performing them and to bring behavior under verbal control. Typically, the teacher first models the use of the verbal routine while solving the problem. Then he or she closely supervises the students using the verbal routine while doing the task, and then the students do it on their own.

One study using self-instruction as an integral feature of instruction involved fifth- and sixth-grade students with learning disabilities solving math word problems (Case, Harris, & Graham, 1992). The five-step strategy the students learned to use involved saying the problem out loud, looking for important words and circling them, drawing pictures to help explain what was happening, writing the math sentence, and writing the answer. Furthermore, students were prompted to use the following self-instructions:

1. *Problem definition:* "What do I have to do?"
2. *Planning:* "How can I solve this problem?"

Self-instruction.
A type of cognitive training technique that requires individuals to talk aloud and then to themselves as they solve problems.

3. *Strategy use:* "The five-step strategy will help me look for important words."
4. *Self-evaluation:* "How am I doing?"
5. *Self-reinforcement:* "Good job. I got it right."

Self-monitoring.
A type of cognitive training technique that requires individuals to keep track of their own behavior.

Self-Monitoring   **Self-monitoring** involves students keeping track of their own behavior. Self-monitoring often consists of two components—*self-evaluation* and *self-recording*. The student evaluates his or her behavior and then records whether the behavior occurred. For example, after working on several math problems, the student can check his or her answers and then record on a graph how many of the answers were correct. After several days, the student and teacher have an observable record of the student's progress. Teachers and students can use self-monitoring for various academic tasks in addition to math. For example, self-monitoring has been used to increase the number of words spelled correctly and to increase the length and the quality of written stories (Harris, Graham, Reid, McElroy, & Hamby, 1994).

In addition to monitoring academic performance, teachers have also had students monitor their on- and off-task behavior. The students are instructed to ask themselves "Was I paying attention?" every time they hear a tone on a tape recorder. (The teacher has prepared a tape with tones that occur randomly every thirty seconds to one and a half minutes.) Not only has the students' on-task behavior increased, but their academic productivity has also increased (Lloyd, Hallahan, Kauffman, & Keller, 1998; Mathes & Bender, 1997).

Scaffolded instruction.
A cognitive approach to instruction in which the teacher provides temporary structure or support while students are learning a task; the support is gradually removed as the students are able to perform the task independently.

Scaffolded Instruction   In **scaffolded instruction**, assistance is provided to students when they are first learning tasks and then is gradually reduced, so that eventually students do the tasks independently. For example, in one study, the teacher modeled a three-step strategy for writing, saying the steps aloud:

1. *Think*, who will read this, and why am I writing it?
2. *Plan* what to say using *TREE* (note *Topic* sentence, note *Reasons*, *Examine* reasons, note *Ending*).
3. *Write* and *Say More*. (Sexton, Harris, & Graham, 1998, p. 300)

In scaffolded instruction, assistance is provided to students when they are first learning tasks and then is gradually reduced, so that eventually students perform tasks independently. ■

While modeling the strategy, the students and teacher discussed various aspects of it, and the students gradually memorized the strategy and implemented it on their own.

Reciprocal Teaching   Like scaffolded instruction, **reciprocal teaching** involves an interactive dialogue between the teacher and students in which the teacher–student relationship is similar to that of an expert (teacher) and an apprentice (student). The teacher gradually relinquishes her or his role as the sole instructor and allows the student to assume the role of co-instructor for brief periods. The teacher models and then encourages and prompts the students to use four strategies: (1) predicting, (2) questioning, (3) summarizing, and (4) clarifying:

> During reciprocal teaching, teachers begin reading selections by having students make predictions based on story titles, headings, or other appropriate passage features. In this way, students are encouraged to activate background knowledge and information and to set a purpose for reading. Teachers then foster practice of good questioning strategies by requiring students to ask "teacher-like" questions rather than fill-in-the-blank questions. In addition, if students are unable to ask a question, the teacher might provide an appropriate question word as a prompt. Summarizing strategies for students include finding the main idea and supporting details and stating this information in their own words without looking at the text. Students are told to look for a topic sentence or to give a name to a list of items as ways to identify main ideas. Finally, students point out information that is unclear or unknown as they clarify new vocabulary, unfamiliar expressions, or ambiguous information. (Meese, 2001, p. 318)

DIRECT INSTRUCTION

The **Direct Instruction (DI)** method focuses on the details of the instructional process. Advocates of Direct Instruction stress a systematic analysis of the concept to be taught, rather than analysis of the characteristics of the student. A critical component of DI is task analysis. **Task analysis** involves breaking down academic problems into their component parts so that teachers can teach the parts separately and then teach the students to put the parts together in order to demonstrate the larger skill.

A variety of DI programs are available for reading, math, and language (Engelmann, Carnine, Engelmann, & Kelly, 1991; Engelmann, Carnine, Johnson, & Meyers, 1988, 1989). These programs consist of precisely sequenced, fast-paced lessons taught to small groups of four to ten. There is a heavy emphasis on drill and practice. The teacher teaches from a well-rehearsed script, and pupils follow the lead of the teacher, who often uses hand signals to prompt participation. The teacher offers immediate corrective feedback for errors and praise for correct responses.

Direct Instruction programs are among the most well-researched commercial programs available for students with learning disabilities. Use of these programs not only results in immediate academic gains but may also bring long-term academic gains (see Lloyd, 1988, for a review of this research).

BEST PRACTICES IN TEACHING STUDENTS WITH LEARNING DISABILITIES

Authorities have concluded that neither cognitive training nor DI, by itself, is *the* answer to instructing all students with learning disabilities. Instead, teachers should be prepared to use both. Students need teachers to teach them strategies and skills directly through DI, but they also need the chance to practice these strategies on their own using cognitive training techniques such as self-instruction, self-monitoring, scaffolded instruction, and reciprocal teaching (Rosenshine & Meister, 1994; Swanson, 2001; Swanson & Hoskyn, 1998; Vaughn, Gersten, & Chard, 2000).

Reciprocal teaching.
A cognitive teaching strategy whereby the student gradually assumes the role of co-instructor for brief periods; the teacher models four strategies for the students to use: (1) predicting, (2) questioning, (3) summarizing, and (4) clarifying.

Direct Instruction (DI).
A method of teaching academics, especially reading and math; emphasizes drill and practice and immediate feedback; lessons are precisely sequenced, fast-paced, and well-rehearsed by the teacher.

Task analysis.
The procedure of breaking down an academic task into its component parts for the purpose of instruction; a major feature of Direct Instruction.

For more information on DI, visit the Association for Direct Instruction Web site: http://www.adihome.org/ ■

RESPONSIVE INSTRUCTION

Meeting the Needs of Students with Learning Disabilities

Direct Instruction

What Is Direct Instruction?

Direct Instruction (DI) is a highly structured, teacher-directed method of instruction. The main features of DI programs are:

- Field-tested, scripted lesson plans
- Curriculum based upon the theory of mastery learning (i.e., students do not move on until they have mastered the concept)
- Rapid pace of instruction highly dependent upon frequent teacher questioning and student response
- Achievement grouping
- Frequent assessments

Siegfried Englemann developed DI in the 1960s based on studies of beginning reading. Since the development of his early DI programs such as DISTAR (Direct Instructional System for Teaching and Remediation), published in 1968, DI programs have been developed in the areas of reading, language arts, mathematics, science, and social studies. One of the defining features of DI programs is that virtually every aspect of instruction undergoes careful evaluation before it is approved for inclusion in the program. Researchers evaluate everything from group size to teacher directions to method of student response in order to achieve optimal effectiveness. As a result, DI programs have received the highest ranking for program effectiveness in an independent analysis of instructional programs (Ellis, 2001).

What the Research Says

In order to obtain an idea of the overall effectiveness of a program, researchers conduct what is called a meta-analysis. To conduct a meta-analysis, researchers identify all studies that have been conducted on a specific technique or program and statistically determine how effective the technique is as a whole. Since the inception of DI, several of these comprehensive evaluations have been conducted in regard to DI curriculum. A recent meta-analysis made over 173 comparisons between DI and other programs. Results showed: (1) 64 percent of the comparisons resulted in statistically significant differ-

ences in favor of the groups using DI, (2) 35 percent of the comparisons showed no differences among programs, and (3) 1 percent showed differences in favor of programs other than DI (Adams & Englemann, 1996). In short, the overall effectiveness of DI programs is among the highest in the field of education.

Implementing the Curriculum

In order to implement DI, teachers need to receive training in the program. Due to the highly structured nature of DI materials, many educators and administrators incorrectly assume that DI is "teacher-proof." That is, anyone could be effective using the materials. Nothing could be farther from the truth. Using the materials with ease, understanding the rationale for each component and therefore being able to communicate that to students, and pacing the instruction to meet the unique needs of a group of students requires teaching skills that cannot come from a script. After initial training, coaches or facilitators provide ongoing support for teachers who use DI programs to ensure that teachers are maximizing the effectiveness of the curriculum.

EXERCISE 3

Say the Sounds
Note: **Do not write the words on the board. This is an oral exercise.**

1. Listen: **fffēēē.** (Hold up a finger for each sound.)
2. Say the sounds in (pause) **fffēēē.** Get ready. (Hold up a finger for each sound.) *fffēēē.* (Repeat until the students say the sounds without stopping.)
3. Say it fast. (Signal.) *Fee.*
4. What word? (Signal.) *Fee.* Yes, **fee.**
5. (Repeat steps 2–4 for **if, fish, sam, at, me, rim, she, we, ship, fat, miff.**)

FIGURE A

What Does DI Look Like?

The sample script in Figure A is an excerpt from Corrective Reading, an accelerated reading program for students in grades 3.5 through 12 who have not mastered the basics of decoding and comprehension. In this decoding lesson, students work on phonemic awareness, letter-symbol identification, and sounding out words. The use of choral response increases opportunities for student engagement, and individual questioning ensures individual mastery.

—By Kristin L. Sayeski

SERVICE DELIVERY MODELS

For many years, the most common form of educational placement for students with learning disabilities was the resource room. In the mid-1990s, however, in keeping with the trend toward inclusion, the regular classroom surpassed the resource room as the most popular placement. In addition, the number of placements in separate classrooms has gradually diminished. Forty-four percent of students with learning disabilities between the ages of six and twenty-one are educated primarily in the regular classroom, with 39 percent in resource rooms and 16 percent in separate classrooms (U.S. Department of Education, 2000).

As we discussed in Chapter 2, more and more schools are moving toward some kind of cooperative teaching arrangement, in which regular and special education teachers work together in the regular classroom. Some believe this model is particularly appropriate for students with learning disabilities, since it allows them to stay in the regular classroom for all or almost all of their instruction. However, the research base for cooperative teaching is still in its infancy (Murawski & Swanson, 2001).

Because students with learning disabilities make up the largest category of special education and because their academic and behavioral problems are not as severe as those of students with mental retardation or behavior disorders, they are often candidates for full inclusion. However, all the major professional and parent organizations have developed position papers against placing all students with learning disabilities in full-inclusion settings. And there is evidence that students with learning disabilities themselves prefer

Direct Instruction programs, which consist of precisely sequenced, fast-paced lessons taught to small groups of four to ten students, may bring both immediate and long-term academic gains in students with learning disabilities. ■

The most accurate predictors of learning problems that may show up later are preacademic skills, such as counting and identifying letters, numbers, shapes, and colors. ■

resource placements over full inclusion, although many of them also think that inclusion meets their needs (Klingner, Vaughn, Schumm, Cohen, & Forgan, 1998). Research on the effectiveness of inclusion for students with learning disabilities also argues against using full inclusion for all students with learning disabilities (Klingner, Vaughn, Hughes, Schumm, & Elbaum, 1998; Vaughn, Elbaum, & Boardman, 2001). In conclusion, evidence indicates that the legal mandate of IDEA requiring the availability of a full continuum of placements is sound policy for students with learning disabilities.

Early Intervention

Very little preschool programming is available for children with learning disabilities because of the difficulties in identifying them at such a young age. When we talk about testing preschool children for learning disabilities, we are really talking about *prediction* rather than *identification* (Keogh & Glover, 1980). In other words, because preschool children do not ordinarily engage in academics, it is not possible, strictly speaking, to say that they are "behind" academically. Unfortunately, all other things being equal, prediction is always less precise than identification.

At least two factors make predicting later learning disabilities particularly difficult at the preschool age:

1. In many cases of learning disabilities, the problems are relatively mild. Many of these children seem bright and competent until faced with a particular academic task, such as reading or spelling. Unlike many other children with disabilities, children with learning disabilities are not so immediately identifiable.

MAKING IT WORK

Collaboration and Co-Teaching for Students with Learning Disabilities

"How can she help me if she doesn't know science like I do?"

Co-teaching with a special educator to meet the needs of students with learning disabilities (LD) can and should take many forms in the classroom. Experts on co-teaching have identified at least five different models for use in the classroom, many of them incorporating the special educator as an equal partner in instruction (see Vaughn, Schumm, & Arguelles, 1997). But how can this work if the special educator is not as much of a content area specialist as the general educator, often an occurrence at the secondary level? Though you might think that would mean an end to equal collaboration in, say, a biology or advanced literature course, teachers of students with learning disabilities have knowledge and skills about learning that can be used across content areas to make them an active part of any co-teaching team.

What Does It Mean to Be a Teacher of Students with Learning Disabilities?

Most training programs for teachers of students with learning disabilities do not focus on content area information. Rather, they focus on understanding learning and effective strategies to promote learning across the content areas. Specifically, the Council for Exceptional Children (2001) has identified the following skills as those necessary for beginning teachers of students with learning disabilities:

1. Modify the pace of instruction and provide organizational cues
2. Identify and teach basic structures and relationships within and across curricula

2. It is often difficult to determine what is a true developmental delay and what is merely maturational slowness. Many nondisabled children show slow developmental progress at this young age, but they soon catch up with their peers.

There has been growing sentiment among some professionals not to use the "learning disability" label with preschoolers. Noting that this label implies deficits in academics, which are not ordinarily introduced until kindergarten or first grade, these professionals favor using more generic labels for preschool children, such as "developmentally delayed" or "at risk." Those who favor using the "learning disability" label argue that the sooner a child's specific problems can be identified, the sooner teachers and parents can make plans for the long-term nature of the condition.

To aid parents and professionals, research is needed on developing better predictive tests at the preschool level. At present, we know that the most accurate predictors are pre-academic skills (Foorman, Francis, Shaywitz, Shaywitz, & Fletcher, 1997; Lerner, 2000). **Preacademic skills** are behaviors that are needed before formal instruction can begin, such as identification of numbers, shapes, and colors. A particularly important preacademic skill for reading is phonological awareness (Torgesen, 2001), a skill we discussed earlier (see p. 162). Phonological awareness is the ability to understand that speech flow can be broken into smaller sound units such as words, syllables, and phonemes. Nondisabled children generally develop phonological awareness in the preschool years. Preschoolers who exhibit problems in phonological awareness are at risk to have reading disabilities after they enter elementary school.

Preacademic skills. Behaviors that are needed before formal academic instruction can begin (e.g., ability to identify letters, numbers, shapes, and colors).

The Coordinated Campaign for Learning Disabilities, consisting of the major professional and parent organizations in learning disabilities, has focused on public awareness of learning disabilities. In particular, it has emphasized making parents of young children aware of the benefits of early identification of learning disabilities: http://www.aboutld.org/ ■

Transition to Adulthood

At one time professionals thought that children outgrew their learning disabilities by adulthood. We now know that this is far from the truth. Although the long-term prognosis for individuals with learning disabilities is generally more positive than that for

3. Use instructional methods to strengthen and compensate for deficits in perception, comprehension, memory, and retrieval
4. Identify and teach essential concepts, vocabulary, and content across the general curriculum
5. Implement systematic instruction in teaching reading comprehension and monitoring strategies
6. Teach learning strategies and study skills to acquire academic content

Most of these skills can help all students in the classroom. These skills are supported by instructional strategies that have been researched and used in the general education classroom for students with learning disabilities and others—strategies that each co-teacher can use to improve learning in his or her classroom.

Successful Strategies for Co-Teaching

Peer-Assisted Learning Strategies (PALS) is a form of peer tutoring that has been shown to improve reading skills for students with LD, as well as low- and average-achieving students in grades 2 through 6 and in high school (Fuchs, et al., 2001). Students are organized in pairs and given specific tasks (partner reading, paragraph shrinking, and prediction relay) to complete as both tutor and tutee, all of which are upper-level skills necessary in content area reading through high school. In partner reading, pairs take turns reading text and correcting errors. In paragraph shrinking, students take turns reading text and summarizing it. During prediction relay, pairs take turns reading text, summarizing it, and then predicting what the next block of text will be about. For all tasks, tutors provide feedback for tutees. Students are taught how to complete the tasks, how to give corrective and appropriate feedback, and how to interact appropriately. The dyads are also on teams, and points are awarded for correct or corrected responses that help the team. In the general education classroom, the teacher of students with LD could be responsible for teaching and implementing the component pieces of PALS on an ongoing basis, while the general educator could be responsible for providing the content area reading material and the extension of the information read to projects, etc. There would also be double the sets of hands to put peer tutoring in motion! More information about PALS is available at www.vanderbilt.edu/kennedy/pals.

—By Margaret P. Weiss

RESPONSIVE INSTRUCTION

Meeting the Needs of Students with Learning Disabilities

PALS—Peer-Assisted Learning Strategies

What the Research Says

In response to increasing student academic diversity within general education settings, researchers at Vanderbilt University have developed a framework for instruction that results in increased individualization, higher levels of student engagement, and greater teacher accountability for student learning (Fuchs & Fuchs, 1998). The program, Peer-Assisted Learning Strategies (PALS), is based upon research-proven, best practices in reading, such as phonological awareness, decoding, and comprehension activities. PALS curriculum is effective for students with and without learning disabilities at all grade levels (Fuchs, Fuchs, & Burish, 2000).

Overview of First-Grade PALS

All PALS programs involve the pairing of a higher-performing student with a lower-performing student. The pairs participate in three highly structured tutoring sessions lasting thirty-five minutes each per week. During each session, students take turns being the Coach (the tutor) and the Reader (the tutee).

The first-grade PALS curriculum includes two main activities—working with sounds and words and reading connected text. During the sounds-and-words part of the lesson, there is both a teacher-directed component and the partnering component. Teacher-directed instruction involves instruction in sounds, segmenting, and blending (i.e., breaking words apart into their individual sounds and blending individual sounds into words). Partnering activities include: saying sounds, sounding out, identifying sight words, and reading PALS stories. For the final activity, students take turns reading out of big books or other trade books.

Implementing the Curriculum

To implement PALS in the classroom, teachers first rank order all of their students from lowest to highest, then divide the class into high performers and low performers. The highest performer is matched to the highest student in the low-performer group. This matching continues until all students are matched. In addition to rank, teachers should consider student personality when making these matches. After the pairs are assigned, the teacher then assigns the pairs to one of two teams. The pairs earn points during each session and these points are added to overall team points. Students stay with their partner for about four weeks.

During the first couple of weeks of implementation, the students are taught how to work with their partner using the PALS materials. Teachers use scripts to assist them in teaching students the rules for PALS, correcting mistakes, and assigning points for the various activities.

Sample Script

The following is part of the script a teacher would use when teaching students the PALS procedures. The sample comes from Training Lesson 3, the "Saying Sounds" part of the lesson (Mathes, et al., 2001).

SAYING SOUNDS

Teacher: You did a nice job of saying sounds in words and reading them. Now you're going to practice "Saying Sounds" with your partner. Readers, open your folders and take out Lesson 3. [*Place the PALS Lesson 3 transparency on the overhead.*] We have a new sound today. The new sound today is /sss/. What sound?

Students: sss

Teacher: Coaches, when there is a new sound in a box, remember to tell your partner the new sound for the day. You should say, "The new sound for today is /sss/. What sound?" Then Readers will say the sounds. Coaches, use a soft voice to tell your partners the new sound for the day. Readers, say the sound in a soft voice. [*Award points to pairs following directions.*] Great job saying the new sound. If I'm the Coach, what do I say as I touch each letter?

Students: What sound?

Teacher: Great! And what do I say when I point to a star?

Students: Good job! Great! Super!

Teacher: Great! You're ready to practice with your partner. You'll do "Saying Sounds." Remember to make some mistakes so your partner can practice helping you. Don't forget to mark your happy faces and 5 points, then switch jobs. Stop when the timer rings.

Begin. [*Set the timer for 4 minutes. Monitor and give points. Stop when the timer rings.* (See Figure A.)]

After about two weeks, students should be able to follow the PALS procedures with less teacher support. Teachers, however, should continue to move around the classroom and support pairs as well as assign points to reinforce appropriate behaviors.

In summary, the PALS components—partnering of high and low performers, structured sessions, effective reading practices, and frequent positive reinforcement—result in a comprehensive approach to address critical reading skills for all students.

—*By Kristin L. Sayeski*

		LESSON 3				Coach says:
s	t	s	a	★	m	"What sound?"
s	m	t	a	s	★	
t	m	a	t	s	★	
				☺	☺	
				5 points	5 points	

FIGURE A

children with some other disabilities (e.g., behavior disorders), there is still the potential for difficulty. There is a danger, for example, that students with learning disabilities will drop out of school in their teenage years. The majority of students with learning disabilities do not drop out of school. Nonetheless, their futures can be uncertain. Many adults with learning disabilities have persistent problems in learning, socializing, holding jobs, and living independently (Blackorby & Wagner, 1997; Gerber, 1997; Goldstein, Murray, & Edgar, 1998; Witte, Philips, & Kakela, 1998). And even those individuals who are relatively successful in their transition to adulthood often must devote considerable energy to coping with daily living situations.

For example, in an intensive study of adults with learning disabilities, one of the subjects (S3), an assistant dean of students at a large urban university, found it

> essential that organization and routines remain constant. For example, she recounted that her kitchen is arranged in a specific fashion. Most implements are visible rather than put away because she would not be able to remember where to find them. Once, when her roommate changed the kitchen setup, S3 had great difficulty finding anything, and when she did, she couldn't remember where to return it. She had to reorganize the kitchen to her original plan. When she moved from her home state to the New Orleans area, she kept her kitchen set up in exactly the same way as previously. "I don't know if that's just because I'm stubborn or because it's comfortable."
>
> The need for organization and structure seems to pervade her daily living. She mentioned that she imposes structure on everything from the arrangement of her medicine cabinet to her professional life. She has her work day carefully organized and keeps close track of all her appointments. She has trouble coping with unannounced appointments, meetings or activities. She said that if her work routine is interrupted in such a fashion, "I can't get it together." (Gerber & Reiff, 1991, p. 113)

FACTORS RELATED TO SUCCESSFUL TRANSITION

How any particular adult with learning disabilities will fare depends on a variety of factors and is difficult to predict. Several researchers have addressed the topic of what contributes

For more information on PALS, visit their Web site: http://www.vanderbilt.edu/kennedy/pals/index.html ■

to successful adjustment of adults with learning disabilities (Gerber, Ginsberg, & Reiff, 1992; Kavale, 1988; Raskind, Goldberg, Higgins, & Herman, 1999; Reiff, Gerber, & Ginsberg, 1997; Spekman, Goldberg, & Herman, 1992). Although it would seem that IQ and achievement would be the best predictors of success, according to successful adults with learning disabilities, the things that set them apart from those who are not as successful are:

- An extraordinary degree of perseverance
- The ability to set goals for oneself
- A realistic acceptance of weaknesses coupled with an attitude of building on strengths
- Access to a strong network of social support from friends and family
- Exposure to intensive and long-term educational intervention
- Being able to take control of their lives

The latter attribute, in particular, is a consistent theme among the successful. They have not let their disability rule them, but rather they have taken the initiative to control their own destiny. As one adult remarked on looking back at his days in secondary school:

> Having an LD is much akin to being blind or losing the use of an appendage; it affects all aspects of your life. In dealing with this, you have two choices. One, you can acknowledge the parasitic relationship the LD has with you and consciously strive to excel despite its presence. . . . The other path let[s] the LD slowly dominate you and become[s] the scapegoat for all your failings. Can't find a good job? Must be the LD. Relationships always fail? It's the LD. If you follow this destructive path, you spend the remainder of your life being controlled by your LD. (Queen, 2001, p. 15)

SECONDARY PROGRAMMING

Approaches to educating students with learning disabilities at the secondary level differ, depending on whether the goal is to prepare students for college or work. In general, there are seven different program options for students with learning disabilities at the secondary level: functional skills, work-study, basic skills remediation, tutorial in subject areas, learning strategies, inclusion or co-teaching, and consultation (Bender, 2001). The first two are oriented more toward preparing students for the world of work than the others. However, schools often offer a blend of these models.

Functional Skills   The functional skills model concentrates on adaptive skills, such as on-the-job behavior, filling out job applications, balancing a checkbook, and so forth. It is often combined with a work-study and/or basic skills model.

Work-Study   The work-study option provides supervised work experiences during the school day. Ideally, the student is able to explore a variety of jobs of interest to her or him.

Basic Skills   With this approach, the special education teacher provides instruction in basic academic skills in math, language arts, and reading. The amount of instruction, delivered by a special educator in a separate classroom, varies according to need.

Tutorial   The special education teacher tutors the student in the content areas—history, math, English, and so forth. One disadvantage is that the special educator is "stretched" to teach in areas in which he or she may not have a great deal of expertise.

Learning Strategies   The learning strategies model was developed at the University of Kansas Center for Research on Learning and focuses on teaching students to overcome their metacognitive deficits by using learning strategies (Deshler et al., 2001). The Kansas

For more information on the University of Kansas Center for Research on Learning visit: http://www.ku-crl.org/htmlfiles/core.html
For specific information on the Strategic Instruction Model developed for adolescents with learning disabilities, visit: http://www.ku-crl.org/htmlfiles/sim.html ■

group has developed a variety of strategies that students can use to help them organize information and learn it more efficiently.

Co-Teaching   In this model, the special and general educator teach together in the general education classroom. As we noted in Chapter 2, there are various co-teaching models, ranging from the general educator delivering the main content and the special educator supplementing the instruction with tutorial help, to both teachers taking turns delivering the content.

Consultation   In the consultation model, the special education teacher consults with the general education teacher on ways to modify the general education curriculum to meet the needs of students with learning disabilities. The general educator delivers the instruction rather than the special educator.

POSTSECONDARY PROGRAMMING

Postsecondary programs include vocational and technical programs as well as community colleges and four-year colleges and universities. More and more individuals with learning disabilities are enrolling in colleges and universities, and more and more universities are establishing special programs and services for these students. In the decade of the 1990s, for example, the percentage of entering first-year college students with learning disabilities nearly tripled—from 1.2 percent to 3.5 percent (Henderson, 1999, as cited in Hitchings et al., 2001).

One of the major difficulties students with learning disabilities face in the transition from high school to college is the decrease in the amount of guidance provided by adults. Many students find this greater emphasis on self-discipline particularly difficult. The greater demands on writing skills (Gajar, 1989) and note taking also present major problems for many college students with learning disabilities.

Secondary-school teachers should prepare their students to make the right choices of colleges, as well as help them delineate what accommodations they will need in their programs. Students and their families may take advantage of published guides to college programs for students with learning disabilities (Cobb, 2001; Kravets & Wax, 2001; Strichart & Mangrum, 2001). Also, students can avail themselves of the special accommodations available for students who are learning disabled when they take the Scholastic Aptitude Test (SAT) and the American College Test (ACT).

In selecting a college, students and their families should explore what kinds of student support services are offered. Section 504 of the Vocational Rehabilitation Act of 1973 (Public Law 93–112) requires that colleges make reasonable accommodations for students with disabilities so that they will not be discriminated against because of their disabilities. Some typical accommodations are extended time on exams, allowing students to take exams in a distraction-free room, providing tape recordings of lectures and books, and assigning volunteer note-takers for lectures. In addition, two key ingredients are *comprehensiveness* and *individualization*.

> With these support services in mind, there are two overall considerations in selecting a college program: comprehensiveness and individualization. The prospective student should consider the comprehensiveness of services offered. A service plan that includes some type of summer orientation and training program, tutoring in various classes, assessment as needed, emotional support, and accommodations in program planning should meet the needs of most students. However, even when comprehensive services are provided, an individually tailored program is critical. Students should not settle for a program that attempts to fit all students with learning disabilities into one standard program. Rather, case managers should meet with the student with learning disabilities to individually plan appropriate services. (Bender, 2001, p. 370)

A major difficulty faced by students with learning disabilities in the transition from high school to college is the decrease in the amount of guidance provided by adults, and the greater demand on self-discipline. ■

A potentially useful skill for college students with learning disabilities can be self-advocacy, the ability to understand one's disability, be aware of one's legal rights, and communicate one's rights and needs to professors and administrators (Hitchings et al., 2001). Although self-advocacy skills ideally should be taught to students with learning disabilities in secondary school, many students come to college in need of guidance in how to go about advocating for themselves in a confident but nonconfrontational manner.

There is little doubt that much remains to be learned about programming effectively for students with learning disabilities at the postsecondary level. However, the field has made great strides in opening windows of opportunity for these young adults. Authorities have noted that many college applicants with learning disabilities attempt to hide their disabilities for fear they will not be admitted (Skinner, 1998). If the burgeoning interest in postsecondary programming for individuals who are learning disabled continues, we may in the near future see the day when students and colleges routinely collaborate to use information concerning students' learning disabilities in planning their programs.

Summary

The three most common factors in definitions of learning disabilities are (1) presumption of central nervous system (CNS) dysfunction, (2) psychological processing problems, and (3) IQ–achievement discrepancy. The most commonly used definition is that of the federal government, which includes all three factors. Another popular definition, that of the National Joint Committee for Learning Disabilities, does not include psychological processing problems and includes the assertion that learning disabilities may continue into adulthood.

Policy makers are struggling with the definition of learning disabilities, in general, and identification procedures, in particular. The major issue centers on the use of IQ–achievement discrepancy. Several authorities have questioned using discrepancy on theoretical and practical grounds. At this time the future of identification procedures for learning disabilities is uncertain.

The prevalence of students identified as learning disabled has increased dramatically, more than doubling since 1976–1977. Some believe this growth indicates that teachers are too quick to label students as learning disabled; others argue that social-cultural factors (e.g., increased poverty, increased stress on families) have contributed to the growth of learning disabilities. Boys outnumber girls in the learning disabilities category by three to one; researchers do not agree on the reasons for this difference in prevalence, however.

More and more evidence is accumulating that many persons with learning disabilities have CNS dysfunction. Possible reasons for the CNS dysfunction include genetic, teratogenic, and medical factors.

Practitioners use four general types of assessment with students with learning disabilities: standardized, formative, informal, and authentic assessment. Standardized instruments compare the student with a normative group. Formative evaluation methods have five features: (1) the teacher usually does the assessment; (2) the teacher assesses classroom behaviors directly; (3) the measures are taken frequently and over a period of time; (4) the assessment is done in conjunction with the setting of educational goals; and (5) the teacher uses the assessment information to decide whether the educational program for an individual student is effective. Curriculum-based assessment is a type of formative evaluation. Informal assessment includes having students do academic work in order to analyze where they have problems. Doing an error analysis can help identify what skills need to be remediated. Authentic assessment methods, such as portfolios, evaluate students' critical-thinking and problem-solving abilities in real-life situations.

Persons with learning disabilities exhibit a great deal of inter- and intraindividual variation in their psychological and behavioral characteristics. The interindividual variation is reflected in the heterogeneity of this population. Intraindividual variation means that persons with learning disabilities often have uneven profiles of abilities.

Academic deficits are the hallmarks of learning disabilities. Reading disabilities are often related to poor phonological skills. Students with learning disabilities can also have problems in written or spoken language and math. Some persons with learning disabilities have problems in perceptual, perceptual-motor, or general coordination.

Persons with learning disabilities often have problems with attention. And some have attentional problems serious enough to also have attention deficit hyperactivity disorder (ADHD).

Many individuals with learning disabilities demonstrate memory deficits. In particular, they can have problems with short-term memory and working memory, the ability to keep information in mind while also doing another cognitive task. In addition, they have cognitive problems that lead to disorganization and metacognitive problems that interfere with their ability to recognize task requirements, select and use appropriate strategies, and monitor and adjust performance.

Persons with learning disabilities tend to be rejected by their peers and to have poor self-concepts. Some students are identified as having nonverbal learning disabilities, which involve problems with social behavior, math, visual-spatial tasks, tactual tasks, and self-regulation and organization. These problems are thought to be associated with dysfunction of the right hemisphere of the brain.

Persons with learning disabilities frequently have difficulty being motivated enough to perform. They often have an external locus of control and display learned helplessness.

Some authorities believe that a composite of many of the preceding characteristics indicates that many students with learning disabilities are passive rather than active learners. Many of their problems, such as a propensity to have problems with homework, may be due to this inactive approach to learning.

Educational methods for alleviating the academic problems of students with learning disabilities include cognitive training and Direct Instruction.

Cognitive training focuses on (1) changing thought processes, (2) providing strategies for learning, and (3) teaching self-initiative. Self-instruction, self-monitoring, scaffolded instruction, and reciprocal teaching are examples of cognitive training. Direct Instruction focuses even more directly on academics than does cognitive training. It concentrates on instructional processes and a systematic task analysis of the concept to be taught, rather than on characteristics of the student. Research indicates that teachers should use a combination of cognitive training and Direct Instruction techniques.

The regular classroom has surpassed the resource room as the most common placement for students with learning disabilities. Cooperative teaching, in which regular and special education teachers work together in the regular classroom, is gaining in popularity, although the research supporting this approach is still developing. Students with learning disabilities are often seen as the most likely candidates for full-inclusion programs, although many professional and parent organizations have resisted overuse of this approach.

Most professionals are cautious about establishing programs for children with learning disabilities at the preschool level because it is so hard to predict at that age which children will develop later academic problems. Some prefer to label preschoolers as "at risk" or "developmentally delayed." We do know that certain preacademic skills—such as letter, shape, and color recognition and especially phonological awareness—are the best predictors of later academic learning.

The importance of educational programming at the secondary level and beyond is underscored by evidence that persons with learning disabilities do not automatically outgrow their problems as adults. For example, students with learning disabilities are at risk to drop out of school. The majority who stay in school are still at risk of having problems in learning, socializing, holding jobs, and performing daily living skills. The most important factors related to successful transition to adulthood are: (1) perseverance, (2) goal setting, (3) realistic acceptance of weaknesses coupled with building on strengths, (4) a supportive social network, (5) intensive and long-term educational intervention, and especially (6) the ability to take control of one's life.

Educational programming at the secondary level varies according to whether the goal is preparation for college or work. Generally, educators can use seven models alone or in combination: functional skills, work-study, basic skills, tutorial, learning strategies, co-teaching, and consultation.

Postsecondary programming has taken on more importance as the number of students with learning disabilities attending college has nearly tripled in the past few years. The most important components of postsecondary programs for students with learning disabilities are comprehensiveness and individualization.

Roger Swike

Untitled (00–99), Ink, Marker on paper. 12 × 18 in.

Mr. Swike, who was born in 1962 in Boston Massachusetts, has codified and organized the world at large through his artwork since he was a child. He is a relentless fan of broadband TV and popular culture. In his work he associated specific colors and themes with specific numbers.

Learners with Attention Deficit Hyperactivity Disorder

Let me see if Philip can
Be a little gentleman.
Let me see, if he is able
To sit still for once at table;
Thus Papa bade Phil behave;
And Mamma look'd very grave.
But fidgety Phil,
He won't sit still;
He wriggles
And giggles,
And then, I declare
Swings backwards and forwards
And tilts up his chair,
Just like any rocking horse;
"Philip! I am getting cross!"
See the naughty restless child
Growing still more rude and wild
Till his chair falls over quite.
Philip screams with all his might.
Catches at the cloth, but then
That makes matters worse again.

Down upon the ground they fall.
Glasses, plates, knives, forks and all.
How Mamma did fret and frown
When she saw them tumbling down!
And Papa made such a face!
Philip is in sad disgrace.
Where is Philip, where is he?
Fairly cover'd up you see!
Cloth and all are lying on him;
He has pull'd down all upon him.
What a terrible to-do!
Dishes, glasses, snapt in two!
Here a knife, and there a fork!
Philip, this is cruel work.
Table all so bare, and ah!
Poor Papa, and poor Mamma
Look quite cross, and wonder how
They shall make their dinner now.

HEINRICH HOFFMANN
"The Story of Fidgety Philip"

For more information on Heinrich Hoffman see: http://www.ricochetjeunes.org/eng/biblio/author/hoffmanh.html

You can see the "Fidgety Philip" and "Johnny-Head-in-Air" nursery rhymes complete with illustrations at http://www.fln.vcu.edu/struwwel/philipp_e.html and at http://www.fln.vcu.edu/struwwel/guck_e.html ■

In 1998, The National Institutes of Health brought together a panel of experts from a variety of disciplines, including medicine, psychology, and special education, to arrive at consensus regarding identification and treatment of ADHD. Although they concluded that more research was needed on various issues, they affirmed the validity of ADHD: "Although an independent diagnostic test for ADHD does not exist, there is evidence supporting the validity of the disorder." To see the complete NIH consensus statement go to: //http:odp.od.nih.gov/consensus/cons/110/110_statement.htm ■

idgety Phil, the character in the poem by the German physician Heinrich Hoffmann (see p. 185) is generally considered one of the first allusions in Western literature to what today is referred to as attention deficit hyperactivity disorder (ADHD) (Barkley, 1998). Phil's lack of impulse control bears an uncanny similarity to today's conceptualization of ADHD as not so much a matter of inattention as primarily a matter of regulating one's behavior. We discuss this conceptualization more fully later, but it is also important to point out here that Phil's excessive motor activity, or hyperactivity, may be characteristic of many children with ADHD, but not all. Interestingly, Hoffman also wrote another poem, "The Story of Johnny Head-in-Air," about a child who fits to a tee children with ADHD who do not have problems with hyperactivity.

The fact that the condition was recognized as early as the mid-nineteenth century, albeit only in the form of a "poetic case study," is important. Today, ADHD is often the subject of criticism, being referred to as a "phantom" or "bogus" condition—sort of a fashionable, trendy diagnosis for persons who are basically lazy and unmotivated. Such thinking is probably behind some of the reasons why ADHD is not recognized as its own separate category (as are mental retardation, learning disabilities, and so forth) by the U.S. Department of Education; students with ADHD are served by special education under the category of "other health impaired."

Although there are undoubtedly a few persons who hide behind an inappropriate diagnosis of ADHD, evidence indicates that the condition is extremely real for those who have it. And as we point out in the next section, ADHD is not a recently "discovered," trendy diagnosis.

Brief History

In addition to Hoffmann's account of Fidgety Phil, published in the mid-nineteenth century, we have more scientific evidence of the existence of ADHD, dating back to the beginning of the twentieth century.

STILL'S CHILDREN WITH "DEFECTIVE MORAL CONTROL"

Dr. George F. Still, a physician, is credited with being one of the first authorities to bring the condition we now call ADHD to the attention of the medical profession. Still delivered three lectures to the Royal College of Physicians of London in 1902 in which he described cases of children who displayed spitefulness, cruelty, disobedience, impulsivity, and problems of attention and hyperactivity. He referred to them as having "defective moral control." Moral control involves inhibitory volition—the ability to refrain from engaging impulsively in inappropriate behavior:

> Volition, in so far as it is concerned in moral control, may be regarded as inhibitory; it is the overpowering of one stimulus to activity—which in this connection is activity contrary to the good of all—by another stimulus which we might call the moral idea, the idea of the good of all. There is, in fact, a conflict between stimuli, and in so far as the moral idea prevails the determining or volitional process may be regarded as inhibiting the impulse which is opposed to it. (Still, 1902, p. 1088)

Although Still's words are more than a century old, they still hold currency. For example, one of the most influential current psychological theories is based on the notion that the essential impairment in ADHD is a deficit involving behavioral inhibition (Barkley, 1997, 1998).

Learners with Attention Deficit Hyperactivity Disorder

MYTH All children with ADHD are hyperactive.	**FACT** Psychiatric classification of ADHD includes (1) ADHD, Predominantly Inattentive Type, (2) ADHD, Predominantly Hyperactive-Impulsive Type, or (3) ADHD, Combined Type. Some children with ADHD exhibit no hyperactivity and are classified as ADHD, Predominantly Inattentive.
MYTH The primary symptom of ADHD is inattention.	**FACT** Although the psychiatric classification includes an Inattentive Type, recent conceptualizations of ADHD place problems with behavioral inhibition and executive functions as the primary behavioral problems of ADHD.
MYTH ADHD is a fad, a trendy diagnosis of recent times with little research to support its existence.	**FACT** Reports of cases of ADHD go back to the mid- nineteenth century and the beginning of the twentieth century. Serious scientific study of it began in the early and mid-twentieth century. There is now a firmly established research base supporting its existence.
MYTH ADHD is primarily the result of minimal brain injury.	**FACT** In most cases of ADHD there is no evidence of actual damage to the brain. Most authorities believe that ADHD is the result of neurological dysfunction, which is often linked to hereditary factors.
MYTH The social problems of students with ADHD are due to their not knowing how to interact socially.	**FACT** Most persons with ADHD know how to interact, but their problems with behavioral inhibition make it difficult for them to implement socially appropriate behaviors.
MYTH Using psycho-stimulants, such as Ritalin, can easily turn children into abusers of other substances, such as cocaine and marijuana.	**FACT** There is no evidence that using psychostimulants for ADHD leads directly to drug abuse. In fact, there is evidence that those who are prescribed Ritalin as children are less likely to turn to illicit drugs as teenagers. However, care should be taken to make sure that children or others do not misuse the psychostimulants prescribed for them.
MYTH Psychostimulants have a "paradoxical effect" in that they subdue children rather than activate them. Plus, they have this effect only on those with ADHD.	**FACT** Psychostimulants, instead of sedating children, actually *activate* parts of the brain responsible for behavioral inhibition and executive functions. In addition, this effect occurs in persons without ADHD, too.
MYTH Because students with ADHD react strongly to stimulation, their learning environments should be highly unstructured in order to take advantage of their natural learning styles.	**FACT** Most authorities recommend a highly structured classroom for students with ADHD, especially in the early stages of instruction.
MYTH ADHD largely disappears in adulthood.	**FACT** Authorities now hold that about two-thirds of children diagnosed with ADHD in childhood will continue to have the condition as adults.

Still's cases were also similar to today's population of persons with ADHD in at least five ways:

1. Still speculated that many of these children had mild brain pathology
2. Many of the children had normal intelligence
3. The condition was more prevalent in males than females
4. There was evidence that the condition had a hereditary basis
5. Many of the children and their relatives also had other physical problems, such as depression and tics

We return later to Barkley's theory and to the above five points. Suffice it to say here that Still's children with "defective moral control" today would very likely be diagnosed as having ADHD by itself, or ADHD with **conduct disorder.** (Conduct disorder, which we discuss more fully in Chapter 7, is characterized by a pattern of aggressive, disruptive behavior.)

GOLDSTEIN'S BRAIN-INJURED SOLDIERS OF WORLD WAR I

Kurt Goldstein reported on the psychological effects of brain injury in soldiers who had suffered head wounds in combat in World War I. Among other things, he observed in his patients the psychological characteristics of disorganized behavior, hyperactivity, perseveration, and a "forced responsiveness to stimuli" (Goldstein, 1936, 1939). **Perseveration,** the tendency to repeat the same behaviors over and over again, is often cited today by clinicians as a characteristic of persons with ADHD. Goldstein found that the soldiers' forced responsiveness to stimuli was evident in their inability to concentrate perceptually on the "figure" without being distracted by the "ground." For example, instead of focusing on a task in front of them (the figure), they were easily distracted by objects on the periphery (the background).

THE STRAUSS SYNDROME

Goldstein's work laid the foundation for the investigations of Heinz Werner and Alfred Strauss in the 1930s and 1940s. Having emigrated from Germany to the United States after Hitler's rise to power, they teamed up to try to replicate Goldstein's findings. Werner and Strauss noted the same behaviors of distractibility and hyperactivity in some children with mental retardation.

In addition to clinical observations, Werner and Strauss also used an experimental task consisting of figure/background slides presented at very brief exposure times. The slides depicted figures (e.g., a hat) embedded in a background (e.g., wavy lines). They found that the children with supposed brain damage, when asked what they saw, were more likely than those without brain damage to say they had seen the background (e.g., "wavy lines") rather than the figure (e.g., "a hat") (Strauss & Werner, 1942; Werner & Strauss, 1939, 1941). After these studies, professionals came to refer to children who were apparently hyperactive and distractible as exhibiting the **Strauss syndrome.**

CRUICKSHANK'S WORK

William Cruickshank, using Werner and Strauss's figure/background task, found that children with cerebral palsy were also more likely to respond to the background rather than the figure (Cruickshank, Bice, & Wallen, 1957). There were two important ways in which this research extended the work of Werner and Strauss. First, whereas Werner and Strauss had largely *assumed* that their children were brain damaged, Cruickshank's children all had **cerebral palsy**—a condition that is relatively easy to diagnose. Cerebral palsy is characterized by brain damage that results in impairments in movement (see Chapter 12). Second, the children studied were largely of normal intelligence, thus demonstrating that children without mental retardation could display distractibility and hyperactivity.

Conduct disorder.
A disorder characterized by overt, aggressive, disruptive behavior or covert antisocial acts such as stealing, lying, and fire setting; may include both overt and covert acts.

Perseveration.
A tendency to repeat behaviors over and over again; often found in persons with brain injury, as well as those with ADHD.

Strauss syndrome.
Behaviors of distractibility, forced responsiveness to stimuli, and hyperactivity; based on the work of Alfred Strauss and Heinz Werner with children with mental retardation.

Cerebral palsy.
A condition characterized by paralysis, weakness, incoordination, and/or other motor dysfunction because of damage to the brain before it has matured.

Cruickshank is also important historically because he was one of the first to establish an educational program for children who today would meet the criteria for ADHD. (We discuss his educational program later in the chapter.) At the time (the late 1950s), however, many of these children were referred to as "minimally brain injured."

MINIMAL BRAIN INJURY AND HYPERACTIVE CHILD SYNDROME

At about the same time as Cruickshank's extension of Werner and Strauss's work to children of normal intelligence, the results of a now classic study were published (Pasamanick, Lilienfeld, & Rogers, 1956). This study of the aftereffects of birth complications revived Still's notion that subtle brain pathology could result in behavior problems, such as hyperactivity and distractibility. Professionals began to apply the label of minimal brain injury to children who were of normal intelligence but who were inattentive, impulsive, and/or hyperactive. Although popular in the 1950s and 1960s, the label of **minimal brain injury** fell out of favor, with professionals pointing out that it was difficult to document actual tissue *damage* to the brain (Birch, 1964).

Minimal brain injury was replaced in the 1960s by the label "hyperactive child syndrome" (Barkley, 1998). **Hyperactive child syndrome** was preferred because it was descriptive of *behavior* and did not rely on vague and unreliable diagnoses of subtle brain damage. This label's popularity extended into the 1970s. By the 1980s, however, it too had fallen out of favor as research began to point out that inattention, and not hyperactivity, was the major behavioral problem experienced by these children. In fact, some exhibited attention problems without excessive movement.

This recognition of inattention as more important than hyperactivity is reflected in today's definition of ADHD and its immediate predecessors. However, as we discuss later, some authorities are now recommending that deficits in behavioral inhibition replace inattention as the primary deficit in ADHD. In any case, most authorities do not view hyperactivity as the primary deficit in ADHD.

Minimal brain injury. A term used to refer to children who exhibit inattention, impulsivity, and/or hyperactivity; popular in the 1950s and 1960s.

Hyperactive child syndrome. A term used to refer to children who exhibit inattention, impulsivity, and/or hyperactivity; popular in the 1960s and 1970s.

Definition

Most professionals rely on the American Psychiatric Association's (APA's) *Diagnostic and statistical manual of mental disorders (DSM)* for the criteria used to determine whether an individual has ADHD. Over the years, researchers and practitioners have debated whether ADHD was a single syndrome or whether there were subtypes. Partly as a result of this debate the name for the condition has changed from time to time. For example, for several years the APA used the general term *attention deficit disorder (ADD)* to refer to all people with the condition. It then allowed for the subtypes of ADD with Hyperactivity and ADD without Hyperactivity.

The current DSM uses ADHD as the general term and subdivides individuals into: (1) ADHD, Predominantly Inattentive Type; (2) ADHD, Predominantly Hyperactive-Impulsive Type; and (3) ADHD, Combined Type (American Psychiatric Association, 2000). See Table 6.1.

Prevalence

ADHD is widely recognized as one of the most frequent reasons, if not the most frequent reason, why children are referred for behavioral problems to guidance clinics. From one-third to one-half of cases referred to guidance clinics are for ADHD (Richters et al., 1995). Most authorities estimate that from 3 to 5 percent of the school-age population have ADHD (National Institutes of Health, 1998). However, because ADHD is not recognized

TABLE 6.1   Diagnostic Criteria for Attention Deficit Hyperactivity Disorder

A. Either (1) or (2):

    (1) six (or more) of the following symptoms of *inattention* have persisted for at least 6 months to a degree that is maladaptive and inconsistent with developmental level:

    Inattention

      (a) often fails to give close attention to details or makes careless mistakes in schoolwork, work, or other activities

      (b) often has difficulty sustaining attention in tasks or play activities

      (c) often does not seem to listen when spoken to directly

      (d) often does not follow through on instructions and fails to finish schoolwork, chores, or duties in the workplace (not due to oppositional behavior or failure to understand instructions)

      (e) often has difficulty organizing tasks and activities

      (f) often avoids, dislikes, or is reluctant to engage in tasks that require sustained mental effort (such as schoolwork or homework)

      (g) often loses things necessary for tasks or activities (e.g., toys, school assignments, pencils, books, or tools)

      (h) is often easily distracted by extraneous stimuli

      (i) is often forgetful in daily activities

    (2) six (or more) of the following symptoms of hyperactivity-impulsivity have persisted for at least 6 months to a degree that is maladaptive and inconsistent with developmental level:

    Hyperactivity

      (a) often fidgets with hands or feet or squirms in seat

      (b) often leaves seat in classroom or in other situations in which remaining seated is expected

      (c) often runs about or climbs excessively in situations in which it is inappropriate (in adolescents or adults, may be limited to subjective feelings of restlessness)

      (d) often has difficulty playing or engaging in leisure activities quietly

      (e) is often "on the go" or often acts as if "driven by a motor"

      (f) often talks excessively

    Impulsivity

      (g) often blurts out answers before questions have been completed

      (h) often has difficulty awaiting turn

      (i) often interrupts or intrudes on others (e.g., butts into conversations or games)

B. Some hyperactive-impulsive or inattentive symptoms that caused impairment were present before age 7 years.

C. Some impairment from the symptoms is present in two or more settings (e.g., at school [or work] and at home).

D. There must be clear evidence of clinically significant impairment in social, academic, or occupational functioning.

E. The symptoms do not occur exclusively during the course of a Pervasive Developmental Disorder, Schizophrenia, or other Psychotic Disorder and are not better accounted for by another mental disorder (e.g., Mood Disorder, Anxiety Disorder, Dissociative Disorder, or a Personality Disorder),

Code based on type

    314.01   Attention-Deficit/Hyperactivity Disorder, Combined Type: if both Criteria A1 and A2 are met for the past 6 months

    314.00   Attention-Deficit/Hyperactivity Disorder, Predominantly Inattentive Type: if Criterion A1 is met but Criterion A2 is not met for the past 6 months

    314.01   Attention-Deficit/Hyperactivity Disorder, Predominantly Hyperactive-Impulsive Type: if Criterion A2 is met but Criterion A1 is not met for the past 6 months

Coding note: For individuals (especially adolescents and adults) who currently have symptoms that no longer meet full criteria, "In Partial Remission" should be specified.

SOURCE: Reprinted with permission from the *Diagnostic and Statistical Manual of Mental Disorders, Fourth Edition, text revision*, pp. 92–93. Copyright 2000 American Psychiatric Association.

How Many Students with ADHD Are Served in Special Education?

Because ADHD is such a prevalent condition, one would think that it would be relatively easy to find out how many students with ADHD receive special education services. Federal law, after all, requires that schools report how many students with a given disability have been identified for special education services. However, when Public Law 94–142 (the Education for All Handicapped Children Act) was passed in 1975, ADHD was not included as one of the separate categories of special education. This was due in part to two interrelated factors: (1) the research on this condition was still in its infancy, and (2) the advocacy base for children with ADHD was not yet well developed. For example, the *Diagnostic and Statistical Manual of Mental Disorders* in effect at the time, the *DSM-II* (American Psychiatric Association, 1968), was vague in its criteria for identifying children with these problems. And the major advocacy organization for people with ADHD, CHADD (Children and Adults with Attention Deficit Disorder) was not founded until 1987.

By the time of the reauthorization of the law as the Individuals with Disabilities Education Act (IDEA) in 1990, however, there was substantial research on ADHD, and CHADD's membership was well on its way to its present level of 22,000 members. CHADD lobbied hard for ADHD to be considered a separate category, arguing that children with ADHD were being denied services because they could qualify for special education only if they also had another disability, such as learning disabilities or emotional disturbance. Their lobbying was unsuccessful. However, the U.S. Department of Education, in 1991, determined that students with ADHD would be eligible for special education under the category other health impaired (OHI) "in instances where the ADD is a chronic or acute health problem that results in limited alertness, which adversely affects educational performance." And students with ADHD can also qualify for accommodations under another law (Section 504).

Many professionals are still disappointed with the decision not to include ADHD as a separate category because they say that using the OHI category is too roundabout a means of identification, and Section 504 is not completely satisfactory because it does not require an individualized education program (IEP). (See pp. 30–34 in Chapter 1 for a discussion of IEPs.)

However, the growth of the OHI category since 1991 suggests that more and more students with ADHD are being identified as OHI (see Figure A). Although numbers in the OHI category have more than tripled in ten years, the 0.35 percent reported for 1998–99 is still well below the prevalence estimates of 3 to 5 percent. Many authorities think that fewer than half of students with ADHD are receiving special education services. As long as ADHD is not recognized as a separate category of special education, however, it will be virtually impossible to know exactly how many school-age children with ADHD are receiving special education services.

FIGURE A

Percentage of students aged 6 to 21 receiving special education services in the category of "other health impaired."

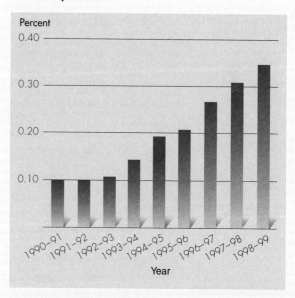

SOURCE: U.S. Department of Education. (1992, 1993, 1994, 1995, 1996, 1997, 1998, 1999, 2000). *Fourteenth, Fifteenth, Sixteenth, Seventeenth, Eighteenth, Nineteenth, Twentieth, Twenty-first, and Twenty-second annual reports to Congress on the implementation of the Individuals with Disabilities Education Act.* Washington, DC: Author.

as a separate category of special education by the U.S. Department of Education, it is difficult to estimate how many students with ADHD are served in special education. (See the box on p. 191.)

ADHD occurs much more frequently in boys than girls, with estimates ranging from about 2.5:1 to 5.1:1 in community-based samples (Barkley, 1998). This has led some to suggest that boys may be overidentified as ADHD and/or that girls may be underidentified as ADHD. They hypothesize that boys tend to exhibit more aggressive behavior, which causes them to be more noticeable. Some gender bias in referral may exist, but our best research evidence suggests that it is not enough to account for the wide disparity in prevalence rates between boys and girls. Gender differences are likely due to constitutional, or biological, differences (Barkley, 1998).

Some critics have asserted that ADHD is primarily a U.S. phenomenon, a result of our society's emphasis on achievement and conformity. However, statistics do not bear this out. Although it is difficult to compare prevalence rates cross-culturally because of differing diagnostic criteria, sampling techniques, and cultural expectations, the evidence strongly suggests that several countries have prevalence rates at least as high as that of the United States. For example, researchers have found prevalence rates of about 6 percent in Brazil (Rohde et al., 1999), 9 percent for boys and 3.3 percent for girls in Canada (Szatmari, 1992), 6 to 9 percent in China (Leung et al., 1996), 19.8 percent for boys and 12.3 percent for girls in Columbia (Pineda et al., 1999), from 4 to over 10 percent in Germany (Baumgaertel, Wolraich, & Dietrich, 1995; Esser, Schmidt, & Woerner, 1990), about 8 percent in Japan (Kanbayashi, Nakata, Fujii, Kita, & Wada, 1994), 1 to 2 percent in the Netherlands (Verhulst, van der Ende, Ferdinand, & Kasius, 1997), and 2 to 6 percent in New Zealand (Fergusson, Horwood, & Lynskey, 1993; Schaughency, McGee, Raja, Freehan, & Silva, 1994).

Assessment

Most authorities agree that there are three important components to assessing whether a student has ADHD: (1) a medical examination, (2) a clinical interview, and (3) teacher and parent rating scales (Barkley, 1998). The medical examination is necessary in order to rule out medical conditions, such as brain tumors, thyroid problems, or seizure disorders, as the cause of the inattention and/or hyperactivity.

The clinical interview of the parent(s) and the child provides information about the child's physical and psychological characteristics, as well as family dynamics and interaction with peers. Although essential to the diagnosis of ADHD, clinicians need to recognize the subjective nature of the interview situation. Some children with ADHD can look surprisingly "normal" in their behavior when in the structured and novel setting of a doctor's office. In fact, researchers have referred to this Jekyll and Hyde–like phenomenon, wherein children who are hyperactive and inattentive at home and school appear to be perfect angels in the physician's office, as the **doctor's office effect** (Cantwell, 1979; Sleator & Ullman, 1981).

Doctor's office effect. The observation that children with ADHD often do not exhibit their symptoms when seen by a clinician in a brief office visit.

In an attempt to bring some quantification to the identification process, researchers have developed rating scales to be filled out by teachers, parents, and in some cases, the child. Some of the most reliable and popular are the Conners scales and the ADHD-Rating Scale–IV. There are now several versions of the Conners scale for parents or teachers in use (Conners, 1989a, 1989b, 1997). The ADHD-Rating Scale–IV (DuPaul, Power, Anastopoulos, & Reid, 1998) is based on the *DSM-IV* criteria. Raters, who can be either parents or teachers, rate the child on items pertaining to each of the eighteen criteria listed in the *DSM-IV* (see Table 6.1). For example, for the first item, "Fails to give close attention to details or makes careless mistakes in his/her work," they rate 0 (never or rarely), 1 (sometimes), 2 (often), or 3 (very often), and so forth. Assessment scales for adults are more recent. An example is the Conners Adult ADHD Rating Scales (Conners, 1999).

In addition to medical exams and clinical interviews, rating scales filled out by teachers, parents, and in some case children, can help quantify the process of identifying children who might have ADHD. ■

The American Academy of Pediatrics has issued clinical practice guidelines for primary care physicians to use in diagnosing and evaluating children for possible ADHD (American Academy of Pediatrics, Committee on Quality Improvement, Subcommittee on Attention-Deficit/Hyperactivity Disorder, 2000). See Table 6.2.

Causes

As noted earlier, authorities in the early and mid-part of the twentieth century attributed problems of inattention and hyperactivity to neurological problems resulting from brain damage. When researchers were unable to verify actual tissue damage in cases of ADHD, many professionals soured on the idea that ADHD was neurologically based. However, as noted in our discussion of learning disabilities (see Chapter 5), the invention of neuroimaging techniques such as MRIs, PET scans, and fMRIs in the 1980s and 1990s allowed scientists for the first time to obtain more detailed and reliable measures of brain functioning. Using these techniques, researchers have made great strides in documenting the neurological basis of ADHD. Like learning disabilities, the research indicates that ADHD most likely results from neurological dysfunction rather than actual brain damage. Again like learning disabilities, evidence points to heredity as playing a very strong role in causing the neurological dysfunction, with teratogenic and other medical factors also implicated to a lesser degree.

The magazine, *Scientific American*, has an excellent article on causes by the noted ADHD authority, Russell Barkley: http://www.sciam.com/1998/0998issue/0998barkley.html ■

AREAS OF THE BRAIN AFFECTED: FRONTAL LOBES, BASAL GANGLIA, AND CEREBELLUM

Using neuroimaging techniques, several teams of researchers have found consistent abnormalities in three areas of the brain in persons with ADHD—the frontal lobes, basal ganglia (specifically, the caudate and the globus pallidus), and cerebellum (Aylward et al., 1996; Berquin et al., 1998; Castellanos et al., 1996; Filipek et al., 1997; Hynd, Semrud-Clikeman, Lorys, Novey, & Eliopulos, 1990; Hynd et al., 1993; Teicher et al., 2000). (See Figure 6.1.) Specifically, researchers have found that the size of each of these areas is

Frontal lobes.
Two lobes located in the front of the brain; responsible for executive functions; site of abnormal development in people with ADHD.

Prefrontal lobes.
Two lobes located in the very front of the frontal lobes; responsible for executive functions; site of abnormal development in people with ADHD.

Basal ganglia.
A set of structures within the brain that include the caudate, globus pallidus, and putamen, the first two being abnormal in people with ADHD; generally responsible for the coordination and control of movement.

Caudate.
A structure in the basal ganglia of the brain; site of abnormal development in persons with ADHD.

Globus pallidus.
A structure in the basal ganglia of the brain; site of abnormal development in persons with ADHD.

TABLE 6.2   American Academy of Pediatrics Clinical Practice Guidelines: Diagnosis and Evaluation of the Child with ADHD

The guidelines contain the following recommendations for the diagnosis of ADHD:

1. in a child 6 to 12 years old who presents with inattention, hyperactivity, impulsivity, academic underachievement, or behavior problems, primary care physicians should initiate evaluation for ADHD;

2. the diagnosis of ADHD requires that a child meet *Diagnostic and Statistical Manual of Mental Disorders, Fourth Edition* criteria;

3. the assessment of ADHD requires evidence directly obtained from parents or caregivers regarding the core symptoms of ADHD in various settings, the age of onset, duration of symptoms, and degree of functional impairment;

4. the assessment of ADHD requires evidence directly obtained from the classroom teacher (or other school professional) regarding the core symptoms of ADHD, duration of symptoms, degree of functional impairment, and associated conditions;

5. evaluation of the child with ADHD should include assessment for associated (coexisting) conditions;

6. other diagnostic tests are not routinely indicated to establish diagnosis of ADHD but may be used for the assessment of other coexisting conditions (e.g., learning disabilities and mental retardation).

SOURCE: Used with permission of the American Academy of Pediatrics, Committee on Quality Improvement, Subcommittee on Attention-Deficit/Hyperactivity Disorder. (2000). *Pediatrics, 105,* p. 1158.

smaller in children and adults with ADHD compared to those who are nondisabled. Although not always consistent, several of the studies point to the abnormality occurring on the right side of the brain, especially the right basal ganglia (Castellanos, 1997). In addition, PET scans suggest reduced metabolic activity in the frontal lobes and basal ganglia in persons with ADHD (Lou, Henriksen, & Bruhn, 1984; Lou, Henriksen, Bruhn, Borner, & Nielsen, 1989).

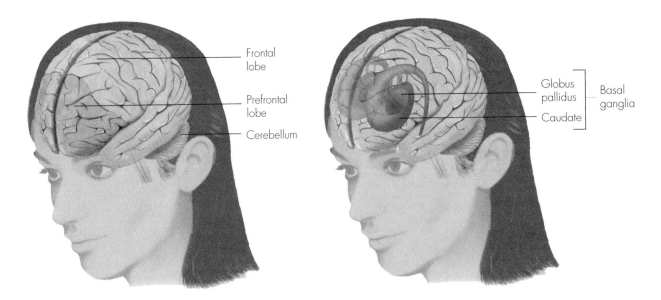

FIGURE 6.1
Areas of the brain (frontal lobes, prefrontal lobes, cerebellum, globus pallidus and caudate of the basal ganglia) identified by some researchers as abnormal in persons with ADHD.

Frontal Lobes   Located in the front of the brain, the **frontal lobes,** and especially the very front portion of the frontal lobes—the **prefrontal lobes**—are responsible for what are referred to as executive functions. Executive functions, among other things, involve the ability to regulate one's own behavior. (We discuss executive functions more fully later.)

Basal Ganglia   Buried deep within the brain, the **basal ganglia** consist of several parts, with the **caudate** and the **globus pallidus** being the structures that are abnormal in persons with ADHD. The basal ganglia are responsible for the coordination and control of motor behavior (Pinel, 2000).

Cerebellum   The **cerebellum** is also responsible for the coordination and control of motor behavior. Although it is relatively small, constituting only about 10 percent of the mass of the brain, the fact that it contains more than half of all the brain's neurons attests to its complexity (Pinel, 2000).

NEUROTRANSMITTER INVOLVED: DOPAMINE

Much exciting research is being conducted on what neurotransmitter abnormalities might cause ADHD. **Neurotransmitters** are chemicals that help in the sending of messages between neurons in the brain. One team of researchers, for example, has pointed to **serotonin** as being the key neurotransmitter involved in ADHD (Gainetdinov et al., 1999). Others, however, have identified **dopamine** as being the culprit (Castellanos, 1997; Ernst, Zametkin, Matochik, Jons, & Cohen, 1998; Ernst et al., 1999; Sagvolden & Sergeant, 1998). Evidence points to the levels of dopamine being too low in the frontal cortex, thus interfering with executive functioning, and too high in the basal ganglia, thus resulting in hyperactivity and impulsivity (Castellanos, 1997). More research is needed to determine if one or both of these neurotransmitters is abnormal in persons with ADHD.

HEREDITARY FACTORS

Most authorities agree that there is a hereditary basis to ADHD. Evidence for the genetic transmission of ADHD comes from at least three sources: family studies, twin studies, and molecular genetic studies.

Family Studies   Generally, studies indicate that if a child has ADHD, the chance of his or her sibling having ADHD is about 32 percent (Barkley, 1998). Children of adults with ADHD run a 57 percent risk of having ADHD (Biederman et al., 1995). In addition, several studies demonstrate that parents of children with ADHD are two to eight times more likely to also be ADHD than are parents of non-ADHD children (Faraone & Doyle, 2001).

Twin Studies   There are several studies comparing the prevalence of ADHD in identical (monozygotic, from the same egg) versus fraternal (dizygotic, from two eggs) twins, when one of the members of the pair has ADHD. These studies consistently show that if an identical twin and a fraternal twin each have ADHD, the second identical twin is much more likely to have ADHD than the second fraternal twin (Gillis, Gilger, Pennington, & DeFries, 1992; Sherman, Iacono, & McGue, 1997; Stevenson, 1992).

Molecular Genetic Studies   With the mapping of the human genome have come advances in **molecular genetics,** the study of the molecules (DNA, RNA, and protein) that regulate genetic information. Molecular genetic research on ADHD is in its early stages, but several studies have already implicated several genes as possibly being involved in causing ADHD (Faraone & Doyle, 2001).

TOXINS AND MEDICAL FACTORS

In Chapters 4 and 5 we discussed **toxins**—agents that can cause malformations in the developing fetus of a pregnant woman—as the cause of some cases of mental retardation

Cerebellum.
An organ at the base of the brain responsible for coordination and movement; site of abnormal development in persons with ADHD.

Neurotransmitters.
Chemicals involved in sending messages between neurons in the brain.

Serotonin.
A neurotransmitter, the levels of which may be abnormal in persons with ADHD.

Dopamine.
A neurotransmitter, the levels of which may be too low in the frontal lobes and too high in the basal ganglia of persons with ADHD.

Molecular genetics.
The study of the organization of DNA, RNA, and protein molecules containing genetic information.

Toxins.
Poisons in the environment that can cause fetal malformations; can result in cognitive impairments.

CW The American Academy of Pediatrics is an excellent Web site containing information on all kinds of medical and health-related conditions. For example, the Academy issues policy statements and press releases on diagnosis and treatment of various disabilities, e.g., blindness, deafness, ADHD, and so forth. It also provides synopses of selected articles appearing in its journal, *Pediatrics* at http://www.aap.org/ ■

Behavioral inhibition.
The ability to stop an intended response, to stop an ongoing response, to guard an ongoing response from interruption, and to refrain from responding immediately; allows executive functions to occur; delayed or impaired in those with ADHD.

Executive functions.
The ability to regulate one's behavior through working memory, inner speech, control of emotions and arousal levels, and analysis of problems and communication of problem solutions to others; delayed or impaired in those with ADHD.

Inner speech.
An executive function; internal language used to regulate one's behavior; delayed or impaired in those with ADHD.

or learning disabilities. Although the evidence is not as strong as it is for heredity, some of these same substances have been shown to be related to ADHD. For example, exposure to lead and the abuse of alcohol or tobacco (Faraone & Doyle, 2001) by pregnant women does place the unborn child at increased risk of developing ADHD.

Other medical conditions may also place children at risk for having ADHD. Again, the evidence is not as strong as it is for heredity, but complications at birth and/or low birthweight are associated with ADHD (Levy, Barr, & Sunohara, 1998; Milberger, Biederman, Faraone, Guite, & Tsuang, 1997).

Psychological and Behavioral Characteristics

One can use the *DSM-IV* criteria discussed earlier (see Table 6.1) to get a sense of some of the typical behaviors of students with ADHD. Although most people think that inattention is the key characteristic of ADHD, there is a growing consensus that inattention, as well as hyperactivity and impulsivity, are actually the result of problems in behavioral inhibition.

BARKLEY'S MODEL OF ADHD

There is an abundance of research pointing to problems with behavioral inhibition in persons with ADHD (Barkley, 1997, 1998; Semrud-Clikeman et al., 2000; Schachar, Mota, Logan, Tannock, & Klim, 2000; Willcutt et al., 2001). As we noted earlier, Russell Barkley (1997, 1998), in particular, has proposed a model of ADHD in which behavioral inhibition is key. In its simplest form this model proposes that problems in behavioral inhibition set the stage for problems in executive functions, which then disrupt the person's ability to engage in persistent goal-directed behavior.

Behavioral Inhibition   **Behavioral inhibition** refers to the ability to "withhold a planned response; to interrupt a response that has been started; to protect an ongoing activity from interfering activities; and to delay a response" (Rubia, Oosterlaan, Sergeant, Brandeis, & van Leeuwen, 1998). This can be reflected in the ability to wait one's turn, to refrain from interrupting in conversations, to resist potential distractions while working, or to delay immediate gratification in order to work for larger, long-term rewards (Tripp & Alsop, 2001). In addition, there is evidence that problems with behavioral inhibition in children with ADHD is related to abnormalities of the caudate in the brain that we discussed earlier (Semrud-Clikeman et al., 2000).

Executive Functions   The delay allowed by behavioral inhibition permits the individual to self-regulate his or her behavior. This ability to engage in a variety of self-directed behaviors involves what are referred to as **executive functions.** The fact that there is a wealth of evidence that executive functions are controlled by the prefrontal and frontal lobes of the brain fits nicely with the neuroimaging studies pointing to these areas of the brain being abnormal in persons with ADHD.

In Barkley's model, persons with ADHD can exhibit problems with executive function in four general ways. First, they often have problems with working memory (WM). As we noted in Chapter 5, WM refers to a person's ability to keep information in mind that "can be used to guide one's actions either now or in the near future" (Barkley & Murphy, 1998, p. 2). In the case of students with ADHD, deficiencies in WM can result in forgetfulness, a lack of hindsight and forethought, and problems with time management.

Second, persons with ADHD frequently have delayed inner speech. **Inner speech** is the inner "voice" that allows people to "talk" to themselves about vari-

Poor concentration, distractibility, and an inability to process or follow instructions are common problems for children with ADHD. ■

RESPONSIVE INSTRUCTION

Meeting the Needs of Students with Attention Deficit Hyperactivity Disorder

Task Switching: Preparing Students with ADHD for Change

What the Research Says

Many researchers contend that the primary deficit of students with attention deficit hyperactivity disorder (ADHD) is deficient behavioral inhibition (see p. 196). In other words, once a student with ADHD begins a task it is difficult for him or her to mentally switch to a new activity. Researchers hypothesize that the executive controls needed to "inhibit" the current activity and "start up" the next are different for students with ADHD compared to students without ADHD.

Research Study

A group of researchers examined task-switching ability of students with and without ADHD (Cepeda, Cepeda, & Kramer, 2000). Results from the study indicated that clear performance deficits existed for unmedicated students with ADHD in the first trial after a "task switch," even when the tasks were considered compatible, such as both tasks involving numbers. All students with ADHD, unmedicated or medicated, had higher "switch costs"—increased response time—when the new task was incompatible with the old task (e.g., switching from a number-identification task to a word-identification task). This type of task required the inhibition of thinking about numbers and the preparation for thinking about letters

and sounds. The findings suggest that differences *do* exist between students with and without ADHD in the ability to efficiently and effectively task switch.

Applying the Research to Teaching

Studies such as the one presented here indicate the need to support students with ADHD as they transition from one activity to another. Cognitive support for such transitions can include:

- Allowing for time between asking a student to do or say something and expecting the response (i.e., increasing wait time)
- Avoiding overloading a students' working memory (Barkley, Murphy, & Kwasnik, 1996) by limiting the number of steps or sequence of procedures a student must keep in working memory or by providing a visual for students to refer to
- Creating routinized procedures for daily transitions
- Preparing students for the type of response that will be required when asking a question
- Dividing instruction into consistent, predictable sequences throughout the day

—By Kristin L. Sayeski

---

ous solutions when in the midst of solving a problem. Students with ADHD who have deficient inner speech have problems in guiding their behavior in situations that demand the ability to follow rules or instructions.

Third, children and adults have problems controlling their emotions and their arousal levels. They often overreact to negative or positive experiences. Upon hearing good news, for example, they may scream loudly, unable to keep their emotions to themselves. Likewise, they are often quick to show their temper when confronted with frustrating experiences.

Fourth, children and adults with ADHD have difficulty analyzing problems and communicating solutions to others. They are less flexible when faced with problem situations, often responding impulsively with the first thing that comes to mind.

Persistent Goal-Directed Behavior   The many problems with executive functions experienced by persons with ADHD lead to deficits in engaging in sustained goal-directed activities:

The National Institutes of Health has funded several studies on the genetics of ADHD. One team of researchers at UCLA has created a Web site that summarizes its findings in layperson's language. This Web site is useful for both professionals and families. For families, it provides opportunities to participate in the research effort: http://www.adhd.ucla.edu/ ■

> The poor sustained attention that apparently characterizes those with ADHD probably represents an impairment in goal- or task-directed persistence arising from poor inhibition and the toll it takes on self-regulation. And the distractibility ascribed to those with ADHD most likely arises from poor interference control that allows other external and internal events to disrupt the executive functions that provide for self-control and task persistence. The net effect is an individual who cannot persist in effort toward tasks that provide little immediate reward and who flits from one uncompleted activity to another as disrupting events occur. The inattention in ADHD can now be seen as not so much a primary symptom as a secondary one; it is the consequence of the impairment that behavioral inhibition and interference control create in the self-regulation or executive control of behavior. (Barkley, 1997, p. 84)

With diminished self-regulation or executive control abilities, students with ADHD find it exceedingly difficult to stay focused on tasks that require effort or concentration but which are not inherently exciting (e.g., many school-related activities).

ADAPTIVE SKILLS

Adaptive skills.
Skills needed to adapt to one's living environment (e.g., communication, self-care, home living, social skills, community use, self-direction, health and safety, functional academics, leisure, and work); usually estimated by an adaptive behavior survey; one of two major components (the other is intellectual functioning) of the AAMR definition.

The concept of **adaptive skills** (e.g., self-help, community use, home use, and so forth) has traditionally been associated with the area of mental retardation. The AAMR definition, for example, stipulates that mental retardation be defined as impairments in intelligence and adaptive behavior (see Chapter 4). In recent years, authorities in the ADHD field have discovered that many children and adults with ADHD also have difficulties in adaptive behavior (Barkley, 1998). A good example is that they have more problems related to driving as adolescents and young adults, more accidents and traffic violations (Cox, Merkel, Kovatchev, & Seward, 2000; Woodward, Fergusson, & Horwood, 2000). Furthermore, those who do have problems with adaptive skills run a much greater risk of having a variety of learning and behavioral problems at school and home (Shelton et al., 2000).

PROBLEMS SOCIALIZING WITH PEERS

Some authorities have argued that the social problems experienced by students with ADHD are so common that they should be considered the defining characteristic of the condition (Landau, Milich, & Diener, 1998). Although the evidence may not warrant asserting that all persons with ADHD experience problems getting along with others, it is probably safe to say that the majority experience significant problems in peer relations. In fact, it usually does not take long for others to find students with ADHD uncomfortable to be around. For example, one team of researchers found that after just one day in a summer camp, many children with ADHD were rejected by other campers (Erhardt & Hinshaw, 1994).

Unfortunately, the negative social status experienced by students with ADHD is difficult to overcome and is usually long lasting. The enduring nature of social rejection leads easily to social isolation. The result is that many children and adults with ADHD have few friends even though they may desperately want to be liked. This can set up a vicious circle in which they attempt to win friends by latching onto the least chance for interaction with others. But their frantic need for friendship, coupled with their deficient impulse control, ends up leading them to bother or pester the very persons they are trying to befriend.

Given the problems in behavioral inhibition, it is not surprising that so many children and adults with ADHD end up socially ostracized. Unable to regulate their behavior and emotions, they are viewed as rude by others. It may not be that they do not know how to behave appropriately so much as that they are unable to do so (Landau et al., 1998). In other words, if asked what the appropriate behavior in a given situation should be, they can often give the socially acceptable answer. But when faced with choices in the actual

Some authorities believe that students with ADHD need considerable classroom structure and teacher direction, especially in the early stages of educational programming. ■

situation, their deficits in behavioral inhibition lead them to make choices impulsively and to overreact emotionally.

COEXISTING CONDITIONS

ADHD often occurs simultaneously with other behavioral and/or learning problems, such as learning disabilities or emotional or behavioral disorders. In addition, persons with ADHD run a higher risk than the general population for substance abuse.

Learning Disabilities   Studies using careful diagnostic criteria have found an overlap of 10 to 25 percent between ADHD and learning disabilities (Forness & Kavale, 2002). And some authorities maintain that the relationship is strongest for students who have ADHD, Predominantly Inattentive Type (Marshall, Hynd, Handwerk, & Hall, 1997; Willcutt, Chhabildas, & Pennington, 2001).

Emotional or Behavioral Disorders   Estimates of the overlap with ADHD vary widely, but it is safe to say that 25 to 50 percent of those with ADHD also exhibit some form of emotional or behavioral disorder (Hallahan & Cottone, 1997; Forness & Kavale, 2002). Some persons with ADHD can exhibit aggressive, acting-out behaviors, whereas others can have withdrawn behaviors that accompany anxiety or depression.

Substance Abuse   Adults with ADHD are about twice as likely as the general population to abuse alcohol or to become dependent on drugs, such as cocaine (Biederman, Wilens, Mick, Faraone, & Spencer, 1998; Lambert & Hartsough, 1998). And children with ADHD who also have externalizing types of behavior disorders are especially vulnerable for early drug use (Chilcoat & Breslau, 1999). In addition, adults with ADHD are about twice as likely to be cigarette smokers (Lambert & Hartsough, 1998). Some reports in the popular media have claimed that the treatment of ADHD with psychostimulants such as Ritalin leads children to take up the use of illegal substances. However, there is no research to back up this claim (DuPaul, Barkley, & Connor, 1998).

Exactly why ADHD co-occurs with so many other learning and behavioral disabilities remains largely a mystery. Researchers are just beginning to attempt to tease out which of several possibilities are the most likely reasons for so much overlap between ADHD and other disabilities. For example, does having ADHD put one at risk for developing another disability, such as learning disabilities or depression? Or do ADHD and the other disability occur independent of each other? And is there a genetic basis to the coexistence of so many of these conditions? Research over the next few years should begin to provide more definitive answers to these questions.

Educational Considerations

In this section we consider two aspects of effective educational programming for students with ADHD:

- Classroom structure and teacher direction
- Functional behavioral assessment and contingency-based self-management

SUCCESS STORIES
Special Educators at Work

Salem, VA: High school sophomore **Josh Bishop** hopes to play football on a team in the National Collegiate Athletic Association's Division I, despite his struggles with organization and time management. Like many students with ADHD, Josh does not find his schoolwork difficult to do, but finds it hard to get done. **Jane Warner** coordinates services for students with disabilities at a large university with a Division I football team. She guides many students like Josh and encourages all incoming freshman with ADHD to begin their self-advocacy early. Josh's mother, Joni Poff, a special education supervisor, agrees and encourages her son to seek out structures to support his success.

Special educator Jane Warner coordinates services for postsecondary students with disabilities at Virginia Polytechnic Institute and State University, better known as Virginia Tech. Jane is a proponent of self-advocacy skills and encourages schools to teach students at all grade levels about their disabilities. "Students need to know what their disability means, how it affects them academically and socially, and how to articulate this information to someone else. Students need to understand that disclosing their learning needs is not going to stigmatize them."

Josh Bishop hopes to play football for Virginia Tech and major in engineering. At age sixteen, he has been playing football for six years. "I played on the varsity team last year when I was a freshman," he says with pride. As a wrestler, a hurdler, and a discus thrower, Josh is a successful high school athlete. In the classroom, he has faced different challenges: "I never have been very organized. I got by in elementary school, but middle school was a real wake-up call

with much more work to do. In sixth grade, I'd get all my homework done *in* class. In seventh grade, I had homework due for *every* class." According to his mother, Joni Poff, "Josh talked early, but when written language came into play, he had trouble. Written work is what he'll avoid at school."

Josh was diagnosed by his pediatrician with ADHD when he was seven years old. "Josh always had a high activity level," recalls his mother. "In kindergarten, he was put on a behavior contract with stickers as positive reinforcement, but his first-grade teacher didn't follow through with his behavior management." By grade two, medication was recommended and Josh's family moved to a small school district. "The secondary school Josh attends has about 650 students in grades six through twelve, with less than one hundred students at each grade level," says Joni. Josh has not been identified for special services under either IDEA or Section 504. Fortunately for Josh and his family, contact

CLASSROOM STRUCTURE AND TEACHER DIRECTION

William Cruickshank, whom we discussed earlier, was one of the first to establish a systematic educational program for children who today would meet the criteria for ADHD. Two hallmarks of Cruickshank's program were: (1) reduction of stimuli irrelevant to learning and enhancement of materials important for learning, and (2) a structured program with a strong emphasis on teacher direction.

Because Cruickshank assumed that children with attention problems were susceptible to distraction, irrelevant stimuli were reduced as much as possible. For example, students' workspaces consisted of three-sided cubicles to reduce distractions. On the other hand, teachers were encouraged to use attractive, brightly colored teaching materials.

The emphasis on classroom structure and teacher direction can be summed up by the following:

> Specifically, what is meant by a structured program? For example, upon coming into the classroom the child will hang his hat and coat on a given hook—not on

---

between home and school has been close, but his mother remarks that high school has brought more difficulties. "Josh has made tremendous social gains since elementary school, but as the academic demands have increased over the last five to six years, it is harder to deal with the ADHD issues than when he was younger and more emotionally immature."

Josh keeps an assignment book but admits that he does not use it faithfully. "When I've missed a deadline, sometimes I don't turn the work in at all. I know that I need to do homework and I keep saying I'm going to do it, and then I don't get my homework in and I get a zero. It's not like it's hard; it's just getting it done! I can get work done at school, but I just can't get it done at home." Says Joni, "Josh does better with shorter time segments in a more structured setting. After school, he has trouble following through with sustained work. His pediatrician told me to back off. Josh takes medication during the day and it's harder for him to concentrate in the evening."

Josh mentioned his medication, but did not refer to his difficulties with completing written work, organizational skills, or attentiveness as being out of the ordinary. He would rather not be treated differently from other students, but he acknowledges that only a few teachers have provided the kind of structured instruction that benefits him. "Miss Mauney, in seventh grade, didn't make exceptions. She always made an effort to organize every kid in the class!" added Josh. Joni Poff thinks the most successful teachers for Josh have been those who were very structured and made their expectations very clear. "They weren't wishy-washy. They were sympathetic that some things were difficult for Josh. They understood that he wasn't being purposefully lazy or disrespectful, but they still held high expectations for him," says Joni. "Recently, I've asked Josh to take advantage

of a tutor or some structured support, but he seems determined to do it alone."

Going it alone is not always the answer, says Jane Warner. Students with ADHD frequently need support when they move from high school to college. Says Jane, "Study skills and time management are troublesome for students with ADHD. Things can start to fall apart. Students might miss several classes and think they can never go back, so they just sit out and their grades go down, their self-esteem starts to slip, and they hit the wall." Warner encourages students to disclose their learning needs confidently and make contact with the office for disability services on campus. Students with ADHD who have not received special services in high school are advised to get the documentation they need for colleges to provide them with appropriate accommodations. "We prefer current comprehensive evaluations that have been done by a qualified professional within the previous three years," says Warner. Every accommodation recommended by an evaluator must be accompanied by a rationale based on the student's current level of functioning. "Documentation completed in grade school or middle school doesn't reflect developmental changes or tell us what the student can do now. IEPs are part of the puzzle, but you still can't use an IEP as the only documentation for post-secondary accommodations."

Warner points out that evaluations for students with ADHD can provide a clear picture of their strengths and weaknesses, especially if the professional evaluator explains what the results mean in laymen's terms and makes specific educational recommendations. "Sometime between now and high school graduation," suggests Jane Warner, "getting a current clinical evaluation will be a very important part of fostering self-advocacy for Josh."

—By Jean Crockett

RESPONSIVE INSTRUCTION

Meeting the Needs of Students with Attention Deficit Hyperactivity Disorder

Planning for Students with ADHD in the General Education Classroom

What the Research Says

The majority of students with ADHD are served in general education classrooms. Through adding key modifications or supports to their traditional instructional routines, teachers can address the needs of students with ADHD without taking away from the instruction of students without disabilities in their class.

The following lesson sequence includes a description of research-supported supports that can be provided at each stage of instruction and a rationale for how those supports meet the needs of students with ADHD.

Applying the Research to Teaching

Stage I: Pre-planning—Divide Instruction into Meaningful "Chunks"

Description Prior to instruction, break your instructional sequence into meaningful chunks or steps (Rosenshine, 1995). By dividing your instructional sequence into small, meaningful sections, you ensure that all students do not move on until they understand and that ample practice and teacher feedback has been provided at each step (Hudson, 1997).

Rationale Long tasks can be overwhelming for students with ADHD. Chunking allows for shorter periods of focused attention, activity changes as you move through the instructional sequence, focused practice, and reduced reliance on working memory (Kemp, Fister, & McLaughlin, 1995).

Stage II: Introduction

Description During this stage the teacher introduces the day's instructional objectives. Information or activities that should be included in the introduction are: (1) a rationale for the lesson, (2) an explanation or presentation of a model of what the end result of the lesson will be, and (3) an advance organizer that informs students of the sequence of instructional activity (Allsopp, 1999).

Rationale These activities provide a "road map" for students to follow. For students with ADHD who have difficulty focusing on the main task or goal (Barkley, 1997),

explicit identification of lesson goals or outcomes and clearly delineated steps create an external goal-setting guide.

Stage III: Instruction and Modeling

Description After the teacher has set the stage for learning, the instructional part of the lesson begins. During this stage, a teacher may demonstrate a procedure or phenomenon, present students with a problem scenario to be solved, or have students engage in an activity that will then be linked to key instructional concepts. Regardless of the particular method the teacher is using to teach, students should have a clear understanding of what the teacher is doing and what they should be doing in response. Strategies for effective teaching include the teacher: (1) "thinking aloud" as he or she presents the initial part of the lesson, (2) modeling the exact steps the students will complete, and (3) soliciting feedback from students during the instructional phase (Mercer & Mercer, 1998).

Rationale A student with ADHD may have difficulty making connections between the instructional phase of a lesson and the activity, assignment, or worksheet that follows. By providing a clear model of what needs to be done, demonstrating the type of "inner speech" that should be guiding their thinking (via the "think aloud"), and checking students for understanding, the teacher increases the likelihood of students making connections between the instruction and the practice/application of the concept (Kucan & Beck, 1997).

Stage IV: Guided Practice

Description The guided practice (GP) stage is the critical transition stage between instruction and independent practice (IP). During GP, students have the opportunity to practice or work with the concept being taught while the teacher is actively providing feedback (Allsopp, 1999; Kemp et al., 1995). GP can consist of students working several problems at the board or on white boards at their desks, students explaining (in their own words) to the class what was previously presented, or groups of students doing the first part of a task and reporting their work to the class. The key element of GP is that the teacher has the opportunity to correct or reteach before students are engaged in IP.

Rationale The GP stage provides an important bridge for students with ADHD who may need to be actively engaged in the task to be receptive to instructional guidelines or recommendations provided during instruction (Kemp et al., 1995). GP also provides an opportunity for positive reinforcement as the student makes initial attempts at understanding. Given the "chunking" of the lesson, teachers could go through the Instruction/Modeling and GP stages two to three times during a given lesson. Providing frequent shifts in activity creates additional support for such ADHD characteristics as short attention span, task-completion difficulty, and short-term memory problems (Rooney, 1995).

Stage V: Independent Practice

Description Independent practice (IP) comes in many forms, ranging from individual to pair or small-group work to homework. The purpose of IP is for students to apply what was taught. At this point in the instructional sequence, students should understand the task requirements and be able to perform the task with competence (Rosenshine, 1995).

Rationale Work presented at students' frustration level can be a trigger for common ADHD behaviors—out of seat or verbal or physical disruptions. By establishing clear expectations for IP, ensuring students are capable of the work, and providing support, teachers increase the likelihood of meaningful student engagement.

Stage VI: Closure and Review

Description At the end of every lesson, time should be permitted to "recap" the main ideas of the lesson. For closure, teachers can review key vocabulary, have students state something they learned, or have students complete a brief journal activity. During closure, the lesson's "big idea" should be reinforced as well as connections made to past and future learning (Kameenui & Carnine, 1998).

Rationale Students with ADHD may have difficulty with synthesizing information (Barkley, 1994). Providing closure at the end of a lesson creates the support necessary for students to make connections among the day's concepts (Rosenshine, 1995).

In summary, teachers can serve many students with ADHD effectively within the general education setting, providing the instruction is responsive to their unique needs.

—*By Kristin L. Sayeski*

any hook of his choice, but on the same hook every day. He will place his lunch box, if he brings one, on a specific shelf each day. He will then go to his cubicle, take his seat, and from that point on follow the teacher's instructions concerning learning tasks, use of toilet, luncheon activities, and all other experiences until the close of the school day. The day's program will be so completely simplified and so devoid of choice (or conflict) situations that the possibility of failure experience will be almost completely minimized. The learning tasks will be within the learning capacity and within the limits of frustration and attention span of the child. . . . If it is determined that he has an attention span of four minutes, then all teaching tasks should be restricted to four minutes. (Cruickshank, Bentzen, Ratzeburg, & Tannhauser, 1961).

It is rare today to see teachers using all the components of Cruickshank's program, especially the cubicles. Many authorities now believe that not all children with ADHD are distracted by things in their environment. For those who are distractible, however, some authorities recommend the use of such things as cubicles to reduce extraneous stimulation.

The *degree* of classroom structure and teacher direction advocated by Cruickshank is also rarely seen today. First, this intensity of structure could only be achieved in a self-contained classroom. As we discuss later, most students with ADHD are in general education settings. Second, most authorities today believe that a structured program is important in the early stages of working with many students with ADHD but that these students gradually need to learn to be more independent in their learning.

Nevertheless, many of the ideas of Cruickshank are still alive in the educational recommendations of today's professionals. For example:

Teacher-directed general education classes, with colorful visual aids, enclosed teaching areas, and proximity to the teacher have been successful learning environments. ■

All children, and particularly, those with ADHD, benefit from clear, predictable, uncomplicated routine and structure. It helps if the day is divided into broad units of time and if this pattern is repeated daily. Within each block of lesson time there should be a similar breaking down of tasks and activities into subtasks/activities. Presenting the student with an enormously detailed list of tasks and subtasks should be avoided. An important goal should be to create a simple overarching daily routine that the student will eventually learn by heart. The number of tasks should be kept small and tight timelines should be avoided. Complexities of timetabling and working structures merely confuse students with ADHD, because a major difficulty that goes with this condition is a poorly developed ability to differentiate between and organize different bits of information. This clearly makes the formal curriculum difficult to manage, without having to struggle with the organizational arrangements that surround the curriculum. Once a workable daily timetable has been established this should be publicly displayed and/or taped to the student's desk or inside his or her homework diary. (Cooper, 1999, p. 146)

FUNCTIONAL ASSESSMENT AND CONTINGENCY-BASED SELF-MANAGEMENT

Functional behavioral assessment (FBA). The practice of determining the consequences (what purpose the behavior serves), antecedents (what triggers the behavior), and setting events (in what contexts the behavior occurs) of inappropriate behavior.

Contingency-based self-management. Educational techniques that involve having students keep track of their own behavior, for which they then receive consequences (e.g., reinforcement).

As we noted in Chapter 4, **functional behavioral assessment (FBA)** is an important aspect of dealing with behavioral problems of students with mental retardation. It is also extremely useful in educational programming for students with ADHD. FBA involves determining the consequences, antecedents, and setting events that maintain inappropriate behaviors (Horner & Carr, 1997). Examples of typical functions of inappropriate behavior of students with ADHD are (1) to avoid work and (2) to gain attention from peers or adults (DuPaul & Ervin, 1996).

Contingency-based self-management approaches usually involve having persons keep track of their own behavior and then receive consequences, usually in the form of rewards, based on their behavior (Davies & Witte, 2000; Shapiro, DuPaul, & Bradley-

Programs that allow students to monitor their own behavior and performance may encourage them to maintain appropriate behavior at school. ■

Klug, 1998). For example, the teacher might have students use **self-monitoring** (see Chapter 5) to record how many times they left their seats during a class period.

A combination of FBA and contingency-based self-management techniques has proven successful in increasing appropriate behavior of elementary and secondary students with ADHD (DuPaul, Eckert, & McGoey, 1997; Ervin, DuPaul, Kern, & Friman, 1998; Shapiro et al., 1998). In one study, for instance, a combination of FBA and contingency-based self-management increased the on-task behavior of two adolescents with ADHD. For example, for one of the students the FBA phase consisted of interviews with the teacher and observations in the classroom, which led the researchers and teachers to conclude that an adolescent boy's disruptive behavior was a function of gaining peer attention (Ervin et al., 1998). They based this assumption on evidence that the antecedents to his inattentive behavior consisted of such things as peers looking his way, calling out his name, making gestures toward him, and that the consequences of his inattention were such things as the peers laughing or returning comments to him.

The contingency-based self-management phase involved the student evaluating his on-task behavior on a 5-point scale (0 = unacceptable to 5 = excellent) at the end of each math class. The teacher also rated his behavior, and the student was awarded points based on how closely the ratings matched. During writing class, the teacher awarded negative or positive points to members of the class depending on whether or not they responded to attention-seeking behaviors from any member of the class. In both classes, the points could be used for privileges.

The Role of Reinforcement   Authorities have pointed to the crucial role that *contingency* plays in contingency-based self-management. In other words, they point out that reinforcement of some kind, such as social praise or points that can be traded for privileges, is especially important in order for self-management techniques to be effective. For example, an extensive review of research found that contingency-based self-management strategies were more effective than self-management strategies without contingencies in leading to positive behavioral changes in students with ADHD (DuPaul & Eckert, 1997).

Although the use of behavioral procedures such as reinforcement and punishment is somewhat controversial—that is, there are those who are opposed to their use (Kohn, 1993)—many authorities consider them almost indispensable in working with students

Self-monitoring.
A self-management technique in which students monitor their own behavior, such as attention to task, and then record it on a sheet.

Meeting the Needs of Students with Attention Deficit Hyperactivity Disorder

The Benefits of Self-Monitoring and Group Contingency

What the Research Says

Many students with ADHD lack the ability to self-monitor. Self-monitoring requires the ability to appraise a situation and consider alternative ways of responding as well as possible outcomes associated with the various forms of responding (Shapiro, DuPaul, & Bradley-Klug, 1998). This inability to "think" before acting creates problems for students with ADHD in the areas of paying attention in class, responding to social situations appropriately, and finishing assigned tasks. To address these issues, teachers can teach students to use self-management procedures wherein the student monitors, records, analyzes, and reinforces her or his own behavior (Davies & Witte, 2000). Many studies have been conducted in the area of self-management and these studies have repeatedly demonstrated the effectiveness of teaching students such strategies (Cole & Bambara, 1992; Lloyd, Hallahan, Kauffman, & Keller, 1998; Mathes & Bender, 1997; Reid & Harris, 1993; Shimabukuro, Prater, Jenkins, & Edelen-Smith, 1999; Smith, Nelson, Young, & West, 1992).

Although teaching self-management to students with ADHD has been proven to be effective, many teachers prefer whole-class or group-contingency plans. Within a group-contingency model the behavior of one student is tied to the outcome of the whole group. Group-contingency models promote interdependence as group members must work together to meet their goal (Tankersley, 1995). Under a group contingency, teachers can use the same behavior-management approach for all students and do not have to differentiate their treatment of the few students who need help with self-management. Thus, group contingencies can be very effective for general education teachers who have students with ADHD in their classrooms.

Research Study

One study examined the effects of a management program with third-graders that included both self-management and group contingency on the behaviors of students with ADHD in a general education classroom (Davies & Witte, 2000). All students—those with ADHD as well as nondisabled students—were responsible for monitoring their own behavior, and contingencies were established for group performance. Sample procedures for the group intervention were:

1. If any student displayed the target behavior [inappropriate verbalizations], she or he moved one dot from his/her group's chart from the green section into the blue section. If the child did not move the dot after about 10 seconds, then the teacher moved a dot into the red section of the chart.

2. The rewards a group received were related to how many dots the group had in the green section of their chart at the end of the intervention period. Each group needed to have at least one dot left in the green section at the end of the intervention period to receive the reinforcer. [Each group started with five dots.] (Davies & Witte, 2000, p. 141)

Research Findings

Results from the study demonstrated a decrease in the talking out behaviors of the four students with ADHD. In addition, there was no evidence of possible negative side effects of peer-pressure, such as threats or negative verbal comments (Davies & Witte, 2000).

Applying the Research to Teaching

Findings from this study demonstrate the effectiveness of using self-management within the context of a group contingency. Teachers can implement similar management strategies through: (1) targeting specific undesirable behaviors to be eliminated or specific desirable behaviors to be reinforced, (2) creating a chart for students to use for self-management, (3) communicating the procedures for recording behaviors on the chart (e.g., "If you do X, mark your chart" or "When the beeper beeps, check to see if you are doing X, then mark your chart accordingly"), or (4) connecting the self-management procedures to a group contingency (e.g., "If all students get over X points during the lesson, all students will get a homework pass").

—By Kristin L. Sayeski

with ADHD. For example, they are an integral part of a set of intervention principles advocated by one team of authorities (see Table 6.3 on p. 208).

SERVICE DELIVERY MODELS

Because ADHD is not recognized as a separate special education category by the U.S. Department of Education, we do not have statistics on how many students are served in different classroom environments. It is safe to assume, however, that one can find students with ADHD across the entire continuum, from residential schools to full inclusion in general education classrooms. But because, as we noted earlier, there is reason to believe that fewer than half receive any special education services (Forness & Kavale, 2002), it is logical to assume that most students with ADHD spend most of their time in general education classrooms.

As with all students with disabilities, the best placement for students with ADHD should be determined on an individual basis. Although full inclusion in a general education classroom may be appropriate for some students with ADHD, the estimate that over half do not receive any special education services can be viewed with some concern. This is especially true in light of the fact that studies have shown that positive behavioral changes in students with ADHD are much more likely to occur in special education than in general education settings (DuPaul & Eckert, 1997).

Medication Considerations

One of the most controversial topics in all of special education is the treatment of ADHD with medication. **Psychostimulants,** which stimulate or activate neurological functioning, are by far the most frequent type of medication prescribed for ADHD. The most common stimulant prescribed for ADHD is methylphenidate, or **Ritalin.** The fact that physicians would prescribe a psychostimulant for someone who exhibits hyperactivity is, at first blush, counterintuitive. In fact, for years professionals referred to the **paradoxical effect of Ritalin** because its effects appeared to be the opposite of those one would expect in the case of someone *without* ADHD. Researchers have concluded, however, that Ritalin influences the release of the neurotransmitter dopamine, thus enabling the brain's executive functions to operate more normally (Swanson, Castellanos, Murias, LaHoste, & Kennedy, 1998; Swanson et al., 1998). Furthermore, it is now believed that Ritalin has the same chemical and behavioral effect on persons without ADHD as it does on those with ADHD (Solanto, 1998).

Ordinarily, Ritalin takes about one hour to take effect, with the optimal effect occurring at about two hours. The effects of Ritalin usually wear off after about four hours. Responsiveness to Ritalin is highly individualistic, so the dosage level and number of doses per day vary from person to person. A relatively new stimulant, **Adderall,** is growing in popularity because it is at least as effective and its effects are longer lasting, meaning that it does not have to be administered as often (Faraone, Pliszka, Olvera, Skolnik, & Biederman, 2001; Manos, Short, & Findling, 1999; Pliszka, Browne, Olvera, & Wynne, 2000).

OPPOSITION TO RITALIN

Not all professionals, parents, and laypeople are in favor of using Ritalin. In fact, Ritalin has been the subject of numerous assaults by the media. Starting in the late 1980s and continuing into the 1990s, several critics appeared on nationally broadcast television shows, such as *Oprah, Donahue, and Geraldo,* and *20/20,* as well as evening and morning news shows. And while some criticisms have been relatively mild, others have ranged from assertions that ADHD is a bogus diagnosis to claims that professionals are trying to control children and make them overly docile.

CW Researchers and other professionals have begun to fight back against what they consider inappropriate media coverage of ADHD. In January, 2002, an international consensus statement, signed by 85 researchers from 12 countries, was posted on the World Wide Web to counteract inaccurate portrayals of ADHD in the media: http://www.chadd.org/consensusexpertstatement.pdf

On February 7, 2002, the National Attention Deficit Disorder Association issued a statement on the media and ADHD: http://www.add.org/content/research/media.htm ■

Psychostimulants.
Medications that activate dopamine levels in the frontal and prefrontal areas of the brain that control behavioral inhibition and executive functions; used to treat persons with ADHD.

Ritalin.
The most commonly prescribed psychostimulant for ADHD; generic name is methylphenidate.

Paradoxical effect of Ritalin.
The now discredited belief that Ritalin, even though a stimulant, acts to subdue a person's behavior and that this effect of Ritalin is evident in persons with ADHD but not in those without ADHD.

Adderall.
A psychostimulant for ADHD; effects are longer acting than Ritalin.

Collaboration and Co-Teaching for Students with ADHD

What Does It Mean to Be a Teacher of Students with Attention Deficit Hyperactivity Disorder?

Currently, the Council for Exceptional Children does not have specific competencies for teachers of students with attention deficit hyperactivity disorder. Often, these students have comorbid disabling conditions, such as a learning disability or an emotional/behavioral disorder, and are served by teachers with expertise in those areas.

Successful Strategies for Co-Teaching

There are a variety of co-teaching classroom configurations that will give teachers "more hands" to meet the needs of students with ADHD. Vaughn, Schumm, and Arguelles (1997) describe five basic models of co-teaching that provide co-teachers with opportunities to use the instructional strategies described in this chapter and in Table 6.3.

One Teach, One Drift In this model, one teacher is responsible for instruction and the other teacher drifts, monitoring students. This model allows the drifting teacher to redirect students who may be off task, to observe and mark student monitoring forms, to provide feedback on individual students' attention and participation, and to deliver reinforcers or consequences on a frequent basis.

Station Teaching In station teaching, co-teachers split content into two parts and students into three groups. Each teacher teaches one of the two content pieces at a station to a small group of students and the other group works independently. The student groups move to each station. In this model, teachers can break content down to smaller tasks that maintain the attention of all students. Each teacher is able to work with a small group of students, making it easier to ensure that they are focused and learning. It is also easier to help students work together and to provide reinforcers and consequences more frequently. The difficulty lies in

More recently, some of the most extreme critics of Ritalin have turned to the courts to make their case, claiming that the pharmaceutical industry, the psychiatric profession, and the major parent and advocacy organization have colluded to promote more sales of Ritalin (see the box on p. 210). In emotionally charged debates like this, it is advisable that we turn to research for guidance.

THE RESEARCH EVIDENCE

Dozens of research teams around the world have been studying the effects of several medications on ADHD. Most of this research has focused on the psychostimulant, Ritalin.

TABLE 6.3   Pfiffner and Barkley's Intervention Principles for ADHD

1. Rules and instructions must be clear, brief, and often delivered through more visible and external modes of presentation.

2. Consequences must be delivered swiftly and immediately.

3. Consequences must be delivered more frequently [than for students without ADHD].

4. The types of consequences must often be of a higher magnitude, or more powerful [than for students without ADHD].

5. An appropriate and often richer degree of incentives must be provided.

6. Reinforcers, or particularly, rewards must be changed or rotated more frequently.

7. Anticipation is the key. Teachers must be mindful of planning ahead, particularly during phases of transition across activities or classes, to ensure that the children are cognizant of the shift in rules (and consequences) that is about to occur.

SOURCE: Condensed from L.J. Pfiffner & R.A. Barkley, Treatment of ADHD in school settings. In R.A. Barkley, Attention-deficit hyperactivity disorder: A handbook for diagnosis and treatment, 2nd ed. (New York: Guilford Press, 1998), pp. 462–464. Reprinted with permission.

making sure that students with ADHD can work appropriately in the independent station.

Parallel Teaching In parallel teaching, the two teachers split the class into two groups and teach the same content to a smaller group of students. This model provides the same opportunities as station teaching, along with the chance to modify the instructional delivery of the same content material to meet the needs of the student.

Alternative Teaching The alternative teaching model includes content instruction by one teacher to a large group of students and remedial or supplementary instruction by the other teacher to a small group of students. In this model, the teacher of the small group can modify delivery of content, control the delivery of consequences and rewards, and closely monitor and observe students. In addition, the teacher of the small group can incorporate instruction in strategies such as self-monitoring.

Team Teaching In team teaching, co-teachers alternate or "tag team" in delivering instruction to the entire class. In this model, co-teachers can both be on the lookout for misconceptions, confusion, inattention, and disruption. These can then be addressed in the flow of instruction rather than afterward or on an individual basis. In addition, co-teachers can work together to both present content and learning strategies in unison to better meet the needs of all students.

In All Models Teachers working together can discuss and better evaluate whether rules and instructions are clear, brief, and delivered in appropriate formats for students with ADHD. Co-teachers can also work together to better anticipate "rough spots" for students with ADHD, particularly during transition times, changes in routines, or complex tasks (see Table 6.3). The varying models of co-teaching provide the flexibility for teachers to adjust instructional delivery to meet the objectives of the teachers and the needs of the students with ADHD.

Cautionary Note All too often, co-teachers fall into the habit of using one model to the exclusion of others. This is unfortunate in that it may mean that one teacher does not participate actively in instruction and/or planning. This nonparticipation can lead to a lack of interest on the teacher's part and a disregard for that teacher on the students' part. The models of co-teaching were developed to match the needs of instruction. Both teachers should participate in instruction in a way that matches their expertise.

—By Margaret P. Weiss

Effectiveness Despite all the negative publicity in the media, most authorities in the area of ADHD are in favor of Ritalin's use. After hundreds of studies, the research is overwhelmingly positive on its effectiveness in helping students have more normalized behavioral inhibition and executive functioning (Barkley, 1998; Crenshaw, Kavale, Forness, & Reeve, 1999; Evans et al., 2001; Forness, Kavale, & Crenshaw, 1999). Moreover, Ritalin not only results in better ratings on parent- and teacher-rating scales, but it leads to improved performance in academic achievement as well as classroom behavior, such as better note-taking, on-task behavior, quiz scores, homework completion, and written-language work (Evans et al., 2001).

In fact, even though there had been a wealth of evidence showing the effectiveness of Ritalin and other medications, the National Institute of Mental Health decided to play it safe because of the controversy surrounding medication for ADHD. It embarked on a large-scale, well-controlled, extensive study on the effects of medication and behavioral management treatments (see the box on p. 211). Again, the results demonstrated the effectiveness of medication.

Psychostimulants, especially Ritalin, have sparked a national controversy over the treatment of ADHD. Although Ritalin is not effective for everyone and can have side effects, the bulk of research evidence supports its effectiveness. ■

Nonresponders and Side Effects Ritalin is not effective for everyone. Somewhere around 30 percent of those who take Ritalin do not have a favorable response (Spencer et al., 1996). In addition, some side effects are possible, including insomnia, reduction in appetite, abdominal pain, headaches, and irritability. There has also been speculation on the possibility that in a very small number of cases Ritalin may cause tics or increase their intensity in those who already have tics (DuPaul, Barkley, & Connor, 1998). There have also been many anecdotal reports of a "rebound effect," in which a child exhibits irritability as the Ritalin wears off. In most cases, these side effects are mild and can be controlled. For example, in the case of the two most common side effects—insomnia and reduction in

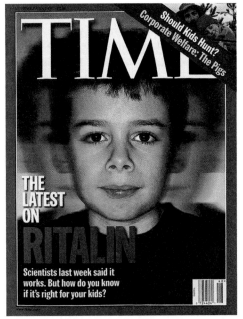

TIME

Should Kids Hunt?
Corporate Welfare: The Pigs

THE LATEST ON RITALIN

Scientists last week said it works. But how do you know if it's right for your kids?

Use of Ritalin Leads to Lawsuits

The following are two news releases pertaining to several lawsuits brought against Novartis AG (the manufacturer of Ritalin), the American Psychiatric Association, and Children and Adults with Attention-Deficit/Hyperactivity Disorder (CHADD). Thus far, the courts have ruled in favor of defendants.[1]

AD/HD Drug Ritalin Faces Court, Capitol Hill, Marketplace Skirmishes[2]

Washington—Ritalin manufacturer Novartis AG is under fire from several directions this month as the longstanding debate over medicating children with Attention-Deficit/Hyperactivity Disorder rages on. In the wake of two new class-action lawsuits filed Sept. 13 against Novartis and the American Psychiatric Association, the House Education and Workforce Subcommittee on Oversight and Investigations has scheduled a hearing for Friday on the use of Ritalin in schools. Meanwhile, two Novartis competitors have stepped up their efforts to unseat the top-selling medication.

The lawsuits, led by Washington, D.C., attorney John Coale and Pascagoula, Miss., attorney Richard Scruggs, who won fame for leading similar lawsuits against the tobacco industry in the late 1990s, allege Novartis and the APA conspired to create a bloated market for Ritalin, the most prescribed drug for AD/HD. The suits were filed in a federal court in California and a state court in New Jersey; they mirror a suit filed last spring in a state court in Texas. . . . That suit also names the national advocacy group, Children and Adults with AD/HD, as a defendant.

Novartis called any allegations that it conspired with APA, CHADD or any other organization "unfounded and preposterous." A company spokeswoman said Wednesday Novartis had not yet seen the lawsuits filed in New Jersey and California. However, the company said, "any charge that ADHD is not a medically valid disorder is contrary to medical evidence and scientific consensus." Forty years of research, documented in the *New England Journal of Medicine* and the *Journal of the American Medical Association,* as well as acknowledgements by the National Institutes of Health and the U.S. Food and Drug Administration that ADHD "is a commonly diagnosed behavioral disorder of childhood," validates Novartis' development of Ritalin to treat it, the company added.

CHADD Vindicated by Lawsuit Dismissals and Withdrawal[3]

Landover, MD—CHADD, the nation's leading advocacy organization serving children and adults with Attention-Deficit/Hyperactivity Disorder (AD/HD) is pleased by recent developments confirming that lawsuits filed against it, Novartis and the American Psychiatric Association are completely without merit or basis. Plaintiffs withdrew their complaint in Florida and decided not to appeal in Texas.

To date, three of five class action lawsuits filed in 2000 against the organizations have been eliminated. Two were dismissed (Texas and California) and one was withdrawn entirely (Florida). The suits allege that CHADD conspired with Novartis, the manufacturer of Ritalin, and the American Psychiatric Association (APA) to improperly broaden the diagnostic criteria for [ADHD] and thereby increase Ritalin sales. CHADD has always maintained that the allegations are preposterous, and has vigorously defended these lawsuits.

"CHADD's message has always been one of sharing science-based information about AD/HD," said CHADD Chief Executive Officer E. Clark Ross. "Removing the cloud of doubt created by such baseless claims allows CHADD to continue its science-based education and advocacy."

On March 9, 2001, Judge Rudi Brewster of the United States District Court in San Diego dismissed the lawsuit filed in his court, finding that the plaintiffs had failed to set forth any allegations to support their claims. Although the plaintiffs in this California lawsuit have appealed . . . , CHADD remains optimistic that his decision will be upheld. . . .

On May 17, 2001, Judge G. Tagle of the United States District Court in Brownsville, Texas dismissed the lawsuit pending in her Court, also finding that the plaintiffs . . . had failed to come forward with even the most basic information to support their conspiracy allegations. Notably, the Texas plaintiffs chose not to appeal. . . .

On July 3, 2001, the plaintiffs in a similar action filed in Florida federal court quietly withdrew their lawsuit. Judges in lawsuits filed in Puerto Rico and New Jersey have not yet decided whether the cases pending in their Courts should be dismissed. CHADD is confident that these judges will follow the lead of Judges Brewster and Tagle.

[1]As of the printing of this text, some of the lawsuits were still pending. Moreover, there may be appeals. Interested readers should keep their eye out for further court actions. A good source would be the CHADD Web site: http://www.chadd.org/

[2]© 2001 Special Education News. Retrieved from the World Wide Web: http://www.specialednews.com/disabilities/disabnews/ADHD ritalinsuits092600.html. Used with permission.

[3]CHADD Media Advisory, July 24, 2001. Retrieved from the World Wide Web: http://www.chadd.org/news/press07242001.htm

Is Medication Effective for Children with ADHD?

The National Institute of Mental Health's MTA Study

The NIMH Collaborative Multisite Multimodal Treatment Study of Children with Attention-Deficit/Hyperactivity Disorder (MTA), co-sponsored with the U.S. Department of Education, has been the most ambitious study yet conducted on the efficacy of medication for children with ADHD. It involved a total sample of 579 children between the ages of 7 and 9.9 years from seven sites around North America: Berkeley, CA; Durham, NC; Irvine, CA; Montreal, Quebec; New York City; Pittsburgh, PA; and Queens, NY.

Researchers randomly assigned students to one of four groups:

- Medication Management (MedMgt)—This group received carefully monitored medication. Most received Ritalin, but those who reacted unfavorably to Ritalin were given an alternative medication.
- Behavioral Treatment (Beh)—This intensive behaviorally oriented program involved a school-based intervention, involving teacher training in behavior management, a classroom aide, and a daily report card linked to home consequences; twenty-seven sessions of parent training in child behavior management; individual parent training sessions; child-focused therapy; and an eight-week all-day behaviorally oriented summer program.
- Combined Medication Management and Behavioral Treatment (Comb)
- Community Care (CC)—Families in this group were provided a list of mental health resources in their community. (Sixty-seven percent ended up on medication, at some point; however, the medication was not managed as closely.)

The study lasted for fourteen months, during which an extensive battery of measures and ratings were taken.

Results

Using a composite score of teacher and parent ratings of core ADHD symptoms, the researchers rated whether each of the treatments could be considered a "success" (Swanson et al., 2001). The ranking of the groups with respect to success rates at the end of the fourteen months was:

1. 68%—Comb
2. 56%—MedMgt
3. 34%—Beh
4. 25%—CC

Conclusions

The findings clearly point to the impressive effects of medication. They also suggest that using medication in combination with behavioral method is the most powerful treatment.

The findings are a bit less clear with respect to the value of the behavioral treatment alone. Although a 34 percent success rate is not as high as one would like, some have noted that this is an average of the seven sites studied (Swanson et al., 2001). Some students improved much more than others. Furthermore, there was considerable variability in how intensively the behavioral treatment was delivered from school to school within each site (Pelham, 2000). In other words, it still makes sense for teachers to use behavior management, especially because we know that the behavior problems of many children with ADHD are likely to deteriorate without intensive behavioral interventions.

SOURCE: A 14-Month Randomized Clinical Trial of Treatment Strategies for Attention-Deficit/Hyperactivity Disorder, *Archives of General Psychiatry*, vol. 56, Dec. 1999, pp. 1073–1086. Reprinted with permission.

---

appetite—care should be taken not to take the Ritalin too close to mealtime or bedtime. In the case of the rebound effect, some physicians recommend using a time-release form of Ritalin.

Drug Abuse   A popular misconception is that, by taking Ritalin, children with ADHD are more likely to become abusers of drugs such as marijuana or cocaine as adolescents or young adults. However, there is little, if any, documented evidence that this occurs (Barkley, 1998). In fact, there is suggestive evidence that those with ADHD who are prescribed Ritalin as children are less likely to turn to illicit drugs as teenagers (Biederman, Wilens, Mick, Spencer, & Faraone, 1999). Some have speculated that perhaps those who

GW Two articles in the *Archives of General Psychiatry*, summarizing the results of the NIMH MTA study, are available on-line at http://archpsyc.ama-assn.org/issues/v56n12/toc.html ■

Ritalin Sold in Playgrounds

A black market has grown up in American playgrounds for the attention-deficit drug Ritalin as children trade the pastel-colored prescription pills they call "Smarties."

Legitimate use of the stimulant has surged . . . in the past decade. . . . That growth has been accompanied by soaring abuse. Teenagers say that the drug, also known as methylphenidate, can be popped, snorted and even dissolved and injected for a high comparable with a caffeine-jolt or even a slower-acting form of cocaine. Selling for $2 . . . to $20 a pill on the black market, it is "as easy to get as candy."

A survey of 6,000 Massachusetts children found that nearly 13 per cent of secondary school pupils had used Ritalin without a prescription. Slightly more than 4 per cent of 12- and 13-year-olds admitted doing so. In Wisconsin and Minnesota a third of pupils prescribed attention-deficit drugs were found to have been approached to sell or trade pills. In Chicago two teenagers changed schools after complaining that they were being harassed by classmates. Many children "palm" their pills, pretending to take them so they can then sell them.

Some experts fear that the pills, though safe for overactive six-year-olds, could be a "gateway" to marijuana, cocaine and heroin when taken by those who do not need them. The Drug Enforcement Administration found that 30 to 50 per cent of teenagers in drug-treatment centres in Indiana, South Carolina and Wisconsin had used methylphenidate to get high, although not as their principal drug.

The trade is so extensive that the General Accounting Office, the investigative arm of Congress, has begun an inquiry into the theft and sale of Ritalin in schools. Henry Hyde, Republican chairman of the House Judiciary Committee, which initiated the investigation, said: "Virtually every data source available confirms . . . the widespread theft, diversion and abuse of Ritalin, and drugs like it."

SOURCE: Copyright Times Newspapers Ltd. (November 28, 2000). Retrieved from the World Wide Web: http://www.thetimes.co.uk/article/0,,42518,00.html. Reprinted by permission.

are *not* medicated with Ritalin turn to other drugs to try to find "peace of mind" or to "mellow out."

CAUTIONS REGARDING RITALIN

Although the research is overwhelmingly positive on the effectiveness of Ritalin for increasing appropriate behavior, there are still a number of cautions:

- Ritalin should not be prescribed at the first sign of a behavioral problem. Only after careful analysis of the student's behavior and environment should Ritalin be considered. The use of psychostimulants for ADHD in the United States has doubled every four to seven years since 1971 (Wilens & Biederman, 1992). Furthermore, rates of Ritalin usage vary substantially from one country to another. For example, Ritalin is administered in the United States at more than twice the rate of Great Britain and Australia (Kewley, 1998). Although it is possible that the lower rates of Ritalin usage in other countries indicate that many persons with ADHD are not being treated properly, it is also very likely that at least some children in the United States are being medicated inappropriately.
- Although research has demonstrated the effectiveness of Ritalin on behavioral inhibition and executive functions, the results for academic outcomes have not been as dramatic. Although important academic measures, such as work completed or accuracy on assignments, have improved substantially, the impact on achievement tests has been much less (Forness et al., 1999). Thus, teachers should not assume that Ritalin will take care of all the academic problems these students face.
- Parents, teachers, and physicians should monitor dosage levels closely so that the dose used is effective but not too strong. Proper dosage levels vary considerably (Hale et al., 1998).

For learners with ADHD, coaching beyond high school, through either a job coach, therapist, or teacher counselor is highly recommended. ■

- Teachers and parents should not lead children to believe that the medication serves as a substitute for self-responsibility and self-initiative.
- Teachers and parents should not view the medication as a panacea; they, too, must take responsibility and initiative in working with the child.
- Parents and teachers should keep in mind that Ritalin is a controlled substance. There is the potential for siblings, peers, or the child himself or herself, to attempt to "experiment" with it. (See the box on p. 212.)
- The final key to the effective use of Ritalin is *communication* among parents, physicians, teachers, and the child himself or herself.

Early Intervention

Diagnosis of young children with ADHD is particularly difficult because many children without ADHD tend to exhibit a great deal of motor activity and a lack of impulse control. For the very reason that excessive activity and impulsivity are relatively normal for young children, preschoolers with ADHD can be particularly difficult to manage. Thus, those preschoolers who really do have ADHD are a great challenge to parents and teachers.

Because of the severity of the symptoms of preschoolers who have been diagnosed with ADHD, the importance of the educational principles of classroom structure, teacher direction, functional behavioral assessment, and contingency-based self-management that we discussed above are all the more important. Given that even young children without ADHD do not have fully developed self-management skills, most recommend an even stronger emphasis on the use of contingencies in the form of praise, points, and tangible rewards.

In the case of preschoolers with ADHD and high rates of aggression, even implementing very intensive early intervention procedures, including highly structured classrooms with strong contingencies, leads only to limited behavioral and academic improvements that do not endure (Shelton et al., 2000). In other words, even high-quality early intervention is not likely to remediate completely the symptoms of children with ADHD and severe aggression. Such children need long-term programming.

An Adult with ADHD: Ann's Story

I grew up not feeling very good about myself. In school, it was hard for me to stay on the subject or to finish anything. . . . Teachers would be on my back. They said I was such a good child—they couldn't understand it. And I tried so hard. I just couldn't finish anything. . . . I was distracted very easily by practically everything. If someone sneezed, I'd look at him and my mind would go off in a million directions. I'd look out the window, wondering why he had sneezed. . . .

The situation has persisted into adulthood. I'm very disorganized. Take housekeeping, for example. After dinner, when I start the dishes, I'll wash a little, then run and wipe off the table, wipe the cabinet, talk on the phone, and never get anything completed. I have to really concentrate and tell myself "You are going to get the dishes done." Then they get done, but I still get the urge to stop and go wash off the dining room table. Just like someone is pulling me. My closet and drawers are still a mess, just like when I was a kid.

What's really hard is to stay with any kind of paper work—bills, for example. It's my husband's job to do the bills. If it were mine, we'd probably be in jail. . . . Only recently at age forty-five have I been able to sit down and write a letter. I usually write small postcards.

I'm the most impulsive person in the world. It gets me in trouble. If I see something I know I shouldn't buy, I'll buy it anyway. Or, I'll say something that I know the minute it comes out of my mouth I'm going to regret. . . .

I wish I could just slow down and relax. I have problems sitting still. . . . People say I make them nervous, but I don't even realize I'm doing anything. That hurts my feelings. I don't want to be different.

My dream has always been to be some kind of counselor, but I felt like I wasn't college material, so I got married and had two children. I have a real estate license now. I don't know how I passed the test. I must have guessed right. What I like about selling is that I'm always on the move and I love people. I'm tuned into them. But I'm too sensitive to have a sense of humor. I think I have a thin skin. I get my feelings hurt easily. When that happens, I cry and go into my shell.

My mood swings from high to low. I either feel very good or very down. I feel up if the house looks good. If I get everything done that I think I should, it makes me feel good about myself. I feel responsible for a lot of people. If my husband is in a bad mood, or if things aren't going right for my kids, my mother, or my sister, I feel bad. I don't know what's wrong with me.

—Ann Ridgley

SOURCE: Weiss, L. (1992). *Attention deficit disorder in adults* (pp. 11–14). Lanham, MD: Taylor Publishing Co. Reprinted by permission.

Transition to Adulthood

CW Adults and children with ADHD, as well as parents of children with ADHD, can find a wealth of useful information from organizations devoted to ADHD. The oldest organization devoted to ADHD is the Children and Adults with Attention-Deficit/Hyperactivity Disorder (CHADD). A more recent organization is the National Attention Deficit Disorder Association (National ADDA). Their respective Web sites are: http://www.chadd.org/ and http://www.add.org/

For more personal stories about ADHD visit the following link on the National ADDA Web site: http://www.add.org/content/stories1.htm ■

It was not too long ago that most professionals assumed that ADHD diminished in adolescence and usually disappeared by adulthood. Authorities now recognize about two-thirds of individuals diagnosed with ADHD in childhood will continue to have significant symptoms in adulthood (Faraone & Doyle, 2001). And with the greater recognition of ADHD by the scientific community as well as by the popular media, many persons are being diagnosed with ADHD in adulthood. The few studies of prevalence that have been conducted report a prevalence rate of about 4 to 5 percent (Barkley, 1998), which mirrors that for children.

DIAGNOSIS IN ADULTHOOD

The diagnosis of ADHD in adults is controversial. Because of the long-held assumption that ADHD did not persist into adulthood, there is not a very long history of research on ADHD in adults. In recent years, however, professionals have begun to make progress in identifying and treating ADHD in adults. Because there is no "test" for ADHD, most authorities hold that the person's history is of utmost importance. As one authoritative team has put it:

This is old-fashioned medicine, not high-tech. This is a doctor talking to a patient, asking questions, listening to answers, drawing conclusions based on getting to know the patient well. These days we often don't respect or trust anything medical that doesn't depend upon fancy technology. Yet the diagnosis of [ADHD] depends absolutely upon the simplest of all medical procedures: the taking of a history. (Hallowell & Ratey, 1994, pp. 195–196)

The best test for [ADHD] is the oldest test in the history of medicine: the patient's own story. . . . If possible, the history should always be taken from at least two people—the identified patient plus a parent or spouse or friend. (Hallowell & Ratey, 1996, p. 188)

An abbreviated history of an adult with ADHD is presented in the box on page 214.

As crucial as the history is, however, its subjective nature does make it vulnerable to misinterpretation. Thus, clinicians have come up with guidelines for diagnosis. Table 6.4 below contains a set of suggested diagnostic criteria for adults.

TABLE 6.4   Suggested Diagnostic Criteria for Attention Deficit Disorder in Adults

Note: Consider a criterion met only if the behavior is considerably more frequent than that of most people of the same mental age.

A. A chronic disturbance in which at least twelve of the following are present:
- A sense of underachievement, of not meeting one's goals (regardless of how much one has actually accomplished).
- Difficulty getting organized.
- Chronic procrastination or trouble getting started.
- Many projects going simultaneously; trouble with followthrough.
- A tendency to say what comes to mind without necessarily considering the timing or appropriateness of the remark.
- A frequent search for high stimulation.
- An intolerance of boredom.
- Easy distractibility, trouble focusing attention, tendency to tune out or drift away in the middle of a page or a conversation, often coupled with an ability to hyperfocus at times.
- Often creative, intuitive, highly intelligent.
- Trouble in going through established channels, following "proper" procedure.
- Impatient; low tolerance of frustration.
- Impulsive, either verbally or in action, as in impulsive spending of money, changing plans, enacting new schemes or career plans, and the like; hot-tempered.
- A tendency to worry needlessly, endlessly; a tendency to scan the horizon looking for something to worry about, alternating with inattention to or disregard for actual dangers.
- A sense of insecurity.
- Mood swings, mood lability, especially when disengaged from a person or a project.
- Physical or cognitive restlessness.
- A tendency toward addictive behavior.
- Chronic problems with self-esteem.
- Inaccurate self-observation.
- Family history of ADD or manic-depressive illness or depression or substance abuse or other disorders of impulse control or mood.

B. Childhood history of ADD. (It may not have been formally diagnosed, but in reviewing the history, one sees that the signs and symptoms were there.)

C. Situation not explained by other medical or psychiatric condition.

SOURCE: From Driven to distraction: Recognizing and coping with attention deficit disorder from childhood through adulthood. by Edward M. Hallowell, M.D. and John J. Ratey, M.D., copyright © 1994 by Edward H. Hallowell, M.D. and John J. Ratey, M.D. Used by permission of Pantheon Books, a division of Random House, Inc.

ADULT OUTCOMES

Many adults with ADHD have antisocial, anxiety, and depression disorders and experience more school failure, employment problems, and automobile accidents than adults without ADHD (Faraone et al., 2000). Those who have a coexisting condition, such as depression or aggression, tend to have less positive outcomes than those who do not. Although persons with ADHD are at risk for poorer outcomes, it is important to point out that there are many adults with ADHD who have highly successful careers and jobs, and many have happy marriages and families.

Employment   One of the keys to successful employment for all people, but especially for persons with ADHD, is to select a job or career that maximizes the individual's strengths and minimizes her or his weaknesses. Success is often dependent on pursuing a job that fits a person's needs for structure versus independence. For those who work best with structure, it is recommended that they look for jobs with organizations that have a clear mission and lines of authority, with an emphasis on oversight from supervisors who have an understanding of ADHD. Those who find formal structures too confining should look for work environments that are flexible, have variety, and allow one to be independent (Hallowell & Ratey, 1996).

Marriage and Family   Given some of the behavioral characteristics of ADHD, it is not surprising that husbands and wives of persons with ADHD frequently complain that their spouse is a poor listener, preoccupied, forgetful, unreliable, messy, and so forth (Murphy, 1998). A person's ADHD can have a negative impact on the entire family. Parents who have ADHD may find it difficult to manage the daily lives of their children. As one parent put it, "I couldn't remember to brush my teeth when I was a kid, and now I can't remember to tell my kid to brush his teeth." (Weiss, Hechtman, & Weiss, 2000, p. 1060)

Many authorities recommend that the first step to treatment is to have all family members become educated about the facts associated with ADHD. Because ADHD is a family issue, they also recommend that all members of the family should be partners in its treatment:

> Unlike some medical problems, [ADHD] touches everybody in the family in a daily, significant way. It affects early-morning behavior, it affects dinner-table behavior, it affects vacations, and it affects quiet time. Let each member of the family become a part of the solution, just as each member of the family has been a part of the problem. (Hallowell & Ratey, 1996, p. 303)

Table 6.5 provides twenty-five tips on the management of ADHD in couples, when one of the partners has ADHD. With current high rates of divorce and single-parent families in the United States, many of these suggestions would also be applicable to the general population.

IMPORTANCE OF COACHING

Coaching.
A technique whereby a friend or therapist offers encouragement and support for a person with ADHD.

One highly recommended therapeutic technique is that of coaching (Hallowell & Ratey, 1994). **Coaching** involves identifying someone whom the person with ADHD can rely on for support. The term *coach* is used because this person can be visualized as someone "standing on the sidelines with a whistle around his or her neck barking out encouragement, directions, and reminders to the player in the game" (Hallowell & Ratey, 1994, p. 226). The coach, who can be a therapist or a friend, is someone who spends ten to fifteen minutes each day helping to keep the person with ADHD focused on his or her goals. The coach provides the structure needed to plan for upcoming events and activities, and heaps on praise when tasks are accomplished.

Although ADHD is a lifelong struggle for most people with the condition, with the appropriate combination of medical, educational, and psychological counseling, satisfac-

TABLE 6.5   Twenty-Five Tips on the Management of ADHD in Couples

1. Make sure you have an accurate diagnosis. Once you are sure of the diagnosis, learn as much as you can about ADHD.

2. Keep a sense of humor! At that psychological branch point we all know so well when the split-second options are to get mad, cry, or laugh, go for the laughter. Humor is a key to a happy life with ADHD.

3. Declare a truce. After you have made the diagnosis and have done some reading, take a deep breath and wave the white flag.

4. Set up a time for talking.

5. Spill the beans. Tell each other what is on your mind. Tell each other just how you are being driven crazy, what you like, what you want to change, what you want to preserve. Try to say it all before you both start reacting. People with ADHD have a tendency to bring premature closure to discussions, to go for the bottom line. In this case, the bottom line is the discussion itself.

6. Write down your complaints and your recommendations. Otherwise you'll forget.

7. Make a treatment plan. You may want some professional help with this phase, but it is a good idea to try starting it on your own.

8. Follow through on the plan. Remember, one of the hallmarks of ADHD is insufficient follow-through.

9. Make lists for each other. Try to use them constructively, not as threats or evidence in arguments.

10. Use bulletin boards. Messages in writing are less likely to be forgotten.

11. Put notepads in strategic places such as by your bed, in your car, in the bathroom and kitchen.

12. Consider writing down what you want the other person to do. This must be done in the spirit of assistance, not dictatorship. Keep a master appointment book for both of you.

13. Take stock of your sex lives. ADHD can affect sexual interest and performance. It is good to know the problems are due to ADHD, and not something else.

14. Avoid the pattern of mess-maker and cleaner-upper.

15. Avoid the pattern of pesterer and tuner-outer.

16. Avoid the pattern of the victim and the victimizer. You don't want the ADHD partner to present himself or herself as a helpless victim left at the merciless hands of the all-controlling non-ADHD mate.

17. Avoid the pattern of master and slave. In a funny way it can often be the non-ADHD partner who feels like the slave to his or her mate's ADHD.

18. Avoid the pattern of a sadomasochistic struggle as a routine way of interacting. Many couples spend most of their time attacking and counterattacking each other. One hopes to get past that and into the realm of problem solving. What you have to be aware of is the covert pleasure that can be found in the struggle. Try to vent your anger at the disorder, not at the person.

19. In general, watch out for the dynamics of control, dominance, and submission that lurk in the background of most relationships, let alone relationships where ADHD is involved.

20. Break the tapes of negativity. The "tapes of negativity" can play relentlessly, unforgivingly, endlessly in the mind of the person. They play over and over, grinding noises of "You can't," "You're dumb," "It won't work out." The tapes can be playing in the midst of a business deal, or they can take the place of making love. It is hard to be romantic when you are full of negative thoughts.

21. Use praise freely.

22. Learn about mood management. Anticipation is a great way to help anyone deal with the highs and lows that come along. If you know in advance that when you say "Good morning, honey!" the response you get might be "Get off my back, will you!" then it is easier to deal with that response without getting a divorce.

23. Let the one who is the better organizer take on the job of organization.

24. Make time for each other.

25. Don't use ADHD as an excuse. Each member of the couple has to take responsibility for his or her actions.

tory employment and family adjustment are within the reach of most people with ADHD. And now that most authorities recognize that ADHD often continues into adulthood, more and more research will be focused on treatment of ADHD in adults. With this research should come an even more positive outlook for adults with ADHD.

Summary

Attention Deficit Hyperactivity Disorder, or ADHD, was first recognized as early as the mid-nineteenth century, though the term ADHD did not appear until over a hundred years later. Early "cases" of the disorder were represented by children described as impulsive, fidgety, or generally lacking in the ability to control their behavior. In 1902, Dr. George F. Still referred to children whose behavior would now be seen as symptomatic of ADHD as having "defective moral control," or an inability to refrain from inappropriate behavior. To this day, ADHD is considered to be primarily a deficit involving behavioral inhibition.

The concept of ADHD has been subject to criticism, often being referred to as a convenient catchall for persons who are simply lazy, disobedient, or unmotivated. ADHD is not recognized as its own special education category, such as mental retardation, learning disabilities, and so forth. However, many students with ADHD are served by special education under the category of "other health impaired."

Research and clinical observations during the middle part of the last century suggested compelling evidence for a connection between brain injury and the presence of behaviors now associated with ADHD. Professionals began to apply the label of "minimal brain injury" to children who were inattentive, impulsive, and/or hyperactive. However, while clinical evidence seemed to connect brain injuries and ADHD, actual tissue damage in the brain was difficult to document. Thus, labeling and diagnoses of the disorder continued to rely on behavioral observations, with the primary focus being hyperactivity—the "hyperactive" child. By the 1980s, "inattention" began to be recognized as more central than "hyperactivity" in cases of ADHD.

Most professionals rely on the American Psychiatric Association's *Diagnostic and Statistical Manual of Mental Disorders (DSM)* for the criteria used to determine whether an individual has ADHD. The current *DSM* uses ADHD as the general term and subdivides individuals into (1) ADHD, Predominantly Inattentive Type; (2) ADHD, Predominantly Hyperactive-Impulsive Type; and (3) ADHD, Combined Type.

Actual prevalence figures for ADHD are difficult to obtain, though estimates are that 3 to 5 percent of school-age children have ADHD. ADHD is recognized widely as one of the most frequent reasons that children are referred for behavioral problems to guidance clinics. It occurs much more frequently in boys than in girls. There may be some gender bias in referral, with boys being more likely referred because of aggressive behavior. However, the gender differences are also likely due to biological, or constitutional, differences. ADHD also occurs at least as frequently in a variety of other countries.

Assessment of whether a student has ADHD should include three components: (1) a medical examination to rule out other reasons for the child's behavior problems; (2) a clinical interview to obtain as much relevant information as possible about the child's physical and psychological characteristics; and (3) teacher and parent rating scales, as a means of quantifying observations. The American Academy of Pediatrics has published guidelines to help primary care physicians diagnose ADHD. Among other things, they recommend that physicians obtain information from parents and teachers regarding the core symptoms of ADHD, the age of onset, the duration of the symptoms, and the degree of functional impairment.

Advances in neuroimaging techniques during the 1980s and 1990s allowed scientists to more accurately document the neurological basis of ADHD. Research has found abnormalities in three areas of the brain in persons with ADHD: the frontal lobes, the basal ganglia, and the cerebellum. The frontal lobes are responsible for executive functions, or the ability to regulate one's behavior. The basal ganglia and cerebellum are involved in coordination and control of motor behavior. Research has also revealed abnormal levels of the neurotransmitter dopamine in persons with ADHD, suggesting that levels of dopamine are too low in the frontal cortex, thus interfering with executive functioning, and too high in the basal ganglia, resulting in hyperactivity and impulsivity.

Family studies, twin studies, and molecular genetic studies indicate that heredity may also be a significant cause of ADHD. Also involved, though to a lesser degree, are toxic factors such as exposure to lead and abuse of alcohol and tobacco, as well as medical factors such as complications at birth and low birthweight.

While the most obvious psychological and behavioral characteristics of ADHD are inattention, hyperactivity, and impulsivity, the more basic problem is the inability to inhibit or regulate one's own behavior. The inability to withhold, interrupt, or delay responses tends to undermine executive functioning. Persons with ADHD find it difficult to engage in a variety of self-directed behaviors or to stay focused on tasks that require sustained effort or concentration.

Children and adults with ADHD also appear to experience problems in adaptive behavior and in their relationships with peers. It is not uncommon for students with ADHD to experience social isolation, though they desperately might want to be liked. ADHD often occurs simultaneously with other behavioral and/or learning disorders, such as learning disabilities and emotional or behavioral disorders. Persons with ADHD are also at a higher risk for substance abuse, with adults being twice as likely as the general population to become dependent on alcohol, drugs, or tobacco.

Educational programming for students with ADHD usually has two components: (1) classroom structure and teacher direction; and (2) functional assessment and contingency-based self-management. A high degree of classroom structure and teacher direction, first advocated by William Cruickshank, is rarely seen today, partly because the intensity with which Cruickshank thought it should be practiced cannot practically be delivered in general education settings, where most students with ADHD are placed. In addition, today's educators believe that while a high degree of structure is important in the early stages of working with students with ADHD, the ultimate priority is for them to become independent in their learning.

Functional behavioral assessment of students with ADHD involves determining the consequences, antecedents, and setting events that maintain appropriate behaviors. Such approaches might also include self-monitoring or self-management programs, wherein students record their own behaviors. These approaches are often contingency-based, with persons keeping track of their own behavior and then receiving consequences, usually in the form of rewards. Reinforcement in the form of social praise or points that can be traded for privileges plays an important role in the effectiveness of self-management techniques.

The treatment of ADHD with medication is one of the most controversial issues in all of special education. Ritalin and Adderall, psychostimulants, are by far the most commonly prescribed medications for ADHD. Scientific studies support their effectiveness (including a large-scale NIMH-sponsored study), and most authorities in ADHD favor their use. Ritalin and Adderall stimulate the release of the neurotransmitter dopamine, thereby enabling more normal operation of the brain's executive and motor functions. Responsiveness to psychostimulants is highly individualistic, so dosages may vary greatly from person to person. And it may not be effective for some people. Possible side effects, including insomnia and reduction in appetite, can usually be addressed very simply. Psychostimulants should not be prescribed at the "first sign" of behavior problems, nor should they be viewed as a panacea for all of a child's academic and social problems.

Early detection of ADHD is difficult, partly because symptoms of ADHD are hard to distinguish from typical behaviors of very young children. Moreover, even high-quality early interventions have not proven to be very effective in the remediation of ADHD. Long-term programming for such children will in most cases still be needed.

The diagnosis of adult ADHD is controversial. For a long time it was assumed that children "outgrew" ADHD, and there has yet to be developed any real "test" for ADHD. Therefore, an interview or history is most crucial in identifying ADHD in adults, though interviews are subjective in nature and might be vulnerable to misinterpretation. Adults with ADHD tend to have less positive outcomes than the general population in terms of employment, marriage and family, and general social well-being, although many exceptions do exist. A recommended therapeutic technique for adults with ADHD is to establish a relationship with a coach, most likely a therapist or a friend, who will spend time regularly with them and help them keep focused on their goals.

Elizabeth Hughes

Done to Jazz, Acrylic on rag paper. 22 × 30 in.

Ms. Hughes, who was born in 1936 in Boston, Massachusetts, is a serious artist with a track record of exhibitions and involvement in the Boston art scene. She is in love with jazz and often paints while listening to music, attempting to translate her impressions into color and shape.

7

Learners with Emotional or Behavioral Disorders

I t has always been hard for me to have friends. I want friends, but I don't know how to make them. I always think people are being serious when they are just joking around, but I don't figure that out until a lot later. I just don't know how to adapt.

I get into fights with people all the time. I take their teasing seriously and get into trouble. I don't remember having as much trouble getting along with kids when I was little. They seemed to feel sorry for me or thought I was weird. I used to run away from kids and hide in the bathroom at school or under my desk.

After I got back from the hospital, I really couldn't get along with anyone. That was when kids first began calling me "retard." I am not retarded, but I get confused and can't figure out what is going on. At first I couldn't figure out what they were saying to me. Finally one girl in my special education class became my friend. She kind of took care of me. I had another friend in junior high who was also nice and kind to me. But my best friend is my dog Cindie. Even though I give her a hard time, she is always ready to love me.

I like to play by myself best. I make up stories and fantasies. My mother says it is too bad I have such a hard time writing, because with my imagination and all the stories I have created in my mind I could write a book.

ANONYMOUS

Children and youths who have emotional or behavioral disorders are not typically good at making friends. In fact, their most obvious problem is failure to establish close and satisfying emotional ties with other people. As the youth in the excerpt on page 221 describes, it may be easier for these individuals to hide, both physically and emotionally. If they do develop friendships, it is often with deviant peers (Farmer, 2000; Farmer, Farmer, & Gut, 1999; Farmer, Quinn, Hussey, & Holahan, 2001).

Some of these children are withdrawn. Other children or adults may try to reach them, but these efforts are usually met with fear or disinterest. In many cases, this kind of quiet rejection continues until those who are trying to make friends give up. Because close emotional ties are built around reciprocal social responses, people naturally lose interest in individuals who do not respond to social overtures.

Many other children with emotional or behavioral disorders are isolated from others not because they withdraw from friendly advances but because they strike out with hostility and aggression. They are abusive, destructive, unpredictable, irresponsible, bossy, quarrelsome, irritable, jealous, defiant—anything but pleasant. Naturally, other children and adults choose not to spend time with children like this unless they have to, and others tend to strike back at youngsters who show these characteristics. It is no wonder, then, that these children and youths seem to be embroiled in a continuous battle with everyone. The reaction of most other children and adults is to withdraw to avoid battles, but rejected children then do not learn to behave acceptably (Farmer et al., 2001). "In the case of [the] rejected child, parents, teachers, and peers simply withdraw from the child, and 'teaching opportunities' are greatly reduced, along with the opportunity for the rejected child to redeem himself in the eyes of parents, teachers, and mainstream peers" (Ialongo, Vaden-Kiernan, & Kellam, 1998, p. 210).

Where does the problem start? Does it begin with behavior that frustrates, angers, or irritates other people? Or does it begin with a social environment so uncomfortable or inappropriate that the only reasonable response of the child is withdrawal or attack? These questions cannot be answered fully on the basis of current research. The best thinking today is that the problem is not just in the child's behavior or just in the environment. The problem *arises because the social interactions and transactions between the child and the social environment are inappropriate.* This is an *ecological* perspective—an interpretation of the problem as a negative aspect of the child *and* the environment in which he or she lives.

Children with emotional and behavior disorders frequently behave in ways that frustrate adults and others around them. ■

Learners with Emotional or Behavioral Disorders

MYTH Most children and youths with emotional or behavioral disorders are not noticed by people around them.

FACT Although it is difficult to identify the types and causes of problems, most children and youths with emotional or behavioral disorders, whether aggressive or withdrawn, are quite easy to spot.

MYTH Students with emotional or behavioral disorders are usually very bright.

FACT Relatively few students with emotional or behavioral disorders have high intelligence; in fact, most have below-average IQs.

MYTH Youngsters who exhibit shy, anxious behavior are more seriously impaired than those whose behavior is hyperaggressive.

FACT Youngsters with aggressive, acting-out behavior patterns have less chance for social adjustment and mental health in adulthood. Neurotic, shy, anxious children and youths have a better chance of getting and holding jobs, overcoming their problems, and staying out of jails and mental hospitals, unless their withdrawal is extreme. This is especially true for boys.

MYTH Most students with emotional or behavioral disorders need a permissive environment, in which they feel accepted and can accept themselves for who they are.

FACT Research shows that a firmly structured and highly predictable environment is of greatest benefit for most students.

MYTH Only psychiatrists, psychologists, and social workers are able to help children and youths with emotional or behavioral disorders overcome their problems.

FACT Most teachers and parents can learn to be highly effective in helping youngsters with emotional or behavioral disorders, sometimes without extensive training or professional certification. Many of these children and youths do require services of highly trained professionals as well.

MYTH Undesirable behaviors are only symptoms; the real problems are hidden deep in the individual's psyche.

FACT There is no sound scientific basis for belief in hidden causes; the behavior and its social context are the problems. Causes may involve thoughts, feelings, and perceptions.

MYTH Juvenile delinquency and the aggressive behavior known as conduct disorder can be effectively deterred by harsh punishment, if children and youths know that their misbehavior will be punished.

FACT Harsh punishment, including imprisonment, not only does not deter misbehavior but creates conditions under which many individuals become even more likely to exhibit unacceptable conduct.

An ecological perspective on emotional and behavioral disorders focuses on a child's interaction with negative aspects of the environment in which he or she lives. ■

Special education for these students is, in many ways, both confused and confusing. The terminology of the field is inconsistent, and there is much misunderstanding of definitions (Kauffman, 2001). Reliable classifications of children's behavior problems have only recently emerged from research. The large number of theories regarding the causes and the best treatments of emotional and behavioral disorders makes it difficult to sort out the most useful concepts. Thus, study of this area of special education demands more than the usual amount of perseverance and critical thinking. In fact, children and youths with emotional or behavioral disorders present some of the most difficult social problems that our society has to solve (Kauffman, 2001; Walker, Forness, Kauffman, Epstein, Gresham, Nelson, & Strain, 1998).

Terminology

Many different terms have been used to designate children who have extreme social-interpersonal and/or intrapersonal problems, including *emotionally handicapped, emotionally impaired, behaviorally impaired, socially/emotionally handicapped, emotionally conflicted,* having *personal and social adjustment problems,* and *seriously behaviorally disabled.* These terms do not designate distinctly different types of disorders; that is, they do not refer to clearly different types of children and youths. Rather, the different labels appear to represent personal preferences for terms and perhaps slightly different theoretical orientations. The terminology of the field is so variable and confusing that it is possible to pick a label of choice simply by matching words from Column A with words from Column B below (and, if it seems appropriate, adding other qualifiers, such as *serious* or *severe*):

Column A	*Column B*
Emotional	Disturbance
Social	Disorder
Behavioral	Maladjustment
Personal	Handicap
	Impairment

Until 1997, *seriously emotionally disturbed* was the term used in federal special education laws and regulations. *Seriously* was dropped from the terminology in 1997. *Emotionally disturbed* is the term now used in the Individuals with Disabilities Education Act (IDEA), but it has been criticized as inappropriate. *Behaviorally disordered* is consistent with the name of the Council for Children with Behavioral Disorders (CCBD, a division of the Council for Exceptional Children) and has the advantage of focusing attention on the clearly observable aspect of these children's problems—disordered behavior. Many authorities favor terminology indicating that these children may have emotional or behavioral problems or both (Kauffman, 2001).

In 1990, the National Mental Health and Special Education Coalition, representing over thirty professional and advocacy groups, proposed the new terminology *emotional or behavioral disorder* to replace *emotional disturbance* in federal laws and regulations (Forness & Knitzer, 1992). It now appears that *emotional or behavioral disorder* may become the generally accepted terminology of the field, although changes in federal and state laws and regulations may be slow in coming.

Definition

Defining emotional and behavioral disorders has always been problematic. Professional groups and experts have felt free to construct individual working definitions to fit their own professional purposes (Forness & Kavale, 1997; Landrum & Kauffman, 2003). For practical reasons, we might say that someone has had an emotional or behavioral disorder whenever an adult authority has said so. Until recently, no one has come up with a definition that is understandable and acceptable to a majority of professionals.

DEFINITIONAL PROBLEMS

There are valid reasons for the lack of consensus regarding definition. Defining emotional and behavioral disorders is somewhat like defining a familiar experience—anger, loneliness, or happiness, for example. We all have an intuitive grasp of what these experiences are, but forming objective definitions is far from simple. The factors that make it particularly difficult to arrive at a good definition of emotional and behavioral disorders are:

- Lack of precise definitions of mental health and normal behavior
- Differences among conceptual models
- Difficulties in measuring emotions and behavior
- Relationships between emotional or behavioral disorder and other disabilities
- Differences in the professionals who diagnose and serve children and youths

Consider each of these problems in turn. Mental health and normal behavior have been hard to define precisely. It is no wonder, then, that the definition of emotional or behavioral disorder presents a special challenge. Professionals who work with youngsters who have emotional or behavioral disorders have been guided by a variety of conceptual models, as we will discuss further. These conceptual models—assumptions or theories about why people behave as they do and what we should do about it—may offer conflicting ideas about just what the problem is. Thus, people who adopt different conceptual models may define emotional or behavioral disorders in very different terms.

Measurement is basic to any definition, and emotions and behavior—the disorders, in this case—are notoriously difficult to measure in ways that make a precise definition possible. Ultimately, subjective judgment is called for, even with the best measurements of emotions and behavior available. Emotional or behavioral disorders tend to overlap a great deal with other disabilities, especially learning disabilities and mental retardation. It is therefore hard to define emotional or behavioral disorders as disabilities clearly distinct from all others.

Finally, each professional group has its own reasons for serving individuals with emotional or behavioral disorders. For example, clinical psychologists, school psychologists, social workers, teachers, and juvenile justice authorities all have their particular concerns and language. Differences in the focuses of different professions tend to produce differences in definition as well (Forness & Kavale, 1997; Kauffman, 2001).

CURRENT DEFINITIONS

Although the terminology used and the relative emphasis given to certain points vary considerably from one definition to another,

Developing objective criteria for defining emotional and behavioral disorders can be problematic, partly because feelings of unhappiness or anger are familiar—or "normal"—to everyone. ■

it is possible to extract several common features of current definitions. There is general agreement that emotional or behavioral disorder refers to:

- Behavior that goes to an extreme—that is not just slightly different from the usual
- A problem that is chronic—one that does not quickly disappear
- Behavior that is unacceptable because of social or cultural expectations

One definition that must be considered is included in the federal rules and regulations governing the implementation of IDEA. In federal laws and regulations, emotionally disturbed has been defined as follows:

(i) The term means a condition exhibiting one or more of the following characteristics over a long period of time and to a marked extent, which adversely affects educational performance:
(A) An inability to learn that cannot be explained by intellectual, sensory, or health factors;
(B) An inability to build or maintain satisfactory relationships with peers and teachers;
(C) Inappropriate types of behavior or feelings under normal circumstances;
(D) A general pervasive mood of unhappiness or depression; or
(E) A tendency to develop physical symptoms or fears associated with personal or school problems.
(ii) The term includes children who are schizophrenic. The term does not include children who are socially maladjusted unless it is determined that they are emotionally disturbed.

The federal definition is modeled after one proposed by Bower (1981). Bower's definition, however, does not include the statements found in part (ii) of the federal definition. These inclusions and exclusions are, as Bower (1982) and Kauffman (2001) point out, unnecessary. Common sense tells us that Bower's five criteria for emotional disturbance indicate that schizophrenic children *must be included* and that socially maladjusted children *cannot be excluded*. Furthermore, the clause *which adversely affects educational performance* makes interpretation of the definition impossible, unless the meaning of educational performance is clarified. Does educational performance refer only to academic achievement? If so, then children with other characteristics who achieve on grade level are excluded.

In recent years the federal definition has been widely criticized, and the federal government has more than once mandated study of it. One of the most widely criticized and controversial aspects of the definition is its exclusion of children who are socially maladjusted but not emotionally disturbed. Strong moves have been made in some states and localities to interpret *social maladjustment* as **conduct disorder**—aggressive, disruptive, antisocial behavior. This is the most common type of problem exhibited by students who have been identified as having emotional or behavioral disorders. Cline (1990) notes that excluding students with conduct disorder is inconsistent with the history of IDEA. Moreover, the American Psychological Association and the CCBD have condemned this practice, which has no empirical basis (Costenbader & Buntaine, 1999). The controversy about the exclusion of socially maladjusted children will likely continue for many years to come.

A second definition that must be considered is the one proposed in 1990 by the National Mental Health and Special Education Coalition. The coalition's proposed definition is:

(i) The term emotional or behavioral disorder means a disability characterized by behavioral or emotional responses in school so different from appropriate age, cultural, or ethnic norms that they adversely affect educational performance.

Conduct disorder.
A disorder characterized by overt, aggressive, disruptive behavior or covert antisocial acts such as stealing, lying, and fire setting; may include both overt and covert acts.

The Council for Children with Behavioral Disorders (CCBD) maintains a Web site at www.ccbd.net ■

Educational performance includes academic, social, vocational, and personal skills. Such a disability:

(A) is more than a temporary, expected response to stressful events in the environment;

(B) is consistently exhibited in two different settings, at least one of which is school-related; and

(C) is unresponsive to direct intervention in general education, or the child's condition is such that general education interventions would be insufficient.

(ii) Emotional and behavioral disorders can co-exist with other disabilities.

(iii) This category may include children or youths with schizophrenic disorders, **affective disorder, anxiety disorder,** or other sustained disorders of conduct or adjustment when they adversely affect educational performance in accordance with section (i). (Forness & Knitzer, 1992, p. 13)

The coalition is working to have the proposed definition and terminology adopted in federal laws and regulations; the hope is that states will adopt them as well. Advantages of the proposed definition over the federal definition include the following:

- It uses terminology reflecting current professional preferences and concern for minimizing stigma.
- It includes both disorders of emotions and disorders of behavior and recognizes that they may occur either separately or in combination.
- It is school-centered but acknowledges that disorders exhibited outside the school setting are also important.
- It is sensitive to ethnic and cultural differences.
- It does not include minor or transient problems or ordinary responses to stress.
- It acknowledges the importance of prereferral interventions but does not require slavish implementation of them in extreme cases.
- It acknowledges that children and youths can have multiple disabilities.
- It includes the full range of emotional or behavioral disorders of concern to mental health and special education professionals without arbitrary exclusions.

Affective disorder.
A disorder of mood or emotional tone characterized by depression or elation.

Anxiety disorder.
A disorder characterized by anxiety, fearfulness, and avoidance of ordinary activities because of anxiety or fear.

Researchers define the externalizing dimension of disordered behavior as striking out against others, for example fighting, disruptive behavior, or damaging property. ■

Classification

Since emotional or behavioral disorders are evidenced in many ways, it seems reasonable to expect that individuals could be grouped into subcategories according to the types of problems they have. Still, there is no universally accepted system for classifying emotional or behavioral disorders for special education.

Psychiatric classification systems have been widely criticized for several decades. Clearly, the usual diagnostic categories—for example, those found in publications of the American Psychiatric Association—have little meaning for teachers. Many psychologists and educators have recommended relying more on individual assessment of the child's behavior and situational factors than on the diagnostic classifications used by psychiatrists.

An alternative to psychiatric classifications is the use of statistical analyses of behavioral characteristics to establish clusters, or dimensions, of disordered behavior. Using sophisticated statistical procedures, researchers look for patterns of behavior that characterize children who have emotional or behavioral disorders. By using these methods, researchers have been able to derive descriptive categories that are less susceptible to bias and unreliability than the traditional psychiatric classifications (Achenbach, 1985; Richardson, McGauhey, & Day, 1995).

Researchers have identified two broad, pervasive dimensions of disordered behavior: **externalizing** and **internalizing.** Externalizing behavior involves striking out against others. Internalizing behavior involves mental or emotional conflicts, such as depression and anxiety. Some researchers have found more specific disorders, but all of the more specific disorders can be located on these two primary dimensions.

Individuals may show behaviors characteristic of both dimensions; that is, the dimensions are not mutually exclusive. That is, a child or youth might exhibit several behaviors associated with internalizing problems (e.g., short attention span, poor concentration) and several of those associated with externalizing problems as well (e.g., fighting, disruptive behavior, annoying others). Actually, **comorbidity**—the co-occurrence of two or more conditions in the same individual—is not unusual (Tankersley & Landrum, 1997). Few individuals with an emotional or behavioral disorder exhibit only one type of maladaptive behavior. The federal government estimates that about one-third of children with emotional or behavioral disorders have another disability as well (U.S. Department of Education, 2000).

Furthermore, children may exhibit characteristic types of behavior with varying degrees of intensity or severity. That is, either dimension of behavior may be exhibited to a greater or lesser extent; the range may be from normal to severely disordered. For example, an individual might have a severe conduct disorder, an externalizing problem defined by overt, aggressive, disruptive behavior or covert antisocial acts such as stealing, lying, and fire setting.

Severe emotional or behavioral disorders include the extremes of any externalizing or internalizing problem. Individuals with **schizophrenia** have a severe disorder of thinking. They may believe they are controlled by alien forces or have other delusions or hallucinations. Typically, their emotions are inappropriate for the actual circumstances, and they tend to withdraw into their own private worlds (Asarnow, Tompson, & Goldstein, 1994). Childhood schizophrenia is a disorder that typically begins after a normal period of development during early childhood. It is distinguished from **autism** or **autistic spectrum disorder,** which we discuss in Chapter 11, in several ways:

1. Children with schizophrenia usually have delusions (bizarre ideas) and hallucinations (seeing or hearing imaginary things), whereas children with autism usually do not.
2. Children with schizophrenia tend to have psychotic episodes interspersed with periods of near-normal behavior, whereas children with autism tend to have more constant symptoms.

Externalizing.
Acting-out behavior; aggressive or disruptive behavior that is observable as behavior directed toward others.

Internalizing.
Acting-in behavior; anxiety, fearfulness, withdrawal, and other indications of an individual's mood or internal state.

Comorbidity.
Co-occurrence of two or more conditions in the same individual.

Schizophrenia.
A disorder characterized by psychotic behavior manifested by loss of contact with reality, distorted thought processes, and abnormal perceptions.

Autism.
A pervasive developmental disability characterized by extreme withdrawal, cognitive deficits, language disorders, self-stimulation, and onset before the age of thirty months.

Autistic spectrum disorder.
A range of disorders characterized by symptoms of autism that can range from mild to severe.

3. About 25 percent of children with autism have epileptic seizures, whereas children with schizophrenia seldom have seizures (Rutter & Schopler, 1987).

In summary, ambiguity in the federal definition of emotional disturbance has led to persistent controversy regarding the classifications that should be included for special education purposes. The most useful classifications of emotional or behavioral disorders describe behavioral dimensions. Dimensions described in the literature involve a wide range of externalizing and internalizing problems. The typical student with emotional or behavioral disorders has multiple problems—comorbidity is not unusual (Cullinan & Epstein, 2001; Gresham et al., 2001; Tankersley & Landrum, 1997).

Prevalence

Estimates of the prevalence of emotional or behavioral disorders in children and youths have varied tremendously because there has been no standard and reliable definition or screening instrument. For decades, the federal government estimated that 2 percent of the school-age population was emotionally disturbed. The government's estimate was extremely conservative, however. Rather consistently, credible studies in the United States and many other countries have indicated that at least 6 to 10 percent of children and youths of school age exhibit serious and persistent emotional/behavioral problems (Brandenburg, Friedman, & Silver, 1990; Costello, Messer, Bird, Cohen, & Reinherz, 1998; Kauffman, 2001). However, only about 1 percent of schoolchildren in the United States are identified as emotionally disturbed for special education purposes (U.S. Department of Education, 2000). A report on children's mental health from the U.S. Surgeon General has also indicated that a very small percentage of children with serious emotional or behavioral disorders receive mental health services (U.S. Department of Health and Human Services, 2001).

The U. S. Surgeon General's 2001 report on children's mental health is found at www.surgeongeneral.gov/topics/cmh/ ■

The most common types of problems exhibited by students placed in special education for emotional or behavioral disorders are externalizing—that is, aggressive, acting-out, disruptive behavior. Boys outnumber girls in displaying these behaviors by a ratio of 5 to 1 or more. Overall, boys tend to exhibit more aggression and conduct disorder than girls do, although antisocial behavior in girls is an increasing concern (Kazdin, 1997; Talbott & Callahan, 1997).

Juvenile delinquency and the antisocial behavior known as conduct disorder present particular problems in estimating prevalence. Delinquent youths constitute a considerable percentage of the population. About 3 percent of U.S. youths are referred to a juvenile court in any given year, a disproportionate number of whom are African American males (Miller, 1997). Many others engage in serious antisocial behavior but are not referred to the courts (see Siegel & Senna, 1994). One point of view is that all delinquent and antisocial youths should be thought of as having emotional or behavioral disorders. Some argue that most youths who commit frequent antisocial acts are socially maladjusted, not emotionally disturbed. However, we can not clearly distinguish social maladjustment from emotional disturbance (Costenbader & Buntaine, 1999).

Clearly, disabling conditions of various kinds are much more common among juvenile delinquents than among the general population (Henggeler, 1989). Just as clearly, the social and economic costs of delinquency and antisocial behavior are enormous. Adolescent males account for a disproportionately high percentage of serious and violent crime in U.S. society. Those who exhibit serious antisocial behavior are at high risk for school failure as well as other negative outcomes (Kazdin, 1995, 1997; Walker, Colvin, & Ramsey, 1995; Walker, Forness et al., 1998; Walker, Kavanaugh et al., 1998). If schools are to address the educational problems of delinquent and antisocial children and youths, then the number served by special education must increase dramatically.

Causes

The causes of emotional or behavioral disorders have been attributed to four major factors:

1. Biological disorders and diseases
2. Pathological family relationships
3. Undesirable experiences at school
4. Negative cultural influences

Although in the majority of cases there is no conclusive empirical evidence that any of these factors is directly responsible for the disorder in most cases, some factors may give a child a predisposition to exhibit problem behavior and others may precipitate or trigger it. That is, some factors, such as genetics, influence behavior over a long time and increase the likelihood that a given set of circumstances will trigger maladaptive responses. Other factors (such as observing one parent beating the other) may have a more immediate effect and may trigger maladaptive responses in an individual who is already predisposed to problem behavior.

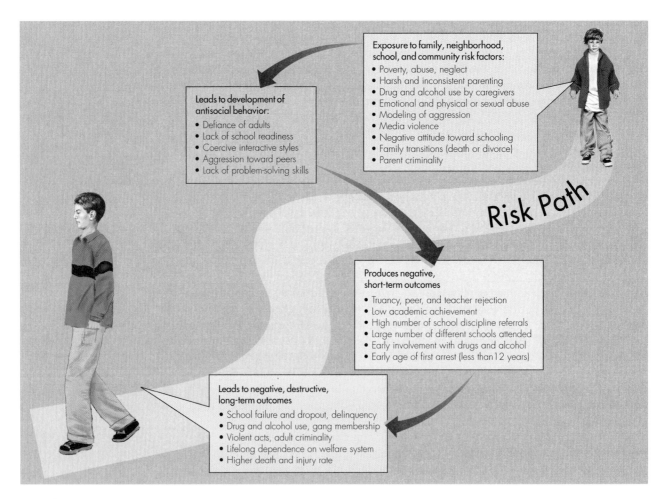

FIGURE 7.1

Risk pathway to antisocial and violent behavior. It reflects the effects of exposure to known risk factors and developmental outcomes.

SOURCE: From *Early identification and intervention for youth with antisocial and violent behavior* by Jeffrey Sprague and Hill Walker. *Exceptional Children, 66,* 371. Copyright © by the Council of Exceptional Children. Reprinted with permission.

Another concept important in all theories is the idea of *contributing factors* that heighten the risk of a disorder. It is extremely unusual to find a single cause that has led directly to a disorder. Usually, several factors together contribute to the development of a problem. In almost all cases, the question of what specifically has caused the disorder cannot be answered because no one really knows. However, we often do know the factors that place children at risk—the circumstances or conditions that increase the chances that a child will develop the disorder. Figure 7.1 illustrates how risk factors accumulate to place children and youths at risk for antisocial and violent behavior—often called conduct disorder—which is one of the most common and troubling emotional-behavioral problems of young people (see also Kazdin, 1997).

BIOLOGICAL FACTORS

Behaviors and emotions may be influenced by genetic, neurological, or biochemical factors or by combinations of these. Certainly, there is a relationship between body and behavior, and it would therefore seem reasonable to look for a biological causal factor of some kind for certain emotional or behavioral disorders. We do know, for example, that prenatal exposure to alcohol can contribute to many types of disability, including emotional or behavioral disorders (U.S. Department of Education, 2000). But only rarely is it possible to demonstrate a relationship between a specific biological factor and an emotional or behavioral disorder.

Many children with emotional or behavioral disorders have no detectable biological flaws that account for their actions, and many behaviorally normal children have serious biological defects. For most children with emotional or behavioral disorders, there simply is no real evidence that biological factors *alone* are at the root of their problems. For those with severe and profound disorders, however, there is evidence to suggest that biological factors may contribute to their conditions (Asarnow, Asamen, Granholm, Sherman, Watkins, & Williams, 1994; Charlop-Christy, Schreibman, Pierce, & Kurtz, 1997; Harris, 1995). Moreover, there is increasing evidence that medications are helpful in addressing the problems of many or most students with emotional or behavioral disorders if they receive state-of-the-art psychopharmacology (Forness & Kavale, 2001).

All children are born with a biologically determined behavioral style, or temperament. Although children's inborn temperaments may be changed by the way they are reared, some have long believed that children with so-called difficult temperaments are predisposed to develop emotional or behavioral disorders (Thomas & Chess, 1984). There is no one-to-one relationship between temperament and disorders, however. A difficult child may be handled so well or a child with an easy temperament so poorly that the outcome will be quite different from what one might predict on the basis of initial behavioral style. Other biological factors besides temperament—disease, malnutrition, and brain trauma, for example—may predispose children to develop emotional or behavioral problems. Substance abuse also may contribute to emotional and behavioral problems. Except in rare instances, it is not possible to determine that these factors are direct causes of problem behavior (see Kauffman, 2001).

As is the case with mental retardation, there is more often evidence of a biological cause among children with severe or profound disabilities. Children with schizophrenia frequently (but not always) show signs of neurological defects. There is convincing evidence that genetic factors contribute to schizophrenia (Gottesman, 1991), although the role of specific biological factors often remains a mystery, even if the disorder is severe. It is now generally accepted that schizophrenia is a brain disorder, but the nature and causes of the problem in the brain are unknown (Kauffman, 2001).

As biological and psychological research has become more sophisticated, it has become apparent that biological factors cause or set the stage for many disorders that formerly were widely assumed to be caused mostly or entirely by social interactions. Schizophrenia is the foremost example. Another example is **Tourette's syndrome (TS),** which is characterized by multiple motor tics (repetitive, stereotyped movements) and verbal tics

GW For a site with links to articles about children's health, including emotional and behavioral problems, see www.mcleanhospital.org/ ■

Tourette's syndrome (TS). A neurological disorder beginning in childhood (about three times more prevalent in boys than in girls) in which stereotyped, repetitive motor movements (tics) are accompanied by multiple vocal outbursts that may include grunting noises or socially inappropriate words or statements (e.g., swearing).

(the individual makes strange noises or says inappropriate words or phrases). Although we now understand that schizophrenia, Tourette's disorder, attention deficit hyperactivity disorder (ADHD), some forms of depression, and many other disorders are caused wholly or partly by brain or biochemical dysfunctions, these biological causal factors remain poorly understood. That is, we do not know exactly how genetic, neurological, and other biochemical factors contribute to these disorders, nor do we know how to correct the biological problems involved in these disorders.

Four points are important to remember about biological causes:

1. The fact that disorders have biological causes does not mean that they are not emotional or behavioral disorders. An emotional or behavioral disorder can have a physical cause; the biological malfunction is a problem because of the disorder it creates in the individual's emotions or behavior.
2. Causes are seldom exclusively biological or psychological. Once a biological disorder occurs, it nearly always creates psychosocial problems that then also contribute to the emotional or behavioral disorder as well.
3. Biological or medical treatment of the disorder is seldom sufficient to resolve the problem. Medication may be of great benefit, but it is seldom the only intervention that is needed (Forness & Kavale, 2001; Forness, Kavale, Sweeney, & Crenshaw, 1999). The psychological and social aspects of the disorder must also be addressed.
4. Medical or biological approaches are sometimes of little or no benefit and the primary interventions are psychological or behavioral, even though the disorder is known to have primarily a biological cause. Medications do not work equally well for all cases, and for some disorders no generally effective medications are known.

FAMILY FACTORS

Mental health specialists have been tempted to blame behavioral difficulties primarily on parent–child relationships because the nuclear family—father, mother, and children—has a profound influence on early development. In fact, some advocates of psychoanalysis believe that almost all severe problems of children stem from early negative interactions between mother and child.

However, empirical research on family relationships indicates that the influence of parents on their children is no simple matter and that children with emotional or behavioral disorders may influence their parents as much as their parents influence them. It is increasingly clear that family influences are interactional and transactional and that the effects parents and children have on one another are reciprocal (Patterson, Reid, & Dishion, 1992). Even in cases of severe emotional or behavioral disorders, it is not possible to find consistent and valid research findings that allow the blame for the children's problem behavior to be placed primarily on their parents (Kauffman, 2001).

The outcome of parental discipline depends not only on the particular techniques used but also on the characteristics of the child (Kazdin, 1997). Generalizations about the effects of parental discipline are difficult to make, for as Becker (1964) commented long ago, "There are probably many routes to becoming a 'good parent' which vary with the personality of both the parents and children and with the pressure in the environment with which one must learn to cope" (p. 202). Nevertheless, sensitivity to children's needs, love-oriented methods of dealing with misbehavior, and positive reinforcement (attention and praise) for appropriate

The quality of parenting may be a factor causing behavior problems in children, but by itself, it is not an adequate or correct explanation. Children, their families, and schools are embedded in cultures that influence them. ■

behavior unquestionably tend to promote desirable behavior in children. Parents who are generally lax in disciplining their children but are hostile, rejecting, cruel, and inconsistent in dealing with misbehavior are likely to have aggressive, delinquent children. Broken, disorganized homes in which the parents themselves have arrest records or are violent are

The home page of the PACER (Parent Advocacy Coalition for Educational Rights) Center is www.pacer.org

For the Federation of Families for Children's Mental Health, see www.ffcmh.org ■

Personal Reflection: Family Factors

Dixie Jordan is the parent of a nineteen-year-old son with an emotional and behavioral disorder, coordinator of the EBD Project at the PACER Center in Minneapolis (a resource center for parents of children with disabilities), and a founding member of the Federation of Families for Children's Mental Health.

Why do you think there is such a strong tendency to hold parents responsible for their children's emotional or behavioral disorders?

I am the parent of two children, the younger of which has emotional and behavioral problems. When my firstborn and I were out in public, strangers often commented on what a "good" mother I was, to have such an obedient, well-behaved, and compliant child. Frankly, I enjoyed the comments, and really believed that those parents whose children were throwing tantrums and generally demolishing their environments were simply not very skilled in child-rearing. I recall casting my share of reproachful glances in those days, and thinking with some arrogance that raising children should be left to those of us who knew how to do it well. Several years later, my second child and I were on the business end of such disdain, and it was a lesson in humility that I shall never forget. Very little that I had learned in the previous 3 years as a parent worked with this child; he was neurologically different, hyperactive, inattentive, and noncompliant even when discipline was consistently applied. His doctors, his neurologist, and finally his teachers referred me to "parenting classes," as though the experiences I had had with my older child were nonexistent; his elementary principal even said that there was nothing wrong that a good spanking wouldn't cure. I expected understanding that this was a very difficult child to raise, but the unspoken message was that I lacked competence in basic parenting skills, the same message that I sent to similarly situated parents just a few years earlier.

Most of us in the world today are parents. The majority of us have children who do not have emotional or behavioral problems. Everything in our experience suggests that when our children are successful and obedient, it is because of our parenting. We are reinforced socially for having a well-behaved child from friends, grandparents, even strangers. It makes sense, then, to attribute less desirable behaviors in children to the failure of their parents to provide appropriate guidance or to set firm limits. Many parents have internalized that sense of responsibility or blame for causing their child's emotional problems, even when they are not able to identify what they might have done wrong. It is a very difficult attitude to shake, especially when experts themselves cannot seem to agree on causation. With most children, the "cause" of an emotional or behavioral disorder is more likely a complex interplay of multiple factors than "parenting styles," "biology," or "environmental influences" as discrete entities, but it is human nature to latch onto a simple explanation—and inadequate parenting is, indeed, a simple explanation. When systems blame parents for causing their child's emotional or behavioral disorders, the focus is no longer on services to help the child learn better adaptive skills or appropriate behaviors, but on rationalizing why such services may not work. When parents feel blamed, their energies shift from focusing on the needs of their child to defending themselves. In either instance, the child is less well served.

Another reason that people hold parents responsible for their children's emotional or behavioral disorders is that parents may be under such unrelenting stress from trying to manage their child's behavior that they may resort to inappropriate techniques because of the failure of more conventional methods. A parent whose 8-year-old hyperactive child smashes out his bedroom window while being timed out for another problem may know that tying the child to a chair is not a good way to handle the crisis, but may be out of alternatives. It may not have been the "right" thing for the parent to do, but [he or she] is hardly responsible for causing the child's problems in the first place. It would be a mistake to attribute the incidence of abuse or neglect as "causing" most emotional or behavioral disorders without consideration that difficult children are perhaps more likely to be abused due to their noncompliant or otherwise difficult behaviors.

SOURCE: Reprinted with the permission of Prentice-Hall Publishing Company from *Characteristics of emotional and behavioral disorders of children and youth* (7th ed.), by James M. Kauffman. Copyright © 2001 by Prentice-Hall Publishing Company.

particularly likely to foster delinquency and lack of social competence (see Reitman & Gross, 1995).

In discussing the combined effects of genetics and environment on behavioral development, Plomin (1989) warns against assuming that the family environment will make siblings similar. "Environmental influences do not operate on a family-by-family basis but rather on an individual-by-individual basis. They are specific to each child rather than general for an entire family" (p. 109). Thus, although we know that some types of family environments (abusive, neglectful, rejecting, and inconsistent, for example) are destructive, we must also remember that each child will experience and react to family relationships in his or her unique way.

In the mid-1990s, Harris (1995) proposed a theory of group socialization, suggesting that the role of parents is minimal in the development of their children's personality or social behavior. Popularization of her theory led many laypersons to the conclusion that family environment has little influence on social development and that the child's peer group is the primary factor in socialization. Although socialization by peers is undeniably an important factor in the development of emotional or behavioral disorders (Farmer et al., 2001), other research already cited indicates that parents and families can have a significant causal influence on some disorders.

Educators must be aware that most parents of youngsters with emotional or behavioral disorders want their children to behave more appropriately and will do anything they can to help them. These parents need support resources—not blame or criticism—for dealing with very difficult family circumstances. The Federation of Families for Children's Mental Health was organized in 1989 to help provide such support and resources, and parents are organizing in many localities to assist each other in finding additional resources (Jordan, Goldberg, & Goldberg, 1991). In the box on page 233, one of the founding members shares her perspective on why parents are so often blamed for their children's emotional or behavioral disorders.

However, we do know that parents can contribute to their children's emotional and behavioral problems through abusive, neglectful, or inadequate caregiving. Conduct problems in early childhood can be a result of deficits in caregiving, and multiple problems are often a result of multiple risk factors that begin during infancy (Shaw, Owens, Giovannelli, & Winslow, 2001). The chronic maltreatment of young children is very likely to lead to aggressive child behavior and peer rejection (Bolger & Patterson, 2001).

SCHOOL FACTORS

Some children already have emotional or behavioral disorders when they begin school; others develop such disorders during their school years, perhaps in part because of damaging experiences in the classroom itself. Children who exhibit disorders when they enter school may become better or worse according to how they are managed in the classroom (Walker, 1995; Walker, Colvin, & Ramsey, 1995). School experiences are no doubt of great importance to children, but as with biological and family factors, we cannot justify many statements regarding how such experiences contribute to the child's behavioral difficulties. A child's temperament and social competence may interact with the behaviors of classmates and teachers in contributing to emotional or behavioral problems. When a child with an already difficult temperament enters school lacking the skills for academic and social success, he or she is likely to get negative responses from peers and teachers (Martin, 1992).

There is a very real danger that such a child will become trapped in a spiral of negative interactions, in which he or she becomes increasingly irritating to and irritated by teachers and peers. The school can contribute to the development of emotional problems in several rather specific ways. For instance, teachers may be insensitive to children's individuality, perhaps requiring a mindless conformity to rules and routines. Educators and parents alike may hold too high or too low expectations for the child's achievement or conduct, and they may communicate to the child who disappoints them that she or he is inadequate or undesirable.

Discipline in the school may be too lax, too rigid, or inconsistent. Instruction may be offered in skills for which the child has no real or imagined use. The school environment may be such that the misbehaving child is rewarded with recognition and special attention (even if that attention is criticism or punishment), whereas the child who behaves is ignored. Finally, teachers and peers may be models of misconduct—the child may misbehave by imitating them (Farmer et al., 2001; Kauffman, 2001; Kauffman, Mostert, Trent, & Hallahan, 2002).

In considering how they may be contributing to disordered behavior, teachers must ask themselves questions about their academic instruction, expectations, and approaches to behavior management (Kauffman et al., 2002; Stein & Davis, 2000). Teachers must not assume blame for disordered behavior to which they are not contributing, yet it is equally important that teachers eliminate whatever contributions they may be making to their students' misconduct.

Questions about the influence of culture on behavior include the degree to which violence in the media affects behavior. This thirteen-year-old boy was convicted of murdering a six-year-old family friend, but said he was only imitating wrestling moves he'd seen on television. ■

CULTURAL FACTORS

Children, their families, and schools are embedded in cultures that influence them (Walker et al., 1995). Aside from family and school, many environmental conditions affect adults' expectations of children and children's expectations of themselves and their peers. Values and behavioral standards are communicated to children through a variety of cultural conditions, demands, prohibitions, and models. Several specific cultural influences come to mind: the level of violence in the media (especially television and motion pictures), the use of terror as a means of coercion, the availability of recreational drugs and the level of drug abuse, changing standards for sexual conduct, religious demands and restrictions on behavior, and the threat of nuclear accidents or war. Peers are another important source of cultural influence, particularly after the child enters the upper elementary grades (Farmer, 2000; Farmer et al., 2001; Harris, 1995).

Undoubtedly, the culture in which a child is reared influences his or her emotional, social, and behavioral development. Case studies of rapidly changing cultures bear this out. Other studies suggest cultural influences on anxiety, depression, and aggression. The level of violence depicted on television and in movies is almost certainly a contributing factor in the increasing level of violence in U.S. society (see Walker et al., 1995).

The changing cultural conditions in the United States may predispose children to develop emotional or behavioral disorders and a variety of other disabling conditions or to be mistakenly identified as having such disorders. Among these changes are increases in the number of children living in poverty and those being born to teenage mothers and to mothers who engage in substance abuse. At the same time, medical and social services available to poor children and their families have been cut substantially. In short, we are living in an era of enormous affluence for some Americans but also a period in which poverty and related problems continue to grow rapidly. Neglect of the problems of poor children and their families has led some to question the importance of the health and welfare of children in U.S. culture (Edelman, 2001; Hodgkinson, 1995; see also Freedman, 1993; Kozol, 1995; Moynihan, 1995). Moreover, dramatic increases in the ethnic diversity of most communities may contribute to the mistaken identification of behavioral differences as behavioral disorders.

Abuse and other forms of extreme trauma are known to contribute significantly to the emotional or behavioral disorders of many children in our society today (see Becker & Bonner, 1997; Saigh, 1997). Racial bias and discrimination are also known to be deeply embedded in our culture and to play a part in the disproportionate imprisonment of African American males. Emphasis on imprisonment and punishment, especially for relatively minor offenses, combined with lack of economic and educational opportunities, appear to perpetuate if not exacerbate the harsh conditions of life that contribute to emotional or behavioral disorders and delinquency (Miller, 1997).

Clearly, cultural influences affect how children behave in school and whether they are identified as having emotional or behavioral disorders. But even when culture is considered as a cause, we must be aware of interactive effects. Schools and families influence culture; they are not simply products of it. Finally, refer back to Chapter 3 and the importance of a multicultural perspective. Consideration of cultural factors in causing emotional or behavioral disorders requires that culturally normative behavior not be construed as disordered.

Identification

It is much easier to identify disordered behaviors than it is to define and classify their types and causes. Most students with emotional or behavioral disorders do not escape the notice of their teachers. Occasionally, such students will not bother anyone and thus be invisible, but it is usually easy for experienced teachers to tell when students need help. Teachers often fail to assess the strengths of students with emotional or behavioral disorders. However, it is important to include assessment of students' emotional and behavioral competencies, not just their weaknesses or deficits (Epstein & Sharma, 1997).

The most common type of emotional or behavioral disorder—conduct disorder, an externalizing problem—attracts immediate attention, so there is seldom any real problem in identification. Students with internalizing problems may be less obvious, but they are not difficult to recognize. Students with emotional or behavioral disorders are so readily identified by school personnel, in fact, that few schools bother to use systematic screening procedures. Also, the availability of special services for those with emotional or behavioral disorders lags far behind the need—and there is not much point in screening for problems when there are no services available to treat them. Children with schizophrenia are seldom mistaken for those who are developing normally. Their unusual language, mannerisms, and ways of relating to others soon become matters of concern to parents, teachers, and even many casual observers. Children with schizophrenia are a very small percentage of those with emotional or behavioral disorders, and problems in their identification are not usually encountered. However, they may first be identified as having another disorder, such as ADHD or depression, and later be diagnosed with schizophrenia.

Even so, do not conclude that there is never any question about whether a student has an emotional or behavioral disorder. The younger the child, the more difficult it is to judge whether his or her behavior signifies a serious problem. And some children with emotional or behavioral disorders are undetected because teachers are not sensitive to their problems or because they do not stand out sharply from other children in the environment who may have even more serious problems. Furthermore, even sensitive teachers sometimes make errors of judgment. Also keep in mind that some students with emotional or behavioral disorders do not exhibit problems at school.

Formal screening and accurate early identification for the purpose of planning educational intervention are complicated by the problems of definition already discussed. In general, however, teachers' informal judgments have served as a fairly valid and reliable means of screening students for emotional or behavioral problems (as compared with judgments of psychologists and psychiatrists). When more formal procedures are used, teachers' ratings of behavior have turned out to be quite accurate.

Walker and his colleagues have devised a screening system for use in elementary schools, based on the assumption that a teacher's judgment is a valid and cost-effective (though greatly underused) method of identifying children with emotional or behavioral disorders (Walker & Severson, 1990; Walker, Severson, & Feil, 1994). Although teachers tend to overrefer students who exhibit externalizing behavior problems (i.e., those with

A teacher's judgment is a valid and cost-effective method of identifying children with emotional or behavioral disorders. ■

conduct disorders), they tend to underrefer students with internalizing problems (i.e., those characterized by anxiety and withdrawal). To make certain that children are not overlooked in screening but that time and effort are not wasted, a three-step process is used:

1. The teacher lists and ranks students with externalizing and internalizing problems. Those who best fit descriptions of students with externalizing problems and those who best fit descriptions of those with internalizing problems are listed in order from "most like" to "least like" the descriptions.
2. The teacher completes two checklists for the three highest-ranked pupils on each list. One checklist asks the teacher to indicate whether each pupil exhibited specific behaviors during the past month (such as "steals," "has tantrums," "uses obscene language or swears"). The other checklist requires the teacher to judge how often (never, sometimes, frequently) each pupil shows certain characteristics (e.g., "follows established classroom rules" or "cooperates with peers in group activities or situations").
3. Pupils whose scores on these checklists exceed established norms are observed in the classroom and on the playground by a school professional other than the classroom teacher (a school psychologist, counselor, or resource teacher). Classroom observations indicate the extent to which the pupil meets academic expectations; playground observations assess the quality and nature of social behavior. These direct observations of behavior, in addition to teachers' ratings, are then used to decide whether the child has problems that warrant classification for special education. Such carefully researched screening systems may lead to improved services for children with emotional or behavioral disorders. Systematic efforts to base identification on teachers' judgments and careful observation should result in services being directed to those students most clearly in need (Walker et al., 1995).

Psychological and Behavioral Characteristics

Describing the characteristics of children and youths with emotional or behavioral disorders is an extraordinary challenge because disorders of emotions and behaviors are extremely varied. We provide a general picture of these children; however, individuals may vary markedly in intelligence, achievement, life circumstances, and emotional and behavioral characteristics.

INTELLIGENCE AND ACHIEVEMENT

The idea that children and youths with emotional or behavioral disorders tend to be particularly bright is a myth. Research clearly shows that the average student with an emotional or behavioral disorder has an IQ in the dull–normal range (around 90) and that relatively few score above the bright–normal range. Compared to the normal distribution of intelligence, more children with emotional or behavioral disorders fall into the ranges of slow learner and mild mental retardation. On the basis of a review of the research on the intelligence of students with emotional or behavioral disorders, Kauffman (2001) hypothesized distributions of intelligence as shown in Figure 7.2.

Of course, we have been referring to children with emotional or behavioral disorders as a group. Some children who have emotional or behavioral disorders are extremely bright and score very high on intelligence tests. We caution, too, that intensive early behavioral intervention may reveal cognitive abilities that have not been apparent. That is, some individuals may have cognitive deficits that early intensive intervention can largely overcome; these individuals may be mistakenly assumed to have permanent cognitive deficits.

There are pitfalls in assessing the intellectual characteristics of a group of children by examining the distribution of their IQs. Intelligence tests are not perfect instruments for measuring what we mean by *intelligence,* and it can be argued that emotional or behavioral difficulties may prevent children from scoring as high as they are capable of scoring. That is, it might be argued that intelligence tests are biased against children with emotional or behavioral disorders and that their true IQs are higher than test scores indicate. Still, the lower-than-normal IQs for these students do indicate lower ability to perform tasks other students perform successfully, and the lower scores are consistent with impairment in other areas of functioning (academic achievement and social skills, for example). IQ is a relatively good predictor of how far a student will progress academically and socially, even in cases of severe disorders.

Most students with emotional or behavioral disorders are also underachievers at school, as measured by standardized tests (Kauffman, 2001). A student with an emotional or behavioral disorder does not usually achieve at the level expected for his or her mental age; seldom are such students academically advanced. In fact, many students with severe disorders lack basic reading and arithmetic skills, and the few who seem to be competent in reading or math are often unable to apply their skills to everyday problems.

SOCIAL AND EMOTIONAL CHARACTERISTICS

Previously, we described two major dimensions of disordered behavior based on analyses of behavior ratings: externalizing and internalizing. The externalizing dimension is

FIGURE 7.2

Hypothetical frequency distribution of IQ for students with emotional or behavioral disorders as compared to a normal frequency distribution.

SOURCE: Reprinted with the permission of Prentice-Hall Publishing Company from *Characteristics of emotional and behavioral disorders of children and youth* (7th ed.) by James M. Kauffman. Copyright ©2001 by Prentice-Hall Publishing Company.

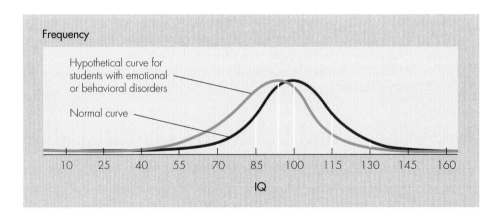

Meeting the Needs of Students with Emotional or Behavioral Disorders

Approaches to Reducing Bullying in Schools

Understanding Bullying

Recent school tragedies directly or indirectly tied to bullying have resulted in increased attention on the part of administrators, teachers, and fellow students to the issue of bullying in schools. One program recommended by researchers addresses bullying through involving key people who can help the aggressor learn more appropriate behaviors and the victim learn options for responding. In addition to bringing all stakeholders together, the program addresses the issue from several vantage points (Garrity et al., 1996, 2000).

A Comprehensive Approach to Reducing Bullying

Garrity and colleagues' program involves the entire school (students, teachers, administrators, staff) as well as students' families. Staff receive training in response procedures and then teachers implement the program within their classes. A summary of this model is presented below.

Who Should Be Involved?

1. Teachers and other staff members. All school personnel need to be informed of standard procedures and be willing to act. Students, both the bully and the victim, must know that teachers will respond.
2. The "caring majority." The caring majority are those students who neither bully nor are bullied. These students know the bullying is occurring but often do not know if or how to respond.
3. The bullies. The bullies need to be addressed in ways that stop their aggression toward other students and direct their need for power into more prosocial directions.
4. The victims. Victims need protection and support, but they also need the social and interpersonal skills critical for seeking outside and internal support.
5. Parents. Parents should be made aware of school policies and procedures. Informed parents will feel more secure about sending their child to school and know the type of response that will occur when their child is either the bully or the victim.

What Is Involved?

1. Staff training. All school personnel are involved in staff training—including bus drivers, after-school workers, media specialists, etc. During staff training, faculty learn about the different manifestations of bullying (e.g., physical aggression, name calling, gossiping, intimidating phone calls, verbal threats, and locking in confined spaces); explore ways to address both the victim and bully; role-play conflict resolution, particularly how to address the bully in a "firm, no-nonsense" approach; generate "antibullying" curriculum, such as selecting literature on bullies and victims or creating skits or artwork with similar themes; and develop a comprehensive school plan for addressing instances of bullying.
2. Classroom intervention. Within the classroom, students are taught rules to eliminate bullying, strategies for reacting to bullying, and steps to follow if they see bullying occurring. The following rules, strategies, and steps are recommended by Garrity et al. (1996, 2000):
   a. Rules for Bully-Proofing Our Classroom
      i. We will not bully other students
      ii. We will help others who are being bullied by speaking out and by getting adult help
      iii. We will use extra effort to include all students in activities at our school
   b. What I Can Do if I Am Being Bullied
      i. HA = Help and Assert
      ii. HA = Humor and Avoid
      iii. SO = Self-Talk and Own It (p. 38)
   c. What I Can Do if I See Someone Being Bullied
      i. Creative Problem Solving
      ii. Adult Help
      iii. Relate and Join
      iv. Empathy

Finally, Garrity and colleagues suggest the following strategies for empowering victims: (1) teach a repertoire of friendship-making skills. (2) develop an understanding that self-esteem affects friendships and how one handles bullying, and (3) teach skills that help victims feel empowered and better able to handle bullies.

—By Kristin Sayeski

characterized by aggressive, acting-out behavior; the internalizing dimension is characterized by anxious, withdrawn behavior. Our discussion here focuses on the aggressive and withdrawn types of behavior typically exhibited by students with emotional or behavioral disorders.

A given student might, at different times, show both aggressive and withdrawn behaviors. Remember that most students with emotional or behavioral disorders have multiple problems (Tankersley & Landrum, 1997; Walker et al., 1995). At the beginning of this chapter, we said that most students with emotional or behavioral disorders are not well liked or identify with deviant peers. Studies of the social status of students in regular elementary and secondary classrooms indicate that those who are identified as having emotional or behavioral disorders may be socially rejected. Early peer rejection as well as aggressive behavior place a child at high risk for later social and emotional problems (Ialongo et al., 1998). Many aggressive students who are not rejected affiliate primarily with others who are aggressive (Farmer, 2000; Farmer et al., 1999, 2001). The relationship between emotional or behavioral disorders and communication disorders is increasingly clear (Rogers-Adkinson & Griffith, 1999). Many children and youths with emotional or behavioral disorders have great difficulty in understanding and using language in social circumstances.

For more information about antisocial children and youth and their management, see www.oslc.org ■

Aggressive, Acting-Out Behavior (Externalizing)　As noted earlier, conduct disorder is the most common problem exhibited by students with emotional or behavioral disorders. Hitting, fighting, teasing, yelling, refusing to comply with requests, crying, destructiveness, vandalism, extortion—these behaviors, if exhibited often, are very likely to earn a child or youth the label "disturbed." Normal children cry, scream, hit, fight, become negative, and do almost everything else children with emotional or behavioral disorders do, only not so impulsively and often. Youngsters of the type we are discussing here drive adults to distraction. These youths are not popular with their peers either, unless they are socialized delinquents who do not offend their delinquent friends. They typically

RESPONSIVE INSTRUCTION

Meeting the Needs of Students with Emotional or Behavioral Disorders

Strategies for Students with Oppositional Defiant Disorder

Understanding ODD

Some children continually act out in specifically defiant ways such as willfully disobeying an adult's request or blaming others for their poor decision making. Often these children are angry and have a difficult time making friends or receiving positive regard from adults. Such behaviors are associated with the psychological category of oppositional defiant disorder (ODD) (American Psychiatric Association, 1994). Obviously, the acting out (externalizing) behaviors associated with ODD place children in a position to have difficulty in school, and many of these children would be considered to have a behavioral disorder.

In order to be diagnosed with ODD, children must exhibit at least four of the following behaviors for at least six months: "often loses temper, often argues with adults, often actively defies or refuses to comply with adults' request or rules, often deliberately annoys people, often blames others for his or her mistakes or misbehavior, is often touchy or easily annoyed by others, is often angry and resentful, and is often spiteful or vindictive" (Knowlton, 1995, p. 6).

It is important for teachers to recognize that all children will go through periods of defiance in the natural course of development. What differentiates children with ODD from their typically developing peers is the persistent nature of the opposition. Many children will "experiment" with being defiant—having a temper tantrum in response to an undesirable situation or choosing not to comply with an adult request. These children eventually abandon the disobedience with more adaptive strategies for getting their needs met (Knowlton, 1995). Children with ODD, on the other hand, continue to use maladaptive responses with adults and their peers even though it leads to alienation and rejection.

Behavior Management and ODD

Ironically, many of the behavior management strategies a teacher would employ with most students do not meet the unique needs of students with ODD. One of the most effective behavior management techniques, positive reinforcement, is one such strategy that can have the opposite effect on students with ODD. The following story illustrates this:

> Billy has always had problems walking down the hall . . . he continually pulls down papers or pictures that other classes have displayed on the walls. Even though he has received several verbal reminders from me and the principal and has as a consequence spent some recess time inside, he continues to exhibit this behavior. On this particular day . . . [w]e walked all the way to the gym without Billy pulling down a single picture . . . I turned to the group and said to Billy that I was very proud of him . . . Billy immediately ran to the closest wall and pulled down several pictures. (Knowlton, 1995, pp. 7–8)

Classroom Suggestions

As you can see from the above example, Billy's desire not to be controlled or to do the opposite of what was expected resulted in positive reinforcement failing. Thus, interventions with students who are oppositional must take into consideration the primary response system for ODD students—public opposition. Knowlton (1995) suggests these "indirect reinforcement" techniques when working with oppositional students:

1. The "walk-by" reinforcement: A brief positive comment or tap as the teacher walks by. This minimizes the need for the student to "publicly" respond and reduces the chance of the student negatively engaging the teacher.
2. Whispering: Providing the student with a private, positive message gives the student the opportunity not to respond.
3. Leaving notes: Similar to the other strategies, leaving a note in the student's desk reduces the likelihood of getting a negative response from the student.
4. Providing rewards: Like all indirect methods, rewards can be delivered but should be done without any amplification or excessive praise. Responses that are delivered in a matter-of-fact manner remove the "emotion" that an oppositional student desires.

Other suggestions include avoiding arguing; reducing perceived teacher control through establishing standardized procedures; offering students choices; anticipating problems; allowing appropriate outlets for anger such as physical, noncompetitive activities; clearly identifying consequences; and providing counseling support from a therapist or trained counselor. The goal of all of these strategies is to retrain the student's negative pattern of interacting, so that someday traditional positive reinforcement is just that—positive.

—By Kristin Sayeski

do not respond quickly and positively to well-meaning adults who care about them and try to be helpful.

Some of these students are considered to have attention deficit hyperactivity disorder (ADHD) or brain injury. Their behavior is not only extremely troublesome but also appears to be resistant to change through typical discipline. Often they are so frequently scolded and disciplined that punishment means little or nothing to them. Because of adult exasperation and their own deviousness, these youths get away with misbehavior a lot of the time. These are children who behave horribly not once in a while, but so often that the people they must live with or be with cannot stand them. Of course, aggressive, acting-out children typically cannot stand the people they have to live and be with either, and often for good reason. Such children are screamed at, criticized, and punished a lot. The problem, then, is not just the individual children's behavior. What must be examined if the child or anyone else is to be helped is the interaction between the child's behavior and the behavior of other people in her or his environment (Walker, Kavanagh et al., 1998).

Meeting the Needs of Students with Emotional or Behavioral Disorders

Strategies for Reducing Cursing

Many students with emotional or behavioral disorders exhibit acting-out behaviors that may include cursing. Student cursing can range from the occasional outburst in reaction to a situation ("D—-, I forgot my homework") to planned insults with a racial or cultural bias. For many teachers, any cursing is undesirable, but assaultive, insulting cursing is simply unacceptable. White and Koorland (1996) recommend twelve strategies for reducing cursing:

1. *Avoid personalizing, accentuating, and usually reinforcing cursing when the misbehavior occurs.* Respond to cursing in a matter-of-fact manner. This reduces the "thrill" associated with offending or shocking a teacher.

2. *Teach students the differences among assaultive cursing, racial insults and slurs, lewd and sexually assaultive insults and slurs, and profanity and epithets.* Explain to students that curses and insults are "verbally assaultive" and can be as harmful as physical assaults. Such verbal assaults should be dealt with more severely than the nonassaultive epithet (Ouch! D—-!) or profanity (S—-!).

3. *Employ developmentally and culturally appropriate verbal or nonverbal reprimands for cursing, to undermine shock value.* Respond to students in an age-appropriate manner that does not invite comment or reaction from peers.

4. *When teaching students about cursing and cursing control, use verbal or written approximations.* Never use the actual curse.

5. *Differentially reinforce less offensive profanity.* Response positively to students when they "depersonalize" their cursing.

6. *Differentially reinforce cursing by setting or place.* Teach students that time and place do matter when cursing, and reinforce them when they choose not to curse in the classroom. This can be "taught" by telling students to go outside the building if they feel the need to curse.

7. *Differentially reinforce lower rates of cursing.* Making students aware of their rate of cursing, charting the cursing occurrences, and reinforcing them when the occurrences are reduced can lead to a reduction or elimination of cursing.

8. *Use response cost to decelerate cursing and token economies to reinforce appropriate verbalizations.* Use a point or token system to provide rewards (earning points for not cursing) and punishments (loss of points for cursing).

9. *Use more intensive aversives only if necessary and always in conjunction with a reinforcement program.* If a student persists in cursing, an aversive such as time-out may be necessary.

10. *Try self-mediated interventions.* Students can self-record their occurrences of cursing and be rewarded for accurately monitoring and reducing or eliminating their cursing.

11. *Implement group-contingent interventions.* Students who are motivated by peer support would benefit from class rewards tied to individual or group reduction in cursing.

12. *use audiovisual recordings for reinforcement and reduction.* Student cursing may decrease when a video camera or audiotape is recording the class session.

—By Kristin Sayeski

Aggression.
Behavior that intentionally causes others harm or that elicits escape or avoidance responses from others.

Aggression has been analyzed from many viewpoints. The analyses that have the strongest support in empirical research are those of social learning theorists, such as Bandura (1973, 1986), and behavioral psychologists, such as Patterson (Patterson et al., 1992; Walker et al., 1995). Their studies take into account the child's experience and his or her motivation, based on the anticipated consequences of aggression. In brief, they view aggression as *learned* behavior, and assume that it is possible to identify the conditions under which it will be learned.

Children who act out aggressively or impulsively with frequent negative confrontations often are not well liked by their peers. ∎

Children learn many aggressive behaviors by observing parents, siblings, playmates, and people portrayed on television and in movies. Individuals who model aggression are more likely to be imitated if they are high in social status and are observed to receive rewards and escape punishment for their aggression, especially if they experience no unpleasant consequences or obtain rewards by overcoming their victims. If children are placed in unpleasant situations and they cannot escape from the unpleasantness or obtain rewards except by aggression, they are more likely to be aggressive, especially if this behavior is tolerated or encouraged by others.

Aggression is encouraged by external rewards (social status, power, suffering of the victim, obtaining desired items), vicarious rewards (seeing others obtain desirable consequences for their aggression), and self-reinforcement (self-congratulation or enhancement of self-image). If children can justify aggression in their own minds (by comparison to the behaviors of others or by dehumanizing their victims), they are more likely to be aggressive. Punishment may actually increase aggression under some circumstances: when it is inconsistent or delayed, when there is no positive alternative to the punished behavior, when it provides an example of aggression, or when counterattack against the punisher seems likely to be successful.

Teaching aggressive children to be less so is no simple matter, but social learning theory and behavioral research do provide some general guidelines. In general, research does not support the notion that it is wise to let children act out their aggression freely. The most helpful techniques include providing examples (models) of nonaggressive responses to aggression-provoking circumstances, helping the child rehearse or role-play nonaggressive behavior, providing reinforcement for nonaggressive behavior, preventing the child from obtaining positive consequences for aggression, and punishing aggression in ways that involve as little counteraggression as possible (e.g., using "time-out" or brief social isolation rather than spanking or yelling) (Walker et al., 1995).

The seriousness of children's aggressive, acting-out behavior should not be underestimated. It was believed for decades that although these children cause a lot of trouble, they are not as seriously disabled as children who are shy and anxious. Research has exploded this myth. When combined with school failure, aggressive, antisocial behavior in childhood generally means a gloomy future in terms of social adjustment and mental health, especially for boys (Ialongo et al., 1998). Shy, anxious children are much more likely to be able to get and hold jobs, overcome their emotional problems, and stay out of jails and mental hospitals than are adults who had conduct problems and were delinquent as children (see Kazdin, 1995).

Of course, there are exceptions to the rule. Nonetheless, there is a high probability that the aggressive child who is a failure in school will become more of a social misfit as an adult than will the withdrawn child. When we consider that conduct disorders and delinquency are highly correlated with school failure, the importance of meeting the needs of acting-out and underachieving children is obvious (Kauffman, 2001; Sprague & Walker, 2000; Walker et al., 1995).

Immature, Withdrawn Behavior (Internalizing)   In noting the seriousness of aggressive, acting-out behavior, we do not intend to downplay the disabling nature of immaturity and withdrawal. In their extreme forms, withdrawal and immaturity may be characteristics of schizophrenia or other severe disorders. Such disorders not only have serious consequences for individuals in their childhood years but also carry a very poor prognosis for adult mental health. The child whose behavior fits a pattern of extreme immaturity and withdrawal cannot develop the close and satisfying human relationships that characterize normal development. Such a child will find it difficult to meet the pressures and demands of everyday life. The school environment is the one in which anxious and withdrawn adolescents in particular experience the most distress (Masia, Klein, Storch, & Corda, 2001).

All children exhibit immature behavior and act withdrawn once in a while. Children who fit the withdrawn, immature description, however, are typically infantile in their ways or reluctant to interact with other people. They are social isolates who have few friends, seldom play with children their own age, and lack the social skills necessary to have fun. Some retreat into fantasy or daydreaming; some develop fears that are completely out of proportion to the circumstances; some complain constantly of little aches and pains and let their supposed illnesses keep them from participating in normal activities; some regress to earlier stages of development and demand constant help and attention; and some become depressed for no apparent reason (see Rabian & Silverman, 1995; Stark, Ostrander, Kurowski, Swearer, & Bowen, 1995).

As in the case of aggressive, acting-out behavior, withdrawal and immaturity may be interpreted in many different ways. Proponents of the psychoanalytic approach are likely to see internal conflicts and unconscious motivations as the underlying causes. Behavioral psychologists tend to interpret such problems in terms of failures in social learning; this view is supported by more empirical research data than other views (Kauffman, 2001). A social learning analysis attributes withdrawal and immaturity to an inadequate environment. Causal factors may include overrestrictive parental discipline, punishment for appropriate social responses, reward for isolated behavior, lack of opportunity to learn and practice social skills, and models (examples) of inappropriate behavior. Immature or withdrawn children can be taught the skills they lack by arranging opportunities for them to learn and practice appropriate responses, showing models engaging in appropriate behavior, and providing rewards for improved behavior.

A particularly important aspect of immature, withdrawn behavior is depression. Only recently have mental health workers and special educators begun to realize that depression is a widespread and serious problem among children and adolescents (Kaslow, Morris, & Rehm, 1997; Sheras, 2001). Today, the consensus of psychologists is that the nature of depression in children and youths is quite similar in many respects to that of depression in adults. The indications of depression include disturbances of mood or feelings, inability to think or concentrate, lack of motivation, and decreased physical well-being. A depressed child or youth may act sad, lonely, and apathetic; exhibit low self-esteem, excessive guilt, and pervasive pessimism; avoid tasks and social experiences; and/or have physical complaints or problems in sleeping, eating, or eliminating. Sometimes depression is accompanied by such problems as bed-wetting (nocturnal **enuresis**), fecal soiling

Enuresis.
Urinary incontinence; wetting oneself.

(**encopresis**), extreme fear of or refusal to go to school, failure in school, or talk of suicide or suicide attempts. Depression also frequently occurs in combination with conduct disorder (Kazdin, 1997; McCracken, Cantwell, & Hanna, 1993).

Suicide increased dramatically during the 1970s and 1980s among young people between the ages of fifteen and twenty-four and is now among the leading causes of death in this age group (Sheras, 2001). Depression, especially when severe and accompanied by a sense of hopelessness, is linked to suicide and suicide attempts. Therefore, it is important for all those who work with young people to be able to recognize the signs. Substance abuse is also a major problem among children and teenagers and may be related to depression.

Depression sometimes has a biological cause, and antidepressant medications have at times been successful in helping depressed children and youths overcome their problems (Pomeroy & Gadow, 1997; Sweeney, Forness, Kavale, & Levitt, 1997). In many cases, however, no biological cause can be found. Depression can also be caused by environmental or psychological factors, such as the death of a loved one, separation of one's parents, school failure, rejection by one's peers, or a chaotic and punitive home environment. Interventions based on social learning theory—instructing children and youths in social interaction skills and self-control techniques and teaching them to view themselves more positively, for example—have often been successful in such cases (Kaslow et al., 1997).

Encopresis.
Bowel incontinence; soiling oneself.

Educational Considerations

Students with emotional or behavioral disorders typically have low grades and other unsatisfactory academic outcomes, have higher dropout and lower graduation rates than other student groups, and are often placed in highly restrictive settings. Moreover, these students are disproportionately from poor and ethnic-minority families and frequently encounter the juvenile justice system (Coutinho, Oswald, Best, & Forness, 2002; Oswald, Coutinho, Best, & Singh, 1999). Consequently, their successful education is among the most important and challenging tasks facing special education today. Finding a remedy for the disproportionate representation of ethnic minorities in programs for students with emotional or behavioral disorders is a critical issue. However, finding effective intervention strategies for diverse students is equally important (Ishii-Jordan, 2000; Landrum & Kauffman, 2003).

Unfortunately, there is not a consensus among special educators about how to meet the challenge of educating students with emotional or behavioral disorders. Although a national agenda has been written for improving services to students with emotional or behavioral disorders, it is so vaguely worded that it is of little value in guiding the design of interventions (Kauffman, 1997).

CONTRASTING CONCEPTUAL MODELS

Several different conceptual models may guide the work of educators. As Kauffman (2001) points out, few practitioners are guided strictly and exclusively by a single model. Nevertheless, a teacher must have a solid grounding in one conceptual orientation to guide competent practice. One of two conceptual models, or a combination of the two, guide most educational programs today: the **psychoeducational** and **behavioral** models. We illustrate these models in action with actual case descriptions. (See Kauffman, 2001, for description and case illustrations of other models.)

Psychoeducational.
Blending psychodynamic (unconscious motivations) and behavioral theories in approaching education and management.

Behavioral.
Focus on behavior itself and the observable conditions and events causing it, rather than unconscious motivations.

Psychoeducational Model   The psychoeducational model acknowledges the existence of unconscious motivations and underlying conflicts, yet also stresses the realistic demands of everyday functioning in school, home, and community. One basic assumption

SUCCESS STORIES
Special Educators at Work

Herndon, VA: Fourteen-year-old **Christina Isaacs** attends a special program for students with emotional and behavioral disorders that is attached to a large, public middle school. Special educator **Teresa Zutter,** principal of this co-facility for seventh- and eighth-graders, knows her sixty students and their families well. She and Christina's mother, Brenda Isaacs, agree that this close community provides Chrissy with the individual support she needs to merge slowly into the mainstream.

Eighth-grader Chrissy Isaacs stood wide-eyed at the principal's door. "I've called you to my office, Chrissy, because you are a star!" said Teresa Zutter. "In the past year, you have made real progress toward your goals."

At Teresa's invitation, a relieved Chrissy sat down at a dark wooden table and talked about all she had accomplished. "I worked hard last year, and by January, my teachers thought I could join a mainstream drama class. I loved it!" "And she was good!" added Zutter.

Chrissy's goals included increasing academic achievement, reducing reliance on adults, and developing friendships as well as confidence in her abilities and performance. This year, Chrissy was included daily in general classes for PE and teen life and sang with the middle school chorus five days a week. She says with pride, her eyes glancing down at her reflection in the glass-topped table, "I want to do well in the mainstream because I want to be a cheerleader and get a regular high school diploma."

According to Teresa Zutter, Chrissy started seventh grade as a girl in distress, but she took advantage of all the resources available to her. Remembers Zutter, "When I first met Chrissy, she gave the impression of being physically frail and frightened. As we walked around her new school, she grabbed my arm and asked, 'Will I like it here?'" Chrissy admits, "I was nervous last year. The school was so big and beautiful!"

The Herndon Center, a co-facility with Herndon Middle School, is two years old and serves sixty students in grades 7 and 8 who have emotional or behavioral disorders and need individual support to prepare for experiences in the mainstream. Each classroom is equipped with a "hot-line" telephone connected to the main office and a carpeted quiet room that serves as a "time-out" area for angry students. There is also frequent communication between Teresa Zutter and parents, who are alerted to misbehaviors, and, in some instances, called to take their sons or daughters home.

of the psychoeducational model is that teachers must understand unconscious motivations if they are to deal most effectively with students' academic failures and misbehaviors. To do so, teachers are not expected to focus on resolving unconscious conflicts, as psychotherapists might. Rather, teachers must focus on how to help students acquire self-control through reflection and planning. Intervention may include therapeutic discussions or *life space interviews (LSIs),* which are designed to help the youth:

1. Understand that what he or she is doing is a problem
2. Recognize his or her motivations
3. Observe the consequences of his or her actions
4. Plan alternative ways of responding to similar circumstances in the future

The emphasis is on the youngster gaining insight that will result in behavioral change, not on changing behavior directly (see Wood, 1990; Wood & Long, 1991). The following case of Andy, drawn from James and Long (1992), illustrates the psychoeducational model in action:

Rules and policies are clear for students, teachers, and families. "There is an absolute need for structure and for individualization to get the trust factor going," says Teresa. "We have so many people here to help and to talk to students, no one has to hit to communicate."

The thrust of the program is to offer a low student–teacher ratio to students who need close attention. In addition to Principal Zutter, there are thirteen teachers and a support staff that includes a psychologist, social worker, guidance counselor, health awareness monitor, and conflict resolution teacher. Weekly clinical staff meetings address the needs of individual students and provide a regular forum for educators and support staff to address problems. As described by Teresa, "This is such a spirited staff. We laugh a lot and take care of each other."

The center assumes a treatment model based on the belief that students thrive on positive reinforcement. Nonphysical punishment is employed briefly and only to the degree necessary, while instruction is geared toward remediation and cultivation of coping mechanisms. "Girls and boys who are stressed can be made to feel better," maintains Teresa. "They [do not just have emotional or behavioral disorders] for a while but have entrenched behaviors; it's a life struggle. They won't be okay without interventions and without being taught how to cope with stress."

Most of the students at the Herndon Center are male, a fact Chrissy Isaacs was quick to note. "I'm at that age where I like boys," she says. When she started grade 7, Chrissy had little sense of her own reality; she often gazed at her reflection and slipped into the protection of fantasy. She was also limited in her awareness of social interactions and needed to learn how to respond to various situations. Lost in her own thoughts, she would have tantrums or provoke other students, not understanding the impact these behaviors had on her relationships. She was also becoming oppositional.

Academically, Chrissy was below grade level in most areas. Although she could easily decode words, she had problems comprehending what she read and organizing her thoughts.

With frequent reassurance and a great deal of help to stay on task, Chrissy made gains and was performing at grade level in all classes by the end of seventh grade. Speech therapy helped her vocabulary development, particularly in using words with multiple meanings, as used in jokes and riddles. Academic supports included receiving extra adult attention, additional time to complete classwork and tests, shortened assignments, and peer/work helpers and having directions stated several times. Although she daydreamed frequently, Chrissy demonstrated two real strengths: a willingness to work hard and an ability to focus when provided with support. She is now described as a conscientious student who worries about the quality of her work.

As long as she is confronted gently and not embarrassed in front of other students, Chrissy is responsive to correction. She takes great pride in her appearance and talents and is still attracted to anything that captures her image. Socially, she tries to be everybody's friend, but peers are still leery of her erratic behavior, which quickly turns antagonistic. "Chrissy tends to be overly sensitive to what others are saying, whether it relates to her or not," says her mother, Brenda Isaacs. And when she is angry, Chrissy resorts to profanity, inappropriate comments, and even physical threats. This year, to her credit, she has managed to develop some stable friendships with a few girls, which she cherishes.

"With all this support, I see my daughter proud and happy and becoming more mature," says Brenda Isaacs. Teresa Zutter agrees: "Chrissy will always have some difficulties, but with help she can be eased from her world of fantasy. Hopefully, she'll value herself and stay in reality."

—By Jean Crockett

Andy

Andy, 14, was referred for special education due to his oppositional and sometimes verbally threatening behavior. In addition to disobeying adults in other ways, he frequently left the classroom without permission and roamed the hallways. He appeared to enjoy confronting his teachers and taunting his peers, especially a deaf peer, Drew, who also had few social skills.

One morning, Drew came to school very agitated, which required that the teacher spend most of her time before lunch calming him down. At lunch, Andy persistently aggravated Drew. When the teacher told Andy to stop and go back to his desk, Andy began yelling that Drew had called him a "fag" and that he (Drew) was the one who should return to his desk. The teacher repeated her instruction. Andy then shoved a desk across the room and left the classroom without permission. In the hall, Andy began pacing and disturbing other students. So the teacher and another staff member then escorted Andy to a quiet room, where he went without resistance. In the quiet room, the teacher used LSI techniques to help Andy think through the reasons for his behavior and how he might behave in more adaptive ways.

Through skillful interviewing about the incident with Drew, the teacher was able to help Andy see that he was jealous and resentful of the time she spent with Drew. Andy lived with his mother and an older sister. His sister had multiple disabilities, was very low functioning, and demanded a lot of his mother's attention. His father had left home when Andy was eight, and his mother was not in good health. This meant that Andy had to take on some adult responsibilities at an early age.

The goals of the teacher's LSI about this particular incident were to get Andy to understand that she cared about him and wanted to prevent him from disrupting the group. Most importantly, she wanted Andy to understand that there were similarities in his situation at home and at school that gave rise to similar feelings and behavior.

Andy's teacher used what James and Long (1992) call a "red flag interview," a discussion that addresses the transfer of problems from home to school. A red flag interview follows a predictable sequence in which a student like Andy is helped to understand that:

1. He experiences a stressful situation at home (e.g., a beating, overstimulation, etc.)
2. His experience triggers intense feelings of anger, helplessness, and the like
3. These feelings are not expressed to the abusive person at home because he is fearful of retaliation
4. He contains his feelings until he gets on the bus, enters school, or responds to a demand
5. He acts out his feelings in an environment that is safer and directs his behavior toward someone else

The LSI may be based on the psychoanalytic notion of defense mechanisms—tactics that people use to avoid dealing with issues, events, or people that may be unpleasant or hurtful. Nonetheless, the LSI also must end with a return to the reality of the situation. In Andy's case, this meant his return to the class and anticipation of future problems. His teacher ended the LSI as follows:

Interviewer: What do you think Drew might do when we walk into the room?
Andy: He will probably point at me and laugh.
Interviewer: That might happen. How can you deal with that?

Educators agree on the importance of collaboration and discussion between the school, community, and family members. ∎

Andy: I can ignore him.

Interviewer: That will not be easy for you. It will take a lot of emotional strength to control your urge to tease him back. And if you do that and Drew teases you, who is going to get into trouble?

Andy: Drew.

Interviewer: That's right. You are now beginning to think more clearly about your actions. Also, I will set up a behavior contract for you. If you are able to ignore Drew's teasing, you will earn positive one-on-one time with me.

Andy: Agreed. (James & Long, 1992, p. 37)

Behavioral Model   Two major assumptions underlie the behavioral model: (1) The essence of the problem is the behavior itself, and (2) behavior is a function of environmental events. Maladaptive behavior is viewed as inappropriate learned responses to particular demands or circumstances. Therefore, intervention should consist of rearranging antecedent events and consequences to teach more adaptive behavior.

Actually, the behavioral model is a natural science approach to behavior, emphasizing precise definition, reliable measurement, careful control of the variables thought to maintain or change behavior, and establishment of replicable cause–effect relationships. Interventions consist of choosing target responses, measuring their current levels, analyzing probable controlling environmental events, and changing antecedent or consequent events until reliable changes are produced in the target behaviors (see Kauffman et al., 2002; Kerr & Nelson, 1998; Walker, 1995; Walker et al., 1995). The following case of Sven, based on a study by Dunlap et al. (1994), illustrates how a behavioral model might guide teaching:

Sven

Sven—an 11-year-old attending a special self-contained class for students with emotional or behavioral disorders—showed inadequate attention to tasks, inappropriate and aggressive talk, and physically aggressive behavior. An observer recorded Sven's behavior during brief (15 second) intervals for 15–30 minutes of his English lesson each day. These observations showed that Sven was engaged in academic tasks less than 60 percent of the time on average and that his behavior was disruptive about 40 percent of the time.

The professionals working with Sven assumed that students who exhibit maladaptive behaviors do so for a variety of reasons, including not only the consequences the behaviors bring but the settings in which they occur and the demands for performance—the antecedents. In this case, the antecedents related to Sven's maladaptive behavior were changed. The antecedents of his off-task, disruptive behavior—what he was assigned to do, especially if it was an assignment he did not like—seemed to be at least as much a problem as the consequences of his behavior. Therefore, the primary strategy used to modify Sven's behavior was to give him his choice of six to eight task options in his English class. The task options were constructed as variations on the work he normally would do, any one of which was acceptable and would lead to the same instructional objective. Under these conditions, Sven engaged in academic tasks about 95 percent of the time, and his disruptive behavior dropped to an average of less than 10 percent.

Clearly, giving Sven assignments about which he had choices—all of them acceptable variations—improved his attention to his tasks and markedly decreased his disruptive behavior. Use of behavioral methods such as rewarding consequences for appropriate behavior and academic performance are critically important. In addition, teachers may also use knowledge of behavior principles to alter the conditions of instruction in ways that defuse task resistance and encourage task attention.

BALANCING BEHAVIORAL CONTROL WITH ACADEMIC AND SOCIAL LEARNING

Some writers have observed that the quality of educational programs for students with emotional or behavioral disorders is often dismal, regardless of the conceptual model underlying practice. The focus is often on rigid external control of students' behavior, and academic instruction and social learning are often secondary or almost entirely neglected (Knitzer, Steinberg, & Fleisch, 1990). Often, teachers do not have knowledge and skills about academic interventions in basic skills such as reading (Coleman & Vaughn, 2000). Although the quality of instruction is undoubtedly low in too many programs, examples can be found of effective academic and social instruction for students at all levels (Peacock Hill Working Group, 1991; Walker, Forness et al., 1998).

Behavioral control strategies are an essential part of educational programs for students with externalizing problems. Without effective means of controlling disruptive behavior, it's extremely unlikely that academic and social learning will occur. Excellent academic instruction will certainly reduce many behavior problems as well as teach important academic skills (Falk & Wehby, 2001; Kauffman et al., 2002; Stein & Davis, 2000; Sutherland & Wehby, 2001). Nevertheless, even the best instructional programs will not eliminate the disruptive behaviors of all students. Teachers of students with emotional or behavioral disorders must have effective control strategies, preferably those involving students as much as possible in self-control. In addition, teachers must offer effective instruction in academic and social skills that will allow their students to live, learn, and work with others (Farmer et al., 2001; Walker et al., 1995). Teachers must also allow stu-

MAKING IT WORK

Collaboration and Co-Teaching for Students with Emotional/Behavioral Disorders

"I don't want him in my classroom if he can't follow the rules!"

Statewide standards to improve educational outcomes and policies of "zero tolerance" to increase the safety of public schools have placed increased pressure on all teachers. These two issues, combined with the fact that many general educators do not receive training in more than routine classroom management, often make a teacher hesitant to collaborate with special educators to include students with emotional/behavioral disorders, even though many students creating discipline problems are not identified as having a disability. The increase in disciplinary concerns in schools is actually a great reason for general educators to collaborate with teachers skilled in assessing and managing behavior.

What Does It Mean to Be a Teacher of Students with Emotional/Behavioral Disorders?

The expertise of a teacher of students with emotional/behavioral disorders includes understanding, assessing, and managing behavior to promote learning across the content areas. Specifically, the Council for Exceptional Children (2001) has identified the following as those skills necessary for beginning teachers of students with emotional/behavioral disorders:

1. Know of prevention and intervention strategies for individuals at risk of emotional/behavioral disorders.
2. Use a variety of nonaversive techniques to control targeted behavior and maintain attention of individuals with emotional/behavioral disorders.
3. Establish a consistent classroom routine and use skills in problem solving and conflict resolution.
4. Plan and implement individualized reinforcement systems and environmental modifications at levels equal to the intensity of the behavior.
5. Integrate academic instruction, affective education, and behavior management for individuals and groups.

dents to make all the choices they can—*manageable* choices that are appropriate for the individual student (Jolivette, Stichter, & McCormick, 2002; Kauffman et al., 2002).

IMPORTANCE OF INTEGRATED SERVICES

Children and youths with emotional or behavioral disorders tend to have multiple and complex needs. For most, life is coming apart in more ways than one. In addition to their problems in school, they typically have family problems and a variety of difficulties in the community (e.g., engaging in illegal activities, an absence of desirable relationships with peers and adults, substance abuse, difficulty finding and maintaining employment). Thus, children or youths with emotional or behavioral disorders may need, in addition to special education, a variety of family-oriented services, psychotherapy or counseling, community supervision, training related to employment, and so on. No single service agency can meet the needs of most of these children and youths, but it is clear that school plays an important role (Farmer & Farmer, 1999). Integrating these needed services into a more coordinated and effective effort is now seen as essential (Edgar & Siegel, 1995; Stein & Davis, 2000; Zanglis, Furlong, & Casas, 2000).

STRATEGIES THAT WORK

Regardless of the conceptual model that guides education, we can point to several effective strategies. Most are incorporated in the behavioral model, but other models may include them as well. Successful strategies at all levels, from early intervention through

6. Assess appropriate and problematic social behaviors of individuals.

Successful Strategies for Co-Teaching

Recent research has validated the use of positive behavioral supports (PBS) for students with chronically challenging behaviors. Lewis (2000) identifies six steps in developing PBS plans for individual students in any classroom. These steps provide a unique opportunity for collaboration among general and special education faculty. Special and general educators can work together on each step to lighten the workload, provide different perspectives, and improve consistency. The first step is to define the behavior operationally. Each teacher can provide feedback to the other to pinpoint exactly what the student is doing in the classroom, not just stating "he's disruptive." Step two includes conducting a functional behavioral assessment (FBA). FBAs are time consuming and include observing, analyzing, and hypothesizing about the behavior. Two (or more) teachers working together can observe the student at different times and in different situations, using both formalized and informal observation systems, without losing time with the rest of the class. They can also analyze data together to move to step three: developing a hypothesis about why the student engages in the behav-

ior. Step four is targeting a replacement behavior—what do the teachers want the student to do instead of the unwanted behavior? Teachers who know the student well then work together to identify this behavior, task analyze it, and describe what skills the student has and does not have in order to set up a teaching scheme for this new behavior (step five). Next, the teachers work together to teach the student the new behavior, reinforce it in the classroom, and verify that it is achieving the goals for both student and teachers. Finally, the last step is to modify the environment enough so that the previous inappropriate behavior does not result in the same outcome. This can be the most difficult part and require the greatest amount of teamwork. The student will probably still try the old behavior. Teachers will hope to not see it again and get discouraged if they do. It is at this point that teachers working together will need to support one another and to enlist other collaborators, such as administrators, parents, and other teachers, to keep the plan going.

More information about positive behavioral supports is available at Office of Special Education Programs' Technical Assistance Center on Positive Behavioral Interventions and Supports at www.pbis.org.

—By Margaret P. Weiss

transition, balance concern for academic and social skills and provide integrated services. These strategies include the following elements (Peacock Hill Working Group, 1991; see also Walker, Forness et al., 1998):

- *Systematic, data-based interventions*—interventions that are applied systematically and consistently and that are based on reliable research data, not unsubstantiated theory
- *Continuous assessment and monitoring of progress*—direct, daily assessment of performance, with planning based on this monitoring
- *Provision for practice of new skills*—skills are not taught in isolation but are applied directly in everyday situations through modeling, rehearsal, and guided practice
- *Treatment matched to the problem*—interventions that are designed to meet the needs of individual students and their particular life circumstances, not general "formulas" that ignore the nature, complexity, and severity of the problem
- *Multicomponent treatment*—as many different interventions as are necessary to meet the multiple needs of students (e.g., social skills training, academic remediation, medication, counseling or psychotherapy, family treatment or parent training)
- *Programming for transfer and maintenance*—interventions designed to promote transfer of learning to new situations, recognizing that "quick fixes" nearly always fail to produce generalized change
- *Commitment to sustained intervention*—interventions designed with the realization that many emotional or behavioral disorders are developmental disabilities and will not be eliminated entirely or cured.

SERVICE DELIVERY MODELS

Only a relatively small percentage of children and youths with emotional or behavioral disorders are officially identified and receive any special education or mental health services. Consequently, those individuals who do receive special education tend to have very serious problems, although most (along with those who have mild mental retardation or learning disabilities) have typically been assumed to have only mild disabilities. That is, the problems of the typical student with an emotional or behavioral disorder who is identified for special education may be more serious than many people have assumed. *Severe* does not apply only to the disorders of autism and schizophrenia; a child can have a severe conduct disorder, for example, and its disabling effects can be extremely serious and persistent (Farmer et al., 2001; Kauffman, 2001; Kazdin, 1997; Patterson et al., 1992).

Compared to students with most other disabilities, a higher percentage of students with emotional or behavioral disorders are educated outside regular classrooms and schools, probably in part because students with these disorders tend to have more serious problems before they are identified. Emotional or behavioral disorders include many different types of behavioral and emotional problems, which makes it hard to make generalizations about how programs are administered.

Even so, the trend in programs for students with emotional or behavioral disorders is toward integration into regular schools and classrooms. Even when students are placed in separate schools and classes, educators hope for reintegration into the mainstream. Integration of these students is typically difficult and requires intensive work on a case-by-case basis (Fuchs, Fuchs, Fernstrom, & Hohn, 1991; Kauffman, Lloyd, Baker, & Riedel, 1995; Walker & Bullis, 1991). Furthermore, some have made the case that students with emotional and behavioral disorders who are at high risk for continued problems need the structure and support of a special class—that being in a separate class *can* be better than being included in a regular classroom (Farmer et al., 2001; Kauffman, Bantz, & McCullough, 2002).

Placement decisions for students with emotional or behavioral disorders are particularly problematic (Kauffman, Lloyd, Hallahan, & Astuto, 1995). Educators who serve stu-

Including students with emotional and behavioral disorders in general education classrooms may sometimes be problematic since social interactions are a primary area of concern. ■

dents with the most severe emotional or behavioral disorders provide ample justification for specialized environments for these children and youths. That is, it is impossible to replicate in the context of a regular classroom in a neighborhood school the intensive, individualized, highly structured environments with very high adult–student ratios offered in special classes and facilities (see Brigham & Kauffman, 1998; Farmer et al., 2001; Kauffman, Bantz, & McCullough, 2002; Kauffman & Hallenbeck, 1996).

Hence it is extremely important that the full continuum of placement options be maintained for students with emotional or behavioral disorders and that placement decisions be made on an individual basis, after an appropriate program of education and related services has been designed. Students must not be placed outside regular classrooms and schools unless their needs require it. The IDEA mandate of placement in the least restrictive environment (LRE) applies to students with behavioral disorders as well as those in all other categories. In other words, they are to be taught in regular schools and classes and with their nondisabled peers to the extent that doing so is consistent with their appropriate education. However, students' needs for appropriate education and safety take priority over placement in a less restrictive environment (Bateman & Chard, 1995; Crockett & Kauffman, 1999).

INSTRUCTIONAL CONSIDERATIONS

Prior to being identified for special education, many students with emotional or behavioral disorders have been in regular classrooms where they could observe and learn from appropriate peer models. In reality, though, these students usually fail to imitate these models. They are unlikely to benefit merely from being with other students who have not been identified as disabled, as incidental social learning is insufficient to address their difficulties (Hallenbeck & Kauffman, 1995; Kauffman & Pullen, 1996; Rhode, Jensen, & Reavis, 1992). In order for students with emotional or behavioral disorders to learn from peer models of appropriate behavior, most will require explicit, focused instruction about whom and what to imitate. In addition, they may need explicit and intensive instruction in social skills, including when, where, and how to exhibit specific types of behavior (Walker et al., 1995).

The academic curriculum for most students with emotional or behavioral disorders parallels that for most students. The basic academic skills have a great deal of survival value for any individual in society who is capable of learning them; failure to teach a student to read, write, and perform basic arithmetic deprives him or her of any reasonable chance for successful adjustment to the everyday demands of life. Students who do not acquire academic skills that allow them to compete with their peers are likely to be socially rejected (Kauffman, 2001; Walker, 1995).

Students with emotional or behavioral disorders may need specific instruction in social skills as well. We emphasize two points: (1) effective methods are needed to teach basic academic skills, and (2) social skills and affective experiences are as crucial as academic skills. How to manage one's feelings and behavior and how to get along with other people are essential features of the curriculum for many students with emotional or behavioral disorders. These children cannot be expected to learn such skills without instruction, for the ordinary processes of socialization obviously have failed (Walker et al., 1995). Enlisting the help of peers—including peers with emotional or behavioral disorders who have learned important social skills themselves—may be an effective strategy in some cases (Blake, Wang, Cartledge, & Gardner, 2000; Farmer et al., 2001; Presley & Hughes, 2000).

Students with schizophrenia and other major psychiatric disorders vary widely in the behaviors they exhibit and the learning problems they have. Some may need hospitalization and intensive treatment; others may remain at home and attend regular public schools. Again, the trend today is away from placement in institutions or special schools and toward inclusion in regular public schools. In some cases, students with major psychiatric disorders who attend regular schools are enrolled in special classes.

Educational arrangements for juvenile delinquents are hard to describe in general terms because *delinquency* is a legal term, not an educational distinction, and because programs for extremely troubled youths vary so much among states and localities. Special classes or schools are sometimes provided for youths who have histories of threatening, violent, or disruptive behavior. Some of these classes and schools are administered under special education law, but others are not because the pupils assigned to them are not considered emotionally disturbed. In jails, reform schools, and other detention facilities housing children and adolescents, wide variation is found in educational practices. Education of incarcerated children and youths with learning disabilities is governed by the same laws that apply to those who are not incarcerated, but the laws are not always carefully implemented. Many incarcerated children do not receive assessment and education appropriate for their needs because of lack of resources, poor cooperation among agencies, and the attitude that delinquents and criminals are not entitled to the same educational opportunities as law-abiding citizens (Katsiyannis & Archwamety, 1999; Kauffman, 2001; Leone, Rutherford & Nelson, 1991).

Given all this, it is clear that teachers of students with emotional or behavioral disorders must be able to tolerate a great deal of unpleasantness and rejection without becoming counteraggressive or withdrawn. Most of the students they teach are rejected by others. If kindness and concern were the only things required to help these students, they probably would not be considered to have disabilities. Teachers cannot expect caring and decency always to be returned. They must be sure of their own values and confident of their teaching and living skills. They must be able and willing to make wise choices for students who choose to behave unwisely (Kauffman, 2001; Kauffman et al., 2002).

SPECIAL DISCIPLINARY CONSIDERATIONS

Disciplining is a controversial topic, especially for students with disabilities, as we discussed in Chapter 2. Many teachers and school administrators are confused about what is legal. Special rules do apply in some cases to students who are identified as having disabilities. In some instances the typical school rules apply, but in others they do not (see Yell, 1998; Yell, Bradley, Katsiyannis, & Rozaliski, 2000; Yell, Rozalski, & Drasgow, 2001). The issues are particularly controversial for students with emotional or behavioral disorders because, although their behavior may be severely problematic, the causes of their misbehavior are often difficult to determine.

Uncertainty or controversy usually involves a change in the student's placement or suspension or expulsion due to very serious misbehavior such as bringing a weapon or illegal drugs to school. The IDEA discipline provisions for students with disabilities are intended to maintain a safe school environment without violating the rights of students with disabilities to fair discipline, taking the effects of their disability into consideration.

However, in 2001 the reauthorization of the Elementary and Secondary Education Act (ESEA) allowed local school officials to discipline a student with disabilities in the same manner as they discipline students without disabilities when it comes to suspension and expulsion. ESEA does not require that schools suspend or expel children with disabilities as they would those without disabilities, but it does allow it. States and localities have the option of following the IDEA rules, which have as a basic purpose continuing the education of a student whose placement is changed to an alternative setting.

FUNCTIONAL BEHAVIORAL ASSESSMENT AND POSITIVE BEHAVIORAL SUPPORTS

The 1997 amendments to IDEA have raised controversial issues regarding the assessment of behavior. The law calls for functional analysis or functional assessment of behavior, but the meaning of these terms is not clear in the context of the law. Precisely what the law now requires of special educators and other school personnel is uncertain (see Gable, 1999; Howell & Nelson, 1999; Nelson, Roberts, Mather, & Rutherford, 1999; Scott & Nelson, 1999; Sugai & Horner, 1999–2000).

One view is that the law simply requires assessment that is meaningful—that helps educators develop effective interventions. Under this assumption, assessment procedures would not need to be changed dramatically in many cases. Educators would need merely to make sure that assessment is meaningfully related to teaching and management. An alternative view is that functional behavioral assessment refers to a specific set of procedures designed to pinpoint the function of the student's behavior—what the student is communicating through her or his behavior, or what the student is trying to accomplish by exhibiting inappropriate behavior. If this meaning is assumed to be correct, then enormous resources will be required to train educators to apply highly technical procedures. These procedures have been researched almost exclusively with students having severe cognitive disabilities, not with students whose school difficulties fit the classification of emotional or behavioral disorder (Sasso, Conroy, Stichter, & Fox, 2001). The controversy about the exact meaning of *functional behavioral assessment* and similar terms will likely continue until the U.S. Department of Education spells out just what the term does and does not mean.

There is now great emphasis on positive behavioral supports (PBS) and behavior intervention plans (BIP) for students with emotional and behavioral disorders (U.S. Department of Education, 2000). Much of the literature on this topic involves schoolwide efforts to focus on support of positive behavior rather than punishment (e.g., Lewis & Sugai, 1999; Sugai et al., 2000). However, it also includes effective instruction in basic skills as a means of positive support (e.g., Stein & Davis, 2000). Increasingly, researchers recognize that problem behavior occurs less frequently in the classroom when the teacher is offering effective instruction (Kauffman et al., 2002). Stein and Davis illustrate the meaning of PBS and offer a definition of the practices it entails:

> Sarah [is] a sixth grader who reads at the second-grade level. . . . She spends a lot of time waiting for assistance, does not make good grades, and is often teased by her peers. During reading instruction, Sarah engages in inappropriate verbal behavior by threatening the teacher or other children around her until she is dismissed from class or given other assignments to complete. Given the context and behavior, her teacher hypothesizes that Sarah's aggressive verbal behavior is an attempt to escape reading instruction. The teacher has determined that in order to develop an effective plan that will decrease Sarah's aggressive behavior, she must target reading instruction.

The principal of Positive Behavioral Supports includes a recognition of the fact that problem behavior occurs less frequently in classrooms where teachers offer consistent, effective instruction. ■

Since the mid-1980s, families, practitioners and researchers have called for more positive and preventive strategies for students with behavioral problems like Sarah's. From this call, the concept of "Positive Behavioral Support" (PBS) emerged. Positive Behavioral Support is a term that includes effective teaching strategies in all areas (e.g., academic, social, and mental health). The components of positive behavioral support are based on empirically validated strategies that focus on developing a positive, stable, and successful environment for all children, not simply those students who engage in problem behavior. (2000, p. 7)

Information about positive behavioral support and its role in schoolwide discipline and teaching may be obtained from www.pbis.org ■

Resources for positive behavior management are increasingly available on the World Wide Web. Many sites are being developed on the Internet, and most provide links to other sites. Some you might want to access:

- The National Center on Education, Disability, and Juvenile Justice at edjj.org
- The Oregon Social Learning Center at oslc.org
- The Technical Assistance Center on Positive Behavioral Interventions and Supports at pbis.org

Early Intervention

Early identification and prevention are basic goals of intervention programs for any category of disability (Sprague & Walker, 2000). For students with emotional or behavioral disorders, these goals present particular difficulties—yet they hold particular promise. The difficulties are related to definition and measurement of emotional or behavioral disorders, especially in young children; the particular promise is that young children's social-emotional behavior is quite flexible, so preventive efforts seem to have a good chance of success (Kaiser, 2000; Kamps, Tankersley, & Ellis, 2000; Kauffman, 1999).

As mentioned previously, defining emotional or behavioral disorders in such a way that children can be reliably identified is a difficult task. Definition and identification involving preschool children are complicated by several additional factors:

1. The developmental tasks that young children are expected to achieve are much simpler than those expected of older children, so the range of normal behaviors

to be used for comparison is quite restricted. Infants and toddlers are expected to eat, sleep, perform relatively simple motor skills, and respond socially to their parents. School-age children, however, must learn much more varied and complex motor and cognitive skills and develop social relations with a variety of peers and adults.

2. There is wide variation in the childrearing practices of good parents and in family expectations for preschool children's behavior in different cultures, so we must guard against inappropriate norms used for comparison. What is described as immature, withdrawn, or aggressive behavior in one family may not be perceived as such in another.

3. In the preschool years children's development is rapid and often uneven, making it difficult to judge what spontaneous improvements might occur.

4. The most severe types of emotional or behavioral disorders often are first observed in the preschool years. But it is frequently difficult to tell the difference between emotional or behavioral disorders and other conditions, like mental retardation or deafness. Often the first signs are difficulty with basic biological functions (e.g., eating, sleeping, eliminating), inadequate social responses (e.g., responding positively to a parent's attempts to offer comfort or "molding" to the parent's body when being held), or delay in learning language. Difficulty with these basic areas or in achieving developmental milestones like walking and talking indicate that the child may have an emotional or behavioral disability. But these difficulties may also be indicators of other conditions, such as mental retardation, sensory impairment, or physical disability. As Thomas and Guskin remarked, "Diagnosis of disruptive behaviors in very young children is challenging because they appear to respond to a variety of risk factors with similar hyperactive, aggressive, and defiant behaviors (2001, p. 50).

The patterns of behavior that signal problems for the preschool child are those that bring them into frequent conflict with, or keep them aloof from, their parents or caretakers and their siblings or peers. Many children who are referred to clinics for disruptive behavior when they are seven to twelve years of age showed clear signs of behavior problems by the time they were three or four—or even younger (Loeber, Green, Lahey, Christ, & Frick, 1992; Shaw et al., 2001). Infants or toddlers who exhibit a very "difficult temperament"—who are irritable; have irregular patterns of sleeping, eating, and eliminating; have highly intense responses to many stimuli and negative reactions toward new situations—are at risk for developing serious behavior problems unless their parents are particularly skillful at handling them. Children of preschool age are likely to elicit negative responses from adults and playmates if they are much more aggressive or much more withdrawn than most children their age. (Remember the critical importance of same-age comparisons. Toddlers frequently grab what they want, push other children down, and throw things and kick and scream when they don't get their way; toddlers normally do not have much finesse at social interaction and often hide from strangers.)

Because children's behavior is quite responsive to conditions in the social environment and can be shaped by adults, the potential for primary prevention—preventing serious behavior problems from occurring in the first place—would seem to be great. If parents and teachers could be taught effective child management skills, perhaps many or most cases could be prevented (Ialongo et al., 1998; Walker et al., 1995; Walker, Kavanagh et al., 1998). Furthermore, one could imagine that if parents and teachers had such skills, children who already have emotional or behavioral disorders could be prevented from getting worse (secondary prevention). But as Bower (1981) notes, the task of primary prevention is not that simple. For one thing, the tremendous amount of money and personnel needed for training in child management are not available. For another, even if the money and personnel could be found, professionals would not always agree on what patterns of behavior should be prevented or on how undesirable behavior could be prevented from developing (Kauffman, 1999; Kazdin, 1995).

Preschool intervention of children with emotional and behavioral disorders has been quite effective in preventing or reducing subsequent problems. However, identifying these disorders between 3 and 5 years can be difficult. ■

If overly aggressive or withdrawn behavior has been identified in a preschooler, what kind of intervention program is most desirable? Behavioral interventions are highly effective (see Peacock Hill Working Group, 1991; Strain & Timm, 2001; Strain et al., 1992; Walker et al., 1995; Walker, Forness et al., 1998). A behavioral approach implies defining and measuring the child's behaviors and rearranging the environment (especially adults' and other children's responses to the problem child) to teach and support more appropriate conduct. In the case of aggressive children, social rewards for aggression should be prevented. For example, hitting another child or throwing a temper tantrum might result in brief social isolation or "time out" instead of adult attention or getting one's own way.

Researchers are constantly seeking less punitive ways of dealing with problem behavior, including aggression. The best way of handling violent or aggressive play or play themes, for example, would be one that effectively reduces the frequency of aggressive play yet requires minimal punishment. In one study with children between the ages of three and five, violent or aggressive theme play (talk or imitation of weapons, destruction, injury, etc.) was restricted to a small area of the classroom defined by a carpet sample (Sherburne, Utley, McConnell, & Gannon, 1988). Children engaging in imaginative play involving guns, for example, were merely told by the teacher, using a pleasant tone of voice, "If you want to play guns, go over on the rug" (p. 169). If violent theme play continued for more than ten seconds after the teacher's warning, the child or children were physically assisted to the rug. They were not required to stay on the rug for a specific length of time; rather, they merely had to go there if they wanted to engage in aggressive play. This simple procedure was quite effective in reducing violent and aggressive themes in the children's play.

In summary, it is possible to identify at an early age those children who are at high risk for emotional or behavioral disorders (Farmer et al., 2001; Walker et al., 1994; Walker, Kavanagh et al., 1998; Wehby, Dodge, & Valente, 1993). These children exhibit extreme aggression or social withdrawal and may be socially rejected or identify with deviant peers. They should be identified as early as possible, and their parents and teachers should learn how to teach them essential social skills and management of their problem behavior using positive, nonviolent procedures (see Kamps et al., 2000; Serna et al., 2000; Strain & Timm, 2001; Timm, 1993; Walker et al., 1995). If children with emotional or behavioral disorders are identified very early and intervention is sufficiently comprehensive, intense, and sustained, then there is a good chance that they can recover and exhibit developmentally normal patterns of behavior (Strain & Timm, 2001; Timm, 1993; Walker et al., 1995).

Nevertheless, research suggests that in practice, early intervention typically does not occur. In fact, intervention does usually not begin until the child has exhibited an extremely disabling pattern of behavior for several years (Duncan, Forness, & Hartsough, 1995). The primary reasons given as to why early, comprehensive, intense, and sustained intervention is so rare include worry about labeling and stigma, optimism regarding the child's development (i.e., the assumption that he or she will "grow out of it"), lack of resources required to address the needs of any but the most severely problematic children, and ignorance about the early signs of emotional or behavioral problems (Kauffman, 1999).

Transition to Adulthood

The programs designed for adolescents with emotional or behavioral disorders have varied widely in aims and structure (Maag & Katsiyannis, 1998). Nelson and Kauffman (1977) describe the following types, which remain the basic options today:

- Regular public high school classes
- Consultant teachers who work with regular teachers to provide individualized academic work and behavior management
- Resource rooms and special self-contained classes to which students may be assigned for part or all of the school day
- Work-study programs in which vocational education and job experience are combined with academic study
- Special private or public schools that offer the regular high school curriculum in a different setting
- Alternative schools that offer highly individualized programs that are nontraditional in both setting and content
- Private or public residential schools

Incarcerated youths with emotional or behavioral disorders are an especially neglected group in special education. One suspects that the special educational needs of many (or most) of these teenagers who are in prison are neglected because incarcerated youths are defined as *socially maladjusted* rather than *emotionally disturbed*. The current federal definition appears to allow denial of special education services to a large number of young people who exhibit extremely serious misbehaviors and have long histories of school failure.

One of the reasons it is difficult to design special education programs at the secondary level for students with emotional or behavioral disorders is that this category of youths is so varied. Adolescents categorized for special education purposes as emotionally disturbed may have behavioral characteristics ranging from autistic-like withdrawn to aggressive delinquency, intelligence ranging from severely retarded to highly gifted, and academic skills ranging from preschool to college level. Therefore, it is hardly realistic to suggest that any single type of program or model will be appropriate for all such youths. In fact, youths with emotional or behavioral disorders, perhaps more than any other category of exceptionality, need a highly individualized, creative, and flexible education. Programs may range from teaching daily living skills in a sheltered environment to advanced placement in college, from regular class placement to hospitalization, and from the traditional curriculum to unusual and specialized vocational training.

Transition from school to work and adult life is particularly difficult for adolescents with emotional or behavioral disorders (Sample, 1998). Many of them lack the basic academic skills necessary for successful employment. In addition, they often behave in ways that prevent them from being accepted, liked, and helped by employers, co-workers, and neighbors. It is not surprising that students with emotional or behavioral disorders are among the most likely to drop out of school and among the most difficult to train in transition programs (Carson, Sitlington, & Frank, 1995; Edgar & Siegel, 1995; Malmgren, Edgar, & Neel, 1998).

Many children and youths with emotional or behavioral disorders grow up to be adults who have real difficulties leading independent, productive lives. The outlook is especially grim for children and adolescents who have conduct disorder. Contrary to popular opinion, the child or youth who is shy, anxious, or neurotic is not the most likely to have psychiatric problems as an adult. Rather, it is the conduct-disordered (hyperaggressive) child or youth whose adulthood is most likely to be characterized by socially intolerable behavior and lack of social competence (Kazdin, 1995, 1997; Walker & Stieber, 1998). About half the children who are hyperaggressive will have problems that require legal intervention or psychiatric care when they are adults.

GW For information about juvenile justice and education, see www.edjj.org ∎

Successful transition to adult life is often complicated by neglectful, abusive, or inadequate family relationships. A high percentage of adolescents with conduct disorder have family relationships of this nature. However, the emphasis on punishment and imprisonment, particularly of African American males, appears to be counterproductive. The emphasis on punishment contributes to family deterioration and harsh conditions of life that perpetuate undesirable conduct (Miller, 1997).

Examples of relatively successful high school and transition programs are available, most of which employ a behavioral approach (Edgar & Siegel, 1995; Peacock Hill Working Group, 1991). However, it is important to stress *relatively* because many adolescents and young adults with severe conduct disorder appear to have a true developmental disability that requires intervention throughout their life span (Wolf, Braukmann, & Ramp, 1987). By the time these antisocial youths reach high school, the aim of even the most effective program is to help them accommodate their disabilities. Rather than focusing on remediation of academic and social skills, these programs attempt to teach youths the skills they will need to survive and cope in school and community, to make a transition to work, and to develop vocations (Walker et al., 1995). Well-planned alternative schools appear to offer important options to students at high risk, including those with emotional or behavioral problems (Duke, Griesdorn, & Kraft, 1998; Tobin & Sprague, 1999).

Summary

Emotional or behavioral disorders are not simply a matter of undesirable or inappropriate behaviors. They involve inappropriate social interactions and transactions between the child or youth and the social environment.

Many different terms have been used for children's emotional or behavioral disorders. In the language of federal laws and regulations, they are *emotionally disturbed*. The term *emotional or behavioral disorder* is becoming widely accepted, due primarily to the work of the National Mental Health and Special Education Coalition, which proposed a new definition and terminology in 1990.

The proposed definition defines emotional or behavioral disorders as a disability characterized by behavioral or emotional responses to school so different from appropriate age, cultural, or ethnic norms that they adversely affect educational performance. Educational performance is defined as more than academic performance; it includes academic, social, vocational, and personal skills. An emotional or behavioral disorder is more than a temporary or expected response to stressful events. It is exhibited in more than one setting, and it is unresponsive to direct intervention in general education. Finally, the proposed definition notes that the term *emotional or behavioral disorders* covers a wide variety of diagnostic groups, including sustained disorders of conduct or adjustment that adversely affect educational performance and can coexist with other disabilities.

Estimates of the prevalence of emotional or behavioral disorders vary greatly, in part because the definition is not precise. Most researchers estimate that 6 to 10 percent of the child population is affected, but only about 1 percent of the school-age population is currently identified as having emotional or behavioral disorders and is receiving special education services. Most children and youths who are identified for special education purposes are boys, and most exhibit externalizing behavior. About 3 percent of U.S. youths are referred to juvenile court in any given year. Relatively few of these receive special education services for emotional or behavioral disorders.

A single, specific cause of an emotional or behavioral disorder can seldom be identified. In most cases, it is possible only to identify causal factors that contribute to the likelihood that a child will develop a disorder or that predispose him or her to developing a disorder. Major contributing factors are found in biological conditions, family relationships, school experiences, and cultural influences. Possible biological factors include genetics, temperament (i.e., an inborn behavioral style), malnutrition, brain trauma, and substance abuse. Most biological causes are poorly understood, and social as well as medical intervention is almost always necessary.

Family disorganization, parental abuse, and inconsistent discipline are among the most important family factors contributing to emotional or behavioral disorders. However, poor parenting is not always or solely the cause. Furthermore, family factors appear to affect each family member in a different way. School factors that may contribute to emotional or behavioral disorders are insensitivity to students' individuality, inappropriate expectations, inconsistent or inappropriate discipline, unintentional rewards for misbehavior, and undesirable models of conduct. Cultural factors include the influences of the media, values and standards of the community and peer group, and social services available to children and their families.

Family, school, and the wider culture create a complex web of cultural causal factors.

Most children and youths with emotional or behavioral disorders—especially those with serious conduct disorder—are easily recognized. Few schools use systematic screening procedures, partly because services would be unavailable for the many students likely to be identified. The most effective identification procedures use a combination of teachers' rankings and ratings and direct observation of students' behavior. Peer rankings or ratings are often used as well.

The typical student with an emotional or behavioral disorder has an IQ in the dull–normal range. The range of intelligence is enormous: A few are brilliant, and more than in the general population have mental retardation. Most children and youths with emotional or behavioral disorders lack, in varying degrees, the ability to apply their knowledge and skills to the demands of everyday living.

Students who express their problems in aggressive, acting-out behavior are involved in a vicious cycle. Their behavior alienates others so that positive interactions with adults and peers become less likely. Children and youths whose behavior is consistently antisocial have less chance of learning to make social adjustments and of achieving mental health in adulthood than do those who are shy, anxious, or neurotic.

Special education is typically guided by one of two conceptual models, or a combination of the two: The psychoeducational model focuses on conscious and unconscious motivations; the behavioral model stresses the fact that behavior is learned as a consequence of environmental events. Both models offer valuable insights into teaching students whose behavior is problematic.

Regardless of the conceptual model guiding intervention or the characteristics of the students involved, the following strategies work: using systematic, data-based interventions; assessing and monitoring progress continuously; providing opportunities to practice new skills; providing treatment matched to the student's problem; offering multicomponent treatment to meet all the student's needs; programming for transfer and maintenance of learning; and sustaining intervention as long as it is needed.

A relatively small percentage of children and youths with emotional or behavioral disorders receive special education and related services. Only those with the most severe problems are likely to be identified, one consequence of which is that many are educated outside regular classrooms and schools. The trend, however, is toward greater integration in regular schools and classes. Because difficulty with social interactions is a hallmark of emotional and behavioral disorders, such placements can be particularly problematic.

Special disciplinary considerations are required by the 1997 amendments to IDEA. In most cases, exceptional learners are subject to the same disciplinary procedures as their nondisabled peers. However, the Elementary and Secondary Education Act of 2001 allowed children with disabilities to be suspended and expelled from school just as are children without disabilities, although states and localities have the option of alternative management. The issues are especially difficult for students with emotional or behavioral disorders because the causes of their misbehavior are often difficult to determine with confidence.

Functional behavioral assessment is required by the 1997 IDEA amendments, but the meaning of the term is not clearly understood. The term may be interpreted to mean using assessment procedures that are useful. It may also be interpreted to mean pinpointing the function or meaning of behavior, which would require extensive technical training of special educators. Positive behavioral interventions and supports are increasingly seen as important in the management of whole schools and children with emotional or behavioral disorders.

Early identification and prevention are goals of early intervention programs. The problem behavior of many children later referred to clinics for emotional or behavioral disorders is evident early in life. Early intervention has been shown to be highly successful; however, it often does not occur due to worry about labeling and stigma, optimism that the child will "grow out of it," lack of resources, and ignorance about the early signs of problems. With early, intensive intervention, great improvements can be seen in nearly all cases.

Programs of special education for adolescents and young adults with emotional or behavioral disorders are extremely varied and must be highly individualized because of the wide differences in students' intelligence, behavioral characteristics, achievements, and circumstances. Transition from school to work and adult life is particularly difficult for students with emotional or behavioral disorders, and they are among those most likely to drop out of school. The outlook for adulthood is particularly poor for youths with severe conduct disorder; many require intervention throughout their lives.

Ronde Allen

Fire Fighter, Pencil, crayon on paper. 14 × 17 in.

An enigmatic individual, Mr. Allen, who was born in 1978 in Boston, Massachusetts, speaks only when it is absolutely necessary. Having grown up in difficult neighborhoods, his work often depicts traumatic events in his life.

8

Learners with Communication Disorders

I said goodbye and turned to go, but she wrapped her purple-green arms around my neck, kissed my cheek, and said, "I love you, Jeremy."

"I'll miss you so much."

"I really, truly love you with all my soul," she said.

"My Dad's waiting. I better go."

She took her arms off me and stepped back, straightened her smock. Then she said, "I've already told you I love you, Jeremy. Can't you say, 'I love you, Faith'?"

"I love you," I said.

"I love you, *Faith*," she insisted.

This little scene in the garage occurred only a few months after my futile attempt to say *Philadelphia* in the living room. Stutterers have a tendency to generalize their fear of one word that begins with a particular sound to a fear of all words that begin with the same sound. In the space of the summer I'd effectively eliminated every *F* from my vocabulary, with the exception of the preposition, "for," which for the time being was too small to incite terror. A few weeks later, my fear of *F* ended when another letter—I think it was *L*—suddenly loomed large. But at the moment, early October 1962, in Faith's garage, I was terrified of *F*s. I simply wasn't saying them. I hadn't called Faith by her first name for nearly a month and had, instead, taken to calling her Carlisle, as if her patronymic had become a term of jocular endearment.

"I can't," I said. "I can't say that."

DAVID SHIELDS
Dead Languages

C ommunication is such a natural part of our everyday lives that we seldom stop to think about it. Social conversation with families, friends, and casual acquaintances is normally so effortless and pleasant that it is hard to imagine having difficulty with it. Most of us have feelings of uncertainty about the adequacy of our speech or language only in stressful or unusual social situations, such as talking to a large audience or being interviewed for a job. If we always had to worry about communicating, we would worry about every social interaction we had.

Communication disorders.
Impairments in the ability to use speech or language to communicate.

Stuttering.
Speech characterized by abnormal hesitations, prolongations, and repetitions; may be accompanied by grimaces, gestures, or other bodily movements indicative of a struggle to speak, anxiety, blocking of speech, or avoidance of speech.

Not all **communication disorders** involve disorders of speech. Not all speech disorders are as handicapping in social interactions as **stuttering,** nor is stuttering the most common disorder of speech. The problem Shields describes (see p. 263) affects only about one person in a hundred, and then usually just during childhood. But stuttering is a mystery, a phenomenon about which theories continue to surface. Its causes and cures remain largely unknown, although for many years it captured a large share of speech-language pathologists' attention (Curlee & Siegel, 1997). Effective interventions have been devised, but they are often ignored or dismissed by those who reject reliable evidence (Conture, 2001; Ratner & Healey, 1999). And the nature and treatment of stuttering continue to be matters of controversy among researchers (e.g., Yairi, Watkins, Ambrose, & Paden, 2001; Wingate, 2001).

In one sense, then, stuttering is a poor example to use in introducing a chapter on communication disorders. It is not the most representative disorder, it is difficult to define precisely, its causes are not fully understood, and only a few of the many suggestions about how to overcome it can be made with confidence. But in another sense, stuttering is the best example. When people think of speech and language disorders, they tend to think first of stuttering. It is a disorder we all have heard and recognized (if not experienced) at one time or another, its social consequences are obvious, and although it *appears* to be a simple problem with obvious logical solutions ("Just slow down"; "Relax, don't worry"; "Think about how to say it"), these seemingly commonsense approaches do not work. The tendency to think of stuttering when speech disorders are mentioned might be illustrated by the fact that Jane Fraser, President of the Stuttering Foundation of America, wrote Ann Landers (letter published May 9, 2001) giving the hotline number (800-992-9392) and Web address (www.stutteringhelp.org) of the Foundation and reminding readers of Ann Landers that the second week in May is National Stuttering Awareness Week.

Today, difficulty such as that described by Shields is viewed within the broad context of communication disorders because of the obstacle it presents to social interaction, which is a major purpose of language. Jeremy's stuttering was an inability to convey his thoughts and feelings to Faith, not just a problem of being fearful and unable to say certain words. In thinking about communication disorders, the context in which communication occurs must be considered in addition to people's reasons for communicating, and the rules that govern the "games" of discourse and dialogue (Haynes & Pindzola, 1998; Nelson, 1998; Plante & Beeson, 1999).

Our points here are simply these: First, all communication disorders carry social penalties. And second, communication is among the most complex human functions, so disorders of this function do not always yield to intuitive or commonsense solutions.

Definitions

An important Web site to visit for more information about communication disorders is the home page of the American Speech-Language-Hearing Association at www.asha.org ■

Speech and language are tools used for communication. Communication requires *encoding* (sending in understandable form) and *decoding* (receiving and understanding) messages. It always involves a sender and a receiver of messages, but it does not always involve language. Animals communicate through movements and noises, for example, but their communication does not qualify as true language. We are concerned here only with communication through language.

MISCONCEPTIONS ABOUT
Learners with Communication Disorders

MYTH Children with language disorders always have speech difficulties as well.

FACT It is possible for a child to have good speech yet not make any sense when he or she talks; however, most children with language disorders have speech disorders as well.

MYTH Individuals with communication disorders always have emotional or behavioral disorders or mental retardation.

FACT Some children with communication disorders are normal in cognitive, social, and emotional development.

MYTH How children learn language is now well understood.

FACT Although recent research has revealed quite a lot about the sequence of language acquisition and has led to theories of language development, exactly how children learn language is still unknown.

MYTH Stuttering is primarily a disorder of people with extremely high IQs. Children who stutter become stuttering adults.

FACT Stuttering can affect individuals at all levels of intellectual ability. Some children who stutter continue stuttering as adults; most, however, stop stuttering before or during adolescence with help from a speech-language pathologist. Stuttering is primarily a childhood disorder, found much more often in boys than in girls.

MYTH Disorders of phonology (or articulation) are never very serious and are always easy to correct.

FACT Disorders of phonology can make speech unintelligible; it is sometimes very difficult to correct phonological or articulation problems, especially if the individual has cerebral palsy, mental retardation, or emotional or behavioral disorders.

MYTH There is no relationship between intelligence and communication disorders.

FACT Communication disorders tend to occur more frequently among individuals of lower intellectual ability, although they may occur in individuals who are extremely intelligent.

MYTH There is not much overlap between language disorders and learning disabilities.

FACT Problems with verbal skills—listening, reading, writing, speaking—are often central features of learning disabilities. The definitions of language disorders and several other disabilities are overlapping.

MYTH Children who learn few language skills before entering kindergarten can easily pick up all the skills they need, if they have good peer models in typical classrooms.

FACT Early language learning is critical for later language development; a child whose language is delayed in kindergarten is unlikely to learn to use language effectively merely by observing peer models. More explicit intervention is typically required.

Language.
An arbitrary code or system of symbols to communicate meaning.

Expressive language.
Encoding or sending messages in communication.

Receptive language.
Decoding or understanding messages in communication.

Speech.
The formation and sequencing of oral language sounds during communication.

Augmentative or alternative communication (AAC).
Alternative forms of communication that do not use the oral sounds of speech or that augment the use of speech.

Speech disorders.
Oral communication that involves abnormal use of the vocal apparatus, is unintelligible, or is so inferior that it draws attention to itself and causes anxiety, feelings of inadequacy, or inappropriate behavior in the speaker.

Articulation.
The movements the vocal tract makes during production of speech sounds; enunciation of words and vocal sounds.

Language is the communication of ideas—sending and receiving them—through an arbitrary system of symbols used according to certain rules that determine meaning. Encoding or sending messages is referred to as **expressive language.** Decoding or understanding messages is referred to as **receptive language.** When people think of language, they typically think of the oral language most of us use. **Speech**—the behavior of forming and sequencing the sounds of oral language—is the most common symbol system used in communication between humans. Some languages, however, are not based on speech. For example, American Sign Language (ASL) does not involve speech sounds; it is a manual language used by many people who cannot hear speech. **Augmentative or alternative communication (AAC)** for people with disabilities involving the physical movements of speech may consist of alternatives to the speech sounds of oral language (see discussion in Chapter 11).

The American Speech-Language-Hearing Association (ASHA) provides definitions of disorders of communication, including speech disorders, language disorders, and variations in communication (differences or dialects and augmentative systems) that are not disorders (see the box on page 267). **Speech disorders** are impairments in the production and use of oral language. They include disabilities in making speech sounds (**articulation**), producing speech with a normal flow (**fluency**), and producing voice.

Language disorders include problems in comprehending and using language for communication, regardless of the symbol system used (spoken, written, or other). The *form, content,* and/or *function* of language may be involved:

- The form of language includes sound combinations (**phonology**), construction of word forms such as plurals and verb tenses (**morphology**), and construction of sentences (**syntax**).
- The content of language refers to the intentions and meanings people attach to words and sentences (**semantics**).
- Language function is the use to which language is put in communication, and it includes nonverbal behavior as well as vocalizations that form the pattern of language use (**pragmatics**).

Differences in speech or language that are shared by people in a given region, social group, or cultural/ethnic group should not be considered disorders. For example, African American English (Ebonics or Black English Vernacular), Appalachian English, and the New York dialect are varieties of English, not disorders of speech or language. Similarly, the use of augmentative or alternative communication systems does not imply that a person has a language disorder. Rather, such systems are used by those who have temporary or permanent inabilities to use speech satisfactorily for communication. Those who use augmentative communication systems may or may not have language disorders in addition to their inability to use speech.

Prevalence

Establishing the prevalence of communication disorders is difficult because they are extremely varied, sometimes difficult to identify, and often occur as part of other disabilities (e.g., mental retardation, brain injury, learning disability, or autism; see Bernstein & Tiegerman-Farber, 1997; Nelson, 1998). Federal data indicate that about a million children—about one-fifth of all children identified for special education—receive services primarily for language or speech disorders (U.S. Department of Education, 2000). Moreover, speech-language therapy is one of the most frequently provided related services for children with other primary disabilities (e.g., mental retardation or learning disability).

Table 8.1 outlines the other categories associated with language disorders of children and youths. The outline suggests the multiple, interrelated causes of language disorders and other disabilities:

TABLE 8.1   Categorical Factors Associated with Childhood Language Disorders

I. **Central factors**	A. Specific language disability
	B. Mental retardation
	C. Autism
	D. Attention-deficit hyperactivity disorder
	E. Acquired brain injury
	F. Others
II. **Peripheral factors**	A. Hearing impairment
	B. Visual impairment
	C. Deaf-blindness
	D. Physical impairment
III. **Environmental and emotional factors**	A. Neglect and abuse
	B. Behavioral and emotional development problems
IV. **Mixed factors**	

SOURCE: From N.W. Nelson, *Childhood language disorders in context: Infancy through adolescence* (2nd ed.). Copyright © 1998 by Allyn & Bacon. Reprinted/adapted by permission.

- *Central factors* refer to causes associated with central nervous system (i.e., brain) damage or dysfunction.
- *Peripheral factors* refer to sensory or physical impairments that are not caused by brain injury or dysfunction but that nonetheless contribute to language disorders.
- *Environmental and emotional factors* refer to language disorders that have their primary origin in the child's physical or psychological environment.
- *Mixed factors* are included because language disorders often have multiple causes—combinations of central, peripheral, and environmental or emotional factors.

Estimates are that about 10 to 15 percent of preschool children and about 6 percent of students in elementary and secondary grades have speech disorders; about 2 to 3 percent of preschoolers and about 1 percent of the school-age population have language disorders (Matthews & Frattali, 1994). Communication disorders of all kinds are predicted to increase during the coming decades, as medical advances preserve the lives of more children and youths with severe disabilities that affect communication. Thus, there is a need for more speech-language pathologists in the schools as well as for greater knowledge of communication disorders by special and general education teachers and greater involvement of teachers in helping students learn to communicate effectively.

Communication disorders cannot be understood and corrected without knowledge of normal language development. So before discussing the disorders of language and speech, we provide a brief description of normal language development. Language disorders are discussed first and more extensively than speech disorders, because the primary focus of speech-language pathologists and other specialists in communicative disorders has shifted from speech to language during the evolution of special education and related services.

Language Development and Language Disorders

The newborn makes few sounds other than cries. The fact that within a few years the human child can form the many complex sounds of speech, understand spoken and written language, and express meaning verbally is one of nature's great miracles. The major milestones in this miraculous ability to use language are fairly well known by child devel-

Fluency.
The flow with which oral language is produced.

Language disorders.
Oral communication that involves a lag in the ability to understand and express ideas, putting linguistic skill behind an individual's development in other areas, such as motor, cognitive, or social development.

Phonology.
The study of how individual sounds make up words.

Morphology.
The study within psycholinguistics of word formation; how adding or deleting parts of words changes their meaning.

Syntax.
The way words are joined together to structure meaningful sentences; grammar.

Semantics.
The study of the meanings attached to words and sentences.

Pragmatics.
The study within psycholinguistics of how people use language in social situations; emphasizes the functional use of language, rather than mechanics.

Definitions of the American Speech-Language-Hearing Association

I. A *communication disorder* is an impairment in the ability to receive, send, process, and comprehend concepts or verbal, nonverbal and graphic symbol systems. A communication disorder may be evident in the processes of hearing, language, and/or speech. A communication disorder may range in severity from mild to profound. It may be developmental or acquired. Individuals may demonstrate one or any combination of communication disorders. A communication disorder may result in a primary disability or it may be secondary to other disabilities.

A. A *speech disorder* is an impairment of the articulation of speech sounds, fluency, and/or voice.

1. *An articulation disorder* is the atypical production of speech sounds characterized by substitutions, omissions, additions, or distortions that may interfere with intelligibility.

2. *A fluency disorder* is an interruption in the flow of speaking characterized by atypical rate, rhythm, and repetitions in sounds, syllables, words, and phrases. This may be accompanied by excessive tension, struggle behavior, and secondary mannerisms.

3. *A voice disorder* is characterized by the abnormal production and/or absences of vocal quality, pitch, loudness, resonance, and/or duration, which is inappropriate for an individual's age and/or sex.

B. A *language disorder* is impaired comprehension and/or use of spoken, written, and/or other symbol systems. The disorder may involve (1) the form of language (phonology, morphology, syntax), (2) the content of language (semantics), and/or (3) the function of language in communication (pragmatics) in any combination.

1. Form of Language

a. *Phonology* is the sound system of a language and the rules that govern the sound combinations.

b. *Morphology* is the system that governs the structure of words and the construction of word forms.

c. *Syntax* is the system governing the order and combination of words to form sentences, and the relationships among the elements within a sentence.

2. Content of Language

a. *Semantics* is the system that governs the meanings of words and sentences.

3. Function of Language

a. *Pragmatics* is the system that combines the above language components in functional and socially appropriate communication.

II. *Communication Variations*

A. *Communication difference/dialect* is a variation of a symbol system used by a group of individuals that reflects and is determined by shared regional, social, or cultural/ethnic factors. A regional, social, or cultural/ethnic variation of a symbol system should not be considered a disorder of speech or language.

B. *Augmentative/alternative communication* systems attempt to compensate and facilitate, temporarily or permanently, for the impairment and disability patterns of individuals with severe expressive and/or language comprehension disorders. Augmentative/alternative communication may be required for individuals demonstrating impairments in gestural, spoken, and/or written modalities.

SOURCE: American Speech-Language-Hearing Association. (1993). "Definitions of communication disorders and variations." *ASHA, 35*(Suppl. 10), pp. 40–41. Reprinted with permission.

opment specialists. The underlying mechanisms that control the development of language are still not well understood, however. What parts of the process of learning language are innate, and what parts are controlled by the environment? What is the relationship between cognitive development and language development? These and many other questions about the origins and uses of language cannot yet be answered definitively (Nelson, 1998).

Comparisons between the language of a normally developing child and one with a language disorder are shown in Table 8.2. Note that, in general, the sequence of development is similar for the two children, but the child with the language disorder reaches milestones at later ages. Although there are other types of language disorders, delayed lan-

ℂ𝕎 For information about normal speech and language development and the difference between speech disorder and language disorder visit the Speech-Language Pathology site at home.ica.net/~fred/ ∎

TABLE 8.2   Pattern of Development Shown by a Child with a Language Disorder and a Child with Normal Language Development

Language-Disordered Child			Normally Developing Child		
Age	Attainment	Example	Age	Attainment	Example
27 months	First words	*this, mama, bye bye, doggie*	13 months	First words	*here, mama, bye bye, kitty*
38 months	50-word vocabulary		17 months	50-word vocabulary	
40 months	First two-word combinations	*this doggie, more apple, this mama, more play*	18 months	First two-word combinations	*more juice, here ball, more TV, here kitty*
48 months	Later two-word combinations	*Mimi purse, Daddy coat, block chair, dolly table*	22 months	Later two-word combinations	*Andy shoe, Mommy ring, cup floor, keys chair*
52 months	Mean sentence length of 2.00 words		24 months	Mean sentence length of 2.00 words / First appearance of *-ing*	*Andy sleeping*
55 months	First appearance of *-ing*	*Mommy eating*			
63 months	Mean sentence length of 3.10 words		30 months	Mean sentence length of 3.10 words / First appearance of *is*	*My car's gone.*
66 months	First appearance of *is*	*The doggie's mad.*	37 months	Mean sentence length of 4.10 words / First appearance of indirect requests	*Can I have some cookies?*
73 months	Mean sentence length of 4.10 words				
79 months	Mean sentence length of 4.50 words / First appearance of indirect requests	*Can I get the ball?*	40 months	Mean sentence length of 4.50 words	

SOURCE: From L. Leonard, "Language disorders in preschool children," in *Human communication disorders: An introduction* (4th ed.), edited by G. H. Shames, E. H. Wiig, and W. A. Secord. Copyright © 1994 by Allyn & Bacon. Reprinted/adapted by permission.

guage—slowness in developing skills and reaching certain milestones—is perhaps the most common type.

No one knows exactly how or why children learn language, but we do know that language development is related in a general way to physical maturation, cognitive development, and socialization. The details of the process—the particulars of what happens physiologically, cognitively, and socially in the learning of language—are still being debated. Nelson (1998) discusses six theories of language that have dominated the study of human communication at various times. The six theories and research based on them have established the following:

- Language learning depends on brain development and proper brain functioning; language disorders are sometimes a result of brain dysfunction, and ways to compensate for the dysfunction can sometimes be taught. The emphasis is on *biological maturation.*
- Language learning is affected by the consequences of language behavior; language disorders can be a result of inappropriate learning, and consequences can sometimes be arranged to correct disordered language. The emphasis is on *behavioral psychology.*
- Language can be analyzed as inputs and outputs related to the way information is processed; faulty processing may account for some language disorders, and more

No one knows exactly how or why children learn language, but we do know that language development is related in a general way to physical maturation, cognitive development, and socialization. ■

effective processing skills can sometimes be taught. The emphasis is on *information processing*.

- Language is based on linguistic rules; language disorders can be described as failures to employ appropriate rules for encoding and decoding messages, and sometimes these disorders can be overcome by teaching the use of linguistic rules. The emphasis is on *induction of linguistic rules*.
- Language is one of many cognitive skills; language disorders reflect basic problems in thinking and learning, and sometimes these disorders can be addressed effectively by teaching specific cognitive skills. The emphasis is on *cognitive development*.
- Language arises from the need to communicate in social interactions; language disorders are a breakdown in ability to relate effectively to one's environment, and the natural environment can sometimes be arranged to teach and support more effective interaction. The emphasis is on *social interaction*.

All these theories contain elements of scientific truth, but none is able to explain the development and disorders of language completely. All six theories have advantages and disadvantages for assessing language disorders and devising effective interventions. Advances in neurological imaging technology may lead to better understanding of the biological bases of language (Foundas, 2001). However, *pragmatic* or *social interaction* theory is widely viewed as having the most direct implications for speech-language pathologists and teachers.

Language involves listening and speaking, reading and writing, technical discourse, and social interaction. Language problems are therefore basic to many of the disabilities discussed in this text, especially hearing impairment, mental retardation, learning disability, and the severe and multiple disorders we discuss in Chapter 11, including traumatic brain injury and autism.

CLASSIFICATION OF LANGUAGE DISORDERS

Language disorders can be classified according to several criteria. The ASHA definitions on page 267 provide a classification scheme involving five subsystems of language: *phonology* (sounds), *morphology* (word forms), *syntax* (word order and sentence structure), *semantics* (word and sentence meanings), and *pragmatics* (social use of language). Difficulty with one of these dimensions of language is virtually certain to be accompanied by difficulty with one or more of the others. However, children with language disorders often have particular difficulty with one dimension. Language disorders involving these subsystems are illustrated in the box on pages 272–273.

Another way of classifying language disorders is based on the presumed cause or related conditions. The literature on language disorders frequently includes chapters and articles on the particular communication disorders of individuals with other specific disabling conditions, such as autism, traumatic brain injury, mental retardation, and cerebral palsy (e.g., Owens, 1995; Shames, Wiig, & Secord, 1994; Szekeres & Meserve, 1995). Owens (1995) discusses seven diagnostic categories of language impairments, each of which tends to present difficulties in particular areas (as shown in Table 8.3): perception, attention, use of symbols, use of language rules, overall mental ability, and social interaction related to communication. In addition, each diagnostic category is characterized by particular problems in the five language subsystems—phonology, morphology, syntax, semantics, and pragmatics—and problems in language comprehension.

Several of the seven conditions included in Table 8.3 are defined in other chapters of this book. **Specific language impairment (SLI)** refers to language disorders that have no identifiable causes. These disorders are not due to mental retardation or to the perceptual problems that characterize language learning disability. Rather, SLI is defined more by the exclusion of other plausible causes than by a clearly defined set of characteristics, and for this reason it is controversial. **Early expressive language delay (EELD)** refers to a significant lag in expressive language that the child will not outgrow (i.e., the child does not have a fifty-word vocabulary or use two-word utterances by age two). About half the children whose language development is delayed at age two *will* gradually catch up developmentally with their age peers; however the other half will not catch up and will continue to have language problems throughout their school years.

A scientific approach to problems demands classification, but human beings and their language are very difficult to categorize. Thus, all classification systems contain ambiguities, and none can account for all cases. Owens (1995) notes:

> Most [college and university] students are in need of a 1-sentence summary statement that once and for all distinguishes each language impairment from the others. Unfortunately, I do not have one forthcoming. We are discussing real human beings who do not like to be placed in boxes and asked to perform in certain ways. (p. 56)

Specific language impairment (SLI).
A language disorder with no identifiable cause; language disorder not attributable to hearing impairment, mental retardation, brain dysfunction, or other plausible cause; also called specific language disability.

Early expressive language delay (EELD).
A significant lag in the development of expressive language that is apparent by age two.

Children with language disorders often have particular difficulty with one dimension of language, be it phonology, morphology, syntax, semantics, or pragmatics. ■

Disorders of the Five Subsystems of Language

Oral language involves communication through a system of sound symbols. Disorders may occur in one or more of the five subsystems of oral language: *phonology* (sounds and sound combinations), *morphology* (words and meaningful word parts), *syntax* (sequences and combinations of words), *semantics* (meanings or content), and *pragmatics* (use for communication). The following interactions illustrate disorders in each of these subsystems. Note that a given illustration may involve more than a single subsystem.

Phonology

Alvin has just turned 6. He is in kindergarten, but has been receiving speech therapy for 2 years. At 4, his parents sought assistance when his speech and language remained unintelligible and he did not appear to be "growing out" of his problem. He has two older siblings whose speech and language are well within the normal range. Alvin substitutes and omits a number of speech sounds, and in addition, he has difficulty with other subsystems of language as shown in the example below:

Clinician: I'd like you to tell me about some words. Here's something that you may have for breakfast: orange juice. What's orange juice?

Alvin: I doh noh. [I don't know.]

Clinician: See if you can guess. What color is orange juice?

Alvin: Ahnge. N you dink i. [Orange. And you drink it.]

Clinician: That's good. Tell me some more about orange juice.

Alvin: Doh noh.

Clinician: Let's try another. What's sugar? Tell me what sugar is.

Alvin: Yukky.

Clinician: Yukky? Why?

Alvin: Cah i wahtuns yer tee. ['Cause it rottens your teeth.]

Morphology

Children with language disorders in the morphological realm will exhibit difficulty in either understanding or producing morphological inflections. These include the ability to add -s to change a word from singular to plural; to include 's to make a word a possessive; -ed to change the tense of a word from present to past; or to use other inflectional endings to differentiate comparatives and superlatives, among others.

Children with morphological difficulties will use inappropriate suffixes. . . . Here are a few . . . examples, taken from the test protocols of school-age children:

Examiner: Anna, say this after me: *cow.*

Anna: (*age 6*) Cow.

Examiner: Good. Now say *boy.*

Anna: Boy.

Examiner: Now put them together. Say *cowboy.*

Anna: Boy.

Examiner: Frank, find two little words in this big word: *outside.*

Frank: (*age 7*) Outside.

Examiner: Not quite right. We need *two* words.

Frank: (*Shrugs and looks around the room*)

Examiner: Well, if one word is *side,* the other would be . . . ?

Frank: Be?

Examiner: Jamie, can you tell me a story?

Jamie: (*age 8*) I can't think of none.

Examiner: What if the story began, "One night I walked into a dark haunted house . . . and . . .

Jamie: I met a ghost. He wanted to kill me. But he couldn't. I ran very, very fastest. And all of a sudden I saw a coffin. I hides in there. And all of a sudden there a ghostes inside there. And I sent out of the coffin. And then there weres a guy named Count. And then he tried to suck my blood. And then he couldn't find me because I hided. And then I met a mummy. And then he wanted to tie me up . . . and . . . that's all.

Syntax

Marie is 8 years old and in a special first-grade class. Her syntactical difficulties are demonstrated in the following story-telling event:

Clinician: Marie, I want you to listen carefully. I am going to tell you a story; listen, and when I'm done, I want you to tell me the story.

Marie: (*interrupting*) I don't know.

Clinician: I haven't told you the story yet. Remember, listen carefully to my story. When I'm done, you are to tell me everything you can remember about the story. One day Mr. Mouse went for a walk. As he was walking, he saw a cat lying in the road. The cat had a stone in his paw so he couldn't walk. Mr. Mouse pulled the stone out of the cat's paw. The cat thanked Mr. Mouse for helping him. They shook hands and walked down the road together.

Marie: Uh, uh, uh . . . Cat was on the road and Mr. Mouse taken out the stone his paw, and then they walked down together the hill and they said thanks, and they walk on the hill, and the mouse chase him.

This task of retelling a story reveals that Marie has difficulty not only in syntax but in the ordering of events and in accurate recall. Indeed, Marie seems unaware that she has modified the story considerably, including giving the story a new ending.

Semantics

Clinician: Burt, tell me about birthday parties.
Burt: (*age 6*) Sing "Happy Birthday," blow away candles, eat a birthday cake, open your presents.
Clinician: All right. Now listen to this story and then say it back to me . . . tell me the whole story: "One day, a little boy went to school. He went up the steps of the school and opened the door. The boy went into his classroom and started playing with his friends. The teacher said, 'Time to come to circle.' The boy put away his toys and sat down on the rug."
Burt: A teacher . . . a boy played with a teacher's toys . . . time for us to come to circle . . . and it's the end.

You will note that Burt does not "blow out" candles; rather, his retrieval of information from semantic memory provides the response "blow away." In addition, it is clear that even the immediate retelling of a story, which in reality represents a string of events well within Burt's everyday experience, is very difficult for Burt. The pauses noted reflect the period of time during which Burt attempted to recall the necessary information.

Pragmatics

Greg, age 7, interacts with his special education teacher. Greg is in a self-contained classroom for mentally retarded children and is one of the more verbal children in the class. Assessment by the speech-language pathol-ogist indicates difficulties in phonology, syntax, morphology, and semantics. He has been identified as suffering from a significant language delay. On most language tests, he functions between 2:7* and 3:6 years of age. His teacher, who has visited his home many times, notes that there are no toys, no books, no playthings, and that there appears to be little communication between Greg and his mother, a single parent. The teacher is eager to draw Greg into conversation and story-telling, and has arranged a "talking and telling time" as part of the daily activities with the seven children who comprise her class.

Teacher: Greg, I'd like you to tell me a story. It can be about anything you like.
Greg: No me.
Teacher: Go ahead, it's your turn.
Greg: (*having had previous instruction on "taking turns"*) No, s'yer turn.
Teacher: You do it. It's your turn.
Greg: I can't. I forget.
Teacher: I bet you can tell me a story about school.
Greg: You eat snack. What we have for snack?

Greg's teacher praises his contribution to the conversation and moves on to another student. She grins to herself; she and Greg have had a running joke about "turns." She feels that Greg tends to use "it's your turn" (when it is inappropriate) to delay the necessity to respond. This time she has enticed him into contributing to the conversation by requesting that he recall something that happens frequently within the school context. Greg attempts to comply, recalling from memory a favored episodic event—a small victory for both Greg and his teacher.

*The age designation 2:7 means "2 years, 7 months" old.

SOURCE: K.G. Butler, *Language disorders in children* (Austin, TX: Pro-Ed, 1986), pp. 13–14, 16–17, 19, 23, 28–29. Reprinted with permission.

STRATEGIES FOR ASSESSMENT AND INTERVENTION

Two general strategies of language assessment are (1) to determine, in as much detail as possible, what the child's current language abilities are, and (2) to observe the ease and speed with which the child learns new language skills (Ruscello, 2001). The first strategy typically involves use of standardized testing, nonstandardized testing, developmental scales, and behavioral observations. Standardized testing has many dangers and is not always useful in planning an intervention program, but it can sometimes be helpful in making crude comparisons of the child's abilities in certain areas. Development scales are ratings or observations that may be completed by direct observation, or based on memory or records of developmental milestones. Nonstandardized tests and behavioral observations are nonnormative in nature, but they may yield the most important assessment information. The subjective judgment of an experienced clinician based on observation of

TABLE 8.3   Language Learning Requirements and the Difficulties of Children with Language Impairment*

Requirements	Language Impairment						
	Mental Retardation	Language Learning Disability	Specific Language Impairment	Autism	Traumatic Brain Injury	Expressive Language Delay	Neglect/ Abuse
Perception	×	×	×	×	×		
Attention		×		×	×		
Use of symbols	×	×	×	×	×	×	×
Use of language rules	×	×	×	×		×	
Overall mental ability	×		×		×		×
Social interaction related to communication				×			

*× represents problem areas in language learning and use.

SOURCE: From R.E. Owens, *Language disorders: A functional approach to assessment and intervention* (2nd ed.). Copyright © 1995 by Allyn & Bacon. Reprinted/adapted by permission.

the child's language in a variety of environments and circumstances may provide the most useful basis for intervention. Because language disorders vary widely in nature and are seen in individuals ranging from early childhood through old age, assessment and intervention are never simple and are always idiosyncratic (Gillam & Hoffman, 2001; Nelson, 1998; Ruscello, 2001).

An intervention plan must consider the content, form, social context, and use of language. That is, it must consider:

1. What the child talks about and should be taught to talk about
2. How the child talks about things and how he or she could be taught to speak of those things more intelligibly
3. How the child functions in the context of his or her linguistic community
4. How the child uses language and how his or her use of it could be made to serve the purposes of communication and socialization more effectively

The causes of communication disorders may be linked to other disabilities, however, many disorders of communication cannot be attributed to specific causes, and must simply be dealt with according to presenting symptoms. ■

In arranging a training sequence, one might base instruction on the normal sequence of language development. Other sequences of instruction might be more effective, however, since children with language disorders obviously have not learned in the normal way and research suggests that different sequences of learning may be more effective. It is more and more apparent that effective language intervention must occur in the child's natural environment and involve parents and classroom teachers, not just speech-language pathologists (Muller, 2000; Nelson, 1998; Prizant, 1999).

The increasing inclusion of children with all types of disabilities in general education means that all teachers must become aware of how they can address language problems in the classroom Throneburg, Calvert, Sturm, Paramboukas, & Paul, 2000). Before discussing the classroom teacher's role in helping students learn to use language more effectively, we consider two special cases: the communication problems of students with delayed language development and students with emotional and behavioral disorders. Other disabilities may present special communication problems as well, and they are discussed in other chapters.

DELAYED LANGUAGE DEVELOPMENT

Children with language disorders may follow the same sequence of development as most children but achieve each skill or milestone at a later-than-average age (review Table 8.2). Some children with language disorders reach final levels of development significantly below those of their peers who do not have disabilities. Still other children may be generally delayed in language development but show great discrepancies in the rate at which they acquire certain features of language.

Some children are "late bloomers" who in time will catch up with their age peers (Owens, 1995; Sowell, 1997). Yet many children whose language development is delayed show a developmental lag that they will not outgrow (Owens, 1997). They are frequently diagnosed as having mental retardation or another developmental disability. Sometimes these children come from environments where they have been deprived of many experiences, including the language stimulation from adults that is required for normal language development, or they have been severely abused or neglected. Regardless of the reasons for a child's delayed language, however, it is important to understand the nature of the delay and to intervene to give him or her the optimal chance of learning to use language effectively.

Some children three years of age or older show no signs that they understand language and do not use language spontaneously. They may make noises, but they use them to communicate in ways that may characterize the communication of infants and toddlers before they have learned speech. In other words, they may use **prelinguistic communication.** For example, they may use gestures or vocal noises to request objects or actions from others, to protest, to request a social routine (e.g., reading), or to greet someone.

When assessing and planning intervention for children with delayed language, it is important to consider what language and nonlanguage behaviors they imitate, what they comprehend, what communication skills they use spontaneously, and what part communication plays in their lives. It is also important, particularly with young children, to provide intervention in contexts in which language is used for normal social interaction. For example, parents or teachers may use a **milieu teaching** approach, "a naturalistic language intervention designed to teach functional language skills" (Kaiser et al., 1995, p. 40). In this approach, teaching is built around the child's interests. When the child requests some action, object, or activity from the adult, the adult prompts the child's language and makes

Prelinguistic communication. Communication through gestures and noises before the child has learned oral language.

Milieu teaching. A naturalistic approach to language intervention in which the goal is to teach functional language skills in a natural environment.

Milieu teaching is an approach that uses naturalistic language to teach function language skills. In this approach, teaching is built around the child's interests. ■

access to what is requested contingent on an attempt to communicate. Milieu teaching is a naturalistic approach, in that it encourages designing interventions that are similar to the conversational interactions that parents and children ordinarily have. Prelinguistic communication may be a good indication of a child's later ability to use language (Calandrella & Wilcox, 2000). The effectiveness of a milieu teaching approach may depend, at least to some extent, on mothers' responsiveness to their children's prelinguistic communication (Yoder & Warren, 2001).

Early intervention with children who have delayed language is critically important for two primary reasons:

1. The older the child is before intervention is begun, the smaller the chance that he or she will acquire effective language skills (other things being equal).
2. Without having functional language, the child cannot become a truly social being (Warren & Abbaduto, 1992). Of all the skills in which a child may be lagging, language—communication—is the most important, as it is the foundation of academic and social learning.

LANGUAGE DISORDERS ASSOCIATED WITH EMOTIONAL AND BEHAVIORAL DISORDERS

Difficulty in using language in social interactions and relationships is now seen as a basic problem in many emotional and behavioral disorders, ranging from social reticence or withdrawal to severe acting out and aggression (Butler, 1999a; Rogers-Adkinson & Griffith, 1999). Young children who have language disorders may have special difficulty in developing skills in social interaction because they do not interpret social circumstances correctly and have difficulty expressing themselves (Guralnick, Connor, Hammond, Gottman, & Kinnish, 1996). Donahue, Hartas, and Cole (1999) provide an example.

In a kindergarten classroom, there are two adjacent (unisex) bathroom doors, each sporting almost identical pumpkin face posters. Almost invisible to the adult eye, one pumpkin has the faintest suggestion of eyelashes (instead of triangle eyes, this pumpkin has rectangles with a jagged top). A boy identified as having a language disorder comes out of this bathroom and goes to his table. Another boy approaches him, saying:

Why did you go to the girls' bathroom? *(pointing to the pumpkin face)*

Huh?

You went to the girls' bathroom.

No—no—. That not girls'.

Yes it is.

No way—boys can too. *(voice rising)*

Yeah, there's a girl pumpkin on it.

But—but . . . that not a girl! *(getting angry)*

Yeah, look at those eyelashes.

But—but . . . NOT! *(Splutters, jumps up and shoves the other boy. The teacher intervenes, and gives the child with the language disorder a time-out for fighting. He sits angrily, muttering to himself, "not a girl!")* (p. 72)

The communication difficulties of students with emotional or behavioral disorders may require special classroom accommodations or programming. First, it is important for teachers of such students to work closely with a speech-language pathologist. Second, special care must be placed on clear teacher-to-student communication, student-to-student communication, and students' self-talk (Audet & Tankersley, 1999).

Perhaps the most important aspect of working with children who have emotional or behavioral problems related to a language disorder is understanding the child's intentions and helping him or her learn to use language to resolve social conflicts and build social relationships. Sowell (1997) provides an example of how a graduate student working in a classroom was able to do this with Billy, a four-year-old.

> Apparently what the graduate student had that the teachers did not always have was common sense and a willingness—and the time—to try to understand a particular child's problem. Billy's biggest problems came out on the playground, where he did not have the skills to negotiate through social encounters. For example, if the graduate student noticed that Billy had his eye on a shovel that another child was using, she would ask him, "Do you want that shovel?" When he nodded, she would then prompt him, "Go ask the child, 'Can I have that shovel please?'" If he was not successful, the graduate student would say, "Ask him, 'Can I have it when you're done?'" Once Billy discovered that using phrases like these in various situations usually got better results than crying, he began to use them on his own. The graduate student also explained to Billy the unspoken social rules of the playground and of life, things that some teachers regard as a nuisance to do. (pp. 59–60)

Language disorders that are associated with emotional or behavioral disorders do not occur only in young children. Older students and adults also may have emotional or behavioral disorders that are in part a consequence of their inability to use language. They may well have language disorders, although their primary diagnosis may be attention deficit hyperactivity disorder, conduct disorder, anxiety disorder, depression, or some other psychiatric designation (Rogers-Adkinson, 1999).

Educational Considerations

Helping children overcome speech and language disorders is not the responsibility of any single profession. Rather, identification is the joint responsibility of the classroom teacher, the speech-language pathologist, and the parents (Nelson, 1997). The teacher can carry

The classroom ought to be a place in which there are continuous opportunities for students and teachers to employ language and obtain feedback in constructive relationships. ■

SUCCESS STORIES
Special Educators at Work

Garden City, NY: College student **Ryan McGarr** has overcome difficulties in speech and language processing as well as problems with memory and organization since being severely injured in a car accident on Thanksgiving Day, 1992. Ryan remained comatose for three days with a traumatic brain injury and fractures to his hip and legs. "I know it happened," says Ryan, "but I still find it hard to believe." His mother, Kathy McGarr, finds it hard to forget. Although Ryan's physical injuries healed quickly, his residual difficulties in language and cognitive processing presented an academic challenge. Fortunately, an innovative special education project came to his assistance, providing a bridge between rehabilitation services and school reentry.

Special educator **Nancy Maher-Maxwell** coordinates the New York State Education Department's TBI (traumatic brain injury) Project for the Board of Cooperative Educational Services of Nassau County. Hospitals, rehabilitation centers, and school districts know to give her name to families who face the maze of issues following their children's head injuries. Since 1991, the project has coordinated services to support families and train teachers to meet the individual needs of students reentering their classrooms.

Kathy McGarr is grateful that someone at the hospital told her about the project: "Just the trauma and trying to take care of your other children—the whole family tends to fall apart. I didn't have the concentration or anything to deal with this." Nancy Maher-Maxwell understands this: "Research is showing that kids who have this connection between rehabilitation and school reentry, as well as the

ongoing staff support once they've returned, have a greater success rate than those who don't. The gulf between rehabilitation and school reentry is too big for families to have to negotiate on their own."

In Ryan's case, several factors combined to make a successful outcome possible, including coordinated services, compensatory instructional strategies, strong support from family and friends, spontaneous neurological recovery, and his own spirit and desire to achieve.

Others were aware of this determination, too. His mother recalls, "The psychologist at the hospital, who evaluated Ryan nine weeks after the accident, told me he would probably never finish school and that I was overwhelming him with academics. But it was what he wanted and I had to let him try to do it." Nancy Maher-Maxwell met Ryan six weeks after the accident and remembers his using crutches and

out specific suggestions for individual cases. By listening attentively and empathetically when children speak, providing appropriate models of speech and language for children to imitate, and encouraging children to use their communication skills appropriately, the classroom teacher can help not only to improve speech and language but also to prevent disorders from developing in the first place.

The primary role of the classroom teacher is to facilitate the *social use of language*. Phonology, morphology, syntax, and semantics are certainly important. Yet the fact that a student has a language disorder does not necessarily mean the teacher or clinician must intensify efforts to teach the student about the form, structure, or content of language. Rather, language must be taught as a way of solving problems by making oneself understood and making sense of what other people say.

The classroom offers many possibilities for language learning. It should be a place in which there are almost continuous opportunities for students and teachers to employ language and obtain feedback in constructive relationships. Language is the basic medium through which most academic and social learning takes place in school. Nevertheless, the language of school, in both classrooms and textbooks, is often a problem for students and teachers (Nelson, 1998; Owens, 1995).

School language is more formal than the language many children use at home and

speaking in a slow, monotone voice. He said he was determined to graduate with his class and wanted tutoring.

To start the process, Nancy contacted Ryan's school district. His former English teacher, Maria Webster, agreed to be his home tutor. Despite Ryan's memory problems and slowness in learning, Maria was optimistic; she remembered Ryan as an expressive writer. With Nancy's help, Maria's lessons were individualized, concentrating on vocabulary and word meanings. She used flash cards and, together with Ryan, made up funny sentences using mnemonics to help him remember information. Instead of giving him a chapter to read in history, Maria "chunked" the material to be learned, breaking it into smaller units. Ryan remembers that being helpful: "It used to be that I even had to reread novels two or three times just to get the meaning."

Kathy McGarr recalls that it was hard to tell if Ryan would regain his language abilities. "In speech therapy, he had a terrible time with categorization skills. His therapist asked him to name five green vegetables, and he couldn't do it! What was even more surprising was that he couldn't imagine that anyone could!"

Ryan returned to school part-time in April 1993. He went to an outpatient rehab for therapies in the morning and then to his local public high school in the afternoon for English, social studies, art, and resource room. He returned full-time for his senior year, carrying a full program of academic courses, with resource room support for forty-five minutes daily.

The TBI project coordinated Ryan's reentry into the regular educational environment by providing inservice workshops as well as personal and continual support for his teachers. They were alerted to changes in Ryan's cognitive processing, such as his memory for sequences used in multistep problem solving. Training emphasized Ryan's need to take in new information in a variety of ways, so teachers were shown techniques to reinforce study skills, like taking notes on lectures, outlining chapters, and organizing projects. As Nancy Maher-Maxwell explains, "Often, the typical high school teacher will lecture on the subject, expect the kids to take good notes, and evaluate them on a test. Because of the disruptions in the learning systems of students with TBI, there may be a slower rate in processing, so extended time is often necessary both in teaching and in testing."

TBI is an acquired injury that demands new adjustments. "If I hadn't spoken with Nancy," says Kathy McGarr, "I wouldn't have known to put Ryan in a resource room, since he never needed special education before." Head injuries can also make the future hard to predict. Nancy recalls, "That early neuropsychological evaluation that said he could forget about his academic aspirations never took into account Ryan's determination and the compensatory strategies that special education could provide. It was devastating to everybody—and look how wrong such a prediction can be with TBI!"

Ryan has been fortunate. He spontaneously regained much of his academic strength, and now he can see how far he has come: "When I look back, I realize how slow I was as a result of the head injury." Ryan still finds that he is more easily distracted than he used to be, and he continues to need extended time on some college exams. Nevertheless, he has emerged confident: "I'll succeed in the world doing whatever I want to do. I have no doubts about that."

—By Jean Crockett

with playmates. It is structured discourse, in which listeners and speakers or readers and writers must learn to be clear and expressive, to convey and interpret essential information quickly and easily. Without skill in using the language of school, a child is certain to fail academically, and virtually certain to be socially unsuccessful as well.

Teachers need the assistance of speech-language specialists in assessing their students' language disabilities and in devising interventions. Part of the assessment and intervention strategy must also examine the language of the teacher. Problems in classroom discourse involve how teachers talk to students as well as how students use language. Learning how to be clear, relevant, and informative and how to hold listeners' attention are not only problems for students with language disorders but also problems for their teachers. Table 8.4 on page 282 lists some general guidelines for how parents and teachers should interact with students to facilitate language development.

One example of the role of the teacher's language in classroom discourse is asking questions. Blank and White (1986) note that teachers often ask students questions in areas of their identified weaknesses. For example, a teacher might ask a preschooler who does not know colors to identify colors repeatedly. Unfortunately, teachers may not know how to modify their questions to teach concepts effectively, so their questions merely add to children's confusion.

The following exchange between a teacher and a child diagnosed as having difficulties with problem solving and causal reasoning illustrates this point:

Teacher: How could grass in a jungle get on fire?

Child: 'Cause they (*referring to animals*) have to stay in the jungle.

Teacher: (*in an incredulous tone*) You mean the grass gets on fire because the animals stay in the jungle?

Child: Yeah.

Teacher: I don't think so. What if there was a fire in somebody's house—

Child: (*interrupting*) Then they're dead, or hurt.

Teacher: Yeah, they'd be hurt. But how would a fire start in somebody's house?

Child: By starting something with matches.

Teacher: A match, okay. Now do you think this could have started with a match?

Child: Yeah.

Teacher: This fire in the jungle? Who would have a match in the jungle? The animals?

Child: A monkey.

Teacher: A monkey would have a match in the jungle?

Child: (*nodding*) I saw that on TV. (Blank & White, 1986, p. 4.)

RESPONSIVE INSTRUCTION

Meeting the Needs of Students with Communication Disorders

Working with the Speech-Language Pathologist

What Is a Speech Language Pathologist?

A speech-language pathologist (SLP) is a specialist in the assessment, treatment, and prevention of communication disorders. Many SLPs work with specific populations or disorders, such as early childhood language development, learning disabilities, developmental delays, autism, articulation/phonology, fluency, voice, swallowing, and acquired brain injury.

Tasks of the SLP can include:

- Administering screening instruments and making recommendations for treatment;
- Adapting interviewing and testing procedures to meet the needs of a student;
- Assisting teachers and other school professionals as to how to identify children who are at risk for developing problems;
- Working with professionals to help prevent problems before they occur by promoting opportunities for success with spoken and written language at home and school;

- Collaborating with other professionals (e.g., classroom teacher, special educator, administration) on issues relevant to case management and service delivery; and
- Providing direct and indirect services. (American Speech-Language-Hearing Association, 2001)

Supporting Speech and Language Goals in the Classroom

Traditionally, SLPs have provided services in a clinical, pull-out model. Students on their caseload would come to them to receive intense, directed therapy. Shifts in ideological perspectives toward inclusion, however, are changing that service delivery model. This trend translates into more therapy being conducted within the classroom (Erhen, 2000). Similar to the tensions that exist in the delivery of special education services within general education settings, SLPs must learn to balance the advantages of creating therapy that is responsive to edu-

After seventeen more exchanges, the teacher gave up.

Alternative question-asking strategies can be used to help students think through problems successfully. When a student fails to answer a higher-order question because it is beyond his or her level of information or skill, the teacher should reformulate the problem at a simpler level. After the intermediate steps are solved, the teacher can return to the question that was too difficult at first, as illustrated by the following dialogue:

Adult: Why do we use tape for hanging pictures?
Child: 'Cause it's shiny.
Adult: Here's a shiny piece of paper and here's a shiny piece of tape. Let's try them both. Try hanging the picture with the shiny paper.
Child: (*does it*)
Adult: Does it work?
Child: No, it's falling.
Adult: Now, try the tape.
Child: (*does it*)
Adult: Does it work?
Child: Yeah, it's not falling.
Adult: So, why do we use the tape for hanging pictures?
Child: It won't fall. (Blank & White, 1986, p. 5)

cational demands with the disadvantages of potentially "watering down" the therapy (Erhen, 2000).

In order to maximize therapy opportunities within classroom settings, SLPs should clearly define their role within the classroom. Role definition should include specific ways in which the SLP will deliver educationally relevant therapy. A guideline for SLPs to follow is:

In providing in-classroom services, the speech-language pathologist's primary responsibility should consist of providing therapeutic services for students on the caseload who need direct service and assisting classroom teachers to meet the needs of these students and others on the caseload who need indirect services. (Erhen, 2000, p. 223)

Examples of therapeutic activities that can be provided in the classroom directly by the SLP include using the classroom text (science, social studies, language arts, etc.) to identify vocabulary, metaphors, idioms, or other language-related concepts; teaching language strategies to all students, while providing cues or guides for students on the caseload to use; and working on therapy goals with a small group of students who may or may not all be on the caseload (Erhen, 2000).

In addition to having the SLP work directly with the classroom, general and special education teachers can support speech and language goals on their own. Through observation, consultation, and collaboration with the SLP, classroom teachers can develop a repertoire of strategies that will maintain the work of the SLP.

Possible strategies may include:

- Developing vocabulary through encouraging naming and describing;
- Promoting comprehension through teaching plot structure, predicting, summarizing strategies, and retelling;
- Creating spelling or reading word lists related to specific articulation goals of a student;
- Connecting speech and written language through having students state responses as well as write them;
- Providing drill and practice in naming objects, following directions, answering questions about stories, etc.;
- Fostering compensatory language skills such as using gestures or writing support or supplant oral communication; or
- Integrating strategies taught by the SLP to encourage language skills such as initiating of conversation, turn-taking, or clarifying communication needs. (American Speech-Language-Hearing Association, 2001)

In summary, many speech and language goals can be addressed within the classroom setting. By understanding the necessary therapeutic role of the SLP, classroom teachers can collaborate with SLPs to identify opportunities for optimal service delivery.

—*By Kristin Sayeski*

TABLE 8.4   Guidelines for Parents' and Teachers' Interactive Styles

1. Talk about things in which the child is interested.
2. Follow the child's lead. Reply to the child's initiations and comments. Share his excitement.
3. Don't ask too many questions. If you must, use questions such as *how did/do . . . , why did/do . . . , and what happened . . .* that result in longer explanatory answers.
4. Encourage the child to ask questions. Respond openly and honestly. If you don't want to answer a question, say so and explain why. (*I don't think I want to answer that question; it's very personal.*)
5. Use a pleasant tone of voice. You need not be a comedian, but you can be light and humorous. Children love it when adults are a little silly.
6. Don't be judgmental or make fun of a child's language. If you are overly critical of the child's language or try to "shotgun" all errors, he will stop talking to you.
7. Allow enough time for the child to respond.
8. Treat the child with courtesy by not interrupting when he is talking.
9. Include the child in family and classroom discussions. Encourage participation and listen to his ideas.
10. Be accepting of the child and of the child's language. Hugs and acceptance can go a long way.
11. Provide opportunities for the child to use language and to have that language work for him to accomplish his goals.

SOURCE: From R. E. Owens, *Language disorders: A functional approach to assessment and intervention* (2nd ed.). Copyright © 1995 by Allyn & Bacon. Reprinted/adapted by permission.

Teachers sometimes do not clearly express their intent in questioning students or fail to explicitly delimit the topic of their questions. Consequently, students become confused. Teachers must learn to clarify the problems under such circumstances. As Blank and White (1986) note, "Teachers do not establish psychological comfort and eagerness to learn by making students spend as much, if not more, energy deciphering the intent than the content of their questions" (p. 8). Teachers must also give unambiguous feedback to students' responses to their questions. Too often, teachers do not tell students explicitly that their answers are wrong, for fear of showing nonacceptance. Lack of accurate, explicit feedback, however, prevents students from learning the concepts involved in instruction.

Our points here are these:

1. The teacher's role is not merely to instruct students *about* language but also to teach them *how to use it*. More specifically, the teacher must help students learn *how to use language in the context of the classroom.*
2. The teacher's own use of language is a key factor in helping students learn effectively, *especially if students have language disorders.*

Teachers need to keep in mind, too, that language disorders can change with the child's development. Just because a child has receptive or expressive language within the normal range at one age does not mean that it will be within the same range at a later age. Figure 8.1 shows the changes with age for Troy, a child whose language problems Plante and Beeson (1999) describe at various ages. Language intervention may change the nature and course of a child's language abilities, but even with therapy a child may have language problems that are persistent. Notice that Troy, who received speech-language services, did not achieve expressive language abilities close to the normal range until age 14, and that only then did his expressive language ability exceed his receptive ability.

Written language is a special problem for many students with language disorders. In fact, as students progress through the grades, written language takes on increasing importance. Students are expected to read increasingly complex and difficult material and understand its meaning. In addition, they are expected to express themselves

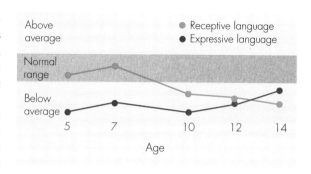

more clearly in writing. The interactions teachers have with students about their writing—the questions they ask to help students understand how to write for their readers—are critical to overcoming disabilities in written language (Graham, Harris, MacArthur, & Schwartz, 1998)

Finally, we note that intervention in language disorders employs many of the same strategies used in intervention in learning disabilities (Mann, 1998; Plante & Beeson, 1999; Seidenberg, 1997). As discussed earlier, the definitions of *specific language disability* and *specific learning disability* are parallel, if not nearly synonymous. Metacognitive training, strategy training, and other approaches that we discuss in Chapter 6 are typically appropriate for use with students who have language disorders (see also Hallahan, Kauffman, & Lloyd, 1999; Wallach & Butler, 1994).

FIGURE 8.1

For children with developmental language disorders, the components of language can change over time. Here we can see receptive and expressive language skills shift over time in a single child relative to typically developing peers.

SOURCE: From Plante, E., & Beeson, P.M. (1999). *Communication and communication disorders: A clinical introduction.* Boston: Allyn & Bacon, p. 155. Copyright © 1999. Reprinted/adapted by permission by Allyn & Bacon.

Communication Variations

As defined earlier in this chapter (see the box on p. 267), *communication variations* include language that is unique to a particular region, ethnic group, or other cultural group. Thus, the fact that a student does not use the language expected in school does not necessarily mean that she or he has a language disorder.

The most important question for a child whose speech or language is different from the standard or expected is whether he or she is an effective communicator in his or her speech and language community. The speech or language of African American children, for example, might mistakenly be judged to indicate disorder when it is merely different from the standard American English. "For purposes of assessing communication disorders, the important question is whether African American children have acquired the dialect (language) of their speech community" (Seymour, Abdulkarim, & Johnson, 1999, p. 75). Oetting and McDonald (2001) noted that differences in Southern White English (SWE) and Southern African American English (SAAE) may lead to the misdiagnosis of specific language impairment (SLI) in either Caucasian or African American children. Of course, an individual may both have a language disorder and exhibit a variation that is not a disorder; such an individual will be unable to communicate effectively even with others who use the same language variation (see Oetting & McDonald, 2001).

Encouraging the communication of children whose cultural heritage or language patterns are not those of the professionals' microculture is of increasing concern to classroom teachers and speech-language clinicians. (See Chapter 3 for a discussion of microculture.) On the one hand, care must be taken not to mistake a cultural or ethnic difference for a disorder; on the other

A child may not have a language disorder yet have a communication difference that demands special teaching. Such differences might be related to culture and/or disability. ∎

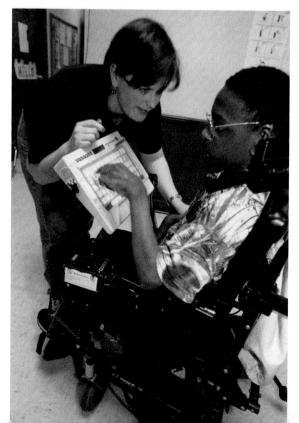

Collaboration and Co-Teaching with Speech-Language Pathologists

"Answer me, Amanda. What? Has the cat got your tongue?"

Though throwaway lines like the one in this title seem to be harmless, to some students with communication disorders this statement brings on feelings of fear, shame, and anxiety. Simple misunderstandings during discussion, reluctance to respond to questions for which they have the answers, and an ability to interpret directions are all problems students may have if they have communication disorders. These characteristics may be incorrectly interpreted by the general classroom teacher. The teacher may think that student is disrespectful, "not getting it," or "hears when he wants to." Language delays are a thread that runs through many disabilities, not just communication disorders. For these reasons, collaboration with a speech-language pathologist or language interventionist is so important for students with communication disorders and their teachers.

What Does It Mean to Be a Teacher of Students with Communication Disorders?

What is a speech-language pathologist? According to the American Speech-Language-Hearing Association (ASHA),

Speech-Language Pathologists help people develop their communication abilities and treat speech, language, and voice disorders. Their services include prevention, identification, evaluation, treatment, and rehabilitation of communication disorders. They

- conduct research to develop new and better ways to diagnose and remediate speech/language problems
- work with children who have language delays and speech problems
- provide treatment to people who stutter and to those with voice and articulation problems
- aid people with foreign or regional accents who want to learn another speech style (www.asha.org/about/)

ASHA, not the Council for Exceptional Children, is the professional organization that oversees the certification of speech-language pathologists. This organization has established a set of standards for the newly trained pathologist. The Certificate of Clinical Competence (CCC) is only given for those with master's or doctoral degrees. The CCC includes requirements in basic science courses, professional course-

hand, disorders existing in the context of a language difference must not be overlooked (Nelson, 1998; Ortiz, 1997; Seymour et al., 1999; Van Keulen, Weddington, & DeBose, 1998). When assessing children's language, the professional must be aware of the limitations of normative tests and other sources of potential bias.

A child may not have a language disorder yet have a communicative difference that demands special teaching. Delpit (1995) and Van Keulen et al. (1998) discuss the need for teaching children of nondominant cultures the rules for effective communication in the dominant culture while understanding and accepting the effectiveness of the children's home languages in their cultural contexts. Failure to teach children the skills they need to communicate effectively according to the rules of the dominant culture will deny them many opportunities. In effect, children of minority language groups may need to learn to live in two worlds—one in which their home language is used and one in which school language is used (Westby & Roman, 1995).

Nelson (1998) and Butler (1999b) note that many students for whom language difference is an issue do not speak entirely different languages, but variations peculiar to certain groups of speakers—that is, *dialects*. For example, one dialect that is different from standard English (and is not a language disorder) is Appalachian English. People in Appalachia speak a variation of English with features not shared by other English dialects. Teachers must understand—and help their students understand—that other dialects are not inferior or limited language systems (Oetting & McDonald, 2001; Seymour, Champion, & Jackson, 1995; Van Keulen et al., 1998). Furthermore, cultural differences must be recognized regardless of the communication device being used. Multicultural issues arise in all communication interactions, including those in which augmentative or alternative communication is used (Soto, Huer, & Taylor, 1997).

Researchers have given attention to how the language of different cultural groups is

work, 375 clock hours of supervised clinical observation/ practice, a clinical fellowship, and a national exam. These requirements include a tremendous amount of coursework in the basics of physiology and audiology, evaluation, and remediation of speech problems.

Successful Strategies for Collaboration

Speech-language pathologists are encouraged to participate in a variety of collaborative structures, such as co-teaching and collaborative consultation. According to McCormick, Loeb, and Schiefelbusch (1997), the speech-language pathologist or language interventionist has the following responsibilities to general educators:

1. Provide information about normal speech and language development.
2. Provide information about delays and disorders of speech, language, or communication.
3. Collect information about speech, language, and communication strengths and intervention needs to maximize participation in the classroom and other school settings.
4. Interpret assessment information to others and help to develop intervention goals and objectives, plan activities, and select appropriate methods and materials.
5. Provide direct instruction for specific speech, language, and communication skills to individuals and small groups.
6. Demonstrate for, teach, and assist others to imple-

ment language and communication intervention procedures.
7. Participate in decision making related to provision of augmentative and alternative communication devices.
8. Evaluate and monitor student progress and program effectiveness.
9. Work collaboratively with others to promote student participation in age-appropriate activities and natural environments. (p. 167)

The general education classroom is one of the environments in which students with language problems must generalize the individual skills they are taught by speech-language pathologists, whether they receive instruction in these skills in that classroom or in separate settings. Therefore, the speech-language pathologist can work with the general education teacher, quite often through the special education teacher, to let that teacher know the specific implications of the speech or language disorder on a student's performance in the classroom. The pathologist can also provide guidance in identifying components of a general educator's instruction that may be causing problems and can help modify those components. And, finally, the speech-language pathologist can work with the general educator to monitor a student's progress, celebrate victories, and work toward a student's independence. For more information, see the American Speech-Language-Hearing Association Web site at www.asha.org.

—By Margaret P. Weiss

related to school learning. Westby (1994) notes that different cultural groups provide very different language environments for infants and young children. However, these differences are more often matters of social class than ethnicity. "Socioeconomic status is more critical to the development of language than race or ethnicity" (Anderson & Battle, 1993, p. 180).

Families also differ greatly in the ways they talk to children and in the language they expect children to use. Conversational interactions—called **narratives**—differ widely in families. Narratives can be classified as **genres,** which are purposes or plans for discourse—for example, to recount recent events, to explain the reason for doing something, or to tell an imaginative story.

Children's experiences with language prior to coming to school are an important factor in determining how they respond to the language demands of the classroom. Although students may not have language *disorders,* their language *variations* may put them at a disadvantage in using language in an academic context. Consequently, some have suggested that children who come to school without mastery of the English of their textbooks should be taught it directly and consistently (e.g., Raspberry, 2001). Consider the cultural variations across narrative genres described by Westby (1994) in Table 8.5 on page 287. The major implication of these differences is that teachers must be able to understand linguistic variations and help students generate narratives through skillful questioning that will help them comprehend and learn to use the language of school. Seymour et al. (1999) recommend that teachers do two things:

1. Understand, accept, and support the dialects that their students bring to school
2. Adapt and devise strategies that accommodate the language backgrounds of their students

Narrative.
Self-controlled, self-initiated discourse; description or storytelling.

Genre.
A plan or map for discourse; type of narrative discourse.

Meeting the Needs of Students with Communication Disorders

Collaboration in an Inner-City Classroom

What the Research Says

Research on early language ability has demonstrated a correlation between early language development and later reading ability (Snow, Burns, & Griffin, 1998). Children from low income homes, with identified language impairments, or who have difficulty speaking English face considerable challenges in learning to read (Snow et al., 1998; Stothard et al., 1998; Walker, Greenwood, Hart, & Carta, 1994).

Given the fact that many inner-city school districts have disproportionately high numbers of students who fall into one of the above "risk factors," school personnel are constantly seeking ways to mediate these risks. Recommendations from professional organizations encourage collaboration among professionals in order to capitalize on specific areas of strength and provide connected interventions across settings. In the area of language, the America Speech-Language-Hearing Association, the professional organization of speech-language pathologists, recommends that speech-language pathologists and the classroom teachers collaborate to intensity language instruction within general education classrooms (American Speech-Language-Hearing Association, 1991).

Research Study

One team of researchers explored the effectiveness of a collaborative, classroom-based intervention to improve the vocabulary and phonological awareness of inner-city kindergartners and first graders (Hadley, Simmerman, Long, & Luna, 2000). Eighty-three percent of the students in this school district were eligible for free or reduced-cost lunch—a marker for low socioeconomic status. In addition, 28 percent of the students were considered limited English proficient.

For the study, four general education classrooms were selected. Two classrooms served as the control groups (i.e., received no intervention) and two served at the experimental groups (i.e., received the intervention). The intervention consisted of the speech-language patholo-

gist teaching language-related lessons two and a half days per week and regularly collaborating with the general education teacher to develop other language-based activities to integrate throughout the day. The control classes followed standard instructional practices with no collaboration or teaching from the speech-language pathologist.

Research Findings

Following the six-month intervention, students in the experimental groups demonstrated greater gains in the areas of receptive vocabulary, expressive vocabulary, beginning sound awareness, and letter-sound associations when compared to students in the control group. Additionally, the findings demonstrated that both native English speakers and students with nonnative backgrounds benefited from the intensive vocabulary and phonemic awareness instruction.

The study demonstrated the ability of speech-language pathologists to collaborate successfully with general education teachers. This collaboration facilitated the teaching of explicit skills within educationally relevant communication and curricular activities.

Applying the Research to Teaching

The results of this study demonstrate potential benefits of collaboration between speech-language pathologists and general educators. Critical are:

- Creating time for joint planning so that intervention activities are planned and roles are clearly established;
- Identifying specific goals to be addressed and allocating intervention activities by expertise;
- Modeling on the part of the speech-language pathologist so that the classroom teacher can use the strategies throughout the day, not just when the speech-language pathologist is present. (Hadley, Simmerman, Long, & Luna, 2000)

—By Kristin L. Sayeski

TABLE 8.5   Cultural Variations in Narrative Genres

Genre	Culture				
	Mainstream	**Mexican American**	**Chinese American**	**White Working Class**	**Black Working Class**
Recounts (Tell Daddy about our trip to . . .)	Common with young children Open-ended scaffolding Invitations to recount decrease with age	Rare	Rare	Predominant genre Tightly scaffolded	Rare
Accounts (Did you hear what happened to . . . ?)	Begun before two years Adults request further explanation Adults suggest alternative outcomes Adults assess attitudes and actions of actor	Frequent Occur especially in family gathering	At home; asked about events of day Not outside the home or with strangers	Not until school Must be accurate Privilege of older adults	Frequent in response to teasing Exaggeration values May be produced cooperatively
Eventcasts (I'm putting the soda in the chest, and then I'll load the car.)	Begun with preverbal Continue throughout the preschool	Almost never in daily events Family may cooperatively plan future events	Occur during ongoing activities More frequent for girls than boys	In play with young children In planning family projects with older children	Rare
Stories (Once upon a time . . .)	Frequent story reading Story comprehension negotiated Produce own imaginative stories	Bruja tales Stories about real events embellished with new details and about historical figures and events Children's literature absent	Tales about historical people and events Prefer informational rather than fictional books	Listen to stories read Comprehension not negotiated	No children's storybooks

SOURCE: From C. E. Westby, "The effects of culture and genre, structure, and style of oral and written texts," in *Language learning disabilities in school-age children and adolescents: Some principles and applications,* edited by G.P. Wallach & K.G. Butler. Copyright © 1994 by Allyn & Bacon. Reprinted/adapted by permission.

A major concern today in both special and general education is teaching children who are learning English as a second language (ESL), who are non-English proficient (NEP), or who have limited English proficiency (LEP). Bilingual education is a field of concern and controversy because of the rapidly changing demographics in many American communities (see Butler, 1999b; Nelson, 1998). Spanish-speaking children comprise a rapidly growing percentage of the students in many school districts. Moreover, a large number of Asian/Pacific children have immigrated to the United States during the past decade. Many of these children have no proficiency or limited proficiency in English, and some have disabilities as well. Bilingual special education is still "an emerging discipline with a brief history" (Baca & Amato, 1989, p. 168). As we discussed in Chapter 3, finding the best way to teach children to become proficient in English, particularly when they have disabilities as well as language differences, is a special challenge for the new century.

Speech Disorders

As we noted at the beginning of the chapter, speech disorders include disorders of voice, articulation, and fluency. Remember that an individual may have more than one speech disorder and that speech and language disorders sometimes occur together.

We provide only brief descriptions of the major speech disorders for two reasons:

1. Compared to language disorders, speech disorders pose a much smaller problem for classroom teachers.
2. Most speech disorders will be treated primarily by speech-language pathologists, not classroom teachers. Teachers are expected to be aware of possible speech disorders and to refer students they suspect of having such disorders for evaluation by speech-language pathologists. Furthermore, teachers are expected to work with speech-language pathologists to help students correct speech as well as language disorders in the classroom (see the box on p. 284).

VOICE DISORDERS

People's voices are perceived as having pitch, loudness, and quality. Changes in pitch and loudness are part of the stress patterns of speech. Vocal quality is related not only to production of speech sounds but also to the nonlinguistic aspects of speech.

Voice disorders, though difficult to define precisely, are characteristics of pitch, loudness, and/or quality that are abusive of the **larynx;** hamper communication; or are perceived as markedly different from what is customary for someone of a given age, sex, and cultural background (Robinson & Crowe, 2001). Voice disorders can result from a variety of biological and nonbiological causes, including growths in the larynx (e.g., nodules, polyps, or cancerous tissue), infections of the larynx (laryngitis), damage to the nerves supplying the larynx, or accidental bruises or scratches on the larynx (Haynes & Pindzola, 1998). Misuse or abuse of the voice also can lead to a quality that is temporarily abnormal. High school cheerleaders, for example, frequently develop temporary voice disorders (Campbell, Reich, Klockars, & McHenry, 1988). Disorders resulting from misuse or abuse

Larynx.
The structure in the throat containing the vocal apparatus (vocal cords); laryngitis is a temporary loss of voice caused by inflammation of the larynx.

Most speech disorders will be treated primarily by speech-language pathologists, not classroom teachers. Teachers should be aware of possible speech disorders in order to be able to refer students properly. ■

The Speech-Language Pathologist

A speech-language pathologist is a highly trained professional capable of assuming a variety of roles in assisting persons who have speech and language disorders. Entering the profession requires rigorous training and demonstration of clinical skills under close supervision. Certification requires completion of a master's degree in a program approved by the American Speech-Language-Hearing Association (ASHA). You may want to write to ASHA, 10801 Rockville Pike, Rockville, MD 20852 for a free booklet, *Careers in Speech-Language Pathology and Audiology.*

Because of the emphasis on *least restrictive environment,* or mainstreaming (see Chapters 1 and 2), speech-language pathologists are doing more of their work in regular classrooms and are spending more time consulting with classroom teachers than they have in the past.

Speech-language pathologists of the future will need more knowledge of classroom procedures and the academic curriculum—especially in reading, writing, and spelling—and will be more involved in the overall education of children with communication disorders. More emphasis will be placed on working as a team member in the schools to see that children with disabilities obtain appropriate educations. Because of legislation and changing population demographics, speech-language pathologists of the future will also probably be more involved with preschool children and those with learning disabilities and severe, multiple disabilities. There will be broader concern for the entire range of communication disorders, including both oral and written communication.

You may want to explore ASHA online at www.professional.asha.org.

---

can damage the tissues of the larynx. Sometimes a person has psychological problems that lead to a complete loss of voice (aphonia) or to severe voice abnormalities.

Voice disorders having to do with **resonance**—vocal quality—may be caused by physical abnormalities of the oral cavity (such as **cleft palate**) or damage to the brain or nerves controlling the oral cavity. Infections of the tonsils, adenoids, or sinuses can also influence how the voice is resonated. Most people who have severe hearing loss typically have problems in achieving a normal or pleasingly resonant voice. Finally, sometimes a person simply has not learned to speak with an appropriately resonant voice. There are no biological or deep-seated psychological reasons for the problem; rather, it appears that she or he has learned faulty habits of positioning the organs of speech (Moore & Hicks, 1994).

When children are screened for speech and language disorders, the speech-language pathologist is looking for problems in voice quality, resonance, pitch, loudness, and duration. If a problem is found, referral to a physician is indicated. A medical report may indicate that surgery or other treatment is needed because of a growth or infection. Aside from the medical evaluation, the speech-language pathologist will evaluate when the problem began and how the individual uses his or her voice in everyday situations and under stressful circumstances. Besides looking for how voice is produced and structural or functional problems, the pathologist also looks for signs of infection or disease that may be contributing to the disorder as well as for signs of serious illness.

ARTICULATION DISORDERS

Articulation disorders involve errors in producing words. Word sounds may be omitted, substituted, distorted, or added. Lisping, for example, involves a substitution or distortion of the [s] sound (e.g., *thunthine* or *shunshine* for *sunshine*). Missing, substituted, added, or poorly produced word sounds may make a speaker difficult to understand or even unintelligible. Such errors in speech production may also carry heavy social penalties, subjecting the speaker to teasing or ridicule.

Resonance.
The quality of the sound imparted by the size, shape, and texture of the organs in the vocal tract.

Cleft palate.
A condition in which there is a rift or split in the upper part of the oral cavity; may include the upper lip (cleft lip).

𝒢𝒲 For information about cleft lip, cleft palate, and other cranio-facial deformities and effects on speech, see SMILES at www.cleft.org ∎

When are articulation errors considered a disorder? That depends on a clinician's subjective judgment, which will be influenced by her or his experience, the number and types of errors, the consistency of these errors, the age and developmental characteristics of the speaker, and the intelligibility of the person's speech.

Young children make frequent errors in speech sounds when they are learning to talk. Many children do not master all the phonological rules of the language and learn to produce all the speech sounds correctly until they are eight or nine years old. Furthermore, most children make frequent errors until after they enter school. The age of the child is thus a major consideration in judging the adequacy of articulation. Another major consideration is the phonological characteristics of the child's community, because children learn speech largely through imitation. For instance, a child reared in the deep South may have speech that sounds peculiar to residents of Long Island, but that does not mean that the child has a speech disorder.

The number of children having difficulty producing word sounds decreases markedly during the first three or four years of elementary school. Among children with other disabilities, especially mental retardation and neurological disorders like cerebral palsy, the prevalence of articulation disorders is higher than in the general population (Schwartz, 1994).

Lack of ability to articulate speech sounds correctly can be caused by biological factors. For example, brain damage or damage to the nerves controlling the muscles used in speech may make it difficult or impossible to articulate sounds (Bernthal & Bankson, 1998; Cannito, Yorkston, & Beukelman, 1998). Furthermore, abnormalities of the oral structures, such as a cleft palate, may make normal speech difficult or impossible. Relatively minor structural changes, such as loss of teeth, may produce temporary errors. Delayed phonological development may also result from a hearing loss.

The parents of a preschool child may refer him or her for assessment if he or she has speech that is really difficult to understand. Most schools screen all new pupils for speech and language problems, and in most cases a child who still makes many articulation errors in the third or fourth grade will be referred for evaluation. Older children and adults sometimes seek help on their own when their speech draws negative attention. A speech-language pathologist will assess not only phonological characteristics but also social and developmental history, hearing, general language ability, and speech mechanism.

Although speech-language pathologists' interest in articulation disorders has appeared to decrease in recent years, with more attention being given to language, persistent articulation disorders may have serious long-term consequences. The decision about whether to include a child in an intervention program will depend on her or his age, other developmental characteristics, and the type and consistency of the articulatory errors (Williams, 2001). Articulation disorders are often accompanied by other disorders of speech or language; thus, the child may need intervention in multiple aspects of communication (Bauman-Waengler, 2000; Hodson & Edwards, 1997; Nelson, 1998). The decision will also depend on the pathologist's assessment of the likelihood that the child will self-correct the errors and of the social penalties, such as teasing and shyness, the child is experiencing. If he or she misarticulates only a few sounds but does so consistently and suffers social embarrassment or rejection as a consequence, an intervention program is usually called for.

FLUENCY DISORDERS

More information about stuttering is available at the following sites: National Center for Stuttering at www.stuttering.com and the Stuttering Foundation of America at www.stuttersfa.org ■

Normal speech is characterized by some interruptions in speech flow. We occasionally get speech sounds in the wrong order (*revalent* for *relevant*), speak too quickly to be understood, pause at the wrong place in a sentence, use an inappropriate pattern of stress, or become *disfluent*—that is, stumble and backtrack, repeating syllables or words, and fill in pauses with *uh* while trying to think of how to finish what we have to say. It is only when the speaker's efforts are so intense or the interruptions in the flow of speech are so frequent or pervasive that they keep him or her from being understood or draw extraordinary attention that they are considered disorders. Besides, listeners have a greater tolerance for some types of disfluencies than others. Most of us will more readily accept speech-flow disruptions we perceive as necessary corrections of what the speaker has said or is planning to say than disruptions that appear to reflect the speaker's inability to proceed with the articulation of what she or he has decided to say (Robinson & Crowe, 2001).

The most frequent type of fluency disorder is stuttering. About 1 percent of children and adults are considered stutterers. More boys than girls stutter. Many children quickly outgrow their childhood disfluencies. These children generally use regular and effortless disfluencies, appear to be unaware of their hesitancies, and have parents and teachers who are unconcerned about their speech patterns. Those who stutter for more than a year and a half or two appear to be at risk for becoming chronic stutterers (Conture, 2001).

A child who is thought to stutter should be evaluated by a speech-language pathologist. Early diagnosis is important if the development of chronic stuttering is to be avoided. Unfortunately, many educators and physicians do not refer potential stutterers for in-depth assessment because they are aware that disfluencies are a normal part of speech-language development. But nonreferral is extremely detrimental to children who are at risk for stuttering. If their persistent stuttering goes untreated, it may result in a lifelong disorder that affects their ability to communicate, develop positive feelings about self, and pursue certain educational and employment opportunities (Conture, 2001; Curlee & Siegel, 1997). "It is now recognized that early intervention is a crucial component of adequate health care provision for stuttering" (Onslow, 1992, p. 983).

SPEECH DISORDERS ASSOCIATED WITH NEUROLOGICAL DAMAGE

The muscles that make speech possible are under voluntary control. When there is damage to the areas of the brain controlling these muscles or to the nerves leading to them, there is a disturbance in the ability to speak normally. These disorders may involve articulation of speech sounds (**dysarthria**) or selecting and sequencing speech (**apraxia**). Difficulties in speaking happen because the muscles controlling breathing, the larynx, the throat, the tongue, the jaw, and/or the lips cannot be controlled precisely. Depending on the nature of the injury to the brain, perceptual and cognitive functions may also be affected; the individual may have a language disorder in addition to a speech disorder (Brookshire, 1997; Robin, Yorkston, & Beukelman, 1996).

In Chapter 12, we discuss the many possible causes of brain injury. Among them are physical trauma, oxygen deprivation, poisoning, diseases, and strokes. Any of these can cause dysarthria or apraxia. Probably the condition that most frequently accounts for these disorders in children is **cerebral palsy**—brain injury before, during, or after birth that results in muscular weakness or paralysis. Vehicular accidents are a frequent cause of traumatic brain injury in adolescence and young adulthood.

The speech-language pathologist will assess the ability of the person with neurological impairment to control breathing, phonation, resonation, and articulatory movements by listening to the person's speech and inspecting his or her speech mechanism. Medical, surgical, and rehabilitative specialists in the treatment of neurological disorders also must evaluate the person's problem and plan a management strategy. In cases in which the neurological impairment makes the person's speech unintelligible, augmentative or alternative communication systems may be required.

Dysarthria.
A condition in which brain damage causes impaired control of the muscles used in articulation.

Apraxia.
The inability to move the muscles involved in speech or other voluntary acts.

Cerebral palsy (CP).
A condition characterized by paralysis, weakness, lack of coordination, and/or other motor dysfunction; caused by damage to the brain before it has matured.

Early Intervention

The study of children's early development has shown that the first several years of life are a truly critical period for language learning. Much of children's language and social development depends on the nature and quantity of the language interactions they have with parents or other caregivers. In the homes of children who come to school ready to learn, the language interactions between parents and children have typically been frequent, focused on encouragement and affirmation of the children's behavior, emphasized the symbolic nature of language, provided gentle guidance in exploring things and relationships, and demonstrated the responsiveness of adults to children. By contrast, children who enter school at a disadvantage tend to have experienced much lower rates of language interaction; heard primarily negative, discouraging feedback on their behavior; and heard language that is harsh, literal, and emotionally detached.

Based on extensive observations in homes, Hart and Risley (1995) compared the language experiences of children of professional parents, working-class parents, and parents on welfare. The contrasts in language experiences and the effects observed in children's academic achievement and behavior are stark, but the differences are unrelated to income or ethnicity. Rather, the differences are related to how and how much the parents talked to their children. As summed up by the authors:

> Our data showed that the magnitude of children's accomplishments depends less on the material and educational advantages available in the home and more on the amount of experience children accumulate with parenting that provides language diversity, affirmative feedback, symbolic emphasis, gentle guidance, and responsiveness. By the time children are 3 years old, even intensive intervention cannot make up for the differences in the amount of such experience children have received from their parents. If children could be given better parenting, intervention might be unnecessary. (Hart & Risley, 1995, p. 210)

Thus, it appears that the key to preventing many disabilities related to language development is to help parents improve how they relate to their children when they are infants and toddlers. Nevertheless, for many young children, intervention in the preschool and primary grades will be necessary. But such intervention must be guided by understanding of children's families, particularly mothers' views of language development (Hammer & Weiss, 2000).

Preschoolers who require intervention for a speech or language disorder occasionally have multiple disabilities that are sometimes severe or profound. Language is closely tied to cognitive development, so impairment of general intellectual ability is likely to have a retarding influence on language development. Conversely, lack of language may hamper cognitive development. Because speech is dependent on neurological and motor development, any neurological or motor problem might impair ability to speak. Normal social development in the preschool years also depends on the emergence of language, so a child with language impairment is at a disadvantage in social learning (Kaiser, Cai, Hancock, & Foster, in press; Prizant, 1999). Therefore, the preschool child's language is seldom the only target of intervention (McCabe, Hernandez, Lara, & Brooks-Gunn, 2000; Nelson, 1998).

Researchers have become increasingly aware that language development has its beginning in the earliest mother-child interactions. Concern for the child's development of the ability to communicate cannot be separated from concern for development in other areas. Therefore, speech-language pathologists are a vital part of the multidisciplinary team that evaluates an infant or young child with disabilities and develops an individualized family service plan (IFSP) (see Chapter 2). Early intervention programs involve extending the role of the parent. This means a lot of simple play with accompanying verbalizations. It means talking to the child about objects and activities in the way most mothers talk to their babies. But it also means choosing objects, activities, words, and consequences for the child's vocalizations with great care so the chances that the child will learn functional language are enhanced (Fey, Catts, & Larrivee, 1995).

Early childhood specialists now realize that *prelinguistic* intervention is critical for language development—that is, intervention should begin *before* the child's language emerges. The foundations for language are laid in the first few months of life through the nonverbal dialogues infants have with their mothers and other caretakers (Nelson, 1998).

In the early years of implementing IFSPs, emphasis was placed on assessing families' strengths and needs and training parents how to teach and manage their children. More recently, professionals have come to understand that assessing families in the belief that professionals know best is often misguided. Parents can indeed be helped by professionals to play an important role in their children's language development. But the emphasis today is on working with parents as knowledgeable and competent partners whose preferences and decisions are respected (Hammer & Weiss, 2000; see also discussion in Chapter 14).

Intervention in early childhood is likely to be based on assessment of the child's behavior related to the content, form, and especially the use of language in social interaction. For the child who has not yet learned language, assessment and intervention will focus on imitation, ritualized and make-believe play, play with objects, and functional use of objects. At the earliest stages in which the content and form of language are interactive, it is important to evaluate the extent to which the child looks at or picks up an object when it is referred to, does something with an object when directed by an adult, and uses sounds to request or refuse things and call attention to objects. When the child's use of language is considered, the earliest objectives involve him or her looking at the adult during interactions; taking turns in and trying to prolong pleasurable activities and games; following the gaze of an adult and directing the behavior of adults; and persisting in or modifying gestures, sounds, or words when an adult does not respond.

In the preschool, teaching **discourse** (conversation skills) is a critical focus of language intervention. In particular, emphasis is placed on teaching children to use the discourse that is essential for success in school. Children must learn, for example, to report their experiences in detail and to explain why things happen, not just add to their vocabularies. They must learn not only word forms and meanings but also how to take turns in conversations and maintain the topic of a conversation or change it in an appropriate way (Johnston, Weinrich, & Glaser, 1991). Preschool programs in which such language

Discourse.

Conversation; the skills used in conversation, such as turn taking and staying on the topic.

The first several years of life are truly critical for language learning. ■

teaching is the focus may include teachers' daily individualized conversations with children, daily reading to individual children or small groups, and frequent classroom discussions.

Current trends are directed toward providing speech and language interventions in the typical environments of young children (Nelson, 1998). This means that classroom teachers and speech-language pathologists must develop a close working relationship. The speech-language pathologist may work directly with children in the classroom and advise the teacher about the intervention that he or she can carry out as part of the regular classroom activities. The child's peers may also be involved in intervention strategies. Because language is essentially a social activity, its facilitation requires involvement of others in the child's social environment—peers as well as adults (Audet & Tankersley, 1999; Fey et al., 1995; Prizant, 1999).

Normally developing peers have been taught to assist in the language development of children with disabilities by doing the following during playtimes: establishing eye contact; describing their own or others' play; and repeating, expanding, or requesting clarification of what the child with disabilities says. Peer tutors can help in developing the speech and language of their classmates who may use different dialects (McGregor, 2000). Another intervention strategy involving peers is *sociodramatic play*. Children are taught in groups of three, including a child with disabilities, to act out social roles such as those people might take in various settings (e.g., a restaurant or shoe store). The training includes scripts that specify what each child is to do and say, which may be modified by the children in creative ways.

Transition to Adulthood

In the past, adolescents and adults in speech and language intervention programs generally fell into three categories: (1) the self-referred, (2) those with other health problems, and (3) those with severe disabilities. Adolescents or adults may refer themselves to speech-language pathologists because their phonology, voice, or stuttering is causing them social embarrassment and/or interfering with occupational pursuits. These are generally persons with long-standing problems who are highly motivated to change their speech and obtain relief from the social penalties their differences impose.

Adolescents and adults with other health problems may have experienced damage to speech or language capacities as a result of disease or injury, or they may have lost part of their speech mechanism through injury or surgical removal. Treatment of these individuals always demands an interdisciplinary effort. In some cases of progressive disease, severe neurological damage, or loss of tissues of the speech mechanism, the outlook for functional speech is not good. However, surgical procedures, medication, and prosthetic devices are making it possible for more people to speak normally. Loss of ability to use language is typically more disabling than loss of the ability to speak. Traumatic brain injury may leave the individual with a seriously diminished capacity for self-awareness, goal setting, planning, self-directing or initiating actions, inhibiting impulses, monitoring or evaluating one's own performance, or problem solving. Recovering these vital language-based skills is a critical aspect of transition of the adolescent or young adult from hospital to school and from school to independent living (Klein & Moses, 1999).

Individuals with severe disabilities may need the services of speech-language pathologists to help them achieve more intelligible speech. They may also need to be taught an alternative to oral language or given a system of augmented communication. One of the major problems in working with adolescents and adults who have severe disabilities is setting realistic goals for speech and language learning. Teaching simple, functional language—such as social greetings, naming objects, and making simple requests—may be realistic goals for some adolescents and adults.

A major concern of transition programming is ensuring that the training and support provided during the school years are carried over into adult life. To be successful, the tran-

Identifying Possible Language-Related Problems

Suggestions for Recognizing the Need for Consultation with a Communicative Specialist for Older Children and Adolescents with Moderate-to-Severe Multiple Disabilities

- **Failure to understand instructions.** When a person has difficulty performing essential job or daily living tasks, consider the possibility that the person may not understand the language of instructions and may not have sufficient communicative skill to ask for repetition or clarification.

- **Inability to use language to meet daily living needs.** When individuals can produce enough words to formulate a variety of utterances, including questions, then they can travel independently, shop independently, use the telephone when they need to, and ask for assistance in getting out of problem situations when they arise. If persons cannot function in a variety of working, shopping, and social contexts, consider that communicative impairments may be limiting their independence.

- **Violation of rules of politeness and other rules of social transaction.** The ability to function well in a variety of contexts with friends, acquaintances, and one-time contacts depends on sensitivity to the unspoken rules of social interaction. One of the most frequently cited reasons for failure of workers with disabilities to "fit in" with fellow workers is their inability to engage in small-talk during work breaks. Examples that might cause difficulty are failure to take communicative turns when offered, or conversely, interrupt-

ing the turns of others; saying things that are irrelevant to the topic; not using politeness markers or showing interest in what the other person says; making blunt requests owing to lack of linguistic skill for softening them; failing to shift style of communication for different audiences (e.g., talking the same way to the boss as to co-workers); and any other communicative behavior that is perceived as odd or bizarre. If people seem to avoid interacting with the target person, referral may be justified.

- **Lack of functional ability to read signs and other symbols and to perform functional writing tasks.** The ability to recognize the communicative symbols of the culture enables people to know how to use public transportation, to find their way around buildings, to comply with legal and safety expectations, and to fill out forms or use bank accounts. Communicative specialists may be able to assist in identifying the best strategies for teaching functional reading and writing skills and encouraging the development of other symbol-recognition and use skills.

- **Problems articulating speech clearly enough to be understood, stuttering, or using an inaudible or inappropriate voice.** Other speech and voice disorders may interfere with the person's ability to communicate. When such problems are noted, the individual should be referred to a speech-language pathologist.

SOURCE: N.W. Nelson, *Childhood language disorders in context: Infancy through adolescence* (2nd ed.). Copyright © 1998 by Allyn & Bacon. Reprinted with permission.

sition must include speech-language services that are part of the natural environment. That is, the services must be community based and integrated into vocational, domestic, recreational, consumer, and mobility training activities. Speech-language interventions for adolescents and young adults with severe disabilities must emphasize functional communication—understanding and making oneself understood in the social circumstances most likely to be encountered in everyday life (Nelson, 1998). Developing appropriate conversation skills (e.g., establishing eye contact, using greetings, taking turns, and identifying and staying on the topic), reading, writing, following instructions related to recreational activities, using public transportation, and performing a job are examples of the kinds of functional speech-language activities that may be emphasized (see Klein & Moses, 1999; Nelson, 1998; Rogers-Adkinson & Griffith, 1999).

Today, much more emphasis is being placed on the language disorders of adolescents and young adults who do not fit into other typical categories of disabilities. Many of these individuals were formerly seen as having primarily academic and social problems that were not language related. But now it is understood that underlying many or most of the school and social difficulties of adolescents and adults are basic disorders of language

(Rogers-Adkinson & Griffith, 1999; Wallach & Butler, 1994). These language disorders are a continuation of difficulties experienced earlier in the person's development.

Classroom teachers are in a particularly good position to identify possible language-related problems and request help from a communication specialist. The box on page 295 describes for teachers several characteristics exhibited by older children and adolescents that may indicate a need for consultation and intervention. Addressing problems like these as early and effectively as possible is important in helping youngsters make successful transitions to more complex and socially demanding environments.

Some adolescents and adults with language disorders are excellent candidates for *strategy training,* which teaches them how to select, store, retrieve, and process information (see Hallahan et al., 1999, and Chapter 5). Others, however, do not have the required reading skills, symbolic abilities, or intelligence to benefit from the usual training in cognitive strategies. Whatever techniques are chosen for adolescents and older students, the teacher should be aware of the principles that apply to intervention with these individuals.

Summary

Communication requires sending and receiving meaningful messages. *Language* is the communication of ideas through an arbitrary system of symbols that are used according to specified and accepted rules. *Speech* is the behavior of forming and sequencing the sounds of oral language. Communication disorders may involve language or speech or both. The prevalence of communication disorders is difficult to determine, but disorders of speech and language are among the most common disabilities of children.

Language development begins with the first mother-child interactions. The sequence of language development is fairly well understood, but relatively little is known about how and why children learn language. Some theories of language development include the following major ideas: (1) Language learning depends on brain development and proper brain functioning; (2) language learning is affected by the consequences of language behavior; (3) language is learned from inputs and outputs related to information processing; (4) language learning is based on linguistic rules; (5) language is one of many cognitive (thinking) skills; (6) language arises from the need to communicate in social interactions. Research supports some aspects of all theories, but social interactional or pragmatic theory is now accepted as having the most important implications for speech-language pathologists and teachers.

Language disorders may be classified according to the five subsystems of language: phonology, morphology, syntax, semantics, and pragmatics. They may also be categorized according to the presumed causes of disorders or related conditions. For example, conditions such as mental retardation, traumatic brain injury, and autism are associated with their own respective communication problems.

Assessment and intervention in language disorders require standardized testing and more informal clinical judgments. An intervention plan must consider what the child talks about and should talk about, how the child talks and should speak to become more intelligible, and how the child uses language for communication and socialization. Helping children learn to use language effectively is not the task of any single professional group. Speech-language pathologists now regularly work with classroom teachers to make language learning an integral part of classroom teaching. Recent approaches to addressing communication problems associated with delayed language have stressed a functional approach, emphasizing social and pragmatic skills that students use frequently.

Dialect or native language differences must not be mistaken for language disorders. However, the language disorders of children with communicative differences must not be overlooked. Bilingual special education is an emerging discipline, as more children have little or no proficiency in English. Research has also begun to focus on differences in socioeconomic status and language development.

Children may have more than one type of speech disorder, and disorders of speech may occur along with language disorders. Voice disorders may involve pitch, loudness, and quality of phonation, which may be unpleasant to the listener, interfere with communication, or abuse the larynx. Articulation or phonological disorders involve omission, substitution, distortion, or addition of word sounds, making speech difficult to understand. The most common fluency disorder is stuttering. Neurological damage can affect people's speech by making it difficult for them to make the voluntary movements required.

Children requiring early intervention for speech and language disorders typically have severe or multiple disabilities. A young child's ability to communicate cannot be separated from other areas of development. Children's language and social interactions with parents and caregivers are being looked at as key factors. Consequently, early language intervention involves all social interactions between a child and his or her caretakers and peers and emphasizes functional communication in the child's natural environment.

Adolescents and young adults with speech and language disorders may be self-referred, have health problems, or have multiple and severe disabilities. Transition programming has provided for the carryover of training and support during the school years into adult life. Emphasis today is on functional communication skills taught in naturalistic settings. Language disorders among young children are the basis for academic and social learning problems in later years.

Frances Benson

Untitled, Acrylic on canvas. 20 × 20 in.

Blind since birth, Ms. Benson, who was born in 1952 in Boston, Massachusetts, has developed a strong tactile sense. An accomplished pianist, with her hands dipped in paint she "plays" her paintings as though they were keyboards.

Learners Who Are Deaf or Hard of Hearing

I was the second of four children. . . . My parents, older brother, Pat, and younger sister, Mary, are all hearing. My younger brother, Dan, and I are deaf. I became deaf at the age of three from measles and mumps, but it wasn't until three years later, at the age of six, that a routine hearing screening offered to my first grade class confirmed this. . . .

. . . My first few years of school, my mother spent hours . . . talking me through my homework. I imagine that she . . . became increasingly concerned when she saw that her efforts to assist me were unsuccessful. Little did she know that I couldn't hear what she was saying, or speechread her. . . .

When I was ten, I reached a turning point. My fifth grade teacher was astute enough to recognize that repeating a grade might help. Embarrassed and hurt . . . , I spent the summer preoccupied with not passing. . . .

My parents transferred me to a smaller school, where I repeated fifth grade. This gave my grades a huge boost and, with this . . . my self-esteem soared. Suddenly I liked school and I discovered learning. . . . I knew I was different, but because I had no framework to describe that difference, no peers, no reference group, and no role models who were also deaf, I didn't understand what that difference was.

Upon transitioning to high school, friends dispersed into separate crowds. The new school was much bigger. . . . I found myself becoming increasingly isolated. One afternoon . . . , I sat on the sofa . . . having a mutually desired but laborious conversation with my mother. Mom would carefully enunciate her words, but she wasn't an easy person to speechread. I'd understand a word here and there and try to pull them all together like . . . a puzzle. I asked her why I didn't have as many friends as the other kids. . . . She looked at me with a surprised expression on her face.

"You don't know why?" she asked.

"No."

"It's because you can't hear, and they don't understand that."

That was a revelation and turning point in my life. Until that moment, I had only understood my deafness in a blur. I had never understood this difference between myself and others to be such a determining factor in my life. . . . But still I did not realize all the implications regarding relationships, my future, language, and education. I did not know this wasn't just a *hearing problem*. The difficulties I faced were not because I had a hearing problem, but because the often-cruel world around me was full of barriers. That understanding was a long way off.

MARTHA SHERIDAN
Inner Lives of Deaf Children: Interviews and Analysis

T o be deaf, or even hard of hearing, often places a person in a difficult place somewhere between the world of the hearing and the world of the Deaf. Martha Sheridan's words (see p. 299) reflect the isolation that can accompany a hearing loss. And as we see from her experience, this isolation is primarily caused by communication problems. As we will see in this chapter, even if the hearing loss is not severe enough for the child to be classified as "deaf," but rather as "hard of hearing," the child with a hearing loss is at a distinct disadvantage in virtually all aspects of English language development. The importance of the English language in U.S. society, particularly in school-related activities, is obvious. Many of the problems that people with hearing loss have in school are primarily due to their deficiencies in English. We explore this issue in some depth in this chapter.

Sign language.
A manual language used by people who are deaf to communicate; a true language with its own grammar.

Another related controversy inherent in Martha Sheridan's words is the debate concerning whether the child who is deaf should be educated to communicate orally or through manual sign language. Sheridan is typical of 90 percent of those who are deaf in that her parents are hearing. Her parents, being hearing, had chosen not to learn **sign language.** Again, this is common. Also common, however, is the fact that Sheridan had difficulty learning to *speechread,* or to use visual information, including lip movements, from a number of sources to understand what is being said.

Again, not unlike others in the same situation, Sheridan eventually went on to immerse herself in the Deaf community. She found her identity as a Deaf person through her experiences at the primary postsecondary institution for students with hearing loss—Gallaudet University:

> Gallaudet was a major gateway for me. It was the pot of gold at the end of my search for self, and it represented the beginning of the rest of my life. It was at Gallaudet that I discovered what it means to be deaf. . . . Here, and with sign language, my love for learning blossomed. (Sheridan, 2001, pp. 7–8)

But not all who are deaf elect to join the Deaf community. Some *do* become fluent enough in spoken English to function in mainstream society. And still others *are* able to straddle both the world of the hearing *and* the Deaf. But no matter what the outcome, virtually all persons who are deaf, as well as their parents, struggle with critical choices about oral versus manual modes of communication and cultural identity. With respect to the latter, in fact, many members of the Deaf community consider themselves part of a cultural minority rather than disabled.

All of these thorny issues make deafness one of the most challenging fields of study in all of special education. And as you would surmise from our discussion of other special education areas, this challenge is manifest in attempts to arrive at a definition of hearing loss.

Definition and Classification

There are many definitions and classification systems of hearing loss. By far the most common division is between *deaf* and *hard of hearing.* And although it is common to think that being deaf means not to be able to hear anything and that being hard of hearing means to be able to hear a little bit, this is generally not true. Most people who are deaf have some residual hearing. Complicating things is the fact that different professionals define the two categories differently. The extreme points of view are represented by those with a physiological orientation versus those with an educational orientation.

Those maintaining a strictly physiological viewpoint are interested primarily in the *measurable degree* of hearing loss. Children who cannot hear sounds at or above a certain intensity (loudness) level are classified as "deaf"; others with a hearing loss are considered

Learners Who Are Deaf or Hard of Hearing

MYTH Persons who are deaf are unable to hear anything.

FACT Most persons who are deaf have some residual hearing.

MYTH Deafness is not as severe a disability as blindness.

FACT Although it is impossible to predict the exact consequences of a disability on a person's functioning, in general, deafness poses more difficulties in adjustment than does blindness. This is largely due to the effects hearing loss can have on the ability to understand and speak oral language.

MYTH It is unhealthy for people who are deaf to socialize almost exclusively with others who are deaf.

FACT Many authorities now recognize that the phenomenon of a Deaf culture is natural and should be encouraged. In fact, some are worried that too much mainstreaming will diminish the influence of the Deaf culture.

MYTH In learning to understand what is being said to them, people with hearing loss concentrate on reading lips.

FACT *Lipreading* refers only to visual cues arising from movement of the lips. Some people who have a hearing loss not only read lips but also take advantage of a number of other visual cues, such as facial expressions and movements of the jaw and tongue. They are engaging in what is referred to as *speechreading*.

MYTH Speechreading is relatively easy to learn and is used by the majority of people with hearing loss.

FACT Speechreading is extremely difficult to learn, and very few people who have hearing loss actually become proficient speechreaders.

MYTH American Sign Language (ASL) is a loosely structured group of gestures.

FACT ASL is a true language in its own right, with its own set of grammatical rules.

MYTH ASL can convey only concrete ideas.

FACT ASL can convey any level of abstraction.

MYTH People within the Deaf community are in favor of mainstreaming students who are deaf into regular classes.

FACT Some within the Deaf community have voiced the opinion that regular classes are not appropriate for many students who are deaf. They point to the need for a critical mass of students who are deaf in order to have effective educational programs for these individuals. They see separate placements as a way of fostering the Deaf culture.

MYTH Families in which both the child and the parents are deaf are at a distinct disadvantage compared to families in which the parents are hearing.

FACT Research has demonstrated that children who are deaf who have parents who are also deaf fare better in a number of academic and social areas. Authorities point to the parents' ability to communicate with their children in ASL as a major reason for this advantage.

A current issue in defining deafness is that many people in the Deaf community do not want to be considered as having a disability. Instead, they want to be thought of as members of a cultural group with its own language—American Sign Language (ASL). ■

Decibels.
Units of relative loudness of sounds; zero decibels (0 dB) designates the point at which people with normal hearing can just detect sound.

Congenitally deaf.
Deafness that is present at birth; can be caused by genetic factors, by injuries during fetal development, or by injuries occurring at birth.

Adventitiously deaf.
Deafness that occurs through illness or accident in an individual who was born with normal hearing.

Prelingual deafness.
Deafness that occurs before the development of spoken language, usually at birth.

Postlingual deafness.
Deafness occurring after the development of speech and language.

"hard of hearing." Hearing sensitivity is measured in **decibels** (units of relative loudness of sounds). Zero decibels (0 dB) designates the point at which the average person with normal hearing can detect the faintest sound. Each succeeding number of decibels that a person cannot detect indicates a certain degree of hearing loss. Those who maintain a physiological viewpoint generally consider people with hearing losses of about 90 dB or greater to be deaf and people with less to be hard of hearing.

People with an educational viewpoint are concerned with how much the hearing loss is likely to affect the child's ability to speak and develop language. Because of the close causal link between hearing loss and delay in language development, these professionals categorize primarily on the basis of spoken language abilities. *Hearing loss* is a broad term that covers those individuals with impairments ranging from mild to profound; it includes those who are deaf or hard of hearing. Following are commonly accepted, educationally-oriented definitions for deaf and hard of hearing:

- A *deaf* person is one whose hearing disability precludes successful processing of linguistic information through audition, with or without a hearing aid.
- A person who is *hard of hearing* generally, with the use of a hearing aid, has residual hearing sufficient to enable successful processing of linguistic information through audition (Brill, MacNeil, & Newman, 1986, p. 67).

Educators are extremely concerned about the age of onset of hearing loss. Again, the close relationship between hearing loss and language delay is the key here. The earlier the hearing loss occurs in a child's life, the more difficulty he or she will have developing the language of the hearing society (e.g., English). For this reason, professionals frequently use the terms **congenitally deaf** (those who are born deaf) and **adventitiously deaf** (those who acquire deafness at some time after birth).

Two other frequently used terms are even more specific in pinpointing language acquisition as critical: **Prelingual deafness** refers to deafness occurring at birth or early in life prior to the development of speech or language. **Postlingual deafness** is deafness occurring after the development of speech and language. Experts differ regarding the dividing point between prelingual and postlingual deafness. Some believe it should be at about eighteen months, whereas others think it should be lower, at about twelve months or even six months (Meadow-Orlans, 1987).

The following hearing threshold classifications are common: mild (26–54 dB), moderate (55–69 dB), severe (70–89 dB), and profound (90 dB and above). These levels of severity according to loss of hearing sensitivity cut across the broad classifications of deaf and hard of hearing. The broader classifications are not directly dependent on hearing sensitivity. Instead, they stress the degree to which speech and language are affected.

Some authorities object to following any of the various classification systems too strictly. Because these definitions deal with events that are difficult to measure, they are not precise. Thus, it is best not to form any hard-and-fast opinions about an individual's ability to hear and speak solely on the basis of a classification of his or her hearing disability.

In considering issues of definition, it is important to point out that there is growing sentiment among people who are deaf that deafness should not even be considered a disability (Lane, Hoffmeister, & Bahan, 1996; Padden & Humphries, 1988). They argue that deafness only renders a person disabled with respect to acquiring the language of the dominant culture (e.g., English in the United States). Supporters of this view note that deafness does not prohibit a person from learning sign language. Furthermore, they object to labels such as "prelingual" and "postlingual" deafness because such distinctions are keyed to spoken language (Andersson, 1994). Proponents argue that instead of being considered disabled, people who are deaf should be considered a cultural minority with a language of their own—sign language.

Later in the chapter we discuss more thoroughly the issues of sign language as a true language and the nature and purpose of the Deaf culture. For now it is enough to be aware of the challenges that have been raised to the very notion of considering deafness a disability.

Prevalence

Estimates of the number of children with hearing loss vary considerably. Such factors as differences in definition, populations studied, and accuracy of testing contribute to the varying figures. The U.S. Department of Education's statistics indicate that about 0.14 percent of the population from six to seventeen years of age is identified as deaf or hard of hearing by the public schools. Although the Department of Education does not report separate figures for the categories of deaf and hard of hearing, some authorities believe that many children who are hard of hearing who could benefit from special education are not being served.

Anatomy and Physiology of the Ear

The ear is one of the most complex organs of the body. The many elements that make up the hearing mechanism are divided into three major sections: the outer, middle, and inner ear. The outer ear is the least complex and least important for hearing; the inner ear is the most complex and most important for hearing. Figure 9.1 shows these major parts of the ear.

THE OUTER EAR

The outer ear consists of the auricle and the external auditory canal. The canal ends with the **tympanic membrane (eardrum),** which is the boundary between the outer and middle ears. The **auricle** is the part of the ear that protrudes from the side of the head. The part that the outer ear plays in the transmission of sound is relatively minor. Sound is collected by the auricle and is funneled through the external auditory canal to the eardrum, which vibrates, sending the sound waves to the middle ear.

CW More information on the anatomy of the ear, including drawings, can be found at a Web site called, Virtual Tour of the Ear: http://www.augie.edu/perry/ear/hearmech.htm

The Virtual Tour of the Ear home page at http://ctl.augie.edu/perry/ar/ar.htm contain dozens of links to Web sites devoted to many topics concerning hearing impairment. Another excellent Web site is maintained by the National Institute on Deafness and Other Communication Disorders of the National Institutes of Health: http://www.nidcd.nih.gov/index.htm. On this site you can access a number of interesting demonstrations, including a video that explains how the ear works. ■

Tympanic membrane (eardrum).
The anatomical boundary between the outer and middle ears; the sound gathered in the outer ear vibrates here.

Auricle.
The visible part of the ear, composed of cartilage; collects the sounds and funnels them via the external auditory canal to the eardrum.

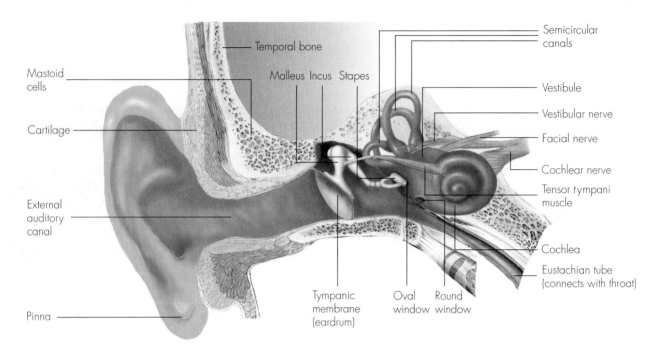

FIGURE 9.1
Illustration of the outer, middle, and inner ear.

Ossicles.
Three tiny bones (malleus, incus, and stapes) that together make possible an efficient transfer of sound waves from the eardrum to the oval window, which connects the middle ear to the inner ear.

Malleus.
The hammer-shaped bone in the ossicular chain of the middle ear.

Incus.
The anvil-shaped bone in the ossicular chain of the middle ear.

Stapes.
The stirrup-shaped bone in the ossicular chain of the middle ear.

Oval window.
The link between the middle and inner ears.

Vestibular mechanism.
Located in the upper portion of the inner ear; consists of three soft, semicircular canals filled with a fluid; sensitive to head movement, acceleration, and other movements related to balance.

THE MIDDLE EAR

The middle ear comprises the eardrum and three very tiny bones (**ossicles**)—called the **malleus** (hammer), **incus** (anvil), and **stapes** (stirrup)—contained within an air-filled space. The chain of the malleus, incus, and stapes conducts the vibrations of the eardrum along to the **oval window,** which is the link between the middle and inner ears. The ossicles function to create an efficient transfer of energy from the air-filled cavity of the middle ear to the fluid-filled inner ear.

THE INNER EAR

About the size of a pea, the inner ear is an intricate mechanism of thousands of moving parts. Because it looks like a maze of passageways and is highly complex, this part of the ear is often called a *labyrinth.* The inner ear is divided into two sections according to function: the vestibular mechanism and the cochlea. These sections, however, do not function totally independently of each other.

The **vestibular mechanism,** located in the upper portion of the inner ear, is responsible for the sense of balance. It is extremely sensitive to such things as acceleration, head movement, and head position. Information regarding movement is fed to the brain through the vestibular nerve.

By far the most important organ for hearing is the **cochlea.** Lying below the vestibular mechanism, this snail-shaped organ contains the parts necessary to convert the mechanical action of the middle ear into an electrical signal in the inner ear that is transmitted to the brain. In the normally functioning ear, sound causes the malleus, incus, and stapes of the middle ear to move. When the stapes moves, it pushes the oval window in and out, causing the fluid in the cochlea of the inner ear to flow. The movement of the fluid in turn causes a complex chain of events in the cochlea, ultimately resulting in excitation of the cochlear nerve. With stimulation of the cochlear nerve, an electrical impulse is sent to the brain, and sound is heard.

Measurement of Hearing Ability

There are four general types of hearing assessment: screening tests, pure-tone audiometry, speech audiometry, and specialized tests for very young children. Depending on the characteristics of the examinee and the use to which the results will be put, the **audiologist** may choose to give any number of tests from any one or a combination of these three categories.

SCREENING TESTS

There are screening tests for infants and screening tests for school-age children. Over half the states now mandate newborn hearing screening programs. These tests, involving the use of computer technology, measure **otoacoustic emissions.** The cochlea not only receives sounds, but it also emits low-intensity sound when stimulated by auditory stimuli. These sounds emitted by the cochlea are known as otoacoustic emissions, and they provide a measure of the how well the cochlea is functioning (Campbell & Derrick, 2001).

Many schools have routine screening programs in the early elementary grades. Hearing screening tests are administered either individually or in groups. These tests, especially those that are group administered, are less accurate than those administered in an audiologist's office. Children detected through screening as having possible problems are referred for more extensive evaluation.

PURE-TONE AUDIOMETRY

Pure-tone audiometry is designed to establish the individual's threshold for hearing at a variety of different frequencies. (Frequency, measured in **hertz (Hz)** units, has to do with the number of vibrations per unit of time of a sound wave; the pitch is higher with more vibrations, lower with fewer.) A person's threshold for hearing is simply the level at which he or she can first detect a sound; it refers to how intense a sound must be before the person can detect it. As mentioned earlier, hearing sensitivity, or intensity, is measured in decibels (dB).

Pure-tone audiometers present tones of varying intensities, or loudness, (dB levels) at varying frequencies, or pitch (Hz). Audiologists are usually concerned with measuring sensitivity to sounds ranging from 0 to about 110 dB. A person with average-normal hearing is barely able to hear sounds at a sound-pressure level of 0 dB. The zero decibel level is frequently called the *zero hearing-threshold level (HTL),* or **audiometric zero.** Because the dB scale is based on ratios, each increment of 10 dB is a tenfold increase in sound level. This means that 20 dB is one hundred times more intense than a 10 dB sound, and 30 dB is one thousand times more intense than a 10 dB sound. Whereas a leaf fluttering in the wind registers about 0 dB, most speech sounds range between 20 and 55 dB, and a power lawnmower would have an intensity of about 100 dB (Schirmer, 2001).

Hertz are usually measured from 125 Hz (low pitch) to 8,000 Hz (high pitch). Frequencies contained in speech range from 80 to 8,000 Hz, but most speech sounds have energy in the 500 to 2,000 Hz range.

Testing each ear separately, the audiologist presents a variety of tones within the range of 0 to about 110 dB and 125 to 8,000 Hz until she or he establishes at what level of intensity (dB) the individual can detect the tone at a number of frequencies—125 Hz, 250 Hz, 500 Hz, 1,000 Hz, 2,000 Hz, 4,000 Hz, and 8,000 Hz. For each frequency, there is a measure of degree of hearing loss. A 50 dB hearing loss at 500 Hz, for example, means the individual is able to detect the 500 Hz sound when it is given at an intensity level of 50 dB, whereas the average person would have heard it at 0 dB.

SPEECH AUDIOMETRY

Because the ability to understand speech is of prime importance, a technique called **speech audiometry** has been developed to test a person's detection and understanding of speech.

The National Institute on Deafness and Other Communication Disorders of the National Institutes of Health has been concerned about the fact that many infants with hearing loss go undetected even though technology exists to identify such impairments. In July of 2001, a working group was convened to focus on early screening of hearing problems. You can keep abreast of the group's work by visiting the Institute's Web site: http://www.nidcd.nih.gov/index.htm ∎

Cochlea.
A snail-shaped organ that lies below the vestibular mechanism in the inner ear; its parts convert the sounds coming from the middle ear into electrical signals that are transmitted to the brain.

Audiologist.
An individual trained in audiology, the science dealing with hearing impairments, their detection, and remediation.

Otoacoustic emissions.
Low-intensity sounds produced by the cochlea in response to auditory stimulation; used to screen hearing problems in infants and very young children.

Pure-tone audiometry.
A test whereby tones of various intensities and frequencies are presented to determine a person's hearing loss.

Hertz (Hz).
A unit of measurement of the frequency of sound; refers to the highness or lowness of a sound.

Audiometric zero.
The lowest level at which people with normal hearing can hear.

Speech audiometry.
A technique that tests a person's detection and understanding of speech, rather than using pure tones to detect hearing loss.

Routine hearing examinations, conducted in schools, often provide the first identification of mild hearing problems. ■

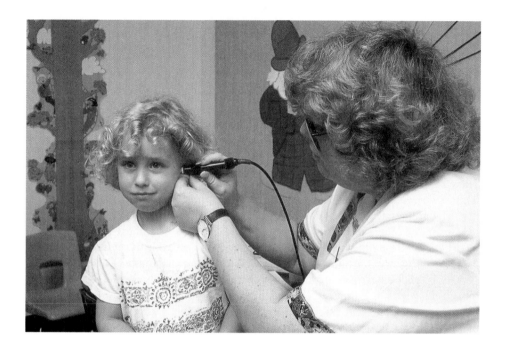

The **speech reception threshold (SRT)** is the dB level at which one is able to understand speech. One way to measure the SRT is to present the person with a list of two-syllable words, testing each ear separately. The dB level at which he or she can understand half the words is often used as an estimate of SRT level.

TESTS FOR YOUNG AND HARD-TO-TEST CHILDREN

A basic assumption for pure-tone and speech audiometry is that the individuals who are being tested understand what is expected of them. They must be able to comprehend the instructions and show with a head nod or raised hand that they have heard the tone or word. None of this may be possible for very young children (under about four years of age) or for children with certain disabilities.

Audiologists use a number of different techniques to test the hearing of young and hard-to-test children. For example, some use the otoacoustic emission testing that we mentioned earlier. Others use **play audiometry.** In a gamelike format, using pure tones or speech, the examiner teaches the child to do various activities whenever he or she hears a signal. The activities are designed to be attractive to the young child. For example, the child may be required to pick up a block, squeeze a toy, or open a book. In **tympanometry,** a rubber-tipped probe is inserted in the ear, sealing the ear canal, and the effects of pressure and sound are then measured to assess the functioning of the middle ear. Still another method is **evoked-response audiometry.** Evoked-response audiometry involves measuring changes in brain-wave activity by using an electroencephalograph (EEG). All sounds heard by an individual result in electrical signals within the brain, so this method has become more popular with the development of sophisticated computers. Evoked-response audiometry can be used during sleep, and the child can be sedated and thus not be aware that he or she is being tested.

Causes

CONDUCTIVE, SENSORINEURAL, AND MIXED HEARING LOSS

Professionals classify causes of hearing loss on the basis of the location of the problem within the hearing mechanism. There are three major classifications: conductive, sen-

Speech reception threshold (SRT).
The decibel level at which a person can understand speech.

Play audiometry.
Use of a game-like format to test hearing of young and hard-to-test children; the examiner teaches the child to respond to sounds.

Tympanometry.
A method of measuring the middle ear's response to pressure and sound.

Evoked-response audiometry.
A technique involving electroencephalograph measurement of changes in brain-wave activity in response to sounds.

sorineural, and mixed hearing losses. A **conductive hearing loss** refers to an interference with the transfer of sound along the conductive pathway of the middle or outer ear. A **sensorineural hearing loss** involves problems in the inner ear. A **mixed hearing loss** is a combination of the two. Audiologists attempt to determine the location of the dysfunction. The first clue may be the severity of the loss. A general rule is that hearing losses greater than 60 or 70 dB involve some inner-ear problem. Audiologists use the results of pure-tone testing to help determine the location of a hearing loss, converting the results to an audiogram—a graphic representation of the weakest (lowest dB) sound the individual can hear at each of several frequency levels. The profile of the audiogram helps determine whether the loss is conductive, sensorineural, or mixed.

HEARING LOSS AND THE OUTER EAR

Although problems of the outer ear are not as serious as those of the middle or inner ear, several conditions of the outer ear can cause a person to be hard of hearing. In some children, for example, the external auditory canal does not form, resulting in a condition known as *atresia*. Children may also develop **external otitis,** or "swimmer's ear," an infection of the skin of the external auditory canal. Tumors of the external auditory canal are another source of hearing loss.

HEARING LOSS AND THE MIDDLE EAR

Although abnormalities of the middle ear are generally more serious than problems of the outer ear, they, too, usually result in a person's being classified as hard of hearing rather than deaf. Most middle-ear hearing losses occur because the mechanical action of the ossicles is interfered with in some way. Unlike inner-ear problems, most middle-ear hearing losses are correctable with medical or surgical treatment.

The most common problem of the middle ear is **otitis media**—an infection of the middle-ear space caused by viral or bacterial factors, among others. For children under six years, it is the most common reason for visits to the physician (Schirmer, 2001). Otitis media is linked to abnormal functioning of the eustachian tubes. If the eustachian tube malfunctions because of a respiratory viral infection, for example, it cannot do its job of ventilating, draining, and protecting the middle ear from infection. Otitis media can result in temporary conductive hearing loss and, if untreated, can lead to rupture of the tympanic membrane.

HEARING LOSS AND THE INNER EAR

The most severe hearing losses are associated with the inner ear. In addition to problems with hearing sensitivity, a person with inner-ear hearing loss can have additional problems, such as sound distortion, balance problems, and roaring or ringing in the ears.

Causes of inner-ear disorders can be hereditary or acquired. Genetic or hereditary factors are a leading cause of deafness in children (Schirmer, 2001). Acquired hearing losses of the inner ear include those due to bacterial infections (e.g., meningitis, the second most frequent cause of childhood deafness), prematurity, viral infections (e.g., mumps and measles), anoxia (deprivation of oxygen) at birth, prenatal infections of the mother (e.g., maternal rubella, congenital syphilis, and cytomegalovirus), Rh incompatibility (which can now usually be prevented with proper prenatal care of the mother), blows to the head, unwanted side effects of some antibiotics, and excessive noise levels.

Two of the above conditions deserve special emphasis because of their relatively high prevalence. **Congenital cytomegalovirus (CMV),** a herpes virus, deserves special mention because it is the most frequent viral infection in newborns, occurring in 1 to 2 percent of all newborns (Hutchinson & Sandall, 1995). CMV can result in a variety of conditions, such as mental retardation, visual impairment, and especially hearing loss. In addition, repeated exposure to such things as loud music, gunshots, or machinery can result in gradual or sudden hearing loss.

Conductive hearing loss.
A hearing loss, usually mild, resulting from malfunctioning along the conductive pathway of the ear (i.e., the outer or middle ear).

Sensorineural hearing loss.
A hearing loss, usually severe, resulting from malfunctioning of the inner ear.

Mixed hearing loss.
A hearing loss resulting from a combination of conductive and sensorineural hearing impairments.

External otitis.
An infection of the skin of the external auditory canal; also called "swimmer's ear."

Otitis media.
Inflammation of the middle ear.

Congenital cytomegalovirus (CMV).
The most frequently occurring viral infection in newborns; can result in a variety of disabilities, especially hearing impairment.

Psychological and Behavioral Characteristics

Hearing loss can have profound consequences for some aspects of a person's behavior and little or no effect on other characteristics. Consider the question: If you were forced to choose, which would you rather be—blind or deaf? On first impulse, most of us would choose deafness, probably because we rely on sight for mobility and because many of the beauties of nature are visual. But in terms of functioning in an English language–oriented society, the person who is deaf is at a much greater disadvantage than someone who is blind.

ENGLISH LANGUAGE AND SPEECH DEVELOPMENT

By far the most severely affected areas of development in the person with a hearing loss are the comprehension and production of the English language. We stress *English* because it is the predominant language in the United States of those who can hear. In other words, people who are hearing impaired are generally deficient in the language used by most people of the hearing society in which they live. The distinction is important, because people who are hearing impaired can be expert in their own form of language. The current opinion is that individuals who use American Sign Language (ASL) produce and comprehend a true language. Furthermore, children who are deaf reach the same language development milestones in sign and do so at the same time as nondisabled children do in spoken language (Lane et al., 1996). For example, they acquire their first words at about 12 to 18 months and two-word phrases at about 18 to 22 months. (We return to a discussion of ASL on p. 322).

Regarding English, however, it is an undeniable fact that individuals with hearing loss are at a distinct disadvantage. This is true in terms of language comprehension, language production, and speech. Speech intelligibility is linked to degree of hearing loss, with 75 percent of children who are profoundly deaf having nonintelligible speech but only 14 percent of children with less-than-severe hearing loss having nonintelligible speech (Wolk & Schildroth, 1986).

In addition, it is much more difficult for children who are prelingually deaf to learn to speak than it is for those who are postlingually deaf. Infants who are able to hear their own sounds and those of adults prior to becoming deaf are at an advantage over those who are born deaf. Babies born deaf begin to babble at the same time as hearing babies, but by eight months their babbling decreases and is qualitatively different from hearing babies (Stoel-Gammon & Otomo, 1986). It is thought that these differences occur because hearing infants are reinforced by hearing their own babbling and by hearing the verbal responses of adults. Children who are unable to hear either themselves or others are not reinforced.

The lack of feedback has also been named as a primary cause of poor speech production in children who are deaf. Children who are deaf are handicapped in learning to associate the sensations they receive when they move their jaws, mouths, and tongues with the auditory sounds these movements produce. In addition, these children have a difficult time hearing the sounds of adult speech, which nonimpaired children hear and imitate. As a result, children who are deaf do not have access to an adequate adult model of spoken English.

Table 9.1 gives general examples of the effects that various degrees of hearing loss may have on English language development. This is only a general statement of these relationships, since many factors interact to influence language development in the child with hearing loss.

INTELLECTUAL ABILITY

Historically, the intellectual ability of children with hearing loss has been a subject of much controversy. For many years professionals believed that the conceptual ability of

TABLE 9.1 Degrees of Hearing Loss and Impact on Communication

Hearing Level	Descriptor	Impact on Communication
–10 to 15 dB	Normal	No impact on communication
16 to 25 dB	Slight	In quiet environments, the individual has no difficulty recognizing speech, but in noisy environments, faint speech is difficult to understand.
26 to 40 dB	Mild	In quiet conversational environments in which the topic is known and vocabulary is limited, the individual has no difficulty in communicating. Faint or distant speech is difficult to hear even if the environment is quiet. Classroom discussions are challenging to follow.
41 to 55 dB	Moderate	The individual can hear conversational speech only at a close distance. Group activities, such as classroom discussions, present a communicative challenge.
56 to 70 dB	Moderate–Severe	The individual can hear only loud, clear conversational speech and has much difficulty in group situations. Often, the individual's speech is noticeably impaired though intelligible.
71 to 90 dB	Severe	The individual cannot hear conversational speech unless it is loud and even then, cannot recognize many of the words. Environmental sounds can be detected, though not always identified. The individual's speech is not altogether intelligible.
91 dB +	Profound	The individual may hear loud sounds but cannot hear conversational speech at all. Vision is the primary modality for communication. The individual's own speech, if developed at all, is not easy to understand.

SOURCE: From Schirmer, B.R. (2001). *Psychological, social, and educational dimensions of deafness.* Boston: Allyn & Bacon. Reprinted/adapted with permission.

individuals who are deaf was deficient because of their deficient spoken language. We now know, however, that we should not assume that persons who cannot speak because they are deaf have no language. They may not have a spoken language, such as English, but if they use American Sign Language, they are using a true language with its own rules of grammar. (Again, we return to this point later.)

Any intelligence testing done with people who are hearing impaired must take into account their English language deficiency. Performance tests, rather than verbal tests, especially if they are administered in sign, offer a much fairer assessment of the IQ of a person with a hearing loss. When these tests are used, there is no difference in IQ between those who are deaf and those who are hearing (Prinz et al., 1996).

ACADEMIC ACHIEVEMENT

Unfortunately, most children with hearing loss have extreme deficits in academic achievement. Reading ability, which relies heavily on English language skills and is probably the most important area of academic achievement, is most affected. Numerous studies paint a bleak picture for the reading achievement of students with hearing loss (Allen, 1986; Kuntze, 1998; Wolk & Allen, 1984). Representative findings are that the growth in reading achievement of students with hearing loss is about one-third that for hearing students. Upon graduation from high school, it is not at all unusual for students who are deaf to be able to read at no more than a fourth-grade level. Even in math, which is their best academic subject, students with hearing loss trail their hearing peers by substantial margins.

Several studies have demonstrated that children who are deaf who have parents who are deaf have higher reading achievement and better language skills than do those who have hearing parents (Bornstein, Selmi, Haynes, Painter, & Marx, 1999). Authorities speculate that this is due to the positive influence of sign language. Parents who are deaf may be able to communicate better with their children through the use of ASL, providing the children with needed support. In addition, children who have parents who are deaf are more likely to be proficient in ASL, and ASL may aid these children in learning written English and reading. There is not much research on this topic, but one study did find a relationship between facility in ASL and academic achievement (Prinz et al., 1996).

Several factors in the home environment are associated with higher achievement in students who are deaf. Families that (1) are more involved in their child's education, (2) seek knowledge about their child's condition in order to provide guidance, (3) have high expectations for achievement, (4) do not try to overprotect their child, and (5) participate along with their child in the Deaf community are likely to have higher achieving children (Schirmer, 2001).

SOCIAL ADJUSTMENT

Social and personality development in the hearing population depend heavily on communication—and the situation is no different for those who are deaf. The hearing person has little difficulty finding people with whom to communicate. The person who is deaf, however, may face problems in finding others with whom he or she can converse. Studies have demonstrated that many students who are deaf are at risk for loneliness (Cambra, 1996; Charlson, Strong, & Gold, 1992). Two factors are important in considering the possible isolation of students who are deaf: inclusion and hearing status of the parents.

Researchers have shown that in inclusionary settings, very little interaction typically occurs between students who are deaf and those who are not (Gaustad & Kluwin, 1992). Furthermore, in inclusionary settings, students who are deaf feel more emotionally secure if they have other students who are deaf with whom they can communicate (Stinson & Whitmire, 1992). This is not always possible, however, because of the low prevalence of hearing loss. Therefore, researchers are trying to come up with programs that directly teach social behaviors to children who are deaf in order to get them to interact with hearing peers (Antia & Kreimeyer, 1997).

Some authorities believe that the child who is deaf who has hearing parents runs a greater risk of being unhappy than if she or he has parents who are deaf. This is because many hearing parents do not become proficient in ASL and are unable to communicate with their children easily. Given that over 90 percent of children who are deaf have hearing parents, this problem in communication may be critical.

The need for social interaction is probably most influential in leading many persons with hearing loss to associate primarily with others with hearing loss. If their parents are deaf, children who are deaf are usually exposed to other deaf families from an early age. Nonetheless, many persons who are deaf end up, as adults, socializing predominantly with others who are deaf, even if they have hearing parents and even if they do not come into contact as children with many other children who were deaf. This phenomenon of socializing with others who are deaf is attributable to the influence of the Deaf culture.

The Deaf Culture   In the past, most professionals viewed isolation from the hearing community on the part of many people who are deaf as a sign of social pathology. But now more and more professionals agree with the many people who are deaf who believe in the value of having their own Deaf culture. They view this culture as a natural condition emanating from the common bond of sign language.

The unifying influence of sign language is the first of six factors noted by Reagan (1990) as demarcating the Deaf community as a true culture: (1) linguistic differentiation, (2) attitudinal deafness, (3) behavioral norms, (4) endogamous marital patterns, (5) historical awareness, and (6) voluntary organizational networks.

Regarding *linguistic differentiation,* most authorities view the Deaf community as bilingual, with individuals possessing varying degrees of fluency in ASL and English (Reagan, 1990). People who are deaf are continually shifting between ASL and English, as well as between the Deaf culture and that of the hearing (Padden, 1996).

Attitudinal deafness refers to whether a person thinks of himself or herself as deaf. It may not have anything to do with a person's hearing acuity. For example, a person with a relatively mild hearing loss may think of herself or himself as deaf more readily than does someone with a profound hearing loss.

The Deaf community has its own set of *behavioral norms*. A few examples of these norms, according to Lane et al. (1996), are that people who are deaf value informality and physical contact in their interactions with one another, often giving each other hugs when greeting and departing. And their departures, or leave-takings, often take much longer than those of hearing society. Also, they are likely to be frank in their discussions, not hesitating to get directly to the point of what it is they want to communicate.

Endogamous marriage patterns are evident from surveys showing rates of ingroup marriage as high as 90 percent. And "mixed marriages" between persons who are deaf and those who are hearing tend to be frowned upon by the Deaf community.

The Deaf community has a long history that has contributed to its *historical awareness* of significant people and events pertaining to people who are deaf. They are often deferential to elders and value their wisdom and knowledge pertaining to Deaf traditions.

Finally, there is an abundance of *voluntary organizational networks* for the Deaf community, such as the National Association of the Deaf, the World Games for the Deaf (Deaf Olympics), and the National Theatre of the Deaf (see the box below).

The National Theatre of the Deaf

The Oldest Continuously Producing Touring Theatre Company in the United States

About NTD

Through its thirty-four year history, the National Theatre of the Deaf stands as testimony to the artistry and capability of its actors. There have been 64 national tours, performances in all 50 states, all the continents, 31 international tours and over 8,000 performances earning NTD its place in theatrical history as the oldest continually-producing touring theatre company in the United States. . . . Through NTD's signature style of visual language, American Sign Language, the audience enjoys a greater appreciation that no other theatre company can approach. Through its art, the NTD has created profound social change. The magic of it all has been the National Theatre of the Deaf's remarkable ability to entertain and inform at the same time. As one critic has praised, "sculpture in the air."

History/Timeline

In 1967, the National Theatre of the Deaf was founded by David Hays at the Eugene O'Neill Memorial Theatre Center in Waterford, Connecticut. With federal grants from the U.S. Department of Health, Education, and Welfare in 1965, this valiant troupe of actors, directors, and designers laid the ground work and in 1967, with additional funds from the U.S. Office of Education, created its Professional Training School and mounted its first National Tour. The following year, the Little Theatre of the Deaf, NTD's theatre for young audiences troupe, was created and began touring as well.

In 1983, NTD moved its home to Chester, Connecticut and in 1994, the National and Worldwide Deaf Theatre Conference had its inaugural session, to facilitate communication, develop techniques, and encourage the work of deaf playwrights from the over 40 theatres of the deaf around the world that NTD was instrumental in founding. In 2000, NTD moved its home to the Connecticut State Capitol, Hartford. . . .

NTD has received critical acclaim for its adaptations of classic literature (Chekhov, Voltaire, Homer, Moliere, Ibsen, and Puccini) as well as for original works by the Company. NTD has collaborated with artists such as Chita Rivera, Jason Robards, Arvin Brown, Bill Irwin, Peter Sellers, Colleen Dewhurst, and Marcel Marceau. NTD productions provide the opportunity for the majority hearing community to be stimulated by the skills and artistry of the minority Deaf community.

Presentations by NTD do more than just make theatre accessible to the Deaf. They enable the Deaf to share with the hearing members of the audience a cultural and social event. This sharing promotes pride in the culture and artistry of the Deaf. The impact of NTD is realized nationwide and around the world through its principle product: theatre. [More information about the NTD can be found on their Web site. See Figure 9.2.]

SOURCE: The National Theatre of the Deaf. (2001, March 19). "About NTD." Retrieved August 25, 2001 from the World Wide Web: http://www.ntd.org/about.htm. The National Theatre of the Deaf. (2001, February 5). "About NTD: History/Timeline." Retrieved August 25, 2001 from the World Wide Web: http://www.ntd.org/about_history.htm. Reprinted with permission.

FIGURE 9.2

Home page for the National Theatre of the Deaf

SOURCE: The National Theatre of the Deaf. (2001, March 19). Retrieved August 25, 2000 from the World Wide Web: http://www.ntd.org. Reprinted with permission.

 Visit the National Theatre of the Deaf Web site to look for upcoming performances in your area: http://www. NTD. org/ ■

Deaf clubs.

Gathering spots where people who are deaf can socialize; on the decline in the United States.

Concern for the Erosion of Deaf Culture　Many within the Deaf community and some within professional ranks are concerned that the cultural status of children who are deaf is in peril (Gaustad & Kluwin, 1992; Janesick & Moores, 1992; Lane et al., 1996). They believe that the increase in inclusion is eroding the cultural values of the Deaf culture. In the past, much of Deaf culture was passed down from generation to generation through contacts made at residential schools, but today's children who are deaf may have little contact with other children who are deaf, if they attend local schools. Many authorities now recommend that schools involve members of the Deaf community in developing classes in Deaf history and culture for students who are deaf who attend local schools.

Further evidence of the erosion of the Deaf culture is the fact that Deaf clubs are on the decline (Lane et al., 1996). **Deaf clubs** are a gathering place wherein people who are deaf can socialize and participate in leisure activities and entertainment. With the increase in inclusion and the growing popularity of the Internet as a means of gathering information, it will be interesting to see what the future holds for Deaf clubs.

Deaf Activism　Even though some may think the Deaf community is in peril of losing its identity, it is still very active in advocating a variety of social, educational, and medical policies. A prominent and historic example of Deaf activism occurred in 1988 at Gallaudet University—a liberal arts college for the deaf and hard of hearing—where students and faculty protested the board of trustees' selection of a hearing president. Since its founding in 1864, Gallaudet had never had a deaf president. After students shut down the university for several days, the school's administration acquiesced to their demands for a deaf president and a reconfiguration of the board to include a majority of members who are deaf.

Deaf activists have also been aggressive in attacking what they consider an oppressive medical and educational establishment. An example of just how much this segment of the Deaf community is at odds with many professionals is its opposition to the medical procedure of **cochlear implantation.** A cochlear implant involves surgically implanting electronic elements under the skin behind the ear and in the inner ear. A small microphone worn behind the ear picks up sounds and sends them to a small computerized speech processor worn by the person. The speech processor sends coded signals back to an external coil worn behind the ear, which sends them through the skin to the implanted internal coil. The internal coil then sends the signals to electrodes implanted in the inner ear, and these signals are sent on to the auditory nerve. (See Figure 9.3.)

Ever since the U.S. Food and Drug Administration (FDA) approved the use of cochlear implants for young children in 1990, there have been thousands of operations both in the United States and the rest of the world, especially Australia. The technology is advancing rapidly, but currently not everyone with hearing loss is a candidate for implantation. Generally, it is recommended for those who have a severe to profound sensorineural loss in both ears. In the case of children, medical opinions vary, but it is usually not recommended before the age of 18 months (Listening Center at Johns Hopkins, 2001).

Although the manufacturers of these devices, as well as many within the medical community, have viewed cochlear implants as miraculous, they have engendered vociferous objections from many within the Deaf community, where they are viewed as physically and culturally invasive:

> I expect that most Americans would agree that our society should not seek the scientific tools or use them, if available, to change a child biologically so he or she will belong to the majority rather than the minority—even if we believe that this biological engineering might reduce the burdens the child will bear as a member of a minority. Even if we could take children destined to be members of the African American, or Hispanic American, or Native American, or Deaf American communities and convert them with bio-power into white, Caucasian, hearing males—even if we could, we should not. We should likewise refuse cochlear implants for young deaf children even if the devices were perfect. (Lane, 1992, p. 237)

Until recently, the Deaf community has not had to even come close to confronting the issue, raised by Lane, of whether to have the surgery even if it were to result in perfect hearing. Although perfect hearing through cochlear implants may not be just around the

Cochlear implantation. A surgical procedure that allows people who are deaf to hear some environmental sounds; an external coil fitted on the skin by the ear picks up sound from a microphone worn by the person and transmits it to an internal coil implanted in the bone behind the ear, which carries it to an electrode implanted in the cochlea of the inner ear.

CW As noted in the feature, "Making Peace with a Threat to 'Deaf Culture,'" on p. 314 of the textbook, the National Association of the Deaf had for years been opposed to cochlear implants. However, in the fall of 2000, it issued a policy statement that was much more neutral in tone. You can see the policy on the NAD Web site: http://www.nad.org/infocenter/newsroom/positions/CochlearImplants.html

The Public Broadcasting Service (PBS) has established an excellent Web site focused on the documentary, "Sound and Fury": http://www.pbs.org/wnet/soundandfury. Although the site focuses on the issue of cochlear implants, it also contains useful information pertaining to the Deaf culture and links to other interesting Web sites. ∎

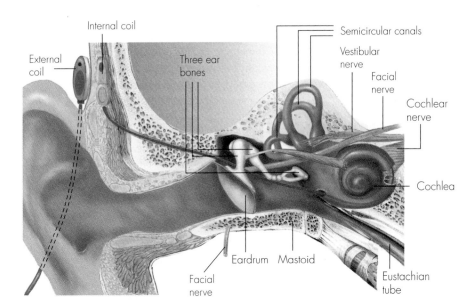

External coil

Internal coil

Three ear bones

Semicircular canals

Vestibular nerve

Facial nerve

Cochlear nerve

Cochlea

Eardrum   Mastoid

Facial nerve

Eustachian tube

FIGURE 9.3
A cochlear implant.

Making Peace with a Threat to "Deaf Culture"

Jamie Weinstein-Delahunt, a deaf toddler from Jamaica Plain, is a born communicator and a symbol of the profound changes now sweeping the world of the deaf.

Hands flying, the 2½-year-old can communicate in American Sign Language, or ASL. But she is also learning to hear and speak standard English, thanks to a controversial device called a cochlear implant that surgeons put in her ear nearly a year ago.

Before long, Jamie and other deaf children who can both speak and sign may accomplish what many of their elders could or would not: Straddle the fiercely separate worlds of people who talk with their voices and those who talk with their hands.

Until a year or so ago, the idea of "fixing" deafness in a child like Jamie was anathema to many proud members of Deaf (they spell it with a capital "D") culture, who feel that deafness is not a disability and that any attempt to remedy it is tantamount to "ethnocide"—the elimination of deaf people and their minority culture and language.

Harlan Lane, a psychologist and linguist at Northeastern University, puts this view bluntly:

"If you believe, as I do, that a healthy, deaf child is a healthy child like a healthy, short child, it's just plain wrong to operate on that child."

Besides, the whole idea of what constitutes a disability—and who gets to label whom as disabled—is "squishy," he said. "My students don't think needing eyeglasses is a disability but that needing a hearing aid is."

But thanks to better implant technology, more widespread screening of newborns to find the one in every 1,000 children who is born deaf and the government's recent decision to lower the age at which children can get implants to 12 months, the popularity of cochlear implants is exploding.

In the United States last year alone, nearly 4,000 adults and children received implants, says Marilyn Neault, director of audiology at Children's Hospital in Boston. Overall, implantation has been growing 20 percent per year, with the biggest increases in people over 65 and children under 5. The number of implants given to children under 3—the prime language-learning years—grew seven-fold between 1995 and 2000.

Stunningly, last fall, the National Association of the Deaf, which for years had vehemently opposed implants, published a new position paper that did not take sides on the issue and argued instead for "diversity" of attitudes within the deaf community.

Indeed, many deaf children with implants now go to mainstream schools, and schools for the deaf are begin-

ning to accommodate children who can speak as well as sign. "A child who is exposed to both sign language and oral English will have a choice of which world to go to," says Mary Mazzotta, the diagnostic teacher at the Horace Mann School for the Deaf and Hard of Hearing in Boston.

And Gallaudet University, the only liberal arts university for deaf students, is doing what was once unthinkable: opening a cochlear implant center for young children and high school students.

"Three years ago, we weren't even discussing cochlear implants," says Debra Nussbaum, an audiologist and head of the new Gallaudet center. "But as technology has improved, people see that it doesn't have to be an either-or choice, implant or ASL," she says. "Implants are now being seen as providing additional information without trying to change the child's identity."

With earlier versions of the implants, children who had been deaf from birth might hear environmental noise with an implant but never truly master speech. (People who become deaf after having learned to speak generally have an easier time adapting to implants because they retain some auditory memory of spoken language.)

To hearing people like Jamie's parents—and 90 percent of deaf children are born to hearing parents—the deaf culture's attitude toward implants has been difficult to understand. Even the prospect that Jamie would need years of speech and hearing therapy after getting an implant seemed worth the gamble.

"We had been in the midst of so much loss," says her mother, "that the idea that Jamie could talk, despite being deaf, was the most hopeful news we had heard."

But probably the biggest driving force behind the growing acceptance of implants is that they have improved so much. A generation ago, the devices had only one electrode and the results were decidedly mixed.

Today, implants, which cost about $23,000 and are often covered by insurance, have up to 22 electrodes, which allows different sounds to sound truly different.

Unlike hearing aids, which merely amplify sounds, cochlear implants essentially replace the function of the damaged cochlea in a deaf person. The cochlea is a pea-sized, fluid-filled structure through which sound signals are passed to the auditory nerve and the brain, says Dr. Akira Ishiyama, a cochlear implant surgeon at UCLA Medical Center.

In the surgery, doctors carve a tunnel through the mastoid bone behind the ear and cut a hole in the damaged cochlea. Using a microscope, they then implant a wire containing the electrodes into the cochlea.

Each electrode captures sound waves at a certain frequency. Incoming sounds are first collected by a small microphone worn on top of the skin behind the ear like a hearing aid, then encoded by a small speech processor that sends electrical signals to the electrodes. The electrodes in turn stimulate the auditory nerve. As long as there is still some function in the auditory nerve, says Ishiyama, a cochlear implant can help.

Implants "dramatically improve hearing in almost all children and lead to good speech recognition and production in most children who get them before age 4," says Neault of Boston.

"More and more individuals are getting implants for their children at younger ages," agrees Barbara Herrmann, an audiologist at the Massachusetts Eye and Ear Infirmary. A series of large studies in Missouri and Indiana shows "very impressive growth of language for children who receive implants."

To be sure, the implants do not make a deaf child into a hearing one. But children with implants can "perform like children with much less severe hearing loss—not like normal, hearing children, but like children who can use hearing aids successfully," says Herrmann.

Still, the debate over implants—or the "sound and fury," as the excellent TV documentary by that name, which aired earlier this year on PBS, puts it—is far from over, partly because there are still strong arguments on both sides, especially for very young children who are still in their prime language learning years.

The decision to get an implant or not to get one is never easy, says Christine Mitchell, director of the office of ethics at Children's Hospital.

Hearing parents who opt for ASL instead of an implant face not only the burden of learning ASL themselves and teaching it to their child, but the possibility that their child may someday become part of the "deaf community in a way they can't follow or share," Mitchell says.

Since it is "often easier to change the child than the parent," she adds, an implant may give assurance to hearing parents that their child may hear and speak and, therefore, be more like them. It also means that their child may be more likely to become part of mainstream culture.

But is that a good thing? In some ways it is, says Mitchell, but a deaf child with an implant is still deaf, and becoming mainstreamed may not fulfill the deepest yearnings, for "feeling like you genuinely belong."

For Jamie and her parents, it's been a long, but hopeful road. Learning sign language, when Jamie was about a year old, was the first step. "The minute we did that, she completely responded," says Weinstein. "My first story for her was 'Goodnight, Gorilla.' I signed all the animal names. It was so satisfying."

The implant has brought even more joy. Although the family still signs when Jamie gets confused, her hearing, and her speech, grow daily. Now, say Weinstein, "I can call her name from down the street and she turns to me."

Judy Foreman's column appears every other week in Health & Science. Her past columns are available on Boston.com and www.myhealthsense.com. Her e-mail address is foreman@globe.com.

SOURCE: Foreman, J. (2001, August 28). Making peace with a threat to "deaf culture." *The Boston Globe,* pp. C1–2. "Making peace with a threat to 'deaf culture.'" Judy Foreman, nationally syndicated health columnist, http://www.myhealthsense.com. Reprinted with permission.

corner, enormous strides in technology have resulted in many more cases than ever before of greatly improved hearing for people with implants (Spencer, 2001). These more positive results are making it more difficult for those who are deaf, or their parents, to decide whether to undergo cochlear implantation (see the box on p. 314). But results still do vary enormously from individual to individual. For someone who is profoundly deaf, the most common outcome is improvement to the level of severe hearing loss (i.e., a hearing loss of about 71 to 90 dB) (Blamey et al., 2001; Spencer, 2002). And in order to reap the benefits of the improved hearing, the individual needs to engage in intensive oral instruction of the kind that we discus below. Again, this is a far cry from a cure, but for some it is enough of

Oralism–manualism debate.
The controversy over whether the goal of instruction for students who are deaf should be to teach them to speak or to teach them to use sign language.

an improvement to elect to undergo the surgery. At this point, it is perhaps best not to take an extreme position on this issue:

> If the greatest hope of conventional wisdom is that the implant will be a bionic ear, curing deafness, and if the worst fear is that implants will eliminate Deaf culture altogether, then implants are a resounding failure, as neither scenario has resulted. In reality, the truth of the matter lies somewhere in between. (Easterbrooks & Mordica, 2000, p. 55)

Educational Considerations

Formidable problems face the educator working with students who are deaf or hard of hearing. As we would expect, one major problem is communication. Dating back to the

SUCCESS STORIES
Special Educators at Work

New York, NY: **Najia Elyoumni-Pinedo** will turn six on Christmas Day. Her mother, Esther Pinedo, is from Peru, and her father, Ahmed Elyoumni, is from Morocco. Her parents met in an English language class in Manhattan one year before Najia's birth. When she was two, Najia was diagnosed as profoundly deaf. Since she had no extended family in the United States, a special day school for students who are deaf or hearing impaired became Najia's second home.

It was snack time, and the six kindergarten children decided to crush their cookies and eat crumbs. Their teacher, **Wanda Frankel**, and her assistant, Maria Diaz-Schwartz, readied chairs for the morning meeting, while Raihiem silently made a mountain. Suddenly, hands flew as another child signed, "Look! Raihiem has the most crumbs!" Warding off further comparisons, Wanda signed for the children to clean up and come to the circle. "Najia," she signed, "what is your job this week?" A dark-haired girl went to get paper towels as she signed back, "To wash the table."

Wanda Frankel is certified as a Teacher of the Deaf. She has taught at the Lexington School for the Deaf for twelve years. Effortlessly, she signs and speaks with her students, using a loud voice to facilitate what hearing some might have. "Usually, I wear a microphone, or an FM system as it's called. Then I don't need to speak so loudly, since I can set the mike to amplify my voice a little louder than other

sounds coming through individual hearing aids. Today, it's broken!" Fortunately, there is an audiology repair shop on campus to assist with this and other problems, such as when students' hearing aids fail.

It is this kind of service that Najia's parents, Esther and Ahmed, have come to expect at Lexington. "We want to know everything about deafness," says Esther. "We come here for conferences and for sign language classes. We have cried with other parents and shared our experiences at meetings."

In this specialized setting, Najia has benefited from the intensity of instruction in sign language; from the small classes of six children, one teacher, and one assistant; and from the flexibility of a curriculum that focuses on her needs and interests.

Najia's progress is also linked to the school's resources for parental education and support. The school serves a

sixteenth century, there has been a raging debate concerning how individuals who are deaf should converse (Lane, 1984). This controversy is sometimes referred to as the **oralism–manualism debate** to represent two very different points of view: one favors teaching people who are deaf to speak; the other advocates the use of some kind of manual communication. Manualism was the preferred method until the middle of the nineteenth century, when oralism began to gain predominance. Currently, most educational programs involve both oral and manual methods in what is referred to as a **total communication approach** (Meadow-Orlans, Mertens, Sass-Lehrer, & Scott-Olson, 1997). However, many within the Deaf community believe that the total communication approach is inadequate, and they advocate for a **bicultural-bilingual approach,** which promotes American Sign Language (ASL) as a first language and instruction in the Deaf culture.

We first discuss the major techniques that make up the oral approach and the oral portion of the total communication approach; then we take up total communication, followed by a discussion of the bicultural-bilingual approach.

Total communication approach.
An approach for teaching students with hearing impairment that blends oral and manual techniques.

Bicultural-bilingual approach.
An approach for teaching students with hearing impairment that stresses teaching American Sign Language as a first language, English as a second language, and promotes the teaching of Deaf culture.

---

large immigrant community with many parents like Najia's who must learn both English and sign language. For Najia and her parents, sign is their common language. Many mothers and fathers are also taught new skills as hearing parents of a deaf child. Says Wanda Frankel, "Counseling services addressing unique communication issues are available to help these parents learn to better communicate with their deaf child as well as to help deaf children express their feelings and anger in nonphysical ways."

Najia's progress cannot be separated from her parents' struggle to find her help. Najia was eighteen months old when her father finally became convinced that she was deaf. "He said, 'I clapped, I slammed a door, I made a lot of noise,'" recalls Najia's mother. Before that, other reasons seemed to explain why Najia did not answer to her name. Since Najia and her parents lived with three other Moroccan families and their seven children, Esther and Ahmed thought that she was too busy playing to respond. They also thought it was a foreign language issue. "When Najia was with me and my friends, we spoke Spanish," explains Esther. "At home, her father and the other families spoke Arabic."

Since the Elyoumni-Pinedos had no family members in the United States to provide support, they were helped by an American acquaintance to make appointments at two audiology centers in Manhattan. The first evaluation found that Najia had a severe hearing loss. "I cried, 'No, not Najia,'" remembers Esther. She hoped the second evaluation would prove the initial finding false; instead, the results indicated a profound loss. At that point, the Elyoumni-Pinedos were advised to take Najia to the nearby Lexington School for early intervention services. She was two years old.

Now in kindergarten, Najia receives an intense classroom focus on communication. She has developed a strong language base and is acquiring beginning reading skills. She knows the alphabet and can sight-read the days of the week and names of favorite people. Along with her classmates, she participates in hands-on math readiness activities in basic addition and subtraction. Since there is also a school-wide emphasis on developing independent learners, children in all grades learn to prepare and to predict through actual problem solving. "Najia comes up with some great solutions," says Wanda Frankel.

At the morning meeting, Najia and her classmates watch Wanda closely, as her lively hands draw their attention. "Listen," she says as she extends her arms and waves her hands, encouraging the children to watch each other. Raihiem is expressive in sign, and his clowning gestures make Najia laugh. She, in turn, signs that she is proud of her body tracing that hangs on the wall. It is decorated in detail and dressed with a feather belt and silver beads for earrings.

"Najia is so artistic," says Wanda. "Last year, she started to draw pictures using perspective! She's very bright." Says Najia's mother, "My husband and I like to think she will be a professional."

The resources of this special school have built a solid foundation for both Najia and her parents. When Esther and Ahmed's second child was born with a hearing loss, the Lexington School was able to provide his evaluation and referral to another program for children with less intense needs.

Esther Pinedo spoke with emotion and her eyes filled as she said, "We are so lucky to have found this school! We are so lucky to be in America!"

—By Jean Crockett

Meeting the Needs of Students Who Are Deaf or Hard of Hearing

Advances in Instructional Practices

Research-Based Recommendations

Advances in research on effective instructional practices can provide guidance for general education teachers *and* special education teachers who have little or no training in methods for students with hearing loss. Among the most promising practices are: universal teaching materials; media, materials, and technology; collaborative models; and classroom interactions and instruction (Easterbrooks, 1999).

- *Universal Design for Learning:* Universal design, an architectural term referring to the construction of buildings accessible to people with disabilities, denotes instructional materials that meet the needs of diverse learners. Universal Design for Learning includes: multiple ways of representing the content (e.g., electronic text that can be transformed into an outline or linked to graphic supports), strategy prompts built into the instruction to promote active engagement, and options for presentation formats (Pisha & Coyne, 2001). (See universal design, p. 63.)
- *Media, materials, and technology:* Due to the heavy reliance on visual rather than auditory cues for learning, students who are deaf or hard of hearing can make use of media, materials, and technology that provide explicit visual support for learning (Kaplan, Mahshie, Mosely, Singer, & Winston, 1993).
- *Collaborative models:* Collaborative models encourage multiple perspectives, solutions, and approaches vital for the diverse population of students with hearing loss. A "one-size-fits-all" approach can lead to ineffective instruction (i.e., instruction lacking in necessary support) or inappropriate instruction (i.e., when too many supports place unnecessary restrictions or communication limitations and/or burdens on a student).
- *Classroom interactions and instruction:* A student's ability to effectively communicate in a classroom has a direct effect on the amount of learning that will occur. Teachers who can sign fluently or are responsive to student communication needs will increase instructional outcomes.

Classroom Applications

Specific recommendations for the classroom teacher include:

- Modify the classroom environment
  - Place students who use amplification devices away from distracting background noise such as doors or windows.
  - Provide ample lighting, particularly on instructional visual aids.
  - Allow the student access to see the teacher's and classmates' faces and the ability to move around the classroom for optimal placement.

- Create "visual" instruction (Lucker, Bowen, & Carter, 2001)
  - Use sign or fingerspelling or promote speech reading when instructing.
  - Use as many visual supports as possible (bulletin boards, computers, televisions, pictures, graphs, graphic organizers, films with captions, artifacts, etc.).
  - Face students when addressing them. Avoid writing on the chalkboard while talking; use an overhead projector that allows you to face students.
  - Use nonverbal cues to emphasize verbal directions (e.g., gesturing, facial expressions).
  - Avoid note taking. Students who are looking at their desk writing notes will not be able to see an interpreter or read lips.
  - Repeat questions and answers provided by other students.

- Support communication
  - Provide access to student's dominant mode of communication (e.g., manual, cued, or oral).
  - Set up effective communication practices among students. When working in pairs or small groups, students should face each other and have rules for communication, which may include signaling before speaking.

— Pair figurative language with concrete or familiar examples.
— Moderate volume, rate, and complexity of speech.

Finally, the classroom teacher should seek guidance and information from outside experts. Speech-language pathologists, teachers of the deaf and hard of hearing, administrators, and professional organizations can provide a range of instructional recommendations to meet the unique needs of a particular student.

—*By Kristin L. Sayeski*

ORAL APPROACH: AUDITORY-VERBAL APPROACH AND SPEECHREADING

The Auditory-Verbal Approach   The techniques falling under the general category of an oral approach are often referred to as the auditory-verbal approach. The **auditory-verbal approach** stresses auditory habilitation and speech training.

Auditory Habilitation   **Auditory habilitation** stresses encouraging children to make use of what hearing they possess. There are several principles held by advocates of auditory habilitation (Auditory-Verbal International, 2001; Stone, 1997):

- Most children with a hearing loss have enough residual hearing to profit from its use
- Amplification technology, such as hearing aids and cochlear implants, has advanced to the point where most children with a hearing loss can be expected to hear conversational speech
- It is never too early to start training and to use amplification procedures; the longer one waits the harder it is to obtain good results
- Parents, as the primary language models for their children, are a critical part of the treatment plan

Speech Training   Because children with a hearing loss have problems hearing their own speech or that of others and often hear speech in a distorted fashion, they must be explicitly instructed in how to produce speech sounds. Because they do not have access to an appropriate speech model to imitate, they must be taught speech sounds. In addition to making the correct sounds, they also have problems with controlling volume, pitch, and nasality (Schirmer, 2001).

Speechreading   Sometimes inappropriately called lipreading, **speechreading** involves teaching children who are hearing impaired to use visual information to understand what is being said to them. *Speechreading* is a more accurate term than *lipreading* because the goal is to teach students to attend to a variety of stimuli in addition to specific movements of the lips. For example, proficient speechreaders read contextual stimuli so they can anticipate certain types of messages in certain types of situations. They are able to use facial expressions to help them interpret what is being said to them. Even the ability to discriminate the various speech sounds that flow from a person's mouth involves attending to visual cues from the tongue and jaw as well as the lips. For example, to learn to discriminate among vowels, the speechreader concentrates on cues related to the degree of jaw opening and lip shaping.

   Cued speech is a method of augmenting speechreading. In cued speech, the individual uses hand shapes to represent specific sounds while speaking. Eight hand shapes are cues for certain consonants, and four serve as cues for vowels. As we discuss below, some sounds look alike on the lips, and these cues are designed to help the speechreader

Auditory-verbal approach.
Part of the oral approach to teaching students who are hearing impaired; stresses teaching the person to use his or her remaining hearing as much as possible; heavy emphasis on use of amplification; heavy emphasis on teaching speech.

Auditory habilitation.
Part of the auditory-verbal approach for children with hearing loss; stresses children developing their residual hearing to the maximum.

Speechreading.
A method that involves teaching children to use visual information from a number of sources to understand what is being said to them; more than just lipreading, which uses only visual clues arising from the movement of the mouth in speaking.

Cued speech.
A method to aid speechreading in people with hearing impairment; the speaker uses hand shapes to represent sounds.

Homophenes.
Sounds that are different but that look the same with regard to movements of the face and lips (i.e., visible articulatory patterns).

Signing English systems.
Used simultaneously with oral methods in the total communication approach to teaching students who are deaf; different from American Sign Language because they maintain the same word order as spoken English.

Fingerspelling.
Spelling the English alphabet by using various finger positions on one hand.

differentiate these sounds. Although it has some devoted advocates, cued speech is not used widely in the United States.

Criticisms of the Oral Approach   Several authorities have been critical of using an exclusively oral approach with students who have hearing loss (Lane et al., 1996; Padden & Humphries, 1988). In particular, they object to the de-emphasis of sign language in this approach, especially for children who are deaf. These critics assert that for many children with severe or profound degrees of hearing loss, it is unreasonable to assume that they have enough hearing to be of use. As such, denying these children access to ASL is denying them access to a language to communicate.

Critics of the oral approach also point out that speechreading is extremely difficult and good speechreaders are rare. It is easy to overlook some of the factors that make speechreading difficult. For instance, speakers produce many sounds with little obvious movement of the mouth. Another issue is that the English language has many **homophenes**—different sounds that are visually identical when spoken. For example, a speechreader cannot distinguish among the pronunciations of [p], [b], and [m]. There is also variability among speakers in how they produce sounds. Finally, such factors as poor lighting, rapid speaking, and talking with one's head turned are further examples of why good speechreading is a rare skill (Menchel, 1988).

TOTAL COMMUNICATION

As noted previously, most schools have adopted the total communication approach, a combination of oral and manual methods. The shift from exclusively oral instruction to total communication in the 1970s occurred primarily because researchers found that children who were deaf fared better academically and socially if they had parents who were deaf than if they had hearing parents (Moores & Maestas y Moores, 1981). Investigators attributed this difference to the greater likelihood of signing in families in which children and parents were both deaf.

Total communication involves the simultaneous use of speech with one of what are known as Signing English systems. **Signing English systems** refer to approaches that professionals have devised for teaching people who are deaf to communicate. There are several such systems—for example, Signing Exact English, Signed English, and Seeing Essential English (Luetke-Stahlman & Milburn, 1996). **Fingerspelling,** the representation

A total communication approach blends oral and manual methods. ■

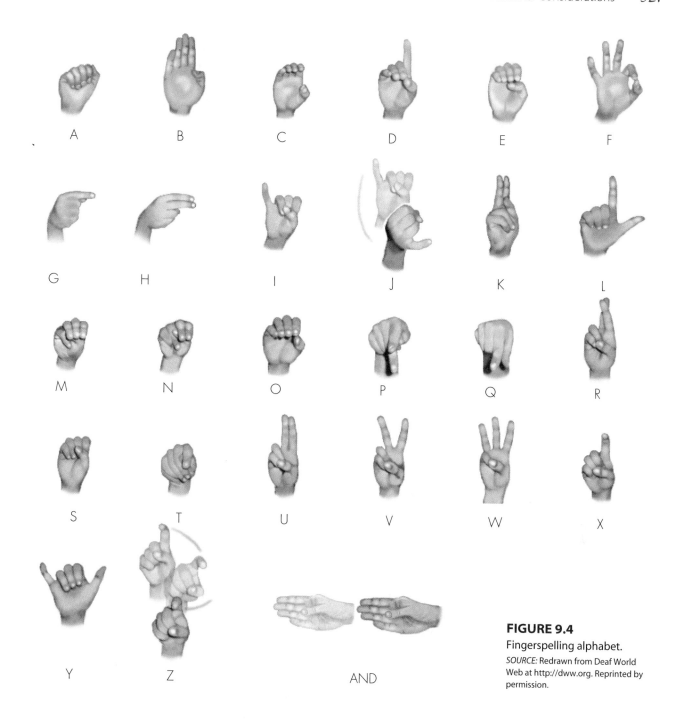

FIGURE 9.4
Fingerspelling alphabet.
SOURCE: Redrawn from Deaf World
Web at http://dww.org. Reprinted by
permission.

of letters of the English alphabet by finger positions, is also used occasionally to spell out
certain words (see Figure 9.4).

There has been growing dissatisfaction with total communication among some professionals and by many within the Deaf community. The focus of the criticism has been on
the use of signing English systems rather than ASL. Unlike ASL, signing English systems
maintain the same word order as spoken English, thereby making it possible to speak and
sign at the same time. Defenders of signing English systems state that the correspondence
in word order between signing English systems and English helps students learn English
better. Advocates of ASL assert that the use of signing English systems is too slow and awkward to be of much benefit in learning English. They argue that word order is not the critical element in teaching a person to use and comprehend English.

The Internet has several sites
with animated finger spelling
or American Sign Language
dictionaries. An example for finger
spelling is: http://www.pbs.org/wnet/
soundandfury/culture/sign_basic.
html. An example for ASL, developed
at Michigan State University, is:
http://commtechlab.msu.edu/
sites/aslweb/ ■

American Sign Language as a True Language

Many people, even some of those working in the area of deaf education, have the misconception that ASL and other sign languages are not true languages. (There is no universal sign language; ASL is only one among many. Most of them are nearly as different from each other as the spoken languages of the world.) Some people believe ASL is merely a loosely constructed system of gestures, and some believe that the signs are so highly pictorial in nature that they limit ASL to the representation of concrete, rather than abstract, concepts. Research has demonstrated that ASL's detractors are wrong on both counts.

ASL Has Its Own Grammar

Far from a disorganized system, ASL has its own very complicated grammar. Linguist William Stokoe first submitted that, analogous to the phonemes of spoken English, each sign in ASL consists of three parts: handshape, location, and movement (Stokoe, 1960; Stokoe, Casterline & Croneberg, 1976). He proposed that there are nineteen different handshapes, twelve locations, and twenty-four types of movements. Scoffed at by his colleagues when he first advanced his theory, Stokoe has come to be regarded as a genius for his pioneering work on the structure of ASL (Sacks, 1989; Wolkomir, 1992).

Research since the pioneering work of Stokoe has further confirmed the grammatical complexity of ASL. For example, researchers have found that young children who are deaf make errors in the early stages of learning ASL that are analogous to those made by hearing children learning English (Bellugi & Klima, 1991; Crowson, 1994). For example, children who are deaf make overgeneralization errors similar to those made by hearing children (e.g., using -ed to form past tenses goed or eated).

One team of researchers compared the signing of (1) individuals fluent in ASL to that of (2) a child who was deaf who had, over a period of years, developed a system of gestures for communicating to his hearing parents to that of (3) a group of previously nonsigning hearing adults and children who were asked to communicate

with each other nonverbally (i.e., to invent a signing system) (Singleton, Morford, & Goldin-Meadow, 1993). These researchers found that, in contrast to the ASL group, the child and final group did not produce sets of signs that were coherent and systematic. In other words, evidence suggested that it is necessary for a signing system to evolve over time, to be passed down from one generation to another, as ASL has. This evolution is needed in order for the signing system to develop the systematic and internally consistent forms that identify it as a true language.

ASL Can Be Used to Convey Abstract Ideas

The misconception that ASL transmits primarily concrete ideas probably comes from the popular belief that signs are made up mostly of pictorial, or iconic, cues. Actually, the origin of some signs is iconic, but over time, even many of these iconic signs have lost their pictorial qualities (Klima & Bellugi, 1979). Sacks (1989) notes that it is the duality of signing—the use of the abstract and the concrete—that contributes to its vividness and aliveness. The following description captures the beauty of signing:

> The creativity can be remarkable. A person can sculpt exactly what he's saying. To sign "flower growing," you delicately place the fingertips at each side of the nose as if sniffing the flower, then you push the fingertips of one hand up through the thumb and first finger of the other. The flower can bloom fast and fade, or, with several quick bursts, it can be a whole field of daffodils. In spoken English, most people would seem silly if they talked as poetically as some supposedly illiterate deaf people sign. With one handshape—the thumb and little finger stretched out, the first finger pointing forward—you can make a plane take off, encounter engine trouble and turbulence, circle an airport, then come in for a bumpy landing. That entire signed sentence takes a fraction of the time than saying it aloud would. (Walker, 1986, p. 48)

Advocates of ASL believe that fluency in ASL provides students with a rich background of information that readies them for the learning of English. Furthermore, they assert that ASL is the natural language of people who are deaf and that it should be fostered because it is the most natural and efficient way for students to learn about the world. To clarify, signing English systems are not true languages, whereas ASL is (see the box above). Signing English systems have been invented by one or a few people in a short period of time, whereas true sign languages such as ASL have evolved over several generations of

The issue of using American Sign Language in general education settings becomes even more complex when the needs of non-English-speaking students are to be considered. ■

users. Many of the critics of the total communication approach advocate the bicultural-bilingual approach.

THE BICULTURAL-BILINGUAL APPROACH

Although there are several variations of a bicultural-bilingual approach, most of them contain three features (Schirmer, 2001):

1. ASL is considered the primary language and English the secondary language.
2. Persons who are deaf play an important role in the development of the program and its curriculum.
3. The curriculum consists of instruction in Deaf culture.

There are two general models of bilingual education for students who are deaf (Drasgow, 1993). One emphasizes allowing children to acquire ASL naturally from teachers who are deaf or truly bilingual before formally teaching them English. This approach is based on the idea that English will be easier to learn if the child first has a solid ASL foundation. Advocates of the second model do not see an advantage to teaching one language before the other. Instead, they stress exposing the child to both ASL and English from as early an age as possible, as long as the two languages are used consistently in separate contexts or by different people. For example, ASL might be used in some subjects and English in others, or ASL might be used by one teacher and English by another.

Lending credence to those advocating ASL instruction are studies showing a relationship between ASL usage and academic performance in English (Prinz et al., 1996; Strong & Prinz, 1997). That is, students who are exposed to ASL at an early age have better English literacy skills regardless of whether their parents are deaf or hearing.

However, research directly bearing on the efficacy of bicultural-bilingual programs is in its infancy. Even though at least one study has found evidence for the effectiveness of bicultural-bilingual programming (Andrews, Ferguson, Roberts, & Hodges, 1997), it is probably safest to conclude that:

No fail-safe, success-guaranteed method exists for educating deaf children, though periodically through the history of deaf education various methods have been proposed as the pedagogical solution. In the 1960s and 1970s, total communication was considered to be the answer. In the 1980s and 1990s, bilingual education was touted as the solution. With the increase in cochlear implants, greater numbers of children are being educated orally/aurally . . . , and oral/aural approaches have seen renewed interest. Ultimately, the profession may recognize that only a range of approaches can meet the needs of a range of deaf children. (Schirmer, 2001, p. 203)

SERVICE DELIVERY MODELS

Students who are deaf or hard of hearing can be found in settings ranging from general education classes to residential institutions. Starting in the mid-1970s, more and more of these students have been attending local schools in self-contained classes, resource rooms, and regular classes. Currently, over 80 percent of students between the ages of 6 and 21 attend classes in local schools, and 39 percent spend the vast majority of their time in the general education classroom (U.S. Department of Education, 2000). Even though students with hearing loss are now included to a very high degree in general education classrooms, they are still served in special schools or residential settings more than any other disability category, with about 7 percent in the former and 9 percent in the latter type of placement. Placement varies considerably, according to severity of hearing loss (students with severest hearing loss are more likely to be in residential schools), hearing level of the parents (students with parents who are deaf are more likely to be in residential schools), and age of the students (older students are more likely to be in residential schools) (Holden-Pitt, 1997).

MAKING IT WORK

Collaboration and Co-Teaching for Students Who Are Deaf or Hard of Hearing

"If he can't hear me, how can I teach him?"

Working with a teacher of students who are deaf or hard of hearing may mean learning a new language or how to work with interpreters. This may cause anxiety and initial reluctance on the part of the general education teacher to try to collaborate, particularly if there is a concern about planning time. In all cases, the general educator who is being asked to collaborate has a right to a thorough understanding of the abilities of the student (not just the disabilities) and of the goals the special educator has set for the collaboration. This initial step is vital in setting up a successful partnership.

What Does It Mean to Be a Teacher of Students Who Are Deaf or Hard of Hearing?

The focus of training for teachers of the deaf or hard of hearing is not in a content area but is on the assessment, characteristics, and management of hearing impairments. Again,

these teachers have special skills that they can offer the general educator, such as:

1. Providing activities to promote literacy in English or American Sign Language.
2. Modifying incidental language experiences to fit visual and other sensory needs.
3. Selecting, adapting, and implementing classroom management strategies.
4. Designing a classroom environment that maximizes opportunities for visual and/or auditory learning.
5. Facilitating independent communication. (Council for Exceptional Children, 2001)

Tapping into these areas of expertise will certainly help in a collaborative situation, but it takes more than expertise in a teaching area to make a collaboration work, as evidenced by the following example.

Many within the Deaf community have been critical of the degree of mainstreaming or inclusion that is occurring (Lane et al., 1996; Padden & Humphries, 1988; Siegel, 2000). They argue that residential schools (and to a lesser extent, day schools) have been a major influence in fostering the concept of a Deaf culture and the use of ASL. Inclusion, they believe, forces students who are deaf to lose their Deaf identity and places them in a hearing and speaking environment in which it is almost impossible to succeed. In particular, critics of inclusion argue that when a student who is deaf is placed in a setting with nondisabled children, he or she is usually the only student with a hearing loss in the class. This lack of a "critical mass" of students who are deaf can lead to two interrelated problems: (1) a lack of peers with whom the student who is deaf can communicate and (2) a high degree of social isolation. Some have argued that the goal of providing optimum opportunities for communication should be the driving force behind where students who are deaf are educated:

> It is time for a new educational paradigm for deaf and hard of hearing children, which must include both a communication "starting point" or conceptual foundation and a formal structure to implement that concept. The paradigm must be a communication-rich and communication-driven system. (Siegel, 2000, p. 72)

Studies of students ranging from preschool (Rodriguez & Lana, 1996) to high school age (Holcomb, 1996) have suggested that inclusion in general education classes runs the risk of making students who are deaf feel isolated. Even though inclusion may present problems for many students who are deaf, by no means is it a negative experience for all students. Research on the effects of integrating students who are deaf with hearing peers

Successful Strategies for Co-Teaching

Cindy Sadonis (a teacher of students who are deaf/hard of hearing) and Connie Underwood (a third-grade teacher) worked collaboratively to include Joe and Brittany. Joe used hearing aids but had language deficits and Brittany had a profound hearing loss and used both sign and oral language.

Cindy: I teach nine students with hearing impairments in grades K through 5. The students receive a range of special education services. All students, however, are mainstreamed for library, music, PE, guidance, and special events.

Connie: I teach a general education third-grade class. There are 17 students. I had worked with students with hearing impairments in my general education classroom in the past, and although the experiences were positive in many ways, I felt that I was connecting with the students "at a distance."

Cindy: We were both apprehensive despite being friends, co-workers, and experienced teachers. I went into Connie's room and she and her third-grade students came into my room.

Connie: I had three main fears. First, was I going to be able to communicate with Joe and Brittany without an interpreter? Yikes! My signing skills were labored, elementary, and painfully wrong at times. Second, how much more planning and time would this take? When I was lead teacher, Cindy interpreted and observed and was ready the following week with lessons on the same theme. I became a support in her room when she became the lead teacher. Third, I was concerned about student relationships. Without prompting, our students began signing as they tried to communicate, and by the latter part of the year it was amazing how much communication was going on at the lunch table, in PE, and even secretively (or so the kids thought) in the classroom. But there were times when Brittany and Joe still felt different and when my students found it much easier to engage in conversations with their friends without hearing losses.

Cindy: It is important to note that collaborative teaching to this degree is often difficult, largely due to schedule. Positive teacher attitudes are required if inclusion is to succeed. Challenges presented themselves along the way for us, too. Social interaction was always an area of need despite our best efforts. As teachers, we have highs and lows too. Working through them has helped us continue to move in the right direction.

—By Margaret P. Weiss

The great majority of students who are deaf or hard of hearing attend local schools, and close to half of that number spend most of their time in general education classrooms. ■

has consistently found that social and academic outcomes vary depending on the individual. For some, full integration is beneficial; for others, a separate setting is best. When students who are deaf are placed in an integrated setting, researchers have found the following to be the elements of effective programming:

- *Time to learn and plan.* . . .
- *Commitment to the model of education.* The professionals and the child's parents must feel committed to making the placement successful and confident about the child's ability to be successful.
- *Support services.* The school principal and school district director of special education play key roles. . . . Examples of support include teacher of the deaf full-time, speech and language specialist, interpreters, paraprofessionals, volunteers, computers, and budget for purchasing materials and equipment.
- *Clarity of program design.* . . . The team of professionals should be engaged in activities that enable them to develop a common understanding of the program design, clarification of their individual roles and responsibilities. . . .
- *Parent participation.* . . .
- *Direct instruction by teachers of the deaf within the regular classroom.* . . . When a teacher of the deaf is teamed with the classroom teacher and they deliver instruction together some of the time, both the hearing and deaf students benefit. (Schirmer, 2001, pp. 189–190)

TECHNOLOGICAL ADVANCES

A number of technological advances have made it easier for persons with hearing loss to communicate with and/or have access to information from the hearing world. This technological explosion has primarily involved five areas: hearing aids, captioning, telephones, computer-assisted instruction, and the Internet.

Hearing Aids   There are three main types of hearing aids—those worn behind the ear, those worn in the ear, and those worn farther down in the canal of the ear. The behind-

Meeting the Needs of Students Who Are Deaf or Hard of Hearing

Assistive Technology

What Is Assistive Technology?

Assistive technology is defined under IDEA as ". . . any item, piece of equipment or product system, whether acquired commercially off the shelf, modified, or customized, that is used to increase, maintain, or improve the functional capabilities of children with disabilities" (*Federal Register*, August 19, 1991, p. 41272). For students with hearing impairments, assistive technology can offer support for receptive and expressive communication, access to visual instruction, and individualization of instruction critical for their success. To make the most of assistive technology in the classroom, teachers need to be aware of how the technology can be integrated into the context of instruction.

Types of Assistive Technology

Students who are deaf or hard of hearing may benefit from the following types of assistive technology:

- Amplification devices such as hearing aids or frequency modulated (FM) systems
- Computer-assisted instruction
- Captioned programming
- Telecommunication devices for the deaf (TDD)
- Speech digitizers and synthesizers

Classroom Applications

Before introducing assistive technology in the classroom, the teacher should identify instructional goals for the student. Guiding questions such as "What is it the student cannot do as a result of his or her disability?" and "Would assistive technology enable the student to meet the goal?" facilitate the identification of instructionally relevant technologies (Chambers, 1997).

When selecting technology, teachers should consider (1) if there is a "low-tech" alternative that would meet the same instructional goals, (2) the level of support necessary to maintain the technology, (3) the skills required to appropriately use the device, and (4) the potential availability of the technology in other environments outside of the classroom (Garrick-Duhaney & Duhaney, 2000).

Finally, teachers should plan for meaningful integration of the technology into the teaching-learning process. Consideration of environmental demands and task expectations help teachers determine where and when to use the technologies. Questions can include:

- What is the physical arrangement?
- What is the instructional context?
- What supports already exist in the environment?
- What activities support the student's curriculum?
- What are the critical elements of the instructional activities?
- How might the activities be modified to accommodate the student's needs?
- How might the technology support the student's participation in those activities? (Chambers, 1997)

—By Kristin L. Sayeski

the-ear hearing aid is the most powerful and is thus used by those with the most severe hearing losses. It is also the one that children most often use because it can be used with FM systems available in some classrooms. With an FM system, the teacher wears a wireless lapel microphone and the student wears an FM receiver (about the size of a cigarette package). The student hears the amplified sound either through a hearing aid that comes attached to the FM receiver or by attaching a behind-the-ear hearing aid to the FM receiver. Whether a student will be able to benefit from a hearing aid by itself depends a great deal on the acoustic qualities of the classroom.

Rear Window Captioning Systems display captions on transparent acrylic panels that movie patrons can attach to their seats. ■

Although hearing aids are an integral part of educational programming for students with hearing loss, some children who are deaf cannot benefit from them because of the severity and/or nature of their hearing loss. Generally, hearing aids make sounds louder, not clearer, so if a person's hearing is distorted, a hearing aid will merely amplify the distorted sound.

For those who can benefit from hearing aids, it is critical for the student, parents, and teachers to work together to ensure the maximum effectiveness of the device. This means that the teacher should be familiar with its proper operation and maintenance.

Television, Video, and Movie Captioning   At one time viewers needed a special decoder to access captioned programs. Federal law now requires that TVs over 13 inches must contain a chip to allow one to view captions without a decoder. Federal law stipulates that television shows caption a certain percentage of their shows: 50 percent of new programming must be captioned starting in January 2002; 75 percent by January 2004; and 100 percent by January 2006 (National Association of the Deaf, 2001).

Many videotapes available from rental stores are captioned as well. And the most recent innovation in captioning is the Rear Window Captioning System, which displays captions on transparent acrylic panels that movie patrons can attach to their seats (National Center for Accessible Media, 1998). The captions are actually displayed in reverse at the rear of the theater, and the viewer sees them reflected on his or her acrylic screen.

Some educators also recommend using captions as a teaching tool. Table 9.2 lists some ways parents can use captions to help their children develop better language and reading skills.

Text telephone (TT).
A device connected to a telephone by a special adapter; allows communication over the telephone between persons who are hearing impaired and those with hearing; sometimes referred to as a TTY (teletype) or TTD (telecommunication device for the deaf).

Telephone Adaptations   At one time persons with hearing loss had problems using telephones, either because their hearing loss was too great or because of acoustic feedback (noise caused by closeness of the telephone receiver to their hearing aids). However, the invention of **text telephones (TT),** sometimes referred to as TTYs (teletypes) or TTDs (telecommunication devices for the deaf). A person can use a TT connected to a telephone to type a message to anyone else who has a TT, and a special phone adaptation allows someone without a TT to use the pushbuttons on his or her phone to "type" messages to someone with a TT.

TABLE 9.2 Tips for Parents About Captioned Programs

Even the best of readers can experience difficulty understanding all of the captions on TV or video. Moreover, if a child does not have strong reading skills then he or she might be inclined to watch a TV or video program without the captions so that there is no interference with the picture. Indeed, reading captions, like reading books, is a skill that must be nurtured. Following are some tips to guide parents to help their deaf child meet the challenges of reading captions:

1. Leave the captions turned on at all times. Show that captioning is a part of the family's TV culture and not just something that is turned on in the presence of deaf children. Leaving the captioning on whenever the TV is turned on demonstrates to deaf children that their communication needs are a valued part of how the family functions.

2. Watch TV and videos with your deaf child. Find out which programs are your child's favorites and take the time to watch some of them. If the timing of the program does not allow you to watch the program, then you might wish to tape the program and watch it later. Taping a program gives you the opportunity to watch a program more than once, to stop the program at any time to talk about what is happening, and to review words and sentences.

3. Explain to your deaf child what is happening in a show. This will make it easier for the child to understand the captioning, and it will certainly make it easier fro him or her to follow the show.

4. Explain the meaning of visual cues that appear as a part of the captioning. These cues come in a variety of forms such as musical notes to indicate music or text in parentheses to describe action that can be heard occurring elsewhere, such as a dog barking or a siren blaring.

5. If the captions help you understand what is being said on TV, then tell this to your deaf child. Provide real examples, such as the captions helped you learn the spelling of a name or word or it helped you understand what was being said because you could not understand what the speaker was saying.

6. Use captioned programs as a way of directly communicating with your deaf child. Captioned TV by itself is not an adequate substitute for direct communication. However, the time you spend with your child discussing a program is an excellent language-learning opportunity.

SOURCE: From Stewart, D.A., & Kluwin, T.N. (2001). *Teaching deaf and hard of hearing students: Content, strategies, and curriculum* (p. 326). Boston: Allyn & Bacon. Reprinted/adapted with permission.

The federal government now requires each state to have a relay service for use by people with TTs. A relay service allows a person with a TT to communicate with anyone through an operator, who conveys the message to a person who does not have a TT. The TT user can carry on a conversation with the non-TT user, or the TT user can leave a message. The latter is useful for carrying out everyday activities, such as scheduling appointments. More and more people with hearing losses are also making use of another telephone device—the fax.

Computer-Assisted Instruction (CAI)   The explosion of microcomputer and related technology (e.g., videodiscs, CD-ROMs) is expanding learning capabilities for people who are deaf and their families. For example, visual displays of speech patterns on a computer screen can help someone with hearing loss learn speech. Videodisc programs showing people sign are also available for use in learning ASL.

Another example of computer-based technology is C-Print (Stinson & Stuckless, 1998). With C-Print, a hearing person transcribes on a computer what is being said by, for example, someone lecturing. The student who is deaf can read a real-time text display on her or his computer as well as receive a printout of the text at a later time (Kelly, 2000).

The Internet   The information superhighway has opened up a variety of communication possibilities for people who are deaf. For example, electronic mail allows people who are deaf to communicate with one another as well as with hearing individuals. People who are deaf may also subscribe to online lists, connect to newsgroups, and participate in "chat rooms" devoted to deafness, along with a multitude of other subjects. The ever-expanding World Wide Web provides access to a variety of information sources.

In addition to providing people who are deaf with a way to access information, educators can also use the Internet to help students who are deaf practice reading and writing skills. For instance, teachers can set up newsgroups through which students can communicate with others in the class, the school, or even worldwide.

Early Intervention

Two examples of publications devoted to issues of concern to the Deaf community are the magazines, Silent News and Deaf Life. The former also has a Web version: http://www.silentnews.com/index.html. On the site, it presents itself as "a good glimpse into the deaf community." Deaf Life's Web site at http://www.deaflife.com/ has chat rooms for adults and just for children. ■

Education for infants and preschoolers with hearing losses is of critical importance. Because language development is such an issue with children who are hearing impaired and because early childhood is such an important time for the development of language, it is not surprising that many of the most controversial issues surrounding early intervention in the area of deafness focus on language. As indicated in the earlier discussion of oralism versus manualism, some people maintain that English language should be the focus of intervention efforts, and others hold that ASL should be used starting in infancy. Among English-language advocates, some professionals recommend a total communication approach, combining spoken English and some kind of signed English system.

Children who are deaf who have parents who are deaf are likely to do better than children who are deaf who have hearing parents. For example, in infancy they develop ASL at a rate similar to the rate at which hearing infants of hearing parents develop English. But infants who are deaf who have hearing parents do not develop either English or ASL at as fast a rate. This may be due to the fact that day-to-day interactions between mothers and infants are more facilitative and natural when both the infant and parents are deaf than when the infant is deaf and the parents are hearing. Hearing mothers of infants who are deaf tend to be more directive in their interactions with their infants—that is, they are more likely to start interactions that are unrelated to the child's activity or expressed interest (Bornstein et al., 1999; Spencer & Meadow-Orlans, 1996).

Because they lack a language model, deaf children of hearing parents sometimes resort to physical gestures and other "tricks" (e.g., pulling on clothing, stamping the feet) to try to capture their parents' attention and get what they want (Lane et al., 1996). This frustration in communication is probably the reason why hearing parents of children who are deaf often exhibit high degrees of stress (Meadow-Orlans, 1995). Also, parents who use sign with their children are more likely to have cohesive families, with a high degree of emotional bonding and sharing of interests (Kluwin & Gaustad, 1994).

In addition to facility with ASL, parents who are deaf also have the advantage of being better prepared to cope with their infant's deafness (Meadow-Orlans, 1990). Parents who are hearing are unprepared for the birth of a child with hearing loss, whereas parents who are deaf can draw on their own experiences in order to offer helpful support to their child who is deaf.

Hearing parents, especially if they desire to teach their infants sign language, may need help in understanding the importance of the visual modality in communicating with their infants (Bornstein et al., 1999). Hearing parents need to understand, for example, that the eye gaze of the infant who is deaf is extremely important because it is his or her way of expressing interest and motivation. These parents also need to be aware that, just as hearing babies babble vocally, babies who are deaf engage in babbling with their hands as they begin to acquire sign language.

Hearing parents of children who are deaf face a quandary over how to provide their children with appropriate sign language models. Both signed English and ASL, especially the latter, are difficult to learn to a high degree of fluency in a relatively short period of time. And like any language, ASL is harder to acquire as an adult and can rarely be learned to the same degree of fluency as that possessed by a native ASL signer.

The fact that over 90 percent of children who are deaf have parents who are hearing underscores the importance of intervention for many infants who are deaf. In fact, many authorities believe that there is a far greater need for early intervention for families with hearing parents of a child who is deaf than for families where both the parents and the child are deaf (Andrews & Zmijewski, 1997).

Educators have established preschool intervention projects in order to teach the basics of sign language to the parents of children who are deaf as well as to the children themselves. Such projects are generally successful at teaching the rudiments of sign to parents and infants. Once the child is ready to progress beyond one- and two-word signed utterances, however, it is important that native signers be available as models. Authorities recommend a practice that is popular in Sweden—that adults who are deaf be part of early intervention efforts because they can serve as sign language models and can help hearing parents form positive expectations about their children's potential (Lane et al., 1996). Even though hearing parents may never be able to communicate fluently in sign language, it is important that they continue to sign with their child. Not only does signing allow parents a means of communicating with the child; it also demonstrates that they value the child's language and the Deaf culture.

Transition to Adulthood

Unemployment and underemployment (being overqualified for a job) have been persistent problems for persons with a hearing loss, especially women (Schirmer, 2001). There is some evidence, however, that this bleak picture is slowly beginning to change. And the primary reason for this change has been the expansion of postsecondary programming for students with hearing loss. A 15-year follow-up of graduates with hearing loss from two-year or four-year colleges found that a college education made a substantial difference in having a satisfying career and life (Schroedel & Geyer, 2000).

While most agree on the advantages of having sign language interpreters in a variety of settings, there is some debate over the use of transliteration, rather than ASL, by the many interpreters. ■

Tips for Working with Sign Language Interpreters

In an article for the journal *College Teaching,* Linda Siple (1993) provides some practical tips for working with sign language interpreters. She notes that first the entire class must have a trusting relationship with the interpreter. His or her job is to translate *everything* that is said in the presence of the student who is deaf, which may include irrelevant or inappropriate comments made during class breaks—even jokes or negative remarks about the student for whom the interpreter is signing.

The interpreter also is expected to maintain confidentiality with regard to sensitive information about the student who is deaf. For example, if the same individual also interprets for the student in other situations (e.g., student health services, financial aid, etc.), any information revealed must be maintained in confidence.

Siple offers the following suggestions for instructors and their classes:

- The interpreter should have copies of all handouts and, if possible, copies of textbooks.
- If a fellow student or the instructor wishes to speak to the student who is deaf, he or she should speak directly to the student, not to the interpreter.

- It is more difficult to interpret in a class in which there is a lot of discussion. Participants should try to talk one at a time, and the instructor should realize that the time lag between what is spoken and when it is signed will put the student who is deaf at a disadvantage during discussion.
- In a lecture class, the instructor should be aware of the pace of his or her delivery, perhaps pausing more frequently than usual.
- If the instructor is comfortable, he or she may request that the interpreter stop the class if something becomes too complicated to interpret. In fact, the interpreter's need to clarify may very well be an indication that the rest of the students do not understand the information either.
- The interpreter should not be considered a participant in the class. Questions for him or her should not be addressed when he or she is not interpreting.

SOURCE: Based on L.A. Siple, "Working with the sign language interpreter in your classroom," *College Teaching, 41,* 139–142, 1993. Reprinted with permission of the Helen Dwight Reid Educational Foundation. Published by Heldref Publications, 1319 Eighteenth St., N.W., Washington, D.C. 20036–1802. Copyright © 1993.

POSTSECONDARY EDUCATION

Before the mid-1960s, the only institution established specifically for the postsecondary education of students with hearing loss was Gallaudet College (now Gallaudet University). Except for this one institution, these students were left with no choice but to attend traditional colleges and universities. However, traditional postsecondary schools were generally not equipped to handle the special needs of students with hearing loss. It is little wonder, then, that a study by Quigley, Jenne, and Phillips (1968) was able to identify only 224 persons with hearing loss who were graduates of regular colleges and universities in the United States between 1910 and 1965.

Findings such as these led to the expansion of postsecondary programs. The federal government has now funded a wide variety of postsecondary programs for students with hearing loss. The two most well-known ones are Gallaudet University and the National Technical Institute for the Deaf (NTID) at the Rochester Institute of Technology. The NTID program, emphasizing training in technical fields, complements the liberal arts orientation of Gallaudet University. At NTID, some students with hearing loss also attend classes with hearing students at the Rochester Institute of Technology.

In addition to Gallaudet and NTID, there are now well over 100 postsecondary programs in the United States and Canada for students with hearing loss. By law, Gallaudet and NTID are responsible for serving students from all fifty states and territories. Others serve students from several states, from one state only, or from specific districts only.

Although many people who are deaf who enroll in higher education choose to attend Gallaudet, NTID, or colleges with special programs, some go to traditional colleges and universities. These students usually take advantage of the expanding roles of university programs that have been established to facilitate the academic experiences of students with disabilities. One of the accommodations often recommended is to provide sign language interpreters in the classes of students with hearing loss.

The role of interpreters generates a debate comparable to the one in total communication classrooms concerning ASL versus signed English (discussed earlier). The central conflict is over the use of transliteration, rather than ASL, by the majority of interpreters. **Transliteration,** which is similar to signed English, maintains the same word order as spoken English. ASL, on the other hand, requires the interpreter to digest the meaning of what is said before conveying it through signs. Although interpreters find it more difficult to use ASL, research has shown that it is more effective than transliteration (Livingston, Singer, & Abrahamson, 1994).

Most college instructors have limited, if any, experience in working with sign language interpreters. Even so, it is critical that instructors and interpreters work closely together in order to provide the optimum learning experience for students who are deaf, while not disrupting other students in the class (Siple, 1993). The box on p. 332 provides some tips for working with sign language interpreters.

Sign language interpreters are also used in elementary and secondary schools, where the issues concerning their use are no less severe. There is a tremendous shortage of qualified interpreters for the public schools. And there is often disagreement over role definition. For example, teachers sometimes treat interpreters like teacher aides, asking them to help grade papers and tutor students (Jones, Clark, & Soltz, 1997).

FAMILY ISSUES

With regard to raising a family, persons who are deaf often face unique challenges. National statistics indicate that 95 percent of adults who are deaf choose deaf spouses, and 90 percent of the offspring of these marriages have normal hearing (Buchino, 1993). These hearing children often serve as interpreters for their parents. Being called on to interpret for one's parents can help develop self-confidence around adult authority figures (e.g., doctors, lawyers, insurance agents), but it can also force one to face some unpleasant biases, as the following story from a hearing child of deaf parents demonstrates:

> Curled up in the seat, chin dug into my chest, I noticed there was a lull in the conversation. Dad was a confident driver, but Mom was smoking more than usual.
> "Something happened? That gas station?" Mom signed to me.
> "No, nothing," I lied.
> "Are you sure?"
> "Everything is fine." Dad and I had gone to pay and get directions. The man behind the counter had looked up, seen me signing and grunted, "Huh, I didn't think mutes were allowed to have driver's licenses." Long ago I'd gotten used to hearing those kind of comments. But I never could get used to the way it made me churn inside. (Walker, 1986, p. 9)

These children also sometimes admit to resenting the fact that being called on to interpret for their parents interfered with their social lives (Buchino, 1993).

There has been a long tradition of preparing students who are deaf for manual trades (Lane, 1992). But today, unskilled and semiskilled trades are fast disappearing from the workforce in favor of jobs requiring higher-level skills. As a result, adults who are deaf face even greater obstacles when they enter the job market. Although the educational, work, and social opportunities for adults who are deaf are often limited, there are reasons to be optimistic about the future. With the continued expansion of transition programming, postsecondary education, and greater public awareness of the potential of people who are deaf should come a brighter outlook for more adults who are deaf.

Transliteration.
A method used by sign language interpreters in which the signs maintain the same word order as that of spoken English; although used by most interpreters, found through research not to be as effective as American Sign Language (ASL).

℘ Children of Deaf Adults (CODA) is an organization devoted to children of adults who are deaf. You can visit its Web site at http://www.coda-international.org/
As stated on the Web site, "CODA is an organization established for the purpose of promoting family awareness and individual growth in hearing children of deaf parents. This purpose is accomplished through providing educational opportunities, promoting self-help, organizing advocacy efforts, and acting as a resource for the membership and various communities." ■

Summary

In defining hearing loss, educators are concerned primarily with the extent to which hearing loss affects the ability to speak and understand spoken language. They refer to people who cannot process linguistic information as *deaf* and those who can as *hard of hearing*. In addition, those who are deaf at birth or before language develops are referred to as having *prelingual deafness,* and those who acquire their deafness after spoken language starts to develop are referred to as having *postlingual deafness*. Professionals favoring a physiological viewpoint define deaf children as those who cannot hear sounds at or above a certain intensity level; they call others with hearing impairment "hard of hearing." Many people who are deaf resent being defined as "disabled" at all; they prefer to be considered a cultural or language minority.

The three most commonly used types of tests for hearing acuity are pure-tone audiometry, speech audiometry, and specialized tests for very young and hard-to-test children. The examiner uses pure tones or speech to find the intensity of sound (measured in decibels) the person can hear at different frequency levels (measured in hertz). Audiologists can test very young children, using otoacoustic, play, or evoked-response audiometry.

Professionals often classify causes of hearing loss according to the location of the problem within the hearing mechanism. *Conductive* losses are impairments that interfere with transfer of sound along the conductive pathway of the ear. *Sensorineural* problems are confined to the complex inner ear and are apt to be more severe and harder to treat.

Impairments of the outer ear are caused by such things as infections of the external canal or tumors. Middle-ear troubles usually occur because of some malfunction of one or more of the three tiny bones called ossicles in the middle ear. Otitis media, a condition stemming from eustachian tube malfunctioning, is the most common problem of the middle ear. The most common inner-ear troubles are linked to hereditary factors. Acquired hearing losses of the inner ear include those due to bacterial infections (such as meningitis), viral infections (such as mumps and measles), prenatal infections of the mother (such as cytomegalovirus, maternal rubella, and syphilis), and deprivation of oxygen at birth. Exposure to loud noises can also result in damage to the inner ear.

Hearing loss can have a profound effect on people, largely because of the emphasis on spoken language in U.S. society. By far, the greatest impact of a hearing loss is on the ability to speak and understand language. However, authorities now recognize that sign language is as true a language as spoken language. They recommend that people who are deaf be tested in sign language and/or with nonverbal tests of intelligence.

In general, the academic achievement of students with hearing loss is very low. Even in math, their best academic area, they demonstrate severe underachievement. Several studies have shown that children who are deaf who have parents who are deaf have higher reading achievement than children who are deaf who have hearing parents. This is probably because parents who are deaf are able to communicate more easily with their children through sign language. There is some evidence that students who have more facility with ASL also have higher academic achievement.

Because of problems finding people with whom to communicate, students who are deaf are at risk for loneliness. This problem is particularly acute in inclusive settings, in which there are few students with hearing loss with whom to communicate. Some authorities also believe that students who are deaf who have hearing parents may experience more unhappiness because of the difficulty they have in communicating with their parents.

Because of these problems in communicating with the larger society, many people who are deaf socialize almost exclusively with others who have hearing loss. At one time many professionals viewed this tendency toward isolation as negative. More and more authorities are pointing out the potential benefits of a Deaf culture. The Deaf culture is built on six features: linguistic differentiation, attitudinal deafness, behavioral norms, endogamous marriage patterns, historical awareness, and voluntary organizational networks.

Some believe that the cultural status of students who are deaf is vulnerable because of the current emphasis on inclusion in the schools. They cite the decline in Deaf clubs as evidence of the erosion of the Deaf culture. Deaf activists have increasingly decried what they consider to be an oppressive medical and educational establishment, pointing to cochlear implants as an example. However, the use of cochlear implantation has continued to increase, and advances in technology have increased its effectiveness, although it is a far cry from being a cure for deafness.

For many years there were two basic approaches to teaching students with hearing impairment: *oralism* and *manualism*. Today, most educators of students who are deaf favor *total communication*, a blend of oralism and manualism. Most educators who use total communication stress the auditory-verbal approach, speechreading, and signing English systems.

Some within the Deaf community are dissatisfied with total communication because it uses a signing English system rather than American Sign Language (ASL). Signing English systems are not true languages, in that they follow the word order of spoken English. Proponents of American Sign Language (ASL) argue that it is a grammatically sophisticated, highly evolved language of its own. Moreover, these proponents believe that deaf children should be proficient in ASL and that their education should be based on bilingual models. This *bicultural-bilingual approach* involves using ASL as the primary language in academic instruction and using English as the second language. It also promotes instruction in the history of the Deaf culture.

Students with hearing loss can be found in a variety of settings, ranging from inclusion in general education classrooms to residential settings. Although the likelihood of inclusion in general education is greater for those with less severe hearing loss, those who are younger, and those who have parents who are hearing, the overall increase in inclusion has been viewed with skepticism by many in the Deaf community and other professionals.

Numerous technological advances are helping persons with hearing loss. These innovations are occurring primarily in the areas of hearing aids, television and movie captioning, telephones, computer-assisted instruction (CAI), and the Internet.

There are now many programs for infants and preschoolers with hearing loss. Research indicates that the families of children who are deaf who have hearing parents may be in greater need of intervention than are families of children who are deaf who have parents who are also deaf. One reason for this is that hearing parents generally are not proficient in ASL, which is difficult to learn quickly.

In addition to Gallaudet University and the National Technical Institute for the Deaf, which focus on the education of students who are deaf or hard of hearing, there are now several postsecondary programs for students with hearing loss. Deaf students enrolled in traditional colleges can take advantage of the increasing presence of sign language interpreters and other university programs. Transition programming for students who do not intend to take part in postsecondary programs is also expanding. Unemployment and the number of persons who are overqualified for their jobs among people who have hearing loss are improving, but they are still exceedingly high.

June Sibley

Cat, Marker on paper. 14 × 17 in.

Ms. Sibley, who was born in 1946 in Melrose, Massachusetts, is proud of her Native American ancestors. She loves working on nature themes, especially animals. She is very attached to her pets, specifically her hamster named Snowball.

Learners with Blindness or Low Vision

No two blind people are alike. I, for instance, grew up wearing chains like Houdini, trying to pull off a magic trick. Not everyone with vision loss goes through this long struggle with self-consciousness. There are those who lose their vision suddenly and find tremendous powers of resilience. They give hope to the people around them, both the sighted and the blind.

We are, all of us, ecstatic creatures, capable of joyous mercy to the self and to others. The strong blind move like modern dancers, their every gesture means something. The newly blind or the lifelong blind often possess an art of living, an invisible, delicate vessel they carry. The sighted can have it too: Jose Carreras comes to mind. After his bout with leukemia, he still sings, and though some critics say that the great tenor's voice is not the same, I say it is more thrilling, touched as it is with buds of darkness. Sometimes roses grow on the sheer banks of the sea cliff.

STEPHEN KUUSISTO
The Planet of the Blind: A Memoir

Stephen Kuusisto's struggle to embrace a blind identity (see quote on p. 337) is not that unusual. Although blind from birth, Kuusisto was well into his adult years before he stopped the charade of trying to "pass" as a sighted person. Once at peace with his blindness, he was able to turn his energies to more productive endeavors, such as being a successful author. As Kuusisto points out, people vary in their response to being blind. Some may actually gain an inner strength from adversity. However, a major impediment to being able to accept one's blindness is society's reactions to people who are blind. Visual impairments seem to evoke more awkwardness than most other disabilities. Why are we so uncomfortably aware of blindness? For one thing, blindness is visible. We often do not realize that a person has impaired hearing, for example, until we actually talk to him or her. The person with visual impairment, however, usually has a variety of symbols—cane, thick or darkened glasses, a guide dog.

Another possible reason for being self-conscious around people who are blind is the role that eyes play in social interaction. Poets, playwrights, and songwriters have long recognized how emotionally expressive the eyes can be for people who are sighted. We all know how uncomfortable it can be to talk with someone who does not make eye contact with us. Think how often we have heard someone say or have ourselves said that we prefer to talk "face to face" on an important matter, rather than over the telephone.

Another reason we fear loss of vision is that the sense of sight is linked so closely with the traditional concept of beauty. We derive great pleasure from our sight. Our feelings about others are often based largely on physical appearances that are visually perceived.

Finally, our use of language reinforces a negative view of blindness:

> The word *blind* has always meant more than merely the inability to see. . . . Throughout history of the language and in common usage today, the word [*blind*] connotes a lack of understanding . . . , a willful disregard or obliviousness, a thing meant to conceal or deceive. In fact, when you stop to listen, the word is far more commonly used in its figurative than its literal sense. And it comes up so often: blind faith, blind devotion, blind luck, . . . blind alley, . . . blind taste test, double-blind study, flying blind, . . . blind submission, blind side, blind spot. . . . Pick up any book or magazine and you will find dozens of similes and metaphors connecting blindness and blind people with ignorance, confusion, indifference, ineptitude. (Kleege, 1999, p. 21)

So, despite the fact that blindness is the least prevalent of all disabilities, at least in children, people dread it. It is reportedly the third most feared condition, with only cancer and AIDS outranking it (Jernigan, 1992). With a bit of reflection, however, it becomes obvious that our anxieties about blindness are irrational. Most of our apprehension can be attributed to our lack of experience in interacting with individuals with visual impairment. It is not until we talk to people who are blind or read about their appreciation of sounds, smells, and touch that we begin to realize that sight is not the only sense that enables us to enjoy beauty or interact socially with other people.

Like anyone with a disability, the person who is blind wants to be treated like everyone else. Most people who are blind do not seek pity or unnecessary help. In fact, they can be fiercely protective of their independence. See the box on p. 340 for tips of etiquette on interacting with someone who is blind.

In this chapter we hope to dispel several myths about blindness. We start by presenting a fact that most sighted people do not know: The majority of people who are blind can actually see.

MISCONCEPTIONS ABOUT
Persons with Blindness or Low Vision

MYTH   People who are legally blind have no sight at all.

FACT   Only a small percentage of people who are legally blind have absolutely no vision. Many have a useful amount of functional vision.

MYTH   People who are blind have an extra sense that enables them to detect obstacles.

FACT   People who are blind do not have an extra sense. Some can develop an "obstacle sense" by noting the change in pitch of echoes as they move toward objects.

MYTH   People who are blind automatically develop better acuity in their other senses.

FACT   Through concentration and attention, individuals who are blind can learn to make very fine discriminations in the sensations they obtain. This is not automatic but rather represents a better use of received sensations.

MYTH   People who are blind have superior musical ability.

FACT   The musical ability of people who are blind is not necessarily better than that of sighted people; however, many people who are blind pursue musical careers as one way in which they can achieve success.

MYTH   Stereotypic behaviors (e.g., body rocking, head swaying) are always maladaptive and should be totally eliminated.

FACT   Although more research is needed, there are some authorities who maintain that these behaviors, except when they are extreme, can help persons who are blind regulate their levels of arousal.

MYTH   Braille is not very useful for the vast majority of people who are blind; it should only be tried as a last resort.

FACT   Very few people who are blind have learned braille, primarily due to fear that using it is a sign of failure and to a historical professional bias against it. Authorities acknowledge the utility of braille for people who are blind.

MYTH   Braille is of no value for those who have low vision.

FACT   Some individuals with low vision have conditions that will eventually result in blindness. More and more, authorities think that these individuals should learn braille to be prepared for when they cannot read print effectively.

MYTH   If people with low vision use their eyes too much, their sight will deteriorate.

FACT   Only rarely is this true. Visual efficiency can actually be improved through training and use. Wearing strong lenses, holding books close to the eyes, and using the eyes often cannot harm vision.

MYTH   Mobility instruction should be delayed until elementary or secondary school.

FACT   Many authorities now recognize that even preschoolers can take advantage of mobility instruction, including the use of a cane.

MYTH   The long cane is a simply constructed, easy-to-use device.

FACT   The National Academy of Sciences has drawn up specifications for the manufacture of the long cane and its proper use.

MYTH   Guide dogs take people where they want to go.

FACT   The guide dog does not "take" the person anywhere; the person must first know where he or she is going. The dog is primarily a protection against unsafe areas or obstacles.

MYTH   Technology will soon replace the need for braille and for mobility aids such as the long cane and guide dogs. In addition, a breakthrough for restoring complete sight through technology is just around the corner.

FACT   As amazing as some of the technology is in the field of vision impairment, it is doubtful that it will be as effective as braille, the long cane, or guide dogs anytime soon. Research on artificial vision is exciting, but it too does not promise to have huge practical benefits for some time.

Legally blind.
A person who has visual acuity of 20/200 or less in the better eye even with correction (e.g., eyeglasses) or has a field of vision so narrow that its widest diameter subtends an angular distance no greater than 20 degrees.

Low vision.
A term used by educators to refer to individuals whose visual impairment is not so severe that they are unable to read print of any kind; they may read large or regular print, and they may need some kind of magnification.

Definition and Classification

The two most common ways of describing someone with a visual disability are the legal and educational definitions. The former is the one laypeople and medical professionals use; the latter is the one educators favor. The two major classifications are blindness and low vision.

LEGAL DEFINITION

The legal definition involves assessment of visual acuity and field of vision. A person who is **legally blind** has visual acuity of 20/200 or less in the better eye even with correction (e.g., eyeglasses) or has a field of vision so narrow that its widest diameter subtends an angular distance no greater than 20 degrees. The fraction 20/200 means that the person sees at 20 feet what a person with normal vision sees at 200 feet. (Normal visual acuity is thus 20/20.) The inclusion of a narrowed field of vision in the legal definition means that a person may have 20/20 vision in the central field but severely restricted peripheral vision. Legal blindness qualifies a person for certain legal benefits, such as tax advantages and money for special materials.

In addition to this medical classification of blindness, there is also a category referred to as low vision (sometimes referred to as partially sighted). According to the legal classification system, persons who have **low vision** have visual acuity falling between 20/70 and 20/200 in the better eye with correction.

Social Interaction with People Who Are Blind: Points of Etiquette

The following letter to "Dear Abby" from the president of the American Foundation for the Blind lists some appropriate ways that the sighted can interact with those who are blind. Suggestions such as these help to avoid awkward social situations.

Dear Abby:

You recently ran a letter from a woman who gave a few tips on what sighted people should do when they meet a blind person. As president of the American Foundation for the Blind, and a blind person myself, I believe I can add a few more points of etiquette your readers may find helpful.

1. Speak to people who are blind or visually impaired using a natural conversational tone and speed. Do not speak loudly and slowly unless the person also has a hearing impairment.
2. Address blind people by name when possible. This is especially important in crowded places.
3. Immediately greet blind people when they enter a room or service area. This lets them know you are present and ready to assist.
4. Indicate the end of a conversation with a blind per-

son in order to avoid the embarrassment of leaving a person speaking when no one is actually there.
5. Feel free to use words that refer to vision when conversing with blind people. Words such as "look," "see," "watching TV," are part of everyday communication. The words "blind" and "visually impaired" are also acceptable in conversation.
6. Do not leave a blind person standing in "free space" when you serve as a guide. Also, be sure that the person you guide has a firm grasp on your arm or is leaning against a chair or a wall if you have to be separated momentarily.
7. Be calm and clear about what to do if you see a blind person about to encounter a dangerous situation. For example, if the person is about to bump into something, calmly and firmly call out, "Wait there for a moment; there is an obstruction in your path." . . .

Carl R. Augusto, President
American Foundation for the Blind, New York.

SOURCE: Letter reprinted with permission of the American Foundation for the Blind.

EDUCATIONAL DEFINITION

Many professionals, particularly educators, have found the legal classification scheme inadequate. They have observed that visual acuity is not a very accurate predictor of how people will function or use whatever remaining sight they have. Although a small percentage of individuals who are legally blind have absolutely no vision, the majority are able to see to some degree.

Many who recognize the limitations of the legal definition of blindness and low vision favor the educational definition, which stresses the method of reading instruction. For educational purposes, individuals who are blind are so severely impaired they *must* learn to read braille or use aural methods (audiotapes and records). (**Braille,** a system of raised dots by which blind people read with their fingertips, consists of quadrangular cells containing from one to six dots whose arrangement denotes different letters and symbols.) Educators often refer to those individuals who can read print, even if they need magnifying devices or large-print books, as having low vision. For example, the following educator's definition states that a person with low vision is someone:

> *who has difficulty accomplishing visual tasks, even with prescribed corrective lenses, but who can enhance his or her ability to accomplish these tasks with the use of compensatory visual strategies, low vision or other devices, and environmental modifications.* (italics in the original) (Corn & Koenig, 1996, p. 4)

It is important to note that, even though persons with low vision can read print, many authorities believe that some of them can benefit from using braille. (We discuss this later in the chapter.) This is why we emphasized above that those who are considered blind *must* use braille in order to read.

Prevalence

Blindness is primarily an adult disability. Most estimates indicate that blindness is approximately one-tenth as prevalent in school-age children as in adults. Only about .05 percent of the population ranging from six to seventeen years of age is classified by the federal government as "visually impaired," which includes those who are blind or who have low vision. This makes visual impairment one of the least prevalent disabilities in children.

Anatomy and Physiology of the Eye

The anatomy of the visual system is extremely complex, so our discussion here will focus only on basic characteristics. Figure 10.1 shows the functioning of the eye. The physical object being seen becomes an electrical impulse sent through the optic nerve to the visual center of the brain, the occipital lobes. Before reaching the optic nerve, light rays reflecting off the object being seen pass through several structures within the eye. The light rays:

1. pass through the **cornea** (a transparent cover in front of the iris and pupil), which performs the major part of the bending (refraction) of the light rays so that the image will be focused
2. pass through the **aqueous humor** (a watery substance between the cornea and lens of the eye)
3. pass through the **pupil** (the contractile opening in the middle of the **iris,** the colored portion of the eye that contracts or expands, depending on the amount of light striking it)

Braille.
A system in which raised dots allow people who are blind to read with their fingertips; each quadrangular cell contains from one to six dots, the arrangement of which denotes different letters and symbols.

Cornea.
A transparent cover in front of the iris and pupil in the eye; responsible for most of the refraction of light rays in focusing on an object.

Aqueous humor.
A watery substance between the cornea and lens of the eye.

Pupil.
The contractile opening in the middle of the iris of the eye.

Iris.
The colored portion of the eye; contracts or expands, depending on the amount of light striking it.

CW Several Web sites contain sample Snellen charts. Some examples are:

http://www.gimbel.com/check-yv.htm

http://www.saoa.co.za/chart.htm

http://www.vision3k.com/snellen.asp

http://www.thomson-software-solutions.com/snellen_charts.html

The Web site of Prevent Blindness America contains an example of a Web-based measure of near vision: http://www.preventblindness.org/eye_tests/near_vision_test.html

Prevent Blindness America, founded in 1908, is a voluntary organization devoted to eye health and safety. Its Web site at http://www.preventblindness.org/ contains a variety of information on blindness prevention. ■

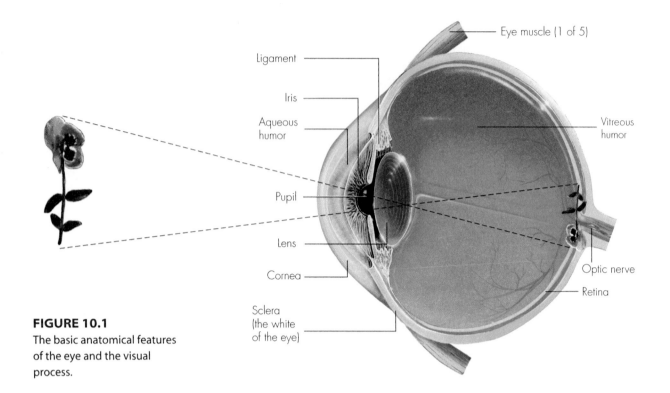

FIGURE 10.1
The basic anatomical features of the eye and the visual process.

Lens.
A structure that refines and changes the focus of the light rays passing through the eye.

Vitreous humor.
A transparent, gelatinous substance that fills the eyeball between the retina and the lens of the eye.

Retina.
The back portion of the eye, containing nerve fibers connected to the optic nerve.

Optic nerve.
The nerve at the back of the eye, which sends visual information back to the brain.

Snellen chart.
Used in determining visual acuity; consists of rows of letters or Es arranged in different positions; each row corresponds to the distance at which a normally sighted person can discriminate the letters; does not predict how accurately a child will be able to read print.

4. pass through the **lens,** which refines and changes the focus of the light rays before they pass through the **vitreous humor** (a transparent gelatinous substance that fills the eyeball between the retina and lens)
5. come to a focus on the **retina** (the back portion of the eye, containing nerve fibers connected to the **optic nerve,** which carries the information back to the brain)

Measurement of Visual Ability

Visual acuity is most often measured with the **Snellen chart,** which consists of rows of letters (for individuals who know the alphabet) or Es (for the very young and or those who cannot read). In the latter case, the Es are arranged in various positions, and the person's task is to indicate in what direction the "legs" of the Es face. Each row corresponds to the distance at which a person with normal vision can discriminate the directions of the Es. (There are eight rows, one corresponding to each of the following distances: 15, 20, 30, 40, 50, 70, 100, and 200 feet.) People are normally tested at the 20-foot distance. If they can distinguish the direction of the letters in the 20-foot row, they are said to have 20/20 central visual acuity for far distances. If they can distinguish only the much larger letters in the 70-foot row, they are said to have 20/70 central visual acuity for far distances.

Although the Snellen chart is widely used and can be very useful, it has at least three limitations:

1. It measures visual acuity for distant but not near objects—which is why it is necessary to report the results in terms of central visual acuity for *far* distances. Many educational activities, particularly reading, require visual acuity at close distances. There are small cards containing different sizes of print that can be used to measure near acuity (Minnesota Laboratory for Low-Vision Research, 1997; Wilkinson, 1996).

2. Visual acuity, as measured by the Snellen chart, does not always correspond with visual efficiency. **Visual efficiency** refers to the ability, for example, to control eye movement, discriminate objects from their background, and pay attention to important details. Barraga and colleagues have developed the Diagnostic Assessment Procedure (DAP) to assess visual efficiency (Barraga, 1983).

3. Visual acuity does not always correspond with how a student actually uses her or his vision in natural settings, which have variable environmental conditions (fluorescent lighting, windows that emit sunshine, highly reflective tile floors, and so forth).

To determine how students use their vision in everyday situations, the vision teacher performs a **functional vision assessment.** The vision teacher observes the student in his or her daily activities, taking note of how he or she functions under a variety of conditions (e.g. in sunny or cloudy weather), and on a variety of tasks (e.g., reading books, navigating within the classroom or from class to class) (Wilkinson, 1996).

As part of this assessment, teachers should be alert to signs that children might have visual disabilities. Prevent Blindness America (1998–2000) has listed a number of signs of possible eye problems on their Web site (see the box on below).

Causes

The most common visual problems are the results of errors of refraction. **Refraction** refers to the bending of the light rays as they pass through the various structures of the eye.

Visual efficiency.
A term used to refer to how well one uses his or her vision, including such things as control of eye movements, attention to visual detail, and discrimination of figure from background; believed by some to be more important than visual acuity alone in predicting a person's ability to function visually.

Functional vision assessment.
An appraisal of an individual's use of vision in everyday situations.

Refraction.
The bending of light rays as they pass through the structures (cornea, aqueous humor, pupil, lens, vitreous humor) of the eye.

Signs of Possible Eye Troubles in Children

It is possible for your child to have a serious vision problem without your being aware of it. Any concern about abnormalities in the appearance of the eyes or vision should be investigated. If you have any questions about your child's vision, see an eye doctor. In any case, start early to provide your child with a regular schedule of professional eye exams.

Signs of possible eye trouble in children include:

Behavior

- Rubs eyes excessively
- Shuts or covers one eye
- Tilts or thrusts head forward
- Has difficulty with reading or other close-up work
- Holds objects close to eyes
- Blinks more than usual or is irritable when doing close-up work
- Is unable to see distant things clearly
- Squints eyelids together or frowns

Appearance

- Crossed or misaligned eyes
- Red-rimmed, encrusted or swollen eyelids

- Inflamed or watery eyes
- Recurring styes (infections) on eyelids
- Color photos of eyes show white reflection instead of typical red or no reflection

Complaints

- Eyes itch, burn, or feel scratchy
- Cannot see well
- Dizziness, headaches or nausea following close-up work
- Blurred or double vision

If a child exhibits one or more of these signs, please seek professional eye care. A professional eye exam is recommended shortly after birth, by six months of age, before entering school (four or five years old) and periodically throughout school years. Regular eye exams are important since some eye problems have no signs or symptoms.

SOURCE: Retrieved April 20, 1998 from the World Wide Web: http://www.prevent-blindness.org/children/trouble_signs.html. Reprinted with permission from Prevent Blindness America®. Copyright © 1997.

FIGURE 10.2
Visual problems: (a) myopia,
(b) hyperopia.

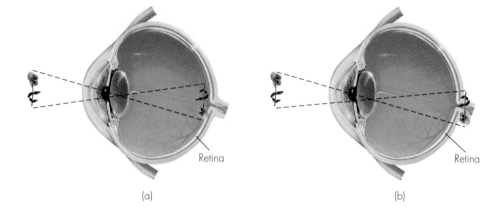

(a)   (b)

Myopia.
Nearsightedness; vision for
distant objects is affected;
usually results when eyeball is
too long.

Hyperopia.
Farsightedness; vision for near
objects is affected; usually
results when the eyeball is too
short.

Astigmatism.
Blurred vision caused by an
irregular cornea or lens.

Glaucoma.
A condition of excessive
pressure in the eyeball; the
cause is unknown; if untreated,
blindness results.

Cataracts.
A condition caused by
clouding of the lens of the eye;
affects color vision and
distance vision.

Diabetic retinopathy.
A condition resulting from
interference with the blood
supply to the retina; the fastest-
growing cause of blindness.

Retinitis pigmentosa.
A hereditary condition resulting
in degeneration of the retina;
causes a narrowing of the field
of vision and affects night
vision.

Tunnel vision.
A condition characterized by
problems in peripheral vision,
or a narrowing of the field of
vision.

Night blindness.
A condition characterized by
problems in seeing at low
levels of illumination; often
caused by retinitis pigmentosa.

Myopia (nearsightedness), **hyperopia** (farsightedness), and **astigmatism** (blurred vision) are examples of refraction errors that affect central visual acuity. Although each can be serious enough to cause significant impairment (myopia and hyperopia are the most common impairments of low vision), wearing glasses or contact lenses usually can bring vision within normal limits.

Myopia results when the eyeball is too long. In this case, the light rays from the object in Figure 10.2a would be in focus in front of, rather than on, the retina. Myopia affects vision for distant objects, but close vision may be unaffected. When the eyeball is too short, hyperopia (farsightedness) results (see Figure 10.2b). In this case, the light rays from the object in the diagram would be in focus behind, rather than on, the retina. Hyperopia affects vision for close objects, but far vision may be unaffected. If the cornea or lens of the eye is irregular, the person is said to have astigmatism. In this case, the light rays from the object in the figure would be blurred or distorted.

Among the most serious impairments are those caused by glaucoma, cataracts, and diabetes. These conditions occur primarily in adults, but each, particularly the latter two, can occur in children.

Glaucoma is a group of eye diseases that causes damage to the optic nerve. At one time it was thought to be due exclusively to excessive pressure inside the eyeball; we now know that some cases of glaucoma occur with normal pressure (Glaucoma Research Foundation, 2001; Glaucoma Foundation, 2001). It is referred to as the "sneak thief of sight" because it often occurs with no symptoms. However, glaucoma can be detected through an eye exam; and because it occurs more frequently in older persons (and in African Americans), professionals recommend increasingly frequent checkups, starting at age thirty-five (and even more frequently for African Americans.

Cataracts are caused by a clouding of the lens of the eye, which results in blurred vision. In children, the condition is called *congenital cataracts,* and distance and color vision are seriously affected. Surgery can usually correct the problems caused by cataracts. Diabetes can cause **diabetic retinopathy,** a condition resulting from interference with the blood supply to the retina.

Several other visual impairments primarily affect children. Visual impairments of school-age children are often due to prenatal causes, many of which are hereditary. We have already discussed congenital (meaning *present at birth*) cataracts and glaucoma. Another congenital condition is retinitis pigmentosa, a hereditary disease resulting in degeneration of the retina. It can start in infancy, early childhood, or the teenage years. **Retinitis pigmentosa** usually causes the field of vision to narrow (**tunnel vision**) and also affects one's ability to see in low light (**night blindness**). Included in the "prenatal" category are infectious diseases that affect the unborn child, such as syphilis and rubella.

A condition that can occur in childhood or adulthood is **cortical visual impairment (CVI).** CVI results from damage or dysfunction in the parts of the brain responsible for

Consider how people with certain visual impairments see the world: (a) normal vision; (b) glaucoma; (c) cataracts; (d) diabetic retinopathy; (e) retinitis pigmentosa ■

vision. The damage or dysfunction can be the result of a variety of causes, such as infection or stroke. Children who have it are characterized by wide fluctuations from day to day in their visual abilities. They often start out blind, with their vision tending to improve over time (Blind Babies Foundation, 2000a).

One of the most dramatic medical discoveries of a cause of blindness involved a condition now referred to as **retinopathy of prematurity (ROP)**. ROP, which results in abnormal growth of blood vessels in the eye, began to appear in the 1940s in premature infants. In the 1950s, researchers determined that excessive concentrations of oxygen often administered to premature infants were causing blindness. The oxygen was necessary to prevent brain damage, but it was often given at too high a level. Since then, hospitals have been careful to monitor the amount of oxygen administered to premature infants. With medical advances, many more premature babies are surviving, but they need very high levels of oxygen and are thus at risk for ROP. Furthermore, many authorities now believe that ROP can result from factors other than excessive oxygen that are related to being born very prematurely (Blind Babies Foundation, 2000b).

Two other conditions resulting in visual problems can be grouped because both are caused by improper muscle functioning. **Strabismus** is a condition in which one or both eyes are directed inward (crossed eyes) or outward. Left untreated, strabismus can result in permanent blindness because the brain will eventually reject signals from a deviating eye. Fortunately, most cases of strabismus are correctable with eye exercises or surgery. Eye exercises sometimes involve the person wearing a patch over the good eye for periods of time in order to force use of the eye that deviates. Surgery involves tightening or

Cortical visual impairment (CVI).
A poorly understood childhood condition that apparently involves dysfunction in the visual cortex; characterized by large day-to-day variations in visual ability.

Retinopathy of prematurity (ROP).
A condition resulting in abnormal growth of blood vessels in the eye; caused by factors related to premature birth, including the administration of an excessive concentration of oxygen at birth.

Strabismus.
A condition in which the eyes are directed inward (crossed eyes) or outward.

Nystagmus.
A condition in which there are rapid involuntary movements of the eyes; sometimes indicates a brain malfunction and/or inner-ear problems.

loosening the muscles that control eye movement. **Nystagmus** is a condition in which there are rapid involuntary movements of the eyes, usually resulting in dizziness and nausea. Nystagmus is sometimes a sign of brain malfunctioning and/or inner-ear problems.

Psychological and Behavioral Characteristics

LANGUAGE DEVELOPMENT

Most authorities believe that lack of vision does not have a very significant effect on the ability to understand and use language. They point to the many studies showing that students who are visually impaired do not differ from sighted students on verbal intelligence tests. Because auditory more than visual perception is the sensory modality through which we learn language, it is not surprising that studies have found that people who are blind are not impaired in language functioning. The child who is blind is still able to hear language and may even be more motivated than the sighted child to use language because it is the main channel through which he or she communicates with others.

There are, however, a few subtle differences in the way in which language usually develops in children, especially infants, who are visually impaired (Perez-Pereira & Conti-Ramsden, 1999). There appears to be a delay in the very earliest stages of language for some infants with visual impairment; their first words tend to come later. Once they start producing words, however, their vocabulary expands rapidly.

INTELLECTUAL ABILITY

Performance on Standardized Intelligence Tests   At one time it was popular for researchers to compare the intelligence of sighted persons with that of persons with blindness. Samuel P. Hayes pioneered the intelligence testing of people who are blind (Hayes, 1942, 1950). He took verbal items from a commonly used IQ test to assess individuals with blindness. His rationale was that people without sight would not be disadvantaged by a test that relied on verbal items: therefore, this kind of test would be a more accurate measure of intelligence than tests containing items of a visual nature.

Most authorities now believe that such comparisons are virtually impossible because finding comparable tests is so difficult (Warren, 1994). From what is known, there is no reason to believe that blindness results in lower intelligence.

Conceptual Abilities   It is also very difficult to assess the performance of children with visual impairment on laboratory-type tasks of conceptual ability. Many researchers, using conceptual tasks originally developed by noted psychologist Jean Piaget, have concluded that infants and very young children who are blind lag behind their sighted peers. This is usually attributed to the fact that they rely more on touch to arrive at conceptualizations of many objects, and touch is less efficient than sight. However, these early delays do not last for long, especially once they begin to use language to gather information about their environment (Perez-Pereira & Conti-Ramsden, 1999). Touch, however, remains a very critical sense throughout life for those who are blind. As one person who is blind described it, he "sees with his fingers" (Hull, 1990).

An important difference between individuals with and without sight is that the latter need to take much more initiative in order to learn what they can from their environment. Sighted infants and children can pick up a lot of visual information incidentally. In a sense, the world comes to them, whereas children who are visually impaired need to extend themselves out to the world in order to pick up some of the same information. Exploring the environment motorically, however, does not come easily for infants and young children with visual impairment, especially those who are blind. Many have serious delays in motor skills, such as sitting up, crawling, and walking (Perez-Pereira & Conti-Ramsden, 1999). Authorities recommend that adults do as much as possible to encourage

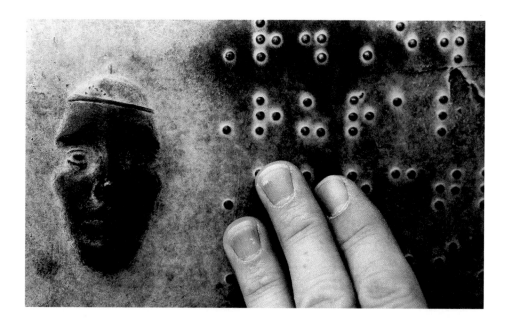

A bas-relief bronze wall of the FDR Memorial includes braille characters that many people who are blind find difficult to read because they are too big. ∎

infants and young children who are blind to explore their environment (Wheeler, Floyd, & Griffin, 1997).

In addition to fostering a sense of exploration in children who are visually impaired, it is also critical that teachers and parents provide intensive and extensive instruction in order to help them develop their conceptual abilities:

> Children with severe visual impairments can build concepts that are just as elaborate as a sighted person's visualizations, but this will inevitably be a longer and less direct process. . . . The point is that for children with visual impairments, less can be gained from direct observation, requiring adults and other interactive partners to be more systematic and structured in their explanations and information-giving. (Webster & Roe, 1998, p. 70)

ORIENTATION AND MOBILITY

Orientation and mobility skills are very important for the successful adjustment of people with vision loss. **Orientation and mobility (O & M) skills** refer to the ability to have a sense of where one is in relation to other people, objects, and landmarks (orientation) and to move through the environment (mobility). O & M skills depend to a great extent on spatial ability. The spatial abilities of persons who are blind continue to develop throughout childhood and adolescence; full development does not occur until well into the teenage years (Ochaita & Huertas, 1993).

Authorities have identified two ways in which persons with visual impairment process spatial information—as a sequential route, or as a map depicting the general relation of various points in the environment (Webster & Roe, 1998). The latter method, referred to as **cognitive mapping,** is preferable because it offers more flexibility in navigating. Consider three sequential points—A, B, and C. A sequential mode of processing spatial information restricts a person's movement so she or he can move from A to C only by way of B. But a person with a cognitive map of points A, B, and C can go from A to C directly without going through B. Although not impossible, it is more difficult for persons who are blind to build these cognitive maps. Vision allows us to:

> construct a coherent sense of the physical environment and our place in it, without struggling to remember. On entering an unfamiliar classroom, a sighted child is able to take in something of the whole at a glance, and perhaps work out

Orientation and mobility (O & M) skills. The ability to have a sense of where one is in relation to other people, objects, and landmarks and to move through the environment.

Cognitive mapping. A nonsequential way of conceptualizing the spatial environment that allows a person who is visually impaired to know where several points in the environment are simultaneously; allows for better mobility than does a strictly sequential conceptualization of the environment.

the overall position of the room in relation to more familiar places, such as the library, computer room. . . . For the child with a visual impairment, constructing an inner map of this new classroom presents a problem of synthesizing information from the interrogation of small, local details to achieve a functional sense of the whole, which must then be largely memorised. (Webster & Roe, 1998, p. 69)

Mobility skills vary greatly among people with visual impairment. It is surprisingly difficult to predict which individuals will be the best travelers. For example, common sense seems to tell us that mobility would be better among those who have more residual vision and those who lose their vision later in life, but this is not always the case. How much motivation and how much proper instruction one receives are critical to becoming a proficient traveler.

Obstacle Sense   Some persons who are blind have the ability to detect physical obstructions in the environment. Walking along the street, they often seem able to sense an object in their path. This ability has come to be known as the **obstacle sense**—an unfortunate term in some ways, because many laypeople have taken it to mean that people who are blind somehow develop an extra sense. It is easy to see why this misconception exists. Even people who are blind have a very difficult time explaining the phenomenon (Hull, 1990). A number of experiments have shown that, with experience, people who are blind come to be able to detect subtle changes in the pitches of high-frequency echoes as they move toward objects. Actually, they are taking advantage of the **Doppler effect,** a physical principle that says the pitch of a sound rises as a person moves toward its source.

Although obstacle sense can be important for the mobility of someone without sight, by itself it will not make its user a highly proficient traveler. It is merely an aid. Extraneous noises (traffic, speech, rain, wind) can render obstacle sense unusable. Also, it requires walking at a fairly slow speed to be able to react in time.

The Myth of Sensory Acuteness   Along with the myth that people with blindness have an extra sense is the general misconception that they automatically develop better acuity in their other senses. However, people who are blind do not have lowered thresholds of sensation in touch or hearing. What they are able to do is make better use of the sensations they obtain. Through concentration and attention, they learn to make very fine discriminations.

Another common belief is that people who are blind automatically have superior musical talent. Some do follow musical careers, but this is because music is an area in which they can achieve success.

ACADEMIC ACHIEVEMENT

Most professionals agree that direct comparisons of the academic achievement of students who are blind with that of sighted students must be interpreted cautiously because the two groups must be tested under different conditions. There are, however, braille and large-print forms of some achievement tests. The few studies that have been done suggest that both children with low vision and those who are blind are sometimes behind their sighted peers (Rapp & Rapp, 1992). Most authorities believe that, when low achievement does occur, it is not due to the blindness itself, but to such things as low expectations or lack of exposure to braille.

SOCIAL ADJUSTMENT

At one time the prevailing opinion of professionals was that people with visual impairment were at risk to exhibit personality disturbances. Most authorities now agree that personality problems are not an inherent condition of blindness. What social difficulties may

Obstacle sense.
A skill possessed by some people who are blind, whereby they can detect the presence of obstacles in their environments; research has shown that it is not an indication of an extra sense, as popularly thought; it is the result of being able to detect subtle changes in the pitches of high-frequency echoes.

Doppler effect.
A term used to describe the phenomenon of the pitch of a sound rising as the listener moves toward its source.

arise are more likely due to society's inappropriate reaction to blindness than to personality flaws of people without sight.

Much of this inappropriateness may be caused by the average person's unfamiliarity with people who are blind. Because we do not have many acquaintances who are blind, we are not used to their usual patterns of social interaction. Social skills that come naturally to the sighted may be difficult for some people with visual impairment. One good example is smiling. Smiling is a strong visual cue used by sighted people to provide feedback to one another. For some people with visual impairment, however, smiling is not as spontaneous a social response as it is for those who are sighted. John M. Hull, whose eyesight deteriorated gradually over several years, kept a diary of his experiences. The following entry pertains to smiling:

> Nearly every time I smile, I am conscious of it. I am aware of the muscular effort; not that my smiles have become forced, as if I were pretending, but it has become a more or less conscious effort. Why is this? It must be because there is no reinforcement. There is no returning smile. . . . Most smiling is responsive. You smile spontaneously when you receive a smile. For me it is like sending dead letters. Have they been received, acknowledged? Was I even smiling in the right direction? (Hull, 1990, p. 34)

Unfortunately, some people who are blind feel like they need to go to great lengths to appear "normal." The following account, written by the National Federation of the Blind's president, himself blind, of one man's attempt not to appear different is humorous, but poignant:

> Dr. Schroeder became a teacher and an administrator of public programs of education, but he was still affected by his beliefs about blindness. With the acquisition of the new job, Dr. Schroeder had the money to buy a house. He faced the problem of how to get the lawn mowed. He thought he might hire somebody to do it, but (he reasoned) if he asked a sighted person to mow his lawn, the neighbors would believe he was not able to do it himself because he was blind. This would reinforce their assessment of him as inferior. However, he was also afraid to mow the lawn himself because the neighbors might watch him do it, and if he

CW The National Federation of the Blind is probably the leading organization devoted to advocacy for people who are blind: http://www.nfb.org/
    Another important organization is the American Foundation for the Blind: http://www.afb.org/ ∎

A stereotypic view of people who are blind is that they do not adjust well socially. This stereotype is no more valid than any other stereotype. ∎

missed a patch of grass, they would conclude that he was incompetent. He could, of course, cover the lawn in such a way that he would not miss any grass—going over it repeatedly in narrow strips—but this would look unusual and peculiar to the neighbors.

Dr. Schroeder did not want to look peculiar. He decided that the best solution was for him to mow his lawn when the neighbors were not likely to observe. He decided to cut the grass at night. I cannot say how the neighbors reacted to this plan. However, if the objective is to seem normal, I doubt that mowing the lawn at night is the best way to accomplish this purpose.

The efforts of Dr. Fred Schroeder to avoid looking conspicuous and to appear normal remind me of my own embarrassing experiences. How great a premium there is on seeming normal! (Maurer, 2000, p. 294)

An important point is that it should not be only up to people who are visually impaired to change their ways of interacting socially. Sighted people should also be

SUCCESS STORIES
Special Educators at Work

Charlottesville, VA: Nineteen-year-old **Patrick Pugh** has no vision in his left eye and only partial sight in his right. His speech is slurred, and he does not have functional use of his left arm or leg. Patrick's disabilities were caused by being born prematurely. For fourteen years, Patrick's mother, Audrey Pugh, and special educator **Ricki Curry** have been partners in Patrick's education. They know that, over time, parents and professionals must collaborate and compromise to help students meet their goals.

Patrick Pugh likes to read braille and translate printed sentences with a unimanual brailler. Now, instead of awkwardly holding a book two inches from his right eye, he reads with a relaxed posture as his fingers scan the brailled page of his easy reader. Ricki Curry, an itinerant teacher of students with visual impairment, taught Patrick to braille two years ago. She is proud of his achievements. "Patrick keeps exceeding everybody's expectations. Every time we've taught him something, he's had some success in learning it. We've come to believe in him, and to set our expectations higher, as a result."

This description of her second son does not surprise Audrey Pugh. "Opportunity is the main thing," she says. "All I want anyone to do is give Patrick a fair chance. I think it would be easier if he were either blind or physically disabled, but he's both, and that makes it even harder."

Patrick's progress is the result of his own persistence, the collaboration of his family and teachers, and the continuity of specialized personnel, instruction, and equipment over many years. Ricki and Audrey also credit much of Patrick's progress to a key ingredient: time. Patrick's story is an example of special education not as a fix-it model or cure-all but as a means of providing services over time to persons whose abilities often take much longer than usual to develop.

Patrick started vision and physical therapy when he was two years old. "The physical therapist asked me why he didn't have therapy before," recalls Audrey, "but no one ever told us it was available to infants or that Patrick needed it."

Ricki remembers the youngster whose eyes would lift aimlessly to the ceiling, not using what vision he had. "Our basic goal was for Patrick to learn to use his sight by tracking objects and looking at pictures, but as a five-year-old he was

responsible for instances of faulty communication with people who are blind. Not only may some people with visual impairment profit from instruction in using appropriate visually based cues (e.g., facial expressions, head nods, and gestures), but sighted people also can learn to use their natural telephone skills when communicating with persons who are blind. Two sighted people talking on the telephone use a variety of auditory cues to help them communicate, even though they cannot see each other (e.g., assenting with "uh-hum" or "yeah," asking for more information, adjusting tone of voice) (Fichten et al., 1991). If sighted individuals consciously try to use these strategies when interacting with people who are blind, communication may be smoother.

STEREOTYPIC BEHAVIORS

An impediment to good social adjustment for some students with visual impairment is **stereotypic behaviors:** repetitive, stereotyped movements such as body rocking, poking or rubbing the eyes, repetitive hand or finger movements, and grimacing. They can begin as

Stereotypic behaviors. Any of a variety of repetitive behaviors (e.g., eye rubbing) that are sometimes found in individuals who are blind, severely retarded, or psychotic; sometimes referred to as *stereotypies* or *blindisms*.

stubborn, difficult, and noncompliant." Despite his reluctance, Patrick successfully learned literal information and concrete routines. To be sure, he was highly distractible and progress was very slow. His parents hoped all he needed was extra time, so he stayed in a preschool for children with special needs until he was seven.

Audrey had problems with the school district when Patrick was ready for first grade. "They told me there was no place for him in the public schools, so I said, 'Well, find one!'" Patrick was placed in a self-contained class for children with learning disabilities in the nearest physically accessible elementary school. Ricki continued to provide weekly sessions and to supervise Patrick's vision services. He was also given a personal aide to assist with mobility and visual modifications. As Ricki points out, "In some ways, kids with personal aides never have any problems, so they don't learn any problem-solving skills! On the other hand, there are some effective strategies that can be used with close attention." Since Patrick's hand use is limited, Ricki trained his aide to assist him as a scribe. In addition, Patrick's math was broken down into small steps, his reading was individualized, and he was taught to write using a large-print word processor.

Patrick finished elementary school two years older than most of his classmates. Yet he was only able to do rote math and was similarly concrete in reading; he could decode text but remained literal in his understanding of the material. "He could answer factual questions, but he couldn't make that leap to the abstract," recalls Ricki. "Patrick was in a middle school science class, learning about mitochondria. That's when it really hit me: Sure, he could learn the definition of mitochondria, but was this functional for him? He'd never use this word again!"

Patrick was thirteen when his mother was told that he needed a class that emphasized functional academics, such as money skills. Audrey agreed to the placement, but it was devastating because it seemed an admission that her son was mentally retarded. "At that point, we all knew this was what he needed," says Ricki. "Patrick has multiple learning needs, and it takes him a long time to learn; it takes intensive care and a lot of specific teaching. This class gave him the right information at the right pace. We forgot about the mitochondria and were now reading for *comprehension.*"

Patrick started high school when he was seventeen, and a creative program was crafted for him, blending functional academics, work experience, and independent living skills. He spent his mornings in two periods of functional English and math. He then boarded a van for the vocational center three afternoons a week, where he ate lunch with co-workers. He spent two afternoons a week at an independent living center, learning to clean, shop, and travel about the community.

Patrick works with Ricki sixty minutes a day on braille skills that are geared toward vocational goals. Ricki is optimistic. "I think there's a job out there for Patrick. We've got two years to get those skills really sharp."

Patrick's odyssey has not been easy for his mother, Audrey. She knows Ricki respects her high expectations, yet she has come to trust that alternate routes hold promise for Patrick's future. Audrey says, "I'd like to think of him living happily in a group home someday, with friends, and, of course, with some supervision and support. I think it's only realistic to imagine he'd need that."

—By Jean Crockett

Blindisms.
Repetitive, stereotyped movements (e.g., rocking or eye rubbing); characteristic of some persons who are blind, severely retarded, or psychotic; more appropriately referred to as *stereotypic behaviors.*

early as a few months of age. For many years, the term **blindisms** was used to refer to these behaviors because it was thought that they were manifested only in people who are blind; however, they are also sometimes characteristic of children with normal sight who are severely retarded or disturbed.

Several competing theories concern the causes of stereotypic behaviors (Warren, 1994). For example, some believe they are an attempt to provide oneself with more stimulation to make up for a relative lack of sensory or social stimulation. Others believe them to be an attempt to self-regulate one's stimulation in the face of overstimulation. In either case, most authorities believe that these behaviors serve to stabilize the person's arousal level.

There is even some disagreement about how much one should intervene to reduce or eliminate stereotypic behaviors. On the one hand, when done to the extreme, they can interfere with learning and socialization, and even be physically injurious. On the other hand, if not done to the extreme, such behaviors might help maintain an appropriate level of arousal (Warren, 1994).

One thing that all agree on is that it is very difficult to reduce stereotypic behaviors. Cognitive and metacognitive training has been somewhat successful in decreasing stereotypic behaviors (Estevis & Koenig, 1994; McAdam, O'Cleirigh, & Cuvo, 1993; Ross & Koenig, 1991; Van Reusen & Head, 1994). One team of researchers, for example, had a student clasp his hands together and tell himself, whenever he began to rock, that he did not want to rock. This procedure resulted in reduced rocking, presumably due to the student's exerting cognitive control over his behavior.

Educational Considerations

Lack of sight can severely limit a person's experiences because a primary means of obtaining information from the environment is not available. What makes the situation even more difficult is that educational experiences in the typical classroom are frequently visual. Nevertheless, most experts agree that students who are visually impaired should be educated in the same general way as sighted children. Teachers need to make some modifications, but they can apply the same general educational principles. The important difference is that students with visual impairment will have to rely on other sensory modalities to acquire information.

The Web site at http://www. nbp.org/alph.html shows the braille alphabet. This Web site, maintained by the National Braille Press, allows the user to type in a word or name and have it translated into braille. ■

The student with little or no sight will possibly require special modifications in four major areas: (1) braille, (2) use of remaining sight, (3) listening skills, and (4) orientation and mobility training. The first three pertain directly to academic education, particularly reading; the last refers to skills needed for everyday living.

BRAILLE

Literary braille.
Braille symbols used for most writing situations.

Nemeth Code.
Braille symbols used for mathematics and science.

Unified Braille Code.
A combination of literary braille and braille codes for technical fields, such as the Nemeth Code for science and mathematics; not yet widely adopted.

In nineteenth-century France, Louis Braille introduced a system of reading and writing for people who, like him, were blind. Although not the first to have developed such a method, Braille's was the one that became widely used. Even his system, however, was not adopted for several years after he invented it. (See the box on p. 354.)

One braille code, called **literary braille,** is used for most everyday situations; other codes are available for more technical reading and writing. The **Nemeth Code,** for example, is used for mathematical and scientific symbols. Some people support adoption of a **Unified Braille Code** that would combine these several codes into one. These proponents argue that in our ever more technological society most people, sighted or blind, often need to read and write using technical as well as everyday language (Chong, 2000; Mangold, 2000; Sullivan, 1997). At this point, the Unified Braille Code has not been adopted widely.

The basic unit of braille is a quadrangular cell, containing from one to six dots (see Figure 10.3). Different patterns of dots represent letters, numbers, and even punctuation

Meeting the Needs of Students with Blindness or Low Vision

Instructional Adaptations

Research-Based Recommendations

Classroom teachers can accommodate and address the needs of students with visual impairment in a variety of ways. The following guidelines provide information about how general education teachers can promote successful inclusion of students with blindness or low vision through effective adaptations (Cox & Dykes, 2001):

- Understand where and when "incidental learning" is not taking place and create supports to address students' lack of access to visual cues. For example, students with visual impairment may be unable to pick up cues from schedules written on the board, the classroom clock, or activities taking place around them. For these students, teachers need to explicitly teach classroom routines, cues for changes in daily events, and even how to identify classmates.

- Promote independent movement around the classroom and school. Students need to be free to move about the classroom as well as the school to have access to a variety of school experiences. Teaching students school landmarks; the layout of the classroom and building; popular areas such as the cafeteria, library, main office, and gym; and emergency procedures helps students successfully navigate their environment. Different types of mobility systems can support this instruction further (e.g., sighted guides, canes, guide dogs, electronic devices).

- Collaborate with the vision specialist to identify resources and design instructional and curricular adaptations. Strategies for instruction can include: designating priority seating, providing copies of notes in large print or braille, reading notes aloud while writing them, providing audiotapes of written materials, enlarging books or worksheets, and creating hands-on activities.

- Provide tactile support for learning whenever possible. Students with visual impairment will learn more from charts, maps, graphs, and models that can be "read" through the sense of touch. In addition, teachers should allow students to work with any manipulatives or equipment prior to an activity so that the student can focus on the concept being taught, rather than the material.

- Check for comprehension of auditory information. Although students with visual impairment can hear, they may not interpret the information in the same way as their sighted peers. Comprehending auditory language involves creating corresponding mental pictures associated with past verbal input. Frequent checks for understanding, opportunities to develop background knowledge, and provision of auditory cues to emphasize important information can aid in student comprehension of the material.

- Make use of any vision capacity. Most students with visual impairment are not totally blind. They can benefit from braille materials or large-print books, an easel to bring the text closer, felt-tip pens and soft lead pencils for greater contrast, or extra light at their work area.

- Teach social skills such as shaking hands, conversational skills (smiling, nodding, and making eye contact), and using hand movements in conversation.

Through understanding the various domains in which students with visual impairment may need support, general education teachers can appropriately plan for making key adaptations and identifying instructional supports.

—By Kristin L. Sayeski

marks. Generally, the best method of reading braille involves using both hands, "with the left reading from the beginning of the line as the right returns from reading the end of the previous line and both meeting in approximately the middle of the line and then separating" (Wormsley, 1996, p. 280).

Two basic means of writing in braille are the Perkins Brailler and the slate and stylus. The **Perkins Brailler** has six keys, one for each of the six dots of the cell (see Figure 10.4).

Perkins Brailler.
A system that makes it possible to write in braille; has six keys, one for each of the six dots of the cell, which leave an embossed print on the paper.

Captain Charles Barbier de la Serre and Louis Braille

The first person to develop a system of reading and writing for persons who are blind was Captain Charles Barbier de la Serre. However, his original reason for inventing the system was for military purposes. Only after his system was rejected by the military establishment did he suggest it as a system for people who are blind. But they, too, turned his offer down. And, ironically, one of his biggest critics was Louis Braille:

In 1882, Captain Charles Barbier de la Serre came to present his night-writing code to the [National Institute for the Young Blind]. He was a career military officer of aristocratic background, presumably full of indignation that his code had been rejected by the army, forcing him to offer it instead to this nearly destitute and decidedly distasteful institution. Children at the institute read texts with embossed Roman characters. Since they had to trace each letter with their fingers, reading was slow and inefficient. Barbier's code used patterns of raised dots to represent phonic units, which would reduce the number of characters required for each word and make reading quicker and more accurate. Among the collection of children selected to test the Barbier system was one skinny, pale, thirteen-year-old boy with reddish brown curls above a high "spiritual" forehead. This boy, when prodded to speak, not only criticized Barbier's code as inferior to the embossed texts already in use but actually enumerated its flaws. . . .

And Barbier must have been an imposing figure, with a voice accustomed to giving orders. To him, this boy Braille, this son of a saddler, this runty bag of bones was the sort of boy one routinely ignored except to have him stoop to give one a leg up onto a horse.

But Braille spoke up anyway. As he analyzed the flaws in Barbier's code it set into motion the thought process that would lead to his own code. Two years later Braille perfected his own system. He used six dots instead of Barbier's twelve. He made each character represent a letter in the alphabet so that a child who learned to read would also learn to spell. And he made provisions for punctuation, numbers, and musical notation. When he proposed his code to the institute's director they rejected it too. They cited the same common objections they had to Barbier's system (the same objections still raised against braille instruction today). But what seemed particularly threatening about Braille's code was that he produced it himself. When the blind learned to write at all, they used a sort of stencil to make Roman letters. But they could not read what they wrote. Braille's code was easy to write, requiring only a couple of simple tools. It would allow blind children to send messages to each other and to read them without sighted intervention. To give blind children a method of communication that their sighted custodians would not be able to oversee meant trouble. Who knew what messages those blind children might write—"Teacher is a big meany," or worse, "We have nothing to lose but our chains"? It was not until 1847 that Braille's code was authorized for use in the institute. During the twenty-three-year interim, students secretly used and trained each other in the forbidden code even though discovery meant punishment, even expulsion.

SOURCE: Kleege, G. (1999). *Sight unseen*. New Haven, CT: Yale University Press, pp. 223–225. Reprinted with permission.

Slate and stylus.
A method of writing in braille in which the paper is held in a slate while a stylus is pressed through openings to make indentations in the paper.

When depressed simultaneously, the keys leave an embossed print on the paper. More portable than the Perkins Brailler is the **slate and stylus** (see Figure 10.5). The stylus—a pen-shaped instrument—is pressed through the opening of the slate, which holds the paper between its two halves.

Perhaps the most hotly debated topic in the field of visual impairment concerns whether students who are blind should be taught to use braille or one of the other methods of communication, such as a tape recorder or voice-activated computer. At one time it was fairly common for students with blindness to use braille, but over the past several years its usage has declined dramatically. For example, the percentage of students who are blind who use braille has steadily declined since the mid-1960s, when nearly half used braille; the most recent estimates indicate that fewer than 10 percent now use braille (P. Mauer, personal communication, June 29, 2001; Schroeder, 1996).

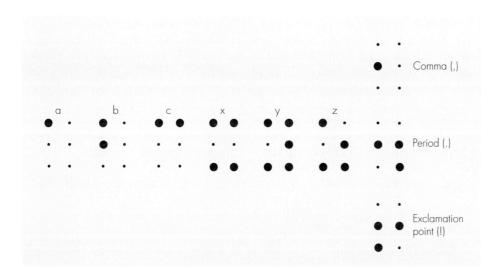

FIGURE 10.3
Examples of symbols from braille.

Many within the community of blind people are alarmed at the reduced availability of braille and assert that it has led to a distressing rate of illiteracy (Foulke, 1996; Hatlen, 1993; Ianuzzi, 1992; Koenig & Holbrook, 2000; Omvig, 1997; Whittle, 1999). They charge that too few sighted teachers are proficient in braille and that they do little to discourage the notion held by some that using braille indicates inferiority.

Whether a person is comfortable in identifying himself or herself as blind is critical to whether that person will be motivated to learn braille:

> Legally blind children who regard themselves as blind may find that Braille facilitates and intensifies group identification and thus leads to the development of self-confidence and self-esteem. . . . Children who do not regard themselves as blind may reject Braille because of its relationship to blindness. (Schroeder, 1996, p. 217)

Many authorities are concerned that, even when students do receive braille instruction, it is often not intense enough. In a survey of experts on braille usage, the respondents stated that in the early stages of braille acquisition, in particular, students need daily instruction for several years (Koenig & Holbrook, 2000). The need for intensive braille instruction presents a dilemma for school systems because of the lack of qualified braille instructors.

The American Foundation for the Blind has a Web site, Braille Bug Site, devoted to encouraging young children to learn braille: http://www.afb.org/braillebug/ ■

FIGURE 10.4
A Perkins Brailler.

FIGURE 10.5
A slate and stylus in use.

Braille bills.
Legislation passed in several states to make braille more available to students with visual impairment; specific provisions vary from state to state, but major advocates have lobbied for (1) making braille available if parents want it, and (2) ensuring that teachers of students with visual impairment are proficient in braille.

Advocates of braille also point out that it is essential for most students who are legally blind to learn braille in order to lead independent lives. Bolstering their argument is research indicating that adults who had learned braille in childhood as their primary medium for reading were employed at twice the rate of those who had used print as their primary medium (Ryles, 1996). A way of ensuring that braille becomes more readily available is through **braille bills.** As of June 2001, thirty-two states had braille bills on the books (J. Gashel, personal communication, June 29, 2001). Although the specific provisions of these bills vary from state to state, the National Federation of the Blind, a major proponent of braille bills, has drafted a model bill that specifies two important components:

1. Braille must be available for students if any members of the individualized program (IEP) team, including parents, indicate that it is needed.
2. Teachers of students with visual impairment need to be proficient in braille.

Federal law now reinforces the first component above. The Individuals with Disabilities Education Act (IDEA) specifies that braille services and instruction are to be a part of the IEP, unless all members of the team, including parents, agree that braille should not be used. To provide a way of determining the braille proficiency of licensed teachers of students who are blind, the Library of Congress has developed the National Braille Literacy Competency Test.

Authorities now recommend that some students with low vision who are able to read large print or print with magnification should also be taught braille. There are many students with low vision whose condition dictates that their vision will worsen over the years. Learning braille at an early age prepares them for the time when their eyesight no longer allows them to read print.

USE OF REMAINING SIGHT

For many years there was a great deal of resistance to having children with visual impairment use their sight in reading and some other activities. Many myths contributed to this reluctance, including beliefs that holding books close to the eyes is harmful, strong lenses hurt the eyes, and using the eyes too much injures them.

It is now recognized that this is true only in very rare conditions. In fact, some professionals believe teachers can actually train students to use what visual abilities they do

Computer monitors that provide large-print images can aid some individuals with visual impairments. ▪

This is an example of 10-pt. type.

This is an example of 18-pt. type.

This is an example of 24-pt. type.

have to better advantage (Barraga & Collins, 1979; Collins & Barraga, 1980). Even though some question the efficacy of such vision training (Ferrell & Muir, 1996), most agree on the importance of encouraging people with visual impairment to use what sight they do have, but not to the exclusion of braille for those who need it.

Two visual methods of aiding children with visual impairment to read print are large-print books and magnifying devices. **Large-print books** are simply books printed in larger-size type. The text in this book, printed primarily for sighted readers, is printed in 10-point type. Figure 10.6 shows print in 18-point type, one of the most popular sizes for large-print materials. Type sizes for readers with visual impairment may range up to 30-point type.

The major difficulty with large-print books is that they are bigger than usual and thus require a great deal of storage space. In addition, they are of limited availability, although, along with the American Printing House for the Blind, a number of commercial publishers are now publishing and marketing large-print books.

Magnifying devices range from glasses and handheld lenses to closed-circuit television scanners that present enlarged images on a TV screen. These devices can be used with normal-size type or large-print books.

Large print books.
Books having a font-size that is larger than the usual 10-point type; a popular size for large print books is 18-point type.

LISTENING SKILLS

The importance of listening skills for children who are blind cannot be overemphasized. The less a child is able to rely on sight for gaining information from the environment, the more crucial it is that he or she become a good listener. Some professionals still assume that good listening skills will develop automatically in children who are blind. This belief is unfortunate, for it is now evident that children do not spontaneously compensate for poor vision by magically developing superior powers of concentration. In most cases, they must be taught how to listen. Teachers should also provide a classroom environment as free from auditory distractions as possible (Webster & Roe, 1998).

Listening skills are becoming more important than ever because of the increasing accessibility of recorded material. The American Printing House for the Blind and the Library of Congress are major sources for these materials. Listeners can simply play the material at normal speed, or they can use a compressed-speech device that allows them to read at about 250 to 275 words per minute. This method works by discarding very small segments of the speech. Some of the more sophisticated compressed-speech devices use a computer to eliminate those speech sounds that are least necessary for comprehension.

ORIENTATION AND MOBILITY (O & M) TRAINING

How well the person with a visual disability can navigate her or his environment will greatly determine how independent and socially integrated she or he will be. There are three general methods to aid the orientation and mobility of people with visual impairment: (1) the long cane, (2) guide dogs, and (3) human guides.

The Long Cane
Professionals most often recommend the long cane for those individuals with visual impairments in need of a mobility aid. It is called a **long cane** because

Long cane.
A mobility aid used by individuals with visual impairment, who sweep it in a wide arc in front of them; proper use requires considerable training; the mobility aid of choice for most travelers who are blind.

It usually takes considerable training to learn how to use a long cane. ■

it is longer than the canes typically used for support or balance. Research has determined that the long cane should extend at least from the floor to the user's armpit (Plain-Switzer, 1993). By moving the cane along the ground, the user is provided with auditory and tactual information about the environment. It can alert the user to drop-offs, such as potholes or stairs, and can help protect the lower part of the body from collision with objects.

Although the long cane looks like a simple device, scientists and O & M specialists working under the auspices of the National Academy of Sciences have drawn up specifications for its construction. And although watching a skilled user of the long cane may give the impression that it is easy to manipulate, intensive training in its proper use is often required. The traveler holds the butt or crook of the long cane at about the height of the navel and sweeps it in an arc wide enough to protect the body, lightly touching the ground in front with the cane tip (Plain-Switzer, 1993). Considerable coordination between the sweeping of the cane and the movement of the feet is required for proper touch technique.

At one time, O & M teachers thought that young children were not old enough to be taught mobility skills. Parents, especially sighted parents, may have seen the use of a cane as too stigmatizing. As one person who is blind said:

> The cane was the thing that my parents put off for as long as they could, and they did it with the support of educators. For them the cane was the symbol. It transformed me from being their blind son—which was okay—to being somebody who might grow up to be a blind man. That wasn't okay. So I didn't see a cane until I was about eleven years old. (Wunder, 1993, p. 568)

Today, however, more and more preschoolers are learning cane techniques.

Currently, there is considerable debate about whether people who are themselves blind should be allowed to be mobility instructors. Those who oppose this practice mainly focus on safety concerns, asking, for example, whether instructors who are blind would be able to warn their students of potential dangers in the environment such as hanging tree limbs, icy sidewalks, or construction sites (Millar, 1996). Those in favor of instructors who are blind view such concerns as overprotection. They state that such potential dangers are part of the frequently faced realities of cane travel, and that instructors who are blind are more likely to allow their pupils to encounter such obstacles in training and thereby learn to cope with them (Hill, 1997).

Guide Dogs   Guide dogs are not as popular an option as most people tend to think. Extensive training is required to learn how to use guide dogs properly. The extended training—as well as the facts that guide dogs are large, walk relatively fast, and need to be cared for—make them particularly questionable for children. Also contrary to what most people think, the guide dog does not "take" the person who is blind anywhere. The person

CW The Web site, HowStuffWorks.com, has a section devoted to guide dogs: http://www.howstuffworks.com/guide-dog.htm ■

Stephen Kuusisto and His Guide Dog, Corky

Stephen Kuusisto has been almost totally blind since birth as the result of retinopathy of prematurity (ROP). In his memoir, *Planet of the Blind,* Kuusisto chronicles how he spent all of childhood and much of adult life in denial of his blindness. Instrumental in his eventual acceptance of a blind identity has been the freedom of mobility provided by Corky, his guide dog. Kuusisto has also discovered that "guide dogs are still wondrous creatures in the public's imagination, and more than fifty years after their introduction to the United States, they remain a novelty." This novelty serves to attract numerous interactions with the public. Although these interactions are usually positive, at times they highlight the misunderstandings that the sighted have about people who are blind:

How strange it is, sometimes, to be Corky's human appendage. Often people stop our forward progress and speak only to her, as if I do not exist, then, after much baby talk, they vanish. Others are drawn to us because we are totemic. Early one morning I meet two boys with developmental disabilities.

"Hi!" one says. "I knew a blind guy, but he died!"

"He was bigger than you," the other adds. "He had a heart attack!" Then they sweep away down the sidewalk on their Rollerblades, and through it all Corky advances without distraction, my familiar, my Pavlova.

In the supermarket we're spotted by a small child.

"Look, Mommy, there's a dog in the store!"

"Shhhh! Be quiet, dear!"

Stephen Kuusisto and his guide dog Corky. ■

"But Mommy, that man has a *dog!*"

"That's a blind man! The dog helps him."

"Is the dog blind too?"

"No, the dog sees for the man!"

"What happens if the dog is blind?"

"The dog isn't blind, honey, the dog can see. It's the man who can't see!"

"The man can't see?"

"That's right, blind people can't see."

"If he can't see, how does he know when it's morning?"

"Shhhh! Be quiet! The man gets up because he has to have breakfast!"

The woman hurries her little boy down the cleaning products aisle. I hear his thin voice from some distance.

"How does he eat?"

I'm standing beside an enormous pyramid of cans. Corky has decided to sit down. I have an evangelical desire, a need to reassure these two. I want to recite something from Psalms to them: "The Lord is gracious, and full of compassion; slow to anger, and of great mercy."

I want to follow this mother and child through the tall laundry soap displays and tell them that the world doesn't end. I imagine telling them that the blind are not hungry for objects. I want to take strangers by the hand and tell them there is no abyss.

SOURCE: From *Planet of the Blind: A Memoir* by Stephen Kuusisto, 1998, New York: The Dial Press, pp. 176–177, 179–180. Copyright © 1998 by Stephen Kuusisto. Used by permission of The Dial Press/Dell Publishing, a division of Random House, Inc.

A number of organizations and companies focus on raising and training guide dogs and helping people who are blind learn to use guide dogs. Following are some examples:

The Seeing Eye, Inc.:
http://www.seeingeye.org/

Guide Dogs of America:
http://www.guidedogsofamerica.org/

Guiding Eyes for the Blind, Inc.:
http://www.guiding-eyes.org/

Guide Dog Foundation for the Blind, Inc.: http://www.guidedog.org/

Guide Dogs for the Blind, Inc.:
http://www.guidedogs.com/ ■

must first know where he or she is going; the dog is primarily a safeguard against walking into dangerous areas.

For some adults, however, guide dogs have proven to be valuable aides and companions. Some users of guide dogs point out that the dogs are able to alert their owners to potential hazards in the environment—such as stairways, entrances, exits, and elevators—sooner than can be detected by a cane (Gabias, 1992). One person who has found a guide dog especially rewarding is author Stephen Kuusisto (see the box on p. 359).

People who are sighted should keep in mind a few guidelines pertaining to guide dogs and their owners (Ulrey, 1994):

1. Although it may be tempting to pet a guide dog, you should do so only after asking the owner's permission. Guide dogs are not just pets—they are working for their owner.
2. If someone with a guide dog appears to need help, approach on his or her right side (guide dogs are almost always on the left side) and ask if he or she needs assistance.
3. Do not take hold of the dog's harness, as this may confuse the dog and the owner.

In recent years, the use of guide horses as alternatives to guide dogs has received considerable attention in the press and on TV, with the first ones receiving their training and being delivered to their owners in the spring of 2001. (Certain to add to the attention is the fact that best-selling author Patricia Cornwell has announced that she plans to incorporate a blind person with a guide horse in her upcoming novel *Isle of Dogs* [Guide Horse Foundation, 2001]). The Guide Horse Foundation (www.guidehorse.com), which is not sanctioned by any guide dog organization, claims that these miniature horses can have advantages over guide dogs, including having better sight (because they have better peripheral vision), a longer life span, and being more appropriate for horse lovers. However, thus far, many within the community of the blind have been skeptical about the practicality of guide horses (Firth, 2001).

Human Guides   Human guides undoubtedly enable people with visual impairment to have the greatest freedom in moving about safely. However, most O & M specialists do not recommend that this be the primary means of navigation because it fosters too much dependence on other people. There are times, however, when the use of a human guide is warranted. Most people who are blind who travel unaccompanied do not need help from those around them. However, if a person with visual impairment looks as though he or she needs assistance, you should first ask if help is wanted. If physical guidance is required, allow the person to hold onto your arm above the elbow and to walk a half-step behind you. Sighted people tend to grasp the arms of persons without sight and to sort of push them in the direction they are heading. (See Figure 10.7.)

TECHNOLOGICAL AIDS

Visual impairment is perhaps the disability area wherein the most technological advances have been made. The infusion of technology has occurred primarily in two general areas: (1) communication and (2) orientation and mobility. In addition, there has been some highly experimental research on artificial vision.

Technological Aids for Communication   There are now computers and software available that convert printed material into synthesized speech or braille. One such device is the **Kurzweil 1000.** The user places the material on a scanner that

The guide dog is still used with success by some individuals, although using a guide dog requires extensive training and would be difficult for children. ■

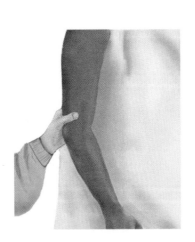

(a)   (b)   (c)

FIGURE 10.7

Human guide technique. (a) The child maintains a constant grip on the guide's arm while following the guide around obstacles as they travel through the environment. To maintain a grip that allows active participation in travel, the child must grasp the guide's arm so the thumb is placed on the outside, with the remaining fingers gripping the inside of the arm (b). The child is a half-step behind and to the side of the guide.

A common adaptation for smaller students is to have the student grasp the guide's extended fingers, wrist, or forearm rather than maintaining a grip above the elbow (c). Effective guided travel involves a partnership between guide and child with both participants actively involved.

SOURCE: Gense, D. J., & Gense, M. (1999, May). The importance of orientation and mobility skills for students who are deaf-blind. *DB-LINK Fact Sheet.* Retrieved July 2, 2001 from the World Wide Web: http://www.tr.wou.edu/dblink/o&m2.htm. Copyright © 1999 DB-LINK. Reprinted with permission. Figure adapted from illustration by Rebecca Marsh-McCannell

reads the material with an electronic voice or renders it in braille. The machines are compatible with the basic editing features of Microsoft Word and WordPerfect (Andrews, 2001) so the user can edit text for customized use. Although they are still relatively expensive (around $1,000), school systems can also use them for students with reading disabilities.

Portable **braille notetakers,** such as BrailleMate and Braille 'n Speak, can serve the same function as the Perkins Brailler or slate and stylus but offer additional speech-synthesizer and word-processing capabilities. The user enters information with a braille keyboard and can transfer the information into a larger computer, review it using a speech synthesizer or braille display, or print it in braille or text. These products are priced at between $1,000 and $1,500.

There is now available a product similar to Palm personal organizers for people who are blind—the Voice Mate. The Voice Mate (around $250) has a talking phone book, a voice note pad, an appointment book that beeps to notify the user of an appointment, a talking alarm clock, and a talking calculator.

Kurzweil 1000.
A computerized device that converts print into speech for persons with visual impairment; the user places the printed material over a scanner that then reads the material aloud by means of an electronic voice.

Braille notetakers.
Portable devices that can be used to take notes in braille, which are then converted to speech, braille, or text.

A popular electronic braille device for taking notes is the Braille 'n Speak. It has full word processing capabilities and notes can be printed out in braille or in print. The device can also review the brailled notes for the user by reading them aloud. ■

Newsline.
A service allowing access via touch-tone phone to several national newspapers; available free of charge to those who are visually impaired.

Descriptive Video Service.
A service for use of people with visual impairment that provides audio narrative of key visual elements; available for several public television programs and some videos of movies.

Two services available for those who are visually impaired are Newsline and Descriptive Video Service. **Newsline,** a free service, allows individuals to access several national newspapers (including *USA Today,* the *Chicago Tribune,* the *New York Times,* the *Wall Street Journal,* the *Washington Post,* the *Los Angeles Times,* and the *Toronto Globe and Mail*), as well as nearly fifty local newspapers. The user can access the information 24 hours a day from any touch-tone telephone. **Descriptive Video Service** inserts a narrated description of key visual features of programs on TV. It is also available with some movies on videotape.

Technological Aids for Orientation and Mobility   Researchers are working on a number of sophisticated electronic devices for sensing objects in the environment. Most are still experimental, and most are expensive. Therefore, they are far less useful than the communication devices we discussed above. Representative examples that have been under development for some time are the laser cane and the Sonic Pathfinder. These devices operate on the principle that human beings can learn to locate objects by means of echoes, much as bats do.

The laser cane can be used in the same way as the long cane or as a sensing device that emits beams of infrared light which are converted into sound after they strike objects in the path of the traveler. The Sonic Pathfinder, which is worn on the head, emits ultrasound and converts reflections from objects into audible sound (Heyes, 1998). It provides advance warning of objects in the traveler's path. Thus far, research on the effectiveness of the Sonic Pathfinder is inconclusive (La Grow, 1999).

A variety of other technological developments can be helpful for individuals who are visually impaired. For example, some communities now have acoustic signaling systems, which emit infrared beams. When the user points a receiver toward a transmitter, he or she receives a message identifying the location. And work is being done to develop external speaker systems for buses that can help commuters who are blind identify incoming buses (Wiener, Ponchilla, Joffee, Rutberg-Kuskin, & Brown, 2001). Also, in the fall of 2000, the National Federation of the Blind partnered with Diebold, Inc., the leading manufacturer of automated teller machines (ATMs) to begin developing voice-guided ATMs that are easily used and provide privacy for users who are blind.

Cautions About Technology   Words of caution are in order in considering the use of computerized and electronic devices. Supporters of braille argue that although tape recorders, computers, and other technological devices can contribute much to reading and acquiring information, these devices cannot replace braille. For example, finding a specific section of a text or "skimming" are difficult with a tape recording, but these kinds of activities are possible when using braille. Taking notes for class, reading a speech, or looking up words in a dictionary is easier when using braille than when using a tape recorder. Braille proponents are especially concerned that the slate and stylus be preserved as a viable method of taking notes. They point out that just as computers have not replaced the pen and pencil for people who are sighted, neither can they take the place of the slate and stylus for people who are blind. The words of author Georgina Kleege are instructive:

Technological advances such as this voice guided ATM machine are a boon for individuals with disabilities participating in everyday activities. ■

> On my desk at this moment there is a computer, a closed-circuit TV, and a number of magnifiers meant to allow me to read print visually, however ineptly, and thus to preserve what the sighted presume to be so valuable—my identity as sighted. There are also three different tape recorders that allow me to experience texts aurally when the inefficiency and strain of reading visually become intolerable. Braille will not replace these things. But braille offers me a freedom I have not known since childhood. With braille, I can take a book under my arm and read it anywhere, without electricity, without a mediating voice in my ear, without pain. (Kleege, 1999, p. 226)

Technological devices designed for orientation and mobility also have limitations. They are best viewed as potential secondary O & M aids. They are not appropriate as substitutes for the long cane, for example.

There has also been remarkable progress in developing an artificial vision system for people who are blind. This involves surgically attaching a digital camera and computer hardware to the visual cortex of the brain (Dobelle, 2000). However, contrary to reports in the popular media, the degree of vision such surgery affords is very far from what sighted people can see. This research may one day prove practical. In the meantime, however, it can lead to false optimism and misunderstanding:

> Since the *New York Times* article, among others, how many of us have been told by well meaning acquaintances that a cure for blindness now exists? How many of us have been encouraged to write a letter or otherwise make contact with someone who can give us the gift of artificial vision? Keep in mind that the present so-called gift of artificial vision is described by its creator as being not yet as useful as a long white cane or guide dog. Also note that the artificial vision enjoyed by Jerry [the patient] requires surgical implantation of electrodes into one's brain.
>
> I believe that we should thank Dr. Dobelle as well as Jerry and other volunteer patients for their hard work and personal sacrifice. They are doing groundbreaking work in a field that in perhaps the twenty-second century will eliminate blindness for most people. It is profoundly unfortunate that their work may in the short term produce increased misunderstanding of blindness and the capabilities of blind people. (Scialli, 2000)

Although technology may not be *the* answer to all the difficulties faced by persons who are blind, there is no doubt that technology can make their lives easier and more productive. And as technologies develop for society in general, it is important that those who are visually impaired be able to take advantage of them. There is a very real danger of a "digital divide" developing between those who are sighted and those who are not.

Collaboration and Co-Teaching for Students with Blindness or Low Vision

"I don't have time to learn braille!"

What Does It Mean to Be a Teacher of Students with Visual Impairments?

Collaboration for students with visual impairments often takes the form of working with itinerant special education teachers. This can be frustrating for general educators in that they are left "on their own" when the special educator is at another building. Therefore, in planning for collaboration, it is important that the general educator and itinerant teacher have time to plan for student needs that may arise at any time. Working with the general educator to plan for instruction, the teacher of students with visual impairments can offer expertise in:

1. Designing multisensory learning environments that encourage active participation in group and individual activities.
2. Creating learning environments that encourage self-advocacy and independence.
3. Teaching individuals with visual impairments to use thinking, problem-solving, and other cognitive strategies.
4. Preparing individuals with visual impairments to respond constructively to societal attitudes and actions.
5. Obtaining and organizing special materials (including technologies) to implement instructional goals. (Council for Exceptional Children, 2001)

Successful Strategies for Co-Teaching

Ricki Curry (an itinerant teacher) and Jenny Garrett (a fourth-grade teacher) talk about how they collaborated to fully include Dennis, a student with a severe visual impairment.

Jenny: My fourth-grade class consisted of 23 nine- and ten-year-old students, including two children with learning disabilities, one with severe behavior disorders, and Den-

A particular problem for those who are blind is their ability to access the wealth of information that is now available via computers and the World Wide Web. As computers have moved more and more toward graphic displays of information on the screen, users with visual impairments have become concerned about how this affects their access to that information. For example, a graphics-based interface requires the user to move a mouse to a relatively precise position on the screen in order to click on the desired function. There are screen-reading programs available that allow those who are visually impaired to access information nonvisually, but cooperation is required from Web site developers to ensure that their Web sites are compatible with these programs (Wunder, 2000). Some progress has been made on this front. The National Federation of the Blind filed a lawsuit against America Online (AOL) and then withdrew it, in July of 2000, after reaching an agreement that AOL would make its service and content accessible to those who are blind.

Educational Placement Models

The four major educational placements for students with visual impairment, from most to least segregated, are (1) residential school, (2) special class, (3) resource room, and (4) regular class with itinerant teacher help. In the early 1900s virtually all children who were blind were educated in residential institutions. Today, however, **itinerant teacher services,** wherein a vision teacher visits several different schools to work with students and their general education classrooms, is the most popular placement for students with visual impairment. The fact is, there are so few students with visual impairment that most schools find it difficult to provide services through special classes or resource rooms.

Residential placement, however, is still a relatively popular placement model compared to other areas of disability. For example, about 7 percent of students with vision loss between the ages of six and twenty-one years are placed in a residential institution,

Itinerant teacher services. Services for students who are visually impaired in which the special education teacher visits several different schools to work with students and their general education teachers; the students attend their local schools and remain in general education classrooms.

nis. They began the year reading anywhere from a first- to a sixth-grade level.

Ricki: Although he has some usable vision, Dennis can see no details from a distance of more than about two feet and uses large-print texts for reading.

Jenny: Dennis has some difficulty making friends because of his immaturity, his compulsive talking, and his inability to listen. On the other hand, Dennis has a good sense of humor and is quick with language. Dennis was in my class all day long for every academic subject. Ricki worked with him during language arts block, teaching braille. She would come to school during the last half of my planning period, which gave us a daily opportunity to discuss assignments, homework, curricular adaptations, equipment, and the like. Homework was an enormous issue. Ricki helped him set up a notebook with a homework contract enclosed and a special highlighter, which he used to mark off completed assignments. He had to write down the assignments himself, remember to take the notebook home, complete the assignments, get a parent's signature, and get it back to school. The hardest part of working with Dennis was the start-up period. I had to get to know him, his visual capabilities, his

strengths and weaknesses, his coping strategies. I began adapting my teaching style, using an easel rather than the blackboard so that he could scoot up to it. I had to decide how hard to push, what to expect from his parents, and what to demand from Dennis.

Ricki: I often found myself overwhelmed by the number of things that Jenny and/or Dennis needed help with in the short time that I was in the building. And so many things seemed to go wrong in the time between when I left one day and arrived again the next day! Although I was frustrated by the limitations imposed by time constraints, the beauty of the inclusion model was that I was very aware of the true gestalt of Dennis's program and knew exactly what he was involved in all the time. Had I not had an almost daily view of Dennis's classroom performance, I might not have believed how hard it was to integrate this very bright, verbal, personable child into Jenny's class.

Jenny: Collaboration works best when there is a match of personalities as well as energy, enthusiasm for teaching, and professionalism.

—By Margaret P. Weiss

whereas only about .5 percent of students with mental retardation are so placed. The advantage of residential placement is that services can be concentrated to this relatively low-incidence population. In the past, most children who were blind attended institutions for several years; today some may attend on a short-term basis (e.g., one to four years). The prevailing philosophy of integrating children with visual impairments with the sighted is also reflected in the fact that many residential facilities have established cooperative arrangements with local public schools wherein the staff of the residential facility usually concentrates on training for independent living skills such as mobility, personal grooming, and home management, while local school personnel emphasize academics.

Early Intervention

For many years psychologists and educators believed that the sighted infant was almost totally lacking in visual abilities during the first half-year or so of life. We now know that the young sighted infant is able to take in a great deal of information through the visual system. This fact makes it easy to understand why intensive intervention should begin as early as possible to help the infant with visual impairment begin to explore the environment. As we noted earlier, many infants who are blind lag behind their peers in motor development. Consequently, O & M training should be a critical component of preschool programming.

Although many advocate that preschoolers with visual impairments should be educated in inclusive settings with sighted children, it is critical that teachers facilitate interactions between the children. We know from research that merely placing preschoolers who are visually impaired with sighted preschoolers does not lead to their interacting with one another (McGaha & Farran, 2001).

Most authorities agree that it is extremely important to involve parents of infants with visual impairment in early intervention efforts. Parents can become actively involved in

RESPONSIVE INSTRUCTION

Meeting the Needs of Students with Blindness or Low Vision

Strategies for Working with Young Children

What Research Says

Children with blindness or low vision learn best through active engagement with their environment. Because these children do not receive visual stimuli to support what they hear, they are dependent upon tactile interactions to promote learning. Research on infants with visual impairment, however, indicates they spend less time exploring and interacting with the environment than infants without visual disabilities (Chen, 2001). As a result, natural understanding of people, objects, activities, and the environment is limited.

Research-Based Recommendations in Early Childhood Settings

To promote cognitive skills, children with visual impairment require direct instruction (Chen, 2001). Structured experiences that allow children to have repeated interactions with objects, people, or situations promote understanding of cause and effect. For example, an infant with a visual impairment drops a spoon. If someone were to hand the spoon back to the child, the infant would not understand (1) where the spoon went, (2) how the spoon returned to him, and (3) that similar phenomena occur every time something is dropped. Repeated exposure to the act of dropping items and showing the child where the item fell will teach the concept of gravity and reinforce the difficulty involved in locating dropped items!

In addition to systematic, repeated learning opportunities, children with visual impairment should interact with real objects rather than models (Chen & Dote-Kwan, 1999). A child who has not previously developed the concept of a banana will be unable to make the connection between a plastic banana and a real one. Instruction,

therefore, should include opportunities for conceptual development through repeated interactions with real objects.

Concepts involving spatial relationship can be difficult to learn because they are dependent upon a visual reference to a physical object. For example, concepts of "in front of" and "behind" are frequently taught in relationship to one's body. Similarly, understanding of physical characteristics such as color, size, shape, and texture can be challenging without a visual reference. Children with visual impairment will need many opportunities to manipulate objects to reinforce these abstract concepts. Even the concepts of outside and inside can be misunderstood if children are not explicitly exposed to the differentiating characteristics of each (e.g., walls, ceilings, doors, streets, sidewalks, grass) (Chen, 2001).

Although children with visual impairment develop language in a similar manner as those without vision loss, they have greater difficulty mastering nuances of language that are visually dependent, such as pronouns (Chen, 2001). Imagine how difficult it would be to interpret pronouns if you could not see the person talking, what is being talked about, or other people who are being referenced! Again, direct instruction in language skills is recommended.

Finally, much of what young children learn about the world comes from watching and imitation. The development of play, adaptive behaviors, and social interactions is largely dependent upon modeling. Hand-over-hand modeling, hand-under-hand modeling, play or social interaction modeling, and participatory modeling all foster social and emotional development.

—By Kristin L. Sayeski

working at home with their young children, helping them with fundamental skills such as mobility and feeding, as well as being responsive to their infants' vocalizations (Chen, 1996). Parents, too, sometimes need support in coping with their reactions to having a baby with visual impairment. There may be an overwhelming sense of grief. Professionals working in early intervention programs for infants who are blind often recommend that initial efforts should focus on helping parents cope with their own reactions to having a child who is blind (Maloney, 1981).

Children with visual impairment should be given many opportunities to explore and learn about their environments. Touchtown is a program used to develop children's sense of orientation and to stimulate all their senses by providing a "palpable city." ■

Transition to Adulthood

Two closely related areas are difficult for some adolescents and adults with visual impairment—independence and employment.

INDEPENDENT LIVING

When working with adolescents and adults with visual impairment, it is extremely important to keep in mind that achieving a sense of independence is often difficult for them. Many authorities point out that much of the problem of dependence is because of the way society treats persons without sight. A common mistake is to assume that such individuals are helpless. Many people think of blindness as a condition to be pitied. People with visual impairment have a long history of arguing against paternalistic treatment by sighted society. In the early 1900s, for example, the idea of a federally supported college for students who were blind (similar to Gallaudet for students with deafness) was quashed because it would add to the prevailing notion that they needed a protected environment to succeed (Kudlick, 2001).

The following account of a trip taken by students from the O & M Program of Louisiana Tech University to the World Trade Center in New York City points out with considerable irony, given the tragedy of September 11, 2001, how misguided special treatment toward those who are blind can be. Presumably because of their blindness, the group experienced lax security in their trip up to the top of the center. Afterwards, in the words of one of the students,

> we made jokes about lax security. If you want to bomb the trade center, just walk in with a white cane, and they will welcome you with open arms. There was a bit of irony in this. In 1993 the World Trade Center had been bombed, but at the moment I had forgotten one important detail about that event. . . .
>
> The thing which I had forgotten about that event was brought back to my attention. I don't remember if it was a graduate student, a center student, or a staff member who said it, but as soon as the words were out, a little piece of irony clicked into place. In a federal penitentiary outside my home town of Springfield,

Erik Weihenmayer. ■

Missouri, sits a blind man. His crime? He masterminded the bombing of the World Trade Center. When will they ever learn?

Society too loses something when it offers undeserved privileges to people it believes inferior. The general public loses the chance to experience the distinctiveness that we can add to society. Each minority has something to add—to contribute to the mosaic of life. With the mixture we all become stronger. By refusing to acknowledge that we are only a cross section of themselves, those members of society who believe we need special treatment are missing out as much as we are when we accept their charity. Because of this charity these people expect us all to be the same. They cannot tell the good guys from the bad guys in the blind minority. (Lansaw, 2000, pp. 964–965)

Compounding the problem of paternalism, the public also has a tendency to make superheroes out of people who are blind when they accomplish relatively mundane tasks. Although climbing mountains such as Mt. McKinley or Mt. Everest (see p. 8 in Chapter 1) are no mundane feats, the sentiments of Erik Weihenmayer point out that the accolades can sometimes be way over the top:

Not all of my time leading up to the climb [of Mount McKinley] was spent on the mountain; as part of their public-education campaign, the [American Foundation for the Blind] asked me to do some TV interviews. One was a cheesy daytime talk show, on which I was showcased among a group of blind people deemed "amazing and inspirational." All the blind people were led onto the stage, canes tapping and dogs' tails wagging, and seated in a row in front of the crowd. I was featured first, and the host opened with, "A blind mountain climber. Isn't that incredible? Even I, who can see just fine, wouldn't think of climbing a mountain." This wasn't the first time I had heard the "even I" statement. It was always meant as a compliment, but it never failed to annoy me. There might be a dozen other factors that prevented the host from excelling in the sport of mountain climbing. She might be fifty pounds overweight, wheezing with every breath, and might never have even set foot on a mountain, but in her mind, success or failure was automatically attributed to one factor: sight or no sight . . .

Throughout the rest of the segment, I squirmed in my seat. I should have been proud to be picked out as "amazing and inspirational," but strangely I felt more embarrassed and even a little sick. I was no more accomplished than the others. I was simply a blind person who planned to climb a mountain and nothing more. But people sensationalize the lives of blind people when, often, all they did was exhibit a semblance of normalcy. I had been receiving these accolades my whole life: give someone directions to my house—incredible. Make eye contact in a conversation—amazing. Pour a glass of milk without spilling it all over the table—inspiring. Each of us on the panel was being honored for our heroic tales, but the recognition spoke more loudly of low expectations than of accomplishment. My heart burned with the memory of my heroes, people like Helen Keller, who took the world's perceptions about the disabled and shattered them into a million pieces, people whose stories made me hunger for the courage to live in their image. (Weihenmayer, 2001, pp. 166–168)

Even though people who are blind can achieve virtually the same degree of independence as people who are sighted, it would be a mistake to assume that this comes naturally or easily. Many independent living skills that are learned incidentally by sighted people need to be taught explicitly to those who are visually impaired. The National Federation of the Blind publishes a book that can be useful in this regard (Jernigan, 1994). It has chapters, for example, on cooking, sewing, marking dials and tactile labeling, and shopping ideas.

In some ways it is more important for people with visual impairment to learn to be independent than it is for those who are sighted. Adults with visual impairment often find that they need to take more initiative to achieve the same level of success as people who are sighted. As one job counselor put it when speaking to a group of college students with visual impairment: "As blind students, you will need to spend time on activities your sighted peers never think about—recruiting and organizing readers, having textbooks prepared in alternative media, getting an early start on term papers" (Rovig, 1992, p. 239).

EMPLOYMENT

Many working-age adults with visual impairment are unemployed, and those who do work are often overqualified for the jobs they hold. For example, the employment rate for adults aged 21 to 64 who have severe functional limitation in seeing (defined as being unable to see words and letters) was only 26 percent (Kirchner & Schmeidler, 1997). This unfortunate situation is due to a history of inadequate transition programming at the secondary school level rather than to the visual impairment itself. Said another way, with proper transition programming, students with visual impairment, even those who are totally blind, can go on to hold jobs at every level of preparation—teachers, laborers, physicians, engineers. Proper transition programming, however, must be intensive and extensive, including numerous well-supervised work experiences, or internships, while still in secondary school.

With IDEA's emphasis on transition services, anecdotal reports of adults with visual impairment who achieve successful independent living and employment are becoming more and more common—although they are still not as common as one would hope. Innovative programs are being developed to meet the transition needs of students with visual impairment. For example, one successful program involves having adolescents and young adults with visual impairment come together with professionals for a three-week summer training session devoted to issues of transition (Sacks & Pruett, 1992). Among other things, this project uses "job shadowing," in which each student is paired with an adult with a similar visual disability and a job that matches the student's interest. The students spend a couple of days with their partners, observing them on the job.

High on the list of ways to improve employment possibilities for those who are blind are job accommodations. Employees who are blind report that relatively minor adjustments

Obtaining gainful, fulfilling employment should not be an unrealistic goal for someone with visual impairment. ■

can go a long way toward making it easier for them to function in the workplace. A sample of suggested adaptations are improved transportation (such as carpools), better lighting, tinted office windows to filter light, prompt snow removal, regularly scheduled fire drills to ensure spatial orientation, hallways free of obstacles, and computer software (such as screen magnification programs) and PC-based reading machines that convert print into braille (Rumrill, Roessler, Battersby-Longden, & Schuyler, 1998; Rumrill, Schuyler, & Longden, 1997).

Visual impairment no doubt poses a real challenge for adjustment to everyday living, but remember Stephen Kuusisto's comments in the introduction to the chapter (p. 337). People with visual impairment share many similarities with people in the rest of society. Special and general educators need to achieve the delicate balance between providing special programming for students with visual impairment and treating them in the same manner as they do the rest of their students.

Summary

There are two definitions of *visual impairment*—legal and educational. The legal definition depends on the measurement of visual acuity and field of vision. A person who is legally blind has visual acuity of 20/200 or less in the better eye, even with correction, or has a very narrow (less than 20 degrees) field of vision. Individuals who have low vision have visual acuity between 20/70 and 20/200 in the better eye with correction.

Educators, however, prefer to define blindness according to how well the person functions, especially in reading. For the educator, blindness indicates the need to read braille or to use aural methods. Those who can read print, even though they may need magnification or large-print books, have *low vision*. The majority of those who are legally blind have some vision. Many students who are legally blind are not educationally blind because they can read print.

Blindness is one of the least prevalent disabling conditions in childhood but is much more prevalent in adults.

The Snellen chart, consisting of rows of letters or of Es arranged in different positions, measures visual acuity for far distances. Special charts measure visual acuity for near distances. In addition to these measures of acuity, educators are often interested in students' visual efficiency and their functional vision.

Most visual problems are the results of errors of refraction. That is, because of faulty structure and/or malfunction of the eye, light rays do not focus on the retina. The most common visual impairments are myopia (nearsightedness), hyperopia (farsightedness), and astigmatism (blurred vision). Eyeglasses or contact lenses can usually correct these problems. More serious impairments include glaucoma, cataracts, diabetic retinopathy, retinitis pigmentosa, cortical visual impairment (CVI), retinopathy of prematurity (ROP), strabismus, and nystagmus. Many serious visual impairments in school-age students are due to hereditary factors. When scientists first discovered that ROP was caused by high levels of oxygen administered to premature newborns, incidents of this condition decreased. However, ROP is on the rise due to medicine's efforts to keep more premature babies alive. In addition, researchers now believe that ROP can also be the result of factors related to prematurity other than excessive oxygen.

Most authorities believe that visual impairment may result in a few subtle language differences but not in deficient language skills. Also, blindness does not result in intellectual retardation. There are some differences in language and conceptual development because children with visual impairment rely more on touch to learn about the world. Infants who are blind may lag behind their sighted peers conceptually, but these delays do not usually last for long. However, infants and young children who are visually impaired need to be directly taught many things that are learned incidentally by sighted children.

A very important ability for the successful adjustment of people with visual impairment is orientation and mobility. As infants, they often experience serious delays in motor development and need direct encouragement to explore their world. There is no one-to-one relationship between the age at onset and the degree of visual loss and mobility skills. Mobility is greatly affected by motivation. Mobility skills depend largely on spatial ability. Those who are able to conceptualize their environments as cognitive maps have better mobility skills than do those who process their environments sequentially.

People who are blind do not, as is commonly thought, have an inherent obstacle sense. But some can develop the ability to detect obstacles by detecting changes in the pitches of echoes as they approach obstacles. Another myth is that people who are blind automatically develop better acuity in other senses. What they actually do is become adept at picking up other sensory cues in their surroundings, thus making better use of their intact senses.

Comparing the academic achievement of students with visual impairment to that of students who are sighted is difficult because the two are tested under different conditions. Evidence suggests, however, that students with visual impairment are behind their sighted peers in achievement. Some believe that this is due to a lack of early exposure to braille.

Personality problems are not an inherent condition of visual impairment. Any social adjustment problems that students with visual impairment have are usually due to society's reaction to blindness. The stereotypic behaviors (e.g., eye poking and body rocking) exhibited by a few persons who are blind can be an impediment to social acceptance, but researchers are working on developing techniques to diminish their occurrence. Some researchers, however, believe that these behaviors serve to stabilize the person's arousal level and speculate that they should not be entirely eliminated.

Educational experiences in regular classrooms are frequently visual. But with some modifications, teachers can usually apply the same general principles of instruction to students both with and without visual impairment. The primary modifications occur in (1) braille, (2) use of remaining sight, (3) listening skills, and (4) orientation and mobility training.

Since the mid-1960s there has been a sharp decline in the use of braille. Many professionals are now decrying this decrease because they believe it has led to a high rate of illiteracy. The National Federation of the Blind has lobbied for braille bills to increase the availability of braille and to establish braille competency for all teachers of students with visual impairment.

Many authorities believe it important to train students to use whatever remaining sight they have. Two methods of doing this are through large-print books and magnifying devices.

Many authorities also emphasize the importance of training students to use their listening skills to access more information from their environment. Listening skills do not develop automatically; they must be taught. Increasingly, recorded material is becoming available for persons who are blind as well as for those with severe reading problems.

Orientation and mobility training can involve the use of the long cane, guide dogs, and human guides. Most O & M instructors recommend the long cane for the majority of individuals who are blind. At one time, O & M instruction for children did not begin until elementary or secondary school. Now most authorities recommend that mobility instruction should begin in preschool. Guide dogs are generally not recommended for children, but some adults find them very helpful. Generally, using a human guide should not be the primary source of aid because it creates dependency.

There has been an explosion in technology to aid children and adults who are blind in communicating and navigating the environment. Examples are the Kurzweil 1000, which converts print to braille or speech, and portable braille notetakers, which allow one to take notes in braille. Newsline is a service whereby users have access to several daily newspapers via a touch-tone phone. Descriptive Video Service provides narration of action taking place in movies or on videotapes.

Technological aids for mobility (e.g., the laser cane and Sonic Pathfinder) are still highly experimental. There are also technological adaptations to the environment, including acoustic signaling systems, external bus speaker systems, and voice-guided ATMs.

We should be cautious about many of these technological advances, however. It is doubtful that they will replace basic tools such as braille and the long cane anytime soon, if ever. In addition, the blind community remains vigilant to make sure that technologies that are now available to the public (e.g., the World Wide Web) are also accessible to those with visual impairments.

The four basic educational placements for students with visual impairment, from most to least segregated, are residential school, special class, resource room, and regular class with itinerant teacher services. Residential placement, at one time the most popular alternative, is now recommended much less frequently than regular classrooms with itinerant services. And many residential schools have adopted a more inclusive philosophy. Some residential schools coordinate their programs with local public schools. The relatively low incidence of visual impairment makes the use of resource rooms and special classrooms less practical.

Without special attention, infants with visual impairment may have restricted interaction with their environment, and mobility in particular may be affected. Early intervention often focuses on parental interaction with the child and parental reaction to the child's disability.

Education for the adolescent and adult stresses independent living and employment skills. Independence is a particularly important area because society often mistakenly treats people with visual impairment as helpless. Many adults with visual impairment are unemployed or overqualified for their jobs. Professionals are attempting to overcome the bleak employment picture by using innovative approaches. Job accommodations—for example, better transportation and computer software applications—can greatly improve the employment outlook for those who are visually impaired.

Yasmin Arshad

Portrait of Shehime, Ink, marker on paper. 17 × 14 in.

Ms. Arshad, who was born in 1974 in Florence, Italy, enjoys swimming, horseback riding, making large jigsaw puzzles, and eating in Italian restaurants. She loves color, especially shades of blue, and has devised a personal way of sequencing colors onto grids. She also likes to sequence numbers and is fascinated by the millennium.

Learners with Low Incidence, Multiple, and Severe Disabilities:

Autistic Spectrum, Traumatic Brain Injury, and Deaf-Blindness

But Jessy's life, and life with Jessy, is not all strangeness. Indeed, it is less strange every year, more ordinary, more like other people's lives. We work, we shop, we do errands. So consider this recent incident, at the little post office on the island where we spend our summers. The parking lot is full. I'll park at the curb and rush inside while she waits in the car.

She doesn't like that. "We could ask someone to move so we can park," she says.

"We can't do that," I tell her.

She confirms this. "We can't ask them because they were there first." She was just hoping; she really does know the rule. She learned it years ago, when she asked some people to move from her favorite table and had to leave the restaurant. Now I counter-sink the lesson: "How would you feel if someone asked us to move so they could park?"

"Hurt my *feelings*."

Still, evidently, more work to be done. "No, it wouldn't hurt your feelings. Feelings get hurt when somebody does something or says something and you think they don't like you. Or criticize you." (This is

getting complicated.) "It's not when they do something *you* don't like; then you get *irritated*, or *angry*. That's different."

That was a year ago. This week, at the supermarket, the lesson resurfaces. Near the checkout, I've met a friend; we get talking. Too long, thinks Jessy; the shopping's done, time to go. She waits a minute, two, then pushes our friend's cart with an abruptness just on the edge of aggression. She's caught herself, but she knows she's been rude. Later, as we talk it over, she plugs in the familiar, all-purpose phrase: "Hurt his feelings." Has there been any progress at all?

I begin to correct her. But she anticipates me. "Not hurt his feelings, *irritated!*" She remembered! This is the first time she's ever made the distinction. Except, except . . . except that he wasn't irritated. He's known Jessy from childhood, and makes allowances. How to explain *that* and still convey the necessity of self-control? Words, feelings, contexts, human meanings. We'll be working on these for years to come.

CLARA CLAIBORNE PARK
Exiting Nirvana: A Daughter's Life with Autism

The definition of every category of exceptionality is controversial. Severe and multiple disabilities are no exception. The Association for Persons with Severe Handicaps (TASH) uses the following definition of severe disabilities:

individuals of all ages who require extensive ongoing support in more than one major life activity in order to participate in integrated community settings and to enjoy a quality of life that is available to citizens with fewer or no disabilities. Support may be required for life activities such as mobility, communication, self-care, and learning as necessary for independent living, employment, and self-sufficiency (as quoted in Brown & Snell, 2000, p. 71).

Severe and multiple disabilities are often linked conceptually because nearly any severe disability will involve extensive and ongoing support in more than one major life activity. That is, *severe* and *multiple* tend to go together. True, one can find a severe disability that involves a single life activity (e.g., profound deafness that involves only manual-visual rather than vocal-aural communication) or multiple disabilities, none of which is severe (e.g., relatively mild orthopedic impairment, mild visual impairment, and mild mental retardation). Nevertheless, people with a severe disability in any area *typically* have more than one disability. Furthermore, a combination of mild disabilities may present severe educational problems, as noted in federal law (the Individuals with Disabilities Education Act, IDEA): "Multiple disabilities means concomitant impairments . . . the combination of which causes such severe educational problems that they cannot be accommodated in special education programs solely for one of the impairments" [34 CFR, Sec. 300 (b)(6)]. IDEA also includes language stating that:

The term "children with severe disabilities" refers to children with disabilities who, because of the intensity of their physical, mental, or emotional problems, need highly specialized education, social, psychological, and medical services in order to maximize their full potential for useful and meaningful participation in society and for self-fulfillment. The term includes those children with severe emotional disturbance (including schizophrenia), autism, severe and profound mental retardation, and those who have two or more serious disabilities, such as deaf-blindness, mental retardation and blindness, and cerebral palsy and deafness. Children with severe disabilities may experience severe speech, language, and/or perceptual-cognitive deprivations, and evidence abnormal behaviors, such as failure to respond to pronounced social stimuli, self-mutilation, self-stimulation, manifestation of intense and prolonged temper tantrums, and the absence of rudimentary forms of verbal control, and may also have intensely fragile physiological conditions. [34 CFR, Sec. 315.4(d)]

With these considerations in mind, in this chapter we discuss the following categories and problems: autism and related disorders, traumatic brain injury (TBI), deaf-blindness, augmented and alternative communication, and self-stimulation, self-injury, and other behavior problems. We discussed severe and profound mental retardation in Chapter 4, Learners with Mental Retardation. However, much of what we talk about in this chapter applies to this population as well.

CW An important and comprehensive report on autism and autistic spectrum disorder is available from the National Academy of Sciences at www.nap.edu/books/0309072697/html/

For information about the search for the genetics of autism, see www.nih.gov/news/pr/mar2002/nimh11.htm ■

Autism.
A pervasive developmental disability characterized by extreme withdrawal, cognitive deficits, language disorders, self-stimulation, and onset before the age of thirty months.

Autistic spectrum disorder.
A range of disorders characterized by symptoms of autism that can range from mild to severe.

Pervasive developmental disorder (PDD).
A severe developmental disorder characterized by abnormal social relations, including bizarre mannerisms, inappropriate social behavior, and unusual or delayed speech and language.

Autism and Related Disorders—Autistic Spectrum Disorder

Although **autism** has been a separate category under IDEA since 1990, other disorders similar to it in many ways are now typically discussed under a broader term, **autistic spectrum disorder.** A similar term is **pervasive developmental disorder (PDD).** The

MISCONCEPTIONS ABOUT
Learners with Low Incidence, Multiple, and Severe Disabilities

---

MYTH Persons with severe and multiple disabilities have problems so severe that the best they can hope for is employment in a sheltered workshop.

FACT With intensive and extensive instruction, many persons with severe and multiple disabilities are now able to be employed in more integrated work settings.

MYTH Persons with severe and multiple disabilities have problems so severe that the best they can hope for is to live under close supervision in a large residential facility.

FACT With intensive and extensive instruction, many persons with severe and multiple disabilities are now able to live independently or semi-independently by themselves or in a small community residential facility (CRF).

MYTH Autism is a single, well-defined category of disability.

FACT Autism is a wide spectrum of disorders and ranges from very severe to very mild. Autistic spectrum disorder includes conditions that may be difficult to identify with great accuracy.

MYTH Persons with autism are mentally retarded and cannot be expected to be involved in higher education or professions.

FACT People with autism have the full range of intellectual capacity. Although a high percentage of people with severe autism do have mental retardation as an additional disability, many with milder forms of autism are highly intelligent, earn graduate degrees, and are successful professionals.

MYTH A person with traumatic brain injury (TBI) can be expected, with time, to recover completely and function without disabilities.

FACT Some people with TBI do recover completely, but many do not. Usually, a person with TBI has long-term disabilities that may be compensated for in many ways, but these disabilities do not ordinarily disappear completely, even with the best treatment and rehabilitation.

MYTH For students with Usher syndrome whose vision will deteriorate over time, it is best not to introduce Braille and training with the long cane while their vision is still relatively good because to do so stigmatizes them.

FACT Braille and orientation and mobility training should not wait until the later stages of vision loss. Getting a head start on learning these complex skills almost always outweighs any stigmatization that might occur.

MYTH Someone who cannot speak will have extreme difficulty making himself or herself understood to others.

FACT With an appropriate augmentative or alternative communication (AAC) system, a person who cannot speak will be able to carry on a normal conversation, sometimes very near the rate at which nondisabled speakers talk. The flexibility, speed, and usefulness in communication of AAC are increasing rapidly with new technologies, and they now often allow a user to approximate the typical verbal exchanges between speakers.

MYTH The only really effective way of controlling the undesirable behavior of people with severe and multiple disabilities, such as severe autism, is to use punishment.

FACT Functional behavioral assessment and positive behavioral supports are finding more and more ways of replacing undesirable with desirable behavior without the use of punishment. Often, the key is finding out what the person with severe and multiple disabilities is trying to communicate and helping them find a more effective, efficient way of communicating that to others.

Jesse Park is a 43-year-old artist with autism. Aside from a few art classes during her school years, she is largely self-taught, and creates most of her highly detailed paintings from memory. ■

Asperger syndrome (AS).
A developmental disability in which language and cognitive development are normal but the child may show a lag in motor development and impairment in emotional and social development; included in *autistic spectrum disorder*.

Rett's disorder.
Apparently normal development through at least age five months, followed by deceleration of head growth between ages five months and forty-eight months, loss of psychomotor skills, and severe impairment of expressive and receptive language; usually associated with severe mental retardation.

Childhood disintegrative disorder.
Normal development followed by significant loss, after age two but before age ten, of previously acquired social, language, self-care, or play skills with qualitative impairment in social interaction or communication and stereotyped behavior.

spectrum of autistic disorders includes not only specific related syndromes but also *pervasive developmental disorder not otherwise specified (PDD-NOS)*.

Both autistic spectrum disorder and PDD involve delays in the development of social relationships, communication of ideas and feelings, self-care, and participation in typical family, school, or community activities (National Research Council, 2001). The symptoms of autism and similar disorders are often noticed soon after birth and are first observed in most cases before the child is two years old. Autism and related disorders are distinguished by their early onset. In fact, a diagnostic criterion for autism is that it is diagnosed by the time the child is thirty months old (American Psychiatric Association, 1994). The consequences of autism and similar disorders are lifelong, usually requiring continued support and transition services through adolescence and adulthood (National Research Council, 2001).

Definition and Characteristics

Traditionally, autism is said to be a pervasive developmental disorder (PDD) with onset before age three. Related disorders may be diagnosed later, and often there is uncertainty at first about just what disorder the child has. Autistic spectrum disorder implies a qualitative impairment of social interaction and communication. It also is often characterized by restricted, repetitive, stereotyped patterns of behavior, interests, and activities. Besides autism, autistic spectrum disorders include the following:

- **Asperger syndrome (AS),** or Asperger's disorder—much like mild autism, but usually without significant delays in cognition and language
- **Rett's disorder**—normal development for five months to four years, followed by regression and mental retardation
- **childhood disintegrative disorder**—normal development for at least 2 and up to 10 years, followed by significant loss of skills
- **pervasive developmental disorder not otherwise specified (PDD-NOS)**—pervasive delay in development that does not fit into any of the other diagnostic cate-

gories (see American Psychiatric Association, 1994; National Research Council, 2001)

Another subset of autistic spectrum disorder is **autistic savant**. An autistic savant may have relatively severe autism, in that the individual shows serious developmental delays in overall social and intellectual functioning. However, the individual with this condition also shows remarkable ability or apparent talent in particular splinter skills—skills that exist in apparent isolation from the rest of the person's abilities to function. An autistic savant might have extraordinary capabilities in playing music, drawing, or calculating. For example, the character in the movie *Rain Man* was an autistic savant. (See Sacks, 1995, for other examples.)

Because all of these disorders are rare, even when combined into a single category, and because their characteristics overlap considerably, we do not discuss them under separate headings. The American Psychiatric Association (1994) offers specific diagnostic criteria for autism and other disorders in its *Diagnostic and Statistical Manual*. However, the following very important caution is offered by the National Research Council (2001):

> Autism is best characterized as a spectrum of disorders that vary in severity of symptoms, age of onset, and associations with other disorders (e.g., mental retardation, specific language delay, epilepsy). The manifestations of autism vary considerably across children and within an individual child over time. There is no single behavior that is always typical of autism and no behavior that would automatically exclude an individual child from a diagnosis of autism, even though there are strong and consistent commonalities, especially in social deficits. (p. 9)

With this caution in mind, we summarize some of the primary characteristics of individuals who have autism and related disorders. Our following discussion of autism should be interpreted to apply generally to individuals who may be said to exhibit autistic spectrum disorder.

Pervasive developmental disorder not otherwise specified (PDD-NOS). A severe developmental disorder that does not fit into any existing subcategory.

Autistic savant. A person with severe autism whose social and language skills are markedly delayed but who also has advanced skills in a particular area, such as calculation or drawing.

At the age of 2, Temple Grandin was diagnosed with autism. Grandin used her exceptional powers of logic, observation, and focus to become an accomplished scientist. She went on to earn a Ph.D. in Animal Science (University of Illinois, 1989). Her area of expertise is the care and handling of livestock, including their processing in meat plants. ■

IMPAIRED SOCIAL RESPONSIVENESS

Impaired social responsiveness is the prime characteristic of autism. Parents of children with autism often notice that their babies or toddlers do not respond normally to being picked up or cuddled. They may show little or no interest in other people but be preoccupied with objects. They may not learn to play normally. These characteristics persist and prevent the child from developing typical attachments to their parents or friendships with their peers. Some children with autism, but not all, improve somewhat in their ability to relate to other people as they progress through later childhood and adolescence. However, even those who do improve may seem unable to catch the nuances of social relationships or comprehend many ordinary social meanings. They may remain socially "distant" and unable to develop intimate relationships.

IMPAIRED COMMUNICATION

Autism also often involves impaired verbal and nonverbal communication. About half of the population of children with autism have no functional language. Autism often includes failure to establish normal eye-to-face gaze or inability to perceive and interpret the emotions and intentions expressed by other people's eyes and facial expressions. Children with autism may lack facial expressions that communicate their own feelings effectively or accurately. Those who do develop speech typically show abnormalities in intonation, rate, volume, and content of their oral language. Their speech may sound "robotic," or they may exhibit **echolalia,** a parroting of what they hear. They may reverse pronouns (e.g., confuse "you" and "I," or refer to themselves as "he" or "she" rather than "I" or "me"). Using language as a tool for social interaction is particularly difficult for most people with autism. If they do acquire language, they may have considerable difficulty using it in social interactions because they are unaware of the reactions of their listeners. For example, they may not realize that the people they are talking to are not interested in all the details of stock quotes that they have committed to memory.

Echolalia.
The parroting repetition of words or phrases either immediately after they are heard or later; usually observed in individuals with *autistic spectrum disorder.*

STEREOTYPED AND RITUALISTIC BEHAVIOR

Stereotyped, ritualistic behavior is a common feature of many individuals with autism. So is aggression directed at others and self-injury. In fact, the behavior problems associated with autism are legion. In more severe cases of autism, these behavior problems are prominent features and severely limit the child's options for learning and social interaction. We discuss behavior problems in more detail later in this chapter because they are not peculiar to autism.

PREOCCUPATION WITH OBJECTS AND RESTRICTED RANGE OF INTERESTS

Another characteristic frequently seen in autism and related disorders is extreme fascination or preoccupation with objects and a very restricted range of interests. Children with autism may play ritualistically with an object for hours at a time or show excessive interest in objects of a particular type. They may be upset by any change in the environment (e.g., something out of place or something new in the home or classroom) or any change in routine. That is, some individuals with autism seem intent on the preservation of sameness and have extreme difficulty with change or transition (Adreon & Stella, 2001; Myles & Simpson, 2001).

Cerebral palsy (CP).
A condition characterized by paralysis, weakness, lack of coordination, and/or other motor dysfunction; caused by damage to the brain before it has matured.

RANGE OF SEVERITY OF SYMPTOMS

As previously noted, the symptoms of autism may range from mild to severe. Autism is something one may have in degrees, just as people may have varying degrees of conduct disorder, **cerebral palsy (CP)**, mental retardation or any other special ability or disabling condition (see Charlop-Christy & Kelso, 1999; Charlop-Christy, Schreibman, Pierce, & Kurtz, 1998; National Research Council, 2001; Newsom, 1998; Simpson & Myles, 1998). Children with autism differ greatly in their specific abilities and disabilities. Many have mental retardation as an additional disability. Yet some are highly intelligent and high achieving. For example, Lee Alderman, a young man with autism, was the 2001 valedictorian of Cardozo High School in Washington, DC (Mathews, 2001). He may be the first student with a severe disability to have graduated as a high school valedictorian. Steven Shore has done advanced graduate work in music and special education (Brownell & Walther-Thomas, 2001).

Until relatively recently, children with severe autism have been the focus of the autistic spectrum—those with mental retardation, extreme preoccupation with objects and self-stimulation, serious self-injurious behavior, and lack of social responsiveness. But these children represent the rarest, smallest group in the spectrum of autism. A far larger number have milder forms of the disorder and are able to function much more normally in society. Since the mid-1990s, much more emphasis has been placed on mild autism and, especially, on the autistic spectrum disorder known as Asperger syndrome (AS). For example, an entire issue of *Intervention in School and Clinic* (Volume 36, Number 5, 2001) was devoted to AS.

ASPERGER SYNDROME (AS)

The central problem in Asperger syndrome (AS), as in all autistic spectrum disorders, is qualitative impairment of social interaction. In AS, the main problem seems to be that the student does not understand what Myles and Simpson (2001) call the "hidden curriculum"—the social skills that are not taught directly but that people are assumed to know, social rules or conventions that most of us learn incidentally. This makes them vulnerable to anger from adults and rejection by peers, who do not understand the "oddball" or socially obtuse behavior that may characterize the child or youth with AS. Examples of hidden curriculum in which students with AS may need instruction include these:

- Do not tell the principal that if she listened better more kids would like her.
- You should not have to pay students to be your friends.
- When you are with classmates you don't know very well and you are the center of attention, do not pass gas, pick your nose, or scratch a private body part.
- Do not tell classmates about all of the "skeletons in your parents' closets."
- During a conversation, face the speaker and position your body in that direction. (Myles & Simpson, 2001, p. 282)

Students with AS need explicit instruction in social skills that most students pick up through indirect or incidental learning. Myles and Simpson summarize as follows:

> Students with AS are at a disadvantage because they do not understand the hidden curriculum. As a result, they inadvertently break the rules associated with the hidden curriculum and either get in trouble with adults or are further ostracized or hurt by peers. Instruction and interpretation of hidden curriculum items should be an integral part of the education of children and youth with AS. It is through these types of activities that individuals with this exceptionality can learn to understand and function in the world around them. (2001, p. 285)

INTERNAL STATES

Individuals with the full spectrum of autistic disorders experience anxiety, stress, and the other internal states that all of us share as human beings (Groden, Cautela, Prince, & Berrryman, 1994). In fact, anxiety and depression may commonly be seen in individuals with Asperger syndrome (Williams, 2001). A few people with autism in some form have described their personal experiences, and these can help us understand more about the nature of this disorder as well. For example, Steven Shore shared his experiences and recommendations for teachers of students with autistic spectrum disorder in an interview in *Intervention in School and Clinic* (Brownell & Walther-Thomas, 2001; see also Grandin, 1995; Sacks, 1995). At the time of the interview, Shore was a doctoral student in special education at Boston University. He told his interviewers the following:

> I was diagnosed with strong autistic tendencies (as well as other things) when I was 2½ years old. Until the age of 18 months, I had been progressing normally, and then, all of a sudden, the development stopped and even slipped backwards. Within a short period, I lost most of my verbal abilities and had developed some other classic autistic tendencies. This is a common pattern of behavior change in children with autism. Parents report a sudden and significant change in their child's language, motor, and social skills. When this happens to the "normal" toddler and his or her family, it represents an "autism bomb" in their lives—nothing is ever the same again. (Brownell & Walther-Thomas, 2001, pp. 293–294)

Prevalence

Typical autism probably accounts for about 7.5 cases per 10,000 children. It is more often diagnosed in boys than in girls. It is not a phenomenon of American culture, as autism occurs among all nations of the world. It occurs across the full range of intelligence, although the majority of individuals with autism (perhaps as high as 80 percent) exhibit mental retardation as well. Besides mental retardation, autism may be accompanied by a variety of other disabilities such as learning disabilities, epilepsy, or conduct disorder.

All autistic spectrum disorders together probably occur in about 20 cases per 10,000 children (i.e., about 0.2 percent of the child population). Asperger's disorder probably occurs in about one or two cases per 10,000 children. Concern about apparent increases in autism and related disorders probably can be accounted for by better diagnosis and a broader definition, not dramatic changes in actual occurrence of these disorders. If anything, the incidence estimates given here are likely too low (National Research Council, 2001).

Causes

Psychoanalytic.
Related to psychoanalysis, including the assumptions that emotional or behavioral disorders result primarily from unconscious conflicts and that the most effective preventive actions and therapeutic interventions involve uncovering and understanding unconscious motivations.

For decades, **psychoanalytic** ideas attributed autism to parental attitudes or behavior (e.g., Bettelheim, 1967). However, we now know that the psychoanalytic explanation was wrong and that autistic spectrum disorders are caused by a brain malfunction. We do know that the families and parents of children with autistic spectrum disorder typically experience considerable stress because they are suddenly and unexpectedly confronted by the child's disability. Usually, their child does not look any different from the typical child, and often the child has gone through a short period of months or years of apparently normal development before the parents recognize that something is wrong. It is thus understandable that parents would behave in ways that reflect stress and concern. Children with autistic spectrum disorder require more than the typical parenting skills.

Scientists do not yet know precisely what is wrong with the brain in autistic spectrum disorder, but they have established unequivocally that the cause is neurological, not interpersonal (Kauffman, 2001; National Research Council, 2001). Given the range of symptoms and levels of severity of autistic spectrum disorder, it is a reasonable guess that there is no single neurological cause.

People are always looking for a simple explanation for autism and related disorders. Predictably, hypotheses about various causes, such as inoculation against childhood

Information for and about families and autism can be found at the Autism Society of America: www.autism-society.org/ ■

RESPONSIVE INSTRUCTION

Meeting the Needs of Students with Autistic Spectrum Disorders

Instructional Strategies

What the Research Says

Students identified as having autistic spectrum disorders will exhibit great variability in their specific strengths, interests, characteristics, behavioral challenges, and academic needs. In general, however, researchers have found that students with autistic spectrum disorders will require instructional programming to address many of the following areas: desire for routine; limited social awareness; restricted range of interests; problems focusing on toys, people's faces, or information-providing prompts; poor motor coordination; academic difficulties; and emotional vulnerability (Barnhill, 2001; Williams, 2001).

Applying the Research to Teaching

To address these characteristics, teachers will need to consider how the learning environment they create and the instructional strategies they choose will affect student growth. Specific suggestions for promoting student success include:

- Create a predictable environment built upon consistent routines.
- Teach students how to read and respond to social cues. Often, students with autism will need to be taught how to "read" emotions, tone of voice, nonverbal gestures, and idioms or abstract expressions. Teachers can use role-play, cue cards, and peers to help teach students these valuable social cues.
- Encourage other students in the class to engage the student with autism. Students with autism can be introverted and prefer their own company. By teaching other students in the class ways to engage and participate with the student with autism, the number of opportunities for learning will be increased.
- Create rules for engaging in discussions or activities that fall within the student's limited interests. Children with Asperger syndrome can have extreme interests and desire to seek only information on that topic. Similarly, a student with autism may want only to play with a certain object. Teachers should establish "time and place" rules for allowing engagement of those topics or activities so that other interests and learning can be developed.

- Use structured, positive reinforcement to shape desired social interactions and behaviors. For example, giving specific praise (or providing another desired response) to a student who joins a group activity or makes a request will lead the student to more frequently engage in those activities. By shaping a student's behavior in this way, the student will begin to act in ways determined by the teacher to result in increased learning or positive long-term outcomes.
- Divide instructional tasks into meaningful components and create overt, external stimuli to guide the student. Students with autistic spectrum disorders can be distracted by nonrelevant stimuli (e.g., the pattern on the teacher's dress, the lawn mower outside, the colors in the book) or internal stimuli (e.g., daydreaming). To support focus on the task at hand, teachers can create physical cues, such as a chart that is divided into the components of the lesson or a cue card the student selects as he or she finishes each step, to direct the student.
- Create academic experiences that build upon success. Students with autistic spectrum disorders can have intellectual capacities that range from severe and profound mental retardation to giftedness, yet all students will need support in the areas of understanding the nuances of language, multiple levels of meaning, and abstract connections. Explicit and structured instruction create cognitive support for student learning, retention, and concept integration.
- Teach students coping mechanisms to use when confronted with stress or anxiety. Routines and scripts can be helpful in allowing the student to feel as though she or he has regained control (Matson, Benavidez, Compton, Paclwaskyj, & Baglio, 1996; McClannahan & Krantz, 1999; Williams, 2001).

—By Kristin L. Sayeski

diseases or the presence or absence of a substance in the bloodstream, have been proposed at various times. Sometimes these hypotheses are also connected to speculation about prevention or cure. So far, all simple or single explanations have been proven false by careful scientific study.

Educational Considerations

As we have mentioned, the characteristics of autistic spectrum disorder are quite varied. When these characteristics are severe, they typically carry a very guarded prognosis, even with early, intensive intervention. A significant percentage of children with severe symptoms are unlikely to recover completely, although they may make substantial progress (Charlop-Christy et al., 1998; National Research Council, 2001).

The education of children with autistic spectrum disorder must begin early and be intensive and sustained. Intervention for a couple of hours per day is not effective. The most effective education starts when the child is an infant or toddler, is implemented for at least twenty-five hours per week throughout the calendar year in multiple settings (school and home), and involves the parents. It is intensively and relentlessly focused on helping the child overcome his or her greatest disability: inability to communicate effectively (Charlop-Christy & Kelso, 1999; National Research Council, 2001).

Children with autistic spectrum disorder have social and behavioral problems that need attention, but it is increasingly clear that communication skills are at the heart of the disability. Communication skills are essential for establishing and maintaining social relatedness. Furthermore, many of the behavior problems associated with autistic spectrum disorder may be ineffective or inefficient attempts to communicate with others. Communication disorders are typically a prominent part of autistic spectrum disorder, although they are a common problem of children with a wide range of developmental disabilities.

Many children and youths with autistic spectrum disorder require intensive instruction in daily living skills (Charlop-Christy & Kelso, 1999; Simpson & Myles, 1998). Effective instruction usually requires a highly structured, directive approach that uses basic principles of behavioral psychology for analyzing tasks and how best to teach them (see Charlop-Christy et al., 1998; Newsom, 1998).

Educators of students with autistic spectrum disorder are putting increasing emphasis on applying behavioral psychology in *natural* settings and in *natural* interactions—the kinds of settings and interactions that nondisabled children enjoy. Researchers are constantly trying to make better instructional use of the natural interactions by which children normally learn language and other social skills. At the preschool level, teachers are putting emphasis on natural interactions with normal peers in regular classrooms. At the elementary level, educators are including more children with autistic spectrum disorder in cooperative learning groups with their nondisabled peers in regular classrooms. Educators are looking for ways to help students with autistic spectrum disorder learn self-management skills at any age, including the teen years (Charlop-Christy et al., 1998). Partly because of the emphasis on more natural ways of teaching children with autistic spectrum disorder, an increasing percentage of such students are being taught in neighborhood schools and general education classrooms, especially at younger ages. Nevertheless, some of the effective instruction of children with autistic spectrum disorder requires one-on-one teaching or teaching in very small groups, and this often cannot be done effectively in the regular classroom. Even when such intensive instruction is offered in specialized settings, state-of-the-art teaching emphasizes the most natural possible human interactions.

Better understanding of the parental role has led to having parents work together with others as co-therapists in many treatment programs. If early intervention is to be as intensive and pervasive as required, then family involvement is essential. Without parental participation in training, children are unlikely to acquire and maintain the communication and daily living skills they need for social development and eventual independence.

Psychopharmacological interventions in autism and related disorders consist of a wide variety of experimental drugs, including **neuroleptics** (antipsychotic drugs) such as Haldol (haloperidol) and **psychostimulants** such as Ritalin (methylphenidate) (Forness, Kavale, Sweeney, & Crenshaw, 1999). Although these medications may give symptomatic relief in some cases (e.g., reducing self-injurious behavior or hyperactivity), responses to these drugs are idiosyncratic. That is, the effects tend to be unpredictable and depend on individual sensitivities. Even when drugs are helpful, behavior management and instruction by parents and teachers are still critical. Medications may sometimes make the individual more tractable or teachable, but they are not sufficient themselves to address the disorder.

Jamie Mangum, a member of the Bolivar Country Riding Club, shows off "Ox," a quarter horse who works with children with all types of mild and severe disabilities, including autism, cerebral palsy, and spina bifida. ■

To reiterate, education and related interventions for students with autism must be early, intensive, highly structured, and involve families, if they are to be most effective. Early, intensive intervention may produce remarkable gains in many young children with autistic spectrum disorder, although no intervention yet can claim universal success in enabling these children to overcome their disabilities completely. Education increasingly focuses on using natural interactions to teach students in natural environments, including regular classrooms to the extent possible. The National Research Council (2001) reviewed research and practice and found strong consensus that the following are essential features of effective educational programs, at least at the preschool level:

- entry into intervention programs as soon as an autism spectrum diagnosis is seriously considered;
- active engagement in intensive instructional programming for a minimum of the equivalent of a full school day, 5 days (at least 25 hours) a week, with full year programming varied according to the child's chronological age and developmental level;
- repeated, planned teaching opportunities generally organized around relatively brief periods of time for the youngest children (e.g., 15–20 minute intervals), including sufficient amounts of adult attention in one-to-one and very small group instruction to meet individualized goals;
- inclusion of a family component, including parent training;
- low student/teacher ratios (no more than two young children with autistic spectrum disorders per adult in the classroom); and
- mechanisms for ongoing program evaluation and assessments of individual children's progress, with results translated into adjustments in programming. (p. 175)

These are all recommendations about *how* children with autistic spectrum disorder should be taught. There is also the question of *what* they should be taught, and the National Research Council recommends that six areas of skill should be given priority in education:

1. Functional, spontaneous communication
2. Social skills that are age-appropriate (e.g., with very young children, responding to mother)
3. Play skills, especially play with peers
4. Cognitive (thinking) skills that are useful and applied in everyday life
5. Appropriate behavior to replace problem behavior
6. Functional academic skills, when appropriate to the needs of the child

Neuroleptics.
Antipsychotic drugs; drugs that suppress or prevent symptoms of psychosis; major tranquilizers.

Psychostimulants.
Medications that activate dopamine levels in the frontal and prefrontal areas of the brain that control behavioral inhibition and executive functions; used to treat persons with ADHD.

The National Research Council (2001) stressed the importance of family participation as one essential feature of effective educational programs for children with autism. ■

Not just anyone can be a successful teacher of students with autistic spectrum disorder. Teaching such children requires extensive training and guided experience. As the National Research Council noted, "Personnel preparation remains one of the weakest elements of effective programming for children with autistic spectrum disorders and their families" (2001, p. 180).

Traumatic Brain Injury (TBI)

In Chapter 1 we noted that in 1990 the Individuals with Disabilities Education Act (IDEA) created the category of **traumatic brain injury (TBI),** under which students may be found eligible for special education and related services. Today there is much greater understanding of the nature of TBI and the educational needs of students who acquire it. Unlike cerebral palsy, TBI is brain damage that is acquired by trauma after a period of normal neurological development. It presents unique educational problems that often have been poorly understood and mismanaged. Recent medical advances have greatly improved diagnosis and treatment.

Definition and Characteristics

Commonly accepted definitions of TBI specify that:

1. There is injury to the brain caused by an external force
2. The injury is not caused by a degenerative or congenital condition
3. There is a diminished or altered state of consciousness
4. Neurological or neurobehavioral dysfunction results from the injury

Most definitions also specify that the injury is followed by impairments in abilities required for school learning and everyday functioning.

Traumatic brain injury (TBI).
Injury to the brain (not including conditions present at birth, birth trauma, or degenerative diseases or conditions) resulting in total or partial disability or psychosocial maladjustment that affects educational performance; may affect cognition, language, memory, attention, reasoning, abstract thinking, judgment, problem solving, sensory or perceptual and motor disabilities, psychosocial behavior, physical functions, information processing, or speech.

Open head injury.
A brain injury in which there is an open wound in the head, such as a gunshot wound or penetration of the head by an object, resulting in damage to brain tissue.

Closed head injury.
Damage to the brain that occurs without penetration of the skull; might be caused by a blow to the head or violent shaking by an adult.

TBI can result from two categories of injury: open or closed. **Open head injuries** involve a penetrating head wound, from such causes as a fall, gunshot, assault, vehicular accident, or surgery. In **closed head injuries,** there is no open head wound but brain damage is caused by internal compression, stretching, or other shearing motion of neural tissues within the head (Adelson & Kochanek, 1998).

The educational definition of TBI focuses on impairments in one or more areas important for learning. The federal (IDEA) definition of TBI states that it is

> an acquired injury to the brain caused by an external physical force, resulting in total or partial functional disability or psychosocial impairment, or both, that adversely affects a child's educational performance. The term applies to open or closed head injuries resulting in impairments in one or more areas, such as cognition; language; memory; attention; reasoning; abstract thinking; judgment; problem-solving; sensory, perceptual, and motor abilities; psychosocial behavior; physical functions; information processing; and speech. The term does not apply to injuries that are congenital or degenerative, or brain injuries induced by birth trauma. [34 CFR, Sec. 300.7(6)(12)]

The various consequences of TBI create a need for special education; the injury itself is a medical problem. The effects of TBI may range from very mild to profound and may be temporary or permanent. Often the effects are immediate, and these immediate effects set TBI apart from most other disabilities—the child or youth is literally changed overnight (Council for Exceptional Children, 2001). The sudden change presents particular difficulties to families and teachers, not to mention the individual sustaining the injury (Dell Orto & Power, 2000). However, sometimes the effects of TBI are not seen immediately after the injury but appear months or even years afterward.

Depending on the age of onset of traumatic brain injury (TBI), personal adjustment problems may be a major concern. Even after recovering, victims may live in fear of injuring themselves again, as is the case with this young boy. ■

The possible effects of TBI include a long list of learning and psychosocial problems, including the following:

- Problems remembering things
- Problems learning new information
- Speech and/or language problems
- Difficulty sequencing things
- Difficulty in processing information (making sense of things)
- Extremely uneven abilities or performance (able to do some things but not others)
- Extremely uneven progress (quick gains sometimes, no gains other times)
- Inappropriate manners or mannerisms
- Failure to understand humor or social situations
- Becoming easily tired, frustrated, or angered
- Unreasonable fear or anxiety
- Irritability
- Sudden, exaggerated swings of mood
- Depression
- Aggression
- Perseveration (persistent repetition of one thought or behavior)

One of the great difficulties with TBI is that it is often "invisible." Like a learning disability, it is not something that one necessarily notices about a person at first. True, in

TBI: Often a Hidden Disability

Yesterday Bill and Alan met with Al's employers at the First Union Bank. All systems seem go for a return to work part-time some time in January, and at this point the folks at the bank say they understand Alan's limitations. Part of Bill's job is to act as an advocate and explain brain injury to Al's bosses and coworkers. He will also go to work with Al every day, functioning as a job coach. The biggest accommodation the bank will have to make is to allow Alan to work part-time, at the beginning only twelve hours a week. Alan looks just fine—that's why TBI is often dubbed "the hidden disability"—but everyone must understand why he has to take it slow. The hardest concept to get across is that brain injury is a *physical* condition. "If Al were in a wheelchair or had a cast on his leg, people would understand that something happened," says Crystal Mangir. "But no one can see a broken brain."

SOURCE: Crimmins, C. (2000). *Where is the mango princess?* (p. 199). New York: Knopf.

More information about TBI may be found at the Brain Injury Association of America: www.biausa.org ■

some cases a person with TBI has paralysis or slurred speech or some other indicator of brain damage that is quickly apparent. But in many cases the person with TBI looks just like everyone else. In the box above, Cathy Crimmins describes in detail her experiences following the TBI of her husband, Alan. He acquired his brain injury in a speedboat accident in 1996. Her book vividly illustrates not only the sudden change in abilities and behavior with which individuals and families must cope, but also the hidden nature of TBI. In the excerpt reprinted in the box, Bill is Alan's counselor from the Office of Vocational Rehabilitation.

Prevalence

The exact prevalence of TBI is difficult to determine, but we do know that TBI occurs at an alarming rate among children and youths. Estimates are that each year about 0.5 percent of school-age children acquire a brain injury. And by the time they graduate from high school, nearly 4 percent of students may have TBI (Savage & Wolcott, 1994). Of about a million children and adolescents who receive head injuries each year, roughly 15,000 to 20,000 will experience lasting effects (Council for Exceptional Children, 2001).

Males are more prone to TBI than females, and the age range in which TBI is most likely to occur for both males and females is late adolescence and early adulthood (Christensen, 1996). The Council for Exceptional Children (2001) refers to TBI as a "silent epidemic." It is considered an epidemic because of its increasing prevalence; "silent" because many serious head injuries are unreported and many cases of TBI are undetected or are mistaken for other disabilities. The prevalence of TBI is disconcerting because so many of the causes of TBI are entirely preventable or avoidable by following ordinary safety precautions (see Christensen, 1996).

Causes

Under age five, accidental falls are the dominant cause of TBI, with vehicular accidents and child abuse causing substantial injuries as well. After age five, and increasingly through adolescence, vehicular accidents (including accidents involving pedestrians, bicycles, motorcycles, and cars) account for the majority of TBI; assaults and gunshot wounds are increasingly prevalent among youths at older ages (McDonald, Togher, & Code, 1999b). Closed head injuries may be caused by a variety of events besides vehicular accidents, including a fall or abuse such as violent shaking of a child by an adult.

The prevalence of TBI is disconcerting because so many of the causes of TBI are entirely preventable or avoidable by following ordinary safety precautions, such as properly securing infants and children in car safety seats. ■

Educational Considerations

The educational implications of TBI can be extremely varied, depending on the nature and severity of the injury and the age and abilities of the individual at the time of injury. A significant issue in educating someone who has experienced TBI is helping family members, teachers, and peers respond appropriately to the sudden and sometimes dramatic changes that may occur in the student's academic abilities, appearance, behavior, and emotional states (Dell Orto & Power, 2000). Both general and special education teachers need training about TBI and its ramifications if students are to be reintegrated successfully into the schools and classrooms they attended before the injury (Tyler & Mira, 1999).

The following characteristics are essential features of appropriate education for students with TBI:

1. Transition from a hospital or rehabilitation center to the school
2. A team approach, involving regular and special educators, other special teachers, guidance counselor, administrators, and the student's family
3. An individualized education program (IEP) concerned with cognitive, social/behavioral, and sensory-motor domains
4. Educational procedures to help students solve problems in focusing and sustaining attention for long periods, remembering previously learned facts and skills, learning new things, dealing with fatigue, and engaging in appropriate social behavior
5. Emphasis on the cognitive processes through which academic skills are learned, not just curriculum content
6. Plans for addressing long-term needs in addition to immediate and annual IEP goals (Savage, 1988; Tyler & Mira, 1999)

TBI is a special case of neurological impairment, in which there is a sudden alteration in abilities; this can often cause frustration in the student and teachers who must cope with this loss. The student must undergo medical treatment to address the biophysical aspects of the injury, and it is critical that educators understand the implications of the injury for structuring the student's psychological and social environments in school (Heller, Alberto, Forney, & Schwartzman, 1996; Dell Orto & Power, 2000; Tyler & Mira, 1999).

The teacher must focus on helping the student with TBI to recover cognitive abilities, as these are most critical to academic and social progress. The abilities to remember and to make sense of academic information and social circumstances are key to the student's long-term success. The teacher must help the student learn to use coping mechanisms and alternative strategies, such as using a tape recorder, a planner, or other organizational devices and memory aids for whatever abilities cannot be recovered. TBI also presents particular challenges to teachers in areas of assessment and educational planning. As the Council for Exceptional Children has noted,

> the educational needs of the child with TBI will change quickly after the injury. Therefore, the child's IEP goals and objectives must be developed initially for achievement over short periods of time, 4–6 weeks, rather than six months to a year as is traditionally done. Likewise, the child may need more frequent assessments than other children with disabilities. (2001, p. 15)

A major problem in reentry to school after TBI—at least if the consequences are serious—is that the student tends to see himself or herself as not having changed, whereas peers and teachers may notice that the student with TBI is not the same. Orto and Power (2000) note that our societal emphasis on productiveness, organization, independence, and achievement may contribute to negative attitudes toward a student with TBI. "Academic deficits displayed by survivors of TBI conflict with achievement values, not only causing discomfort in teachers, but frustration and perhaps a sense of rejection in the young person" (p. 22). Many teachers apparently do not want students with TBI in their classrooms, probably because these students exhibit characteristics that teachers find troublesome (just consider the bulleted list on p. 385). Thus a student's returning to school following TBI is a major issue that typically requires a team approach involving a variety of professionals, as mentioned in our list of essential features of appropriate educational programs.

The assessment of a student's academic and social skills following TBI is tricky, due to the fact that it is often difficult or impossible to separate physiological causes or reasons for difficulty with a task from other causes. More important than knowing precisely what difficulties have a physiological cause is pinpointing just what the student's academic and social learning difficulties are. Here again, a team approach is essential. Neurologists can often provide information about the consequences of TBI that helps teachers set reasonable expectations and teach coping skills that help the student compensate for abilities that will not return.

LANGUAGE DISORDERS

A student with TBI may acquire a language disorder after a period of normal development, or she or he may acquire a more severe language disorder than existed prior to the injury. Individuals with TBI are a very diverse population, although a disproportionate number of students with TBI have a pretrauma history of learning problems or delayed speech and language (Beukelman & Mirenda, 1998; McDonald, Togher, & Code, 1999a; Nelson, 1998).

Language or speech disorders may be the greatest complicating factor in most students' return to school following TBI. A loss of ability to understand and formulate language due to brain injury is sometimes referred to as **acquired aphasia.** The student with aphasia may have trouble finding or saying words or constructing sentences that are appropriate for the topic of conversation or social context. Problems like these are a source of frustration, anger, and confusion for some students with TBI.

The language problems acquired with TBI are primarily related to the cognitive and social demands of communication. The student may have problems with tasks that

Acquired aphasia.
Loss or impairment of the ability to understand or formulate language because of accident or illness.

demand responding quickly, organizing, dealing with abstractions, sustaining attention (especially if there are distractions), learning new skills, responding appropriately in social situations, and showing appropriate affect. In fact, TBI can potentially disrupt all aspects of the give-and-take of social interaction that are required for effective communication.

The effects of TBI on language are extremely variable, and careful assessment of the given individual's abilities and disabilities is critically important. Interventions may range from making special accommodations—such as allowing more response time or keeping distractions to a minimum—to focusing on instruction in the social uses of language.

Depending on the site and degree of brain damage, a person with TBI may have motor control problems that interfere with communication, with or without the cognitive and social aspects of communication (McDonald, Togher, & Code, 1999a). Some students with TBI are not able to communicate orally using the muscles of speech and must rely on alternative or augmentative communication systems, which we describe later.

SOCIAL AND EMOTIONAL PROBLEMS

Brain injury may be accompanied by a variety of serious social and emotional effects. We know that TBI can cause violent aggression, hyperactivity, impulsivity, inattention, and a wide range of other emotional or behavioral problems, depending on just what parts of the brain are damaged. The possible effects of TBI include a long list of other psychosocial problems, some of which we listed previously as general characteristics (see Light et al., 1998; Dell Orto & Power, 2000; Tyler & Mira, 1999):

The emotional and behavioral effects of TBI are determined by more than the physical damage. These effects also depend on the student's age at the time of injury and the social environment before and after the injury occurs. Home, community, or school environments that foster misbehavior of any child or youth are known to be associated with increased risk for acquiring TBI. Such environments are extremely likely to worsen any emotional or behavioral problem resulting from TBI. Creating an environment that is conducive to and supportive of appropriate behavior is one of the great challenges of dealing effectively with the sequelae of brain injury (Bergland & Hoffbauer, 1996; Tyler & Mira, 1999).

Many of the typical **behavior modification** or **behavior management** strategies used with other students who have emotional or behavioral difficulties are appropriate for use

Behavior modification. Systematic control of environmental events, especially of consequences, to produce specific changes in observable responses. May include reinforcement, punishment, modeling, self-instruction, desensitization, guided practice, or any other technique for strengthening or eliminating a particular response.

Behavior management. Strategies and techniques used to increase desirable behavior and decrease undesirable behavior. May be applied in the classroom, home, or other environment.

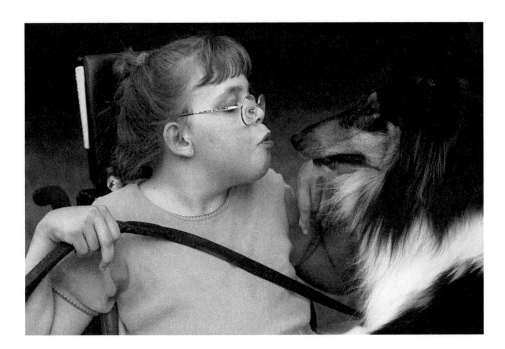

The emotional issue involved in TBI can be especially complex. Eileen Vosper, 12, enjoys holding "Kelli," a six-year-old collie who serves in a pet therapy program for children and adults with brain-injury related disabilities. The visits with the dogs are short, but meaningful. ■

Special Educators at Work

Albertson, NY: Sixteen-year-old **David Womack** is in the ninth grade at an academic day school for students with severe physical disabilities. He has been dependent on a ventilator since a spinal cord injury nine years ago. A collaborative team of teachers and therapists work closely with David and his parents, Brenda and David Womack, Sr., to maximize his independence through technology.

O n the second day of second grade, seven-year-old David Womack was hit by a car as he stepped from the school bus in front of his home. The accident injured David's spinal cord, leaving him a quadriplegic, with no movement below his neck and no ability for spontaneous respiration.

During David's two-year rehabilitation in a Baltimore hospital, his father, David Womack, Sr., traveled four hours every other weekend to be with his son and his wife, Brenda, who rented a nearby apartment. Their twelve-year-old daughter stayed behind with her grandmother in the Long Island community that rallied in support to raise funds for a home computer system for David and to help his family buy and renovate an accessible home.

Upon David's release from the hospital, his parents and educators from their school district made the decision to enroll nine-year-old David in Henry Viscardi School, a special day school for students with intense medical and physical needs. Unlike most schools, Viscardi is equipped with a large medical and therapeutic staff. Nurses as well as physical and occupational therapists team with teachers, so that students benefit from closely monitored physical and instructional management.

In 1989, David was the first student dependent on a ventilator to attend the school. He made his third-grade entrance in a large electronic "sip-and-puff" wheelchair, directed by airflow he provided through a strawlike mouth-piece. "The vent," as this life-support system is also called, was mounted on the back of his chair and detected by its rhythmic sound. Never more than several feet away was a private-duty nurse, who monitored him at all times. "It was so scary," recalls Brenda Womack. "I could tell everybody was nervous."

The school's task included helping all the Womacks adjust to a different life and stimulating David to discover his new potential. Before the first day of school, staff occupational therapist Ginette Howard worked closely with David to ready him for classroom technology, as well as with his teachers, all of whom were certified in both special and general education. Even though the staff was experienced in dealing with difficult physical issues, David presented a challenge, and the presence of the ventilator, necessary equipment, and private nurse emphasized his fragility. Says Ginette, "Before long, we realized we had to raise everybody's expectations and start treating David like a student instead of a patient!"

David's progress has been built slowly but steadily on a foundation of trust, and his achievements are the result of both sophisticated instructional technology and effective collaboration among teachers, therapists, nurses, and his home community. It was the school's team approach to technology that supported David's classroom learning. Ginette Howard and computer teacher Maryann Cicchillo

with students who have TBI. Consistency, predictability, and reinforcement (praise, encouragement, and other rewards) are particularly important. So is developing rapport with the student. Developing a good personal relationship with a student with TBI may be particularly challenging, as such students can be unpredictable, irritable, and angry at those who are trying to help (see Kauffman, Mostert, Trent, & Hallahan, 2002; Tyler & Mira, 1999).

TBI often shatters an individual's sense of self. Recovering one's identity may require a long period of rehabilitation and may be a painstaking process requiring multidisciplinary efforts (Fraser & Clemmons, 2000; Dell Orto & Power, 2000). Effective education and treatment often require not only classroom behavior management but family therapy, medication, cognitive training, and communication training (Light et al., 1998; Tyler & Mira, 1999).

combined their knowledge of instructional software and sophisticated electronics to provide David with the tools to read, write, and compute. Classroom teachers followed their lead, and so did his nurse, Gail Nolan, who was committed to his academic and social growth.

"The first year, we needed to overcome fear and develop trust," recalls Ginette Howard. David was frightened to leave the hospital, so the first task was to secure his ventilator equipment for school mobility and classroom use. "We made sure there was a plastic casing over the dials since he was afraid someone might play with the settings," Ginette explains. The second year, David became more confident and was willing to try out new pieces of educational technology. Over six years, Ginette and Maryann have seen David progress from being withdrawn and fearful, to trusting, to finally developing real interest in computer applications. Providing him with computer access has been the challenge.

"David has chin supports to keep his head erect, and he can move his mouth," says Ginette. She and Maryann selected a small alternative-access keyboard, worked by an electronic mouthstick called a *wand*. With much effort, David would clench the mouthstick in his teeth and gently tap the attached wand on the miniature impulse-sensitive keyboard set on a height-adjustable table in front of him. The classroom computer would directly respond, and Maryann ensured that appropriate software was available to David's teacher through the school's network. Very gradually, David became accustomed to the awkwardness of the mouthstick and to the expectation that he was independently responsible for his schoolwork. As Ginette remembers, "David is extremely artistic, and he increased his facility by using adapted paintbrushes. By his second and third year, I was making mouthsticks like you wouldn't believe!"

Now in ninth grade, David no longer needs the adapted access of the miniature system, since he has developed greater facial mobility. Having used mouthsticks for numerous functional tasks, he has the flexibility and range of motion to use one with an angled standard keyboard. "My goal for David is for him to become an independent thinker via technology," says his science teacher, Dorothy Vann.

"This direct keyboard access gives him much more freedom in class."

Since David tires easily, he uses a word-prediction and abbreviation/expansion program to reduce the number of keystrokes and increase his speed in writing assignments. He also has started to use a laptop computer with a trackball, further challenging his accuracy and increasing his speed. David's technology sessions have been used to increase his independence as a student. "I can't tell you how many times we've explored technology to support homework assignments, to take tests, or complete a paper," says Maryann. "Last year, we used the word-prediction and abbreviation/expansion program to write formal letters," recalls Ginette Howard. "David learned to program the abbreviations for salutations and common phrases, such as 'DS' for 'Dear Sir,' or 'YT' for 'Yours Truly.' When he keyed in the abbreviations, the phrases would appear."

"Science is my favorite subject," says David, now a quiet young man who speaks in a soft, breathy voice. Dorothy Vann's science lab is fully accessible to him, with adjustable tables and low sinks; it is also equipped with instructional technology that David needs to fully participate. In biology, he views slides through a stereo microscope, which utilizes a small attached video camera to project images onto a TV monitor. "I knew David was capable of doing more than he initially showed us," says Dorothy. "Now he uses the video microscope in labs, and in the future, he will use the computerized video laser disc player for independent research on science topics."

Working with David has been an evolving process for each of the collaborators. "When some teachers see and hear that ventilator, their tendency is to pamper the child," observes Brenda Womack. "But I have a sixteen-year-old son and I want him treated like any other student."

In reflecting on their work with David, Ginette Howard and Maryann Cicchillo think there is a breaking-in period, in which teachers and the child who is newly ventilator dependent have to overcome their fears. Says Dorothy Vann, "It also takes a while for the child to accept goals for achievement and believe in his or her own success."

—By Jean Crockett

A great deal of information is now available about TBI on the World Wide Web. For further information, you may want to visit the Web site of the Brain Injury Association.

Deaf-Blindness

In previous chapters we noted that, depending on the level of severity, blindness or deafness can have a substantial impact on a person's ability to function independently. For those who are both deaf *and* blind, however, the impact can be even more profound than

Ⓦ A variety of information about deaf-blindness is found at www.deafblind.com and at www.tr.wou.edu/dblink/ ∎

simply adding the effects of each disability. Because the primary avenues for receiving information—sight and sound—are limited, those who are deaf-blind are at risk for having extensive problems in communicating and in navigating their environments.

Although being cut off from the sights and sounds of daily life makes deaf-blindness one of the most challenging of all multiple disabilities (Scheetz, 2001), this does not mean that a person with deaf-blindness is doomed to a life of low quality. In general, outcomes for individuals with deaf-blindness are dependent on at least three things:

1. The quality and intensity of instruction the person receives is critical. Teachers of students with deaf-blindness "must make the most of every opportunity for learning. All interactions with adults and all aspects of the environment will be harnessed to help the child overcome the restrictions imposed by sensory impairments" (Hodges, 2000, p. 167).

2. The degree and type of visual impairment and auditory impairment can vary dramatically in individuals with deaf-blindness. The term *deaf-blindness* covers those with visual impairments ranging from low vision (20/70 to 20/200 in the better eye with correction) to those who are totally blind. Likewise, the term covers those with hearing impairments ranging from mild to profound. Although there are some very notable exceptions in general, the more severe the impairments, the greater the impact on a person's ability to adapt.

3. The vast majority of students who are deaf-blind have other disabilities and medical conditions. For example, approximately 11 percent of children between birth and age twenty-two who are deaf-blind also have mental retardation (Hembree, 2000). In general, the more numerous and severe these other disabilities, the greater the impact on a person's ability to adapt.

Definition

As we discussed in Chapters 9 and 10, there is considerable controversy over definitions of deafness and blindness. As one might expect, this means that defining deaf-blindness is even more controversial than defining deafness or blindness by itself. Following is the federal government's definition of deaf-blindness contained in IDEA:

Deaf-blindness means concomitant hearing and visual impairments, the combination of which causes such severe communication and other developmental and educational needs that they cannot be accommodated in special education programs solely for children with deafness or children with blindness. (U.S. Department of Education, 1999, p. 12422)

Many states, however, have found this definition too vague and have either developed their own definitions or have added other criteria to the federal definition. For example, Alaska has added the following criteria:

Vision:

Visual acuity of 20/70 or less in the better eye with correction; visual field restriction of 20 degrees or less; functional vision which is virtually absent or unmeasurable for purposes of learning; need for special services requiring the use of non-standard instructional materials or aids designed to facilitate the child's learning; temporary impairment or loss of vision due to illness, accidents, temporary treatments; a diagnosis of a syndrome or disorder associated with progressive vision loss.

Hearing:

Hearing impairment of 30dB or greater unaided in the better ear; recurrent otitis media or documented history of recurrent otitis media affecting language or learning abilities; functional hearing which is absent or unmeasurable for purposed of learning; diagnosis of a syndrome or disorder associated with a progressive hearing loss. (National Information Clearinghouse on Children Who Are Deaf-Blind, 2001)

Prevalence

The fact that definitions and criteria vary from state to state, coupled with the fact that so many students with deaf-blindness also have other disabling conditions, has made it very difficult to get an accurate picture of prevalence rates. The National Technical Assistance Consortium for Children and Young Adults Who Are Deaf-Blind (NTAC) at Western Oregon University keeps the most accurate figures. Each year, they take a census of the deaf-blind student population. The most recent census indicates that there are about 10,000 individuals from birth to twenty-two years of age who are deaf-blind (Hembree, 2000). The number of adults with deaf-blindness is estimated to be about 35,000 to 40,000 (Baldwin, 1994, as cited in Miles, 1998).

Causes

Causes of deaf-blindness can be grouped into three broad categories: (1) genetic/chromosomal syndromes, (2) prenatal conditions, and (3) postnatal conditions.

GENETIC/CHROMOSOMAL SYNDROMES

As we discussed in Chapter 4, researchers are making enormous strides in discovering genetic/chromosomal mental retardation syndromes. Some of these syndromes are inherited and some result from damaged genetic and/or chromosomal material. This is also the case with respect to deaf-blindness. There are now over fifty genetic/chromosomal syndromes associated with deaf-blindness. The most common are **CHARGE syndrome, Usher syndrome,** and **Down syndrome.**

CHARGE Syndrome

CHARGE syndrome is characterized by a number of physical anomalies present at birth. The exact cause of CHARGE is still being debated, but there is growing evidence that it results from a genetic abnormality (Aitken, 2000; Oley, 2001). The reason for the uncertainty is probably due to the fact that the condition was not identified in the medical literature until 1979 (Hall, 1979). The letters in CHARGE refer to some of the most common characteristics of this condition: C = coloboma, cranial nerves; H = heart defects; A = atresia of the choanae; R = retardation in growth and mental development; G = genital abnormalities; E = ear malformation and/or hearing loss.

Coloboma refers to a condition in which the child is born with an abnormally shaped pupil and/or abnormalities of the retina or optic nerve (CHARGE Syndrome Foundation, 2001). Coloboma can result in a variety of visual problems, including deficits in visual acuity and extreme sensitivity to light.

The **cranial nerves** supply information between the brain and various muscles and glands in the body. Individuals with CHARGE syndrome often have paralysis or weakness of facial muscles as well as swallowing problems because of abnormal development of some of the cranial nerves.

CHARGE syndrome.
A genetic syndrome resulting in deaf-blindness; characterized by physical anomalies, often including coloboma (abnormalities of the pupil, retina and/or optic nerve), cranial nerves, heart defects, atresia (absence or closure) of the chonae (air passages from nose to throat), retardation in growth and mental development, genital abnormalities, ear malformation and/or hearing loss.

Usher syndrome.
An inherited syndrome resulting in hearing loss and retinitis pigmentosa, a progressive condition characterized by problems in seeing in low light and tunnel vision; there are three different types of Usher syndrome, differing with respect to when it occurs developmentally and the range of the major symptoms of hearing loss, vision loss, and balance problems.

Down syndrome.
A condition resulting from a chromosomal abnormality; characterized by mental retardation and such physical signs as slanted-appearing eyes, hypotonia, a single palmar crease, shortness, and a tendency toward obesity; the most common type of Down syndrome is trisomy 21.

Coloboma.
A condition of the eye in which the pupil is abnormally shaped and/or there are abnormalities of the retina or optic nerve; can result in loss of visual acuity and extreme sensitivity to light.

Cranial nerves.
Twelve pairs of nerves that connect the brain with various muscles and glands in the body.

Atresia.
Absence or closure of a part of the body that is normally open.

Choanae.
Air passages from the nose to the throat.

Retinitis pigmentosa.
A hereditary condition resulting in degeneration of the retina; causes a narrowing of the field of vision and affects night vision.

Night blindness.
A condition characterized by problems in seeing at low levels of illumination; often caused by retinitis pigmentosa.

Tunnel vision.
A condition characterized by problems in peripheral vision, or a narrowing of the field of vision.

Prenatal.
Occurring or developing in the fetus before birth.

Rubella.
(German measles).
A serious viral disease, which, if it occurs during the first trimester of pregnancy, is likely to cause a deformity in the fetus.

Cytomegalovirus (CMV).
A herpes virus; can cause a number of disabilities.

Postnatal.
Occurring in an infant after birth.

Meningitis.
A bacterial or viral infection of the linings of the brain or spinal cord; can cause a number of disabilities.

The vast majority of children with CHARGE syndrome are born with heart defects. Some of these problems are relatively minor, but some are life threatening and require surgery (CHARGE Syndrome Foundation, 2001).

An **atresia** is the absence or closure of a body opening present at birth. The **choanae** are air passages from the nose to throat. When the choanae are blocked or narrowed, the ability to breathe is affected. Surgery can help correct these breathing problems.

Most children with CHARGE syndrome are of normal size at birth, but may experience growth problems because of nutrition, heart problems, and/or growth hormone abnormalities (CHARGE Syndrome Foundation, 2001). In addition, some are mentally retarded.

Genital anomalies include incomplete or underdeveloped genitals. This is more common in males than females (Brown, 1996).

CHARGE syndrome can result in a variety of structural abnormalities of the outer, middle, and/or inner ear. The consequent hearing loss may be conductive, sensorineural, or mixed (both conductive and sensorineural).

Usher Syndrome   Usher syndrome, an inherited condition, is characterized by hearing loss and **retinitis pigmentosa.** As you recall from Chapter 10, retinitis pigmentosa can result in vision problems starting in infancy, early childhood, or the teenage years, with the condition becoming progressively worse. It results in problems in seeing in low light, referred to as **night blindness,** and as it progresses it results in a narrowing of the field of vision, referred to as **tunnel vision.**

There are three types of Usher syndrome, varying with respect to the type and time of occurrence of the major symptoms of hearing loss, vision loss, and balance problems. For example, depending on the type of Usher syndrome, the person can be born profoundly deaf, hard of hearing, or with normal hearing that deteriorates over time. Some experience night blindness starting in infancy, whereas others have night blindness starting in the teenage years. Some have severe balance problems, due to inner-ear problems, starting in infancy; some have no balance problems; and some are born with normal balance that deteriorates over time.

Genetic researchers have been finding more and more genes that cause the three types of Usher syndrome. As of February 2001, researchers had localized six genes causing six subtypes of Usher I, three genes causing three subtypes of Usher II, and one gene causing Usher III (Boys Town National Research Hospital Genetics Department, 2001).

Although Usher syndrome is one of the most common hereditary conditions causing deaf-blindness, its overall prevalence is very low. There are only about 300 persons from birth to age twenty-two identified as having Usher syndromes I–III (Hembree, 2000). However, the genetics of Usher syndrome show an interesting demographic pattern (see the box on p. 395).

Down Syndrome   Most often noted as a cause of mental retardation (see Chapter 4), Down syndrome is also sometimes associated with deaf-blindness. Unlike Usher syndrome, which is inherited, Down syndrome results from damaged chromosomal material.

PRENATAL CONDITIONS

Like Down syndrome, two of the most common types of **prenatal** conditions—**rubella** and congenital **cytomegalovirus (CMV)**—can cause mental retardation and/or deaf-blindness. Rubella, sometimes referred to as **German measles**, occurring in a pregnant woman, especially in the first trimester, can lead to a variety of disabilities, including deaf-blindness. Children born with CMV, a herpes virus, are also at risk for a variety of disabilities, including deaf-blindness.

POSTNATAL CONDITIONS

Among the most common **postnatal** conditions that can cause deaf-blindness are **meningitis** and traumatic brain injury (TBI). As we learned in Chapter 4, meningitis, which is an

The Genetics of Usher Syndrome and Its Geographic Distribution

About one in seventy-five persons carries an Usher gene, but most do not realize they have it. Usher syndrome is an *autosomal recessive disorder,* meaning that in order for a child to have the condition, both parents must be carriers of the gene. And with each pregnancy, there is a one-in-four chance of the child having Usher syndrome. Thus, the chance of having a child with Usher syndrome is relatively rare even among those carrying the gene, and that is why the prevalence of Usher syndrome is so low. However, the odds of producing an offspring with Usher syndrome rise dramatically among people who are related:

> Each of us, regardless of family history, is thought to silently carry five or more recessive genes that have the potential to cause genetic disorders in the next generation. But the chance of conceiving a child with a recessive disorder is low because most unrelated couples do not carry the exact same recessive genes. Conversely, because members of one's immediate or extended family share a similar genetic makeup, it becomes easier for two autosomal recessive genes to match up to cause a particular disorder. Thus, children conceived by parents who are related to each other are at higher than average risk for being affected by autosomal recessive disorders. And in certain cultures in which marriages between relatives are the norm or in which many people preferentially choose partners with the same inherited trait (e.g., marriage between two people with deafness), recessive conditions occur more commonly than expected. (Dykens, Hodapp, & Finucane, 2000, p. 46)

Unfortunately, social forces have operated historically to make the likelihood of intermarriage higher among a certain cultural group—the Acadian French of south Louisiana. This has resulted in a relatively higher number of persons with Usher syndrome in this area of the country. Following is an excerpt from a retired teacher who had worked at the Louisiana School for the Deaf for twenty-seven years:

> To begin with, Usher syndrome among the Acadian French people in south Louisiana was something people knew the "about" of, but not the "what" or "why" of. They knew that generation after generation of children were struck mysteri-

ously with deafness and eventually with partial-to-full blindness. It was something that was dreaded, but had to be endured. Again and again, cousins, aunts, uncles, and sometimes two or three children in a family were found to have the condition, but no one knew what to do, or what to call it.

> The "what" and "why" of it was that the Acadian parishes of south Louisiana have a far higher percentage of Usher syndrome than anywhere else in the United States. This extraordinarily high percentage has been documented in several studies. . . . For example, [Kloepfer, Laguaite, and McLaurin, 1966] estimated that 30 percent of the deaf population in the parishes of Lafayette, Vermillion, and Acadia had Usher syndrome. The high incidence is a result of several hundred years of intermarriage among this close-knit ethnic group. Inevitably, two individuals, both carrying a recessive gene for Usher syndrome transmitted to them by a common ancestor, marry and have children with this condition.

> The Acadians, or Cajuns, as they are called, were originally from Acadia (Nova Scotia) in Canada. In the 1700s they were expelled from that area by the English. They moved down along the east coast of America, finally settling along the bayous of several south Louisiana parishes. At first they were not readily accepted by people in the area and were somewhat isolated both by language and by culture. With time, however, the Cajuns came into their own and have won admirers around the world for their music, love of fun, and never-to-be-forgotten cuisine.

> Many students at the Louisiana School for the Deaf (LSD) come from the Acadian parishes resulting in a high incidence of Usher syndrome at the school. . . . Fifteen to twenty percent of children on the Louisiana deaf-blind census for children birth through age 21 are known to have Usher syndrome [Type I] as compared to an average of 3 percent for all other states in the nation. (Melancon, 2000, p. 1)

The high prevalence of Usher syndrome in south Louisiana is also the subject of a video narrated by the well-known neurologist Oliver Sacks, *The Ragin' Cajun: Usher Syndrome,* produced by the British Broadcasting Company.

infection of the covering of the brain, can also cause mental retardation. And TBI, as discussed earlier in this chapter, can result in a variety of other disabilities, as well as deaf-blindness.

Psychological and Behavioral Characteristics

Persons who are deaf-blind can have significant problems in at least three areas: (1) accessing information, (2) communicating, and (3) navigating the environment (Aitken, 2000).

PROBLEMS ACCESSING INFORMATION

People who are sighted and have hearing are able to access a variety of information about their world, whether it be from the media (newspapers, television, the Internet) or other people. For persons who are deaf-blind, however, access to this information is much harder to obtain. And because communication is largely dependent on the availability of information, restricted access to information can have a negative impact on the ability to communicate:

> The consequence of not being able to access information is that life experiences are reduced. Lack of everyday ordinary experiences—how to make a sandwich, knowing that water comes from a tap—makes it more difficult for the person who is deaf-blind to build up a store of world knowledge. Without that store of world knowledge what is there to communicate about? (Aitken, 2000, p. 3)

PROBLEMS COMMUNICATING

Most authorities agree that the biggest obstacle faced by persons with deaf-blindness is communication (Aitken, 2000; Ford & Fredericks, 1995; Miles, 1998). Without a strong commitment by teachers and other professionals and parents to providing a variety of opportunities for communication, the child who is deaf-blind can easily become a social isolate. The pattern for this isolation can begin at birth. The baby

> may not be able to make and sustain eye contact or to respond to a soothing voice. His mother's face may be invisible or only a blur and her speech only a low sound which he cannot pick out from the background of other noises. The deaf-blind baby may register little of the world around him, or may find it a frightening place full of half-registered shapes and sounds. He will not hold his mother's attention with a ready gaze and will not be able to play the games of sight, sound and movement which other babies enjoy. If his vision and hearing are so seriously damaged that he cannot use visual or auditory cues to warn him that someone is coming to pick him up, or that a particular activity is about to happen, contact with other people may even become threatening. (Pease, 2000, p. 38)

Once this pattern of isolation is established it is difficult to reverse it. Therefore, it is critical that professionals and parents work together to provide an environment as supportive and rich in communication opportunities as possible.

No better example of the importance of providing a language-rich environment exists than the classic case of Helen Keller (1880–1968) and her teacher Annie Sullivan (1866–1936). Popularized by the now classic movie *The Miracle Worker*, Helen Keller's accomplishments are now familiar to most of us. Having lost her sight and hearing at the age of nineteen months, Keller went on to extraordinary achievements, including graduating cum laude from Radcliffe College in 1904; authoring essays and books (including the much acclaimed *The Story of My Life*, written while in college and available in over fifty languages); touring the country lecturing on blindness; being a spokesperson for women's right to vote; and receiving the Presidential Medal of Freedom, the nation's highest civilian award.

Helen Keller is testimony to the power of the human spirit to overcome overwhelming odds. However, just as important, she is testimony to the power of intensive and extensive special education instruction. As remarkable as she was, it is doubtful Keller would have conquered her condition without the prolonged instruction from Annie Sullivan, who devoted nearly fifty years to being Keller's teacher and constant companion. Sullivan, herself born blind, had had some of her sight restored through several operations. She arrived at the home of the Kellers in 1887 to meet a not yet seven-year-old Helen, who had some rudiments of communication but who was prone to severe tantrums. Through persistence and intensive instruction, Sullivan was able to set Helen's mind free to learn language and higher concepts.

Sullivan and Keller are not the only famous teacher-student team to demonstrate the importance of intensive instruction of the deaf-blind. See the box on p. 398 for the story of Laura Bridgman and Samuel Gridley Howe.

PROBLEMS NAVIGATING THE ENVIRONMENT

As we discussed in Chapter 10, persons who are blind or who have low vision can have significant difficulties with mobility. For persons who are deaf-blind, these problems are often even more pronounced. Individuals who are blind and hearing are able to pick up auditory cues that help them in navigation. For example, being able to hear approaching traffic can be very helpful when crossing an intersection, or being able to hear such things as buses, trains, construction noises, and so forth, can help a person who is blind identify her or his location. However, persons who are both deaf and blind are restricted in their ability to make use of auditory signals useful for navigating the environment.

Educational Considerations

The major educational needs of infants and preschoolers, as well as older students, who are deaf-blind fall generally under the categories of communication and orientation and mobility. In addressing these needs, there are at least two important principles that practitioners and parents should keep in mind: the importance of direct teaching and the importance of structured routines.

THE IMPORTANCE OF DIRECT TEACHING

Many students with disabilities (e.g., mental retardation, learning disabilities, blindness, deafness) are more reliant than those without disabilities on having teachers teach them directly. Whereas students without disabilities can learn a great deal *incidentally* (e.g., from seeing or hearing things that happen around them), students with disabilities are often in greater need of having material *taught to them directly*. As we mentioned in connection with Helen Keller and Laura Bridgman, because of their restricted sensory input, this need for direct teaching of information is even more pronounced for students who are deaf-blind than it is for children with other disabilities.

THE IMPORTANCE OF STRUCTURED ROUTINES

In order to create a successful environment for learning, it is also critical that teachers and other professionals and parents provide a sense of security for students who are deaf-blind. One of the best ways to create this sense of security is through the use of *structured routines* (Chen, Alsop, & Minor, 2000; Miles, 1998), discussed in detail in the box on p. 400.

For information on Helen Keller, including many of her letters and papers, visit the Web site maintained by the American Foundation for the Blind: http://www.afb.org/info_documents.asp?collectionid=1 ■

Laura Bridgman and Her Teacher, Samuel Gridley Howe

Although most people are familiar with the story of Helen Keller, Laura Bridgman (1829–1889) was actually the first documented case of a deaf–blind person to learn language. Laura was struck at the age of two with scarlet fever and left deaf and blind.

Samuel Gridley Howe (1801–1876) was one of the nineteenth century's most daring social activists, reforming schools, prisons, and mental institutions, as well as being a member of the "Secret Six" who leant financial support to John Brown's campaign to end slavery in the United States with his ill-fated launching of the raid at Harper's Ferry in 1859. Howe received his medical degree from Harvard University in 1824. After serving a seven-year stint as a surgeon in the Greek civil conflict, he returned to Boston. In 1832, he was named head of the Perkins Institution and Massachusetts School for the Blind (now named the Perkins School for the Blind).

After reading a newspaper account of Laura, Howe visited her parents and convinced them to send the eight-year-old to Perkins in 1837. There, he and his teachers worked painstakingly with Laura for several years. In addition to the goals of teaching her to communicate, Howe viewed Bridgman as a philosophical and religious experiment. By showing that she could learn to communicate, he was debunking the materialists, who held that sensory input was necessary in order to form concepts: "As Laura reached out to the world around her, Howe thrilled to witness the triumph of mind over matter" (Freeberg, 2001, p. 41). With respect to religion, Howe hoped to show that Laura possessed an innate moral consciousness that was intact despite her sensory losses.

Howe held open houses for the public to see the accomplishments of the students at Perkins. Laura soon became the major attraction, drawing hundreds of onlookers. One of the early visitors was Charles Dickens, whose account of his meeting with Laura, which he described in *American Notes,* further publicized the accomplishments of Howe's work with her.

Howe eventually became discouraged because Laura did not progress as far as he had hoped. Although she was able to communicate well, her personality, charac-terized by immaturity and occasional fits of rage, kept her from becoming the ideal case to prove his philosophical and theological theories.

Although her achievements were not as spectacular as Keller's, Bridgman's accomplishments were extraordinary for the time, a time when many authorities believed that to be deaf-blind was to be mentally retarded. Furthermore, had it not been for Bridgman, Keller might never have received the instruction that unlocked her intellect. Helen's parents were alerted to the potential of teaching their own daughter after reading about Bridgman's accomplishments. Furthermore, Helen's teacher, Annie Sullivan, herself a former student at Perkins, consulted Howe's reports on Laura before embarking on her journey to tutor Helen.

Perhaps most important,

Laura Bridgman's dramatic story drew the public's attention to the wider reform movement that was transforming the lives of many disabled people in nineteenth century America. Howe and other educators invented teaching tools, experimented with curriculum, and built new institutions that helped thousands of people with sensory handicaps to overcome the physical barriers that had always deprived them of an education. . . . Chipping away at centuries of accumulated prejudice and misunderstanding, these students and their teachers began to dismantle one of the greatest barriers faced by the blind and the deaf, the deep-rooted misconception that people with sensory handicaps are unreachable and somehow less than fully human. In the crucial early years of this important reform movement, no person did more to challenge those assumptions and inspire new respect for the disabled than Laura Bridgman. (Freeberg, 2001, pp. 220–221)

SOURCE: Reprinted by permission of the publisher from *The Education of Laura Bridgman: First Deaf and Blind Person to Learn Language* by E. Freeberg, Cambridge, Mass.: Harvard University Press, Copyright © 2001 by the President and Fellows of Harvard College.

Braille.
A system in which raised dots allow people who are blind to read with their fingertips; each quadrangular cell contains from one to six dots, the arrangement of which denotes different letters and symbols.

COMMUNICATION

The hands play a critical role in communication for most students who are deaf-blind. In effect they become the "voice, or the primary means of expression" (Miles, 1999, p. 1). There are a number of modes of communication used with persons who are deaf-blind that involve touch. **Braille** is the most obvious one. Some other common tactile learning strategies are: **hand-over-hand guidance, hand-under-hand guidance, adapted signs,** and **touch cues** (Chen, Downing, & Rodriguez-Gil, 2000/2001).

Hand-Over-Hand Guidance   Hand-over-hand guidance involves the adult placing his or her hand(s) over the child's hand(s) while exploring an object or signing. Although this technique may be necessary, especially for children who have physical disabilities that interfere with movement of their hands, it does have some disadvantages (Chen et al., 2000/2001; Miles, 1999). Some children are resistant to this technique, apparently because they do not like the feeling of loss of control over their hands. Furthermore, some children can become too passive, waiting for someone else's hands to be placed over theirs rather than reaching out on their own.

Hand-Under-Hand Guidance   Hand-under-hand guidance is often recommended as an alternative to hand-over-hand guidance. This technique involves the adult gently slipping his or her hand(s) underneath part of the child's hand(s) while the child is exploring an object. It becomes the tactile equivalent to pointing (Miles, 1999). One of the main advantages of hand-under-hand guidance is that it is noncontrolling, and some authorities believe that when children and adults explore objects and movements together it lays a foundation for language (Miles, 1999).

Laura Bridgman with Samuel Gridley Howe. ■

Adapted Signs   Signs used by the Deaf community, such as American Sign Language and Signed English, are visually based, which makes them difficult or impossible to use by persons who are deaf-blind, depending on the severity of their vision loss. For this reason, a variety of tactual versions of signing have been created (Chen et al., 2000/2001). For example, for the reception of signs, the person who is deaf-blind can place his or her hands on the hands of the signer; for the expression of signs, the teacher or parent can hold the hands of the person who is deaf-blind and guide him or her to produce signs.

Touch Cues   Touch cues are tactual signals that can convey a number of messages depending on the situation and context. It is important that the touch cues be consistent:

> A child will not be able to decipher the meaning of a touch cue if different people use it for a variety of messages. For example, patting or tapping a child on the shoulder may express any of the following:
> - positive feedback ("Great job")
> - a request or directive ("Sit down")
> - information ("Your turn")
> - comfort or reassurance ("Don't cry, you're OK)
>
> . . . Touch cues should be used selectively, conservatively, and consistently so that the child can develop an understanding of what they represent. (Chen et al., 2000/2001, p. 3)

ORIENTATION AND MOBILITY

As we learned in Chapter 10, orientation and mobility (O & M) training is critical for those who are blind or who have low vision. The more a person with vision loss is able to navigate the environment, the more she or he is able to become independent. For persons who have both vision loss and hearing loss, the need for mobility training is even more important

Hand-over-hand guidance.
A tactile learning strategy for persons who are deaf-blind; the teacher places his or her hands over those of the person who is deaf-blind and guides them to explore objects.

Hand-under-hand guidance.
A tactile learning strategy for persons who are deaf-blind; the teacher places his or her hands underneath part of the student's hand or hands while the child is exploring objects.

Adapted signs.
Signs adapted for use by people who are deaf-blind; tactually-based rather than visually-based, such as American Sign Language for those who are deaf but sighted.

Touch cues.
Tactual signals used to communicate with persons who are deaf-blind; can be used to signify a variety of messages.

RESPONSIVE INSTRUCTION

Meeting the Needs of Students with Multiple or Severe Disabilities

The Importance of Establishing Structured Routines

What the Research Says

Researchers and practitioners from Project PLAI* (Promoting Learning Through Active Interaction) have developed several modules for working with infants who have multiple disabilities and their families (Chen, Alsop, & Minor, 2000; Klein, Chen, & Haney, 2000). One of the modules focuses on establishing predictable routines. Specifically for infants who are deaf-blind, they have recommended the following objectives:

- Create a predictable routine by identifying at least five daily activities that can be scheduled in the same sequence each day.
- Identify predictable sequences within specific activities (i.e., "subroutines").
- Identify and use specific auditory, visual, tactile, olfactory, and kinesthetic cues to help the infant anticipate familiar activities. (Chen et al., 2000, p. 6)

The following describes how they implemented these objectives with fourteen-month-old Michael, his mother, Cecilia, and older sister, Kate. Michael was born prematurely and only weighed one pound, eight ounces at birth. He was diagnosed with severe ROP (retinopathy of prematurity), cerebral palsy, and a hearing loss of undetermined severity.

An early interventionist helped Cecelia realize that Michael could better understand what was going on around him if his daily events were more predictable. In addition to the early morning and evening routines, Cecelia decided to try to increase the predictability of Michael's routines in several ways. After he finished his morning bottle, he would always get a bath. After the bath, Cecelia would put lotion on him and give him a shoulder and back massage. At bedtime, she would give him his bottle and then Kate would rock him while watching TV. Cecelia also realized that she and Michael had developed "subroutines." For example, after removing Michael's diaper and cleaning him, she would blow on his tummy and say, "Okay, all dry. All dry." Then she would sprinkle powder and put a new diaper on him, say "All done," and give him a kiss while picking him up.

Other predictable routines and subroutines followed. Before going into Michael's room, Cecelia would always announce loudly, "Here comes Mommy." She would touch his shoulders before picking him up. Before putting him in the bath, she would put his foot in the water a couple of times, which helped him to stop screaming when he was placed in the tub. Before Cecelia gave Michael his back massage, she would rub some lotion on her fingers and let him smell it. (Chen, Hodges, & Minor, 2000, pp. 6–7)

Applying the Research to Teaching

Although the above example pertains to infants, structured routines are no less important for school-age children who have multiple disabilities, including deaf-blindness. School routines are particularly important for the student who is deaf-blind because the only way for that child to learn is by doing. The student will be unable to learn through visually observing or hearing stimuli that will assist her or him in making sense of the world. Therefore, the student will be dependent upon the creation of a safe learning environment and trust with the primary instructor (Moss & Hagood, 1995). School routines that would benefit the student who is deaf-blind are:

- *Turn-taking routines.* By keeping interactions balanced ("me, then you"), the student will consistently know when to respond and be more active in his or her learning.
- *Travel or movement routines.* If the student does not feel comfortable moving around the classroom or school, he or she may choose to not move. Lack of mobility decreases opportunities for exploration, social interaction, and independence.
- *Communication routines.* The student who is deaf-blind will rely on tactile communication. The student will be unable to make connections among input without direct interaction with others. Therefore, it is important to establish routines for communication as the student moves from objects to gestures for communication.

*Project PLAI was a four-year collaborative project involving California State University-Northridge, SKI-HI Institute at Utah State University, and several early intervention programs, funded by the Office of Special Education Programs, U.S. Department of Education.

because they are at even greater risk of being unable to navigate their environment.

O & M training for persons who have both vision and hearing loss differs in at least two ways from O & M training for those with only vision loss. First, adaptations are needed in order to communicate with persons with deaf-blindness (Gense & Gense, 1999). The O & M instructor might need to use such adaptations as an interpreter, adapted signs, and/or touch cues to communicate with the student who is deaf-blind.

Second, it is sometimes necessary to alert the public that the traveler is deaf-blind. Even the best travelers with deaf-blindness occasionally become temporarily disoriented and need assistance. Hearing persons with vision loss can ask for assistance relatively easily. However, persons who have both hearing and vision loss may have a more difficult time communicating

This blind child is assisted by a teacher who is using the hand-over-hand technique to help him explore a tray of potato sticks. ■

their needs to the public, and it will not always be obvious to the public that the person has both a vision and a hearing loss. A long cane can signal vision loss, but it does not indicate hearing loss. Therefore, some professionals advocate the use of **assistance cards.** Assistance cards are usually relatively small (e.g., 3″ × 6″) and can be held up by the person who is deaf-blind at a busy or unfamiliar intersection. The words on the card indicate that the person is asking for assistance—for example, "Please help me to CROSS STREET. I am both DEAF <u>and</u> VISUALLY IMPAIRED, so TAP ME if you can help. Thank you." (Franklin & Bourquin, 2000, p. 175).

SPECIAL CONSIDERATIONS FOR STUDENTS WITH USHER SYNDROME

Assistance card.
A relatively small card containing a message that alerts the public that the user is deaf-blind and needs assistance crossing the street.

Students with Usher syndrome present some special educational challenges because most of them have progressive vision loss. They may start out having relatively good vision, but their vision inevitably declines to the point where they are legally, if not totally, blind. The effects of retinitis pigmentosa, which accompanies Usher syndrome, can sometimes be erratic and change rapidly, thus catching the student and his or her family off guard (Miner & Cioffi, 1999). And even when the deterioration occurs slowly over the course of several years, parents and teachers of children with Usher syndrome may neglect the importance of preparing the child for the fact that he or she will one day have substantial vision loss. Sometimes, they fear that early introduction of braille and O & M training will stigmatize the child and damage his or her self-concept (see the box on p. 402). However, most authorities now agree that braille and O & M training should not wait until the student can no longer function as a seeing individual.

Considerations for All Low Incidence, Multiple, and Severe Disabilities

Some of the devices and methods we describe here may apply to any of the disabilities we discuss in this chapter. Communication, behavior management, early intervention, transition, employment, family involvement, and normalization are all concerns frequently encountered with any of these disabilities.

Braille Is Not Just for People Who Are Already Blind

There are many individuals whose visual impairment is not severe enough in childhood to require learning braille but whose condition will worsen in time to the point where using braille will be a desirable option. For these students, it makes sense to start braille instruction before they actually need to rely on it extensively. Unfortunately, as the following vignette shows, one of the barriers to beginning Braille instruction with these students is the social stigma attached to using braille:

> I grew up in a small farming town in Iowa. By the time I was fifteen years of age, I was so blind that I could no longer even pretend to function successfully in the public school, so I was enrolled in the Iowa Braille and Sight-Saving School to complete my last three-and-a-half years of high school.
>
> Unbelievable as it sounds, even though I could read no more than fifteen or twenty words a minute of very large-print material for no more than fifteen or twenty minutes at a sitting and, further, even though everyone knew I would be totally blind one

day, I was not taught Braille at this remarkable institution. The attitude of the school was "Let him be normal (sighted) as long as he can."

> My parents knew, of course, that I would be totally blind one day, so they were justifiably concerned about my lack of training. However, when my mother wrote to the school requesting that I be taught Braille, she was told, "He can always learn Braille when he really needs it."
>
> Therefore, since I was unable to read my own school books and papers, I got through high school by having literate students (using either Braille or print) read aloud to me. By the time I graduated, I was nearly totally blind and therefore could read neither print nor Braille at all.

SOURCE: Omvig, J.H. (1997, November) From bad philosophy to bad policy: The American Braille illiteracy crisis. *Braille Monitor*, pp. 723–728. Reprinted with permission from the National Federation of the Blind.

Augmentative and Alternative Communication

Augmentative or alternative communication (AAC). Alternative forms of communication that do not use the oral sounds of speech or that augment the use of speech.

For some individuals with severe and multiple disabilities, oral language is out of the question; they have physical or cognitive disabilities, usually as a result of neurological damage, that preclude their learning to communicate through normal speech. A system of **augmentative or alternative communication (AAC)** must be designed for them.

AAC includes any manual or electronic means by which such a person expresses wants and needs, shares information, engages in social closeness, or manages social etiquette (Beukelman & Mirenda, 1998; Beukelman, Yorkston, & Reichle, 2000; Lloyd, Fuller, & Arvidson, 1997). Students for whom AAC must be designed range in intelligence from highly gifted to profoundly retarded, but they all have one characteristic in common—the inability to communicate effectively through speech because of a physical impairment. Some of these individuals may be unable to make any speech sounds at all; others need a system to augment their speech when they cannot make themselves understood because of environmental noise, difficulty in producing certain words or sounds, or unfamiliarity with the person with whom they want to communicate.

Manual signs or gestures may be useful for some individuals. But many individuals with severe physical limitations are unable to use their hands to communicate through the usual sign language; they must use another means of communication, usually involving special equipment. However, a University of Virginia undergraduate student who intends to become an orthopedic surgeon, Nikki Kissane, has developed a simplified sign language

ᏇᏔ Simplified signs are shown at www.simplifiedsigns.org
For augmentative and alternative communication, see www.isaac-online.org/ ∎

system. Her simplified signs can be learned and used more easily than traditional signs by children and adults with limited speech capabilities (see the box and photos below).

The problems to be solved in helping individuals communicate in ways other than signing include selecting a vocabulary and giving them an effective, efficient means of indicating elements in their vocabularies. Although the basic ideas behind AAC are quite simple, selecting the best vocabulary and devising an efficient means of indication for many individuals with severe disabilities are extraordinarily challenging. As one AAC user put it, "The AAC evaluation should be done with the AAC user involved in the process from step one. It is the augmented speaker who will be using the device every day, both personally and professionally, not the AAC specialist" (Cardona, 2000, p. 237).

Simplified Sign Language

Figuring out how to communicate effectively with simple gestures has not been an easy task for U.Va. student Nikki Kissane. But thanks to her research efforts, mute children and adults or those with limited speech capabilities have a new simplified communication system that is easier to learn, produce and understand than existing sign languages. . . .

After witnessing her grandfather suffer a series of strokes and seeing the physiological and emotional difficulties he experienced, Kissane approached psychology professor John Bonvillian to see if she could participate in his ongoing research on sign-language communication for nonspeaking but hearing individuals. . . .

Kissane studied more than 20 sign language dictionaries to identify signs that are "iconic," those clearly resembling the object or action they represent, or "transparent," those that easily convey their meaning. To illustrate, cradling one's arms while gently rocking back and forth would be a transparent sign for "baby," whereas gesturing throwing a ball would be an iconic gesture for "throw."

From her research, Kissane identified about 900 signs

for such everyday words as "comb," "book" and "reach" that have the potential of being easily understood and communicated through simple hand and arm gestures. She also created numerous new signs to supplement those she found in her search.

To determine if such signs could be incorporated into a simplified system, she had volunteer U.Va. students view different groups of signs to see which ones they could remember and repeat easily. All signs recalled perfectly by at least 70 percent of the participants were added to a lexicon.

Kissane also observed some classes led by her mother, who teaches elementary school art to children, including several with autism. She gained pointers from her mother on how to draw the gestures.

"I observed a few of the classes to see where autistic children struggle in motor and cognitive skills," Kissane said.

SOURCE: Wooten, I.L. (2001, May 18). Student develops new sign language system. *Inside UVA, 31*(18), 12. Reprinted with permission. Photos from *The Daily Progress,* Charlottesville, VA. Reprinted with permission.

Eye ■

Celebrate ■

Sleep ■

A variety of approaches to AAC have been developed, some involving relatively simple or so-called low-technology solutions and some requiring complex or high-technology solutions (Lloyd et al., 1997). Many different direct-selection and scanning methods have been devised for AAC, depending on individual capabilities. The system used may involve pointing with the hand or a headstick, eye movements, or operation of a microswitch by foot, tongue, head movement, or breath control. Sometimes, the individual can use a typewriter or computer terminal fitted with a key guard, so that keys are not likely to be pressed accidentally, or use an alternative means for selecting keystrokes. Often, communication boards are used. A communication board is an array of pictures, words, or other symbols that can be operated with either a direct-selection or scanning strategy. The content and arrangement of the board will vary, depending on the person's capabilities, preferences, and communication needs.

Speed, reliability, portability, cost, and overall effectiveness in helping a person communicate independently are factors to be considered in designing and evaluating AAC (Beukelman & Mirenda, 1998; Lloyd et al., 1997). Some AAC systems are very slow, unreliable (either because of the equipment or a poor match with the abilities of the user), cumbersome, or useful only in very restricted settings. Although people typically think of the equipment and material costs involved in AAC, the real costs must include intensive and extensive instruction. A communication board will not necessarily be useful just because it is available. And the most sophisticated technological solution to communication is not always the one that will be most useful in the long run.

Today, researchers are finding increasingly innovative and creative technological solutions to the problem of nonvocal communication. At the same time, they are recognizing the importance of making decisions on a highly individual basis. Until rather recently, many saw AAC primarily as a means of allowing users to demonstrate the language skills they have already acquired. But now researchers and practitioners increasing

Life with Cerebral Palsy

By Chris Featherly

My name is Christopher Glen Featherly, and I'm going to try to give you a little overview of life with cerebral palsy as I know it.

I'm 18 years old and was born in Fort Worth, Texas. I'm currently attending Bremen High School in Midlothian, Illinois. . . .

When I came from Texas to live with my grandparents at the age of 5, I only had five generic signs for communication. My grandmom wouldn't put up with that, and so she went to the library for a sign language book. Now she learned that there really was something upstairs! The school system wanted me to use a 48-page, three-ring binder of pictures for my communication. Can you see me, using my right hand, to flip between 48 pages to talk to someone? I don't think so! My grandmom took me to Siegel Institute in downtown Chicago for a speech evaluation. They said, "This kid needs a TouchTalker [an AAC device; see www.prentrom.com for descriptions of other devices]. . . ." Well, guess what! The school speech clinician said, "No. He doesn't have language, and if he has it

[TouchTalker] he won't use his own voice to talk." So guess what grandmom did? She took me to Homewood to see another speech therapist. What do you think she said? You got it! She said, "TouchTalker." So back to school, and again the answer was, "No." Grandmom then told them she was going to take me to Shriners. If they said TouchTalker, that would be the mode of communication I would have. Well, what do you think they said? Yup! It was TouchTalker. Now, we knew how school felt about it, which meant it was in our ball park. It was time to save money and purchase it so that I could get stuff out of my head and stuff into it. By now, do you sorta have an idea what kind of grandmom I have?

[Chris's story goes on to describe software and hardware upgrades that he needed as he progressed, and his use of online resources.]

SOURCE: Featherly, C. (2000). Life with cerebral palsy. In M. Oken-Fried & H.A. Bersani (Eds.), *Speaking up and spelling it out: Personal essays on augmentative and alternative communication* (pp. 189–193). Baltimore: Paul H. Brookes.

emphasis on how AAC can be a tool for teaching language—for helping AAC users not only to give voice to what they feel and know about specific tasks but also to acquire increasingly sophisticated language skills (Nelson, 1998; Oken-Fried & Bersani, 2000; Yoder, 2001).

Researchers are attempting to make it possible for young AAC users to talk about the same kinds of things that other youngsters do (Marvin, Beukelman, Brockhaus, & Kast, 1994). Other efforts are directed at training AAC users to tell those with whom they communicate how to interact with them more effectively—that is, to train AAC users in pragmatics. The box on page 404 was written by Chris Featherly as an 18-year-old high school student. His story and others written by AAC users (Fried-Oken & Bersani, 2000) illustrate the value of AAC and issues involved in its use. The fact that Chris Featherly has cerebral palsy, a congenital neurological condition discussed in Chapter 12, is beside the point here. The important thing is that some people have physical limitations that preclude their efficient use of oral language and need an augmented or alternative means of communicating.

Users of AAC encounter three particular challenges not faced by natural communicators:

1. AAC is much slower than natural communication—perhaps one-twentieth the typical rate of speech. This can result in great frustration for both the AAC users and natural communicators.
2. Users of AAC who are not literate must rely on a vocabulary and symbols that are selected by others. If the vocabulary and symbols, as well as other features of the system, are not well chosen, AAC will be quite limited in the learning and personal relationships it allows.
3. AAC must be constructed to be useful in a variety of social contexts, allow accurate and efficient communication without undue fatigue, and support the individual's learning of language and academic skills.

Progress in the field of AAC requires that all of these challenges be addressed simultaneously. AAC is increasingly focused on literacy and the right to use print, including writing, for communication. In many ways the emphasis on basic literacy skills parallels the emphasis on literacy for all students, regardless of disabilities (Yoder, 2001).

The need for AAC is increasing as more people with severe disabilities, including those with TBI and other disabilities, are surviving and taking their places in the community. As more students with severe disabilities are integrated into regular educational programs at all levels, the availability and appropriate use of AAC in such classrooms become more critical issues (Beukelman & Mirenda, 1998; Lloyd et al., 1997). Whatever system of AAC is devised, it must be relatively easy to use, efficient, mechanically reliable, and reliable in communicating the user's thoughts and intentions, not someone else's. One type of AAC that burst upon the scene in the early 1990s is called facilitated communication (FC). FC requires that a "facilitator" physically assist the user in typing out messages on a keyboard. Although FC quickly became very popular and still may be used by some, it has been called into serious question because it appears to communicate the facilitator's words, not the words of the person with disabilities. In fact, FC appears to have been discredited by research (Mostert, 2001; National Research Council, 2001). Beukelman and Mirenda, noting that a very small number of people around the world appear to be typing independently after being taught with FC, concluded, "we do not believe that FC works for everyone or even with *most* people" (1998, p. 329). Any AAC device that misrepresents the user's communication demeans the user through pretense. This is not acceptable, as all people with disabilities should be treated with dignity and respect (Yoder, 2001). The goal of AAC should be independent communication in which there is no doubt about the authenticity of the messages, as the National Research Council (2001) points out.

The remarkable increase in the power and availability of microcomputers is radically changing our ability to provide AAC and make sure that the user's words are communicated.

Temple University electrical engineering student Scott Stoffel holds his senior design project. Stoffel, who is legally deaf and blind, designed a device to assist deaf and blind people to communicate. He also developed software to enable people with visual impairments to read braille off the computer screen (rear). ∎

New applications of microcomputers may lead to breakthroughs that will allow people with severe disabilities to communicate more effectively, even if they have extremely limited muscle control. Furthermore, existing microcomputer software suggests ways of encouraging children to use their existing language skills. Technological developments will no doubt revolutionize AAC within a few years (Fried-Oken & Bersani, 2000). Loncke (2001) predicts that electronic communication will lead to globalization of AAC, which seems consistent with Chris Featherly's on-line communication (see the box on p. 404).

Much information about AAC is now available on various Web sites. The International Society for Augmentative and Alternative Communication (ISAAC) publishes the professional journal *Augmentative and Alternative Communication*. ISACC also maintains a Web site that you may want to explore.

Behavior Problems

Some individuals who have certain severe or multiple disabilities engage in problematic behaviors. Their behaviors may include self-stimulation, self-injury, tantrums, aggression toward others, or some combination of these. In fact, as the federal (IDEA) definition states, self-stimulation, self-mutilation, tantrums, and failure to respond to social stimuli are prominent features of many severe and multiple disabilities.

We caution that not all persons with severe or multiple disabilities exhibit the behavior problems we discuss here. Many people who are deaf and blind and many who have TBI, autism, or other severe or multiple disabilities do not engage in these behaviors. Nevertheless, most of the people who do show these problems to a significant extent have severe and multiple disabilities. Moreover, behaviors of the type we discuss here add a level of complexity and seriousness to any disability. Thus, finding solutions to these behavior problems is critical to treating the individual with respect and helping the person to participate in typical school and community activities.

SELF-STIMULATION

Self-stimulation may be defined as any repetitive, stereotyped behavior that seems to have no immediately apparent purpose other than providing sensory stimulation. Self-stimulation may take a wide variety of forms, such as swishing saliva, twirling objects, hand-flapping, fixed staring, and the like. Repetitive, stereotyped behavior (sometimes called *stereotypy*) may have multiple causes, including social consequences, in addition to sensory stimulation (Kennedy, Meyer, Knowles, & Shukla, 2000; Rapp, Miltenberger, Galensky, Ellingson, & Long, 1999).

Nearly everyone engages in some form of self-stimulation, such as lip-biting, hair-stroking, nail-biting, and so on, but not at the high rate that characterizes a disability. Nondisabled infants engage in self-stimulation, and so do nondisabled adults, particularly when they are tired or bored. Only the high rate, lack of subtlety, and social inappropriateness of such self-stimulation differentiates it from the norm.

Self-stimulation becomes problematic when it occurs at such a high rate that it interferes with learning or social acceptability or when it occurs with such intensity that it does injury. Some individuals with autism or other pervasive developmental disability engage in self-stimulation to the exclusion of academic and social learning. In most of these cases,

Self-stimulation.
Any repetitive, stereotyped activity that seems only to provide sensory feedback.

it appears that only intrusive, directive intervention will be successful in helping the individual learn academic and social skills (Kauffman, 2001).

SELF-INJURY

Self-injurious behavior (SIB) is repeated physical self-abuse, such as biting, scratching, or poking oneself, head-banging, and so on. Unchecked, SIB often results in self-mutilation. Self-stimulation can be so frequent and intense that it becomes SIB. For example, Worsdell, Iwata, Conners, Kahng, and Thompson (2000) studied SIB characterized by hand-biting, head- or body-hitting, hand-mouthing, and skin-picking. Hand-mouthing is self-stimulation of the kind that all infants do; even some nondisabled adults can be seen occasionally mouthing their hands. However, hand-mouthing becomes self-injurious for some people with severe developmental disabilities, resulting in serious skin lesions.

TANTRUMS

Severe tantrums can include a variety of behaviors, including, self-injury, screaming, crying, throwing or destroying objects, and aggression toward others. Sometimes the event that sets off a tantrum is unknown, at least to the causal observer. Often, however, a tantrum is precipitated by a request or demand that the individual do something (perhaps a self-care task or some academic work) and the consequence of the tantrum is that the demand is withdrawn.

Tantrums impose a handicap on the individual who uses them to avoid learning or doing important things. They stymie socialization, as most people want to avoid interacting with someone who is likely to tantrum. Teachers and others who work most successfully with individuals who have tantrums do not withdraw reasonable demands for performance. What they do is modify their demand or circumstances in some way or alternate their demands for performance in ways that are less likely to set off a tantrum.

AGGRESSION TOWARD OTHERS

Not all aggression toward others is associated with tantrums. Some individuals with severe or multiple disabilities engage in calculated physical attacks that threaten or injure others. Sometimes these attacks come without warning or only after subtle indications of imminent assault that only someone who knows the individual well is likely to perceive. Aggression toward others is disabling because it limits social interactions. For understandable reasons, people tend to avoid those they believe are likely to endanger or hurt them. Research suggests that aggression and other undesirable behavior such as SIB may be followed by attention or other rewarding consequences for individuals with severe and multiple disabilities (Thompson & Iwata, 2001).

LACK OF DAILY LIVING SKILLS

Lack of **daily living skills** refers to the absence or significant impairment of the ability to take care of one's basic needs, such as dressing, feeding, or toileting. Many persons with severe and multiple disabilities must be taught the adaptive behavior that is expected of older children and adults. These adaptive behaviors include a wide variety of tasks involving clothing selection and dressing, food preparation and eating, grooming, socializing, using money, using public transportation, playing games or other recreation, and so on (Brown & Snell, 2000).

FUNCTIONAL BEHAVIORAL ASSESSMENT AND POSITIVE BEHAVIORAL SUPPORT

Problem behaviors are often related to a brain disorder or brain injury, even if the disorder is not understood. An example is severe autism, which often includes self-stimulation, self-injury, tantrums, or all of these. However, there is increasing emphasis on analyzing

Self-injurious behavior (SIB).
Behavior causing injury or mutilation of oneself, such as self-biting or head-banging; usually seen in individuals with severe and multiple disabilities.

Daily living skills.
Skills required for living independently, such as dressing, toileting, bathing, cooking, and other typical daily activities of nondisabled adults.

Functional behavioral assessment (FBA).
Evaluation that consists of finding out the consequences (purposes), antecedents (what triggers the behavior), and setting events (contextual factors) that maintain inappropriate behaviors; this information can help teachers plan educationally for students.

Positive behavioral support (PBS).
Systematic use of the science of behavior to find ways of supporting the desirable behavior of an individual rather than punishing undesirable behavior.

CW For management of behavior problems, see www.pbis.org ■

and changing the environments in which problem behavior is exhibited—increasing focus on the immediate and alterable influences on behavior rather than on immutable or historical reasons for behavior (Horner, Albin, Sprague, & Todd, 2000).

In earlier chapters, we introduced the ideas of **functional behavioral assessment (FBA)** and **positive behavioral support (PBS),** primarily as they apply to students with less severe disabilities (see Chapters 2, 4, and 7). However, these procedures may be particularly important for students with severe and multiple disabilities. FBA entails finding out why or under what circumstances problem behavior is exhibited, and PBS involves creating an environment that supports appropriate behavior. Horner and his colleagues have provided a particularly clear description of the four major components of FBA, along with examples that include a student named Darin. Darin is 19 years old and has autism and severe intellectual disabilities. He lives at home and can communicate in one- or two-word phrases. Left alone, he will play for long periods with a Slinky. He has a history of slapping his own face (SIB), screaming, and physically attacking adults who try to work with him. Here are examples of the four steps in FBA and what these steps revealed about Darin:

1. Description of problem behaviors . . . Darin's team agreed that his behaviors of concern were slapping his own face, screaming, and hitting or kicking (attacking) others. . . .
2. Consequences maintaining problem behaviors . . . Darin's functional assessment indicated that his problem behaviors were maintained by escape from activities and situations that he found aversive. These aversive situations included activities involving writing, speaking in front of the class, and transitions that were confusing and unpredictable. . . .
3. Antecedent events that trigger problem behaviors . . . For Darin, confusing transitions, requests to speak in front of the class, and tasks involving writing were identified as antecedent events that preceded problem behaviors. . . .
4. Setting events that exaggerate the likelihood of problem behaviors . . . Being tired, defined as less than 6 hours of sleep, was identified as a powerful setting event for Darin. When he was tired, escape from aversive tasks was an even stronger reinforcer, so problem behaviors that produced "escape" were more likely to occur. (Horner et al., 2000, pp. 209–211)

FBA often reveals how a student "uses" self-stimulation, SIB, tantrums, or aggression against others. A student may behave inappropriately to escape or avoid unpleasant or nonpreferred activities or tasks (McCord, Thomson, & Iwata, 2001). In many instances, researchers and practitioners find that the student has no other effective and efficient means of communication. The task, therefore, is to figure out how the student is "using" unacceptable communication and teach him or her a more effective and efficient and acceptable means of letting others know what he or she wants or is feeling. FBA has led to the discovery that sometimes people with severe and multiple disabilities use inappropriate behavior to communicate a variety of their wants or needs (e.g., "Pay attention to me," "Let me out of here," "There's nothing to do," "There's too much to do," or "I don't want to do that now").

Positive behavioral support (PBS) is the vehicle for teaching a student how to behave more appropriately—making appropriate behavior "work" for their communication. In the case of students with severe and multiple disabilities, making PBS a part of managing behavior across school, home, neighborhood, and community is particularly important (*Families and Disability Newsletter,* 2001; Horner et al., 2000).

Early Intervention

Most children with multiple and severe disabilities are identified at birth or soon thereafter because their disabilities are very noticeable to parents, physicians, and/or nurses. Some newborns with severe and multiple disabilities require extensive medical treatment

Meeting the Needs of Students with Multiple or Severe Disabilities

Positive Behavioral Support

What Is Positive Behavioral Support?

Recent amendments to the Individuals with Disabilities Education Act require teachers, school systems, and those involved with students who exhibit challenging behaviors to approach problematic behavior through a mechanism called "positive behavioral support." Positive behavioral support (PBS) refers to the process of identifying alternative, acceptable ways to communicate through teaching more appropriate behaviors and/or changing the environment to reduce the likelihood of prompting the undesirable behavior (Kogel, Kogel, & Dunlap, 1996). This approach to behavior management differs fundamentally from traditional behavioral modification plans that focus on the elimination of target behaviors, yet do not take into account possible environmental or personal triggers when doing so. For example, a student's undesirable behavior of banging his head on his desk may be eliminated by placing a baseball cap on his head. Although this may appear to be an acceptable solution, if the student's banging was a sign of boredom or an anxiety-producing peer in the vicinity, the baseball cap solution does not address the function of the behavior and it is likely that another behavior will manifest in response to the original source of the behavior.

PBS, on the other hand, is guided by two fundamental assumptions: (1) each behavior carries a communicative intent, and (2) typically, multiple factors influence the presence of specific behavior. Interventions based upon these assumptions, therefore, include a functional behavioral assessment (FBA) (Horner, Vaughn, Day, Ard, 1996). FBA seeks to identify the purpose of the behavior and supporting environmental conditions. The results of such assessment lead to the development of multifaceted plans that can include changing situational events, altering events that immediately precede the behavior, teaching alternative responses to the situation, and providing meaningful reinforcers to promote acceptable responses (Horner et al., 1996).

Applying the Research to Teaching

Support strategies such as removing "high frustration" activities (e.g., difficult assignments, undesirable directives), selecting functional and meaningful (from the student's perspective) curricula, reducing fear or anxiety about a situation through precorrection (e.g., a teacher may suggest what to do when feeling frustrated), teaching more appropriate ways to make requests or express oneself, using behavior modification to reinforce desired behaviors and communicate nonacceptability, and creating activities that build upon student interest and strength are all a part of implementing PBS.

Based upon a synthesis of studies that included PBS, the U.S. Office of Special Education Programs makes the following recommendations to support the behavioral needs of individuals with significant disabilities:

- *Respond to individual needs.* Services and programs should be responsive to the preferences, strengths, and needs of individuals with challenging behavior. In addition, students may benefit from instruction in self-determination skills, social skills, goal-setting, and independent learning skills.
- *Alter environments.* If something in the individual's environment influences the challenging behavior, it is important to organize the environment for success. For example, clearly defined work spaces and quiet work areas may assist a child who is noise-sensitive.
- *Teach new skills to the individual with challenging behavior and members of his or her social network.* Individuals need to be taught alternative, appropriate responses that serve the same purpose as the challenging behavior.
- *Appreciate positive behaviors.* It is important to reinforce and acknowledge all positive behaviors consistently. (U.S. Office of Special Education Programs, 1998, p. 1)

—By Kristin L. Sayeski

Authorities agree that parents should be encouraged to spend as much time as possible with their infants being cared for in neonatal intensive care units (NICUs). ■

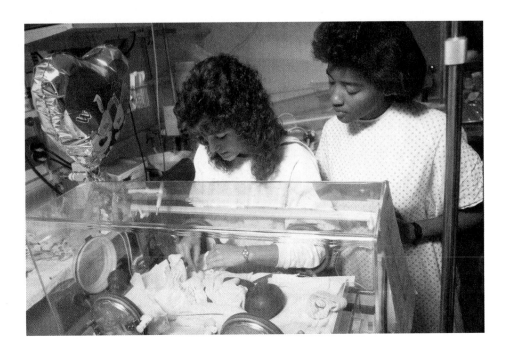

Neonatal intensive care units (NICUs).
A special unit in a hospital designed to provide around the clock monitoring and care of newborns who have severe physical problems; staffed by professionals from several disciplines, e.g., nursing, social work, occupational therapy, respiratory therapy, medicine; similar to an intensive care unit for older children and adults.

and therefore are immediately placed in **neonatal intensive care units (NICUs).** NICUs are the equivalent of intensive care units (ICUs) for older children and adults, providing around-the-clock monitoring of bodily functions. The NICU staff consists of several specialists, often including specially trained nurses, physicians, respiratory care practitioners, occupational therapists, and social workers. Because NICUs are expensive to staff and administer, not all hospitals have them; therefore, newborns are sometimes transported from one hospital to another that has a NICU. Even though the infant may be under constant medical supervision, most authorities agree that parents should be allowed to spend as much time as possible with their newborns so that bonding can take place between the parents and infant. Some NICUS allow parents to "room in" with their babies.

Others with severe and multiple disabilities may seem typical at birth but are recognized as having pervasive developmental disabilities within the first couple of years of their lives. For example, children with autism may not be perceived to have autism at birth, but before they are thirty months old their parents notice that their responses to social stimuli are not developing as expected. In the case of very serious TBI, an individual may actually be developing normally until the event that severely damages her or his brain. Therefore, early intervention should be seen as having two meanings: (1) early in the child's life and (2) as soon as possible after the disability is detected.

The Division for Early Childhood (DEC) of the Council for Exceptional Children (CEC) has established a set of recommended practices for early intervention special education programs (Odom & McLean, 1996; Sandall, McLean, & Smith, 2000). The task force that developed these recommendations relied on six criteria it considered essential to early intervention programs in special education: (1) research- or value-based practices, (2) family-centered practices, (3) a multicultural perspective, (4) cross-disciplinary collaboration, (5) developmentally and chronologically age-appropriate practices, and (6) adherence to the principle of normalization (McLean & Odom, 1996).

RESEARCH- OR VALUE-BASED PRACTICES

Early intervention programs should be based as much as possible on techniques shown to be effective by research. Unfortunately, it is not always possible to conduct all the necessary research before an approach or technique is adopted. The task force recommended that, when research has not provided definitive evidence of an approach's effectiveness, that the approach be based on values held by the early childhood special education community. Some of these value-based practices are providing individualized practices for each child and family, communicating with family members in a nonpaternalistic manner and with mutual respect and caring, making center environments safe and clean, and providing opportunities for families to have access to medical decision-making (Strain, Smith, & McWilliam, 1996).

FAMILY-CENTERED PRACTICES

At one time the prevailing philosophy in early childhood special education programming ignored parents and families, at best, or viewed them primarily as potential negative influences on the child with disabilities. When early intervention programs did involve parents, the assumption often was that the parents had little to offer and were in need of training to improve their parenting skills. Although it is true that some parents do need to be educated about how to be better parents, to assume that this is always the case is paternalistic and off-putting to the majority of parents, who are very capable. For this reason, authorities now recommend that one not assume that parents have little or nothing to offer with respect to how to work with their children. Instead, they emphasize that parents, and siblings too, can be a valuable and integral part of the educational process for young children with disabilities.

As we discussed in Chapters 1 and 2, the federal law, IDEA, also recognizes that parents and families should be central to the educational process for infants and toddlers. The Individualized Family Service Plan (IFSP), in fact, dictates that the family be central in the decision-making process for the child. A family-centered philosophy means taking into account the particular priorities and needs of the family when developing an educational intervention plan for the child.

MULTICULTURAL PERSPECTIVE

Given the changing ethnic demographics in the United States, it is critical that all special education programming be culturally sensitive. It is particularly important that early intervention professionals adopt a multicultural perspective because parents are often still coping with the stress of having had their child diagnosed with a disability (McLean & Odom, 1996).

In order to provide early intervention from a multicultural perspective, the task force recommended practices such as ensuring that:

- someone in the program or immediately available to the program speaks the family's preferred language . . .
- staff base their communication with family members on principles of mutual respect, caring, and sensitivity . . .
- and services ensure an unbiased, nondiscriminatory curriculum with regard to disability, gender, race, religion, and ethnic and cultural orientation. (Strain et al., 1996, p. 105)

CROSS-DISCIPLINARY COLLABORATION

Because infants and young children with multiple and severe disabilities, by definition, have needs in *multiple* areas, best practice dictates that professionals from several discipline should be involved. Furthermore, it is critical that these professionals *collaborate* in a coordinated way to provide high-quality services. There are different kinds of cross-disciplinary models, but the most critical feature for success is that the professionals in each of the disciplines work collaboratively and not independently. Some authorities also recommend that professionals should be willing to share roles (Strain et al., 1996). For

Developmentally appropriate practice (DAP).
Educational methods for young children that are compatible with their developmental levels and that meet their individual needs; coined by the National Association for the Education of Young Children (NAEYC).

example, the early childhood special education teacher might engage in training activities that are typically conducted by the speech therapist, and vice versa.

DEVELOPMENTALLY AND CHRONOLOGICALLY AGE-APPROPRIATE PRACTICES

The term **developmentally appropriate practice (DAP)** was first used by the National Association for the Education of Young Children (NAEYC), an organization focused on early childhood education for children without disabilities. DAP refers to the practice of using educational methods that are at the developmental levels of the child and that meet the child's individual needs (Bredekamp & Rosegrant, 1992). Many early childhood special educators are in agreement with the notion of DAP, but they believe that it should be balanced with the need for using educational methods that are also chronologically age appropriate. They believe that young children with disabilities should be educated as much as possible alongside their same-age nondisabled peers rather than with much younger nondisabled peers.

PRINCIPLE OF NORMALIZATION

As we discussed in Chapter 2, normalization is the philosophical principle that all persons with disabilities should have educational and living environments that are as similar as possible to those who do not have disabilities. The DEC of CEC has adopted the philosophy of inclusion wholeheartedly in their statement on inclusion:

> Inclusion, as a value, supports the right of all children, regardless of their diverse abilities, to participate actively in natural settings within their communities. A

MAKING IT WORK

Collaboration and Co-Teaching for Students with Severe and Profound Disabilities

"We may have different goals for students. How can we solve that problem?"

Successful Strategies for Collaboration

Students with severe disabilities often require a wide range of services at school. Many professionals, including teachers, nurses, aides, etc., must collaborate to provide those services. With so many people involved in a student's education, problems are likely to arise and everyone should be ready to engage in collaborative problem solving.

Partners in collaborative settings should develop a plan to attack problems before they arise. Problems can be related to the student response to settings and personnel, the student's environment, differences in professional goals, discrepancies in professional philosophies, etc. Though the causes may be different, a similar step-by-step process can be used to address each one. Mostert (1998) describes the following steps for successful problem solving:

1. *Is there a problem to solve?* This step involves reflection on the questions: Is there really a problem here? Who owns it? Is the problem solvable?

2. *What is the problem?* Once a problem is identified, participants define it in specific, objective terms. Statements such as "I don't like his attitude" must be refined to describe the situation specifically: "John makes inappropriate comments about other students when I ask him a question in class." After the problem is defined, partners gather data on the frequency, duration, and degree of the problem in a variety of environments.

3. *How can the problem be solved?* All participants generate solutions to the problem. This is the brainstorming step, so all suggestions should be welcomed.

4. *Which solution or combination is best?* Personnel working

natural setting is one in which the child would spend time had he or she not had a disability. (Division for Early Childhood, 1993, p. 4, as cited in McLean & Odom, 1996, p. 12)

Transition to Adulthood

Transition to adulthood is a critical time for most persons with severe and multiple disabilities. Fortunately, as we noted in Chapter 2, the field of special education has made great strides in developing transition services for persons with disabilities. Much of this progress has been made because of a change in philosophy about how persons with disabilities are treated, and this change is nowhere more evident than in the treatment of persons with severe and multiple disabilities. For example, not too long ago, with respect to employment the best one hoped for was to be able to place such individuals in a **sheltered workshop.** Now, however, a much wider range of options is available, including for some persons **competitive employment** alongside workers who are nondisabled.

CHANGING PHILOSOPHY

We can point to at least two principles of current transition programming that reflect the change in philosophy toward treating persons with severe disabilities with more dignity (Westling & Fox, 2000). First, there is an emphasis on **self-determination.** Self-determination

> has been described as "acting as the primary causal agent in one's life and making choices and decisions regarding one's quality of life, free from undue external influence or interference" (Wehmeyer, 1992, p. 305). Self-determination

Sheltered workshop.
A facility that provides a structured environment for persons with disabilities in which they can learn skills; can be either a transitional placement or a permanent arrangement.

Competitive employment.
A workplace that provides employment that pays at least minimum wage and in which most workers are nondisabled.

Self-determination.
Having control over one's life, not having to rely on others for making choices about one's quality of life; develops over one's life span.

together must be able to discuss the solutions presented and evaluate them without emotional attachment. Interventions for students should be judged as to whether there is evidence of previous success (research-based, not anecdotal), whether there are appropriate supports and resources, whether the participants can/will fully implement it, and whether the intervention is truly appropriate for the student. Solutions that do not fit these criteria should be abandoned.

5. *Which solution should we select?* After evaluating all solutions, the partners choose the one to implement.
6. *How will we implement the solution?* This step requires delegating responsibilities for the solution to members of the team. It means specifically stating what the team hopes will happen, setting up how the partners will know if the solution worked, and scheduling a time to reconvene to share data.
7. *Did it work?* This step requires data collection again. Partners must be able to present information as to whether the solution achieved its goals. If not, it is time to start the process again. If the solution worked, the team can move on to another problem!

Problem solving with other professionals requires that participants develop an environment with open communication, overcoming barriers by using effective communication skills. According to Walther-Thomas, Korinek, McLaughlin, and Williams (2000), these skills include:

1. *Listening.* Attending to the speaker, paraphrasing content, reflecting feelings, and summarizing.
2. *Repetition.* Sending the same message to partners repeatedly and through different channels.
3. *Empathy.* Making predictions about how a partner will respond to a message you send.
4. *Understanding.* Making sure that the language you use is clear and concise.

When collaborating with other professionals and even with students, there is no way to avoid problems. But, to avoid conflict, partners should discuss and set up problem-solving strategies *before* these situations occur. Problem-solving strategies, along with effective communication skills, will help collaborators provide continuous, appropriate services to students.

—*By Margaret P. Weiss*

Person-centered plan.
A method of planning for persons with disabilities that places the person and his family at the center of the planning process.

Natural supports.
Resources in a person's environment that can be used for support, such as friends, family, co-workers.

Job coach.
A person who assists adult workers with disabilities (especially those with mental retardation), providing vocational assessment, instruction, overall planning, and interaction assistance with employers, family, and related government and service agencies.

develops over the life span and is associated with reaching adulthood. . . . Issues such as accessibility, employment rights, community living, inclusive schooling, mobility, and personal care assistance all stem from the desire of individuals with disabilities to access the activities and lifestyles they desire. (Westling & Fox, 2000, p. 473)

As part of this emphasis on self-determination, professionals have developed a number of what are called **person-centered plans.** Person-centered plans focus on the student's preferences and those of her or his family in planning for the student's future (Brown & Snell, 2000; Giangreco, Cloninger, & Iverson, 1993; Mount & Zwernik, 1988; Vandercook, York, & Forest, 1989).

Second, authorities now recommend that **natural supports** be an integral part of transition planning. Rather than always creating new services for a person's particular needs, the notion of natural supports is to try first to find available resources that already exist in the workplace or the community. With respect to work, this might mean training co-workers to provide assistance rather than immediately assuming a **job coach** is required. With respect to community living, this might mean having the person with a disability living in an apartment, with assistance in daily living skills from a neighbor, family member, or paid attendant, rather than living in a residential facility with attendants.

VOCATIONAL PROGRAMMING

As we stated in Chapter 2, each student's **individualized education program (IEP)** must contain a transition plan, beginning no later than age 16; and it should begin by age 14, when appropriate. The transition plan should contain recommendations for how to ready the student for the world of work and/or for postsecondary education or training.

For many students with severe and multiple disabilities, it is advisable that vocational training actually begin in elementary school because it may take several years to acquire all the skills they will need in order to hold down a job successfully. In elementary school, the training might consist of such things as learning to keep on schedule, building social skills, performing worklike tasks (e.g., helping to take attendance, collecting lunch money), and beginning to learn about different types of jobs.

There is a growing range of employment options available to persons with severe and multiple disabilities, including sheltered workshops, but also in competitive environments alongside workers who do not have disabilities. ■

In secondary school the focus shifts to involving the student in actual work situations in the community with the help of a job coach. The student should be involved in selecting these placements, and there should be enough variety in the jobs so that the student gets a good sample of what kinds of jobs are available and what he or she is good at and likes. In the early stages, this may involve the student volunteering in several different types of placements. Later, it is preferable that the student engage in paid work placements. Being paid adds to the "reality" of the experience and also provides an opportunity for the student to learn how to handle finances.

COMMUNITY AND DOMESTIC LIVING SKILLS

As we noted in Chapter 4, community living skills involve such things as using transportation, shopping, using telephones, managing money, and using the Internet. And domestic living skills include such things as preparing meals, doing laundry, housekeeping, yard maintenance, and so forth.

At one time community living skills were taught primarily, or solely, in classroom settings. In other words, teachers arranged their classroom to simulate a community setting, such as an aisle in a grocery store. Authorities now believe that simulations are much inferior to using real community settings (Westling & Fox, 2000). The best place to teach domestic living skills, however, is not necessarily in the student's home. Because students are not that far away from the time when they will move out of their parents' home and because teaching domestic skills is often done in small groups, there are some advantages to using a setting other than their own home. Thus, domestic living skills are often taught in a school setting, such as the home economics classroom and the school cafeteria (Westling & Fox, 2000).

Another reason for using the school as the instructional setting some of the time is to ensure that the student with disabilities has a chance to interact with same-age peers who do not have disabilities (Browder & Bambara, 2000; Moon & Inge, 2000). Inclusion in regular school programs provides opportunities for students with disabilities to interact socially with nondisabled peers. And social skills are critical for successful integration into the community and workplace.

The last thirty to forty years have seen enormous strides in preparing persons with multiple and severe disabilities to lead productive lives as adults. It was not that long ago that persons with multiple and severe disabilities were housed in large residential institutions and had minimal contact with the public. Today, with intensive and extensive instruction and the support of professionals and the community, many of them can aspire to work alongside nondisabled persons and live independently or semi-independently by themselves or in a small **community residential facility (CRF).**

Individualized education program (IEP). IDEA requires an IEP to be drawn up by the educational team for each exceptional child; the IEP must include a statement of present educational performance, instructional goals, educational services to be provided, and criteria and procedures for determining that the instructional objectives are being met.

Community residential facility (CRF). A place, usually a group home, in an urban or residential neighborhood where about three to ten adults with retardation live under supervision.

Summary

The definition of *severe and multiple disabilities,* as with every category of exceptionality, is controversial. The Association for Persons with Severe Handicaps (TASH) defines individuals with severe disabilities as requiring extensive ongoing support in more than one major life activity such as mobility, communication, self-care, and learning as necessary for independent living, employment, and self-sufficiency.

Severe and multiple disabilities tend to go together; people with a severe disability in any area typically have more than one disability. Furthermore, a combination of mild disabilities may present severe educational problems.

As noted in IDEA, children with severe and multiple disabilities include those with autism, severe and profound mental retardation, and those who have two or more serious disabilities, such as deaf-blindness, mental retardation and blindness, and cerebral palsy and deafness.

Autism has been a separate IDEA category since 1990, though disorders similar to it are discussed under a broader term, *autistic spectrum disorder* or *pervasive developmental disorder (PDD).* Autistic spectrum disorder and PDD involve delays in the development of social relationships, communication of ideas and feelings, self-care, and participation in everyday activities. Symptoms of autism and similar disorders are noticed soon after birth, usually before the child is two years old. Besides autism, autistic spectrum disorders include Asperger syndrome, Rett's disorder, childhood disintegrative disorder, and pervasive developmental disorder. Another subset is autistic savant, in which an individual shows remarkable ability in a specific skill that exists in isolation from the rest of the person's ability to function.

There is no single behavior that is always typical of autism and no behavior that would automatically preclude its diagnosis. In general, primary characteristics include impaired social responsiveness, impaired communication, and stereotyped and ritualistic behavior. Autism may range from mild to severe, and children with autism differ greatly in their specific abilities and disabilities. Although the majority of children with severe autism also have moderate to severe mental retardation, those with mild autism may have superior intelligence. While children with severe autism have been the focus of the autistic spectrum, a far larger number have milder forms of the disorder and are able to function much more normally in society. Autism accounts for about 7.5 cases per 10,000 children, is diagnosed more often in boys than in girls, occurs among all nations of the world, and crosses the full range of intelligence.

For decades, psychoanalytic ideas attributed autism to parental attitudes or behavior. It is now known that the causes are neurological rather than interpersonal, and are related to some sort of brain malfunction. Education and related interventions for students with autism must be early, intensive, highly structured, and involve families. Efforts must focus relentlessly on deficits in communication skills, which lie at the heart of the disability. Intensive instruction in daily living skills may also be required. Emphasis on applying behavioral psychology in natural settings has increased, though one-on-one or small-group teaching may sometimes be preferable. Psychopharmacological interventions can give symptom relief in some cases, but they are not sufficient themselves to address the disorder.

Traumatic brain injury (TBI) is brain damage that is acquired by trauma after a period of normal neurological development and presents unique educational problems. Definitions of TBI specify that injury to the brain is caused by an external force, not a degenerative or congenital condition. It is associated with a diminished or altered state of consciousness and neurological or neurobehavioral dysfunction. TBI can result from two categories of injury: open head injuries, in which there is a penetrating head wound, and closed head injuries, in which brain damage is caused by internal compression, stretching, or other shearing motion of neural tissues. The educational definition of TBI focuses on impairments in one or more areas important for learning, such as cognition; language; memory; attention; reasoning; abstract thinking; judgment; problem-solving; sensory, perceptual, and motor abilities; psychosocial behavior; physical functions; information processing; and speech. The effects of TBI may range from very mild to profound, may be temporary or permanent, and include a long list of learning and psychological problems.

The exact prevalence of TBI is difficult to determine, though it is certain that it occurs at an alarming rate among children and youths, and that many will experience lasting effects. Males are more prone to TBI than females, and it is most likely to occur in late adolescence and early adulthood for both males and females. Many of the causes of TBI are preventable or avoidable. Under age five, accidental falls are the dominant cause of TBI. After age five, vehicular accidents account for the majority of TBI. Other causes include violence and abuse.

A significant issue in educating someone who has experienced TBI is helping family members, teachers, and peers respond appropriately to the sudden, dramatic changes in a student's academic abilities, appearance, behavior, and emotional state. Teachers must focus on helping students with TBI recover cognitive abilities and learn to use coping mechanisms and alternative strategies. Challenges in the areas of assessment and educational planning should also be expected. A team approach involving a variety of professionals is typically required.

Language or speech disorders may be the greatest complicating factor in students' return to school following TBI. Loss of ability to understand or formulate language due to TBI is referred to as *acquired aphasia*. The effects of TBI on language are extremely variable, and careful assessment of the given individual's abilities and disabilities is critical. TBI may be accompanied by a variety of serious social and emotional effects, including aggression, hyperactivity, impulsivity, inattention, and others. Behavior modification or behavior management strategies are appropriate for students who have TBI. Effective education and treatment often require not only classroom behavior management but family therapy, medication, cognitive training, and communication training.

Deaf-blindness is one of the most challenging of all multiple disabilities. Outcomes for individuals with deaf-blindness are dependent on at least three things: quality and intensity of instruction; degree and type of visual and auditory impairment; and presence of other disabilities and medical conditions. IDEA states: "Deaf-blindness means concomitant hearing and visual impairments, the combination of which causes such severe communication and other developmental and educational needs that they cannot be accommodated in special education programs solely for children with deafness or children with blindness." There are about 10,000 students from birth to 22 years of age who are deaf-blind. The number of adults with deaf-blindness is estimated to be 35,000 to 40,000. Causes of deaf-blindness can be grouped into three broad categories: (1) genetic/chromosomal syndromes, (2) prenatal conditions, and (3) postnatal conditions. The most common genetic/chromosomal syndromes associated with deaf-blindness are CHARGE syndrome, Usher syndrome, and Down syndrome. Among the most common postnatal conditions that can cause deaf-blindness are meningitis and traumatic brain injury (TBI).

Persons who are deaf-blind can have significant problems in at least three areas: (1) accessing information, (2) communicating, and (3) navigating the environment. Reliance on direct and intensive teaching methods is pronounced for students who are deaf-blind. It is also critical that teachers, professionals, and parents provide a sense of security for students who are deaf-blind through the use of structured routines. There are a number of modes of communication used with persons who are deaf-blind that involve touch. Braille is the most obvious one. Others include hand-over-hand guidance, hand-under-hand guidance, adapted signs, and touch cues. The need for mobility training is critical for persons who are deaf-blind, and differs in at least two ways from O & M training for those with only vision loss: adaptations are needed in order to communicate with persons with deaf-blindness; and it is sometimes necessary to alert the public that the traveler is deaf-blind.

Augmentative or alternative communication (AAC) includes any manual or electronic means by which a person who is unable to communicate through speech because of a physical impairment expresses wants and needs, shares information, and interacts socially with others. Manual signs or gestures may be useful for some individuals, but individuals who are unable to use their hands to communicate must use other means, often involving special equipment. A variety of approaches to AAC have been developed, some involving relatively simple or so-called low-technology solutions and some requiring complex or high-technology solutions. Speed, reliability, portability, cost, and overall effectiveness in helping a person communicate independently are factors to be considered in designing and evaluating AAC. The need for AAC is increasing as more people with severe disabilities, including those with TBI and other disabilities, are surviving and taking their places in the community. The goal of AAC should be independent communication in which there is no doubt about the authenticity of the messages.

Some individuals who have severe or multiple disabilities may engage in problematic behaviors, including self-stimulation, self-injury, tantrums, aggression, or some combination thereof. Self-stimulation is any repetitive, stereotyped behavior that seems to have no purpose other than providing sensory stimulation. It becomes problematic when it interferes with learning or social acceptability or causes injury. Self-injurious behavior (SIB) is repeated physical self-abuse, such as biting, scratching, or poking oneself, head-banging, and so on. Unchecked, SIB often results in self-mutilation. Self-stimulation can be so frequent and intense that it becomes SIB. Severe tantrums can include a variety of behaviors, including self-injury, screaming, crying, throwing or destroying objects, and aggression toward others. Lack of daily living skills refers to the absence or significant impairment of the ability to take care of one's basic needs, such as dressing, feeding, or toileting. Such deficits require that adaptive behaviors be taught.

There is increasing emphasis on analyzing and changing the environments in which problems behavior is exhibited—increasing focus on the immediate and alterable influences on behavior rather than on immutable or historical reasons. Functional behavioral assessment (FBA) and positive behavioral support (PBS) may be particularly important for students with severe and multiple disabilities. FBA entails finding out why or under what circumstances problem behavior is exhibited, and PBS involves creating an environment that supports appropriate behavior.

Most multiple and severe disabilities are identified at birth or soon therefore. In many of these cases children are placed in neonatal intensive care units (NICUs) where they receive treatment from a variety of specialists. Experts agree that even at this stage parents should be allowed as much time as possible with their infants. Other children may seem typical at birth but are recognized as having disabilities within the first years of their lives. In these cases early intervention should be enacted as soon as possible after the disability is detected. The Division for Early Childhood (DEC) of the Council for Exceptional Children (CEC) has established recommended practices for early intervention programs which rely on six essential criteria: (1) research- or value-based practices, (2) family-centered practices, (3) a multicultural perspective, (4) cross-disciplinary collaboration, (5) developmentally and chronologically age-appropriate practices, and (6) adherence to the principle of normalization.

Transition to adulthood is a critical time for most persons with severe and multiple disabilities. Two principles of current transition programming reflect a change in philosophy toward treating persons with severe disabilities with more dignity: an emphasis on self-determination and the use of natural supports as an integral part of transition planning. It is advised that vocational training for students with multiple and severe disabilities begin during elementary school because it could take several years to acquire all the skills that will be needed in order to hold down a job successfully. In secondary school the focus shifts to involving students in actual work situations in the community with the help of a job coach. It is felt that classroom simulations are inferior to using real community settings for vocational training. With intensive and extensive instruction and the support of professionals and the community, many persons with multiple and severe disabilities can aspire to work alongside nondisabled persons and live independently or semi-independently.

Joanne O'Connell

Lady Godiva, Ink, watercolor on rag paper. 15 × 15 in.

Ms. O'Connell, who was born in 1968 in Brighton, Massachusetts, has a daring and unconventional approach to life and art. Her work juxtaposes the natural and man-made worlds and speaks about her favorite subjects, people, and relationships.

Learners with Physical Disabilities

He followed her out the back door and onto a covered mud porch. The yard sloped away toward a small creek. Two rocking chairs faced the creek, and Penn sat in one of the chairs. Jim stopped uneasily at the top of the steps. "Is he okay?" he asked.

Mrs. Carson tilted her head and smiled at Jim as if he were the one she felt sorry for.

"I think he's just fine," she said. "Why don't you go see for yourself? He's been waiting for you."

Jim trudged down the steps and across the yard. He felt mad at the world. He was angry at the uncles for bringing him up here, and mad at Mama for letting him come. He thought about going to wait in the truck for the uncles to come back, but his legs wouldn't stop moving down the slope of the yard. Penn had been to the top of the Empire State Building. Penn had been to Independence Hall. Jim had no idea what to say to a boy who had seen the things Penn had seen. And he had no idea what to say to a boy who had polio. When he walked past the rocking chairs, his stomach dropped as if he had jumped off of something high. He took a deep breath and turned around. "Hey, Penn," he said.

"Hey, Jim," said Penn.

The two boys stared at each other and grinned, then shook hands awkwardly, as if a grown-up were making them do it. Jim looked down at Penn's legs before he could stop himself. Penn slapped his right leg twice with an open palm.

"It's this one," he said. "I can't move this one."

"Oh," Jim said. "I'm sorry."

Penn shrugged. "It's okay," he said. "It could've been a lot worse." He kicked his left leg straight out. "This one's fine."

"At first, down in town, they said you were going to die."

"That's what they said up here, too."

"Did you think you were going to die?"

"Not really. I don't remember."

Jim rolled a stick back and forth with his toe. "Will you . . . ?"

"Maybe," Penn said.

"Really?"

"The doctor in Winston-Salem says it might come back. You can't ever tell." . . .

"You get used to it, though."

"What does it feel like?"

"Sometimes it hurts. Mostly it just feels asleep."

Penn slapped his leg again and stared at it. Jim stared at it, too. "Oh, well," Penn said.

"Oh, well," said Jim.

TONY EARLEY
Jim the Boy

Congenital anomaly.
An irregularity (anomaly) present at birth; may or may not be due to genetic factors.

In Western culture, many people are almost obsessed with their bodies. They don't just want to be healthy and strong; they want to be beautiful—well formed and attractive to others. In fact, some people seem to be more concerned about the impression their bodies make than they are about their own well-being. They may even endanger their health in an effort to become more physically alluring. It is not really surprising, then, that people with physical disabilities must fight two battles—first, the battle to overcome the limitations imposed by their physical conditions and then the battle to be accepted by others.

Individuals with physical disabilities or differences are often stared at, feared, teased, socially rejected, or treated cruelly. Sometimes people feel embarrassed about a disability that isn't theirs, not seeming to understand the feelings of the person who has the disability. Or people may feel that an acquired physical disability must change someone's personality dramatically. In Tony Earley's story about Jim and his friend Penn, who had polio, we see Jim's mixed feelings of anger and fear when seeing his pal for the first time after Penn was paralyzed (see p. 419). We probably expect Jim's mixture of anger, fear, and inquisitiveness from a 10-year-old—wondering about death, the permanence of disability, how it feels to have the disability, and so on. But most of us have such feelings and questions, regardless of our age. And most people with physical disabilities share Penn's matter-of-factness and eagerness to be accepted and get on with life.

Although polio has been virtually eradicated by vaccination, many other causes of partial paralysis and other physical disabilities have not been eliminated. Attitudes toward physical disabilities have not changed much in many ways, and in many ways neither have the problems of having physical disabilities. Children with physical disabilities often face more than the problem of acceptance. For many, accomplishing the seemingly simple tasks of everyday living is a minor—or major—miracle.

Definition and Classification

In this chapter we consider children whose primary distinguishing characteristics are health or physical problems. For the purposes of this book, *children with physical disabilities* are defined as those whose physical limitations or health problems interfere with school attendance or learning to such an extent that special services, training, equipment, materials, or facilities are required. Children who have physical disabilities may also have other disabilities of any type, or special gifts or talents. Thus, the characteristics of children with physical disabilities are extremely varied. The child's physical condition is the proper concern of the medical profession—but when physical problems have obvious implications for education, teaching specialists are needed.

The fact that the primary distinguishing characteristics of children with physical disabilities are medical conditions, health problems, or physical limitations highlights the necessity of interdisciplinary cooperation. There simply must be communication between physicians and special educators to maintain the child's health and at the same time develop whatever capabilities he or she has (Bigge, Best, & Heller, 2001; Heller, Alberto, Forney, & Schwartzman, 1996; Kurtz, Dowrick, Levy, & Batshaw, 1996).

Physical disabilities occur with tremendous range and variety. Children may have **congenital anomalies** (defects they are born with), or they may acquire disabilities through accident or

In the past, physical disabilities kept children from engaging in many everyday activities, but today they are encouraged to participate to the fullest extent possible. ■

Learners with Physical Disabilities

MYTH Cerebral palsy is a contagious disease.	**FACT** Cerebral palsy is not a disease. It is a nonprogressive neurological injury. It is a disorder of muscle control and coordination caused by injury to the brain before or during birth or in early childhood.
MYTH Physical disabilities of all kinds are decreasing because of medical advances.	**FACT** Because of advances in medical technology, the number of children with severe disabilities is increasing. The number of survivors of serious medical conditions who develop normally or have mild impairments, such as hyperactivity and learning disabilities, is also increasing.
MYTH The greatest educational problem involving children with physical disabilities is highly specialized instruction.	**FACT** The greatest educational problem is teaching people without disabilities about what it is like to have a disability and how disabilities can be accommodated.
MYTH The more severe a person's physical disability, the lower his or her intelligence.	**FACT** A person may be severely physically disabled by cerebral palsy or another condition but have a brilliant mind.
MYTH People with epilepsy are mentally ill.	**FACT** People with epilepsy (seizure disorder) are not any more or less disposed to mental illness than those who do not have epilepsy.
MYTH Arthritis is found only in adults, particularly those who are elderly.	**FACT** Arthritic conditions are found in people of any age, including young children.
MYTH People with physical disabilities have no need for sexual expression.	**FACT** People with physical disabilities have sexual urges and need outlets for sexual expression.
MYTH Physical disabilities shape people's personalities.	**FACT** People with physical disabilities have the full range of personality characteristics found among those who do not have physical disabilities. There are no particular personality characteristics associated with physical disability.
MYTH If a child with a physical disability like cerebral palsy or spina bifida learns to walk as a young child, then he or she will maintain that ability throughout life.	**FACT** Continuing intervention through adolescence and adulthood—the entire life span—is required in many cases. Adolescents or adults may find walking much more difficult or give up walking, even if they learned to walk as children, unless they have continued support for ambulation.

Acute.
A serious state of illness or injury from which someone often recovers with treatment.

Chronic.
A permanent condition; not temporary.

Episodic.
Occurring in episodes; a temporary condition that will pass but may recur.

Progressive.
A disease or condition that worsens over time and from which one seldom or never recovers with treatment.

Traumatic brain injury (TBI).
Injury to the brain (not including conditions present at birth, birth trauma, or degenerative diseases or conditions) resulting in total or partial disability or psychosocial maladjustment that affects educational performance; may affect cognition, language, memory, attention, reasoning, abstract thinking, judgment, problem solving, sensory or perceptual and motor disabilities, psychosocial behavior, physical functions, information processing, or speech.

disease after birth. Some physical disabilities are comparatively mild and transitory; others are profound and progressive, ending in total incapacitation and early death. It is difficult to discuss physical disabilities in general, so this chapter is organized around specific conditions falling under one of three categories: neuromotor impairments, orthopedic and musculoskeletal disorders, and other conditions affecting health or physical ability.

It is important to make distinctions among conditions that are *acute* or *chronic* and those that are *episodic* or *progressive*. An **acute** illness or condition may be very serious or severe, but with treatment (which may include hospitalization or medication) it resolves and the person recovers. Someone with a serious infection or who has a serious accident may, for example, become acutely ill or be in critical condition for a time but recover. However, a **chronic** condition is one that is ongoing. It does not resolve, even with the best treatment; it is an incurable condition. Cerebral palsy is chronic; it cannot be cured. An **episodic** condition is one that recurs, although most of the time the individual may function quite normally. Its occurrence is limited primarily to successive episodes. The episodes do not necessarily become more serious or severe over time. Asthma and seizure disorders (epilepsy), for example, tend to be episodic. However, a **progressive** condition in one that becomes more and more serious or severe over time, usually involving more and more complications or deterioration. Muscular dystrophy is an example of a physical problem that is usually progressive.

Prevalence and Need

Roughly 290,000 students in U.S. public schools are being served under two special education categories related to physical disabilities. About 70,000 of these have orthopedic disabilities, and about 220,000 have other health problems (see U.S. Department of Education, 2000). This does not include students with traumatic brain injury or multiple disabilities or young children who are said to have a developmental delay. The needs of many students with physical disabilities appear to be unmet for a number of reasons, including the fact that the population of children and youths with physical disabilities is growing but the availability of health and social service programs is not (see Heller, Alberto, Forney, & Schwartzman, 1996)

Part of the increase in the prevalence of physical disabilities may be due to improvements in the identification of, and medical services to, children with certain conditions. Ironically, medical advances have not only improved the chances of preventing or curing certain diseases and disorders; they have also assured the survival of more children with severe medical problems (Blum, 1992; Brown, 1993; Kurtz et al., 1996). Many children with severe and multiple disabilities and those with severe, chronic illnesses or severe injuries, who in the past would not have survived long, today can have a normal lifespan. So declining mortality rates do not necessarily mean there will be fewer individuals with disabilities. Moreover, improvements in medical care may not lower the number of individuals with disabilities unless there is also a lowering of risk factors in the environment—factors such as accidents, toxic substances, poverty, malnutrition, disease, and interpersonal violence (Baumeister, Kupstas, & Klindworth, 1990; Pless, 1994).

Neuromotor Impairments

Neuromotor impairments are the result of injury to the brain or spinal cord (neurological damage) that also affects the ability to move parts of one's body (motor impairment). It may be associated with injury to the brain before, during, or after birth. **Traumatic brain injury (TBI),** which we discussed in Chapter 11, involves brain damage with an identifiable external cause (trauma) after the birth process. However, brain injury can be acquired from a variety of nontraumatic causes as well: hypoxia (reduced oxygen to the brain, as might occur in near drowning), infection of the brain or its linings, stroke, tumor, metabolic disorder (such as may occur with diabetes, liver disease, or kidney disease), or toxic chemicals or drugs.

In many cases of brain damage, it is impossible to identify the exact cause of the neuromotor impairment. The important point is that *when a child's nervous system is damaged, no matter what the cause, muscular weakness or paralysis is almost always one of the symptoms*. And because these children cannot move about like most others, their education typically requires special equipment, special procedures, or other accommodations for their disabilities.

CEREBRAL PALSY

Cerebral palsy (CP) is not a disease. It is not contagious, it is not progressive (except that improper treatment may lead to complications), and there are no remissions. Although it is often thought of as a motor problem associated with brain damage at birth, it is actually more complicated. For practical purposes, cerebral palsy can be considered part of a syndrome that includes motor dysfunction, psychological dysfunction, seizures, or emotional or behavioral disorders due to brain damage.

Some individuals with CP show only one indication of brain damage, such as motor impairment; others may show combinations of symptoms. The usual definition of CP refers to a condition characterized by paralysis, weakness, lack of coordination, and/or other motor dysfunction because of damage to the child's brain before it has matured (Batshaw & Perret, 1986; Capute & Accardo, 1996a, 1996b). Symptoms may be so mild that they are detected only with difficulty, or so profound that the individual is almost completely incapacitated. Because CP includes such a heterogeneous group of children, the label "cerebral palsy" has been called into question by some. Others have noted that the label "defines groups of children who are desperately in need of a service, and this seems an adequate ground" for continuing to use the label (Bax, 2001, p. 75).

Although there is no cure for CP, advances in medical and rehabilitation technology offer increasing hope of overcoming the disabilities imposed by neurological damage. For example, intensive long-term physical therapy in combination with a surgical procedure called *selective posterior rhizotomy*—in which the surgeon cuts selected nerve roots below

Cerebral palsy (CP).
A condition characterized by paralysis, weakness, lack of coordination, and/or other motor dysfunction; caused by damage to the brain before it has matured.

The United Cerebral Palsy Association provides information and resources for people with CP and their families: www.ucpa.org ■

Advances in medical and rehabilitation technology offer increasing hope of overcoming disabilities associated with cerebral palsy. ■

the spinal cord that cause spasticity in the leg muscles—allows some children with spastic CP to better control certain muscles. Such treatment allows some nonambulatory children to walk and helps others walk more normally (Dyar, 1988). However, the fact that children are enabled to walk does not mean that they will be able to walk all their lives. Continued services may be required if they are to continue walking as adults (Bottos, Feliciangeli, Sciuto, Gericke, & Vianello, 2001).

Causes and Types   Anything that can cause brain damage during the brain's development can cause CP. Before birth, maternal infections, chronic diseases, physical trauma, or maternal exposure to toxic substances or X rays, for example, may damage the brain of the fetus. During the birth process, the brain may be injured, especially if labor or birth is difficult or complicated. Premature birth, hypoxia, high fever, infections, poisoning, hemorrhaging, and related factors may cause harm following birth. In short, anything that results in oxygen deprivation, poisoning, cerebral bleeding, or direct trauma to the brain can be a possible cause of CP.

Although CP occurs at every social level, it is more often seen in children born to mothers in poor socioeconomic circumstances. Children who live in such circumstances have a greater risk of incurring brain damage because of such factors as malnutrition of the mother, poor prenatal and postnatal care, environmental hazards during infancy, and low birthweight (see Baumeister et al., 1990; Nelson, 1996; Stanley & Blair, 1994).

The two means of classification that have been most widely accepted specify the limbs involved and the type of motor disability. Classification according to the extremities involved applies not just to CP but to all types of motor disability or paralysis. The most common classifications may be summarized as follows:

- **Hemiplegia:** One-half (right or left side) of the body is involved
- **Diplegia:** Legs are involved to a greater extent than arms
- **Quadriplegia:** All four limbs are involved
- **Paraplegia:** Only the legs are involved

CP may involve problems of voluntary movement or **spasticity**—stiffness or tenseness of muscles and inaccurate voluntary movement. Other types are characterized by abrupt, involuntary movements and difficulty maintaining balance, known as **choreoathetoid** movements, or muscles that give the appearance of floppiness, known as atonic muscles. Some individuals have a mixture of various types of CP.

The important point about CP is that the brain damage affects strength and the ability to move parts of the body normally. The difficulty of movement may involve the limbs as well as the muscles used to control facial expressions and speech. As a result, someone with CP may have difficulty moving or speaking or may exhibit facial contortions or drooling. But these results of brain damage do not necessarily mean that the person's intelligence or emotional sensitivity has been affected by the damage affecting muscle control.

Associated Disabilities and Educational Implications   Research during the past few decades has made it clear that CP is a developmental disability—a multidisabling condition far more complex than a motor disability alone (Capute & Accardo, 1996b; Heller, Alberto, Forney, & Schwartzman, 1996). When the brain is damaged, sensory abilities, cognitive functions, and emotional responsiveness as well as motor performance are usually affected. A high proportion of children with CP are found to have hearing impairments, visual impairments, perceptual disorders, speech problems, emotional or behavioral disorders, mental retardation, or some combination of several of these disabling conditions, in addition to motor disability. They may also exhibit such characteristics as drooling or facial contortions.

Some individuals with CP have normal or above-average intellectual capacity, and a few test within the gifted range. The average tested intelligence of children with CP, however, is clearly lower than the average for the general population (Batshaw & Perret, 1986).

Hemiplegia.
A condition in which one half (right or left side) of the body is paralyzed.

Diplegia.
A condition in which the legs are paralyzed to a greater extent than the arms.

Quadriplegia.
A condition in which all four limbs are paralyzed

Paraplegia.
A condition in which both legs are paralyzed.

Spasticity.
Characterized by muscle stiffness and problems in voluntary movement; associated with spastic cerebral palsy.

Choreoathetoid.
Characterized by involuntary movements and difficulty with balance; associated with choreoathetoid cerebral palsy.

However, we must be very cautious in interpreting the test results of children with CP, as many standardized tests of intelligence and achievement may be inappropriate for individuals with special difficulties in perception, movement, or response speed. Furthermore, the movement problems of a child with CP may become more apparent in a state of emotional arousal or stress; this can complicate using typical testing procedures, which tend to be demanding and stressful.

The educational problems of children who have CP are as multifaceted as their disabilities. Not only must special equipment and procedures be provided because the children have physical disabilities, but the same special educational procedures and equipment required to teach children with vision, hearing, or communication disorders, learning disabilities, emotional or behavioral disorders, or mental retardation are often needed. Careful and continuous educational assessment of the individual child's capabilities is particularly important. Teaching the child who has CP demands competence in many aspects of special education and experience in working with a variety of disabling conditions in a multidisciplinary setting (Bigge et al., 2001; Heller, Alberto, Forney, & Schwartzman, 1996; Tyler & Colson, 1994).

SEIZURE DISORDER (EPILEPSY)

A person has a **seizure** when there is an abnormal discharge of electrical energy in certain brain cells. The discharge spreads to nearby cells, and the effect may be loss of consciousness, involuntary movements, or abnormal sensory phenomena. The effects of the seizure will depend on the location of the cells in which the discharge starts and how far the discharge spreads.

People with **epilepsy** have recurrent seizures (Engel, 1995). About 6 percent of the population will have a seizure at some time during life, but most of them will not be diagnosed as having epilepsy because they do not have repeated seizures (Batshaw & Perret, 1986). Seizures reflect abnormal brain activity, so it is not surprising that they occur more often in children with developmental disabilities (e.g., mental retardation or cerebral palsy) than in children without disabilities (Bigge et al., 2001; Coulter, 1993; Vining & Freeman, 1996).

Causes and Types   Seizures apparently can be caused by almost any kind of damage to the brain. As brain imaging and molecular biology advance, scientists are arriving at a better understanding of risk for epilepsy (Avoli, Rogawski, & Avanzini, 2001). The most common immediate causes include lack of sufficient oxygen (hypoxia), low blood sugar (hypoglycemia), infections, and physical trauma. Certain conditions, like those named, tend to increase the chances that neurochemical reactions will be set off in brain cells (Vining & Freeman, 1996). In many cases the causes are unknown. Some types of seizures may be progressive; that is, they may damage the brain or disrupt its functioning in such a way that having a seizure increases the probability of having another (Girvin, 1992). Even though the cause of seizures is not well understood, it is important to note that with proper medication most people's seizures can be controlled.

Seizures may take many forms, and the best way to classify seizures is a matter of debate among neurologists (e.g., Parra, Augustijn, Geerts, & Boas, 2001). However, educators should note that seizures may differ along at least the following dimensions:

- *Duration:* They may last only a few seconds or for several minutes.
- *Frequency:* They may occur as frequently as every few minutes or only about once a year.
- *Onset:* They may be set off by certain identifiable stimuli or be unrelated to the environment, and they may be totally unexpected or be preceded by certain internal sensations.
- *Movements:* They may cause major convulsive movements or only minor motor symptoms (e.g., eye blinks).

Seizure (convulsion).
A sudden alteration of consciousness, usually accompanied by motor activity and/or sensory phenomena; caused by an abnormal discharge of electrical energy in the brain.

Epilepsy.
A pattern of repeated seizures.

ᴳᵂ More information about epilepsy is available at www.efa.org/
    At Adrian's Adaptive Closet you will find clothes adapted for individuals who use wheel chairs: www.adrianscloset.com/
    The site for Wheelchair Net is a community for people who have a common interest in wheelchair technology and its improvement and successful application: www.wheelchairnet.org/index2.html ■

- *Causes:* They may be caused by a variety of conditions, including high fever, poisoning, trauma, and other conditions mentioned previously; but in many cases the causes are unknown.
- *Associated disabilities:* They may be associated with other disabling conditions or be unrelated to any other medical problem or disability.
- *Control:* They may be controlled completely by drugs, so that the individual has no more seizures, or they may be only partially controlled.

Educational Implications   About half of all children with seizure disorders have average or higher intelligence, just as is true for the general population. Among those without mental retardation, however, there seems to be a higher-than-usual incidence of learning disabilities (Besag, 1995). Although many children who have seizure disorders have other disabilities, some do not. Consequently, both general and special education teachers may expect to encounter children who have seizures (see Spiegel, Cutler, & Yetter, 1996). Besides obtaining medical advice regarding management of the child's particular seizure disorder, teachers should know first aid for epileptic seizures (see the box below). Ignorance about the causes of seizures and about first aid are among the most common misconceptions about epilepsy (Gouvier, Brown, Prestholdt, Hayes, & Apostolas, 1995).

Seizures are primarily a medical problem and require primarily medical attention. Educators are called on to deal with the problem in the following ways:

1. General and special teachers need to help dispel ignorance, superstition, and prejudice toward people who have seizures and provide calm management for the occasional seizure the child may have at school (Spiegel et al., 1996).
2. Special education teachers who work with students with severe mental retardation or teach children with other severe developmental disabilities need to be prepared to manage more frequent seizures as well as to handle learning problems. The teacher should record the length of a child's seizure and the type of activity the child was engaged in before it occurred. This information will help physicians in diagnosis and treatment. If a student is being treated for a seizure

First Aid for Epileptic Seizures

A major epileptic seizure is often dramatic and frightening. It lasts only a few minutes, however, and does not require expert care. These simple procedures should be followed:

- Remain calm. You cannot stop a seizure once it has started. Let the seizure run its course. Do not try to revive the child.
- If the child is upright, ease him to the floor and loosen his clothing.
- Try to prevent the child from striking his head or body against any hard, sharp, or hot objects; but do not otherwise interfere with his movement.
- Turn the child's face to the side so that saliva can flow out of his mouth.
- *Do not insert anything between the child's teeth.*

- Do not be alarmed if the child seems to stop breathing momentarily.
- After the movements stop and the child is relaxed, allow him to sleep or rest if he wishes.
- It isn't generally necessary to call a doctor unless the attack is followed almost immediately by another seizure or the seizure lasts more than ten minutes.
- Notify the child's parents or guardians that a seizure has occurred.
- After a seizure, many people can carry on as before. If, after resting, the child seems groggy, confused, or weak, it may be a good idea to accompany him or her home.

SOURCE: Courtesy of Epilepsy Foundation of America.

disorder, the teacher should know the type of medication and its possible side effects (Bigge et al., 2001).

Some children who do not have mental retardation but have seizures exhibit learning and behavior problems (Michael, 1995). These problems may result from damage to the brain that causes other disabilities as well, or they may be the side effects of anticonvulsant medication or the result of mismanagement by parents and teachers. Teachers must be aware that seizures of any type may interfere with the child's attention or the continuity of education (McCarthy, Richman, & Yarbrough, 1995). Brief seizures may require the teacher to repeat instructions or allow the child extra time to respond. Frequent major convulsions may prevent even a bright child from achieving at the usual rate.

"Many students with epilepsy show very few or no learning problems" (Michael, 1995, p. 81). However, some do have learning disabilities, and children with epilepsy more often have emotional or behavioral disorders than do those without epilepsy (Michael, 1995). In fact, *Epilepsia*, the journal of the International League Against Epilepsy, devoted an entire special issue to learning disabilities (Ayala, Elia, Cornaggia, & Trimble, 2001). If children with epilepsy do have problems in school, their school adjustment can be improved dramatically if they are properly assessed, placed, counseled, taught about seizures, and given appropriate work assignments (Heller, Alberto, Forney, & Schwartzman, 1996).

SPINA BIFIDA AND OTHER SPINAL CORD INJURIES

Neurological damage may involve only the spinal cord, leaving the brain unaffected. Spinal cord injury may occur before or after birth, affecting the individual's ability to move or control bodily functions below the site of the injury (Bigge et al., 2001).

During early fetal development, the two halves of the embryo grow together or fuse at the midline. When the closure is incomplete, a congenital midline defect is the result. Cleft lip and cleft palate are examples of such midline defects. **Spina bifida** is a congenital midline defect resulting from failure of the bony spinal column to close completely during fetal development. The defect may occur anywhere from the head to the lower end of the spine. Because the spinal column is not closed, the spinal cord (nerve fibers) may protrude, resulting in damage to the nerves and paralysis and/or lack of function or sensation below the site of the defect.

Spina bifida is often accompanied by paralysis of the legs and of the anal and bladder sphincters because nerve impulses are not able to travel past the defect. Surgery to close the spinal opening is performed in early infancy, but this does not repair the nerve damage. Although spina bifida is one of the most common birth defects resulting in physical disability, its causes are not known.

Spinal cord injuries resulting from accidents after birth are also a major cause of paralysis. The basic difference between spina bifida and other spinal cord injuries is that the individual who is injured after birth has gone through a period of normal development and must adjust to an acquired disability.

Educational Implications   The extent of the paralysis resulting from a spinal cord injury depends on how high or low on the spinal column it is. Some children with spinal cord injuries are able to walk independently, some need braces, and others have to use wheelchairs. Lack of sensation and ability to control bodily functions, too, will depend on the nature of the injury. Thus, the implications for education are extremely varied. However, factors other than muscle weakness or paralysis alone affect a child's ability to walk (Bartonek & Saraste, 2001). Thus careful analysis of motivation and other environmental inducements to walk are critically important.

Some children will have acute medical problems, which may lead to repeated hospitalizations for surgery or treatment of infections. Lack of sensation in certain areas of the skin may increase the risk of burns, abrasions, and pressure sores. The child may need to

Spina bifida.
A congenital midline defect resulting from failure of the bony spinal column to close completely during fetal development.

For more information about spina bifida, see the Web site of the National Spina Bifida Association of America: www.sbaa.org
    See also the National Spinal Cord Injury Association: www.spinalcord.org ■

Catheterization.
The insertion of a tube into the urethra to drain the bladder.

Muscular dystrophy.
A hereditary disease characterized by progressive weakness caused by degeneration of muscle fibers.

Juvenile rheumatoid arthritis.
A systemic disease with major symptoms involving the muscles and joints.

Scoliosis.
An abnormal curvature of the spine.

Asthma.
A lung disease characterized by episodic difficulty in breathing, particularly exhaling, due to inflammation or obstruction of the air passages.

be positioned periodically during the school day and monitored carefully during some activities in which there is risk of injury.

Because the student with spina bifida has deficiencies in sensation below the defect, she or he may have particular problems in spatial orientation, spatial judgment, sense of direction and distance, organization of motor skills, and body image or body awareness. Lack of bowel and bladder control in some children will require periodic **catheterization.** Many children can be taught to do the procedure known as *clean intermittent catheterization* themselves, but teachers should know what to do or obtain help from the school nurse.

Orthopedic and Musculoskeletal Disorders

Some children are physically disabled because of defects or diseases of the muscles or bones. Even though they do not have neurological impairments, their ability to move is affected. Most of the time, muscular and skeletal problems involve the legs, arms, joints, or spine, making it difficult or impossible for the child to walk, stand, sit, or use his or her hands. The problems may be congenital or acquired after birth, and the causes may include genetic defects, infectious diseases, accidents, or developmental disorders.

Two of the most common musculoskeletal conditions affecting children and youths are **muscular dystrophy** and **juvenile rheumatoid arthritis.** Muscular dystrophy is a hereditary disease that is characterized by progressive weakness caused by degeneration of muscle fibers (Batshaw & Perret, 1986). The exact biological mechanism responsible for muscular dystrophy is not known, nor is there any cure at present. Juvenile rheumatoid arthritis is a potentially debilitating disease in which the muscles and joints are affected; the cause and cure are unknown (Bigge et al., 2001). It can be a very painful condition and is sometimes accompanied by complications such as fever, respiratory problems, heart problems, and eye infections. Among children with other physical disabilities, such as cerebral palsy, arthritis may be a complicating factor that affects the joints and limits movement. These and other conditions can significantly affect a student's social and academic progress at school.

A wide variety of other congenital conditions, acquired defects, and diseases also can affect the musculoskeletal system, such as the spinal curvature known as **scoliosis** or missing or malformed limbs (see Bigge et al., 2001; Heller, Alberto, Forney, & Schwartzman, 1996). In all these conditions, as well as in cases of muscular dystrophy and arthritis, the student's intelligence is unaffected, unless there are additional associated disabilities. Regarding the musculoskeletal problem itself, special education is necessary only to improve the student's mobility, to see that proper posture and positioning are maintained, to provide for education during periods of confinement to hospital or home, and otherwise to make the educational experience as normal as possible.

ᏟᎳ Children with special health needs and their families face common problems. Family Voices (National Coalition for Children with Special Healthcare Needs) provides information at www.familyvoices.org

A variety of Web sites contain information about specific diseases and conditions:

The Asthma and Allergy Foundation of America: www.aafa.org

The National Cystic Fibrosis Society: www.cff.org

The National Multiple Sclerosis Foundation: www.nmss.org

The National Association for Rare Disorders: www.rarediseases.org ∎

Other Conditions Affecting Health or Physical Ability

In addition to those discussed so far, an extremely wide array of diseases, physiological disorders, congenital malformations, and injuries may affect students' health and physical abilities and create a need for special education and related services. The cataloging of these conditions is not important, but special educators should understand the range of physical disabilities and the types of accommodations that may be necessary to provide an appropriate education and related services.

Asthma is a lung disease characterized by episodic inflammation or obstruction of the air passages such that the person has difficulty in breathing. Usually, the difficulty in breathing is reversible (i.e., is responsive to treatment). Severe asthma can be life-threatening, and in some cases it severely restricts a person's activities. The disease can also get better or worse for poorly understood reasons, and the unpredictability of the condition can be difficult to deal with. In the box on page 430, Kathryn Hegarty describes some of her experiences with asthma. Note that she received important support from both her family and her school. Without the special resource class for students with special needs, which she describes as "The Base," she doesn't think she would have been able to go to school.

Congenital malformations and disorders may occur in any organ system, and they may range from minor to fatal flaws in structure or function. In many cases the cause of the malformation or disorder is not known, but in others it is known to be hereditary or caused by maternal infection or substance use by the mother during pregnancy. For instance, **fetal alcohol syndrome (FAS)**, which is now one of the most common syndromes involving malformations and mental retardation, is caused by the mother's use of alcohol during pregnancy. Worldwide, FAS is now seen in about 1 in 1000 live births, and the prevalence of other disorders related to alcohol use of women during pregnancy is a serious problem (Archibald, Fennema-Notestine, Gamst, Riley, Mattson, & Jernigan, 2001).

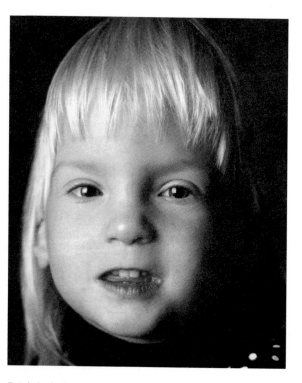

Fetal alcohol syndrome, associated with mothers' alcohol use during pregnancy, results in distinct physical and developmental abnormalities. ■

More children die in accidents each year than are killed by all childhood diseases combined. Millions of children and youths in the United States are seriously injured and disabled temporarily or permanently in accidents each year. Many of those who do not acquire traumatic brain injury receive spinal cord injuries that result in partial or total paralysis below the site of the injury. Others undergo amputations or are incapacitated temporarily by broken limbs or internal injuries.

Acquired immune deficiency syndrome (AIDS) is often thought to be a disease that merely makes one susceptible to fatal infections. However, children with AIDS often acquire neurological problems as well, including mental retardation, cerebral palsy, seizures, and emotional or behavioral disorders. AIDS is caused by the human immunodeficiency virus (HIV). Although HIV infections can be spread in other ways, the primary means of transmission is through sexual contact Most of the reported new cases of HIV infections are in minority populations, and almost three-fourths of the new infections in the group aged thirteen to nineteen years are in minority populations. Thus it is clear that "HIV infection in American adolescents has not received the attention it merits over the years" (Rogers, 2001, p. 1).

As children and youths with AIDS and other viral and bacterial infections live longer due to improved medical treatments, there will be an increasing need for special education and related services. Teachers should be aware that if reasonable procedures are followed for preventing infections, there is no serious concern regarding transmission of HIV in the classroom (Ainsa, 2000; Bigge et al., 2001; Heller, Alberto, Forney, & Schwartzman, 1996; Lerner, Lowenthal, & Egan, 1998).

We have already mentioned fetal alcohol syndrome, which results in disabilities acquired by children of mothers who abuse alcohol during pregnancy. The abuse of other substances by mothers also has negative implications for their children. If the mother is a substance abuser, then there is also a high probability of neglect and abuse by the mother after her baby is born. Many women who are intravenous drug users not only risk chemical damage to their babies but also give them venereal diseases such as syphilis, which can result in disabilities. If the number of substance-abusing mothers increases, then the number of infants and young children with severe and multiple disabilities will increase as well. In spite of the multiple causal factors involved, the prospects of effective early intervention

Fetal alcohol syndrome (FAS).
Abnormalities associated with the mother's drinking alcohol during pregnancy; defects range from mild to severe, including growth retardation, brain damage, mental retardation, hyperactivity, anomalies of the face, and heart failure; also called alcohol embryopathy.

Acquired immune deficiency syndrome (AIDS).
A virus-caused illness resulting in a breakdown of the immune system; currently, no known cure exists.

For many Web sites related to FAS, simply enter fetal alcohol syndrome as a search term in your Web browser. The American Autoimmune and Related Diseases Association provides information about AIDs and related disorders at www. aarda.org ■

The Importance of Family and School in Coping with Asthma

I was diagnosed with asthma at the age of two so I don't remember what life was like without it. Fortunately, throughout my younger years the illness never affected me significantly and I was able to do everything other children my age did.

I was lucky to have a supportive family, we had always been very close, but things changed when my asthma got worse. My older brother, Andrew, was very protective, although he had quite a tough time as he was always told to look after me. My Mum and Dad were often shouted at when I was feeling fed up or if I was begging them to discharge me from the hospital.

It was when I hit puberty that things started to go wrong. I woke up one morning feeling a bit breathless and I found that my inhaler wasn't helping. My Mum took me to hospital where I was put on a nebuliser. It was the same medication as my inhaler but it was delivered through a breathing mask. I soon felt better and was sent home, although it started to become a regular occurrence. I was put on a very high dose of steroids. The list of possible side effects included weight gain, high blood pressure and brittle bones. . . .

Over the following months my asthma got progressively worse, which involved my having short but frequent stays in the hospital. My school had a facility called "The Base" for pupils who needed to work out of their usual class for a variety of reasons. This meant that on days I was not feeling well I could go there and work would be brought down from my classes so that I could work quietly at my own pace. I could also use this facility if the [elevators] were out of use since it was difficult for

me to use the stairs around the school as I would become so breathless.

I certainly wouldn't have been at school half as much without "The Base." I became very friendly with one of the teachers who worked there. She provided not only educational support, but emotional support as well. I would often go in feeling fed up and frustrated. She would sit down and listen while I poured my heart out and told her how awful my life was.

Some days, even walking to the bus stop was too much for me, so the school provided a taxi to take me between home and school. It meant that if I was unwell while I was at school, I could telephone the taxi to pick me up early, or if I hadn't been well during the night I could go in to school later. It gave me a lot of freedom but I didn't abuse it. The school knew that I wanted to be there so I didn't have to feel guilty if I was late or even if I didn't go in at all. . . . [Kathryn also describes her worsening condition, some classmates' misunderstanding, and her lack of social life due to her illness.]

I think the fact that I have such a supportive family has kept me going. I am also extremely grateful to my school. If it hadn't been for "The Base" I would hardly have been there at all. I could have given up a long time ago, but I didn't. I am a fighter because I have had to be. I will always have asthma. It is part of my life but, hopefully, I am over the worst of it. From now on things can only get better.

SOURCE: Hegarty, K., Lyke, T., Docherty, R., & Douglas, S. (2000). "I didn't ask to have this:" First-person accounts of young people. In A. Closs (Ed.), *The education of children with medical conditions* (pp. 15–17). London: David Fulton.

with children exposed prenatally to drugs are much better than previously thought. Although the consequences of any drug use during pregnancy may be serious, the near hysteria of the 1980s about the irreversible effects of crack cocaine on infants was not justified (see Hanson, 1996; Lerner et al., 1998; Lockhart, 1996). True, many children exposed prenatally to drugs will have developmental disabilities. Like the developmental disabilities having other causes, however, those of children exposed before birth to drugs are amenable to modification (Heller, Alberto, Forney, & Schwartzman, 1996; Lerner et al., 1998; Lockhart, 1996).

Some students have conditions that require particularly careful treatment because seemingly minor mistakes or oversights can have very serious consequences for them. Programs for students who are *medically fragile* must be particularly flexible and open to revision. Daily health care plans and emergency plans are essential, as are effective lines of communication among all who are involved with the student's treatment, care, and schooling. Decisions regarding placement of these students must be made by a team including health care providers and school personnel as well as the student and his or her parents.

An increasing number of children are returning home from hospitalization able to breathe only with the help of a ventilator (a mechanical device forcing oxygen into the lungs through a tube inserted into the trachea). Many of these children are also returning to public schools, sometimes with the assistance of a full-time nurse. It is debatable as to whether it is appropriate for children who are dependent on ventilators or other medical technology to attend regular classrooms. Educators and parents together must make decisions in each individual case, weighing medical judgment regarding danger to the child as well as the interest of the child in being integrated into as many typical school activities as possible with her or his peers (see Heller, Alberto, Forney, & Schwartzman, 1996).

Prevention of Physical Disabilities

Although some physical disabilities are not preventable by any available means, many or most are. For instance, failure to wear seat belts and other safety devices accounts for many disabling injuries. Likewise, driving under the influence of alcohol or other drugs, careless storage of drugs and other toxic substances, use of alcohol and other drugs during pregnancy, and a host of unsafe and unhealthful practices that could be avoided cause many disabilities (Hanson, 1996).

Teenage girls are more likely than older women to give birth to premature or low-birthweight babies, who will be at high risk for learning problems when they reach school age. ■

Teenage mothers are more likely than older women to be physically battered (*Shelter News*, 2001). Teens are also more likely than older women to give birth to premature or low-birthweight babies, and these babies are at high risk for a variety of psychological and physical problems when they reach school age (Cowden & Funkhouser, 2001). Thus, preventing adolescent pregnancies would keep many babies from being born with disabilities. Inadequate prenatal care, including maternal infections and inadequate maternal nutrition during pregnancy, also contributes to the number of babies born with disabilities. And for young children, immunization against preventable childhood diseases could lower the number of those who acquire disabilities (Hanson, 1996).

Child abuse is a significant contributing factor in creating physical disabilities in the United States, and its prevention is a critical problem. Many thousands of children, ranging from newborns to adolescents, are battered or abused each year. Teachers can play an extremely important role in detecting, reporting, and preventing child abuse and neglect because, next to parents, they are the people who spend the most time with children. If they suspect abuse or neglect, teachers must report it to child protective services under state and local regulations. These vary from one area and state to another, but ordinarily the teacher is required to report suspected cases of child abuse or neglect to a school administrator, law enforcement officer, or social services official. A professional who fails to report child abuse or neglect may be held legally liable.

Children who are already disabled physically, mentally, or emotionally are more at risk for abuse than are nondisabled children (Crosse, Kaye, & Ratnofsky, n.d.). Because children with disabilities are more vulnerable and dependent, abusive adults find them easy targets. Moreover, some of the characteristics of children with disabilities are sources of additional stress for their caretakers and may be contributing factors in physical abuse—they often require more time, energy, money, and patience than children without disabilities. Parenting any child is stressful; parenting a child with a disability can demand more than some parents are prepared to give. It is not surprising that children with disabilities are disproportionately represented among abused children and that the need for training is particularly great for parents of children with disabilities.

Psychological and Behavioral Characteristics

ACADEMIC ACHIEVEMENT

It is impossible to make many valid generalizations about the academic achievement of children with physical disabilities because they vary so widely in the nature and severity of their conditions. The environmental and psychological factors that determine what a child will achieve academically also are extremely varied (Bigge et al., 2001; Heller, Alberto, & Meagher, 1996).

Many students with physical disabilities have erratic school attendance because of hospitalization, visits to physicians, the requirement of bed rest at home, and so on. Some learn well with ordinary teaching methods; others require special methods because they have mental retardation or sensory impairments in addition to physical disabilities. Because of the frequent interruptions in their schooling, some fall considerably behind their age-mates in academic achievement, even though they have normal intelligence and motivation. The two major effects of a physical disability, especially if it is severe or prolonged, are that a child may be deprived of educationally relevant experiences and that he or she may not be able to learn to manipulate educational materials and respond to educational tasks the way most children do.

Some children with mild or transitory physical problems have no academic deficiencies at all; others have severe difficulties. Some students who have serious and chronic health problems still manage to achieve at a high level. Usually these high-achieving children have high intellectual capacity, strong motivation, and teachers and parents who make every possible special provision for their education. Children with neurological impairments are, as a group, most likely to have intellectual and perceptual deficits and therefore to be behind their age-mates in academic achievement (see Bigge et al., 2001; Heller, Alberto, Forney, & Schwartzman, 1996).

PERSONALITY CHARACTERISTICS

Research does not support the notion that there is a certain personality type or self-concept associated with any physical disability (Llewellyn & Chung, 1997). Children and youths with physical disabilities are as varied in their psychological characteristics as nondisabled children, and they are apparently responsive to the same factors that influence the psychological development of other children. How children adapt to their physical limitations and how they respond to social-interpersonal situations greatly depends on how parents, siblings, teachers, peers, and the public react to them (Bigge et al., 2001; Lerner et al., 1998; Heller, Alberto, & Meagher, 1996; Myers, 1996).

Public Reactions   Public attitudes can have a profound influence on how children with physical disabilities see themselves, and on their opportunities for psychological adjustment, education, and employment. If the reaction is one of fear, rejection, or discrimination, they may spend a great deal of energy trying to hide their stigmatizing differences. If the reaction is one of pity and an expectation of helplessness, people with disabilities will tend to behave in a dependent manner. To the extent that other people can see children with physical disabilities as persons who have certain limitations but are otherwise just like everyone else, children and youths with disabilities will be encouraged to become independent and productive members of society (see Bigge et al., 2001; Closs, 2000; Powers, Singer, & Sowers, 1996).

Several factors seem to be causing greater public acceptance of people with physical disabilities. Professional and civic groups encourage support and decrease fear of people who are disabled through information and public education. Government insistence on the elimination of architectural barriers that prevent citizens with disabilities from using public facilities serves to decrease discrimination. Programs to encourage hiring workers with disabilities help the public see those with physical disabilities as constructive, capable people. Laws that protect every child's right to public education bring more individuals into contact with people who have severe or profound disabilities. But there is no doubt that many children with physical disabilities are still rejected, feared, pitied, or discriminated against. The more obvious the physical flaw, the more likely it is that the person will be perceived in negative terms by the public.

Public policy regarding children's physical disabilities has not met the needs of most such children and their families. Particularly, as successful medical treatment prolongs the lives of more and more children with severe, chronic illnesses and other disabilities, issues of who should pay the costs of treatment and maintenance (which are often enormous) and which children and families should receive the limited available resources are becoming critical.

Children's and Families' Reactions   As suggested earlier, children's reactions to their own physical disabilities are largely a reflection of how they have been treated by others. Shame and guilt are learned responses; children will have such negative feelings only if others respond to them by shaming or blaming them (and those like them) for their physical differences. Children will be independent and self-sufficient (within the limits of their physical disabilities), rather than dependent and demanding, only to the extent that they learn how to take care of their own needs. And they will have realistic self-perceptions and set realistic goals for themselves only to the extent that others are honest and clear in appraising their conditions.

However, certain psychological reactions are inevitable for the child with physical disabilities, no matter how she or he is treated. The wish to be nondisabled and participate in the same activities as most children and the fantasy that the disability will disappear are to be expected. With proper management and help, the child can be expected eventually to accept the disability and live a happy life, even though he or she knows the true nature of the condition. Fear and anxiety, too, can be expected. It is natural for children to be afraid

Children's feelings about their own disabilities are largely a reflection of how they are treated by others, and also of the attitude that their own families take toward them. They are more likely to see themselves as "normal" if they are treated that way, and encouraged to participate in regular activities. ◼

Overcoming a Health Challenge

Jessie Skinner

I was 3 when I was first diagnosed with diabetes. My Mom gave me my shots until I was 8. The first few times I gave myself shots, it was scary! It got easier as I got older. I went to camp and everyone else was doing their own shots, so I decided to start doing it myself.

My diabetes is hard to control. I remember being in the hospital when I was in seventh grade because my blood sugar was high. Close to the end of seventh grade I changed doctors because I didn't feel comfortable adjusting my own insulin. My new doctor was really nice when my Mom was in the room; she'd always compliment me. But when my Mom left the room, she'd tell me, "You'd better start taking your insulin!" I'd tell her, "I *am* taking my insulin!" I never really felt that she believed me. Once when I was in the hospital, the same thing happened—my blood sugar was really high, but *they* were doing my shots for me. From that point on, she believed that I was doing my shots on a regular basis.

Once my doctor started believing me, we got closer and I could talk to her better. I wasn't afraid to tell her that I forgot my insulin on a day. Now she wants me to write some things down to help other kids with hard-to-control diabetes. One suggestion is for kids to always tell the truth about skipping their insulin. I learned that the hard way. One day I was mad at my Mom and I skipped my insulin, thinking that I was going to hurt her. The only one I hurt was myself. I got really sick and ended up in the hospital. Then I had to tell the truth.

If your doctors say that you're skipping your insulin and you're not, keep telling them that you aren't—sooner or later, they'll listen! Also, try to be involved in the decisions about your insulin. They tried to get me to four shots a day, but I told them I only wanted to do three. I would rather do the regular shots less often and the booster shots more often.

I think it's important for kids to learn to take care of their medical issues because it makes you more responsible and it helps you to better understand what you have. If you need help, don't be afraid to ask. For me, if my blood sugar is really high, my vision isn't very good. It's good to take a break once in a while and let someone else do the shot, to make sure it's the right dosage. I'll sometimes ask the nurse at school for help.

Another suggestion I have is in dealing with adults who don't understand. My softball coach found out that I had diabetes. This changed my relationship with her a whole lot. The positions that I was good at she no longer let me play. She put me in right field where no balls ever come. I think she was scared and didn't know anything about diabetes. I ended up talking to her and asking her what her problem was. Her response was, "Your diabetes." I asked her why she was holding me back, because it was something that I couldn't help. She told me that she didn't realize that she was treating me any differently than the other kids. Talking with her turned our relationship around. Now we're best friends. We even go skiing together! And now I play all the positions on my softball team.

When kids feel that they're being treated differently, I suggest they talk to the person and ask what's bothering him or her. Don't give up! I didn't, even though I wanted to give up. I now feel good that I didn't. I was so nervous when I approached my coach, because I thought she was going to kick me off the team. I'm afraid to tell other people that I have diabetes because I'm afraid they'll treat me differently. Even though I have a good relationship with my coach now, I still wonder if she looks at me differently.

Health professionals need to be honest with teens. For example, they need to help teens schedule their medications based on their own personal lifestyles. If a teen is a late sleeper on weekends, let her take her medications later on Friday evening, so she can sleep late the next day. Another suggestion is to believe in your patient. Help build a relationship with the person you're treating. If possible, provide a mentor for the teenager who had similar problems when she was her age, because it helps kids realize they're not the only ones who are going through problems.

Employers need to recognize people as individuals. If you find that an employee has a health challenge, DON'T treat him any differently than you would if he didn't have the challenge! My boss recently found out that I have diabetes. Since then, he's been driving me crazy by calling me to the front of the store every half hour to ask me if I'm feeling okay. If kids learn to be responsible for their medical care and other people listen to and respect what kids say they need and don't need, managing a health challenge will be a lot easier for everyone.

SOURCE: Skinner, J. (1996). Overcoming a health challenge. In Powers, L.E., Singer, G.H.S., & Sowers, J. (Eds.). (1996). *On the road to autonomy: Promoting self-competence in children and youth with disabilities* (pp. 255–256). Baltimore: Paul H. Brookes. Reprinted with permission.

when they are separated from their parents, hospitalized, and subjected to medical examinations and procedures that may be painful. In these situations, too, proper management can minimize emotional stress. Psychological trauma is not a necessary effect of hospitalization. The hospital environment may, in fact, be better than the child's home in the case of abused and neglected children.

Other important considerations regarding the psychological effects of a physical disability include the age of the child and the nature of the limitation (e.g., whether it is congenital or acquired, progressive or not). But even these factors are not uniform in their effects. A child with a relatively minor and short-term physical disability may become more maladjusted, anxious, debilitated, and disruptive than another child with a terminal illness because of the way the child's behavior and feelings are managed. Certainly, understanding the child's and the family's feelings about the disability are important. But it is also true that managing the consequences of the child's behavior is a crucial aspect of education and rehabilitation. Adolescence is a difficult time for most parents, and the fact that a child has a physical disability does not necessarily mean that the family will find a youngster's adolescence more difficult or less difficult (Magill-Evans, Darrah, Pain, Adkins, & Kratochvil, 2001).

The box on page 434 illustrates how family support, school experiences, medical treatment, and public attitudes affect the life of a child with a chronic health problem (diabetes). Besides the school and society at large, the family and its cultural roots are important determinants of how and what children with physical disabilities will learn; thus, it is important to take cultural values into account in teaching children not only about the academic curriculum but about their disability as well (Walker, 1995).

Prosthetics, Orthotics, and Adaptive Devices for Daily Living

Many individuals with physical disabilities use prosthetics, orthotics, and other adaptive devices to help them better function on a daily basis. A **prosthesis** is an artificial replacement for a missing body part (e.g., an artificial hand or leg); an **orthosis** is a device that enhances the partial function of a part of a person's body (a brace or a device that allows a person to do something). **Adaptive devices** for daily living include a variety of adaptations of ordinary items found in the home, office, or school—such as a device to aid bathing or hand washing or walking—that make performing the tasks required for self-care and employment easier for the person who has a physical disability.

The most important principles to keep in mind are use of residual function, simplicity, and reliability. For example, the muscles of the arm, shoulder, or back operate an artificial hand. This may be too complicated or demanding for an infant or young child with a missing or deformed upper limb. Depending on the child's age, the length and function of the amputated limb, and the child's other abilities, a passive "mitt" or a variety of other prosthetic devices might be more helpful. Choice of the most useful prosthesis will depend on careful evaluation of each individual's needs. A person without legs may be taught to use his or her arms to move about in a wheelchair, or to use his or her torso and arms to get about on artificial legs (perhaps using crutches or a cane in addition). Again, each individual's abilities and preferences must be evaluated in designing the prosthesis (see Bigge et al., 2001; Heller, Alberto, Forney, & Schwartzman, 1996).

Two points regarding prosthetics, orthotics, and residual function must be kept in mind:

1. Residual function is often important even when a prosthesis, orthosis, or adaptive device is not used. For example, it may be crucial for the child with cerebral

Prosthesis.
A device designed to replace, partially or completely, a part of the body (e.g., artificial teeth or limbs).

Orthosis.
A device designed to restore, partially or completely, a lost function of the body (e.g., a brace or crutch).

Adaptive devices.
Special tools that are adaptations of common items to make accomplishing self-care, work, or recreation activities easier for people with physical disabilities.

(a)

(b)

Use of residual function is a key factor in the design of prosthetic devices. The man in photo (a) uses an artificial hand that he controls by flexing the muscles in his residual limb. Photo (b) shows a new system that enables the patient to sense how hard he is grasping this bottle. ■

The Northwestern University Prosthetics Research Laboratory and Rehabilitation Engineering Program is dedicated to the improvement of prostheses and orthoses: http://www.repoc.northwestern.edu/
Rehabilitation tools and assistive devices may be researched at www.rehabtool.com ■

palsy or muscular dystrophy to learn to use the affected limbs as well as possible without the aid of any special equipment because using residual function alone will make the child more independent and may help prevent or retard physical deterioration. Moreover, it is often more efficient for a person to learn not to rely completely on a prosthesis or orthosis, as long as he or she can accomplish a task without it.

2. Spectacular technological developments often have very limited meaning for the immediate needs of the majority of individuals with physical disabilities. It may be years before expensive experimental equipment is tested adequately and marketed at a cost most people can afford, and a given device may be applicable only to a small group of individuals with an extremely rare condition (Moore, 1985). Even though a device may provide greater ability to participate in ordinary childhood activities, the current cost of some technological devices is clearly a barrier to their common use. Thus, for a long time to come, common standby prostheses, orthoses, and other equipment adapted to the needs of individuals will be the most practical devices.

We do not mean to downplay the importance of technological advances for people with physical disabilities. Advances in computer technology and applications have provided extraordinary help for many students with disabilities (DeFord, 1998; Lindsey, 2000). Our point here is that the greatest significance of a technological advance often lies in how it changes seemingly ordinary items or problems. For example, technological advances in metallurgy and plastics have led to the design of much more functional braces and wheelchairs. The heavy metal-and-leather leg braces formerly used by many children with cerebral palsy or other neurological disorders—cumbersome, difficult to apply, and not very helpful in preventing deformity or improving function—have been largely supplanted by braces constructed of thermoform plastic. Wheelchairs are being built of lightweight metals and plastics and redesigned to allow users to go places inaccessible to the typical wheelchair (see Figure 12.1). And an increasing number of computerized devices are improving the movement and communication abilities of people with disabilities.

The greatest problem today is not devising new or more sophisticated assistive technology but rather accurately evaluating children and youths to determine what would be most useful and then making that technology available. As Lynne Anderson-Inman has noted, "The potential for using technology is way beyond what's used in most schools" (quoted in DeFord, 1998, p. 30). Many children and youths who need prostheses or other assistive devices, such as computers, special vehicles, and self-help aids, are not carefully evaluated and provided with the most appropriate equipment (Bigge, 2001; Heller, Alberto, Forney, & Schwartzman, 1996; Lindsey, 2000).

(a)

(b)

FIGURE 12.1
Rehabilitation engineers are redesigning wheelchairs for use in off-the-street recreational and work environments: (a) chairs suitable for use at the beach or in other soft terrain; (b) a chair specially designed for racing.

Educational Considerations

Too often we think of people who have physical disabilities as being helpless or unable to learn. It is easy to lower our expectations for them because we know that they are indeed unable to do some things. We forget, though, that many people with physical disabilities can learn to do many or all the things most nondisabled persons do, although sometimes they must perform these tasks in different ways (e.g., a person who does not have the use of the hands may have to use the feet or mouth). Accepting the limitations imposed by physical disabilities without trying to see how much people can learn or how the environment can be changed to allow them to respond more effectively is an insulting and dehumanizing way of responding to physical differences.

Educating students with physical disabilities is not so much a matter of special instruction for children with disabilities as it is of educating the nondisabled population (Closs, 2000). People with physical disabilities solve many of their own problems, but their lives are often needlessly complicated because the nondisabled give no thought to what life is like for someone with specific physical limitations. Design adaptations in buildings,

This inclusive first grade classroom makes it possible for a young student with cerebral palsy to participate as fully as every other student. ■

Meeting the Needs of Students with Physical Disabilities

Adapted Physical Education

What Is Adapted Physical Education?

Adapted physical education (APE) is an instructional service, not a setting or placement. Students receive APE when their disability necessitates a physical education program different from their peers. The difference can be in the form of an alternative activity, an instructional modification or adaptation, or different criteria for success. APE can be part of an integrated program, for students with and without physical disabilities, or can be a stand-alone program for students with disabilities only.

Who Qualifies for Adapted Physical Education?

Any student with an IEP may be eligible for APE. IDEA requires "physical education services, specially designed if necessary, must be made available to every child with a disability receiving a free appropriate public education." Necessary adaptations are determined by IEP team members. Any student with gross motor skill deficits or limitations in strength, flexibility, or physical fitness should be considered for APE services.

Strategies for Making Accommodations

Strategies for making accommodations to general physical education classes include (Auxter, Pyfer, & Huettig, 2001):

- Reducing the size of the playing field through reducing the size of the soccer field, goal area, basketball court, or length of a race
- Changing the size of equipment by using larger or more colorful balls, increasing the size of the bat but decreasing weight, using larger rackets, lighter bows, or scoops for catching
- Reducing the playing area by adding more players to the field or court
- Modifying basic rules such as everyone plays seated, less mobile players get two or three bounces to get to the ball in tennis, rest periods or frequent substitutions are allowed, shorten the game, or partner activities
- Using specialized equipment such as a ramp or bumpers for bowling, a batting tee, or a sit-ski for skiing

The overarching aim for APE is for students to have access to activities that will support physical, recreational, and/or leisure goals. APE should take place in the least restrictive environment (LRE). Determining LRE involves consideration of safety as well as opportunities for meaningful participation. For many students the LRE will be the general education physical education class.

—By Kristin L. Sayeski

furniture, household appliances, and clothing can make it possible for someone with a physical disability to function as efficiently as a nondisabled person in a home, school, or community.

The objectives of educators and other professionals who work with children and youths with physical disabilities should include autonomy and self-advocacy (Bigge et al., 2001; Bullock & Mahon, 2000; Powers et al., 1996). Children with physical disabilities typically want to be self-sufficient, and they should be encouraged and taught the skills needed to take care of themselves to the maximum extent possible. This requires knowledge of the physical limitations created by the disability and sensitivity to the child's social and academic needs and perceptions—understanding of the environmental and psychological factors that affect classroom performance and behavior. The box on page 439 illustrates how adaptations can be made in the classroom to accommodate the needs of a student with a chronic health impairment in ways that encourage achievement, self-advocacy, and psychological growth.

INDIVIDUALIZED PLANNING

Students with complex physical disabilities typically require a wide array of related services as well as special education. The IEPs (individualized education programs) for such students tend to be particularly specific and detailed. The instructional goals and objectives often include seemingly minute steps, especially for young children with severe disabilities (see Bigge et al., 2001; Hanson, 1996; Heller, Alberto, Forney, & Schwartzman, 1996; Lerner et al., 1998). Many of the children under the age of three years who need special education and related services are children with physical disabilities. These children are required by law to have an **individualized family service plan (IFSP)** rather than an IEP. These plans must specify how the family will be involved in intervention as well as what other services will be provided. It is clear that parents of children with chronic health conditions may wish that their children did not exist, could be cured, or would improve significantly, although their expectations are more realistic (Wolman, Garwick, Kohrman, & Blum, 2001).

Individualized family service plan (IFSP).
A plan mandated by PL 99–457 to provide services for young children with disabilities (under three years of age) and their families; drawn up by professionals and parents; similar to an IEP for older children.

EDUCATIONAL PLACEMENT

Children with physical disabilities may be educated in any one of several settings, depending on the type and severity of the condition, the services available in the community, and the medical prognosis for the condition. If such children ordinarily attend regular public school classes but must be hospitalized for more than a few days, they may be included in a class in the hospital itself. If they must be confined to their homes for a time, a visiting or homebound teacher may provide tutoring until they can return to regular classes. In these cases—which usually involve children who have been in accidents or who have conditions that are not permanently and severely disabling—relatively minor, commonsense adjustments are required to continue the children's education and keep them from falling behind their classmates. At the other extreme—usually involving serious or chronic disabilities—the child may be taught for a time in a hospital school or a special public school class designed specifically for children with physical disabilities. Today, most are being integrated into the public schools because of advances in medical

Accommodations and Self-Advocacy in the Classroom

Tonya is 8 years old and has juvenile rheumatoid arthritis. The primary environmental factor affecting her performance is pain and the primary psychological factor affecting performance is self-advocacy. Due to her condition, Tonya is unable to sit for long periods of time without experiencing pain upon getting up from her chair to go to another class. Tonya would try to hide the fact that she was in pain and minimize her arm movement, which only worsened the condition. Her lack of participation in writing, art, and activities requiring arm movement was erroneously attributed to a motivational problem. The staff was given an inservice as to her condition; upon identifying she was in pain, a specific pain management plan was written. In the plan are given activities that she is to engage in at regular intervals that encourage her to use her affected joints, such as helping to get materials, passing papers out in class,

and sharpening pencils. This is programmed in such a way so that she is not singled out, but other students are performing the same tasks. If she is in pain, she is to move a special item to the corner of her desk. Tonya prefers this method to decrease drawing attention to herself. After Tonya signals the teacher with the special item, the teacher comes over and the treatment plan is followed. A specific time has been arranged for teaching Tonya any missed material. In the area of self-advocacy, a teacher certified in orthopedic impairments spends time with Tonya role playing situations to assist her in explaining her condition and her needs to significant others.

SOURCE: Heller, K.W., Alberto, P.A., & Meagher, T.M. (1996). The impact of physical impairments on academic performance. *Journal of Developmental and Physical Disabilities, 8,* p. 243. Reprinted with permission.

SUCCESS STORIES
Special Educators at Work

Roanoke, VA: **Danielle Durrance,** who has cerebral palsy, has received early intervention services and early childhood special education since she was nine months old. Her mother, Jennifer Durrance, communicates frequently with special educator **Leigh-Anne Williams** and special education administrator Beth Umbarger to ensure that Danielle receives appropriate instruction and related services in her county's newly initiated inclusive public preschool program.

Four-year-old Danielle Durrance peered out from under the wide brim of a witch's hat and giggled as her preschool classmates sang "Danielle has a hat. What do you think of that!" Danielle rocked to the rhythm of the music and smiled with delight as she passed the hat to the next child with the help of an instructional assistant. Danielle has cerebral palsy (CP), a neurological condition that limits her mobility, her speech, and her social interactions. She is the only child in the class who uses a wheelchair. Her walker, other adaptive equipment, and supplementary aids and supports are on hand to foster her participation and educational progress.

"We've started an inclusive preschool at Green Valley Elementary School this year," said Roanoke County Public Schools special education preschool coordinator Beth Umbarger. "We used to send our young children with disabilities to private preschools in order to meet IDEA's least restrictive environment requirements. Now we've opened a preschool class designed to serve both typically developing youngsters as well as most of our three- and four-year-olds with disabilities or developmental delays." According to early childhood special educator Leigh-Anne Williams, eight of the preschoolers require the individualized support of special education and related services. The other two students are developing typically. "This year, most of the children in the class have special needs. We hope to increase the proportion of children without disabilities in the future."

Leigh-Anne Williams's classroom is large, with generous space for movement, sand-play, computers, and specialized equipment. On the day before Halloween her classroom was alive with art and music. Sponge paintings of autumn leaves adorned the walls as her ten students dabbed white finger-painted ghosts and goblins on sheets of black paper. Danielle Durrance finished her creation at her standing table, a piece of adaptive equipment that provides her with vertical support for up to sixty minutes each day. While her classmates washed their hands, Danielle transferred to her wheelchair with the help of another one of the classroom's three instructional assistants. "We take turns lifting Danielle and positioning her to use her walker or the vestibular swing that hangs from the classroom ceiling," said Ms. Williams. "The instructional assistants also help Danielle with her personal hygiene and we keep a chart on the bathroom door to be sure we're sharing her physical support."

Danielle has attended the Green Valley Preschool Program since August 1999, two years before it started enrolling children without disabilities. According to evaluations using the Carolina Curriculum for Preschoolers with

treatment: new developments in bioengineering, allowing them greater mobility and functional movement; decreases in or removal of architectural barriers and transportation problems; and the movement toward public education for all children (Bigge et al., 2001; Closs, 2000; Heller, Alberto, Forney, & Schwartzman, 1996; Lerner et al., 1998).

Any placement has positive and negative features, and the best decision for a particular child requires weighing the pros and cons. Sometimes the benefits of a particular type of placement are either greatly exaggerated or almost completely dismissed. The box on page 442 is an excerpt from the personal story of Tanya Lyke, a girl with a very "aggressive" type of juvenile arthritis, which caused her a lot of physical pain and required extensive treatment. Her reflections on placement should give pause to any idea that all of the benefits are found in one type of placement or the other.

Special Needs, Danielle has progressed in all developmental areas, although her delays in cognition and social adaptation place her approximately one year to one and a half years behind her age peers. She remembers objects that have been hidden and understands concepts like empty/full and add one more. Socially, she follows directions, expresses enthusiasm for work or play, plays games with supervision, and enjoys being with other children. According to her IEP, Danielle's social interactions are limited by her physical delays. Danielle's fine and gross motor skills place her closer to two years behind her age peers. She receives occupational and physical therapy to enhance her manipulative and visual motor skills and to improve her mobility and endurance. She also receives speech-language therapy. Receptively, Danielle appears to understand many age-appropriate concepts and vocabulary, but she doesn't often initiate communication, nor does she imitate consistently.

Jennifer Durrance, who works in the school's cafeteria, describes her daughter as a happy and outgoing child. "She's curious about things, although her speech is somewhat hard to understand. She's very determined and really wants to walk. Sometimes she gets on her belly at home and slides across the floor." Mr. and Mrs. Durrance have worked closely with medical and educational professionals over the past four years. Danielle was delivered prematurely at thirty-four weeks' gestation when doctors found that her twin sister's heart had stopped beating. Although her twin was stillborn, Danielle survived the traumatic birth but experienced a lack of oxygen during delivery. She weighed only four pounds, four ounces at birth and spent eleven days in the hospital before her parents could bring her home. Mr. and Mrs. Durrance became suspicious that something was wrong when Danielle was four months old. "She couldn't roll over and find a toy that was near her in the crib. You know how babies look at their hands a lot? Well, she would mostly look at one hand; she kept her other hand down." At six months, Danielle was not sitting up and it was clear that her eyes were crossed. "The pediatrician was a little concerned but suggested that we wait until she turned nine months old," remembers Mrs. Durrance. "I wish he had been more aggressive. I wish he had said 'I think there might be a problem' so that we might have

understood what he was waiting to see. Just telling us to wait seemed so impersonal when our child's development was so very personal to us." When she was nine months old, development tests, including an MRI, confirmed that Danielle had CP and early intervention services began. A special education teacher came to the house to work with Danielle. In addition, her parents drove her to physical and occupational therapy several times a week, and made periodic visits to an ophthalmologist.

Jennifer Durrance credits Danielle's smooth transition from early intervention services to early childhood special education to clear communication among the many professionals involved in her care. "At the transition meeting, someone asked if I had a picture of Danielle with me. I really appreciated that. There was nothing in particular that caused me to feel stressed, but I think teachers should know that many parents feel very nervous at these meetings." Leigh-Anne Williams made Mrs. Durrance feel welcome at the Green Valley Preschool Program: "I felt she understood. She made the transition so nice. She wrote me notes daily because she knew that Danielle couldn't tell me about her day."

In spring, the IEP team will make decisions for Danielle's programming for the next school year. Together, her parents and her multidisciplinary team will consider if Danielle should start kindergarten with her age peers or whether she would benefit more from extended preschool support. Danielle has learned much from her early intervention services and her preschool special education. Jennifer Durrance has learned a great deal, too, and she has important things to say to teachers who might have a student like Danielle in their class.

First of all, *know the IEP,* especially when a child is served in the regular classroom. Second, *keep communication a priority.* Teachers need to make the time to know the parents of the child, too. Third, *seek information.* Know that parents are knowledgeable about their child's disability. Learn as much as you can about how the child's disability affects her life and her learning.

—*By Jean Crockett*

EDUCATIONAL GOALS AND CURRICULA

It is not possible to prescribe educational goals and curricula for children with physical disabilities as a group because their individual limitations vary so greatly. Even among children with the same condition, goals and curricula must be determined after assessing each child's intellectual, physical, sensory, and emotional characteristics. A physical disability, especially a severe and chronic one that limits mobility, may have two implications for education: (1) the child may be deprived of experiences that nondisabled children have, and (2) the child may find it impossible to manipulate educational materials and respond to educational tasks the way most children do. For example, a child with severe cerebral palsy cannot take part in most outdoor play activities and travel experiences and

Weighing the Issue of Placement: One Student's Perspective

There were gains and losses at special school. Some of the positives were small classes and individual tuition to catch up on work I missed when absent, on-site paramedical therapy and medical specialists who visited school, so saving time, energy and having to be off school. There was more specialist equipment available too, some of my own, some for the use of anyone who needed it at any time. The school was fully accessible. I suppose the other thing was that there was less feeling of isolation or difference in relation to being ill or disabled: that was the norm.

On the negative side, special schools then didn't really encourage assertiveness and pride about being disabled, there really was a prevailing medical model of "caring" that could result in childlike dependency. In mainstream

schools there is an understanding that kids will experiment with so-called bad habits such as smoking and sex, but staff were horribly shocked and dismayed when I was found smoking. . . . It is ironic that when I was in special school so many of us would have benefited from more liberal and "normal" approaches with opportunities for mainstreaming, but now, when so many of the children who attend special school seem to have far more complex and profound disabilities, they can't take advantage of the progress fully.

SOURCE: Hegarty, K., Lyke, T., Docherty, R., & Douglas, S. (2000). "I didn't ask to have this:" First-person accounts of young people. In A. Closs (Ed.), *The education of children with medical conditions* (p. 18). London: David Fulton.

may not be able to hold and turn pages in books, write, explore objects manually, or use a typewriter without special equipment.

For children with an impairment that is only physical, curriculum and educational goals should ordinarily be the same as for nondisabled children: reading, writing, arithmetic, and experiences designed to familiarize them with the world about them. In addition, special instruction may be needed in mobility skills, daily living skills, and occupational skills. That is, because of their physical impairments, these children may need special, individualized instruction in the use of mechanical devices that will help them perform tasks that are much simpler for those without disabilities. For children with other disabilities in addition to physical limitations, curricula will need to be further adapted (Bigge et al., 2001; Hanson, 1996; Heller, Alberto, Forney, & Schwartzman, 1996).

Educational goals for students with severe or profound disabilities must be related to their functioning in everyday community environments. Only recently have educators begun to address the problems of analyzing community tasks (e.g., crossing streets, using money, riding public transportation, greeting neighbors) and planning efficient instruction for individuals with severe disabilities. Efficient instruction in such skills requires that teaching occur in the community environment itself.

The range of educational objectives and curricula for children with physical disabilities is often extended beyond the objectives and curricula typically provided for other students in school. For example, very young children and those with severe neuromuscular problems may need objectives and curricula focusing on the most basic self-care skills (e.g., swallowing, chewing, self-feeding). Older students may need not only to explore possible careers in the way all students should, but to consider the special accommodations their physical limitations demand for successful performance as well (see Bigge et al., 2001).

Although all students may profit from a discussion of death and dying, education about these topics may be particularly important in classrooms in which a student has a terminal illness. Teachers should be direct and open in their discussion of death and dying. Death should not be a taboo subject, nor should teachers deny their own feelings or squelch the feelings of others. Confronted with the task of educating a child or youth with a terminal illness, teachers should seek available resources and turn to professionals in other disciplines for help (Heller, Alberto, Forney, & Schwartzman, 1996; Leaman, 2000).

Meeting the Needs of Students with Physical Disabilities

Integrating Physical and Occupational Therapy in General Education Settings

The majority of students with physical disabilities receive related services as a part of their educational program. Related services can include anything from speech-language pathology to counseling to transportation. Two common related services for students with physical disabilities are occupational and physical therapy. Researchers have found that the more integrated these types of services are into education settings, the more effective the outcomes (Karnish, Bruder, & Rainforth, 1995).

Physical and Occupational Therapy

Understanding the differences between physical and occupational therapy can be confusing. Yet a clear understanding of the skills that are supported through these therapies is fundamental for creating the necessary bridge between "out of class" therapy and integrated therapy that supports student learning.

Physical therapy addresses sensory and gross motor functions. Physical therapists can assist students by identifying optimal positions for various tasks, teach students how to move within the classroom and school environment, and develop students' movement, strength, and coordination. Occupational therapists provide support for daily living skills such as dressing, bathing, and toileting as well as fine motor skills (handling small objects, handwriting, oral-motor skills).

Classroom Implications

Despite the different focuses of the two groups, their services can overlap. As a classroom teacher, multidisciplinary collaboration among all services providers is a must. When planning for the integration of physical or occupational services in the classroom, the classroom teacher should consider:

- What are educationally relevant services versus medically relevant services? For example, an educationally relevant service would be to work on transfer and handling techniques with the teacher and parapro-

fessional to position a student for instruction. A medically relevant therapy would be strength building (Szabo, 2000).

- What are the educationally relevant IEP goals and how can therapy support progress towards those goals? For example, mobility independence, ability to operate assistive technology, improved posture, and improved upper extremity coordination are all therapy goals that directly relate to improved educational outcomes.

- What type of service is necessary—direct, indirect, or both? Direct services involve hands-on treatment provided directly by the therapist. Preferably, these treatments occur within the natural environment (classroom, playground, gym) where the skill is expected. Indirect services, on the other hand, involve consultation or monitoring support. Under a consultation model, the therapist makes recommendations for instructional modifications, activity enhancement, environmental modifications, adaptation of materials, or schedule alterations. It may even include training the classroom teacher in ways to provide direct services. Monitoring involves periodic evaluations of student progress and related training for team members. A combination of direct and indirect services provides both direct services for certain goals or skills and consultation support for others.

- Is peer support appropriate? As students become more skilled, peer support can be solicited. This reduces the dependence a student has on any one individual and encourages interdependence—an important skill as students get older.

By working with therapists to identify ways to support therapy within the classroom, teachers learn ways to reduce the physical challenges students can encounter within general education settings, while fostering the development of necessary physical and occupational skills.

—By Kristin L. Sayeski

LINKS WITH OTHER DISCIPLINES

In the opening pages of this chapter we made two points: (1) children with physical disabilities have medical problems, and (2) interdisciplinary cooperation is necessary in their education. It is important for the teacher to know what other disciplines are involved in the child's care and treatment and to be able to communicate with professionals in these areas about the child's physical, emotional, and educational development.

It goes almost without saying that knowing the child's medical status is crucial. Many children with physical disabilities will need the services of a physical therapist and/or occupational therapist. Both can give valuable suggestions about helping the child use his or her physical abilities to the greatest possible extent, continuing therapeutic management in the classroom, and encouraging independence and good work habits. The teacher should be particularly concerned about how to handle and position the child so that the risk of further physical disability will be minimized and independent movement and manipulation of educational materials can be most efficiently learned.

Specialists in prosthetics and orthotics design and build artificial limbs, braces, and other devices that help individuals who are physically disabled function more conventionally. By conferring with such specialists, the teacher will get a better grasp of the function and operation of a child's prosthesis or orthosis and understand what the child can and cannot be expected to do.

Social workers and psychologists are the professionals with whom most teachers are quite familiar. Cooperation with them may be particularly important in the case of a child with a physical disability. Work with the child's family and community agencies is often necessary to prevent lapses in treatment. The child may also be particularly susceptible to psychological stress, so the school psychologist may need to be consulted to obtain an accurate assessment of intellectual potential.

MAKING IT WORK

Collaboration and Co-Teaching for Students with Physical Disabilities

"But I'm not a nurse!"

Students with physical disabilities often require complex systems of care, including services from health care professionals, related service personnel, and special educators. It is easy for everyone to forget about the students' cognitive and social needs because of the day-to-day physical needs. Even though a student with physical disabilities may have a wide range of services, the least restrictive environment for them may be the general education classroom. It is in this situation that collaboration with a special educator is important for the general education teacher to understand and meet the needs of these students.

What Does It Mean to Be a Teacher of Students with Physical Disabilities?

Special educators who work with students with physical disabilities must have skills related to learning and instruction, as well as skills in determining appropriate assistive technology devices, positioning, and socialization. According to the Council for Exceptional Children (2001), they should be adept at:

1. Using adaptations and assistive technology to provide individuals with physical and health disabilities full participation and access to the general curriculum
2. Using techniques of physical management to ensure participation in academic and social environments
3. Integrating an individual's health care plan into daily programming
4. Participating in the selection and implementation of augmentative or alternative communication systems

These skills require a broad range of training for special educators, including medical management and extensive collaboration with health care providers and families. With this knowledge, special educators can collaborate with general

Speech-language therapists are often called on to work with children with physical disabilities, especially those with cerebral palsy. The teacher will want advice from the speech-language therapist on how to maximize the child's learning of speech and language.

Individuals of all ages need access to play and recreation, regardless of their physical abilities. Any adequate program for children or youths with physical disabilities will provide toys, games, and physical exercise to stimulate, amuse, and teach recreation skills and provide the youngster with options for productive leisure (Bullock & Mahon, 2000). Physical education that is adapted to the abilities and disabilities of students is an important part of every sound school program.

Early Intervention

All who work with young children with physical disabilities have two concerns: (1) early identification and intervention, and (2) development of communication (see Bigge et al., 2001; Hanson, 1996). Identifying signs of developmental delay so intervention can begin as early as possible is important in preventing further disabilities that can result from lack of teaching and proper care. Early intervention is also important for maximizing the outcome of therapy. Communication skills are difficult for some children with physical disabilities to learn, and they are one of the critical objectives of any preschool program (see Chapter 8).

Probably the first and most pervasive concerns of teachers of young children with physical disabilities, in addition to communication, should be handling and positioning. Handling refers to how the child is picked up, carried, held, and assisted; positioning refers to providing support for the child's body and arranging instructional or play

education teachers to adjust instruction, change the physical environment of the classroom, and communicate successfully with students.

Successful Strategies for Co-Teaching

Jo is a special education teacher of five- and six-year-olds with cerebral palsy and spina bifida. Charlotte is a general education teacher with a group of twenty-eight kindergarten-aged students, some of whom had never had any school experiences. They describe their collaboration experiences.

Jo: We combined the children into two groups. Each group was made up of half my children and half of Charlotte's children. We'd occasionally put the two groups together. I became an expert in a certain content area. I taught it to two groups and Charlotte did the same.

Charlotte: Our classes are scheduled for music together because of our collaboration. We had a music teacher come in who taught music to both classes as a large group; however, Jo and I did stay in the classroom to facilitate management needs because it was such a large group for one teacher to handle. In fact, we had to teach the music teacher some management ideas.

It was a good experience for her (the music teacher); she was able to see how you can work with a range and variety of children. It's important to find someone who has a similar philosophy and treats children the way you do, but it also must be someone you can get along with, who has the same tolerance that you do. Had we not been friendly, liked each other, and respected the way each other did things, we would not have been successful. We have seen collaborations that were not as successful as ours because they did not develop out of commonalities.

Jo: One of the most demanding things about our collaboration was keeping up with the kids, keeping them on pace, and trying to make it valuable for them educationally. As much as I want this very worthwhile social experience for my special-needs kids, am I giving them the multisensory nuts-and-bolts special education that they need? I constantly have to try and strike a balance between the social needs of the children and the intense requirements of their special needs.

Charlotte: The most demanding thing about our collaboration was not working together ourselves, but effectively meeting the needs of the children. That's really the most demanding thing: living up to them.

—By Margaret P. Weiss

People with physical disabilities can learn to do many of the things most nondisabled persons do, although sometimes they must perform these tasks in different ways. Educating students with physical disabilities is often as much a matter of educating the nondisabled population of this fact. ■

materials in certain ways. Proper handling makes the child more comfortable and receptive to education. Proper positioning maximizes physical efficiency and ability to manipulate materials; it also inhibits undesirable motor responses while promoting desired growth and motor patterns (Bigge et al., 2001; Heller, Alberto, Forney, & Schwartzman, 1996; Kurtz et al., 1996).

What constitutes proper positioning for one child may not be appropriate for another. It is important that teachers of children who are physically disabled be aware of some general principles of positioning and handling; in addition, they must work closely with physical therapists and physicians so that each child's particular needs are met. The physical problems that most often require special handling and positioning involve muscle tone. Some children have **spastic** muscles—that is, chronic increased muscle tone. As a result, their limbs may be either flexed or extended all the time. If nothing is done to counteract the effects of the chronic imbalance of muscle tone, the child develops **contractures,** permanent shortening of muscles and connective tissues that results in deformity and further disability. Other children have **athetosis,** or fluctuating muscle tone, that results in almost constant uncontrolled movement. If these movements are not somehow restrained, the child cannot accomplish many motor tasks successfully. Still other children have muscles that are **hypotonic.** These children appear floppy, as their muscles are flaccid and weak. The hypotonia may prevent them from learning to hold up their heads or to sit or stand. All these muscle tone problems can occur together in the same child, they can occur with varying degrees of severity, and they can affect various parts of the body differently.

The teacher of young children with physical disabilities must know how to teach gross motor responses—such as head control, rolling over, sitting, standing, and walking—and understand how abnormal reflexes that may be a part of developmental disabilities may interfere with learning basic motor skills. If the child has severe neurological and motor impairments, the teacher may need to begin by focusing on teaching the child to eat (e.g., how to chew and swallow) and to make the oral movements required for speech (Bigge et al., 2001; Heller, Alberto, Forney, & Schwartzman, 1996). Fine motor skills, such as pointing, reaching, grasping, and releasing, may be critically important. These motor skills are best taught in the context of daily lessons that involve self-help and communication. That is, motor skills should not be taught in isolation but as part of daily living and learning activities that will increase the child's communication, independence, creativity, motivation, and future learning.

Motor and communication skills necessary for daily living are not the only areas in which the teacher must provide instruction. Learning social responsiveness, appropriate social initiation, how to play with others, and problem solving, for example, are important goals for which the teacher must develop instructional strategies. Some children who are well beyond the typical preschooler's age may still be functioning at a very early developmental level. Consequently, the muscle tone, posture, and movement problems discussed here (as well as the approach to teaching just described) apply to some older students too.

Transition to Adulthood

Transition involves a turning point, a change from one situation or environment to another. When special educators speak of transition, they typically refer to change from school to work or from adolescence to adulthood. For children with physical disabilities, however, transition is perhaps a more pervasive concern than it is for children with other disabilities. It may involve discharge from intensive care or transition from hospital to home at any age. In fact, transition begins for some newborns immediately after they have been treated with sophisticated medical procedures. Nevertheless, we focus here on the transition concerns of adolescents and young adults with physical disabilities. Clearly, transition planning for many students with physical disabilities, including those supported by medical technology, is inadequate (Morningstar, Turnbull, Lattin, Umbarger, Reichard, & Moberly, 2001).

Two areas of concern for transition stand out clearly for adolescents and young adults with physical disabilities: careers and sociosexuality. Adolescents begin contemplating and experimenting with jobs, social relations, and sexuality in direct and serious ways. For the adolescent with a physical disability, these questions and trial behaviors are often especially perplexing, not just to themselves but to their families as well: Can I get and hold a satisfying job? Can I become independent? Will I have close and lasting friendships? Will anyone find me physically attractive? How can I gratify my sexual needs? Ordinary adolescents have a hard time coming to grips with these questions and the developmental tasks they imply; adolescents with physical disabilities often have an even harder time.

As we pointed out in discussing psychological characteristics, there is no formula for predicting the emotional or behavioral problems a person with a given physical disability will have. Much depends on the management and training the person has received and continues to receive as an adolescent and as an adult. Bottos et al. provide the following caution about interventions for cerebral palsy: "Services for individuals with CP should be planned keeping in mind an entire life perspective rather than just the child-focused approach. Reduced contact when children grow up often results in a general deterioration of the quality of life of adults with disabilities and their careers" (2001, p. 526). Andersson and Mattsson (2001) drive the point home. In their study, 35 percent of adults with CP reported decreased walking ability, and 9 percent had stopped walking altogether.

CHOOSING A CAREER

For the adolescent or young adult with physical disabilities, career considerations are extremely important (Bigge et al., 2001; Johnson, 1996; Ward, 1996). In working out an occupational goal, it is vital to realistically appraise the individual's specific abilities and disabilities and to assess motivation carefully. Postsecondary education must be considered in light of the individual's interests, strengths, demands, and accessibility. Some disabilities clearly rule out certain occupational choices. With other disabilities, high motivation and full use of residual function may make it possible to achieve unusual professional status.

One of the greatest problems in dealing with adolescents who have physical disabilities is helping them attain a realistic employment outlook. Intelligence, emotional characteristics, motivation, and work habits must be assessed at least as carefully as physical limitations. Furthermore, the availability of jobs and the demands of certain occupations must be taken into account. The child who has moderate mental retardation and severe spastic quadriplegia, for instance, is highly unlikely to have a career as a lawyer, a laboratory technician, or a clerk-typist. But what of one who has severe spastic quadriplegia and a bright mind? Such a person may well overcome both the physical limitation and the associated social stigma and be successful in a wide variety of fields in which the work is more mental than physical.

There are no simple conclusions regarding the occupational outlook for students with physical disabilities. Those with mild or transitory disabling conditions may not be affected at all in their occupational choices. Yet some with relatively mild physical disabilities may be unemployed or even unemployable because of inappropriate social and emotional behavior or poor work habits; they may need vocational rehabilitation training to function even in a vocation with limited demands. Some people with severe physical

Spastic.
A term describing a sudden, involuntary contraction of muscles that makes accurate, voluntary movement difficult.

Contractures.
Permanent shortenings of muscles and connective tissues and consequent distortion of bones and/or posture because of neurological damage.

Athetosis.
A type of cerebral palsy that involves fluctuating muscle tone and almost constant uncontrolled movement.

Hypotonic.
A term describing low muscle tone that sometimes occurs as a result of cerebral palsy.

A wide variety of Web sites provide ideas and guidance for independent living. These include:

Canine Companions for Independence, a nonprofit organization providing assistance dogs: www.caninecompanions.org

A collection of computer related products and services available to assist persons with disabilities: www.closingthegap.com

The Independent Living Research Utilization Center: www.ilru.org

The Institute on Independent Living: www.independentliving.org ■

disabilities are able to use their intelligence, social skills, and residual physical abilities to the fullest and become competitive employees (or employers) in demanding occupations.

The outlook for employment of students with physical or multiple and severe disabilities has been improved dramatically by legislation and research and demonstration projects. As mentioned in Chapter 1, the Americans with Disabilities Act (ADA) of 1990 requires that reasonable accommodations be made to create equal employment opportunities for people with disabilities. More accessible transportation and buildings, increased skill in using technology to allow people to accomplish tasks at work, and greater commitment to preparing people with disabilities for work are resulting in more personal independence, economic self-sufficiency, and social acceptance—which benefit not only people with disabilities but the economy and society as well.

We now recognize that preparing for work begins in childhood. Long before adolescence, children—including those with physical disabilities—need to be taught about and to explore various careers. They need to be thinking about what they like to do, as well as what they are particularly good at, and the demands and rewards of various kinds of jobs. The objective should be to help students select training and enter a career that makes maximum use of their abilities in ways that they find personally gratifying.

Supported employment.
A method of integrating people with disabilities who cannot work independently into competitive employment; includes use of an employment specialist, or job coach, who helps the person with a disability function on the job.

Supported employment for people with severe disabilities is a relatively new concept that is being adopted widely. In this approach, a person with a severe disability works in a regular work setting. He or she becomes a regular employee, performs a valued function in the same workplace as nondisabled employees, and receives fair remuneration. Training and continued support are necessary; hence the term *supported* employment.

New technologies, especially in computing and other electronic devices, offer great promise for enabling students with physical disabilities to achieve personal independence, to acquire education and training that will make them employable, and to find employment. Following is one example:

> Last year Justin Dolan, an 18-year-old junior at Falls Church High School, began using a computer that takes dictation, in addition to using an AlphaSmart word processor for class notes. Dolan, who has cerebral palsy and is in a wheelchair, has so improved his ability to keep up with classwork that he's thinking about going to college. "I have a better shot than I did three or four years ago," he said. (DeFord, 1998, p. 30)

In some cases, the technology is readily available and educators need only to become aware of the software (e.g., software that allows the functions of keys to be altered), find ways in which keystrokes can be saved through subprogramming routines (e.g., macro or find-and-replace features in word processing), or provide substitutions for physical manipulation of materials (e.g., computer graphics programs as substitutes for paper paste-ups or model construction) (Heller, Alberto, Forney, & Schwartzman, 1996; Lindsey, 2000).

Sometimes an individual's ability to use standard equipment is greatly enhanced by a simple modification such as orientation or location. Figure 12.2 shows how simply placing a keyboard in a vertical position over a monitor may enhance the ability of someone who uses a headstick to use a computer. A headstick is an adaptive device that allows someone who cannot use hands or feet, but who has control of neck muscles, to use a computer or accomplish other tasks. Teachers must always look for simple, virtually cost-free ways to facilitate the performance of students with disabilities—to prevent an environment designed for people without disabilities from handicapping those who must do things a different way. Overlooking the seemingly obvious is perhaps the way in which we most frequently handicap people with disabilities.

SOCIOSEXUALITY

Until fairly recently, physical disabilities were assumed to cancel human sexuality (see Edmonson, 1988). People who were not typical physically, especially if they had limited

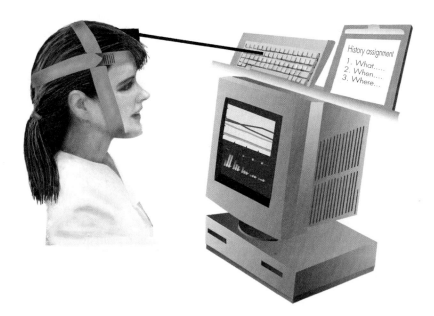

FIGURE 12.2

A keyboard positioned for efficient use with a headstick.

SOURCE: Teaching individuals with physical and multiple disabilities, 3rd ed. by Bigge, June L. Copyright © 1991, p. 486. Reprinted by permission of Pearson Education, Inc., Upper Saddle River, New Jersey.

mobility, were thought of as having no sex appeal for anyone and as having little or no ability or right to function sexually.

Fortunately, attitudes and experiences are changing. It is now recognized that people with disabilities have a right to family life education, including sex education, and to a full range of human relationships, including appropriate sexual expression. Sociosexual education for students with physical disabilities, as with such education for all other children and youths, should begin early, continue through adulthood, and include information about the structures and functions of the body, human relationships and responsibilities, and alternative modes of sexual gratification.

Youths with physical disabilities need to experience close friendships and warm physical contact that is not sexually intimate. But it is neither realistic nor fair to expect people with physical disabilities to keep all their relationships platonic or to limit themselves to fantasy. Most physical disability, even if severe, does not in itself kill sexual desire or prevent sexual gratification, nor does it preclude marriage and children. The purpose of special education and rehabilitation is to make exceptional individuals' lives as full and complete as possible. In the case of youths with physical disabilities, this may involve teaching or providing alternative means of sexual stimulation and accepting sexual practices and relationships that are different from the norm. With sensitive education and rehabilitation, satisfying sociosexual expression can be achieved by all but a small minority.

Summary

Children with physical disabilities have physical limitations or health problems that interfere with school attendance or learning to such an extent that special services, training, equipment, materials, or facilities are required. They may have disabilities they are born with (congenital disabilities) or acquire disabilities through accident or disease. Their disabilities may be acute or chronic, episodic or progressive. These children may also have other disabilities, such as mental retardation and emotional or behavioral disorders, or they may have special gifts or talents. The medical nature of the problem highlights the need for interdisciplinary cooperation in special education.

Less than 0.5 percent of the child population in the United States receives special education and related services for physical disabilities. About half of these students have multiple disabilities, about one-fourth have orthopedic impairments, and about a fourth have chronic health problems. Because of advances in medical technology, more children with severe disabilities are surviving and many more are living with disease or injury with mild impairments, such as hyperactivity and learning disabilities. Three major categories of physical disabilities are (1) neuromotor impairments, (2) orthopedic and musculoskeletal disorders, and (3) other conditions affecting health or physical ability.

Individuals with neuromotor impairments have experienced damage to the brain that affects their ability to move parts of the body. The injury may occur prior to, during, or after birth. The causes of neuromotor impairments include trauma, infections, diseases, hypoxia, poisoning, congenital malformations, and child abuse. Neurological impairments include cerebral palsy (CP), a condition characterized by paralysis, weakness, uncoordination, and/or other motor dysfunction. It is nonprogressive brain damage that occurs before or during birth or in early childhood. Classification of CP is generally made according to the limbs involved and the type of motor disability. The educational problems associated with CP are varied because of the multiplicity of symptoms; a careful clinical appraisal must be made of each individual to determine the type of special education needed.

Seizures are caused by abnormal discharges of electrical energy in the brain. Recurrent seizures are referred to as epilepsy. Most people with seizure disorders are able to function normally, except when having seizures. Intelligence is not directly affected by a seizure disorder, so educational procedures consist chiefly of attaining knowledge of the disorder and how to manage seizures, as well as a commitment to help dispel the ignorance and fear connected with seizures. Spina bifida is a congenital midline defect resulting from failure of the bony spinal column to close completely during fetal development. The resulting damage to the nerves generally causes paralysis and lack of sensation below the site of the defect. The cause of spina bifida is not known. Educational implications of spina bifida are determined by the extent of the paralysis and medical complications as well as the child's cognitive and behavioral characteristics.

Some physical disabilities are orthopedic or musculoskeletal disorders, in which there are defects or diseases of the muscles or bones. Children with such disabilities have a range of difficulties in walking, standing, sitting, or using their hands. Muscular dystrophy is a degenerative disease causing a progressive weakening and wasting away of muscle tissues. Juvenile rheumatoid arthritis is a disease that causes acute inflammation around the joints and may cause chronic pain and other complications. These and other musculoskeletal conditions do not cause lowered intelligence, so educational considerations include overcoming

the child's limited mobility so that she or he can continue learning in as normal a way as possible.

A wide variety of other conditions may affect health and physical ability, including congenital malformations, diseases, and injuries. Fetal alcohol syndrome (FAS), which is now one of the most common causes of malformation and mental retardation, is caused by the mother's abuse of alcohol during pregnancy. Although maternal substance abuse during pregnancy may have serious consequences for the fetus, the near hysteria of the 1980s about the irreversible effects of crack cocaine was not justified. Accidents that result in neurological impairment, disfigurement, or amputation are an important cause of physical disabilities among children and youths. AIDS, a life-threatening viral infection, also involves neurological complications such as mental retardation, seizures, cerebral palsy, and emotional or behavioral disorders.

Children who are medically fragile or dependent on ventilators are being returned home from hospitals in increasing numbers. Many of these children are returning to public schools. Careful consideration of the mainstreaming of these children is required.

Many physical disabilities—including those that result from accidents, substance use, and poisoning—are fully preventable. Preventing adolescent pregnancies also would reduce the number of children born with disabilities. Teenage mothers are more likely than older women to give birth to premature or low-birthweight babies, and the babies of teens will remain at risk for developing a range of physical and psychological problems when they reach school age. Abused and neglected children represent a large number of those with physical disabilities. Children who already have disabilities are more likely to be abused than those without disabilities. Teachers must be especially alert to signs of possible child abuse and neglect, and must be aware of reporting procedures in their states.

As a group, children with physical disabilities represent the total range of impairment, and their behavioral and psychological characteristics vary greatly. The necessity for hospitalization, bed rest, prosthetic devices, and so on means that their academic achievement depends on individual circumstances, motivation, and the caliber of care received both at home and at school. A child with a physical disability may be deprived of educationally relevant experiences or not be able to learn to manipulate educational materials and respond to educational tasks the way most children do.

There does not appear to be a certain personality type associated with any particular physical disability. The reactions of the public, family, peers, and educational personnel—as well as the child's own reactions to the disability—are all closely interwoven in the determination of his or her personality, motivation, and progress. Given ample opportunity to develop educationally, socially, and emotionally in as normal a fashion as possible, many children with physical disabilities are able to make healthy adjustments to their impairments.

Many individuals with physical disabilities use prosthetics, orthotics, and other adaptive devices to improve functioning. A *prosthesis* replaces a missing body part. An *orthosis* is a device that enhances the partial function of a body part. An *adaptive device* aids a person's daily activity. Important considerations in choosing prostheses, orthoses, and adaptive devices are simplicity, reliability, and the use of residual function. Advances in technology are providing more useful devices for those with physical disabilities. The greatest problem is accurately evaluating needs and making existing technology available.

Education for students with physical disabilities must focus on making the most of their assets. The student's individual characteristics (intellectual, sensory, physical, and emotional) must be considered when developing educational plans. Plans for young children must include services for the family.

Increasingly, students with physical disabilities are being placed in regular classrooms. The problem of educating students with physical disabilities is often a problem of educating students *without* disabilities about the needs of people with disabilities. Along with scholastic education, the child may need special assistance in daily living, mobility, and occupational skills. Education should serve the goals of autonomy and self-advocacy. The major considerations are to help each child become as independent and self-sufficient in daily activities as possible, to provide basic academic skills, and to prepare her or him for advanced education and work. Links with other disciplines are crucial.

Besides early identification and intervention to develop communication, handling and positioning are important considerations. Motor skills must be taught as part of daily lessons in self-help and communication, and intervention must be continued in adolescence and adulthood to make sure that abilities are not lost.

Career choice and sociosexuality are two primary concerns of youths with physical disabilities. Career considerations must include careful evaluation of the young person's intellectual, emotional, and motivational characteristics as well as physical capabilities. Young people with physical disabilities have the right to the social relationships and modes of sexual expression afforded others in society.

Ruby Pearl

Ruby Shoes, Acrylic on rag paper. 22 × 30 in.

Ms. Pearl, who was born in 1949 in Weymouth, Massachusetts, is a very popular self-taught artist. She has survived homelessness and now lives in her dream apartment in an historic building in Brookline. She is dedicated to portraying the lives of women through her work.

Learners with Special Gifts and Talents

I think Jim Gillis was a much more remarkable person than his family and his intimates ever suspected. He had a bright and smart imagination and it was of the kind that turns out impromptu work and does it well, does it with easy facility and without previous preparation, just builds a story as it goes along, careless of whither it is proceeding, enjoying each fresh fancy as it flashes from the brain and caring not at all whether the story shall ever end brilliantly and satisfactorily or shan't end at all. Jim was born a humorist and a very competent one. When I remember how felicitous were his untrained efforts, I feel a conviction that he would have been a star performer if he had been discovered and had been subjected to a few years of training with a pen. A genius is not very likely to ever discover himself; neither is he very likely to be discovered by his intimates; they are so close to him that he is out of focus to them and they can't get at his proportions; they cannot perceive that there is any considerable difference between his bulk and their own. They can't get a perspective on him and it is only by a perspective that the difference between him and the rest of their limited circle can be perceived.

The Autobiography of Mark Twain

People who have special gifts, or at least have the potential for gifted performance, can go through life unrecognized. As Mark Twain pointed out (see p. 453), they may seem unremarkable to their closest associates. Sometimes children and youths with special talents or gifts are not discovered because their families and intimates simply place no particular value on their special abilities. And sometimes they are not recognized because they are not given the necessary opportunities or training. Especially in the case of individuals who are poor or members of minority groups, children with extraordinary gifts or talents may be deprived of chances to demonstrate and develop their potential. How many more outstanding artists and scientists would we have if every talented child had the opportunity and the training necessary to develop his or her talents to the fullest possible extent? There is no way of knowing, but it is safe to say we would have more.

Unlike mental retardation and other disabling conditions, giftedness is something to be fostered deliberately. Yet giftedness is not something a child can show without risk of stigma and rejection. Many people have a low level of tolerance for those who eclipse the ordinary individual in some area of achievement. A child who achieves far beyond the level of her or his average peers may be subject to criticism or social isolation by other children or their parents (Coleman & Cross, 2000; Cross, 1997; Swiatek, 1998). Had Jim Gillis been discovered, given a few years of training with a pen, and become a gifted writer, it is possible that some of his intimates would have found his giftedness hard to accept.*

Some of the problems presented by giftedness parallel those presented by the disabling conditions discussed in the other chapters of this book. For instance, the definition and identification of children with special gifts or talents involve the same sort of difficulties that exist in the case of children with mental retardation or emotional or behavioral disorders. But there is an underlying philosophical question regarding giftedness that makes us think differently about this exceptionality: Most of us feel a moral obligation to help those who are at some disadvantage compared to the average person, who have a difference that prevents them from achieving ordinary levels of competence unless they are given special help. But in the case of a person who is has special gifts, we may wonder about our moral obligation to help someone who is already accelerated become even better, to distinguish himself or herself further by fulfilling the highest promise of his or her extraordinary resources. It is on this issue—the desirability or necessity of helping the most high achieving children become even better—that special education for students who have special gifts or talents is likely to founder (Gallagher, 2000b). Today, the emphasis is on programs to develop the talents of *all* students, with less special attention to those who may be identified as gifted or talented. As some researchers have noted, this trend toward downplaying giftedness may not be very wise (Gallagher, 2000b).

Definition

Children with special gifts excel in some way compared to other children of the same age. Beyond this almost meaningless statement, however, there is little agreement about how giftedness should be defined. Local school systems often have widely differing practices regarding the education of students with special gifts or talents, as "gifted" has no clear-cut definition (Mathews, 1998; Ziegler & Heller, 2000).

The disagreements about definition are due primarily to differences of opinion regarding the following questions:

1. *In what ways do children with a special gift or talent excel?* Do they excel in general intelligence, insight, creativity, special talents, and achievements in academic

*We are indebted to Dr. Carolyn M. Callahan of the University of Virginia for her invaluable assistance in preparing this chapter.

MISCONCEPTIONS ABOUT
Learners with Special Gifts or Talents

MYTH People with special intellectual gifts are physically weak, socially inept, narrow in interests, and prone to emotional instability and early decline.

FACT There are wide individual variations, and most individuals with special intellectual gifts are healthy, well adjusted, socially attractive, and morally responsible.

MYTH Those who have special gifts or talents are in a sense superhuman.

FACT People with special gifts or talents are not superhuman; rather, they are human beings with extraordinary gifts in particular areas. And like everyone else, they may have particular faults.

MYTH Children with special gifts or talents are usually bored with school and antagonistic toward those who are responsible for their education.

FACT Most children with special gifts like school and adjust well to their peers and teachers, although some do not like school and have social or emotional problems.

MYTH People with special gifts or talents tend to be mentally unstable.

FACT Those with special gifts or talents are about as likely to be well adjusted and emotionally healthy as those who do not have such gifts.

MYTH We know that 3 to 5 percent of the population has special gifts or talents.

FACT The percentage of the population that is found to have special gifts or talents depends on the definition of *giftedness* used. Some definitions include only 1 or 2 percent of the population; others, over 20 percent.

MYTH Giftedness is a stable trait, always consistently evident in all periods of a person's life.

FACT Some of the remarkable talents and productivity of people with special gifts develop early and continue throughout life; in other cases, a person's gifts or talents are not noticed until adulthood. Occasionally, a child who shows outstanding ability becomes a nondescript adult.

MYTH People who have special gifts do everything well.

FACT Some people characterized as having a special gift have superior abilities of many kinds; others have clearly superior talents in only one area.

MYTH A person has special intellectual gifts if he or she scores above a certain level on intelligence tests.

FACT IQ is only one indication of one kind of giftedness. Creativity and high motivation are as important as indications as general intelligence. Gifts or talents in some areas, such as the visual and performing arts, are not assessed by IQ tests.

MYTH Students who have a true gift or talent for something will excel without special education. They need only the incentives and instruction that are appropriate for all students.

FACT Some children with special gifts or talents will perform at a remarkably high level without special education of any kind, and some will make outstanding contributions even in the face of great obstacles to their achievement. But most will not come close to achieving at a level commensurate with their potential unless their talents are deliberately fostered by instruction that is appropriate for their advanced abilities.

subjects or in a valued line of work, moral judgment, or some combination of such factors? Perhaps nearly everyone is gifted in some way or other. What kind of giftedness is most important? What kind of giftedness should be encouraged?

2. *How is giftedness measured?* Is it measured by standardized tests of aptitude and achievement, teacher judgments, past performance in school or everyday life, or by some other means? If it is measured in one particular way, some individuals will be overlooked. If past performance is the test, giftedness is being defined after the fact. What measurement techniques are valid and reliable? What measurements will identify those children who have the potential to develop special gifts or talents?

3. *To what degree must a child excel to be considered to have a special gift or talent?* Must the child do better than 50 percent, 80 percent, 90 percent, or 99 percent of the comparison group? The number of individuals with special gifts will vary depending on the criterion (or criteria) for giftedness. What percentage of the population should be considered to have special gifts?

4. *Who should make up the comparison group?* Should it be every child of the same chronological age, the other children in the child's school, all children of the same ethnic or racial origin, or some other grouping? Almost everyone is the brightest or most capable in some group. What group should set the standard?

5. *Why should students with special gifts be identified?* What social or cultural good is expected to come from their identification? Is it important to meet individual students' educational needs? Are national economic or security issues at stake? Does identifying these individuals maintain an elite group or social power? By providing special educational opportunities for these students, will others reap personal or social benefits? What criteria will be used to judge whether identifying students with special gifts or talents pays off?

You may have concluded already that giftedness or talentedness, just like mental retardation, is whatever we choose to make it. Someone can be considered gifted (or retarded) one day and not the next, simply because an arbitrary definition has been changed. There is no inherent rightness or wrongness in the definitions professionals use. Some definitions may be more logical, more precise, or more useful than others, but we are still unable to say they are more correct in some absolute sense. We have to struggle with the concepts of gift and talent and the reasons for identifying individuals with these gifts or talents before we can make any decisions about definition (Borland, 1997; Callahan, 1997; Gallagher, 2000a, 2000b). Our definition of giftedness will be shaped, to a large extent, by what our culture believes is most useful or necessary for its survival. Giftedness is invented, not discovered (Heller, Monks, Sternberg, & Subotnik, 2000; Howley, Howley, & Pendarvis, 1995).

Even the terminology of giftedness can be rather confusing. Besides the word *gifted*, a variety of other terms have been used to describe individuals who are superior in some way: *talented, creative, insightful, genius,* and *precocious,* for example.

- **Precocity** refers to remarkable early development. Many children with extraordinary gifts show precocity in particular areas of development, such as language, music, or mathematical ability, and the rate of intellectual development of all children with special intellectual gifts exceeds that for typically developing children.
- **Insight** may be defined as separating relevant from irrelevant information, finding novel and useful ways of combining relevant bits of information, or relating new and old information in a novel and productive way.
- **Genius** has sometimes been used to indicate a particular aptitude or capacity in any area. More often, it has been used to indicate extremely rare intellectual powers (often assumed to be indicated by IQ) or creativity.
- **Creativity** refers to the ability to express novel and useful ideas, to sense and elucidate novel and important relationships, and to ask previously unthought of, but crucial, questions.

Precocity.
Remarkable early development.

Insight.
The ability to separate and/or combine various pieces of information in new, creative, and useful ways.

Genius.
A word sometimes used to indicate a particular aptitude or capacity in any area; rare intellectual powers.

Creativity.
The ability to express novel and useful ideas, to sense and elucidate new and important relationships, and to ask previously unthought-of but crucial questions.

- **Talent** ordinarily has been used to indicate a special ability, aptitude, or accomplishment.
- **Giftedness,** as we use the term in this chapter, refers to cognitive (intellectual) superiority (not necessarily of genius caliber), creativity, and motivation in combination and of sufficient magnitude to set the child apart from the vast majority of age-mates and make it possible for her or him to contribute something of particular value to society.

The lack of consensus about what *giftedness* means poses enormous problems for government definitions. No federal law requires special education for students with special gifts or talents as it does for students with disabilities, although federal legislation encourages states to develop programs for such students and support research. Most states have mandatory programs for students with special gifts or talents. The most common elements of state definitions are (1) general intellectual ability, (2) specific academic aptitude, (3) creative thinking ability, (4) advanced ability in the fine arts and performing arts, and (5) leadership ability.

Giftedness (or genius) appears to involve both quantitative and qualitative differences in thinking. "People who are gifted typically work really hard (i.e., they are highly motivated). Of course, quantity alone does not make one a genius. The quality of the quantity matters" (Shermer, 2001, p. 268). Gifted people may think and work more, but they also think and work better than most of us (Heller et al., 2000). Table 13.1 illustrates some of the myths and countermyths about intelligence and its measurement and offers truths to replace these myths.

The field of special education is beginning to appreciate the many different ways in which giftedness can be expressed in various areas of human endeavor. Likewise, educators are starting to acknowledge the extent to which the meaning of giftedness is rooted in cultural values (Karnes & Bean, 2001; Sternberg, 1998, 2000).

Whereas the usual tests of intelligence assess the ability to think deductively and arrive at a single answer that can be scored right or wrong, tests of creativity suggest many different potential answers. Creativity has become an extremely appealing topic of commentary and research in the early twenty-first century (see Lynch & Harris, 2001; Sternberg, 2001; Sternberg & Dess, 2001). A special section of *American Psychologist* featured articles on the creative talents of writer John Irving (Amabile, 2001), physicist Linus Pauling (Nakamura & Csikszentmihalyi, 2001), scientists Thomas Young (Martindale, 2001) and Charles Darwin (Gruber & Wallace, 2001), writer Stephen Donaldson (Ward, 2001), and painter Claude Monet (Stokes, 2001).

Recognizing the many facets of human intelligence has led to dissatisfaction with previous conceptualizations of general intelligence that reduced it to a single number (IQ) (Gould, 1996). Sternberg (1997) describes a theory of intelligence that suggests three main kinds of giftedness: analytic, synthetic, and practical.

- *Analytic giftedness* involves being able to take a problem apart—to understand the parts of a problem and how they are interrelated, which is a skill typically measured by conventional intelligence tests.
- *Synthetic giftedness* involves insight, intuition, creativity, or adeptness at coping with novel situations, skills typically associated with high achievement in the arts and sciences.
- *Practical giftedness* involves applying analytic and synthetic abilities to the solution of everyday problems, the kinds of skills that characterize people who have successful careers.

Other researchers are finding evidence of multiple intelligences, such as logical-mathematical, linguistic, musical, spatial, bodily-kinesthetic, interpersonal, and intrapersonal (Gardner & Hatch, 1989; Ramos-Ford & Gardner, 1997). However, the concept of multiple intelligences is sometimes misunderstood and misused to indicate that everyone

Talent.
A special ability, aptitude, or accomplishment.

Giftedness.
Refers to cognitive (intellectual) superiority, creativity, and motivation of sufficient magnitude to set the child apart from the vast majority of age-mates and make it possible for him or her to contribute something of particular value to society.

Anne Mulcahy is president and chief operating officer of Xerox Corporation. ■

Ray Charles, the legendary soul and R&B artist, has been blind since 9 years old from glaucoma. ■

Joseph Seiglitz was awarded the Nobel Prize in Economics in 2001. ■

Susan Stroman is the Tony award-winning director and choreographer of such Broadway hits as *Contact* and *The Producers*. ■

Tiger Woods is one of the most successful golf champions of all time. ■

is equally intelligent (Delisle, 1996; White & Breen, 1998). Whether intelligence should be considered as a general characteristic or identified as having distinctive qualities is an ongoing debate with significant implications for defining giftedness. Intelligence may be a developing form of expertise in a given area, not a static characteristic or trait that can be measured accurately by a test (Gould, 1996; Sternberg, 1998, 2000). Regardless of how the debate is ultimately resolved, it is clear that we have come a long way since the invention of the IQ in conceptualizing human intelligence.

Old stereotypes of giftedness die hard. For example, many still hold the myth that people with special gifts or talents are superior in every way, that they comprise a distinct category of human beings. This myth may account, in part, for the general public's fascination with particularly creative people and the tendency to fawn over those who distinguish themselves in glamorous lines of work.

Today most experts in education of those with special gifts and talents suggest that giftedness refers to superior abilities in specific areas of performance, which may be exhibited under some circumstances but not others. So even though giftedness is believed to be a remarkable ability to do something valued by society, it is not an inherent, immutable trait that a person necessarily carries for life. Moreover, having a special gift at one thing does not mean that a person is good at everything.

Condoleeza Rice is the national security advisor and a member of President George W. Bush's cabinet. ■

Robert Ballard, an explorer and anthropologist, broadcasts live from his expeditions down the Amazon River via satellite and the Internet to students all over the world. ■

Jody Williams is coordinator of the International Campaign to Ban Landmines and winner of the Nobel Peace Prize in 1997. ■

Stephen Hawking, world-renowned cosmologist and author, has had ALS, a form of motor neuron disease, all of his adult life. ■

Marion Jones won five Olympic medals (3 golds, 2 bronzes) in track and field at the summer games in 2000 in Sydney, Australia. ■

Another significant issue in reconceptualizing giftedness is recognizing that it, like beauty, is something defined by cultural consensus. Accordingly, Sternberg and Zhang (1995) propose five criteria for judging whether someone exhibits giftedness:

1. *Excellence*, meaning that the individual must be superior to the peer group in one or more specific dimensions of performance
2. *Rarity*, meaning that very few members of the peer group exhibit the characteristic or characteristics
3. *Demonstrability*, meaning that the person must be able to actually exhibit the excellent and rare ability through some type of valid assessment (i.e., he or she cannot just claim to have it)
4. *Productivity*, meaning that the person's performance must lead to or have the potential to lead to producing something
5. *Value*, meaning that the person's performance is highly valued by society

Sternberg and Zhang also suggest that most people intuitively believe that each of these five criteria is necessary and all five together are sufficient to define giftedness.

TABLE 13.1   Myths, Mythical Countermyths, and Truths About Intelligence

Myth	Mythical Countermyth	Truth
Intelligence is one thing, *g* (or IQ)	Intelligence is so many things you can hardly count them.	Intelligence is multidimensional but scientifically tractable.
The social order is a natural outcome of the IQ pecking order.	Tests wholly create a social order.	The social order is partially but not exclusively created by tests.
Intelligence cannot be taught to any meaningful degree.	We can perform incredible feats in teaching individuals to be more intelligent.	We can teach intelligence in at least some degree, but cannot effect radical changes at this point.
IQ tests measure virtually all that's important for school and job success.	IQ tests measure virtually nothing that's important for school and job success.	IQ tests measure skills that are of moderate importance in school success and of modest importance in job success.
We are using tests too little, losing valuable information.	We're overusing tests and should abolish them.	Tests, when properly interpreted, can serve a useful but limited function, but often they are not properly interpreted.
We as a society are getting stupider because of the dysgenic effects of stupid superbreeders.	We have no reason at all to fear any decline in intellectual abilities among successive generations.	We have some reason to fear loss of intellectual abilities in future generations, but the problem is not stupid superbreeders.
Intelligence is essentially all inherited except for trivial and unexplainable variance.	Intelligence is essentially all environmental except for trivial and unexplainable variance.	Intelligence involves substantial heritable and environmental components in interaction.
Racial differences in IQ clearly lead to differential outcomes.	Racial differences in IQ have nothing to do with differential environmental outcomes.	We don't really understand the relationships among race, IQ, and environmental outcomes.
We should write off stupid people.	There's no such thing as a stupid person. Everyone is smart.	We need to rethink what we mean by "stupid" and "smart."

SOURCE: Sternberg, R.J. (1996). Myths, countermyths, and truths about intelligence. *Educational Researcher, 25*(2), p. 12. Copyright 1996 by the American Educational Research Association. Reprinted by permission of the publisher.

Children who are gifted may have superior cognitive abilities that allow them to compete with adults of average intellect. ■

Similar intuitive, consensual definitions appear to have existed in all cultures throughout history (see Hunsaker, 1995; Tannenbaum, 1993, 2000a). Some researchers have suggested that we should speak of people who exhibit gifted *behavior,* rather than of gifted *people,* because people typically demonstrate special gifts only under particular circumstances (Reis & Renzulli, 2001; Renzulli & Reis, 1997, 2000).

Prevalence

It has been assumed in federal reports and legislation that 3 to 5 percent of the U.S. school population could be considered to have special gifts or talents. Obviously the prevalence of giftedness is a function of the definition chosen. If giftedness is defined as the top x percent on a given criterion, the question of prevalence has been answered. Of course, if x percent refers to a percentage of a national sample, the prevalence of gifted pupils in a given school or cultural group may vary from that of the comparison group regardless of the criteria used to measure performance (Gagne, 2000).

See ERIC Clearinghouse on Disabilities & Gifted Education, www.ericed.org

Origins of Giftedness

As defined today, giftedness is not something that sets people apart in every way from those who are average. Instead, it refers to specific, valued, and unusual talents that people may exhibit during some periods of their lives. Therefore, the main factors that contribute to giftedness are really much the same as those that foster any type of behavior, whether typical or exceptional:

1. Genetic and other biological factors, such as neurological functioning and nutrition
2. Social factors, such as family, school, the peer group, and community

We are all combinations of the influences of our genetic inheritances and social and physical environments; to say otherwise is to deny reality (see Gould, 1996; Heller et al., 2000; Shermer, 2001; Sternberg, 1998). Having said this, we must focus on environments that foster gifted performance.

As one proponent of special education for students with special gifts suggested, attempts to assign racial or class superiority or inferiority are unacceptable and have no place in a society in which equal opportunity and justice are valued: "In an interdependent, pluralistic, complex and multifaceted world, we are all our brothers' keepers" (Roeper, 1994, p. 150). Although giftedness may be determined in part by one's genetic inheritance, whatever genetic combinations are involved are exceedingly complex and not distributed by race or social class. Genetic differences in abilities apply within various ethnic groups and social classes, not between them (see Gould, 1996; Plomin, 1997; Thompson & Plomin, 2000). However, the fact that children are not born with equal capabilities is obvious:

> So, we can conclude there is evidence to support the following statement: There are some youngsters who are born with the capability to learn faster than others those ideas or concepts that modern societies value in children and adults. Such youngsters and their abilities are subject to many social influences and must interact with their environmental context. Therefore, it often becomes difficult to find students with these special talents in a multicultural society. (Gallagher, 2000b, p. 6)

Research has shown that the home and family, especially in a child's younger years, are extremely important. ■

Families, schools, peer groups, and communities obviously have a profound influence on the development of giftedness. Stimulation, opportunities, expectations, demands, and rewards for performance all affect children's learning. For decades, researchers have found a correlation between socioeconomic level and IQ, undoubtedly in part because the performances measured by standard intelligence tests are based on what families, schools, and communities of the upper classes expect and teach. As definitions of intelligence and giftedness are broadened to include a wider range of skills and abilities that are not so specific to socio-economic class, we will no doubt see changes in how environmental effects on giftedness are viewed (Borland, Schnur, & Wright, 2000; Clark, 1997; Subotnik & Arnold, 1994, 2000; Tannenbaum, 1997, 2000a, 2000b).

How can families, schools, and the larger culture nurture children's giftedness? Research has shown that parents differ greatly in their attitudes toward and management of the giftedness of their children (Silverman, 1997). A study of individuals who have been successful in a variety of fields has shown that the home and family, especially in the child's younger years, are extremely important (Subotnik & Arnold, 1994). The following were found to occur in the families of highly successful persons:

- Someone in the family (usually one or both parents) had a personal interest in the child's talent and provided great support and encouragement for its development.
- Most of the parents were role models (at least at the start of their child's development of talent), especially in terms of lifestyle.
- There was specific parental encouragement of the child to explore, to participate in home activities related to the area of developing talent, and to join the family in related activities. Small signs of interest and capability by the child were rewarded.
- Parents took it for granted that their children would learn in the area of talent, just as they would learn language.
- Expected behaviors and values related to the talent were present in the family. Clear schedules and standards for performance appropriate for the child's stage of development were held.
- Teaching was informal and occurred in a variety of settings. Early learning was exploratory and much like play.
- The family interacted with a tutor/mentor and received information to guide the child's practice. Interaction included specific tasks to be accomplished, information or specific points to be emphasized or problems to be solved, a set time by which the child could be expected to achieve specific goals and objectives, and the amount of time to be devoted to practice.
- Parents observed practice, insisted that the child put in the required amount of practice time, provided instruction where necessary, and rewarded the child whenever something was done especially well or when a standard was met.
- Parents sought special instruction and special teachers for the child.
- Parents encouraged participation in events (recitals, concerts, contests, etc.) in which the child's capabilities were displayed in public.

How schools may nurture children's giftedness has received too little attention (Borland et al., 2000; Heller et al., 2000; Lynch & Harris, 2001). Yet the ways in which schools identify giftedness, group children for instruction, design curricula, and reward performance have a profound effect on what the most able students achieve. When schools facilitate the performance of all students who are able to achieve at a superior level in specific areas, giftedness is found among children of all cultural and socioeconomic groups.

Identification of Giftedness

Measurement of giftedness is a complicated matter. Some components cannot be assessed by traditional means; in addition, the particular definition of giftedness will determine how test scores are interpreted. But if it is indeed important to identify giftedness early so that children with special talents will achieve self-fulfillment and be aided in the development of their special potential to make a unique and valuable contribution to society, it is important that appropriate methods be used.

The most common methods of identification include IQ (based on group or individual tests), standardized achievement test scores, teacher nominations, parent nominations, peer nominations, self-nominations, and evaluations of students' work or performances. Typically, some combination of several of these methods is used. Identification practices have been extremely controversial, and best practices have frequently been ignored.

In devising identification procedures that are fair to individuals from all cultural and ethnic groups and all social classes, educators must take into account the varied definitions of giftedness and recognize the effects of cultural variation on children's behavior (Borland et al., 2000; Feldhusen & Jarwan, 2000; Ford, 1998; Frasier & Passow, 1994; Heller et al., 2000). In addressing multicultural differences, it is important to recognize the variations of socioeconomic status, language, and values that occur within various ethnic and cultural groups, not just between them. Hunsaker and Callahan (1995) propose eight general identification principles that will help ensure fairness:

1. Assessments go beyond a narrow conception of talent.
2. Separate and appropriate identification strategies are used to identify different aspects of giftedness.
3. Reliable and valid instruments and strategies are used to assess talent.
4. Appropriate instruments are employed for underserved populations.
5. Each child is viewed as an individual, recognizing the limits of a single score on any measure.
6. A multiple-measure/multiple-criteria approach is followed.
7. Appreciation is shown for the value of the individual case study and the limitations of combinations of scores.
8. Identification and placement are based on individual students' needs and abilities rather than on the numbers who can be served.

The focus of identification methods should be on balancing concern for identifying only those students whose capabilities are markedly above average with concern for including all who show promise for gifted performance.

Psychological and Behavioral Characteristics

Giftedness has been recognized in some form in every society throughout recorded history (Heller et al., 2000; Hunsaker, 1995; Morelock & Feldman, 1997; Tannenbaum, 2000a, 2000b). In many societies, individuals with special gifts have been stereotyped in one of two ways: (1) as physically weak, socially inept, narrow in interests, and prone to emotional instability and early decline or, in the opposite direction, (2) as superior in intelligence, physique, social attractiveness, achievement, emotional stability, and moral character and immune to ordinary human frailties and defects. Although it may be possible to find a few individuals who seem to fit one stereotype or the other, the vast majority of people with special gifts or talents fit neither.

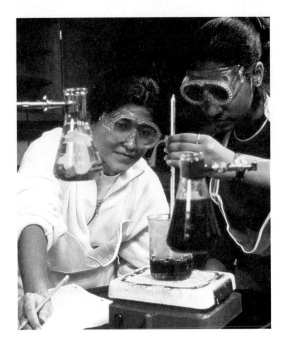

Contrary to myth, most students who are gifted are not constantly bored with and antagonistic toward school, if they are given work that is challenging. ■

Nevertheless, stereotypes persist. A still-common misperception is that genius predisposes people to mental illness. For example, in the movie *A Beautiful Mind*, Russell Crowe plays the role of a mathematician, John Nash, about whom one movie critic wrote: "John Nash was one of those men both blessed and cursed by genius. It made him smart, it made him fragile" (Hunter, 2001, p. C1). People with special gifts and talents sometimes accomplish remarkable things *in spite of, not because of,* mental illness or physical disability.

The box on pages 466–467 summarizes some of what we know about the development of child prodigies—children whose development and accomplishments meet or exceed those of adults with extraordinary talent. The article by Burge (1998) illustrates that giftedness occurs in many different fields of performance and among students of both sexes and all cultural identities. Besides those prodigies depicted in the box, Burge (1998) describes Chris Sharma (who won the World Cup in rock climbing at age fifteen), Jennifer Baybrook (who became the first female national yo-yo champion at age seventeen), Alexandra Nechita (who at age twelve showed her paintings in fifty galleries), Sara Chang (who at age eight was a guest violin soloist with Zubin Mehta and the New York Philharmonic), and Justin Miller (a globe-trotting gourmet who by age eight had cooked three times on the David Letterman show).

Students with special gifts tend to be far ahead of their age-mates in specific areas of performance. Most children carrying the label "gifted" learn to read easily, often before entering school. They may be far advanced in one area, such as reading or math, but not in another, such as writing or art (i.e., skills requiring manual dexterity). Contrary to popular opinion, most such students are not constantly bored with and antagonistic toward school, if they are given work that is reasonably challenging for them (Gallagher & Gallagher, 1994). Some, however, become uninterested in school and perform poorly in the curriculum or drop out (Baker, Bridger, & Evans, 1998). Not surprisingly, they become upset and maladjusted when they are discriminated against and prevented from realizing their full potential. But such a reaction is not unique to any group of children, exceptional or average along any dimension.

Perhaps it should not be surprising that the majority of students who show giftedness enter occupations that demand greater-than-average intellectual ability, creativity, and motivation. Most find their way into the ranks of professionals and managers, and many distinguish themselves among their peers in adulthood. But not all such students enjoy occupational success in demanding jobs; some choose career paths that do not make use of their talents or otherwise fail to distinguish themselves (Manstetten, 2000).

The self-concepts, social relationships, and other psychological characteristics of students with special gifts or talents have been matters of considerable interest. Many of these students are happy, well liked by their peers, emotionally stable, and self-sufficient. They may have wide and varied interests and perceive themselves in positive terms (Coleman & Cross, 2000; Coleman & Fultz, 1985; Ford & Harris, 1997). However, the links between many aspects of self-concept and giftedness are uncertain. For example, placing students in homogeneous classes, in which all students are selected because of their advanced abilities, appears to lower academic self-concept but not self-concept related to such things as appearance and peer relations (Marsh, Chessor, Craven, & Roche, 1995). However, self-concept appears to be related to specific areas of performance, such as math or verbal skills. Moreover, gifted students appear to make internal as well as external comparisons of their performance—to see their own *relative* strengths and weaknesses. "For example, a student with high mathematics achievement will probably have a high math self-concept, but her verbal self-concept may be depressed as a result—*regardless of her verbal achievement*" (Plucker & Stocking, 2001, p. 542).

Students with intellectual gifts are often acutely sensitive to their own feelings and those of others and highly concerned about interpersonal relationships, intrapersonal states, and moral issues. Using their advanced cognitive abilities appears to help many of these children develop at a young age the social and emotional adjustment strategies used by most adults. In short, many (but not all) students with high intellectual gifts are self-aware, self-assured, socially skilled, and morally responsible. However, assuming that gifted students do not need education in morality is a terrible mistake. Individuals can and have used their special gifts for nightmarish purposes, as Tannenbaum (2000b) has described. Therefore, it is important to recognize the enormous potential for both good and evil to which special gifts and talents can be put and to help individuals who have such gifts and talents see the value of using them in the service of what is morally right.

Giftedness includes a wide variety of abilities and degrees of difference from average. Moreover, the nature and degree of an individual's giftedness may affect his or her social and emotional adjustment and educational and psychological needs. Consider, for example, that categorizing only people with IQs of 180 or higher as "gifted" is roughly like categorizing as "mentally retarded" only those individuals with IQs of 20 or less. In fact, children who are exceptionally precocious—those whose talents are extremely rare—may constitute a group for which extraordinary adaptations of schooling are required (just as extraordinary adaptations are required for children with very severe mental retardation) (see Gross, 1992, 1993, 2000; Lovecky, 1994).

Cultural Values Regarding Students with Special Gifts or Talents and Their Education

In American culture, it is relatively easy to find sympathy for children with disabilities but more than a little difficult to turn that sympathy into public support for effective educational programs. However, for children with special gifts, especially intellectual gifts, it is difficult to elicit sympathy and next to impossible to arrange sustained public support for education that meets their needs (Clark, 1997; Gallagher, 2000a).

This is not a peculiarly American problem, but there is something self-limiting, if not self-destructive, about a society that refuses to acknowledge and nourish the special talents of its children who have the greatest gifts (see deHahn, 2000; Tannenbaum, 1993, 2000a). Hunsaker (1995) has examined the perception and treatment of giftedness in traditional West African, Egyptian, Greco-Roman, Semitic, Chinese, Mesoamerican, and European Renaissance cultures. He found that few of these cultures used the term *gifted*. Nevertheless, as in contemporary American society, individuals with advanced abilities were viewed with ambivalence:

> They were considered exceptional because of the hopes people had that they would ensure the continued existence of their culture. Their ability was seen as a divine or inherited gift. Great efforts personally and societally were needed to develop their abilities, and special opportunities were generally not available to the socially disadvantaged. Finally, the exceptional were the objects of ambivalent feelings directed toward them as persons and toward their knowledge. Beliefs and feelings about individuals of exceptional ability have not changed a great deal from those we inherited from other cultures. (Hunsaker, 1995, pp. 265–266)

Gallagher (2000a) describes American society's ambivalence toward students with special gifts or talents. Our society loves the good things that people with extraordinary gifts produce, but it hates to acknowledge superior intellectual performance. Opponents of special education for students with special gifts argue that it is inhumane and un-American to segregate such students for instruction, and to allocate special resources for

Prodigies

The Scientist

Considering her predicament, Carrie Shilyansky's phone voice is surprisingly amiable. "I've got some frozen slugs in my hand, so let me just put them in the freezer quick," she says. As her nonchalance testifies, Carrie knows sea slugs. At 16, she has already studied the creatures for three years, and her research has given scientists insight into the cellular processes behind memory and learning.

Her work with the mollusk—*Aplysia californica* when she talks to her lab buddies—won her second place at the national level in the prestigious Westinghouse Science Talent Search last year. "She is absolutely brilliant," says John Armstrong of Westinghouse. In October, Carrie presented her research, which she hopes eventually to publish, at an annual meeting among thousands of neuroscientists in New Orleans. "It was just amazingly exciting," says Carrie, who lives in San Marino, California.

Her interest in memory began as a child, when she started reading scientific literature to understand how memory works and how information is stored. "People always talk about information and memory," she says. "But they're just sort of these general concepts floating around." She started sitting in on neurobiology seminars at the California Institute of Technology when she was 11. Last fall, when she showed up as a freshman at CalTech, Carrie's advisor remembered her face. "You're the little kid who always used to come sit up front," she said when she met Carrie again.

Carrie began studying sea slugs at a CalTech laboratory where she worked weekends and during breaks at her high school. The creatures, with their simple central nervous systems, make ideal neurobiology subjects. Carrie wanted to study how memory was encoded in the slugs' nervous systems. She tapped them, causing their gills to retract, until they learned the taps weren't harmful. When she changed the frequency of the taps, however, she observed that the slugs had to learn again that the taps were harmless. Scientists had previously thought that only the strength of stimuli such as taps, and not the frequency, affected learning.

Despite her success, Carrie has learned that a young life built around science has its drawbacks. "A big, huge chunk of your social life is just gone because you don't have the time," she says. "There are a lot of times I need to be there for friends and I can't because I need to be in the lab."

The Humanitarian

When Emily Kumpel was 9, her humanitarian career was born from a newspaper article. As a reporter for the now-defunct WBZ radio show "Kid Company,' she was researching a piece about apartheid in South Africa. She came across a newspaper story that detailed how book shortages in South Africa prevented many black children from getting an education. Then she learned about Dr. Wayne Dudley, a Salem (Massachusetts) State College history professor, who was organizing a book drive for South African children. She joined his effort, eventually becoming the national youth coordinator. In the past four years, she has collected 60,000 books for South African students.

Her motive was simple: "I figured that we have had the opportunity to learn, so why shouldn't they?"

Emily started small. She recruited a few friends to help host a bake sale and collect unused books from their school. Then they performed a skit about South Africa in local elementary schools. Their work won them a $3,000 grant, which they used to pay to ship the first books to South Africa. Emily continued to collect books, writing letters to local newspapers asking for donations. She stored the books in a shed behind her house, until the floors began to buckle beneath the weight of 6,000 books. Last year, after a letter-writing campaign, she convinced a local trucking company to transport her books from her home in Wakefield, Massachusetts, to ships in Boston Harbor free of charge. Until then, she had been recruiting relatives to help her move the books, load by load, in her grandparents' Suburban.

Still, there were setbacks. It was hard to find a company willing to move the books from shed to harbor. And whenever she heard, too late, about schools throwing out old textbooks, her heart sank. Still, she says, "It's kind of an infectious thing." She continues to collect books, but she is thinking ahead to future projects. "My dream is to someday get South Africa hooked up to the Internet," she says, "so our school can talk to them."

The Publisher

When Jason Crowe's grandmother died in 1996, he looked for a way to turn his grief into a meaningful tribute to her. Since his grandmother had always read to him and listened to his stories, he decided a newspaper would be fitting, giving a voice to other children the way his grandmother had nurtured his own voice. Besides, he says, "I was on an entrepreneurial kick, and a newspaper was about the only thing I hadn't done."

Jason, now 11, knocked on his neighbors' doors, telling them about his grandmother and the newspaper. (His mother, haunted by visions of angry neighbors demanding their money back if the paper didn't pan out, convinced Jason to begin with three-month subscriptions.) The Informer started as a newspaper for the neighborhood, written by kids and for kids. But as the paper began to find its way far from his hometown of Newburgh, Indiana, Jason began writing about broader issues: global warming, euthanasia, racial harmony. His work on The Informer, now read in 24 states, the District of Columbia, and four foreign countries, has already won him a $10,000 scholarship. As a tribute to his grandmother, half his profits from the paper go to the American Cancer Society. By the end of this subscription cycle he will have contributed about $170.

Jason does most of the newspaper work himself, although his parents help with spelling, organizing ideas, and photocopying. "It's a lot more fun than most people would think," he says. "You get to get inside people when you interview them. You get to walk into different parts of humanity." The newspaper also gives him school credit. His mother, Cindy Crowe, began home-schooling him when school officials said he was hyperactive—his IQ was off the charts—and suggested the drug Ritalin. "He drove the teachers at regular school crazy because he just has all these ideas and they just keep coming out," she says.

Jason has also won attention for another project: raising money to create a statue of a cellist from Sarajevo who refused to stop playing publicly during the war in Bosnia. Jason has already organized two local events, including a concert, in the cellist's honor. Now he has enlisted former Indiana Congressman Frank McCloskey in his statue project. The two may travel to Sarajevo later this year. "To Jason, it's kind of like food for the soul," says his mother.

The Orator

Adults learned Ayinde Jean-Baptiste had a way with words when he recited part of a sermon by Martin Luther King Jr. to his first-grade class. He was 4 years old. His performance was so powerful that it immediately led to his first gig: delivering the King sermon to a Chicago-area church. In the decade since Ayinde first took the podium, requests for speaking engagements have continued to pour into his Evanston, Illinois, home. He has twice shared a podium with President Clinton—at a celebration of Martin Luther King's birthday and at the inauguration of Kweisi Mfume as president of the National Association for the Advancement of Colored People. At the Million Man March in Washington, D.C., Ayinde addressed hundreds of thousands of men, exhorting them to build their communities and commit themselves to their families.

His speaking, which has helped win him a host of awards—including a $10,000 scholarship and the Chicago NAACP President's Award—takes him around the country to about 25 engagements a year. Said one woman who heard him speak at an awards ceremony: "After two or three sentences, I thought, 'He's really good.' After four or five sentences, he could have sold me swampland."

Ayinde, 15, who has never taken a speech class, practices at home before his family. He memorizes all the speeches he delivers, a strategy (used by the ancient Greeks) that he believes allows the words to flow through him more powerfully. "I enjoy the feeling that I get when people respond to me," he says. "I enjoy being able to spread positivity."

One of the most moving responses came from a young man who approached Ayinde after a 1995 speech in New York City. The man, who remembered Ayinde's talk at the Million Man March, said that in the months after the rally he had conquered his drug addiction and reclaimed his role as a young father.

Ayinde often exhorts young people to value education and to avoid drugs and gangs. "I think the reason that I'm an effective speaker, especially with youth, is that sometimes we listen to each other more readily than we do to adults," he says. "If we're talking with each other about things that we face, it stays with us longer."

SOURCE: K. Burge (1998, April). Prodigies. U.S. Airways Attaché, 82–84.

educating those who are already advantaged; also, there is the danger of leaving some children out, when only the ablest are selected for special programs (see, for example, Kaufman, 1998; Margolin, 1994; Sapon-Shevin, 1994; Treffinger, 1998). However, it seems impossible to argue against special education for students with special gifts and talents without arguing against special education in general, for all special education involves recognizing and accommodating unusual individual differences.

Neglected Groups of Students with Special Gifts or Talents

There has been recent concern for neglected groups of children and youths with special gifts and talents—those who are disadvantaged by economic needs, racial discrimination, disabilities, or gender bias—and it is not misplaced. Two facts cannot be ignored:

1. Children from higher socioeconomic levels already have many of the advantages—such as more appropriate education, opportunities to pursue their interests in depth, and intellectual stimulation—that special educators recommend for those with special gifts or talents.
2. There are far too many individuals with special gifts or talents who are disadvantaged by life circumstances or disabilities and who have been overlooked and discriminated against, resulting in a tremendous waste of human potential.

UNDERACHIEVERS WITH SPECIAL GIFTS OR TALENTS

Students may fail to achieve at a level consistent with their abilities for a variety of reasons. Many females achieve far less than they might because of social or cultural barriers to their selection or progress in certain careers. Students who are members of racial or ethnic minorities also are often underachievers because of bias in identification or programming for their abilities. Likewise, students with obvious disabilities are frequently overlooked or denied opportunities to achieve.

Underachievement of children with special gifts or talents can result from any of the factors that lead to underachievement in any group, such as emotional conflicts or a chaotic, neglectful, or abusive home environment. A frequent cause is inappropriate school programs—schoolwork that is unchallenging and boring because these students have already mastered most of the material or because teachers have low expectations or mark students down for their misbehavior. A related problem is that underachievers with special gifts or talents often develop negative self-images and negative attitudes toward school. And when a student shows negative attitudes toward school and self, any special abilities she or he may have will likely be overlooked (see Montgomery, 2000; Peters, Grager-Loidl, & Supplee, 2000).

One way of preventing or responding to underachievement is allowing students to skip grades or subjects so school becomes more nurturing and provides greater interest and challenge. However, acceleration is not always appropriate, nor is it typically sufficient by itself to address the problems of the underachieving student with exceptional abilities (Jones & Southern, 1991; Rimm & Lovance, 1992). Counseling, individual and family therapy, and a variety of supportive or remedial strategies may be necessary alternatives or additions to acceleration (see Colangelo & Assouline, 2000).

Underachievement must not be confused with nonproductivity. A lapse in productivity does not necessarily indicate that the student is underachieving. The student with extraordinary ability should not be expected to be constantly producing something remarkable. But this points up our difficulty in defining giftedness: How much time must elapse between episodes of creative productivity before we say that someone no longer exhibits giftedness or has become an underachiever? We noted earlier that giftedness is in the performance, not the person. Yet we know that the unrelenting demand for gifted performance is unrealistic and can be inhumane.

STUDENTS WITH SPECIAL GIFTS FROM CULTURAL- AND ETHNIC-MINORITY GROUPS

Three characteristics may be used to define students who have both extraordinary abilities and unique needs because of their cultural or minority status: cultural diversity, socioeconomic deprivation, and geographic isolation. These characteristics may occur singly or in combination.

Some ethnic groups, such as many ethnic minorities from Asian countries, are included in programs for gifted students more often than would be suggested by their percentage of the general population. However, some ethnic groups, especially African Americans and Spanish-speaking students, are underrepresented in programs for gifted students. For example, Swanson (1995) describes the problems of serving African American students in rural areas who have special gifts or talents, and Kitano and Espinosa (1995) discuss the complications of working with such students who are learning English as a second language. Borland et al. (2000) describe economically disadvantaged minority students from central Harlem. Each group has unique needs for different reasons. Children from minority cultural groups may be viewed negatively, or the strengths and special abilities valued in their cultures may conflict with those of the majority. Children reared in poverty may not have toys, reading materials, opportunities for travel and exploration, good nutrition and medical care, and many other advantages typically provided by more affluent families. Lack of basic necessities and opportunities for learning may mask intelligence and creativity. Children living in remote areas may not have access to many of the educational resources that are typically found in more populated regions.

Among the greatest challenges in the field today are identifying culturally diverse and disadvantaged students with special abilities and including and retaining these students in special programs. Some cultural and ethnic groups have been sorely neglected in programs for students with special gifts or talents. The desegregation of public schooling following the landmark 1954 decision of the U.S. Supreme Court in *Brown v. Board of Education* has not yet resulted in racial balance in programs for students with special gifts or talents. Many African American students with special gifts or talents remain underachievers, even if they recognize the importance of achievement in American society (Ford, 1993, 1998). And some, perhaps many, students of color who have exceptional ability feel misunderstood by peers, family, and teachers who are not trained to respond competently to cultural differences in giftedness (see Cropper, 1998; Frasier, 1997). However, African American students identified as having special gifts or talents have been found to have more positive attitudes toward achievement and to be more optimistic about their futures than their African American peers who have not been so identified (Ford & Harris, 1996).

Appropriate identification and programming for students with special gifts or talents

Many gifted individuals have been disadvantaged by life circumstances or other disabilities and thus overlooked and discriminated against, resulting in a tremendous waste of potential. ■

will result in including approximately equal proportions of all ethnic groups. This proportionality will likely be achieved only if renewed efforts are made to:

- Devise and adopt culturally sensitive identification criteria
- Provide counseling to raise the educational and career aspirations of students in underrepresented groups
- Make high-achieving models from all ethnic groups available
- Retain underrepresented ethnic students in programs for gifted students
- Adopt a workable system to ensure the inclusion of underrepresented groups
- Build relationships with the families of minority children

Ultimately, the larger social-environmental issue of making families and communities safe, as well as intellectually stimulating, for children and youths of all cultural and ethnic backgrounds must be addressed (Borland & Wright, 2000; Cropper, 1998; Feldhusen, 1998; Gallagher, 1998, 2000a). Equal opportunity for development outside the school environment would help address the underrepresentation of minority students in programs for students with extraordinary abilities.

STUDENTS WITH DISABILITIES AND SPECIAL GIFTS OR TALENTS

For additional information about children with disabilities who are also gifted or talented, see http://www.uniquelygifted.org ■

The education of students with both disabilities and special gifts or talents is just emerging as a field. The major goals of the field are identification of gifted and talented students with specific disabilities, research and development, preparation of teachers and other professionals to work with such children and youths, improvement of interdisciplinary cooperation for the benefit of such children and youths, and preparation of students for adult living.

Our stereotypic expectations of people with disabilities frequently keep us from recognizing their abilities. For example, if a child lacks the ability to speak or to be physically active or presents the image associated with intellectual dullness (e.g., drooling, slumping, dull eyes staring), we tend to assume that he or she has mental retardation. The fact is, students with physical characteristics typically associated with severe mental retardation may be intellectually brilliant; unless this is acknowledged, however, the talents of students with cerebral palsy and other physical disabilities may be easily overlooked. Students with special gifts or talents and impaired hearing also may be overlooked if their communication skills are poorly developed, if their teachers are not looking for signs of talent, or if they are taught by teachers who have limited competence in communicating with people who are deaf (Rittenhouse & Blough, 1995). Some students with learning disabilities or attention deficit hyperactivity disorder (ADHD) have extraordinarily high intellectual

Students whose disabilities prevent them from speaking or physically expressing themselves may have potential that is not obvious through casual observation. ■

Meeting the Needs of Students with Special Gifts or Talents

Strategies for the Identification and Instruction of Twice Exceptional Students

Who Are "Twice Exceptional" Students?

The term *twice exceptional* refers to any student who is both gifted and has a disability, such as a learning disability or cerebral palsy. Unfortunately, the identification of gifts or talents can be challenging, as the "disability" characteristics often take center stage (see p. 472). Researchers have identified specific barriers to the identification of giftedness in populations of students with disabilities (Cline & Hegeman, 2001). Challenges can include:

- Focus on assessment of the disability without attention to possible talents
- Stereotypic expectations associated with physical or global intelligence expectations
- Developmental delays particularly evident in certain areas of cognitive ability such as abstract thinking or verbal ability
- Lack of "worldly" experiences due to disability limitations
- Narrow views of giftedness as global, high intelligence only
- Disability-specific concerns overshadowing possible gifts or talents

To mediate these barriers, these researchers recommend that: (1) assessment batteries include information about participation in extracurricular activities, (2) patterns of strengths should be noted in addition to disability-specific reporting, (3) ability should be viewed in terms of experiential opportunities, (4) adaptations and accommodations should be made during testing (e.g., omitting questions about color for a blind student or allowing extended time for a student with learning disabilities), (5) comparisons should be made with other students with similar disabilities, and (6) areas unaffected by the disability should be weighed more heavily (Cline & Hegeman, 2001; Willard-Holt, 1999).

Strategies for Meeting the Needs of Twice Exceptional Students

To address the issue of underidentification of giftedness in individuals with disabilities, schools need to become advocates for the identification of gifts in all populations of students. Parents, school personnel, and the community should take an active role in supporting the unique needs of students with gifts.

Instructional strategies to foster the development of gifts in twice exceptional students include:

- Focusing on the development of the strengths, interests, and intellectual gifts
- Teaching and encouraging the use of compensatory strategies
- Reducing communication limitations and developing alternative means for communicating
- Helping students shape a healthy, realistic self-concept in which students acknowledge their strengths and weaknesses through open discussions
- Emphasizing high-level abstract thinking, creativity, and problem-solving approaches
- Providing for individual pacing in areas of giftedness and disability
- Establishing high expectations and promoting avenues for self-direction
- Offering instructional options that capitalize on students' strengths (Willard-Holt, 1999)

—*By Kristin L. Sayeski*

abilities, yet their talents will be missed if those abilities are not properly assessed (Baum, Olenchak, & Owen, 1998; Kaufmann & Castellanos, 2000; Moon, Zentall, Grskovic, Hall, & Stormont, 2001). Shaywitz et al. (2001) found that boys with very high IQs and boys with learning disabilities exhibited similar types of behavior problems, strongly suggesting that gifted students are a very heterogeneous group.

Disabilities Do Not Preclude Giftedness

The Unbeatable Drummer

For those who would experience the ultimate synthesis of mental, physical and musical harmony, let me prescribe the Evelyn Glennie Workout—if you can keep up with her, you're in terrific shape. On Thursday night at the Kennedy Center, Glennie played the Washington premiere of Joseph Schwantner's Percussion Concerto with the National Symphony Orchestra under Leonard Slatkin and she was magnificent—a thrilling, hyperkinetic wild woman racing about the stage, striking her many and variegated instruments with the ritualized, poetic violence of a martial artist.

Over the course of the concerto's 20 minutes, Glennie leapt repeatedly from one instrument to another—now rapid-fire ostinato patterns for marimba, now a bright explosion of chimes, now a series of mortal whacks to the guts of the tuned drums. Still, for all of Glennie's stamina, dexterity and strength, her sheer musicianship is what lingers in the memory—the subtle gradations of sound and color she brings to every phrase, the assurance with which she controls the whole vast tintinnabulation.

The concerto itself makes an extraordinarily exciting first impression; how well it will stand up to repeated listenings—without the spectacle of Glennie's physical presence—is, to this taste, still open to question. Fortunately, we shall have an opportunity to find out, as RCA Red Seal is recording this series of concerts for release on disc next year.[1]

Blind Valedictorian Is Headed to Med School

Sure but sightless, Timothy Cordes arrived on the University of Notre Dame's campus four years ago, an 18-year-old freshman from Eldridge, Iowa, who wanted to enroll in the biochemistry program. Faculty members tried, politely, to dissuade him. Just how, they wondered aloud, could a blind student keep up with the rigorous courses and demanding laboratory work of biochemistry?

Cordes graduated today from Notre Dame with a degree in biochemistry and a 3.991 grade-point average. He was the last of Notre Dame's 2,000 seniors to enter the crowded auditorium for commencement. His German shepherd, Electra, led him to the lectern to deliver the valedictory speech as his classmates rose, cheered, applauded and yelled his name affectionately.

Cordes starts medical school in two months, only the second blind person ever admitted to a U.S. medical school. He does not plan to practice medicine. His interest is in research, he said: "I've just always loved science."

His life has been both an act of open, mannerly defi-ance and unshakable faith. And this unassuming, slightly built young man with a choirboy's face awes acquaintances and friends.

Armed with Electra, a high-powered personal computer and a quick wit, Cordes managed a near-perfect academic record, an A-minus in a Spanish class the only blemish. Two weeks ago, he earned a black belt in the martial arts tae kwon do and jujitsu.

"He is really a remarkable young man," said Paul Helmquist, a Notre Dame biochemistry professor. Helmquist at first had doubts but ultimately recommended Cordes for medical school. "He is by far the most brilliant student I've ever come across in my 24 years of teaching," Helmquist said.

If others find some noble lessons in his life, Cordes perceives it more prosaically: He's merely shown up for life and done what was necessary to reach his goals.

"I don't see myself as some sort of 'Profiles in Courage' story," he said. "If people are inspired by what I've done, that's great, but the truth is that I did it all for me. It was just hard work. It's like getting the black belt. It's not like I just took one long lesson. It was showing up every day, and sweating and learning and practicing. You have your bad days and you just keep going." . . .

Cordes has Leber's disease, a genetic condition that gradually diminished his vision until he was blind at age 14.

When doctors at the University of Iowa first diagnosed the disease when he was 2, "it was the saddest moment of my life." said his mother, Therese, 50.

"The doctors . . . told us: 'He won't be able to do this, and don't expect him to be able to do this,'" Therese Cordes recalled. "So I went home and just ignored everything they said."

The ability to conceptualize images has greatly helped Cordes in his studies, Helmquist said. The study of biochemistry relies heavily on graphics and diagrams to illustrate complicated molecular structures. Cordes compensated for his inability to see by asking other students to describe the visual aides or by using his computer to recreate the images in three-dimensional forms on a special screen he could touch.

Cordes applied to eight medical schools. Only the University of Wisconsin accepted him. (The first blind medical student was David Hartman who graduated from Temple in 1976 and is a psychiatrist in Roanoke, Va.)[2]

SOURCES: (1) Page, T. (1996, Oct. 12). The unbeatable drummer. *The Washington Post,* p. C–1; (2) Jeter, J. (1998, May 18). Blind valedictorian is headed to med school. *The Washington Post,* p. A–6. © **1996, 1998 The Washington Post. Reprinted with permission.**

In fact, giftedness can occur in combination with disabilities of nearly every description, as depicted in cases described by Sacks (1995) and as illustrated in the following:

"Alec (a pseudonym) reads. He reads all the time."

"What does he read?"

"*Scientific American, National Geographic, Omni, Air and Space,* Isaac Asimov."

Alec's mother paused briefly. "For hours at a time he just disappears into books and magazines. He comprehends well. His science vocabulary is incredible."

"How old did you say he is?"

"Eleven."

"And he doesn't go to school?"

"We've kept him home because of his health problems."

As the case conference progressed, it became apparent that Alec was an extraordinary child. His disabilities included asthma, severe food and chemical sensitivities, poor motor skills, difficulties with perception and orientation, hyperactivity, and learning disabilities. In spite of all these problems, Alec had special verbal gifts. (Moon & Dillon, 1995, p. 111)

Consider also the individuals featured in the box on page 472. Evelyn Glennie, a deaf percussionist, and Timothy Cordes, a blind medical student, do not fit the stereotypes we hold of people who are deaf or blind. True, they are not typical of people with their disabilities, or of people who do not have their disabilities, for that matter. Fortunately, their disabilities were not allowed to preclude their pursuit of their areas of special talent.

We do not want to foster the myth that giftedness is found as often among students with disabilities as among those who do not have disabilities. But clearly, students with special gifts or talents and disabilities have been a neglected population. A key factor in meeting these students' needs is the collaboration of a variety of disciplines and institutions to provide appropriate technology and training (Dale, 2000; Johnson, Karnes, & Carr, 1997).

FEMALES WITH SPECIAL GIFTS OR TALENTS

Clearly, females comprise the largest group of neglected students with special gifts or talents. As Callahan (1991) and Kerr (1997, 2000) point out, some aspects of the way females are treated in U.S. society are undergoing rapid change. Females with extraordinary capabilities today have many opportunities for education and choice of careers that were denied to females a generation ago. "Yet, there is certainly convincing data that suggest that this particular group of students with special gifts or talents is facing inequities, they are still not achieving at the levels we would expect, and they are not choosing career options commensurate with their abilities" (Callahan, 1991, p. 284).

Cultural factors work against the development and recognition of females with special gifts or talents. Females simply have not been provided with equal opportunity and motivation to enter many academic disciplines or careers that have, by tradition, been dominated by males, such as chemistry, physics, medicine, and dentistry. When females have entered these fields, they have often been rewarded inappropriately (according to irrelevant criteria or with affection rather than promotion) for their performance. English literature has tended to portray females as wives, mothers, or "weaker" sisters, who are either dependent on males or sacrifice themselves for the sake of males. These barriers to giftedness in females have only recently been brought forcefully to public attention.

Females lag behind males in many measures of achievement and aptitude (e.g., professional and career achievement, standardized test scores, grades) and tend not to pursue courses of study or careers involving science, engineering, and math (Lubinski, Benbow, & Morelock, 2000). In short, they are underrepresented in many fields of advanced study and in professions and careers that carry high status, power, and pay. We can only presume to know the reasons for their underrepresentation (Callahan, 1991; Kerr, 2000).

Collaboration and Co-Teaching for Students with Special Gifts and Talents

"How can I challenge him when half of my students have difficulty reading?"

Working with students with gifts and talents can be especially challenging for classroom teachers, considering the wide range of achievement levels in today's classrooms. Collaboration with a teacher of students with special gifts and talents can help general education teachers challenge all students.

What Does It Mean to Be a Teacher of Students with Special Gifts and Talents?

The Council for Exceptional Children (2001) identifies the following skills as important for teachers of the gifted and talented:

1. Teach individuals to use self-assessment, problem solving, and other cognitive strategies
2. Use procedures to increase the individual's self-awareness, self-management, self-control, self-reliance, self-esteem, and self-advocacy
3. Create a safe, equitable, positive, and supportive learning environment in which diversities are valued
4. Create an environment that encourages self-advocacy and increased independence

Successful Strategies for Co-Teaching or Collaboration

Instruction in a differentiated classroom is based upon student readiness and includes constant assessment of student skill and knowledge, varying of activities or assignments for individuals, and the active exploration of topics at varying levels by individuals or groups of students (Tomlinson, 1995). Assignments vary, instructional support needs vary, and groupings vary. This can be quite difficult to manage as a single classroom teacher with between twenty and thirty students with a wide variety of skills. Teachers of students

Factors contributing to the situation may include lower parental expectations for females, overemphasis on and glamorization of gender differences, school and societal stereotypes of gender roles, and educational practices detrimental to achievement (e.g., less attention to high-achieving girls, expectations of less independence of girls).

Research reviewed by Callahan (1991), Kerr (1997, 2000), and Lubinski et al. (2000) suggests that the problems of neglect and underrepresentation of females with exceptional abilities are much more complex than previously believed. Like underrepresentation of ethnic and cultural minorities, the problems involving females are closely tied to cultural, social, and political issues, and they do not have simple or easy solutions. Nevertheless, the education of females with special gifts or talents might be improved by encouraging females to take risks by enrolling in challenging courses, to make career choices appropriate for their abilities, and to explore avenues that break stereotypical female roles.

Educational Considerations

The focus of education is now on talent development across the full spectrum of abilities in particular areas of functioning (see Gentry & Owen, 1999; Heller et al., 2000). However, this point of view includes the recognition by many that special education for some is necessary to provide equity for students with special gifts or talents. Although there is no federal requirement of special education for gifted students, the National Association for Gifted Children has published program standards that states and localities can use to assess the quality of their services (Landrum, Callahan, & Shaklee, 2001).

All students at all ages have relative talent strengths, and schools should help students identify and understand their own best abilities. Those whose talents are at levels exceptionally higher than those of their peers should have access to instructional resources and activities that are commensurate with their talents. The one-size-fits-all mentality that is at least partly an outgrowth of the inclusion movement reflects a mistaken view of human development. Highly talented young people suffer boredom and negative peer pressure in

GW Educational programming ideas for gifted and talented students can be obtained at www.cloudnet. com/~edrbsass/edexc.htm ▪

with gifts and talents can facilitate this process by helping to manage the classroom when groups and individuals are working, by helping to assess student progress, and by helping to collect resources. For example, the following lesson involving "fractured fairy tales" could be very successful with two teachers working together.

Using fractured fairy tales to explore fiction. Fractured fairy tales are designed to be humorous by changing a familiar story in an unexpected way, such as altering the plot, a character, or setting. One student might decide to make Little Red Riding Hood a tough, strong girl, completely unafraid of the wolf and able to save her grandmother. Another student may select a fictional superhero and create a humorous flaw that causes problems when he/she has to save the day. When the teacher presents a fractured fairy tale, asking a series of questions helps the children think through the changes and what they mean. Examples include: (1) What characters in this story differ from the original and how? (2) Which events occur in the new one that don't in the original? (3) How do the changes in characters and plot in the new version change the meaning and/or the way you feel about the characters? (4) How does this change the overall effect? When students are asked to change the nature of even a few characters in a fairy tale, they will dis-cover that the smallest change can affect plot. If their changes remove the conflict and suspense from the story, the teacher can take them back to the original story. What moment in the story held the most tension for them? What kept them riveted to the story? This process can apply to the simplest stories as well as to the most advanced novels and plays. The key is to discuss the relationships across story elements and to examine what is gained or lost with each change (Smutny, 2001).

This lesson can be used with students of all achievement and grade levels; however, the instructional support necessary for all students to understand the lesson varies. For example, the collaborating teachers could split students into groups by their understanding of plot, conflict, resolution, and character and the two teachers could work with the groups to either help clarify these concepts and their application to creation of a new fairy tale or to help push students' thinking of perspective and the influence of small changes on these concepts. Together, the teachers can challenge all students to actively explore literature while providing the support that each needs to be successful—an often impossible task for a teacher working alone.

—By Margaret P. Weiss

heterogeneous classrooms. Students at all ages and grade levels are entitled to challenging and appropriate instruction if they are to develop their talents fully.

The common belief that students with special gifts or talents do not need education designed for their needs works against talent development. "Contrary to popular belief, talented individuals do not make it on their own. Not only is the process of talent development lengthy and rigorous, but the need for support from others is crucial for ultimate success" (Van Tassel-Baska, 1998, p. 762). As noted earlier, family support plays a crucial role in the development of talent (Freeman, 2000). However, special school supports as well are needed for many students if they are to achieve to their full potential. The consensus of leaders in the field is that special education for students with special gifts or talents should have three characteristics:

1. A curriculum designed to accommodate the students' advanced cognitive skills
2. Instructional strategies consistent with the learning styles of students with extra-ordinary abilities in the particular content areas of the curriculum
3. Administrative arrangements facilitating appropriate grouping of students for instruction (see Callahan, 2000, 2001; Feldhusen, 1998; Landrum et al., 2001; Lynch & Harris, 2001; Moon & Rosselli, 2000).

States and localities have devised a wide variety of plans for educating students with special gifts or talents. Generally, the plans can be described as providing **enrichment** (additional experiences provided to students without placing them in a higher grade) or **acceleration** (placing the students ahead of their age-mates).

Many variations of enrichment and acceleration have been invented, however, ranging from regular classroom placement, with little or no assistance for the teacher, to special schools offering advanced curricula in special areas such as science and mathematics or the arts. Between these extremes are consulting teacher programs, resource rooms, community mentor programs (in which highly talented students work individually with professionals), independent study programs, special classes, and rapid advancement of students through the usual grades, including early admission to high school or college.

Enrichment.
An approach in which additional learning experiences are provided for students with special gifts or talents while they remain in the grade levels appropriate for their chronological ages.

Acceleration.
An approach in which students with special gifts or talents are placed in grade levels ahead of their age peers in one or more academic subjects.

Not every community offers all possible options. In fact, there is great variation in the types of services offered within the school systems of given states and from state to state. As one might expect, large metropolitan areas typically offer more program options than small towns or rural areas. New York City, for example, has a long history of special high schools for students with extraordinary gifts and talents.

Some of the educational options for students with high ability, such as acceleration and inclusion, are extremely controversial. Some educators argue that when students with extraordinary abilities are pulled out of regular classes, there is a negative impact on the attitudes and perceptions of the students who are not pulled out (e.g., Sapon-Shevin, 1994); research findings contradict this assumption, however (Shields, 1995). Others have found that offering a variety of program options for students with special gifts and talents

SUCCESS STORIES

Special Educators at Work

Palo Alto, CA: **Noshua Watson** is enrolled in the Ph.D. program in economics at Stanford University. Just eighteen years old, she recently completed high school and college through a residential acceleration program for students with special gifts or talents. Along with her parents, Aremita and Rudy Watson, and program director **Celeste Rhodes**, Noshua is satisfied that, for her, this educational alternative makes sense.

At age thirteen, Noshua Watson enrolled in the Program for the Exceptionally Gifted, known as PEG, which is an acceleration program at Mary Baldwin College in Virginia. "The intellectual challenges I had as a young teenager blew my mind. It was so exciting to realize what I could do!" she remembers. "It was the first time I felt part of a school community."

Noshua's parents saw her academically challenged beyond what was possible with the high school curriculum and in a supportive environment that encouraged her personal growth. Noshua thrived on the stimulation of campus activities, including lacrosse, theater, music, and the college's judicial review board. She assisted with institutional research and helped to teach an economics course during her senior year.

"Acceleration programs like PEG challenge our culture," says Celeste Rhodes, the program's director. "Parents and students must be courageous in their ability to accept uniqueness." Noshua's mother, Aremita Watson, explains, "My husband and I feel it's our responsibility to provide opportunities for our girls, and PEG was something Noshua

really wanted to do. Most children don't get the chance to be their best because too often we teach them to be like others, instead of encouraging them to be motivated by a belief about life that can shape their dreams and aspirations."

Celeste describes this ten-year-old program as an alternative for the motivated student who may have teenage interests but demonstrates what she calls "a serious sense of purpose." "You see it in the interviews," she says. "There is an energy, a spark, a drive."

To Celeste, giftedness is not defined narrowly by IQ but includes multiple measures, including consistent achievement over time. "We are accelerating students by four years. That requires a history of discipline, hard work, and high grades." Through a lengthy essay and interview process, an optimal match is sought between student and program. Explains Celeste, "Since we are residential, emotional stability is extremely important." Noshua agrees. "As PEG students, we were ready and eager for the academic rigors, but emotionally and physically we were not as mature. We were still teenagers with a lot of special needs."

produces good outcomes and that no single type of program option meets the needs of all such students (Delcourt, Loyd, Cornell, & Goldberg, 1994; Feldhusen, 1998).

Ideally, assessment, identification, and instruction are closely linked, whether students have disabilities or special gifts and talents. Sternberg has proposed a model that uses the three kinds of intelligence he has identified—analytic, synthetic, and practical (see page 457)—as the basis for assessing, identifying, and teaching students who have special gifts (Sternberg & Clinkenbeard, 1995). According to this model, students' ability to exhibit the three types of intelligence would be assessed, and those who showed extraordinary facility in using a particular form of intelligence in a given area of the curriculum then would be provided instruction that emphasized their unusual strengths. Although

In this acceleration program, Noshua was supported by an individualized, integrated curriculum that addressed her advanced cognitive skills. Small-group instruction with college students and PEG peers was combined with personal mentoring and alternatives such as independent study and accelerated pacing. According to Noshua, "I was intellectually challenged, but I could socially mature at my own rate, and for me, that was really key."

For her first two years in the program, Noshua lived in a special dormitory for younger PEG students, along with residential coordinators sensitive to the needs of adolescents. Social activities were sponsored and friendships nurtured through residence life, and the coordinators also served as academic advisors to first-year students. Noshua was free to choose among the college's liberal arts offerings but was required to take two specific PEG-level courses: one in literature and one in mathematics. She also took several study skills workshops. Celeste explains, "Study skills is taught by older PEG students and directed toward how to organize for college-level learning. These tutors, or 'near peers,' help acculturate the younger students to life at the college." For her last two years, Noshua lived independently in a regular dorm, and her academic advisor was a faculty member in her chosen major of economics.

Selecting educational alternatives is a familiar practice for Noshua and her family. As a youngster, she attended a magnet school and was described as an avid learner who was strong willed and knew her own mind. Her first experience with education for students with special gifts or talents came from a centralized public school program for third- through fifth-graders. Noshua remembers hoping that when the family moved, she would attend a similar school, but there were no separate programs in her new district. Enrichment classes were held before and after school, but her parents opted not to enroll her because of transportation problems.

Aremita Watson remembers that junior high was not a positive experience for her daughter, who has bad memories. "I was frustrated academically because my guidance counselor said if I wanted to take both French and Spanish, I also had to take an honors math course one level beyond my grade. Socially, I was frustrated because most kids at school just wanted to 'hang out.' My parents wouldn't allow me to do this, and it was hard for me to relate. I guess you could say I was sort of a geek!"

Through a talent search at a local university, Noshua discovered a residential camp for gifted students and happily attended for three summers. "I felt I could finally be myself," she says. In eighth grade, a national search service identified programs offering alternatives to conventional high schools. "That's where I heard about PEG, and so did a fellow camper. We graduated from college together last June."

Noshua is the recipient of a National Science Foundation Graduate Fellowship. As a doctoral student, she is part of a minority on several counts: At eighteen, she is younger than her peers and considered to be gifted. She is also female and African American. Undaunted, her voice is filled with energy when she says, "I just love being at Stanford! I have more in common with graduate students, since most people my age are just starting to live away from home for the first time. My life experience has been different, and I'm used to a lot more independence."

For Noshua, getting an early start on education and career has been satisfying. But as the oldest of three sisters, she believes that everyone has to make her own choices. Her sister Tenea is now a PEG student, and twelve-year-old Cambria will decide soon if she wants to take the same route. "My parents never pressure us to do things the same way," says Noshua. "They've done so much to provide us with unique experiences."

—By Jean Crockett

Meeting the Needs of Students with Special Gifts or Talents

Acceleration

What the Research Says

Recent conceptualizations of gifted education focus on the "talent identification and development" aspects of this educational process (Van Tassel-Baska, 1998). This trend has come about as a result of expanded views of giftedness. Giftedness, once narrowly defined in terms of overall intellectual prowess, now encompasses students with talents in specific academic and nonacademic areas. For example, a student may be gifted in the area of mathematics but not verbal abilities (specific academic giftedness) or a student may be gifted in music or art (nonacademic giftedness). Expanded definitions recognize each of these forms of giftedness and current research has explored ways to promote and foster the development of those specific talents.

One line of research showing promising benefits involves acceleration models of service delivery for highly gifted students. Students in accelerated programs take advanced coursework. Common forms of acceleration are early entrance to school, advanced placement in certain subjects, grade skipping, curriculum compacting (rapid, focused curriculum), college course enrollment while in high school, grade telescoping (reorganizing high school or junior high to reduce the number of years required to finish), and early enrollment into college (Rogers & Kimpston, 1992). Research on acceleration shows that students who took accelerated coursework as preteens selected advanced coursework in high school and college, were accepted to schools with good reputations, maintained acceleration into graduate-level programs, and identified productive career paths early (Swiatek & Benbow, 1991).

Skepticism about the efficacy of acceleration can be reduced to two overarching concerns: (1) acceleration leads to academic burnout or academic challenges due to gaps in knowledge, and (2) acceleration has negative social and emotional consequences. Large-scale research on these issues involving many studies, however, dispels wholesale acceptance of these concerns (Rogers & Kimpston, 1992; Swiatek & Benbow, 1991). Researchers do recommend that decisions about acceleration should be made on an individual basis and different forms of acceleration should be considered. Specific forms of acceleration associated with positive consequences are early entrance to school; grade skipping, particularly in grades 3–6; nongraded or multigraded classrooms; curriculum compacting; grade telescoping; subject acceleration in mathematics; and early admission to college (Rogers & Kimpston, 1992).

Applying the Research to Teaching

Research on acceleration reveals three critical program elements: (1) flexible philosophy in regard to age and student placement, (2) implementation of diagnostic/prescriptive testing, and (3) strong commitment on behalf of administration and teachers (Van Tassel-Baska, 1998).

Schools can foster talent development through:

- Embracing national and state content standards that emphasize higher-level concepts, skills, and ideas
- Conducting testing closely linked to instructional practices
- Ensuring that content knowledgeable and skilled teachers provide instruction
- Allowing access to advanced curriculum at whatever age readiness is demonstrated
- Establishing College Board Advanced Placement classes in a range of disciplines
- Offering a variety of acceleration options (Van Tassel-Baska, 1998)

—*By Kristin L. Sayeski*

this three-dimensional model might be applicable to all program options and areas of the curriculum, its validity for program design has not yet been established.

Advances in telecommunications, the presence of microcomputers in the home and classroom, and the call for excellence in American education are three developments with implications for educating the most able students. Telecommunications—including instructional television, telephone conferencing, and electronic mail—are technological means of facilitating the interaction of particularly able students and their teachers over wide geographical areas. These communication systems are important for extending appropriate education to students with special gifts or talents who live in rural and remote areas. The possible uses of microcomputers for enhancing the education of extraordinarily high-performing students are enormous (Dale, 2000). Using software tutorials, accessing data banks, playing or inventing computer games that are intellectually demanding, writing and editing in English and foreign languages, learning computer languages, and solving advanced problems in mathematics are only a few of the possibilities.

ACCELERATION

Acceleration involves moving a student ahead of her or his age peers in one or more areas of the curriculum. It may mean skipping one or more grades or attending classes with students in higher grades for one or a few specific subjects. Acceleration has not been used frequently, especially in rural areas (Jones & Southern, 1992). It has been used primarily with students who are extremely intellectually precocious (i.e., those scoring 160 or higher on individually administered intelligence tests). Radical acceleration of extremely precocious students, combined with enrichment at each stage of their school careers, appears to offer many of these students the best social experiences as well as academic progress commensurate with their abilities (Charlton, Marolf, & Stanley, 1994; Gross, 2000).

Opponents of acceleration fear that children who are grouped with older students will suffer negative social and emotional consequences or that they will become contemptuous of their age peers. Proponents of acceleration argue that appropriate curricula and instructional methods are available only in special schools or in regular classes for students who are older than the child with special gifts or talents. Furthermore, proponents argue that by being grouped with other students who are their intellectual peers in classes in which they are not always first or correct, students acquire more realistic self-concepts and learn tolerance for others whose abilities are not so great as their own.

Research on the effects of acceleration does not clearly indicate that it typically has negative effects, but neither does it clearly indicate benefits in *all* cases (Jones & Southern, 1991; Van Tassel-Baska, 2000). Acceleration appears to be a plan that can work very well but demands careful attention to the individual case and to specific curriculum areas.

ENRICHMENT

Renzulli and his colleagues have developed an enrichment model based on the notion that children exhibit gifted behaviors in relation to particular projects or activities to which they apply their above-average ability, creativity, and task commitment (Reis & Renzulli, 2001; Renzulli & Reis, 2000). Students selected into a "talent pool" through case-study identification methods are engaged in enrichment activities that involve individual or small-group investigation of real-life problems; they become practicing pollsters, politicians, geologists, editors, and so on. The teacher (1) helps students translate and focus a general concern into a solvable problem, (2) provides them with the tools and methods necessary to solve the problem, and (3) assists them in communicating their findings to authentic audiences (i.e., consumers of information). Students may stay in the enrichment program as long as they have the ability, creativity, and motivation to pursue productive activities that go beyond the usual curriculum for students their age. The model has become known as the *schoolwide enrichment model*. The purpose is to make special programming for students who have such abilities a more integral part of general education.

Early Intervention

The giftedness of young children presents special problems of definition, identification, programming, and evaluation (Jackson & Klein, 1997; Perleth, Schatz, & Monks, 2000).

Although progress has been made in building model programs and providing better services for young children with special gifts, negative attitudes toward such efforts persist. Barriers inhibiting the development of better education for these children include lack of parental advocacy, lack of appropriate teacher training, an emphasis on older students of extraordinary ability, financial constraints, and legal roadblocks such as laws preventing early admission to school. The barriers to early identification and programming for students with special gifts or talents include school policies and ideologies that refuse to advance students in grade beyond their chronological age peers.

Many questions regarding the education of young children who have special gifts remain unanswered. Relatively little is known about how advantageous it is to identify and program for such children before they are in third or fourth grade or how best to train parents and teachers to work with preschoolers with special abilities. Yet some statements can be made with a high degree of confidence, as Karnes and Johnson (1991) point out:

1. We have not been committed to early identification and programming for the young gifted.
2. We have few advocates for young gifted children.
3. We do not have institutions of higher learning training personnel in gifted education to work with our young gifted children.
4. We are in need of financial resources to: conduct research with young gifted children and their families, develop more effective and efficient procedures and instruments for screening and assessing young gifted children, determine the most effective strategies for meeting their unique needs, including ways of differentiating instruction, and follow-up data that will give us insights into the effectiveness of our identification and programming.
5. We don't have the legislation we need to permit public schools to serve young gifted children below the age of five, nor to help public schools finance programming.
6. There is little awareness among educators and parents alike of the importance of early identification and programming for the gifted.
7. Procedures and instruments for identification of children who have disabilities and those who come from low income homes must compare children of like kind rather than expect children to demonstrate or score on instruments at the level of their more affluent peers or peers without disabilities.
8. Identification of young gifted children must be an ongoing process. This is particularly true for children from low-income and minority groups as well as children with disabilities because these children need time and the opportunity to display their special gifts and talents. (pp. 279–280)

Although not a panacea, early admission to school and acceleration through grades and subjects offer significant advantages for some young students with special gifts or talents. What many young children with special abilities need most is the freedom to make full and appropriate use of school systems as they now exist. They need the freedom to study with older children in specific areas where their abilities are challenged. Such children need to be able to get around the usual eligibility rules so they can go through the ordinary curriculum at an accelerated rate. Unfortunately, relatively few preschoolers with special gifts receive the kind of educational programming appropriate for their abilities. This is especially the case for young children with extraordinary abilities who are also from minority or poor families or have disabilities (Gallagher & Gallagher, 1994).

Preschoolers with special gifts or talents may be intellectually superior and have above-average adaptive behavior and leadership skills, as well. Their advanced abilities in many areas, however, do not mean that their development will be above average across the board. Emotionally, they may develop at an average pace for their chronological age. Sometimes their uneven development creates special problems of social isolation, and adults may have unrealistic expectations for their social and emotional skills because their cognitive and language skills are so advanced. They may require special guidance by sensitive adults who not only provide appropriate educational environments for them but also discipline them appropriately and teach them the skills required for social competence. They may need help, for example, in acquiring self-understanding, independence, assertiveness, sensitivity to others, friend-making skills, and social problem-solving skills (Perleth et al., 2000; Robinson, 1993).

Transition to Adulthood

For students with special gifts or talents who are achieving near their potential and are given opportunities to take on adult roles, the transitions from childhood to adolescence to adulthood and from high school to higher education or employment are typically not very problematic. Particularly by adolescence, they tend to be aware of their relative strengths and weaknesses, and they may have lowered self-concepts in their areas of relative weakness even though in those areas they perform as well as or better than the majority of their age peers (Plucker & Stocking, 2001).

In many ways, transitions for these youths tend to mirror the problems in transitions faced by adolescents and young adults with disabilities. Consider the case of Raymond Kurzweil, inventor of the Kurzweil Reading Machine for blind persons (see Chapter 10).

Accelerated educational programs, particularly in mathematics, have been evaluated favorably and may support early college entrance for some students who are gifted. ■

> A summer job, at age 12, involved statistical computer programming. Could a kid comprehend IBM's daunting Fortran manual? He very well could. Soon, in fact, IBM would be coming to young Kurzweil for programming advice. By the time he was graduated from high school, the whiz kid had earned a national reputation, particularly for a unique computer program that could compose original music in the styles of Mozart and Beethoven, among others. After carefully weighing all his options, Kurzweil decided to enroll in the Massachusetts Institute of Technology so that he could mingle with the gurus of the then-emerging science of artificial intelligence. Kurzweil was in his element. He was also rather quickly in the chips. (Neuhaus, 1988, p. 66)

At middle age, Kurzweil was a highly successful entrepreneur and chairman of several of the high-tech corporations he founded.

Not all adolescents and young adults with special gifts or talents take transitions in stride. Many need personal and career counseling and a networking system that links students to school and community resources (Delisle, 1992). Some are well served by an eclectic approach that employs the best features of enrichment and acceleration (Feldhusen & Kolloff, 1986).

If there is a central issue in the education of adolescents with special gifts or talents, it is that of acceleration versus enrichment. Proponents of enrichment feel that these students need continued social contact with their age peers. They argue that such students should follow the curriculum of their age-mates and study topics in greater depth. Proponents of acceleration feel that the only way to provide challenging and appropriate education for those with special gifts and talents is to let them compete with older students. These educators argue that since the cognitive abilities of such students are advanced beyond their years, they should proceed through the curriculum at an accelerated pace.

Acceleration for adolescents with special gifts or talents may mean early entrance to college or enrollment in college courses while attending high school. Acceleration programs, particularly in mathematics, have been evaluated very favorably (Brody & Stanley,

1991; Kolitch & Brody, 1992). In fact, early entrance to college on a full-time or part-time basis appears to work very well for the vast majority of these adolescents, as long as it is done with care and sensitivity to the needs of individual students (Brody & Stanley, 1991; Noble & Drummond, 1992). As Buescher (1991) points out, "Talented adolescents are *adolescents* first and foremost. They experience fully the regression, defensiveness, and relational fluctuations of normal adolescence" (p. 399). Thus, it is important to provide counseling and support services for students who enter college early to ensure that they have appropriate, rewarding social experiences that enhance their self-esteem, as well as academic challenges and successes in the courses they take.

Beyond acceleration and enrichment, adolescents with special gifts or talents need attention to social and personal development if they are to make successful and gratifying transitions to adulthood and careers. Like other groups of students with special characteristics and needs, they may benefit from opportunities to socialize with and learn from other students who have similar characteristics and face similar challenges. They may be able to obtain particular benefit from reflecting on the nature and meaning of life and the directions they choose for themselves. Given proper supports, they can often make use of self-determination and survival skills (Galbraith & Delisle, 1996). Delisle (1992) discusses six realities that adults might use in guiding adolescents with special gifts or talents who are in transition:

1. *Remember that the real basics go beyond reading, writing, and arithmetic.* (They include play and relaxation.) . . .
2. *You can be good at something you don't enjoy doing.* (Just because you're good at something doesn't mean you have to plan your life around doing it.) . . .
3. *You can be good at some things that are unpopular with your friends.* (It's a good idea to connect with others who share your preferences, beliefs, and experiences and to guard against stereotyping yourself or others.) . . .
4. *Life is not a race to see who can get to the end the fastest.* (Don't become preoccupied with performance, work, or success, and don't be afraid to try something at which you might not succeed.) . . .
5. *You have the ability to ask questions that should have answers but don't.* (Look and listen to the world around you, and become involved in making the world a better place.) . . .
6. *It's never too late to be what you might have been.* (Remember that you always have career options and pursue those goals that you want most.) (pp. 137–145)

Summary

Disagreements about how to define giftedness center on the questions of exactly how children excel; how this excellence is measured; the degree to which the individual must excel to be considered to have special abilities; who should make up the comparison group; and why giftedness should be identified at all. Even the terms used can be confusing: *Precocity* indicates remarkable early development; *insight* involves separating relevant from irrelevant information and combining information in novel and productive ways; *genius* refers to rare intellectual powers; *creativity* has to do with the ability to express novel and useful ideas, to see novel relationships, to ask original and crucial questions; and *talent* indicates a special ability within a particular area.

The use of individually administered intelligence tests as the only basis for defining giftedness has met with in-

creasing dissatisfaction. First, traditional intelligence tests are limited in what they measure. Second, intelligence is being reconceptualized. Whether intelligence should be considered a general characteristic or distinguished according to unique areas is an ongoing controversy. Third, children exhibit gifted performance in specific domains. For example, a child with a physical disability might show giftedness in any area not impaired by his or her other specific disability.

A consistent myth is that individuals who show giftedness in particular areas are superior beings. Current thinking suggests that individuals may have extraordinary talents in specific areas but ordinary talents in others. Giftedness is no longer considered to be a fixed human characteristic. Moreover, giftedness may be present or not present at different times in an individual's life. Thus, prevalence figures are difficult to establish.

As with some other exceptionalities, the causes of gifted behavior are varied and most likely represent a combination of biological and environmental factors. Although genetic inheritance may be a factor, giftedness is not specific to any socioeconomic or cultural or ethnic-minority group. A culturally consensual definition of giftedness includes five criteria: excellence, rarity, demonstrability, productivity, and value. For the purposes of education this definition would be expanded to include high ability, high creativity, and high task commitment.

Identification and selection of students for special programs must be based on multiple criteria to avoid bias against neglected groups of students with special gifts or talents. To ensure fairness, principles of identification must take into account the varied definitions of giftedness and recognize the effects of cultural variation—both among and within cultures—on children's behavior.

Giftedness has been recognized in every society throughout history, and individuals with special gifts and talents have been stereotyped as either physically and socially inept or as superhuman. Most individuals with special gifts fit neither category. Identification of giftedness based on IQ scores has often been flawed or biased in favor of physically superior or economically privileged children. Students with special gifts or talents tend to be far ahead of their age-mates in specific areas of academic performance, and the majority of students who show giftedness enter occupations that demand greater-than-average intellectual ability, creativity, and motivation.

The link between giftedness and self-concept is uncertain. Many students who have special gifts or talents are self-aware, self-assured, and socially skilled. Gifted students, like others, tend to compare their relative strengths and weaknesses in forming self-concepts about particular abilities. Those who have truly unusual gifts or talents or who are precocious children may constitute a group for which extraordinary adaptations of schooling are required. American societal attitudes toward giftedness reflect ambivalence: We love the good things giftedness can produce but hate to acknowledge superior intelligence.

Neglected groups of students with special gifts and talents include underachievers—those who fail to achieve at a level consistent with their abilities, for whatever reason. Underachievement is often a problem of minority students and those with disabilities, whose special abilities tend to be overlooked because of biased expectations and/or the values of the majority. Students who display physical characteristics typically associated with severe mental retardation may be intellectually brilliant; unless this is acknowledged, however, the talents of students with cerebral palsy and other physical disabilities may be easily overlooked. Females of extraordinary ability are the largest single group of neglected students with special gifts or talents.

Education of students with special gifts or talents should be based on three characteristics: (1) curriculum designed to accommodate advanced cognitive skills, (2) instructional strategies consistent with learning styles in particular curriculum areas, and (3) administrative facilitation of grouping for instruction. Programs and practices in the education of students with special gifts and talents are extremely varied and include special schools, acceleration, special classes, tutoring, and enrichment during the school year or summer. Administrative plans for modifying the curriculum include enrichment in the classroom, use of consultant teachers, resource rooms, community mentors, independent study, special classes, and special schools.

Acceleration has not been a popular plan for educating exceptionally able students, although considerable research supports it. Enrichment includes a schoolwide plan in which students continue to engage in enrichment activities for as long as they are able to go beyond the usual curriculum of their age-mates. This model is designed to improve the learning environment for all students.

Early intervention entails early identification of special abilities, providing stimulation to preschool children to foster giftedness, and special provisions such as acceleration to make education appropriate for the young child's advanced skills. Young children with special gifts appear to have particular skills much like those of older children who do not have such special abilities. Special care is needed not to assume that a child's emotional and social development are advanced just because his or her language and cognitive skills are advanced.

Transitions to adolescence, adulthood, and higher education and employment are typically not the problems for high-achieving children that they are for children with disabilities. Nevertheless, many highly talented adolescents do need personal and career counseling and help in making contacts with school and community resources. A major issue is acceleration versus enrichment. Programs of acceleration (especially in mathematics, in which students skip grades or complete college-level work early) have been evaluated very positively.

Shifra–Lilith Freewoman

Bird Woman, Mixed mediums on wood. 33 × 25.5 in.

A feminist, Ms. Freewoman, who was born in 1961 in Lynn, Massachusetts, imbues her work with the spirit of womanhood and nature. Her work often depicts creation stories and uses symbolism from traditional societies.

Parents and Families

Worn out, I toss my purse under the seat and look absently out the window onto the dark tarmac. Last to board, a woman and a girl of about ten struggle to get into the small, crowded plane. The girl flaps her hand frantically near her face. The pair move in a sort of lunging, shuffling duet. The mother's eyes are firmly fixed toward the rear of the plane and her hand is vise-gripped to the girl's wrist. I know this scenario: mother and child with autism traveling. Small world.

Loud guttural sounds, almost a moan, almost a scream, come from the girl. Her first utterance causes the people near me to shift around in their seats and nervously clear their throats.

I glance back. The mother is working overtime to get her daughter to settle down and stay calm as we take off and gain altitude. It is hard for anyone to stay calm on a little airplane. I look down as the brightly lit buildings of Portland give way to the faint lights of small towns and farms.

The girl's sounds begin to escalate as the plane hits some turbulence. Fellow passengers murmur. To me, of course, this feels like home. . . .

More NOISE. The child is obviously upset and uncomfortable. At least that's obvious to me. The pressure in her ears is probably giving her excruciating pain. I am jarred from my internal reflection by a man's cold remark.

"Why can't she make her be quiet?" the passenger behind me complains loudly.

"Why the hell did she bring her on a plane," hisses the other. Passengers in the seats next to them chuckle.

It's all I can do not to turn around and shout, "Be glad that you aren't that uncomfortable. Be glad that you aren't that child's caretaker, having to dread taking a short, forty minute flight because of cutting remarks from jerks like you. Aren't you glad she isn't your child because if she was you couldn't just get off a plane and walk away from her!" But I stew in silence.

The plane is descending. We will touch ground soon. The people behind me will get off the plane and glide down to their baggage and their cars. Perhaps they will stop for a martini before they go home, with only themselves to worry about.

The mother in the rear of the plane will wait until everyone else is off, struggle down the rickety steps, carrying too many bags and trying to keep her grip on the tired, crotchety girl. A week from now the others will not even remember this flight or the girl who was making so much noise. I will not be able to forget her.

ELIZABETH KING GERLACH
Just This Side of Normal: Glimpses into Life with Autism

There is little doubt that society is now much more accepting of persons with disabilities. As more and more individuals with disabilities have been integrated into schools, the workplace, and the community, many prejudicial barriers and the fear on which they are invariably based have crumbled. However, as Elizabeth King Gerlach's experience points out (see. p. 485), we still have a long way to go. King's quote also illustrates that it is often the family members of people with disabilities who take the brunt of insensitive comments from others. Her anger is not atypical. As we discuss, it is one of the common reactions, along with shock, denial, sadness, anxiety and fear, and guilt experienced by parents of children with disabilities. But none of these reactions is universal. Parents can experience some, none, or all of them. Reactions of family members to the individual with a disability can run the gamut from absolute rejection to absolute acceptance, from intense hate to intense love, from total neglect to overprotection. And, most important, a child with disabilities does not always threaten the well-being of a family. In fact, some parents and siblings assert that having a family member with a disability has actually strengthened the family.

In this chapter we explore the dynamics of families with children who are disabled and discuss parental involvement in their treatment and education. Before proceeding further, however, it is instructive to consider the role of parents of children who are disabled from a historical perspective.

Professionals' Changing Views of Parents

Eugenics movement.
A popular movement of the late nineteenth and early twentieth centuries that supported the selective breeding of humans; resulted in laws restricting the marriage of individuals with mental retardation and sterilization of some of them.

Today, knowledgeable professionals who work with exceptional learners are aware of the importance of the family. They now recognize that the family of the person with a disability, especially the parents, can help in their educational efforts. To ignore the family is shortsighted because it can lessen the effectiveness of teaching.

Even though we now recognize how crucial it is to consider the concerns of parents and families in treatment and educational programs for individuals who are disabled, this was not always the case. Professionals' views of the role of parents have changed dramatically. In the not too distant past, some professionals pointed to the parents as the primary cause of the child's problems or as a place to lay blame when practitioners' interventions were ineffective. According to one set of authorities, negative views of parents were in some ways a holdover from the **eugenics movement** of the late nineteenth and early twentieth centuries (Turnbull & Turnbull, 1997). Professionals associated with the eugenics movement believed in the selective breeding of humans. For example, they proposed sterilization of people with mental retardation because they erroneously believed that virtually all causes of mental retardation were hereditary.

Although the eugenics movement had largely died out by the 1930s and few professionals any longer blamed disabilities primarily on heredity, the climate was ripe for some of them to blame a variety of disabilities, especially emotional problems, on the childrearing practices of parents. For example, until the 1970s and 1980s, when research demonstrated a biochemical basis for autism, it was quite popular to pin the blame for this condition on the parents, especially the mother. The leading proponent of this viewpoint, Bruno Bettelheim, asserted that mothers who were cold and unresponsive toward their children—"refrigerator moms"—produced autism in their children (Bettelheim, 1950, 1967).

Federal law stipulates that schools must make a concerted effort to involve parents and families in the education of their children with disabilities. ■

MISCONCEPTIONS ABOUT
Parents and Families of Persons with Disabilities

MYTH Parents are to blame for many of the problems of their children with disabilities.

FACT Parents can influence their children's behavior, but so, too, can children affect how their parents behave. Research shows that some children with disabilities are born with difficult temperaments, which can affect parental behavior.

MYTH Parents must experience a series of reactions—shock and disruption, denial, sadness, anxiety and fear, and anger—before adapting to the birth of a child with a disability.

FACT Parents do not go through emotional reactions in lockstep fashion. They may experience some, or all, of these emotions but not necessarily in any particular order.

MYTH Many parents of infants with disabilities go from physician to physician, "shopping" for an optimistic diagnosis.

FACT Just the opposite is often true. Parents frequently suspect that something is wrong with their baby but are told by professionals not to worry—that the child will outgrow the problem. Then they seek another opinion.

MYTH The father is unimportant in the development of the child with a disability.

FACT Although they are frequently ignored by researchers and generally do experience less stress than mothers, fathers can play a critical role in the dynamics of the family.

MYTH Parents of children with disabilities are destined for a life of stress and misery.

FACT Some parents may experience high degrees of disruption and stress, but over time many come to learn to cope. And some actually gain unanticipated positive benefits from having a child with a disability.

MYTH Siblings are usually unaffected by the addition of a child with a disability to the family.

FACT Siblings often experience the same emotional reactions as parents, and their lack of maturity can make coping with these emotions more difficult.

MYTH The primary role of the early intervention professional should be to provide expertise for the family.

FACT Many authorities now agree that professionals should help parents become more involved in making decisions for the family.

MYTH The typical family in the United States has two parents, is middle class, and has only the father working outside the home.

FACT Demographics are changing rapidly. There are now many more families with both parents working as well as more single-parent families and families living in poverty.

MYTH Parents who elect not to be actively involved in their child's education and treatment are neglectful.

FACT Although it is desirable for parents to be involved, it is sometimes very difficult for them to do so because of their commitments to other family functions (e.g., work and child care).

MYTH Professionals are always in the best position to help families of people with disabilities.

FACT Informal sources of support, such as extended family and friends, are often more effective than formal sources of support, such as professionals and agencies, in helping families adapt to a family member with a disability.

MYTH Teachers should respect the privacy of parents and communicate with them only when absolutely necessary—for example, when their child has exhibited serious behavior problems.

FACT Teachers should initiate some kind of contact with parents as soon as possible, so that if something like a serious behavior infraction does occur, some rapport with the parents will already have been established.

In the late 1970s and early 1980s, professionals became less likely to blame parents automatically for the problems of their children. There were at least two reasons for this more positive view:

1. Researchers forwarded the notion that the direction of causation between child and adult behavior is a two-way street (Bell & Harper, 1977). Sometimes the parent changes the behavior of the child or infant; sometimes the reverse is true. With specific regard to children who are disabled, some researchers point out that these children, even as infants, sometimes possess difficult temperaments, which influence how parents respond to them (Brooks-Gunn & Lewis, 1984; Mahoney & Robenalt, 1986). Some infants who are disabled, for example, are relatively unresponsive to stimulation from their parents, making it more difficult to interact with them. With an understanding of the reciprocal nature of parent–child interaction, we are thus more likely, for example, to sympathize with a mother's frustration in trying to cuddle an infant with severe mental retardation or a father's anger in attempting to deal with his teenager who has an emotional or behavior disorder.

2. Professionals began to recognize the potentially positive influence of the family in the educational process. Although at first many authorities tended to think that parents needed training to achieve a positive effect on their children, more and more now have recognized that parents often have as much, or more, to offer than professionals regarding suggestions for the treatment of their children. The prevailing philosophy now dictates that, whenever possible, professionals should seek the special insights that parents can offer by virtue of living with their children. Furthermore, authorities today are less likely to view the purpose of early intervention to be training parents to assume the role of quasi-therapist or quasi-teacher (Berry & Hardman, 1998). Instead, many believe the goal should be to develop and preserve the natural parent–child relationship as much as possible. In sum, a healthy parent–child relationship is inherently beneficial.

    The fact is that parents and teachers have a symbiotic relationship. Each group can benefit enormously from each other. (See Table 14.1).

Individualized family service plan (IFSP). A plan for services for young children with disabilities (under three years of age) and their families; drawn up by professionals and parents; similar to an IEP for older children; mandated by PL 99–457.

Recognizing the importance of the family, Congress has passed several federal laws stipulating that schools make a concerted effort to involve parents and families in the education of their children with disabilities. Current law mandates that schools attempt to include parents in crafting their children's individualized education programs (IEPs) (see Chapter 1). In the case of children under three years of age, schools must involve parents in developing **individualized family service plans (IFSPs).** The focus of the IFSP is to be family-centered. In other words, the IFSP not only addresses the needs of the individual child who has a disability, but it also focuses on his or her family by specifying what services the family needs to enhance the child's development.

The Effects of a Child with a Disability on the Family

The birth of any child can have a significant effect on the dynamics of the family. The parents and other children must undergo a variety of changes to adapt to the presence of a new member. The effects on the family of the birth of a child who has a disability can be even more profound.

The everyday routines that most families take for granted are frequently disrupted in families with children who are disabled (Keogh, Garnier, Bernheimer, & Gallimore, 2000). For example, the child with a disability may require alterations in housing (e.g., the family may decide to move closer to therapists), household maintenance schedules (e.g., chores

TABLE 14.1   Importance of Families to Teachers and Teachers to Families

Importance of Families to Teachers	Importance of Teachers to Families
• Families provide teachers with personal information that may explain why certain student behaviors are occurring in the classroom.	• Teachers provide families with documented evidence of their children's progress and successes.
• Families provide background information and medical histories to teachers and to the school that may help teachers understand why a student behaves or learns in certain ways.	• Teachers can help families become more actively involved in their children's education. • Teachers can help families determine where a student's interests lay so that appropriate long-term goals can be established.
• Families can reinforce directives that teachers give their students, especially on homework assignments.	
• Families can support teachers, such as through serving as chaperones or volunteers in the classroom.	• Teachers can teach and reinforce social skills that are needed for students to be successful, contributing members of the communities in which families live.
• Families can help teachers determine students' interests so that long-term education or vocation goals can be established.	• Teachers can let families know whether their children exhibit inappropriate behaviors or academic needs in the classroom.
• Families can relay information to teachers about which types of discipline and learning strategies work best with their children.	• Teachers can locate and disseminate important educational and community data to help families stay current and knowledgeable about opportunities available for children.
• Families can help teachers find out what each student's strengths and needs are so that appropriate instructional goals are created.	• Teachers can lend a helping hand, a supportive ear, and a friendly face to all families served.

SOURCE: O'Shea, D.J., & O'Shea, L.J. (2001). Why learn about students' families? In D.J. O'Shea, L.J. O'Shea, R. Algozzine, D.J. Hammitte (Eds.), *Families and teachers of individuals with disabilities: Collaborative orientations and responsive practices* (pp. 5–24). Boston: Allyn & Bacon. Copyright © 2001. Reprinted/adapted by permission by Allyn & Bacon.

may not be done as quickly because of lack of time), and even parents' career goals (e.g., a parent may pass up a promotion in order to spend more time with the child).

Moreover, the child with a disability can have an impact on both parents and siblings and in different ways. We discuss parental reactions first and then sibling reactions.

PARENTAL REACTIONS

A Stage Theory Approach   Traditionally, researchers and clinicians have suggested that parents go through a series of stages after learning they have a child with a disability. Some of these stages parallel the proposed sequence of responses that accompany a person's reactions to the death of a loved one. Based on interviews of parents of infants with serious physical disabilities, a representative set of stages includes shock and disruption, denial, sadness, anxiety and fear, anger, and finally adaptation (Drotar, Baskiewicz, Irvin, Kennell, & Klaus, 1975).

Several authorities have questioned the wisdom of this stage approach in understanding parental reactions. It is clear that parents should not be thought of as marching through a series of stages in lockstep fashion. It would be counterproductive, for example, to think, "This mother is now in the anxiety and fear stage; we need to encourage her to go through the anger stage, so she can finally adapt."

One argument against a strict stage model comes from the fact that many parents report that they do *not* engage in denial. In fact, they are often the first to suspect a problem. It is largely a myth that parents of children who are disabled go from physician

The birth of any child has a profound effect on his or her family, and when the child is born with a disability, the effect is even more so. ■

to physician, "shopping" for a more favorable diagnosis. In fact, all too frequently they have to convince the doctor that there is something wrong with their child.

Although parents may not go through these reactions in a rigid fashion, some do experience some or all these emotions at one time or another. A commonly reported reaction is guilt.

The Role of Guilt The parents of a child with a disability frequently wrestle with the terrifying feeling that they are in some way responsible for their child's condition. Even though in the vast majority of cases there is absolutely no basis for such thoughts, guilt is one of the most commonly reported feelings of parents of exceptional children.

The high prevalence of guilt is probably due to the fact that the primary cause of so many disabilities is unknown. Uncertainty about the cause of the child's disability creates an atmosphere conducive to speculation by the parents that they themselves are to blame. Mothers are particularly vulnerable. As Featherstone (1980), the mother of a boy who was blind and had hydrocephaly, mental retardation, cerebral palsy, and seizures, stated:

> Our children are wondrous achievements. Their bodies grow inside ours. If their defects originated in utero, we blame our inadequate bodies or inadequate caution. If . . . we accept credit for our children's physical beauty (and most of us do, in our hearts), then inevitably we assume responsibility for their physical defects.
>
> The world makes much of the pregnant woman. People open doors for her, carry her heavy parcels, offer footstools and unsolicited advice. All this attention seems somehow posited on the idea that she is creating something miraculously fine. When the baby arrives imperfect, the mother feels she has failed not only herself and her husband, but the rest of the world as well.
>
> Soon this diffuse sense of inadequacy sharpens. Nearly every mother fastens on some aspect of her own behavior and blames the tragedy on that. (pp. 73–74)

Dealing with the Public In addition to ambivalence concerning the cause of the child's disability, parents can feel vulnerable to criticism from others about how they deal with their child's problems. Parents of children with disabilities sometimes sense, whether deservedly or not, that others are scrutinizing their decisions about their child's treatment, educational placement, and so forth.

The public sometimes can be cruel in their reactions to people with disabilities (recall the chapter opening quote from Elizabeth King Gerlach). People with disabilities—especially those who have disabilities that are readily observable—are inevitably faced with inappropriate reactions from those around them. John Hockenberry, holder of an Emmy award and currently a correspondent for *Dateline NBC* and MSNBC.com, who has been in a wheelchair since the age of nineteen years due to an automobile accident, talks about how total strangers sometimes ask him inappropriate questions:

> Once on a very hot day on the Washington, D.C., subway a woman sat looking at me for a long time. She was smiling. I suspected that she knew me from the radio, that she had some picture of me somewhere. I am rarely recognized in public, but it was the only plausible explanation for why she kept watching me with a look of some recognition. Eventually, she walked up to me when the train stopped, said hello, then proceeded in a very serious voice.
>
> "Your legs seem to be normal."
>
> "They are normal, I just can't move them."
>
> "Right, I know that. I mean, I can see that you are paralyzed." I was beginning to wonder where she was going with this. "Why aren't you shriveled up more?" she asked, as though she was inquiring about the time of day. "I notice that your legs aren't shrunken and all shriveled up. Why is that?" I was wearing shorts. She looked at my legs as though she was pricing kebab at the market. "I mean, I thought paralyzed legs got all shriveled up after a while. Were you injured recently?"

"Uh . . . twelve years ago."

This was a line of questioning I was unprepared for. I continued to smile and listen. I wondered under what circumstances I would ever roll up to a perfect stranger and ask the question, "Why aren't you shriveled up more?". . .

Perhaps the correct answer to the woman . . . was to take a deep breath and calmly explain the details of my legs and muscles as I understood them. Yet to do so I would have had to admit that there was a category of shriveled-up people, and that I was not one of them. I would also have had to concede that it was perfectly permissible for her to walk up to me and say something outrageous when that was the last thing I believed. (Hockenberry, 1995, pp. 93–95)

Hockenberry, an adult, had a difficult time knowing how to handle interactions with insensitive people. So think about how much more difficult it would be for a child. Understandably, parents often assume the burden of responding to inappropriate or even cruel reactions from the public.

Dealing with the Child's Feelings   In addition to dealing with the public's reactions to their child's disability, parents are also faced with the delicate task of talking with their child about his or her disability. This can be a difficult responsibility because the parents need to address the topic without making the disability seem more important than it actually is. In other words, the parents do not want to alarm the child or make her or him more concerned about the disability than is necessary.

Along with learning how to proceed when a family member has a disability, families must learn to handle reactions from the public. ■

Nevertheless, the child with a disability usually has questions about it: How did I get it? Will it go away? Will it get worse? Will I be able to live independently as an adult? If possible, parents should wait for the child to ask specific questions to which they can respond, rather than lecturing about generalities. However, it is a good idea for parents to talk with the child at as early an age as possible, especially before the teenage years, when so many parents and children have problems communicating. Finally, most authorities recommend that parents be honest in their responses. Here is advice from an adult with cerebral palsy:

Some parents have a tendency to hold back information, wanting to spare their son's or daughter's feelings. What they fail to realize is that, in the long term, being given correct information at an early age is very good for healthy development. And, if kids are informed, they can answer questions themselves, rather than depending on Mom or Dad to speak up for them. (Pierro, 1995, p. 92)

Parental Adjustment   Evidence is abundant that parents of children with disabilities undergo more than the average amount of stress (Beckman, 1991; Duis, Summers, & Summers, 1997; Dumas, Wolf, Fisman, & Culligan, 1991; Dyson, 1997; Gavidia-Payne & Stoneman, 1997). The stress usually is not the result of major catastrophic events but rather the consequence of daily responsibilities related to child care. A single event, such as a family member coming down with a serious illness, may precipitate a family crisis, but its effects will be even more devastating if the family was already under stress because of a multitude of "daily hassles."

There is not a clear consensus on whether mothers and fathers of children with disabilities experience the same degree of stress. Earlier studies suggested that fathers are not under as much stress as mothers, but as fathers have assumed more child-care responsibilities than was once the case, there appears to be a trend toward fathers and mothers experiencing relatively equal amounts of stress (Dyson, 1997).

The Fathers Network is a Web site devoted to information for fathers of children with disabilities and special health needs: http://www.fathersnetwork.org/ ■

Parental Reaction to Stress   There is no universal parental reaction to the added stress of raising a child with a disability. Although one would think that stress would be strongly related to the severity of the disability, there is little evidence to support this assumption. For example, parents of children with more severe disabilities may have greater child-care burdens, but parents of children with milder disabilities may be more likely to experience additional stress related to that felt by parents of children without disabilities (e.g., stress pertaining to school achievement, dating, driving a car).

Two factors that appear to be most predictive of how parents will cope with the stress are (1) their prior psychological makeup and marital happiness and (2) the quality and degree of informal support they receive from others. Although there are exceptions, it is fair to say that parents who were well adjusted and happily married before the birth of the child have a better chance of coping with the situation than those who were already having psychological or marital problems.

Social support that parents receive from each other, extended family members, friends, and others can be critical in helping them cope with the stress of raising a child with a disability (D'Asaro, 1998; Duis et al., 1997; Gavidia-Payne & Stoneman, 1997). The support can be physical, such as offering child care, or it can be psychological. Just having someone to talk to about problems can be helpful.

Changing Views of Parental Adjustment   At one time, most professionals assumed that parents of children with disabilities were destined for a life of stress and misery. In recent years, however, authorities have begun to find that many parents of children with disabilities end up adjusting quite well. This more positive view may be due to advances in educational and social programming for persons with disabilities that have come about in the last twenty to thirty years. In the early years of raising a child with a disability, some may experience high degrees of disruption and stress, but over time many come to learn to cope (Seltzer, Greenberg, Floyd, Pettee, & Hong, 2001).

Some parents, in fact, report that adding a child with a disability to the family actually has some unanticipated positive results (Scorgie & Sobsey, 2000; Skinner, Bailey, Correa, & Rodriguez, 1999). They report undergoing transformational, or life-changing, experiences, which include becoming:

- More tolerant of differences in other people
- More concerned about social issues

Some parents report that having a child with disability in the family has unanticipated positive results, including greater tolerance of differences in other people, being better parents, and having a closer-knit family. ■

- Better parents
- A closer-knit family
- More philosophical or spiritual about life

Elizabeth King Gerlach's philosophical outlook on society's obsession with normalcy was undoubtedly shaped by her having a child with a disability:

> Society views disability as a "tragedy." In fact, the greater tragedy is society's larger and erroneous view that there is such a state as "normal." This view, in itself, sometimes feels like a greater burden than the disability.
>
> "Normal" does exist, but you have to look for it. It is a place that is somewhere between the middle of two extremes. For instance, there are shampoos for oily, normal, or dry hair. Another good example of normal can be found on my clothes dryer, between "fluff," and "shrink it." This area is marked "normal." I use this setting because it is the closest to normal that my life usually gets.
>
> The truth is, "normal" is not a word that should apply to the human condition. People are different, and they constantly change. A close approximation to "normal" might be "balanced." For example, the body will work overtime to fight an infection and return to a healthful state. Balance is a state of being we often strive for—a sort of happy comfortableness. And some of us endeavor to maintain a balanced state within ourselves, our families, and our communities. We have to discover what this means for ourselves, and this too changes over time.
>
> I used to think there was such a thing as a "normal, happy family" and that it was something attainable. I hadn't experienced that as a child, so I set out to create it as an adult. Autism bombed that notion. Just as well. I'm not pretending that autism, in its varying degrees of severity, isn't painful in many ways for everyone involved. It is. I'm simply saying that some of that pain is relieved with understanding and acceptance. Having a child with a disability has shown me how precious life really is and that being human means learning to love. The simplicity and complexity of this understanding never cease to amaze me. (Gerlach, 1999, pp. 4–6)

This is not to minimize the fact that the added stress a child with a disability often brings can have a devastating impact on the stability of the family. It is dangerous to assume, though, that the birth of a child with a disability automatically spells doom for the psychological well-being of the parents or for the stability of their marriage.

SIBLING REACTIONS

Although a relatively large body of literature pertains to parental reactions, there is much less information about siblings of persons with disabilities. What is available, however, indicates that siblings can and frequently do experience the same emotions—fear, anger, guilt, and so forth—that parents do. In fact, in some ways, siblings may have an even more difficult time than their parents in coping with some of these feelings, especially when they are younger. Being less mature, they may have trouble putting some of their negative sensations into proper perspective. And they may be uncomfortable asking their parents the questions that bother them. Table 14.2 provides examples of sibling concerns.

Although some feelings about their siblings' disabilities may not appear for many years, a substantial number of accounts indicate that nondisabled siblings are aware at an early age that their brothers or sisters are different in some way. For example, in the box on page 496, Abby recalls feeling the sting of prejudice toward her brother when she was only about five or six years old. Even though young children may have a vague sense that their siblings with disabilities are different, they may still have misconceptions about the nature of their siblings' conditions, especially regarding what caused them.

As nondisabled siblings grow older, their concerns often become more focused on how society views them and their siblings who are disabled. Adolescence can be a

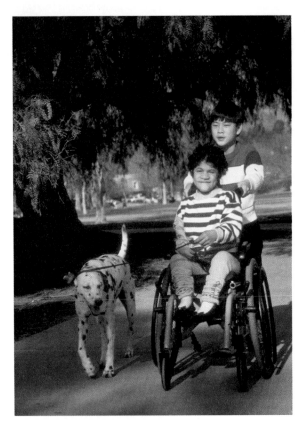

Siblings of children with disabilities often recount being aware at a very early age that something was different about their brothers or sisters. Siblings' attitudes change at different stages of their own lives; for example, adolescents become more concerned about public perception of themselves and their siblings with disabilities. ■

particularly difficult period. Teens, fearing rejection by peers, often do not want to appear different. And having a sibling with a disability can single a person out.

Siblings' Adjustment   Children, like parents, can adapt well or poorly to having family members with disabilities. Research indicates that some siblings have trouble adjusting, some have no trouble adjusting, and some actually appear to benefit from the experience. Like parents, however, siblings of children with disabilities are at a greater risk than siblings of nondisabled children to have difficulties in adjustment.

Why some individuals respond negatively, whereas others do not, is not completely understood. Although not definitive, there is some evidence that birth order, gender, and age differences between siblings have some bearing on adjustment (Berry & Hardman, 1998). A nondisabled sister who is older than her sibling who has a disability is likely to have a negative attitude when she reaches adolescence because she often has to shoulder child-care responsibilities. Siblings of the same gender and siblings who are close in age are more likely to experience conflicts. At older ages, however, when siblings are adults, there is evidence that women show more favorable attachments than men to their sibling with a disability, and adults who are the same gender as their sibling with a disability experience more favorable emotional responses (Orsmond & Seltzer, 2000).

Access to information is one key to adjustment for siblings of children with disabilities. As noted in Table 14.2, siblings have myriad questions pertaining to their sibling's disability. Straightforward answers to these questions can help them cope with their fears.

Teachers, as well as parents, can provide answers to some of these questions. Teachers, for example, can talk with students about the materials and contents of programs for their siblings with disabilities (Powell & Gallagher, 1993). Another excellent resource for providing information and support to siblings is "**sibshops**" (Meyer & Vadasy, 1994). Sibshops are workshops specifically designed to help siblings of children with disabilities.

Family Involvement in Treatment and Education

As noted earlier, today's professionals are more likely to recognize the positive influence parents can have on their exceptional children's development. This more positive attitude toward parents is reflected in how parents are now involved in the treatment and education of their children.

At one time, most early intervention programs for families who had children with disabilities operated according to the philosophy that the professionals had the expertise and that the families needed that expertise to function. Most authorities today, however, advocate a **family-centered model.** A family-centered model:

> can be defined as a friendly respectful partnership between educators and families that includes: giving emotional and educational support; ensuring that families have opportunities to make decisions; and providing support to enable families to meet their own goals. (Kraus, Maxwell, & McWilliam, 2001, p. 63)

Sibshops.
Workshops for siblings of children with disabilities; designed to help siblings answer questions about the disability and learn to adjust to having a sister or brother with a disability.

Family-centered model.
A type of early intervention program; consumer-driven in that professionals are viewed as working for families; views family members as the most important decision makers.

TABLE 14.2   Examples of Sibling Concerns

Concerns about a sibling with a disability	• What caused the disability? • Why does my brother behave so strangely? • Will my sister ever live on her own?
Concerns about parents	• Why do they let my brother get away with so much? • Why must all their time be given to my sister? • Why do they always ask me to babysit?
Concerns about themselves	• Why do I have such mixed feelings about my sister? • Will I catch the disability? • Will we have a normal brother-sister relationship?
Concerns about friends	• How can I tell my best friend about my brother? • Will my friends tell everyone at school? • What should I do when other kids make fun of people with disabilities?
Concerns about school and the community	• What happens in special education classes? • Will I be compared with my sister? • What should I tell strangers?
Concerns about adulthood	• Will I be responsible for my brother when my parents die? • Do I need genetic counseling? • Should I join a parents' and/or siblings' group?

SOURCE: Adapted from *Brothers & sisters—A special part of exceptional families* (2nd ed.), by T.H. Powell & P.A. Gallagher, 1993, Baltimore, MD: Paul H. Brookes (P. O. Box 10624, Baltimore, MD 21285–0624).

Another way of describing the family-centered approach is to say that it is a model in which the professionals work *for* the family. The use of family-centered models reflects a change from viewing parents as passive recipients of professional advice to equal partners in the development of treatment and educational programs for their children. The notion is that, when professionals do not just provide direct services but encourage the family to help themselves and their children, the family takes more control over their own lives and avoids the dependency sometimes associated with typical professional-family relationships. Situations in which the family looks to professionals for all its help can result in family members becoming dependent on professionals and losing their feelings of competence and self-esteem. Table 14.3 lists several tips for teachers that are consistent with a family-centered approach.

The effort to build professional–parent partnerships is consistent with the thinking of child development theorists who stress the importance of the social context within which child development occurs. Urie Bronfenbrenner (1979, 1995), a renowned child development and family theorist, has been most influential in stressing that an individual's behavior cannot be understood without understanding the influence of the family on that behavior. Furthermore, the behavior of the family cannot be understood without considering the influence of other social systems (e.g., the extended family, friends, and professionals) on the behavior of the family. The interaction between the family and the surrounding social system is critical to how the family functions. A supportive network of professionals (and especially friends) can be beneficial to the family with a child who has a disability.

FAMILY SYSTEMS THEORY

The emphasis on the individual's behavior being understood in the context of the family and the family's behavior being understood in the context of other social systems are the basic principles underlying **family systems theory** (Lambie, 2000). There are several family system theories, all of which assume that the more treatment and educational programs take into account the relationships and interactions among family members, the more

Family systems theory. Stresses that the individual's behavior is best understood in the context of the family and the family's behavior is best understood in the context of other social systems.

Fighting Prejudice

My older brother, Justin, 19, was born with Down syndrome. When he was young he learned a little more slowly than others, but he could do a lot of things. When he was 2 he had a blood clot in his brain and had a stroke. After that he needed to use a walker, and he couldn't talk. The clot killed the left side of his brain. Now he can only make noises because he uses a trache to breathe. When he got older, his legs got worse, and he needed a wheelchair to get around. I remember something else that happened to Justin a few years ago. He experienced prejudice.

One day, when I was about 5 or 6, my mom and dad took Justin, my friend, Tony, and me to McDonald's. After we ate we went to the restaurant playroom. As we played there was a group of boys that began to laugh at Justin. They were calling him a pig, a loser, an idiot, retarded, and stupid. Justin didn't know they were being mean to him so he laughed right along.

I was dumbstruck. I didn't know what to do. I wanted to yell at them and tell them they didn't know him—that they should be quiet. When we left the restaurant, I told my mom and she told me about prejudice. That day I learned that people should try to get to know other people before they make fun of them. After that, I was always protective of my brother.

To this day, Justin still doesn't know if people are making fun of him. If I saw anyone doing that to him again, I would go up to them and tell them that if they knew him, and knew what a great friend he is, they wouldn't make fun of him. Then I'd ask if they would like to meet him.

What happened to my brother was very mean, and it still makes me feel like crying when I think about it. Prejudice is so cruel. Nobody makes fun of him anymore: my friends have gotten to know him and they like him, and some of them are even learning to sign so they can talk with him. Next time you think of making fun of someone different, think about my brother Justin.

Mom's Turn

Cynthia Seaver knows how much her daughter cares for Justin, and that this compassion is the result of the connection the children share. "Abby and Justin are very close. She can communicate with him better than anyone else and has taken signing classes to be able to help him with his signing at home."

Thoughts from Dad

Though proud of his entire family, David Seaver feels that Abby's experience taught her one of life's most important lessons: "She'll always know that whatever outward differences a person may have, physical or cognitive, there is so much more to be gained from being able to look beyond the difference while getting to know the person."

SOURCE: Abigail Seaver. (2001). Fighting prejudice. *Exceptional Parent, 31*(4), 116. Reprinted with the expressed consent and approval of *Exceptional Parent,* a monthly magazine for parents and families of children with disabilities and special health care needs. Subscription cost is $39.95 per year for 12 issues; call (877) 372-7368. Offices at 65 E. Rte. 4, River Edge, N.J. 07661.

Abigail, 10, and Justin live with their parents, Cynthia and David, in Wallingford, CT. Abigail attends Rock Hill School and Justin works at a local Wal-Mart. ■

Family characteristics. A component of the Turnbulls' family systems model; includes type and severity of the disability as well as such things as size, cultural background, and socioeconomic background of the family.

likely they will be successful. One model that has been developed specifically with persons with disabilities in mind is that of the Turnbulls. Their model includes four interrelated components: **family characteristics, family interaction, family functions,** and **family life cycle** (Turnbull & Turnbull, 1997).

Family Characteristics   Family characteristics provide a description of basic information related to the family. They include characteristics of the exceptionality (e.g., the

TABLE 14.3   Suggestions for Teachers to Incorporate Family Involvement into Class and School Activities

- Consider varied family compositions and living arrangements that differ from the teacher's personal experiences.

- Empathize with students and family members to understand what they may be experiencing and act according to their needs instead of personal needs.

- Value individual families, cultures, and their uniqueness instead of trying to categorize and stereotype families.

- Consider that all children will not suffer from abuse or divorce situations in the same way. For example, all foster parents do not parent their children the same way. Consider the entire picture and all of the issues, before acting.

- Take time each morning to speak with students. Communicate regularly with family members.

- Allow options when communicating with families. Use a variety of contacts, including phone, face to face, notebook, or home visits. Determine the school professional with whom the family members may feel most comfortable: the teacher, counselor, principal, or other school professional.

- Demonstrate a genuine interest in what is happening on the home front and communicate with both households when there is a joint custody arrangement. Don't assume the information from school is reaching both parents.

- Be considerate of home arrangement facts when assigning homework. There may be no one at home to help with projects or difficult assignments that would need adult supervision. There may not be anyone checking to see whether homework is complete or done correctly.

- Plan alternative conference times in addition to school hour conferences: Think convenience for the families instead of teachers only. Hold conferences frequently. Seek to be helpful to everyone involved (teacher, student, and parents). Avoid talking over or under parents' heads: Avoid educational jargon.

- Make every conference meaningful and productive. Include the student in some of the conferences: Begin and end every conference, conversation, meeting, with a positive fact or work sample.

- Invite families into the classroom as much as possible. Value any and all contributions or suggestions family members make. Incorporate into the lessons family issues that can be helpful. Assume families are not teaching these skills at home. Use lessons to incorporate family customs, rituals, and traditions.

- Value the diversity of all students and their family compositions. Even though a family composition may seem unstructured or confusing, there are lessons and a contribution they can make to the class. Set up programs that benefit all students and all types of households.

- Get educated about the families of the students. Know what is going on at home. Find out more about each students' family and living arrangements.

SOURCE: O'Shea, D.J., & Riley, J.E. (2001). Typical families: Fact or fiction? In D.J. O'Shea, L.J. O'Shea, R. Algozzine, D.J. Hammitte (Eds.), *Families and teachers of individuals with disabilities: Collaborative orientations and responsive practices* (pp. 25–50). Boston: Allyn & Bacon. Copyright © 2001. Reprinted/adapted by permission by Allyn & Bacon.

Family interaction.
A component of the Turnbulls' family systems model; refers to how cohesive and adaptable the family is.

Family functions.
A component of the Turnbulls' family systems model; includes such things as economic, daily care, social, medical, and educational needs.

Family life cycle.
A component of the Turnbulls' family systems model; consists of birth and early childhood, childhood, adolescence, and adulthood

type and severity), characteristics of the family (e.g., size, cultural background, socioeconomic status, and geographic location), personal characteristics of each family member (e.g., health and coping styles), and special conditions (e.g., child or spousal abuse, maternal depression, and poverty). Family characteristics help determine how family members interact with themselves and with others outside the family. It will probably make a difference, for example, whether the child with a disability is mentally retarded or hearing impaired, whether he or she is an only child or has five siblings, whether the family is upper middle class or lives in poverty, and so forth.

Recent trends in U.S. society make it even more important for teachers and other professionals who work with families to take into account family characteristics. In particular, teachers should be attentive to the expanding ethnic diversity in the United States. (See box on p. 498 for suggestions on facilitating involvement of culturally and linguistically diverse families in the education of their children.) In addition to wider diversity with

Facilitating Involvement of Culturally and/or Linguistically Diverse Families

The increasing ethnic diversity of schools has resulted in a wider mismatch between the ethnicity of teachers and students, especially students in special education. (See Chapter 3.) One of the things that many special education teachers, who are often white, have difficulty with is knowing how to involve families from a different culture. Here are several suggestions based on the work of Howard Parette and Beverly Petch-Hogan, two professors at Southeast Missouri State University.

Contacts with Families

- *Problem:* Families from culturally and/or linguistically diverse backgrounds often defer to professionals as the "experts." *Possible solution:* Do not assume that school personnel should always take the lead in providing information or contacting families.
- *Problem:* Some families mistrust school personnel. *Possible solutions:* Identify trusted people in the community (e.g., a minister, physician, retired teacher) to contact the family; establish a Family Advisory Council where parents can present issues; make use of interpreters in the case of parents who are English language learners.

Location of Meetings

- *Problem:* Meetings typically take place in a school building, which can present parents with transportation problems and may be perceived as aversive or intimidating. *Possible solutions:* Provide transportation, or hold the meeting at a neutral site, e.g., neighborhood church or community center.

Supports During the Meeting

- *Problem:* Child care for families can make it difficult to attend a meeting. *Possible solution:* Provide child care.

Provision of Information/Training

- *Problem:* Professionals often deliver information to families via lectures and printed materials. *Potential solution:* Consider that culturally and linguistically diverse families are often more comfortable obtaining information in less formal settings, such as parent support groups.
- *Problem:* Typically, parents alone are the targets of information and training. *Potential solution:* Consider involving siblings or extended family members because they often assume significant responsibility for childcare.

Knowledge of Family Priorities, Needs, Resources

- *Problem:* Some families may find the implementation of intervention programs results in too much stress for the family. *Potential solution:* Be sensitive to families' desire not to get involved too deeply in intervention efforts.
- *Problem:* Some families do not view time in the same way as many professionals do. *Potential solution:* Be flexible in scheduling meeting times and consider video- or audio-taping parts of meetings missed by families.

SOURCE: Parette, H.P., & Petch-Hogan, B. (2000). Approaching families: Facilitating culturally/linguistically diverse family involvement. *Teaching Exceptional Children, 33*(2), 4–10.

Fiesta Educativa is a project focused on providing information for Spanish speaking families that have a child with a disability: http://www.fiestaeducativa.org/ ■

regard to ethnicity, there are also increases in the numbers of families in which both parents work outside the home, single-parent families, and families who are living in poverty.

Coupled with these demographic changes—and to a certain extent influenced by them—families today live under a great deal more stress. Adding to this stress is the threat of terrorism subsequent to the bombing of the World Trade Center on September 11, 2001. On the one hand, children need attention and reassurance more than ever; but on the other hand, because of pressures to earn a living, parents have fewer resources to draw upon to provide comfort to their children.

These dramatic societal changes present formidable challenges for teachers and other professionals working with families of children with disabilities. As the configuration of families changes, professionals will need to alter their approaches. For example, the same approaches that are successful with two-parent families may not be suitable for single mothers. Also, professionals need to understand that today's parent is living under more and more stress and may find it increasingly difficult to devote time and energy to working on behalf of his or her child.

Family Interaction   Family members can have a variety of functional and dysfunctional ways of relating to one another. Some authorities point to the degree of responsiveness of the parent to the child as key to healthy child development (Mahoney, Boyce, Fewell, Spiker, & Wheeden, 1998). The more the parent responds appropriately to the young child's body language, gestures, facial expressions, and so forth, the more the child's development will flourish.

In the Turnbulls' model, they point to family cohesion and adaptability as important determinants of how family members interact with each other. In general, families are healthier if they have moderate degrees of cohesion and adaptability.

Adults with mental retardation, especially those who live at home, often have special problems finding the right degree of independence from their families. When they do live away from home, parents are often concerned about providing enough support so their children don't become socially isolated. ■

Cohesion   *Cohesion* refers to the degree to which an individual family member is free to act independently of other family members. An appropriate amount of family cohesion permits the individual to be his or her own person while at the same time drawing on other family members for support as needed. Families with low cohesion may not offer the child with a disability the necessary support, whereas the overly cohesive family may be overprotective.

It is frequently very difficult for otherwise healthy families to find the right balance of cohesion. They sometimes go overboard in wanting to help their children and, in so doing, limit their children's independence. A particularly stressful time can be adolescence, when the teenager strives to break some of the bonds that have tied him or her to the family. This need for independence is normal behavior. What makes the situation difficult for many families of children with disabilities is that the child, because of her or his disability, has often by necessity been more protected by parents. In fact, there is research to suggest that, in the early years, the more supportive the parent is with the child the better. For example, in one study mothers of toddlers with Down syndrome who during play engaged in more helpful behaviors such as steadying objects and otherwise making it more likely that the children would experience success had children who were more likely to play and vocalize (Roach, Barratt, Miller, & Leavitt, 1998).

As the child matures, however, the issue of independence usually takes on more importance. One way to help children feel more connected to the family, without infringing on their freedom, is to give them family-based responsibilities such as chores. For some children with physical limitations, this may mean making accommodations so they can perform the tasks successfully.

Cohesion can also be an issue for adults with disabilities. Current thinking dictates that persons with learning disabilities should live in the community, but many will also need support from their families in order to do this successfully. For example, parents of young adults with learning disabilities and/or ADHD are often faced with the decision of whether their children are ready to live on their own (Smith & Strick, 2000). They will need a number of daily living skills, such as managing personal finances, keeping to a work schedule, planning and preparing meals, that do not always come easily even to nondisabled young adults.

Adults with mental retardation, especially those who live at home, often have special problems finding the right degree of independence from their families. And when they do live away from home, their parents are often concerned about providing enough support so that their grown children do not become socially isolated. One mother who was interviewed about future living arrangements for her daughter, who is severely mentally retarded, explained:

> I would like to see her live fairly close so that she can come over and visit when she wants to or if she needed help. She's going to have to have some support, I know that. There are lots of apartments close by that I think she can handle . . . and I would like to see her close enough so that we always have the constant, not constant, [*sic*] but we will always be there if she needs us. And both Tim and I agree that that's something we will always do. We will be here. But, on the other hand, if we want to go away for a month, we'll know there are other people that can be called upon to give her the support she needs. (Lehmann & Baker, 1995, p. 30)

Adaptability   *Adaptability* refers to the degree to which families are able to change their modes of interaction when they encounter unusual or stressful situations. Some families are so chaotic that it is difficult to predict what any one member will do in a given situation. In such an unstable environment, the needs of the family member who is disabled may be overlooked or neglected. At the other end of the continuum are families characterized by extreme rigidity. Each family member has his or her prescribed role in the family. Such rigidity makes it difficult for the family to adjust to the addition of a member with a disability. The addition of any child requires adjustment on the part of the family, but it is even more important if the child has special needs. For example, it may be that the mother's involvement in transporting the child with a disability from one therapy session to another will necessitate that the father be more involved than previously in household chores and taking care of the other children.

Family Functions   Family functions are the numerous routines in which families engage to meet their many and diverse needs. Economic, daily care, social, medical, and educational needs are just a few examples of the functions to which families need to attend.

An important point for teachers to consider is that education is only one of several functions in which families are immersed. And for some students, especially those with multiple disabilities, several professionals may be vying for the time of the parents. It is only natural, of course, that teachers should want to involve parents in the educational programming of their children as much as possible. Teachers know the positive benefits that can occur when parents are part of the treatment program. At the same time, however, teachers need to respect the fact that education is just one of the many functions to which families must attend.

Several authorities have reported that many families of students with disabilities prefer a passive, rather than active, degree of involvement in their children's education (Turnbull & Turnbull, 2000). Parents often have very legitimate reasons for playing a more passive role. For example, in their culture, it may be customary for parents to refrain from interfering with the roles of school personnel in educational matters. Furthermore, some parents may simply be so busy attending to other family functions that they are forced to delegate most of the educational decisions for their children to teachers. Respecting the parents' desire to play a relatively passive role in their child's education does not mean that teachers should discourage or discount parental involvement for those who desire it.

Family Life Cycle   Several family theorists have noted that the impact of a child with a disability on the family changes over time (Berry & Hardman, 1998; O'Shea, O'Shea, Algozzine, & Hammitte, 2001). For this reason, some have pointed to the value of looking at families with children with a disability from a life-cycle perspective. Most family theorists consider four stages in the lives of families: (1) early childhood, (2) childhood, (3) adolescence, and (4) adulthood.

Transitions between stages in the life cycle are particularly stressful for families, especially families with children who are disabled. We have already mentioned the difficulties facing families at the transition point when their child, as an adult, moves into more independent work and living settings. A particularly difficult issue for some parents of children with disabilities who are entering adulthood is that of mental competence and guardianship. These parents must struggle with how much self-determination to allow their children given their ability to make reasoned choices (Berry & Hardman, 1998). Parents who decide that their children are not competent to make rational choices without endangering themselves can go through legal channels to obtain guardianship of their children. **Guardianship** means that one person has the authority, granted by the courts, to make decisions for another person. Guardianship can range in degree from total to more limited, or temporary, authority to make decisions.

Another particularly troublesome transition can be from the relatively intimate confines of an infant or preschool program to the larger context of a kindergarten setting. For the child, the transition often requires a sudden increase in independent functioning (Fowler, Schwartz, & Atwater, 1991). For the parents, it often means giving up a sense of security for their child. As one parent relates:

The impact of a child with a disability on the family changes over time. Family theorists have begun to look at issues that are unique to children with disabilities as they approach adulthood. ■

> As my daughter's third birthday approached, I lived in dread, not wishing to leave the familiar, comfortable environment of her infant program. The infant program had become home away from home for me. It was supportive and intimate. I had made some lifelong friendships, as well as having established a comfortable routine in our lives. I saw making the transition to a preschool program in the school district as an extremely traumatic experience, second only to learning of Amy's diagnosis.
>
> What were my fears? First, I was concerned that my husband and I, along with professionals, would be deciding the future of our child. How could we play God? Would our decisions be the right ones? Second, I feared loss of control, as I would be surrendering my child to strangers—first to the school district's intake assessment team and then to the preschool teacher. The feeling of being at the mercy of professionals was overwhelming. In addition, I had more information to absorb and a new system with which to become familiar. Finally, I feared the "label" that would be attached to my child and feared that this label would lower the world's expectations of her. (Hanline & Knowlton, 1988, p. 116)

Transitions between stages are difficult because of the uncertainty that each new phase presents to the family. One of the reasons for the uncertainty pertains to replacements of the professionals who work with the child who is disabled. In particular, parents of a child with multiple disabilities, who requires services from multiple professionals, can be anxious about the switches in therapists and teachers that occur many times throughout the child's life, especially at transition points.

SOCIAL SUPPORT FOR FAMILIES

Authorities now recognize that families can derive tremendous benefit from social support provided by others (Dunst, Trivette, & Jodry, 1997). **Social support** refers to emotional, informational, or material aid provided to persons in need. In contrast to assistance that comes from professionals and agencies, social support is informal, coming from such

Guardianship.
A legal term that gives a person the authority to make decisions for another person; can be full, limited, or temporary; applies in cases of parents who have children who have severe cognitive disabilities.

Social support.
Emotional, informational, or material aid provided to a person or a family; this informal means of aid can be very valuable in helping families of children with disabilities.

There are several projects, many of which are funded by the federal government, focused on providing information and support to families of children with disabilities. Following are some examples:

PACER Center: http://www.pacer.org/

Beach Center: http://www.beachcenter.org/

Federation for Children with Special Needs: http://www.fcsn.org/

Family Village of the Waisman Center, U of Wisconsin: http://www.familyvillage.wisc.edu/index.htmlx

Through the Looking Glass: http://www.lookingglass.org/

National Center for Infants, Toddlers and Families: Zero to Three: http://www.zerotothree.org/

The U.S. Department of Education has a Web site that provides information on publications focused on parents: http://www.ed.gov./pubs/parents/

And *Exceptional Parent* is a magazine focused on families with children with disabilities. It also contains useful information on its Web site: http://www.eparent.com/ ◼

sources as extended family, friends, church groups, neighbors, and social clubs. We discuss two methods of providing social support: parental support groups and the Internet.

Parental Support Groups   One common type of social support, especially for parents of recently diagnosed children, is parental support groups that consist of parents of children with the same or similar disabilities. Such groups can be relatively unstructured, meeting infrequently with unspecified agendas, or they can be more structured. In any case, parental groups can provide a number of benefits, "including (1) alleviating loneliness and isolation, (2) providing information, (3) providing role models, and (4) providing a basis for comparison" (Seligman & Darling, 1989, p. 44).

Parental support groups, however, are not of benefit to everyone. Some parents may actually experience more stress from sharing problems and listening to the problems of others (Berry & Hardman, 1998). The impact of support groups on parents is probably dependent on the particular personalities of the parents involved.

Internet Resources for Parents   The Internet has become an excellent resource for parents of children with disabilities. Dozens of electronic mailing lists, newsgroups, and World Wide Web sites are now devoted to disability-related topics. Through mailing lists and newsgroups, parents of children with disabilities can communicate with each other, with people who have disabilities, and with professionals concerning practical as well as theoretical issues. Lists and newsgroups are available regarding specific disabilities (e.g., Down syndrome, attention deficit hyperactivity disorder, cerebral palsy, cystic fibrosis) as well as more general ones.

Via Web sites, parents can access information on disabilities. A good example is The Office of Special Education, based at the University of Virginia. (The address for this site is http://curry.edschool.virginia.edu/curry/dept/cise/ose/.) This site provides information and links to other Web sites on such topics as legislation, legal issues, documented teaching techniques, parent resources, and upcoming articles in special education journals.

COMMUNICATION BETWEEN PARENTS AND PROFESSIONALS

Virtually all family theorists agree that, no matter what particular approach one uses to work with parents, the key to the success of a program is how well parents and professionals are able to work together. Even the most creative, well-conceived model is doomed to fail if professionals and parents are unable to communicate effectively.

Unfortunately, special education does not have a long tradition of excellent working relationships between parents and teachers (Michael, Arnold, Magliocca, & Miller, 1992). This is not too surprising, considering the ingredients of the situation. On the one hand, there are the parents, who may be trying to cope with the stresses of raising a child with a disability in a complex and changing society. On the other hand, there are the professionals—teachers, speech therapists, physicians, psychologists, physical therapists, and so forth—who may be frustrated because they do not have all the answers to the child's problems.

One of the keys to avoiding professional–parent misunderstandings is *communication*. It is critical that teachers attempt to communicate with the parents of their students. There are advantages to receiving information from parents as well as imparting information to them. Given that the parents have spent considerably more time with the child and have more invested in the child emotionally, they can be an invaluable source of information regarding his or her characteristics and interests. And by keeping parents informed of what is going on in class, teachers can foster a relationship in which they can call on parents for support should the need arise. Even those parents mentioned earlier, who do not want to be actively involved in making decisions regarding their child's educational program, should receive periodic communication from their child's teacher.

One area in particular that requires the cooperation of parents is homework. For mainstreamed students who are disabled, homework is often a source of misunderstanding and conflict. The box on page 505 offers some strategies for enhancing the homework experience for students with disabilities.

Most authorities agree that the communication between the teacher and parents should take place as soon as possible and that it should not be initiated only by negative behavior on the part of the student. Parents, especially those of students with behavior disorders, often complain that the only time they hear from school personnel is when their child has misbehaved (Hallahan & Martinez, 2002). To establish a degree of rapport with parents, some teachers make a practice of sending home a brief form letter at the beginning of the school year, outlining the goals for the year. Others send home periodic newsletters or make occasional phone calls to parents. Even if teachers do not choose to use some of these techniques, authorities recommend that they be open to the idea of communicating with parents as soon as possible in the school year. By establishing a line of communication with parents early in the year, the teacher is in a better position to initiate more intensive and focused discussions should the need arise. Three such methods of communication are parent–teacher conferences, home-note programs, and traveling notebooks.

Parent–Teacher Conferences   Parent–teacher conferences can be an effective way for teachers to share information with parents. Likewise, they are an opportunity for teachers to learn from parents more about the students from the parents' perspective. In addition to regularly scheduled meetings open to all parents, teachers may want to hold individual conferences with the parents of particular students. A key to conducting successful parent–teacher conferences is planning. How the teacher initiates the meeting, for example, can be crucial. Some recommend that the first contact be a telephone call that proposes the need for the meeting, without going into great detail, followed by a letter reminding the parents of the time and place of the meeting (Hallahan & Martinez, 2002). Table 14.4 presents some suggestions for effective parent–teacher conferences.

If the focus of the meeting is the student's poor work or misbehavior, the teacher will need to be as diplomatic as possible. Most authorities recommend that the teacher find something positive to say about the student, while still providing an objective account of what the student is doing that is troubling. The teacher needs to achieve a delicate balance

TABLE 14.4 Guidelines for Parent–Teacher Meetings and Conferences

Lay the Foundation

- Review the student's cumulative records.
- Familiarize yourself with the student and family's culture.
- Consult with other professionals about the student.
- Establish rapport with the parents and keep them informed.
- Collect information to document the student's academic progress and behavior.
- Share positive comments about the student with parents.
- Invite the parents to observe or volunteer in your classroom.

Before the Meeting

- Discuss the goals of the meeting with the parents and solicit their input.
- Involve the student, as appropriate.
- Schedule a mutually convenient day and time for the meeting.
- Provide written notice prior to the meeting.

During the Meeting

- Welcome the parents and speak informally with them before beginning.
- Reiterate the goals of the meeting.
- Begin with a discussion of the student's strengths.
- Support your points with specific examples and documentation.
- Encourage the parents to ask questions.
- Encourage parents to share insights.
- Ask open-ended questions.
- Avoid jargon.
- Practice active listening (e.g., show interest, paraphrase comments, avoid making judgments, etc.).
- Review the main points of the meeting and determine a course of action.
- Provide additional resources (e.g., support groups, family resource centers, websites).

After the Meeting

- Document the results of the meeting.
- Share results with colleagues who work with the student.
- Follow up with the parents as needed to discuss changes.

SOURCE: Hallahan, D.P., & Martinez, E.A. (2002). Working with families. In J.M. Kauffman, M. Mostert, S.C. Trent, & D.P. Hallahan (Eds.), *Managing classroom behavior: A reflective case-based approach* (3rd ed., pp. 124–140). Boston: Allyn & Bacon. Copyright © 2002. Reprinted/adapted by permission by Allyn & Bacon.

of providing an objective account of the student's transgressions or poor work while demonstrating advocacy for the student. Conveying only bad or good news can lose the parents' sense of trust:

> Conveying only good news skews their perspective . . . just as much as conveying only negative information. If a serious incident arises, they have no sense of background or warning. [This] may lead them to conclude that the teacher is withholding information and provoke a sense of mistrust. When telling parents unpleasant information, it helps not only to be as objective as possible, but also state the case in a way that clearly conveys your advocacy of the student. When it is obvious to the parents that the teacher is angry or upset with their child, parents become apprehensive about the treatment the child may receive. A common response to this sense of dread is a defensiveness which polarizes parent–teacher relationships. (Hallahan & Martinez, 2002, p. 135)

Homework: Tips for Teachers

Homework is often a source of conflict among teachers, parents, and students with disabilities. Over the past several years, the U. S. Department of Education's Office of Special Education Programs has funded several projects focused on enhancing the homework experience for students with disabilities. A summary of this effort has arrived at five general recommendations, as excerpted from Warger (2001):

Give Clear and Appropriate Assignments

If the homework is too hard, is perceived as busy work, or takes too long to complete, students might tune out and resist doing it. Never send home any assignment that students cannot do. Homework should be an extension of what students have learned in class.

- Make sure students and parents have information regarding the policy on missed and late assignments, extra credit, and available adaptations.
- Assign homework in small units.
- Explain the assignment clearly.
- Write the assignment on the chalkboard and leave it there until the assignment is due.
- Remind the students of due dates periodically.
- Coordinate with other teachers to prevent homework overload.
- Establish a routine at the beginning of the year for how homework will be assigned.
- Assign homework at the beginning of class.
- Relate homework to classwork or real life.
- Explain how to do the homework, provide examples, and write directions on the chalkboard.
- Have students begin the homework in class, check that they understand, and provide assistance as necessary.

Make Homework Accommodations

- Provide additional one-on-one assistance to students.
- Monitor students' homework more closely.
- Allow alternative response formats (e.g., allow the student to audiotape an assignment).
- Adjust the length of the assignment.
- Provide a peer tutor or assign the student to a study group.
- Provide learning tools (e.g., calculators).
- Adjust evaluation standards.
- Give fewer assignments.

Teach Study Skills

[Consider teaching students to:]

- Identify a location for doing homework that is free of distractions.
- Have all materials available and organized.
- Allocate enough time to complete activities and keep on schedule.
- Take good notes.
- Check assignments for accuracy and completion before turning them in.

Use a Homework Calendar

Just as adults use calendars, schedulers, lists, and other devices to self-monitor activities, students can benefit from these tools as well. Students with disabilities can monitor their own homework using a planning calendar to keep track of homework assignments. Homework planners can also double as home–school communication tools if they include space next to each assignment for messages from teachers and parents.

Ensure Clear Home/School Communication

Recommended ways that teachers can improve communications with parents include

- Providing a list of suggestions on how parents might assist with homework. For example, ask parents to check with their children about homework daily.
- Providing parents with frequent written communication about homework.

Ways that administrators can support teachers in improving communication include

- Supplying teachers with the technology needed to aid communication (e.g., telephone answering systems, email, homework hotlines).
- Providing incentives for teachers to participate in face-to-face meetings with parents (e.g., release time, compensation).
- Suggesting that the school district offer after school and/or peer tutoring sessions to give students extra help with homework.

Resources

Bryan, Nelson, & Mathur (1995); Bryan & Sullivan-Burstein (1997); Epstein, Munk, Bursuck, Polloway, & Jayanthi (1999); Jayanthi, Bursuck, Epstein, & Polloway (1997); Jayanthi, Sawyer, Nelson, Bursuck, & Epstein (1995); Klinger & Vaughn (1999); Polloway, Bursuck, Jayanthi, Epstein, & Nelson (1996)

SOURCE: Warger, C. (2001, March). *Five homework strategies for teaching students with disabilities.* ERIC Clearinghouse on Disabilities and Gifted Education. Retrieved October 20, 2001 from the World Wide Web: http://www.ericec.org/digests/e608.html. Reprinted by permission.

Parent-teacher conferences can be an effective way for teachers and parents to share perspectives and learn from one another about any student. Effective conferences are particularly valuable for students with disabilities ■

Home-note program.
A system of communication between the teacher and parents; the teacher evaluates the behavior of the student using a simple form, the student takes the form home, gets the parents' signatures, and returns the form the next day.

Traveling notebook.
A system of communication in which parents and professionals write messages to each other by way of a notebook or log that accompanies the child to and from school.

Advocacy.
Action that is taken on behalf of oneself or others; a method parents of students with disabilities can use to obtain needed or improved services.

Home-Note Programs   Sometimes referred to as *home-contingency programs,* **home-note programs** are a way of communicating with parents and having them reinforce behavior that occurs at school (Cottone, 1998; Kelley, 1990; Kelley & McCain, 1995; McCain & Kelley, 1993). By having parents dispense the reinforcement, the teacher takes advantage of the fact that parents usually have a greater number of reinforcers at their disposal than do teachers.

There are a number of different types of home-notes. A typical one consists of a simple form on which the teacher records "yes," "no," or "not applicable" to certain categories of behavior (e.g., social behavior, homework completed, homework accurate, in-class academic work completed, in-class academic work accurate). The form also may contain space for the teacher and the parents to write a few brief comments. The student takes the form home, has his or her parents sign it, and returns it the next day. The parents deliver reinforcement for the student's performance. The teacher often starts out sending a note home each day and gradually decreases the frequency until he or she is using a once-a-week note.

Although home-note programs have a great deal of potential, researchers have pointed out that they require close communication between the teacher and parents (Cottone, 1998). Additionally, both teachers and parents need to agree philosophically with a behavioral approach to managing student behavior. If either is opposed to using reinforcement as a means of shaping behavior, the home-note program is unlikely to succeed.

Traveling Notebooks   Less formal than home-notes and particularly appropriate for students who see multiple professionals are traveling notebooks. A **traveling notebook** goes back and forth between school and home. The teacher and other professionals, such as the speech and physical therapists, can write brief messages to the parents and vice versa. In addition, a traveling notebook allows the different professionals to keep up with what each is doing with the student. See Figure 14.1 for excerpts from a traveling notebook of a two-year-old with cerebral palsy.

Another important way that parents and other family members can communicate with professionals is through advocacy. **Advocacy** is action that results in benefit to one or more persons (Alper, Schloss, & Schloss, 1996). Advocacy can be a way of gaining needed or improved services for children while helping parents gain a sense of control over outcomes for their children. Although sometimes associated with the notion of confronta-

Lyn,   9/7

   Lauren did *very* well — We had several criers, but — She played & worked very nicely. She responds so well to instruction — that's such a plus!

   She fed herself crackers & juice & did a good job. She was very vocal & enjoyed the other children too. She communicated with me very well for the 1st day. Am pleased with her first day.

                                                                          Sara

Sara,   9/15

   Please note that towel, toothbrush/paste and clean clothes may be removed from bag today — Wed. We witnessed an apparently significant moment in her oral communication: She'll try to say "all done" after a meal. The execution is imperfect, to say the least, but she gets an "A" for effort. Could you please reinforce this after snack? Just ask her, "What do you say after you finish your snack?"

                                                                      Thanks,
                                                                          Lynn

9/28

   Lauren had an esp. good day! She was jabbering a lot! Being very expressive with her vocalness & jabbering. I know she said "yes," or an approximate thereof, several times when asked if she wanted something. She was so cute with the animal sounds esp. pig & horse — she was really trying to make the sounds. It was the first time we had seen such a response. Still cruising a lot! She walked with me around the room & in the gym. She used those consonant and vowel sounds: dadada, mamama — her jabbering was just so different & definitely progressive. I am sending her work card with stickers home tomorrow for good working.

   Several notes:

   1. Susie (VI) came today & evaluated Lauren. She will compile a report & be in touch with you and me. She seemed very pleased with Lauren's performance.

   2. Marti (speech) will see Lauren at 11 AM for evaluation. She'll be in touch afterwards.

   3. Susie informed me about the addition to the IEP meeting on Mon. Oct. 4 at 10 AM here at Woodbrook.

   How are the tape & cards working at home? I know you both are pleased with her jabbering. She seems so ready to say "something" — we are very, very pleased. See you tomorrow.

                                                                          Sara

9/29

   Lauren was a bit fussy during O.T. today — she stopped fussing during fine motor reaching activities (peg board, block building) but wasn't too pleased with being handled on the ball. She did a great job with the peg board & and readily used her left hand.

   I want to bring in some different spoons next week to see if she can become more independent in scooping with a large handle spoon or a spoon that is covered.

                                                                          Joan

Joan —   10/1

   Although Lauren would very much approve of your idea for making her more independent during feeding, we'd rather not initiate self-feeding with an adaptive spoon at this time. Here's why:

   1. When I feed Lauren or get her to grip a spoon and then guide her hand, I can slip the entire bowl of the spoon into her mouth and get her to close her lips on it. When Lauren uses a spoon without help, she turns it upside-down to lick it or inserts just the tip of it into her mouth and then sucks off the food …

   2. Lauren has always been encouraged to do things "normally." She never had a special cup or a "Tommy Tippee," for instance. Of course it took a year of practice before she could drink well from a cup, and she still dribbles a little occasionally; but she's doing well now. We really prefer to give Lauren practice in using a regular spoon so that she doesn't get dependent on an adaptive utensil.

   I'd like to assure you that we appreciate your communication about sessions with Lauren and ideas for her therapy. Coordinating her school, home, and CRC programs is going to be a challenge, to say the least.

                                                                          Lynn

2/26

   Good news! Lauren walked all the way from the room to the gym & back — She also walked up & down the full length of the gym!

   Several other teachers saw her and were thrilled. She fell maybe twice! But picked herself right up —

                                                                          Sara

3/2

   Lauren had a great speech session! We were playing with some toys and she said "I want help" as plain as day. Later she said "I want crackers" and at the end of the session, she imitated "Cindy, let's go." Super!

                                                                          Marti

FIGURE 14.1

A traveling notebook. These short excerpts are taken at random from a notebook that accompanies two-year-old Lauren, who has cerebral palsy, back and forth to her special class for preschoolers. The notebook provides a convenient mode for an ongoing dialogue among her mother, Lyn; her teacher, Sara; her occupational therapist, Joan; and her speech therapist, Marti. As you can see from this representative sample, the communication is informal but very informative in a variety of items relating to Lauren.

The National Information Center for Children and Youth with Disabilities, funded by the U.S. Department of Education's Office of Special Education Programs, has information on the IEP process that parents should find valuable: http://www.nichcy.org/basicpar.htm

There are now several Web sites focused on helping parents and advocates understand special education and the law. Following are some examples:

http://www.reedmartin.com/

http://www.wrightslaw.com/

http://www.edlaw.net/

http://www.specialedlaw.net/index.mv

http://www.cleweb.org/ ■

tions between parents and professionals, advocacy need not be adversarial. In fact, ideally, parents and professionals should work together in their advocacy efforts.

Parents can focus their advocacy on helping their own children, as well as other persons with disabilities. The latter may involve volunteering for advisory posts with schools and agencies as well as political activism—for example, campaigning for school board members who are sympathetic to educational issues pertinent to students with disabilities.

One of the most common ways of advocating for one's own child is by means of the IEP meeting. Table 14.5 lists several ways that parents can help make IEP meetings more effective. And the box on p. 509 offers suggestions on how parents can prepare themselves to advocate for their child.

As important as advocacy is, not all parents have the personalities or the time to engage in such activities. Also, engaging in advocacy may be more or less suitable to some parents at various stages in their child's development. For example, some parents may be heavily involved in such efforts when their children are young but become exhausted over the years and, thus, reduce their involvement. Likewise, some parents may not see the need for intervening on behalf of their children until they encounter problems later on— for example, in transition programming in the teenage years. The best advice for teachers is to encourage parents to be advocates for their children but respect their hesitancy to take on such responsibilities.

In Conclusion

Today's knowledgeable educators recognize the tremendous impact a child with a disability can have on the dynamics of a family. They appreciate the negative as well as the positive influence such a child can exert. Today's knowledgeable educators also realize that the family of a child with a disability can be a bountiful reservoir of support for the child as well as an invaluable source of information for the teacher. Although tremendous advances have been made, we are just beginning to tap the potential that families have for

TABLE 14.5 Hints for Parents for a More Effective IEP Meeting

- Take the initiative to set the date, time, and place of the meeting. Consider holding the meeting in your own home or in a community setting that feels comfortable to you.

- Before the meeting, ask the organizer to clarify the purpose and provide you with information you may need ahead of time. Also, find out who will be attending the meeting so that you may suggest other potential team members.

- Call the organizers to let them know what items you would like to have included on the agenda.

- Write down ideas about your child's present and future goals, interests, and needs, and bring these with you to share at the meeting.

- During the meeting, ask to have discussion items and lists of actions written down on large pieces of flip-chart paper so that all team members can see them.

- Be a "jargon buster"—ask to have unfamiliar terms clarified for you and other team members during the meeting.

- Ask team members to set a regular meeting schedule (e.g., monthly, bimonthly, semiannually, etc.) for the purpose of reviewing and evaluating your child's progress.

- After the meeting, ask to have the minutes sent to you and other team members.

- Help promote ongoing communication by asking other team members to call or write you on a regular basis.

SOURCE: Salembier, G. B., & Furney, F. S. (1998). Speaking up for your child's future. *Exceptional Parent, 28*(7), 62–64. Reprinted with permission.

Advocacy in Action: You Can Advocate for Your Child

Get All the Information You Can

The first step to successful advocacy is to gather information. Learn what is happening in the school; get copies of school records, as well as information about any tests or evaluations affecting your child; and talk with your child's teacher to learn his or her view of areas of concern.

You should also learn about special education law and its protections. You can obtain this information from the school's special education or guidance director, state departments of education, or parent information and training centers, as well as organizations such as CEC (Council for Exceptional Children). Because the law can be complex and difficult to understand, you might want to work with a parent advocate, who can explain the law, as well as special education procedures.

Last but not least, talk with your child to learn his or her view of the situation and what he or she thinks will help. Even young children have a keen sense of their stress points and what could be done to make it easier for them to succeed.

What Do You Want the School to Do?

As your child's advocate, you need to be clear about what you want the school to do. Be able to explain what you are happy with, unhappy with, what you want changed, and how you want it changed. For example, if a child is having difficulty completing homework, you should say whether you would like the assignment to be changed or for it to be provided on tape.

To learn about the different options available, you could talk with other parents who have children with similar problems. Ask the school for contact names.

Be a Good Communicator

Communicating well with your child's teacher and other school personnel is essential to your advocacy efforts. Keep in mind that the school's interest is the same as yours—you both want the best for your child. In your dealings with the school, be honest and develop a positive relationship with the teacher and other staff. Start where the concern is, usually the classroom teacher. Only move up the chain of command if you must.

Being diplomatic can be hard when you are concerned about your child's welfare—you want to get feisty. But, get feisty only if that is what it takes.

Bring a Companion to Meetings

Bring a companion, a friend or advocate, with you to school meetings. This person can help you listen, take notes so you are free to concentrate on what is happening, and help you understand what happened afterwards. In addition, your companion can help slow you down if things get too emotional.

Don't Be Afraid to Say No

Don't be pressured into making a bad decision. You can always say no, ask for more information, or for more time to consider a proposed solution. Take the time to consult with experts and people you trust in the community, then get back to the school with your decision.

Due Process

If your child has a disability, you can use due process to resolve disputes with the school, but it should be a last resort. Often, due process proceedings turn the school and parents into adversaries. It is much more beneficial to maintain a positive relationship with the individuals who will work with your child.

Making Your Voice Stronger

One of the best ways to make your voice stronger is to band together with other parents facing similar situations. To learn of other parents who share your concern, give the school a sheet of labels containing your name and address and a statement that you would like to meet other parents facing a similar issue.

When you meet with other parents, share your experiences. As a group, develop some proposals to solve the problem. The parents should then meet with the individual(s) who will be affected. For example, a group of parents who wanted to get computers in the resource room would meet first with the resource room teacher. This approach allows the parents to build a strong partnership with the teachers. Then teachers and parents can build an alliance, which can be particularly effective in creating change.

SOURCE: Osher, T. (1997). Advocacy in action: You can advocate for your child! *CEC Today, 4*(4).

contributing to the development of their children with disabilities. We are just beginning to enable families to provide supportive and enriching environments for their children. And we are just beginning to harness the expertise of families so we can provide the best possible programs for their children.

Summary

At one time the prevailing attitude toward parents of persons with disabilities was negative. Professionals viewed them as causes of their children's problems, at worst, or as roadblocks to educational efforts, at best. Two factors have contributed to a much more positive attitude toward parents: First, current theory dictates that children, even young infants, can cause changes in adults' behavior. Professionals now view adult–child interaction as a two-way street—sometimes adults affect children, and sometimes the reverse is true. Second, professionals began to see parents as a potential source of information about how to educate their children. Most authorities now believe that parents should not be viewed as quasi-therapists or quasi-teachers—the goal should be to preserve the natural parent–child relationship. Current law also recognizes the central role the family plays—in particular, individualized family service plans (IFSPs) stress the need for family-centered programming.

Many theorists believe that parents go through a series of stages after learning that they have a child with a disability. There are limitations to a stage approach, however, including the tendency to view all parents as going through all the stages in the same order. Nevertheless, many parents do have emotional reactions; for example, guilt.

Parents of children with disabilities must deal with a number of sources of stress, including the reactions of the public toward them and the feelings of the children themselves. How parents cope with the stress varies. Although very few experience major psychological disturbances, they are at risk for mild forms of depression. How well they deal with stress is dependent upon two factors: (1) their prior psychological makeup and marital satisfaction and (2) the quality and degree of informal support. There is not clear consensus on whether the impact of having a child with a disability results in the same amount of stress in mothers and fathers, but there is apparently a trend for fathers to have more stress than was once the case.

At one time, professionals focused on the negative impact on parents of having a child with a disability. Today, professionals are more aware that the impact is not always totally negative. In fact, some parents report undergoing positive changes, such as being more tolerant of differences in others, being more concerned about social issues, being better parents, and having a closer-knit family.

Siblings of children with disabilities experience some of the same emotions that parents do. Because they are less mature, may not have a broad base of people with whom to talk, and may be hesitant to talk over sensitive issues with their parents, siblings may have a difficult time coping with their emotions. There is suggestive evidence that birth order, gender, and age differences interact to influence how well one adjusts to having a sibling with disabilities. During adolescence, children's feelings often become centered on how society views them and their family. Nondisabled older girls, siblings of the same gender, and siblings close in age appear to have more difficulties. However, in adulthood, women tend to have more positive relationships with their siblings with disabilities than do men. Like their parents, most children are able to adjust to siblings with disabilities.

Current family practitioners advocate a family-focused or family-centered approach, in which professionals work for families, helping them obtain access to nonprofessional (e.g., family and friends) as well as formal sources of support. Families are encouraged to be active in decision making. Current theorists also stress the influence of the social context on child development. They note that the family, as a whole, affects individual family members and that society affects the family. Family systems theory is a family-centered approach to families that considers the social context.

The Turnbulls' family systems model includes four components: family characteristics, family interaction, family functions, and family life cycle. *Family characteristics* comprise the type and severity of the disability as well as such things as the size, cultural background, and socioeconomic background of the family. *Family interaction* refers to how cohesive and adaptable the family is. *Family functions* include such things as economics, daily care, social, medical, and educational needs. It is important for teachers to keep in mind that education is just one of many needs to which the family must attend; some parents prefer more passive than active involvement in educational programming. The *family life cycle* is made up of birth and early childhood, childhood, adolescence, and adulthood. Transitions between stages, especially between preschool and school and between adolescence and adulthood, can be very difficult for families with children who are disabled. With regard to the latter, some families must deal with the complex issue of guardianship.

Current family-centered approaches stress the importance of social support—the emotional, informational, or material aid provided informally by such persons as the extended family, friends, neighbors, and church groups.

One source of social support is that of parent support groups, made up of parents who have children with similar disabilities. The Internet has grown into an excellent resource for parents, as well. A social systems program is built on the assumption that it is better to enable families to help themselves than to provide only direct services to them.

Family theorists agree that the key to working with and involving parents is *communication*. The parent–teacher conference is one of the most common avenues, and preparation is the key to a successful conference. A home-note program, in which teachers send home brief checklists of students' behavior that they have filled out, can keep parents informed and involve them in reinforcing the students' behavior. A traveling notebook is a log that accompanies the child to and from school, in which the parent, teacher, and other professionals can write messages to one another concerning the child's progress. Parents can also stay in touch with professionals through advocacy activities.

Glossary

Acceleration. An approach in which students with special gifts or talents are placed in grade levels ahead of their age peers in one or more academic subjects.

Acquired aphasia. Loss or impairment of the ability to understand or formulate language because of accident or illness.

Acquired immune deficiency syndrome (AIDS). A virus-caused illness resulting in a breakdown of the immune system; currently, no known cure exists.

Acute. A serious state of illness or injury from which someone often recovers with treatment.

Adapted signs. Signs adapted for use by people who are deaf-blind; tactually-based rather than visually-based, such as American Sign Language for those who are deaf but sighted.

Adaptive devices. Special tools that are adaptations of common items to make accomplishing self-care, work, or recreation activities easier for people with physical disabilities.

Adaptive skills. Skills needed to adapt to one's living environment (e.g., communication, self-care, home living, social skills, community use, self-direction, health and safety, functional academics, leisure, and work); usually estimated by an adaptive behavior survey; one of two major components (the other is intellectual functioning) of the AAMR definition.

Adderall. A psychostimulant for ADHD; effects are longer acting than Ritalin.

Adventitiously deaf. Deafness that occurs through illness or accident in an individual who was born with normal hearing.

Advocacy. Action that is taken on behalf of oneself or others; a method parents of students with disabilities can use to obtain needed or improved services.

Affective disorder. A disorder of mood or emotional tone characterized by depression or elation.

Aggression. Behavior that intentionally causes others harm or that elicits escape or avoidance responses from others.

Americans with Disabilities Act (ADA). Civil rights legislation for persons with disabilities ensuring nondiscrimination in a broad range of activities.

Amniocentesis. A medical procedure that allows examination of the amniotic fluid around the fetus; sometimes recommended to determine the presence of abnormality.

Anoxia. Deprivation of oxygen; can cause brain injury.

Anxiety disorder. A disorder characterized by anxiety, fearfulness, and avoidance of ordinary activities because of anxiety or fear.

Apraxia. The inability to move the muscles involved in speech or other voluntary acts.

Aqueous humor. A watery substance between the cornea and lens of the eye.

Articulation. The movements the vocal tract makes during production of speech sounds; enunciation of words and vocal sounds.

Asperger syndrome (AS). A developmental disability in which language and cognitive development are normal but the child may show a lag in motor development and impairment in emotional and social development; included in *autistic spectrum disorder*.

Assistance card. A relatively small card containing a message that alerts the public that the user is deaf-blind and needs assistance crossing the street.

Asthma. A lung disease characterized by episodic difficulty in breathing, particularly exhaling, due to inflammation or obstruction of the air passages.

Astigmatism. Blurred vision caused by an irregular cornea or lens.

Athetosis. A type of cerebral palsy that involves fluctuating muscle tone and almost constant uncontrolled movement.

Atresia. Absence or closure of a part of the body that is normally open.

Attention deficit hyperactivity disorder (ADHD). A condition characterized by severe problems of inattention, hyperactivity, and/or impulsivity; often found in persons with learning disabilities.

Audiologist. An individual trained in audiology, the science dealing with hearing impairments, their detection, and remediation.

Audiometric zero. The lowest level at which people with normal hearing can hear.

Auditory habilitation. Part of the auditory-verbal approach for children with hearing loss; stresses children developing their residual hearing to the maximum.

Auditory-verbal approach. Part of the oral approach to teaching students who are hearing impaired; stresses teaching the person to use his or her remaining hearing as much as possible; heavy emphasis on use of amplification; heavy emphasis on teaching speech.

Augmentative or alternative communication (AAC). Alternative forms of communication that do not use the oral sounds of speech or that augment the use of speech.

Auricle. The visible part of the ear, composed of cartilage; collects the sounds and funnels them via the external auditory canal to the eardrum.

Authentic assessment. A method that evaluates a student's critical-thinking and problem-solving ability in real-life situations in which he or she may work with or receive help from peers, teachers, parents, or supervisors.

Autism. A pervasive developmental disability characterized by extreme withdrawal, cognitive deficits, language disorders, self-stimulation, and onset before the age of thirty months.

Autistic savant. A person with severe autism whose social and language skills are markedly delayed but who also has advanced skills in a particular area, such as calculation or drawing.

Autistic spectrum disorder.   A range of disorders characterized by symptoms of autism that can range from mild to severe.

Autosomal recessive disorder.   A genetically transmitted disorder in which both parents must carry the gene; Usher syndrome is an example of such a disorder.

Basal ganglia.   A set of structures within the brain that include the caudate, globus pallidus, and putamen, the first two being abnormal in people with ADHD; generally responsible for the coordination and control of movement.

Behavior management.   Strategies and techniques used to increase desirable behavior and decrease undesirable behavior. May be applied in the classroom, home, or other environment.

Behavior modification.   Systematic control of environmental events, especially of consequences, to produce specific changes in observable responses. May include reinforcement, punishment, modeling, self-instruction, desensitization, guided practice, or any other technique for strengthening or eliminating a particular response.

Behavioral inhibition.   The ability to stop an intended response, to stop an ongoing response, to guard an ongoing response from interruption, and to refrain from responding immediately; allows executive functions to occur; delayed or impaired in those with ADHD.

Behavioral phenotype.   A collection of behaviors, including cognitive, language, and social behaviors as well as psychopathological symptoms that tend to occur together in persons with a specific genetic syndrome.

Behavioral.   Focus on behavior itself and the observable conditions and events causing it, rather than unconscious motivations.

Bicultural-bilingual approach.   An approach for teaching students with hearing impairment that stresses teaching American Sign Language as a first language, English as a second language, and promotes the teaching of Deaf culture.

Blindisms.   Repetitive, stereotyped movements (e.g., rocking or eye rubbing); characteristic of some persons who are blind, severely retarded, or psychotic; more appropriately referred to as *stereotypic behaviors.*

Braille.   A system in which raised dots allow people who are blind to read with their fingertips; each quadrangular cell contains from one to six dots, the arrangement of which denotes different letters and symbols.

Braille bills.   Legislation passed in several states to make braille more available to students with visual impairment; specific provisions vary from state to state, but major advocates have lobbied for (1) making braille available if parents want it, and (2) ensuring that teachers of students with visual impairment are proficient in braille.

Braille notetakers.   Portable devices that can be used to take notes in braille, which are then converted to speech, braille, or text.

Cataracts.   A condition caused by clouding of the lens of the eye; affects color vision and distance vision.

Catheterization.   The insertion of a tube into the urethra to drain the bladder.

Caudate.   A structure in the basal ganglia of the brain; site of abnormal development in persons with ADHD.

Center-based.   A program implemented primarily in a school or center, not in the student's home.

Cerebellum.   An organ at the base of the brain responsible for coordination and movement; site of abnormal development in persons with ADHD.

Cerebral palsy (CP).   A condition characterized by paralysis, weakness, lack of coordination, and/or other motor dysfunction; caused by damage to the brain before it has matured.

Childhood disintegrative disorder.   Normal development followed by significant loss, after age two but before age ten, of previously acquired social, language, self-care, or play skills with qualitative impairment in social interaction or communication and stereotyped behavior.

Choanae.   Air passages from the nose to the throat.

Choreoathetoid.   Characterized by involuntary movements and difficulty with balance; associated with choreoathetoid cerebral palsy.

Chorionic villus sampling (CVS).   A method of testing the unborn fetus for a variety of chromosomal abnormalities, such as Down syndrome; a small amount of tissue from the chorion (a membrane that eventually helps form the placenta) is extracted and tested; can be done earlier than amniocentesis but the risk of miscarriage is slightly higher.

Chromosomal disorder.   Any of several syndromes resulting from abnormal or damaged chromosome(s); can result in mental retardation.

Chromosome.   A rod-shaped entity in the nucleus of the cell; contains genes, which convey hereditary characteristics; each cell in the human body contains 23 pairs of chromosomes.

Chronic.   A permanent condition; not temporary.

Chronological age.   Refers to how old a person is; used in comparison to mental age to determine IQ. IQ = (mental age ÷ chronological age) ∞ 100.

Classwide peer tutoring (CWPT).   An instructional procedure in which all students in the class are involved in tutoring and being tutored by classmates on specific skills as directed by their teacher.

Cleft palate.   A condition in which there is a rift or split in the upper part of the oral cavity; may include the upper lip (cleft lip).

Closed head injury.   Damage to the brain that occurs without penetration of the skull; might be caused by a blow to the head or violent shaking by an adult.

Coaching.   A technique whereby a friend or therapist offers encouragement and support for a person with ADHD.

Cochlea.   A snail-shaped organ that lies below the vestibular mechanism in the inner ear; its parts convert the sounds coming from the middle ear into electrical signals that are transmitted to the brain.

Cochlear implantation.   A surgical procedure that allows people who are deaf to hear some environmental sounds; an external coil fitted on the skin by the ear picks up sound from a microphone worn by the person and transmits it to an internal coil implanted in the bone behind the ear, which carries it to an electrode implanted in the cochlea of the inner ear.

Cognition.   The ability to solve problems and use strategies; an area of difficulty for many persons with learning disabilities.

Cognitive mapping.   A nonsequential way of conceptualizing the spatial environment that allows a person who is visually impaired to know where several points in the environment are simultaneously; allows for better mobility than does a strictly sequential conceptualization of the environment.

Cognitive training.   A group of training procedures designed to change thoughts or thought patterns.

Collaborative consultation.   An approach in which a special educator and a general educator collaborate to come up with teaching strategies for a student with disabilities. The relationship between the two professionals is based on the premises of shared responsibility and equal authority.

Coloboma.   A condition of the eye in which the pupil is abnormally shaped and/or there are abnormalities of the retina or optic nerve; can result in loss of visual acuity and extreme sensitivity to light.

Communication disorders.   Impairments in the ability to use speech or language to communicate.

Community residential facility (CRF).   A place, usually a group home, in an urban or residential neighborhood where about three to ten adults with mental retardation live under supervision.

Comorbidity.   Co-occurrence of two or more conditions in the same individual.

Competitive employment.   A workplace that provides employment that pays at least minimum wage and in which most workers are nondisabled.

Comprehension monitoring.   The ability to keep track of one's own comprehension of reading material and to make adjustments to comprehend better while reading; often deficient in students with learning disabilities.

Computerized axial tomographic (CAT) scans.   A neuroimaging technique whereby X rays of the brain are compiled by a computer to produce a series of pictures of the brain.

Conceptual intelligence.   The traditional conceptualization of intelligence, emphasizing problem solving related to academic material; what IQ tests primarily assess.

Conduct disorder.   A disorder characterized by overt, aggressive, disruptive behavior or covert antisocial acts such as stealing, lying, and fire setting; may include both overt and covert acts.

Conductive hearing loss.   A hearing loss, usually mild, resulting from malfunctioning along the conductive pathway of the ear (i.e., the outer or middle ear).

Congenital anomaly.   An irregularity (anomaly) present at birth; may or may not be due to genetic factors.

Congenital cytomegalovirus (CMV).   The most frequently occurring viral infection in newborns; can result in a variety of disabilities, especially hearing impairment.

Congenitally deaf.   Deafness that is present at birth; can be caused by genetic factors, by injuries during fetal development, or by injuries occurring at birth.

Constant time delay.   An instructional procedure whereby the teacher makes a request while simultaneously prompting the student and then over several occasions makes the same request and waits a constant period of time before prompting; often used with students with mental retardation.

Contingency-based self-management.   Educational techniques that involve having students keep track of their own behavior, for which they then receive consequences (e.g., reinforcement).

Continuum of alternative placements (CAP).   The full range of alternative placements, from those assumed to be least restrictive to those considered most restrictive; the continuum ranges from regular classrooms in neighborhood schools to resource rooms, self-contained classes, special day schools, residential schools, hospital schools, and home instruction.

Contractures.   Permanent shortenings of muscles and connective tissues and consequent distortion of bones and/or posture because of neurological damage.

Cooperative learning.   A teaching approach in which the teacher places students with heterogeneous abilities (for example, some might have disabilities) together to work on assignments.

Cooperative teaching.   An approach in which general educators and special educators teach together in the general classroom; it helps the special educator know the context of the regular classroom better.

Cornea.   A transparent cover in front of the iris and pupil in the eye; responsible for most of the refraction of light rays in focusing on an object.

Cortical visual impairment (CVI).   A poorly understood childhood condition that apparently involves dysfunction in the visual cortex; characterized by large day-to-day variations in visual ability.

Cranial nerves.   Twelve pairs of nerves that connect the brain with various muscles and glands in the body.

Creativity.   The ability to express novel and useful ideas, to sense and elucidate new and important relationships, and to ask previously unthought-of but crucial questions.

Criterion-referenced testing.   Assessment wherein an individual's performance is compared to a goal or standard of mastery, differs from norm-referenced testing wherein an individual's performance is compared to the performance of others.

Cued speech.   A method to aid speechreading in people with hearing impairment; the speaker uses hand shapes to represent sounds.

Cultural-familial mental retardation.   Today, a term used to refer to mild mental retardation due to an unstimulating environment and/or hereditary factors.

Curriculum-based assessment (CBA).   A formative evaluation method designed to evaluate performance in the particular curriculum to which students are exposed; usually involves giving students a small sample of items from the curriculum in use in their schools; proponents argue that CBA is preferable to comparing students with national norms or using tests that do not reflect the curriculum content learned by students.

Cystic fibrosis.   An inherited disease affecting primarily the gastrointestinal (GI) tract and respiratory organs; characterized by thick, sticky mucous that often interferes with breathing or digestion.

Cytomegalovirus (CMV).   A herpes virus; can cause a number of disabilities.

Daily living skills.   Skills required for living independently, such as dressing, toileting, bathing, cooking, and other typical daily activities of nondisabled adults.

Deaf clubs.   Gathering spots where people who are deaf can socialize; on the decline in the United States.

Decibels.   Units of relative loudness of sounds; zero decibels (0 dB) designates the point at which people with normal hearing can just detect sound.

Deinstitutionalization.   A social movement of the 1960s and 1970s whereby large numbers of persons with mental retardation and/or mental illness were moved from large mental institutions into smaller community homes or into the homes of their families; recognized as a major catalyst for integrating persons with disabilities into society.

Descriptive Video Service. A service for use of people with visual impairment that provides audio narrative of key visual elements; available for several public television programs and some videos of movies.

Developmental delay. A term often used to encompass a variety of disabilities of infants or young children indicating that they are significantly behind the norm for development in one or more areas such as motor development, cognitive development, or language.

Developmentally appropriate practice (DAP). Educational methods for young children that are compatible with their developmental levels and that meet their individual needs; coined by the National Association for the Education of Young Children (NAEYC).

Diabetic retinopathy. A condition resulting from interference with the blood supply to the retina; the fastest-growing cause of blindness.

Diplegia. A condition in which the legs are paralyzed to a greater extent than the arms.

Direct Instruction (DI). A method of teaching academics, especially reading and math; emphasizes drill and practice and immediate feedback; lessons are precisely sequenced, fast-paced, and well-rehearsed by the teacher.

Disability rights movement. Patterned after the civil rights movement of the 1960s, this is a loosely organized effort to advocate for the rights of people with disabilities through lobbying legislators and other activities. Members view people with disabilities as an oppressed minority.

Discourse. Conversation; the skills used in conversation, such as turn taking and staying on the topic.

Doctor's office effect. The observation that children with ADHD often do not exhibit their symptoms when seen by a clinician in a brief office visit.

Dopamine. A neurotransmitter, the levels of which may be too low in the frontal lobes and too high in the basal ganglia of persons with ADHD.

Doppler effect. A term used to describe the phenomenon of the pitch of a sound rising as the listener moves toward its source.

Down syndrome. A condition resulting from an abnormality with the twenty-first pair of chromosomes; the most common abnormality is a triplet rather than a pair (the condition sometimes referred to as trisomy 21); characterized by mental retardation and such physical signs as slanted-appearing eyes, hypotonia, a single palmar crease, shortness, and a tendency toward obesity.

Dysarthria. A condition in which brain damage causes impaired control of the muscles used in articulation.

Early expressive language delay (EELD). A significant lag in the development of expressive language that is apparent by age two.

Echolalia. The parroting repetition of words or phrases either immediately after they are heard or later; usually observed in individuals with *autistic spectrum disorder*.

Education for All Handicapped Children Act. Also known as Public Law 94–142, which became law in 1975 and is now known as the Individuals with Disabilities Education Act (IDEA).

Encephalitis. An inflammation of the brain; can affect the child's mental development adversely.

Encopresis. Bowel incontinence; soiling oneself.

Enrichment. An approach in which additional learning experiences are provided for students with special gifts or talents while they remain in the grade levels appropriate for their chronological ages.

Enuresis. Urinary incontinence; wetting oneself.

Epilepsy. A pattern of repeated seizures.

Episodic. Occurring in episodes; a temporary condition that will pass but may recur.

Error analysis. An informal method of teacher assessment that involves the teacher noting the particular kinds of errors a student makes when doing academic work.

Eugenics movement. A popular movement of the late nineteenth and early twentieth centuries that supported the selective breeding of humans; resulted in laws restricting the marriage of individuals with mental retardation and sterilization of some of them.

Evoked-response audiometry. A technique involving electroencephalograph measurement of changes in brain-wave activity in response to sounds.

Executive functions. The ability to regulate one's behavior through working memory, inner speech, control of emotions and arousal levels, and analysis of problems and communication of problem solutions to others; delayed or impaired in those with ADHD.

Expressive language. Encoding or sending messages in communication.

External otitis. An infection of the skin of the external auditory canal; also called "swimmer's ear."

Externalizing. Acting-out behavior; aggressive or disruptive behavior that is observable as behavior directed toward others.

Familiality studies. A method of determining the degree to which a given condition is inherited; looks at the prevalence of the condition in relatives of the person with the condition.

Family-centered model. A type of early intervention program; consumer-driven in that professionals are viewed as working for families; views family members as the most important decision makers.

Family characteristics. A component of the Turnbulls' family systems model; includes type and severity of the disability as well as such things as size, cultural background, and socioeconomic background of the family.

Family functions. A component of the Turnbulls' family systems model; includes such things as economic, daily care, social, medical, and educational needs.

Family interaction. A component of the Turnbulls' family systems model; refers to how cohesive and adaptable the family is.

Family life cycle. A component of the Turnbulls' family systems model; consists of birth and early childhood, childhood, adolescence, and adulthood.

Family systems theory. Stresses that the individual's behavior is best understood in the context of the family and the family's behavior is best understood in the context of other social systems.

Fetal alcohol syndrome (FAS). Abnormalities associated with the mother's drinking alcohol during pregnancy; defects range from mild to severe, including growth retardation, brain damage, mental retardation, hyperactivity, anomalies of the face, and heart failure; also called alcohol embryopathy.

Fingerspelling.   Spelling the English alphabet by using various finger positions on one hand.

Fluency.   The flow with which oral language is produced.

Formative assessment.   Measurement procedures used to monitor an individual student's progress; they are used to compare how an individual performs in light of his or her abilities, in contrast to standardized tests, which are primarily used to compare an individual's performance to that of other students.

Fragile X syndrome.   A condition in which the bottom of the X chromosome in the twenty-third pair of chromosomes is pinched off; can result in a number of physical anomalies as well as mental retardation; occurs more often in males than females; thought to be the most common hereditary cause of mental retardation.

Free appropriate public education (FAPE).   The primary intent of federal special education law, that the education of all children with disabilities will in all cases be free of cost to parents (i.e., at public expense) and appropriate for the particular student.

Frontal lobes.   Two lobes located in the front of the brain; responsible for executive functions; site of abnormal development in people with ADHD.

Full inclusion.   All students with disabilities are placed in their neighborhood schools in general education classrooms for the entire day; general education teachers have the primary responsibility for students with disabilities.

Functional academics.   Practical skills (e.g., reading a newspaper or telephone book) rather than academic learning skills.

Functional behavioral assessment (FBA).   Evaluation that consists of finding out the consequences (what purpose the behavior serves), antecedents (what triggers the behavior), and setting events (contextual factors) that maintain inappropriate behaviors; this information can help teachers plan educationally for students.

Functional magnetic resonance imaging (fMRI).   An adaptation of the MRI used to detect changes in the brain while it is in an active state; unlike a PET scan, it does not involve using radioactive materials.

Functional magnetic resonance spectroscopy (fMRS).   An adaptation of the MRI used to detect changes in the brain while it is in an active state; unlike a PET scan, it does not involve using radioactive materials.

Functional vision assessment.   An appraisal of an individual's use of vision in everyday situations.

Genius.   A word sometimes used to indicate a particular aptitude or capacity in any area; rare intellectual powers.

Genre.   A plan or map for discourse; type of narrative discourse.

Giftedness.   Refers to cognitive (intellectual) superiority, creativity, and motivation of sufficient magnitude to set the child apart from the vast majority of age-mates and make it possible for him or her to contribute something of particular value to society.

Glaucoma.   A condition of excessive pressure in the eyeball; the cause is unknown; if untreated, blindness results.

Globus pallidus.   A structure in the basal ganglia of the brain; site of abnormal development in persons with ADHD.

Guardianship.   A legal term that gives a person the authority to make decisions for another person; can be full, limited, or temporary; applies in cases of parents who have children who have severe cognitive disabilities.

Hand-over-hand guidance.   A tactile learning strategy for persons who are deaf-blind; the teacher places his or her hands over those of the person who is deaf-blind and guides them to explore objects.

Hand-under-hand guidance.   A tactile learning strategy for persons who are deaf-blind; the teacher places his or her hands underneath part of the student's hand or hands while the child is exploring objects.

Handicapism.   A term used by activists who fault the unequal treatment of individuals with disabilities. This term is parallel to the term *racism*, coined by those who fault unequal treatment based on race.

Hemiplegia.   A condition in which one half (right or left side) of the body is paralyzed.

Heritability studies.   A method of determining the degree to which a condition is inherited; a comparison of the prevalence of a condition in identical (i.e., monozygotic, from the same egg) twins versus fraternal (i.e., dizygotic, from two eggs) twins.

Herpes simplex.   A viral disease that can cause cold sores or fever blisters; if it affects the genitals and is contracted by the mother-to-be in the later stages of fetal development, it can cause mental subnormality in the child.

Hertz (Hz).   A unit of measurement of the frequency of sound; refers to the highness or lowness of a sound.

Home-based.   A program delivered primarily in a student's home rather than in a school or center.

Home-note program.   A system of communication between the teacher and parents; the teacher evaluates the behavior of the student using a simple form, the student takes the form home, gets the parents' signatures, and returns the form the next day.

Homophenes.   Sounds that are different but that look the same with regard to movements of the face and lips (i.e., visible articulatory patterns).

Hydrocephalus.   A condition characterized by enlargement of the head because of excessive pressure of the cerebrospinal fluid.

Hydrocephalus.   A condition characterized by enlargement of the head because of excessive pressure of the cerebrospinal fluid.

Hyperactive child syndrome.   A term used to refer to children who exhibit inattention, impulsivity, and/or hyperactivity; popular in the 1960s and 1970s.

Hyperopia.   Farsightedness; vision for near objects is affected; usually results when the eyeball is too short.

Hypotonic.   A term describing low muscle tone that sometimes occurs as a result of cerebral palsy.

Inborn errors of metabolism.   Deficiencies in enzymes used to metabolize basic substances in the body, such as amino acids, carbohydrates, vitamins, or trace elements; can sometimes result in mental retardation; PKU is an example.

Inclusive schools movement.   A reform movement designed to restructure general education schools and classrooms so they better accommodate all students, including those with disabilities.

Incus.   The anvil-shaped bone in the ossicular chain of the middle ear.

Individualized education program (IEP).   IDEA requires an IEP to be drawn up by the educational team for each exceptional child; the IEP must include a statement of present educational performance, instructional goals, educational services to be provided, and criteria and procedures for determining that the instructional objectives are being met.

Individualized family service plan (IFSP).   A plan mandated by PL 99–457 to provide services for young children with disabilities (under three years of age) and their families; drawn up by professionals and parents; similar to an IEP for older children.

Individuals with Disabilities Education Act (IDEA).   The Individuals with Disabilities Education Act of 1990 and its amendments of 1997; replaced PL 94–142. A federal law stating that to receive funds under the act, every school system in the nation must provide a free, appropriate public education for every child between the ages of three and twenty-one, regardless of how or how seriously he or she may be disabled.

Informal reading inventory (IRI).   A method of assessing reading in which the teacher has the student read progressively more difficult series of passages or word lists; the teacher notes the difficulty level of the material read and the types of errors the student makes.

Inner speech.   An executive function; internal language used to regulate one's behavior; delayed or impaired in those with ADHD.

Insight.   The ability to separate and/or combine various pieces of information in new, creative, and useful ways.

Intellectual functioning.   The ability to solve problems related to academics; usually estimated by an IQ test; one of two major components (the other is adaptive skills) of the AAMR definition.

Internalizing.   Acting-in behavior; anxiety, fearfulness, withdrawal, and other indications of an individual's mood or internal state.

IQ–achievement discrepancy.   Academic performance markedly lower than would be expected based on a student's intellectual ability.

Iris.   The colored portion of the eye; contracts or expands, depending on the amount of light striking it.

Itinerant teacher services.   Services for students who are visually impaired in which the special education teacher visits several different schools to work with students and their general education teachers; the students attend their local schools and remain in general education classrooms.

Job coach.   A person who assists adult workers with disabilities (especially those with mental retardation), providing vocational assessment, instruction, overall planning, and interaction assistance with employers, family, and related government and service agencies.

Juvenile rheumatoid arthritis.   A systemic disease with major symptoms involving the muscles and joints.

Kurzweil 1000.   A computerized device that converts print into speech for persons with visual impairment; the user places the printed material over a scanner that then reads the material aloud by means of an electronic voice.

Language disorders.   Oral communication that involves a lag in the ability to understand and express ideas, putting linguistic skill behind an individual's development in other areas, such as motor, cognitive, or social development.

Language.   An arbitrary code or system of symbols to communicate meaning.

Large print books.   Books having a font-size that is larger than the usual 10-point type; a popular size for large print books is 18-point type.

Larynx.   The structure in the throat containing the vocal apparatus (vocal cords); laryngitis is a temporary loss of voice caused by inflammation of the larynx.

Learned helplessness.   A motivational term referring to a condition wherein a person believes that no matter how hard he or she tries, failure will result.

Least restrictive environment (LRE).   A legal term referring to the fact that exceptional children must be educated in as normal an environment as possible.

Legally blind.   A person who has visual acuity of 20/200 or less in the better eye even with correction (e.g., eyeglasses) or has a field of vision so narrow that its widest diameter subtends an angular distance no greater than 20 degrees.

Lens.   A structure that refines and changes the focus of the light rays passing through the eye.

Levels of support.   The basis of the AAMR classification scheme; characterizes the amount of support needed for someone with mental retardation to function as competently as possible as (1) intermittent, (2) limited, (3) extensive, or (4) pervasive.

Literary braille.   Braille symbols used for most writing situations.

Locus of control.   A motivational term referring to how people explain their successes or failures; people with an internal locus of control believe they are the reason for success or failure, whereas people with an external locus of control believe outside forces influence how they perform.

Long cane.   A mobility aid used by individuals with visual impairment, who sweep it in a wide arc in front of them; proper use requires considerable training; the mobility aid of choice for most travelers who are blind.

Low birthweight (LBW).   Babies who are born weighing less than 5.5 pounds; usually premature; at risk for behavioral and medical conditions, such as mental retardation.

Low vision.   A term used by educators to refer to individuals whose visual impairment is not so severe that they are unable to read print of any kind; they may read large or regular print, and they may need some kind of magnification.

Macroculture.   A nation or other large social entity with a shared culture.

Magnetic resonance imaging (MRI).   A neuroimaging technique whereby radio waves are used to produce cross-sectional images of the brain; used to pinpoint areas of the brain that are dysfunctional.

Mainstreaming.   The placement of students with disabilities in general education classes for all or part of the day and for all or only a few classes; special education teachers maintain the primary responsibility for students with disabilities.

Malleus.   The hammer-shaped bone in the ossicular chain of the middle ear.

Mandatory sentencing.   Laws requiring specific sentences for specific violations, removing the discretion of the judge in sentencing based on circumstances of the defendant or other considerations.

Manifestation determination.   Determination that a student's misbehavior is or is not a manifestation of a disability.

Maternal serum screening (MSS).   A method of screening the fetus for developmental disabilities such as Down syndrome or spina bifida; a blood sample is taken from the mother and analyzed; if it is positive, a more accurate test such as amniocentesis or CVS is usually recommended.

Meningitis.   A bacterial or viral infection of the linings of the brain or spinal cord; can cause a number of disabilities.

Mental age.   Age level at which a person performs on an IQ test; used in comparison to chronological age to determine IQ. IQ = (mental age ÷ chronological age) ∞ 100.

Metacognition.   A person's (1) awareness or understanding of what strategies are necessary to perform a task and (2) the ability to use self-regulation strategies to complete the task.

Microcephalus.   A condition causing development of a small, conical-shaped head; proper development of the brain is prevented, resulting in mental retardation.

Microculture.   A smaller group existing within a larger cultural group and having unique values, style, language, dialect, ways of communicating nonverbally, awareness, frame of reference, and identification.

Mild mental retardation.   A classification used to specify an individual whose IQ is approximately 55–70.

Milieu teaching.   A naturalistic approach to language intervention in which the goal is to teach functional language skills in a natural environment.

Minimal brain injury.   A term used to describe a child who shows behavioral but not neurological signs of brain injury; the term is not as popular as it once was, primarily because of its lack of diagnostic utility (i.e., some children who learn normally show signs indicative of minimal brain injury). A term popular in the 1950s and 1960s to refer to children who exhibit inattention, impulsivity, and/or hyperactivity.

Mixed hearing loss.   A hearing loss resulting from a combination of conductive and sensorineural hearing impairments.

Mnemonics.   Techniques that aid memory, such as using rhymes, songs, or visual images to remember information.

Moderate mental retardation.   A classification used to specify an individual whose IQ is approximately 40–55.

Molecular genetics.   The study of the organization of DNA, RNA, and protein molecules containing genetic information.

Morphology.   The study within psycholinguistics of word formation; how adding or deleting parts of words changes their meaning.

Multicultural education.   Aims to change educational institutions and curricula so they will provide equal educational opportunities to students regardless of their gender, social class, ethnicity, race, disability, or other cultural identity.

Muscular dystrophy.   A hereditary disease characterized by progressive weakness caused by degeneration of muscle fibers.

Myopia.   Nearsightedness; vision for distant objects is affected; usually results when eyeball is too long.

Narrative.   Self-controlled, self-initiated discourse; description or storytelling.

Native-language emphasis.   An approach to teaching language-minority pupils in which the student's native language is used for most of the day and English is taught as a separate subject.

Natural supports.   Resources in a person's environment that can be used for support, such as friends, family, co-workers.

Nemeth Code.   Braille symbols used for mathematics and science.

Neonatal intensive care units (NICUs).   A special unit in a hospital designed to provide around the clock monitoring and care of newborns who have severe physical problems; staffed by professionals from several disciplines, e.g., nursing, social work, occupational therapy, respiratory therapy, medicine; similar to an intensive care unit for older children and adults.

Neuroleptics.   Antipsychotic drugs; drugs that suppress or prevent symptoms of psychosis; major tranquilizers.

Neurotransmitters.   Chemicals involved in sending messages between neurons in the brain.

Newsline.   A service allowing access via touch-tone phone to several national newspapers; available free of charge to those who are visually impaired.

Night blindness.   A condition characterized by problems in seeing at low levels of illumination; often caused by retinitis pigmentosa.

Nonverbal learning disabilities.   A term used to refer to individuals who have a cluster of disabilities in social interaction, math, visual-spatial tasks, and tactual tasks.

Normalization.   A philosophical belief in special education that every individual, even the most disabled, should have an educational and living environment as close to normal as possible.

Nystagmus.   A condition in which there are rapid involuntary movements of the eyes; sometimes indicates a brain malfunction and/or inner-ear problems.

Obstacle sense.   A skill possessed by some people who are blind, whereby they can detect the presence of obstacles in their environments; research has shown that it is not an indication of an extra sense, as popularly thought; it is the result of being able to detect subtle changes in the pitches of high-frequency echoes.

Open head injury.   A brain injury in which there is an open wound in the head, such as a gunshot wound or penetration of the head by an object, resulting in damage to brain tissue.

Optic nerve.   The nerve at the back of the eye, which sends visual information back to the brain.

Oralism–manualism debate.   The controversy over whether the goal of instruction for students who are deaf should be to teach them to speak or to teach them to use sign language.

Orientation and mobility (O & M) skills.   The ability to have a sense of where one is in relation to other people, objects, and landmarks and to move through the environment.

Orthosis.   A device designed to restore, partially or completely, a lost function of the body (e.g., a brace or crutch).

Ossicles.   Three tiny bones (malleus, incus, and stapes) that together make possible an efficient transfer of sound waves from the eardrum to the oval window, which connects the middle ear to the inner ear.

Otitis media.   Inflammation of the middle ear.

Otoacoustic emissions.   Low-intensity sounds produced by the cochlea in response to auditory stimulation; used to screen hearing problems in infants and very young children.

Oval window.   The link between the middle and inner ears.

Paradoxical effect of Ritalin.   The now discredited belief that Ritalin, even though a stimulant, acts to subdue a person's behavior and that this effect of Ritalin is evident in persons with ADHD but not in those without ADHD.

Paraplegia.   A condition in which both legs are paralyzed.

Partial participation.   An approach in which students with disabilities, while in the general education classroom, engage in the same activities as nondisabled students but on a reduced basis; the teacher adapts the activity to allow each student to participate as much as possible.

Peer tutoring. A method that can be used to integrate students with disabilities in general education classrooms, based on the notion that students can effectively tutor one another. The role of learner or teacher may be assigned to either the student with a disability or the nondisabled student.

Peer-mediated instruction. The deliberate use of a student's classroom peer(s) to assist in teaching an academic or social skill.

Perinatal causes of mental retardation. Causes at birth; some examples are anoxia, low birthweight, and infections such as syphilis and herpes simplex.

Perkins Brailler. A system that makes it possible to write in braille; has six keys, one for each of the six dots of the cell, which leave an embossed print on the paper.

Perseveration. A tendency to repeat behaviors over and over again; often found in persons with brain injury, as well as those with ADHD.

Person-centered plan. A method of planning for persons with disabilities that places the person and his family at the center of the planning process.

Person-centered planning. Planning for a person's self-determination; planning activities and services based on a person's dreams, aspirations, interests, preferences, strengths, and capacities.

Pervasive developmental disorder (PDD). A severe developmental disorder characterized by abnormal social relations, including bizarre mannerisms, inappropriate social behavior, and unusual or delayed speech and language.

Pervasive developmental disorder not otherwise specified (PDD-NOS). A severe developmental disorder that does not fit into any existing subcategory.

Phenylketonuria (PKU). A metabolic genetic disorder caused by the inability of the body to convert phenylalanine to tyrosine; an accumulation of phenylalanine results in abnormal brain development.

Phonological awareness. The ability to understand grapheme-phoneme correspondence—the rules by which sounds go with letters to make up words; generally thought to be the reason for the reading problems of many students with learning disabilities.

Phonology. The study of how individual sounds make up words.

Play audiometry. Use of a game-like format to test hearing of young and hard-to-test children; the examiner teaches the child to respond to sounds.

Portfolios. A collection of samples of a student's work done over time; a type of authentic assessment.

Positive behavioral intervention (PBI) or Positive behavioral intervention and supports (PBIS). Positive reinforcement (rewarding) procedures intended to support a student's appropriate or desirable behavior.

Positive behavioral support (PBS). Systematic use of the science of behavior to find ways of supporting the desirable behavior of an individual rather than punishing the undesirable behavior.

Positron emission tomography (PET) scans. A computerized method for measuring bloodflow in the brain; during a cognitive task, a low amount of radioactive dye is injected in the brain; the dye collects in active neurons, indicating which areas of the brain are active.

Postlingual deafness. Deafness occurring after the development of speech and language.

Postnatal causes of mental retardation. Causes occurring after birth; can be biological (e.g., traumatic brain injury, infections) or psychosocial (an unstimulating environment).

Postnatal. Occurring in an infant after birth.

Practical intelligence. The ability to solve problems related to activities of daily living.

Prader-Willi syndrome. Caused by inheriting from one's father a lack of genetic material on the fifteenth pair of chromosomes; leading genetic cause of obesity; degree of mental retardation varies, but the majority fall within the mildly mentally retarded range.

Pragmatics. The study within psycholinguistics of how people use language in social situations; emphasizes the functional use of language, rather than mechanics.

Preacademic skills. Behaviors that are needed before formal academic instruction can begin (e.g., ability to identify letters, numbers, shapes, and colors).

Preassessment teams (PATs). Teams made up of a variety of professionals, especially regular and special educators, who work with regular class teachers to devise strategies for teaching difficult-to-teach children before they are formally assessed for special education.

Precocity. Remarkable early development.

Prefrontal lobes. Two lobes located in the very front of the frontal lobes; responsible for executive functions; site of abnormal development in people with ADHD.

Prelingual deafness. Deafness that occurs before the development of spoken language, usually at birth.

Prelinguistic communication. Communication through gestures and noises before the child has learned oral language.

Prenatal. Occurring or developing in the fetus before birth.

Prenatal causes of mental retardation. Causes occurring during fetal development; some examples include chromosomal disorders, inborn errors of metabolism, developmental disorders affecting brain formation, and environmental influences.

Prereferral teams (PRTs). Teams made up of a variety of professionals, especially regular and special educators, who work with regular class teachers to come up with strategies for teaching difficult-to-teach children. Designed to influence regular educators to take ownership of difficult-to-teach students and to minimize inappropriate referrals to special education.

Profound mental retardation. A classification used to specify an individual whose IQ is below approximately 25.

Progressive. A disease or condition that worsens over time and from which one seldom or never recovers with treatment.

Progressive time delay. An instructional procedure whereby the teacher makes a request while simultaneously prompting the student and then over several occasions gradually increases the latency between the request and the prompt; often used with students with mental retardation.

Prosthesis. A device designed to replace, partially or completely, a part of the body (e.g., artificial teeth or limbs).

Psychoanalytic. Related to psychoanalysis, including the assumptions that emotional or behavioral disorders result primarily from unconscious conflicts and that the most effective preventive actions and therapeutic interventions involve uncovering and understanding unconscious motivations.

Psychoeducational. Blending psychodynamic (unconscious motivations) and behavioral theories in approaching education and management.

Psychostimulants. Medications that activate dopamine levels in the frontal and prefrontal areas of the brain that control behavioral inhibition and executive functions; used to treat persons with ADHD.

Pull-out programs. Special education programs in which students with disabilities leave the general education classroom for part or all of the school day (e.g., to go to special classes or resource room).

Pupil. The contractile opening in the middle of the iris of the eye.

Pure-tone audiometry. A test whereby tones of various intensities and frequencies are presented to determine a person's hearing loss.

Quadriplegia. A condition in which all four limbs are paralyzed

Readiness skills. Skills deemed necessary before academics can be learned (e.g., attending skills, ability to follow directions, knowledge of letter names).

Receptive language. Decoding or understanding messages in communication.

Reciprocal teaching. A cognitive teaching strategy whereby the student gradually assumes the role of co-instructor for brief periods; the teacher models four strategies for the students to use: (1) predicting, (2) questioning, (3) summarizing, and (4) clarifying. A method in which students and teachers are involved in a dialogue to facilitate learning.

Refraction. The bending of light rays as they pass through the structures (cornea, aqueous humor, pupil, lens, vitreous humor) of the eye.

Regular education initiative (REI). A philosophy that maintains that general education, rather than special education, should be primarily responsible for the education of students with disabilities.

Resonance. The quality of the sound imparted by the size, shape, and texture of the organs in the vocal tract.

Retina. The back portion of the eye, containing nerve fibers connected to the optic nerve.

Retinitis pigmentosa. A hereditary condition resulting in degeneration of the retina; causes a narrowing of the field of vision and affects night vision.

Retinopathy of prematurity (ROP). A condition resulting from administration of an excessive concentration of oxygen at birth; causes scar tissue to form behind the lens of the eye.

Rett's disorder. Apparently normal development through at least age five months, followed by deceleration of head growth between ages five months and forty-eight months, loss of psychomotor skills, and severe impairment of expressive and receptive language; usually associated with severe mental retardation.

Ritalin. The most commonly prescribed psychostimulant for ADHD; generic name is methylphenidate.

Rubella (German measles). A serious viral disease, which, if it occurs during the first trimester of pregnancy, is likely to cause deformity in the fetus.

Scaffolded instruction. A cognitive approach to instruction in which the teacher provides temporary structure or support while students are learning a task; the support is gradually removed as the students are able to perform the task independently.

Schizophrenia. A disorder characterized by psychotic behavior manifested by loss of contact with reality, distorted thought processes, and abnormal perceptions.

Scoliosis. An abnormal curvature of the spine

Seizure (convulsion). A sudden alteration of consciousness, usually accompanied by motor activity and/or sensory phenomena; caused by an abnormal discharge of electrical energy in the brain.

Self-determination. The ability to make personal choices, regulate one's own life, and be a self-advocate; a prevailing philosophy in education programming for persons with mental retardation. Having control over one's life, not having to rely on others for making choices about one's quality of life; develops over one's life span.

Self-injurious behavior (SIB). Behavior causing injury or mutilation of oneself, such as self-biting or head-banging; usually seen in individuals with severe and multiple disabilities.

Self-instruction. A type of cognitive training technique that requires individuals to talk aloud and then to themselves as they solve problems.

Self-monitoring. A type of cognitive training technique that requires individuals to keep track of their own behavior; students monitor their own behavior, such as attention to task, and then record it on a sheet.

Self-regulation. Refers generally to a person's ability to regulate his or her own behavior (e.g., to employ strategies to help in a problem-solving situation); an area of difficulty for persons who are mentally retarded.

Self-stimulation. Any repetitive, stereotyped activity that seems only to provide sensory feedback.

Semantics. The study of the meanings attached to words and sentences.

Sensorineural hearing loss. A hearing loss, usually severe, resulting from malfunctioning of the inner ear.

Serotonin. A neurotransmitter, the levels of which may be abnormal in persons with ADHD.

Severe mental retardation. A classification used to specify an individual whose IQ is approximately 25–40.

Sheltered workshop. A facility that provides a structured environment for persons with disabilities in which they can learn skills; can be either a transitional placement or a permanent arrangement.

Sheltered-English approach. A method in which language-minority students are taught all their subjects in English at a level that is modified constantly according to individuals' needs.

Short-term memory. The ability to recall information after a short period of time.

Sibshops. Workshops for siblings of children with disabilities; they are designed to help siblings answer questions about the disability and learn to adjust to having a sister or brother with a disability.

Sign language. A manual language used by people who are deaf to communicate; a true language with its own grammar.

Signing English systems. Used simultaneously with oral methods in the total communication approach to teaching students who are deaf; different from American Sign Language because they maintain the same word order as spoken English.

Slate and stylus. A method of writing in braille in which the paper is held in a slate while a stylus is pressed through openings to make indentations in the paper.

Sleep apnea.   Cessation of breathing while sleeping.

Snellen chart.   Used in determining visual acuity; consists of rows of letters or Es arranged in different positions; each row corresponds to the distance at which a normally sighted person can discriminate the letters; does not predict how accurately a child will be able to read print.

Social intelligence.   The ability to understand social expectations and to cope in social situations.

Social support.   Emotional, informational, or material aid provided to a person or a family; this informal means of aid can be very valuable in helping families of children with disabilities.

Sociocultural theory.   The theory that the individual, interpersonal or social experiences, and community or institution are all important and inseparable causes of human behavior and that language ties all of these aspects of development together.

Sonography.   A medical procedure in which high-frequency sound waves are converted into a visual picture; used to detect major physical malformations in the unborn fetus.

Spastic.   A term describing a sudden, involuntary contraction of muscles that makes accurate, voluntary movement difficult.

Spasticity.   Characterized by muscle stiffness and problems in voluntary movement; associated with spastic cerebral palsy.

Specific language impairment (SLI).   A language disorder with no identifiable cause; language disorder not attributable to hearing impairment, mental retardation, brain dysfunction, or other plausible cause; also called specific language disability.

Speech.   The formation and sequencing of oral language sounds during communication.

Speech audiometry.   A technique that tests a person's detection and understanding of speech, rather than using pure tones to detect hearing loss.

Speech disorders.   Oral communication that involves abnormal use of the vocal apparatus, is unintelligible, or is so inferior that it draws attention to itself and causes anxiety, feelings of inadequacy, or inappropriate behavior in the speaker.

Speech reception threshold (SRT).   The decibel level at which a person can understand speech.

Speechreading.   A method that involves teaching children to use visual information from a number of sources to understand what is being said to them; more than just lipreading, which uses only visual clues arising from the movement of the mouth in speaking.

Spina bifida.   A congenital midline defect resulting from failure of the bony spinal column to close completely during fetal development.

Standardized achievement assessment.   A method of evaluating a person that has been applied to a large group so that an individual's score can be compared to the norm, or average.

Stapes.   The stirrup-shaped bone in the ossicular chain of the middle ear.

Stereotypic behaviors.   Any of a variety of repetitive behaviors (e.g., eye rubbing) that are sometimes found in individuals who are blind, severely retarded, or psychotic; sometimes referred to as *stereotypies* or *blindisms*.

Strabismus.   A condition in which the eyes are directed inward (crossed eyes) or outward.

Strauss syndrome.   Behaviors of distractibility, forced responsiveness to stimuli, and hyperactivity; based on the work of Alfred Strauss and Heinz Werner with children with mental retardation.

Stuttering.   Speech characterized by abnormal hesitations, prolongations, and repetitions; may be accompanied by grimaces, gestures, or other bodily movements indicative of a struggle to speak, anxiety, blocking of speech, or avoidance of speech.

Supported competitive employment.   A workplace where adults who are disabled earn at least minimum wage and receive ongoing assistance from a specialist or job coach; the majority of workers in the workplace are nondisabled.

Supported employment.   A method of integrating people with disabilities who cannot work independently into competitive employment; includes use of an employment specialist, or job coach, who helps the person with a disability function on the job.

Supported living.   An approach to living arrangements for those with mental retardation that stresses living in natural settings rather than institutions, big or small.

Syntax.   The way words are joined together to structure meaningful sentences; grammar.

Syphilis.   A venereal disease that can cause mental subnormality in a child, especially if it is contracted by the mother-to-be during the latter stages of fetal development.

Systematic instruction.   Teaching that involves instructional prompts, consequences for performance, and transfer of stimulus control; often used with students with mental retardation.

Talent.   A special ability, aptitude, or accomplishment.

Task analysis.   The procedure of breaking down an academic task into its component parts for the purpose of instruction; a major feature of Direct Instruction.

Teratogens.   Agents, such as chemicals, that can disrupt the normal development of the fetus; a possible cause of learning disabilities and other learning and behavioral problems.

Text telephone (TT).   A device connected to a telephone by a special adapter; allows communication over the telephone between persons who are hearing impaired and those with hearing; sometimes referred to as a TTY (teletype) or TTD (telecommunication device for the deaf).

Total communication approach.   An approach for teaching students with hearing impairment that blends oral and manual techniques.

Touch cues.   Tactual signals used to communicate with persons who are deaf-blind; can be used to signify a variety of messages.

Tourette's syndrome (TS).   A neurological disorder beginning in childhood (about three times more prevalent in boys than in girls) in which stereotyped, repetitive motor movements (tics) are accompanied by multiple vocal outbursts that may include grunting noises or socially inappropriate words or statements (e.g., swearing).

Toxins.   Poisons in the environment that can cause fetal malformations; can result in cognitive impairments.

Transliteration.   A method used by sign language interpreters in which the signs maintain the same word order as that of spoken English; although used by most interpreters, found through research not to be as effective as American Sign Language (ASL).

Traumatic brain injury (TBI).   Injury to the brain (not including conditions present at birth, birth trauma, or degenerative diseases or conditions) resulting in total or partial disability or psychosocial maladjustment that affects educational performance; may affect cognition, language, memory, attention, reasoning, abstract thinking, judgment, problem solving, sensory or perceptual and motor disabilities, psychosocial behavior, physical functions, information processing, or speech.

Traveling notebook.   A system of communication in which parents and professionals write messages to each other by way of a notebook or log that accompanies the child to and from school.

Trisomy 21.   A type of Down syndrome in which the twenty-first chromosome is a triplet, making forty-seven, rather than the normal forty-six, chromosomes in all.

Tunnel vision.   A condition characterized by problems in peripheral vision, or a narrowing of the field of vision.

Tympanic membrane (eardrum).   The anatomical boundary between the outer and middle ears; the sound gathered in the outer ear vibrates here.

Tympanometry.   A method of measuring the middle ear's response to pressure and sound.

Unified Braille Code.   A combination of literary braille and braille codes for technical fields, such as the Nemeth Code for science and mathematics; not yet widely adopted.

Universal design.   The design of new buildings, tools, and instructional programs to make them useable by the widest possible population of potential users.

Usher syndrome.   An inherited syndrome resulting in hearing loss and retinitis pigmentosa, a progressive condition characterized by problems in seeing in low light and tunnel vision; there are three different types of Usher syndrome, differing with respect to when it occurs developmentally and the range of the major symptoms of hearing loss, vision loss, and balance problems.

Vestibular mechanism.   Located in the upper portion of the inner ear; consists of three soft, semicircular canals filled with a fluid; sensitive to head movement, acceleration, and other movements related to balance.

Visual efficiency.   A term used to refer to how well one uses his or her vision, including such things as control of eye movements, attention to visual detail, and discrimination of figure from background; believed by some to be more important than visual acuity alone in predicting a person's ability to function visually.

Vitreous humor.   A transparent, gelatinous substance that fills the eyeball between the retina and the lens of the eye.

Williams syndrome.   A condition resulting from deletion of material in the seventh pair of chromosomes; often results in mild to moderate mental retardation, heart defects, and elfin facial features; people affected often display surprising strengths in spoken language and sociability while having severe deficits in spatial organization, reading, writing, and math.

Working memory.   The ability to remember information while also performing other cognitive operations.

Zero tolerance.   A school policy, supported by federal and state laws, that having possession of any weapon or drug on school property will automatically result in a given penalty (usually suspension or expulsion) regardless of the nature of the weapon or drug or any extenuating circumstances.

References

CHAPTER 1

Bateman, B.D., & Linden, M.A. (1998). *Better IEPs: How to develop legally correct and educationally useful programs* (3rd ed.). Longmont, CO: Sopris West.

Bolger, K.E., & Patterson, C.J. (2001). Developmental pathways from child maltreatment to peer rejection. *Child Development, 72,* 549–568.

Clark, D.L., & Astuto, T.A. (1988). Education policy after Reagan—What next? Occasional paper No. 6, Policy Studies Center of the University Council for Educational Administration, University of Virginia, Charlottesville.

Council for Exceptional Children. (1998). *What every special educator must know* (3rd ed.). Reston, VA: Author.

Council for Exceptional Children (2001). *Performance-Based Standards.* Retrieved June 5, 2001 from www.cec.sped.org/ps/perf_based_stds/index.html <http://www.cec.sped.org/ps/perf_based_stds/index.html>

Crockett, J.B., & Kauffman, J.M. (1999). *The least restrictive environment: Its origins and interpretations in special education.* Mahwah, NJ: Erlbaum.

Crockett, J.B., & Kauffman, J.M. (2001). The concept of the least restrictive environment and learning disabilities: Least restrictive of what? Reflections on Cruickshank's 1977 guest editorial for the *Journal of Learning Disabilities.* In D.P. Hallahan & B.K. Keogh (Eds.), *Research and global perspectives in learning disabilities: Essays in honor of William M. Cruickshank.* (pp 147–166). Mahwah, NJ: Erlbaum.

Cruickshank, W.M. (1977). Guest editorial. *Journal of Learning Disabilities, 10,* 193–194.

Dupre, A.P. (1997). Disability and the public schools: The case against "inclusion." *Washington Law Review, 72*(3), 775–858.

Finn, C.E., Jr., Rotherham, A.J., & Hokanson, C.R., Jr. (Eds.). (2001). *Rethinking special education for a new century.* New York: Thomas B. Fordham Foundation.

Fuchs, D., & Fuchs, L.S. (1994). Inclusive schools movement and the radicalization of special education reform. *Exceptional Children, 60,* 294–309.

Goodman, J.F., & Bond, L. (1993). The individualized education program: A retrospective critique. *Journal of Special Education, 26,* 408–422.

Hallahan, D.P., & Kauffman, J.M. (1977). Labels, categories, behaviors: ED, LD, and EMR reconsidered. *Journal of Special Education, 11,* 139–149.

Hallahan, D.P., Kauffman, J.M., & Lloyd, J.W. (1999). *Introduction to learning disabilities* (2nd ed.). Boston: Allyn & Bacon.

Hart, B., & Risley, T.R. (1995). *Meaningful differences in the everyday experience of young American children.* Baltimore: Paul H. Brookes.

Hockenbury, J.C., Kauffman, J.M., & Hallahan, D.P. (1999–2000). What's right about special education? *Exceptionality, 8*(1), 3–11.

Hendrick, I.G., & MacMillan, D.L. (1989). Selecting children for special education in New York City: William Maxwell, Elizabeth Farrell, and the development of ungraded classes, 1900–1920. *Journal of Special Education, 22,* 395–417.

Howe, K.R., & Miramontes, O.B. (1992). *The ethics of special education.* New York: Teachers College Press.

Huefner, D.S. (1994). The mainstreaming cases: Tensions and trends for school administrators. *Educational Administration Quarterly, 30,* 27–55.

Huefner, D.S. (2000). *Getting comfortable with special education law: A framework for working with children with disabilities.* Norwood, MA: Christopher Gordon.

Hungerford, R. (1950). On locusts. *American Journal of Mental Deficiency, 54,* 415–418.

Itard, J.M.G. (1962). *The wild boy of Aveyron.* (George & Muriel Humphrey, Trans.). Englewood Cliffs, NJ: Prentice-Hall.

Kanner, L. (1964). *A history of the care and study of the mentally retarded.* Springfield, IL: Charles C. Thomas.

Kauffman, J.M. (1976). Nineteenth century views of children's behavior disorders: Historical contributions and continuing issues. *Journal of Special Education, 10,* 335–349.

Kauffman, J.M. (1995). Why we must celebrate a diversity of restrictive environments. *Learning Disabilities Research and Practice, 10,* 225–232.

Kauffman, J.M. (1999a). Today's special education and its messages for tomorrow. *The Journal of Special Education, 32,* 244–254.

Kauffman, J.M. (1999b). How we prevent the prevention of emotional and behavioral disorders. *Exceptional Children, 65,* 448–468.

Kauffman, J.M. (1999–2000). The special education story: Obituary, accident report, conversion experience, reincarnation, or none of the above? *Exceptionality, 8*(1), 61–71.

Kauffman, J.M., & Hallahan, D.P. (Eds.). (1995). *The illusion of full inclusion: A comprehensive critique of a current special educational bandwagon.* Austin, TX: Pro-Ed.

Kauffman, J.M., & Hallahan, D.P. (1997). A diversity of restrictive environments: Placement as a problem of social ecology. In J.W. Lloyd, E.J. Kameenui, & D. Chard (Eds.), *Issues in educating students with disabilities* (pp. 325–342). Hillsdale, NJ: Erlbaum.

Kauffman, J.M., Mostert, M.P., Trent, S.C., & Hallahan, D.P. (2002). *Managing classroom behavior: A reflective case-based approach* (3rd ed.). Boston: Allyn & Bacon.

Kuusisto, S. (1998). *The planet of the blind: A memoir.* New York: Dial Press.

Lloyd, J.W., Forness, S.R., & Kavale, K.A. (1998). Some methods are more effective. *Intervention in School and Clinic, 33*(1), 195–200.

Lloyd, J.W., Singh, N.N., & Repp, A.C. (Eds.). (1991). *The regular education initiative: Alternative perspectives on concepts, issues, and models.* Sycamore, IL: Sycamore Publishing.

MacMillan, D.L., & Forness, S.R. (1998). The role of IQ in special education placement decisions: Primary and determinative or peripheral and inconsequential? *Remedial and Special Education, 19,* 239–253.

MacMillan, D.L., & Hendrick, I.G. (1993). Evolution and legacies. In J.I. Goodlad & T.C. Lovitt (Eds.), *Integrating general and special education.* Columbus, OH: Merrill/Macmillan.

Martin, E.W. (1995). Case studies of inclusion: Worst fears realized. *The Journal of Special Education, 29,* 192–199.

Mock, D.R., & Kauffman, J.M. (in press). Preparing teachers for full inclusion: Is it possible? *The Teacher Educator.*

Morse, W.C. (1984). Personal perspective. In B. Blatt & R. Morris (Eds.), *Perspectives in special education: Personal orientations.* Glenview, IL: Scott, Foresman.

National Center on Educational Restructuring and Inclusion (1995). National study on inclusion: Overview and summary report. *National Center on Educational Restructuring and Inclusion Bulletin, 2*(2), 1–10.

National Research Council. (2001). *Educating children with autism.* Committee on Educational Interventions for Children with Autism. Division of Behavioral and Social Sciences and Education. Washington, DC: National Academy Press.

Patterson, G.R., Reid, J.B., & Dishion, T.J. (1992). *Antisocial boys.* Eugene, OR: Castalia.

Pierce, B. (2001). Weihenmayer reaches the top. *Braille Monitor, 44,* 497–514.

Richards, P.L., & Singer, G.H.S. (1998). "To draw out the effort of his mind": Educating a child with mental retardation in early-nineteenth-century America. *The Journal of Special Education, 31,* 443–466.

Safford, P.L., & Safford, E.H. (1998). Visions of the special class. *Remedial and Special Education, 19,* 229–238.

Sarason, S.B. (1990). *The predictable failure of educational reform: Can we change course before it's too late?* San Francisco: Jossey-Bass.

Smith, J.D. (1998a). Histories of special education: Stories from our past, insights for our future. *Remedial and Special Education, 19,* 196–200.

Smith, J.D. (Ed.). (1998b). The history of special education: Essays honoring the bicentennial of the work of Jean Itard. [Special issue]. *Remedial and Special Education, 19*(4).

Taylor, H. (1995, July 18). Louis Harris/N.O.D. survey finds employers overwhelmingly support the ADA—and jobs. *The Washington Post,* p. A10.

Stein, M., & Davis, C.A. (2000). Direct instruction as a positive behavioral support. *Beyond Behavior, 10*(1), 7–12.

Trent, J.W. (1998). Defectives at the World's Fair: Constructing disability in 1904. *Remedial and Special Education, 19,* 201–211.

U.S. Department of Education. (1995). *Seventeenth annual report to Congress on implementation of the Individuals with Disabilities Education Act.* Washington, DC: Author.

U.S. Department of Education. (1997). *Nineteenth annual report to Congress on implementation of the Individuals with Disabilities Education Act.* Washington, DC: Author.

U.S. Department of Education. (2000). *Twenty-second annual report to Congress on implementation of the Individuals with Disabilities Education Act.* Washington, DC: Author.

Verstegen, D.A., & Clark, D.L. (1988). The diminution of federal expenditures for education during the Reagan administration. *Phi Delta Kappan, 70,* 134–138.

Werner, E.E. (1986). The concept of risk from a developmental perspective. In B.K. Keogh (Ed.), *Advances in special education:*

Vol. 5. Developmental problems in infancy and the preschool years. Greenwich, CT: JAI Press.

Winzer, M.A. (1986). Early developments in special education: Some aspects of Enlightenment thought. *Remedial and Special Education, 7*(5), 42–49.

Winzer, M.A. (1993). *The history of special education: From isolation to integration.* Washington, DC: Gallaudet University Press.

Winzer, M.A. (1998). A tale often told: The early progression of special education. *Remedial and Special Education, 19,* 212–218.

Yell, M.L. (1998). *The law and special education.* Upper Saddle River, NJ: Prentice-Hall.

Yell, M.L., Rogers, D., & Rogers, E.L. (1998). The legal history of special education: What a long, strange trip it's been! *Remedial and Special Education, 19,* 219–228.

Zelder, E.Y. (1953). Public opinion and public education for the exceptional child—Court decisions 1873–1950. *Exceptional Children, 18,* 187–198.

Zigmond, N. (1997). Educating students with disabilities: The future of special education. In J.W. Lloyd, E.J. Kameenui, & D. Chard (Eds.), *Issues in educating students with disabilities* (pp. 377–390). Mahwah, NJ: Erlbaum.

Zigmond, N., & Baker, J.M. (1995). Concluding comments: Current and future practices in inclusive schooling. *Journal of Special Education, 29,* 245–250.

CHAPTER 2

Abt Associates. (1976–1977). *Education as experimentation: A planned variation model* (Vols. 3A and 4). Cambridge, MA: Author.

Agran, M., Blanchard, C., & Wehmeyer, M.L. (2000). Promoting transition goals and self-determination through student self-directed learning: The self-determined learning model of instruction. *Education and Training in Mental Retardation and Developmental Disabilities, 35,* 351–364.

Arizona Easter Seal Society. (n.d.). *The first step. Friends who care. Friends who count.* Phoenix, AZ: Author.

Artesani, A.J., & Millar, L. (1998). Positive behavior supports in general education settings: Combining person-centered planning and functional analysis. *Intervention in School and Clinic, 34,* 33–38.

Bailey, D.B. (2000). The federal role in early intervention: Prospects for the future. *Topics in Early Childhood Special Education, 20,* 71–78.

Baker, J.M., & Zigmond, N. (1995). The meaning and practice of inclusion for students with learning disabilities: Themes and implications from the five cases. *Journal of Special Education, 29,* 163–180.

Bank-Mikkelsen, N.E. (1969). A metropolitan area in Denmark: Copenhagen. In R.B. Kugel & W. Wolfensberger (Eds.), *Changing patterns of residential services for the mentally retarded* (pp. 227–254). Washington, DC: President's Committee on Mental Retardation.

Bateman, B.D., & Linden, M.A. (1998). *Better IEPs: How to develop legally correct and educationally useful programs* (3rd ed.). Longmont, CO: Sopris West.

Baxter, J.A., Woodward, J., & Olson, D. (2001). Effects of reform-based mathematics instruction on low achievers in five third-grade classrooms. *Elementary School Journal, 101,* 529–547.

Bock, S.J., Tapscott, K.E., & Savner, J.L. (1998). Suspension and expulsion: Effective management for students? *Intervention in School and Clinic, 34,* 50–52.

Bogdan, R. (1986). The sociology of special education. In R.J. Morris & B. Blatt (Eds.), *Special education: Research and trends* (pp. 344–359). New York: Pergamon Press.

Bogdan, R., & Biklen, D. (1977). Handicapism. *Social Policy, 7*(5), 14–19.

Bowman, B.T. (1994). The challenge of diversity. *Phi Delta Kappan, 76,* 218–225.

Bradley, M.R. (Ed.) (2001). Positive behavior supports: Research to practice. *Beyond Behavior, 11*(1), [special feature].

Bricker, D.D. (1986). An analysis of early intervention programs: Attendant issues and future directions. In R.J. Morris & B. Blatt (Eds.), *Special education: Research and trends* (pp. 28–65). New York: Pergamon Press.

Bricker, D. (1995). The challenge of inclusion. *Journal of Early Intervention, 19,* 179–194.

Browder, D.M., Wood, W.M., Test, D.W., Karvonen, M., & Algozzine, B. (2001). Reviewing resources on self-determination: A map for teachers. *Remedial and Special Education, 22,* 233–244.

Bruder, M.B. (2000). Family-centered early intervention: Clarifying our values for the new millennium. *Topics in Early Childhood Special Education, 20,* 105–115, 122.

Buck, G.H., Polloway, E.A., Kirkpatrick, M.A., Patton, J.R., & Fad, K.M. (2000). Developing behavioral intervention plans: A sequential approach. *Intervention in School and Clinic, 36,* 3–9.

Carpenter, B., & Bovair, K. (1996). Learning with dignity: Educational opportunities for students with emotional and behavioral difficulties. *Canadian Journal of Special Education, 11*(1), 6–16.

Carta, J.J. (1995). Developmentally appropriate practice: A critical analysis as applied to young children with disabilities. *Focus on Exceptional Children, 27*(8), 1–14.

Carta, J.J., & Greenwood, C.R. (1997). Barriers to the implementation of effective educational practices for young children with disabilities. In J.W. Lloyd, E.J. Kameenui, & D. Chard (Eds.), *Issues in educating students with disabilities* (pp. 261–274). Mahwah, NJ: Erlbaum.

Chadsey-Rusch, J., & Heal, L.W. (1995). Building consensus from transition experts on social integration outcomes and interventions. *Exceptional Children, 62,* 165–187.

Collet-Klingenberg, L.L. (1998). The reality of best practices in transition: A case study. *Exceptional Children, 65,* 67–78.

Condon, K.A., & Tobin, T.J. (2001). Using electronic and other new ways to help students improve their behavior: Functional behavioral assessment at work. *Teaching Exceptional Children, 34*(1), 44–51.

Cook, B.G., Gerber, M.M., & Semmel, M.I. (1997). Are effective school reforms effective for all students? The implications of joint outcome production for school reform. *Exceptionality, 7,* 77–95.

Crissey, M.S., & Rosen, M. (Eds.). (1986). *Institutions for the mentally retarded: A changing role in changing times.* Austin, TX: Pro-Ed.

Crockett, J.B., & Kauffman, J.M. (1998). Taking inclusion back to its roots. *Educational Leadership, 56*(2), 74–77.

Crockett, J.B., & Kauffman, J.M. (1999). *The least restrictive environment: Its origins and interpretations in special education.* Mahwah, NJ: Erlbaum.

Crockett, J.B., & Kauffman, J.M. (2001). The concept of the least restrictive environment and learning disabilities: Least restrictive of what? Reflections on Cruickshank's 1977 guest editorial for the *Journal of Learning Disabilities.* In D.P. Hallahan & B.K. Keogh (Eds.), *Research and global perspectives in learning disabilities: Essays in honor of William M. Cruickshank* (pp. 147–166). Mahwah, NJ: Erlbaum.

Cronin, M.E. (2000). Instructional strategies. In P.L. Sitlington, G.M. Clark, & O.P. Kolstoe (Eds.), *Transition education and services for adolescents with disabilities* (3rd ed., pp. 255–283). Boston: Allyn & Bacon.

Cruickshank, W.M. (1977). Guest editorial. *Journal of Learning Disabilities, 10,* 193–194.

Duhaney, L.M.G., & Salend, S.J. (2000). Parental perceptions of inclusive educational placements. *Remedial and Special Education, 21,* 121–128.

Dupre, A.P. (1997). Disability and the public schools: The case against "inclusion." *Washington Law Review, 72,* 775–858.

Dupre, A.P. (2000). A study in double standards, discipline, and the disabled student. *Washington Law Review, 75*(1).

Dwyer, K.P., Osher, D., & Hoffman, C.C. (2000). Creating responsive schools: Contextualizing early warning, timely response. *Exceptional Children, 66,* 347–365.

Eiserman, W.D., Weber, C., & McCoun, M. (1995). Parent and professional roles in early intervention: A longitudinal comparison of the effects of two intervention configurations. *Journal of Special Education, 29,* 20–44.

Falk, K.B., & Wehby, J.H. (2001). The effects of peer-assisted learning strategies on the beginning reading skills of young children with emotional or behavioral disorders. *Behavioral Disorders, 26,* 344–359.

Feil, E.G., Walker, H.M., Severson, H., & Ball, A. (2000). Proactive screening for emotional/behavioral concerns in Head Start preschools: Promising practices and challenges in applied research. *Behavioral Disorders, 26,* 13–25.

Fennick, E. (2001). Coteaching: An inclusive curriculum for transition. *Teaching Exceptional Children, 33*(6), 60–66.

Fiedler, C.R., & Simpson, R.L. (1987). Modifying the attitudes of nonhandicapped high school students toward handicapped peers. *Exceptional Children, 53,* 342–349.

Finn, C.E., Jr., Rotherham, A.J., & Hokanson, C.R., Jr. (Eds.). (2001). *Rethinking special education for a new century.* New York: Thomas B. Fordham Foundation.

Fox, N., & Ysseldyke, J.E. (1997). Implementing inclusion at the middle school level: Lessons from a negative example. *Exceptional Children, 64,* 81–98.

Fuchs, D., & Fuchs, L.S. (1991). Framing the REI debate: Abolitionists versus conservationists. In J.W. Lloyd, N.N. Singh, & A.C. Repp (Eds.), *The regular education initiative: Alternative perspectives on concepts, issues, and models* (pp. 241–255). Sycamore, IL: Sycamore Publishing.

Fuchs, D., & Fuchs, L.S. (1992). Limitations of a feel-good approach to consultation. *Journal of Educational and Psychological Consultation, 3,* 93–97.

Fuchs, D., & Fuchs, L.S. (1994). Inclusive schools movement and the radicalization of special education reform. *Exceptional Children, 60,* 294–309.

Fuchs, D., Fuchs, L.S., Thompson, A., Svenson, E., Yanb, L., Otaiba, S.A., Yang, N., McMaster, K.N., Prentice, K., Kazdan, S., & Saenz, L. (2001). Peer-assisted learning strategies in reading: Extensions for kindergarten, first grade, and high school *Remedial and Special Education, 22,* 15–21.

Fulk, B.M., & King, K. (2001). Classwide peer tutoring at work. *Teaching Exceptional Children, 34*(2), 49–53.

Furney, K.S., Hasazi, S.B., & DeStefano, L. (1997). Transition policies, practices, and promises: Lessons from three states. *Exceptional Children, 63,* 343–355.

Gallagher, J.J. (1972). The special education contract for mildly handicapped children. *Exceptional Children, 38,* 527–535.

Gallagher, J.J. (1994). The pull of societal forces on special education. *Journal of Special Education, 27,* 521–530.

Gallagher, J.J. (2000). The beginnings of federal help for young children with disabilities. *Topics in Early Childhood Special Education, 20,* 3–6.

Gardner, R., Cartledge, G., Seidl, B., Woolsey, M.L., Schley, G.S., & Utley, C.A. (2001). Mt. Olivet after-school program: Peer-mediated interventions for at-risk students. *Remedial and Special Education, 22,* 22–33.

Garrett, J.N., Thorp, E.K., Behrmann, M.M., & Denham, S.A. (1998). The impact of early intervention legislation: Local perceptions. *Topics in Early Childhood Special Education, 18,* 183–189.

Gartner, A., & Joe, T. (1986). Introduction. In A. Gartner & T. Joe (Eds.), *Images of the disabled/disabling images.* New York: Praeger.

Greenwood, C.R., Arrega-Mayer, C., Utley, C.A., Gavin, K.M., & Terry, B. (2001). Classwide peer tutoring learning management system: Applications with elementary-level English language learners. *Remedial and Special Education, 22,* 34–47.

Grigal, M., Test, D.W., Beattie, J., & Wood, W.M. (1997). An evaluation of transition components of individualized education programs. *Exceptional Children, 63,* 357–372.

Gronna, S.S., Jenkins, A.A., & Chin-Chance, S.A. (1998). Who are we assessing: Determining state-wide participation rates for students with disabilities. *Exceptional Children, 64,* 407–418.

Guterman, B.R. (1995). The validity of categorical learning disabilities services: The consumer's view. *Exceptional Children, 62,* 111–124.

Hallahan, D.P., & Kauffman, J.M. (1994). Toward a culture of disability in the aftermath of Deno and Dunn. *Journal of Special Education, 27,* 496–508.

Hallahan, D.P., Kauffman, J.M., & Lloyd, J.W. (1999). *Introduction to learning disabilities* (2nd ed.). Boston: Allyn & Bacon.

Halpern, A.S. (1993). Quality of life as a conceptual framework for evaluating transition outcomes. *Exceptional Children, 59,* 486–498.

Heal, L.W., & Rusch, F.R. (1995). Predicting employment status for students who leave special education high school programs. *Exceptional Children, 61,* 472–487.

Hendrick, I.G., MacMillan, D.L., & Balow, I.H. (1989, April). *Early school leaving in America: A review of the literature.* Riverside: University of California, California Educational Research Cooperative.

Holbrook, P.J. (2001). When bad things happen to good children: A special educator's views of MCAS. *Phi Delta Kappan, 82,* 781–785.

Huefner, D.S. (2000). *Getting comfortable with special education law: A framework for working with children with disabilities.* Norwood, MA: Christopher Gordon.

Jakubecy, J.J., Mock, D.R., & Kauffman, J.M. (in press). Special education: Current trends. In J.W. Guthrie (Ed.), *Encyclopedia of education* (2nd ed.). New York: Macmillan Reference.

Kaiser, A.P. (Ed.) (2000). Special issue: Assessing and addressing problems in children enrolled in Head Start. *Behavioral Disorders, 26*(1).

Kastor, E. (1997, June 19). Ready, willing, and disabled: Women at global forum turn the wheelchairs of progress. *The Washington Post,* p. D1.

Katsiyannis, A., & Magg, J.W. (2001). Manifestation determination as a golden fleece. *Exceptional Children, 68,* 85–96.

Katz, L.G. (1994). Perspectives on the quality of early childhood programs. *Phi Delta Kappen, 76,* 200–205.

Kauffman, J.M. (1989). The regular education initiative as a Reagan-Bush education policy: A trickle-down theory of education of the hard-to-teach. *Journal of Special Education, 2,* 256–278.

Kauffman, J.M. (1999a). Today's special education and its messages for tomorrow. *Journal of Special Education, 32,* 244–254.

Kauffman, J.M. (1999b). How we prevent the prevention of emotional and behavioral disorders. *Exceptional Children, 65,* 448–468.

Kauffman, J.M. (1999–2000). The special education story: Obituary, accident report, conversion experience, reincarnation, or none of the above? *Exceptionality, 8*(1), 61–71.

Kauffman, J.M. (2001). *Characteristics of emotional and behavioral disorders of children and youth* (7th ed.). Upper Saddle River, NJ: Prentice-Hall.

Kauffman, J.M., Bantz, J., & McCullough, J. (in press). Separate and better: A special public school class for students with emotional and behavioral disorders. *Exceptionality.*

Kauffman, J.M., & Brigham, F.J. (2000). Editorial: Zero tolerance and bad judgment in working with students with emotional or behavioral disorders. *Behavioral Disorders, 26,* 5–6.

Kauffman, J.M., & Hallahan, D.P. (1992). Deinstitutionalization and mainstreaming exceptional children. In M.C. Alkin (Ed.), *Encyclopedia of educational research* (6th ed., Vol. 1, pp. 299–303). New York: Macmillan.

Kauffman, J.M., & Hallahan, D.P. (1993). Toward a comprehensive delivery system: The necessity of identity, focus, and authority for special education and other compensatory programs. In J.I. Goodlad & T.C. Lovitt (Eds.), *Integrating general and special education* (pp. 73–102). Columbus, OH: Merrill.

Kauffman, J.M., & Hallahan, D.P. (1997). A diversity of restrictive environments: Placement as a problem of social ecology. In J.W. Lloyd, E.J. Kameenui, & D. Chard (Eds.), *Issues in educating students with disabilities* (pp. 325–342). Hillsdale, NJ: Erlbaum.

Kauffman, J.M., & Lloyd, J.W. (1995). A sense of place: The importance of placement issues in contemporary special education. In J.M. Kauffman, J.W. Lloyd, D.P. Hallahan, & T.A. Astuto (Eds.), *Issues in educational placement: Students with emotional and behavioral disorders* (pp. 3–19). Hillsdale, NJ: Erlbaum.

Kauffman, J.M., Lloyd, J.W., Hallahan, D.P., & Astuto, T.A. (1995). Toward a sense of place for special education in the twenty-first century. In J.M. Kauffman, J.W. Lloyd, D.P. Hallahan, & T.A. Astuto (Eds.), *Issues in educational placement: Students with emotional and behavioral disorders* (pp. 379–385). Hillsdale, NJ: Erlbaum.

Kauffman, J.M., Mostert, M.P., Trent, S.C., & Hallahan, D.P. (2002). *Managing classroom behavior: A reflective case-based approach* (3rd ed.) Boston: Allyn & Bacon.

Kavale, K.A., & Forness, S.R. (2000). History, rhetoric, and reality: Analysis of the inclusion debate. *Remedial and Special Education, 21,* 279–296.

King-Sears, M.E. (2001). Institutionalizing peer-mediated instruction and interventions in schools: Beyond "train and hope." *Remedial and Special Education, 22,* 89–101.

Klinger, J.K., & Vaughn, S. (1998). Using collaborative strategic reading. *Teaching Exceptional Children, 30*(6), 32–37.

Klinger, J.K., Vaughn, S., Schumm, J.S., Cohen, P., & Forgan, J.W. (1998). Inclusion or pull-out: Which do students prefer? *Journal of Learning Disabilities, 31,* 148–158.

Klobas, L. (1985, January–February). TV's concept of people with disabilities: Here's lookin' at you. *The Disability Rag,* pp. 2–6. Louisville, KY: Advocado Press.

Kohler, P.D. (1998). Implementing a transition perspective of education: A comprehensive approach to planning and delivering secondary education and transition services (pp. 179–205). In F.R. Rusch & J.G. Chadsey (Eds.), *Beyond high school: Transition from school to work.* Belmont, CA: Wadsworth.

Landesman, S., & Butterfield, E.C. (1987). Normalization and de-institutionalization of mentally retarded individuals: Controversy and facts. *American Psychologist, 42,* 809–816.

Laski, F.J. (1991). Achieving integration during the second revolution. In L.H. Meyer, C.A. Peck, & L. Brown (Eds.), *Critical issues in the lives of people with severe disabilities* (pp. 409–421). Baltimore, MD: Paul H. Brookes.

Lerner, W., Lowenthal, B., & Egan, R. (1998). *Preschool children with special needs: Children at-risk, children with disabilities.* Boston: Allyn & Bacon.

Lieberman, L.M. (1992). Preserving special education . . . for those who need it. In W. Stainback & S. Stainback (Eds.), *Controversial issues confronting special education: Divergent perspectives* (pp. 13–25). Boston: Allyn & Bacon.

Longmore, P.K. (1985). Screening stereotypes: Images of disabled people. *Social Policy, 16,* 31–37.

Longmore, P.K., & Umansky, L. (Eds.). (2001). *The new disability history: American perspectives.* New York: New York University Press.

MacMillan, D.L., Widaman, K.F., Balow, I.H., Borthwick-Duffy, S., Hendrick, I.G., & Hemsley, R.E. (1992). Special education students exiting the educational system. *Journal of Special Education, 26*(1), 20–36.

Maheady, L., Harper, G.F., & Mallette, B. (2001). Peer-mediated instruction and interventions with students with mild disabilities. *Remedial and Special Education, 22,* 4–14.

Martin, E.W. (1994). Case studies on inclusion: Worst fears realized. *Journal of Special Education, 29,* 192–199.

Mathiason, C.S. (1997, February 15). *DPI advocates for a "disability-friendly" International Classification of Impairment, Disability and Handicap (ICIDH).* Retrieved from http://www.escape.ca/~dpi/icicdh.html

McCabe, L.A., Hernandez, M., Lara, S.L., & Brooks-Gunn, J. (2000). Assessing preschoolers' self-regulation in homes and classrooms: Lessons from the field. *Behavioral Disorders, 26,* 53–69.

McConnell, M.E., Hilvitz, P.B., & Cox, C.J. (1998). Functional assessment: A systematic process for assessment and intervention in general and special education classrooms. *Intervention in School and Clinic, 34,* 10–20.

McCray, A.D., Vaughn, S., & Neal, L.I. (2001). Not all students learn to read by third grade: Middle school students speak out about their reading disabilities. *Remedial and Special Education, 35,* 17–30.

McDonnell, L.M., McLaughlin, M.J., & Morison, P. (Eds.). (1997). *Educating one and all: Students with disabilities and standards-based reform.* Washington, DC: National Academy Press.

McLean, M.E., & Odom, S.L. (1993). Practices for young children with and without disabilities: A comparison of DEC and NAEYC identified practices. *Topics in Early Childhood Special Education, 13,* 274--292.

McNeil, L.M. (2000). Creating new inequalities: Contradictions of reform. *Phi Delta Kappan, 81,* 729–734.

Mills, P.E., Cole, K.N., Jenkins, J.R., & Dale, P.S. (1998). Effects of differing levels of inclusion on preschoolers with disabilities. *Exceptional Children, 65,* 79–90.

Mock, D.R., Jakubecy, J.J., & Kauffman, J.M. (in press). Special education, history of. In J.W. Guthrie (Ed.), *Encyclopedia of education* (2nd ed.). New York: Macmillan Reference.

Mock, D.R., & Kauffman, J.M. (in press). Preparing teachers for full inclusion: Is it possible? *The Teacher Educator.*

Moody, S.W., Vaughn, S., Hughes, M.T., & Fischer, M. (2000). Reading instruction in the resource room: Set up for failure. *Exceptional Children, 66,* 305–316.

Moon, M.S., & Inge, K. (2000). Vocational preparation and transition. In M.E. Snell & F. Brown (Eds.), *Instruction of students with severe disabilities* (5th ed., pp. 591–628). Upper Saddle River, NJ: Merrill.

Nelson, J.R., Martella, R., & Galand, B. (1998). The effects of teaching school expectations and establishing a consistent consequence on formal office disciplinary actions. *Journal of Emotional and Behavioral Disorders, 6,* 153–161.

Nelson, J.R., Roberts, M., Mather, S., & Rutherford, R.J. (1999). Has public policy exceeded our knowledge base? A review of the functional behavioral assessment literature. *Behavioral Disorders, 24,* 169–179

Noell, G.H., Witt, J.C., LaFleur, L.H., Mortenson, B.P., Rainer, D.D., & LeVelle, J. (2000). Increasing intervention implementation in general education following consultation: A comparison of two follow-up strategies. *Journal of Applied Behavior Analysis, 33,* 271–284.

Odom, S.L. (2000). Preschool inclusion: What we know and where we go from here. *Topics in Early Childhood Special Education, 20,* 20–27.

Ogletree, B.T., Bull, J., Drew, R., & Lunnen, K.Y. (2001). Team-based service delivery for students with disabilities: Practice option and guidelines for success. *Intervention in School and Clinic, 36,* 138–145.

Ormsbee, C.K. (2001). Effective preassessment team procedures: Making the process work for teachers and students. *Intervention in School and Clinic, 36,* 146–153.

Palmer, D.S., Fuller, K., Arora, T., & Nelson, M. (2001). Taking sides: Parent views on inclusion for their children with severe disabilities. *Exceptional Children, 67,* 467–484.

Pisha, B., & Coyne, P. (2001). Smart from the start: The promise of universal design for learning. *Remedial and Special Education, 22,* 197–203.

Pomplun, M. (1997). When students with disabilities participate in cooperative groups. *Exceptional Children, 64,* 49–58.

Position Statement of National Association for the Education of Young Children and National Association of Early Childhood Specialists in State Departments of Education. (1991). *Young Children, 46*(3), 21–38.

Pugach, M.C., & Warger, C.L. (2001). Curriculum matters: Raising expectations for students with disabilities. *Remedial and Special Education, 22,* 194–196.

Raynes, M., Snell, M., & Sailor, W. (1991). A fresh look at categorical programs for children with special needs. *Phi Delta Kappan, 73*(4), 326–331.

Rueda, R., Gallego, M.A., & Moll, L.C. (2000). The least restrictive environment: A place or a context? *Remedial and Special Education, 21,* 70–78.

Ruef, M.B., Higgins, C., Glaeser, B.J.C., & Patnode, M. (1998). Positive behavioral support: Strategies for teacher. *Intervention in School and Clinic, 34,* 21–32.

Safran, S.P. (1998). Disability portrayal in film: Reflecting the past, directing the future. *Exceptional Children, 64,* 227–238.

Safran, S.P. (2001). Movie images of disability and war: Framing history and political ideology. *Remedial and Special Education, 22,* 223–232.

Sailor, W. (1991). Special education in the restructured school. *Remedial and Special Education, 12*(6), 8–22.

Sainato, D.M., & Strain, P.S. (1993). Increasing integration success for preschoolers with disabilities. *Teaching Exceptional Children, 25*(2), 36–37.

Sale, P., & Carey, D.M. (1995). The sociometric status of students with disabilities in a full-inclusion school. *Exceptional Children, 62,* 6–19.

Sasso, G.M. (2001). The retreat from inquiry and knowledge in special education. *Journal of Special Education, 34,* 178–193.

Sasso, G.M., Conroy, M.A., Stichter, J.P., & Fox, J.J. (2001). Slowing down the bandwagon: The misapplication of functional assessment for students with emotional and behavioral disorders. *Behavioral Disorders, 26,* 269–281.

Schwartz, A.A., Jacobson, J.W., & Holburn, S.C. (2000). Defining person centeredness: Results of two consensus methods. *Education and Training in Mental Retardation and Developmental Disabilities, 35,* 235–249.

Scruggs, T.E., & Mastropieri, M.A. (1996). Teacher perceptions of mainstreaming/inclusion, 1958–1995: A research synthesis. *Exceptional Children, 63,* 59–74.

Semmel, M.I., Abernathy, T.V., Butera, G., & Lesar, S. (1991). Teacher perceptions of the regular education initiative. *Exceptional Children, 58*(1), 9–24.

Serna, L., Nielsen, E., Lambros, K., & Forness, S. (2000). Primary prevention with children at risk for emotional or behavioral disorders: Data on a universal intervention for Head Start classrooms. *Behavioral Disorders, 26,* 70–84.

Sinclair, M.F., Christenson, S.L., Evelo, D.L., & Hurley, C.M. (1998). Dropout prevention for youth with disabilities: Efficacy of a sustained school engagement procedure. *Exceptional Children, 65,* 7–21.

Sitlington, P.L., Clark, G.M., & Kolstoe, O.P. (2000). *Transition education and services for adolescents with disabilities* (3rd ed.). Boston: Allyn & Bacon.

Skiba, R.J., & Peterson, R.L. (2000). School discipline at a crossroads: From zero tolerance to early response. *Exceptional Children, 66,* 335–346.

Smith, B.J. (2000). The federal role in early childhood special education policy in the next century: The responsibility of the individual. *Topics in Early Childhood Special Education, 20,* 7–13.

Smith, J.D. (Ed.). (1998). The history of special education: Essays honoring the bicentennial of the work of Jean Itard [Special issue]. *Remedial and Special Education, 19*(4).

Sprague, J., & Walker, H. (2000). Early identification and intervention for youth with antisocial and violent behavior. *Exceptional Children, 66,* 367–379.

Stainback, S., & Stainback, W. (1992). Schools as inclusive communities. In W. Stainback & S. Stainback (Eds.), *Controversial issues confronting special education: Divergent perspectives* (pp. 29–43). Boston: Allyn & Bacon.

Stancliffe, R.J., Abery, B.H., & Smith, J. (2000). Personal control and the ecology of community living settings: Beyond living-unit size and type. *American Journal on Mental Retardation, 105,* 431–454.

Strain, P.S. (2001). Empirically-based social skills intervention: A case for quality of life improvement. *Behavioral Disorders., 27,* 30–36.

Strain, P.S., & Timm, M.A. (2001). Remediation and prevention of aggression: An evaluation of the Regional Intervention Program over a quarter century. *Behavioral Disorders, 26,* 297–313

Strauss, D., & Kastner, T.A. (1996). Comparative mortality of people with mental retardation in institutions and the community. *American Journal on Mental Retardation, 101,* 26–40.

Strauss, D., Shavelle, R., Baumeister, A., & Anderson, T.W. (1998). Mortality in persons with developmental disabilities after transfer into community care. *American Journal on Mental Retardation, 102,* 569–581.

Sugai, G. (1996). Providing effective behavior support to all students: Procedures and processes. *SAIL, 11*(1), 1–4.

Sugai, G., & Horner, R.H. (Eds.). (1999–2000). Functional behavioral assessment. *Exceptionality, 8*(3) [special issue].

Sugai, G., Sprague, J.R., Horner, R.H., & Walker, H.M. (2000). Preventing school violence: The use of office discipline referrals to assess and monitor school-wide discipline interventions. *Journal of Emotional and Behavioral Disorders, 8,* 94–101.

Thompson, B. (1993). *Words can hurt you: Beginning a program of anti-bias education.* Reading, MA: Addison-Wesley.

Thompson, L., Lobb, C., Elling, R., Herman, S., Jurkiewicz, T., & Hulleza, C. (1998). Pathways to family empowerment: Effects of family-centered delivery of early intervention services. *Exceptional Children, 64,* 99–113.

Thurlow, M.L. (2000). Standards-based reform and students with disabilities: Reflections on a decade of change. *Focus on Exceptional Children, 33*(3), 1–16.

Thurlow, M.L., Nelson, J.R., Teelucksingh, W., & Draper, I.L. (2001). Multiculturalism and disability in a results-based educational system: Hazards and hopes for today's schools. In C.A. Utley & F.E. Obiakor (Eds.), *Special education, multicultural education, and school reform: Components of quality education for learners with mild disabilities* (pp. 155–172). Springfield, IL: Charles C. Thomas.

Tindal, G., Heath, B., Hollenbeck, K., Almond, P., & Harniss, M. (1998). Accommodating students with disabilities on large-scale tests: An experimental study. *Exceptional Children, 64,* 439–450.

U.S. Department of Education. (2000). *Twenty-second annual report to Congress on implementation of the Individuals with Disabilities Education Act.* Washington, DC: Author.

University of Minnesota. (1999, October). Behavioral outcomes of deinstitutionalization for people with intellectual disabilities: A review of studies conducted between 1980 and 1999. *Policy Research Brief, 10*(1), 1–11.

Utley, C.A., Mortweet, S.L., & Greenwood, C.R. (1997). Peer-mediated instruction and interventions. *Focus on Exceptional Children, 29*(5), 1–23.

Vanderwood, M., McGrew, K.S., & Ysseldyke, J.E. (1998). Why we can't say much about students with disabilities during education reform. *Exceptional Children, 64*, 359–370.

Vaughn, S., Bos, C., & Schumm, J.S. (1997). *Teaching mainstreamed, diverse, and at-risk students in the general education classroom.* Boston: Allyn & Bacon.

Vaughn, S., Moody, S.W., & Schumm, J.S. (1998). Broken promises: Reading instruction in the resource room. *Exceptional Children, 64*, 211–225.

Vaughn, S., Schumm, J.S., & Arguelles, M.E. (1997). The ABCDEs of co-teaching. Teaching *Exceptional Children, 30*(2), 4–10.

Vaughn, S., Elbaum, B., & Boardman, A.G. (2001). The social functioning of students with learning disabilities: Implications for inclusion. *Exceptionality, 9*, 47–65.

Wehmeyer, M.L., Palmer, S.B., Agran, M., Mithaug, D.E., & Martin, J.E. (2000). Promoting causal agency: The self-determined learning model of instruction. *Exceptional Children, 66*, 439–453.

Wolfensberger, W. (1972). *The principle of normalization in human services.* Toronto: National Institute on Mental Retardation.

Wyer, K. (2001, Spring). The Great Equalizer: Assistive technology launches a new era in inclusion. *Teaching Tolerance,* Number 19.

Yell, M.L. (1998). *The law and special education.* Upper Saddle River, NJ: Prentice-Hall.

Yell, M.L., Rozalski, M.E., & Drasgow, E. (2001). Disciplining students with disabilities. *Focus on Exceptional Children, 33*(9), 1–20.

Yell, M.L., & Shriner, J.G. (1997). The IDEA amendments of 1997: Implications for special and general education teachers, administrators, and teacher trainers. *Focus on Exceptional Children, 30*(1), 1–19.

Zigler, E., Hodapp, R.M., & Edison, M.R. (1990). From theory to practice in the care and education of mentally retarded individuals. *American Journal on Mental Retardation, 95*(1), 1–12.

Zigler, E., & Styfco, S.J. (2000). Pioneering steps (and fumbles) in developing a federal preschool intervention. *Topics in Early Childhood Special Education, 20*, 67–70, 78.

Zigmond, N. (1995). An exploration of the meaning and practice of special education in the context of full inclusion of students with learning disabilities. *Journal of Special Education, 29*, 109–115.

Zigmond, N., & Baker, J.M. (1995). Concluding comments: Current and future practices in inclusive schooling. *Journal of Special Education, 29*, 245–250.

Zigmond, N., Jenkins, J., Fuchs, L.S., Deno, S., Fuchs, D., Baker, J.N., Jenkins, L., & Couthino, M. (1995). Special education in restructured schools: Findings from three multi-year studies. *Phi Delta Kappan, 76*, 531–540.

Zigmond, N., & Miller, S.E. (1992). Improving high school programs for students with learning disabilities: A matter of substance as well as form. In F.R. Rusch, L. DeStefano, J. Chadsey-Rusch, L.A. Phelps, & E. Szymanski (Eds.), *Transition from school to adult life* (pp. 17–31). Sycamore, IL: Sycamore Publishing.

Zurkowski, J.K., Kelly, P.S., & Griswold, D.E. (1998). Discipline and IDEA 1997: Instituting a new balance. *Intervention in School and Clinic, 34*, 3–9.

CHAPTER 3

Artiles, A.J., & Trent, S.C. (Eds.). (1997a). Building a knowledge base on culturally diverse students with learning disabilities: The need to enrich research with a sociocultural perspective [Special issue]. *Learning Disabilities Research and Practice, 12*(2).

Artiles, A., & Trent, S.C. (1997b). Forging a research program on multicultural preservice teacher education in special education: A proposed analytic scheme. In J.W. Lloyd, E.J. Kameenui, & D. Chard (Eds.), *Issues in educating students with disabilities* (pp. 275–304). Mahwah, NJ: Erlbaum.

Artiles, A.J., Trent, S.C., Hoffman-Kipp, P., & Lopez-Torres, L. (2000). From individual acquisition to cultural-historical practices in multicultural teacher education. *Remedial and Special Education, 21*, 79–89, 120.

Artiles, A.J., & Zamora-Duran, G. (Eds.). (1997). *Reducing disproportionate representation of culturally diverse students in special education.* Reston, VA: Council for Exceptional Children.

Ascher, C. (1992). School programs for African-American males . . . and females. *Phi Delta Kappan, 73*, 777–782.

Banks, J.A. (1993). *Introduction to multicultural education.* Boston: Allyn & Bacon.

Banks, J.A. (1994). *Multiethnic education: Theory and practice* (3rd ed.). Boston: Allyn & Bacon.

Banks, J.A. (1997). *Teaching strategies for ethnic studies* (6th ed.). Boston: Allyn & Bacon.

Banks, J.A., & Banks, C.A.M. (Eds.). (1997). *Multicultural education: Issues and perspectives* (3rd ed.). Boston: Allyn & Bacon.

Bateman, B.D. (1994). Who, how, and where: Special education's issues in perpetuity. *Journal of Special Education, 27*, 509–520.

Bennett, L. (2000). Equality by design: Three charter schools try new approaches to integration. *Teaching Tolerance, 17*, 43–49.

Caplan, N., Choy, M.H., & Whitmore, J.K. (1992, February). Indochinese refugee families and academic achievement. *Scientific American, 266*(2), 36–42.

Cartledge, G., & Loe, S.A. (2001). Cultural diversity and social skill instruction. *Exceptionality, 9*, 33–46.

Cho, S., Singer, G.H.S., & Brenner, M. (2000). Adaptation and accommodation to young children with disabilities: A comparison of Korean and Korean American parents. *Topics in Early Childhood Special Education, 20*, 236–249.

Choate, J.S., Enright, B.E., Miller, L.J., Poteet, J.A., & Rakes, T.A. (1995). *Curriculum-based assessment programming* (3rd ed.). Boston: Allyn & Bacon.

Cohn, D., & Cohen, S. (2001, August 6). Census sees vast change in language, employment: More people work at home, more speak little English. *The Washington Post,* pp. A1, A5.

Collins, K. (2000, Spring). No place for bigotry: An anti-bias club changes the atmosphere at a suburban high school. *Teaching Tolerance,* Number 17.

Council for Exceptional Children. (1997). Making assessments of diverse students meaningful. *CEC Today, 4*(4), 1, 9.

Council for Exceptional Children. (2000, Fall). Improving results for culturally and linguistically diverse students. *Research Connections in Special Education,* Number 7.

Coutinho, M.J., & Oswald, D.P. (2000). Disproportionate representation in special education: A synthesis and recommendations. *Journal of Child and Family Studies, 9,* 135–156.

Delpit, L.D. (1988). The silenced dialogue: Power and pedagogy in educating other people's children. *Harvard Educational Review, 58,* 280–298.

Delpit, L. (1995). *Other people's children: Cultural conflict in the classroom.* New York: New Press.

Edelman, M.W. (1992). *The measure of our success: A letter to my children and yours.* New York: Beacon Press.

Edgar, E., & Siegel, S. (1995). Postsecondary scenarios for troubled and troubling youth. In J.M. Kauffman, J.W. Lloyd, D.P. Hallahan, & T.A. Astuto (Eds.), *Issues in educational placement: Students with emotional and behavioral disorders* (pp. 251–283). Hillsdale, NJ: Erlbaum.

Elksnin, L.K., & Elksnin, N. (2000). Teaching parents to teach their children to be prosocial. *Intervention in School and Clinic, 36,* 27–35.

Elliot, B. (2000). Finding my stride: A gay student takes the bold step of being true to himself. *Teaching Tolerance, 17,* 40–41.

Ford, B.A., Obiakor, F.E., & Patton, J.M. (Eds.). (1995). *Effective education of African American exceptional learners: New perspectives.* Austin, TX: Pro-Ed.

Ford, D.Y. (1998). The under-representation of minority students in gifted education: Problems and promises in recruitment and retention. *Journal of Special Education, 32,* 4–14.

Franklin, M.E. (1992). Culturally sensitive instructional practices for African-American learners with disabilities. *Exceptional Children, 59,* 115–122.

Fuchs, L.S., & Fuchs, D. (1977). Use of curriculum-based measurement in identifying students with disabilities. *Focus on Exceptional Children, 30*(3), 1–16.

Fujiura, G.T., & Yamaki, K. (2000). Trends in demography of childhood poverty and disability. *Exceptional Children, 66,* 187–199.

Fulk, B.M., & King, K. (2001). Classwide peer tutoring at work. *Teaching Exceptional Children, 34*(2), 49–53.

Gallucci, J.P. (2000). Signs of remembrance: A school for the deaf celebrates Dia de los Muertos. *Teaching Tolerance, 18,* 30–31.

Gerber, P.J., Ginsberg, R., & Reiff, H.B. (1992). Identifying alterable patterns in employment success for highly successful adults with learning disabilities. *Journal of Learning Disabilities, 25,* 475–487.

Gersten, R., & Baker, S. (2000). What we know about effective instructional practices for English-language learners. *Exceptional Children, 66,* 454–470.

Gersten, R., Brengelman, S., & Jimenez, R. (1994). Effective instruction for culturally and linguistically diverse students: A reconceptualization. *Focus on Exceptional Children, 27*(1), 1–16.

Gersten, R., & Woodward, J. (1994). The language-minority student and special education: Issues, trends, and paradoxes. *Exceptional Children, 60,* 310–322.

Glazer, N. (1997). *We are all multiculturalists now.* Cambridge, MA: Harvard University Press.

Glazer, N. (1998). In defense of preference. *The New Republic, 218*(14), 18–21, 24–25.

Gollnick, D.M., & Chinn, P.C. (1994). *Multicultural education in a pluralistic society* (4th ed.). New York: Macmillan.

Greenwood, C.R., Arrega-Mayer, C., Utley, C.A., Gavin, K.M., & Terry, B. J. (2001). Classwide peer tutoring learning management system: Applications with elementary-level English language learners. *Remedial and Special Education, 22,* 34–47.

Hallahan, D.P., & Kauffman, J.M. (1994). Toward a culture of disability in the aftermath of Deno and Dunn. *Journal of Special Education, 27,* 496–508.

Hallahan, D.P., Kauffman, J.M., & Lloyd, J.W. (1999). *Introduction to learning disabilities* (2nd ed.). Boston: Allyn & Bacon.

Harrison, M.M. (2000). Stories waiting to be told: Refugee students find their voices in two Midwestern communities. *Teaching Tolerance, 18,* 39–44.

Harry, B., Torguson, C., Katkavich, J., & Guerrero, M. (1993). Crossing social class and cultural barriers in working with families. *Teaching Exceptional Children, 26*(1), 48–51.

Hilliard, A.G. (1992). The pitfalls and promises of special education practice. *Exceptional Children, 59,* 168–172.

Hirsch, E.D. (1987). *Cultural literacy: What every American needs to know.* Boston: Houghton Mifflin.

Hirsch, E.D. (1996). *The schools we need and why we don't have them.* New York: Doubleday.

Horwitz, S. (1998, April 5). Lessons in black and white; crossing color lines in room 406 with Miss Kay and her kids. *The Washington Post,* p. F1.

Ishii-Jordan, S. (1997). When behavior differences are not disorders. In A.J. Artiles & G. Zamora-Duran (Eds.), *Reducing disproportionate representation of culturally diverse students in special and gifted education* (pp. 27–46). Reston, VA: Council for Exceptional Children.

Jones, C.J. (2001a). CBAs that work: Assessing students' math content-reading levels. *Teaching Exceptional Children, 34*(1), 24–28.

Jones, C.J. (2001b). Teacher-friendly curriculum-based assessment in spelling. *Teaching Exceptional Children, 34*(2), 32–38.

Kalyanpur, M., & Harry, B. (1997). A posture of reciprocity: A practical approach to collaboration between professionals and parents of culturally diverse backgrounds. *Journal of Child and Family Studies, 6,* 487–509.

Katsiyannis, A. (1994). Pre-referral practices: Under Office of Civil Rights scrutiny. *Journal of Developmental and Physical Disabilities, 6,* 73–76.

Kauffman, J.M. (1999). How we prevent the prevention of emotional and behavioral disorders. *Exceptional Children, 65,* 448–468.

Kauffman, J.M. (2001). *Characteristics of emotional and behavioral disorders of children and youths* (7th ed.). New York: Merrill/Macmillan.

Kauffman, J.M., Mostert, M.P., Trent, S.C., & Hallahan, D.P. (2002). *Managing classroom behavior: A reflective case-based approach* (3rd ed.). Boston: Allyn & Bacon.

Kennedy, R. (1997). My race problem—and ours. *Atlantic Monthly, 279*(5), 55–66.

Keogh, B.K., Gallimore, R., & Weisner, T. (1997). A sociocultural perspective on learning and learning disabilities. *Learning Disabilities Research and Practice, 12,* 107–113.

Kidder, J.T. (1989). *Among schoolchildren.* Boston: Houghton Mifflin.

Kline, S.A., Simpson, R.L., Blesz, D.P., Myles, B.S., & Carter, W.J. (2001). School reform and multicultural learners with emotional and behavioral disorders: Issues, challenges, and solutions. In C.A. Utley & F.E. Obiakor (Eds.), *Special education, multicultural education, and school reform: Components of quality education for learners with mild disabilities* (pp. 118–129). Springfield, IL: Charles C. Thomas.

Leake, D., & Leake, B. (1992). African-American immersion schools in Milwaukee: A view from inside. *Phi Delta Kappan, 73,* 783–785.

Lopez-Reyna, N.A., & Bay, M. (1997). Enriching assessment using varied assessments for diverse learners. *Teaching Exceptional Children, 29*(4), 33–37.

MacMillan, D.L., & Reschly, D.J. (1998). Overrepresentation of minority students: The case for greater specificity or reconsideration of the variables examined. *Journal of Special Education, 32,* 15–24.

MacMillan, D.L., Gresham, F.M., Lopez, M.F., & Bocian, K.M. (1996). Comparison of students nominated for prereferral interventions by ethnicity and gender. *Journal of Special Education, 30,* 133–151.

McAfee, M. (2000). Welcome to Park Day School: A bay area teacher shares her independent school's commitment to community. *Teaching Tolerance, 18,* 24–29.

McBride, J. (1996). *The color of water: A black man's tribute to his white mother.* New York: Riverhead Books.

McDonnell, L.M., McLaughlin, M.J., & Morison, P. (Eds.). (1997). *Educating one and all: Students with disabilities and standards-based reform.* Washington, DC: National Academy Press.

McIntyre, T. (1992). The "invisible culture" in our schools: Gay and lesbian youth. *Beyond Behavior, 3*(3), 6–12.

McNergney, R.F. (1992). *Teaching and learning in multicultural settings: The case of Hans Christian Anderson School.* Video cassette. Boston: Allyn & Bacon.

Minow, M. (1985). Learning to live with the dilemma of difference: Bilingual and special education. In K.T. Bartlett & J.W. Wegner (Eds.), *Children with special needs* (pp. 375–429). New Brunswick, NJ: Transaction Books.

Morgan, J.H. (2001, Fall). The rhetoric of hate: An AP English class unmasks racist propaganda on the internet. *Teaching Tolerance,* Number 20.

Ogbu, J.U. (1992). Understanding cultural diversity and learning. *Educational Researcher, 21*(8), 5–14.

Ortiz, A.A. (1997). Learning disabilities occurring concomitantly with linguistic differences. *Journal of Learning Disabilities, 30,* 321–332.

Oswald, D.P., & Coutinho, M.J. (2001). Trends in disproportionate representation: Implications for multicultural education. In C.A. Utley & F.E. Obiakor (Eds.), *Special education, multicultural education, and school reform: Components of quality education for learners with mild disabilities* (pp. 53–73). Springfield, IL: Charles C. Thomas.

Ovando, C.J. (1997). Language diversity and education. In J.A. Banks & C.A.M. Banks (Eds.), *Multicultural education: Issues and perspectives* (3rd ed., pp. 272–296). Boston: Allyn & Bacon.

Padden, C., & Humphries, T. (1988). *Deaf in America: Voices from a culture.* Cambridge, MA: Harvard University Press.

Patterson, O. (1993, February 7). Black like all of us: Celebrating multiculturalism diminishes blacks' role in American culture. *The Washington Post,* p. C2.

Patton, J.M. (1997). Disproportionate representation in gifted programs: Best practices for meeting this challenge. In A.J. Artiles & G. Zamora-Duran (Eds.), *Reducing disproportionate representation of culturally diverse students in special and gifted education* (pp. 59–85). Reston, VA: Council for Exceptional Children.

Pavri, S. (2001). Loneliness in children with disabilities: How teachers can help. *Teaching Exceptional Children, 33*(6), 52–58.

Price, H.B. (1992). Multiculturalism: Myths and realities. *Phi Delta Kappan, 74,* 208–213.

Reschly, D.J. (2001, July 13). *Overrepresentation, it's not what you think it is: Equal treatment studies.* Presentation at the Office of Special Education Programs Annual Research Project Directors' Conference, Washington, DC.

Rodriguez, R. (1982). *Hunger of memory: The education of Richard Rodriguez. An autobiography.* Boston: D.R. Godine.

Rodriguez, R. (1992). *Days of obligation: An argument with my Mexican father.* New York: Viking.

Rogoff, B., & Morelli, G. (1989). Culture and American children. *American Psychologist, 44,* 341–342.

Rueda, R. (1997). Changing the context of assessment: The move to portfolios and authentic assessment. In A.J. Artiles & G. Zamora-Duran (Eds.), *Reducing disproportionate representation of culturally diverse students in special and gifted education* (pp. 7–25). Reston, VA: Council for Exceptional Children.

Rueda, R., & Garcia, E. (1997). Do portfolios make a difference for diverse students? The influence of type of data on making instructional decisions. *Learning Disabilities Research and Practice, 12,* 114–122.

Rueda, R., & Kim, S. (2001). Cultural and linguistic diversity as a theoretical framework for understanding multicultural learners with mild disabilities. In C.A. Utley & F.E. Obiakor (Eds.), *Special education, multicultural education, and school reform: Components of quality education for learners with mild disabilities* (pp. 74–89). Springfield, IL: Charles C. Thomas.

Russell, K.Y. (1992). *The color complex: The "last taboo" among African Americans.* San Diego, CA: Harcourt Brace Jovanovich.

Schofield, J.W. (1997). Causes and consequences of the colorblind perspective. In J.A. Banks & C.A.M. Banks (Eds.), *Multicultural education: Issues and perspectives* (3rd ed., pp. 251–271). Boston: Allyn & Bacon.

Singh, N.N. (1996). Cultural diversity in the 21st century: Beyond E Pluribus Unum. *Journal of Child and Family Studies, 5,* 121–136.

Singh, N.N., Baker, J., Winton, A.S.W., & Lewis, D.K. (2000). Semantic equivalence of assessment instruments across cultures. *Journal of Child and Family Studies, 9,* 123–134.

Singh, N.N., Ellis, C.R., Oswald, D.P., Wechsler, H.A., & Curtis, W.J. (1997). Value and address diversity. *Journal of Emotional and Behavioral Disorders, 5,* 24–35.

Spencer, J.M. (1997). *The new colored people: The mixed-race movement in America.* New York: New York University Press.

Takaki, R. (1994). Interview: Reflections from a different mirror. *Teaching Tolerance, 3*(1), 11–15.

Taylor, R.L. (1997). *Assessment of exceptional students: Educational and psychological procedures* (4th ed.). Boston: Allyn & Bacon.

Teach English. (2001, August 9). *The Washington Post,* p. A18.

Terwilliger, J. (1997). Semantics, psychometrics, and assessment reform: A close look at "authentic" assessments. *Educational Researcher, 26*(8), 24–27.

Thomas, C. (1998, April 22). Do we education our children or preserve an institution? *Charlottesville Daily Progress,* p. A8.

Thurlow, M.L., Nelson, J.R., Teelucksingh, W., & Draper, I.L. (2001). Multiculturalism and disability in a results-based educational system: Hazards and hopes for today's schools. In C.A.

Utley & F.E. Obiakor (Eds.), *Special education, multicultural education, and school reform: Components of quality education for learners with mild disabilities* (pp. 155–172). Springfield, IL: Charles C. Thomas.

Trent, S.C., & Artiles, A.J. (Eds.). (1998). Multicultural teacher education in special education [Special issue]. *Remedial and Special Education, 19*(1).

Uribe, V., & Harbeck, K.M. (1992). *Coming out of the classroom closet: Gay and lesbian students, teachers, and curricula.* Binghamton, NY: Hayworth Press.

Utley, C.A., & Obiakor, F.E. (Eds.). (2001a). *Special education, multicultural education, and school reform: Components of quality education for learners with mild disabilities.* Springfield, IL: Charles C. Thomas.

Utley, C.A., & Obiakor, F.E. (2001b). Learning problems or learning disabilities of multicultural learners: Contemporary perspectives. In C.A. Utley & F.E. Obiakor (Eds.), *Special education, multicultural education, and school reform: Components of quality education for learners with mild disabilities* (pp. 90–117). Springfield, IL: Charles C. Thomas.

Utley, C.A., & Obiakor, F.E. (2001c). Multicultural education and special education: Infusion for better schooling. In C.A. Utley & F.E. Obiakor (Eds.), *Special education, multicultural education, and school reform: Components of quality education for learners with mild disabilities* (pp. 3–29). Springfield, IL: Charles C. Thomas.

U.S. Department of Education. (1992). *Fourteenth annual report to Congress on the implementation of the Individuals with Disabilities Education Act.* Washington, DC: Author.

U.S. Department of Education. (1996). *Eighteenth annual report to Congress on the implementation of the Individuals with Disabilities Education Act.* Washington, DC: Author.

U.S. Department of Education. (1997). *Nineteenth annual report to Congress on the implementation of the Individuals with Disabilities Education Act.* Washington, DC: Author.

U.S. Department of Education. (2000). *Twenty-second annual report to Congress on the implementation of the Individuals with Disabilities Education Act.* Washington, DC: Author

Van Keulen, J.E., Weddington, G.T., & DeBose, C.E. (1998). *Speech, language, learning, and the African American child.* Boston: Allyn & Bacon.

Walker, T. (2000). Street smart: Sidewalk libraries open a world of learning for urban youth. *Teaching Tolerance, 17,* 22–25.

Wilkins, R. (2001). *Jefferson's pillow: The founding fathers and the dilemma of black patriotism.* Boston: Beacon.

Williams, P.J. (1998a). In living black and white. *Washington Post Magazine,* pp. 19–20, 30.

Williams, P.J. (1998b). *Seeing a color-blind future.* New York: Noonday Press.

Wortham, A. (1992, September). Afrocentrism isn't the answer for black students in American society. *Executive Educator, 14,* 23–25.

www.tolerance.org/teach/ could replace www.teachingtolerance.com as a web address (teachingtolerance.com actually now defaults to tolerance.org/teach/)

CHAPTER 4

AAMR Ad Hoc Committee on Terminology and Classification. (1992). *Mental retardation: Definition, classification, and systems of support* (9th ed.). Washington, DC: American Association on Mental Retardation.

American Association on Mental Retardation. (1998, May; revised 2000, May). Self-determination policy statement. Retrieved July 21, 2001, from http://www.aamr.org/Policies/Pol_self_determination.shtml

American Psychiatric Association. (2000). *Diagnostic and statistical manual of mental disorders* (4th ed., text revision). Washington, DC: Author.

The Arc. (2001, April 10). Phenylketonuria (PKU). Retrieved July 18, 2001, from http://www.thearc.org/faqs/pku.html

Baumeister, A.A., & Woodley-Zanthos, P. (1996). Prevention: Biological factors. In J.W. Jacobson & J.A. Mulick (Eds.), *Manual of diagnosis and professional practice in mental retardation* (229–242). Washington, DC: American Psychological Association.

Bebko, J.M., & Luhaorg, H. (1998). The development of strategy use and metacognitive processing in mental retardation: Some sources of difficulty. In J.A. Burack, R.M. Hodapp, & E. Zigler (Eds.), *Handbook of mental retardation and development* (pp. 382–407). New York: Cambridge University Press.

Beirne-Smith, M., Ittenbach, R.F., & Patton, J.R. (1998). *Mental retardation* (5th ed.). Upper Saddle River, NJ: Merrill.

Belser, R.C., & Sudhalter, V. (2001). Conversational characteristics of children with fragile X syndrome: Repetitive speech. *American Journal on Mental Retardation, 106,* 28–38.

Blackorby, J., & Wagner, M. (1996). Longitudinal postschool outcomes of youth with disabilities: Findings from the National Longitudinal Transition Study. *Exceptional Children, 62,* 399–413.

Bray, N.W., Fletcher, K.L., & Turner, L. (1997). Cognitive competencies and strategy use in individuals with mental retardation. In W.E. MacLean (Ed.), *Ellis' handbook of mental deficiency, psychological theory, and research* (pp. 197–217). Mahwah, NJ: Erlbaum.

Browder, D., & Snell, M.E. (2000). Teaching functional academics. In M.E. Snell & F. Brown (Eds.), *Instruction of students with severe disabilities* (5th ed.). Columbus, OH: Merrill.

Brown, L., Shiraga, B., Ford, A., Nisbet, J., Van Deventer, P., Sweet, M., York, J., & Loomis, R. (1986). Teaching severely handicapped students to perform meaningful work in nonsheltered vocational environments. In R.J. Morris & B. Blatt (Eds.), *Special education: Research and trends* (pp. 131–189). New York: Pergamon Press.

Bryant, B.R., Taylor, R.L., & Rivera, D.P. (1996). *Assessment of Adaptive Areas.* Austin, TX: Pro-Ed.

Butler, F.M., Miller, S.P., Lee, K., & Pierce, T. (2001). Teaching mathematics to students with mild-to-moderate mental retardation: A review of the literature. *Mental Retardation, 39,* 20–31.

Butterworth, J., & Strauch, J.D. (1994). The relationship between social competence and success in the competitive work place for persons with mental retardation. *Education and Training in Mental Retardation and Developmental Disabilities, 29,* 118–133.

Campbell, F.A., & Pungello, E. (2000). High quality child care has long-term educational benefits for poor children. Paper presented at the Head Start National Research Conference, Washington, DC, June 28–July 1, 2000.

Carr, J. (1994). Annotation: Long term outcome for people with Down's syndrome. *Journal of Child Psychology and Psychiatry, 35,* 425–439.

Council for Exceptional Children (2001). Performance-based Standards. Retrieved June 5, 2001 from www.cec.sped.org/ps/perf_based_stds/index.html <http://www.cec.sped.org/ps/perf_based_stds/index.html>

Cronin, M.E. (2000). Instructional strategies. In P.L. Sitlington, G.M. Clark, & O.P. Kolstoe, *Transition education and services for adolescents with disabilities* (3rd ed., pp. 255–283). Boston: Allyn & Bacon.

Davis, P.K., & Cuvo, A.J. (1997). Environmental approaches to mental retardation. In D.M. Baer & E.M. Pinkerston (Eds.), *Environment and behavior* (pp. 231–242). Boulder, CO: Westview Press.

Davis, S. (1997). *The Human Genome Project: Examining the Arc's concerns regarding the Human Genome Project's ethical, legal, and social implications.* An address presented at the DOE Human Genome Program Contractor-Grantee Workshop VI. Posted on the World Wide Web by the Human Genome Management Information System. Retrieved July 29, 2001, from http://www.ornl.gov/hgmis/resource/arc.html

Delquadri, J., Greenwood, C.R., Stretton, K., & Hall, R.V. (1983). The peer tutoring spelling game: A classroom procedure for increasing opportunity to respond and spelling performance. *Education and Treatment of Children, 6,* 225–239.

Dimitropoulos, A., Feurer, I.D., Butler, M.G., & Thompson, T. (2001). Emergence of compulsive behavior and tantrums in children with Prader-Willi syndrome. *American Journal on Mental Retardation, 106,* 39–51.

Dykens, E. (2001). Introduction to special issue. *American Journal on Mental Retardation, 106,* 1–3.

Dykens, E.M., Hodapp, R.M., & Finucane, B.M. (2000). *Genetics and mental retardation syndromes: A new look at behavior and interventions.* Baltimore, MD: Paul H. Brookes.

Evenhuis, H.M. (1990). The natural history of dementia in Down's syndrome. *Archives of Neurology, 47,* 263–267.

Finegan, J.A. (1998). Study of behavioral phenotypes: Goals and methodological considerations. *American Journal of Medical Genetics, 81,* 148–155.

Frank, A.R., & Sitlington, P.L. (2000). Young adults with mental disabilities—Does transition planning make a difference? *Education and Training in Mental Retardation and Developmental Disabilities, 35,* 119–134.

Fraser, J., & Mitchell, A. (1876). Kalmuc idiocy: Report of a case with autopsy, with notes on sixty-two cases. *Journal of Mental Science, 22,* 161–179.

Greenspan, S. (1997). Dead manual walking? Why the 1992 AAMR definition needs redoing. *Education and Training in Mental Retardation and Developmental Disabilities, 32,* 179–190.

Greenwood, C.R. (1991). Longitudinal analysis of time, engagement, and achievement of at-risk versus non-risk students. *Exceptional Children, 57,* 521–532.

Guralnick, M.J., Connor, R.T., & Hammond, M. (1995). Parent perspectives of peer relationships and friendships in integrated and specialized programs. *American Journal on Mental Retardation, 99,* 457–476.

Hagerman, R.J. (2001). Fragile X syndrome. In S.B. Cassidy & J.E. Allanson (Eds.), *Management of genetic syndromes* (pp. 165–183). New York: Wiley-Liss.

Heal, L.W., Gonzalez, P., Rusch, F.R., Copher, J.I., & DeStefano, L. (1990). A comparison of successful and unsuccessful placements of youths with mental handicaps into competitive employment. *Exceptionality, 1,* 181–195.

Hodapp, R.M., & Fidler, D.J. (1999). Special education and genetics: Connections for the 21st century. *Journal of Special Education, 33,* 130–137.

Hof, P.R., Bouras, C., Perl, D.P., Sparks, L., Mehta, N., & Morrison, J.H. (1995). Age-related distribution of neuropathologic changes in the cerebral cortex of patients with Down's syndrome. *Archives of Neurology, 52,* 379–391.

Horner, R.H., Albin, R.W., Sprague, J.R., & Todd, A.W. (2000). Positive behavior support. In M.E. Snell & F. Brown (Eds.), *Instruction of students with severe retardation* (5th ed., pp. 207–243). Upper Saddle River, NJ: Prentice-Hall.

Howe, J., Horner, R.H., & Newton, J.S. (1998). Comparison of supported living and traditional residential services in the state of Oregon. *Mental Retardation, 36,* 1–11.

Hughes, C., & Agran, M. (1993). Teaching persons with severe disabilities to use self-instruction in community settings: An analysis of applications. *Journal of the Association for Persons with Severe Handicaps, 18,* 261–273.

Human Genome Management Information System. (1998, July 5). Human genome project information. Retrieved July 5, 1998 from http://www.ornl.gov/TechResources/Human_Genome/home.html

Hunter, A.G.W. (2001). Down syndrome. In S.B. Cassidy & J.E. Allanson (Eds.), *Management of genetic syndromes* (pp. 103–129). New York: Wiley-Liss.

Jacobson, J.W., & Mulick, J.A. (1996). Definition of mental retardation. In J.W. Jacobson & J.A. Mulick (Eds.), *Manual of diagnosis and professional practice in mental retardation* (pp. 13–53). Washington, DC: American Psychological Association.

Kamphaus, R.W., & Reynolds, C.R. (1987). *Clinical and research applications of the K-ABC.* Circle Pines, MN: American Guidance.

Kasari, C., & Bauminger, N. (1998). Social and emotional development in children with mental retardation. In J.A. Burack, R.M. Hodapp, & E. Zigler (Eds.), Handbook of mental retardation and development (pp. 411–433). New York: Cambridge University Press.

Kasari, C., Freeman, S.F.N., & Hughes, M.A. (2001). Emotion recognition by children with Down syndrome. *American Journal on Mental Retardation, 106,* 59–72.

Kaufman, A.S., & Kaufman, N.L. (1983). *Kaufman Assessment Battery for Children.* Circle Pines, MN: American Guidance Service.

Kaufman, S.Z. (1999). *Retarded isn't stupid, mom!* (Rev. ed.). Baltimore: MD: Paul H. Brookes.

Kuna, J. (2001). The Human Genome Project and eugenics: Identifying the impact on individuals with mental retardation. *Mental Retardation, 39,* 158–160.

Lambert, N., Nihira, K., & Leland, H. (1993). *AAMD Adaptive Behavior Scale–School, 2nd Edition.* Austin, TX: Pro-Ed.

Luckasson, R. (2000, September/October). New draft definition of mental retardation proposed. *American Association on Mental Retardation News & Notes,* pp. 1, 12.

Luckasson, R., & Reeve, A. (2001). Naming, defining, and classifying in mental retardation. *Mental Retardation, 39,* 47–52.

MacMillan, D.L., Gresham, F.M., & Siperstein, G.N. (1993). Conceptual and psychometric concerns about the 1992 AAMR definition of mental retardation. *American Journal on Mental Retardation, 98,* 325–335.

MacMillan, D.L., Gresham, F.M., Bocian, K.M., & Lambros, K.M. (1998). Current plight of borderline students: Where do they belong? *Education and Training in Mental Retardation and Developmental Disabilities, 33,* 83–94.

Mank, D., Cioffi, A., & Yovanoff, P. (2000). Direct support in supported employment and its relation to job typicalness, coworker involvement, and employment outcomes. *Mental Retardation, 38,* 506–516.

McCaughrin, W.B., Ellis, W.K., Rusch, F.R., & Heal, L.W. (1993). Cost-effectiveness of supported employment. *Mental Retardation, 31,* 41–48.

Mercer, J.R., & Lewis, J.F. (1982). *Adaptive Behavior Inventory for Children.* San Antonio, TX: Psychological Corporation.

Mervis, C.B., Klein-Tasman, B.P., & Mastin, M.E. (2001). Adaptive behavior of 4- through 8-year-old children with Williams syndrome. *American Journal on Mental Retardation, 106,* 82–93.

Moldavsky, M., Lev, D., & Lerman-Sagie, T. (2001). Behavioral phenotypes of genetic syndromes: A reference guide for psychiatrists. *Journal of the American Academy of Child and Adolescent Psychiatry, 40,* 749–761.

Morse, T.E., & Schuster, J.W. (2000). Teaching elementary students with moderate intellectual disabilities how to shop for groceries. *Exceptional Children, 66,* 273–288.

Mortweet, S.L., Utley, C.A., Walker, D., Dawson, H.L., Delquadri, J.C., Reddy, S.S., Greenwood, C.R., Hamilton, S., & Ledford, D. (1999). Classwide peer tutoring: Teaching students with mild mental retardation in inclusive classrooms. *Exceptional Children, 65,* 524–536.

MR/DD Data Brief. (2001, April). Characteristics of service use by persons with MR/DD living in their own homes or with family members: NHIS-D analysis. Research and Training Center on Community Living, Institute on Community Integration, University of Minnesota.

National Institute of Neurological Disorders and Stroke. (2001, July 1). NINDS microcephaly information page. Retrieved July 18, 2001, from http://www.ninds.nih.gov/health_and_medical/disorders/microcephaly.htm

Nietupski, J., Hamre-Nietupski, S., VanderHart, N.S., & Fishback, K. (1996). Employer perceptions of the benefits and concerns of supported employment. *Education and Training in Mental Retardation and Developmental Disabilities, 31,* 310–323.

Nihira, K., Leland, H., & Lambert, N. (1993). *AAMR Adaptive Behavior Scale–Residential and Community* (2nd ed.). Austin, TX: Pro-Ed.

Olney, M.F., & Kennedy, J. (2001). National estimates of vocational service utilization and job placement rates for adults with mental retardation. *Mental Retardation, 39,* 32–39.

Palmer, D.S., Borthwick-Duffy, S.A., & Widaman, K. (1998). Parent perceptions of inclusive practices for their children with significant cognitive disabilities. *Exceptional Children, 64,* 271–282.

Parmar, R.S., Cawley, J.F., & Miller, J.H. (1994). Differences in mathematics performance between students with learning disabilities and students with mental retardation. *Exceptional Children, 60,* 549–563.

Patton, R.S., Smith, T.E., Clark, G.M., Polloway, E.A., Edgar, E., & Lee, S. (1996). Individuals with mild mental retardation: Postsecondary outcomes and implications for educational policy. *Education and Training in Mental Retardation and Developmental Disabilities, 31,* 75–85.

Pinel, P.J. (2000). *Biopsychology* (4th ed.). Boston: Allyn & Bacon.

Ramey, C.T., & Campbell, F.A. (1984). Preventive education for high-risk children: Cognitive consequences of the Carolina Abecedarian Project. *American Journal of Mental Deficiency, 88,* 515–523.

Ramey, C.T., & Campbell, F.A. (1987). The Carolina Abecedarian Project: An educational experiment concerning human malleability. In J.J. Gallagher & C.T. Ramey (Eds.), *The malleability of children* (pp. 127–139). Baltimore, MD: Paul H. Brookes.

Revell, W.G., Wehman, P., Kregel, J., West, M., & Rayfield, R. (1994). Supported employment for persons with severe disabilities: Positive trends in wages, models, and funding. *Education and Training in Mental Retardation and Developmental Disabilities, 29,* 256–264.

Reynolds, A.J., Temple, J.A., Robertson, D.L., & Mann, E.A. (2001). Long-term effects of an early childhood intervention on educational achievement and juvenile arrest. *Journal of the American Medical Association, 285,* 2339–2346.

Salzberg, C.L., Lignugaris/Kraft, B., & McCuller, G.L. (1988). Reasons for job loss: A review of employment termination studies of mentally retarded workers. *Research in Developmental Disabilities, 9,* 153–170.

Schuster, J.W., Morse, T.E., Ault, M.J., Doyle, P.M., Crawford, M.R., & Wolery, M. (1998). Constant time delay with chained tasks: A review of the literature. *Education and Treatment of Children, 21,* 74–106.

Schweinhart, L.J., & Weikart, D.P. (1993). Success by empowerment: The High/Scope Perry Preschool Study through age 27. *Young Children, 49,* 54–58.

Scott, M.S., Greenfield, D.B., & Partridge, M.F. (1991). Differentiating between two groups that fail in school: Performance of learning disabled and mildly retarded students on an oddity problem. *Learning Disabilities Research and Practice, 6,* 3–11.

Skeels, H.M. (1966). Adult status of children with contrasting early life experiences. *Monographs of the Society for Research in Child Development, 31* (serial no. 105). University of Chicago Press.

Skeels, H.M., & Dye, H.B. (1939). A study of the effects of differential stimulation on mentally retarded children. *Convention Proceedings, American Association on Mental Deficiency, 44,* 114–136.

Slomka, G.T., & Berkey, J. (1997). Aging and mental retardation. In P.D. Nussbaum (Ed.), *Handbook of neuropsychology and aging* (pp. 331–347). New York: Plenum Press.

Smith, J.D. (1994). The revised AAMR definition of mental retardation: The MRDD position. *Education and Training in Mental Retardation and Developmental Disabilities, 29,* 179–183.

Smith, J.D., & Mitchell, A.L. (2001). "Me? I'm not a drooler. I'm an assistant": Is it time to abandon mental retardation as a classification? *Mental Retardation, 39,* 144–146.

Sparrow, S.S., Balla, D.A., & Cicchetti, D.V. (1984). *Vineland Adaptive Behavior Scales.* Circle Pines, MN: American Guidance Service.

Stancliffe, R.J., Abery, B.H., & Smith, J. (2000). Personal control and the ecology of community living settings: Beyond living-unit size and type. *American Journal on Mental Retardation, 105,* 431–454.

Stodden, R.A., & Browder, P.M. (1986). Community-based competitive employment preparation of developmentally disabled persons: A program description and evaluation. *Education and Training of the Mentally Retarded, 21,* 43–53.

Sugai, G., Horner, R., Dunlap, G., Lewis, T., Nelson, C.M., Scott, T., Liaupsin, C., Ruef, M., Sailor, W., Turnbull, A.P., Turnbull, H.R., Wickham, D., & Wilcox, B.L. (2000). Applying positive behavior support and functional behavioral assessment in schools. *Journal of Positive Behavior Interventions, 2,* 131–143.

Taylor, H.G., Klein, N., Minich, N.M., & Hack, M. (2000). Middle-school-age outcomes in children with very low birthweight. *Child Development, 71,* 1495–1511.

Test, D.W., Carver, T., Ewers, L., Haddad, J., & Person, J. (2000). Longitudinal job satisfaction of persons in supported employment. *Education and Training in Mental Retardation and Developmental Disabilities, 35,* 365–373.

Thomas, C.L. (Ed.). (1985). *Taber's cyclopedic medical dictionary* (15th ed.). Philadelphia: F. A. Davis Co.

Thorndike, R.L., Hagen, E.P., & Sattler, J.M. (1986). *Technical manual, Stanford-Binet Intelligence Scale* (4th ed.). Chicago: Riverside.

Tomporowski, P.D., & Tinsley, V. (1997). Attention in mentally retarded persons. In W. E. MacLean (Ed.), *Ellis' handbook of mental deficiency, psychological theory, and research* (pp. 219–244). Mahwah, NJ: Erlbaum.

Turner, G., Webb, T., Wake, S., & Robinson, H. (1996). Prevalence of fragile X syndrome. *American Journal of Medical Genetics, 64,* 196–197.

Visser, F.E., Aldenkamp, A.P., vanHuffelen, A.C., Kuilman, M., Overweg, J., & vanWijk, J. (1997). Prospective study of the prevalence of Alzheimer-type dementia in institutionalized individuals with Down syndrome. *American Journal on Mental Retardation, 101,* 400–412.

Wagner, B.R. (2000). Presidential Address 2000—Changing visions into reality. *Mental Retardation, 38,* 436–443.

Warren, S., & Yoder, P.J. (1997). Communication, language, and mental retardation. In W.E. MacLean (Ed.), *Ellis' handbook of mental deficiency, psychological theory, and research* (pp. 379–403). Mahwah, NJ: Erlbaum.

Wechsler, D. (1991). *Wechsler Intelligence Scale for Children* (3rd ed.). San Antonio, TX: Psychological Corporation.

Wehmeyer, M.L., Palmer, S.B., Agran, M., Mithaug, D.E., & Martin, J.E. (2000). Promoting causal agency: The Self-Determined Learning Model of Instruction. *Exceptional Children, 66,* 439–453.

Westling, D.L., & Fox, L. (2000). *Teaching students with severe disabilities* (2nd ed.). Upper Saddle River, NJ: Merrill.

Wisniewski, H.M., Silverman, W., & Wegiel, J. (1994). Aging, Alzheimer disease, and mental retardation. *Journal of Intellectual Disability Research, 38,* 233–239.

Wolery, M., & Schuster, J.W. (1997). Instructional methods with students who have significant disabilities. *Journal of Special Education, 31,* 61–79.

Zigler, E., & Hodapp, R.M. (1986). *Understanding mental retardation.* New York: Cambridge University Press.

CHAPTER 5

Adams, G.L., & Engelmann, S. (1996). *Research on Direct Instruction: 25 years beyond DISTAR.* Seattle: Educational Achievement Systems.

American Psychiatric Association. (1994). *Diagnostic and statistical manual of mental disorders* (4th ed.). Washington, DC: Author.

Baumeister, A.A., Kupstas, F., & Klindworth, L.M. (1990). New morbidity: Implications for prevention of children's disabilities. *Exceptionality, 1,* 1–16.

Beichtman, J.H., Hood, J., & Inglis, A. (1992). Familial transmission of speech and language impairment: A preliminary investigation. *Canadian Journal of Psychiatry, 37,* 151–156.

Bender, W.N. (2001). *Learning disabilities: Characteristics, identification, and teaching strategies* (4th ed.). Boston: Allyn & Bacon.

Bender, W.N., Rosenkrans, C.B., & Crane, M.K. (1999). Stress, depression, and suicide among students with learning disabilities: Assessing the risk. *Learning Disability Quarterly, 22,* 143–156.

Blackorby, J., & Wagner, M. (1997). The employment outcomes of youth with learning disabilities: A review of findings from NLTS. In P.J. Gerber & D.S. Brown (Eds.), *Learning disabilities and employment* (pp. 57–74). Austin, TX: Pro-Ed.

Brunswick, N., McCrory, E., Price, C.J., Frith, C.D., & Frith, U. (1999). Explicit and implicit processing of words and pseudo-words by adult developmental dyslexics: A search for Wernicke's Wortschatz? *Brain, 122*(Part 10), 1901–1917.

Bryan, T.H., Donahue, M., Pearl, R., & Sturm, C. (1981). Learning disabled children's conversational skills—The "TV Talk Show." *Learning Disability Quarterly, 4,* 250–260.

Bryan, T.H., & Sullivan-Burstein, K. (1998). Teacher-selected strategies for improving homework completion. *Remedial and Special Education, 19,* 263–275.

Butler, D.L. (1998). Metacognition and learning disabilities. In B.Y.L. Wong (Ed.), *Learning about learning disabilities* (2nd ed., pp. 277–307). San Diego, CA: Academic Press.

Case, L.P., Harris, K.R., & Graham, S. (1992). Improving the mathematical problem-solving skills of students with learning disabilities. *Journal of Special Education, 26,* 1–19.

Cawley, J.F., Parmar, R.S., Yan, W., & Miller, J.H. (1998). Arithmetic computation performance of students with learning disabilities: Implications for the curriculum. *Learning Disabilities Research and Practice, 13,* 68–74.

Choate, J.S., Enright, B.E., Miller, L.J., Poteet, J.A., & Rakes, T.A. (1995). *Curriculum-based assessment programming* (3rd ed.). Boston: Allyn & Bacon.

Clarizio, H.F., & Phillips, S.E. (1986). Sex bias in the diagnosis of learning disabled students. *Psychology in the Schools, 23,* 44–52.

Cobb, J. (2001). *Learning how to learn: Getting into and surviving college when you have a learning disability.* Washington, DC: Child Welfare League of America Press.

Connolly, A.J. (1997). *Key Math revised/normative update: A diagnostic inventory of essential mathematics.* Circle Pines, MN: American Guidance Service.

Council for Exceptional Children (2001). Performance-based Standards. Retrieved June 5, 2001 from www.cec.sped.org/ps/perf_based_stds/index.html <http://www.cec.sped.org/ps/perf_based_stds/index.html>

DeFries, J.C., Gillis, J.J., & Wadsworth, S.J. (1993). Genes and genders: A twin study of reading disability. In A.M. Galaburda (Ed.), *Dyslexia and development: Neurobiological aspects of extra-ordinary brains* (pp. 187–294). Cambridge, MA: Harvard University Press.

Deno, S.L. (1985). Curriculum-based measurement: The emerging alternative. *Exceptional Children, 52,* 219–232.

Deshler, D.D., Schumaker, J.B., Lenz, B.K., Bulgren, J.A., Hock, M.F., Knight, J., & Ehren, B.J. (2001). Ensuring content-area learning by secondary students with learning disabilities. *Learning Disabilities Research and Practice, 16,* 96–108.

Ellis, A. (2001). *Research on educational innovations* (3rd ed.). Larchmont, New York: Eye On Education.

Engelmann, S., Carnine, D., Engelmann, O., & Kelly, B. (1991). *Connecting math concepts.* Chicago: Science Research Associates.

Engelmann, S., Carnine, L., Johnson, G., & Meyers, L. (1988). *Corrective reading: Decoding.* Chicago: Science Research Associates.

Engelmann, S., Carnine, L., Johnson, G., & Meyers, L. (1989). *Corrective reading: Comprehension.* Chicago: Science Research Associates.

Epstein, M.H., Munk, D.D., Bursuck, W.D., Polloway, E.A., & Jayanthi, M. (1998). Strategies for improving home-school communication about homework for students with disabilities. *Journal of Special Education, 33,* 166–176.

Fletcher, J.M., Lyon, G.R., Barnes, M., Stuebing, K.K., Francis, D.J., Olson, R.K., Shaywitz, S.E., & Shaywitz, B.A. (2001, August). *Classification of learning disabilities: An evidence-based evaluation.* Paper presented at the LD Summit. Washington, DC: U.S. Department of Education.

Flowers, D.L. (1993). Brain basis for dyslexia: A summary of work in progress. *Journal of Learning Disabilities, 26,* 575–582.

Flowers, D.L., Wood, F.B., & Naylor, C.E. (1991). Regional cerebral blood flow correlates of language processes in reading disability. *Archives of Neurology, 48,* 637–643.

Foorman, B.R., Francis, D.J., Shaywitz, S.E., Shaywitz, B.A., & Fletcher, J.M. (1997). The case for early reading intervention. In B. Blachman (Ed.), *Foundations of reading acquisition and dyslexia: Implications for early intervention* (pp. 243–264). Mahwah, NJ: Erlbaum.

Forness, S.R., & Kavale, K.A. (2002). Impact of ADHD on school systems. In P. Jensen & J.R. Cooper (Eds.) (in press), *NIH consensus conference on ADHD.*

Frostig, M., & Horne, D. (1964). *The Frostig program for the development of visual perception: Teacher's guide.* Chicago: Follett.

Fuchs, D., Fuchs, L., & Burish, P. (2000). Peer-Assisted Learning Strategies: A evidence-based practice to promote reading achievement. *Learning Disabilities Research and Practice, 15*(2), 85–91.

Fuchs, D., Fuchs, L.S., Mathes, P.G., Lipsey, M.W., & Roberts, P.H. (2001, August). *Is "learning disabilities" just a fancy term for low achievement? A meta-analysis of reading differences between low achievers with and without the label.* Paper presented at the LD Summit. Washington, DC: U.S. Department of Education.

Fuchs, D., Fuchs, L.S., Thompson, A., Svenson, E., Yen, L. Otaiba, S., Yang, N., McMaster, K.N., Prentice, K., & Kazdan, S. (2001). Peer-assisted learning strategies in reading: Extensions for kindergarten, first grade, and high school. *Remedial and Special Education, 22,* 15–21.

Fuchs, L.S., Deno, S.L., & Mirkin, P.K. (1984). The effects of frequent curriculum-based measurement and evaluation of pedagogy, student achievement and student awareness of learning. *American Educational Research Journal, 24,* 449–460.

Fuchs, L.S., & Fuchs, D. (1997). Use of curriculum-based measurement in identifying students with disabilities. *Focus on Exceptional Children, 30*(3), 1–16.

Fuchs, L.S., & Fuchs, D. (1998a). Treatment validity: A unifying concept for reconceptualizing the identification of learning disabilities. *Learning Disabilities Research and Practice, 13,* 204–219.

Fuchs, L.S., & Fuchs, D. (1998b). General educators' instructional adaptation for students with learning disabilities. *Learning Disabilities Quarterly, 21,* 23–33.

Gajar, A.H. (1989). A computer analysis of written language variables and a comparison of compositions written by university students with and without learning disabilities. *Journal of Learning Disabilities, 22,* 125–130.

Georgiewa, P., Rzanny, R., Hopf, J.M., Knab, R., Glauche, V., Kaiser, W.A., & Blanz, B. (1999). fMRI during word processing in dyslexic and normal reading children. *Neuroreport, 10,* 3459–3465.

Gerber, P.J. (1997). Life after school: Challenges in the workplace. In P.J. Gerber & D.S. Brown (Eds.), *Learning disabilities and employment* (pp. 3–18). Austin, TX: Pro-Ed.

Gerber, P.J., Ginsberg, R., & Reiff, H.B. (1992). Identifying alterable patterns in employment success for highly successful adults with learning disabilities. *Journal of Learning Disabilities, 25,* 475–487.

Gerber, P.J., & Reiff, H.B. (1991). *Speaking for themselves: Ethnographic interviews with adults with learning disabilities.* Ann Arbor, MI: University of Michigan Press.

Goldstein, D.E., Murray, C., & Edgar, E. (1998). Employment earning and hours of high school graduates with learning disabilities through the first decade after graduation. *Learning Disabilities Research and Practice, 13,* 53–64.

Gresham, F. (2001, August). *Reponsiveness to intervention: An alternative approach to the identification of learning disabilities.* Paper presented at the LD Summit. Washington, DC: U.S. Department of Education.

Hagman, J.O., Wood, F., Buchsbaum, M.S., Tallal, P., Flowers, L., & Katz, W. (1992). Cerebral metabolism in adult dyslexic subjects assessed with positron emission tomography during performance on an auditory task. *Archives of Neurology, 49,* 734–739.

Hallahan, D.P. (1975). Comparative research studies on the psychological characteristics of learning disabled children. In W.M. Cruickshank & D.P. Hallahan (Eds.), *Perceptual and learning disabilities in children. Vol. 1: Psychoeducational practices* (pp. 29–60). Syracuse, NY: Syracuse University Press.

Hallahan, D.P. (1992). Some thoughts on why the prevalence of learning disabilities has increased. *Journal of Learning Disabilities, 25,* 523–528.

Hallahan, D.P., & Bryan, T.H. (1981). Learning disabilities. In J.M. Kauffman & D.P. Hallahan (Eds.), *Handbook of special education* (pp. 141–164). Englewood Cliffs, NJ: Prentice-Hall.

Hallahan, D.P., & Cruickshank, W.M. (1973). *Psychoeducational foundations of learning disabilities.* Englewood Cliffs, NJ: Prentice-Hall.

Hallahan, D.P., Gajar, A.H., Cohen, S.B., & Tarver, S.G. (1978). Selective attention and locus of control in learning disabled and normal children. *Journal of Learning Disabilities, 4,* 47–52.

Hallahan, D.P., Kauffman, J.M., & Ball, D.W. (1973). Selective attention and cognitive tempo of low achieving and high achieving sixth grade males. *Perceptual and Motor Skills, 36,* 579–583.

Hallahan, D.P., Kauffman, J.M., & Lloyd, J.W. (1999). *Introduction to learning disabilities* (2nd ed.). Boston: Allyn & Bacon.

Hallahan, D.P., & Mercer, C.D. (2001, August). *Learning disabilities: Historical perspectives.* Paper presented at the LD Summit. Washington, DC: U.S. Department of Education.

Hallahan, D.P., & Reeve, R.E. (1980). Selective attention and distractibility. In B.K. Keogh (Ed.), *Advances in special education.*

Vol. 1: Basic constructs and theoretical orientations (pp. 141–181). Greenwich, CT: JAI Press.

Hallgren, B. (1950). Specific dyslexia (congenital word blindness: A clinical and genetic study). *Acta Psychiatrica et Neurologica, 65,* 1–279.

Hammill, D.D. (1990). On defining learning disabilities: An emerging consensus. *Journal of Learning Disabilities, 23,* 74–84.

Hammill, D.D., & Larsen, S. (1974). The effectiveness of psycholinguistic training. *Exceptional Children, 41,* 5–15.

Hammill, D., & Larsen, S. (1996). *Test of Written Language, Third Edition.* Austin, TX: Pro-Ed.

Hammill, D.D., Leigh, J.E., McNutt, G., & Larsen, S.C. (1981). A new definition of learning disabilities. *Learning Disability Quarterly, 4,* 336–342.

Harris, K.R., Graham, S., Reid, R., McElroy, K., & Hamby, R.S. (1994). Self-monitoring of attention versus self-monitoring of performance: Replication and cross-task comparison studies. *Learning Disability Quarterly, 17,* 121–139.

Helmuth, L. (2001). Dyslexia: Same brains, different languages. *Science, 291,* 264–265.

Henderson, C. (1999). *1999 college freshmen with disabilities: A biennial statistical profile.* Washington, DC: American Council on Education, HEATH Resource Center.

Hitchings, W.E., Luzzo, D.A., Ristow, R., Horvath, M., Retish, P., & Tanners, A. (2001). The career development needs of college students with learning disabilities: In their own words. *Learning Disabilities Research and Practice, 16,* 8–17.

Jenkins, J., & O'Connor, R. (2001, August). *Early identification and intervention for children with reading/learning disabilities.* Paper presented at the LD Summit. Washington, DC: U.S. Department of Education.

Kavale, K.A. (1988). The long-term consequences of learning disabilities. In M.C. Wang, M.C. Reynolds, & H.J. Walberg (Eds.), *Handbook of special education: Research and practice. Vol. 2: Mildly handicapped conditions.* New York: Pergamon Press.

Kavale, K.A. (2001, August). *Discrepancy models in the identification of learning disability.* Paper presented at the LD Summit. Washington, DC: U.S. Department of Education.

Keogh, B.K., & Glover, A.T. (1980, November). Research needs in the study of early identification of children with learning disabilities. *Thalamus (Newsletter of the International Academy for Research in Learning Disabilities).*

Kephart, N.C. (1971). *The slow learner in the classroom* (2nd ed.). Columbus, OH: Merrill.

Kibby, M.Y., & Hynd, G.W. (2001). Neurological basis of learning disabilities. In D.P. Hallahan & B.K. Keogh (Eds.), *Research and global perspectives in learning disabilities: Essays in honor of William M. Cruickshank* (pp. 25–42). Mahwah, NJ: Lawrence Erlbaum Associates.

Kirk, S.A., & Kirk, W.D. (1971). *Psycholinguistic learning disabilities: Diagnosis and remediation.* Urbana: University of Illinois Press.

Klingner, J.K., Vaughn, S., Hughes, M.T., Schumm, J.S., & Elbaum, B. (1998). Outcomes for students with and without learning disabilities in inclusive classrooms. *Learning Disabilities Research and Practice, 13,* 153–161.

Klingner, J.K., Vaughn, S., Schumm, J.S., Cohen, P., & Forgan, J. (1998). Inclusion or pull-out: Which do students prefer? *Journal of Learning Disabilities, 31,* 148–158.

Kotkin, R.A., Forness, S.R., & Kavale, K.A. (2001). Comorbid ADHD and learning disabilities: Diagnosis, special education,

and intervention. In D.P. Hallahan & B.K. Keogh (Eds.), *Research and global perspectives in learning disabilities: Essays in honor of William M. Cruickshank* (pp. 43–63). Mahwah, NJ: Lawrence Erlbaum Associates.

Kravets, M., & Wax, I.F. (2001). *The K & W guide to colleges: For students with learning disabilities or attention deficit disorder* (6th ed.). New York: Princeton Review.

Kushch, A., Gross-Glenn, K., Jallad, B., Lubs, H., Rabin, M., Feldman, E., & Duara, R. (1993). Temporal lobe surface area measurements on MRI in normal and dyslexic readers. *Neuropsychologia, 31,* 811–821.

Lasley II, T.J., Matczynski, T.J., & Rowley, J.B. (2002). *Instructional models: Strategies for teaching in a diverse society.* Belmont, CA: Wadsworth/Thomas Learning.

Leinhardt, G., Seewald, A., & Zigmond, N. (1982). Sex and race differences in learning disabilities classrooms. *Journal of Educational Psychology, 74,* 835–845.

Lerner, J.W. (2000). *Learning disabilities: Theories, diagnosis, and teaching strategies* (8th ed.). Boston: Houghton Mifflin.

Levin, J.R. (1993). Mnemonic strategies and classroom learning: A twenty year report card. *Elementary School Journal, 27,* 301–321.

Lewis, B.A. (1992). Pedigree analysis of children with phonology disorders. *Journal of Learning Disabilities, 25,* 586–597.

Lewis, B.A., & Thompson, L.A. (1992). A study of development of speech and language disorders in twins. *Journal of Speech and Hearing Research, 35,* 1086–1094.

Lloyd, J.W. (1988). Direct academic interventions in learning disabilities. In M.C. Wang, M.C. Reynolds, & H.J. Walberg (Eds.), *Handbook of special education: Research and practice. Vol. 2: Mildly handicapped conditions.* New York: Pergamon Press.

Lloyd, J.W., Hallahan, D.P., Kauffman, J.M., & Keller, C.E. (1998). Academic problems. In G. Stoner, M.R. Shinn, & H.M. Walker (Eds.), *Intervention for achievement and behavior problems* (pp. 201–239). Silver Spring, MD: National Association of School Psychologists.

Lopez-Reyna, N.A., & Bay, M. (1997). Enriching assessment using varied assessments for diverse learners. *Teaching Exceptional Children, 29*(4), 33–37.

MacMillan, D.L., Gresham, F.M., & Bocian, K.M. (1998). Discrepancy between definitions of learning disabilities and school practices: An empirical investigation. *Journal of Learning Disabilities, 31,* 314–326.

MacMillan, D.L., & Siperstein, G.N. (2001, August). *Learning disabilities as operationally defined by schools.* Paper presented at the LD Summit. Washington, DC: U.S. Department of Education.

Mastropieri, M.A., & Scruggs, T.E. (1998). Constructing more meaningful relationships in the classroom: Mnemonic research into practice. *Learning Disabilities Research and Practice, 13,* 138–145.

Mastropieri, M.A., Sweda, J., & Scruggs, T.E. (2000). Putting mnemonics to work in an inclusive classroom. *Learning Disabilities Research & Practice, 15,* 69–74.

Mathes, M.Y., & Bender, W.N. (1997). The effects of self-monitoring on children with attention-deficit/hyperactivity disorder. *Remedial and Special Education, 18,* 121–128.

Mathes, P., Torgesen, J.K., Allen, S.H., & Allor, J.H. (2001). *First grade PALS (Peer-Assisted Literacy Strategies).* Longmont, CO: Sopris West.

McCrory, E., Frith, U., Brunswick, N., & Price, C. (2000). Abnormal functional activation during a simple word repetition task: A PET study of adult dyslexics. *Journal of Cognitive Neuroscience, 12,* 753–762.

McGrady, H.J., Lerner, J.W., & Boscardin, M.L. (2001). The educational lives of students with learning disabilities. In P. Rodis, A. Garrod, & M.L. Boscardin (Eds.), *Learning disabilities and life stories* (pp. 177–193). Boston: Allyn & Bacon.

Meese, R.L. (2001). *Teaching learners with mild disabilities: Integrating research and practice.* (2nd ed.). Stamford, CT: Wadsworth.

Montague, M. (1997). Student perception, mathematical problem solving, and learning disabilities. *Remedial and Special Education, 18,* 46–53.

Montague, M., & Graves, A. (1992). Teaching narrative composition to students with learning disabilities. In M. Pressley, K. Harris, & J.T. Guthrie (Eds.), *Promoting academic competence and literacy in schools* (pp. 261–276). New York: Academic Press.

Murawski, W.W., & Swanson, H.L. (2001). A meta-analysis of co-teaching research: Where are the data? *Remedial and Special Education, 22,* 258–267.

National Joint Committee on Learning Disabilities. (1989, September 18). Letter from NJCLD to member organizations. Topic: Modifications to the NJCLD definition of learning disabilities. Washington, DC: Author.

Olson, R., Wise, B., Conners, F., Rack, J., & Fulker, D. (1989). Specific deficits in component reading and language skills: Genetic and environmental influences. *Journal of Learning Disabilities, 22,* 339–348.

Paulesu, E., Demonet, J.F., Fazio, F., McCrory, E., Chanonine, V., Brunswick, N., Cappa, S.F., Cossu, G., Habib, M., Frith, C.D., & Frith, U. (2001). Dyslexia: Cultural diversity and biological unity. *Science, 291,* 2165–2167.

Pelkey, L. (2001). In the LD bubble. In P. Rodis, A. Garrod, & M.L. Boscardin (Eds.), *Learning disabilities and life stories* (pp. 17–28). Boston: Allyn & Bacon.

Pennington, B.F. (1990). Annotation: The genetics of dyslexia. *Journal of Child Psychology and Child Psychiatry, 31,* 193–201.

Psychological Corporation. (1992). *Wechsler Individual Achievement Test.* San Antonio, TX: Author.

Pugh, K.R. Mencl, W.E., Shaywitz, B.A., Shaywitz, S.E., Fulbright, R.K., Constable, R.T., Skudlarski, P., Marchione, K.E., Jenner, A.R., Fletcher, J.M., Liberman, A.M., Shankweiler, D.P., Katz, L., Lacadie, C., & Gore, J.C. (2000). Task-specific differences in functional connections within the posterior cortex. *Psychological Science, 11,* 51–56.

Queen, O. (2001). Blake Academy and the Green Arrow. In P. Rodis, A. Garrod, & M.L. Boscardin (Eds.), *Learning disabilities and life stories* (pp. 3–16). Boston: Allyn & Bacon.

Raskind, M.H., Goldberg, R.J., Higgins, E.L., & Herman, K.L. (1999). Patterns of change and predictors of success in individuals with learning disabilities: Results from a twenty-year longitudinal study. *Learning Disabilities Research and Practice, 14,* 35–49.

Raskind, W.H. (2001). Current understanding of the genetic basis of reading and spelling disability. *Learning Disability Quarterly, 24,* 141–157.

Reiff, H.B., Gerber, P.J., & Ginsberg, R. (1997). *Exceeding expectations: Successful adults with learning disabilities.* Austin, TX: Pro-Ed.

Reynolds, C.A., Hewitt, J.K., Erickson, M.T., Silberg, J.L., Rutter, M., Simonoff, E., Meyer, J., & Eaves, L.J. (1996). The genetics of children's oral reading performance. *Journal of Child Psychology and Psychiatry, 37,* 425–434.

Richards, T.L. (2001). Functional magnetic resonance imaging and spectroscopic imaging of the brain: Application of fMRI and fMRS to reading disabilities and education. *Learning Disability Quarterly, 24,* 189–203.

Rosenshine, B., & Meister, C. (1994). Reciprocal teaching: A review of research. *Review of Educational Research, 64,* 479–530

Rourke, B.P. (1995). *Syndrome of nonverbal learning disabilities: Neurodevelopmental manifestations.* New York: Guilford Press.

Rueda, R., & Garcia, E. (1997). Do portfolios make a difference for diverse students? The influence of type of data on making instructional decisions. *Learning Disabilities Research and Practice, 12,* 114–122.

Rumsey, J.M., Horwitz, B., Donohue, B.C., Nace, K.L., Maisog, J.M., & Andreason, P. (1999). A functional lesion in developmental dyslexia: Left angular gyral blood flow predicts severity. *Brain and Language, 70*(2), 187–204.

Schulte-Korne, G., Deimel, W., Muller, K., Gutenbrunner, C., & Remschmidt, H. (1996). Familial aggregation of spelling disability. *Journal of Child Psychology and Psychiatry, 37,* 817–822.

Seligman, M.E. (1992). *Helplessness: On depression, development and death.* San Francisco: W.H. Freeman.

Sexton, M., Harris, K.R., & Graham, S. (1998). Self-regulated strategy development and the writing process: Effects on essay writing and attributions. *Exceptional Children, 64,* 295–311.

Shaywitz, S.E., Shaywitz, B.A., Fletcher, J.M., & Escobar, M.D. (1990). Prevalence of reading disability in boys and girls: Results of the Connecticut Longitudinal Study. *Journal of the American Medical Association, 264,* 998–1002.

Shaywitz, S.E., Shaywitz, B.A., Pugh, K.R., Fulbright, R.K., Constable, R.T., Mencl, W.E., Shankweiler, D.P., Liberman, A.M., Skudlarski, P., Fletcher, J.M., Katz, L., Marchione, K.E., Lacadie, C., Gatenby, C., & Gore, J.C. (1998). Functional disruption in the organization of the brain for reading in dyslexia. *Neurobiology, 95,* 2636–2641.

Short, E.J., & Weissberg-Benchell, J. (1989). The triple alliance for learning: Cognition, metacognition, and motivation. In C.B. McCormick, G.E. Miller, & M. Pressley (Eds.), *Cognitive strategy research: From basic research to educational applications* (pp. 33–63). New York: Springer-Verlag.

Skinner, M.E. (1998). Promoting self-advocacy among college students with learning disabilities. *Intervention in School and Clinic, 33,* 278–283.

Spekman, N.J., Goldberg, R.J., & Herman, K.L. (1992). Learning disabled children grow up: A search for factors related to success in the young adult years. *Learning Disabilities Research and Practice, 7,* 161–170.

Sridhar, D., & Vaughn, S. (2001). Social functioning of students with learning disabilities. In D.P. Hallahan & B.K. Keogh (Eds.), *Research and global perspectives in learning disabilities: Essays in honor of William M. Cruickshank* (pp. 65–91). Mahwah, NJ: Lawrence Erlbaum Associates.

Strichart, S.S., & Mangrum, C.T. (2001). *Peterson's colleges with programs for students with learning disabilities or attention deficit disorders* (6th ed.). Princeton, NJ: Petersons Guides.

Swanson, H.L. (Ed.). (1987). *Memory and learning disabilities: Advances in learning and behavioral disabilities.* Greenwich, CT: JAI Press.

Swanson, H.L. (2001). Research on interventions for adolescents with learning disabilities: A meta-analysis of outcomes related to higher-order processing. *Elementary School Journal, 101,* 331–348.

Swanson, H.L., & Hoskyn, M. (1998). Experimental intervention research for students with learning disabilities: A meta-analysis of treatment outcomes. *Review of Educational Research, 68,* 277–321.

Swanson, H.L., & Sachse-Lee, C. (2001). A subgroup analysis of working memory in children with reading disabilities: Domain-general or domain-specific deficiency? *Journal of Learning Disabilities, 34,* 249–263.

Torgesen, J.K. (1977). The role of nonspecific factors in the task performance of learning disabled children: A theoretical assessment. *Journal of Learning Disabilities, 10,* 27–34.

Torgesen, J.K. (1988). Studies of children with learning disabilities who perform poorly on memory span tasks. *Journal of Learning Disabilities, 21,* 605–612.

Torgesen, J.K. (2001, August). *Empirical and theoretical support for direct diagnosis of learning disabilities by assessment of intrinsic processing weaknesses.* Paper presented at the LD Summit. Washington, DC: U.S. Department of Education.

Torgesen, J.K., & Kail, R.V. (1980). Memory processes in exceptional children. In B.K. Keogh (Ed.), *Advances in special education. Vol. 1: Basic constructs and theoretical orientations.* Greenwich, CT: JAI Press.

U.S. Department of Education. (2000). *Twenty-second annual report to Congress on the implementation of the Individuals with Disabilities Education Act.* Washington, DC: Author.

U.S. Department of Education. (1997). *Nineteenth annual report to Congress on the implementation of the Individuals with Disabilities Education Act.* Washington, DC: Author.

Vaughn, S., Elbaum, B., & Boardman, A.G. (2001). The social functioning of students with learning disabilities: Implications for inclusion. *Exceptionality, 9,* 47–65.

Vaughn, S., Gersten, R., & Chard, D.J. (2000). The underlying message in LD intervention research: Findings from research syntheses. *Exceptional Children, 67,* 99–114.

Vaughn, S., Schumm, J.S., & Arguelles, M.E. (1997). The ABCDEs of Co-teaching. *Teaching Exceptional Children, 30,* 4–10.

Werner, H., & Strauss, A.A. (1941). Pathology of figure-background relation in the child. *Journal of Abnormal and Social Psychology, 36,* 236–248.

Willows, D.M. (1998). Visual processes in learning disabilities. In H.L. Swanson (Ed.), *Handbook of assessment of learning disabilities: Theory, research, and practice* (pp. 147–175). Austin, TX: Pro-Ed.

Wise, B.W., & Snyder, L. (2001, August). *Judgments in identifying and teaching children with language-based reading difficulties.* Paper presented at the LD Summit. Washington, DC: U.S. Department of Education.

Witte, R.H., Philips, L., & Kakela, M. (1998). Job satisfaction of college graduates with learning disabilities. *Journal of Learning Disabilities, 31,* 259–265.

Woodward, J., & Baxter, J. (1997). The effects of an innovative approach to mathematics on academically low-achieving students in inclusive settings. *Exceptional Children, 63,* 373–388.

Worling, D.E., Humphries, T., & Tannock, R. (1999). Spatial and emotional aspects of language inferencing in nonverbal learning disabilities. *Brain and Language, 70,* 220–239.

CHAPTER 6

American Academy of Pediatrics, Committee on Quality Improvement, Subcommittee on Attention-Deficit/Hyperactivity Disorder. (2000). *Pediatrics, 105,* 1158–1170.

Allsopp, D.H. (1999). Using modeling, manipulatives, and mnemonics with eighth-grade math students. *Teaching Exceptional Children, 32*(2), 74–81.

American Psychiatric Association. (2000). *Diagnostic and statistical manual of mental disorders* (4th ed., text rev.). Washington, DC: Author.

Aylward, E.H., Reiss, A.L., Reader, M.J., Brown, J.E., & Denckla, M.B. (1996). Basal ganglia volumes in children with attention-deficit hyperactivity disorder. *Journal of Child Neurology, 11,* 112–115.

Barkley, R.A. (1994). Impaired delayed responding: A unified theory of attention-deficit hyperactivity disorder. In D.K. Routh (Ed.), *Disruptive behavior disorders in childhood* (pp. 11–57). New York: Plenum.

Barkley, R.A. (1997). Behavioral inhibition, sustained attention, and executive functions: Constructing a unifying theory of ADHD. *Psychological Bulletin, 121,* 65–94.

Barkley, R.A. (1998). *Attention-deficit hyperactivity disorder: A handbook for diagnosis and treatment.* New York: Guilford Press.

Barkley, R.A., & Murphy, K.R. (1998). *Attention-deficit hyperactivity disorder: A clinical workbook* (2nd ed.). New York: Guilford Press.

Barkley, R.A., Murphy, K.R., & Kwasnik, D. (1996). Psychological adjustment and adaptive impairments in young adults with ADHD. *Journal of Attention Disorders, 1,* 41–54.

Baumgaertel, A., Wolraich, M.L., & Dietrich, M. (1995). Comparison of diagnostic criteria for attention deficit disorders in a German elementary school sample. *Journal of the Academy of Child and Adolescent Psychiatry, 34,* 629–638.

Berquin, M.D., Giedd, J.N., Jacobsen, L.K., Hamburger, S.D., Krain, A.L., Rapoport, J.L., & Castellanos, F.X. (1998). Cerebellum in attention-deficit hyperactivity disorder. *Neurology, 50,* 1087–1093.

Biederman, J., Faraone, S.V., Mick, E., Spencer, T., Wilens, T., Kiely, K., Guite, J., Ablon, J.S., Reed, E., & Warburton, R. (1995). High risk for attention deficit hyperactivity disorder among children of parents with childhood onset of the disorder: A pilot study. *American Journal of Psychiatry, 152,* 431–435.

Biederman, J., Wilens, T., Mick, E., Faraone, S.V., & Spencer, T. (1998). Does attention-deficit hyperactivity disorder impact the developmental course of drug and alcohol abuse and dependence? *Biological Psychiatry, 44,* 269–273.

Biederman, J., Wilens, T., Mick, E., Spencer, T., & Faraone, S.V. (1999). Pharmacotherapy of attention-deficit/hyperactivity disorder reduces risk for substance abuse disorder. *Pediatrics, 104,* 20.

Birch, H.G. (1964). *Brain damage in children: The biological and social aspects.* Baltimore: Williams & Wilkins.

Cantwell, D.P. (1979). The "hyperactive child." *Hospital Practice, 14,* 65–73.

Castellanos, F.X. (1997). Toward a pathophysiology of attention-deficit/hyperactivity disorder. *Clinical Pediatrics, 36,* 381–393.

Castellanos, F.X., Giedd, J.N., Marsh, W.L., Hamburger, S.D., Vaituzis, A.C., Dickstein, D.P., Sarfatti, S.E., Vauss, Y.C., Snell, J.W., Lange, N., Kaysen, D., Krain, A.L., Ritchie, G.F.,

Rajapakse, J.C., & Rapoport, J.L. (1996). Quantitative brain magnetic resonance imaging in attention-deficit hyperactivity disorder. *Archives of General Psychiatry, 53*, 607–616.

Cepeda, N.J., Cepeda, M.L., & Kramer, A.F. (2000). Task switching and attention deficit hyperactivity disorder. *Journal of Abnormal Child Psychology, 28*, 213–226.

Chilcoat, H.D., & Breslau, N. (1999). Pathways from ADHD to early drug use. *Journal of the American Academy of Child and Adolescent Psychiatry, 38*, 1347–1354.

Cole, C.L., & Bambara, L.M. (1992). Issues surrounding the use of self-management interventions in the school. *School Psychology Review, 21*, 193–201.

Conners, C.K. (1989a). *Conners Teacher Rating Scale–28.* Tonawanda, NY: Multi-Health Systems.

Conners, C.K. (1989b). *Conners Teacher Rating Scale–39.* Tonawanda, NY: Multi-Health Systems.

Conners, C.K. (1997). *Conners Rating Scales—Revised (CSR-R).* North Tonawanda, NY: Multi-Health Systems.

Conners, C.K. (1999). *Conners Adult ADHD Rating Scales (CAARS).* North Tonawanda, NY: Multi-Health Systems.

Cooper, P. (1999). ADHD and effective learning: Principles and practical approaches. In P. Cooper & K. Bilton (Eds.), *ADHD: Research, practice and opinion* (pp. 138–157). London: Whurr.

Cox, D.J., Merkel, R.L., Kovatchev, B., & Seward, R. (2000). Effect of stimulant medication on driving performance of young adults with attention-deficit hyperactivity disorder. *Journal of Nervous and Mental Disease, 188*, 230–234.

Crenshaw, T.M., Kavale, K.A., Forness, S.R., & Reeve, R.E. (1999). Attention deficit hyperactivity disorder and the efficacy of stimulant medication: A meta-analysis. In T. Scruggs & M. Mastropieri (Eds.), *Advances in learning and behavioral disabilities, Vol. 13* (pp. 135–165). Greenwich, CT: JAI Press.

Cruickshank, W.M., Bentzen, F.A., Ratzeburg, F.H., & Tannhauser, M.T. (1961). *A teaching method of brain-injured and hyperactive children.* Syracuse, NY: Syracuse University Press.

Cruickshank, W.M., Bice, H.V., & Wallen, N.E. (1957). *Perception and cerebral palsy.* Syracuse, NY: Syracuse University Press.

Davies, S., & Witte, R. (2000). Self-management and peer-monitoring within a group contingency to decrease uncontrolled verbalizations of children with attention-deficit/hyperactivity disorder. *Psychology in the Schools, 37*, 135–147.

DuPaul, G.J., Barkley, R.A., & Connor, D.F. (1998). Stimulants. In R.A. Barkley (Ed.), *Attention-deficit hyperactivity disorder: A handbook for diagnosis and treatment* (pp. 510–551). New York: Guilford Press.

DuPaul, G.J., & Eckert, T.L. (1997). The effects of school-based interventions for attention deficit hyperactivity disorder: A meta-analysis. *School Psychology Review, 26*, 5–27.

DuPaul, G.J., Eckert, T.L., & McGoey, K.E. (1997). Interventions for students with attention-deficit/hyperactivity disorder: One size does not fit all. *School Psychology Review, 26*, 369–381.

DuPaul, G.J., & Ervin, R.A. (1996). Functional assessment of behaviors related to attention-deficit hyperactivity disorder: Linking assessment to intervention design. *Behavior Therapy, 27*, 601–622.

DuPaul, G.J., Power, D.T.J., Anastopolos, A.D., & Reid, R. (1998). *ADHD Rating Scale–IV: Checklists, norms, and clinical interpretations.* New York: Guilford Press.

Erhardt, D., & Hinshaw, S.P. (1994). Initial sociometric impressions of attention-deficit hyperactivity disorder and comparison boys: Predictions from social behaviors and from nonbehavioral variables. *Journal of Consulting and Clinical Psychology, 62*, 833–842.

Ernst, M., Zametkin, A.J., Matochik, J.A., Jons, P.H., & Cohen, R.M. (1998). DOPA decarboxylase activity in attention deficit hyperactivity disorder adults. A [fluorine-18]fluorodopa positron emission tomographic study. *The Journal of Neuroscience, 18*, 5901–5907.

Ernst, M., Zametkin, A.J., Matochik, J.A., Pascualvaca, D., Jons, P.H., & Cohen, R.M. (1999). High midbrain [18F] DOPA accumulation in children with attention deficit hyperactivity disorder. *American Journal of Psychiatry, 156*, 1209–1215.

Ervin, R.A., DuPaul, G.J., Kern, L., & Friman, P.C. (1998). Classroom-based functional and adjunctive assessments: Proactive approaches to intervention selection for adolescents with attention deficit hyperactivity disorder. *Journal of Applied Behavior Analysis, 31*, 65–78.

Esser, G., Schmidt, M.H., & Woerner, W. (1990). Epidemiology and course of psychiatric disorders in school-age children—Results of a longitudinal study. *Journal of Child Psychology and Psychiatry, 31*, 243–263.

Evans, S.W., Pelham, W.E., Smith, B.H., Bukstein, O., Gnagy, E.M., Greiner, A.R., Altenderfer, L., & Baron-Myak, C. (2001). Dose-response effects of methylphenidate on ecologically valid measures of academic performance and classroom behavior in adolescents with ADHD. *Experimental and Clinical Pharmacology, 9*, 163–175.

Faraone, S.V., Biederman, J., Spencer, T., Wilens, T., Seidman, L.J., Mick, E., & Doyle, A.E. (2000). Attention-deficit/hyperactivity disorder in adults: An overview. *Biological Psychiatry, 48*, 9–20.

Faraone, S.V., & Doyle, A.E. (2001). The nature and heritability of attention-deficit/hyperactivity disorder. *Child and Adolescent Psychiatric Clinics of North America, 10*, 299–316.

Faraone, S.V., Pliszka, S.R., Olvera, R.L., Skolnik, R., & Biederman, J. (2001). Efficacy of Adderall and methylphenidate in attention deficit hyperactivity disorder: A reanalysis using drug-placebo and drug-drug response curve methodology. *Journal of Child and Adolescent Psychopharmacology, 11*, 171–180.

Fergusson, D.M., Horwood, L.J., & Lynskey, M.T. (1993). Prevalence and comorbidity of DSM-III-R diagnoses in a birth cohort of 15 year olds. *Journal of the American Academy of Child and Adolescent Psychiatry, 32*, 1127–1134.

Filipek, P.A., Semrud-Clikeman, M., Steingard, R.J., Renshaw, P.F., Kennedy, D.N., & Biederman, J. (1997). Volumetric MRI analysis comparing subjects having attention-deficit hyperactivity disorder with normal controls. *Neurology, 48*, 589–601.

Forness, S.R., Kavale, K.A. (2002). Impact of ADHD on school systems. In P. Jensen & J.R. Cooper (Eds.), *NIH consensus conference on ADHD.* In press.

Forness, S.R., Kavale, K.A., & Crenshaw, T.M. (1999). Stimulant medication revisited: Effective treatment of children with ADHD. *Journal of Emotional and Behavioral Problems, 7*, 230–235.

Gainetdinov, R.R., Wetsel, W.C., Jones, S.R., Levin, E.D., Jaber, M., & Caron, M.G. (1999). Role of Seratonin in the paradoxical calming effect of psychostimulants on hyperactivity. *Science, 283*(5400), 397–401.

Gillis, J.J., Gilger, J.W., Pennington, B.F., & DeFries, C. (1992). Attention deficit disorder in reading-disabled twins: Evidence for a genetic etiology. *Journal of Abnormal Child Psychology, 20,* 303–315.

Goldstein, K. (1936). The modification of behavior consequent to cerebral lesions. *Psychiatric Quarterly, 10,* 586–610.

Goldstein, K. (1939). *The organism.* New York: American Book Co.

Hale, J.B., Hoeppner, J.B., DeWitt, M.B., Coury, D.L., Ritacco, D.G., & Trommer, B. (1998). Evaluating medication response in ADHD: Cognitive, behavioral, and single-subject methodology. *Journal of Learning Disabilities, 31,* 595–607.

Hallahan, D.P., & Cottone, E.A. (1997). Attention deficit hyperactivity disorder. In T.E. Scruggs & M.A. Mastropieri (Eds.), *Advances in learning and behavioral disabilities, Vol. 11* (pp. 27–67). Greenwich, CT: JAI Press.

Hallowell, E.M., & Ratey, J.J. (1994). *Driven to distraction.* New York: Touchstone.

Hallowell, E.M., & Ratey, J.J. (1996). *Answers to distraction.* New York: Bantam Books.

Hoffmann, H. (1865). Die Geschichte vom Zappel-Philipp [The Story of Fidgety Philip]. *Der Struwwelpeter.* Germany: Pestalozzi-Verlag.

Horner, R.H., & Carr, E.G. (1997). Behavioral support for students with severe disabilities: Functional assessment and comprehensive intervention. *Journal of Special Education, 31,* 1–11.

Hudson, P. (1997). Using teacher-guided practice to help students with learning disabilities acquire and retain social studies content. *Learning Disabilities Quarterly, 20,* 23–32.

Hynd, G.W., Hern, K.L., Novey, E.S., Eliopulos, D., Marshall, R., Gonzalez, J.J., & Voeller, K.K. (1993). Attention deficit hyperactivity disorder and asymmetry of the caudate nucleus. *Journal of Child Neurology, 8,* 339–347.

Hynd, G.W., Semrud-Clikeman, M., Lorys, A.R., Novey, E.S., & Eliopulos, D. (1990). Brain morphology in developmental dyslexia and attention deficit/hyperactivity. *Archives of Neurology, 47,* 919–926.

Kameenui, E.J., & Carnine, D.W. (1998). *Effective teaching strategies that accommodate diverse learners.* Columbus, OH: Prentice-Hall.

Kanbayashi, Y., Nakata, Y., Fujii, K., Kita, M., & Wada, K. (1994). ADHD-related behavior among non-referred children: Parents' ratings of DSM-III-R symptoms. *Child Psychiatry and Human Development, 25*(1), 13–29.

Kemp, K., Fister, S., & McLaughlin, P.J. (1995). Academic strategies for children with ADD. *Intervention in School and Clinic, 30,* 203–210.

Kewley, G.D. (1998). Personal paper: Attention deficit hyperactivity disorder is underdiagnosed and undertreated in Britain. *British Medical Journal, 316,* 1594–1596.

Kohn, A. (1993). *Punished by rewards: The trouble with gold stars, incentive plans, A's, praise, and other bribes.* Boston: Houghton Mifflin.

Kucan, L., & Beck, I.L. (1997). Thinking aloud and reading comprehension research: Inquiry, instruction, and social interaction. *Review of Educational Research, 67,* 271–299.

Lambert, N.M., & Hartsough, C.S. (1998). Prospective study of tobacco smoking and substance dependencies among samples of ADHD and non-ADHD participants. *Journal of Learning Disabilities, 31,* 533–544.

Landau, S., Milich, R., & Diener, M.B. (1998). Peer relations of children with attention-deficit hyperactivity disorder. *Reading and Writing Quarterly: Overcoming Learning Difficulties, 14,* 83–105.

Leung, P.W.L., Luk, S.L., Ho, T.P., Taylor, E., Mak, F.L., & Bacon-Shone, J. (1996). The diagnosis and prevalence of hyperactivity in Chinese schoolboys. *British Journal of Psychiatry, 168,* 486–496.

Levy, F., Barr, C., & Sunohara, G. (1998). Directions of aetiologic research on attention deficit hyperactivity disorder. *Australian and New Zealand Journal of Psychiatry, 32,* 97–103.

Lloyd, J.W., Hallahan, D.P., Kauffman, J.M., & Keller, C.E. (1998). Academic problems. In R.J. Morris & T.R. Kratochwill (Eds.), *The practice of child therapy* (pp. 167–198). Boston: Allyn & Bacon.

Lou, H.C., Henriksen, L., & Bruhn, P. (1984). Focal cerebral hypoperfusion in children with dysphasia and/or attention deficit disorder. *Archives of Neurology, 41,* 825–829.

Lou, H.C., Henriksen, L., Bruhn, P., Borner, H., & Nielsen, J.B. (1989). Striatal dysfunction in attention deficit and hyperkinetic disorder. *Archives of Neurology, 46,* 48–52.

Manos, M.J., Short, E.J., & Findling, R.L. (1999). Differential effectiveness of methylphenidate and Adderall in school-age youths with attention-deficit/hyperactivity disorder. *Journal of the American Academy of Child and Adolescent Psychiatry, 38,* 813–819.

Marshall, R.M., Hynd, G.W., Handwerk, M.J., & Hall, J. (1997). Academic underachievement in ADHD subtypes. *Journal of Learning Disabilities, 30,* 635–642.

Mathes, M.Y., & Bender, W.N. (1997). The effects of self-monitoring on children with attention-deficit/hyperactivity disorder who are receiving pharmacological interventions. *Remedial and Special Education, 18,* 121–128.

Mercer, C.D., & Mercer, A.R. (1998). *Teaching students with learning problems* (5th ed.). Columbus, OH: Prentice-Hall.

Milberger, S., Biederman, J., Faraone, S.V., Guite, J., & Tsuang, M.T. (1997). Pregnancy, delivery and infancy complications and attention deficit hyperactivity disorder: Issues of gene-environment interaction. *Biological Psychiatry, 41,* 65–75.

Murphy, K.R. (1998). Psychological counseling of adults with ADHD. In R.A. Barkley (Ed.), *Attention-deficit hyperactivity disorder: A handbook for diagnosis and treatment* (pp. 582–591). New York: Guilford Press.

National Institutes of Health (November, 1998). Diagnosis and treatment of attention deficit hyperactivity disorder. *NIH Consensus Statement, 16*(2).

Pasamanick, B., Lilienfeld, A.M., & Rogers, M.E. (1956). Pregnancy experience and the development of behavior disorders in children. *American Journal of Psychiatry, 112,* 613–617.

Pelham, W.E. (2000). Implications of the MTA Study for behavioral and combined treatments. *ADHD Report, 8*(4), 9–13, 16.

Pfiffner, L.J., & Barkley, R.A. (1998). Treatment of ADHD in school settings. In R.A. Barkley (Ed.), *Attention-deficit hyperactivity disorder: A handbook for diagnosis and treatment* (pp. 458–490). New York: Guilford Press.

Pineda, D., Ardila, A., Rosselli, M., Arias, B.E., Henao, G.C., Gomez, L.F., Mejia, S.E., & Miranda, M.L. (1999). Prevalence of attention-deficit/hyperactivity disorder symptoms in 4- to 17-year-old children in the general population. *Journal of Abnormal Child Psychology, 27,* 455–462.

Pinel, J.P.J. (2000). *Biopsychology* (4th ed.). Boston: Allyn & Bacon.

Pliszka, S.R., Browne, R.G., Olvera, R.L., & Wynne, S.K. (2000). A double-blind, placebo-controlled study of Adderall and methylphenidate in the treatment of attention deficit/

hyperactivity disorder. *Journal of the American Academy of Child and Adolescent Psychiatry, 39,* 619–626.

Reid, R., & Harris, K.R. (1992). Self-monitoring of attention versus self-monitoring of performance: Effects on attention and academic performance. *Exceptional Children, 60,* 29–40.

Richters, J.E., Arnold, L.E., Abikoff, H., Conners, C.K., Greenhill, L.L., Hechtman, L., Hinshaw, S.P., Pelham, W.E., & Swanson, J.M. (1995). NIMH collaborative multisite multimodal treatment study of children with ADHD: Background and rationale. *Journal of the Academy of Child and Adolescent Psychiatry, 34,* 987–1000.

Rohde, L.A., Biederman, J., Busnello, E., Zimmerman, H., Schmitz, M., Martins, S., & Tramontina, S. (1999). ADHD in a sample of Brazilian adolescents: A study of prevalence, comorbid conditions, and impairments. *Journal of the Academy of Child and Adolescent Psychiatry, 38,* 716–722.

Rooney, K.J. (1995). Teaching students with attention disorders. *Intervention in School and Clinic, 30,* 221–225.

Rosenshine, R. (1995). Advances in research on instruction. *Journal of Educational Research, 88,* 262–268.

Rubia, K., Oosterlann, J., Sergeant, J.A., Brandeis, D., & Van-Leeuwen, T. (1998). Inhibitory dysfunction in hyperactive boys. *Behavioural Brain Research, 94,* 25–32.

Sagvolden, T., & Sergeant, J.A. (1998). Attention deficit/hyperactivity disorder—from brain dysfunctions to behaviour. *Behavioural Brain Research, 94,* 1–10.

Schachar, R., Mota, V.L., Logan, G.D., Tannock, R., & Klim, P. (2000). Confirmation of an inhibitory control deficit in attention-deficit/hyperactivity disorder. *Journal of Abnormal Child Psychology, 28,* 227–235.

Schaughency, E.A., McGee, R., Raja, S.N., Freehan, M., & Silva, P. (1994). Self-reported inattention, impulsivity, and hyperactivity in ages 15 and 18 years in the general population. *Journal of the Academy of Child and Adolescent Psychiatry, 33,* 173–183.

Semrud-Clikeman, M., Steingard, R.J., Filipek, P., Biederman, J., Bekken, K., & Renshaw, P.F. (2000). Using MRI to examine brain-behavior relationships in males with attention deficit disorder with hyperactivity. *Journal of the American Academy of Child and Adolescent Psychiatry, 39,* 477–484.

Shapiro, E.S., DuPaul, G.J., & Bradley-Klug, K.L. (1998). Self-management as a strategy to improve the classroom behavior of adolescents with ADHD. *Journal of Learning Disabilities, 31,* 545–555.

Shelton, T.L., Barkley, R.A., Crosswait, C., Moorehouse, M., Fletcher, K., Barrett, M.S., Jenkins, L., & Metevia, L. (2000). Multimethod psychoeducational intervention for preschool children with disruptive behavior: Two-year post-treatment follow-up. *Journal of Abnormal Child Psychology, 28,* 253–266.

Sherman, D.K., Iacono, W.G., & McGue, M.K. (1997). Attention-deficit hyperactivity disorder dimensions: A twin study of inattention and impulsivity-hyperactivity. *Journal of the American Academy of Child and Adolescent Psychiatry, 36,* 745–753.

Shimabukuro, S.M., Prater, M.A., Jenkins, A., & Edelen-Smith, P. (1999). The effects of self-monitoring of academic performance on students with learning disabilities and ADD/ADHD. *Education and Treatment of Children, 22,* 397–414.

Sleator, E.K., & Ullmann, R.K. (1981). Can the physician diagnose hyperactivity in the office? *Pediatrics, 67,* 13–17.

Smith, D.J., & Nelson, J.R., Young, K.R., & West, R.P. (1992). The effect of a self-management procedure on the classroom and academic behavior of students with mild handicaps. *School Psychology Review, 21,* 59–72.

Solanto, M.V. (1998). Neuropsychopharmacological mechanisms of stimulant drug action in attention-deficit hyperactivity disorder: A review and integration. *Behavioural Brain Research, 94,* 127–152.

Spencer, T., Biederman, J., Wilens, T., Harding, M., O'Donnell, D., & Griffin, S. (1996). Pharmacotherapy of attention-deficit hyperactivity disorder across the life cycle. *Journal of the American Academy of Child and Adolescent Psychiatry, 35,* 409–432.

Stevenson, J. (1992). Evidence for a genetic etiology in hyperactive children. *Behavior Genetics, 22,* 337–344.

Still, G.F. (1902). Some abnormal psychical conditions in children. *The Lancet, 1,* 1008–1012, 1077–1082, 1163–1168.

Strauss, A.A., & Werner, H. (1942). Disorders of conceptual thinking in the brain-injured child. *Journal of Nervous and Mental Disease, 96,* 153–172.

Swanson, J., Castellanos, F.X., Murias, M., LaHoste, G., & Kennedy, J. (1998). Cognitive neuroscience of attention deficit hyperactivity disorder and hyperkinetic disorder. *Current Opinion in Neurobiology, 8,* 263–271.

Swanson, J.M., Kraemer, H.C., Hinshaw, S.P., Arnold, L.E., Conners, C.K., Abikoff, H.B., Clevenger, W., Davies, M., Elliott, G.R., Greenhill, L.L., Hechtman, L., Hoza, B., Jensen, P., March, J.S., Newcorn, J.H., Owens, E.B., Pelham, W.E., Schiller, E., Severe, J.B., Simpson, S., Vitiello, B., Wells, K., Wigal, T., & Wu, M. (2001). Clinical relevance of the primary findings of the MTA: Success rates based on severity of ADHD and ODD symptoms at the end of treatment. *Journal of the American Academy of Child and Adolescent Psychiatry, 40,* 168–179.

Swanson, J.M., Sergeant, J.A., Taylor, E., Sonuga-Barke, E.J.S., Jensen, P.S., & Cantwell, D.P. (1998). Attention-deficit hyperactivity disorder and hyperkinetic disorder. *The Lancet, 351,* 429–433.

Szatmari, P. (1992). The epidemiology of attention-deficit/hyperactivity disorder. In G. Weiss (Ed.), *Child and adolescent psychiatry clinics of North America: Attention deficit disorder* (pp. 361–372). Philadelphia: Saunders.

Tankersley, M. (1995). A group-oriented contingency management program: A review of research on the good behavior game and implications for teachers. *Preventing School Failure, 40,* 59–72.

Teicher, M.H., Anderson, C.M., Polcarl, A., Glod, C.A., Maas, L.C., & Renshaw, P.F. (2000). Functional deficits in basal ganglia of children with attention-deficit/hyperactivity disorder shown with functional magnetic resonance imaging relaxometry. *Nature Medicine, 6,* 470–473.

Tripp, G., & Alsop, B. (2001). Sensitivity to reward delay in children with attention deficit hyperactivity disorder (ADHD). *Journal of Child Psychology and Psychiatry, 42,* 691–698.

Vaughn, S., Schumm, J.S., & Arguelles, M.E. (1997). The ABCDEs of Co-teaching. *Teaching Exceptional Children, 30,* 4–10.

Verhulst, F.C., van der Ende, J., Ferdinand, R.F., & Kasius, M.C. (1997). The prevalence of DSM-III-R diagnoses in a national sample of Dutch adolescents. *Archives of General Psychiatry, 54,* 329–336.

Weiss, M., Hechtman, L., & Weiss, G. (2000). ADHD in parents. *Journal of the American Academy of Child and Adolescent Psychiatry, 39,* 1059–1061

Werner, H., & Strauss, A.A. (1939). Types of visuo-motor activity in their relation to low and high performance ages. *Proceedings of the American Association on Mental Deficiency, 44,* 163–168.

Werner, H., & Strauss, A.A. (1941). Pathology of figure-background relation in the child. *Journal of Abnormal and Social Psychology, 36,* 236–248.

Wilens, T.E., & Biederman, J. (1992). Pediatric psychopharmacology: The stimulants. *Pediatric Clinics of North America, 15*(1), 191–222.

Willcutt, E.G., Chhabildas, N., & Pennington, B.F. (2001). Validity of the DSM-IV subtypes of ADHD. *ADHD Report, 9*(1), 2–5.

Willcutt, E.G., Pennington, B.F., Boada, R., Ogline, J.S., Tunick, R.A., Chhabildas, N.A., & Olson, R.K. (2001). A comparison of the cognitive deficits in reading disability and attention-deficit/hyperactivity disorder. *Journal of Abnormal Psychology, 110,* 157–172.

Woodward, L.J., Fergusson, D.M., & Horwood, L.J. (2000). Driving outcomes for young people with attentional difficulties in adolescence. *Journal of the American Academy of Child and Adolescent Psychiatry, 39,* 627–634.

CHAPTER 7

Achenbach, T.M. (1985). *Assessment and taxonomy of child and adolescent psychopathology.* Newbury Park, CA: Sage.

American Psychiatric Association. (1994). *Diagnostic and statistical manual of mental disorders* (4th ed.). Washington, DC: Author.

Asarnow, R.F., Asamen, J., Granholm, E., Sherman, T., Watkins, J.M., & Williams, M.E. (1994). Cognitive/neuropsychological studies of children with a schizophrenic disorder. *Schizophrenia Bulletin, 20,* 647–669.

Asarnow, J.R., Tompson, M.C., & Goldstein, M.J. (1994). Childhood-onset schizophrenia: A follow-up study. *Schizophrenia Bulletin, 20,* 599–617.

Bandura, A. (1973). *Aggression: A social learning analysis.* Englewood Cliffs, NJ: Prentice-Hall.

Bandura, A. (1986). *Social foundations of thought and action: A social cognitive theory.* Englewood Cliffs, NJ: Prentice-Hall.

Bateman, B.D., & Chard, D.J. (1995). Legal demands and constraints on placement decisions. In J.M. Kauffman, J.W. Lloyd, D.P. Hallahan, & T.A. Astuto (Eds.), *Issues in educational placement: Students with emotional and behavioral disorders* (pp. 285–316). Hillsdale, NJ: Erlbaum.

Becker, J.V., & Bonner, B. (1997). Sexual and other abuse of children. In R.J. Morris & T.R. Kratochwill (Eds.), *The practice of child therapy* (3rd ed., pp. 367–389). Boston: Allyn & Bacon.

Becker, W.C. (1964). Consequences of different kinds of parental discipline. In M.L. Hoffman & L.W. Hoffman (Eds.), *Review of child development research* (Vol. 1). New York: Russell Sage Foundation.

Blake, C., Wang, W., Cartledge, G., & Gardner, R. (2000). Middle school students with serious emotional disturbances serve as social skills trainers and reinforcers for peers with SED. *Behavioral Disorders, 25,* 280–298.

Bolger, K.E., & Patterson, C.J. (2001). Developmental pathways from child maltreatment to peer rejection. *Child Development, 72,* 549–568.

Bower, E.M. (1981). *Early identification of emotionally handicapped children in school* (3rd ed.). Springfield, IL: Charles C. Thomas.

Bower, E.M. (1982). Defining emotional disturbance: Public policy and research. *Psychology in the Schools, 19,* 55–60.

Brandenburg, N.A., Friedman, R.M., & Silver, S.E. (1990). The epidemiology of childhood psychiatric disorders: Prevalence findings from recent studies. *Journal of the American Academy of Child and Adolescent Psychiatry, 29,* 76–83.

Brigham, F.J., & Kauffman, J.M. (1998). Creating supportive environments for students with emotional or behavioral disorders. *Effective School Practices, 17*(2), 25–35.

Carson, R.R., Sitlington, P.L., & Frank, A.R. (1995). Young adulthood for individuals with behavioral disorders: What does it hold? *Behavioral Disorders, 20,* 127–135.

Charlop-Christy, M.H., Schreibman, L., Pierce, K., & Kurtz, P.F. (1997). Childhood autism. In R.J. Morris & T.R. Kratochwill (Eds.), *The practice of child therapy* (3rd ed., pp. 271–389). Boston: Allyn & Bacon.

Cline, D.H. (1990). A legal analysis of policy initiatives to exclude handicapped/disruptive students from special education. *Behavioral Disorders, 15,* 159–173.

Coleman, M., & Vaughn, S. (2000). Reading interventions for students with emotional/behavioral disorders. *Behavioral Disorders, 25,* 93–104.

Costello, E.J., Messer, S.C., Bird, H.R., Cohen, P., & Reinherz, H.Z. (1998). The prevalence of serious emotional disturbance: A re-analysis of community studies. *Journal of Child and Family Studies, 7,* 411–432.

Costenbader, V., & Buntaine, R. (1999). Diagnostic discrimination between social maladjustment and emotional disturbance: An empirical study. *Journal of Emotional and Behavioral Disorders, 7,* 1–10.

Council for Exceptional Children (2001). Performance-based Standards. Retrieved June 5, 2001 from *www.cec.sped.org/ps/perf_based_stds/index.html.*

Coutinho, M.J., Oswald, D.P., Best, A.M., & Forness, S.R. (2002). Gender and socio-demographic factors and the disproportionate identification of minority students as emotionally disturbed. *Behavioral Disorders, 27,* 109–125.

Crockett, J.B., & Kauffman, J.M. (1999). *The least restrictive environment: Its origins and interpretations in special education.* Mahwah, NJ: Erlbaum.

Cullinan, D., & Epstein, M.H. (2001). Comorbidity among students with emotional disturbance. *Behavioral Disorders, 26,* 200–213.

Duke, D.L., Griesdorn, J., & Kraft, M. (1998, March). *A school of their own: A status check of Virginia's alternative high schools for at-risk students.* Charlottesville, VA: Thomas Jefferson Center for Educational Design.

Duncan, B.B., Forness, S.R., & Hartsough, C. (1995). Students identified as seriously emotionally disturbed in school-based day treatment: Cognitive, psychiatric, and special education characteristics. *Behavioral Disorders, 20,* 238–252.

Dunlap, G., dePerczel, M., Clarke, S., Wilson, D., Wright, S., White, R., & Gomez, A. (1994). Choice making to promote adaptive behavior for students with emotional and behavioral challenges. *Journal of Applied Behavior Analysis, 27,* 505–518.

Edelman, P. (2001). *Searching for America's heart: RFK and the renewal of hope.* Boston: Houghton Mifflin.

Edgar, E., & Siegel, S. (1995). Postsecondary scenarios for troubled and troubling youth. In J.M. Kauffman, J.W. Lloyd, D.P. Hallahan, & T.A. Astuto (Eds.), *Issues in educational placement:*

Students with emotional or behavioral disorders (pp. 251–283). Hillsdale, NJ: Erlbaum.

Epstein, M.H., & Sharma, J. (1997). Behavioral and Emotional Rating Scale (BERS): A strength-based approach to assessment. Austin, TX: Pro-Ed.

Falk, K.B., & Wehby, J.H. (2001). The effects of peer-assisted learning strategies on the beginning reading skills of young children with emotional/behavioral disorders. *Behavioral Disorders, 26,* 344–359.

Farmer, E.M.Z., & Farmer, T.W. (1999). The role of schools in outcomes for youth: Implications for children's mental health services research. *Journal of Child and Family Studies, 8,* 377–396.

Farmer, T.W. (2000). Misconceptions of peer rejection and problem behavior: Understanding aggression in students with mild disabilities. *Remedial and Special Education, 21,* 194–208.

Farmer, T.W., Farmer, E.M.Z., & Gut, D. (1999). Implications of social development research for school based intervention for aggressive youth with emotional and behavioral disorders. *Journal of Emotional and Behavioral Disorders, 7,* 130–136.

Farmer, T.W., Quinn, M.M., Hussey, W., & Holahan, T. (2001). The development of disruptive behavioral disorders and correlated constraints: Implications for intervention. *Behavioral Disorders, 26,* 117–130.

Forness, S.R., & Kavale, K.A. (1997). Defining emotional or behavioral disorders in school and related services. In J.W. Lloyd, E.J. Kameenui, & D. Chard (Eds.), *Issues in educating students with disabilities* (pp. 45–61). Mahwah, NJ: Erlbaum.

Forness, S.R., & Kavale, K.A. (2001). Ignoring the odds: Hazards of not adding the new medical model to special education decisions. *Behavioral Disorders, 26,* 269–281.

Forness, S.R., & Knitzer, J. (1992). A new proposed definition and terminology to replace "serious emotional disturbance" in Individuals with Disabilities Act. *School Psychology Review, 21,* 12–20.

Forness, S.R., Kavale, K.A., Sweeney, D.P., & Crenshaw, T.M. (1999). The future of research and practice in behavioral disorders: Psychopharmacology and its school implications. *Behavioral Disorders, 24,* 305–318.

Freedman, J. (1993). *From cradle to grave: The human face of poverty in America.* New York: Atheneum.

Fuchs, D., Fuchs, L.S., Fernstrom, P., & Hohn, M. (1991). Toward a responsible reintegration of behaviorally disordered students. *Behavioral Disorders, 16,* 133–147.

Gable, R.A. (1999). Functional assessment in school settings. *Behavioral Disorders, 24,* 246–248.

Garrity, C., Jens, K., Porter, W., Sager, N., & Short-Camilli, C. (1996). Bully-proofing your school: A comprehensive approach. *Reclaiming Youth and Children, 5*(1), 35–39.

Garrity, C., Jens, K., Porter, W., Sager, N., & Short-Camilli, C. (2000). *Bully-proofing your school: A comprehensive approach* (2nd ed.). Longmont, CO: Sopris West.

Gottesman, I.I. (1991). *Schizophrenia genesis: The origins of madness.* New York: W.H. Freeman.

Gresham, F.M., Lane, K.L., McIntyre, L.L., Olson-Tinker, H., Dostra, L., MacMillan, D.M., Lambros, K.M., & Bocian, K. (2001). Risk factors associated with the co-occurrence of hyperactivity-impulsivity-inattention and conduct problems. *Behavioral Disorders, 26,* 189–199.

Hallenbeck, B.A., & Kauffman, J.M. (1995). How does observational learning affect the behavior of students with emotional or behavioral disorders? A review of research. *Journal of Special Education, 29,* 45–71.

Harris, J.R. (1995) Where is the child's environment? A group socialization theory of development. *Psychological Review, 102,* 458–489.

Henggeler, S.W. (1989). *Delinquency in adolescence.* Newbury Park, CA: Sage.

Hodgkinson, H.L. (1995). What should we call people? Race, class, and the census for 2000. *Phi Delta Kappan, 77,* 173–179.

Horner, R.H., Vaughn, B.J., Day, H.M., & Ard, W.R. (1996). The relationship between setting events and problem behavior: Expanding our understanding of behavioral supports. In L.K. Kogel, R.L. Kogel, & G. Dunlap (Eds.), *Positive behavioral support: Including people with difficult behavior in the community* (pp. 381–402). Baltimore, MD: Paul H. Brookes.

Howell, K.W., & Nelson, K.L. (1999). Has public policy exceeded our knowledge base? This is a two part question. *Behavioral Disorders, 24,* 331–334.

Ialongo, N.S., Vaden-Kiernan, N., & Kellam, S. (1998). Early peer rejection and aggression: Longitudinal relations with adolescent behavior. *Journal of Developmental and Physical Disabilities, 10,* 199–213.

Ishii-Jordan, S.R. (2000). Behavioral interventions used with diverse students. *Behavioral Disorders, 25,* 299–309.

James, M., & Long, N. (1992). Looking beyond behavior and seeing my needs: A red flag interview. *Journal of Emotional and Behavioral Problems, 1*(2), 35–38.

Jolivette, K., Stichter, J.P., & McCormick, K.M. (2002). Making choices—improving behavior—engaging in learning. *Teaching Exceptional Children, 34*(3), 24–30.

Jordan, D., Goldberg, P., & Goldberg, M. (1991). *A guidebook for parents of children with emotional or behavioral disorders.* Minneapolis: Pacer Center.

Kaiser, A.P. (Ed.). (2000). Special issue: Assessing and addressing problems in children enrolled in Head Start. *Behavioral Disorders, 26*(1).

Kamps, D.M., Tankersley, M., & Ellis, C. (2000). Social skills interventions for young at-risk students: A 2-year follow-up study. *Behavioral Disorders, 25,* 310–324.

Kaslow, N.J., Morris, M.K., & Rehm, L.P. (1997). Childhood depression. In R.J. Morris & T.R. Kratochwill (Eds.), *The practice of child therapy* (3rd ed., pp. 48–90). Boston: Allyn & Bacon.

Katsiyannis, A., & Archwamety, T. (1999). Academic remediation/achievement and other factors related to recidivism rates among delinquent youths. *Behavioral Disorders, 24,* 93–101.

Kauffman, J.M. (1997). Conclusion: A little of everything, a lot of nothing is an agenda for failure. *Journal of Emotional and Behavioral Disorders, 5,* 76–81.

Kauffman, J.M. (1999). How we prevent the prevention of emotional and behavioral disorders. *Exceptional Children, 65,* 448–468.

Kauffman, J.M. (2001). *Characteristics of emotional and behavioral disorders of children and youth* (7th ed.). Upper Saddle River, NJ: Merrill Prentice-Hall.

Kauffman, J.M., Bantz, J., & McCullough, J. (2002). Separate and better: A special public school class for students with emotional and behavioral disorders. *Exceptionality.*

Kauffman, J.M., & Hallenbeck, B.A. (Eds.). (1996). Why we need to preserve specialized placements for students with emotional or behavioral disorders [Special issue]. *Canadian Journal of Special Education, 11*(1).

Kauffman, J.M., Lloyd, J.W., Baker, J., & Riedel, T.M. (1995). Inclusion of all students with emotional or behavioral disorders? Let's think again. *Phi Delta Kappan, 76,* 542–546.

Kauffman, J.M., Lloyd, J.W., Hallahan, D.P., & Astuto, T.A. (Eds.). (1995). *Issues in educational placement: Students with emotional and behavioral disorders.* Hillsdale, NJ: Erlbaum.

Kauffman, J.M., Mostert, M.P., Trent, S.C., & Hallahan, D.P. (2002). *Managing classroom behavior: A reflective case-based approach* (3rd ed.). Boston: Allyn & Bacon.

Kauffman, J.M., & Pullen, P.L. (1996). Eight myths about special education. *Focus on Exceptional Children, 28*(5), 1–16.

Kazdin, A.E. (1995). *Conduct disorders in childhood and adolescence* (2nd ed.). Newbury Park, CA: Sage.

Kazdin, A.E. (1997). Conduct disorder. In R.J. Morris & T.R. Kratochwill (Eds.), *The practice of child therapy* (3rd ed., pp. 199–270). Boston: Allyn & Bacon.

Kerr, M.M., & Nelson, C.M. (1998). *Strategies for managing behavior problems in the classroom* (3rd ed.). Upper Saddle River, NJ: Prentice-Hall.

Knitzer, J., Steinberg, Z., & Fleisch, F. (1990). *At the schoolhouse door: An examination of programs and policies for children with behavioral and emotional problems.* New York: Bank Street College of Education.

Knowlton, D. (1995). Managing children with oppositional behavior. *Beyond Behavior, 6*(3), 5–10.

Kogel, L.K., Kogel, R.L., & Dunlap, G. (Eds.). (1996). *Positive behavioral support: Including people with difficult behavior in the community.* Baltimore, MD: Paul H. Brookes.

Kozol, J. (1995, October 1). The kids that society forgot. *Washington Post,* pp. C1, C4.

Landrum, T.J., & Kauffman, J.M. (2003). Emotionally disturbed, education of. In J.W. Guthrie (Ed.), *Encyclopedia of education* (2nd ed.). New York: Macmillan Reference.

Leone, P.E., Rutherford, R.B., & Nelson, C.M. (1991). *Special education in juvenile corrections.* Reston, VA: Council for Exceptional Children.

Lewis, T. (2000). Establishing and promoting disciplinary practices at the classroom and individual student level that ensure safe, effective, and nurturing learning environments. In L.M. Bullock and R.A. Gable (Eds.), *Positive academic and behavioral supports: Creating safe, effective, and nurturing schools for all students.* Reston, VA: Council for Exceptional Children.

Lewis, T.J., & Sugai, G. (1999). Effective behavior support: A systems approach to proactive schoolwide management. *Focus on Exceptional Children, 31*(6), 1–24.

Loeber, R., Green, S.M., Lahey, B.B., Christ, M.A.G., & Frick, P.J. (1992). Developmental sequences in age of onset of disruptive child behaviors. *Journal of Child and Family Studies, 1,* 21–41.

Maag, J.W., & Katsiyannis, A. (1998). Challenges facing successful transition for youths with E/BD. *Behavioral Disorders, 23,* 209–221.

Malmgren, K., Edgar, E., & Neel, R.S. (1998). Postschool status of youths with behavioral disorders. *Behavioral Disorders, 23,* 257–263.

Martin, R.P. (1992). Child temperament effects on special education: Process and outcomes. *Exceptionality, 3,* 99–115.

Masia, C.L., Klein, R.G., Storch, E.A., & Corda, B. (2001). School-based behavioral treatment for social anxiety disorder in adolescents: Results of a pilot study. *Journal of the American Academy of Child and Adolescent Psychiatry, 40,* 780–786.

McCracken, J.T., Cantwell, D.P., & Hanna, G.L. (1993). Conduct disorder and depression. In E. Klass & H.S. Koplewica (Eds.), *Depression in children and adolescents* (pp. 121–132). New York: Harwood.

Miller, J.G. (1997). African American males in the criminal justice system. *Phi Delta Kappan, 79,* K1–K12.

Moynihan, D.P. (1995, September 21). "I cannot understand how this could be happening." *Washington Post,* p. A31.

Nelson, C.M., & Kauffman, J.M. (1977). Educational programming for secondary school age delinquent and maladjusted pupils. *Behavioral Disorders, 2,* 102–113.

Nelson, J.R., Roberts, M., Mather, S., & Rutherford, R.J. (1999). Has public policy exceeded our knowledge base? A review of the functional behavioral assessment literature. *Behavioral Disorders, 24,* 169–179.

Oswald, D.P., Coutinho, M.J., Best, A.M., & Singh, N.N. (1999). Ethnic representation in special education: The influence of school-related economic and demographic variables. *Journal of Special Education, 32,* 194–206.

Patterson, G.R., Reid, J.B., & Dishion, T.J. (1992). *Antisocial boys.* Eugene, OR: Castalia.

Peacock Hill Working Group. (1991). Problems and promises in special education and related services for children and youth with emotional or behavioral disorders. *Behavioral Disorders, 16,* 299–313.

Plomin, R. (1989). Environment and genes: Determinants of behavior. *American Psychologist, 44,* 105–111.

Pomeroy, J.C., & Gadow, K.D. (1997). In R.J. Morris & T.R. Kratochwill (Eds.), *The practice of child therapy* (3rd ed., pp. 419–470). Boston: Allyn & Bacon.

Presley, J.A., & Hughes, C. (2000). Peers as teachers of anger management to high school students with behavioral disorders. *Behavioral Disorders, 25,* 114–130.

Rabian, B., & Silverman, W.K. (1995). Anxiety disorders. In M. Hersen & R.T. Ammerman (Eds.), *Advanced abnormal child psychology* (pp. 235–252). Hillsdale, NJ: Erlbaum.

Reitman, D., & Gross, A.M. (1995). Familial determinants. In M. Hersen & R.T. Ammerman (Eds.), *Advanced abnormal child psychology* (pp. 87–104). Hillsdale, NJ: Erlbaum.

Rhode, G., Jensen, W.R., & Reavis, H.K. (1992). *The tough kid book: Practical classroom management strategies.* Longmont, CO: Sopris West.

Richardson, G.A., McGauhey, P., & Day, N.L. (1995). Epidemiologic considerations. In M. Hersen & R.T. Ammerman (Eds.), *Advanced abnormal child psychology* (pp. 37–48). Hillsdale, NJ: Erlbaum.

Rogers-Adkinson, D., & Griffith, P. (Eds.). (1999). *Communication disorders and children with psychiatric and behavioral disorders.* San Diego: Singular.

Rutter, M., & Schopler, E. (1987). Autism and pervasive developmental disorders: Concepts and diagnostic issues. *Journal of Autism and Developmental Disabilities, 17,* 159–186.

Saigh, P.A. (1997). Posttraumatic stress disorder. In R.J. Morris & T.R. Kratochwill (Eds.), *The practice of child therapy* (3rd ed., pp. 390–418). Boston: Allyn & Bacon.

Sample, P.L. (1998). Postschool outcomes for students with significant emotional disturbance following best-practice transition services. *Behavioral Disorders, 23,* 231–242.

Sasso, G.M., Conroy, M.A., Stichter, J.P., & Fox, J.J. (2001). Slowing down the bandwagon: The misapplication of functional assessment for students with emotional and behavioral disorders. *Behavioral Disorders, 26,* 282–296.

Scott, R.M., & Nelson, C.M. (1999). Functional behavioral assessment: Implications for training and staff development. *Behavioral Disorders, 24,* 249–252.

Serna, L.A., Lambros, K., Nielsen, E., & Forness, S.R. (2000). Head Start children at-risk for emotional or behavioral disorders: Behavioral profiles and clinical implications of a primary prevention program. *Behavioral Disorders, 26,* 70–84.

Shaw, D.S., Owens, E.B., Giovannelli, J., & Winslow, E.B. (2001). Infant and toddler pathways leading to early externalizing disorders. *Journal of the American Academy of Child and Adolescent Psychiatry, 40,* 36–43.

Sheras, P.L. (2001). Depression and suicide in adolescence. In C.E. Walker & M.C. Roberts (Eds.), *Handbook of clinical child psychology* (3rd ed.) (pp. 657–673). New York: Wiley.

Sherburne, S., Utley, B., McConnell, S., & Gannon, J. (1988). Decreasing violent and aggressive theme play among preschool children with behavior disorders. *Exceptional Children, 55,* 166–172.

Siegel, L.J., & Senna, J.J. (1994). *Juvenile delinquency: Theory, practice, and law* (5th ed.). St. Paul, MN: West.

Sprague, J., & Walker, H. (2000). Early identification and intervention for youth with antisocial and violent behavior. *Exceptional Children, 66,* 367–379.

Stark, K.D., Ostrander, R., Kurowski, C.A., Swearer, S., & Bowen, B. (1995). Affective and mood disorders. In M. Hersen & R.T. Ammerman (Eds.), *Advanced abnormal child psychology* (pp. 253–282). Hillsdale, NJ: Erlbaum.

Stein, M., & Davis, C.A. (2000). Direct instruction as a positive behavioral support. *Beyond Behavior, 10*(1), 7–12.

Strain, P.S., McConnell, S.R., Carta, J.J., Fowler, S.A., Neisworth, J.T., & Wolery, M. (1992). Behaviorism in early intervention. *Topics in Early Childhood Special Education, 12*(1), 121–141.

Strain, P.S., & Timm, M.A. (2001). Remediation and prevention of aggression: An evaluation of the Regional Intervention Program over a quarter century. *Behavioral Disorders, 26,* 297–313.

Sugai, G., & Horner, R.H. (Ed.). (1999–2000). Special issue: Functional behavioral assessment. *Exceptionality, 8*(3).

Sugai, G., Horner, R., Dunlap, G., Lewis, T., Nelson, C.M., Scott, T., Liaupsin, C., Ruef, M., Sailor, W., Turnbull, A.P., Turnbull, H.R., Wickham, D., & Wilcox, B.L. (2000). Applying positive behavior support and functional behavioral assessment in schools. *Journal of Positive Behavior Interventions, 2,* 131–143.

Sutherland, K.S., & Wehby, J.H. (2001). Exploring the relationship between increased opportunities to respond to academic requests and the academic and behavioral outcomes of students with EBD. *Remedial and Special Education, 22,* 113–121.

Sweeney, D.P., Forness, S.R., Kavale, K.A., & Levitt, J.G. (1997). An update on psychopharmacologic medication: What teachers, clinicians, and parents need to know. *Intervention in School and Clinic, 33,* 4–21, 25.

Talbott, E., & Callahan, K. (1997). Antisocial girls and the development of disruptive behavior disorders. In J.W. Lloyd, E.J. Kameenui, & D. Chard (Eds.), *Issues in educating students with disabilities* (pp. 305–322). Mahwah, NJ: Erlbaum.

Tankersley, M., & Landrum, T.J. (1997). Comorbidity of emotional and behavioral disorders. In J.W. Lloyd, E.J. Kameenui, & D. Chard (Eds.), *Issues in educating students with disabilities* (pp. 153–173). Mahwah, NJ: Erlbaum.

Thomas, A., & Chess, S. (1984). Genesis and evolution of behavioral disorders: From infancy to early adult life. *American Journal of Psychiatry, 141,* 1–9.

Thomas, J.M., & Guskin, K.A. (2001). Disruptive behavior in young children: What does it mean? *Journal of the American Academy of Child and Adolescent Psychiatry, 40,* 44–51.

Timm, M.A. (1993). The Regional Intervention Program: Family treatment by family members. *Behavioral Disorders, 19,* 34–43.

Tolbin, T., & Sprague, J. (1999). Alternative education programs for at-risk youth: Issues, best practice, and recommendations. *Bulletin of the Oregon School Study Council, 42*(4).

U.S. Department of Education. (2000). *Twenty-second annual report to Congress on implementation of the Individuals with Disabilities Education Act.* Washington, DC: Author.

U.S. Department of Health and Human Services. (2001). *Report of the Surgeon General's Conference on Children's Mental Health: A National Action Agenda.* Washington, DC: Author.

U.S. Office of Special Education Programs. (1998). *Positive behavioral support: Helping students with challenging behaviors succeed.* Reston, VA: ERIC/OSEP Special Project, the ERIC Clearinghouse on Disabilities and Gifted Education, the Council for Exceptional Children.

Walker, H.M. (1995). *The acting-out child: Coping with classroom disruption.* Longmont, CO: Sopris West.

Walker, H.M., & Bullis, M. (1991). Behavior disorders and the social context of regular class integration: A conceptual dilemma? In J.W. Lloyd, N.N. Singh, & A.C. Repp (Eds.), *The regular education initiative: Alternative perspectives on concepts, issues, and models.* Sycamore, IL: Sycamore Publishing.

Walker, H.M., Colvin, G., & Ramsey, E. (1995). *Antisocial behavior in school: Strategies and best practices.* Pacific Grove, CA: Brooks/Cole.

Walker, H.M., Forness, S.R., Kauffman, J.M., Epstein, M.H., Gresham, F.M., Nelson, C.M., & Strain, P.S. (1998). Macro-social validation: Referencing outcomes in behavioral disorders to societal issues and problems. *Behavioral Disorders, 24,* 7–18.

Walker, H.M., Kavanagh, K., Stiller, B., Golly, A., Severson, H., & Feil, E.G. (1998). First Step to Success: An early intervention approach for preventing school antisocial behavior. *Journal of Emotional and Behavioral Disorders, 6,* 66–80.

Walker, H.M., & Severson, H.H. (1990). *Systematic screening for behavior disorders (SSBD): A multiple gating procedure.* Longmont, CO: Sopris West.

Walker, H.M., Severson, H.H., & Feil, E.G. (1994). *The early screening project: A proven child-find process.* Longmont, CO: Sopris West.

Walker, H.M., & Stieber, S. (1998). Teacher ratings of social skills as longitudinal predictors of long-term arrest status in a sample of at-risk males. *Behavioral Disorders, 23,* 222–230.

Wehby, J.H., Dodge, K.A., & Valente, E. (1993). School behavior of first grade children identified as at-risk for development of conduct problems. *Behavioral Disorders, 19,* 67–78.

White, R.B., & Koorland, M.A. (1996). Curses! What do we do about cursing? *Teaching Exceptional Children, 28,* 48–51.

Wolf, M.M., Braukmann, C.J., & Ramp, K.A. (1987). Serious delinquent behavior as part of a significantly handicapping condition. *Journal of Applied Behavior Analysis, 20,* 347–359.

Wood, F.H. (Ed.). (1990). When we talk with children: The life space interview [Special section]. *Behavioral Disorders, 15,* 110–126.

Wood, M.M., & Long, N.J. (1991). *Life space intervention: Talking with children and youth in crisis.* Austin, TX: Pro-Ed.

Yell, M.L. (1998). *The law and special education.* Upper Saddle River, NJ: Prentice-Hall.

Yell, M.L., Bradley, R., Katsiyannis, A., & Rozalski, M.E. (2000). Ensuring compliance with the discipline provisions of IDEA '97. *Journal of Special Education Leadership, 13*(1), 3–18.

Yell, M.L., Rozalski, M.E., & Drasgow, E. (2001). Disciplining students with disabilities. *Focus on Exceptional Children, 33*(9), 1–20.

Zanglis, I., Furlong, M.J., & Casas, J.M. (2000). Case study of a community mental health collaborative: Impact on identification of youths with emotional or behavioral disorders. *Behavioral Disorders, 25,* 359–371.

CHAPTER 8

American Speech-Language-Hearing Association. (1991, March). Guidelines for speech-language pathologists serving persons with language, socio-communicative, and/or cognitive-communicative impairments. *ASHA, 33,* 21–25.

American Speech-Language-Hearing Association. (1993). Definitions of communication disorders and variations. *ASHA, 35*(Suppl. 10), 40–41.

American Speech-Language-Hearing Association. (2001). Retrieved September 2001 from http://www.asha.org.

Anderson, N.B., & Battle, D.E. (1993). Cultural diversity in the development of language. In D.E. Battle (Ed.), *Communication disorders in multicultural populations* (pp. 158–185). Boston: Andover Medical Publishers.

Audet, L.R., & Tankersley, M. (1999). Implications of communication and behavioral disorders for classroom management: Collaborative intervention techniques. In D. Rogers-Adkinson & P. Griffith (Eds.), *Communication disorders and children with psychiatric and behavioral disorders* (pp. 403–440). San Diego: Singular.

Baca, L., & Amato, C. (1989). Bilingual special education: Training issues. *Exceptional Children, 56,* 168–173.

Bauman-Waengler, J. (2000). *Articulatory and phonological impairments: A clinical focus.* Boston: Allyn & Bacon.

Bernstein, D.K., & Tiegerman-Farber, E. (1997). *Language and communication disorders in children* (4th ed.). Boston: Allyn & Bacon.

Bernthal, J.E., & Bankson, N.W. (1998). *Articulation and phonological disorders* (4th ed.). Boston: Allyn & Bacon.

Blank, M., & White, S.J. (1986). Questions: A powerful form of classroom exchange. *Topics in Language Disorders, 6*(2), 1–12.

Brookshire, R.H. (1997). *Introduction to neurogenic communication disorders* (5th ed.). St. Louis: Mosby.

Butler, K.G. (Ed.). (1999a). Children's language, behavior, and emotional problems [Special issue]. *Topics in Language Disorders, 19*(2).

Butler, K.G. (Ed.). (1999b). Many voices, many tongues: Accents, dialects, and variations [Special issue]. *Topics in Language Disorders, 19*(4).

Calandrella, A.M., & Wilcox, M.J. (2000). Predicting language outcomes for young prelinguistic children with developmental delay. *Journal of Speech, Language and Hearing Research, 43,* 1061–1071.

Campbell, S.L., Reich, A.R., Klockars, A.J., & McHenry, M.A. (1988). Factors associated with dysphonia in high school cheerleaders. *Journal of Speech and Hearing Disorders, 53,* 175–185.

Cannito, M.P., Yorkston, K.M., & Beukelman, D.R. (Eds.). (1998). *Neuromotor speech disorders: Nature, assessment, and management.* Baltimore: Paul H. Brookes.

Conture, E.G. (2001). *Stuttering: Its nature, diagnosis, and treatment.* Boston: Allyn & Bacon.

Curlee, R.F., & Siegel, G.M. (Eds.). (1997). *Nature and treatment of stuttering: New directions* (2nd ed.). Boston: Allyn & Bacon.

Delpit, L. (1995). *Other people's children: Cultural conflict in the classroom.* New York: New Press.

Donahue, M.L., Hartas, D., & Cole, D. (1999). Research on interactions among oral language and emotional/behavioral disorders. In D. Rogers-Adkinson & P. Griffith (Eds.), *Communication disorders and children with psychiatric and behavioral disorders* (pp. 69–97). San Diego: Singular.

Erhen, B.J. (2000). Maintaining a therapeutic focus and sharing responsibility for student success: Keys to in-classroom speech-language services. *Language, Speech, and Hearing in Schools, 31,* 219–229.

Fey, M.E., Catts, H.W., & Larrivee, L.S. (1995). Preparing preschoolers for academic and social challenges of school. In M.E. Fey, J. Windsor, & S.F. Warren (Eds.), *Language intervention: Preschool through the elementary years* (pp. 3–37). Baltimore: Paul H. Brookes.

Foundas, A.L. (2001). The anatomical basis of language. *Topics in Language Disorders, 21*(3), 1–19.

Gillam, R.B., & Hoffman, L.M. (2001). Language assessment during childhood. In D.M. Ruscello (Ed.), *Tests and measurements in speech-language pathology* (pp. 77–117). Boston: Butterworth-Heinemann.

Graham, S., Harris, K.R., MacArthur, C., & Schwartz, S. (1998). Writing instruction. In B.Y.L. Wong (Ed.), *Learning about learning disabilities* (2nd ed., pp. 391–424). San Diego: Academic Press.

Guralnick, M., Connor, R., Hammond, M., Gottman, J., & Kinnish, K. (1996). The peer relations of preschool children with communication disorders. *Child Development, 67,* 471–489.

Hadley, P.A., Simmerman, A., Long, M., & Luna, M. (2000). Facilitating language development for inner-city children: Experimental evaluation of a collaborative, classroom-based intervention. *Language, Speech, and Hearing in Schools, 31,* 280–295.

Hallahan, D.P., Kauffman, J.M., & Lloyd, J.W. (1999). *Introduction to learning disabilities* (2nd ed.). Boston: Allyn & Bacon.

Hammer, C.S., & Weiss, A.L. (2000). African American mothers' views of their infants' language development and language-learning environment. *American Journal of Speech-Language Pathology, 9,* 126–140.

Hart, B., & Risley, T.R. (1995). *Meaningful differences in the everyday experience of young American children.* Baltimore: Paul H. Brookes.

Haynes, W.O., & Pindzola, R.H. (1998). *Diagnosis and evaluation in speech pathology* (5th ed.). Boston: Allyn & Bacon.

Hodson, B.W., & Edwards, M.L. (1997). *Perspectives in applied phonology.* Gaithersburg, MD: Aspen.

Johnston, E.B., Weinrich, B.D., & Glaser, A.J. (1991). *A sourcebook of pragmatic activities: Theory and intervention for language therapy (PK–6)* (Rev. ed.). Tucson, AZ: Communication Skill Builders.

Kaiser, A.P., Cai, X., Hancock, T.B., & Foster, E.M. (in press). Teacher-reported behavior problems and language delays in boys and girls enrolled in Head Start. *Behavioral Disorders.*

Kaiser, A.P., Hemmeter, M.L., Ostrosky, M.M., Alpert, C.L., & Hancock, T.B. (1995). The effects of training and individual feedback on parent use of milieu teaching. *Journal of Childhood Communication Disorders, 16,* 39–48.

Klein, H.B., & Moses, N. (1999). *Intervention planning for adults with communication problems: A guide for clinical practicum and professional practice.* Boston: Allyn & Bacon.

Mann, V. (1998). Language problems: A key to early reading problems. In B.Y.L. Wong (Ed.), *Learning about learning disabilities* (2nd ed., pp. 163–202). San Diego: Academic Press.

Matthews, J., & Frattali, C. (1994). The professions of speech-language pathology and audiology. In G.H. Shames, E.H. Wiig, & W.A. Secord (Eds.), *Human communication disorders: An introduction* (4th ed., pp. 2–33). New York: Merrill/Macmillan.

McCabe, L.A., Hernandez, M., Lara, S.L., & Brooks-Gunn, J. (2000). Assessing preschoolers' self-regulation in homes and classrooms: Lessons from the field. *Behavioral Disorders, 26,* 53–69.

McCormick, L., Loeb, D.F., & Schiefelbusch, R.L. (1997). *Supporting children with communication difficulties in inclusive settings: School-based language intervention.* Boston: Allyn & Bacon.

McGregor, K.K. (2000). The development and enhancement of narrative skills in a preschool classroom: Towards a solution to clinician-client mismatch. *American Journal of Speech-Language Pathology, 9,* 55–71.

Moore, G.P., & Hicks, D.M. (1994). Voice disorders. In G.H. Shames, E.H. Wiig, & W.A. Secord (Eds.), *Human communication disorders: An introduction* (4th ed., pp. 292–335). New York: Merrill/Macmillan.

Muller, N. (Ed.). (2000). *Pragmatics in speech and language pathology.* Philadelphia: John Benjamins.

Nelson, N.W. (1997). Language intervention in school settings. In D.K. Bernstein & E. Tiegerman-Farber (Eds.), *Language and communication disorders in children* (4th ed., pp. 324–381). Boston: Allyn & Bacon.

Nelson, N.W. (1998). *Childhood language disorders in context: Infancy through adolescence* (2nd ed.). Boston: Allyn & Bacon.

Oetting, J.B., & McDonald, J.L. (2001). Nonmainstream dialect use and specific language impairment. *Journal of Speech, Language and Hearing Research, 44,* 207–223.

Onslow, M. (1992). Choosing a treatment procedure for early stuttering: Issues and future directions. *Journal of Speech and Hearing Research, 35,* 983–993.

Ortiz, A.A. (1997). Learning disabilities occurring concomitantly with linguistic differences. *Journal of Learning Disabilities, 30,* 321–332.

Owens, R.E. (1995). *Language disorders: A functional approach to assessment and intervention* (2nd ed.). Boston: Allyn & Bacon.

Owens, R.E. (1997). Mental retardation: Difference and delay. In D.K. Bernstein & E. Tiegerman-Farber (Eds.), *Language and communication disorders in children* (4th ed., pp. 457–523). Boston: Allyn & Bacon.

Plante, E., & Beeson, P.M. (1999). *Communication and communication disorders: A clinical introduction.* Boston: Allyn & Bacon.

Prizant, B.M. (1999). Early intervention: Young children with communication and emotional/behavioral problems. In D. Rogers-Adkinson & P. Griffith (Eds.), *Communication disorders and children with psychiatric and behavioral disorders* (pp. 295–342). San Diego: Singular.

Raspberry, W. (2001, August 21). Bi-English education: Low-income children might benefit from early immersion in standards. *Charlottesville Daily Progress,* p. A6.

Ratner, N.B., & Healey, E.C. (Eds.). (1999). *Stuttering research and practice: Bridging the gap.* Mahwah, NJ: Erlbaum.

Robin, D.A., Yorkston, K.M., & Beukelman, D.R. (Eds.). (1996). *Disorders of motor speech: Assessment, treatment, and clinical characterization.* Baltimore: Paul H. Brookes.

Robinson, R.L., & Crowe, T.A. (2001). Fluency and voice. In D.M. Ruscello (Ed.), *Tests and measurements in speech-language pathology* (pp. 163–183). Boston: Butterworth-Heinemann.

Rogers-Adkinson, D.L. (1999). Psychiatric disorders in children. In D. Rogers-Adkinson & P. Griffith (Eds.), *Communication disorders and children with psychiatric and behavioral disorders* (pp. 39–68). San Diego: Singular.

Rogers-Adkinson, D., & Griffith, P. (Eds.). (1999). *Communication disorders and children with psychiatric and behavioral disorders.* San Diego: Singular.

Ruscello, D.M. (2001). Use of tests and measurements in speech-language pathology: An introduction to diagnosis. In D.M. Ruscello (Ed.), *Tests and measurements in speech-language pathology* (pp. 1–29). Boston: Butterworth-Heinemann.

Schwartz, R.G. (1994). Phonological disorders. In G.H. Shames, E.H. Wiig, & W.A. Secord (Eds.), *Human communication disorders: An introduction* (4th ed., pp. 251–290). New York: Merrill/Macmillan.

Seidenberg, P.L. (1997). Understanding learning disabilities. In D.K. Bernstein & E. Tiegerman-Farber (Eds.), *Language and communication disorders in children* (4th ed., pp. 411–456). Boston: Allyn & Bacon.

Seymour, H.N., Abdulkarim, L., & Johnson, V. (1999). The Ebonics controversy: An educational and clinical dilemma. *Topics in Language Disorders, 19*(4), 66–77.

Seymour, H.N., Champion, T., & Jackson, J. (1995). The language of African American learners: Effective assessment and instructional programming for children with special needs. In B.A. Ford, F.E. Obiakor, & J.M. Patton (Eds.), *Effective education of African American exceptional learners* (pp. 89–121). Austin, TX: Pro-Ed.

Shames, G.H., Wiig, E.H., & Secord, W.A. (Eds.). (1994). *Human communication disorders: An introduction* (4th ed.). New York: Merrill/Macmillan.

Snow, C., Burns, M., & Griffin, P. (1998). *Preventing reading difficulties in young children.* Washington, DC: National Academy Press.

Soto, G., Huer, M.B., & Taylor, O. (1997). Multicultural issues. In L.L. Lloyd, D.R. Fuller, & H.H. Arvidson (Eds.), *Augmentative and alternative communication: A handbook of principles and practices* (pp. 406–413). Boston: Allyn & Bacon.

Sowell, T. (1997). *Late-talking children.* New York: Basic Books.

Stothard, S., Snowling, M., Bishop, D., Chipchase, B., & Kaplan, C. (1998). Language impaired preschoolers: A follow-up into adolescence. *Journal of Speech, Language and Hearing Research, 41,* 407–418.

Szekeres, S.F., & Meserve, N.F. (1995). Collaborative intervention in schools after traumatic brain injury. *Topics in Language Disorders, 15*(1), 21–36.

Throneburg, R.N., Calvert, L.K., Sturm, J.J., Paramboukas, A.A., & Paul, P.J. (2000). A comparison of service delivery models: Effects on curricular vocabulary skills in the school setting. *American Journal of Speech-Language Pathology, 9,* 10–20.

U.S. Department of Education. (2000). *Twenty-second annual report to Congress on the implementation of the Individuals with Disabilities Education Act.* Washington, DC: Author.

Van Keulen, J.E., Weddington, G.T., & DeBose, C.E. (1998). *Speech, language, learning, and the African American child.* Boston: Allyn & Bacon.

Walker, D., Greenwood, C., Hart, B., & Carta, J. (1994). Prediction of school outcomes based on early language production and socioeconomic factors. *Child Development, 65,* 606–621.

Wallach, G.P., & Butler, K.G. (Eds.). (1994). *Language learning disabilities in school-age children and adolescents: Some principles and applications.* New York: Merrill/Macmillan.

Warren, S.F., & Abbaduto, L. (1992). The relation of communication and language development to mental retardation. *American Journal on Mental Retardation, 97,* 125–130.

Westby, C.E. (1994). The effects of culture and genre, structure, and style of oral and written texts. In G.P. Wallach & K.G. Butler (Eds.), *Language learning disabilities in school-age children and adolescents: Some principles and applications* (pp. 180–218). New York: Merrill/Macmillan.

Westby, C.E., & Roman, R. (1995). Finding the balance: Learning to live in two worlds. *Topics in Language Disorders, 15*(4), 68–88.

Williams, A.L. (2001). Phonological assessment of child speech. In D.M. Ruscello (Ed.), *Tests and measurements in speech-language pathology* (pp. 31–76). Boston: Butterworth-Heinemann.

Wingate, M.E. (2001). SLD is not stuttering. *Journal of Speech, Language and Hearing Research, 44,* 381–383.

Yairi, E., Watkins, R., Ambrose, N., & Paden, E. (2001). What is stuttering? *Journal of Speech, Language and Hearing Research, 44,* 585–597.

Yoder, P.J., & Warren, S.F. (2001). Relative treatment effects of two prelinguistic communication interventions on language development of toddlers with developmental delays vary by maternal characteristics. *Journal of Speech and Hearing Research, 44,* 224–237.

CHAPTER 9

Allen, T.E. (1986). Patterns of achievement among hearing-impaired students: 1974 and 1983. In A.N. Schildroth & M.A. Karchmer (Eds.), *Deaf children in America* (pp. 161–206). San Diego, CA: College-Hill Press.

Andersson, Y. (1994). Comment on Turner. *Sign Language Studies, 83,* 127–131.

Andrews, J.F., & Zmijewski, G. (1997). How parents support home literacy with deaf children. *Early Child Development and Care, 127,* 131–139.

Andrews, J.F., Ferguson, C., Roberts, S., & Hodges, P. (1997). What's up, Billy Jo? Deaf children and bilingual-bicultural instruction in East-Central Texas. *American Annals of the Deaf, 142,* 16–25.

Antia, S.D., & Kreimeyer, K.H. (1997). The generalization and maintenance of the peer social behaviors of young children who are deaf or hard of hearing. *Language, Speech, and Hearing Services in Schools, 28,* 59–69.

Auditory-Verbal International. (2001, February 24). *Existing evidence that supports the rationale for auditory-verbal practice.* Re-

trieved September 4, 2001 from the World Wide Web: http://ww.auditory-verbal.org/About_Rationale.htm

Bellugi, U., & Klima, E. (1991). What the hands reveal about the brain. In D.S. Martin (Ed.), *Advances in cognition, education, and deafness.* Washington, DC: Gallaudet University Press.

Blamey, P.J., Sarant, J.Z., Paatsch, L.E., Barry, J.G., Bow, C.P., Wales, R.J., Wright, M., Psarros, C., Rattigan, K., & Tooer, R. (2001). Relationships among speech perception, production, language, hearing loss, and age in children with impaired hearing. *Journal of Speech, Language, and Hearing Research, 44,* 264–285.

Bornstein, M.H., Selmi, A.M., Haynes, O.M., Painter, K.M., & Marx, E.S. (1999). Representational abilities and the hearing status of child/mother dyads. *Child Development, 70,* 833–852.

Brill, R.G., MacNeil, B., & Newman, L.R. (1986). Framework for appropriate programs for deaf children. *American Annals of the Deaf, 131,* 65–77.

Buchino, M.A. (1993). Perceptions of the oldest hearing child of deaf parents. *American Annals of the Deaf, 138,* 40–45.

Cambra, C. (1996). A comparative study of personality descriptors attributed to the deaf, the blind, and individuals with no sensory disability. *American Annals of the Deaf, 141,* 24–28.

Campbell, K.C.M., & Derrick, G. (2001). Otoacoustic emissions. *eMedicine Journal, 2*(7).

Chambers, A.C. (1997). *Has technology been considered? A guide for IEP teams.* Reston, VA: Technology and Media Division/Council of Administrators of Special Education, Council for Exceptional Children.

Charlson, E., Strong, M., & Gold, R. (1992). How successful deaf teenagers experience and cope with isolation. *American Annals of the Deaf, 137,* 261–270.

Council for Exceptional Children (2001). Performance-based standards. Retrieved June 5, 2001 from the World Wide Web: www.cec.sped.org/ps/perf_based_stds/index.html

Crowson, K. (1994). Errors made by deaf children acquiring sign language. *Early Child Development and Care, 99,* 63–78.

Drasgow, E. (1993). Bilingual/bicultural deaf education: An overview. *Sign Language Studies, 80,* 243–266.

Easterbrooks, S. (1999). Improving practices for students with hearing impairments. *Exceptional Child, 65,* 537–554.

Easterbrooks, S.R., & Mordica, J.A. (2000). Teachers' ratings of functional communication in students with cochlear implants. *American Annals of the Deaf, 145,* 54–59.

Foreman, J. (2001, August 28). Making peace with a threat to 'deaf culture.' *Boston Globe,* pp. C1–2.

Garrick-Duhaney, L.M., & Duhaney, D.C. (2000). Assistive technology: Meeting the needs of learners with disabilities. *Journal of Instructional Media, 27,* 393–401.

Gaustad, M.G., & Kluwin, T.N. (1992). Patterns of communication among deaf and hearing adolescents. In T.N. Kluwin, D.F. Moores, & M.G. Gaustad (Eds.), *Toward effective public school programs for deaf students: Context, process, and outcomes* (pp. 107–128). New York: Teachers College Press.

Holcomb, T.K. (1996). Social assimilation of deaf high school students: The role of the school environment. In I. Parasnis (Ed.), *Cultural and language diversity and the deaf experience* (pp. 181–198). Cambridge, England: Cambridge University Press.

Holden-Pitt, L. (1997). A look at residential school placement patterns for students from deaf- and hearing-parented families: A ten-year perspective. *American Annals of the Deaf, 142,* 108–114.

Hutchinson, M.K., & Sandall, S.R. (1995). Congenital TORCH infections in infants and young children: Neurodevelopmental sequelae and implications for intervention. *Topics in Early Childhood and Special Education, 15,* 65–82.

Janesick, V.J., & Moores, D.F. (1992). Ethnic and cultural considerations. In T.N. Kluwin, D.F. Moores, & M.G. Gaustad (Eds.), *Toward effective public school programs for deaf students: Context, process, and outcomes* (pp. 49–65). New York: Teachers College Press.

Jones, B.E., Clark, G.M., & Soltz, D.F. (1997). Characteristics and practices of sign language interpreters in inclusive education programs. *Exceptional Children, 63,* 257–268.

Kaplan, H., Mahshie, J., Mosely, M., Singer, B., & Winston, E. (1993). *Research synthesis on design of effective media, materials, and technology for deaf and hard-of-hearing students* (Tech. Report No. 2). Eugene, OR: National Center to Improve the Tools of Education. (ERIC Document Reproduction Service No. 386 851).

Kelly, (2000). Individuals with hearing and vision impairments. In J.D. Lindsey (Ed.), *Technology and exceptional individuals* (3rd ed., pp. 359–374). Austin: TX: Pro-Ed.

Klima, E.S., & Bellugi, U. (1979). *The signs of language.* Cambridge, MA: Harvard University Press.

Kluwin, T.N., & Gaustad, M.G. (1994). The role of adaptability and communication in fostering cohesion in families of deaf adolescents. *American Annals of the Deaf, 139,* 329–335.

Kuntze, M. (1998). Literacy and deaf children: The language question. *Topics in Language Disorders, 18*(4), 1–15.

Lane, H. (1984). *When the mind hears: A history of the deaf.* New York: Random House.

Lane, H. (1992). *The mask of benevolence: Disabling the Deaf community.* New York: Knopf.

Lane, H., Hoffmeister, R., & Bahan, B. (1996). *A journey into the Deaf world.* San Diego, CA: Dawn Sign Press.

Listening Center at Johns Hopkins. (2001, August 17). Frequently Asked Questions. Retrieved August 31, 2001 from the World Wide Web: http://www.thelisteningcenter.com/faq.html

Livingston, S., Singer, B., & Abrahamson, T. (1994). Effectiveness compared: ASL interpretation vs. transliteration. *Sign Language Studies, 82,* 1–54.

Lucker, J., Bowen, S., & Carter, K. (2001). Visual teaching strategies for students who are deaf or hard of hearing. *Teaching Exceptional Children, 33*(3), 38–44.

Luetke-Stahlman, B., & Milburn, W.O. (1996). A history of Seeing Essential English (SEE I). *American Annals of the Deaf, 141,* 29–33.

Meadow-Orlans, K.P. (1987). An analysis of the effectiveness of early intervention programs for hearing-impaired children. In M.J. Guralnick & F.C. Bennett (Eds.), *The effectiveness of early intervention for at-risk and handicapped children* (pp. 325–362). New York: Academic Press.

Meadow-Orlans, K.P. (1990). Research on developmental aspects of deafness. In D.F. Moores & K.P. Meadow-Orlans (Eds.), *Educational and developmental aspects of deafness* (pp. 283–298). Washington, DC: Gallaudet University Press.

Meadow-Orlans, K.P. (1995). Sources of stress for mothers and fathers of deaf and hard of hearing infants. *American Annals of the Deaf, 140,* 352–357.

Meadow-Orlans, K.P., Mertens, D.M., Sass-Lehrer, M.A., & Scott-Olson, K. (1997). Support services for parents and their children who are deaf or hard of hearing. *American Annals of the Deaf, 142,* 278–288.

Menchel, R.S. (1988). Personal experience with speechreading. *Volta Review, 90*(5), 3–15.

Moores, D.F., & Maestas y Moores, J. (1981). Special adaptations necessitated by hearing impairments. In J.M. Kauffman & D.P. Hallahan (Eds.), *Handbook of special education.* Englewood Cliffs, NJ: Prentice-Hall.

National Association of the Deaf. (2001, March 26). Newsroom: NAD Statement on Captioning. Retrieved September 4, 2001 from the World Wide Web: http://www.nad.org/infocenter/newsroom/nadnews/NADstatementCaptioning.html.

National Center for Accessible Media. (1998, April 7). Motion picture access. Retrieved June 5, 1998 from the World Wide Web: http://www.wgbh.org/wgbh/pages/ncam/currentprojects/mopix.html

National Theatre of the Deaf. (2001, March 19). About NTD. Retrieved August 25, 2001 from the World Wide Web: http://www.ntd.org/about.htm. National Theatre of the Deaf. (2001, February 5). About NTD: History/Timeline. Retrieved August 25, 2001 from the World Wide Web: http://www.ntd.org/about_history.htm.

Padden, C.A. (1996). Early bilingual lives of Deaf children. In I. Parasnis (Ed.), *Cultural and language diversity and the Deaf experience.* (pp. 99–116). Cambridge, England: Cambridge University Press.

Padden, C., & Humphries, T. (1988). *Deaf in America: Voices from a culture.* Cambridge, MA: Harvard University Press.

Pisha, B., & Coyne, P. (2001). Smart from the start: The promise of Universal Design for Learning. *Remedial and Special Education, 22,* 197–203.

Prinz, P.M., Strong, M., Kuntze, M., Vincent, M., Friedman, J., Moyers, P., & Helman, E. (1996). A path to literacy through ASL and English for Deaf children. In C.E. Johnson & J.H.V. Gilbert (Eds.), *Children's language* (Vol. 9, pp. 235–251). Mahwah, NJ: Erlbaum.

Quigley, S., Jenne, W., & Phillips, S. (1968). *Deaf students in colleges and universities.* Washington, DC: Alexander Graham Bell Association for the Deaf.

Reagan, T. (1990). Cultural considerations in the education of deaf children. In D.F. Moores & K.P. Meadow-Orlans (Eds.), *Educational and developmental aspects of deafness* (pp. 73–84). Washington, DC: Gallaudet University Press.

Rodriguez, M.S., & Lana, E.T. (1996). Dyadic interactions between deaf children and their communication partners. *American Annals of the Deaf, 141,* 245–251.

Sacks, O. (1989). *Seeing voices: A journey into the world of the deaf.* Berkeley: University of California Press.

Schirmer, B.R. (2001). *Psychological, social, and educational dimensions of deafness.* Boston: Allyn & Bacon.

Schroedel, J.G., & Geyer, P.D. (2000). Long-term career attainments of deaf and hard of hearing college graduates: Results from a 15-year follow-up survey. *American Annals of the Deaf, 145,* 303–314.

Sheridan, M. (2001). *Inner lives of deaf children: Interviews and analysis.* Washington, DC: Gallaudet University Press

Siegel, L. (2000). The educational and communication needs of deaf and hard of hearing children: A statement of principle on fundamental educational change. *American Annals of the Deaf, 145,* 64–77.

Singleton, J.L., Morford, J.P., & Goldin-Meadow, S. (1993). Once is not enough: Standards of well-formedness in manual communication created over three different timespans. *Language, 69*, 683–715.

Siple, L. (1993). Working with the sign language interpreter in your classroom. *College Teaching, 41*, 139–142.

Spencer, P. (2001). *Cochlear implants for children: Language, culture, and education.* Paper presented at the 2001 Office of Special Education Program Research Project Directors' Conference, Washington, DC, July 12, 2001.

Spencer, P. (2002). Language development of children with cochlear implants. In J. Christiansen & I. Leigh (Eds.), *Cochlear implants in children: Ethics and choices.* Washington, DC: Gallaudet University Press.

Spencer, P.E., & Meadow-Orlans, K.P. (1996). Play, language, and maternal responsiveness: A longitudinal study of deaf and hearing infants. *Child Development, 67*, 3176–3191.

Stewart, D.A., & Kluwin, T.N. (2001). *Teaching deaf and hard of hearing students: Content, strategies, and curriculum.* Boston: Allyn & Bacon.

Stinson, M.S., & Stuckless, R. (1998). Recent developments in speech-to-print transcription systems for deaf students. In A. Weisel (Ed.), *Deaf education in the 1990s: International perspectives.* Washington, DC: Gallaudet University Press.

Stinson, M.S., & Whitmire, K. (1992). Students' views of their social relationships. In T.N. Kluwin, D.F. Moores, & M.G. Gaustad (Eds.), *Toward effective public school programs for deaf students: Context, process, and outcomes* (pp. 149–174). New York: Teachers College Press.

Stoel-Gammon, C., & Otomo, K. (1986). Babbling development of hearing-impaired and normally hearing subjects. *Journal of Speech and Hearing Disorders, 51*, 33–41.

Stokoe, W.C. (1960). *Sign language structure.* Silver Spring, MD: Linstok Press.

Stokoe, W.C., Casterline, D.C., & Croneberg, C.G. (1976). *A dictionary of American Sign Language on linguistic principles* (2nd ed.). Silver Spring, MD: Linstok Press.

Stone, P. (1997, August). *Educating children who are deaf or hard of hearing: Auditory-oral.* The ERIC Clearinghouse on Disabilities and Gifted Education. Retrieved September 4, 2001 from the World Wide Web: http://ericec.org/digests/e551.html

Strong, M., & Prinz, P.M. (1997). A study of the relationship between American Sign Language and English literacy. *Journal of Deaf Studies and Deaf Education, 2*, 37–46.

U.S. Department of Education. (2000). *Twenty-second annual report to Congress on the implementation of the Individuals with Disabilities Education Act.* Washington, DC: Author.

Walker, L.A. (1986). *A loss for words: The story of deafness in a family.* New York: Harper & Row.

Wolk, S., & Allen, T.E. (1984). A five-year follow-up of reading comprehension achievement of hearing-impaired students in special education programs. *Journal of Special Education, 18*, 161–176.

Wolk, S., & Schildroth, A.N. (1986). Deaf children and speech intelligibility: A national study. In A.N. Schildroth & M.A. Karchmer (Eds.), *Deaf children in America* (pp. 139–159). San Diego: College-Hill Press.

Wolkomir, R. (1992). American Sign Language: "It's not mouth stuff—it's brain stuff." *Smithsonian, 23*(4), 30–38, 40–41.

CHAPTER 10

Andrews, D. (2001, February). Comparing the Openbook and the Kurzweil 1000. *Braille Monitor,* 112–131.

Barraga, N.C. (1983). *Visual handicaps and learning* (Rev. ed.). Austin, TX: Exceptional Resources.

Barraga, N.C., & Collins, M.E. (1979). Development of efficiency in visual functioning: Rationale for a comprehensive program. *Journal of Visual Impairment and Blindness, 73*, 121–126.

Blind Babies Foundation. (2000a, April 18). Cortical visual impairment. Retrieved June 26, 2001 from the World Wide Web: http://www.blindbabies.org/factsheet_cvi.htm

Blind Babies Foundation. (2000b, April 18). Retinopathy of prematurity. Retrieved June 26, 2001 from the World Wide Web: http://www.blindbabies.org/factsheet_rop.htm

Chen, D. (1996). Parent-infant communication: Early intervention for very young children with visual impairment or hearing loss. *Infants and Young Children, 9*(2), 1–12.

Chen, D. (2001). *Visual impairment in young children: A review of the literature with implications for working with families of diverse cultural and linguistic backgrounds* (CLAS Tech. Rep. No. 7). Champaign, IL: University of Illinois at Urbana-Champaign, Early Childhood Research Institute on Culturally and Linguistically Appropriate Services.

Chen, D., & Dote-Kwan, J. (1999). The preschool years. In K.E. Wolffe (Ed.), *Skills for success: A career education handbook for children and adolescents with visual impairments* (pp. 44–158). New York: AFB Press.

Chong, C. (2000, Fall). Technology, Braille, the Nemeth Code, and jobs. *Future Reflections, 19*(4). Retrieved June 29, 2001 from the World Wide Web: http://www.nfb.org/FR/FR4/FRFA0010.htm

Collins, M.E., & Barraga, N.C. (1980). Development of efficiency in visual functioning: An evaluation process. *Journal of Visual Impairment and Blindness, 74*, 93–96.

Corn, A.L., & Koenig, A.J. (1996). Perspectives on low vision. In A.L. Corn & A.J. Koenig (Eds.), *Foundations of low vision: Clinical and functional perspectives* (pp. 3–25). New York: AFB Press.

Council for Exceptional Children (2001). Performance-based Standards. Retrieved June 5, 2001 from www.cec.sped.org/ps/perf_based_stds/index.html

Cox, P.R., & Dykes, M.K. (2001). Effective classroom adaptations for students with visual impairments. *Teaching Exceptional Children, 33*(6), 68–74.

Dobelle, W.H. (2000). Artificial vision for the blind by connecting a television camera to the visual cortex of the brain. *Journal of the American Society of Artificial Internal Organs, 46*, 3–9.

Estevis, A.H., & Koenig, A.J. (1994). A cognitive approach to reducing stereotypic body rocking. *RE:view, 26*, 119–125.

Ferrell, K.A., & Muir, D.W. (1996). A call to end vision stimulation training. *Journal of Visual Impairment and Blindness, 90*, 364–366.

Fichten, C.S., Judd, D., Tagalakis, V., Amsel, R., & Robillard, K. (1991). Communication cues used by people with and without visual impairments in daily conversations and dating. *Journal of Visual Impairment and Blindness, 85*, 371–378.

Firth, E. (2001, April). The Guide Horse Foundation: Joke or jeopardy? *Braille Monitor,* 252–257.

Foulke, E. (1996, November). Is it too late for braille literacy? *Braille Monitor*, 588–600.

Gabias, P. (1992, July). Unique features of guide dogs: Backtracking and homing. *Braille Monitor*, 392–399.

Gense, D.J., & Gense, M. (1999, May). The importance of orientation and mobility skills for students who are deaf-blind. *DB-LINK Fact Sheet*. Retrieved July 2, 2001 from the World Wide Web: http://www.tr.wou.edu/dblink/o&m2.htm

Glaucoma Foundation. (2001, March 15). About glaucoma. Retrieved June 26, 2001 from the World Wide Web: http://www.glaucomafoundation.org.about.htm

Glaucoma Research Foundation. (2001, January 10). About glaucoma. Retrieved June 26, 2001 from the World Wide Web: http://www.glaucoma.org/faq.html.

Guide Horse Foundation. (2001). Patricia Cornwell announces guide horse in forthcoming novel, *Isle of Dogs*. Retrieved June 30, 2001 from the World Wide Web: http://www.guidehorse.com//PC.html.

Hatlen, P.H. (1993). A personal odyssey on schools for blind children. *Journal of Visual Impairment and Blindness, 87*, 171–174.

Hayes, S.P. (1942). Alternative scales for the mental measurement of the visually handicapped. *Outlook for the Blind and the Teachers Forum, 36*, 225–230.

Hayes, S.P. (1950). Measuring the intelligence of the blind. In P.A. Zahl (Ed.), *Blindness*. Princeton, NJ: Princeton University Press.

Heyes, T. (1998, February 18). The Sonic Pathfinder: An electronic travel aid for the vision impaired. Retrieved March 1, 1998 from the World Wide Web: http://ariel.ucs.unimelb.EDU.AU:80/~heyes/pf_blerb.html

Hill, A. (1997, April). Teaching can travel blind? *Braille Monitor*, 222–225.

Hull, J.M. (1990). *Touching the rock*. New York: Pantheon Books.

Ianuzzi, J.W. (1992, May). Braille or print: Why the debate? *Braille Monitor*, 229–233.

Jernigan, K. (1992, June). Equality, disability, and empowerment. *Braille Monitor*, 292–298.

Jernigan, K. (1994). *If blindness comes*. Baltimore, MD: National Federation of the Blind.

Kirchner, C., & Schmeidler, E. (1997). Prevalence and employment of people in the United States who are blind or visually impaired. *Journal of Visual Impairment and Blindness, 91*, 508–511.

Kleege, G. (1999). *Sight unseen*. New Haven, CT: Yale University Press.

Koenig, A.J., & Holbrook, M.C. (2000). Ensuring high-quality instruction for students in braille literacy programs. *Journal of Visual Impairment and Blindness, 94*, 677–694.

Kudlick, C.J. (2001). The outlook of *The Problem* and the problem of *The Outlook:* Two advocacy journals reinvent blind people in turn-of-the-century America. In P.K. Longmore & L. Umansky (Eds.), *The new disability history: American perspectives* (pp. 187–213). New York: New York University Press.

Kuusisto, S. (1998). *The planet of the blind: A memoir*. New York: Dial Press.

La Grow, S. (1999). The use of the Sonic Pathfinder as a secondary mobility aid for travel in business environments: A single-subject design. *Journal of Rehabilitation Research and Development, 3*(4). Retrieved from the World Wide Web: http://www.vard.org/jour/99/36/4/lagro364.htm

Lansaw, J. (2000, December). Citizenship and the irony at the top of the world. *Braille Monitor*, 963–965.

Maloney, P.L. (1981). *Practical guidance for parents of the visually handicapped preschooler*. Springfield, IL: Thomas.

Mangold, S.S. (2000, October). Trends in the use of braille contractions in the United States: Implications for UBC decisions. *Braille Monitor*, 813–819.

Maurer, M. (2000, April). Blindness, quotas, and the disadvantages of civil rights. *Braille Monitor*, 287–296.

McAdam, D.B., O'Cleirigh, M., & Cuvo, A.J. (1993). Self-monitoring and verbal feedback to reduce stereotypic body rocking in a congenitally blind adult. *RE:view, 24*, 163–172.

McGaha, C.G., & Farran, D.C. (2001). Interactions in an inclusive classroom: The effects of visual status and setting. *Journal of Visual Impairment and Blindness, 95*, 80–93.

Millar, D. (1996). A consumer's perspective. *Journal of Visual Impairment and Blindness, 90*, 9.

Minnesota Laboratory for Low-Vision Research. (1997). MN-READ acuity charts. Retrieved June 25, 2001, http://vision.psych.umn.edu/mnread.html.

Ochaita, E., & Huertas, J.A. (1993). Spatial representation by persons who are blind: A study of the effects of learning and development. *Journal of Visual Impairment and Blindness, 87*, 37–41.

Omvig, J.H. (1997, November). From bad philosophy to bad policy: The American braille illiteracy crisis. *Braille Monitor*, 723–728.

Perez-Pereira, M. & Conti-Ramsden, G. (1999). *Language development and social interaction in blind children*. East Sussex, England: Psychology Press, Ltd.

Plain-Switzer, K. (1993). A model for touch technique and computation of adequate cane length. *International Journal of Rehabilitation Research, 16*, 66–71.

Prevent Blindness America. (1998–2000). Signs of possible eye trouble in children. Retrieved June 25, 2001 from the World Wide Web: http://www.prevent-blindness.org/children/trouble_signs.html.

Rapp, D.W., & Rapp, A.J. (1992). A survey of the current status of visually impaired students in secondary mathematics. *Journal of Visual Impairment and Blindness, 86*, 115–117.

Ross, D.B., & Koenig, A.J. (1991). A cognitive approach to reducing stereotypic head rocking. *Journal of Visual Impairment and Blindness, 85*, 17–19.

Rovig, L. (1992, May). Ideas for increasing your chance of job success while still in college. *Braille Monitor*, 238–244.

Rumrill, P.D., Roessler, R.T., Battersby-Longden, J.C., & Schuyler, B.R. (1998). Situational assessment of the accommodation needs of employees who are visually impaired. *Journal of Visual Impairment and Blindness, 92*, 42–54.

Rumrill, P.D., Schuyler, B.R., & Longden, J.C. (1997). Profiles of on-the-job accommodations needed by professional employees who are blind. *Journal of Visual Impairment and Blindness, 91*, 66–76.

Ryles, R. (1996). The impact of braille reading skills on employment, income, education, and reading habits. *Journal of Visual Impairment and Blindness, 90*, 219–226.

Sacks, S.Z., & Pruett, K.M. (1992). Summer transition training project for professionals who work with adolescents and young adults. *Journal of Visual Impairment and Blindness, 86*, 211–214.

Schroeder, F.K. (1996). Perceptions of braille usage by legally blind adults. *Journal of Visual Impairment and Blindness, 90*, 210–218.

Scialli, P.M. (2000, November). Looking into artificial vision for the blind. *Braille Monitor*, 882–886.

Sullivan, J.E. (1997, October). A perspective on braille unification. *Braille Monitor*, 648–657.

Ulrey, P. (1994). When you meet a guide dog. *RE:view, 26*, 143–144.

Van Reusen, A.K., & Head, D.N. (1994). Cognitive and metacognitive interventions: Important trends for teachers of students who are visually impaired. *RE:view, 25,* 153–162.

Warren, D.H. (1994). *Blindness and children: An individual differences approach.* New York: Cambridge University Press.

Webster, A., & Roe, J. (1998). *Children with visual impairments: Social interaction, language, and learning.* London: Routledge.

Weihenmayer, E. (2001). *Touch the top of the world: A blind man's journey to climb farther than the eye can see.* E.P. Dutton.

Wheeler, L.C., Floyd, K., & Griffin, H.C. (1997). Spatial organization in blind children. *RE:view, 28*, 177–181.

Whittle, J. (1999, March). The vitality of braille. *Braille Monitor*, 182–184.

Wiener, W.R., Ponchilla, P., Joffee, E., Rutberg-Kuskin, J., & Brown, J. (2001). The effectiveness of external bus speaker systems for persons who are visually impaired. *Journal of Visual Impairment and Blindness, 95*, 421–433.

Wilkinson, M.E. (1996). Clinical low vision services. In A.L. Corn & A.J. Koenig (Eds.), *Foundations of low vision: Clinical and functional perspectives* (pp. 143–175). New York: AFB Press.

Wormsley, D.P. (1996). Reading rates of young braille-reading children. *Journal of Visual Impairment and Blindness, 90*, 278–282.

Wunder, G. (1993, March). Mobility: Whose responsibility is it? *Braille Monitor*, 567–572.

Wunder, G. (2000, May). NFB testifies on internet access and the ADA. *Braille Monitor*, 315–321.

CHAPTER 11

Adelson, P.D., & Kochanek, P.M. (1998). Head injury in children. *Journal of Child Neurology, 13*, 2–15.

Adreon, D., & Stella, J. (2001). Transition to middle and high school: Increasing the success of students with Asperger syndrome. *Intervention in School and Clinic, 36*, 266–271.

Aitken, S. (2000). Understanding deafblindness. In S. Aitken, M. Buultjens, C. Clark, J.T. Eyre, & L. Pease (Eds.), *Teaching children who are deafblind: Contact, communication, and learning* (pp. 1–34). London: David Fulton Publishers.

American Psychiatric Association. (1994). *Diagnostic and statistical manual of mental disorders* (4th ed.). Washington, DC: Author.

Baldwin, V. (1994). *Annual Deaf-Blind Census.* Monmouth: Teaching Research Division. DB-LINK: The National Clearinghouse on Children Who Are Deaf-Blind.

Barnhill, G.P. (2001). What is Asperger syndrome? *Intervention in School and Clinic, 36*, 259–265.

Bergland, M., & Hoffbauer, D. (1996). New opportunities for students with traumatic brain injuries. *Teaching Exceptional Children, 28*(2), 54–56.

Bettelheim, B. (1967). *The empty fortress.* New York: Free Press.

Beukelman, D.R., & Mirenda, P. (1998). *Augmentative and alternative communication: Management of severe communication disorders in children and adults* (2nd ed.). Baltimore, Paul H. Brookes.

Beukelman, D.R., Yorkston, K.M., & Reichle, J. (Eds.). (2000). *Augmentative and alternative communication for adults with acquired neurologic disorders.* Baltimore: Paul H. Brookes.

Boys Town National Research Hospital Genetics Department. (2001, February 21). The Collaborative Usher Syndrome Project. Retrieved May 15, 2001 from the World Wide Web: http://www.boystown.org/btnrh/genetics/usher.htm

Bredekamp, S., & Rosegrant, T. (Eds.). (1992). *Reaching potentials: Appropriate curriculum and assessment for young children.* Washington, DC: National Association for the Education of Young Children.

Browder, D.M., & Bambara, L.M. (2000). Home and community. In M.E. Snell & F. Brown (Eds.), *Instruction of students with severe disabilities* (5th ed., pp. 543–589). Upper Saddle River, NJ: Merrill.

Brown, D. (1996, February). CHARGE. Retrieved May 15, 2001 from the A-Z to Deafblindness on the World Wide Web: http://www.deafblind.com/chargedb.html

Brown, F., & Snell, M.E. (2000). Meaningful assessment. In M.E. Snell & F. Brown (Eds.), *Instruction of students with severe disabilities* (pp. 67–114). Upper Saddle River, NJ: Prentice-Hall.

Brownell, M.T., & Walther-Thomas, C. (2001). Steven Shore: Understanding the autism spectrum—what teachers need to know. *Intervention in School and Clinic, 36*, 293–305.

Cardona, G.W. (2000). Spaghetti talk. In M. Oken-Fried & H.A. Bersani (Eds.), *Speaking up and spelling it out: Personal essays on augmentative and alternative communication* (pp. 237–244). Baltimore: Paul H. Brookes.

CHARGE Syndrome Foundation, Inc. (2001, April 18). Home page. Retrieved May 15, 2001 from the World Wide Web: http://www.chargesyndrome.org/

Charlop-Christy, M.H., & Kelso, S.E. (1999). Autism. In V.L. Schwean & D.H. Saklofske (Eds.), *Handbook of psychosocial characteristics of exceptional children* (pp. 247–273). New York: Plenum.

Charlop-Christy, M.H., Schreibman, L., Pierce, K., & Kurtz, P.F. (1998). Childhood autism. In R.J. Morris & T.R. Kratochwill (Eds.), *The practice of child therapy* (3rd ed., pp. 271–302). Boston: Allyn & Bacon.

Chen, D., Alsop, L., Minor, L. (2000). Lessons from Project PLAI in California and Utah: Implications for early intervention services to infants who are deaf-blind and their families. *Deaf-Blind Perspectives, 7*(3), 1–8.

Chen, D., Downing, J., & Rodriguez-Gil, G. (2000/2001). Tactile learning strategies for children who are deaf-blind: Concerns and considerations from Project SALUTE. *Deaf-Blind Perspectives, 8*(2), 1–6.

Christensen, J.R. (1996). Pediatric traumatic brain injury. In A.J. Capute & P.J. Accardo (Eds.), *Developmental disabilities in infancy and childhood: Vol. I. Neurodevelopmental diagnosis and treatment* (2nd ed., pp. 245–260). Baltimore: Paul H. Brookes.

Council for Exceptional Children. (2001). Traumatic brain injury—the silent epidemic. *CEC Today, 7*(7), 1, 5, 15.

Crimmins, C. (2000). *Where is the mango princess?* New York: Knopf.

Dell Orto, A.E., & Power, P.W. (2000). *Brain injury and the family: A life and living perspective* (2nd ed.). Washington, DC: CRC Press.

Division for Early Childhood. (1993). DEC position statement on inclusion. *DEC Communicator, 19*(4), 4.

Dykens, E.M., Hodapp, R.M., & Finucane, B.M. (2000). *Genetics and mental retardation syndromes: A new look at behavior and interventions.* Baltimore: MD: Paul H. Brookes.

Families and Disability Newsletter. (2001, June). Positive behavioral support (PBS). Lawrence, KS: University of Kansas Life Span Institute Beach Center on Families and Disability.

Featherly, C. (2000). Life with cerebral palsy. In M. Oken-Fried & H.A. Bersani (Eds.), *Speaking up and spelling it out: Personal essays on augmentative and alternative communication* (pp. 189–193). Baltimore: Paul H. Brookes.

Ford, J., & Fredericks, B. (1995). Perceptions of inclusion by parents of children who are deaf-blind. In N.G. Haring & L.T. Romer (Eds.), *Welcoming students who are deaf-blind into typical classrooms: Facilitating school participation, learning, and friendships* (pp. 37–53). Baltimore, MD: Paul H. Brookes.

Forness, S.R., Kavale, K.A., Sweeney, D.P., & Crenshaw, T.M. (1999). The future of research and practice in behavioral disorders: Psychopharmacology and its school implications. *Behavioral Disorders, 24,* 305–318.

Franklin, P., & Bourquin, E. (2000). Picture this: A pilot study for improving street crossings for deaf-blind travelers. *RE:view, 31,* 173–179.

Fraser, R.T., & Clemmons, D.C. (Eds.). (2000). *Traumatic brain injury rehabilitation: Practical, vocational, neuropsychological, and psychotherapy interventions.* Boca Raton, FL: CRC Press.

Freeberg, E. (2001). *The education of Laura Bridgman: First deaf and blind person to learn language.* Cambridge, MA: Harvard University Press.

Gense, D.J., & Gense, M. (1999). The importance of orientation and mobility skills for students who are deaf-blind. Retrieved May 15, 2001 from the DB-LINK Web site on the World Wide Web: http://www.tr.wou.edu/dblink/o&m2.htm

Giangreco, M.F., Cloninger, C.J., & Iverson, V.S. (1993). *Choosing options and accommodations for children: A guide to planning inclusive education.* Baltimore: Paul H. Brookes.

Grandin, T. (1995). How people with autism think. In E. Schopler & G.B. Mesibov (Eds.), *Learning and cognition in autism* (pp. 137–156). New York: Plenum.

Groden, J., Cautela, J., Prince, S., & Berryman, J. (1994). The impact of stress and anxiety on individuals with autism and developmental disabilities. In E. Schopler & G.B. Mesibov (Eds.), *Behavioral issues in autism* (pp. 177–194). New York: Plenum.

Hall, B.D. (1979). Choanal atresia and associated multiple anomalies. *Journal of Pediatrics, 95,* 395–398.

Heller, K.W., Alberto, P.A., Forney, P.E., & Schwartzman, M.N. (1996). *Understanding physical, sensory, and health impairments: Characteristics and educational implications.* Pacific Grove, CA: Brooks/Cole.

Hembree, R. (2000). National deaf-blind child count summary: December 1, 1999 count. Monmouth, OR: National Technical Assistance Consortium for Children and Young Adults who are Deaf-Blind (NTAC), Teaching Research Division, Western Oregon University.

Hodges, L. (2000). Effective teaching and learning. In S. Aitken, M. Buultjens, C. Clark, J.T. Eyre, & L. Pease (Eds.), *Teaching children who are deafblind: Contact, communication, and learning* (pp. 167–199). London: David Fulton Publishers.

Horner, R.H., Albin, R.W., Sprague, J.R., & Todd, A.W. (2000). Positive behavior support. In M.E. Snell & F. Brown (Eds.), *Instruction of students with severe disabilities* (pp. 207–243). Upper Saddle River, NJ: Prentice-Hall.

Horner, R.H., Vaughn, B.J., Day, H.M., & Ard, W.R. (1996). The relationship between setting events and problem behavior: Expanding our understanding of behavioral supports. In L.K.

Kogel, R.L. Kogel, & G. Dunlap (Eds.). *Positive behavioral support: Including people with difficult behavior in the community* (pp. 381–402). Baltimore: Paul H. Brookes.

Kauffman, J.M. (2001). *Characteristics of emotional and behavioral disorders of children and youth* (7th ed.). Upper Saddle River, NJ: Prentice-Hall.

Kauffman, J.M., Mostert, M.P., Trent, S.C., & Hallahan, D.P. (2002). *Managing classroom behavior: A reflective case-based approach* (3rd ed.) Boston: Allyn & Bacon.

Kennedy, C.H., Meyer, K.A., Knowles, T., & Shukla, S. (2000). Analyzing the multiple functions of stereotypical behavior for students with autism: Implications for assessment and treatment. *Journal of Applied Behavior Analysis, 33,* 559–571.

Klein, M.D., Chen, D., & Haney, M. (2000). *Promoting learning through active interaction: A guide to early communication for young children who have multiple disabilities.* Baltimore: MD: Paul H. Brookes.

Kloepfer, H.W., Laguaite, J.K., & McLaurin, J.W. (1996). The hereditary syndrome of congenital deafness and retinitis pigmentosa (Usher's syndrome). *Laryngoscope, 76,* 850–862.

Kogel, L.K., Kogel, R.L., & Dunlap, G. (1996). *Positive behavioral support: Including people with difficult behavior in the community.* Baltimore: Paul H. Brookes.

Light, R., McCleary, C., Asarnow, R., Zaucha, K., & Lewis, R. (1998). Mild closed-head injury in children and adolescents: Behavior problems and academic outcomes. *Journal of Consulting and Clinical Psychology, 66,* 1023–1027.

Lloyd, L.L., Fuller, D.R., & Arvidson, H.H. (Eds.). (1997). *Augmentative and alternative communication: A handbook of principles and practices.* Boston: Allyn & Bacon.

Loncke, F. (2001). Augmentative and alternative communication in the 21st century. *Augmentative and Alternative Communication, 17,* 61.

Marvin, C.A., Beukelman, D.R., Brockhaus, J., & Kast, L. (1994). "What are you talking about?" Semantic analysis of preschool children's conversational topics in home and preschool settings. *Augmentative and Alternative Communication, 10,* 75–86.

Mathews, J. (2001, June 10). Autistic public school teen shatters myths, grade book. *Washington Post,* pp. C1, C8.

Matson, J.L., Benavidez, D.A., Compton, L.S., Paclwaskyj, T., & Baglio, C. (1996). Behavioral treatment of autistic persons: A review of research from 1980 to the present. *Research in Developmental Disabilities, 7,* 388–451.

McClannahan, L.E., & Krantz, P.J. (1999). *Activity schedules for children with autism: Teaching independent behavior.* Bethesda, MD: Woodbine House.

McCord, B.E., Thomson, R.J., & Iwata, B.A. (2001). Functional analysis and treatment of self-injury associated with transition. *Journal of Applied Behavior Analysis, 34,* 195–210.

McDonald, S., Togher, L., & Code, C. (Eds.). (1999a). *Communication disorders following traumatic brain injury.* East Sussex, UK: Psychology Press.

McDonald, S., Togher, L., & Code, C. (1999b). The nature of traumatic brain injury: Basic features and neuropsychological consequences. In S. McDonald, L. Togher, & C. Code (Eds.), *Communication disorders following traumatic brain injury* (pp. 19–54). East Sussex, UK: Psychology Press.

McLean, M.E., & Odom, S.L. (1996). Establishing recommended practices in early intervention/early childhood special education. In S.L. Odom & M.E. McLean (Eds.), *Early intervention/*

early childhood special education: Recommended practices (pp. 1–22). Austin, TX: Pro-Ed.

Melancon, F. (2000). A group of students with Usher syndrome in south Louisiana. *Deaf-Blind Perspectives, 8*(1), 1–3.

Miles, B. (1998). Overview of deaf-blindness. Retrieved May 15, 2001 from the DB-LINK Web site on the World Wide Web: http://www.tr.wou.edu/dblink/Overview2.htm.

Miles, B. (1999, March 9). Talking the language of the hands. Retrieved June 1, 2001 from the DB-LINK Web site on the World Wide Web: http://www.tr.wou.edu/dblink/hands2.htm

Miner, I., & Cioffi, J. (1999, October 25). Usher syndrome in the school setting. Retrieved May 15, 2001 from the DB-LINK Web site on the World Wide Web: www.tr.wou.edu/dblink/usherfulltext.htm

Moon, M.S., & Inge, K. (2000). Vocational preparation and transition. In M.E. Snell & F. Brown (Eds.), *Instruction of students with severe disabilities* (5th ed., pp. 591–628). Upper Saddle River, NJ: Merrill.

Moss, K., & Hagood, L. (1995, January). Teaching strategies and content modifications for the child with deaf-blindness. *PS News.* Retrieved June 20, 2001 from http://www.tsbvi.edu/outreach/seehear/archive/strategies.html

Mostert, M.P. (1998). *Interprofessional collaboration in schools.* Boston: Allyn & Bacon.

Mostert, M.P. (2001). Facilitated communication since 1995: A review of published studies. *Journal of Autism and Developmental Disorders, 31,* 287–313.

Mount, B., & Zwernik, K. (1988). *It's never too early; it's never too late.* St. Paul, MN: Metropolitan Council.

Myles, B.S., & Simpson, R.L. (2001). Understanding the hidden curriculum: An essential social skill for children and youth with Asperger syndrome. *Intervention in School and Clinic, 36,* 279–286.

National Information Clearinghouse On Children Who Are Deaf-Blind. (2001, May 18). State definitions of deaf-blindness. Retrieved June 9, 2001 from the DB-LINK Web site on the World Wide Web: http://www.tr.wosc.osshe.edu/dblink/data/definitions.htm

National Research Council. (2001). *Educating children with autism.* Washington, DC: National Academy Press.

Nelson, N.W. (1998). *Childhood language disorders in context: Infancy through adolescence* (2nd ed.). Boston: Allyn & Bacon.

Newsom, C. (1998). Autistic disorder. In E.J. Mash & R.A. Barkley (Eds.), *Treatment of childhood disorders* (2nd ed., pp. 416–467). New York: Guilford Press.

Odom, S.L., & McLean, M.E. (Eds.), (1996). *Early intervention/early childhood special education: Recommended practices.* Austin, TX: Pro-Ed.

Oken-Fried, M., & Bersani, H.A. (Eds.). (2000). *Speaking up and spelling it out: Personal essays on augmentative and alternative communication.* Baltimore: Paul H. Brookes.

Oley, C.A. (2001). CHARGE association. In S.B. Cassidy & J.E. Allanson (Eds.), *Management of genetic syndromes* (pp. 71–84). New York: Wiley-Liss.

Omvig, J.H. (1997, November) From bad philosophy to bad policy: The American Braille illiteracy crisis. *Braille Monitor,* pp. 723–728.

Park, C.C. (2001). *Exiting nirvana: A daughter's life with autism.* Boston: Little, Brown.

Pease, L. (2000). Creating a communicating environment. In S. Aitken, M. Buultjens, C. Clark, J.T. Eyre, & L. Pease (Eds.),

Teaching children who are deafblind: Contact, communication, and learning (pp. 35–82). London: David Fulton Publishers.

Rapp, J.T., Miltenberger, R.G., Galensky, T.L., Ellingson, S.A., & Long, E.S. (1999). A functional analysis of hair-pulling. *Journal of Applied Behavior Analysis, 32,* 329–337.

Sacks, O. (1995). *An anthropologist on Mars.* New York: Knopf.

Sandall, S., McLean, M.E., & Smith, B.J. (Eds.). (2000). *DEC recommended practices in early intervention/early childhood special education.* Longmont, CO: Sopris West.

Savage, R.C. (1988). *Introduction to educational issues for students who have suffered traumatic brain injury. An educator's manual: What educators need to know about students with traumatic brain injury.* Southborough, MA: Author.

Savage, R.C., & Wolcott, G.F. (1994). (Eds.). *Educational dimensions of acquired brain injury.* Austin, TX: Pro-Ed.

Scheetz, N.A. (2001). *Orientation to deafness* (2nd ed.). Boston: Allyn & Bacon.

Simpson, R.L., & Myles, B.S. (Eds.). (1998). *Educating children and youth with autism: Strategies for effective practice.* Austin, TX: Pro-Ed.

Strain, P.S., Smith, B.J., & McWilliam, R.A. (1996). The widespread adoption of service delivery recommendations: A systems change perspective. In S.L. Odom & M.E. McLean (Eds.), *Early intervention/early childhood special education: Recommended practices* (pp. 101–123). Austin, TX: Pro-Ed.

Thompson, R.H., & Iwata, B.A. (2001). A descriptive analysis of social consequences following problem behavior. *Journal of Applied Behavior Analysis, 34,* 169–178.

Tyler, J.S., & Mira, M.P. (1999). *Traumatic brain injury in children and adolescents: A sourcebook for teachers and other school personnel* (2nd ed.). Austin, TX: Pro-Ed.

U.S. Department of Education (1999, March 12). Assistance to the States for the Education of Children with Disabilities and the Early Intervention Program for Infants and Toddlers with Disabilities: Final Regulations. *Federal Register, 64*(48), 12422.

U.S. Office of Special Education Programs. (1998). *Positive behavioral support: Helping students with challenging behaviors succeed.* Reston, VA: ERIC/OSEP Special Project, the ERIC Clearinghouse on Disabilities and Gifted Education, the Council for Exceptional Children.

Vandercook, T., York, J., & Forest, M. (1989). The McGill Action Planning System (MAPS): A strategy for building the vision. *Journal of the Association for Persons with Severe Handicaps, 14,* 205–215.

Walther-Thomas, C., Korinek, L., McLaughlin, V.L., & Williams, B.T. (2000). *Collaboration for inclusive education: Developing successful programs.* Boston: Allyn & Bacon.

Wehmeyer, M. (1992). Self-determination and the education of students with mental retardation. *Education and Training in Mental Retardation, 27,* 303–314.

Westling, D.L., & Fox, L. (2000). *Teaching students with severe disabilities* (2nd ed.). Upper Saddle River, NJ: Merrill.

Williams, K. (2001). Understanding the student with Asperger syndrome: Guidelines for teachers. *Intervention in School and Clinic, 36,* 287–292.

Worsdell, A.S., Iwata, B.A., Conners, J., Kahng, S.W., & Thompson, R.H. (2000). Relative influences of establishing operations and reinforcement contingencies on self-injurious behavior during functional analysis. *Journal of Applied Behavior Analysis, 33,* 451–461.

Yoder, D.E. (2001). Having my say. *Augmentative and Alternative Communication, 17,* 2–10.

CHAPTER 12

Ainsa, P. (2000). *Teaching children with AIDS.* Lampeter, Ceredigion, Wales, UK: Edwin Mellen Press.

Andersson, C., & Mattsson, E. (2001). Adults with cerebral palsy: A survey describing problems, needs, and resources, with special emphasis on locomotion. *Developmental Medicine and Child Neurology, 43,* 76–82.

Archibald, S.L., Fennema-Notestine, C., Gamst, A., Riley, E.P., Mattson, S.N., & Jernigan, T.L. (2001). Brain dysmorphology in individuals with prenatal alcohol exposure. *Developmental Medicine and Child Neurology, 43,* 148–154.

Auxter, D., Pyfer, J., & Huettig, C. (2001). *Principles and methods of adapted physical education* (9th ed.). Boston, MA: McGraw Hill.

Avoli, M., Rogawski, M.A., & Avanzini, G. (2001). Generalized epileptic disorders: An update. *Epilepsia, 42,* 445–457.

Ayala, G.F., Elia, M., Cornaggia, C.M., & Trimble, M.M. (Eds.). (2001). Epilepsy and learning disabilities. *Epilepsia, 42*(Suppl. 1).

Bartonek, A., & Saraste, H. (2001). Factors influencing ambulation in myelomeningocele: A cross-sectional study. *Developmental Medicine and Child Neurology, 43,* 253–260.

Batshaw, M.L., & Perret, Y.M. (1986). *Children with handicaps: A medical primer.* Baltimore: Paul H. Brookes.

Baumeister, A.A., Kupstas, F., & Klindworth, L.M. (1990). New morbidity: Implications for prevention of children's disabilities. *Exceptionality, 1,* 1–16.

Bax, M. (2001). Editorial: What's in a name? *Developmental Medicine and Child Neurology, 43,* 75.

Besag, F.M.C. (1995). Epilepsy, learning, and behavior in children. *Epilepsia, 36,* 58–63.

Bigge, J.L., Best, S.J., & Heller, K.W. (2001). *Teaching individuals with physical, health, or multiple disabilities* (4th ed.). Upper Saddle River, NJ: Merrill/Prentice-Hall.

Blum, R.W. (1992). Chronic illness and disability in adolescence. *Journal of Adolescent Health, 13,* 364–368.

Bottos, M., Feliciangeli, A., Sciuto, L., Gericke, C., & Vianello, A. (2001). Functional status of adults with cerebral palsy and implications for treatment of children. *Developmental Medicine and Child Neurology, 43,* 516–528.

Brown, R.T. (1993). An introduction to the special series: Pediatric chronic illness. *Journal of Learning Disabilities, 26,* 4–6.

Capute, A.J., & Accardo, P.J. (Eds.). (1996a). *Developmental disabilities in infancy and childhood: Vol. 1. Neurodevelopmental diagnosis and treatment* (2nd ed.). Baltimore: Paul H. Brookes.

Capute, A.J., & Accardo, P.J. (Eds.). (1996b). *Developmental disabilities in infancy and childhood: Vol. 2. The spectrum of developmental disabilities* (2nd ed.). Baltimore: Paul H. Brookes.

Closs, A. (Ed.). (2000). *The education of children with medical conditions.* London: David Fulton.

Coulter, D.L. (1993). Epilepsy and mental retardation: An overview. *American Journal on Mental Retardation, 98,* 1–11.

Council for Exceptional Children (2001). Performance-based Standards. Retrieved June 5, 2001 from www.cec.sped.org/ps/perf_based_stds/index.html.

Cowden, A.J., & Funkhouser, E. (2001). Adolescent pregnancy, infant mortality, and source of payment for birth: Alabama residential live births, 1991–1994. *Journal of Adolescent Health, 29,* 37–45.

Crosse, S.B., Kaye, E., & Ratnofsky, A.C. (n.d.). *A report on the maltreatment of children with disabilities.* Washington, DC: National Center on Child Abuse and Neglect.

DeFord, S. (1998, July 26). High tech for the disabled. *Washington Post Education Review, 4,* 30.

Dyar, S.E. (1988). A step in the right direction. *Helix: The University of Virginia Health Sciences Quarterly, 6*(3), 5–11.

Earley, T. (2000). *Jim the Boy* (pp. 203–205). Boston: Little, Brown.

Edmonson, B. (1988). Disability and sexual adjustment. In V.B. Van Hasselt, P.S. Strain, & M. Hersen (Eds.), *Handbook of developmental and physical disabilities* (pp. 91–106). New York: Pergamon Press.

Engel, J. (1995). Concepts of epilepsy. *Epilepsia, 36,* 23–29.

Girvin, J.P. (1992). Is epilepsy a progressive disorder? *Journal of Epilepsy, 5,* 94–104.

Gouvier, W.D., Brown, L.M., Prestholdt, P.H., Hayes, J.S., & Apostolas, G. (1995). A survey of common misconceptions about epilepsy. *Rehabilitation Psychology, 40,* 51–59.

Hanson, M.J. (Ed.). (1996). *Atypical infant development* (2nd ed.). Austin, TX: Pro-Ed.

Heller, K.W., Alberto, P.A., Forney, P.E., & Schwartzman, M.N. (1996). *Understanding physical, sensory, and health impairments: Characteristics and educational implications.* Pacific Grove, CA: Brooks/Cole.

Heller, K.W., Alberto, P.A., & Meagher, T.M. (1996). The impact of physical impairments on academic performance. *Journal of Developmental and Physical Disabilities, 8,* 233–245.

Johnson, C.P. (1996). Transition in adolescents with disabilities. In A.J. Capute & P.J. Accardo (Eds.), *Developmental disabilities in infancy and childhood: Vol. 1. Neurodevelopmental diagnosis and treatment* (2nd ed., pp. 549–564). Baltimore: Paul H. Brookes.

Karnish, K., Bruder, M., & Rainforth, B. (1995). A comparison of physical therapy in two school based treatment contexts. *Physical and Occupational Therapy in Pediatrics, 15*(4), 1–25.

Kurtz, L.A., Dowrick, P.W., Levy, S.E., & Batshaw, M.L. (Eds.). (1996). *Handbook of developmental disabilities: Resources for interdisciplinary care.* Gaithersburg, MD: Aspen.

Leaman, O. (2000). Schools and death. In A. Closs (Ed.), *The education of children with medical conditions* (pp. 155–168). London: David Fulton.

Lerner, J.W., Lowenthal, B., & Egan, R. (1998). *Preschool children with special needs: Children at risk, children with disabilities.* Boston: Allyn & Bacon.

Lindsey, J.E. (Ed.). (2000). *Technology and exceptional individuals* (3rd ed.). Austin, TX: Pro-Ed.

Llewellyn, A., & Chung, M.C. (1997). The self-esteem of children with physical disabilities—Problems and dilemmas of research. *Journal of Developmental and Physical Disabilities, 9,* 265–275.

Lockhart, P.J. (1996). Infants of substance-abusing mothers. In A.J. Capute & P.J. Accardo (Eds.), *Developmental disabilities in infancy and childhood: Vol. 1. Neurodevelopmental diagnosis and treatment* (2nd ed., pp. 215–229). Baltimore: Paul H. Brookes.

Magill-Evans, J., Darrah, J., Pain, K., Adkins, R., & Kratochvil, M. (2001). Are families with adolescents and young adults with cerebral palsy the same as other families? *Developmental Medicine and Child Neurology, 43,* 466–472.

McCarthy, A.M., Richman, L.C., & Yarbrough, D. (1995). Memory, attention, and school problems in children with seizure disorders. *Developmental Neuropsychology, 11,* 71–86.

Michael, R.J. (1995). *The educator's guide to students with epilepsy.* Springfield, IL: Charles C. Thomas.

Moore, J. (1985). Technology is not magic. *Exceptional Parent, 15*(7), 41–42.

Morningstar, M.E., Turnbull, H.R., Lattin, D.L., Umbarger, G.T., Reichard, A., & Moberly, R. (2001). Students supported by medical technology: Making the transition from school to adult life. *Journal of Developmental and Physical Disabilities, 13,* 229–259.

Myers, B.A. (1996). Coping with developmental disabilities. In A.J. Capute & P.J. Accardo (Eds.), *Developmental disabilities in infancy and childhood: Vol. 1. Neurodevelopmental diagnosis and treatment* (2nd ed., pp. 473–483). Baltimore: Paul H. Brookes.

Nelson, K.B. (1996). Epidemiology and etiology of cerebral palsy. In A.J. Capute & P.J. Accardo (Eds.), *Developmental disabilities in infancy and childhood: Vol. 2. The spectrum of developmental disabilities* (2nd ed., pp. 73–79). Baltimore: Paul H. Brookes.

Parra, J., Augustijn, P.B., Geerts, Y., & Boas, W. (2001). Classification of epileptic seizures: a comparison of two systems. *Epilepsia, 42,* 476–482.

Pless, I.B. (Ed.). (1994). *The epidemiology of childhood disorders.* New York: Oxford University Press.

Powers, L.E., Singer, G.H.S., & Sowers, J. (Eds.). (1996). *On the road to autonomy: Promoting self-competence in children and youth with disabilities.* Baltimore: Paul H. Brookes.

Rogers, A.S. (2001). HIV research in American youth. *Journal of Adolescent Health, 29*(Suppl. 3S), 1–4.

Shelter News. (2001, Fall). Battering and teen pregnancy: A connection too real to ignore. Charlottesville, VA: Shelter for Help in Emergency.

Spiegel, G.L., Cutler, S.K., & Yetter, C.I. (1996). What every teacher should know about epilepsy. *Intervention in School and Clinic, 32,* 34–38.

Stanley, F.J., & Blair, E. (1994). Cerebral palsy. In I.B. Pless (Ed.), *The epidemiology of childhood disorders* (pp. 473–497). New York: Oxford University Press.

Szabo, J.L. (2000). Maddie's story: Inclusion through physical and occupational therapy. *Teaching Exceptional Children, 33*(2), 12–18.

Tyler, J.S., & Colson, S. (1994). Common pediatric disabilities: Medical aspects and educational implications. *Focus on Exceptional Children, 27*(4), 1–16.

U.S. Department of Education. (2000). *Twenty-second annual report to Congress on the implementation of the Individuals with Disabilities Education Act.* Washington, DC: Author.

Vining, E.P.G., & Freeman, J.M. (1996). Epilepsy and developmental disabilities. In A.J. Capute & P.J. Accardo (Eds.), *Developmental disabilities in infancy and childhood: Vol. 2. The spectrum of developmental disabilities* (2nd ed., pp. 511–520). Baltimore: Paul H. Brookes.

Walker, B. (1995, June). African-American fathers: In raising a child with disabilities, believe only the best, demand only the best, give only the best. *Pacesetter,* 14–15.

Ward, K.M. (1996). School-based vocational training. In L.A. Kurtz, P.W. Dowrick, S.E. Levy, & M.L. Batshaw (Eds.), *Handbook of developmental disabilities: Resources for interdisciplinary care* (pp. 237–248). Gaithersburg, MD: Aspen.

Weihenmayer, E. (2001). *Touch the top of the world: A blind man's journey to climb farther than the eye can see.* New York: E.P. Dutton.

Wolman, C., Garwick, A., Kohrman, C., & Blum, R. (2001). Parents' wishes and expectations for children with chronic conditions. *Journal of Developmental and Physical Disabilities, 13,* 261–277.

CHAPTER 13

Amabile, T.M. (2001). Beyond talent: John Irving and the passionate craft of creativity. *American Psychologist, 56,* 333–336.

Baker, J.A., Bridger, R., & Evans, K. (1998). Models of underachievement among gifted preadolescents: The role of personal, family, and school factors. *Gifted Child Quarterly, 42,* 5–15.

Baum, S.M., Olenchak, F.R., & Owen, S.V. (1998). Gifted students with attention deficits: Fact and/or fiction? Or, can we see the forest for the trees? *Gifted Child Quarterly, 42,* 96–104.

Borland, J.H. (1997). The construct of giftedness. *Peabody Journal of Education, 72*(3&4), 6–20.

Borland, J.H., Schnur, R., & Wright, L. (2000). Economically disadvantaged students in a school for the academically gifted: A postpositivist inquiry into individual and family adjustment. *Gifted Child Quarterly, 44,* 13–32.

Borland, J.H., & Wright, L. (2000). Identifying and educating poor and under-represented gifted students. In K.A. Heller, F.J. Monks, R.J. Sternberg, & R.F. Subotnik (Eds.), *International handbook of giftedness and talent* (2nd ed., pp. 587–594). New York: Pergamon.

Brody, L.E., & Stanley, J.C. (1991). Young college students: Assessing factors that contribute to success. In W.T. Southern & E.D. Jones (Eds.), *The academic acceleration of gifted children* (pp. 102–132). New York: Teachers College Press.

Buescher, T.M. (1991). Gifted adolescents. In W.T. Southern & E.D. Jones (Eds.), *The academic acceleration of gifted children* (pp. 382–401). New York: Teachers College Press.

Burge, K. (1998, April). Prodigies. *U.S. Airways Attache,* 80–87.

Callahan, C.M. (1991). An update on gifted females. *Journal for the Education of the Gifted, 14,* 284–311.

Callahan, C.M. (1997). The construct of talent. *Peabody Journal of Education, 72*(3&4), 21–35.

Callahan, C.M. (2000). Evaluation as a critical component of program development and implementation. In K.A. Heller, F.J. Monks, R.J. Sternberg, & R.F. Subotnik (Eds.), *International handbook of giftedness and talent* (2nd ed., pp. 537–548). New York: Pergamon.

Callahan, C.M. (2001). Evaluating learner and program outcomes in gifted education. In F.A. Karnes & S.M. Bean (Eds.), *Methods and materials for teaching the gifted* (pp. 253–298) Waco, TX: Prufrock Press.

Charlton, J.C., Marolf, D.M., & Stanley, J.C. (1994). Follow-up insights on rapid educational acceleration. *Roeper Review, 17,* 123–130.

Clark, B. (1997). *Growing up gifted: Developing the potential of children at home and at school* (5th ed.). Upper Saddle River, NJ: Prentice-Hall.

Cline, S., & Hegeman, K. (2001). Gifted children with disabilities. *Gifted Child Today, 24*(3), 16–24.

Coleangelo, N., & Assouline, S.G. (2000). Counseling gifted students. In K.A. Heller, F.J. Monks, R.J. Sternberg, & R.F. Subotnik (Eds.), *International handbook of giftedness and talent* (2nd ed., pp. 595–608). New York: Pergamon.

Coleman, J.M., & Fultz, B.A. (1985). Special class placement, level of intelligence, and the self-concepts of gifted children: A social comparison perspective. *Remedial and Special Education, 6*(1), 7–12.

Coleman, L.J., & Cross, T.L. (2000). Social-emotional development and the personal experience of giftedness. In K.A. Heller, F.J. Monks, R.J. Sternberg, & R.F. Subotnik (Eds.), *International handbook of giftedness and talent* (2nd ed., pp. 203–212). New York: Pergamon.

Council for Exceptional Children (2001). Performance-based Standards. Retrieved June 5, 2001 from www.cec.sped.org/ps/perf_based_stds/index.html.

Cropper, C. (1998). Fostering parental involvement in the education of the gifted minority student. *Gifted Child Today, 21*(1), 20–24, 46.

Cross, T.L. (1997). Psychological and social aspects of educating gifted students. *Peabody Journal of Education, 72*(3&4), 180–200.

Dale, E.J. (2000). Technology for individuals with gifts and talents. In J.E. Lindsey (Ed.), *Technology and exceptional individuals* (3rd ed., pp. 375–407). Austin, TX: Pro-Ed.

DeHahn, E.L.H. (2000). Cross-cultural studies in gifted education. In K.A. Heller, F.J. Monks, R.J. Sternberg, & R.F. Subotnik (Eds.), *International handbook of giftedness and talent* (2nd ed., pp. 549–561). New York: Pergamon.

Delcourt, M.A.B., Loyd, B.H., Cornell, D.G., & Goldberg, M.D. (1994, October). *Evaluation of the effects of programming arrangements on student learning outcomes.* Storrs, CT: National Research Center on the Gifted and Talented, University of Connecticut.

Delisle, J.R. (1992). *Guiding the social and emotional development of gifted youth: A practical guide for educators and counselors.* New York: Longman.

Delisle, J.R. (1996). Multiple intelligences: Convenient, simple, wrong. *Gifted Child Today, 19*(6), 12–13.

Feldhusen, J.F. (1998). Programs for the gifted few or talent development for the many? *Phi Delta Kappan, 79,* 735–738.

Feldhusen, J.R., & Jarwan, F.A. (2000). Identification of gifted and talented youth for educational programs. In K.A. Heller, F.J. Monks, R.J. Sternberg, & R.F. Subotnik (Eds.), *International handbook of giftedness and talent* (2nd ed., pp. 271–282). New York: Pergamon.

Feldhusen, J.F., & Kolloff, P.B. (1986). The Purdue secondary model for gifted and talented youth. In J.S. Renzulli (Ed.), *Systems and models for developing programs for the gifted and talented.* Mansfield, CT: Creative Learning Press.

Ford, D.Y. (1993). An investigation of the paradox of underachievement among gifted black students. *Roeper Review, 16,* 78–84.

Ford, D.Y. (1998). The under-representation of minority students in gifted education: Problems and promises in recruitment and retention. *Journal of Special Education, 32,* 4–14.

Ford, D.Y., & Harris, J.J. (1996). Perceptions and attitudes of black students toward school, achievement, and other educational variables. *Child Development, 67,* 1141–1152.

Ford, D.Y., & Harris, J.J. (1997). A study of the racial identity and achievement of black males and females. *Roeper Review, 20,* 105–110.

Frasier, M.M. (1997). Gifted minority students: Reframing approaches to their identification and education. In N. Colangelo & G.A. Davis (Eds.), *Handbook of gifted education* (2nd ed., pp. 498–515). Boston: Allyn & Bacon.

Frasier, M.M., & Passow, A.H. (1994, December). *Toward a new paradigm for identifying talent potential.* Storrs, CT: National Research Center on the Gifted and Talented, University of Connecticut.

Freeman, J. (2000). Families: The essential context for gifts and talents. In K.A. Heller, F.J. Monks, R.J. Sternberg, & R.F. Subotnik (Eds.), *International handbook of giftedness and talent* (2nd ed., pp. 573–586). New York: Pergamon.

Gagne, F. (2000). Understanding the complex choreography of talent development through DMGT-based analysis. In K.A. Heller, F.J. Monks, R.J. Sternberg, & R.F. Subotnik (Eds.), *International handbook of giftedness and talent* (2nd ed., pp. 67–79). New York: Pergamon.

Galbraith, J., & Delisle, J. (1996). *The gifted kids' survival guide: A teen handbook* (Rev. ed.). Minneapolis: Free Spirit Publishing.

Gallagher, J.J. (1998). Accountability for gifted students. *Phi Delta Kappan, 79,* 739–742.

Gallagher, J.J. (2000a). Changing paradigms for gifted education in the United States. In K.A. Heller, F.J. Monks, R.J. Sternberg, & R.F. Subotnik (Eds.), *International handbook of giftedness and talent* (2nd ed., pp. 681–693). New York: Pergamon.

Gallagher, J.J. (2000b). Unthinkable thoughts: Education of gifted students. *Gifted Child Quarterly, 44,* 5–12.

Gallagher, J.J., & Gallagher, S.A. (1994). *Teaching the gifted child* (4th ed.). Boston: Allyn & Bacon.

Gardner, H., & Hatch, T. (1989). Multiple intelligences go to school: Educational implications of the theory of multiple intelligences. *Educational Researcher, 18*(8), 4–9.

Gentry, M., & Owen, S.V. (1999). An investigation of the effects of total school flexible cluster grouping on identification, achievement, and classroom practices. *Gifted Child Quarterly, 43,* 224–243.

Gould, S.J. (1996). *The mismeasure of man* (Rev. ed.). New York: Norton.

Gross, M.U.M. (1992). The use of radical acceleration in cases of extreme intellectual precocity. *Gifted Child Quarterly, 36,* 91–99.

Gross, M.U.M. (1993). *Exceptionally gifted children.* London: Routledge.

Gross, M.U.M. (2000). Issues in the cognitive development of exceptionally and profoundly gifted individuals. In K.A. Heller, F.J. Monks, R.J. Sternberg, & R.F. Subotnik (Eds.), *International handbook of giftedness and talent* (2nd ed., pp. 179–192). New York: Pergamon.

Gruber, H.E., & Wallace, D.B. (2001). Creative work: The case of Charles Darwin. *American Psychologist, 56,* 346–349.

Heller, K.A., Monks, F.J., Sternberg, R.J., & Subotnik, R.F. (Eds.). (2000). *International handbook of giftedness and talent* (2nd ed.). New York: Pergamon.

Howley, C.B., Howley, A., & Pendarvis, E.D. (1995). *Out of our minds: Anti-intellectualism and talent development in American schooling.* New York: Teachers College Press.

Hunsaker, S.L. (1995). The gifted metaphor from the perspective of traditional civilizations. *Journal for the Education of the Gifted, 18,* 255–268.

Hunsaker, S.L., & Callahan, C.M. (1995). Creativity and giftedness: Published instrument uses and abuses. *Gifted Child Quarterly, 39,* 110–114.

Hunter, S. (2001, December 21). Fragile genius of "A Beautiful Mind:" The human enigma within the known patterns of the universe. *Washington Post,* C1, C5.

Jackson, N.E., & Klein, E. (1997). Gifted performance in young children. In N. Colangelo & G.A. Davis (Eds.), *Handbook of gifted education* (2nd ed., pp. 460–474). Boston: Allyn & Bacon.

Johnson, L.J., Karnes, M.B., & Carr, V.W. (1997). Providing services to children with gifts and disabilities: A critical need. In N. Colangelo & G.A. Davis (Eds.), *Handbook of gifted education* (2nd ed., pp. 516–527). Boston: Allyn & Bacon.

Jones, E.D., & Southern, W.T. (1991). Conclusions about acceleration: Echoes of debate. In W.T. Southern & E.D. Jones (Eds.), *The academic acceleration of gifted children* (pp. 223–228). New York: Teachers College Press.

Jones, E.D., & Southern, W.T. (1992). Programming, grouping, and acceleration in rural school districts: A survey of attitudes and practices. *Gifted Child Quarterly, 36,* 112–117.

Karnes, M.B., & Bean, S.M. (Eds.). (2001). *Methods and materials for teaching the gifted.* Waco, TX: Prufrock Press.

Karnes, M.B., & Johnson, L.J. (1991). The preschool/primary gifted child. *Journal for the Education of the Gifted, 14,* 267–283.

Kaufman, M. (1998, February 2). The best for the brightest. *Washington Post Magazine,* pp. 18–20, 32–35.

Kaufmann, F.A., & Castellanos, F.X. (2000). Attention deficit/hyperactivity disorder in gifted students. In K.A. Heller, F.J. Monks, R.J. Sternberg, & R.F. Subotnik (Eds.), *International handbook of giftedness and talent* (2nd ed., pp. 621–632). New York: Pergamon.

Kerr, B. (1997). Developing talents in girls and young women. In N. Colangelo & G.A. Davis (Eds.), *Handbook of gifted education* (2nd ed., pp. 475–482). Boston: Allyn & Bacon.

Kerr, B. (2000). Guiding gifted girls and young women. In K.A. Heller, F.J. Monks, R.J. Sternberg, & R.F. Subotnik (Eds.), *International handbook of giftedness and talent* (2nd ed., pp. 649–658). New York: Pergamon.

Kitano, M.K., & Espinosa, R. (1995). Language diversity and giftedness: Working with gifted English language learners. *Journal for the Education of the Gifted, 18,* 234–254.

Kolitch, E.R., & Brody, L.E. (1992). Mathematics acceleration of highly talented students: An evaluation. *Gifted Child Quarterly, 36,* 78–86.

Landrum, M.S., Callahan, C.M., & Shaklee, B.D. (Eds.). (2001). *Aiming for excellence: Gifted program standards.* Waco, TX: Prufrock Press.

Lovecky, D.V. (1994). Exceptionally gifted children: Different minds. *Roeper Review, 17,* 116–120.

Lubinski, D., Benbow, C.P., & Morelock, M.J. (2000). Gender differences in engineering and the physical sciences among the gifted: An inorganic-organic distinction. In K.A. Heller, F.J. Monks, R.J. Sternberg, & R.F. Subotnik (Eds.), *International handbook of giftedness and talent* (2nd ed., pp. 633–648). New York: Pergamon.

Lynch, M.D., & Harris, C.R. (Eds.). (2001). *Fostering creativity in children K–8: Theory and practice.* Boston: Allyn & Bacon.

Manstetten, R. (2000). Promotion of the gifted in vocational training. In K.A. Heller, F.J. Monks, R.J. Sternberg, & R.F. Subotnik (Eds.), *International handbook of giftedness and talent* (2nd ed., pp. 439–446). New York: Pergamon.

Margolin, L. (1994). *Goodness personified: The emergence of gifted children.* New York: Aldine de Gruyter.

Marsh, H.W., Chessor, D., Craven, R., & Roche, L. (1995). The effects of gifted and talented programs on academic self-concept: The big fish strikes again. *American Educational Research Journal, 32,* 285–319.

Martindale, C. (2001). Oscillations and analogies: Thomas Young, MD, FRS, genius. *American Psychologist, 56,* 342–345.

Mathews, J. (1998, June 7). Across area, "gifted" has no clear-cut definition: School guidelines mystify many parents. *Washington Post,* pp. A1, A16.

Montgomery, D. (Ed.). (2000). *Able underachievers.* London: Whurr.

Moon, S.M., & Dillon, D.R. (1995). Multiple exceptionalities: A case study. *Journal for the Education of the Gifted, 18,* 111–130.

Moon, S.M., & Rosselli, H.C. (2000). Developing gifted programs. In K.A. Heller, F.J. Monks, R.J. Sternberg, & R.F. Subotnik (Eds.), *International handbook of giftedness and talent* (2nd ed., pp. 499–521). New York: Pergamon.

Moon, S.M., Zentall, S., Grskovic, J.A., Hall, A., & Stormont, M. (2001). Emotional and social characteristics of boys with AD/HD and giftedness: A comparative case study. *Journal for the Education of the Gifted, 24,* 207–247.

Morelock, M.J., & Feldman, D.H. (1997). High IQ children, extreme precocity, and savant syndrome. In N. Colangelo & G.A. Davis (Eds.), *Handbook of gifted education* (2nd ed., pp. 439–459). Boston: Allyn & Bacon.

Nakamura, J., & Csikszentmihalyi, M. (2001). Catalytic creativity: The case of Linus Pauling. *American Psychologist, 56,* 337–341.

Neuhaus, C. (1988). Genius at work. *US Air, 10*(2), 64–68.

Noble, K.D., & Drummond, J.E. (1992). But what about the prom? Students' perceptions of early college entrance. *Gifted Child Quarterly, 36,* 106–111.

Perleth, C., Schatz, T., & Monks, F.J. (2000). Early identification of high ability. In K.A. Heller, F.J. Monks, R.J. Sternberg, & R.F. Subotnik (Eds.), *International handbook of giftedness and talent* (2nd ed., pp. 297–316). New York: Pergamon.

Peters, W.A.M., Grager-Loidl, H., & Supplee, P. (2000). Underachievement in gifted children and adolescents: Theory and practice. In K.A. Heller, F.J. Monks, R.J. Sternberg, & R.F. Subotnik (Eds.), *International handbook of giftedness and talent* (2nd ed., pp. 609–620). New York: Pergamon.

Plomin, R. (1997). Genetics and intelligence. In N. Colangelo & G.A. Davis (Eds.), *Handbook of gifted education* (2nd ed., pp. 67–74). Boston: Allyn & Bacon.

Plucker, J.A., & Stocking, V.B. (2001). Looking outside and inside: Self-concept development of gifted adolescents. *Exceptional Children, 67,* 535–548.

Ramos-Ford, V., & Gardner, H. (1997). Giftedness from a multiple intelligences perspective. In N. Colangelo & G.A. Davis (Eds.), *Handbook of gifted education* (2nd ed., pp. 54–66). Boston: Allyn & Bacon.

Reis, S.M., & Renzulli, J.S. (2001). The schoolwide enrichment model: Developing students' creativity and talents. In M.D. Lynch & C.R. Harris (Eds.), *Fostering creativity in children, K–8: Theory and practice* (pp. 15–39). Boston: Allyn & Bacon.

Renzulli, J.S., & Reis, S.M. (1997). The schoolwide enrichment model: New directions for developing high-end learning. In N. Colangelo & G.A. Davis (Eds.), *Handbook of gifted education* (2nd ed., pp. 136–154). Boston: Allyn & Bacon.

Renzulli, J.S., & Reis, S.M. (2000). The schoolwide enrichment model. In K.A. Heller, F.J. Monks, R.J. Sternberg, & R.F. Subotnik (Eds.), *International handbook of giftedness and talent* (2nd ed., pp. 367–382). New York: Pergamon.

Rimm, S.B., & Lovance, K.J. (1992). The use of subject and grade skipping for the prevention and reversal of underachievement. *Gifted Child Quarterly, 36,* 100–105.

Rittenhouse, R.K., & Blough, L.K. (1995). Gifted students with hearing impairments: Suggestions for teachers. *Teaching Exceptional Children, 27*(4), 51–53.

Robinson, N.M. (1993). Identifying and nurturing gifted, very young children. In K.A. Heller, F.J. Monks, & A.H. Passow (Eds.), *International handbook of research and development of giftedness and talent* (pp. 507–524). New York: Pergamon.

Roeper, A. (1994). Gifted education must take a stand on The Bell Curve. *Roeper Review, 17*, 150.

Rogers, K.B., & Kimpston, R.D. (1992). Acceleration: What we do vs. what we know. *Educational Leadership, 50*(2), 58–61.

Sacks, O. (1995). *An anthropologist on Mars: Seven paradoxical tales.* New York: Knopf.

Sapon-Shevin, M. (1994). *Playing favorites: Gifted education and the disruption of community.* Albany: State University of New York Press.

Shaywitz, S.E., Holahan, J.M., Freudenheim, D.A., Fletcher, J.M., Makuch, R.W., & Shaywitz, B.A. (2001). Heterogeneity within the gifted: Higher IQ boys exhibit behaviors resembling boys with learning disabilities. *Gifted Child Quarterly, 45*, 16–23.

Shermer, M. (2001). *The borderlands of science: Where sense meets nonsense.* New York: Oxford University Press.

Shields, C.M. (1995). A comparison study of student attitudes and perceptions in homogeneous and heterogeneous classrooms. *Roeper Review, 17*, 234–238.

Silverman, L.K. (1997). Family counseling with the gifted. In N. Colangelo & G.A. Davis (Eds.), *Handbook of gifted education* (2nd ed., pp. 382–397). Boston: Allyn & Bacon.

Smutny, J.F. (2001). *Creative strategies for teaching language arts to gifted students* (K–8). (ERIC Digest No. E612). Retrieved October 30, 2001 from http://www.ericec.org.

Sternberg, R.J. (1996). Myths, countermyths, and truths about intelligence. *Educational Researcher, 25*(2), 11–16.

Sternberg, R.J. (1997). A triarchic view of giftedness: Theory and practice. In N. Colangelo & G.A. Davis (Eds.), *Handbook of gifted education* (2nd ed., pp. 43–53). Boston: Allyn & Bacon.

Sternberg, R.J. (1998). Abilities are forms of developing expertise. *Educational Researcher, 27*(3), 11–20.

Sternberg, R.J. (2000). Giftedness as developing expertise. In K.A. Heller, F.J. Monks, R.J. Sternberg, & R.F. Subotnik (Eds.), *International handbook of giftedness and talent* (2nd ed., pp. 23–54). New York: Pergamon.

Sternberg, R.J. (2001). What is the common thread of creativity? Its dialectical relation to intelligence and wisdom. *American Psychologist, 56*, 360–362.

Sternberg, R.J., & Clinkenbeard, P.R. (1995). The triarchic model applied to identifying, teaching, and assessing gifted children. *Roeper Review, 17*, 255–260.

Sternberg, R.J., & Dess, N.K. (2001). Creativity for the new millennium. *American Psychologist, 56*, 332.

Sternberg, R.J., & Zhang, L. (1995). What do we mean by giftedness? A pentagonal implicit theory. *Gifted Child Quarterly, 39*, 88–94.

Stokes, P.D. (2001). Variability, constraints, and creativity: Shedding light on Claude Monet. *American Psychologist, 56*, 355–359.

Subotnik, R.F., & Arnold, K.D. (Eds.). (1994). *Beyond Terman: Contemporary longitudinal studies of giftedness and talent.* Norwood, NJ: Albex.

Subotnik, R.F., & Arnold, K.D. (2000). Addressing the most challenging questions in gifted education and psychology: A role

best suited to longitudinal research. In K.A. Heller, F.J. Monks, R.J. Sternberg, & R.F. Subotnik (Eds.), *International handbook of giftedness and talent* (2nd ed., pp. 423–252). New York: Pergamon.

Swanson, J.D. (1995). Gifted African-American children in rural schools: Searching for the answers. *Roeper Review, 17*, 261–266.

Swiatek, M.A. (1998). Helping gifted adolescents cope with social stigma. *Gifted Child Today, 21*(1), 42–46.

Swiatek, M.A., & Benbow, C.P. (1991). Ten-year longitudinal follow-up of ability-matched accelerated and unaccelerated gifted students. *Journal of Educational Research, 83*, 528–538.

Tannenbaum, A.J. (1993). History of giftedness and "gifted education" in world perspective. In K.A. Heller, F.J. Monks, & A.H. Passow (Eds.), *International handbook of research and development of giftedness and talent* (pp. 3–27). New York: Pergamon.

Tannenbaum, A.J. (1997). The meaning and making of giftedness. In N. Colangelo & G.A. Davis (Eds.), *Handbook of gifted education* (2nd ed., pp. 27–42). Boston: Allyn & Bacon.

Tannenbaum, A.J. (2000a). A history of giftedness in school and society. In K.A. Heller, F.J. Monks, R.J. Sternberg, & R.F. Subotnik (Eds.), *International handbook of giftedness and talent* (2nd ed., pp. 23–54). New York: Pergamon.

Tannenbaum, A.J. (2000b). Giftedness: The ultimate instrument for good and evil. In K.A. Heller, F.J. Monks, R.J. Sternberg, & R.F. Subotnik (Eds.), *International handbook of giftedness and talent* (2nd ed., pp. 447–466). New York: Pergamon.

Thompson, L.A., & Plomin, R. (2000). Genetic tools for exploring individual differences in intelligence. In K.A. Heller, F.J. Monks, R.J. Sternberg, & R.F. Subotnik (Eds.), *International handbook of giftedness and talent* (2nd ed., pp. 157–164). New York: Pergamon.

Tomlinson, C. (1995). *Differentiating instruction for advanced learners in the mixed-ability middle school classroom.* (ERIC Digest No. E536). Retrieved October 30, 2001 from http://www.ericec.org.

Treffinger, D.J. (1998). From gifted education to programming for talent development. *Phi Delta Kappan, 79*, 752–755.

Van Tassel-Baska, J. (1998). The development of academic talent: A mandate for educational best practice. *Phi Delta Kappan, 79*, 760–763.

Van Tassel-Baska, J. (2000). Theory and research on curriculum development for the gifted. In K.A. Heller, F.J. Monks, R.J. Sternberg, & R.F. Subotnik (Eds.), *International handbook of giftedness and talent* (2nd ed., pp. 345–365). New York: Pergamon.

Ward, T.B. (2001). Creative cognition, conceptual combination, and the creative writing of Sephen R. Donaldson. *American Psychologist, 56*, 350–354.

White, D.A., & Breen, M. (1998). Edutainment: Gifted education and the perils of misusing multiple intelligences. *Gifted Child Today, 21*(2), 12–17.

Willard-Holt, C. (1999). *Dual exceptionalities.* (ERIC Digest No. E574.) Alexandria, VA: ERIC Clearinghouse on Disabilities and Gifted Education.

Ziegler, A., & Heller, K.A. (2000). Conceptions of giftedness from a meta-theoretical perspective. In K.A. Heller, F.J. Monks, R.J. Sternberg, & R.F. Subotnik (Eds.), *International handbook of giftedness and talent* (2nd ed., pp. 203–212). New York: Pergamon.

CHAPTER 14

Alper, S., Schloss, P.J., & Schloss, C.N. (1996). Families of children with disabilities in elementary and middle school: Advocacy models and strategies. *Exceptional Children, 62,* 261–270.

Beckman, P.J. (1991). Comparison of mothers' and fathers' perceptions of the effect of young children with and without disabilities. *American Journal on Mental Retardation, 95,* 585–595.

Bell, R.Q., & Harper, L.V. (1977). *Child effects on adults.* Hillsdale, NJ: Erlbaum.

Berry, J.O., & Hardman, M.L. (1998). *Lifespan perspectives on the family and disability.* Boston: Allyn & Bacon.

Bettelheim, B. (1950). *Love is not enough.* New York: Macmillan.

Bettelheim, B. (1967). *The empty fortress.* New York: Free Press.

Bronfenbrenner, U. (1979). *The ecology of human development: Experiments by nature and design.* Cambridge, MA: Harvard University Press.

Bronfenbrenner, U. (1995). Developmental ecology through space and time: A future perspective. In P. Moen, G.H. Elder, & K. Luscher (Eds.), *Examining lives in context: Perspectives on the ecology of human development* (pp. 619–647). Washington, DC: American Psychological Association.

Brooks-Gunn, J., & Lewis, M. (1984). Maternal responsivity in interactions with handicapped infants. *Child Development, 55,* 858–868.

Bryan, T.H., Nelson, C., & Mathur, S. (1995). Homework: A survey of primary students in regular, resource, and self-contained classrooms. *Learning Disabilities Research and Practice, 10,* 85–90.

Bryan, T.H., & Sullivan-Burstein, K. (1997). Homework how-to's. *Teaching Exceptional Children, 29*(6), 32–37.

Cottone, E. (1998). *Home-school collaboration: Evaluating the effectiveness of a school-home note program for children with ADHD.* Unpublished doctoral dissertation, University of Virginia, Charlottesville.

D'Asaro, A. (1998). Caring for yourself is caring for your family: Methods of coping with the everyday stresses of care giving. *Exceptional Parent, 28*(6), 38–40.

Drotar, D., Baskiewicz, A., Irvin, N., Kennell, J., & Klaus, M. (1975). The adaptation of parents to the birth of an infant with a congenital malformation: A hypothetical model. *Pediatrics, 56,* 710–717.

Duis, S.S., Summers, M., & Summers, C.R. (1997). Parent versus child stress in diverse family types: An ecological approach. *Topics in Early Childhood and Special Education, 17,* 53–73.

Dumas, J.E., Wolf, L.C., Fisman, S.N., & Culligan, A. (1991). Parenting stress, child behavior problems, and dysphoria in parents of children with autism, Down syndrome, behavior disorders, and normal development. *Exceptionality, 2,* 97–110.

Dunst, C.J., Trivette, C.M., & Jodry, W. (1997). Influences of social support on children with disabilities and their families. In M.J. Guralnick (Ed.), *The effectiveness of early intervention* (pp. 499–522). Baltimore: Paul H. Brookes.

Dyson, L.L. (1997). Fathers and mothers of school-age children with developmental disabilities: Parental stress, family functioning, and social support. *American Journal on Mental Retardation, 102,* 267–279.

Epstein, M., Munk, D., Bursuck, W., Polloway, E., & Jayanthi, M. (1999). Strategies for improving home-school communication about homework for students with disabilities. *Journal of Special Education, 33,* 166–176.

Featherstone, H. (1980). *A difference in the family: Life with a disabled child.* New York: Basic Books.

Fowler, S.A., Schwartz, I., & Atwater, J. (1991). Perspectives on the transition from preschool to kindergarten for children with disabilities and their families. *Exceptional Children, 58,* 136–145.

Gavidia-Payne, S., & Stoneman, Z. (1997). Family predictors of maternal and paternal involvement in programs for young children with disabilities. *Child Development, 68,* 701–717.

Gerlach, E.K. (1999). *Just this side of normal: Glimpses into life with autism.* Eugene, OR: Four Leaf Press.

Hallahan, D.P., & Martinez, E.A. (2002). Working with families. In J.M. Kauffman, M. Mostert, S.C. Trent, & D.P. Hallahan (Eds.), *Managing classroom behavior: A reflective case-based approach* (3rd ed., pp. 124–140). Boston: Allyn & Bacon.

Hanline, M.F., & Knowlton, A. (1988). A collaborative model for providing support to parents during their child's transition from infant intervention to preschool special education public school programs. *Journal of the Division for Early Childhood, 12,* 116–125.

Hockenberry, J. (1995). *Moving violations: War zones, wheelchairs, and declarations of independence.* New York: Hyperion.

Jayanthi, M., Bursuck, W., Epstein, M., & Polloway, E. (1997). Strategies for successful homework. *Teaching Exceptional Children, 30*(1), 4–7.

Jayanthi, M., Sawyer, V., Nelson, J., Bursuck, W., & Epstein, M. (1995). Recommendations for homework-communication problems: From parents, classroom teachers, and special education teachers. *Remedial and Special Education, 16,* 212–225.

Kelley, M.L. (1990). *School-home notes: Promoting children's classroom success.* New York: Guilford Press.

Kelley, M.L., & McCain, A.P. (1995). Promoting academic performance in inattentive children. *Behavior Modification, 19,* 357–375.

Keogh, B.K., Garnier, H.E., Bernheimer, L.P., & Gallimore, R. (2000). Models of child-family interactions for children with developmental delays: Child-driven or transactional? *American Journal on Mental Retardation, 105,* 32–46.

Klinger, J., & Vaughn, S. (1999). Students' perceptions of instruction in inclusion classrooms: Implications for students with learning disabilities. *Exceptional Children, 66,* 23–37.

Kraus, S., Maxwell, K., & McWilliam, R.A. (2001). "Practice" makes perfect: Research looks at family-centered practices in early elementary grades. *Exceptional Parent, 31*(3), 62–63.

Lambie, R. (2000). *Family systems within educational contexts: Understanding at-risk and special-needs students.* Denver, CO: Love Publishing Co.

Lehmann, J.P., & Baker, C. (1995). Mothers' expectations for their adolescent children: A comparison between families with disabled adolescents and those with non-labeled adolescents. *Education and Training in Mental Retardation and Developmental Disabilities, 30,* 27–40.

Mahoney, G., & Robenalt, K. (1986). A comparison of conversational patterns between mothers and their Down syndrome and normal infants. *Journal of the Division for Early Childhood, 10,* 172–180.

Mahoney, G., Boyce, G., Fewell, R.R., Spiker, D., & Wheeden, C.A. (1998). The relationship of parent-child interaction to the effectiveness of early intervention services for at-risk children and children with disabilities. *Topics in Early Childhood and Special Education, 18,* 5–17.

McCain, A.P., & Kelley, M.L. (1993). Managing the classroom behavior of an ADHD preschooler: The efficacy of a school-home note intervention. *Child and Family Behavior Therapy, 15*(3), 33–44.

Meyer, D.J., & Vadasy, P.F. (1994). *Sibshops: Workshops for siblings of children with special needs.* Baltimore: Paul H. Brookes.

Michael, M.G., Arnold, K.D., Magliocca, L.A., & Miller, S. (1992). Influences on teachers' attitudes of the parents' role as collaborator. *Remedial and Special Education, 13,* 24–30, 39.

Orsmond, G.I., & Seltzer, M.M. (2000). Brothers and sisters of adults with mental retardation: Gendered nature of the sibling relationship. *American Journal on Mental Retardation, 105,* 486–508.

O'Shea, D.J., & O'Shea, L.J. (2001). Why learn about students' families? In D.J. O'Shea, L.J. O'Shea, R. Algozzine, D.J. Hammitte (Eds.), *Families and teachers of individuals with disabilities: Collaborative orientations and responsive practices* (pp. 5–24). Boston: Allyn & Bacon.

O'Shea, D.J., O'Shea, L.J., Algozzine, R., & Hammitte, D.J. (Eds.). (2001). *Families and teachers of individuals with disabilities: Collaborative orientations and responsive practices.* Boston: Allyn & Bacon.

O'Shea, D.J., & Riley, J.E. (2001). Typical families: Fact or fiction? In D.J. O'Shea, L.J. O'Shea, R. Algozzine, D.J. Hammitte (Eds.), *Families and teachers of individuals with disabilities: Collaborative orientations and responsive practices* (pp. 25–50). Boston: Allyn & Bacon.

Osher, T. (1997). Advocacy in action: You can advocate for your child! *CEC Today, 4*(4).

Parette, H.P., & Petch-Hogan, B. (2000). Approaching families: Facilitating culturally/linguistically diverse family involvement. *Teaching Exceptional Children, 33*(2), 4–10.

Pierro, C. (1995). Talking with your child about disabilities. *Exceptional Parent, 25*(6), 92.

Polloway, E., Bursuck, W., Jayanthi, M., Epstein, M., & Nelson, J. (1996). Treatment acceptability: Determining appropriate interventions within inclusive classrooms. *Intervention in School and Clinic, 31,* 133–144.

Powell, T.H., & Gallagher, P.A. (1993). *Brothers & sisters—A special part of exceptional families* (2nd ed.). Baltimore: Paul H. Brookes.

Roach, M.A., Barratt, M.S., Miller, J.F., & Leavitt, L.A. (1998). The structure of mother-child play: Young children with Down syndrome and typically developing children. *Developmental Psychology, 34,* 77–87.

Salembier, G.B., & Furney, F.S. (1998). Speaking up for your child's future. *Exceptional Parent, 28*(7), 62–64.

Scorgie, K., & Sobsey, D. (2000). Transformational outcomes associated with parenting children who have disabilities. *Mental Retardation, 38,* 195–206.

Seaver, A. (2001). Fighting prejudice. *Exceptional Parent, 31*(4), 116.

Seligman, M., & Darling, R.B. (1989). *Ordinary families, special children: A systems approach to childhood disability.* New York: Guilford Press.

Seltzer, M.M., Greenberg, J.S., Floyd, F.J., Pettee, Y., & Hong, J. (2001). Life course impacts of parenting a child with a disability. *American Journal on Mental Retardation, 106,* 265–286.

Skinner, D., Bailey, D.B., Correa, V., & Rodriguez, P. (1999). Narrating self and disability: Latino mothers' construction of identities vis-à-vis their child with special needs. *Exceptional Children, 65,* 481–495.

Smith, C.R., & Strick, L. (2000). Is your child ready to leave home? *Their World,* pp. 41–43, New York: National Center for Learning Disabilities.

Turnbull, A.P., & Turnbull, H.R. (1997). *Families, professionals, and exceptionality: A special partnership* (3rd ed.). Upper Saddle River, NJ: Prentice-Hall.

Turnbull, A.P., & Turnbull, H.R. (2000). Fostering family-professional partnerships. In M.E. Snell & F. Brown (Eds.), *Instruction of students with severe disabilities* (5th ed., pp. 31–66). Columbus, OH: Merrill/Prentice-Hall.

Warger, C. (2001, March). *Five homework strategies for teaching students with disabilities.* ERIC Clearinghouse on Disabilities and Gifted Education. Retrieved October 20, 2001 from the World Wide Web: http://www.ericec.org/digests/e608.html

Name Index

AAMR AD Hoc Committee on Terminology and Classification, 112, 113, 115
Abbaduto, L., 276
Abdulkarim, L., 283, 284, 285
Abernathy, T. V., 51
Abery, B. H., 43, 141
Abikoff, H., 189
Abikoff, H. B., 211
Ablon, J. S., 195
Abrahamson, T., 331
Abt Associates, 67
Accardo, P. J., 423, 424
Achenbach, T. M., 228
Adams, G. L., 174
Adelson, P. D., 385
Adkins, R., 435
Adreon, D., 378
Agran, M., 43, 129, 140
Ainsa, P., 429
Aitken, S., 393, 396
Alberto, P. A., 388, 420, 422, 424, 425, 427, 428, 429, 430, 431, 432, 435, 436, 439, 440, 442, 446, 448
Albin, R. W., 134, 408, 410
Aldenkamp, A. P., 117
Algozzine, B., 43
Algozzine, R., 500
Allen, S. H., 178
Allen, T. E., 309
Allor, J. H., 178
Allsopp, D. H., 202
Almond, P., 61
Alper, S., 506
Alpert, C. L., 275
Alsop, B., 196
Alsop, L., 397, 400
Altenderfer, L., 209
Amabile, T. M., 457
Amato, C., 287
Ambrose, N., 264
American Academy of Pediatrics, Committee on Quality Improvement, Subcommittee on Attention-Deficit/Hyperactivity Disorder, 193, 194
American Association on Mental Retardation, 130
American Psychiatric Association, 114, 165, 190, 240, 376, 377
American Speech-Language-Hearing Association, 267, 280–281, 281, 286

Amsel, R., 351
Anastopoulos, A. D., 192
Anderson, C. M., 193
Anderson, N. B., 285
Anderson, T. W., 43
Andersson, C., 447
Andersson, Y., 303
Andreason, P., 157
Andrews, D., 361
Andrews, J. F., 323, 330
Antia, S. D., 310
Apostolas, G., 426
The Arc, 119
Archibald, S. L., 429
Archwamety, T., 254
Ard, W. R., 409
Ardila, A., 192
Arguelles, M. E., 56, 176, 208
Arias, B. E., 192
Arizona Easter Seal Society, 57
Arnold, K. D., 462, 502
Arnold, L. E., 189, 211
Arora, T., 52, 53, 54
Arrega-Mayer, C., 58, 98
Artesani, A. J., 74
Artiles, A. J., 85, 91, 92, 94, 99
Arvidson, H. H., 402, 404, 405
Asamen, J., 231
Asarnow, J. R., 228
Asarnow, R., 389, 390
Asarnow, R. F., 231
Ascher, C., 98
Assouline, S. G., 468
Astuto, T. A., 27, 54, 252
Atwater, J., 501
Audet, L. R., 276, 294
Auditory-Verbal International, 319
Augustijn, P. B., 425
Augusto, Carl R., 340
Ault, M. J., 140
Auxter, D., 438
Avanzini, G., 425
Avoli, M., 425
Ayala, G. F., 427
Aylward, E. H., 193

Baca, L., 287
Bacon-Shone, J., 192
Baglio, C., 381
Bahan, B., 303, 308, 311, 312, 320, 325, 329, 330
Bailey, D. B., 63, 492
Baker, C., 500
Baker, J., 94, 252
Baker, J. A., 464

Baker, J. M., 23, 55
Baker, J. N., 55
Baker, S., 90, 97, 102
Baldwin, V., 393
Ball, A., 63
Ball, D. W., 165
Balla, D. A., 124
Balow, I. H., 68
Bambara, L. M., 206, 415
Bandura, A., 242
Bank-Mikkelsen, N. E., 40
Banks, C.A.M., 80, 106
Banks, J. A., 80, 85, 86, 90, 99, 102, 103, 104, 106
Bankson, N. W., 290
Bantz, J., 45, 252, 253
Barcus, J. M., 139
Barkley, R. A., 186, 189, 192, 195, 196, 197, 198, 199, 202, 203, 208, 209, 211, 213, 214
Barnes, M., 152, 153
Barnhill, G. P., 381
Baron-Myak, C., 209
Barr, C., 196
Barraga, N. C., 343, 357
Barratt, M. S., 499
Barrett, M. S., 198, 213
Barry, J. G., 315
Baskiewicz, A., 489
Bateman, B. D., 22, 106, 253
Batshaw, M. L., 420, 422, 423, 424, 425, 428, 446
Battersby-Longden, J. C., 370
Battle, D. E., 285
Baum, S. M., 471
Bauman-Waengler, J., 290
Baumeister, A., 43
Baumeister, A. A., 120, 155, 422, 424
Baumgaertel, A., 192
Bauminger, N., 124
Bax, M., 423
Baxter, J., 164
Baxter, J. A., 54
Bay, M., 94, 161
Bean, S. M., 457
Beattie, J., 70
Bebko, J. M., 124
Beck, I. L., 202
Becker, J. V., 235
Becker, W. C., 232
Beckman, P. J., 491
Beeson, P. M., 264, 282, 283
Behrmann, M. M., 67
Beichtman, J. H., 157–158
Beirne-Smith, M., 117, 118

Bekken, K., 196
Bell, R. Q., 488
Bellugi, U., 127, 322
Benavidez, D. A., 381
Benbow, C. P., 473, 474, 478
Bender, W. N., 167, 172, 180, 181, 206
Bennett, L., 99
Bentzen, F. A., 203
Bergland, M., 389
Berkey, J., 117
Bernheimer, L. P., 488
Bernstein, D. K., 266
Bernthal, J. E., 290
Berquin, M. D., 193
Berry, J. O., 488, 494, 500, 501, 502
Berryman, J., 379
Bersani, H. A., 405, 406
Besag, F.M.C., 426
Besler, R. C., 126
Best, A. M., 245
Best, S. J., 420, 425, 427, 428, 429, 432, 435, 436, 438, 439, 440, 442, 445, 446, 447
Bettelheim, B., 380, 486
Beukelman, D. R., 290, 291, 388, 402, 404, 405
Bice, H. V., 188
Biederman, J., 192, 193, 195, 196, 199, 207, 209, 211, 212, 216
Bigge, J. L., 420, 425, 427, 428, 429, 432, 435, 436, 438, 439, 440, 442, 445, 446, 447
Biklen, D., 48
Birch, H. G., 189
Bird, H. R., 229
Bishop, D., 286
Blackorby, J., 141, 179
Blair, E., 424
Blake, C., 254
Blamey, P. J., 315
Blanchard, C., 43
Blank, M., 279, 282
Blanz, B., 157
Blesz, D. P., 103
Blind Babies Foundation, 345
Blough, L. K., 470
Blum, R., 439
Blum, R. W., 422
Boada, R., 196
Boardman, A. G., 54, 55, 176
Boas, W., 425
Bocian, K., 229
Bocian, K. M., 94, 115, 155

Bock, S. J., 73
Bogdan, R., 45, 48
Bolger, K. E., 6, 234
Bond, L., 31, 32
Bonner, B., 235
Borland, J. H., 456, 462, 463, 469, 470
Borner, H., 194
Bornstein, M. H., 309, 330
Borthwick-Duffy, S., 68
Borthwick-Duffy, S. A., 136
Bos, C., 56, 57
Boscardin, M. L., 166
Bottos, M., 424, 447
Bouras, C., 117
Bourquin, E., 401
Bovair, K., 45
Bow, C. P., 315
Bowen, B., 244
Bowen, S., 318
Bower, E. M., 226, 257
Bowman, B. T., 67
Boyce, G., 499
Boys Town National Research Hospital Genetics Department, 394
Bradley, M. R., 74
Bradley, R., 254
Bradley-Klug, K. L., 205, 206
Brandeis, D., 196
Brandenburg, N. A., 229
Braukmann, C. J., 260
Bray, N. W., 124
Bredekamp, S., 412
Breen, M., 458
Brengelman, S., 90, 102
Brenner, M., 99
Breslau, N., 199
Bricker, D., 47, 67
Bricker, D. D., 63
Bridger, R., 464
Brigham, F. J., 73, 253
Brill R. G., 302
Brockhaus, J., 405
Brody, L. E., 481–482, 482
Bronfenbrenner, U., 495
Brooks-Gunn, J., 66, 292, 488
Brookshire, R. H., 291
Browder, D., 132, 140
Browder, D. M., 43, 415
Browder, P. M., 141
Brown, D., 394
Brown, F., 374, 407, 414
Brown, J., 362
Brown, J. E., 193
Brown, L., 141
Brown, L. M., 426
Brown, R. T., 422
Browne, R. G., 207
Brownell, M. T., 379, 380
Bruder, M., 443
Bruder, M. B., 66
Bruhn, P., 194
Brunswick, N., 157, 163

Bryan, T. H., 164, 167, 168, 505
Bryant, B. R., 124
Buchino, M. A., 332
Buchsbaum, M. S., 157
Buck, G. H., 74
Buescher, T. M., 482
Bukstein, O., 209
Bulgren, J. A., 180
Bull, J., 57
Bullis, M., 252
Buntaine, R., 226
Burge, K., 464, 466–467
Burish, P., 178
Burns, M., 286
Bursuck, W., 505
Bursuck, W. D., 168
Busnello, E., 192
Butera, G., 51
Butler, D. L., 165, 166
Butler, F. M., 133
Butler, K. G., 273, 276, 283, 284, 287, 296
Butler, M. G., 126
Butterfield, E. C., 43
Butterworth, J., 141

Cai, X., 292
Calandrella, A. M., 276
Callahan, C. M., 456, 463, 473, 474, 475
Callahan, K., 229
Calvert, L. K., 274
Cambra, C., 310
Campbell, F. A., 138
Campbell, K.C.M., 305
Campbell, S. L., 288
Cantwell, D. P., 192, 207, 245
Caplan, N., 87
Cappa, S. F., 157, 163
Cardona, G. W., 403
Carey, D. M., 54
Carnine, D., 173
Carnine, D. W., 203
Carnine, L., 173
Caron, M. G., 195
Carpenter, B., 45
Carr, E. G., 204
Carr, J., 117
Carr, V. W., 473
Carson, R. R., 259
Carta, J., 286
Carta, J. J., 67, 258
Carter, K., 318
Carter, W. J., 103
Cartledge, G., 58, 103, 254
Carver, T., 142
Casas, J. M., 251
Case, L. P., 171
Castellanos, F. X., 193, 194, 195, 207, 471
Casterline, D. C., 322
Catts, H. W., 292, 294
Cautela, J., 379
Cawley, J. F., 133, 164

Cepeda, M. L., 197
Cepeda, N. J., 197
CHADD Media Advisory, 210
Chadsey-Rusch, J., 69
Chambers, A. C., 327
Champion, T., 284
Chanonine, V., 157, 163
Chard, D. J., 173, 253
CHARGE Syndrome Foundation, 393, 394
Charlop-Christy, M. H., 231, 379, 382
Charlson, E., 310
Charlton, J. C., 479
Chen, D., 366, 397, 399, 400
Chess, S., 231
Chessor, D., 464
Chhabildas, N., 199
Chhabildas, N. A., 196
Chilcoat, H. D., 199
Chin-Chance, S. A., 60
Chinn, P. C., 93
Chipchase, B., 286
Cho, S., 99
Choate, J. S., 95, 159
Chong, C., 352
Choy, M. H., 87
Christ, M.A.G., 257
Christensen, J. R., 386
Christenson, S. L., 68
Chung, M. C., 432
Cicchetti, D. V., 124
Cioffi, A., 142
Cioffi, J., 401
Clarizio, H. F., 155
Clark, B., 462, 465
Clark, D. L., 27
Clark, G. M., 68, 70, 72, 140, 333
Clarke, S., 249
Clemmons, D. C., 390
Clevenger, W., 211
Cline, D. H., 226
Cline, S., 471
Clinkenbeard, P. R., 477
Cloninger, C. J., 414
Closs, A., 432, 437, 440
Cobb, J., 181
Code, C., 386, 388, 389
Cohen, P., 51, 176, 229
Cohen, R. M., 195
Cohen, S., 86
Cohen, S. B., 167
Cohn, D., 86
Colangelo, N., 468
Cole, C. L., 206
Cole, D., 276
Cole, K. N., 47, 54, 67
Coleman, J. M., 464
Coleman, L. J., 454, 464
Coleman, M., 250
Collet-Klingenberg, L. L., 68
Collins, K., 99
Collins, M. E., 357

Colson, S., 425
Colvin, G., 229, 234, 235, 237, 240, 242, 243, 244, 249, 250, 253, 254, 257, 258, 260
Compton, L. S., 381
Condon, K. A., 63, 74
Conners, C. K., 189, 192, 211
Conners, F., 157
Conners, J., 407
Connolly, A. J., 159
Connor, D. F., 199, 209
Connor, R., 276
Connor, R. T., 136
Conroy, M. A., 74, 255
Constable, R. T., 157
Conti-Ramsden, G., 346
Conture, E. G., 264, 291
Cook, B. G., 54
Cooper, P., 204
Copher, J. I., 141
Corda, B., 244
Corn, A. L., 341
Cornaggia, C. M., 427
Cornell, D. G., 477
Correa, V., 492
Cossu, G., 157, 163
Costello, E. J., 229
Costenbader, V., 226
Cottone, E., 506
Cottone, E. A., 199
Coulter, D. L., 425
Council for Exceptional Children, 23, 94, 95, 98, 136, 176–177, 250, 324, 364, 385, 386, 388, 444, 474
Coury, D. L., 212
Couthino, M., 55
Coutinho, M. J., 92, 93, 245
Cowden, A. J., 431
Cox, C. J., 74
Cox, D. J., 198
Cox, P. R., 353
Coyne, P., 63, 318
Crane, M. K., 167
Craven, R., 464
Crawford, M. R., 140
Crenshaw, T. M., 209, 212, 232, 383
Crimmins, C., 386
Crissey, M. S., 43
Crockett, J. B., 15, 19, 22, 30, 44, 45, 54, 55, 253
Crockett, Jean, 128–129, 227, 278–279, 316–317, 350–351, 390–391, 409, 440–441, 476–477
Croneberg, C. G., 322
Cronin, M. E., 44, 131
Cropper, C., 469, 470
Cross, T. L., 454, 464
Crosse, S. B., 431
Crosswait, C., 198, 213
Crowe, T. A., 288, 291
Crowson, K., 322

Cruickshank, W. M., 15, 45, 151, 162, 188, 203
Csikszentmihalyi, M., 457
Culligan, A., 491
Cullinan, D., 229
Curlee, R. F., 264, 291
Curtis, W. J., 98
Cutler, S. K., 426
Cuvo, A. J., 132, 352

Dale, E. J., 473, 479
Dale, P. S., 47, 54, 67
Darling, R. B., 502
Darrah, J., 435
D'Asaro, A., 492
Davies, M., 211
Davies, S., 205, 206
Davis, C. A., 6, 250, 251, 255–256
Davis, P. K., 132
Davis, S., 116
Dawson, H. L., 135
Day, H. M., 409
Day, N. L., 228
Deaf World Web, 321
DeBose, C. E., 94, 97, 102, 284
DeFord, S., 436, 448
DeFries, C., 195
DeFries, J. C., 158
deHahn, E.L.H., 465
Deimel, W., 158
Delcourt, M.A.B., 477
Delisle, J., 482
Delisle, J. R., 458, 481, 482
Dell Orto, A. E., 385, 387, 388, 389, 390
Delpit, L. D., 96
Delpit, L., 103, 284
Delquadri, J., 135
Delquadri, J. C., 135
Demonet, J. F., 157, 163
Denckla, M. B., 193
Denham, S. A., 67
Deno, S., 55
Deno, S. L., 159, 160
dePerczel, M., 249
Derrick, G., 305
Deshler, D. D., 180
Dess, N. K., 457
DeStefano, L., 70, 141
DeWitt, M. B., 212
Dickstein, D. P., 193
Diener, M. B., 198
Dietrich, M., 192
Dillon, D. R., 473
Dimitropoulos, A., 126
Dishion, T. J., 6, 232, 242, 252
Division for Early Childhood, 413
Dobelle, W. H., 363
Docherty, R., 430, 442
Dodge, K. A., 258
Donahue, M., 164
Donahue, M. L., 276

Donohue, B. C., 157
Dostra, L., 229
Dote-Kwan, J., 366
Douglas, S., 430, 442
Downing, J., 399
Dowrick, P. W., 420, 422, 446
Doyle, A. E., 195, 196, 214, 216
Doyle, P. M., 140
Draper, I. L., 59, 61, 62, 94
Drasgow, E., 72, 73, 254, 323
Drew, R., 57
Drotar, D., 489
Drummond, J. E., 482
Duara, R., 157
Duhaney, D. C., 327
Duhaney, L.M.G., 52
Duis, S. S., 491, 492
Duke, D. L., 260
Dumas, J. E., 491
Duncan, B. B., 258
Dunlap, G., 134, 249, 255, 409
Dunst, C. J., 501
DuPaul, G. J., 192, 199, 204, 205, 206, 207, 209
Dupre, A. P., 29, 54, 72, 74
Dwyer, K. P., 72
Dyar, S. E., 424
Dye, H. B., 122
Dykens, E. M., 117, 118, 119, 122, 123, 125, 126, 395
Dykens, E., 125
Dykes, M. K., 353
Dyson, L. L., 491

Earley, T., 419–420
Easterbrooks, S., 318
Easterbrooks, S. R., 316
Eaves, L. J., 158
Eckert, T. L., 205, 207
Edelen-Smith, P., 206
Edelman, M. W., 79, 82
Edelman, P., 235
Edgar, E., 105–106, 140, 179, 251, 259, 260
Edison, M. R., 43
Edmonson, B., 448
Edwards, M. L., 290
Egan, R., 66, 68, 429, 430, 432, 439, 440
Ehren, B. J., 180
Eiserman, W. D., 66
Elbaum, B., 54, 55, 176
Elia, M., 427
Eliopulos, D., 193
Elksnin, L. K., 104
Elksnin, N., 104
Elling, R., 66
Ellingson, S. A., 406
Elliot, B., 105
Elliott, G. R., 211
Ellis, A., 174
Ellis, C., 256, 258
Ellis, C. R., 98
Ellis, W. K., 142

Engel, J., 425
Engelmann, O., 173
Engelmann, S., 173
Englemann, S., 174
Enright, B. E., 95, 159
Epilepsy Foundation of America, 426
Epstein, M., 505
Epstein, M. H., 168, 224, 229, 236, 250, 252, 258
Erhardt, D., 198
Erhen, B. J., 280
Erickson, A., 101
Erickson, M. T., 158
Ernst, M., 195
Ervin, R. A., 204, 205
Escobar, M. D., 155
Espinosa, R., 469
Esser, G., 192
Estevis, A. H., 352
Evans, K., 464
Evans, S. W., 209
Evelo, D. L., 68
Evenhuis, H. M., 117
Everson, J. M., 139
Ewers, L., 142

Fad, K. M., 74
Falk, K. B., 58, 250
Families and Disabilities Newsletter, 408
Faraone, S. V., 195, 196, 199, 207, 211, 214, 216
Farmer, E.M.Z., 222, 251
Farmer, T. W., 222, 234, 235, 240, 250, 251, 252, 253, 254, 258
Farran, D. C., 365
Fazio, F., 157, 163
Featherly, C., 404
Featherstone, H., 490
Federal Register, 327
Feil, E. G., 63, 229, 236, 241, 257, 258
Feldhusen, J. F., 470, 475, 477, 481
Feldhusen, J. R., 463
Feldman, D. H., 463
Feldman, E., 157
Feliciangeli, A., 424, 447
Fennema-Notestine, C., 429
Fennick, E., 56, 71
Ferdinand, R. F., 192
Ferguson, C., 323
Fergusson, D. M., 192, 198
Fernstrom, P., 252
Ferrell, K. A., 357
Feurer, I. D., 126
Fewell, R. R., 499
Fey, M. E., 292, 294
Fichten, C. S., 351
Fidler, D. J., 125
Fiedler, C. R., 46
Fietcher, J. M., 471

Filipek, P., 196
Filipek, P. A., 193
Findling, R. L., 207
Finegan, J. A., 125
Finn, C. E., Jr., 34, 59
Finucane, B. M., 117, 118, 119, 122, 123, 125, 126, 395
Firth, E., 360
Fischer, M., 55, 59
Fishback, K., 141, 143
Fisman, S. N., 491
Fister, S., 202, 203
Fleisch, F., 250
Fletcher, J. M., 152, 153, 155, 157, 177
Fletcher, K., 198, 213
Fletcher, K. L., 124
Flowers, D. L., 157
Flowers, L., 157
Floyd, F. J., 492
Floyd, K., 347
Foorman, B. R., 177
Ford, A., 141
Ford, B. A., 97
Ford, D. Y., 94, 95, 103, 463, 464, 469
Ford, K., 396
Foreman, J., 314–315
Forest, M., 414
Forgan, J., 176
Forgan, J. W., 51
Forness, S., 63
Forness, S. R., 6, 30, 51, 54, 165, 199, 207, 209, 212, 224, 225, 227, 229, 231, 232, 245, 250, 252, 258, 383
Forney, P. E., 388, 420, 422, 424, 425, 427, 428, 429, 430, 431, 432, 435, 436, 439, 440, 442, 446, 448
Foster, E. M., 292
Foulke, E., 355
Foundas, A. L., 270
Fowler, S. A., 258, 501
Fox, J. J., 74, 255
Fox, L., 126, 128, 129, 413, 414, 415
Fox, N., 54
Francis, D. J., 152, 153, 177
Frank, A. R., 143, 259
Franklin, M. E., 97
Franklin, P., 401
Fraser, J., 117
Fraser, R. T., 390
Frasier, M. M., 463, 469
Frattali, C., 268
Fredericks, B., 396
Freeberg, E., 398
Freedman, J., 235
Freehan, M., 192
Freeman, J., 475
Freeman, J. M., 425
Freeman, S.F.N., 126
Freudenheim, D. A., 471

Frick, P. J., 257
Friedman, J., 309, 323
Friedman, R. M., 229
Friman, P. C., 205
Frith, C. D., 157, 163
Frith, U., 157, 163
Frostig, M., 151
Fuchs, D., 19, 52, 54, 55, 58, 95, 153, 159, 177, 178, 252
Fuchs, L., 178
Fuchs, L. S., 19, 52, 54, 55, 58, 95, 153, 159, 160, 177, 178, 252
Fujii, K., 192
Fujiura, G. T., 86
Fulbright, R. K., 157
Fulk, B. M., 58, 98
Fulker, D., 157
Fuller, D. R., 402, 404, 405
Fuller, K., 52, 53, 54
Fultz, B. A., 464
Funkhouser, E., 431
Furlong, M. J., 251
Furney, F. S., 508
Furney, K. S., 70

Gabias, P., 360
Gable, R. A., 255
Gadow, K. D., 245
Gagne, F., 461
Gainetdinov, R. R., 195
Gajar, A. H., 167, 181
Galand, B., 73
Galbraith, J., 482
Galensky, T. L., 406
Gallagher, J. J., 47, 55, 63, 454, 456, 461, 464, 465, 470, 480
Gallagher, P. A., 494, 495
Gallagher, S. A., 464, 480
Gallego, M. A., 45
Gallimore, R., 88, 488
Gallucci, J. P., 105
Gamst, A.A., 429
Gannon, J., 258
Garcia, E., 95, 161
Gardner, H., 457
Gardner, R., 58, 254
Garnier, H. E., 488
Garrett, J. N., 67
Garrick-Duhaney, L. M., 327
Garrity, C., 239
Gartner, J. N., 48, 50
Garwick, A., 439
Gashel, J., 356
Gatenby, C., 157
Gaustad, M. G., 310, 312, 330
Gavidia-Payne, S., 491, 492
Gavin, K. M., 58, 98
Geerts, Y., 425
Gense, D. J., 361, 401
Gense, M., 361, 401
Gentry, M., 474
Georgiewa, P., 157
Gerber, M. M., 54

Gerber, P. J., 105, 179, 180
Gericke, C., 424, 447
Gerlach, E. K., 485, 486, 493
Gersten, R., 90, 97, 102, 173
Geyer, P. D., 330
Giangreco, M. F., 414
Giedd, J. N., 193
Gilger, J. W., 195
Gillam, R. B., 274
Gillis, J. J., 158, 195
Ginsberg, R., 105, 180
Giovannelli, J., 234, 257
Girvin, J. P., 425
Glaeser, B.J.C., 74
Glaser, A. J., 293
Glauche, V., 157
Glaucoma Foundation, 344
Glaucoma Research Foundation, 344
Glazer, N., 80, 83
Glod, C. A., 193
Glover, A. T., 176
Gnagy, E. M., 209
Gold, R., 310
Goldberg, M., 234
Goldberg, M. D., 477
Goldberg, P., 234
Goldberg, R. J., 180
Goldin-Meadow, S., 322
Goldstein, D. E., 179
Goldstein, K., 188
Goldstein, M. J., 228
Gollnick, D. M., 93
Golly, A., 229, 241, 257, 258
Gomez, A., 249
Gomez, L. F., 192
Gonzalez, J. J., 193
Gonzalez, P., 141
Goodman, J. F., 31, 32
Gore, J. C., 157
Gottesman, I. I., 231
Gottman, J., 276
Gould, S. J., 457, 458, 461
Gouvier, W. D., 426
Grager-Loidl, H., 468
Graham, S., 171, 172, 283
Grandin, T., 380
Granholm, E., 231
Graves, A., 162
Green, S. M., 257
Greenberg, F., 127
Greenberg, J. S., 492
Greenfield, D. B., 133
Greenhill, L. L., 189, 211
Greenspan, S., 114
Greenwood, C., 286
Greenwood, C. R., 58, 67, 98, 135
Greiner, A. R., 209
Gresham, F., 153
Gresham, F. M., 94, 114, 115, 155, 224, 229, 250, 252, 258
Gresham, T., 9
Griesdorn, J., 260

Griffin, H. C., 347
Griffin, P., 286
Griffin, S., 209
Griffith, P., 240, 276, 295, 296
Grigal, M., 70
Griswold, D. E., 73
Groden, J., 379
Gronna, S. S., 60
Gross, A. M., 234
Gross, M.U.M., 465, 479
Gross-Glenn, K., 157
Grskovic, J. A., 471
Gruber, H. E., 457
Guerrero, M., 99, 100
Guide Horse Foundation, 360
Guite, J., 195, 196
Guralnick, M., 276
Guralnick, M. J., 136
Guskin, K. A., 257
Gut, D., 222
Gutenbrunner, C., 158
Guterman, B. R., 51, 52

Habib, M., 157, 163
Hack, M., 121
Haddad, J., 142
Hadley, P. A., 286, 296
Hagen, E. P., 123
Hagerman, R. J., 119
Hagman, J. O., 157
Hagood, L., 400
Hale, J. B., 212
Hall, A., 471
Hall, B. D., 393
Hall, J., 199
Hall, R. V., 135
Hallahan, D. P., 6, 19, 22, 25, 42, 47, 54, 56, 57, 84, 95, 100, 101, 103, 105, 106, 151, 153, 155, 161, 162, 163, 164, 165, 167, 171, 172, 199, 206, 235, 249, 250, 251, 252, 254, 255, 283, 390, 503, 504
Hallenbeck, B. A., 253
Hallgren, B., 157
Hallowell, E. M., 215, 216, 217
Halpern, A. S., 69
Hamburger, S. D., 193
Hamby, R. S., 172
Hamilton, S., 135
Hammer, C. S., 292, 293
Hammill, D. D., 150, 154, 159, 162
Hammitte, D. J., 500
Hammond, M., 136, 276
Hamre-Nietupski, S., 141, 143
Hancock, T. B., 275, 292
Handwerk, M. J., 199
Haney, M., 400
Hanline, M. F., 501
Hanna, G. L., 245
Hanson, M. J., 430, 431, 439, 442, 445
Harding, M., 209

Hardman, M. L., 488, 494, 500, 501, 502
Harniss, M., 61
Harper, G. F., 58
Harper, L. V., 488
Harris, C. R., 457, 462, 475
Harris, J. J., 464, 469
Harris, J. R., 231, 234, 235
Harris, K. R., 171, 172, 206, 283
Harrison, M. M., 86
Harry, B., 99, 100, 101
Hart, B., 6, 286, 292
Hartas, D., 276
Hartsough, C., 258
Hartsough, C. S., 199
Hasazi, S. B., 70
Hatch, T., 457
Hatlen, P. H., 355
Hayes, J. S., 426
Hayes, S. P., 346
Haynes, O. M., 309, 329, 330
Haynes, W. O., 264, 288
Head, D. N., 352
Heal, L. W., 68, 69, 141, 142
Healey, E. C., 264
Heath, B., 61
Hechtman, L., 189, 211, 216
Hegarty, K., 430, 442
Hegeman, K., 471
Heller, K. A., 454, 456, 457, 461, 462, 463, 474
Heller, K. W., 388, 420, 422, 424, 425, 427, 428, 429, 430, 431, 432, 435, 436, 438, 439, 440, 442, 445, 446, 447, 448
Helman, E., 309, 323
Helmuth, L., 163
Hembree, R., 392, 393, 394
Hemmeter, M. L., 275
Hemsley, R. E., 68
Henao, G. C., 192
Henderson, C., 181
Hendrick, I. G., 25, 68
Henggeler, S. W., 229
Henriksen, L., 194
Herman, K. L., 180
Herman, S., 66
Hern, K. L., 193
Hernandez, M., 66, 292
Hewitt, J. K., 158
Heyes, T., 362
Hicks, D. M., 289
Higgins, C., 74
Higgins, E. L., 180
Hill, A., 358
Hilliard, A. G., 98
Hilvitz, P. B., 74
Hinshaw, S. P., 189, 198, 211
Hirsch, E. D., 82
Hitchings, W. E., 181, 182
Ho, T. P., 192
Hock, M. F., 180
Hockenberry, J., 490–491
Hockenbury, J. C., 19

Hodapp, R. M., 43, 117, 118, 119, 121, 122, 123, 125, 126, 395
Hodges, L., 392
Hodges, P., 323
Hodgkinson, H. L., 235
Hodson, B. W., 290
Hoeppner, J. B., 212
Hof, P. R., 117
Hoffbauer, D., 389
Hoffman, C. C., 72
Hoffman, L. M., 274
Hoffman-Kipp, P., 91
Hoffmann, H., 185, 186
Hoffmeister, R., 303, 308, 311, 312, 320, 325, 329, 330
Hohn, M., 252
Hokanson, C. R., Jr., 34, 59
Holahan, J. M., 471
Holahan, T., 222, 234, 235, 240, 250, 252, 253, 254, 258
Holbrook, M. C., 355
Holbrook, P. J., 62
Holburn, S. C., 43
Holcomb, T. K., 325
Holden-Pitt, L., 324
Hollenbeck, K., 61
Hong, J., 492
Hood, J., 157–158
Hopf, J. M., 157
Horne, D., 151
Horner, R., 134, 255
Horner, R. H., 74, 134, 141, 204, 255, 408, 409, 410
Horvath, M., 181, 182
Horwitz, B., 157
Horwitz, S., 83
Horwood, L. J., 192, 198
Hoskyn, M., 173
Howe, J., 141
Howe, K. R., 22
Howell, K. W., 255
Howley, A., 456
Howley, C. B., 456
Hoza, B., 211
Hudson, P., 202
Huefner, D. S., 26, 30, 60, 68, 73
Huer, M. B., 284
Huertas, J. A., 347
Huettig, C., 438
Hughes, C., 140, 254
Hughes, M. A., 126
Hughes, M. T., 55, 59, 176
Hull, J. M., 346, 348, 349
Hulleza, C., 66
Human Genome Management Information System, 116
Humphries, T., 93, 167, 303, 320, 325
Hunsaker, S. L., 461, 463
Hunter, A.G.W., 117
Hunter, S., 464
Hurley, C. M., 68

Hussey, W., 222, 234, 235, 240, 250, 252, 253, 254, 258
Hutchinson, M. K., 307
Hynd, G. W., 156, 193, 199

Iacono, W. G., 195
Ialongo, N. S., 222, 240, 243, 257
Ianuzzi, J. W., 355
Inge, K., 70, 71, 72, 415
Inglis, A., 157–158
Irvin, N., 489
Ishii-Jordan, S., 104
Ishii-Jordan, S. R., 245
Itard, J.M.G., 23–24
Ittenbach, R. F., 117, 118
Iverson, V. S., 414
Iwata, B. A., 407, 408, 410

Jaber, M., 195
Jackson, J., 284
Jackson, N. E., 479
Jacobsen, L. K., 193
Jacobson, J. W., 43, 114
Jakubecy, J. J., 40
Jallad, B., 157
James, M., 246–249
Janesick, V. J., 312
Jarwan, F. A., 463
Jayanthi, M., 168, 505
Jenkins, A., 206
Jenkins, A. A., 60
Jenkins, J., 55, 153
Jenkins, J. R., 47, 54, 67
Jenkins, L., 55, 198, 213
Jenne, W., 332
Jenner, A. R., 157
Jens, K., 239
Jensen, P., 211
Jensen, P. S., 207
Jensen, W. R., 253
Jernigan, K., 338, 368
Jernigan, T. L., 429
Jimenez, R., 90, 102
Jodry, W., 501
Joe, T., 48, 50
Joffee, E., 362
Johnson, C. P., 447
Johnson, G., 173
Johnson, L. J., 473, 480
Johnson, V., 283, 284, 285
Johnston, E. B., 293
Jolivette, K., 251
Jones, B. E., 331
Jones, C. J., 95
Jones, E. D., 468, 479
Jones, S. R., 195
Jons, P. H., 195
Jordan, D., 234
Judd, D., 351
Jurkiewicz, T., 66

Kahn, Joseph P., 9
Kahng, S. W., 407

Kail, R. V., 165
Kaiser, A. P., 63, 256, 275, 292
Kaiser, W. A., 157
Kakela, M., 179
Kalyanpur, M., 101
Kameenui, E. J., 203
Kamphaus, R. W., 123
Kamps, D. M., 256, 258
Kanbayashi, Y., 192
Kanner, L., 23
Kaplan, C., 286
Kaplan, H., 318
Karnes, M. B., 457, 473, 480
Karnish, K., 443
Karvonen, M., 43
Kasari, C., 124, 126
Kasius, M. C., 192
Kaslow, N. J., 244, 245
Kast, L., 405
Kastner, T. A., 43
Kastor, E., 48
Katkavich, J., 99, 100
Katsiyannis, A., 74, 94, 254, 259
Katz, L., 157
Katz, L. G., 67
Katz, W., 157
Kauffman, J. M., 6, 8, 11, 15, 18, 19, 22, 23, 25, 30, 40, 42, 44, 45, 47, 54, 55, 56, 57, 58, 68, 73, 84, 95, 100, 101, 103, 105, 106, 155, 161, 162, 163, 165, 171, 172, 206, 224, 225, 226, 229, 231, 232, 233, 235, 238, 244, 245, 249, 250, 251, 252, 253, 254, 255, 256, 257, 258, 259, 283, 380, 390, 407
Kaufman, A. S., 123
Kaufman, M., 467
Kaufman, N. L., 123
Kaufmann, F. A., 471
Kavale, K. A., 6, 51, 54, 152, 153, 165, 180, 199, 207, 209, 212, 225, 231, 232, 245, 383
Kavanagh, K., 229, 241, 257, 258
Kaye, E., 431
Kaysen, D., 193
Kazdan, S., 58, 177
Kazdin, A. E., 229, 231, 232, 244, 245, 252, 257, 259
Kellam, S., 222, 240, 243, 257
Keller, C. E., 172, 206
Kelley, M. L., 506
Kelly, B., 173
Kelly, P. S., 73
Kelly, R. R., 328
Kelso, M. H., 379, 382
Kemp, K., 202, 203
Kennedy, C. H., 406
Kennedy, D. N., 193
Kennedy, J., 143, 207
Kennedy, R., 82, 85
Kennell, J., 489

Keogh, B. K., 88, 176, 488
Kephart, N. C., 151
Kern, L., 205
Kerr, B., 473, 474
Kerr, M. M., 249
Kewley, G. D., 212
Kibby, M. Y., 156
Kidder, T., 104–105
Kiely, K., 195
Kim, S., 87, 95
Kimpston, R. D., 478
King, K., 58, 98
King-Sears, M. E., 58
Kinnish, K., 276
Kirchner, C., 369
Kirk, S. A., 151
Kirk, W. D., 151
Kirkpatrick, M. A., 74
Kita, M., 192
Kitano, M. K., 469
Klaus, M., 489
Kleege, G., 338, 354, 363
Klein, E., 479
Klein, H. B., 294, 295
Klein, M. D., 400
Klein, N., 121
Klein, R. G., 244
Klein-Tasman, B. P., 126
Klim, P., 196
Klima, E. S., 322
Klindworth, L. M., 155, 422, 424
Kline, S. A., 103
Klinger, J., 505
Klinger, J. K., 51, 58
Klingner, J. K., 176
Klobas, L., 50
Klockars, A. J., 288
Kluwin, T. N., 310, 312, 330
Knab, R., 157
Knight, J., 180
Knitzer, J., 224, 227, 250
Knowles, T., 406
Knowlton, A., 501
Knowlton, D., 240, 241
Kochanek, P. M., 385
Koenig, A. J., 341, 352, 355
Kogel, L. K., 409
Kogel, R. L., 409
Kohler, P. D., 70
Kohn, A., 205
Kohrman, C., 439
Kolitch, E. R., 482
Kolloff, P. B., 481
Kolstoe, O. P., 68, 70, 72
Koorland, M. A., 242
Korinek, L., 413
Kotin, R. A., 165
Kozol, J., 235
Kovatchev, B., 198
Kozol, J., 235
Kraemer, H. C., 211
Kraft, M., 260
Krain, A. L., 193
Kramer, A. F., 197

Krantz, P. J., 381
Kratochvil, M., 435
Kraus, S., 494
Kravets, M., 181
Kregel, J., 142
Kreimeyer, K. H., 310
Kucan, L., 202
Kudlick, C. J., 367
Kuilman, M., 117
Kuna, J., 116
Kuntze, M., 309, 323
Kupstas, F., 155, 422, 424
Kurowski, C. A., 244
Kurtz, L. A., 420, 422, 446
Kurtz, P. F., 231, 379, 382
Kushch, A., 157
Kuusisto, S., 7, 337–338, 359
Kwasnik, D. D., 197

La Grow, S., 362
Lacadie, C., 157
LaFleur, L. H., 56
Lahey, B. B., 257
LaHoste, G., 207
Lambert, N., 124
Lambert, N. M., 199
Lambie, R., 495
Lambros, K., 63, 258
Lambros, K. M., 115, 229
Lana, E. T., 325
Landau, S., 198
Landesman, S., 43
Landrum, M. S., 474, 475
Landrum, T. J., 225, 228, 229,
    240, 245
Lane, H., 303, 308, 311, 312,
    313, 317, 320, 325, 330, 331,
    333
Lane, K. L., 229
Lange, N., 193
Lansaw, J., 368
Lara, S. L., 66, 292
Larrivee, L. S., 292, 294
Larsen, S., 159, 162
Larsen, S. C., 154
Laski, F. J., 44
Lasley II, T. J., 170
Lattin, D. L., 447
Leake, B., 98
Leake, D., 98
Leaman, O., 442
Leavitt, L. A., 499
Ledford, D., 135
Lee, K., 133
Lee, S., 140
Lehmann, J. P., 500
Leigh, J. E., 154
Leinhardt, G., 155
Leland, H., 124
Lenhoff, H. M., 127
Lenz, B. K., 180
Leonard, L., 269
Leone, P. E., 254
Lerman-Sagie, T., 125, 126

Lerner, J. W., 66, 68, 166, 177,
    429, 430, 432, 439, 440
Lesar, S., 51
Leung, P.W.L., 192
Lev, D., 125, 126
LeVelle, J., 56
Levin, E. D., 195
Levin, J. R., 170
Levitt, J. G., 245
Levy, F., 196
Levy, S. E., 420, 422, 446
Lewis, B. A., 158
Lewis, D. K., 94
Lewis, J. F., 124
Lewis, M., 488
Lewis, R., 389, 390
Lewis, T., 134, 251, 255
Lewis, T. J., 255
Liaupsin, C., 134, 255
Liberman, A. M., 157
Lieberman, L. M., 54
Light, R., 389, 390
Lignugaris/Kraft, B., 141
Lilienfeld, A. M., 189
Linden, M. A., 22, 26, 30, 31,
    32, 35, 36, 52, 56, 60, 64, 68,
    73
Lindsey, J. E., 436, 448
Lipsey, M. W., 153
Listening Center at Johns
    Hopkins, 313
Livingston, S., 333
Llewellyn, A., 432
Lloyd, J. W., 6, 19, 54, 56, 95,
    155, 161, 162, 163, 171, 172,
    173, 206, 252, 283
Lloyd, L. L., 402, 404, 405
Lobb, C., 66
Lockhart, P. J., 430
Loe, S. A., 103
Loeb, D. F., 285
Loeber, R., 257
Logan, G. D., 196
Loncke, F., 406
Long, E. S., 406
Long, M., 286, 296
Long, N., 246–249
Long, N. J., 246
Longden, J. C., 370
Longmore, P. K., 50
Loomis, R., 141
Lopez, M. F., 94
Lopez-Reyna, N. A., 94, 161
Lopez-Torres, L., 91
Lorys, A. R., 193
Lou, H. C., 194
Lovance, K. J., 468
Lovecky, D. V., 465
Lowenthal, B., 66, 68, 429, 430,
    432, 439, 440
Loyd, B. H., 477
Lubinski, D., 473, 474
Lubs, H., 157
Luckasson, R., 110, 114

Lucker, J., 318
Luetke-Stahlman, B., 320
Luhaorg, H., 124
Luk, S. L., 192
Luna, M., 286, 296
Lunnen, K. Y., 57
Luzzo, D. A., 181, 182
Lyke, T., 430, 442
Lynch, M. D., 457, 462, 475
Lynskey, M. T., 192
Lyon, G. R., 152, 153

Maag, J. W., 74, 259
MacArthur, C., 283
MacMillan, D. L., 25, 30, 68,
    92, 94, 114, 115, 153, 155
MacMillan, D. M., 229
MacNeil, B., 302
Maestas y Moores, J., 320
Magill-Evans, J., 435
Magliocca, L. A., 502
Maheady, L., 58
Mahoney, G., 488, 499
Mahshie, J., 318
Maisog, J. M., 157
Mak, F. L., 192
Makuch, R. W., 471
Mallette, B., 58
Malmgren, K., 259
Maloney, P. L., 366
Mangold, S. S., 352
Mangrum, C. T., 181
Mank, D., 142
Mann, E. A., 137
Mann, V., 283
Manos, M. J., 207
Manstetten, R., 464
March, J. S., 211
Marchione, K. E., 157
Margolin, L., 467
Marolf, D. M., 479
Marsh, H. W., 464
Marsh, W. L., 193
Marshall, R., 193
Marshall, R. M., 199
Martella, R., 73
Martin, E. W., 19, 55
Martin, J. E., 43, 129
Martin, R. P., 234
Martindale, C., 457
Martinez, E. A., 503, 504
Martins, S., 192
Marvin, C. A., 405
Marx, E. S., 309, 329, 330
Masia, C. L., 244
Mass, L. C., 193
Mastin, M. E., 126
Mastropieri, M. A., 53, 170, 171
Matczynski, T. J., 170
Mather, S., 74, 255
Mathes, M. Y., 172, 206
Mathes, P., 178
Mathes, P. G., 153
Mathews, J., 89, 379, 454

Mathiason, C. S., 42
Mathur, S., 505
Matochik, J. A., 195
Matson, J. L., 381
Matthews, J., 268
Mattson, S. N., 429
Mattsson, E., 447
Mauer, P., 354
Maurer, M., 350
Maxwell, K., 494
McAdam, D. B., 352
McAfee, M., 99
McBride, J., 83
McCabe, L. A., 66, 292
McCain, A. P., 506
McCarthy, A. M., 427
McCaughrin, W. B., 142
McClannahan, L. E., 381
McCleary, C., 389, 390
McConnell, M. E., 74
McConnell, S., 258
McConnell, S. R., 258
McCord, B. E., 408
McCormick, K. M., 251
McCormick, L., 285
McCoun, M., 66
McCracken, J. T., 245
McCray, A. D., 55
McCrory, E., 157, 163
McCuller, G. L., 141
McCullough, J., 45, 252, 253
McDonald, J. L., 283, 284
McDonald, S., 386, 388, 389
McDonnell, L. M., 60, 93
McElroy, K., 172
McGaha, C. G., 365
McGauhey, P., 228
McGee, R., 192
McGoey, K. E., 205
McGrady, H. J., 166
McGregor, K. K. 00, 294
McGrew, K. S., 60
McGue, M. K., 195
McHenry, M. A., 288
McIntyre, L. L., 229
McIntyre, T., 105
McLaughlin, M. J., 60, 93
McLaughlin, P. J., 202, 203
McLaughlin, V. L., 413
McLean, M. E., 67, 410, 411
McMaster, K. N., 58, 177
McNeil, L. M., 61
McNergney, R. F., 82
McNutt, G., 154
McWilliam, R. A., 411, 494
Meadow-Orlans, K. P., 302,
    317, 330
Meagher, T. M., 432, 439
Meese, R. L., 160, 161, 173
Mehta, N., 117
Meister, C., 173
Mejia, S. E., 192
Melancon, F., 395
Menchel, R. S., 320

Mencl, W. E., 157
Mercer, A. R., 202
Mercer, C. D., 153, 202
Mercer, J. R., 124
Merkel, R. L., 198
Mertens, D. M., 317
Mervis, C. B., 126
Meserve, N. F., 271
Messer, S. C., 229
Metevia, L., 198, 213
Meyer, D. J., 494
Meyer, J., 158
Meyer, K. A., 406
Meyers, L., 173
Michael, M. G., 502
Michael, R. J., 427
Mick, E., 195, 199, 211, 216
Milberger, S., 196
Milburn, W. O., 320
Miles, B., 393, 396, 397, 398, 399
Milich, R., 198
Millar, D., 358
Millar, L., 74
Miller, J. F., 499
Miller, J. G., 229, 236, 260
Miller, J. H., 133, 164
Miller, L. J., 95, 159
Miller, S., 502
Miller, S. E., 72
Miller, S. P., 133
Mills, P. E., 47, 54, 67
Miltenberger, R. G., 406
Miner, I., 401
Minich, N. M., 121
Minnesota Laboratory for Low-Vision Research, 342
Minor, L., 397, 400
Minow, M., 96, 101
Mira, M. P., 387, 388, 389, 390
Miramontes, O. B., 22
Miranda, M. L., 192
Mirenda, P., 388, 402, 404, 405
Mirkin, P. K., 160
Mitchell, A., 117
Mitchell, A. L., 110
Mithaug, D. E., 43, 129
Moberly, R., 447
Mock, D. R., 18, 19, 40, 45, 54
Moldavsky, M., 125, 126
Moll, L. C., 45
Monks, F. J., 456, 457, 461, 462, 463, 474, 479, 481
Montague, M., 162, 167
Montgomery, D., 468
Moody, S. W., 47, 55, 59
Moon, M. S., 70, 71, 72, 139, 415
Moon, S. M., 471, 473, 475
Moore, G. P., 289
Moore, J., 436
Moorehouse, M., 198, 213
Moores, D. F., 312, 320
Mordica, J. A., 316

Morelli, G., 82
Morelock, M. J., 463, 473, 474
Morford, J. P., 322
Morison, P., 60, 93
Morningstar, M. E., 447
Morris, M. K., 244, 245
Morrison, J. H., 117
Morse, T. E., 132, 140
Morse, W. C., 15
Mortenson, B. P., 56
Mortweet, S. L., 58, 135
Mosely, M., 318
Moses, N., 294, 295
Moss, K., 400
Mostert, M. P., 6, 22, 57, 100, 101, 103, 106, 249, 250, 251, 254, 255, 390, 405, 412
Mota, V. L., 196
Mount, B., 414
Moyers, P., 309, 323
Moynihan, D. P., 235
MR/DD Data Brief, 141
Muir, D. W., 357
Mulick, J. A., 114
Muller, K., 158
Muller, N., 274
Munk, D., 505
Munk, D. D., 168
Murawski, W. W., 175
Murias, M., 207
Murphy, K. R., 196, 197, 216
Murray, C., 179
Myers, B. A., 432
Myles, B. S., 103, 378, 379, 382

Nace, K. L., 157
Nakamura, J., 457
Nakata, Y., 192
National Association of the Deaf, 328
National Center for Accessible Media, 328
National Center on Educational Restructuring and Inclusion, 27
National Early Intervention Longitudinal Study, 65
National Information Clearing House on Children Who Are Deaf-Blind, 393
National Institute of Neurological Disorders and Stroke, 119
National Institutes of Health, 189
National Joint Committee on Learning Disabilities, 154
National Research Council, 13, 376, 377, 379, 380, 382, 383–384, 405
National Theatre of the Deaf, 311
Naylor, C. E., 157
Neal, L. I., 55

Neel, R. S., 259
Neisworth, J. T., 258
Nelson, C., 505
Nelson, C. M., 134, 224, 229, 249, 250, 252, 254, 255, 258, 259
Nelson, J., 505
Nelson, J. R., 59, 61, 62, 73, 74, 94, 206
Nelson, K. B., 424
Nelson, K. L., 255
Nelson, M., 52, 53, 54
Nelson, N. W., 264, 266, 268, 269, 274, 277, 278, 284, 287, 290, 292, 293, 294, 295, 388, 405
Neuhaus, C., 481
Newcorn, J. H., 211
Newman, L. R., 302
Newsom, C., 379, 382
Newton, J. S., 141
Nielsen, E., 63, 258
Nielsen, J. B., 194
Nietupski, J., 141, 143
Nihira, K., 124
Nisbet, J., 109, 141
Noble, K. D., 482
Noell, G. H., 56
Novey, E. S., 193

Obiakor, F. E., 80, 85, 93, 94, 95, 97, 99, 106
Ochaita, E., 347
O'Cleirigh, M., 352
O'Connor, R., 153, 158
Odom, S. L., 67, 410, 411
O'Donnell, D., 209
Oetting, J. B., 283, 284
Ogbu, J. U., 87
Ogletree, B. T., 57
Ogline, J. S., 196
Oken-Fried, M., 405, 406
Olenchak, F. R., 471
Oley, C. A., 393
Olney, M. F., 143
Olson, D., 54
Olson, R., 157
Olson, R. K., 152, 153, 196
Olson-Tinker, H., 229
Olvera, R. L., 207
Omvig, J. H., 355, 402
Onslow, M., 291
Oosterlaan, J., 196
Ormsbee, C. K., 56
Ormsond, G. I., 494
Ortiz, A. A., 94, 102, 284
O'Shea, D. J., 489, 497, 500
O'Shea, L. J., 489, 500
Osher, D., 72
Osher, T., 508
Ostrander, R., 244
Ostrosky, M. M., 275
Oswald, D. P., 92, 93, 98, 245
Otaiba, S., 177

Otaiba, S. A., 58
Otomo, K., 308
Ovando, C. J., 102
Overweg, J., 117
Owen, S. V., 471, 474
Owens, E. B., 211, 234, 257
Owens, R. E., 271, 274, 275, 278, 281

Paatsch, L. E., 315
Paclwaskyj, T., 381
Padden, C., 93
Padden, C. A., 303, 310, 320, 325
Paden, E., 264
Page, T., 472
Pain, K., 435
Painter, K. M., 309, 329, 330
Palmer, D. S., 52, 53, 54, 136
Palmer, S. B., 43, 129
Paramboukas, A. A., 274
Parette, H. P., 498
Park, C. C., 373
Parmar, R. S., 133, 164
Parra, J., 425
Partridge, M. F., 133
Pasamanick, B., 189
Pascualvaca, D., 195
Passow, A. H., 463
Patnode, M., 74
Patterson, C. J., 6, 234
Patterson, G. R., 6, 232, 242, 252
Patterson, O., 85
Patton, J. M., 95, 97, 103
Patton, J. R., 74, 117, 118
Patton, R. S., 140
Paul, P. J., 274
Paulesu, E., 157, 163
Pavri, S., 105
Peacock Hill Working Group, 250, 252, 258, 260
Pearl, R., 164
Pease, L., 396
Pelham, W. E., 189, 209, 211
Pelkey, L., 148
Pendarvis, E. D., 456
Pennington, B. F., 157, 195, 196, 199
Perez-Pereira, M., 346
Perl, D. P., 117
Perleth, C., 479, 481
Perret, Y. M., 423, 424, 425, 428
Person, J., 142
Petch-Hogan, B., 498
Peters, W.A.M., 468
Peterson, R. L., 72, 73
Pettee, Y., 492
Pfiffner, L. J., 208
Philips, L., 179
Phillips, S., 332
Phillips, S. E., 155
Pierce, B., 7, 8
Pierce, K., 231, 379, 382
Pierce, T., 133

Pierro, C., 491
Pindzola, R. H., 264, 288
Pineda, D., 192
Pinel, J. P. J. , 195
Pinel, P. J., 117, 122
Pisha, B., 63, 318
Plain-Switzer, K., 358
Plante, E., 264, 282, 283
Pless, I. B., 422
Pliszka, S. R., 207
Plomin, R., 234, 461
Plucker, J. A., 464, 481
Polcarl, A., 193
Polloway, E., 505
Polloway, E. A., 74, 140, 168
Pomeroy, J. C., 245
Pomplun, M., 58
Ponchilla, P., 362
Porter, W., 239
Position Statement of National
    Association for the
    Education of Young
    Children and National
    Association of Early
    Childhood Specialists in
    State Departments of
    Education, 57
Poteet, J. A., 95, 159
Powell, T. H., 494, 495
Power, D.T.J., 192
Power, P. W., 385, 387, 388,
    389, 390
Powers, L. E., 432, 438
Prater, M. A., 206
Prentice, K., 58, 177
Presley, J. A., 254
Prestholdt, P. H., 426
Prevent Blindness America, 343
Price, C., 157
Price, C. J., 157
Price, H. B., 82, 85
Prince, S., 379
Prinz, P. M., 309, 323
Prizant, B. M., 274, 292, 294
Pruett, K. M., 369
Psarros, C., 315
Psychological Corporation, 158
Pugach, M. C., 59, 60
Pugh, K. R., 157
Pullen, P. L., 11, 253
Pungello, E., 138
Pyfer, J., 438

Queen, O., 166, 180
Quigley, S., 332
Quinn, M. M., 222, 234, 235,
    240, 250, 252, 253, 254, 258

Rabian, B., 244
Rabin, M., 157
Rack, J., 157
Rainer, D. D., 56
Rainforth, B., 443
Raja, S. N., 192

Rajapakse, J. C., 193
Rakes, T. A., 95, 159
Ramey, C. T., 138
Ramos-Ford, V., 457
Ramp, K. A., 260
Ramsey, E., 229, 234, 235, 237,
    240, 242, 243, 244, 249, 250,
    253, 254, 257, 258, 260
Rapoport, J. L., 193
Rapp, A. J., 348
Rapp, D. W., 348
Rapp, J. T., 406
Raskind, M. H., 180
Raskind, W. H., 157, 158
Raspberry, W., 285
Ratey, J. J., 215, 216, 217
Ratner, N. B., 264
Ratnofsky, A. C., 431
Rattigan, K., 315
Ratzeburg, F. H., 203
Rayfield, R., 142
Raynes, M., 58
Reader, M. J., 193
Reavis, H. K., 253
Reddy, S. S., 135
Reed, E., 195
Reeve, A., 110
Reeve, R. E., 167, 209
Rehm, L. P., 244, 245
Reich, A. R., 288
Reichard, A., 447
Reichle, J., 402
Reid, J. B., 6, 232, 242, 252
Reid, R., 172, 192, 206
Reiff, H. B., 105, 179, 180
Reinherz, H. Z., 229
Reis, S. M., 461, 479
Reiss, A. L., 193
Reitman, D., 234
Remschmidt, H., 158
Renshaw, P. F., 193, 196
Renzulli, J. S., 461, 479
Repp, A. C., 19
Reschly, D. J., 92
Retish, P., 181, 182
Revell, W. G., 142
Reynolds, A. J., 137
Reynolds, C. A., 158
Reynolds, C. R., 123
Rhode, G., 253
Richards, P. L., 25
Richards, T. L., 156, 157
Richardson, G. A., 228
Richman, L. C., 427
Richters, J. E., 189
Riedel, T. M., 252
Riley, E. P., 429
Riley, J. E., 497
Rimm, S. B., 468
Risley, T. R., 6, 292
Ristow, R., 181, 182
Ritacco, D. G., 212
Ritchie, G. F., 193
Rittenhouse, R. K., 470

Rivera, D. P., 124
Roach, M. A., 499
Robenalt, K., 488
Roberts, M., 74, 255
Roberts, P. H., 153
Roberts, S., 323
Robertson, D. L., 137
Robillard, K., 351
Robin, D. A., 291
Robinson, H., 119
Robinson, N. M., 481
Robinson, R. L., 288, 291
Roche, L., 464
Rodriguez, M. S., 325
Rodriguez, P., 492
Rodriguez, R., 82
Rodriguez-Gil, G., 399
Roe, J., 347, 348, 357
Roeper, A., 461
Roessler, R. T., 370
Rogawski, M. A., 425
Rogers, A. S., 429
Rogers, D., 27
Rogers, E. L., 27
Rogers, K. B., 478
Rogers, M. E., 189
Rogers-Adkinson, D., 240
Rogers-Adkinson, D. L., 276,
    277, 295, 296
Rogoff, B., 82
Rohde, L. A., 192
Roman, R., 284
Rooney, K. J., 203
Rosegrant, T., 412
Rosen, M., 43
Rosenkrans, C. B., 167
Rosenshine, B., 173
Rosenshine, R., 202, 203
Ross, D. B., 352
Rosselli, H. C., 475
Rosselli, M., 192
Rotherham, A. J., 34, 59
Rourke, B. P., 167
Rovig, L., 369
Rowley, J. B., 170
Rozalski, M. E., 72, 73, 254
Rubia, K., 196
Rueda, R., 45, 87, 95, 161
Ruef, M., 134, 255
Ruef, M. B., 74
Rumrill, P. D., 370
Rumsey, J. M., 157
Ruscello, D. M., 273, 274
Rusch, F. R., 68, 141, 142
Russell, K. Y., 82
Rutberg-Kuskin, J., 362
Rutherford, R. B., 254
Rutherford, R. J., 74, 255
Rutter, M., 158, 229
Ryles, R., 356
Rzanny, R., 157

Sachse-Lee, C., 165
Sacks, O., 322, 377, 380, 473

Sacks, S. Z., 369
Saenz, L., 58
Safford, E. H., 25
Safford, P. L., 25
Safran, S. P., 50
Sager, N., 239
Sagvolden, T., 195
Saigh, P. A., 235
Sailor, W., 44, 58, 134, 255
Sainato, D. M., 67
Sale, P., 54
Salembier, G. B., 508
Salend, S. J., 52
Salzberg, C. L., 141
Sample, P. L., 259
Sandall, S., 410
Sandall, S. R., 307
Sapon-Shevin, M., 467, 476
Sarant, J. Z., 315
Sarason, S. B., 34
Saraste, H., 427
Sarfatti, S. E., 193
Sass-Lehrer, M. A., 317
Sasso, G. M., 51, 54, 74, 255
Sattler, J. M., 123
Savage, R. C., 386, 387
Savner, J. L., 73
Sawyer, V., 505
Schachar, R., 196
Schatz, T., 479, 481
Schaughency, E. A., 192
Scheetz, N. A., 392
Schiefelbusch, R. L., 285
Schildroth, A. N., 308
Schiller, E., 211
Schirmer, B. R., 305, 307, 309,
    310, 319, 323, 324, 326, 330
Schley, G. S., 58
Schloss, C. N., 506
Schloss, P. J., 506
Schmeidler, E., 369
Schmidt, M. H., 192
Schmitz, M., 192
Schnur, R., 462, 463, 469
Schofield, J. W., 83
Schopler, E., 229
Schreibman, L., 231, 379, 382
Schroedel, J. G., 331
Schroeder, F. K., 354, 355
Schulte-Korne, G., 158
Schumaker, J. B., 180
Schumm, J. S., 47, 51, 56, 57,
    59, 176, 208
Schuster, J. W., 132, 140
Schuyler, B. R., 370
Schwartz, A. A., 43
Schwartz, I., 501
Schwartz, R. G., 290
Schwartz, S., 283
Schwartzman, M. N., 388, 420,
    422, 424, 425, 427, 428, 429,
    430, 431, 432, 435, 436, 439,
    440, 442, 446, 448
Schweinhart, L. J., 137

Scialli, P. M., 363
Sciuto, L., 424, 447
Scorgie, K., 492
Scott, M. S., 133
Scott, R. M., 255
Scott, T., 134, 255
Scott-Olson, K., 317
Scruggs, T. E., 53, 170, 171
Seaver, A., 496
Secord, W. A., 271
Seewald, A., 155
Seidenberg, P. L., 283
Seidl, B., 58
Seidman, L. J., 216
Seligman, M., 502
Seligman, M. E., 167
Selmi, A. M., 309, 329, 330
Seltzer, M. M., 492, 494
Semmel, M. I., 51, 54
Semrud-Clikeman, M., 193, 196
Senna, J. J., 229
Sergeant, J. A., 195, 196, 207
Serna, L., 63
Serna, L. A., 258
Severe, J. B., 211
Severson, H., 63, 229, 241, 257, 258
Severson, H. H., 236, 258
Seward, R., 198
Sexton, M., 172
Seymour, H. N., 283, 284, 285
Shaklee, B. D., 474, 475
Shames, G. H., 271
Shankweiler, D. P., 157
Shapiro, E. S., 205, 206
Sharma, J., 236
Shavelle, R., 43
Shaw, D. S., 234, 257
Shaywitz, B. A., 152, 153, 155, 157, 177, 471
Shaywitz, S. E., 152, 153, 155, 157, 177, 471
Shelter News, 431
Shelton, T. L., 198, 213
Sheras, P. L., 244, 245
Sherburne, S., 258
Sheridan, M., 299–300
Sherman, D. K., 195
Sherman, T., 231
Shermer, M., 461
Shields, C. M., 476
Shields, D., 263
Shimabukuro, S. M., 206
Shiraga, B., 141
Short, E. J., 167, 207
Short-Camilli, C., 239
Shriner, J. G., 60, 61, 73
Shukla, S., 406
Siegel, G. M., 264, 291
Siegel, L., 325
Siegel, L. J., 229
Siegel, S., 105–106, 251, 259, 260
Silberg, J. L., 158

Silva, P., 192
Silver, S. E., 229
Silverman, L. K., 462
Silverman, W., 117
Silverman, W. K., 244
Simmerman, A., 286, 296
Simonoff, E., 158
Simpson, R. L., 46, 103, 378, 379, 382
Simpson, S., 211
Sinclair, M. F., 68
Singer, B., 318, 331
Singer, G.H.S., 25, 99, 432, 438
Singh, N. N., 19, 94, 98, 99, 245
Singleton, J. L., 322
Siperstein, G. N., 114, 153, 155
Siple, L. A., 331, 332
Sitlington, P. L., 68, 70, 72, 143, 259
Skeels, H. M., 122
Skiba, R. J., 72, 73
Skinner, D., 492
Skinner, J., 434
Skinner, M. E., 182
Skolnik, R., 207
Sleator, E. K., 192
Slomka, G. T., 117
Smith, B. H., 209
Smith, B. J., 63, 72, 410, 411
Smith, C. R., 499
Smith, D. J., 206
Smith, J., 43, 141
Smith, J. D., 23, 110, 114
Smith, T. E., 140
Smith J. D., 40
Smutny, J. F., 475
Snell, J. W., 193
Snell, M., 58
Snell, M. E., 132, 140, 374, 407, 414
Snow, C., 286
Snowling, M., 286
Snyder L., 153
Sobsey, D., 492
Solanto, M. V., 207
Soltz, D. F., 333
Sonuga-Barke, E.J.S., 207
Soto, G., 284
Southern, W. T., 468, 479
Sowell, T., 275, 277
Sowers, J., 432, 438
Sparks, L., 117
Sparrow, S. S., 124
Spekman, N. J., 180
Spencer, J. M., 80, 82, 83
Spencer, P., 315
Spencer, P. E., 330
Spencer, T., 195, 199, 209, 211, 216
Spiegel, G. L., 426
Spiker, D., 499
Sprague, J., 63, 64, 72, 230, 244, 256, 260

Sprague, J. R., 74, 134, 408, 410
Sridhar, D., 166
Stainback, S., 44, 48, 51
Stainback, W., 44, 48, 51
Stancliffe, R. J., 43, 141
Stanley, F. J., 424
Stanley, J. C., 479, 481–482
Stark, K. D., 244
Stein, M., 6, 250, 251, 255–256
Steinberg, Z., 250
Steingard, R. J., 193, 196
Stella, J., 378
Sternberg, R. J., 456, 457, 458, 460, 461, 462, 463, 474, 477
Stevenson, J., 195
Stewart, D. A., 329
Stichter, J. P., 74, 251, 255
Stieber, S., 259
Still, G. F., 186
Stiller, B., 229, 241, 257, 258
Stinson, M. S., 310, 328
Stocking, V. B., 464, 481
Stodden, R. A., 141
Stoel-Gammon, C., 308
Stokes, P. D., 457
Stokoe, W. C., 322
Stone, P., 319
Stoneman, Z., 491, 492
Storch, E. A., 244
Stormont, M., 471
Stothard, S., 286
Strain, P. S., 64, 66, 67, 224, 229, 250, 252, 258, 411
Strauch, J. D., 141
Strauss, A. A., 151, 188
Strauss, D., 43
Stretton, K., 135
Strichart, S. S., 181
Strick, L., 499
Strong, M., 309, 310, 323
Struck, D., 10
Stuckless, R., 329
Stuebing, K. K., 152, 153
Sturm, C. C., 164
Sturm, J. J., 274
Styfco, S. J., 63
Subotnik, R. F., 456, 457, 461, 462, 463, 474
Sudhalter, V., 126
Sugai, G., 73, 74, 134, 255
Sullivan, J. E., 352
Sullivan-Burstein, K., 168, 505
Summers, C. R., 491, 492
Summers, M., 491, 492
Sunohara, G., 196
Supplee, P., 468
Sutherland, K. S., 250
Svenson, E., 58, 177
Swanson, H. L., 165, 173, 175
Swanson, J., 207
Swanson, J. D., 469
Swanson, J. M., 189, 207, 211
Swearer, S., 244
Sweda, J., 171

Sweeney, D. P., 232, 245, 383
Sweet, M., 141
Swiatek, M. A., 454, 478
Szabo, J. L., 443
Szatmari, P., 192
Szekeres, S. F., 271

Tagalakis, V., 351
Takaki, Ronald, 99
Talbott, E., 229
Tallal, P., 157
Tankersley, M., 206, 228, 229, 240, 256, 258, 276, 294
Tannenbaum, A. J., 461, 462, 463, 465
Tanners, A., 181, 182
Tannhauser, M. T., 203
Tannock, R., 167, 196
Tapscott, K. E., 73
Tarver, S. G., 167
Taylor, E., 192, 207
Taylor, H., 28
Taylor, H. G., 121
Taylor, O., 284
Taylor, R. L., 93, 94, 124
Teach English, 96
Teelucksingh, W., 59, 61, 62, 94
Teicher, M. H., 193
Temple, J. A., 137
Terry, B. J., 58, 98
Terwilliger, J., 95
Test, D. W., 43, 70, 142
Thomas, A., 231
Thomas, C., 82
Thomas, C. L., 119
Thomas, J. M., 257
Thompson, A., 58, 177
Thompson, B., 57
Thompson, L., 66
Thompson, L. A., 158, 461
Thompson, R. H., 407, 408
Thompson, T., 126
Thomson, R. J., 410
Thorndike, R. L., 123
Thorp, E. K., 67
Throneburg, R. N., 274
Thurlow, M. L., 59, 60, 61, 62, 94
Tiegerman-Farber, E., 266
Timm, M. A., 64, 66, 258
Tindal, G., 61
Tinsley, V., 124
Tobin, T., 260
Tobin, T. J., 63, 74
Todd, A. W., 134, 408, 410
Togher, L., 386, 388, 389
Tomlinson, C., 474
Tomporowski, P. D., 124
Tompson, M. C., 228
Tooer, R., 315
Torgesen, J. K., 151, 153, 162, 165, 167, 177, 178
Torguson, C., 99, 100
Tramontina, S., 192

Treffinger, D. J., 467
Trent, J. W., 25
Trent, S. C., 6, 22, 57, 85, 91, 100, 101, 103, 106, 249, 250, 251, 254, 255, 390
Trimble, M. M., 427
Tripp, G., 196
Trivette, C. M., 501
Trommer, B., 212
Tsuang, M. T., 196
Tunick, R. A., 196
Turnbull, A. P., 134, 255, 486, 496, 500
Turnbull, H. R., 134, 225, 447, 486, 496, 500
Turner, G., 119
Turner, L., 124
Tyler, J. S., 387, 388, 389, 390, 425

Ullman, R. K., 192
Ulrey, P., 360
Umansky, L., 50
Umbarger, G. T., 447
University of Minnesota, 43
Uribe, V., 105
U.S. Department of Education, 12, 16, 26, 66, 67, 68, 92, 93, 94, 102, 155, 175, 191, 228, 229, 231, 255, 266, 324, 392, 422
U.S. Department of Health and Human Services, 229
U.S. Office of Special Education Programs, 409
Utley, B., 258
Utley, C. A., 58, 80, 85, 93, 94, 95, 98, 99, 106, 135

Vadasy, P. F., 494
Vaden-Klernan, N., 222, 240, 243, 257
Vaituzis, A. C., 193
Valente, E., 258
van der Ende, J., 192
Van Deventer, P., 141
van Huffelen, A. C., 117
Van Keulen, J. E., 94, 97, 102, 284
Van Reusen, A. K., 352
Van Tassel-Baska, J., 475, 478, 479
Vandercook, T., 414
VanderHart, N. S., 141, 143
Vanderwood, M., 60
vanLeeuwen, T., 196
vanWijk, J., 117
Vaughn, B. J., 409
Vaughn, S., 47, 51, 54, 55, 56, 57, 58, 59, 166, 173, 176, 208, 250, 505

Vauss, Y. C., 193
Verhulst, F. C., 192
Verstegen, D. A., 27
Vianello, A., 424, 447
Vincent, M., 309, 323
Vining, E.P.G., 425
Visser, F. E., 117
Vitiello, B., 211
Voeller, K. K., 193

Wada, K., 192
Wadsworth, S. J., 158
Wagner, B. R., 131
Wagner, M., 141, 179
Wake, S., 119
Wales, R. J., 315
Walker, B., 435
Walker, D., 135, 286
Walker, H., 63, 64, 72, 230, 244, 256
Walker, H. M., 63, 74, 224, 229, 234, 235, 236, 237, 240, 241, 242, 243, 244, 249, 250, 252, 253, 254, 257, 258, 259, 260
Walker, L. A., 322, 333
Walker, T., 86
Wallace, D. B., 457
Wallach, G. P., 283, 296
Wallen, N. E., 188
Walther-Thomas, C., 379, 380, 413
Wang, P. P., 127
Wang, W., 254
Warburton, R., 195
Ward, K. M., 447
Ward, T. B., 457
Warger, C., 505
Warger, C. L., 59, 60
Warren, D. H., 346, 352
Warren, S., 124
Warren, S. F., 276
Watkins, J. M., 231
Watkins, R., 264
Wax, I. F., 181
Webb, T., 119
Weber, C., 66
Webster, A., 347, 348, 357
Wechsler, D., 123
Wechsler, H. A., 98
Weddington, G. T., 94, 97, 102, 284
Wegiel, J., 117
Wehby, J. H., 58, 250, 258
Wehman, P., 139, 142
Wehmeyer, M., 413
Wehmeyer, M. L., 43, 129
Weihenmayer, E., 368
Weikart, D. P., 137
Weinrich, B. D., 293
Weisner, T., 88
Weiss, A. L., 292, 293

Weiss, G., 216
Weiss, L., 214
Weiss, M., 216
Weissberg-Benchell, J., 167
Wells, K., 211
Werner, E. E., 6
Werner, H., 151, 188
West, M., 142
West, R. P., 206
Westby, C. E., 284, 285, 287
Westling, D. L., 126, 128, 129, 413, 414, 415
Wetsel, W. C., 195
Whedon, C., 171
Wheeden, C. A., 499
Wheeler, L. C., 347
White, D. A., 458
White, R., 249
White, R. B., 242
White, S. J., 279, 282
Whitmire, K., 310
Whitmore, J. K., 87
Whittle, J., 355
Wickham, D., 134, 255
Widaman, K., 136
Widaman, K. F., 68
Wiener, W. R., 362
Wigal, T., 211
Wiig, E. H., 271
Wilcox, B. L., 134, 255
Wilcox, M. J., 276
Wilens, T., 195, 199, 209, 211, 216
Wilens, T. E., 212
Wilkins, R., 80, 99
Wilkinson, M. E., 342, 343
Willard-Holt, C., 471
Willcutt, E. G., 196, 199
Williams, A. L., 290
Williams, B. T., 413
Williams, K., 379, 381
Williams, M. E., 231
Williams, P. J., 83, 84
Willows, D. M., 164
Wilson, D., 249
Wingate, M. E., 264
Winslow, E. B., 234, 257
Winston, E., 318
Winton, A.S.W., 94
Winzer, M. A., 23
Wise, B., 157
Wise, B. W., 153
Wisniewski, H. M., 117
Witt, J. C., 56
Witte, R., 205, 206
Witte, R. H., 179
Woerner, W., 192
Wolcott, G. F., 386
Wolery, M., 132, 140, 258
Wolf, L. C., 491
Wolf, M. M., 260

Wolfensberger, W., 40
Wolk, S., 308, 309
Wolkomir, R., 322
Wolman, C., 439
Wolraich, M. L., 192
Wood, F., 157
Wood, F. B., 157
Wood, F. H., 246
Wood, M. M., 246
Wood, W., 139
Wood, W. M., 43, 70
Woodley-Zanthos, P., 120
Woodward, J., 54, 102, 164
Woodward, L. J., 198
Woolsey, M. L., 58
Wooten, I.L., 403
Worling, D. E., 167
Wormsley, D. P., 353
Worsdell, A. S., 407
Wortham, A., 97
Wright, L., 462, 463, 469, 470
Wright, M., 315
Wright, S., 249
Wu, M., 211
Wunder, G., 358, 364
Wyer, K., 63
Wynne, S. K., 207

Yairi, E., 264
Yamaki, K., 86
Yan, W., 164
Yanb, L., 58
Yang, N., 58, 177
Yarbrough, D., 427
Yell, M. L., 22, 26, 27, 30, 60, 61, 68, 72, 73, 254
Yen, L., 177
Yetter, C. I., 426
Yoder, D. E., 405
Yoder, P. J., 124, 276
York, J., 141, 414
Yorkston, K. M., 290, 291, 402
Young, K. R., 206
Yovanoff, P., 142
Ysseldyke, J. E., 54, 60

Zametkin, A. J., 195
Zamora-Duran, G., 92, 94, 99
Zanglis, I., 251
Zaucha, K., 389, 390
Zelder, E. Y., 28
Zentall, S., 471
Zhang, L., 458
Ziegler, A., 454
Zigler, E., 43, 63, 121
Zigmond, N., 22, 23, 55, 72, 155
Zimmerman, H., 192
Zmijewski, G., 331
Zurkowski, J. K., 73
Zwernik, K., 414

Subject Index

Page numbers followed by *t* and *f* refer to tables and figures respectively. Page numbers in bold indicate the page on which the subject is defined in a marginal note.

AAC. *See* Augmented or alternative communication
AAMR. *See* American Association on Mental Retardation
AAMR Adaptive Behavior Scale-Residential and Community Edition, 124
AAMR Adaptive Behavior Scale-School, Second Edition, 124
Abecedarian Project, 137–138
Abuse. *See* Neglect and abuse
Academic skills/achievement. *See also* Intelligence; Intelligence quotient (IQ) tests; IQ-achievement discrepancies
  and culture, 87–88
  in hearing impairment, 309–310
  in mental retardation, 131–132
  in physical disabilities, 432
  preacademic skills and, 177
  in visual impairment, 348
Acadians, Usher syndrome and, 395
Acceleration, **475–479**
Accessibility, of Internet, 62–63
  in hearing impairment, 328
  in visual impairment, 364
Accommodation of exceptionality
  in giftedness, 465–467
  in homework, 505
  in learning disabilities, 181
  in physical disabilities, 438–439, 445
  in standardized testing, 60–61, 61*t*
  teacher's role in, 19
  in visual impairment, 353
Acquired aphasia, **388–389**
Acquired immune deficiency syndrome (AIDS), **429**
Acute, **422**
ADA. *See* Americans with Disabilities Act
Adapted physical education (APE), 438
Adapted signs, **399,** 402–403
Adaptive Behavior Inventory for Children, 124
Adaptive devices, **435–436**
Adaptive skills, **198**
  in ADHD, 198
  in mental retardation, **112**
    assessment of, 123
Adderall, **207**
ADHD. *See* Attention-deficit hyperactivity disorder
ADHD-Rating Scale–IV, 192
Adventitiously deaf, **302**
Advocacy, 10, 506–509
Affective disorder, **227**
African Americans. *See also* Communication variations (dialects); Minorities

African-American immersion schools, 98
  and Afrocentric instruction, 97
  and assessment fairness, 93–95
  emotional/behavioral disorders in, 260
  giftedness and, 469
  percentage in special education, 92–93, 92*f*
Aggression, **241**
  in emotional/behavioral disorders, 240–244
  as learned behavior, 241–242
  in multiple severe disabilities, 407–408
AIDS (acquired immune deficiency syndrome), **429**
Alcohol. *See also* Fetal alcohol syndrome
  emotional/behavioral disorders and, 231
Alzheimer's Disease, Down syndrome and, 117
American Academy of Pediatrics, ADHD diagnostic criteria, 194*t*
American Association on Mental Retardation (AAMR), 44
  classifications for severity of retardation, 113–114, 113*t*
  definition of mental retardation, 112–114
  on self-determination, 127, 130
American Printing House for the Blind, 357
American Psychiatric Association
  definition of ADHD, 189
  definition of autism, 377
  definition of mental retardation, 114
American Psychological Association
  definition of emotional/behavioral disorders, 226
  definition of mental retardation, 114
American School of the Deaf, 24
American Sign Language (ASL), **266**
  deaf culture and, 310–311, 317, 323–324
  as true language, 301, 309, 322
American Speech-Language-Hearing Association (ASHA), 284–285, 289
  definitions of communication disorders, 266–267, 270–271
Americans with Disabilities Act (1990) [ADA], **26,** 27–28, 35, 448
Amniocentesis, **118**
Anoxia, **120**
Antecedents, in functional behavior assessment, 134
Anxiety disorder, **227**
Aphasia, acquired, **388–389**
Appropriate education, legal right to, 30
Apraxia, **291**
Aqueous humor, **341,** 342*f*
The ARC (formerly the Association for Retarded Citizens), 26
  in Human Genome Project, 116
  on self-determination, 127
Arthritis, misconceptions about, 421
Articulation, **266**
  disorders of, 267, 289–290
AS. *See* Asperger syndrome

ASHA. *See* American Speech-Language-Hearing Association

Asian/Pacific Islanders, percentage in special education, 92, 92*f*

ASL. *See* American Sign Language

Asperger syndrome (AS), **376,** 379
 prevalence of, 380

Assessment. *See also* Functional behavioral assessment;
  Standardized testing; *individual disorders*
 of adaptive areas, 124
 authentic, **161**
 classroom teacher's role in, 19–22
 curriculum-based, **95, 160**–161
 definition of, 93
 discrimination in, and federal law, 29
 fairness to minorities, 29, 93–95, 101–102, 110, 124
 federal law on, 29, 60, 255
 formative, **159**–161
 IEPs requirements for, 60
 of instructional environment, 95
 preassessment teams, **56**
 standards-based reforms in, 59–62, 72
 of vision, 343

Assessment of Adaptive Areas, 124

Assistance cards, **401**

Assistive technology. *See* Technology, assistive

Association for Children with Learning Disabilities, 150

Association for Persons with Severe Handicaps (TASH), 374

Association for Retarded Citizens. *See* [The] ARC

Asthma, **428**–430

Astigmatism, **344**

At-risk students, 19

Athetosis, 446, **447**

ATMs, voice-guided, 362, 363*f*

Atresia, **394**

Attention deficit disorder (ADD), 189

Attention-deficit hyperactivity disorder (ADHD)
 adult persistence of, 187, 214–215
  management of, 216–218, 217*t*
 assessment of, 187, 192–193, 194*t*
  in adults, 214–215, 215*t*
 Barkley's model of, 196–198
 brain areas affected in, 193–195, 194*f*
 causes of, 187, 193–196
 coexisting conditions, 199–200
 conduct disorder and, 188
 definition of, 189
 diagnostic criteria for, 190
 early intervention in, 213
 educational programming for, 200–204
 emotional/behavioral problems in, 188–189, 199–200, 241
 and gender, 192
 in gifted children, 470–471
 hereditary factors in, 195
 history of, 186–189
 hyperactivity in, 187, 189–190
 and inclusion, 202–203
 instructional methods for, 197, 204–209, 208*t*
 in learning disabilities, 165
 management in adults, 216–218, 217*t*
 medication for, 207–213
 misconceptions about, 187

numbers served in special education, 191, 191*f*
 perseveration in, 188
 prevalence of, 189–192
 psychological and behavioral characteristics, 196–200
 reality of, 186–187
 service delivery models, 207
 social skills/development in, 187, 198–199
 substance abuse and, 187, 199–200, 211–213
 toxins and medical factors in, 195–196
 transition programs in, 214–218
 treatment of, 187
 types of, 189–190

Attitudinal deafness, 310

Audiologist, **305**–306

Audiometric zero, **305**

Audiometry, **305**–306

Auditory habilitation, **319**

Auditory-verbal approach, **319**

Augmented or alternative communication (AAC), **266,** 267
 in multiple severe disabilities, 402–406

Auricle, **303**

Authentic assessment, in learning disabilities, **161**

Autism, **228**–229, **374.** *See also* Autistic spectrum disorder
 behavioral characteristics of, 406–407
 incidence of, 12–13, 12*t*
 language learning in, 274*t*
 medications for, 383
 misconceptions about, 375
 prevalence of, 380

Autism Society of America, 26

Autistic savant, 377, 377*f*

Autistic spectrum disorder, **228**–229, **374**–376
 behavioral characteristics in, 377–379
 causes of, 380–382
 definition and included disorders, 376–377
 early intervention in, 382–383
 educational considerations in, 382–384
 instructional strategies in, 381
 internal states in, 379–380
 language development in, 274*t*, 378
 medications for, 383
 prevalence of, 380
 severity range and symptoms, 378–379
 social skills/development in, 378
 treatment of, 382–383

Barbier de la Serre, Charles, 354

Barkley, Russell, 196–198

Basal ganglia, in ADHD, **194,** 195

Bedwetting, and depression, 244–245

Behavior management. *See also* Disciplining of exceptional
  students; Functional behavioral assessment; Positive
  behavioral support
 in ADHD, 206
 of bullying, 239
 of cursing, 241–242
 in emotional/behavioral disorders, 240–260
 in mental retardation, 134
 in multiple severe disabilities, 408–410
 in oppositional defiant disorder, 241

as teacher responsibility, 22
in traumatic brain injury, **389**–390
Behavioral disorders. *See* Emotional and behavioral disorders
Behavioral inhibition, in ADHD, **196**
Behavioral intervention plans (BIPs), 255
Behavioral model, in emotional/behavioral disorders, **245**, 249
Behavioral phenotype, in chromosomal disorders, **125**–126, 126*t*
Bettelheim, Bruno, 486
Bicultural-bilingual approach, **317**, 323–324
Bilingual education. *See also* Language-minority students;
        Multicultural education
    and deaf biculturalism, **317**, 323–324
    efficacy of, 89, 96–97
    giftedness and, 469
    issues in, 81, 89
    language disorders and, 287
BIPs. *See* Behavioral intervention plans
Blindisms, **351**–352
Blindness. *See* Visual impairment
Braille, **341**, 352–356, 355*f*
    advance learning of, 402
    on computers, 406*f*
    in deaf-blindness, 398–399
    literacy rate in, 8
    literary, **352**
    utility of, 339
Braille, Louis, 354
Braille 'n Speak, 361, 362*f*
Braille notetakers, **361**
BrailleMate, 361
Bridgman, Laura, 24, 397–398, 399*f*
Brown v. *Board of Education* (1954), 469
Bullying, approaches to, 239

CAI. *See* Computer-assisted instruction
Cajuns, Usher syndrome and, 395
CAP. *See* Continuum of alternative placements
Captioning, 326–327, 329*t*
CAT (computerized axial tomographic) scans, in learning
        disabilities, **156**
Cataracts, **344**, 345*f*
Catheterization, **428**
Caudate, in ADHD, **194**, 195
Causes of disabilities, progress in discovering, 4–6
CBA. *See* Curriculum-based assessment
CCBD. *See* Council for Children with Behavioral Disorders
CEC. *See* Council for Exceptional Children
Center-based early intervention programs, **65**–66
Central nervous system dysfunction, in learning disabilities, 151,
        155–157, 163
Cerebellum, in ADHD, **195**
Cerebral palsy (CP), **423**–425
    assistive technology in, 404
    associated disabilities, 424–425
    athetosis, 446
    case study, 440–441
    causes and types, 424
    characteristics of, 422
    distractibility and hyperactivity in, **188**
    educational implications, 424–425

misconceptions about, 421
speech disorders and, **291**
transition programs in, 447
CHADD. *See* Children and Adults with Attention Deficit Disorder
CHARGE syndrome, **393**–394
Chicago Child-Parent Center (CPC) Program, 137
Childhood disintegrative disorder, **376**
Children and Adults with Attention Deficit Disorder (CHADD),
        191
Choanae, **394**
Choreoathetoid movements, in cerebral palsy, **424**
Chorionic villus sampling (CVS), **118**
Chromosome(s), **117**
    disorders of, **115**. *See also* Genetic factors
        behavioral phenotype in, 125–126, 126*t*
        and mental retardation, 117–119
        screening for, 118
Chronic, **422**
Chronological age, **123**
Classroom teachers. *See also* Collaborative consultation (co-
        teaching)
    and assessment, role in, 19–22
    communication with parents, 502–508
    in emotional/behavioral disorders, 236–237
    family involvement strategies for, 497*t*
    on full inclusion, 53–54
    importance of families to, 489*t*
    in language disabilities, 277–283, 295–296
    multicultural education for, 91, 91*f*, 104
    role in special education, 13–14, 16*t*, 19–22
    training for, as legal requirement, 29
Classwide peer tutoring (CWPT), **58**
    in bilingual instruction, **98**
    in mental retardation, 135
Cleft palate, **289**
Closed head injury, **384**–385
CMV. *See* Cytomegalovirus
Co-teaching. *See* Collaborative consultation
Coaching, **216**
    in ADHD, 216–218
    job coaches, **69**, 142, 213*f*, **414**
Cochlea, 304–**305**
Cochlear implantation, **62**, **313**–315, 313*f*
    and deaf activism, 313–315
Cognition, **165**
    in learning disabilities, 165
Cognitive mapping, 347–348
Cognitive training, **169**–173
Cohesion, in family system theory, 499–500
Collaborative consultation (co-teaching), **56**
    in ADHD, 208–209
    in communication disorders, 280, 284–286
    in emotional/behavioral disorders, 250–251
    in giftedness, 474–475
    in hearing impairment, 324–326
    in learning disabilities, 175–177
    in mental retardation, 136–137
    in multiple severe disabilities, 412–413
    in physical disabilities, 443–445
    in visual impairment, 364–365

Collaborative Multisite Multimodal Treatment Study of Children with Attention-Deficit/Hyperactivity Disorder (MTA), 210
Coloboma, **393**
Communication disorders. *See also* Language disorders; Speech disorders
  in adults, 294–295
  in autistic spectrum disorder, 382
  causes of, 266–268, 268*t*
  definition of, 264–267, 270–271
  vs. dialects, 266–267, 283–284
  early intervention in, 265, 291–294
  identification in adults, 295
  instructional strategies in, 280, 284–286
  misconceptions about, 265
  prevalence of, 266–268
  prevention of, 292
  social skills/development in, 263–264
  transition programs in, 294–296
  types of, 266
Communication variations (dialects)
  vs. communication disorders, 266–267, 283–284
  instructional strategies in, 284–287
Community-based instruction, in mental retardation, 138–141, 139*t*
Community residential facility (CRF), **141, 415**
Comorbidity, in emotional/behavioral disorders, **228**–229
Competitive employment, **413**
  in mental retardation, **142**
  in multiple severe disabilities, 413
Comprehension monitoring, in learning disabilities, **166**
Computer-assisted instruction (CAI), in hearing impairment, 328
Computerized axial tomographic (CAT) scans, in learning disabilities, **156**
Conceptual intelligence, **114**
Conduct disorder. *See also* Emotional and behavioral disorders
  in ADHD, **188**
  definition of, **226**
  identification of, 236
  transition to adulthood, 259–260
Conductive hearing loss, 306–**307**
Conferences, parent-teacher, 503–504, 504*t*
Confidentiality, as legal right, 29
Congenital anomalies, **420**–421
Congenital cytomegalovirus (CMV), **307**
  hearing impairment and, 307
Congenitally deaf, **302**
Conners Adult ADHD Rating Scales, 192
Conners scales, 192
Consequences, in functional behavior assessment, 134
Constant time delay, in mental retardation, **132**
Consultation model, in learning disabilities, 181
Contingency-based self-management, in ADHD, **204**–206
Continuum of alternative placements (CAP), **44**
  vs. full inclusion, 44–55
  satisfaction with, 51–53, 55
  service options, 13–15, 16*t*–17*t*
Contractures, 446, **447**
Convulsion (seizure), **425**
  first aid for, 426

Cooperative learning, **58, 104**–105
Cooperative teaching, **56**–57
  in ADHD, 208–209
  challenges of, 26–27
  in learning disabilities, 175–177, 181
  in mental retardation, 136–137
Cornea, **341**, 342*f*
Cortical visual impairment (CVI), 344–**345**
Council for Children with Behavioral Disorders (CCBD), 224, 226
Council for Exceptional Children (CEC), 25, 27, 208, 410
CP. *See* Cerebral palsy
CPC Program. *See* Chicago Child-Parent Center (CPC) Program
Cranial nerves, **393**
Creativity, **456**
CRF. *See* Community residential facility
Criterion-referenced testing, in learning disabilities assessment, **160**
Cued speech, **319**–320
Cultural-familial mental retardation, **121**–123
Cultural sensitivity, and exceptionalities, 90–93, 91*f*, 104, 106
Culture(s). *See also* Bilingual education; Communication variations (dialects); Deaf culture; Minorities; Multicultural education
  definitions of, 85–86
  macrocultures, **86**
  microcultures, **86**, 86*f*
    academic performance of, 87–88
  U.S.
    diversity of, 86–87, 497–498
    and emotional/behavioral disorders, 235–236
Culture-specific instruction, 96–99
Curricula. *See also* educational programming *and* transition programs *under individual disabilities*
  for mainstreaming, 57–58
  multicultural education and, 95–99
  standards-based reforms and, 59–61
  vocational training and, 41, 71–72
Curriculum-based assessment (CBA), **95**
  in learning disabilities, **160**–161
Cursing, strategies for, 241–242
CVI. *See* Cortical visual impairment
CVS. *See* Chorionic villus sampling
CWPT. *See* Classwide peer tutoring
Cystic fibrosis, **6**
Cytomegalovirus (CMV), **394**
  congenital, **307**
  and deaf-blindness, 394

Daily living skills, **408**
  in multiple severe disabilities, 408
DAP. *See* Developmentally appropriate practice
Deaf activism, 312–316
Deaf-blindness
  causes of, 393–396
  communication in, 398–399
  definition of, 392–393
  educational programming in, 397–401
  incidence of, 12–13, 12*t*
  orientation and mobility in, 399–401

outcomes in, 391–392
prevalence of, 393
psychological and behavioral characteristics of, 396–397
Deaf clubs, 312
Deaf culture
    activism of, 312–316
    American Sign Language and, 310–311, 317, 323–324
    challenges to, 312, 314–315
    on disability, 303
    family and, 332–333
    inclusion and, 325–326
    and resistance to prevention, 90
    and social development, 310–311
Deaf/hard of hearing. *See* Hearing impairment
Death, discussion of, 442
DEC of CEC. *See* Division for Early Childhood of Council for
        Exceptional Children
Decibels, **302**
Deinstitutionalization, **42–43**
Delayed language development, 275–276
Depression, in emotional/behavioral disorders, 244–245
Descriptive Video Service, **362**
Developmental delay, **64**
Developmentally appropriate practice (DAP), **412**
    in multiple severe disabilities, 412
DI. *See* Direct Instruction (DI) method
Diabetic retinopathy, **344**, 345*f*
Diagnostic and Statistical Manual of Mental Disorders (DSM),
        189, 377
    Fourth Edition (DSM-IV), 190
    Second Edition (DSM-II), 191
Diagnostic-prescriptive centers, 14, 17*t*
Dialects. *See* Communication variations
Diplegia, in cerebral palsy, **424**
Direct Instruction (DI) method, in learning disabilities, **173**–175
Direct Instructional System for Teaching and Remediation
        (DISTAR), 174
Direct teaching, in deaf-blindness, 397
Disabilities. *See* Exceptionalities
The Disability Rag (periodical), 50
Disability rights movement, **48–50**
Disciplining of exceptional students, 72–75. *See also* Behavior
        management; Functional behavioral assessment; Positive
        behavioral support
    cultural sensitivity in, 106
    current trends in, 73–74
    in emotional and behavioral disorders, 223, 232–234,
        238–244, 250–251, 254–256
    issues in, 74–75
    law and, 41, 73–74, 255
    and mandatory sentencing, 73
    manifestation determination in, 74
    in multiple severe disabilities, 375
    and zero tolerance policies, 72–73
Discourse, **293**
    in language learning, 293–294
Discrimination, 83. *See also* Prejudice
    in assessment, 29, 93–95, 101–102, 110, 124
    inadvertent, 91, 91*f*, 104
    as persistent problem, 82–85

DISTAR. *See* Direct Instructional System for Teaching and
        Remediation
Division for Early Childhood of Council for Exceptional
        Children (DEC of CEC), 410, 412–413
Doctor's office effect, in ADHD, **192**
Dopamine, in ADHD, **195**
Dopper effect, **348**
Down syndrome, **117**–118, 118*f*
    and Alzheimer's Disease, 117
    and behavioral phenotype, 125, 126*t*
    deaf-blindness in, **393**–394
Drug abuse. *See* Substance abuse
DSM. *See Diagnostic and Statistical Manual of Mental Disorders*
Due process hearings
    classroom teacher's role in, 20
    right to, 29
Dysarthria, **291**
Dyslexia, 163
    and brain function, 156

Ear(s). *See also entries under* Hearing
    anatomy and physiology of, 303–304, 304*f*
    cochlear implantation, 62, 313–315, 313*f*
Early expressive language delay (EELD), **271**
Early intervention, 63–68. *See also* Individualized family service
        plans; Preschoolers; *specific disabilities*
    advantages of, 8, 63–64
    child- *vs.* teacher-directed, 41, 66–67
    current trends in, 66–67
    in emotional and behavioral disorders, 64, 256–258
    family role in, 66
    federal law on, 26–27, 29, 64–65, 64*f*
    resistance to, 67–68
    types of programs, 16–17, 65–66
    in visual impairment, 365–366
Easter Seal Society, 57
Echolalia, **378**
Ecological perspective, in emotional and behavioral disorders,
        222–224
Education, as legal right, 28–30
Education for All Handicapped Children Act (1975) [PL 94-
        142], **26**, 27, 30, 34–35, 191
    amendments to (PL 99-457), 21–22, 33, 64*f*
EELD. *See* Early expressive language delay
Elementary and Secondary Education Act (ESEA), 255
Eligibility requirements, federal, 10
Emotional and behavioral disorders. *See also* Attention-deficit
        hyperactivity disorder; Autistic spectrum disorder;
        Conduct disorder
    behavioral assessment and support in, 251, 255–256
    causes of, 222–223, 230–236, 230*f*
    classification of, 228–229
    comorbidity in, 228–229
    definition of, 225–227
    delinquents and incarcerated youths, 254, 259
    depression in, 244–245
    discipline in, 223, 232–234, 238–244, 250–251, 254–256
    early intervention and, 64, 256–258
    educational considerations in, 224, 234–235, 245–256
    and environment, 6

Emotional and behavioral disorders *(Cont.)*
  identification of, 236–237
    in preschoolers, 256–257
  inclusion in, 252–253
  instructional methods in, 223, 250–254
  intelligence and achievement in, 238
  language disorders in, 276–277
  medication for, 231
  in minorities, 245, 260
  misconceptions about, 223
  in multiple severe disabilities, 406–410
  prevalence of, 229
  prevention of, 257
  service delivery models, 251–253
  social and emotional characteristics in, 221–222, 234,
    238–245, 276–277
  terminology of, 224
  transition to adulthood, 243–244, 259–260
Empirical evidence, *vs.* ethics, in inclusion, 50–51, 54–55
Employment
  in hearing impairment, 330, 333
  in learning disabilities, 180–181
  in mental retardation, 111, 139*t*, 141–143
  in multiple severe disabilities, 375, 413–415
  in physical disabilities, 443, 447–449
  supported, **69**
    in mental retardation, **142**
    in physical disabilities, **448**
  in visual impairment, 369–370
  vocational education issues, 41, 71–72
Encephalitis, **121**
  and mental retardation, 121
Encopresis, and depression, 244–245
Enuresis, and depression, 244–245
Environmental influences
  in emotional/behavioral disorders, 6
  in learning disabilities, 158
  in mental retardation, 120–121
Epilepsy, **425–427**
  causes and types, 425–426
  educational implications, 426–427
  misconceptions about, 421
Episodic, **422**
Error analysis, in learning disabilities assessment, **161**
ESEA. *See* Elementary and Secondary Education Act
Ethics
  and full inclusion, 50–51, 54–55
  gene therapy and, 116
  Human Genome Project and, 116
  and multicultural education, 98–99
  technology and, 62–63
Ethnic group(s). *See also* Language-minority students;
    Minorities; Multicultural education
  definition of, 90
  and diversity awareness, 86–87, 497–498
  and genetic disability, 81
Eugenics movement, 486
Evoked-response audiometry, **306**
Exceptionalities
  acceptance of, 6

  characteristics of, 7–10
  cultural sensitivity and, 90–93, 91*f,* 104, 106
  definition of, 7
  giftedness and, 470–473
  vs. handicap, 5–7
  impact on family, 488–494
  incidence of, 12–13, 12*t,* 67–68
  misconceptions about, 5, 41
  need for special education, 7–10
  and parental guilt, 490
  prevalence of, 10–13, 12*t*
  public reaction to, 485–486, 490–491, 496
  theories of, history of, 486–488
Exceptionality group
  definition of, 90
  as minority, 47–50, 54
Executive functions, in ADHD, **196**–197
Expressive language, **266**
  changes in, 283*f*
  delay in, 274*t*
External otitis, **307**
Externalizing behavior, **228**
  aggressiveness in, 240–244
Eye(s). *See also entries under* Visual
  anatomy and physiology of, 341–342, 342*f*
  trouble signs in, 343

Facilitated communication (FC), 405
Familiality studies, in learning disabilities, **157**–158
Family. *See also* Parents
  and deaf culture, 332–333
  in early intervention, role of, 66
  emotional/behavioral disorders and, 232–234
  ethnic diversity and, 86–87, 497–498
  hearing impairment and, 333
  impact of disabled child on, 488–494
  importance of teachers to, 489*t*
  independence from, 499–500
  involvement in treatment/education, 494–508, 497*t*
    family-centered model of, **494**–495
    family systems theory, **495**–501, 497*t*
    history of, 486–488
  misconceptions about, 487
  in multicultural education, 99–101
  sibling reactions to disabled child, 493–494, 495*t,* 496
  social support for, **501**–502
  stress and, 491–493, 498
Family-centered model, **494**–495
Family characteristics, in family system theory, **497**–499
Family functions, in family system theory, **497,** 500
Family interaction, in family system theory, **497,** 499–501
Family life cycle, in family system theory, **497,** 500–501
Family systems theory, **495**–501, 497*t*
FAPE. *See* Free appropriate education
FAS. *See* Fetal alcohol syndrome
FBA. *See* Functional behavioral assessment
FC. *See* Facilitated communication
FDA. *See* U.S. Food and Drug Administration
Federal law
  on assessment, 29, 60, 255

and disciplining of exceptional students, 41, 73–74, 255
on early intervention, 26–27, 29, 64–65, 64*f*
eligibility requirements for special education, 10
on free appropriate education, 5, 26–27, 29
history of, 26–28
on individualized education plans (IEPs), 30–34
on individualized family service plans (IFSPs), 33, 64–65
intent of, 30
knowledge of, as teacher responsibility, 22
on least restrictive environment, 5, 29–30, 44
and litigation, trends in, 28–30, 32–33
on parental involvement, 29, 486*f*, 488
on transition plans, 68–70
Federation of Families for Children's Mental Health, 26, 233–234
Feedback, importance of, 103
Feelings of disabled child, dealing with, 491
Fetal alcohol syndrome (FAS), **429**
    and learning disabilities, 158
    and mental retardation, **120**
Fingerspelling, 320–321, 321*f*
Fluency, 266, **227**
    disorders of, 267, 290–291
fMRI (functional magnetic resonance imaging), in learning disabilities, **156**
Formative assessment, in learning disabilities, **159**–161
Fragile X syndrome, **119**
    and behavioral phenotype, 125, 126*t*
Free appropriate education (FAPE)
    federal law on, 5, 26–27, 29
    least restrictive environment standard and, 44–45
Frontal lobes, **194**
    in ADHD, 194–195, 194*f*
Full inclusion, **44**–55. *See also* Inclusion; Mainstreaming
    arguments against, 51–55
    arguments for, 45–51
    ethics *vs.* evidence in, 50–51, 54–55
Functional academics, in mental retardation, **131**–132
Functional behavioral assessment (FBA)
    in ADHD, **204**–205
    in disciplining of exceptional students, **74**
    in emotional/behavioral disorders, 251, 255–256
    in mental retardation, **134**
    in multiple severe disabilities, 408
Functional magnetic resonance imaging (fMRI), in learning disabilities, **156**
Functional vision assessment, **343**

Gallaudet, Thomas Hopkins, 24, 25*f*
Gallaudet University, 24, 300, 313–314, 330–331
Gay and lesbian students, and tolerance, 105
Gender
    and ADHD, 192
    and giftedness, 468, 473–474
    and learning disabilities, 155
    and representation in special education, 92, 92*f*
    and stuttering, 291
    and traumatic brain injury, 386
Gene therapy, ethics of, 116
General education teachers. *See* Classroom teachers

Genetic factors. *See also* Chromosome(s), disorders of; Human Genome Project
    in ADHD, 195
    in deaf-blindness, 393–395
    in emotional/behavioral disorders, 231–232
    eugenics movement and, 486
    in learning disabilities, 157–158
Genius, **456**. *See also* Giftedness
Genres, **285**
    cultural variation in, 285, 287*t*
German measles. *See* Rubella
Giftedness, **457**
    case studies in, 466–467, 476–477
    definition of, 454–461
    in disabled students, 470–473
    early intervention in, 479–481
    educational programming, 462, 465–467, 474–479
    gender and, 468, 473–474
    identification of, 463
    minorities and, 468–470
    misconceptions about, 455, 458, 460*t*, 464
    origins of, 461–462
    prevalence of, 461
    psychological and behavioral characteristics, 463–465
    transition to adulthood, 481–482
    and underachievement, 468
Glaucoma, **344,** 345*f*
Globus pallidus, in ADHD, **194,** 195
Goal-directed activities, in ADHD, 197–198
Graduation rate, high school, 68*f*
Group contingency, in ADHD, 206
Guardianship, **501**
Guide dogs, 339, 359–360
Guide Horse Foundation, 360
Guide horses, 360
Guilt, parental, 490
Gun-Free School Act (1994), 72–73

Haldol (haloperidol), for autistic spectrum disorder, 383
Hand-over-hand guidance, **399,** 401*f*
Hand-under-hand guidance, **399**
Handicap, *vs.* disability, 5–7
Handicapism, **48**. *See also* Prejudice
Handwriting difficulties, in learning disabilities, 162
Hard of hearing. *See* Hearing impairment
Headsticks, 448*f*, 449
Hearing aids, 326–328
Hearing impairment. *See also entries under* Deaf
    academic achievement in, 309–310
    and assistive technology, 326–328
        cochlear implantation, **62, 313**–315, 313*f*
    causes of, 306–307
    definition and classification of, 300–303
    ear anatomy and, 303–304, 304*f*
    early intervention in, 330–331
    educational programming in, 316–328
    English language and speech development in, 302, 308, 309*t*
    incidence of, 12–13, 12*t*
    inclusion in, 301, 310, 312, 325–326
    instructional methods, 317–318

Hearing impairment *(Cont.)*
   intellectual ability and, 308–309
   marriage and family issues in, 333
   misconceptions about, 301
   prevalence of, 303
   psychological and behavioral characteristics, 308–316
   service delivery models in, 324–326
   social skills/development in, 299–301, 310–316
   transition programs for, 331–333
Hemiplegia, in cerebral palsy, **424**
Heritability studies, in learning disabilities, **158**
Herpes simplex, **121**
   and mental retardation, 121
Hertz (Hz), **305**
High school graduation rate, 68*f*
Hispanics. *See also* Spanish-speaking students
   percentage in special education, 92, 92*f*
HIV (human immunodeficiency virus), 429
Home-based early intervention programs, **65–66**
Home-contingency programs, 506
Home-note program, **506**
Homebound instruction, 14, 17*t*
Homework, guidelines for, 505
Homophenes, **320**
Horace Mann School for the Deaf and Hard of Hearing, 314
Hospital instruction, 14, 17*t*
Howe, Samuel Gridley, 24, 398, 399*f*
Hudson v. *Rowley* (1982), 30
Human Genome Project
   and causes of mental retardation, 115–116
   and ethics, 116
Human guides, in visual impairment, 360
Human immunodeficiency virus (HIV), 429
Hydrocephalus, **6, 119–120**
Hyperactive child syndrome, **189**
Hyperopia, **344**, 344*f*
Hypotonic, 446, **447**

IDEA. *See* Individuals with Disabilities Education Act
Identification. *See also* Assessment
   of communication disorders, in adults, 295
   of conduct disorder, 236
   of emotional/behavioral disorders, 236–237
     in preschoolers, 256–257
   of giftedness, 463
   of language disorders, in adults, 295
   in language-minority students, 101–102
   of schizophrenia, 236
IEPs. *See* Individualized education plans
IFSPs. *See* Individualized family service plans
Illinois Test of Psycholinguistic Abilities, 162
Inborn errors of metabolism, **119**
Incidence of exceptionalities, 12–13, 12*t*, 67–68. *See also*
     Prevalence
Inclusion. *See also* Collaborative consultation (co-teaching); Full
     inclusion; Mainstreaming
   in ADHD, 202–203
   in emotional/behavioral disorders, 252–253
   in giftedness, 465–467
   in hearing impairment, 301, 310, 312, 325–326

   in learning disabilities, 175–176
   in mental retardation, 126–127, 136
   in multiple severe disabilities, 412–413
   in physical disabilities, 420*f*, 440–441
   of preschoolers, 67
   and standardized testing, 41, 60
   in visual impairment, 365–366
Inclusive schools movement, **18**
Incus, **304**, 304*f*
Independent living
   families and, 499–500
   in multiple severe disabilities, 375
   in visual impairment, 367–369
Individualized education plans (IEPs), 414–**415**
   assessment requirements in, 60
   classroom teacher's role in, 20
   IDEA requirements for, 30–34
   meetings, effective, 508, 508*t*
   in multiple severe disabilities, 414
   sample of, 32*f*–34*f*
   structure and content of, 30–34, 31*t*, 35*t*–36*t*
   transition plan requirements, 69
   in visual impairment, 356
Individualized family service plans (IFSPs), **64**
   age at drafting of, 65*f*
   in communication disorders, 292–293
   federal law on, 33, 64–65
   in multiple severe disabilities, 411
   parental involvement in, **488**
   in physical disabilities, **439**
   requirements for, 64–65
Individuals with Disabilities Education Act (1990, 1997) [IDEA],
     26–27
   assessment requirements of, 60
   assistive technology in, 327
   and behavioral assessment, 255
   and braille, 356
   criticisms of, 31–35
   definition of deaf blindness, 392
   definition of multiple disabilities, 374
   definition of multiple severe disabilities, 406
   definition of traumatic brain injury, 384–385
   discipline procedures and, 73–74
   emotional and behavioral disorders in, 224, 226
   IEP requirements in, 30–34
   impact of, 34–35, 72
   and positive behavioral support, 409
   provisions of, 27, 29
   reauthorization of, 153–154
   and right to choose, 54
   transition plan requirements, 68–70, 369
Informal reading inventories (IRIs), in learning disabilities
     assessment, 159*f*, **161**
Inner speech, in ADHD, **196**–197
Insight, **456**
Instructional environment, and assessment equity, 95
Instructional methods. *See also* Collaborative consultation;
     Cooperative teaching; *specific disabilities*
   acceleration, **475–479**
   advances in, 6

Afrocentric instruction, 97
classwide peer tutoring, **58**
    in bilingual instruction, **98**
    in mental retardation, 135
in communication variations, 284–287
community-based instruction, 138–141, 139*t*
constant time delay, **132**
consultation model, 181
contingency-based self-management, **204**–206
cooperative learning, **58, 104**–105
Direct Instruction method, in learning disabilities, **173**–175
direct teaching, 397
enrichment, **475,** 479
group contingency, 206
homework guidelines, 505
importance of knowing, 22
for language-minority students, 96–98, 101–103
learning strategies model, 180–181
in mathematics, 133
mnemonics, 103, 170–171
in multicultural education, 95–99
native-language emphasis, 96–97, **102**
Peer-Assisted Learning Strategies (PALS), in learning disabilities, 177–179
progressive time delay, **132**
reciprocal teaching, **103, 173**
scaffolding, 102–**103, 172**–173
self-instruction, in learning disabilities, **171**–172
self-monitoring, **172, 205**–206
sheltered-English approach, **102**
systematic instruction, **132**
task switching, 197
Integration into classroom. *See also* Inclusion
    challenges of, 26–27
    rationale for, 18–19
Integration into society, 40–59. *See also* Employment; Self-determination
    deinstitutionalization, **42**–43
    full inclusion, **44**–55
    normalization, **40**–42, 412–413
    person-centered planning and, **43**
Intellectual functioning, in mental retardation, **112**
Intelligence
    in emotional/behavioral disorders, 238
    in hearing impairment, 308–309
    in mental retardation, 112
    misconceptions about, 460*t*
    types of, 114, 457–458
    in visual impairment, 346–347
Intelligence quotient (IQ) tests. *See also* IQ-achievement discrepancies
    cultural bias in, 123
    in emotional/behavioral disorders, 223, 238, 238*f*
    giftedness and, 457, 460*t*, 465
    in hearing impairment, 309
    limitations of, 457, 460*t*
    in mental retardation, 112–115, 115*f,* 117–118, 123
    minorities and, 460*t*
    normal distribution of scores, 114–115, 115*f*
    in visual impairment, 346

in Williams syndrome, 118
Intelligence tests. *See* Intelligence quotient (IQ) tests; Standardized testing; *specific tests*
Internalizing behavior, **228,** 244–245
International Society for Augmentative and Alternative Communication (ISAAC), 406
Internet
    accessibility of, 62–63
        in hearing impairment, 329–330
        in visual impairment, 364
    parent resources on, 502
Interpreters, in hearing impairment, 331–332
IQ-achievement discrepancies
    in emotional/behavioral disorders, 238
    in giftedness, 468–474
    in learning disabilities, 149, **151**–154
IQ tests. *See* Intelligence quotient (IQ) tests
IRIs. *See* Informal reading inventories
Iris, **341,** 342*f*
ISAAC. *See* International Society for Augmentative and Alternative Communication
Itard, Jean-Marc-Gaspard, 23–24, 24*f*
Itinerant services, 13–14, 16*t*
    in visual impairment, 364

Job coach, **69,** 142, 213*f,* **414**
Juvenile delinquents, 254, 259
Juvenile rheumatoid arthritis, **428,** 439

Kaufman Assessment Battery for Children (K-ABC), 123
Keller, Helen, 24, 396–397
Key Math, Revised, 159
Klippel-Trenaunay-Weber syndrome, 28
Kurzweil, Raymond, 481
Kurzweil 1000, **360**–361

Labels. *See also* Identification
    impact of, 41, 45–47, 105–106
    resistance to, 67–68
Language, **266**
    expressive, **266,** 274*t,* 283*f*
    receptive, **266,** 283*f*
Language development, 265
    in autistic spectrum disorder, 274*t,* 378
    delayed, 275–276
    in hearing impairment, 302, 308, 309*t*
    normal *vs.* impaired, 268–270, 269*t*
Language disorders, 266–267. *See also* Speech disorders
    assessment of, 273–274
    changes in, 282–283, 283*f*
    classification of, 270–273
    comorbidities in, 265
    early intervention in, 276, 291–294
    educational considerations, 277–283
    in emotional/behavioral disorders, 276–277
    identification in adults, 295
    incidence of, 12, 12*t*
    intervention strategies, 273–274, 274*t,* 281*t*
    language development and, 268–270, 269*t*
    language-minority students and, 287

Language disorders (Cont.)
  misconceptions about, 265
  prevalence of, 266–268
  prevention of, 292
  transition programs in, 294–296
  in traumatic brain injury, 388–389
  types of, 266
  written language in, 282, 283f
Language-minority students. See also Bilingual education;
      Minorities
  and deaf biculturalism, 317, 323–324
  disabled, misassessment of, 101–102
  instructional methods for, 101–103
    classwide peer tutoring, 98
    native-language emphasis, 96–97, 102
    principles of, 102–103
    scaffolding, 102–103
    sheltered-English approach, 102
  language disorders and, 287
  Spanish-speaking
    giftedness and, 469
    language disorders and, 287
Large print books, 357
Larynx, in speech disorders, 288–289
Law
  federal. See Federal law
  knowledge of, as teacher responsibility, 22
LBW. See Low birthweight
Learned helplessness
  in learning disabilities, 167
  in mental retardation, 125
Learning disabilities
  ADHD and, 165, 199
  adult persistence of, 149, 177–178
  assessment in, 149, 153, 155–161, 176–177
  causes of, 149, 155–158
  definition of, 148–154
    federal, 152–154
    NJCLD, 153–154
  early intervention in, 176–177
  educational programming in, 180–182
  and environment, 6
  incidence of, 12, 12t
  and inclusion, 175–176
  instruction methods in, 168–175
  IQ-achievement discrepancies in, 149, 151–154
  language learning in, 274t
  memory, cognitive, and metacognitive problems in, 165–166
  misconceptions about, 149
  motivational problems in, 167
  perceptual and motor problems in, 164
  prevalence of, 149, 155
  psychological and behavioral characteristics in, 161–168
  service delivery models for, 175–176
  social skills/development in, 149, 166–167
  socio-emotional problems in, 166–167
  strategy deficits in, 167–168
  transition programs in, 177–182
Learning Disabilities Association of America, 26, 150
Learning Disabilities Initiative (Dept. of Education), 153

Learning Disabilities Summit (2001), 153
Learning strategies model, in learning disabilities, 180–181
Least restrictive environment (LRE), 15
  disability type and, 17
  in emotional/behavioral disorders, 253
  federal law on, 5, 29–30, 44
  issues in, 15, 44–45
Legally blind, 340
Legislation. See Federal law
Lens (of eye), 342, 342f
Lesch-Nyhan disease, 116
Levels of support, in mental retardation, 113–114, 113t
Life space interviews, 246–249
Lipreading, 301, 319
Listening skills training, in visual impairment, 357
Literary braille, 352
Litigation
  Ritalin and, 210
  trends in, 28–30, 32–33
Locus of control, in learning disabilities, 167
Long cane, 357–358, 358f
Low birthweight (LBW), 121
Low vision, 340
LRE. See Least restrictive environment

Macrocultures, 87
Magnetic resonance imaging (MRI), in learning disabilities, 156
Mainstreaming, 56
  impact of, 72
  issues in, 58–59
  strategies for, 56–58
Malleus, 304, 304f
Malnutrition, and mental retardation, 120–121
Mandatory sentencing, and disciplining of disabled, 73
Manifestation determination, in disciplining of exceptional
      students, 74
Maternal serum screening, 118
Mathematics
  instruction methods in, 133
  in learning disabilities, 164
Media
  and captioning, 327–328, 329t
  portrayals of exceptionality, 41, 50
  violence in, and emotional/behavioral disorders, 235–236,
      235f
Medically fragile students, 430–431
Medication. See also Ritalin
  for ADHD, 207–213
  for autism and autistic spectrum disorder, 383
  for depression, 245
  for emotional/behavioral disorders, 231
Memory
  in ADHD, 196
  in learning disabilities, 165–166
  in mental retardation, 124
Meningitis
  and deaf-blindness, 394–395
  and mental retardation, 121
Mental age, 123
Mental retardation

adult persistence of, 111–113
assessment in, 110, 123–124, 134
causes of, 111, 115–123
    psychosocial, 121–123
community-based instruction, 138–141, 139*t*
definition of, 111–114
early intervention in, 136–138
educational programming in, 126–136
employment in, 111, 139*t*, 141–143
gene therapy and, 116
incidence of, 12, 12*t*
inclusion in, 126–127, 136
instructional methods in, 131–134
intelligence quotient (IQ) tests and, 112–115, 115*f*, 117–118, 123
language learning in, 274*t*
levels of support in, 113–114, 113*t*
mild, **113**, 131–132
misconceptions about, 111
moderate, **113**
natural supports in, 110
prevalence of, 114–115
prevention of, 137–138
prospects for future, 143
psychological and behavioral characteristics, 124–126
self-concepts in, 125*f*
self-determination in, 127–131
service delivery models, 133–136
services for, 109–110
severe, **113**, 132
severity of (AAMR classifications), 113–114, 113*t*
transition programs in, 138–143, 139*t*, 499–500
vocational education in, 111
Metacognition
    in learning disabilities, **165**
    in mental retardation, **124**
Methylphenidate. *See* Ritalin
Microcephalus, **119**
Microcultures, **87,** 86*f*
    academic performance of, 87–88
Mild mental retardation, **113**
    instructional methods in, 131–132
Milieu teaching, **275–276**
Minimal brain injury, **189**
    in learning disabilities, **150**
Minorities. *See also* African Americans; Communication variations (dialects); Microcultures
    academic performance of, 87–88
    disabled persons as, 47–50, 54
    emotional/behavioral disorders in, 245, 260
    expectionality groups as, 47–50, 54
    giftedness and, 468–470
    and racism, as persistent problem, 82–85
    in special education
        misassessment of, 29, 93–95, 101–102, 110, 124
        representation of, 81, 92–93, 92*f*
    and test bias, 123, 284, 460*t*
Misconceptions about exceptionalities, 5, 41. *See also specific disabilities*
Mixed hearing loss, 306–**307**

Mnemonics
    for language-minority students, **103**
    in learning disabilities, 170–171
Moderate mental retardation, **113**
Morphology, 266, **267**
    disorders of, 267, 272
Motivational problems, in learning disabilities, 167
MRI (magnetic resonance imaging), in learning disabilities, **156**
MTA study (NIH), 210
Multicultural education, 80–106. *See also* Bilingual education; Language-minority students
    and adult success, 96–97
    assessment in, 93–95
    criticisms of, 81–82
    cultural theory in, 85–88
    culture-specific instruction, 95–99
    and deaf bicultural-bilingual approach, 317, 323–324
    ethics and, 98–99
    families and, 99–101
    goals of, 106
    implementation of, 90–106
    instructional methods, 95–99
    issues in, 88–90
    misconceptions about, 81
    in multiple severe disabilities, 411
    need for, 82–85, 98–99
    purpose of, 80–82, 88, 95, 98–99
    socialization skills and, 103–106
    teacher training in, 91, 91*f*, 104
    tolerance, teaching of, 99, 104–106
Multiple severe disabilities. *See also* Autistic spectrum disorder; Deaf-blindness; Traumatic brain injury
    augmented or alternative communication in, 402–406
    behavior problems in, 406–410
    definition of, 374
    discipline in, 375
    early intervention in, 407*f*, 410–413
    educational programming in, 401–402
    employment in, 375, 413–415
    inclusion in, 412–413
    living skills in, 415
    misconceptions about, 375
    multicultural education in, 411
    normalization in, 412–413
    service delivery models in, 411–412
    transition programs in, 413–414
Muscular dystrophy, **428**
Musculoskeletal disorders, 428
Myopia, **344,** 344*f*

NAEYC, National Association for the Education of Young Children, 412
Narratives, **285**
    cultural variation in, 285, 287*t*
National Association for Gifted Children, 26, 197, 204–209, 208*t*, 474
National Association for the Education of Young Children (NAEYC), 412
National Association of the Deaf, 314
National Braille Literacy Competency Test, 356

National Center on Education, Disability, and Juvenile Justice, 256

National Federation of the Blind, 362, 364, 368

National Institute of Mental Health, ADHD treatment study, 209, 211

National Institute on Deafness and Other Communication Disorders, 325

National Joint Committee for Learning Disabilities (NJCLD), 153–154

National Mental Health and Special Education Coalition, 226–227

National Research Council, 377, 383

National Technical Assistance Consortium for Children and Young Adults Who Are Deaf-Blind (NTAC), **393**

National Technical Institute for the Deaf (NTID), 330–331

National Theatre of the Deaf, 311, 312f

Native-language emphasis, 96–97, **102**

Natural supports, **414**

  in mental retardation, **110**

  in multiple severe disabilities, 414

Neglect and abuse, language learning in, 274t

Nemeth Code, **352**

Neonatal intensive care units (NICUs), in multiple severe disabilities, 410

Neuroleptics, **383**

  for autistic spectrum disorder, 383

Neuromotor impairments, 422–428

Neurotransmitters, in ADHD, **195**

Newsline, **362**

NICUs. *See* Neonatal intensive care units

Night blindness, **344**

  in Usher syndrome, **394**

NJCLD. *See* National Joint Committee for Learning Disabilities

Nonverbal learning disabilities, **167**

Normalization, **40**–42

  in multiple severe disabilities, 412–413

Notebooks, traveling, **506**, 507t

NTAC. *See* National Technical Assistance Consortium for Children and Young Adults Who Are Deaf-Blind

NTID. *See* National Technical Institute for the Deaf

Nystagmus, **346**

O & M. *See* Orientation and mobility (O & M) skills

Obstacle sense, **348**

ODD. *See* Oppositional defiant disorder

Office of Special Education, 502, 505

OI (osteogenesis imperfecta), 9

Open head injury, **384**–385

Oppositional defiant disorder (ODD), strategies in, 240–241

Optic nerve, **342**, 342f

Oral approach, in deaf education, 319–320

Oralism-manualism debate, **316**–317

Oregon Social Learning Center, 256

Orientation and mobility (O & M) skills

  in deaf-blindness, 399–401

  in visual impairment, 347–348, 357–360, 362, 365

Orthopedic disorders, 428

  incidence of, 12–13, 12t

Orthosis, **435**–436

Ossicles, **304**

Osteogenesis imperfecta (OI), 9

Otitis, external, **307**

Otitis media, **307**

Otoacoustic emissions, **305**

Oval window, **304**, 304f

PACER Center, 233

PALS. *See* Peer-Assisted Learning Strategies

Paraplegia, in cerebral palsy, **424**

Parent-teacher conferences, 503–504, 504t

Parents. *See also* Family

  advocacy and, 10, 506–509

  on full inclusion, 51–53

  honesty with child, 491

  impact of disabled child on, 489–493

  Internet resources for, 502

  involvement in treatment/education

    classroom teacher's role in, 20–21

    communication and, 502–508

    law on, 29, 486f, 488

  misconceptions about, 487

  organizations for, 25–26

  resistance to special education, 11, 29–30

  social support for, 501–502

  stress and, 491–493, 498

  support groups for, 502

Partial participation, **58**

PASS (Plan to Achieve Self-Support), 70

PATs. *See* Preassessment teams

PBIS. *See* Positive behavioral intervention and supports

PBS. *See* Positive behavioral support

Peer(s), interaction with. *See* Social skills/development

Peer-Assisted Learning Strategies (PALS), in learning disabilities, 177–179

Peer-mediated instruction, **58**

Peer tutoring, **58**

  classwide (CWPT), **58, 98,** 135

Performance-Based Professional Standards (CEC), 27

Perinatal causes of mental retardation, **115,** 120–121

Perkins Brailler, **353**–354, 355f

Perkins School for the Blind, 24, 398

Perry Preschool Project, 137

Perseveration, in ADHD, **188**

Person-centered plan/planning, **43**

  in multiple severe disabilities, **414**

Pervasive developmental disorder (PDD), **374**–376

Pervasive development disorder not otherwise specified (PDD-NOS), **376**–377

PET (positron emission tomography) scans, in learning disabilities, **156,** 163

Phenylketonuria (PKU), **6, 119**

Phonological awareness, **162**

Phonology, **163,** 266, **267**

  disorders of, 265, 267, 272

  in learning disabilities, 163

Physical disabilities

  academic achievement in, 432

  accommodations in, 438–439, 445

  assistive technology in, 435–436, 448–449, 448f

  definition and classification of, 420–422

  early intervention in, 445–446

educational considerations, 437–445
employment in, 443, 447–449
handling and positioning in, 445–446
inclusion in, 420f, 440–441
misconceptions about, 421
prevalence of, 421–422
prevention of, 431–432
psychological and behavioral characteristics in, 421,
    432–435
sociosexuality in, 449
transition programs in, 446–449
Piaget, Jean, 66, 346
PKU. *See* Phenylketonuria
PL. *See entries under* Public Law
Placement. *See also* Continuum of alternative placements;
    Inclusion; Least restrictive environment
guidelines for, 31, 35f, 35t
normalization, 40–42, 412–413
service options, 13–15, 16t–17t
in visual impairment, 364–365
Plan to Achieve Self-Support (PASS), 70
Play audiometry, **306**
Portfolios, in learning disabilities assessment, **161**
Positive behavioral intervention and supports (PBIS), **74**
Positive behavioral support (PBS), **74**
in emotional/behavioral disorders, 251, 255–256
in mental retardation, **134**
in multiple severe disabilities, **408**–409
Positron emission tomography (PET) scans, in learning
    disabilities, **156**, 163
Postlingual deafness, **302**
Postnatal causes
of mental retardation, **115**, 121–123
of severe disabilities, **394**
Practical intelligence, **114**
Prader-Willi syndrome, **119**
and behavioral phenotype, 125, 126t
Pragmatics, 266, **268**
disorders of, 267, 273
in learning disabilities, **163**–164, 164f
Preacademic skills, as predictor for learning disabilities, 177
Preassessment teams (PATs), **56**
Precocity, **456**
Prefrontal lobes, in ADHD, **194**, 195
Prejudice. *See also* Discrimination
case study of, 83–84, 100–101
disarming through humor, 46
and exceptionality as minority status, 47–50, 54
labeling and, 45–46
and racism, as persistent problem, 82–85
Prelingual deafness, **302**
Prelinguistic communication, **275**
Prenatal causes
of mental retardation, **115**–120
of severe disabilities, **394**
Prereferral teams (PRTs), **56**
Preschoolers. *See also* Early intervention; Individualized family
    service plans (IFSPs)
audiometry in, 306
emotional/behavioral disorder identification in, 256–257

incidence of exceptionalities in, 67–68
inclusion and, 67
and prediction of learning disabilities, 177
Prevalence. *See also* Incidence
of Asperger syndrome, 380
of attention-deficit hyperactivity disorder, 189–192
of autism and autistic spectrum disorder, 380
of communication disorders, 266–268
of deaf-blindness, 393
of emotional/behavioral disorders, 229
of exceptionalities, 10–13, 12t
of giftedness, 461
of hearing impairment, 303
of language disorders, 266–268
of learning disabilities, 149, 155
of mental retardation, 114–115
of physical disabilities, 421–422
of speech disorders, 266–268
of traumatic brain injury, 386
of visual impairment, 341
Prevention
of communication disorders, 292
Deaf culture resistance to, 90
early intervention and, 8, 67–68
emotional/behavioral disorders, 257
of language disorders, 292
mental retardation, 137–138
of physical disabilities, 431–432
progress in, 4–6
Professional organizations, 25–27
Profound mental retardation, **113**
Progressive disorder, **422**
Progressive time delay, in mental retardation, **132**
Project PLAI (Promoting Learning Through Active Interaction),
    400
Prosthesis, **435**–436
PRTs. *See* Prereferral teams
Psychoanalytic, **380**
Psychoeducational model, in emotional/behavioral disorders,
    245–249
Psychological processing disorders, in learning disabilities, 151
Psychostimulants
for ADHD, 187, **207**–213
for autistic spectrum disorder, **383**
Public Law 93-112. *See* Vocational Rehabilitation Act
Public Law 94-142. *See* Education for All Handicapped Children
    Act
Public Law 99-457. *See* Education for All Handicapped Children
    Act, amendments to
Public Law 101-476. *See* Individuals with Disabilities Education
    Act
Public's reaction to exceptionalities, 485–486, 490–491, 496
Pull-out programs, **47**
efficacy of, 47
student satisfaction with, 51–52
Punishment. *See* Disciplining of exceptional students
Pupil, **341**, 342f
Pure-tone audiometry, **305**

Quadriplegia, in cerebral palsy, **424**

Racial minorities. *See* Minorities
Racism, as persistent problem, 82–85
Readiness skills, in mental retardation, **131**
Reading skills, in learning disabilities, 159*f*, 161–162
Reagan administration, and deregulation, 27
Rear Window Captioning Systems, 323*f*, 326–327
Receptive language, **266**
   changes in, 283*f*
Reciprocal teaching
   for language-minority students, **103**
   in learning disabilities, **173**
Referral of students for screening
   classroom teacher's role in, 19–22
   evaluation and documentation criteria for, 21
Refraction, **343**
   errors of, 343–344
Regular education initiative (REI), **18**
Reinforcement, in ADHD, 205–207
Residential schools, 15, 17*t*
Resonance, voice disorders and, **289**
Resource teachers, 14, 16*t*
Retina, **342**, 342*f*
Retinitis pigmentosa, **344**, 345*f*
   in Usher syndrome, **394**
Retinopathy of prematurity (ROP), 4–6, **345**
Rett's disorder, **376**
Rhizotomy, selective posterior, 423–424
Ritalin (methylphenidate), **207**
   for ADHD, 207–213
   for autistic spectrum disorder, 383
   cautions regarding, 212–213
   lawsuits on, 210
   paradoxical effect of, **207**
   side effects and nonresponse, 209–211
   and substance abuse, 187, 211–212
ROP. *See* Retinopathy of prematurity
Rubella (German measles)
   and deaf-blindness, **394**
   and mental retardation, **120**

Scaffolding
   for language-minority students, 102–**103**
   in learning disabilities, **172**–173
Schizophrenia, **228**–229
   causes of, 231
   identification of, 236
   instructional methods in, 254
Schools, advocacy and, 10, 506–509
Scoliosis, **428**
   in Prader-Willi syndrome, **119**
Screening, for chromosomal disorders, 118
Séguin, Édouard, 24
Seizure (convulsion), **425**
   first aid for, 426
Seizure disorder. *See* Epilepsy
Selective posterior rhizotomy, 423–424
Self-advocacy
   in learning disabilities, 182
   in physical disabilities, 439
Self-determination, **43**–44

four characteristics of, **128**–129
   in mental retardation, 127–131
   in multiple severe disabilities, **413**–414
Self-esteem, multicultural education and, 105–106
Self-injurious behavior (SIB), 407
Self-instruction, in learning disabilities, **171**–172
Self-monitoring
   in ADHD, **205**–206
   in learning disabilities, **172**
Self-regulation
   in mental retardation, **124**
Self-stimulation, in multiple severe disabilities, **406**–407
Semantics, **163**, 266, **267**
   disorders of, 267, 273
   in learning disabilities, 163
Sensorineural hearing loss, 306–**307**
Sensory acuteness, in visual impairment, 348
Serotonin, in ADHD, **195**
Setting events, in functional behavior assessment, 134
Severe mental retardation, **113**
   instructional methods in, 132
Severe multiple disabilities. *See* Multiple severe disabilities
Sheltered-English approach, **102**
Sheltered workshops, **413**
   in mental retardation, **142**
   in multiple severe disabilities, 413
Short-term memory, in learning disabilities, **165**
SIB. *See* Self-injurious behavior
Siblings of disabled child, reactions of, 493–494, 495*t*, 496
Sibshops, **494**
Sign language, **300**. *See also* American Sign Language
   adapted, **399**, 402–403
   fingerspelling, 320–321, 321*f*
   Signing English systems, 320–321
Slate and stylus, 353–**354**, 355*f*
Sleep apnea, in Prader-Willi syndrome, **119**
SLI. *See* Specific language impairment
SLP. *See* Speech-language pathologist
Snellen chart, **342**–343
Social intelligence, **114**
Social skills/development
   in ADHD, 187, 198–199
   in Asperger syndrome, 379
   in autistic spectrum disorder, 378
   in communications disorders, 263–264
   in emotional/behavioral disorders, 221–222, 234, 238–245, 276–277
   in hearing impairment, 299–301, 310–316
   learning disabilities and, 149, 166–167
   in multicultural education, 103–106
   in traumatic brain injury, 389–391
   in visual impairment, 348–351
Social support for families, **501**–502
Sociocultural theory, 87–88, 87*f*
Sonography, **118**
Spanish-speaking students. *See also* Hispanics
   giftedness and, 469
   language disorders and, 287
Spastic, 446–**447**
Spasticity in cerebral palsy, **424**

Special day schools, 15, 17*t*
Special education
    complexity of issues in, 75
    definition of, 12–13, 12*t*
    goal of, 4*f*
    history of, 23–27
    need for, 7–10
    parental resistance to, 11, 29–30
    progress of, 34–35
    service types, 13–15, 16*t*–17*t*
        percentages of students in, 15–17, 18*t*
Special education teachers. *See also* Collaborative consultation
            (co-teaching)
    communication with parents, 502–508
    family involvement strategies for, 497*t*
    importance of families to, 489*t*
    role in special education, 22–23
    and service alternatives, 13–15, 16*t*–17*t*
    training for, as legal requirement, 29
Special self-contained classes, 14–15, 17*t*
Specific language impairment (SLI), **271**
Speech, **266**
Speech audiometry, **305**–306
Speech disorders, 288–291
    incidence of, 12, 12*t*
    in learning disabilities, 163–164
    misconceptions about, 265
    neurological damage and, 291
    prevalence of, 266–268
    transition programs in, 291–294
    types of, **266,** 267
Speech-language pathologist (SLP)
    certification of, 284–285, 289
    role of, 280–281, 284–285, 289, 294
Speech reception threshold (SRT), **306**
Speechreading, 300, **319**–320
    misconceptions about, 301
Spelling difficulties, in learning disabilities, 162
Spina bifida, **118,** 427–428
Spinal chord injuries, 427–428
SRT. *See* Speech reception threshold
Standardized testing. *See also* Intelligence quotient (IQ) tests
    accommodations in, 60–61, 61*t*
    and eligibility for services, 30
    fairness to minorities, 94–95, 94*f*
    inclusion of disabled in, 41, 60
    in language disabilities, 273, 284
    in learning disabilities, **158**–159
Standards-based reforms in assessment, 59–62
    impact of, 72
Stanford-Binet IQ tests, 123
Stapes, **304,** 304*f*
State law, knowledge of, as teacher responsibility, 22
Stereotypic behaviors (stereotypy)
    in autistic spectrum disorder, 378
    in multiple severe disabilities, 406–407
    in visual impairment, **351**–352
Strabismus, **345**–346
Strategy deficits
    in language disabilities, 296

    in learning disabilities, 167–168
Strauss syndrome, **188**
Stress, parental, 491–493, 498
Stuttering, 265, 291
Stuttering Foundation of America, 264
Substance abuse
    ADHD and, 187, 199–200, 211–213
    and birth defects, 429–430
    emotional/behavioral disorders and, 231
    and mental retardation, 120
    Ritalin and, 187, 211–213
Suicide, depression and, 245
Sullivan, Annie, 396–397
Supported employment, **69**
    in mental retardation, **142**
    in physical disabilities, **448**
Supported living, in mental retardation, **141**
Syntax, **163, 266, 267**
    disorders of, 267, 272–273
    in learning disabilities, 163
Syphilis, **121**
    and mental retardation, 121
Systematic instruction, in mental retardation, **132**

Talent, **457.** *See also* Giftedness
Tantrums, in multiple severe disabilities, 407
TASH. *See* Association for Persons with Severe Handicaps
Task switching, in ADHD, 197
TBI. *See* Traumatic brain injury
Teachers. *See* Classroom teachers; Special education teachers
Team teaching, **56**–57
Technical Assistance Center on Positive Behavioral Interventions
            and Supports, 256
Technology, assistive. *See also* Augmented or alternative
            communication
    advantages and disadvantages of, 41, 62–63
    awareness of, as teacher responsibility, 22
    in cerebral palsy, 404
    ethics of, 62–63
    in hearing impairment, 326–328
        cochlear implantation, **62, 313**–315, 313*f*
    in physical disabilities, 435–436, 448–449, 448*f*
    in visual impairment, 339, 356–357, 360–364
Television. *See* Media
Teratogens, **158**
    and learning disabilities, 158
Terminal illness, approaches to, 442
Test of Written Language, Third Edition, 159
Testing. *See* Assessment; Standardized testing
Text telephones, **328**–329
Tolerance
    importance of, 80
    teaching of, 99, 104–106
Total communication approach, **317,** 320–323
Touch cues, **399**
TouchTalker, 404
Touchtown, 367*f*
Tourette's syndrome (TS), 231
Toxins, **195**
    in ADHD, 195–196

Transition programs, 68–72. *See also* Employment; *specific disabilities*
  case study, 70
  definition of, 68
  family life cycle and, 500–501
  federal requirements for, 68–70, 369
  issues in, 69–72
  for mildly disabled, 71–72
  multicultural education and, 96–97
  for severely disabled, 71
  sheltered work, 71*t*
  typical services, 71*t*
Transliteration, **331**
Traumatic brain injury (TBI), **121, 422**
  causes of, 386
  definition and characteristics of, **384**–386
  educational programming in, 387–391
  incidence of, 12–**13,** 12*t*
  language disorders in, 388–389
  language learning in, 274*t*
  and mental retardation, 121
  misconceptions about, 375
  prevalence of, 386
  social skills/development in, **389**–391
Traveling notebooks, **506,** 507*t*
Trisomy 21, **117**
TTDs (telecommunication devices for the deaf), 327–328
Tunnel vision, **344**
  in Usher syndrome, **394**
Twice exceptional students, 471
Tympanic membrane (eardrum), **303,** 304*f*
Tympanometry, **306**

Underachievers. *See* IQ-achievement discrepancies
Unified Braille Code, **352**
Universal design, 61*f,* **63**
  in deaf education, 318
University of Kansas Center for Research on Learning, 180–181
U.S. Department of Education
  Learning Disabilities Initiative, 153
  Office of Special Education Programs, 502, 505
U.S. Food and Drug Administration (FDA), cochlear implantation and, 313
U.S. Office of Special Education Programs, 409
Usher syndrome, **393**–395
  educational programming in, 401
  misconceptions about, 375

Verbal skills. *See* Language; Speech
Vestibular mechanism, **304**
Vineland Adaptive Behavior Scales, 124
Visual efficiency, **343**
Visual impairment. *See also* Deaf-blindness
  academic achievement in, 348
  assistive technology in, 339, 356–357, 360–364
  and blindisms, 351–352
  braille and. *See* Braille
  causes of, 343–346
  definition and classification of, 340–341
  early intervention in, 365–366
  educational placement models in, 364–365
  educational programming in, 352–364
  employment in, 369–370
  etiquette in, 338
  and eye anatomy, 341–342, 342*f*
  fear of, 339–340
  incidence of, 12–13, 12*t*
  inclusion and, 365–366
  instructional strategies in, 366
  intellectual ability in, 346–347
  language development in, 346
  measurement in, 342–343
  misconceptions about, 339
  orientation and mobility in, 347–348, 357–360, 362, 365
  prevalence of, 341
  psychological and behavioral characteristics in, 346–352
  and remaining sight, use of, 356–357
  social skills/development in, 348–351
  stereotypic behaviors in, 351–352
  transition programs in, 367–369
Vitreous humor, **342,** 342*f*
Vocational education. *See* Employment
Vocational Rehabilitation Act (1973), 181
Voice disorders, 267, 288–289
Voice Mate, 361

Wechsler Individual Achievement Test (WIAT), 158–159
Wechsler Intelligence Scale for Children (WISC), 158–159
Wechsler Intelligence Scale for Children—Revised (WISC-III), 114–115, 123
Whites, percentage in special education, 92, 92*f*
WIAT. *See* Wechsler Individual Achievement Test
Williams syndrome, **118,** 127, 127*f*
  and behavioral phenotype, 125, 126*t*
WISC. *See* Wechsler Intelligence Scale for Children
WISC-III. *See* Wechsler Intelligence Scale for Children—Revised
Withdrawn behavior. *See* Internalizing behavior
Working memory
  in ADHD, 196
  in learning disabilities, **165**
  in mental retardation, 124
World Wide Web. *See* Internet
Writing difficulties. *See also* Communication disorders
  in learning disabilities, 162–163

Zero hearing-threshold level, 305
Zero tolerance policies, and disciplining of disabled, **72**–73